Vito Pirrelli, Ingo Plag, Wolfgang U. Dressler (Eds.)
Word Knowledge and Word Usage

Trends in Linguistics
Studies and Monographs

Editors
Chiara Gianollo
Daniël Van Olmen

Editorial Board
Walter Bisang
Tine Breban
Volker Gast
Hans Henrich Hock
Karen Lahousse
Natalia Levshina
Caterina Mauri
Heiko Narrog
Salvador Pons
Niina Ning Zhang
Amir Zeldes

Editor responsible for this volume
Daniël Van Olmen

Volume 337

Word Knowledge and Word Usage

A Cross-Disciplinary Guide to the Mental Lexicon

Edtited by
Vito Pirrelli, Ingo Plag, Wolfgang U. Dressler

DE GRUYTER
MOUTON

ISBN 978-3-11-077673-7
e-ISBN (PDF) 978-3-11-044057-7
e-ISBN (EPUB) 978-3-11-043244-2
ISBN 1861-4302
DOI https://doi.org/10.1515/9783110440577

This work is licensed under a Creative Commons Attribution-NonCommercial-NoDerivatives 4.0 International License. For details go to http://creativecommons.org/licenses/by-nc-nd/4.0/.

Library of Congress Control Number: 2019956255

Bibliographic information published by the Deutsche Nationalbibliothek
The Deutsche Nationalbibliothek lists this publication in the Deutsche Nationalbibliografie; detailed bibliographic data are available on the Internet at http://dnb.dnb.de.

© 2021 Vito Pirrelli, Ingo Plag, Wolfgang U. Dressler, published by Walter de Gruyter GmbH, Berlin/Boston.
This volume is text- and page-identical with the hardback published in 2020.
The book is published open access at www.degruyter.com.

Typesetting: Integra Software Services Pvt. Ltd.
Printing and binding: CPI books GmbH, Leck

www.degruyter.com

This book is dedicated to the memory of Lavinia Merlini Barbaresi, a pioneering contributor to the field of morphopragmatics and a unique friend, who relentlessly worked on this volume during the hardest stages of her illness.

Contents

Vito Pirrelli, Ingo Plag and Wolfgang U. Dressler
Word knowledge in a cross-disciplinary world —— 1

Part 1: Technologies, tools and data

Vito Pirrelli, Claudia Marzi, Marcello Ferro, Franco Alberto Cardillo,
Harald R. Baayen and Petar Milin
Psycho-computational modelling of the mental lexicon —— 23

Jacolien van Rij, Nemanja Vaci, Lee H. Wurm and Laurie Beth Feldman
**Alternative quantitative methods in psycholinguistics:
Implications for theory and design** —— 83

Paola Marangolo and Costanza Papagno
**Neuroscientific protocols for exploring the mental lexicon:
Evidence from aphasia** —— 127

Emmanuel Keuleers and Marco Marelli
Resources for mental lexicon research: A delicate ecosystem —— 167

Part 2: Topical issues

Sabine Arndt-Lappe and Mirjam Ernestus
Morpho-phonological alternations: The role of lexical storage —— 191

Claudia Marzi, James P. Blevins, Geert Booij and Vito Pirrelli
Inflection at the morphology-syntax interface —— 228

Ingo Plag and Laura Winther Balling
**Derivational morphology: An integrative perspective on some
fundamental questions** —— 295

Gary Libben, Christina L. Gagné and Wolfgang U. Dressler
The representation and processing of compounds words —— 336

Paolo Acquaviva, Alessandro Lenci, Carita Paradis and Ida Raffaelli
Models of lexical meaning —— 353

Lavinia Merlini Barbaresi and Wolfgang U. Dressler
Pragmatic explanations in morphology —— 405

Part 3: **Words in usage**

Antonio Fábregas and Martina Penke
Word storage and computation —— 455

Madeleine Voga, Francesco Gardani and Hélène Giraudo
Multilingualism and the Mental Lexicon —— 506

Marco Marelli, Daniela Traficante and Cristina Burani
Reading morphologically complex words: Experimental evidence and learning models —— 553

Dorit Ravid, Emmanuel Keuleers and Wolfgang U. Dressler
Emergence and early development of lexicon and morphology —— 593

Thomas Berg
Morphological slips of the tongue —— 634

Mila Vulchanova, David Saldaña and Giosué Baggio
Word structure and word processing in developmental disorders —— 680

Index —— 709

Vito Pirrelli, Ingo Plag and Wolfgang U. Dressler
Word knowledge in a cross-disciplinary world

Abstract: This editorial project stemmed from a 4-year period of intense interdisciplinary research networking funded by the **European Science Foundation** within the framework of the **NetWordS** project (09-RNP-089). The project mission was to bring together experts of various research fields (from brain sciences and computing to cognition and linguistics) and of different theoretical inclinations, to advance the current awareness of theoretical, typological, psycholinguistic, computational and neurophysiological evidence on the structure and processing of words, with a view to promoting novel methods of research and assessment for grammar architecture and language usage.

The unprecedented cross-disciplinary fertilization prompted by a wide range of scientific and educational initiatives (three international workshops, two summer schools, one main conference and over a hundred grants supporting short visits and multilateral exchanges) persuaded us to pursue this effort beyond the project lifespan, spawning the idea of an interdisciplinary handbook, where a wide range of central topics on word knowledge and usage are dealt with by teams of authors with common interests and different backgrounds. Unsurprisingly (with the benefit of the hindsight), the project turned out to be more challenging and time-consuming than initially planned. Cross-boundary talking and mutual understanding are neither short-term, nor immediately rewarding efforts, but part of a long-sighted, strategic vision, where stamina, motivation and planning ahead play a prominent role. We believe that this book, published as an **open access volume**, significantly sharpens the current understanding of issues of word knowledge and usage, and has a real potential for promoting novel research paradigms, and bringing up a new generation of language scholars.

Keywords: interdisciplinarity, word knowledge, word usage, language units, statistical and computer modeling, levels of understanding, between-level mapping, linking hypotheses, scale effects

---

Vito Pirrelli, Italian National Research Council (CNR), Institute for Computational Linguistics, Pisa, Italy
Ingo Plag, Heinrich-Heine-Universität Düsseldorf, Department of English, Düsseldorf, Germany
Wolfgang U. Dressler, University of Vienna, Department of Linguistics, Vienna, Austria

∂ Open Access. © 2020 Vito Pirrelli et al., published by De Gruyter. [cc) BY-NC-ND] This work is licensed under a Creative Commons Attribution-NonCommercial-NoDerivatives 4.0 International License.
https://doi.org/10.1515/9783110440577-001

1 Context

Scientists are nowadays faced with a few important discontinuities with the past: (a) an exponentially growing rate of technological innovation, (b) the ever-increasing availability of multimodal data, (c) an increasing disciplinary specialization, involving the danger of being blind to interdisciplinarity, and (d) a pressing demand for problem-oriented interdisciplinarity. 19th century medical practitioners based a diagnosis upon visiting their patients. For a 21st century medical doctor, patient encounters are complemented by a number of sophisticated diagnostic techniques, ranging from radiography, PET and MEG to ECG, EEG and ultrasound. This is what contemporary medicine is about: creating new objects of scientific inquiry by multiplying and integrating different information sources.

21st century language scientists are no exception. They can benefit from an equally large array of technological tools tapping linguistic information at unprecedented levels of range and detail. They know that words, phrases and utterances are not just mental representations or convenient descriptive devices grounded in introspection and informants' intuition. They are multidimensional objects, emerging from interrelated patterns of experience, social interaction and psychological and neurobiological mechanisms. Investigation of these objects calls for integration of manifold information sources at a conceptual and functional level.

In this book, we strive to understand more of words in language by squarely addressing a number of questions underlying the relationship between speakers' knowledge of words, evidence of the way speakers use words in daily communicative exchanges and psychological and neurofunctional correlates of word usage. How are words processed in working memory? Are they stored in long-term memory as a whole or rather composed 'on-line' in working memory from stored sub-lexical constituents? What role is played in this process by knowledge-based factors, such as formal regularity and semantic transparency, and usage-based factors, such as perceptual salience, familiarity and frequency? Does word-level knowledge require parallel development of form and meaning representations, or do they develop independently and at a different pace? How do word meanings function and combine in daily communicative contexts, and evolve through learning? What types of lexical knowledge affect on-line processing? Do the dramatic typological differences in word structure across world languages impact on processing and acquisition? And how will a thorough investigation of such differences change lexical models worked out on the basis of a single language? Finally, what neurobiological patterns of connectivity sustain word processing and storage in the brain? And how can they break down as a result of neurological damage or disorders?

Any serious effort to address these questions needs to ultimately be based upon recognition that words define a multifactorial domain of scientific inquiry, whose thorough investigation requires synergic integration of a wide range of disciplines. Of late, a few independent lines of scientific inquiry appear to lend support to an integrative approach to the study of the mental lexicon:
- In line with a view of word knowledge as an **interface domain**, the architecture of the mental lexicon is better understood as resulting from the dynamic integration of multiple levels of information (Jackendoff 2002); correlation of these levels, albeit indirect and possibly non-linear, enforces constraints and mutual dependencies that are not justified on single-level grounds (Elman 2004, 2009). This view is not incompatible with a principle of representational modularity, segregating linguistic information according to levels of representation (Jackendoff 2000, 2007). Nonetheless, it conceives of lexical knowledge as emerging from the unique, distributed network of stored associations among fragments of disparate representations, including constructions, idioms, proverbs and social routine clichés (e.g. Arnon et al. 2017; Arnon and Snider 2010; Bannard and Matthews 2008; Grimm et al. 2017; Tremblay and Baayen 2010; Siyanova-Chanturia et al. 2017; Vespignani et al. 2009).
- Word processing requires a two-way **interactive perspective**, whereby the speaker can anticipate what the hearer needs to be provided with in order to obtain the intended perlocutionary effects, and, in turn, the hearer can predict what may be offered in the ongoing spoken or written communicative interaction (Huettig 2015; Pickering and Garrod 2013; Riest et al. 2015); communicative factors include Theory-of-Mind states (Milligan et al. 2007; Wellman 2002) and perspective taking (Brown-Schmidt 2009), contextual and co-textual embedding and transparency of words (Marelli et al. 2017; Mikolov et al. 2013; Mitchell and Lapata 2010), especially of neologisms and occasionalisms (Mattiello 2017; Plag 2018), choice between synonyms, lexical and morphological differences between child-directed and adult-directed speech (Kilani-Schoch et al. 2009; Saxton 2008, 2009; Taylor et al. 2009), paraphrases, and simultaneous top-down and bottom-up processing strategies (Ferro et al. 2010; Kuperberg and Jaeger 2016; Pickering and Garrod 2007, 2013; Smith and Levy 2013);
- Accordingly, word processing is modelled as the task of optimal resolution of multiple, parallel and possibly conflicting constraints on complex lexical structures, where top-down expectations, based on past experiences and entrenched memory traces, combine, in on-line processing, with the bottom-up requirements of input stimuli (Berger et al. 1996; Kukona et al. 2011; Seidenberg and MacDonald 1999; Spivey and Tanenhaus 1998; Tabor and Tanenhaus 1999);

- This is in keeping with a **Maximization of Opportunity Principle** for word processing: different processing strategies are applied simultaneously, and preference for one strategy over another is opportunistically given on the basis of task-based requirements, or compensatory mechanisms offsetting contingent failures caused by language impairments or production/perception errors and other types of noise (Libben 2005, 2016);
- All these perspectives are compatible with the hypothesis of an **indirect correspondence** between low-level principles of word processing/organization and their brain localization (Clahsen 2006; Hasson et al. 2018; Pirrelli 2007; Price 2017). On this view, complex language functions are not localized to specific brain regions, but are rather the emergent property of the interaction of parallel distributed networks of densely interconnected regions (D'Esposito 2007; Price 2010, 2012). In this context, the functional anatomy of language cannot be deduced from a high-level conceptualization of the way language is understood to work in the brain, but it requires a deep understanding of the functional interaction of concomitant low-level processing principles and associative mechanisms (Hasson et al. 2018, Pirrelli et al. this volume).
- Over the last 20 years, the anatomy of language has been investigated with neuroimaging techniques (e.g. PET and fMRI) and brain areas associated with language processing have been identified consistently (Ben Shalom and Poeppel 2008; Hickok and Poeppel 2004; Price 2010, 2012, 2017). Future studies will undoubtedly be able to improve the spatial and temporal precision with which functional regions can be located (see Davis 2015, for the neuroanatomy of lexical access). Nonetheless, assuming that our current understanding of the general picture is correct, the main task for future research will be to specify the details of the inter-region organization and computational operations.

2 Content

In this volume, experts of various disciplines look at common topics from complementary standpoints, to discuss and understand what can be learned from integrating different approaches into converging perspectives. Most chapters are jointly authored by at least two experts from different fields, not only to bring together evidence from different domains but, more importantly, to make these domains talk to each other, with a view to gaining a deeper understanding of the issues focused on in the chapter.

The book is structured into three parts. Part 1: Technologies, Tools and Data (covering chapters 2 through to 5) is chiefly devoted to the methodological pre-requisites to interdisciplinary research on languages: technologies, tools and data. Its focus ranges over the contribution, goals and limits of computer simulations, statistical techniques for multidimensional data analysis and modeling, neuroscientific experimental paradigms and tools, and shared data and data infrastructures. Part 2: Topical Issues (including chapters 6 through to 11) deals with topical issues in word inquiry, including the morphology-phonology interface, inflection, derivation, compounding, lexical semantics and morpho-pragmatics. Finally, Part 3: Words in Usage (chapters 12 through to 17) contains an overview of classical theoretical approaches to the dualism between word storage and processing, together with more focused contributions on word usage issues, zooming in on multilingual lexica, word reading, word acquisition, errors in morphological processing and developmental disorders in word competence. In what follows, we provide a concise introduction to the main topics harped on in each chapter, with a view to highlighting converging trends, actual and potential interactions, as well as prospects for cross-fertilization.

2.1 Outline

Chapter 2, on psycho-computational and algorithmic models of the mental lexicon, delineates a clear connection between word frequency distributions and information theoretical measures for word families, statistical correlations over behavioral evidence (e.g. wordlikeness ratings and reaction times), principles of discriminative learning, and integrative algorithmic models of word storage and processing. However tightly interrelated, this heterogeneous bundle of evidence has traditionally been in the purview of distinct domains of scientific inquiry such as corpus linguistics, psycholinguistics, machine language learning, computational linguistics and serial cognition. By going through Marr's (1982) levels of understanding of complex systems, Vito Pirrelli, Marcello Ferro, Claudia Marzi, Franco Alberto Cardillo, Harald Baayen and Petar Milin show that approaching all these issues from a learning perspective sheds light on their potential for integration, while defining a fruitful line of research in the years to come.

Chapter 3, by Jacolien van Rij, Nemanja Vaci, Lee H. Wurm and Laurie Beth Feldman, is a guided tour to some of the most successful statistical techniques for psycholinguistic data modelling to date, from ANOVA to Generalized Additive Models. It addresses, step by step, a wide range of methodological issues that are only occasionally discussed in the technical literature at this level of depth. In spite of its apparent technicality, the chapter will thus be beneficial to non-expert as well as more advanced users of statistical packages for analysis of language data. We believe that these techniques are bound to become part and parcel of the methodological tool-kit of any language scientist, as witnessed by the growing awareness of the importance of quantitative data, even within theoretical frameworks that proved, in the past, more reluctant to accept usage-based data as part of their empirical evidence.

In Chapter 4, Paola Marangolo and Costanza Papagno provide a clear, comprehensive introduction to the best-known protocols and techniques for investigating the neurophysiological reality of words in the brain, using aphasia as a case study. Whereas in earlier times language brain substrates could only be studied indirectly, through correlation of cerebral lesions with dysfunctional behavior, today functional neuroimaging allows direct *in vivo* visualization of cerebral activity. This opens up unprecedented, exciting opportunities in investigating the neurobiology of language, to offer rich evidence that distinct cerebral areas process different word classes. Nonetheless, a couple of caveats are in order here. First, in using neuroimaging methods, one must be aware of their inherent limitations. Methods that are based on the study of perfusion and metabolism (such as PET and fMRI) detect neural activity only indirectly, based on local blood flow. On the contrary, recordings of event-related potentials with electroencephalography can detect neural activity directly, with optimal temporal resolution, but poor spatial precision. A better understanding of the brain dynamics involved in word processing is thus likely to require a combination of techniques with different temporal and spatial resolutions. Secondly, establishing a causal relationship between a language task and the activation of a specific brain region should be assessed with care, since several uncontrolled variables can produce a misinterpretation of results. For example, localization of a verb-specific (as opposed to noun-specific) brain region can in fact be due to effects of morpho-syntactic processing, such as subject-verb agreement checking, rather than to a pure, categorical effect. In fact, language-driven interpretations of the involvement of specific cortical areas in an experimental task could (and, according to some scholars, should) be replaced by more parsimonious explanatory accounts, postulating basic or domain-general computations (Hasson et al. 2018; Price 2017). As the number of linguistic and extra-linguistic variables can be extremely large, Marangolo and Papagno suggest that a closer interaction of neurobiological models with both low-level computer models and high-level cognitive linking hypotheses can provide fruitful, top-down constraints on the interpretation space.

The important issue of producing and sharing high-quality multimodal evidence of elicited as well as unelicited language production/recognition, is addressed in Chapter 5, where Emmanuel Keuleers and Marco Marelli discuss at some length the complex and delicate nature of what they appropriately call "the language data ecosystem". They focus on the often-neglected fact that data are never produced in a vacuum, but are always the by-product of a complex interaction between scientific goals, methodological stances and analytical tools. Awareness of this deep interdependency is key to pushing progress in our field. Only by getting a clearer view of the shortcomings of analyses exclusively based on data that are elicited in tightly controlled experimental conditions, scholars can hope to address fundamental questions concerning the neurobiology of language usage in more ecological settings.

Chapter 6, by Sabine Arndt-Lappe and Mirjam Ernestus, deals with the relation between morpho-phonological alternations and lexical storage and processing. There is a long tradition of structurally and theoretically oriented studies of morpho-phonology that have explained phonological alternations in complex words in the form of rules (or similar mechanisms). More recently, however, a growing body of evidence has accrued that morpho-phonology may be closely linked to how speakers and listeners process complex words. The authors discuss several morpho-phonological alternations and demonstrate what we can learn from these alternations about the storage of complex forms. Existing theoretical and computational models are evaluated in the light of psycholinguistic evidence. Ultimately, it seems that alternations can only be explained if we assume lexical storage of at least some alternants.

In dealing with inflection as a central component of morphological competence, the authors of Chapter 7 set themselves the ambitious goal of focusing on the role of formal contrast in marking functional differences in the syntactic distribution of inflected words. Claudia Marzi, James Blevins, Geert Booij and Vito Pirrelli discuss the way storage of frequent forms can interact with generalization strategies that compensate for lack of input evidence in the low-frequency range. Both morphological and constructional information are assumed to be stored in long-term memory, in keeping with a view of lexical representations as highly context-sensitive. This is in line with recent psycholinguistic evidence reported, among others, in Chapter 6 of this volume, showing how much information is actually accessible in the mental lexicon, both in terms of the phonetic details stored for each word, and in terms of how morphologically-complex words are actually stored as (possibly) independent lexical units.

In Chapter 8, Ingo Plag and Laura Wither Balling cast a very wide net on the extremely rich and variegated evidence on derivatives and derivational processes coming from as diverse research areas in language sciences as phonetics, theoretical linguistics, psycholinguistics, neurolinguistics and computational linguistics. Such a bird's eye view allows for careful assessment of widely held assumptions, as well as more contentious issues, while charting those yet unexplored territories in morphological derivation that may offer fruitful prospects of converging progress in the years to come. In particular, the authors observe that theoretical linguistics has typically over-emphasized representational issues at the expense of processing issues, with psycholinguistics and neurolinguistics being more, if not exclusively, concerned with the latter (i.e. behavioral evidence of the human word processor). Such a discipline-oriented bias made theoretical linguistics relatively blind to the relevance of formal contrast for word recognition irrespective of the formal means by which it is enforced (i.e. whether morphemically or not). On the other hand, more brain-oriented language disciplines turned out to be relatively blind to issues of word production, with comparatively sparser attention being paid to how sublexical constituents are combined to produce whole word meaning in derivatives.

Morphological compounds bear witness to the advantages of taking a multidisciplinary perspective on a common pool of data. In Chapter 9, Gary Libben, Christina Gagné and Wolfgang U. Dressler keep their focus on both representational and processing issues. From this two-fold perspective, compounds appear to be linguistic objects of a quintessentially dual nature. On the one hand, their meaning is intimately associated with their lexical wholes. Such constructional effects are "both greater than the sum of their parts and greater than the division of their wholes", requiring some form of "weak compositionality" (Baroni, Guevara and Pirrelli 2007) mostly dictated by paradigmatic relations holding between overlapping members of the same compound family (as opposed to combinatorial principles of syntactic composition). At the same time, the processing of compounds calls for activation of their constituents as distinct units, with more transparent compounds, i.e. those compounds whose form and meaning are more directly amenable to the form and meaning of their constituent parts, being the easiest to process.

Issues of lexical semantics are the specific focus of Chapter 10, illustrating, in a somewhat exemplary way, the benefit of comparing different perspectives on the same subject area, and weighing up their respective strengths and weaknesses. Paolo Acquaviva, Alessandro Lenci, Carita Paradis and Ida Raffaelli provide a comprehensive overview of very diverse models of lexical meaning. Coverage includes the traditional, structuralist view of word meanings as forming part of a systemic network of value contrasts/oppositions; the symbolic rule-based approach of generativist tradition; the investigation of concept formation as rooted in cognitive primitives like space and geometry; more recent distributional approaches, where meanings are points in a multidimensional space defined by the distribution of words in context. All these models appear to articulate different, and in some cases, irreconcilable answers to fundamental questions about the nature of lexical meaning. It would be rather naïve to claim, however, that they offer just complementary and inevitably incomplete rival perspectives on the vast, elusive realm of lexical semantics. In the end, all these aspects need be reconciled and accounted for within a unitary, analytical framework, able to integrate the results of different approaches, including data of typologically different languages, experientially-based evidence, results of computer simulations using word distributions in context, and results of psycholinguistic and neurolinguistic experimental paradigms.

Chapter 11 focuses on the relation between morphology and pragmatics. In contrast to models that take morphology and pragmatics to be always secondary in being based on the morphosemantics of the respective categories, Lavinia Merlini Barbaresi and Wolfgang U. Dressler argue that at least some of these categories (e.g. evaluatives, such as diminutives and augmentatives) have a basic pragmatic meaning, a claim which is incompatible with the assumption of external modularity between grammar and pragmatics. Although emotion may be heavily involved in the pragmatic meanings of morphopragmatic categories, pragmatic meanings cannot be reduced to the presence of emotion. The chapter goes beyond evaluatives and pragmatic devices of reduplication (both grammatical and extragrammatical) which are most extensively discussed in the literature, to also include honorifics, excessives and pragmatic uses of plurals, as well as many other categories of word formation and inflection. The roles of lexical pragmatics, sociopragmatics, corpus linguistic approaches and new developments in pragmatics are also discussed in some detail.

The dualism between storage and computation in morphology is focused on in Chapter 12, where Martina Penke and Antonio Fábregas scrutinize competing theoretical frameworks of lexical competence, to assess theoretical predictions in the light of some of the major word processing effects that have been identified in psycholinguistic research over the last decades. In particular, they discuss two of the most established behavioral findings to date: (i) the relative insensitivity of regularly inflected forms to token frequency effects in word processing, and (ii) the stronger perception of morphological structure in regulars as opposed to irregulars. Somewhat surprisingly, these findings appear to cut across two of the main theoretical dimensions governing the contemporary debate on morphology: namely, the opposition between lexicalism and neo-constructionism, and the item-and-arrangement vs. item-and-process dualism. According to the authors, both A-morphous Morphology and Minimalist Morphology prove to be compatible with evidence that humans process regulars and irregulars differently. Nonetheless, they appear to take opposite sides on the theoretically crucial question of what morphological units are stored in the mental lexicon and what units are produced by rules. This suggests that the relationship between principles of grammar organization (e.g. lexicon vs. rules) and processing correlates (storage vs. computation) is not as straightforward as the "direct correspondence" hypothesis (Clahsen 2006) has claimed in the past. Differential processing effects may in fact be the complex outcome of the non-linear interaction of uniform learning and processing principles. Since modelling such interaction may well exceed the limits of both theoretical conceptualizations and box-and-arrow models of cognition, settling these theoretical issues will call for advanced sources of experimental evidence (e.g. computational and neuropsychological models of language behavior) and more sophisticated experimental paradigms (e.g. discriminating between morphophonological and morpho-syntactic effects in word processing).

In Chapter 13, Madeleine Voga, Francesco Gardani and Hélène Giraudo investigate multilingualism from a two-fold perspective: the psycholinguistic modeling of the bilingual (and multilingual) lexicon, and the role of language contact in language change. In both domains, the co-existence of lexical items belonging to different languages and, possibly, to different morphological systems, raises a number of non-trivial questions on structural and processing counts. What sort of interaction governs the two sets? Does similarity of forms play a prominent role in this dynamic relationship? Or is rather similarity of meaning involved here? Or just a combination of the two, as with classical accounts of morphological relatedness? Is such a relationship symmetrical or asymmetrical, and what prevents items from one language from interfering with items belonging to the other language in daily communicative practice? The authors go on with establishing an interesting parallelism between the L1–L2 contrast in bilingualism (as well as the factors governing the L1–L2 interaction), and the synergic opposition between a recipient language and a source language in the literature on language contact and change. Interestingly, the two oppositions share a number of properties: (i) the gradient asymmetry of their relationship, accountable in terms of both frequency effects and the entrenchment of connections between the lexical and the conceptual level of speakers' word knowledge, (ii) the prominent role of word families in spreading cross-linguistic activation, and (iii) the sensitivity of systemic co-activation to pragmatic factors. In fact, all these interactive effects appear to be influenced by the specific pragmatic force of speakers' utterances, and their perlocutionary effects. The authors conclude that, in spite of persisting differences in methodology, terminology and goals, the material continuity of multilingual evidence in both domains lends support to a unifying view, and encourages a converging perspective in their scientific investigation.

Chapter 14 focuses on the connection between reading skills and morphological competence from a psycholinguistic, neuropsychological and computational perspective. Marco Marelli, Daniela Traficante and Cristina Burani start with an overview of evidence supporting the classical morpheme-as-unit view of lexical representations in the mental lexicon, together with the developmental literature supporting the idea that morphological awareness is an age-related, emergent aspect of word processing. Effects of both semantic and frequency-sensitive modulation of morpheme access, as well as evidence of the global organization of lexical and sublexical constituents in large word families, and the context-sensitivity and task-dependency of behavioral findings based on established experimental protocols, jointly suggest that morphological effects may not require dedicated processing modules and storage units. Rather, these effects can be accounted for by general-purpose mechanisms for time-serial processing, coupled with the ability to track down and generalize statistically-strong form-meaning patterns. Reading skills can take advantage of these general abilities. At the same time, the age-related development of these abilities can largely benefit from increasing literacy levels. On a more general, methodological note, the authors point out that it is increasingly difficult to explore such a complex interaction of multiple, concurring factors through traditional experimental protocols. Computational simulations can nowadays dynamically model the interaction of several factors in the context of a specific task, thereby allowing one to weigh up and inspect their individual influence as well as their joint, interactive effects, at unprecedented levels of accuracy. It is only to be expected that large-scale computational simulations will play an important role in the investigation of morphological effects in reading in the years to come.

In Chapter 15, Emmanuel Keuleers, Dorit Ravid and Wolfgang U. Dressler deal with morphology and lexicon acquisition in children's first three years of life, by zooming in on a few focal points from an interdisciplinary perspective. The fundamental advantage of taking a broader perspective on issues of morphology acquisition is that integration of different viewpoints can shed light on the inherent limitations of domain-specific findings. Theoretical linguistic frameworks have long offered conceptual scaffolding for describing children's linguistic behavior in a structured, systemic way; and they will likely continue to do so in the near future. However, the further assumption that theoretical concepts and classification criteria developed for descriptive purposes are mapped linearly onto developmental evidence is misconceived. The scientific ability to identify minimal linguistic units and fundamental principles for their combination should not be confused with the hypothesis that language behavior can be understood by only observing the behavior of elementary units. Scale and complexity effects are ubiquitous in complex systems. It would be highly surprising if they were not observed in the acquisition of the most complex communication system in nature. Besides, what theoretical linguists call categories can be mentally structured along a similarity gradient. Likewise, some nearly instantaneous generalization processes in language development, apparently due to rule application, can in fact be the outcome of a continuous process of memory self-organization. Finally, it is difficult to over-estimate the contribution of the information-theoretic notions of entropy and communication code to understanding how children learn words in context, and the proper role that frequency, stimulus discrimination and concept development play in the process.

In Chapter 16, Thomas Berg carries out a fine-grained analysis of morphological errors in speech, by assessing the causal factors involved, and their theoretical implications. Errors may be triggered by morphological competition of the mistaken target with (i) words that appear in the context being uttered (*in praesentia*), or (ii) paradigmatically-related companions of the target (*in absentia*). The author emphasizes the important role played by lexico-semantic factors in weighing up the strength of paradigm relations and, ultimately, the degree of accessibility of morphological structure and the competition between paradigmatically-related words. From this perspective, derivation and inflection are conceptualized as two opposing points in a cline going from the more lexical to the more grammatical end of the language spectrum. The availability of derivational paradigms vs. inflectional paradigms is crucially modulated by lexical semantics. Since members of the same derivational family share less lexico-semantic content than members of the family of inflected forms of the same lemma (or inflectional paradigm), the former belong to "weaker", less accessible "families" than the latter do. A similar line of argument also allows one to draw a principled distinction between phonologically conditioned allomorphs (as with English –s plural marker) and morphologically (and lexically) conditioned allomorphs (as with *foot* and *feet*). Phonological allomorphs require involvement of two processes only: ordering and contextual accommodation of segmental material. Morphological allomorphs, on the other hand, call for an extra process of lexically-conditioned selection, involving a further processing cost, and making morphological allomorphs more prone to errors.

Developmental disorders offer a spacious window onto the neurobiological reality of word knowledge and its complex interaction with general cognition. In Chapter 17, Mila Vulchanova, David Saldaña and Giosué Baggio persuasively show that language disorders can hardly be associated with highly specific grammatical deficits. What may appear as a deceptively selective difficulty in language usage, such as the production of inflected regular forms by children with Language Impairment, are in fact subject to language-specific variation, depending on subtle factors such as the complexity of an inflectional system, the size, formal variety and frequency distribution of its paradigms, or the perceptual salience of morphological markers. Likewise, semantic problems in lexical development may be associated with general receptive deficits, as well as non-verbal IQ, maternal education level and language learning deficits, such as effects of increased lexical competition in the mental lexicon of language impaired children. The general emerging picture seems to suggest that the patterns of dysfunctional language behavior observed in children with language disorders reflect the complexity, subtlety and robustness of the language system, rather than a broad dissociation between language and cognition.

3 Lessons to be learned

The thoughts and evidence offered in this book elucidate a number of non-trivial methodological and theoretical points in word knowledge. By way of a summary, we recap here a few take-home points.

In approaching interdisciplinary issues in language inquiry, there is a common two-way misconception, which scholars should be aware of and warned against. On the one hand, we contend that it is simply wrong to see theoretical language models as inevitably partial and incomplete, waiting for external evidence from mind and brain sciences to validate them. On the other hand, it would be just as wrong to see psychological and neurological methods of language inquiry as invariably in need of linguistic concepts and classification criteria that were developed by theoretical models for different purposes. Both views strike us as the misconstrued, or at best preconceived, by-product of a persisting lack of disciplinary crosstalk.

In too many cases, psycho- and neurocognitive evidence seems to cut across the theoretical frontline between rival linguistic accounts. In the last few pages, we pointed out that the decade-long theoretical confrontation between Item-and-Process and Item-and-Arrangement morphologies, probably the most influential dimension of classificatory variation among competing models of word competence, proves to be orthogonal to the wealth of psycholinguistic and neurolinguistic evidence on human processing behavior accrued over the last decades. No matter whether affixes are conceived of as ontological units existing independently of lexical items and stored alongside with them, or, rather, as on-line processing effects of word production/recognition, both views can be reconciled with evidence of human selective sensitivity to lexical structure and frequency effects. This by no means implies that the theoretical distinction going back to Hockett (1954) is irrelevant. In fact, Hockett's concerns appear to be supported by the mounting awareness that, contrary to classical generative assumptions, knowledge of "what" (stored representations) and knowledge of "how" (processing principles) can hardly be decoupled in the debate on what constitutes human word knowledge (Pirrelli 2018). In the post-Bloomfieldian flourishing of word models, Hockett's prescient concerns have been largely misinterpreted as supporting some architectures for word processing at the expenses of some others.

Likewise, the use of predefined morphological categories and established theoretical frameworks to understand the physiology and development of language skills in children seems to suggest that the role of mind and brain sciences is to simply validate existing linguistic categories and theories. This is another misconception. With a few exceptions, theoretical approaches were established outside the field of child language acquisition, and, in most cases, predate it. Data and categories from linguistics are certainly key to carving out areas of language development and defining scientific objectives. Nonetheless, linguistic terms and categories should be used with extreme care in the context of language acquisition, and should be validated against the specific goals and independent methodological requirements of this research domain. The simplifying assumption that linguistic categories are, as such, a reflection of the child's mind (rather than a working hypothesis) is as dangerous as blatantly ignoring these categories.

Marr's (1982) hierarchy of epistemological levels of understanding of complex systems offers a valid methodological scaffolding for discussing interdisciplinary issues in language sciences on a principled footing. The hierarchy is useful to distinguish between knowledge of what we do when we use language (Marr's "computational" level), knowledge of how we do it (his "algorithmic" level), and knowledge of how this ability is neurobiologically "embodied" in the brain (his "implementational" level). The distinction was intended to emphasize that each such level can, in principle, be investigated independently, through its own concepts and level-specific objects of inquiry. Nonetheless, a full understanding of a complex system ultimately requires integration of multiple perspectives, with each level being assessed on its own merits, for its intended goals and limitations, but with acquisitions from one level constraining acquisitions of all other levels.

To illustrate, due to the dominant focus of theoretical linguistics on the basic units of language and the laws for their combination, linguists have laid more, if not exclusive emphasis on representation issues, with processing issues being comparatively neglected. The approach is in sharp contrast with the psycholinguistic and neurolinguistic prevalent concerns with behavioral and physiological evidence of the human processor. Pace Clahsen (2006), however, it is highly unlikely that the two perspectives can be related mutually through some form of direct correspondence. Evidence of different time-scale effects in the behavior of complex dynamic systems should warn us against the search for straightforward one-to-one relationships between either linguistic representations (Marr's computational level) and their behavioral correlates (Marr's algorithmic level), or observable processing effects (Marr's algorithmic level) and their neuroanatomical localizations (Marr's implementational level). The properties of the whole linguistic system may well be constrained and shaped by the properties of its parts. But its causal dynamics are inherently multileveled (Corning 2004). This means that the performance of each part, and its functional role, can only be understood in terms of its interaction with other parts and the whole system. Inter-level mapping rarely implies the simple extrapolation to level Y of properties holding at level X. More often, it is a matter of discovering entirely new laws and concepts, and requires a creative shift from quantitative to qualitative differentiation (Anderson 1972).

All this may sound somewhat discouraging. After all, direct inter-level relationships would be by far simpler to understand and investigate than multileveled, non-linear relationships. But there is room for some hope when it comes to language. Recent advances in the technological and analytical weaponry of language sciences promise to provide the level of material continuity between empirical data and functional modeling that constitutes an essential precondition to concrete methodological unification of neighboring language domains. Looking at the boundary between cognitive psychology and neuroscience, for example, the advent and development of neuroimaging technology permitted *in vivo* investigation of the functional interconnection between brain data and psychological evidence, thus establishing a direct explanatory link and a causal continuity between observations and hypotheses in the two domains. Likewise, cognitively-motivated computational models of language processing, however admittedly simpler than the still poorly understood human mechanisms they are intended to simulate, may assist scientists in decomposing a complex process into a handful of interacting sub-processes, and may enable carrying out experiments under more favorable and controlled conditions than those holding for experiments with human subjects. Decade-long developments in Recurrent Neural Networks learning complex language units have proved instrumental in addressing a few open issues about the psychological nature of classical linguistic categories and basic units. In particular, the connectionist idea that storage and processing are two interlocked steps of a unique learning dynamic appears to provide an elegant solution to the linguistic conundrum of the appropriate ontological status of sublexical constituents (as either storage or processing units). This unifying view lends support to Poggio's (2010) claim that (language) learning is key to the appropriate methodological unification of Marr's epistemological levels. Accordingly, units in language crucially depend on the way they are acquired, organized and used by humans. Any form of ontological realism is, in this connection, rather dubious.

On a more analytical front, linear and non-linear regression models for the quantitative scrutiny of multifactorial language data, have considerably freed language data collection from the strict methodological constraints of prior hypothesis testing, dispensing with the need for a tightly controlled and balanced protocol of data elicitation based on a clear experimental design. Such freedom in data elicitation, combined with the huge support of information and communication technologies to digital storage and cooperative efforts for data creation, has spawned the innovative development of "megastudies" (Keuleers and Marelli 2020, this volume) specifically designed to maximize utility, availability and reusability of behavioral data.

In our view, all these developments will have an increasingly large impact on data modeling for linguistic and psycholinguistic research. In a similar vein, distributional semantic models (Acquaviva et al. 2020, this volume; Jones et al. 2015; Landauer and Dumais 1997; Mikolov et al. 2013) have proved to be able to quantitatively assess the role of linguistic context in shaping word meanings, and in guiding speakers' expectations about the typical events nouns participate in, and the typical arguments verbs subcategorize for. Accordingly, a distributional, graded interpretation of word meaning similarity is bound to have a considerable impact on psycholinguistic accounts of morpho-semantic opacity/transparency effects in word processing (Dressler 2005; Kilani-Schoch and Dressler 2005; Mayerthaler 1981), moving away from Frege's (1891) logical principle of compositionality, according to which an expression is either fully transparent or opaque. In Marelli, Gagné and Spalding's (2017) CAOSS model, for example, relational effects in compound interpretation are modeled as the by-product of nuanced operations across patterns of word distributions.

Similarly, the information theoretic notion of entropy has been used to model the discriminative power of words in context, thereby offering a quantitative measure of the elusive notion of salience against a background of contextual events (Keuleers et al. 2020, this volume). In addition, the *Low Entropy Conjecture* (Ackerman and Malouf 2013) is based on the role of implicative paradigmatic relations in allowing speakers to infer an unseen inflected form from its paradigm companions. The fact that, cross-linguistically, inflectional paradigms tend to exhibit low expected conditional entropy, i.e. low uncertainty in intra-paradigmatic inference, can thus be interpreted as meeting some basic learnability requirements. Once more, insights from information theory and from computational modeling of usage-based theories have made it possible to see competing views and diverging perspectives subjected to critical assessment on experimental grounds. We welcome this as an important precondition to rapid progress in the field.

To our knowledge, no other existing single publication covers, in such a highly complementary and interdisciplinary way, as many different approaches to word knowledge and usage as the present volume does. We are deeply grateful to all contributing authors for sharing with us the view that interdisciplinary crosstalk is indeed possible, and for taking much of their time and effort to prove its merits. We believe that this book will be beneficial for diverse types of readers and we hope its open access publication will make its impact and influence wide and durable. Young researchers, who already see a clear advantage in the synergic integration of traditionally segregated competences, will find, here, useful material and pointers for developing a truly interdisciplinary curriculum. Single-domain specialists, interested in knowing more about how their expertise can contribute to understanding issues of common interest when approached by other disciplines, will look for methodological guidelines and open issues to be investigated through interdisciplinary cooperation. Finally, both specialist and non-specialist readers will be offered easily accessible, state-of-the-art information, covering interconnected areas of lexical expertise that are rarely discussed and comparatively assessed within a single book.

Acknowledgments: We gratefully acknowledge the European Science Foundation Research Networking Programmes, and the former ESF Standing Committee for the Humanities for their great foresight and support, and for making it possible to publish the present editorial effort as an open access volume with generous funding of the NetWordS project in the years 2011–2015. We express our hope that similar programmes will continue to be launched and funded in Europe in the years to come.

References

Ackerman, Farrell & Robert Malouf. 2013. Morphological organization: the low conditional entropy conjecture. *Language* 89. 429–464.
Arnon, Inbal, Stewart M. McCauley & Morten H. Christiansen. 2017. Digging up the building blocks of language: Age-of-acquisition effect for multiword phrases. *Journal of Memory and Language* 92. 265–280.
Arnon, Inbal & Neal Snider. 2010. More than words: frequency effects for multiword phrases. *Journal of Memory and Language* 62. 67–82.
Anderson, Philip W. 1972. More Is Different. *Science* 4047 (177). 393–396.
Bannard, Colin & Danielle E. Matthews. 2008. Stored word sequences in language learning: the effect of familiarity on children's repetition of four-word combinations. *Psychological Science* 19 (3). 241–248.
Baroni, Marco, Emiliano Guevara and Vito Pirrelli. 2007. NN compounds in Italian: modelling category induction and analogical extension. *Lingue e Linguaggio*, 6 (2). 263–290.
Ben Shalom, Dorit & David Poeppel. 2008. Functional anatomic models of language: assembling the pieces. *The Neuroscientist* 14 (1). 119–127.
Berger, Adam L., Vincent J. Della Pietra & Stephen A. Della Pietra. 1996. A maximum entropy approach to natural language processing. *Computational linguistics* 22 (1). 39–71.

Brown-Schmidt, Sarah. 2009. The role of executive function in perspective taking during online language comprehension. *Psychonomic Bulletin and Review* 16 (5). 893–900.
Clahsen, Harald. 2006. Linguistic perspectives on morphological processing. In Dieter Wunderlich (ed.), *Advances in the Theory of the Lexicon*, 355–388. Mouton De Gruyter.
Corning, Peter A. 2004. *Holistic Darwinism*. University of Chicago Press.
Davis, Matthew H. 2015. The Neurobiology of Lexical Access. In Gregory Hickok & Steven L. Small (eds.), *Neurobiology of Language*, 541–555. Associated Press.
D'Esposito, Mark. 2007. From cognitive to neural models of working memory. *Philosophical Transactions of the Royal Society of London B: Biological Sciences* 362 (1481). 761–772.
Dressler, Wolfgang U. 2005. Word-formation in Natural Morphology. In Pavol Štekauer & Rochelle Lieber (eds.), *Handbook of Word Formation*, 267–284. Springer.
Elman, Jeffrey L. 2004. An alternative view of the mental lexicon. *Trends in Cognitive Sciences* 8 (7). 301–306.
Elman, Jeffrey L. 2009. On the Meaning of Words and Dinosaur Bones: Lexical Knowledge Without a Lexicon. *Cognitive Science* 33. 1–36.
Ferro, Marcello, Dimitri Ognibene, Giovanni Pezzulo & Vito Pirrelli. 2010. Reading as active sensing: a computational model of gaze planning during word recognition. *Frontiers in Neurorobotics* 4 (6).
Frege Gottlob. 1891. *Funktion und Begriff*. Pohle.
Grimm, Robert, Giovanni Cassani, Steven Gillis & Walter Daelemans. 2017. Facilitatory Effects of Multi-Word Units in Lexical Processing and Word Learning: A Computational Investigation. *Frontiers in Psychology* 8 (555).
Hasson, Uri, Giovanni Egidi, Marco Marelli & Roel M. Willems. 2018. Grounding the neurobiology of language in first principles: The necessity of non-language-centric explanations for language comprehension. *Cognition* 180. 135–157.
Hickok, Gregory & David Poeppel. 2004. Dorsal and ventral streams: a framework for understanding aspects of the functional anatomy of language. *Cognition* 92. 67–99.
Hockett, Charles F. 1954. Two models of grammatical description. *Word*, 10. 210–231.
Huettig, Falk. 2015. Four central questions about prediction in language processing. *Brain Research* 1626. 118–135.
Jackendoff, Ray. 2000. Fodorian Modularity and Representational Modularity. In Yosef Grodzinsky, Lewis P. Shapiro & David Swinney (eds.), *Language and the Brain. Representation and Processing*, 3–30. San Diego: Academic Press.
Jackendoff, Ray. 2002. *Foundations of Language: Brain, Meaning, Grammar, Evolution*. Oxford University Press.
Jackendoff, Ray. 2007. *Language, Consciousness, Culture: Essays on Mental Structures*. The MIT Press.
Jones, Michael N., Jon A. Willits & Simon Dennis. 2015. Models of Semantic Memory. In Jerome R. Busemeyer, Zheng Wang, James T. Townsend & Ami Eidels (eds.), *Oxford Handbook of Mathematical and Computational Psychology*, 232–254. (Oxford Library of Psychology). Oxford University Press. https://doi.org/10.1093/oxfordhb/9780199957996.013.11
Kilani-Schoch, Marianne, Ingrida Balčiunienė, Katharina Korecky Kröll, Sabine Laaha & Wolfgang U. Dressler. 2009. On the role of pragmatics in child-directed speech for the acquisition of verb morphology. *Journal of Pragmatics* 41. 219–239.
Kilani-Schoch, Marianne & Wolfgang U. Dressler. 2005. *Morphologie naturelle et flexion du verbe français*. Narr.

Kukona, Anuenue, Shin-Yi Fang, Karen A. Aicher, Helen Chen & James S. Magnuson. 2011. The time course of anticipatory constraint integration. *Cognition* 119 (1). 23–42.

Kuperberg, Gina R. & T. Florian Jaeger. 2016. What do we mean by prediction in language comprehension? *Language, Cognition and Neuroscience* 31 (1). 32–59.

Landauer, Thomas K. & Susan T. Dumais. 1997. A solution to Plato's problem: The latent semantic analysis theory of acquisition, induction, and representation of knowledge. *Psychological Review* 104 (2). 211–240.

Libben Gary. 2005. Everything is psycholinguistics: Material and methodological considerations in the study of compound processing. *Canadian Journal of Linguistics* 50. 267–283.

Libben, Gary. 2016. The quantum metaphor and the organization of words in the mind. *Journal of Cultural Cognitive Science* 1. 49–55.

Marelli, Marco, Christina L. Gagné & Thomas L. Spalding. 2017. Compounding as Abstract Operation in Semantic Space: Investigating relational effects through a large-scale, data-driven computational model. *Cognition* 166. 207–224.

Marr, David (1982). *Vision*. San Francisco: W.H. Freeman.

Mattiello, Elisa. 2017. *Analogy in Word Formation. A study of English neologisms and occasionalisms*. De Gruyter.

Mayerthaler, Willi. 1981. *Morphologische Natuerlichkeit*. Athenaeum.

Mitchell, Jeff & Mirella Lapata. 2010. Composition in distributional models of semantics. *Cognitive science* 34 (8). 1388–1429.

Mikolov, Tomas, Ilya Sutskever, Kai Chen, Greg S. Corrado, & Jeffrey Dean. 2013. Distributed representations of words and phrases and their compositionality. In Christopher J. C. Burges, Leon Bottou, Zoubin Ghahramani & Kilian Q. Weinberger (eds.), *Advances in Neural Information Processing Systems 26: 27th Annual Conference on Neural Information Processing Systems 2013*, 3111–3119.

Milligan, Karen, Janet Wilde Astington & Lisa Ain Dack. 2007. Language and theory of mind: meta-analysis of the relation between language ability and false-belief understanding. *Child Development* 78 (2). 622–646.

Pickering, Martin J. & Simon Garrod. 2007. Do people use language production to make predictions during comprehension? *Trends in Cognitive Sciences* 11 (3). 105–110.

Pickering, Martin J. & Simon Garrod. 2013. An integrated theory of language production and comprehension. *Behavioral and Brain Sciences* 36. 329–392.

Pirrelli, Vito. 2007. Psycho-computational issues in morphology learning and processing. An overture. *Lingue e Linguaggio* 6 (2). 131–138.

Pirrelli, Vito. 2018. Morphological Theory and computational linguistics. In Jenny Audring & Francesca Masini (eds.), *The Oxford Handbook of Morphological Theory*, 573–593. Oxford University Press.

Plag, Ingo. 2018. *Word-formation in English*. Cambridge University Press.

Price, Cathy J. 2010. The anatomy of language: a review of 100 fMRI studies published in 2009. *Annals of the New York Academy of Sciences* 1191 (1). 62–88.

Price, Cathy J. 2012. A review and synthesis of the first 20years of PET and fMRI studies of heard speech, spoken language and reading. *Neuroimage* 62 (2). 816–847.

Price, Cathy J. 2017. The evolution of cognitive models: From neuropsychology to neuroimaging and back. *Cortex* 107. 37–49.

Poggio, Tomaso. 2010. Afterword. Marr's Vision and Computational Neuroscience. In David Marr, *Vision*, 362–367. MIT Press.

Riest, Carina, Annett B. Jorschick & Jan P. de Ruiter. 2015. Anticipation in turn-taking: mechanisms and information sources. *Frontiers in Psychology*, 6: art. 89.

Saxton, Matthew. 2008. What's in a name? Coming to terms with the child's linguistic environment. *Journal of Child Language* 35 (3). 677–686.

Saxton, Matthew. 2009. The inevitability of Child Directed Speech. In Susan Foster-Cohen (ed.), *Language acquisition*, 62–86. Palgrave Macmillan.

Seidenberg, Mark S., Maryellen C. MacDonald. 1999. A Probabilistic Constraints Approach to Language Acquisition and Processing. *Cognitive Science* 23 (4). 569–588.

Siyanova-Chanturia, Anna, Kathy Conklin, Sendy Caffarra & Edith Kaan. 2017. Representation and processing of multi-word expressions in the brain. *Brain and Language* 175. 111–122.

Smith, Nathaniel J. & Roger Levy. 2013. The effect of word predictability on reading time is logarithmic. *Cognition* 128 (3). 302–319.

Spivey, Michael & Michael K. Tanenhaus. 1998. Syntactic ambiguity resolution in discourse: Modelling the effects of referential context and lexical frequency. Journal of Experimental Psychology Learning Memory and Cognition 24 (6). 1521–1543.

Tabor, Whitney & Michael K. Tanenhaus. 1999. Dynamical Models of Sentence Processing. *Cognitive Science* 23 (4). 491–515.

Taylor, Nicole, Wilberta Donovan, Sally Miles & Lewis Leavitt. 2009. Maternal control strategies, maternal language usage and children's language usage at two years. *Journal of Child Language* 36 (2). 381–404.

Tremblay, Antoine & R. Harald Baayen. 2010. Holistic processing of regular four-word sequences: A behavioral and ERP study of the effects of structure, frequency, and probability on immediate free recall. In David Wood (ed.), *Perspectives on formulaic language: Acquisition and communication*, 151–173. Bloomsbury Publishing.

Vespignani, Francesco, Paolo Canal, Nicola Molinaro, Sergio Fonda & Cristina Cacciari. 2009. Predictive Mechanisms in Idiom Comprehension. *Journal of Cognitive Neuroscience* 22 (8). 1682–1700.

Wellman, Henry M. 2002. Understanding the psychological world: Developing a theory of mind. In Usha Goswami (ed.), *Handbook of childhood cognitive development*, 167–187. Oxford, England: Blackwell.

Part 1: **Technologies, tools and data**

Vito Pirrelli, Claudia Marzi, Marcello Ferro,
Franco Alberto Cardillo, Harald R. Baayen and Petar Milin

Psycho-computational modelling of the mental lexicon

A discriminative learning perspective

Abstract: Over the last decades, a growing body of evidence on the mechanisms governing lexical storage, access, acquisition and processing has questioned traditional models of language architecture and word usage based on the hypothesis of a direct correspondence between modular components of grammar competence (lexicon vs. rules), processing correlates (memory vs. computation) and neuro-anatomical localizations (prefrontal vs. temporo-parietal perisylvian areas of the left hemisphere). In the present chapter, we explore the empirical and theoretical consequences of a distributed, integrative model of the mental lexicon, whereby words are seen as emergent properties of the functional interaction between basic, language-independent processing principles and the language-specific nature and organization of the input. From this perspective, language learning appears to be inextricably related to the way language is processed and internalized by the speakers, and key to an interdisciplinary understanding of such a way, in line with Tomaso Poggio's suggestion that the development of a cognitive skill is causally and ontogenetically prior to its execution (and sits "on top of it"). In particular, we discuss conditions, potential and prospects of the epistemological continuity between psycholinguistic and computational modelling of word learning, and illustrate the yet largely untapped potential of their integration. We use David Marr's hierarchy to clarify the complementarity of the two viewpoints. Psycholinguistic models are informative about how speakers learn to use language (interfacing Marr's levels 1 and 2). When we move from the psycholinguistic analysis of the functional operations involved in language learning to an algorithmic description of how they are computed, computer simulations can help us explore the relation between speakers' behavior and general learning principles in more detail. In the end, psycho-computational

---

Vito Pirrelli, Claudia Marzi, Marcello Ferro, Franco Alberto Cardillo, Italian National Research Council (CNR), Institute for Computational Linguistics, Pisa, Italy
Harald R. Baayen, Eberhard Karls University, Seminar für Sprachwissenschaft/Quantitative Linguistics Sprachwissenschaft/Quantitative Linguistics, Tübingen, Germany
Petar Milin, University of Birmingham, Department of Modern Languages, Edgbaston, Birmingham, UK

Open Access. © 2020 Vito Pirrelli et al., published by De Gruyter. This work is licensed under a Creative Commons Attribution-NonCommercial-NoDerivatives 4.0 International License.
https://doi.org/10.1515/9783110440577-002

models can be instrumental to bridge Marr's levels 2 and 3, bringing us closer to understanding the nature of word knowledge in the brain.

Keywords: mental lexicon, word storage and processing, psycholinguistics, computational linguistics, connectionist models, discriminative learning

1 Introduction

1.1 Motivation and historical background

Over the past 30 years, theoretical and applied linguistics, cognitive psychology and neuroscience have gradually shifted their research focus on language knowledge from discipline-specific issues to a broader range of shared interests, questions and goals. This has been particularly true in the domain of lexical knowledge since the mid-eighties, when the Parallel Distributed Processing (PDP) group simulated non-linear developmental trajectories in child acquisition of the English past tense, moving away from traditional box-and-arrow models to data-driven computer simulations of emergent phenomena (Rumelhart and McClelland 1986). The trend was concomitant with other important developments in this area. The dichotomy between data and programming, reflected in the contrast between static lexical items and dynamic rules of grammar (as in Pinker's "Words and Rules" approach, Pinker and Prince 1988, 1994) has progressively given way to more integrative views of the lexicon as a dynamic store of words in context, where basic levels of language representation (sound, syntax and meaning) are interfaced and co-organized into context-sensitive "chunks" (Jackendoff 2002; Goldberg 2006; Booij 2010). Accordingly, human brains must "contain" not only morphologically simple words, but also inflected and derived forms, compound words, light verb constructions, collocations, idioms, proverbs, social routine clichés and all sorts of ready-made, routinized sequences, maximizing processing opportunities (Libben 2005), augmenting the human working memory capacity (Baddeley 1986), and having distinct frequency/familiarity effects on processing (see Baayen et al. 2007; Kuperman et al. 2009; Tremblay and Baayen 2010, among others).

Probably, the best known assumption in morphological inquiry is the hypothesis that word processing is a form of algebraic calculus, based on the combination/composition of sublexical building blocks called "morphemes" (e.g. *will-*, *-ing*, *-ness*, *un-*), traditionally conceived of as minimal linguistic signs, or irreducible form-meaning pairs, according to an influential terminology whose roots can be traced back to Bloomfield's work (1933).[1] Besides, the content of a morphologically complex word is assumed to be a function of the meaningful contribution of each of its internal morphemes. This assumption is part of a very influential view on language processing as the result of a staged sequence of processing steps and intermediate, hierarchically arranged representations: from sounds to syllables, morphemes, words and beyond. At each step, intermediate representations are output and fed into upper representation levels. In particular, morphemes are credited with playing an active role in word recognition and production.

These assumptions are usually bundled together. Effects of morpheme boundaries on word processing are often coupled with the hypothesis that morphemes are stored and accessed as independent, atomic linguistic signs, making the lexicon a redundancy-free store of simple, irreducible items. In addition, morphemes are assumed to be involved in processing prior to word identification/production. In fact, as we will see in the following sections, the involvement of morpheme-like structures in word processing is not necessarily staged prior to word access, and it does not imply, per se, further assumptions such as form-meaning pairing and strong compositionality. Besides, the linguistic status of the morpheme is confronted with a number of theoretical difficulties (Matthews 1991), suggesting that other relations than just the simple position of a sublexical constituent within an input word may influence human word knowledge. In particular, many studies in the framework of Word and Paradigm Morphology have challenged the idea that morphemes are the atomic units of morphological analysis, suggesting that full words represent basic building blocks in their own right (Anderson 1992; Aronoff 1994; Beard 1995; Booij 2010; Blevins 2016; Marzi et al. 2020, this volume). This has led to a radical reconceptualization of the role of morphemes in word processing that received indirect support by work in computational morphology (Pirrelli 2018). As we will see in more detail in the ensuing sections, computer modelling of morphological processes can shed light on dynamic aspects of language organization that would otherwise elude scientific inquiry. For example, the idea that linguistic structure can emerge through self-organization of unstructured input is nowadays key to our understanding of a number of issues in language acquisition (Bybee and Hopper 2001; Ellis and Larsen-Freeman 2006; MacWhinney 1999; MacWhinney and O'Grady 2015). Nonetheless, it had to await the challenging test of successful computer simulations before it could be given wide currency in the acquisitional literature. As will be argued more extensively in the following

---

1 Note, however, that only post-Bloomfieldian accounts translated Bloomfield's idea that complex lexical forms can be analyzed into simple constituents (morphemes) into the hypothesis that lexical forms can be reconstructed starting from their independently stored, simple parts (Blevins 2016; Blevins et al. 2016).

section, by giving center stage to processing issues, computational morphology and psycholinguistic approaches to word knowledge have in fact much more in common than ever acknowledged in the past.

1.2 Computational Linguistics & Psycholinguistics: conditions for a methodological unification

Computational Linguistics (CL) and Psycholinguistics (PL) share a broad range of interests and goals. CL is chiefly concerned with computer-based simulations of how language is understood, produced and learned. Simulations are running models of language performance, implemented as sets of instructions performing specific tasks on a computer. They commonly require a precise algorithmic characterization of aspects of language processing that are often neglected by language theories, such as the encoding of input data, the structure of output representations, the basic operations of word segmentation, storage, access, retrieval and assembly of intermediate representations (e.g. Clark et al. 2010).

In a similar vein, PL focuses on the cognitive mechanisms and representations that are known to underlie language processing in the mind or brain of a speaker. Traditionally, PL uses experiments with human subjects to obtain measures of language behavior as response variables. In a typical lexical decision experiment, a speaker is asked to decide, as quickly and accurately as possible, whether a written form shown on a computer screen for a short time (or, alternatively, its acoustically rendered pronunciation) is a word in her language or not. The researcher controls and manipulates the factors that are hypothesized to be involved in the processing task, to measure the extent to which factor manipulation affects processing performance in terms of response time and accuracy. Of late, PL more and more often incorporates evidence from neural experimentation, measuring brain activity more directly as it unfolds during the task (e.g. Spivey et al. 2012; Marangolo and Papagno 2020, this volume).

In spite of their shared concerns, however, CL and PL have traditionally developed remarkably different approaches, principles and goals. The impact of information and communication technologies on language inquiry has spawned a myriad of successful commercial applications (from speech recognition and speech synthesis, to machine translation, information retrieval and knowledge extraction), laying more emphasis on optimizing the computational properties of parsing algorithms, such as their time and space complexity, and efficiency in task completion. This technological trend has, however, parceled out language usage into a fragmentary constellation of small sub-problems and ad hoc software solutions, proposed independently of one another.

Conversely, psycholinguistic models approach language as resulting from the interaction of both language specific functions (e.g. word co-activation and competition) and general-purpose cognitive functions (e.g. long-term storage, sensory-motor integration, rehearsal, executive control). Different global effects in the operation of low-level interactive processes are investigated as the by-products of specific levels of input representations (e.g. phonological, morpho-syntactic or semantic levels), giving rise to autonomous, self-organizing effects. Psycholinguistic models are also aimed to investigate under what conditions language processing can be found to perform sub-optimally, with inherent limitations, occasional errors and possible breakdowns of the human language processor being just as important to understand as processing efficiency and performance optimization (Berg 2020, this volume; Vulchanova, Saldaña and Baggio 2020, this volume).

The apparent divergence in the way CL and PL are concerned with issues of language performance, however, has not precluded growing awareness of their potential for synergy. We already mentioned the important role that seminal work by Rumelhart, McClelland and the Parallel Distributed Processing (PDP) group played in the mid-eighties in re-orienting the research focus on language processing away from algorithmic issues. We will consider the legacy of connectionism and its persisting influence on current models of lexical competence in the ensuing sections in more detail. Here, we would like to focus very briefly on the implications of the connectionist revolution for the methodological interaction between CL and PL.

Following the PDP success story, the question of how rules carry out computations in language, and what types of rules are needed for linguistic computations, stopped to be the exclusive concern of CL. In fact, emphasis on language learning slowly shifted the research spotlight on the more fundamental issue of how a speaker develops the computations and representations used by the brain from the experience of the natural world. This shift has two important methodological consequences. First, even if we assume (following traditional wisdom) that sentences are made of phrases, phrases of words and words of morphemes, and that language processing is an algebraic calculus combining smaller units into larger ones, the central question that must be addressed is how basic combinatorial units are acquired in the first place. Words, phrases and utterances are not given, but they should be investigated as dynamic processes, emerging from interrelated patterns of sensory experience, communicative and social interaction and psychological and neurobiological mechanisms (Elman 2009). Secondly, if both combinatorial rules and units are acquired, what are the principles underlying (i) rule learning and (ii) the intake/development of input representations during learning? In the scientific pursuit for ultimate explanatory mechanisms, learning principles informing our capacity to adaptively use regularities from experience are better candidates than regularities themselves. In the end, we may ignore what rules consist of and what representations they manipulate, or even wonder whether rules and representations exist at all (questions that have animated much of the contemporary debate on language and cognition). Investigation of the basic neurocognitive functions (e.g., serial perception, storage, alignment, to mention but a few) that allow for the language input to be processed and acquired strikes us as an inescapable precondition to understanding what we know when we know a language. In this connection, learning represents a fundamental level of meta-cognition where PL and CL can successfully meet.

1.2.1 Marr's hierarchy

Tomaso Poggio, one the pioneers of computer vision, has recently suggested (2010, 2012) that *learning* should be added to Marr's classical hierarchy of levels of understanding of complex processing systems (Marr 1982). The original Marr's hierarchy defined three such levels:

(1) the *computational level*, answering the "semantic" question "what does it do?", by providing a precise characterization of what types of functions and operations are to be computed for a specific cognitive process to be carried out successfully;

(2) the *algorithmic level*, answering the "syntactic" question "how does it do it?", by specifying how computation takes place in terms of detailed equations and programming instructions;

(3) the *implementation level*, stating how representations and algorithms are actually realized at the physical level (e.g. as electronic circuits or patterns of neurobiological connectivity).[2]

Poggio argues that learning sits on top of Marr's computational level, as it allows us to replicate the ability of performing a particular task (e.g. object

---

[2] Computer terminology plays, nowadays, a much more pervasive role than it did in the 70s and early 80s. Adjectives like "computational" and "implementational", which are common terminological currency in today's information sciences, were used by Marr in a different, more literal sense. In a contemporary adaptation of Marr's terminology, the "computational level" can arguably be translated into "functional" or "architectural level". Similarly, his "implementational level" could more readily be understood as referring to a "(bio-)physical level". This would avoid, among other things, the potential confusion arising when we ascribe "computer modelling" (and CL) to Marr's "algorithmic level" (rather than to his "computational level"). We decided to stick to Marr's original terminology nonetheless, and tried to avoid terminological clashes by using terms unambiguously in context.

identification) in machines "even without an understanding of which algorithms and specific constraints are exploited". This gives a special status to the study of machine learning and explains much of its influence in various areas of computer science and in today's computational neuroscience (Poggio 2010: 367). From our perspective, machine learning and statistical models of language have made an essential contribution in breaking a relatively new, interdisciplinary middle ground, for CL and PL to meet and profitably interact. But what is the ultimate goal of this interaction? Is it methodologically well founded?

Marr introduced his hierarchy to emphasize that explanations at different levels can be investigated largely independently of each other. A language engineer can automatically process large quantities of text data, disregarding how difficult they are for a human speaker to process. A neuroscientist can describe the biophysics of oscillations in the neural activity of cortical areas, and ignore how these oscillations can possibly map onto higher-level processing functions. However, full understanding of a complex system requires tight inter-level interaction. In the spirit of computational neuroscience, one must eventually understand what kind of computations are performed by oscillations, and what algorithm controls them.

We agree with Poggio (2012) that it is time to clarify the potential for between-level interaction in Marr's hierarchy, and investigate the methodological conditions for their appropriate integration. It has been observed (Alvargonzáles 2011) that interdisciplinary convergence requires operational, material continuity between the objects of investigation of neighboring scientific fields. Trivially, using the same battery of formal/mathematical methods and functions to model as diverse empirical domains as mechanics, economy or epidemiology, does not make the boundaries between these domains any closer. Only if we can clarify the role of formal psycholinguistic models of language processing and computer simulations along Marr's hierarchy, we can establish a material common ground between PL and CL, and, ultimately, assess the potential for their unification.

1.2.2 Complementarity and integration

In a classical psycholinguistic experiment, scholars aim to understand more of the architecture and functioning principles of the human language processor by investigating human language behavior in highly controlled conditions. From this standpoint, the human processor represents a "black box" (the research *explanandum*), whose internal organization and principles are inferred through observation of overt behavioral variables (the *explanans*). The approach of psycholinguistic inquiry can thus be described in terms of *abductive inference*, whereby underlying causes are studied and understood by analyzing their overt effects.[3]

Conversely, experiments conducted by implementing and running computer simulations of a specific language task can be used to understand more of the human processing behavior by testing the mechanisms that are assumed to be the *cause* of this behavior. Suppose that we want to model how speakers learn to process words as a dynamic process of optimal resolution of multiple, parallel (and possibly conflicting) constraints on complex lexical structures (Seidenberg and MacDonald 1999). In this case, a parallel processing architecture represents our *explanans*, designed and implemented to combine top-down expectations (based on past input evidence) with the on-line bottom-up requirements of current input stimuli. If successful, the simulator should be able to replicate aspects of human language behavior.

Such a methodological complementarity between CL and PL enables us to establish an effective continuity between observations and hypotheses. Abductively inferred functions in the human processor can be simulated through a piece of programming code replicating human results on a comparable set of test data. But replicating results is of little explanatory power unless we understand why and how simulations are successful (Marzi and Pirrelli 2015). The real insights often come from examining the way problems are solved algorithmically, how they are affected by changes in data distribution or parameter setting, and by observing the interaction between these changes and principles that were not specified by the original psycholinguistic model, but had to be implemented for the computational model to carry out a specific task. We can then check these new insights back on human subjects, and make abductive reasoning and computer modelling interact for our level of knowledge to scale up along Marr's hierarchy. Ultimately, simulations should be able to incorporate requirements coming from Marr's implementational level, and make processing mechanisms match what is known about the neurophysiological principles supporting language processing. From this perspective, computational modelling cannot only provide a framework for psycholinguistic theories to be tested, but can also bridge the gap between high-level psycholinguistic and cognitive functions, and low-level interactive brain processes.

---

[3] Abductive inference, also known as "inference to the best explanation", must be distinguished from both deductive and inductive inference. Deductive reasoning allows deriving *b* from *a* only when *b* is a formal logical consequence of *a*. Inductive reasoning allows inferring *b* from *a*, by way of a logically unnecessary generalization: if one has experience of white swans only, one can (wrongly) believe that all swans are white. Abductive reasoning allows inferring *a* as a possible explanation of *b*. If you glance an apple falling from a tree, you can abduce (rather uneconomically) that someone hidden in the tree leaves is dropping apples to the ground.

To sum up, by describing and interpreting the behavior of a speaker performing a certain task, psycholinguistic models help us bridge the gap between Marr's computational (i.e. "what the speaker does") and algorithmic level (i.e. "how she does it"). On the other hand, by simulating how the same problems are solved by a computer, machine learning models can help us test psycholinguistic models algorithmically. If algorithmic results prove to match human results, and if the implemented mechanisms can be mapped onto high-level aspects of human behavior to make independent predictions about it, progress is made. Finally, if algorithmic models are implemented to incorporate neurobiologically grounded processing principles, we make progress in filling the gap between Marr's algorithmic and implementation levels.

In this section, we discussed the methodological conditions for a fruitful interaction between PL and CL approaches to language processing, in line with Marr's original idea that a full scientific theory of a complex processing system requires understanding its computational, algorithmic and biophysical levels and making predictions at all such levels. In the following section, we will selectively overview a few psycholinguistic and algorithmic models of the mental lexicon, with a view to exploring concrete prospects for methodological unification in the context of language learning. As a final methodological remark, it is important to be clear on where we agree and where we disagree with Poggio's claims. We think that Poggio is right in emphasizing that, from an ontogenetic perspective, learning how to execute a cognitive task is temporally and causally prior to task execution. Besides, understanding how the task is learned is inextricably related to the way the task is executed, and is key to understanding such a way. However, this hierarchy of (meta-)cognitive levels is concerned with their ontogenetic and possibly phylogenetic relationships (e.g. in connection with evolutionary changes of biological processing systems), and has little to do with Marr's hierarchy. In our view (unlike Poggio's), learning does not sit on top of Marr's levels, but can better be analyzed and understood *through* each of them.

2 Psycho-computational models of the mental lexicon: A selective overview

2.1 Morpheme-based and a-morphous models

For decades, issues of lexical processing, access and organization have been investigated by focusing on aspects of the internal structure of complex words (Bloomfield 1933; Bloch 1947; Chomsky and Halle 1968; Lieber 1980; Selkirk 1984).

According to the classical generative view, words are made up out of morphemes. A repository of sublexical constituents accounts for the ways morphologically complex words are mutually related in the speaker's' mind. For example, the theory of speech production developed by Levelt et al. (1999) assumes that only irreducible forms are stored in the lexicon as separate entries, thus providing a psycholinguistic model of this view.

The generative approach goes back to an "Item and Arrangement" view of morphological competence (Hockett 1954), and was influenced by the dominant computer metaphor of the 50s, equating the human language processor to a processing device coupled with highly efficient retrieval procedures (Baayen 2007). Since morphemes were understood as sign-based units, which capture the minimal patterns of recurrence of form and meaning in our vocabulary, they were conceived of as potential access units of the mental lexicon. These assumptions boil down to what Blevins (2006) termed a *constructive approach* to morphological theory, where roots/stems (and possibly affixes) are the basic building blocks of morphological competence, in a largely redundancy-free lexicon. This is contrasted with an *abstractive approach*, according to which full word forms are the building blocks of morphological competence, and recurrent sublexical parts define *abstractions* over full forms.

Since early work in the lexicalist framework (Halle 1973; Jackendoff 1975; Aronoff 1976; Scalise 1984), it was clear that morphological rules might not be heavily involved in *on-line* word processing (see Fábregas and Penke 2020, this volume). Besides, despite its attractiveness and simplicity, the constructive idea that morphemes play a fundamental role as representational units in the mental lexicon has met a number of theoretical, computational and psycholinguistic difficulties (Blevins 2016). In the psycholinguistic literature, this awareness led to a sweeping reappraisal of the role of morphemes in language usage, and prompted a flourishing number of diverse theoretical perspectives on the mental lexicon.

Psycholinguistic models in the '70s (Becker 1980; Rubenstein et al. 1970, 1971; Snodgrass and Jarvella 1972) investigated the idea that lexical units compete for recognition. Token frequency of single input forms, type frequency of related forms (size of morpho-lexical families) and their relative probabilistic distribution, were shown to affect the way lexical units are matched against an input stimulus, with high-frequency units being checked earlier for matching than low-frequency units are. In line with this evidence, it was suggested that morpheme-based representations do not provide an alternative to full word listing in lexical organization, but are rather complementary access units to whole words. We can mention at least four different views of the role of sublexical units in the morphological lexicon:

(i) as permanent access units to full words, speeding up lexical access/retrieval (Taft and Forster 1975; Taft 1994, 2004);
(ii) as fallback processing routes, in case of failure to access fully-inflected lexical entries (Caramazza et al. 1988);
(iii) as pre-lexical processing routes, running in parallel with full-word access routes, and competing with the latter in a race for lexical access (Schreuder and Baayen 1995);
(iv) as post-lexical meaningful formal cores reflecting inter-word relationships in so-called morphological families (Giraudo and Grainger 2000; Grainger et al. 1991).

As a radical departure from a morpheme-centered view of the mental lexicon, other lexical models were put forward that appeared to dispense altogether with the idea that lexical access is mediated by sublexical constituents. Morton's (1969, 1970, 1979) original logogen model and its updates were apparently influenced by feature detection models of visual object recognition, based on the parallel activation of competing "demons" (neurons), dedicated to perform processing of specific input features, and "yelling" for primacy (Selfridge 1959). Morton's demons, named "logogens", were conceived of as specialized word receptors, accumulating sensory properties of linguistic stimuli and outputting their own response (e.g. a single word form) when accumulated properties (e.g. semantic, visual or acoustic features) rose above a threshold value.

The Parallel Distributed Processing (or PDP) way to connectionism in the eighties (Rumelhart et al. 1986) followed in Morton's footsteps, to popularize the idea that the lexical processor consists of a network of parallel processing nodes (functionally equivalent to neuron clusters) selectively firing in response to sensory stimuli (McClelland and Elman 1986; Norris 1994; Rumelhart and McClelland 1986). Accordingly, word production was modelled as a mapping function between two levels of representation, consisting of the input and output layers of processing nodes in a multi-layered neural network: namely, the level of morpho-lexical content (consisting of lexical meanings and morpho-syntactic features), and the level of surface form (strings of letters or sounds). For example, given an appropriate encoding of the base form *go* and the feature PAST on the input layer, this representation is mapped onto the string *went* on the output layer.

The PDP model explicitly implemented an assumption that was common to most psycholinguistic models of the lexicon; namely the idea that, when a word is input, multiple access units are activated in parallel. Levels of co-activation depend on the degree of fit between the incoming input and each lexical unit represented in the lexicon, and is modulated by the prior probability of input representations, estimated with their relative frequency of occurrence. Word recognition and production are guided by competition among similar representations (or lexical neighbors), whose influence on the process is a function of their number (or neighborhood density), their independent token frequencies, and their uniqueness recognition points in input/output words (Marslen-Wilson 1984).[4]

Each of these principles is quite general, and allows for considerable cross-model variation (Dahan and Magnuson 2006). For example, frequency can directly affect the activation of processing units by modulating either the units' threshold for response (as in Morton's logogen model), or the units' resting activation level (as in Marslen-Wilson's cohort model), or the strength of connections between sublexical and lexical representations (MacKay 1982). Alternatively, frequency can act as a post-activation bias, thus influencing lexical selection, as in the NAM model (Luce 1986; Luce and Pisoni 1998). Besides, theories may differ in their similarity metrics and/or bottom-up activation mechanisms (which determine degree of fit), information flow (e.g. only bottom-up or top-down as well), and the nature of the competition mechanisms they assume (e.g. decision rule, lateral inhibition, or interference).

Differences and similarities notwithstanding, the PDP connectionism brought to the fore a factor missing in all previous models: the temporal dynamic of *learning*. In fact, non-connectionist models simply assumed the existence of a representational level made up out of access units, and an independent access procedure, mapping the input signal onto lexical representations. However, very little was said about how representations develop in the first place: how do children come to the decision of storing an irregular form as an unsegmented access unit, and a regular form as consisting of distinct access units? Even for those approaches where the decision does not have to be yes-or-no (since both hypotheses can be entertained at the same time, as in race models of lexical access), questions about how this is implemented (e.g., how does a child come up with the appropriate segmentation of a word form into sub-lexical units?) are left open.

In classical multi-layered perceptrons, internalized representations develop as the result of learning. The mapping of an input full form onto its morphological constituents is a continuous function of the statistical regularities in the

---

4 A uniqueness point (or UP) refers to the word-internal point (e.g. a sound, or a letter) at which an input form is uniquely identified among all its morphologically unrelated competitors (e.g. *k* in *walk* compared with *wall*). More recently, Balling and Baayen (2008) define a second uniqueness point, or Complex Uniqueness Point (CUP), where morphologically related competitors become incompatible with the input word (e.g. *i* in *walking* compared with *walk, walks, walked* etc.).

form and meaning of different words. Since form-meaning mapping is predicted to be a graded phenomenon, perception of morphological boundaries by a connectionist network may vary as a result of the probabilistic support the boundaries receive from frequency distributions of acquired exemplars (e.g., Hay and Baayen 2005; Plaut and Gonnerman 2000; Rueckl and Raveh 1999). This mechanism is key to what is arguably the most important legacy of connectionism for models of the mental lexicon: both regular and irregular words are processed by the same underlying mechanism and supported by the same memory resources. Pace Pinker and Ullman (2002), perception of morphological structure is not the by-product of the design of the human word processor, purportedly segregating exceptions from rules. Rather, it is an emergent property of the dynamic self-organization of lexical representations, contingent on the processing history of past input word forms.

However, as correctly observed by Baayen (2007), classical connectionist simulations model word acquisition as the mapping of a base input form onto its inflected output form (e.g. *go* → *went*). This protocol is in fact compatible with the view of a redundancy-free lexicon, and seems to adhere to a *derivational* approach to morphological competence, reminiscent of classical generative theories. Nonetheless, since network-internal representations (encoded in hidden layers of processing nodes) are dependent on the temporal dynamics of input-output mapping steps, connectionist principles are conducive to the idea that sublexical constituents dynamically *emerge* from the lexical store. Emergence of morphological structure is the result of morphologically complex words being redundantly memorized and mutually related as full forms.

2.2 Morphological emergence and paradigm-based models

The general idea that word structure emerges from lexical self-organization allows for considerable variation in matters of detail. According to Bybee (1995), stored words presenting overlapping parts with shared meaning are mutually related through lexical connections. Connection strength correlates positively with the number of related words (their family size) and negatively with their token frequency (see Bybee and McClelland 2005 for a more connectionist rendering of these ideas). Burzio (1998) interprets lexical connections as global lexical entailments, which may redundantly specify multiple surface bases. In line with this view, Word and Paradigm Morphology (Matthews 1991; Blevins 2006, 2016) conceives of mastering the morphology of a language as the acquisition of an increasing number of paradigmatic constraints on how paradigm cells are filled in (or *cell-filling problem*: Ackerman et al. 2009; Cardillo et al. 2018; Finkel and

Stump 2007; Pirrelli and Battista 2000; Pirrelli and Yvon 1999). What all these approaches have in common is the assumption that full word forms are the building blocks of morphological competence, and recurrent sublexical parts define *abstractions* over full forms (Blevins 2006).

The extent to which abstracted sublexical parts play a role in word processing remains a highly debated point in the psycholinguistic literature (see Schmidtke et al. 2017, for a recent, concise overview). Nonetheless, there seems to be a general consensus on the idea that the organization of items into morphologically natural classes (be they inflectional paradigms, inflectional classes, derivational families or compound families) has a direct influence on morphological processing, and that surface word relations constitute a fundamental domain of morphological competence. Of late, the emphasis on lexical families prompted a growing interest in information-theoretic measures of their degree of complexity. Once more, the connection between self-organization of word forms into morphological families and Shannon's information theory (Shannon 1948) is mainly provided by the relation between lexical knowledge and learning. Due to the Zipfian distribution of word forms in the speaker's input, inflectional paradigms happen to be attested only partially also for high-frequency lexemes (Blevins et al. 2017). Speakers must then be able to generalize available knowledge, and infer the inflectional class to which a partially attested paradigm belongs, for non-attested cells to be filled in accordingly.

Inferring non-attested forms of a paradigm on the basis of a few attested forms only thus requires that some word forms be diagnostic for inflectional class. Some forms can be more diagnostic than others, but it is often the case that no single form exists in a paradigm from which all other forms of the same paradigm can be inferred. This is not only true of irregular verb paradigms, but also of regular ones, where some inflected forms may neutralize class-membership diacritics (e.g. theme vowels for verb inflectional classes, see Albright 2002). Different forms can be instrumental for filling in specific subsets of paradigm cells (irrespective of their degree of morphological or phonological predictability), and more forms can be interchangeably used to predict the same subclass. On the one hand, this strategy calls for more evidence to be stored (so-called exemplary diagnostic forms, also referred to as "principal parts" in classical grammars). On the other hand, a speaker does not have to wait for one specific form (a "base" form) to be input, or abstract away an appropriate representation from available evidence. More forms can be used interchangeably for class assignment.

2.3 The "disappearing" lexicon

Paradigm-based approaches prompt a significant shift of emphasis away from traditional computational work on morphology, chiefly based on finite state technology and concerned with cognitively neutral, rule-like representations and analyses (Corbett and Fraser 1993; Karttunen 2003; Pirrelli 2018). A way to understand the difference between classical morpheme-based approaches and paradigm-based approaches to morphology is by looking at analogical proportions between paradigmatically-related word forms like the following:

(*drink*, PRES) : (*drank*, PAST) :: (*sink*, PRES) : (*sank*, PAST)

Given some computational constraints, one can infer any of the forms in the proportion above on the basis of the remaining three forms (Pirrelli and Yvon 1999). To illustrate, from the relation between *drink* and *drank*, one can infer that, by changing *i* into *a*, PRES is turned into PAST. Given (*drink*, PRES), (*drank*, PAST) and (*sink*, PRES), we can thus infer (*sank*, PAST). Note that, for a proportion to apply consistently, proportional relations must obtain concurrently and independently *within* each representation level (in our example, lexical form and grammatical content). Nothing explicit is stated about inter-level relations, i.e. about what substring in *drink* is associated with PRES. We could have stated the formal relationship between *drink* and *drank* as a (redundant) change of *ink* into *ank*, and the same inference would obtain. In fact, by the *principle of contrast* (Clark 1987, 1990), any formal difference can be used to mark a grammatical opposition as long as it obtains within one minimal pair of paradigmatically-related forms. This principle solves many of the paradoxes in the traditional notion of morpheme as a minimal linguistic sign: e.g. morphemes with no meanings (or empty morphemes), meanings with no morphemes (or zero morphemes), bracketing paradoxes etc.

It is noteworthy that the time-honored principle of contrast in linguistics is fully in line with principles of *discriminative learning*, whose roots can be traced back to philosophical pragmatism (particularly James 1907, 1909; and later Wittgenstein 1953; Quine 1960), functional psychology (James 1890) and behaviorism (Tolman 1932, 1951; Osgood 1946, 1949, 1966; Skinner 1953, 1957). Discriminative principles received their formal and mathematical modeling in the work of Rescorla and Wagner on classical conditioning, also known as error-driven learning (Rescorla 1988; Rescorla and Wagner 1972). More recently, work of Ramscar and collaborators (Ramscar and Yarlett 2007; Ramscar et al. 2010) and Ellis (2006a, also see Ellis and Larsen-Freeman 2006) laid the foundations of error-driven learning in the context of language learning. Baayen et al. (2011)

and Milin, Feldman et al. (2017) provide the discriminative approach with its computational platform, dubbed Naive Discrimination Learning (NDL).

Unlike strongly compositional and associative approaches to learning, error-driven or discriminative learning assumes that learning "results from exposure to relations among events in the environment", and, as such, it is "a primary means by which the organism represents the structure of its world" (Rescorla 1988: 152). Learning proceeds not by *associating* co-occurring cues and outcomes, but by *discriminating* between multiple cues that are constantly in competition for their predictive value for a given outcome. Furthermore, cues are not fixed in advance, but they emerge dynamically within an environment, shaped up by adaptive pressures. According to this view, human lexical information is never stable, time- or context-independent. Its content is continuously updated and re-shaped as a function of when, why and how often it is accessed and processed, with activation spreading to neighboring patterns of connectivity. Such flowing activation states are more reminiscent of the wave/particle duality in quantum physics (Libben 2016) or the inherently adaptive, self-organizing behavior of biological dynamic systems (Beckner et al. 2009; Larsen-Freeman and Cameron 2008) than ever thought in the past. From this perspective, the very notion of the mental lexicon is challenged; it may represent, at best, a metaphorical device or a convenient terminological shortcut (Elman 2009).

We saw that, from a theoretical linguistic perspective, the discriminative view fits in very well with Word and Paradigm Morphology (Blevins 2016), according to which morphemes and words are set-theoretic constructs. In a more computational perspective, it appears to support the view that storage and processing are not functionally and physically independent components of an information processing architecture (as with familiar desktop computers). Rather, they are better conceived of as two interdependent long-term and short-term dynamics of the same underlying process: learning.

Ultimately, we believe that understanding more of the far-reaching implications of (human) learning and adaptive behavior pushes us into a profound reassessment of traditional linguistic notions and processing requirements. This calls for more advanced computer models of human language behavior. In this section, we reviewed converging evidence of the role of morphological families and paradigmatic relations in the developmental course of lexical acquisition. The evidence bears witness to a fundamental interdependency between mechanisms of lexical activation/competition and effects of lexical token frequency, paradigm frequency, and paradigm regularity in word processing and learning. However, there have been comparatively few attempts to simulate this interdependency algorithmically. Most existing computational models of word recognition and production (Chen and Mirman 2012; Gaskell and Marslen-Wilson 2002;

Levelt et al. 1999; McClelland and Elman 1986; Norris, McQueen and Cutler 1995; among others) either focus on processing issues, by analyzing how input patterns can be mapped onto stored exemplars during processing; or focus on storage, by entertaining different hypotheses concerning the nature of stored representations (e.g. Henson 1998; Davis 2010, among others). Much less work is devoted to more "integrative" (neuro)computational accounts, where (i) "memory units that are repeatedly activated in processing an input word are the same units responsible for its stored representation" (Marzi and Pirrelli 2015: 495), and (ii) "memory units are made develop dynamically as the result of learning" (Marzi et al. 2016: 80). Truly integrative models would lead to an effective implementation and a better understanding of the dynamic interaction between processing and storage, and make room for a careful analysis of the empirical consequences of such a mutual implication on realistically distributed lexical data.

In the ensuing sections, we investigate what can be learned about the impact of principles of discriminative learning on lexical acquisition, access and production, by running computer simulations of models of dynamic lexical storage. We start with a general introduction of the Naive Discriminative Learning framework, its mathematical underpinnings and general philosophy, moving from the basics to advanced applications. Then, we investigate the time-bound dynamics of co-activation and competition in the acquisition of families of inflected forms, with a view to providing a unitary account of paradigm-based lexical acquisition and effects of neighbor families on lexical processing. This will be done using a family of recurrent neural networks known as Temporal Self-Organizing Maps. We will show that self-organizing memories provide a biologically inspired explanatory framework accounting for the interconnection between Word and Paradigm Morphology and principles of Discriminative Learning.

3 Computer models of discriminative learning

3.1 Naive Discriminative Learning

Naive Discriminative Learning (NDL) represents a computational modelling approach to language processing, providing theoretical and methodological grounding of research on diverse language phenomena. The NDL computational model itself implements the simplest possible error-driven learning rule, originally proposed by Rescorla and Wagner (1972), which since then has been shown to make powerful predictions for a range of phenomena in language learning and language comprehension (Ellis 2006a, 2006b; Ramscar, Dye and McCauley 2013;

Ramscar and Yarlett 2007; Ramscar et al. 2010). The first study to apply discrimination learning to predict reaction times by training a network on large corpora is Baayen, Milin et al. (2011), and the term NDL was coined and first used in this study.

3.1.1 NDL – The Basics

The Rescorla-Wagner learning rule updates the weights on connections from input features (henceforth cues) to output classes (henceforth outcomes) in a simple two-layer network. Outcomes are word-like units that are labelled "lexomes" in the NDL terminology (e.g. the unit *something*), cues are typically letter bigrams, trigrams or even word forms (like *#so, som, ome, met, eth, thi, hin, ing, ng#* for the word *something*; with the '#' symbol replacing start-of-word and end-of-word spaces). The relationship between cues and outcomes is incremental, and develops in discrete time steps. Presence of a cue C_i in a given learning event E_t taking place at time t is indicated by $PRESENT(C_i, t)$, and presence of an outcome O_j in E_t by $PRESENT(O_J, t)$. The weight w_{ij}^t is defined on the connection between a given cue C_i and specific outcome O_j at time t, and at the subsequent timestep w_{ij}^{t+1} this weight is defined as:

$$w_{ij}^{t+1} = w_{ij}^t + \Delta w_{ij}^t \tag{1}$$

where the change in weight Δw_{ij}^t is specified as:

$$\Delta w_{ij}^t = \begin{cases} = 0 & ; \quad \text{if } PRESENT(C_{i,t}) \text{ is } \mathbf{false} \\ = \eta_i \left(\lambda_j - \sum_{present(C_k, t)} w_{kj} \right) & ; \text{if } PRESENT(C_{i,t}) \text{ is } \mathbf{true} \ \& \ PRESENT(O_{j,t}) \text{ is } \mathbf{true} \\ = \eta_i \left(0 - \sum_{present(C_k, t)} w_{kj} \right) & ; \text{if } PRESENT(C_{i,t}) \text{ is } \mathbf{true} \ \& \ PRESENT(O_{j,t}) \text{ is } \mathbf{false} \end{cases} \tag{2}$$

Weights on connections from cues that are absent in the input are left unchanged. For cues that are present in the input, the weights to a given outcome are updated, depending on whether the outcome was correctly predicted. The prediction strength or activation a for an outcome is defined as the sum of the weights on the connections from the cues in the input to the outcome. If the outcome is present in a learning event, together with the cues, then the weights are increased by a proportion η of the difference between the maximum prediction strength (λ, set at 1 in *NDL* simulations) and a. The proportionality constant η defines the learning rate of the model. Thus, the adjustment to the weights when the outcome is indeed present is $\eta(\lambda - a)$. When the outcome is not present, the weights are decreased by $\eta(0 - a)$. For networks trained on large corpora, setting η to 0.001 appears optimal. In general, learning rate η should be set to a small value (commonly between 0.1 and 0.001) to allow for learning to be incremental (Rescorla and Wagner 1972; Blough 1975; Baayen et al. 2011; Ghirlanda 2005; Ghirlanda et al. 2017). The learning rate η is the only free parameter of the NDL implementation of the Rescorla-Wagner learning rule.[5]

3.1.2 Current results

Naive Discriminative Learning has been used successfully to model the results of a range of experiments. Baayen, Milin et al. (2011), Pham and Baayen (2015), and Milin, Feldman et al. (2017) investigated primed and unprimed lexical decision. Arnold et al. (2017) developed a model of spoken word recognition using input cues derived from the speech signal. Linke et al. (2017) modeled (supposed) lexical learning in baboons. Geeraert et al. (2017) used NDL to clarify idiom variation; and Ramscar et al. (2014, 2017) used NDL to study the consequences of the accumulation of knowledge over a lifetime.

The 2011 study applying Naive Discriminative Learning to lexical decision latencies used cues consisting of individual letters and letter pairs. It has since been shown that letter triplets provide better cues for modelling reading. In the same paper, outcomes were conceptualized as "semantic units". In subsequent

---

[5] Implementations of NDL are available for R (package ndl, Arppe et al. 2015) and as a Python library (pyndl: Weitz et al. 2017). The first study to explore the potential of discrimination learning for understanding reaction times (Baayen, Milin et al. 2011) did not make use of the Rescorla-Wagner equations themselves, but instead used the equations developed by Danks (2003). Danks developed equations for estimating the weights under the assumption that the system has reached a state of equilibrium in which no further learning takes place. Although the option of using Danks' equilibrium equations is implemented in the available software packages, subsequent research strongly suggests it is preferable to use the original equations and apply them step by step to the sequence of learning events. NDL networks appear quite sensitive to the order in which sets of cues and outcomes are presented for learning. Hence, if order information is available (as when models are trained on corpora), it is advisable to let this order co-determine learning. The available software implements optimized algorithms that can utilize multiple cores in parallel to speed up the incremental updating of the weights. For large data sets, estimating the weights is actually accomplished substantially more quickly for 'incremental' learning as compared to the estimation method based on the Danks equations.

work, the nature of these units was clarified: they are now conceptualized as pointers to locations in a multidimensional semantic space. To avoid confusing these pointers with contentful lexical representations, we labelled these pointers 'lexomes' (c.f., Baayen, Shaoul et al. 2016; Milin, Divjak, and Baayen 2017; Milin, Feldman et al. 2017). Lexomes thus link lexical contrasts in form to lexical contrasts in semantic space. Figure 1 clarifies the role of this theoretical construct in the model. This figure simultaneously represents three discrimination networks, each of which is trained independently. The three networks have all been used for successfully predicting data from experimental studies.

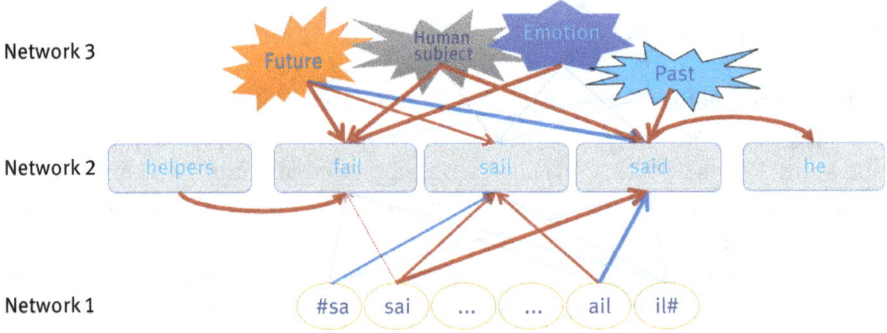

Figure 1: NDL network layout obtained with the iterative application of Rescorla-Wagner rule, for the lexomes *fail*, *sail*, and *said*. Red arrows represent positive associations, while blue arrows represent negative associations. Arrow width reflects the absolute magnitude of the weights on the connections. Networks are trained independently of each other.

Of the three networks in Figure 1, the first one represents bottom-up associations from perceptual input cues (here letter trigrams) to lexomes. This network is referred to as a 'Grapheme-to-Lexome network' (or G2L-network). Milin, Feldman et al. (2017) trained such a network on utterances from a 1.1 billion word corpus of English subtitles (Tiedemann 2012), using letter trigrams such as *#sa, sai, ail* and *il#*, or *#he* and *he#*, to lexomes such as *sail* and *he*. Three measures that can be derived from such G2L networks have been found to be predictive for experimental measures gauging lexical processing costs. First, the *Activation* of a lexome is defined as the sum of the weights on the connections from the cues in the input to that lexome. Second, the *Prior* availability of a lexome is estimated by the L1-norm of the weights on the connections from all cues to that lexome.[6] Whereas the

---

[6] The L1-norm of a numeric vector is the sum of its absolute values. Like the Euclidean distance (the L2-norm), the L1-norm is a distance measure. It is the distance between two points

activation measure, given the network, is determined by the input, the prior availability is a systemic measure that is independent from the input and is determined by the network only. Prior availability can be understood as a measure of network entrenchment, and hence is reminiscent of the priors in Bayesian models of word recognition (Norris 1994, 2006; Norris and McQueen 2008). The activation *Diversity*, finally, is the L1-norm of the activations of all lexomes generated by the input. It gauges the extent to which other lexomes are co-activated by the input. All three measures have been found to be good predictors for a number of experimental tasks across languages (cf. Baayen et al. 2011; Baayen, Milin, and Ramscar 2016 for visual lexical decision; Milin, Divjak et al. 2017 for self-paced reading in Russian, Hendrix, Bolger, and Baayen 2017 for ERPs, and Arnold et al. 2017 for spoken word identification).

The second learning network, partially represented in the middle row in Figure 1, has lexomes both as input cues and as output outcomes. In Figure 1, only two connections are indicated: the connection from the lexome *helpers* (cue) to the lexome *fail* (outcome), and from the cue *said* to the outcome *he*. Weights estimated from the corpus of English subtitles suggest that these two connections have strong and positive association strengths. From this 'Lexome-to-Lexome network' (L2L-network), several further measures can be derived. In parallel to the Diversity and outcome Prior availability based on a G2L network, an L2L Diversity of activations as well as an L2L Prior availability can be derived, again using L1-norms. Both measures are strong predictors of lexical processing costs, alongside the G2L measures.

L2L networks define semantic vector spaces (cf. Baayen, Milin et al. 2016; Milin, Feldman et al. 2017; see Marelli and Baroni 2015; Acquaviva et al. 2020, this volume for an overview of distributed semantic models). The rows of the L2L weight matrix that defines the L2L network constitute the semantic vectors of the model. Importantly, it is these semantic vectors that the lexome units in the G2L and L2L networks identify (or "point" to). From the cosine similarity matrix of the L2L row vectors, two further measures have been derived and tested against empirical data: a lexome's Semantic Density and a lexome's Semantic Typicality. A lexome's Semantic Density is defined as the number of all lexomes that have a very high cosine similarity with the target lexome. Similarly, a lexome's Semantic Typicality is defined as the cosine similarity of that lexome's semantic vector and the average semantic vector (see also Marelli and Baroni 2015; Shaoul

---

on a grid when one can move only in the direction of the axes. Thus, whereas the L2-norm of the point (3,−4) is 5, the L1-norm is 7.

and Westbury 2010). Milin, Feldman et al. (2017) observe inhibition from semantic density and facilitation from semantic typicality for lexical decision latencies.

Milin, Divjak et al. (2017) introduced a third NDL network with content lexomes as outcomes, and as cues what we call 'experiential' lexomes. This third network was labeled the BP2L network. Relying on the Behavioural Profiles developed by Divjak & Gries (2006) and later publications, it indexes dimensions of experience, including those that are marked grammatically, such as aspect, tense, mood and number. The authors show that the activations that lexomes of 'try'- verbs receive from such grammatical lexomes are predictive for reading latencies obtained in self-paced sentence reading in Russian. Statistical analyses also revealed that participants optimized their responses in the course of the experiment: the activations had an inhibitory effect on reading latencies at the beginning of the experiment, that later reversed into facilitation. The results from the Milin, Divjak et al. (2017) study are especially interesting as they show that the linguistic profiling of words or constructions (Divjak and Gries 2006; see also Bresnan et al. 2005) can be integrated within a computationally exact approach to learning to yield novel insights into language processing.

Baayen, Milin, and Ramscar (2016), for example, demonstrated and discussed how empirically well-established yet theoretically neglected frequency effects emerge naturally from discriminative learning. The Activation and Prior availability measure are strongly correlated with frequency of occurrence in the corpus on which the network is trained. They can be viewed as measures of frequency that have been molded by discriminative learning. At the same time, interactive activation models account for frequency effects by coding frequency of use into resting activation levels, and Bayesian models build them in by means of priors. Both approaches in effect assume some kind of counter in the head.

3.1.3 Recent developments

In principle, any activation-based computer model of utterance comprehension should be able to discriminate, based on levels of activation, between the intended words actually found in an input utterance and the tens of thousands of other irrelevant words that are potentially available. For example, upon being exposed to *Bill ate the apple pie*, the model should perceive, as the most highly activated units, the individual forms corresponding to the following lexical and grammatical categories: BILL, EAT_PAST and DEF_APPLEPIE. In practice, the two individual forms *apple* and *pie* may be the most highly activated units, and may (wrongly) be perceived as associated with APPLE and PIE respectively, rather than with APPLEPIE as one 'meaning' contrast. In the context of *Bill ate the apple pie* this would be a case of misclassification of input data. The correct interpretation of an utterance thus requires that all and only its intended word units are classified correctly, by discarding all other irrelevant units that may possibly get activated.

NDL models trained on large corpora may not always achieve this. This is perhaps unsurprising, as a 10 million word corpus such as the TASA (Landauer, Foltz, and Laham 1998) can easily contain 50,000 words that occur at least twice. Hence, classification of these 50,000 words, given their large number and rare occurrence, is a formidable task. In that sense, if these words would be among the first 300 most highly activated candidates, such result would be respectable. Nevertheless, human performance is typically more precise. Baayen et al. (2017) show that classification accuracy can be improved considerably, to human-like levels, by working with coupled error-driven networks. The weights of the two networks are estimated independently, i.e. the same error is 'injected' twice. The first network takes sublexical orthographic or auditory features as input cues, and has lexomes as outcomes. The second network takes as input the output of the first network, i.e. a vector of activations over all lexomes. The outcomes of the second network are again lexomes. The second network thus implements a second try, taking the results from the first network and attempting to predict once again the lexomes that are actually present in the learning event.

We illustrate the coupled networks by means of a simple example, which we also use to lay out the novel way in which the discriminative perspective addresses lexical access. Table 1 lists 10 sentences together with their (randomly generated) frequency of occurrence and a list of the lexomes occurring in each sentence. This list is not intended to be comprehensive, but to illustrate some modelling strategies while keeping the complexity of the example low.

Table 1: Sentences, selected lexomes in the message, and frequency of occurrence, totaling 771.

no.	Sentence	Lexomes (lexical meanings)	Frequency
1	Mary passed away	MARY DIE PAST	40
2	Bill kicked the ball	BILL KICK PAST DEF BALL	100
3	John kicked the ball away	JOHN KICK PAST DEF BALL AWAY	120
4	Mary died	MARY DIE PAST	300
5	Mary bought some flowers	MARY BUY PAST SOME FLOWERS	20
6	Ann bought a ball	ANN BUY PAST INDEF BALL	45
7	John filled the bucket	JOHN FILL PAST DEF BUCKET	100
8	John kicked the bucket	JOHN DIE PAST	10
9	Bill ate the apple pie	BILL EAT DEF APPLEPIE	3
10	Ann tasted an apple	ANN TASTE PAST INDEF APPLE	33

Several aspects of the choice of lexomes are important. First, the sentences with "kicked the bucket", "passed away", and "died", are all associated with the same lexome DIE. This is a many-forms-to-one-lexome mapping (for a discussion of idiom comprehension in this framework, see Geeraert et al. 2017). Second, past-tense word forms such as regular "passed" and irregular "ate" are mapped onto two lexomes, PASS and PAST, and EAT and PAST respectively. One might want to add further grammatical lexomes here, such as a lexomes for person and number. Here, we have a one-form-to-multiple-lexomes mapping. Third, the compound "apple pie" is represented as a single onomasiological entity with the lexome APPLEPIE.

The task of the network is to identify all lexomes that are encoded in the input. This multi-label classification task is one that has to be accomplished solely on the basis of the letter trigrams in the input. For the sentence *John kicked the bucket*, the unique trigraphs that constitute the input cues are #Jo, Joh, ohn, hn#, n#k, #ki, kic, ick, cke, ked, ed#, d#t, #th, the, he#, e#b, #bu, buc, uck, ket, et# (duplicate triplets like *cke* are included only once; again, the # symbol represents the space character).

For this multi-label classification task, we use a coupled network as described above. The first network has the trigram cues as input, and the lexomes as output. A given set of input cues produces a vector of activations over the lexomes. When presented with the sentence *John kicked the bucket*, a network trained on the mini-corpus summarized in Table 1 incorrectly assigns a higher activation to the grammatical lexome DEF than to the lexome DIE (see Figure 2, left upper panel, and related discussion below). A language model bringing in (often implicitly) sophisticated, high-level 'knowledge about the world', could help alleviating this kind of problem for words in utterances, by providing 'hints' to desired outcomes. However, any such language model would give its contribution "for free", as nothing would be revealed about how this knowledge was acquired in the first place.

Classification accuracy is improved by taking the vector of activations produced by the first network, and giving the second network the task of discriminating between the lexomes encoded in the utterance and those that are not part of the message. This second network is a lexome-to-lexome network, but the inputs are no longer dichotomous (1 or 0, depending on whether the lexome is present in the input) but real-valued (see left panels in Figure 2). As a consequence, the Rescorla-Wagner equations cannot be used. Instead, the closely related learning rule of Widrow and Hoff (1960), identical to the Rescorla-Wagner rule under proper parameter selection, can be used for incremental updating of the weights, learning event by learning event. Instead of the Widrow-Hoff learning rule, the weights of the second network can also be estimated by

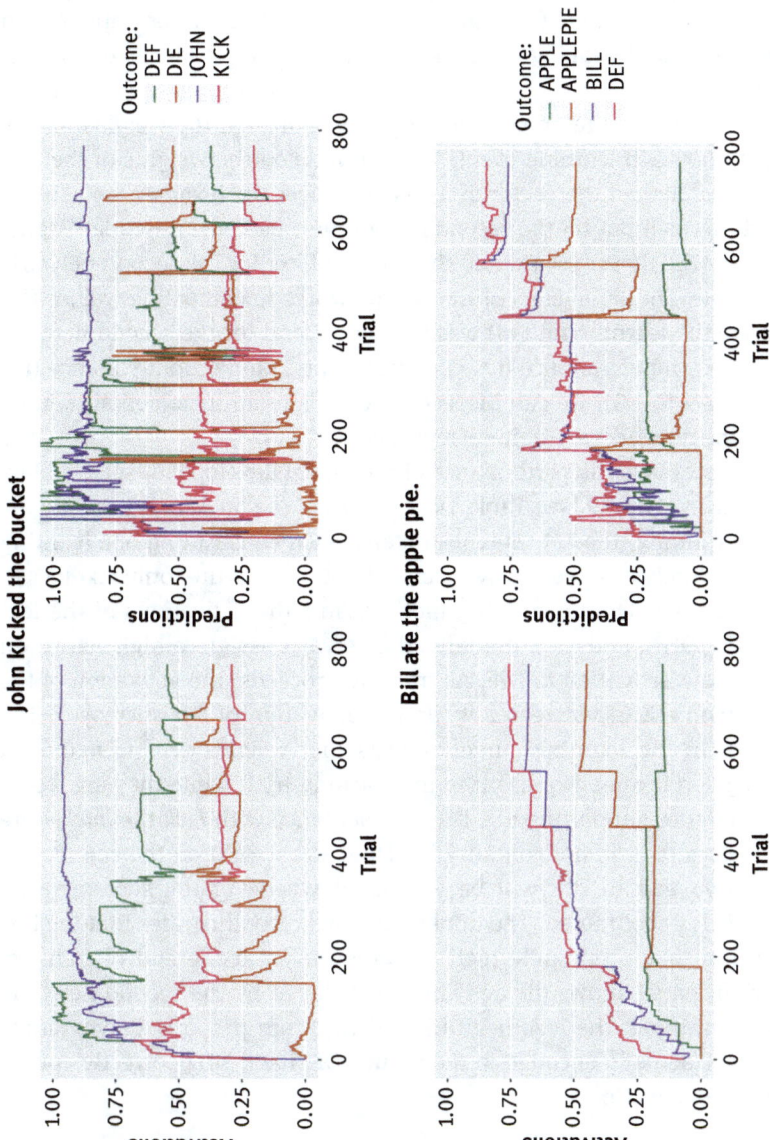

Figure 2: Activations and prediction strengths for selected lexomes in the learning events of sentences 8 and 9 in Table 1, using incremental coupled Rescorla-Wagner and Kalman Filtering. Left panels: activations from the first network; right panel: predictions from the second network. For clarity we are not presenting all of the outcomes.

means of Kalman Filtering (KF: Kalman 1960). The Kalman filter improves on Widrow-Hoff learning by taking the cues' uncertainty (i.e. variance-covariance) into account.[7]

For the mini-corpus presented in Table 1, we estimated the weights for the two networks. For each learning event, we first updated the weights of the first network, then calculated the vector of activations over the lexomes, and subsequently used this as input for the second network; we used the Rescorla-Wagner learning rule for the first network, and the Kalman filter for the second network. By setting all relevant parameters of the two networks to compatible values (for both networks, the learning rate (η) was set to 0.01 and for the second network initial variances – input variance (i.e. cue uncertainty), and output variance (i.e. noise) were all set to 1.0), we can inspect the details of an incremental training regime when the networks are trained in parallel.

Figure 2 shows how the performance of the model develops for selected lexomes in sentences 8 and 9 (see Table 1), *John kicked the bucket* and *Bill ate the apple pie*. For training, the 771 sentence tokens, each constituting one learning event, were randomly ordered. To avoid clogging up the figure, only lexomes of interest are graphed. The upper left panel presents the activations of the lexomes DEF, DIE, JOHN, and KICK. Initially, the network assigns a high activation to KICK and a low activation to DIE. As training proceeds, the activation of the unintended lexome KICK decreases while the activation of DIE increases. The jagged pattern in the learning curves reflects that weights are strengthened only when a given lexome is present in the learning trial, while they are weakened whenever cues supporting e.g. DIE in a sentence with *kick the bucket* are used in sentences that do not contain DIE. Thus, the weight on the connection from the trigram ed# to DIE will be weakened whenever the sentence *Ann tasted an apple* is encountered. The upper left panel also illustrates that the lexome DEF has an inappropriately high activation even at the end of training. The upper right panel shows the activations produced by the second network. By the end of training, the lexomes DEF and KICK are properly downgraded, and the lexomes actually encoded in the input, JOHN and DIE, correctly appear with the highest activations.

---

[7] A computationally efficient implementation of both WH and KF is currently under development by the last author (P. Milin) and his research group (https://outofourminds.bham.ac.uk/). Alternatively, given a set of learning events and the vectors of activations over the outcomes for these learning events, finding the weights of the second network amounts to solving a set of equations, which can be accomplished mathematically with the generalized inverse. In current implementations, this second method is much faster, but, unfortunately, it misses out on the consequences of incremental learning.

The bottom panels present the development of activations for *Bill ate the apple pie*. Here, the relative activations of APPLE and APPLEPIE are of interest. Note that in the initial stages of learning, APPLE receives a higher activation than APPLEPIE. By the end of learning, the first network already succeeds in discriminating apple pies from apples, and the second network enhances the difference in activation even further. The fact that APPLE has not been completely suppressed is, in our opinion, an asset of the model. In a multi-label classification problem, a winner-takes-all set-up, as commonly found in interactive activation models, cannot work. In fact, we think that semantic percepts are co-determined by all lexomes in the system, proportional to their activation. (In the semantic vector space, this hypothesis translates into all lexomes having vectors the length and prominence of which is modulated by their activation.) Thus, according to the present example model, there is an *apple* in *apple pie*, but the model also knows very well that Bill ate an APPLEPIE and not an APPLE. This highlights that in the present approach, the semantics of complex words are not derived from the semantics of their parts by some combinatorial operation.

Comparing the panels in the left and right columns of Figure 2 reveals that the first network (the Rescorla-Wagner network) shows a more stable behavior, which means that it 'learns' faster than the second network trained with the Kalman Filter.[8] Nevertheless, by the end of the learning sequence, only the second network succeeds in giving the intended lexomes higher scores.

3.1.4 Advantages of NDL

An important design property of NDL is that 'lexical access' is defined as a multi-label classification problem driven by low-level, sublexical features. A hierarchy of units, such as letter features, letters, morphemes and words for reading, and phonemes, syllables, morphemes, and words for auditory comprehension, is not part of the model. In fact, such a hierarchy of units is viewed as disadvantageous, because low-level co-occurrence information is a-priori ruled out to influence comprehension. For instance, fine phonetic detail below the phoneme that is present across (co-articulated) syllables is lost when comprehension is filtered first through abstract phonemes and then through abstract syllables. Baayen, Shaoul et al. (2016) show how the word segmentation problem, which is computationally

---

[8] However, the Kalman Filter network learns much faster than a network trained with the Widrow-Hoff learning rule, as can be seen by comparing the present results with those reported in Sering et al. (2018) using a variant of WH.

hard, is no longer an issue in a discrimination-driven approach. Arnold et al. (2017), furthermore, show that an NDL network trained on cues derived from the speech signal achieves an identification accuracy that is within the range of human identification performance.[9]

Inspired by Word and Paradigm Morphology (Matthews 1974; Blevins 2016), NDL likewise avoids the popular idea that the morpheme is a linguistic sign, which goes back to post-Bloomfieldian American structuralism. This does not imply that NDL denies the relevance of all linguistic variables such as tense, aspect, person, or number. In fact, the approach implements such variables through 'experiential' lexomes, as illustrated above in Figure 2. However, form units for morphemes are not part of the model (cf. Milin, Feldman et al. 2017; and also consult Schmidtke et al. 2017). Finally, the discriminative perspective also sheds light on why – often fairly idiosyncratic – allomorphy is widespread in morphological systems. Such allomorphy requires complex adjustment rules (or extensive listing) in classic decompositional approaches, while from the discrimination stance allomorphy renders the base word and the complex word less similar in form, which consequently makes the two easier to distinguish (see also Blevins, Milin, and Ramscar 2017).

In the discriminative framework, NDL is a computational implementation of implicit learning, i.e. the learning that goes on without conscious reflection. This kind of learning is not unique to language. For instance, Marsolek (2008) discusses how error-driven updating of visual features affects cognition. Implicit learning is likely the dominant form of learning in young children, whose cognitive control systems are not well-developed. As prefrontal systems mature, it becomes possible to consider multiple sources of information simultaneously, leading to markedly different performance on a variety of tasks (Ramscar and Gitcho 2007). Indeed, Ramscar, Dye, and Klein (2013) provide an example of the very different performance, on the same novel-object labelling task, of young children on the one hand and adults on the other, with the children following discriminative informativity, and the adults applying logical reasoning. As a

---

[9] The auditory model also takes acoustic reductions in its stride. Standard computational models of auditory comprehension are challenged by strongly reduced forms, which are ubiquitous in spontaneous speech. When reduced forms are added to the inventory of word forms, recognition systems tend not to improve. Although some words may be recognized better, the addition of many short, reduced forms typically increases problems elsewhere (Johnson 2004). From a discriminative perspective, reduced forms simply have different acoustic features, and as the requirement is dropped that comprehension must proceed through an abstract standardized form representation, the acoustic features that are highly specific for the reduced form can straightforwardly support the intended lexomes.

consequence, NDL networks will often not be sufficient for predicting adult behavior in experiments addressing morphological learning using stimuli constructed according to some artificial grammar. For such data, NDL can still be useful for clarifying where human performance deviates from what one would expect if learning were restricted to implicit learning, which in turn is informative about where additional processes of cognitive control addressing response competition are at work. If the goal is to clarify implicit learning in adults, which we think takes place continuously (but not exclusively), great care is required to ensure that participants do not have time to think about the task they are performing or to develop response strategies.

NDL networks provide functional models for tracing the consequences of discriminative learning for lexical processing. Although there is ample neurobiological evidence for error-driven learning (e.g. Schultz 1998), actual neural computation is much more complex than suggested by the architecture of a two-layer artificial neural network. Because of this, the NDL model remains agnostic about possible spatial clustering of cues and outcomes in neural tissue.

Published work using NDL addresses primarily aspects of language comprehension. Much less work has been done on speech production. Ramscar, Dye, and McCauley (2013) show how discrimination learning predicts the U-shaped learning curve often observed for the acquisition of irregular morphology. Hendrix (2015) developed a computational model for word naming that is built on two discrimination networks. Recent studies (Tucker et al. 2017; Lensink et al. 2017) suggest that specifically the activation diversity measure helps predict the acoustic durations with which segments or utterances are realized in speech. Whether a computational model of speech production that eschews representations for phonemes and morphemes can be made to work is currently under investigation.

3.2 Temporal Self-Organizing Maps

Although most recent work in discriminative word learning has primarily focused on form-meaning relationships based on highly-distributed a-morphous representations, a recurrent network variant of discriminative learning has recently been used in one-level self-organizing grids of processing nodes known as Temporal Self-Organizing Maps (TSOMs, Ferro et al. 2011; Marzi et al. 2014; Pirrelli et al. 2015). TSOMs develop Markov-like chains of memory nodes that can mirror effects of gradient morphological structure and emergent paradigmatic organization upon exposure to simple inflected forms. By developing specialized patterns of input receptors through recurrent connections, TSOMs recode *one-level stimuli auto-associatively*, thereby exploiting the formal redundancy of temporal series of symbols. From this perspective, discriminative learning proves to be a powerful strategy for scaffolding the input stream into internalized structured representations, which turn out to be useful for efficient word recognition and production. Here we will show how TSOMs can be used as lexical memories.

3.2.1 Architecture outline

The core of a TSOM consists of an array of nodes with two weighted layers of synaptic connectivity (Figure 3). Input connections link each node to the current

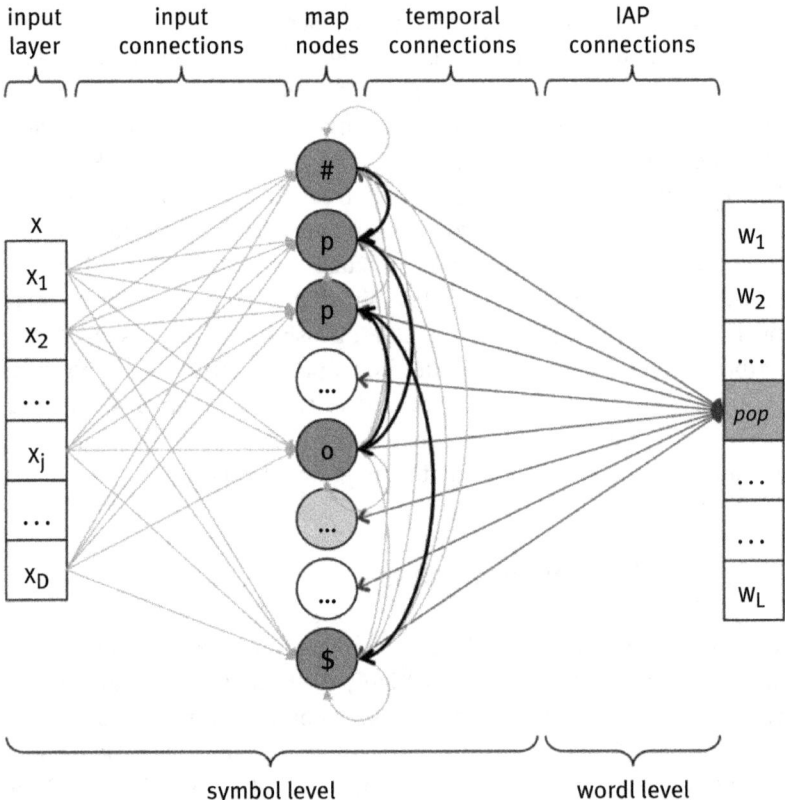

Figure 3: Functional architecture of a Temporal Self-Organizing Map (TSOM). Shades of grey represent levels of activation of map nodes, from low (light grey) to high (dark grey). The figure depicts the integrated level of activation of the map after the word *pop* ('#pop$') is shown in input.

input stimulus (e.g. a letter or a sound), a one-hot vector presented on the input layer at a discrete time tick. Temporal connections link each map node to the pattern of node activation of the same map at the immediately preceding time tick. In Figure 3, these connections are depicted as re-entrant directed arcs, leaving from and to map nodes. Nodes are labelled by the input characters that fire them most strongly. '#' and '$' are special characters, marking the beginning and the end of an input word respectively.

3.2.2 Processing and storage

Storage and processing are traditionally seen as independent, non-interactive functions, carried out by distinct computer components, with data representations defined prior to processing, and processing applied independently of input data. Conversely, in a TSOM storage and processing are two different time-scales of the same underlying process, defined by a unique pool of principles: (i) long-term storage depends on processing, as it consists in routinized time-bound chains of sequentially activated nodes; (ii) processing is memory-based since it consists in the short-term reactivation of node chains that successfully responded to past input. As a result of this mutual interaction, weights on input and temporal connections are adaptively adjusted as a continuous function of the distributional patterns of input data.

Algorithmically, when an input vector $x(t)$ (say the letter o in Figure 3) is input to the map at time t, activation propagates to all map nodes through both input and temporal connections. The most highly activated node at time t is termed Best Matching Unit ($BMU(t)$ for short), and represents the processing response of the map to the current input.

Following this short-term processing step, both input and temporal connections are updated incrementally, for map nodes to be made more sensitive to the current input. In particular, for each jth input value $x_j(t)$ in the input vector, its connection weight $w_{i,j}$ to the ith map node is incremented by *equation 3*:

$$\Delta w_{i,j}(t) = \gamma_I(E) \cdot G_I(d_i(t)) \cdot [x_j(t) - w_{i,j}(t)] \quad (3)$$

Likewise, the temporal connections of the ith node are synchronized to the activation state of the map at time t-1, by increasing the weight $m_{i,BMU(t-1)}$ on the connection from $BMU(t-1)$ to the ith node (*equation 4*), and by decreasing all other temporal connections to the ith node (*equation 5*).

$$\Delta m_{i,h}(t) = \gamma_T(E) \cdot G_T(d_i(t)) \cdot [1 - m_{i,h}(t)]; \quad h = BMU(t-1). \quad (4)$$

$$\Delta m_{i,h}(t) = \gamma_T(E) \cdot G_T(d_i(t)) \cdot [0 - m_{i,h}(t)]; \quad h \neq BMU(t-1). \tag{5}$$

Note that for both input and temporal connections, the resulting long-term increment (respectively $\Delta w_{i,j}(t)$ and $\Delta m_{i,h}(t)$) is an inverse function (respectively $G_I(\cdot)$ and $G_T(\cdot)$) of the topological distance $d_i(t)$ between the ith node and the current $BMU(t)$, and a direct function (respectively $\gamma_I(\cdot)$ and $\gamma_T(\cdot)$) of the map's learning rate at epoch E.[10]

Because of this dynamic, $BMU(t)$ will benefit most from weight adjustment at time t, but information will nonetheless spread radially from $BMU(t)$ to topologically neighbouring nodes. In the end, the map develops a topological organization where nodes responding to the same symbol tend to cluster in a connected area. Figure 4 shows a map trained on German verb inflected forms: each map node is labelled with the input letter it responds most highly to. A node N gets the label L, if the L input vector is at a minimal distance from N's vector of spatial weights. Nodes that are labelled with the same symbol are specialized for responding to that symbol in different temporal contexts. Intuitively, they store long-term information about the typical contexts where the symbol happened to be found in input. Notably, the node that stores specialized information about the L symbol in a specific context is the same node that responds most highly to L when L happens to be input in that particular context.

3.2.3 Information of 'what' and information of 'when'

Input connections store information about the nature of the current input (or 'what' information). The layer of temporal connections encodes the expectation for the current state of map activation given the activation of the map at the previous time tick (or 'when' information). *Equation 4* and *equation 5*, by which 'when' connections are dynamically trained in TSOMs, are strongly reminiscent of Rescorla-Wagner's *equation 2*. Given the input bigram '*ab*', the connection strength between $BMU('a')$ at time *t-1* and $BMU('b')$ at time *t* will
(i) increase every time '*a*' precedes '*b*' in training (entrenchment)
(ii) decrease every time '*b*' is preceded by a symbol other than '*a*' (competition and inhibition).

---

[10] Intuitively the two functions define the degree of *plasticity* of the map, i.e. how readily the map adjusts itself to the current input stimuli. Hence, they are inverse functions of the map's learning epoch E, i.e. their impact decreases as learning progresses.

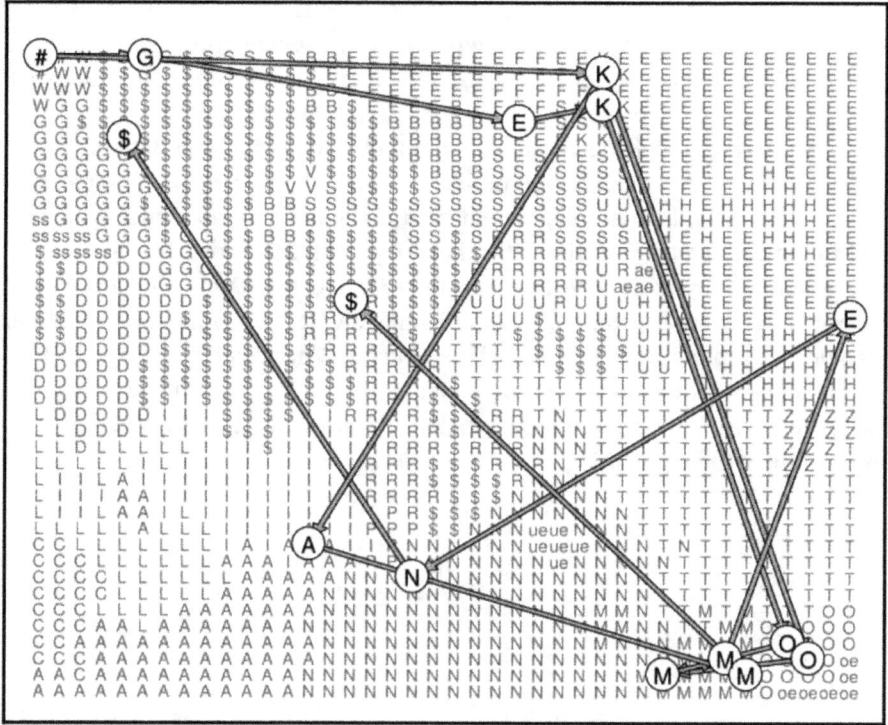

Figure 4: A labelled TSOM trained on German verb inflected forms. Highlighted nodes depict the BMUs activated by the forms *kommen* 'come' (infinitive/1P-3P present indicative), *gekommen* 'come' (past participle) and *kam* 'came' (1S-3S past tense), with directed arrows representing their activation timeline.

Note, however, that *equation 4* and *equation 5* apparently reverse the cue-outcome relationship of *equation 2*: $BMU(t)$ acts as a cue to $BMU(t-1)$ and strengthens the temporal connection from $BMU(t-1)$ to $BMU(t)$ accordingly (entrenchment). At the same time, all the temporal connections to $BMU(t)$ emanating from nodes other than $BMU(t-1)$ are depressed (competition). To understand this apparent reversal, it is useful to bear in mind that the output of a TSOM is an optimal self-organization of map nodes, based on past stimuli. This is done incrementally, by adjusting the weights on temporal connections to optimize processing of the current input string. Ultimately, *equation 4* and *equation 5* concur to develop the most *discriminative* chains of *BMUs* given a set of training data. This means that $BMU(t)$ is not the map's outcome, but the internally encoded cue to the map's optimal self-organization. By differentially adjusting the incoming temporal connections that emanate from $BMU(t-1)$ and non-*BMU*(*t* – 1), the current *BMU*(*t*) is in fact specializing a chain of *BMUs* for them to keep in memory, at each step, as many previous processing steps as possible. The *outcome* of *BMU*(*t*) is thus the incremental step in building such maximally discriminative chain.

The interaction between entrenchment and competition accounts for effects of context-sensitive specialization of map nodes. If the bigram '*ab*' is repeatedly input, a TSOM tends to develop a dedicated node for '*b*' in '*ab*'. Since node specialization propagates with time, if '*c*' is a frequent follower of '*ab*', the map will strengthen a temporal connection to another dedicated *BMU* responding to '*c*' preceded by '*b*' when preceded by '*a*'. Ultimately, the TSOM is biased towards memorizing input strings through *BMUs* structured in a word tree (Figure 5). As we shall see later in the section on serial word processing, a tree-like memory structure favors word recognition by looking for word uniqueness points as early as possible in the input string.

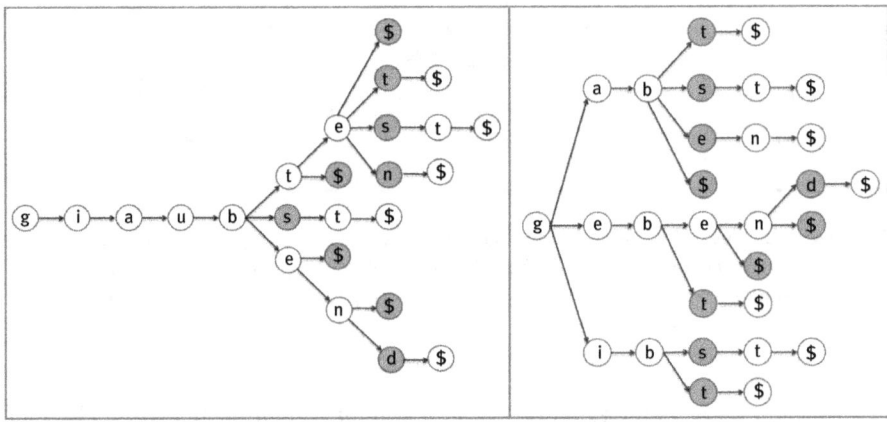

Figure 5: Word-tree representations of sub-paradigms of German *glauben* ('believe') and *geben* ('give'). Shaded nodes represent word Complex Uniqueness Points (see note 2, and the section below on serial word processing).

Figure 6 shows the scatter plot of the number of *BMUs* responding to input symbols in a 40×40 node TSOM trained on 750 German verb forms, regressed on the number of distinct nodes required to represent the same symbols in a word-tree (Pearson's r = .95, p < .00001). On average, the more contexts a symbol is found in during training (accurately approximated by the number of distinct tree nodes associated with the symbol), the more map nodes will be specialized for that symbol. Context-sensitive specialization of *BMUs* allows a TSOM to

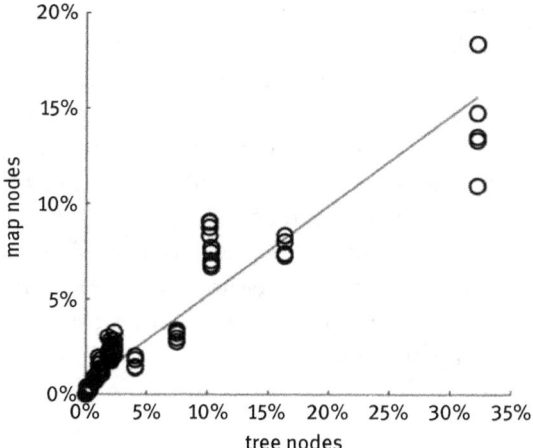

Figure 6: Scatter plot of per-symbol nodes allocated in a map trained on German verb forms. Data are regressed on the number of nodes in a word-tree representing the training data.

allocate specific resources to input symbols that occur at specific points in time. A TSOM develops a growing sensitivity to surface distributional properties of input data (e.g. language-specific constraints on admissible symbol arrangements, as well as probabilistic expectations of their occurrence), turning chains of randomly connected, general-purpose nodes into specialized sub-chains of *BMUs* that respond to specific letter strings in specific contexts. This ability is fundamental to storing symbolic time-series like words.

3.2.4 Using TSOMs as lexical memories

In showing a word like *#pop$* one symbol at a time on the input layer (Figure 3), the activation pattern produced on the map by each symbol in the string is incrementally overlaid with all patterns generated by all other symbols making up the same string. The resulting *Integrated Activation Pattern* (IAP) is shown in Figure 3 by levels of node activation represented as shaded nodes. IAP activation levels are calculated according to the following equation:

$$\hat{y}_i = max_{t=1,\ldots,k}\{y_i(t)\}; i = 1, \ldots, N \tag{6}$$

where *i* ranges over the number of nodes in the map, and *t* ranges over symbol positions in the input string. Intuitively, each node in the *IAP* is associated with the maximum activation reached by the node in processing the whole input word. Note that, in Figure 3, the same symbol 'p', occurring twice in *#pop$*, activates two different BMUs depending on its position in the string. After presentation of *#pop$*, integrated levels of node activation are stored in the weights of a third level of *IAP* connectivity, linking the map nodes to the lexical map proper (rightmost vector structure in Figure 3). The resulting *IAP* is not only the short-term processing response of a map to *#pop$*. The long-term knowledge sitting in the lexical connections makes the current *IAP* a routinized memory trace of the map processing response. Given an *IAP* and the temporal connections between BMUs, a TSOM can thus use this knowledge to predict, for any currently activated BMU in the *IAP*, the most likely upcoming BMU. This makes it possible to test the behavior of a TSOM on two classical lexical tasks: immediate word recall and serial word processing.

3.2.4.1 Word recall

Word recall refers to the process of retrieving lexical information from the long-term word store. We can test the accuracy of the IAPs as long-term lexical representations by simulating a process of recall of a target word from its own IAP. Since an IAP is a synchronous pattern of activated nodes, the task tests how accurately levels of node activation in the IAP encode information about the timing of the symbols that make up the target word. The process of recall consists in the following steps:

(i) initialize:
   a) reinstate the word IAP on the map
   b) prompt the map with the start-of-word symbol '#'
   c) integrate the word IAP with the temporal expectations of '#'
(ii) calculate the current BMU and output its associated label
(iii) if the output label is NOT symbol '$':
   a) integrate the word IAP with the temporal expectations of the current BMU
   b) go back to step (ii)
(iv) stop

A word is recalled correctly from its IAP if all its symbols are output correctly in the appropriate left-to-right order.

There are a number of features that make IAPs interesting correlates of lexical long-term memory traces. First, activation of an IAP makes all its BMUs simultaneously available. This accounts for "buffering effects" (Goldrick and Rapp 2007; Goldrick et al. 2010), where the idea that symbol representations are concurrently maintained while being manipulated for recall explains the distribution of substitution, deletion and transposition errors. Secondly, IAPs encode word letters in a context-sensitive way, allowing for representation of multiple occurrences of one letter type in the same word. In addition, they rely on a predictive bias, capturing facilitative effects of probabilistic expectation on word processing. Finally, they may contain highly activated nodes that are BMUs of other non-target IAPs, causing strong co-activation (and possible interference) of the latter. To illustrate, if two input strings present some symbols in common (e.g. English *write* and *written*, or German *macht* '(s)he makes' and *gemacht* 'made', past participle), they will tend to activate largely overlapping patterns of nodes.

A TSOM can be said to have acquired a new word form when the word form is accurately recalled from its own IAP. Accordingly, the time of acquisition of a word can be defined as the earliest learning epoch since the word is always recalled accurately. Monitoring the pace of acquisition of words through learning epochs thus allows us to observe which factors affect word acquisition. Concurrent memorization of morphologically redundant forms in inflectional paradigms prompts competition for the same memory resources (processing nodes and temporal connections). Due to *equation 4*, at each processing step, weights on the temporal connection between $BMU(t)$ and $BMU(t+1)$ are reinforced (entrenchment). At the same time, *equation 5* depresses presynaptic connections to $BMU(t+1)$ from any other node than $BMU(t)$ (competition). This simple per-node dynamic has far-reaching consequences on the global self-organization of the map at the word level.

First, the number of nodes responding to a specific input symbol is directly proportional to the token frequency of that symbol. As a result of this correlation (Pearson's r = .95, p < .00001), at early learning epochs, high-frequency words are assigned a larger pool of processing resources than low-frequency words are. In addition, entrenchment makes the time taken for a form to develop strong temporal connections an inverse function of the token frequency of the form. The large availability of processing nodes and dedicated connections causes high-frequency words to be acquired (i.e. accurately recalled from their own IAPs) at earlier learning epochs than low-frequency words (Figure 7, right panel).

Figure 7, left panel, shows the pace of acquisition for regular and irregular verb forms in German, focusing on the interaction between word length and inflectional regularity.

Together with word frequency, word length appears to be a major factor delaying the time of acquisition. Longer words are more difficult to recall since more, concurrently-activated BMUs in an IAP are easier to be confused, missed or jumbled than fewer BMUs are. When word length and word frequency are controlled, regularly inflected forms are recalled at earlier stages than irregulars. The evidence

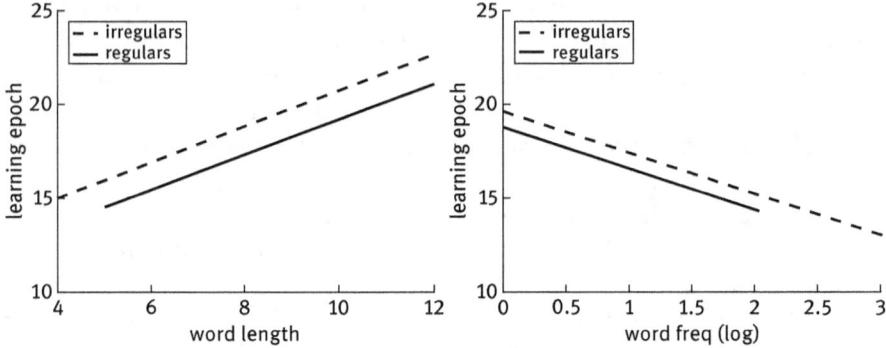

Figure 7: Marginal plots of interaction effects between word length (left panel), word frequency (right panel), and inflectional regularity (solid lines = regulars, dotted lines = irregulars) in an LME model fitting word learning epochs in German.

is in line with the observation that speakers produce words that belong to bigger neighbor families more quickly than isolated words (Chen and Mirman 2012).

3.2.4.2 Serial word processing

Serial word processing involves the processing of an input signal unfolding with time, as is the case with auditory word recognition. Serial lexical access and competition are based on the incremental activation of onset-sharing items, forming a cohort-like set of concurrently activated lexical competitors (Marslen-Wilson 1984; Marslen-Wilson and Welsh 1978). The so-called Uniqueness Point (UP) defines the position in the input string where the cohort of competitors winnows down to unity, meaning that there is only one possible lexical continuation of the currently activated node chain. Figure 5 provides a few examples of Complex Uniqueness Point (or CUP: Balling and Baayen 2008, 2012) for trees of inflectionally related lexical items. Unlike Marslen-Wilson's original definition of UP, which is meant to mark the point in time at which morphologically unrelated words are teased apart, at CUP a target input word is distinguished from the set of its paradigmatically-related companions.

To analyze serial word processing with TSOMs, we monitor the activation state of a map incrementally presented with an input word. Upon each symbol presentation on the input layer at time t, a TSOM is prompted to complete the current input by predicting its most likely lexical continuation. The map propagates the activation of the current $BMU(t)$ through its forward temporal connections, and outputs the label $L_{BMU(t+1)}$ of the most strongly (pre)activated node $BMU(t+1)$:

$$BMU(t+1) = argmax_{i=1,...,N}\{m_{i,h}\}; \quad h = BMU(t), \qquad (7)$$

where $m_{i,h}$ is the weight on the forward temporal connection from node h to node i, and N the overall number of map nodes. Prediction accuracy across the input word is calculated by assigning each correctly anticipated symbol in the input word a 1-point score. Otherwise, the symbol receives a 0-point score. We can then sum up the per-symbol prediction scores in an input word and average the sum by the input word length, to obtain a per-word prediction score; the higher the score, the easier for the map to process the input word.

The panel in Figure 8 shows how prediction scores vary, on average, in 750 German verb forms, as a function of the incremental left-to-right processing of input symbols. Input symbols are plotted by their distance from the word stem-ending boundary ($x = 0$ denotes the first position in the input string after the base stem). Training forms are selected from the 50 top-ranked German verb paradigms by their cumulative frequency in Celex (Baayen et al. 1995), and classified as either regular or irregular.[11]

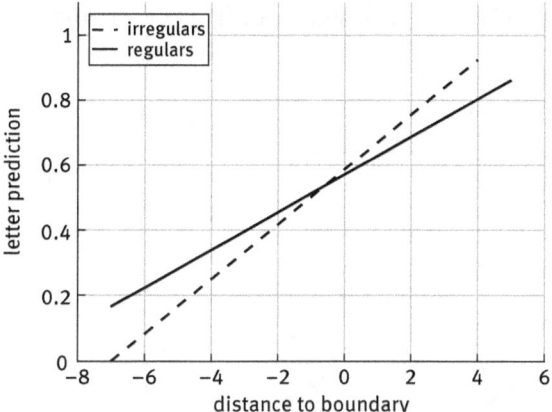

Figure 8: Marginal plot of interaction effects between letter distance to the stem-inflection boundary (x axis, with $x = 0$ marking the first letter in the inflectional ending) and inflectional regularity (regular = solid line vs. irregular = dashed line) in an LME model fitting letter prediction (y axis) in a TSOM trained on German verbs.

---

11 Following a paradigm-based approach to inflection (Aronoff 1994; Blevins 2016; Matthews 1991), all inflected forms belonging to regular paradigms share an invariant base stem (e.g. *walk, walk-s, walk-ed, walk-ing*), whereas irregular paradigms exhibit a more or less wide variety of phonologically unpredictable stems (*sing, sing-s, sang, sung, sing-ing*). Paradigms can thus be classified according to the number of base stems they select, and individual forms are more or less regular depending on the number of their stem-sharing neighbors.

In Figure 8, prediction scores are found to get higher while the end of the form is approached. This is an expected consequence of the reduction in uncertainty for possible lexical continuations at lower nodes in a word-tree. However, the rate of increase follows significantly different slopes in regulars and irregulars.

The evidence is accounted for by the way regularly and irregularly inflected forms are structured in a word-tree (Figure 5). German irregular paradigms (e.g. *geben*) typically present vowel-alternating stems (e.g. *geb-*, *gib-*, *gab-*), which cause their tree-like representation to branch out at higher nodes in the hierarchy (Figure 5). Stems in regular verbs, on the other hand, do not suffer from the competition of other stem alternants within the same paradigm.[12] The general pattern is plotted in Figure 9, depicting the branching-out factor (or node "arity") in the word-tree representation of German verb forms by inflectional regularity and letter distance from the morpheme boundary. Irregulars appear to show a higher branching-out factor at early nodes in the word-tree representation. This factor, however, shrinks further down in the hierarchy more quickly in irregulars than in regulars. This means that processing decisions made on early nodes in the tree-structure reduce the level of processing uncertainty downstream in the lexical tree. Intuitively, once a specific stem alternant is

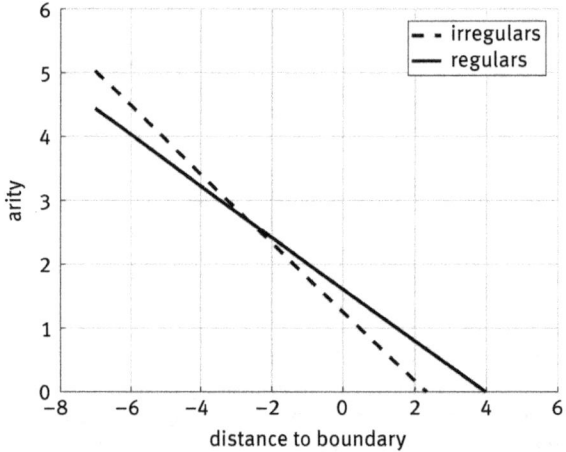

Figure 9: Marginal plot of interaction effects between distance to stem-inflection boundary (x axis) and inflectional regularity (regular = solid line vs. irregular = dashed line) in an LME model fitting node arity (y axis) in a word-tree of German verbs.

---

12 Clearly, both regular and irregular stems can be onset-aligned with other paradigmatically-unrelated stems. Our evidence shows that this extra-paradigmatic "competition" affects both regulars and irregulars to approximately the same extent.

found at the beginning of an irregularly inflected form (e.g. *gab-* in *gaben*), the number of admissible paths branching out at the end of the selected stem goes down dramatically.

These structural properties accord well with evidence that time latencies in processing words out of context are a function of lexical uniqueness points, i.e. the word-internal positions where the human processor can uniquely identify an input word. Balling and Baayen (2008, 2012) show that, in morphologically complex words, lexical processing is paced by two disambiguation points: (i) the uniqueness point distinguishing the input stem form other morphologically-unrelated onset-overlapping stems (or UP1), and (ii) the complex uniqueness point distinguishing the input form from other morphologically-related forms sharing the same stem (or CUP). To illustrate (see Figure 5), in a toy German lexicon containing two paradigms only, namely *geben* ('give') and *glauben* ('believe'), UP1 for *gebt* ('you give', second person plural) is the leftmost letter telling *gebt* from all forms of *glauben*: namely, *e* in second position. Its CUP is the leftmost letter that distinguishes *gebt* from all other forms of *geben*: i.e. *t* in fourth position.

Balling and Baayen show that late UP1s are inhibitory and elicit prolonged reaction times in acoustic word recognition. The evidence challenges the Bayesian decision framework of Shortlist B (Norris and McQueen 2008), where intermediate points of disambiguation play no role in predicting response latencies in auditory comprehension. Balling and Baayen's evidence is nonetheless modelled by a quantitative analysis of the TSOM processing response.

Figure 10 (top panel) depicts average prediction scores in a TSOM processing input symbols in German verb stems, plotted by increasing position values of UP1 in the word form, measured as a distance from the start of the word. Late UP1s slow down processing by decreasing prediction scores. The bottom panel of Figure 10 shows a similar pattern. As expected, late CUPs elicit lower suffix prediction scores than early CUPs.

Finally, when the influence of both UP1 and CUP is taken into account, their joint effect on processing is additive: for any two words with the same CUP position, the word with a later UP1 is processed more slowly by a TSOM than the word with an earlier UP1, in keeping with evidence of human processing (Balling and Baayen 2012).

3.2.5 Competition and entropy

There is a clear connection linking competition among members of a morphological family, and the entropy of the frequency distribution of family members (Baayen et al. 2006; Moscoso del Prado Martín et al. 2004). Milin and colleagues

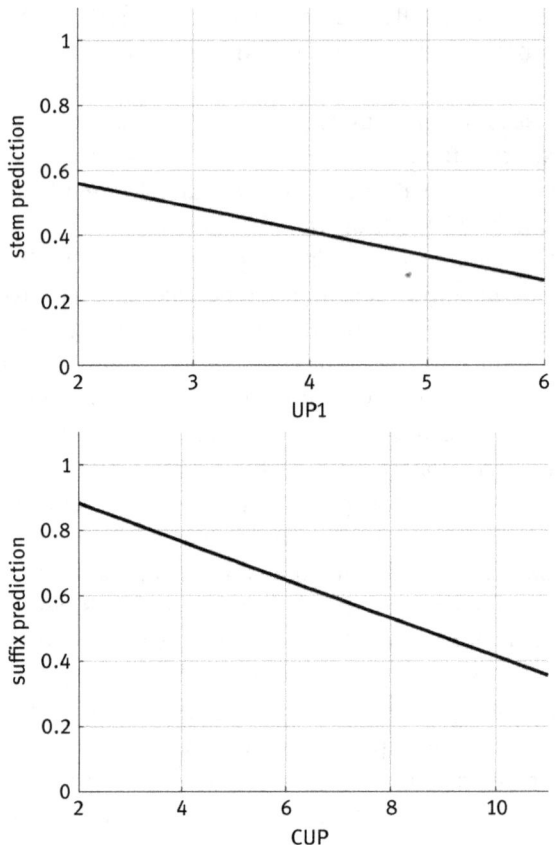

Figure 10: Top panel – marginal plot of interaction effects between UP1 position (x axis) and stem length in an LME model fitting letter prediction in verb stems (y axis) by a TSOM trained on German verbs. Bottom panel – marginal plot of interaction effects between CUP position (x axis) and length of inflectional endings in an LME model fitting letter prediction in verb endings (y axis) by a TSOM trained on German verbs.

(Milin, Filipović Đurđević et al. 2009, Milin, Kuperman et al. 2009) put considerable emphasis on the interactive role of intra-paradigmatic and inter-paradigmatic distributions in accounting for differential effects on visual lexical recognition. In particular, they focus on the divergence between the distribution of inflectional endings within each single paradigm (measured as the entropy of the distribution of paradigmatically-related forms, or Paradigm Entropy), and the distribution of the same endings within their broader inflectional class (measured as the entropy of the distributions of inflectional endings across all paradigms, or Inflectional Entropy). Both entropic scores are known to facilitate visual lexical recognition. If the two distributions differ, however, a conflict may arise, resulting in slower recognition of the words. These effects are the by-product of a model of the lexicon offering more or less explicit mechanisms dealing with the simultaneous existence of potentially competing paradigmatically related forms, and with the simultaneous existence of multiple paradigms. Similar results are reported by Kuperman et al. (2010) on reading times for Dutch derived words, and are interpreted as reflecting an information imbalance between the family of the base word (e.g. *plaats* 'place' in *plaatsing* 'placement') and the family of the suffix (*-ing*).

The difference between Paradigm Entropy and Inflectional Entropy can be expressed in terms of Relative Entropy, or Kullback-Leibler divergence (D_{KL}, Kullback 1987), as follows:

$$D_{KL}(p(e|s)||p(e)) = \sum_{e} p(e|s) \log \frac{p(e|s)}{p(e)}, \qquad (8)$$

where $p(e|s)$ represents the probability of having a specific inflected form (an ending e) given a stem s, and $p(e)$ the probability of encountering e. For any specific paradigm being selected, the larger D_{KL}, the more difficult is, on average, the visual recognition of members of that paradigm.

The relatively simple learning dynamic of TSOMs, expressed by rules (i) and (ii) above, accounts for facilitative effects of paradigm entropy and inflectional entropy on word learning.

To illustrate, we trained a TSOM on three mini-paradigms, whose forms are obtained by combining three stems ('A', 'B' and 'C') with two endings (symbols 'X' and 'Y'). Mini-paradigms were administered to the map on six training regimes (R1-R6, see Table 2), whose distribution was intended to control the comparative probability distribution of 'X' and 'Y', and the comparative probability distribution of the stems 'A', 'B' and 'C' relative to each ending. Across regimes 1–3, we kept the frequency distribution of X constant (but we made it vary across paradigms), while increasing the distribution of Y both within each paradigm (R2), and across paradigms (R3). Across regimes 4-5, the frequency of Y was held constant, while X frequencies were made vary. Finally in R6 all word frequencies were set to 100. Note that in R3 and R6 $p(e|s) = p(e)$: i.e., the distribution of each inflected form within a paradigm equals the distribution of its ending (given its inflection class).

Results of the different training regimes are shown in Figure 11, where we plotted weights on the connection between stems ('A', 'B' and 'C') and endings ('X' and 'Y') by learning epochs, averaged over 100 repetitions of the same experiment on each regime. Results were analyzed with linear mixed-effects models, with stem-ending connection weights as our dependent variable and the

Table 2: Frequency distribution of 3 mini-paradigms (rows) in 6 training regimes (columns).

paradigm id	items	Frequency					
		regime 1	regime 2	regime 3	regime 4	regime 5	regime 6
A	#,A,X,$	5	5	5	5	5	100
A	#,A,Y,$	5	50	50	333	333	100
B	#,B,X,$	10	10	10	10	100	100
B	#,B,Y,$	10	100	100	333	333	100
C	#,C,X,$	85	85	85	85	850	100
C	#,C,Y,$	10	100	850	333	333	100

following three fixed effects: (i) the word probability $p(s, e)$, expressed as a stem-ending combination, (ii) the probability $p(e \mid s)$ of a stem selecting a specific ending (or intra-paradigmatic competition), and (iii) the conditional probability $p(s \mid e)$ of a given ending being selected by a specific stem (inter-paradigmatic competition). Experiment repetitions were used as random effects. We refer the interested reader to Ferro et al. (2018) for a thorough analysis of the effects. Here, we shortly summarize the main results observed, and provide an analytical interpretation of this evidence.

Due to entrenchment (*equation 4*), the strength of each connection at the morpheme boundary tends to be a direct function of the probability of each word form, or $p(s, e)$ (see panel R3 in Figure 11). However, other factors interact with word frequency: connection strengths are affected by the probability of each ending $p(e)$, with low-frequency words that contain high-frequency endings (e.g. "AX" in panel R1) showing a stronger boundary connection than low-frequency words that contain less frequent endings ("AY" in panel R1). This boosting effect is modulated by two further interactions: the conditional probability distribution $p(e|s)$, with connections to 'X' suffering from an increase in the probability mass of 'Y' (panels R2 and R4), and the competition between words selecting the same ending (rule ii), modulated by the entropy of the conditional probability distribution $p(s|e)$, or $H(s|e)$ (panels R4 and R5). In particular, if we control $H(s)$, i.e. the distribution of paradigms in the input data, the entropy $H(s|e)$ is expressed analytically by the following equation:

$$H(s|e) = H(s) - \sum_{s,e} p(s,e) \log \frac{p(s,e)}{p(s)p(e)}. \qquad (9)$$

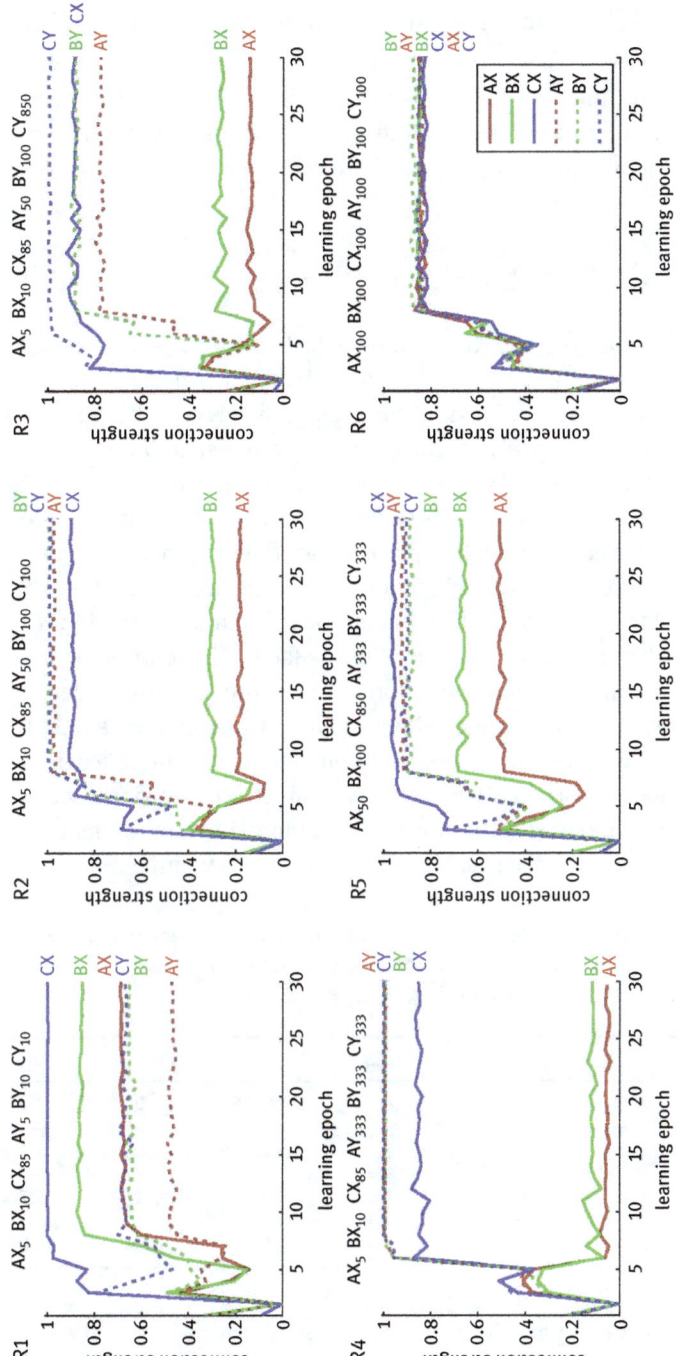

Figure 11: Developmental trends of connection strength at the stem-ending boundary under different training regimes with three mini-paradigms (R1-R6, see Table 2). Weights are plotted against the first 30 learning epochs.

Where $\sum_{s,e} p(s,e) \log \frac{p(s,e)}{p(s)p(e)}$ is known as *Mutual Information*, a measure of the mutual dependence between stems and endings, defined as the divergence of the distribution $p(s,e)$ of the verb forms in our training set from the hypothesis that $p(s,e) = p(s)p(e)$, or independence hypothesis (Manning and Schütze 1999). Using the Bayesian equality $p(s,e) = p(s)p(e|s)$, we can rewrite *equation 9* above as follows:

$$H(s|e) = H(s) - \sum_s p(s) \sum_e p(e|s) \log \frac{p(e|s)}{p(e)}, \qquad (10)$$

where $\sum_s p(s) \sum_e p(e|s) \log \frac{p(e|s)}{p(e)}$ is the Kullback-Leibler divergence between $p(e|s)$ and $p(e)$ in *equation 8* above. *Equation 10* shows that, when $H(s)$ is kept fixed, $H(s|e)$ is maximized by minimizing the average divergence between the intra-paradigmatic distribution $p(e|s)$ of the endings given a stem, and the marginal distribution $p(e)$ of the endings (see Table 3). In other words, verb paradigms are learned more accurately by a TSOM when, on average, the distribution $p(e|s)$ of the forms within each paradigm approximates the marginal distribution of each ending in the corresponding conjugation class (compare R4 and R6). This behavior, accounted for by the interaction of entrenchment and competition/inhibition in discriminative learning, is in line with the facilitation effects reported for visual lexical recognition of inflected words and reading times of derived words (Milin, Filipović Đurđević et al. 2009, Milin, Kuperman et al. 2009; Kuperman et al. 2010). Besides, the evidence is compatible with more extensive experiments on German and Italian verbs (Marzi et al. 2014), showing that, for comparable cumulative frequencies, uniform distributions in training data (R6) facilitate paradigm acquisition (see also Marzi et al. 2020, this volume).

Table 3: Different intra-paradigmatic frequency distributions obtained by keeping marginal distributions fixed. The right-hand distribution is obtained with $p(s,e) = p(s) \cdot p(e)$, to make $D_{KL}(p(e|s)||p(e)) = 0$. For the distribution on the left, $D_{KL}(p(e|s)||p(e)) > 0$.

$p(s,e)$	X	Y	$p(s)$		$p(s,e)$	X	Y	$p(s)$
A	0.04	0.04	0.08		A	0.064	0.016	0.08
B	0.08	0.08	0.16	>	B	0.128	0.032	0.16
C	0.68	0.08	0.76		C	0.608	0.152	0.76
$p(e)$	0.8	0.2	1.00		$p(e)$	0.8	0.2	1.00

Ferro et al. (2018) report comparable results with TSOMs trained on real inflection systems. In two experiments, a TSOM is trained on the same 50 German verb paradigms by varying their frequency distributions: in the first experiment, forms are presented with a uniform frequency distribution (Kullback-Leibler divergence = 0); in the second experiment, the same set of forms was presented with realistic frequency distributions (Kullback-Leibler divergence > 0). For each map, the number of BMUs recruited for the recognition of inflectional ending was counted. The two experiments were repeated 5 times, and results were averaged across repetitions. As shown in Figure 12, in the training regime with uniform distributions, inflectional endings recruit a larger number of *BMUs* than in the realistic training regime.

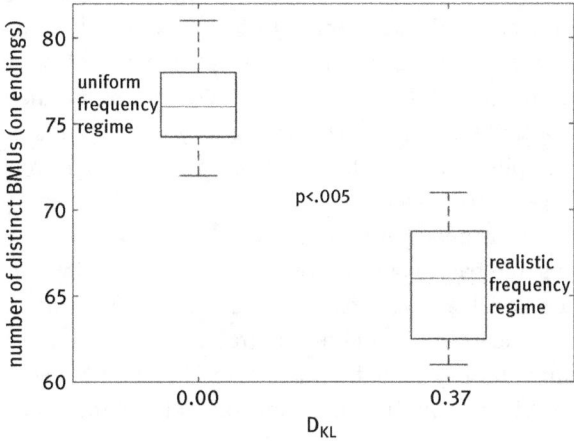

Figure 12: Number of BMUs recruited by inflectional endings, in two experiments where a TSOM is trained with German verb forms with uniform (left) and realistic (right) frequency distributions.

4 Concluding remarks

This chapter provided (i) a selective overview of mathematical and computational approaches to the mental lexicon with a view to prospective unification, (ii) a reappraisal of traditional issues of word storage and processing, and (iii) a novel perspective on these issues from a discriminative learning perspective. In principle, a learning perspective on matters of lexical content, organization and processing crucially can part ways with two alternative views: (i) that lexical representations and word processing strategies are completely predetermined by nature and structure of input data; (ii) that they are completely predetermined by the blueprints of the human word processor. Computer simulations of lexical modelling tell us that both word representations and processing strategies are shaped up by a complex, dynamic interaction between the innate, domain general principles governing the way humans encode and manage input stimuli, and the structure, paradigmatic organization and frequency distribution of the language input. Different global effects in the operation of a pool of low-level interactive processes are the by-products of domain-specific levels of input representations giving rise to a relatively autonomous organization. Likewise, in a neuro-anatomical perspective, words can be investigated as emergent properties of the functional interaction of different brain areas, each participating in multiple functions (Price 2012, 2017).

We believe that the question of how much of a speaker's internalized word knowledge is determined and accounted for by the informativeness of the language input, and how much is due to the operation of innate principles of serial processing and storage is entirely empirical and, according to our current understanding, not yet amenable to a unifying theory. This is why any strongly dualistic view on lexical matters, sharply separating lexicon from rules, storage from processing, exceptions from regularities, declarative from procedural knowledge strikes us as premature if not unwarranted. A more sensible way to make progress in this area is to focus on some basic cognitive operations and their interaction, and investigate how higher-level language functions and operations emerge from them. From this perspective, learning is not only central to language inquiry as such, but it is also a fundamental key to methodological unification between psycholinguistic and cognitive evidence on the one hand, constraining important aspects of algorithmic modelling, and computer simulations on the other hand. In this chapter, we showed that very simple principles of discriminative learning can go a long way to accounting for complex behavioral evidence. Future work will tell us if these accounts are entirely correct, or should be refined or rejected altogether. Nonetheless, we see no serious alternative to a minimalist, bottom-up approach, whereby innatistic assumptions and ad hoc language principles are introduced as cautiously as possible.

This approach shifts the research focus from a "modular" view of lexical storage, segregated and fundamentally independent from processing, to a radically "integrative view", where storage and processing are in fact two different dynamics of the same underlying process. We provide here a list of some criterial features of such an integrative storage-processing framework (adapted from Marzi and Pirrelli 2015):

- **non-enumerative**: there is no such thing as a finite list of stored items in the human brain; there are many more (potential) pathways in our network of partially overlapping lexical items, than those attested in the input; as a result, the notion of "wordlikeness" (or "lexicality") is a gradient one (a

lexical entry can be perceived as more or less "typical"), and is not coextensive with the linguistic notion of "listedness" (Di Sciullo and Williams 1987);
- **parallel**: lexical items are activated simultaneously and accessed globally, through resolution of highly distributed, shared sublexical relations;
- **dynamic**: information is never stable; every time a lexical representation is successfully accessed, its content changes accordingly (e.g. through consolidation of connection strengths); moreover, access of any lexical representation affects, more or less deeply, the activation state of all other representations in the same lexicon;
- **processing-dependent**: a lexical representation is fundamentally grounded in processing principles; in fact, it may consist in the same processing units that are fired by the input word associated with the lexical representation;
- **redundant**: lexical representations consist of highly redundant, distributed relations, subsuming both lexical and sublexical structures;
- **emergent/abstractive**: word structure is not a prior, but the perceived by-product of stored, unsegmented input stimuli (full forms or units larger than full forms); perception of structure eventually feeds back on processing;
- **multidimensional**: the lexicon develops structural units defined over many hierarchically arranged levels of representation, ranging from sounds, syllables and morphemes, to words, phrases and sentences; nonetheless, the hypothesis that complex units are processed through a staged sequence of steps going from irreducible primitives to the whole input, is questioned by the highly interactive nature of representation levels, showing pervasive top-down effects on the processing of lower level units;
- **two-way interaction**: lexical representations affect processing, and are crucially affected by processing.

An important cross-linguistic implication of this view is that not all morphologies are processed equally. They do not give rise to homogenous effects of global self-organization. Differences may depend on differences in morphological structure and degrees of predictability (Bompolas et al. 2017; Marzi et al. 2018; and Marzi et al. 2020, this volume). In turn, perception of morphological structure may vary as a function of word length, frequency, perceptual salience, size of lexical neighborhood, distribution of neighborhood members, valence, age of acquisition, embedding context and yet other factors. Computer simulations have so far only scratched the surface of such a multifaceted dynamic interaction. An important emerging trend in the recent literature is that a comparatively small pool of basic, language-independent principles can account for a number of differential effects that were commonly understood to require different modules and functionally specialized processing routes.

Competition among multiple lexical cues for their discriminative value is key to understanding fundamental aspects of the word learning dynamic (Baayen et al. 2011; Ramscar and Yarlett 2007; Ramscar, Dye, and McCauley 2013; Milin, Feldman et al. 2017). In most discriminative approaches to language learning reviewed here, units defined on one level of representation are understood and modelled to cue units on a different level. For example, forms are cues to either lexical or morpho-syntactic content. Although this is the most intuitive way to conceptualize a cue-outcome relationship in language learning, we saw here that discriminative equations can be used to develop maximally efficient processing structures for symbolic series defined on one representation level only: e.g. sequences of letters/sounds in TSOMs, and lexome-to-lexome discriminative networks for word recognition. One-level, re-entrant discriminative networks prove to be effective in a number of tasks, from prediction-driven processing of upcoming symbols, to context-sensitive filtering of irrelevant units in context. The most efficient way to learn these tasks is to build a maximally discriminative network given the input context. We showed that this straightforward principle can account for complex effects of relative entropy on human processing of verb paradigms.

Finally, in spite of the wide variety of attested self-organizing systems, there seems to be an upper limit on the level of structural complexity they can exhibit, measured as the speaker's uncertainty in making processing predictions about an unknown inflected form in word production (or cell filling problem). Ackerman and Malouf (2013) use Shannon's information entropy to quantify the average conditional entropy of predicting each form in a paradigm on the basis of any other form in the same paradigm, to conjecture that inflectional systems tend to minimize such figure of merit for inflectional complexity. In a discriminative learning framework, Ackerman and Malouf's conjecture can naturally be interpreted in terms of the average degree of predictability of word forms in either recognition or recall. Based on evidence from German and Italian, we showed that processing uncertainty is differently apportioned, depending on the nature of the processing task (Marzi et al. 2016). While irregulars can hardly be predicted when they are unknown because they typically have fewer neighbors than regulars have, irregulars are readily accessed once they are acquired, for exactly the same reason. Thus, existence of irregulars is not dysfunctional, but instrumental to the need to balance processing costs in the two tasks. Similarly, in a typological perspective, non-concatenative morphologies make stems harder to process, due to the variety of their allomorphs, but easier to be completed with their appropriate inflectional endings. Conversely, concatenative morphologies tend to make stems easier to process, but increase processing uncertainty in the selection of the inflectional ending at the morpheme boundary (Marzi et al. 2018; Ferro et al. 2018; Marzi et al. 2019; Marzi et al. 2020, this volume).

Of late, the advent and exponential growth of neuroimaging technology has allowed in-vivo investigation of the connection between brain data and psychological evidence, establishing a level of material continuity between observations and hypotheses in the domains of neuroscience and cognitive psychology. In the near future, further technological progress will be able to improve the spatial and temporal resolution with which functional regions are located anatomically, to provide novel evidence and constraints on computations and word representations in the brain. Nonetheless, the greatest challenge ahead of us is probably to understand "how" processing takes place in each region and how it interacts with information processed in other regions recruited for the same linguistic task. In this connection, computational and mathematical models of behavioral evidence and functionally related anatomic data have a great potential in bridging the persisting gap between low-level, interactive brain processes and high-level, cognitive models of language knowledge and language behavior. We believe that such integrative, multi-scale, performance-based models of word knowledge will provide an important contribution to a deeper understanding of how language works and is implemented in the brain.

References

Ackerman, Farrell, James P. Blevins & Robert Malouf. 2009. Parts and wholes: implicative patterns in inflectional paradigms. In James P. Blevins & Juliette Blevins (eds.), *Analogy in Grammar*, 54–82. Oxford: Oxford University Press.

Acquaviva, Paolo, Alessandro Lenci, Carita Paradis & Ida Raffaelli. 2020. In Vito Pirrelli, Ingo Plag & Wolfgang U. Dressler (eds.), *Word knowledge and word usage: a cross-disciplinary guide to the mental lexicon*, 354–404. De Gruyter.

Ackerman, Farrell & Robert Malouf. 2013. Morphological organization: The low conditional entropy conjecture. *Language* 89 (3). 429–464.

Albright, Adam. 2002. Islands of reliability for regular morphology: Evidence from Italian. *Language* 78 (4). 684–709.

Alvargonzález, David. 2011. Multidisciplinarity, interdisciplinarity, transdisciplinarity, and the sciences. *International Studies in the Philosophy of Science* 25 (4). 387–403.

Anderson, Stephen R. 1992. *A-Morphous Morphology*. Cambridge (UK): Cambridge University Press.

Arnold, Denis, Fabian Tomaschek, Konstantin Sering, Florence Lopez & R. Harald Baayen. 2017. Words from spontaneous conversational speech can be recognized with human-like accuracy by an error-driven learning algorithm that discriminates between meanings straight from smart acoustic features, bypassing the phoneme as recognition unit. *PLoS ONE* 12 (4) e0174623. 1–16.

Aronoff, Mark (1976). *Word Formation in Generative Grammar*. Cambridge (Mass.): MIT Press.
Aronoff, Mark (1994). *Morphology by Itself: Stems and Inflectional Classes*. Cambridge (Mass.): MIT Press.
Arppe, Antti, Peter Hendrix, Petar Milin, R. Harald Baayen, Tino Sering & Cyrus Shaoul. 2015. ndl: Naive Discriminative Learning. R package. Retrieved from https://CRAN.R-project.org/package=ndl
Baayen R. Harald (2007). Storage and computation in the mental lexicon. In Gonia Jarema & Gary Libben (eds.), *The Mental Lexicon: Core Perspectives*, 81–104. Elsevier.
Baayen, R. Harald, Laurie B. Feldman & Robert Schreuder 2006. Morphological influences on the recognition of monosyllabic monomorphemic words. *Journal of Memory and Language* 55 (2). 290–313.
Baayen, R. Harald, Petar Milin, Dušica Filipović Đurđević, Peter Hendrix, Marco Marelli. 2011. An amorphous model for morphological processing in visual comprehension based on naive discriminative learning. *Psychological Review* 118 (3). 438–481.
Baayen, R. Harald, Petar Milin & Michael Ramscar. 2016. Frequency in lexical processing. *Aphasiology 30* (11). 1174–1220.
Baayen, R. Harald, Richard Piepenbrock & Leon Gulikers. 1995. The CELEX Lexical Database (CD-ROM). Philadelphia: Linguistic Data Consortium.
Baayen, R. Harald, Tino Sering, Cyrus Shaoul & Petar Milin. 2017. Language comprehension as a multiple label classification problem. In Marco Grzegorczyk & Giacomo Ceoldo (eds.), *Proceedings of the 32nd International Workshop on Statistical Modelling (IWSM)*, 21–34. Groningen, University of Groningen.
Baayen, R. Harald, Cyrus Shaoul, Jon Willits & Michael Ramscar. 2016. Comprehension without segmentation: A proof of concept with naive discriminative learning. *Language, Cognition and Neuroscience* 31 (1). 106–128.
Baayen, R. Harald, Lee H. Wurm & Joanna Aycock. 2007. Lexical dynamics for low-frequency complex words. A regression study across tasks and modalities. *The Mental Lexicon* 2. 419–463.
Baddeley Alan D. (1986). *Working Memory*. Oxford, Oxford University Press.
Balling, Laura W. & Baayen, R. Harald. 2008. Morphological effects in auditory word recognition: Evidence from Danish. *Language and Cognitive Processes* 23 (7–8). 1159–1190.
Balling, Laura W. & Baayen, R. Harald. 2012. Probability and surprisal in auditory comprehension of morphologically complex words. *Cognition* 125(1). 80–106.
Becker, Curtis A. 1980. Semantic context effects in visual word recognition: An analysis of semantic strategies. *Memory and Cognition* 8. 493–512.
Beckner, Clay, Richard Blythe, Joan Bybee, Morten H. Christiansen, William Croft, Nick C. Ellis, John Holland, Jinyun Ke, Diane Larsen-Freeman & Tom Schoenemann. 2009. Language is a complex adaptive system: Position paper. *Language learning* 59. 1–26.
Beard, Robert. 1995. *Lexeme-Morpheme Base Morphology: A General Theory of Inflection and Word Formation*. SUNY Press.
Berg, Thomas. 2020. Morphological slips of the tongue. In Vito Pirrelli, Ingo Plag & Wolfgang U. Dressler (eds.), *Word knowledge and word usage: a cross-disciplinary guide to the mental lexicon*, 635–679. De Gruyter.
Blevins, James P. 2006. Word-based morphology. *Journal of Linguistics* 42. 531–573.
Blevins, James P. 2016. *Word and paradigm morphology*. Oxford: Oxford University Press.

Blevins, James P., Farrell Ackerman, Robert Malouf & Michael Ramscar. 2016. Morphology as an adaptive discriminative system. In Daniel Siddiqi & Heidi Harley (eds.), *Morphological metatheory*, 271–302. John Benjamins.
Blevins, James P., Petar Milin & Michael Ramscar. 2017. The Zipfian paradigm cell filling problem. In Ferenc Kiefer, James P. Blevins & Huba Bartos (eds.), *Perspectives on Morphological Organization: Data and Analyses*, 139–158. Leiden: Brill.
Bloch, Bernard. 1947. English verb inflection. *Language* 23. 399–418.
Bloomfield, Leonard. 1933. *Language*. New York, Henry Holt.
Blough, Donald S. 1975. Steady state data and a quantitative model of operant generalization and discrimination. *Journal of Experimental Psychology: Animal Behavior Processes* 1 (1). 3.
Bompolas Stavros, Marcello Ferro, Claudia Marzi, Franco Alberto Cardillo & Vito Pirrelli. 2017. For a performance-oriented notion of regularity in inflection: the case of Modern Greek conjugation. *Italian Journal of Computational Linguistics* 3 (1). 77–92.
Booij, Geert. 2010. *Construction Morphology*. Oxford University Press.
Bresnan, Joan, Anna Cueni, Tatiana Nikitina, & R. Harald Baayen. 2005. Predicting the dative alternation. *Proceeding of the (KNAW) Academy Colloquium: Cognitive foundations of interpretation*, Amsterdam.
Burzio, Luigi. 1998. Multiple Correspondence, *Lingua* 104. 79–109.
Bybee Joan. 1995. Regular Morphology and the Lexicon. *Language and Cognitive Processes* 10 (5). 425–455.
Bybee, Joan. 2002. Sequentiality as the basis of constituent structure. In Thomas Givón & Bertram F. Malle (eds.), *The Evolution of Language out of Pre-Language*, 107–132. John Benjamins.
Bybee, Joan & Paul J. Hopper (eds.). 2001. *Frequency and the Emergence of Linguistic Structure*. John Benjamin Publishing Company.
Bybee, Joan & James L. McClelland. 2005. Alternatives to the combinatorial paradigm of linguistic theory based on domain general principles of human cognition. *The Linguistic Review* 22 (2–4). 381–410.
Caramazza, Alfonso, Alessandro Laudanna & Cristina Romani. 1988. Lexical access and inflectional morphology. *Cognition*, 28, 297–332.
Cardillo, Franco Alberto, Marcello Ferro, Claudia Marzi & Vito Pirrelli. 2018. Deep learning of inflection and the Cell-filling problem. *Italian Journal of Computational Linguistics* 4(1). 57–75.
Chen, Qi & Daniel Mirman. 2012. Competition and cooperation among similar representations: toward a unified account of facilitative and inhibitory effects of lexical neighbors. *Psychological review* 119 (2). 417–430.
Chomsky, Noam & Morris Halle. 1968. *The sound pattern of English*. New York, Harper and Row.
Clark, Alexander, Chris Fox & Shalom Lapping (eds.). 2010. *The Handbook of Computational Linguistics and Natural Language Processing*. Wiley Blackwell.
Clark, Eve V. 1987. The Principle of Contrast: A Constraint on Language Acquisition. In Brian MacWhinney (ed.), *Mechanisms of Language Acquisition*, 1–33. Lawrence Elbaum.
Clark, Eve V. 1990. On the pragmatics of contrast. *Journal of child language* 17 (2). 417–431.
Corbett, Greville G. & Norman M. Fraser. 1993. Network Morphology: A DATR account of Russian nominal inflection. *Journal of Linguistics* 29. 113–142.

Dahan, Delphine & James S. Magnuson. 2006. Spoken-word recognition. In Matthew J. Traxler& Morton A. Gernsbacher (eds.), *Handbook of Psycholinguistics*, 249–283. Elsevier.

Danks, David. 2003. Equilibria of the Rescorla–Wagner model. *Journal of Mathematical Psychology* 47 (2). 109–121.

Davis, Colin J. 2010. The Spatial Coding Model of Visual Word Identification, *Psychological Review* 117 (3). 713–758.

Di Sciullo, Anna Maria & Edwin Williams. 1987. *On the Definition of Word*. Cambridge: MIT Press.

Divjak, Dagmar & Stephan T. Gries. 2006. Ways of trying in Russian: Clustering behavioral profiles. *Corpus Linguistics and Linguistic Theory* 2 (1). 23–60.

Ellis, Nick C. 2006a. Language acquisition as rational contingency learning. *Applied linguistics* 27 (1). 1–24.

Ellis, Nick C. 2006b. Selective attention and transfer phenomena in L2 acquisition: Contingency, cue competition, salience, interference, overshadowing, blocking, and perceptual learning. *Applied linguistics* 27 (2). 164–194.

Ellis, Nick C. & Diane Larsen-Freeman. 2006. Language energence: Implications for applied linguistics – Introduction to the special issue. *Applied Linguistics* 27. 558–589.

Elman, Jeffrey L. 2009. On the meaning of words and dinosaur bones: Lexical knowledge without a lexicon. *Cognitive science* 33 (4). 547–582.

Fábregas, Antonio and Martina Penke. 2020. Word storage and computation. In Vito Pirrelli, Ingo Plag & Wolfgang U. Dressler (eds.), *Word knowledge and word usage: a cross-disciplinary guide to the mental lexicon*, 455–505. De Gruyter.

Ferro, Marcello, Claudia Marzi & Vito Pirrelli. 2011. A Self-Organizing Model of Word Storage and Processing: Implications for Morphology Learning. *Lingue e Linguaggio* X (2). 209–226.

Ferro, Marcello, Claudia Marzi & Vito Pirrelli. 2018. Discriminative word learning is sensitive to inflectional entropy. *Lingue e Linguaggio* XVII (2). 307–327.

Finkel, Raphael & Gregory Stump. 2007. Principal parts and morphological typology. *Morphology* 17. 39–75.

Gaskell, M. Gareth & William D. Marslen-Wilson. 2002. Representation and competition in the perception of spoken words. *Cognitive psychology* 45 (2). 220–266.

Geeraert, Kristina, John Newman & R. Harald Baayen. 2017. Idiom variation: Experimental data and a blueprint of a computational model. In Morten Christiansen & Inbal Arnon (eds.), *More than Words: The Role of Multiword Sequences in Language Learning and Use*. Special issue of *Topics in Cognitive Science* 9 (3). 653–669.

Ghirlanda, Stefano (2005) Retrospective revaluation as simple associative learning. *Journal of Experimental Psychology: Animal Behavior Processes*, 31(1), 107.

Ghirlanda, Stefano, Johan Lind & Magnus Enquist. 2017. Memory for stimulus sequences: a divide between humans and other animals? *Royal Society Open Science* 4. 161011. http://dx.doi.org/10.1098/rsos.161011

Giraudo, Hélène & Jonathan Grainger. 2000. Effects of prime word frequency and cumulative root frequency in masked morphological priming. *Language and Cognitive Processes* 15 (4/5). 421–444.

Goldberg, Adele. 2006. *Constructions at work. the nature of generalization in language*. Oxford University Press.

Goldrick, Matthew, Jocelyn R. Folk & Brenda Rapp. 2010. Mrs. Malaprop's neighborhood: Using word errors to reveal neighborhood structure. *Journal of Memory and Language* 62 (2). 113–134.

Goldrick, Matthew & Brenda Rapp. 2007. Lexical and post-lexical phonological representations in spoken production. *Cognition* 102 (2). 219–260.

Grainger, Jonathan, Pascale Colé & Juan Segui, J. (1991). Masked morphological priming in visual word recognition. *Journal of Memory and Language*, 30, 370–384.

Halle, Morris (1973). Prolegomena to a theory of word formation. *Linguistic Inquiry* 4. 451–464.

Hay, Jennifer B. & R. Harald Baayen. 2005. Shifting Paradigms: Gradient structure in morphology. *Trends in Cognitive Sciences* 9 (7). 342–348.

Hendrix, Peter. 2015. Experimental explorations of a discrimination learning approach to language processing. Doctoral dissertation, University of Tuebingen.

Hendrix, Peter, Patrick Bolger & R. Harald Baayen. 2017. Distinct ERP signatures of word frequency, phrase frequency, and prototypicality in speech production. *Journal of Experimental Psychology: Learning, Memory, and Cognition* 43 (1). 128.

Henson, Richard N. 1998. Short-term memory for serial order: The start-end model, *Cognitive Psychology* 36. 73–137.

Hockett, Charles F. 1954. Two models of grammatical description. *Word* 10. 210–231.

Jackendoff, Ray. 1975. Morphological and semantic regularities in the lexicon. *Language* 51. 639–671.

Jackendoff, Ray. 2002. *Foundations of Language. Brain, Meaning, Grammar, Evolution*. Oxford University Press.

James, William. 1890. *Principles of Psychology*. New York: Henry Holt & Company.

James, William. 1907. *Pragmatism: A New Name for Some Old Ways of Thinking*. New York: Longmans, Green, & Co.

James, William. 1909. *The Meaning of Truth: A Sequel to "Pragmatism"*. New York: Longmans, Green, & Co.

Johnson, Keith. 2004. Massive reduction in conversational American English. In *Spontaneous speech: Data and analysis. Proceedings of the 1st session of the 10th international symposium*, 29–54. Tokyo, Japan: The National International Institute for Japanese Language.

Kalman, Rudolph E. 1960. A new approach to linear filtering and prediction problems. *Journal of basic Engineering 82* (1). 35–45.

Karttunen, Lauri. 2003. Computing with realizational morphology. In Alexander Gelbukh (ed.), *Computational Linguistics and Intelligent Text Processing, Proceedings of CICLing 2003*, 203–214. Springer Verlag, Berlin.

Kullback, Solomon. 1987. Letter to the editor: The Kullback-Leibler distance. *The American Statistician* 41 (4), 340–341.

Kuperman, Victor, Raymond Bertram & R. Harald Baayen. 2010. Processing trade-offs in the reading of Dutch derived words. *Journal of Memory and Language* 62(2). 83–97.

Kuperman, Victor, Robert Schreuder, Raymond Bertram & R. Harald Baayen. 2009. Reading of multimorphemic Dutch compounds: towards a multiple route model of lexical processing. *Journal of Experimental Psychology: HPP* 35. 876–895.

Landauer, Thomas K., Peter W. Foltz & Darrell Laham. 1998. An introduction to latent semantic analysis. *Discourse Processes* 25 (2–3). 259–284.

Larsen-Freeman, Diane & Lynne Cameron. 2008. *Complex Systems and Applied Linguistics*. Oxford University Press.

Lensink, S.E., Verhagen, A., Schiller, N. & R. Harald Baayen. 2017. Keeping them apart: on using a discriminative approach to study the nature and processing of multi-word units. Manuscript, University of Leiden.

Levelt, Willem J., Ardi Roelofs & Antje S. Meyer. 1999. A theory of lexical access in speech production. *Behavioral and Brain Sciences* 22. 1–38.

Libben Gary. 2005. Everything is psycholinguistics: Material and methodological considerations in the study of compound processing. *Canadian Journal of Linguistics* 50. 267–283.

Libben, Gary. 2016. The quantum metaphor and the organization of words in the mind. *Journal of Culture Cognitive Science* 1. 49–55.

Lieber, Rochelle 1980. *On the organization of the lexicon*. PhD thesis. Cambridge, MIT.

Linke, Maja, Franziska Bröker, Michael Ramscar & R. Harald Baayen. 2017. Are baboons learning "orthographic" representations? Probably not. *PloS one* 12 (8). e0183876.

Luce, Paul A. 1986. A computational analysis of uniqueness points in auditory word recognition. *Perception & Psychophysics* 39. 155–158.

Luce, Paul A. & David B. Pisoni. 1998. Recognizing spoken words: The neighborhood activation model. *Ear and Hearing* 19. 1–36.

MacKay, Donald G. 1982. The problems of flexibility, fluency, and speed-accuracy trade-off in skilled behavior. *Psychological Review* 89. 483–506.

MacWhinney, Brian (ed.). 1999. *The emergence of language*. Lawrence Erlbaum Associates.

MacWhinney, Brian & William O'Grady. (eds.). 2015. *The Handbook of Language Emergence*. Wiley Blackwell.

Manning, Christopher D. & Hinrich Schütze. 1999. *Foundations of statistical natural language processing*. Cambridge: MIT press.

Marangolo, Paola & Costanza Papagno. 2020. Neuroscientific protocols for exploring the mental lexicon. In Vito Pirrelli, Ingo Plag & Wolfgang U. Dressler (eds.), *Word knowledge and word usage: a cross-disciplinary guide to the mental lexicon*, 127–166. De Gruyter.

Marelli, Marco & Marco Baroni. 2015. Affixation in semantic space: Modeling morpheme meanings with compositional distributional semantics. *Psychological review* 122 (3). 485–515.

Marr, David. 1982. *Vision*. San Francisco: W.H. Freeman.

Marslen-Wilson, William D. 1984. Function and process in spoken word recognition: A tutorial overview. In Herman Bouma & Don G. Bouwhuis (eds.), *Attention and performance X: Control of language processes*, 125–150. Hillsdale: Erlbaum.

Marslen-Wilson, William D. & Alan Welsh. 1978. Processing interactions and lexical access during word recognition in continuous speech. *Cognitive Psychology* 10. 29–63.

Marsolek, Chad J. 2008. What antipriming reveals about priming. *Trends in Cognitive Sciences* 12 (5). 176–181.

Marzi Claudia, James P. Blevins, Geert Booij & Vito Pirrelli. 2020. Inflection at the morphology-syntax interface. In Vito Pirrelli, Ingo Plag & Wolfgang U. Dressler (eds.), *Word Knowledge and Word Usage: a Cross-disciplinary Guide to the Mental Lexicon*, 228–294. De Gruyter.

Marzi, Claudia, Marcello Ferro, Franco Alberto Cardillo & Vito Pirrelli. 2016. Effects of frequency and regularity in an integrative model of word storage and processing. *Italian Journal of Linguistics* 28 (1). 79–114.

Marzi, Claudia, Marcello Ferro, Ouafae Nahli, Patrizia Belik, Stavros Bompolas & Vito Pirrelli. 2018. Evaluating Inflectional Complexity Crosslinguistically: a Processing Perspective. In *Proceedings of 11th LREC 2018*, Miyazaki, Japan. 3860–3866.

Marzi, Claudia, Marcello Ferro & Vito Pirrelli. 2014. Morphological structure through lexical parsability. *Lingue e Linguaggio* XIII (2). 263–290.

Marzi, Claudia, Marcello Ferro & Vito Pirrelli. 2019. A processing-oriented investigation of inflectional complexity. Frontiers in Communication 4. 48, 1–23. https://doi.org/10.3389/fcomm.2019.00048

Marzi, Claudia & Vito Pirrelli. 2015. A neuro-Computational Approach to Understanding the Mental Lexicon. *Journal of Cognitive Science* 16 (4). 491–533.

Matthews, Peter H. 1974. *Morphology. An Introduction to the Theory of Word Structure*. Cambridge University Press.

Matthews Peter H. 1991. *Morphology*. Cambridge, Cambridge University Press.

McClelland, James L. & Elman, Jeffrey L. 1986. The TRACE model of speech perception. *Cognitive Psychology* 18. 1–86.

Milin, Petar, Dagmar Divjak & R. Harald Baayen. 2017. A learning perspective on individual differences in skilled reading: Exploring and exploiting orthographic and semantic discrimination cues. *Journal of Experimental Psychology: Learning, Memory, and Cognition* 43 (11). 1730–1751.

Milin, Petar, Laurie B. Feldman, Michael Ramscar, Peter Hendrix, R. Harald Baayen. 2017. Discrimination in lexical decision. *PloS one* 12 (2). e0171935.

Milin, Petar, Dušica Filipović Đurđević & Fermín Moscoso del Prado Martín. 2009. The simultaneous effects of inflectional paradigms and classes on lexical recognition: Evidence from Serbian. *Journal of Memory and Language* 60 (1). 50–64.

Milin, Petar, Victor Kuperman, Aleksandar Kostić & R. Harald Baayen. 2009. Words and paradigms bit by bit: An information theoretic approach to the processing of paradigmatic structure in inflection and derivation. In James P. Blevins & Juliette Blevins (eds.), *Analogy in grammar: Form and acquisition*, 214–252. Oxford University Press.

Morton, John. 1969. Interaction of information in word recognition. *Psychological review* 76 (2). 165–178.

Morton, John. 1970. A functional model for memory. *Models of human memory*. 203–254.

Morton, John. 1979. Facilitation in word recognition: Experiments causing change in the logogen model. In *Processing of visible language*, Springer, 259–268.

Moscoso del Prado Martín, Fermín, Aleksandar Kostić, & R. Harald Baayen. 2004. Putting the bits together: An information theoretical perspective on morphological processing. *Cognition* 94 (1). 1–18.

Norris, Dennis. 1994. Shortlist: A connectionist model of continuous speech recognition. *Cognition* 52. 189–234.

Norris, Dennis. 2006. The Bayesian reader: explaining word recognition as an optimal Bayesian decision process. *Psychological review* 113 (2). 327.

Norris, Dennis & James M. McQueen. 2008. Shortlist B: a Bayesian model of continuous speech recognition. *Psychological review* 115 (2). 357–395.

Norris, Dennis, James M. McQueen & Anne Cutler. 1995. Competition and segmentation in spoken-word recognition. *Journal of Experimental Psychology: Learning, Memory, and Cognition* 21 (5). 1209–1228.

Osgood, Charles E. 1946. Meaningful similarity and interference in learning. *Journal of Experimental Psychology* 36 (4). 277–301.

Osgood, Charles E. 1949. The similarity paradox in human learning: A resolution. *Psychological Review* 56 (3). 132–143.
Osgood, Charles E. 1966. Meaning cannot be r_m?. *Journal of Verbal Learning and Verbal Behavior* 5 (4). 402–407.
Pham, Hien & R. Harald Baayen. 2015. Vietnamese compounds show an anti-frequency effect in visual lexical decision. *Language, Cognition and Neuroscience* 30. 1077–1095.
Pinker, Steven & Alan Prince. 1988. On language and connectionism: Analysis of a parallel distributed processing model of language acquisition. *Cognition* 29, 195–247.
Pinker, Steven & Alan Prince. 1994. Regular, and Irregular Morphology, and the Psychological Status of Rules of Grammar. In Susan D. Lima, Roberta Corrigan & Gregory K. Iverson (eds.), *The Reality of Linguistic Rules*, 321–351. John Benjamins.
Pinker, Stevan & Michael T. Ullman. 2002. The past and future of the past tense. *Trends in Cognitive Science* 6. 456–463.
Pirrelli, Vito. 2018. Morphological Theory And Computational Linguistics. In Jenny Audring & Francesca Masini (eds.), *The Oxford Handbook of Morphological Theory*, 573–593. Oxford University Press.
Pirrelli, Vito & Marco Battista. 2000. The paradigmatic dimension of stem allomorphy in Italian verb inflection. *Italian Journal of Linguistics* 12. 307–380.
Pirrelli, Vito, Marcello Ferro & Claudia Marzi. 2015. Computational complexity of abstractive morphology. In Matthew Baerman, Dunstan Brown & Greville Corbett (eds.), *Understanding and Measuring Morphological Complexity*, 141–166. Oxford University Press.
Pirrelli, Vito & François Yvon. 1999. The hidden dimension: a paradigmatic view of data-driven NLP. *Journal of Experimental & Theoretical Artificial Intelligence* 11 (3). 391–408.
Plaut, David C. & Laura M. Gonnerman. 2000. Are nonsemantic morphological effects incompatible with a distributed connectionist approach to lexical processing? *Language and Cognitive Processes* 15 (4/5). 445–485.
Poggio, Tomaso. 2010. Afterword. Marr's Vision and Computational Neuroscience. In David Marr, *Vision*, 362–367. The MIT Press.
Poggio, Tomaso. 2012. The levels of understanding framework, revised. *Perception*, 41(9), 1017–1023.
Price, Cathy J. 2012. A review and synthesis of the first 20 years of PET and fMRI studies of heard speech, spoken language and reading. *Neuroimage* 62 (2). 816–847.
Price, Cathy J. 2017. The evolution of cognitive models: From neuropsychology to neuroimaging and back. *Cortex* 107. 37–49.
Quine, Willard V.O. (1960) *Word and object*. Cambridge: MIT Press.
Ramscar, Michael, Melody Dye & Joseph Klein. 2013. Children value informativity over logic in word learning. *Psychological Science* 24 (6). 1017–1023.
Ramscar, Michael, Melody Dye & Stewart M. McCauley. 2013. Error and expectation in language learning: The curious absence of mouses in adult speech. *Language* 89 (4). 760–793.
Ramscar, Michael & Nicole Gitcho. 2007. Developmental change and the nature of learning in childhood. *Trends in cognitive sciences*, 11 (7). 274–279.
Ramscar, Michael, Peter Hendrix, Cyrus Shaoul, Petar Milin & R. Harald Baayen. 2014. The myth of cognitive decline: Non-linear dynamics of lifelong learning. *Topics in cognitive science* 6 (1). 5–42.

Ramscar, Michael, Ching C. Sun, Peter Hendrix & R. Harald Baayen. 2017. The Mismeasurement of Mind: Lifespan Changes in Paired Associate Test Scores Reflect The 'Cost' of Learning, Not Cognitive Decline. *Psychological Science*. 1171–1179.

Ramscar, Michael & Daniel Yarlett. 2007. Linguistic Self-Correction in the Absence of Feedback: A New Approach to the Logical Problem of Language Acquisition. *Cognitive Science* 31 (6). 927–960.

Ramscar, Michael, Daniel Yarlett, Melody Dye, Katie Denny & Kirsten Thorpe. 2010. The Effects of Feature-Label-Order and their Implications for Symbolic Learning. *Cognitive Science* 34 (6). 909–957.

Rescorla, Robert A. 1988. Behavioral Studies of Pavlovian conditioning. *Annual review of neuroscience* 11 (1). 329–352.

Rescorla, Robert A. & Allan R. Wagner. 1972. A theory of Pavlovian conditioning: Variations in the effectiveness of reinforcement and nonreinforcement. *Classical conditioning II: Current research and theory* 2. 64–99.

Rubenstein, Herbert, Lonnie Garfield & Jane A. Millikan. 1970. Homographic entries in the internal lexicon. *Journal of verbal learning and verbal behavior* 9 (5). 487–494.

Rubenstein, Herbert, Spafford S. Lewis & Mollie A. Rubenstein. 1971. Homographic entries in the internal lexicon: Effects of systematicity and relative frequency of meanings. *Journal of Memory and Language* 10 (1). 57.

Rueckl, Jay G. & Michal Raveh. 1999. The influence of morphological regularities on the dynamics of a connectionist network. *Brain and Language* 68. 110–117.

Rumelhart David & James McClelland. 1986. On learning the past tense of English verbs. In David Rumelhart, James McClelland & PDP Research Group, *Parallel distributed processing: Explanations in the microstructure of cognition*, vol. I. 216–271. The MIT Press.

Rumelhart David, James McClelland & PDP Research Group. 1986. *Parallel distributed processing: Explanations in the microstructure of cognition*. Voll. 1 & 2. The MIT Press.

Scalise, Sergio. 1984. *Generative Morphology*. Dordrecht: Foris.

Schmidtke, Daniel, Kazunaga Matsuki & Victor Kuperman. 2017. Surviving blind decomposition: a distributional analysis of the time-course of complex word recognition. *Journal of experimental psychology. Learning, memory, and cognition* 43(11). 1793–1820.

Schreuder, Robert & R. Harald Baayen. 1995. Modeling morphological processing. In Laurie B. Feldman (ed.), *Morphological aspects of language processing*, 131–56. Hillsdale, NJ: Erlbaum.

Schultz, Wolfram. 1998. Predictive reward signal of dopamine neurons. *Journal of neurophysiology* 80 (1). 1–27.

Seidenberg, Mark S. & Maryellen C. MacDonald. 1999. A probabilistic constraints approach to language acquisition and processing. *Cognitive science* 23(4). 569–588.

Selkirk, Elisabeth. 1984. *Phonology and Syntax*. The MIT Press.

Selfridge, Oliver G. 1959. Pandemonium: A paradigm for learning. In D. V. Blake & A. M. Uttley (eds.), *Proceedings of the Symposium on Mechanisation of Thought Processes*, 511–529.

Sering, Konstantin, Petar Milin & R. Harald Baayen. 2018. Language comprehension as a multiple label classification problem. *Statistica Neerlandica* 72 (3). 339–353.

Shannon, Claude. 1948. A mathematical theory of communication. *The Bell System Technical Journal* 27. 379–423, 623–656.

Shaoul, Cyrus & Chris Westbury. 2010. Exploring lexical co-occurrence space using HiDEx. *Behavior Research Methods* 42 (2). 393–413.

Skinner, Burrhus F. 1953. *Science and Human Behavior*. Simon and Schuster.
Skinner, Burrhus F. 1957. *Verbal Behavior*. Copley Publishing Group.
Snodgrass, Joan G. & Robert Jarvella. 1972. Some linguistic determinants of word classification times. *Pyschonomic Science* 27 (4). 220–222.
Spivey, Michael J, Ken McRae & Marc F. Joanisse. 2012. *The Cambridge Handbook of Psycholinguistics*. Cambridge University Press.
Taft, Marcus. 1994. Interactive-activation as a framework for understanding morphological processing. *Language and cognitive processes* 9 (3). 271–294.
Taft, Marcus. 2004. Morphological decomposition and the reverse base frequency effect. *Quarterly Journal of Experimental Psychology Section A* 57 (4). 745–765.
Taft, Marcus & Kenneth I. Forster. 1975. Lexical storage and retrieval of prefixed words. *Journal of Verbal Learning and Verbal Behavior* 14. 638–647.
Tiedemann, Jörg. 2012. Parallel Data, Tools and Interfaces in OPUS. Proceedings of the Eighth International Conference on Language Resources and Evaluation (LREC). 2214–2218. Istanbul, Turkey.
Tolman, Edvard C. 1932. *Purposive behavior in animals and men*. New York: Century.
Tolman, Edvard C. 1951. *Behavior and psychological man: essays in motivation and learning*. Berkeley: University of California Press.
Tremblay, Antoine & R. Harald Baayen. 2010. Holistic processing of regular four-word sequences: A behavioral and erp study of the effects of structure, frequency, and probability on immediate free recall. In David Wood (ed.), *Perspectives on formulaic language: Acquisition and communication*, 151–173. Bloomsbury Publishing.
Tucker, Benjamin V., Michelle Sims & R. Harald Baayen. 2017. *Opposing forces on acoustic duration*. Manuscript, University of Alberta and University of Tübingen.
Vulchanova, Mila, David Saldaña and Giosué Baggio. 2020. Word structure and word processing in developmental disorders. In Vito Pirrelli, Ingo Plag & Wolfgang U. Dressler (eds.), *Word knowledge and word usage: a cross-disciplinary guide to the mental lexicon*, 680–707. De Gruyter.
Weitz, Marc, Konstantin Sering, David-Elias Künstle & Lennard Schneider. 2017. pyndl: Naive Discriminative Learning. Python3 package. Retrieved from https://github.com/quantling/pyndl.
Widrow, Bernard & Marcian E-Hoff. 1960. *Adaptive switching circuits* (No. TR-1553-1). Stanford University, CA Stanford Electronics labs.
Wittgenstein, Ludwig. 1953. *Philosophical Investigations*. Gertrude E. M. Anscombe (*Trans.*), Blackwell Publishing.

Jacolien van Rij, Nemanja Vaci, Lee H. Wurm and Laurie Beth Feldman

Alternative quantitative methods in psycholinguistics: Implications for theory and design

Abstract: We describe three different methods that are appropriate to analyze various types of psycholinguistic data. We discuss some of the strengths and weaknesses of each and their suitability according to characteristics of the data. Methods include analysis of variance (ANOVA), linear mixed-effects modeling (LME) and generalized additive mixed models (GAMM).

Keywords: analysis of variance, ANOVA, linear mixed-effects modeling, LME, generalized additive modeling, GAM, model criticism, collinearity, autocorrelation, experimental design, time course data, mouse tracking

1 Introduction

Statistical analyses are an important tool for interpreting experimental results and generalizing the findings. As many different techniques are being used to investigate the structure and processing of language, there is a large variation in the types of psycholinguistic data that are being generated: for example, grammatical judgements, reaction times, ERP responses, eye gaze fixation durations, and corpus counts. These different types of data impose different constraints on the statistical methods, and consequently one style of statistical analysis is not appropriate for all types of experimental data. To facilitate choosing the appropriate statistical method, this chapter provides an overview of the regression methods that are currently used in psycholinguistics.

Jacolien van Rij, University of Groningen, Department of Artificial Intelligence, Groningen, The Netherlands
Nemanja Vaci, University of Oxford, Department of Psychiatry, Oxford, UK
Lee H. Wurm, Wayne State University, Department of Psychology, Detroit, USA
Laurie Beth Feldman, University at Albany, Department of Psychology, Albany, USA

Open Access. © 2020 Jacolien van Rij et al., published by De Gruyter. This work is licensed under a Creative Commons Attribution-NonCommercial-NoDerivatives 4.0 International License.
https://doi.org/10.1515/9783110440577-003

1.1 Focus of the chapter

The "preferred" statistical method is largely determined by the nature of the data, the structure of the data, and the design of the experiment. Relevant factors are whether they are continuous data, such as reaction times, ERP responses, or fixation durations, or categorical data, such as accuracy data (i.e. binary data), type of morphological construction, or eye gaze fixation area. In this chapter we additionally make a broad distinction between behavioral data and time course data: *Behavioral data* are characterized by a single measure per trial, such as responses, accuracy, or reaction times. *Time course data*, on the other hand, consist of multiple measures per trial, which are ordered in time. Examples are EEG recordings measured while processing a word, eye gaze position during listening to a sentence, pupil size during the trial, or tongue position while producing a word. In practice, time course data are often analyzed as behavioral data by summarizing the measurements in a trial or in a certain time window to arrive at a mean value, but ideally one would like to investigate the changes over time along multiple dimensions of information. The statistical method is also determined by the design of the experiment: in a typical design (factorial experiment investigating the main effects and interactions between manipulations with only a few – often two or three – possible values) all our predictors are categorical, whereas when analyzing natural language we would like to include continuous predictors (henceforth *covariates*; numeric predictors, with an infinite range of potential values). Additionally, we may want to account for structure in the data that we are not interested in. For example, in most experimental studies the participants produce multiple responses. In such data, we would like to account for the variability introduced by the various participants, while our results should generalize over these particular participants and should provide information about the population.

This chapter focuses on the regression methods, and specifically presents linear mixed-effects modeling (LME; e.g. Pinheiro and Bates 2000; Baayen, Davidson, and Bates 2008) and generalized additive mixed modeling (GAMM; Lin and Zhang 1999; Wood 2011, 2017) as two complementary methods for analyzing most types of psycholinguistic data. LME is particularly useful for analyzing data with categorical predictors and/or continuous predictors that are linearly related with the dependent measure. GAMMs are suited for analyzing data with continuous predictors that may show a non-linear relation with the dependent measure, in addition to optional categorical or linear continuous predictors. We will introduce LME and GAMMs using an example data set to demonstrate how these new methods allow us to go beyond the typical factorial design, so as to begin to explore language behavior more dynamically.

The statistical software R version 3.4.0 (2017-04-21) was used for the analyses, with the packages *lme4* (Bates et al. 2015) for the LME analysis, the package *mgcv* version 1.8-17 (Wood 2011, 2017) for the GAMM analysis, and the package *itsadug* version 2.3 (van Rij et al. 2017) for interpretation and visualization of the GAMM analysis. The data, analysis, and code for all the graphs are available in the online Supplementary Materials at [https://www.jacolienvanrij.com/NetWordS-SupplementaryMaterials.html], along with further reading suggestions. In this chapter our aim is to provide an overview of the different methods, without presenting the actual R code.

1.2 Experimental data used as example

The data were collected by Kit Cho, Rachel Brotman and Laurie Feldman. The experiment was designed to test the effect of different accent combinations at study and test on the spoken recognition of English words. The experiment was set up as a factorial within-subjects 2x2x2 design. In a study phase, each participant was presented with pre-recorded English words spoken with either American-English or Chinese (Mandarin) as the native language. All participants were native speakers of American English. In the test phase participants were presented with the same English words, and they had to judge whether those words were produced by the same speaker as in the study phase, or by the other speaker. Thus, two manipulations were introduced in the experiment: *Accent* (accent at test phase: English or Chinese), and *Congruency* (whether or not the accent in the study and test phases matched or mismatched).[1]

Participants indicated whether the speaker was the same or different than in the study phase by moving the mouse and clicking on one of the corresponding words that was presented in the top-right or the top-left corner of the screen. The positions of the words "SAME" and "DIFFERENT" were balanced across participants. The accuracy and the reaction time were recorded, along with the mouse trajectory from the resting position (bottom-center of screen) to the appropriate word. The auditorily presented words were balanced for length (between 3 and 8 characters), with the frequency ranging between 0.044 and 325 per million words (based on the English OpenSubtitle corpus).

---

[1] The experiment contained another manipulation: in the study phase participants had to either listen to the words, or they had to listen and repeat the words. As the effect of study task was very subtle, we ignore this manipulation for the current presentation purposes.

These example data contain the typical psycholinguistic behavioral measures accuracy and reaction time, but also the mouse trajectory (x and y coordinates over time). This time course measure has properties in common with increasingly popular online measures such as EEG, eye tracking, pupil dilation, pitch contours, and articulography. Time course measures potentially provide more information about the processing of the stimuli, but we demonstrate below that without new analytical methods much of that information is lost.

1.3 Outline

In the following sections we will show how we could analyze the responses from the mouse tracking task using traditional ANOVA (analysis of variance) and provide an overview of the more recent methods LME and GAMM in Sections 3 and 4, by using data from the same experiment. On the basis of these analyses, we will provide guidelines on when and how to use these methods. In the final sections of the chapter we will argue that one needs to be extremely careful in the interpretation of statistical results, because each of the currently available analytical methods has severe limitations. In the discussion, we delineate the implications of the statistical methods that we use, the limitations for interpretation and consequences for design.

As all methods discussed in this chapter are basically regression analyses, we will first provide a short introduction to regression analysis and list the assumptions that hold for all regression analyses.

1.4 Basics of regression modeling

Linear regression uses a linear functional relation to describe how a numerical dependent variable varies with the values of predictors. As an example, we could use a simple linear regression model to investigate the effect of *Congruency* (match or mismatch item) on response time:

(1) $y \sim \beta_0 + \beta_1 x + \varepsilon$

The regression model describes the relation (indicated with the symbol '∼') between reaction times (y, the dependent variable that is on the left-side of the '∼') and the predictor Congruency (x, which is on the right-side of the '∼') as a single regression line. The symbol 'ε' represents random noise, deviations from the regression line that are not fitted by the model. The line is characterized by two parameters: β_0, a constant value called the intercept, and β_1, the slope for the effect of Congruency. The intercept specifies the height of the line, because it is the value of the dependent variable y when the predictor x equals the value 0. The slope specifies the direction of the line: it is the increase in y when x increases by 1 unit. If x is a categorical predictor such as Congruency ("match" and "mismatch"), each of the levels is assigned a value: "match" is represented by the value 0, and "mismatch" by 1. As a result, the slope coefficient β_1 actually models the *difference* between the reference level "match" and the level "mismatch", as illustrated in Figure 1.

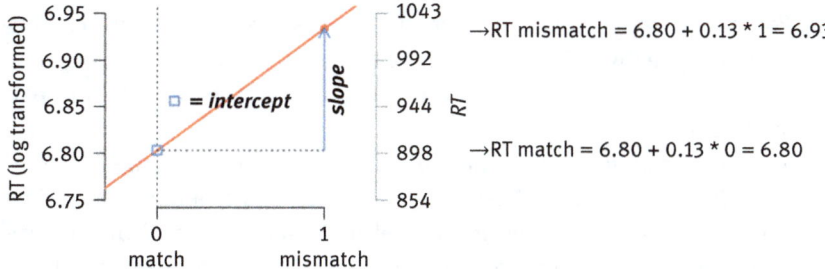

Figure 1: Schematic overview of the interpretation of linear regression coefficients.

Three assumptions for regression analysis:
i. The observations should be independent.
ii. The residuals should follow a normal distribution.
iii. The variances should be equal (often called *homoscedasticity*), which implies that the variances should be independent of the means.

The first assumption, i.e., independent observations, is violated if we do not take into account in our analysis that the data are produced by sets of participants and items. Particular participants or particular items may introduce consistent variation in the data, for example consistently slower response times than average. The assumption is also violated when we do not take into account in our analysis that the data within a time series trial are correlated. For example, in mouse tracking data the position of the mouse at the next timestamp is largely dependent on where the mouse is in the present moment. The second assumption states that the residuals should be normally distributed. The residuals are the difference between the observed data and the fitted values of the regression model. In other words, the residuals are that part of the data that is not explained by the statistical model. The third assumption specifies that the variance does not increase or decrease with an increasing mean. This is often tested by plotting the residuals of the regression model against the fitted values. For example, the assumption of homoscedasticity is violated when the residuals show a wider spread for higher fitted values than for lower fitted values.

A typical property of experimental data collected to study language processing is that the data are structured by participants and items. Participants and items are considered as random samples from the population of speakers and from the population of words in the language. Stated differently, our focus is less on the performance of specific participants, and more on the possibility to make generalization to the whole population. Participants and items may introduce greater variation to the data than do the experimental manipulations of interest. For more precise statistical estimations, the statistical tests used in language processing ideally take into account the variation due to participants and items, so that the experimental effects are not masked by variation in participants and items.

The methods discussed in this chapter, namely repeated-measures ANOVA, linear mixed-effects modeling (LME) and generalized additive mixed modeling (GAMM) are variants of the regression model, but take into account the variability in participants and items. We refer the reader to other textbooks (e.g., Baayen 2008; Gelman and Hill 2007) for a more extensive introduction to linear regression.

2 Traditional methods in psycholinguistic research: ANOVA

This section analyzes the mouse tracking responses and reaction times using repeated-measures ANOVA, which is still one of the most frequently applied analyses in psycholinguistic research. ANOVA (acronym for analysis of variance) is particularly suited for analyzing factorial designs. The section ends with a discussion of how the use of ANOVA has shaped our experimental designs.

2.1 Introduction to ANOVA

An ANOVA tests whether the means of different groups are the same by comparing the variance *between* the groups with the variance *within* the groups using an F-test. The F-test compares the ratio of variances to the F-distribution, while taking into account the number of observations and the number of groups, to test if the groups differ significantly from each other. One could view an ANOVA as a special case of a linear regression analysis with only categorical predictors.

As ANOVA compares group data, it is better suited for analyzing behavioral data than for analyzing on-line time course measures. For example, we could use ANOVA to analyze the accuracy and reaction times of the responses on the mouse tracking task, in order to determine whether the experimental manipulations of study-test Congruency and Accent influence the accuracy and reaction time of the response. Note that in this experiment item order is randomized and location of the match and mismatch box is counterbalanced across participants.

To account for the fact that the responses are not independent and that subsets of the data are produced by different participants and different stimuli, we use a *repeated-measures ANOVA*, which partitions out the variability due to individual differences. The input for a repeated-measures ANOVA is the means for each condition *per participant*. This is generally referred to as an F1 analysis (cf. Clark 1973). To account for the variation in items, an additional repeated-measures ANOVA on the averages *per item* (collapsed over participants) is generally performed. This is referred to as the F2 analysis. The Supplementary Materials provide more details and the code for running the analyses; here we only present the results.

2.2 In practice: Analyzing responses using RM-ANOVA

We analyze the behavioral responses of the mouse tracking data, i.e. accuracy and reaction times, using ANOVA as implemented in the R package *ez* (Lawrence 2016). For visualizing the accuracy data (Figure 2, left) proportions of correct responses were calculated. However, the underlying distribution for accuracy data is *binomial*: the accuracy of a response is correct or incorrect, or has the value 0 or 1. For analyzing binomial data, the logit transformation[2] is preferred over proportions, because ANOVA assumes normally distributed data. The proportion scale has a finite range between 0 and 1, whereas the logit scale is continuous. We included the categorical predictors *Accent*, the accent of the speaker during the test (English or Chinese), and *Congruency*, whether the word was produced by the same speaker in the training phase. *Accent* and *Congruency* are tested within participants.

---

2 The logit transformation is: $logit = \ln((n_{correct} + c) / (n_{incorrect} + c))$, in which $n_{correct}$ and $n_{incorrect}$ are the numbers of correct and incorrect responses and c is an arbitrary constant to avoid undefined numbers when zero counts occur (set to 0.5 here).

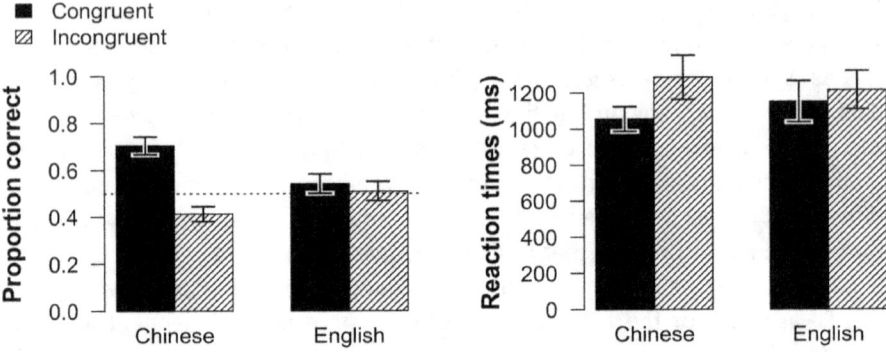

Figure 2: Accuracy (*Left*) and reaction times (*Right*) of the correct responses in the mouse tracking task. The solid bars represent the trials for which the accent in the test phase matched the accent in the study phase, the dashed bars represent the trials for which the accent in the test phase did not match the accent in the study phase. Error bars: ±1SE (i.e. standard error of the participant means).

Accuracy. The F1 ANOVA of the accuracy data indicates a significant interaction of Accent x Congruency ($F(1,32) = 4.71$, $p = .038$), and significant main effects of Congruency ($F(1,32) = 16.02$, $p = .00035$) and of Accent ($F(1,32) = 4.34$, $p = .045$). We speak of an *interaction* when the relation between a predictor and the dependent variable is changed by the value of another predictor. In this example, the effect of Accent changes depending on Congruency of speaker at training and at test. The F2 ANOVA suggests the same significant interaction: Accent x Congruency ($F(1,62) = 52.54$, $p < .001$), along with a significant main effect of Congruency ($F(1,62) = 55.12$, $p < .001$), and a marginal effect of Accent ($F(1,62) = 3.61$, $p = .062$). The effects that are significant in both the F1 and F2 analyses will be labeled as significant, which is the interaction between Accent and Congruency and the main effect of Congruency.

Reaction times. We only included correct answers in the analysis, and the reaction times were log-transformed. Reaction time data are generally not normally distributed, but rather skewed. Therefore, they are commonly transformed by taking the log, inverse, or power transformation. In contrast with the accuracy data, the F1 and F2 ANOVA analyses for the log-transformed reaction times only revealed a significant main effect of Congruency ($F1(1,30) = 8.38$, $p = .007$; $F2 (1,61) = 9.81$, $p = 0.003$); see Figure 2, right.

A disadvantage of ANOVA tables is that they only indicate which predictors are influencing the model estimations significantly. To interpret the direction of the interaction we could look at the accuracy plot (Figure 2, Left panel). The plot reveals that the effect of Congruency is different for the two levels of Accent: The

Chinese accented speech at test seems to result in a significant difference between match and mismatch items, but this difference seems to be absent for items pronounced with an English accent. Thus, with an unfamiliar accent, participants resort to a strategy of selecting "SAME", but with a familiar accent they do not use such a strategy.

2.3 Discussion

The repeated-measures ANOVA provides a relatively simple and quick test to confirm which factorial predictors contribute significantly to the values of the response variables. The results are easy to report, following the standard conventions in the literature. However, a disadvantage of ANOVA tables is that they only indicate which predictors are influencing the model estimations significantly. Post-hoc tests are necessary to interpret the direction of the interaction, because coefficients of the estimated effects are not automatically given. In the accuracy plot (Figure 2, Left panel) the Accent x Congruency interaction is clearly visible. The Chinese accented speech at test seems to result in a significant difference between match and mismatch items, but this difference seems to be absent for items pronounced with an English accent.

As the ANOVA test is performed on averages, it does not provide a straightforward way to deal with missing data or unbalanced designs. This is particularly an issue for our current reaction time data, from which we excluded the incorrectly answered items. Another consequence is that participant and item variation cannot be accounted for at the same time. Instead two analyses (F1 and F2) are generally performed to account for the variation in participants and items (e.g. Clark 1973). The convention is to consider a predictor significant only when the F1 and F2 both indicate that that predictor is significant. The F1 and F2 analyses are not an ideal solution to this problem (e.g. Raaijmakers et al. 1999). Baayen (2008) has pointed out that for a design where items are nested under a condition, such as words presented in an American or a Chinese accent but not both, F1 and F2 may reveal conflicting results and may result in the incorrect (too conservative) conclusion that a predictor is not significant. One more comprehensive analysis, that can account for participants and item variation at the same time, would provide a more coherent solution.

Another important disadvantage is that ANOVA only accepts categorical predictors, which means that covariates have to be converted to be categorical. In our analysis of the behavioral responses we have only included categorical predictors, but in other analyses we may want to include continuous covariates. For example, if we would like to test whether the frequency of the word influences the behavioral response, we need to dichotomize the frequency continuum: for example, words with a frequency lower than the median frequency are labeled as "low", the other words are labeled as "high". Rather than an arbitrary division of the frequencies into two groups, it is generally preferable to treat frequency as continuous and include it as a covariate.[3]

Although the ANOVA analysis still is the most commonly used analysis in language processing research, linear mixed-effects modeling (LME) is quickly gaining in popularity because it provides a solution for many of the disadvantages of the repeated-measures ANOVA.

3 Linear mixed-effects modeling (LME)

Linear mixed-effects modeling (LME) is a linear regression analysis that does not require group averages as input, and can handle the responses of individual trials. LME is preferred over ANOVA (i) when the data result from an unbalanced design, or contain missing observations, (ii) when the dependent variable is not normally distributed, or (iii) when continuous predictors are available. With balanced factorial designs LME has comparable power to repeated-measures ANOVA (e.g. Baayen 2008; Baayen et al. 2008; Barr et al. 2013), but we still recommend LME as it does not require separate analyses for participants and items.

3.1 Introduction to linear mixed-effects modeling

In contrast to the repeated-measures ANOVA, LME accounts for the variability among participants and for the variability among items at the same time rather than in separate analyses. In LME, a distinction is made between random effects and fixed effects. *Fixed effects* are those that are expected to hold for the entire population or expected to apply to other experimental stimuli, whereas *random effects* capture variation introduced by the particular participants and stimuli that were randomly sampled from larger populations (e.g. Pinheiro and Bates 2000; Gelman and Hill 2007; Baayen et al. 2008).

In mixed-models, i.e., models including both fixed and random effects, random effects predictors are each represented by one parameter, namely the

---

[3] We use frequency as our example, but language skill is a measure that often gets treated dichotomously and is subject to similar limitations in the ANOVA.

standard deviation associated with the random effect. The random adjustments for each individual participant (or item) are selected such that when added to the fixed effects they provide an estimate of that participant's (or item's) performance. However, the estimates are not necessarily the same as the participants' means: they are a compromise between the mean over all participants and the participant's mean, weighted for the participant's number of observations and under the constraints that the random adjustments follow a normal distribution with a mean of zero and the estimated standard deviation for the random effect (Gelman and Hill 2007). If the participant contributed only a few observations and much of the data were missing, the estimated mean for that participant will be closer to the mean of all participants than to his or her observed mean, i.e. the random adjustment for that participant will be smaller than expected. The assumption that random effects follow a normal distribution allows for making generalizations: an extremely fast reaction time, much faster than average, is atypical and is not very likely to be observed in a follow-up experiment with different participants. So, the estimated mean for such a fast participant also tends to be closer to the mean of all participants than to the observed mean for that participant. The effect that the estimations for extreme participants are closer to the overall mean than to their observed means is called *shrinkage*.

Two types of random effects can be specified in LME: random adjustments of the intercept, and random adjustments of slopes. Random intercepts adjust the height of regression lines for each participant or item. Random slopes adjust the slope of a regression line for each participant or item. Figure 3 illustrates the regression line in our earlier example, in which we used linear regression to analyze the effect of Congruency on the log transformed reaction times. In the left panel random intercepts are illustrated: the intercept adjustments raise or lower the regression line (black solid line), but do not change the relation between the congruency conditions. In the center panel random slopes are illustrated: the slope adjustments tilt the regression line, in order to change the difference between the two Congruency conditions, but does not change the height of the regression line. The right panel illustrates a combination of random intercepts and random slopes. For one of the participants an increase in intercept but a decrease in slope is estimated (higher gray dashed line). This participant is slower in responding, but does not show much difference in response times between the match and mismatch trials. The lower dashed line represents a faster participant, but with a stronger effect of Congruency: the intercept is much lower than the average intercept, but the slope is increased. In short, random intercepts capture general differences in performance between participants (or items) and random slopes capture variation between conditions for those participants (or items).

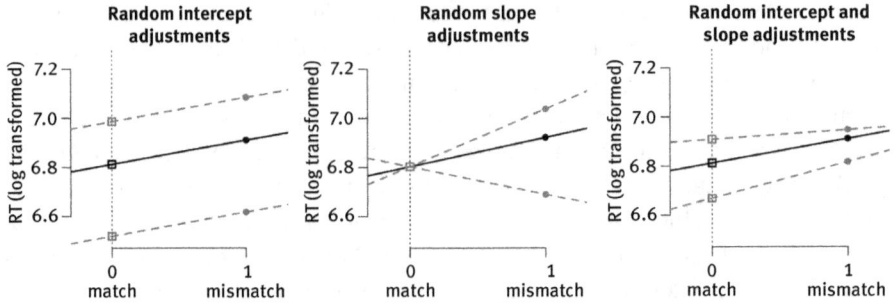

Figure 3: Schematic overview of random intercepts (*left panel*), random slopes (*center panel*), and the combination of random intercepts and slopes (*right panel*).

Different from an ANOVA analysis, LME does not return which predictors or random effects are significantly contributing to the model. Rather, given that these predictors are included, the outcome indicates whether or not the contrasts are different from the intercept and whether or not the slopes are significantly different from zero. A model comparison procedure is necessary to determine which predictors significantly contribute to the model. The collective wisdom is to start by determining the appropriate random effects structure, and then to test which fixed effects are significant. Backward-fitting model comparison procedures, which start with the most complex fixed-effect model and gradually reduce non-significant interactions and predictors, generally reduce the risk of overlooking interactions and main effects (e.g. Barr et al. 2013). R packages are available that facilitate model comparison procedures by automatic model selection.

3.2 In practice: Analyzing responses using LME

Here, we re-analyze the behavioral responses of the mouse tracking data, i.e. accuracy and reaction times, using LME as implemented in the R package *lme4* (Bate et al. 2015), and the R package *multcomp* (Hothorn, Bretz and Westfall 2008) for inspection of the model estimates.

Accuracy. When the raw data rather than averages are being analyzed, LME does not require transformation of binomial data. LME implements generalized algorithms to analyze binomial data, or data from several other non-Gaussian distributions. In our example, backward-fitting model comparison procedures were used to determine the maximum random effects structure that was allowed by the data, and to determine which fixed effects to include. The random effect structure for the accuracy data included random by-participant slopes for Accent and Congruency and the interaction Accent x Congruency. The best-fitting model included a significant interaction between Accent and Congruency ($\chi^2(1) = 4.77$, $p = 0.029$). The model coefficients explain this interaction: Participants do not differ from chance performance on items pronounced with an English accent ($\beta_{intercept} = 0.118$, $SE = 0.214$, z-value = 0.550, $p > 0.1$), and do not show a difference between congruent and incongruent items with an English accent ($\beta_{Mismatch} = -0.081$, $SE = 0.394$, z-value $= -0.204$, $p > 0.1$). However, they do show a significant difference between congruent and incongruent items with an Chinese accent ($\beta_{Mismatch:Chinese} = -1.397$, $SE = 0.621$, z-value $= -2.250$, $p = 0.024$): Participant's performance on congruent items with a Chinese accent is significantly more accurate than English congruent items ($\beta_{Chinese} = 0.920$, $SE = 0.353$, z-value = 2.608, $p = 0.009$), but the performance on incongruent items with an Chinese accent is not significantly different from the performance on incongruent items with English accent ($\beta_{MismatchCH\text{-}MismatchEN} = -0.477$, $SE = 0.301$, z-value $= -1.586$, $p > .1$).

However, the models with this random effects structure were showing difficulties to converge. Therefore, we replaced the random effects by a random intercept adjustment for each combination of Congruency, Accent, and Participant to reduce the number of variance and correlation parameters. This alternative random effects structure yielded the same conclusions.

Reaction times. We analyzed the reaction times of the correct responses. The reaction times are log transformed to improve normality. A backward-fitting model comparison procedure suggested inclusion of a random intercept for participant, and by-participant random slopes for Congruency and Trial (centered and scaled, to facilitate the interpretation of the regression coefficients). The slope for Trial was included to account for correlations between subsequent reaction times (e.g. Baayen and Milin 2010). Only the main effect of Congruency was found to be significant ($\chi^2(1) = 7.850$, $p = 0.005$): the correctly answered incongruent items are responded slower than the correctly answered congruent items ($\beta_{Mismatch} = 0.087$, $SE = 0.030$, t-value = 2.90).

3.3 Discussion

Basically, the LME analyses of behavioral responses lead to the same results as the repeated-measures ANOVA. A large advantage of LME over repeated-measures ANOVA, however, is that it combines the participants and item analysis into a single statistical model. Further advantages are that LME does not require separate post-hoc tests, as the coefficients of the estimated values are provided in the summary, and that covariates can be included in the analysis.

A disadvantage of LME is that one needs to determine the appropriate random effects structure. Only including random intercepts for participants and items without an adjustment for the experimental conditions may result in over-confident estimates of the fixed effects, finding effects that are not really there (e.g. Pinheiro and Bates 2000; Baayen, Davidson and Bates 2008; Barr et al., 2013). For example, it is not uncommon to add measures of vocabulary and spelling knowledge. However, these should be contrasted with simple random slopes and intercepts to make sure that the estimated effects are not caused by random variation between participants and items. To avoid over-confident estimates that are not generalizable, Barr et al. (2013) argue to maximize the random effect structure based on the experimental design. This means including the slopes for all experimental predictors by participants and items in addition to the random intercepts. Recently, Bates et al. (2015) showed that this is in practice not possible for many data sets. Missing data and limited data samples strongly limit the number of random effects that lead to a reliable and converging estimation of the parameters of the model (see also Baayen et al. 2017 and Matuschek et al. 2017). Determining the appropriate random effects structure is one of the challenges when using LME.

As LME can also include covariates, it seems at first glance to be the obvious choice for analyzing the mouse tracking data. LME even allows polynomial functions (or other non-linear functions) for modeling a non-linear relationship between the dependent variable and a covariate (see Supplementary Materials). However, we prefer to use GAMM over LME, as will be explained in Sections 4 and 5. In the next section, we will introduce GAMMs and illustrate how they could be applied to analyze time course data, such as mouse tracking data.

4 Generalized Additive Modeling (GAM)

Language processing research increasingly makes use of time course measures to investigate *online* language processing, i.e. the actual processing of the word or utterance from the moment it is being read or heard. *Time course* measures provide multiple data samples during a trial, often with a fixed sampling rate. Traditionally, time course measures are simplified to one value per trial, for example the mean value in a specific time window or the average deviation of the mouse trajectory, to be able to perform an ANOVA. However, as noted above, this considerably reduces the information these measures provide.

Instead, we prefer to analyze the time course directly. For example, we could analyze how participants in the mouse tracking experiment move their mouse to the response location on the screen. The mouse position is a continuous measure developing over time that may reflect uncertainty and hesitation in the form of pauses and deviations from the ideal trajectory (straight path to answer location). The example data contains 101 samples per trajectory, each of which records the x-position and y-position of the mouse, and the time relative to the offset of the word. For the current data, we normalized the time between the onset of the movement and click/answer, as rate of mouse movement varies along the trajectory. The mouse movement *duration* is the time from the onset of the movement until the participant clicked to respond. Below we present an analysis of the mouse trajectory on correctly answered trials only, to facilitate interpretation. As we do not know the cause of errors, trials that are incorrectly answered were excluded from analysis. Of the 2081 trials 958 were incorrectly answered and excluded (54% of the trials were included in the analysis).

The raw data of the mouse position (x and y coordinates) are presented in the Left panel of Figure 4. Location of match and mismatch responses is counterbalanced across participants. The black dots show one sample mouse trajectory. The Right panel of Figure 4 shows a measure derived from the x and y coordinates, namely the *distance to the clicked target*, with the same sample trajectory in black. For each data point the Euclidean distance to the target, i.e. the answer that participants eventually clicked, was calculated.[4] The idea behind using the Euclidean distance is that when participants are uncertain or change their mind during response selection they take a less direct route to the target than the optimal straight path. For example, participants may initially go toward one of the responses, but, during the mouse movement, change their mind and abruptly shift to the other response, called x-flips (see example trial in Left panel of Figure 4; Freeman, Dale and Farmer 2011; Freeman and Johnson 2016). These hesitations show up in various measure as pauses or increased distance to the target (see Right panel of Figure 4).

---

[4] The choice of distance to target as the dependent variable instead of the X and Y coordinates was made for illustration purposes, to make the analysis more comparable to other psycholinguistic time course measures such as EEG or pupillometry data.

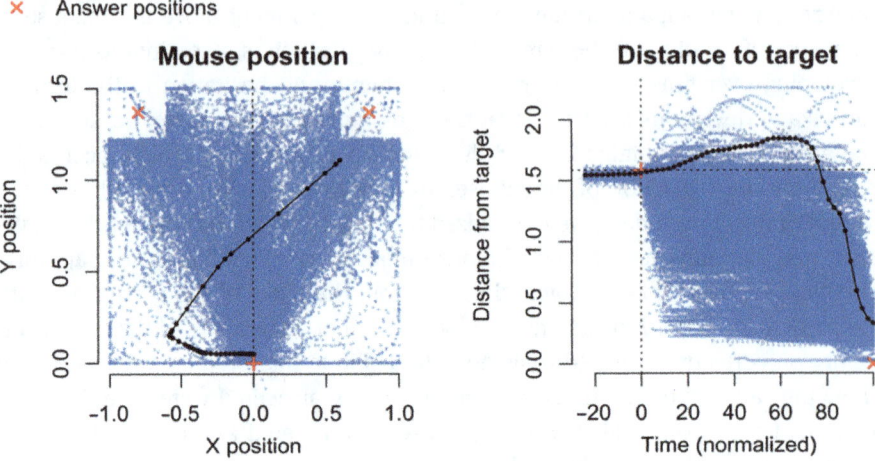

Figure 4: Mouse tracking data exclusively including correctly answered trials included. *Left panel:* Recorded X and Y position of the mouse. The black dots highlight one example trial. *Right panel:* Distance to the clicked target over time. The black dots highlight the same trial as in the left plot.

4.1 Introduction to generalized additive (mixed) modeling

Generalized Additive Mixed Modeling (GAMMs; Lin and Zhang 1999; Wood 2017) is a recently introduced analysis method that is specially designed to model non-linear covariates: it is a non-linear mixed-effects regression method, which can fit non-linear regression lines to the data. GAMMs are implemented in the R package *mgcv* (Wood 2017, 2011). In contrast with LME, the user does not need to specify the shape of the non-linear regression line (e.g., which order polynomial to use), because the model determines the non-linear pattern based on the data. The use and interpretation of GAMMs is slightly different from linear regression models. Where linear regression models aim to explain the data by fitting the *coefficients* in the regression formula, GAMMs try to optimize the smooth function that describes the potentially non-linear relation between the predictor and the dependent variable; see the formulas in Example (2).

(2) Difference between linear regression and non-linear regression (with y the dependent variable, x a predictor, β_0 the intercept, $\beta_{>0}$ the slope(s), and ε the residuals):
 - Linear regression formula: $y \sim \beta_0 + \beta_1 x + \varepsilon$

- Linear regression with nth order polynomial curve: $y \sim \beta_0 + \sum_{i=1}^{n} \beta_i x^i + \varepsilon$
- GAMMs: $y \sim \beta_0 + f(x) + \varepsilon$

The output of a GAMM only presents the coefficients for the linear predictors, including the intercept, i.e. the height adjustment of regression lines, intercept adjustments, and linear slopes. The output does not present a description of the *non-linear* regression lines, because the smooth functions ($f(x)$) often cannot be captured by a few coefficients. Instead the summary provides information on the wiggliness of the regression line, and whether the line is (somewhere) significantly different from zero. Visualization is necessary for interpreting the non-linear terms.

Similar to LME, in GAMMs fixed effects and random effects can be specified. However, the structure of the random effects in GAMMs is different from the random effects in LME: In addition to random intercepts and random slopes, GAMMs also provides the option to include *random smooths*, non-linear random adjustments of a regression line. These random smooths capture also random intercepts and slopes, so they are generally not combined with random intercepts and slopes for the same predictors. Figure 5 illustrates how the random effects of two different participants (Left panel) alter the non-linear fixed effect regression line to generate estimates for these two participants. It is important to realize that the random effects in the Left panel are *adjustments* of the fixed effects, with a negative value indicating a shorter distance than the general trend (represented by the fixed effect), and a positive value indicating a longer distance than the general trend.

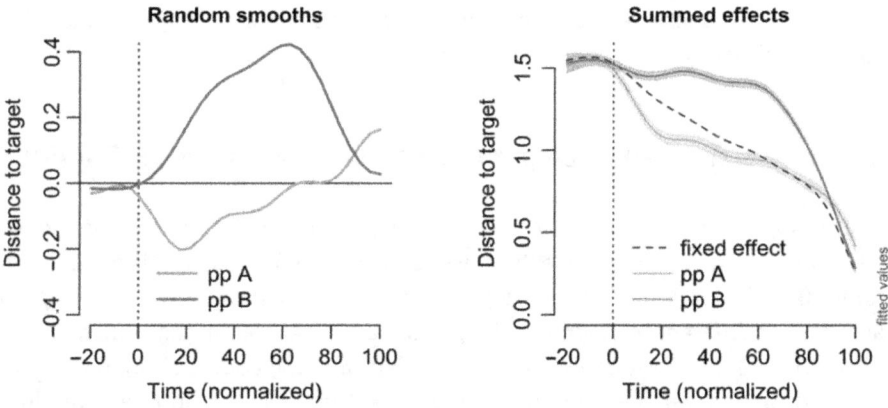

Figure 5: Non-linear random effects in GAMMs. *Left panel:* random smooths for two arbitrary participants in the mouse tracking data. Negative values indicate movement away from target. *Right panel:* summed effects for the same two participants. The random effects (Left panel plot) are added to the fixed effects smooth (dashed line in the Right panel plot) and the intercept.

Another difference with LME is the possibility of GAMMs to add *non-linear interaction surfaces*. For example, in the mouse tracking data we could include a non-linear interaction between Time, the normalized time along the trajectory (ranging between 0 and 100), and Duration, the actual duration of the trajectory in milliseconds (log transformed, ranging between 47 and 6365 ms) starting with the first mouse movement until the response. A linear interaction would imply that the slope of the regression line for Time is increased or decreased with Duration in a constant way. A non-linear interaction allows the shape of the non-linear regression line for Time to change depending on the value of Duration in a non-linear way. An example of a non-linear interaction is provided in the next section.

GAMM provides the same advantages as LME with respect to missing data and unbalanced designs. The method also includes an extensive list of link functions for handling data that is not normally distributed. Similar to LME, model comparison procedures are used to determine the best-fitting model. However, the output tables do not provide precise information on the shape of nonlinear regression lines or interaction surfaces, but visualization is necessary for interpreting the results.

In sum, advantages of GAMMs over LME are the possibilities to fit non-linear regression lines and surfaces without a priori assumptions on the shape of the regression lines. In addition, the visualization methods facilitate interpretation, whereas the polynomial terms in linear regression are rather difficult to interpret (see Supplementary Materials). Moreover, GAMMs also allow for non-linear random variations in time course patterns for individual participants and items, which result in more generalizable time course estimations (Baayen et al. 2018; van Rij et al. 2019).

4.2 In practice: Analyzing mouse tracking data using GAMMs

To investigate whether and how Accent and Congruency influenced the mouse trajectory during response selection, we analyzed the Euclidean distance to the target (see Figure 4, Right) as a dependent variable with a GAMM analysis. To account for differences in strategy by participants and conditions, which are reflected in the paths to the target, we included the time course along the trajectory per participant per condition (predictor Time) as a non-linear random smooth. Similarly, the time course per word per condition was included as a non-linear random effect to account for differences in processing of different words. In addition, we included a random intercept adjustment per *event*, i.e., a unique participant-trial combination. Individual trials are likely to show variation in time series data, as each trial consists of multiple measurements. Including an intercept for each event accounts for the variation between trials.

After determining the random effects structure, a backward-fitting model comparison procedure was used to determine the effect of Accent and Congruency. Model comparison procedures for GAMMs are less easy to interpret than for LME, as the models that differ minimally are not necessarily strictly nested. When doing model comparisons with linear regression, we try to compare two models that differ in only one term: one of the two models contains an additional term, which the other model lacks. These models are called *nested*. However, with GAMMs the difference of one model term does not necessarily mean that the two models are nested, because the shape of the smooth terms may change non-linearly (for example by changing the number of base functions being used) in the presence or absence of other model terms. In other words, the model with fewer model terms does not necessarily end up being the simplest model. Therefore, visualization and checking the summary output provide useful information in addition to the model comparison results themselves.

Visual inspection. We start with a model that includes a three-way interaction between Accent, Congruency, and *Time* along the trajectory (order of mouse positions, with values between 0, indicating the start of the movement, and 1, the response click). As Time is the only continuous predictor of these three, the interaction was implemented as a non-linear regression line for Time split by a four-level grouping predictor representing the two-way interaction between Accent and Congruency. Beside this non-linear interaction, we included the *Duration* (log transformed; the total time duration of the mouse movement until the response click) of the trajectory as a non-linear main effect and the (additive) non-linear interaction between Time and Duration. By normalizing the mouse trajectories, the differences between fast and slow trials are lost. The interaction between Time and Duration captures potential spatial differences in trajectory that are related to the duration of the trajectory (paths tend to be straighter when velocity is high).

Figure 6 plots the estimated effects for Chinese accented words (Left panel) and English accented words (Center panel). The straight solid line indicates a straight ideal path to the target. From timestamp 40 (around 40% of the trajectory) the average mouse trajectories in all conditions deviate significantly from a straight line. The Right panel of Figure 6 plots the estimated differences between the accents for match items (solid line) and mismatch items (dashed line) with 95% confidence interval. A positive difference indicates that the mismatch items deviate more from the ideal trajectory than the match items. A negative difference indicates that the match items deviate more from the ideal trajectory than the mismatch items. Although the difference lines deviate from zero in the second half of the trajectory, the difference between the accents does not become significant as the zero line is always included within the confidence bands. The differences between the Congruency conditions within Accent (not visualized here) are also not significant based on the visualization of the model's estimates.

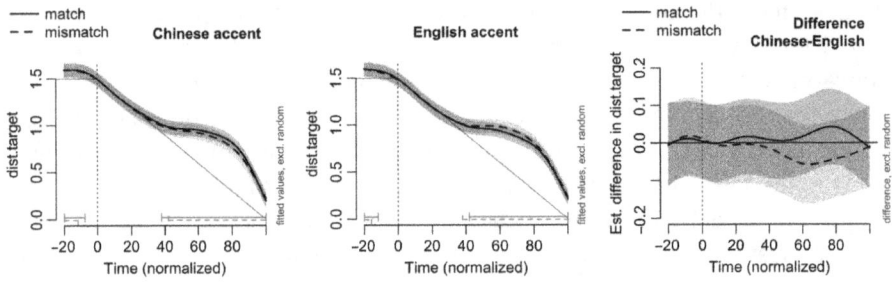

Figure 6: Estimated effects for Chinese accented words (*Left panel*) and English accented words (*Center panel*). The straight diagonal solid line indicates an ideal (straight) path to the target. The red horizontal interval markers indicate at which parts of the trajectory participants significantly deviate from this straight trajectory. The *Right panel* shows the differences between Chinese and English items for the match (solid line) and mismatch items (dashed line) with 95% confidence interval visualized by shading.

Model comparison. Visualization is an important tool for significance testing with GAMMs. Another important tool is a model comparison procedure. Here, we compared the model with the effects of Congruency and Accent (four-level categorical predictor[5]) with a model that does not include these effects using a Chi square test on the fREML scores, i.e. the minimized smoothing parameter selection score, while taking into account the difference in degrees of freedom specified in the model. The model without the effects of Congruency and Accent is preferred, because it has a lower fREML score (difference of 36.863) and lower degrees of freedom (6 df), supporting the earlier conclusion that there is no difference in trajectory for the Congruency and Accent conditions. Note, however, that fREML scores (default selection score in GAMMs) are actually not ideal for comparing different fixed effects structures (see Supplementary Materials). A model comparison based on AIC (Akaike's Information Criterion) prefers the model *with* Congruency and Accent included (AIC difference of 3.10). Sections 4 and 5 explain why

---

[5] We also tested breaking apart the four-level predictor into separate two-level predictors Congruency and Accent, which resulted in the same conclusions. See Supplementary Materials.

different significance tests can point to opposite conclusions and we provide suggestions on how to deal with a situation of inconsistent information.

Non-linear interactions. Besides the effects of Congruency and Accent over Time, we also included a non-linear interaction between Duration and Time, for which the estimated effects are illustrated in Figure 7. The contour plot (Left panel) can be read like a hiking map with the contour lines and the colors indicating the height: blue areas are valleys and the yellow areas hills. The right panel shows the estimated regression lines for mouse trajectories with durations of 5 and 7 (log scale). The two plots suggest that participants use different strategies in short (e.g., Duration of 5) and long trajectories (e.g., Duration of 7.5). The long trajectories move with a direct path (indicated by straight diagonal line) towards the target until half-way, and only then seem to reconsider their choice, i.e. the position does not decrease for quite a while. Short trajectories follow a less straight path initially, but do not seem to hesitate half-way through. Contour plots are a useful instrument to interpret non-linear interactions. Although higher order non-linear interactions (3-way or higher) are possible in GAMMs, they get increasingly more difficult to visualize and interpret.

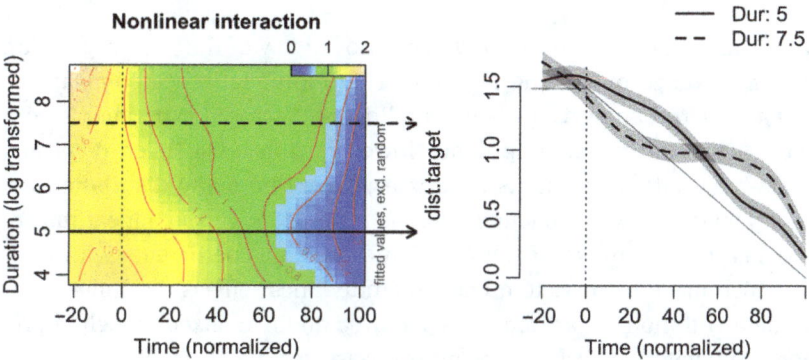

Figure 7: *Left panel:* Contour plot visualizing a non-linear interaction between two continuous predictors (Time and Duration). The colors and contour lines indicate the distance to the target. *Right panel:* estimated distance to target for Durations of 5 (148 MS) and 7.5 (1808 MS) over Time. The straight line indicates the ideal path to the target.

4.3 Discussion

To summarize, GAMMs are particularly suited to analyze non-linear patterns and time course data, because they allow us to fit non-linear regression lines, non-linear interactions, and non-linear random effects. As the non-linear effects are not represented with coefficients, the statistical method necessarily relies on visual inspection of the model estimates, which facilitates interpretation and increases understanding of patterns in the data in comparison with linear regression analyses.

An important contribution of GAMMs for the analysis of time course data is the possibility to investigate different questions, such as investigating at which moment the trajectories of different conditions start to differ, or when trajectories start to deviate from the ideal path to the target. For mouse tracking data, these questions are currently investigated with the calculation of a separate t-test for every time bin or area under the curve between ideal trajectory and observed one (e.g. Freeman and Ambady 2010). Disadvantages of GAMMs are that different sources of information, such as visualization and model comparisons, need to be assessed to determine whether a predictor contributes significantly to the model; that models may take a long time to run; and that the estimated effects often cannot simply be described with a single coefficient.

5 All statistical models are wrong

In the previous sections we have provided an overview of different regression methods for language processing research. The traditional repeated-measures ANOVA is a powerful analysis for behavioral data of factorial experiments with balanced designs and no missing data. However, with unbalanced or nested designs, missing data, continuous covariates, or not normally distributed dependent variables, a mixed-modeling approach is a better choice. Linear mixed-modeling has the advantage of returning interpretable coefficients with their statistics which make it easier to quickly quantify linear effects. For time series data and data with non-linear trends, generalized additive mixed modeling provides more explanatory power and the most precise data fit.

However, no statistical model is perfect. Problems with statistical models are generally detected when evaluating the model. Therefore, *model criticism* is the most important part of statistical analyses. This involves inspection of the residuals and testing the generalizability of the model. The first thing to check is the assumptions of regression models: (i) are the residuals normally distributed? (ii) and are the observations independent? We have already listed disadvantages for all the discussed regression methods, but in the next sections we explain some more fundamental problems with regression models and how they influence the reliability of the analyses.

5.1 Power of the model

In this chapter we have presented the GAMM analysis of the mouse tracking data, on the basis of which we concluded that the mouse tracking trajectories (or rather the Euclidean distance to the target) do not differ significantly between the words with English and Chinese (Accent), nor between the items that were congruent and incongruent in accent in comparison with the study phase (Congruency). However, the absence of a significant effect for Accent and Congruency could have various causes, such as participants' mouse trajectories are really not influenced by Accent or Congruency, or there is not sufficient power to detect the effect, or the model is not a good fit of the data and fails to include important structure in the data. In some cases, some statistical methods may come to another conclusion.

For example, we could run a LME model with Time modeled as a *non-linear* polynomial effect (cf. Growth Curve Analysis; e.g. Mirman, Dixon and Magnuson 2008; Mirman 2014) as an alternative to the GAMM analysis. To fit the non-linear trend of Time, we include a fourth order polynomial. This means that the Euclidian distances over Time are fitted with a quadratic function. This LME model includes the Time variable raised to the power of 1, 2, 3 and 4, and in addition Congruency (match or mismatch), Accent at test (English or Mandarin), and Duration (log transformed duration of the mouse movement) as fixed effects predictors. The complete analysis is part of the Supplementary Materials. In contrast with the GAMM analysis, the LME model with a polynomial effect for Time indicates that the mouse trajectories of the different conditions do vary significantly. The polynomial LME model suggests that the words with an English accent elicit *more* uncertainty with respect to whether or not the accents in the study and test phase match, and also produce a less direct path to the answer compared with Chinese accent, whereas in the GAMM the interaction between Congruency, Accent, and Time does not reach significance. How do we know whether this effect is just an artifact of the analysis or it exists in reality? Stated bluntly, this effect could be a false positive finding where we are wrongly concluding that there is an effect, when there is none (Type I error).

In this case it may be more constructive to ask first the opposite question: assuming that the effect exists in the population, how likely is it for us to detect the effect in the sample and to observe a statistical difference between the trajectories? The statistical procedures that we introduced throughout the chapter differ in how powerful they are to deal with particular types of data. To investigate this question further, we simulated hypothetical trajectories that are similar to the collected data (see Supplementary Materials).

Simulations. The basic shape of the distance function across time was simulated with a logistic curve for every participant, thus, the simulated data observe a sigmoidal shape. More importantly, the intercept of the function differs between subjects. In the next step, we added more noise to the data, but also a categorical predictor that has a small interaction with time course of the experiment, shifting the trajectory of one condition up (0.05 for simulated Euclidean distance over time). Our simulated population comprised 300 subjects, with a two level factor (match or mismatch) and 121 time points for each condition. Five different models were estimated on every subset of the population, starting with a subsample of only two subjects in the analyses and increasing up to the moment when the whole population was sampled. We used the following models:

i. LM Linear: a linear regression model with a linear effect for Time.
ii. LM Polynomial: a linear regression model with polynomial effects for Time.
iii. LME Linear: a LME with a linear effect for Time and a by-subject intercept adjustments.
iv. LME Polynomial: a LME with polynomial effects for Time and by-subject intercept adjustments.
v. GAMM: a GAMM model with a non-linear effect of time and by-subject intercept adjustments.

Finally, for every iteration, that is a subset of the population, we monitored outcomes of the models for 100 separate simulations. These outcomes were used to calculate the proportion of the obtained significant effects, thus, its power.

The results are illustrated in Figure 8. The simulations indicate that the regression models with a linear effect for Time (LM Linear and LME Linear) require vastly more subjects to be powerful enough, that is, to detect the effect in 80% of the simulations (over 300 subjects). The polynomial models in the case of simple regression (LM Polynomial) need to sample relatively fewer subjects, approximately 60 of them. Thus, specifying polynomial effects in the model explains additional variance, making the model more powerful. The most powerful in estimating the simulated interaction are the linear mixed-effects modeling with polynomial effects (LME Polynomial) and GAMMs. They need approximately 55 subjects to have 80% power for the effect estimation. To summarize, these simulations show that for detecting this simulated interaction a non-linear regression line is crucial.

Model criticism. Inspection of the residuals may also reveal that a non-linear predictor should be included instead of a linear predictor. For illustration purposes we modeled one participant's mouse tracking data (Euclidean distance to target) with a GAMM and with a comparable LME model with Time (centered and scaled) included as a linear predictor (LME Linear). Figure 9 (Left

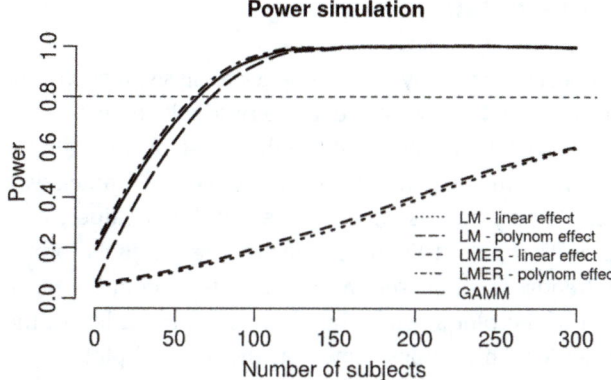

Figure 8: The power estimation for each of the illustrated analysis. X-axis represents number of subjects sampled from the population, while Y-axis represents the percentage of significant tests out of 100 simulations. The dotted horizontal line at the 0.8 value of the Y-axis indicates the moment when the statistical procedure catches the effect in 80% of the simulated times. LM – linear effect: linear regression with specified linear relation between Time course of the experiment and simulated Euclidean distances. LM – polynomial effect: linear regression with specified fourth polynomial relation. LMER – linear effect: linear mixed-effect modeling with linear effect. LMER – polynomial effect: linear mixed-effect modeling with polynomial relation. GAMM: generalized additive modeling with non-linear effect of Time.

and Center panels) plots the residuals against the values of the predictor Time for the GAMM analysis for the LME Linear analysis. Note that the residuals of the GAMM model do not show a trend over the Time values, but the residuals for the LME Linear model do. This indicates that there is unexplained structure in the residuals. The Right panel of Figure 9 shows the same plot for the GAMM model of all mouse trajectories.

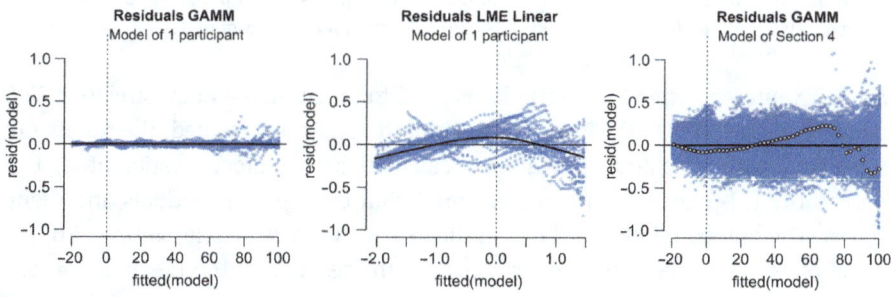

Figure 9: The residuals plotted against the predictor Time. Left: GAMM model of 1 participant. Center: LME model with linear predictors modeling the same participant. The residuals show that the linear predictors did not capture the non-linear trend of Time. Right: GAMM model of all data, as presented in Section 4. The residuals from one specific trial are marked with white dots.

5.2 Autocorrelation of residuals

One of the most important checks, especially for time series analysis, involves inspection of the structure in the residuals. Structure in the residuals indicates that the model fails to account adequately for the structure that exists in the data. In other words, the model does not provide a very good fit of the data. A quick way of checking for structure is plotting the residuals against the fitted values, or a continuous predictor such as Time, as in Figure 9. Ideally, the residuals form a random cloud without any trends. As discussed in the previous section, the black solid line in the Right panel of the plot suggest that there is no trend left in the residuals of the GAMM model for Time values. However, the residual plot clearly shows trial structure in the residuals – sequences of residuals that seem connected. To highlight this, we have colored the residuals for one specific trial white in the right panel of Figure 9 (the same example as in Figure 4). Such structure is called *autocorrelation* in the residuals. The autocorrelation means that the value of a residual is correlated with the residual of the previous data point.

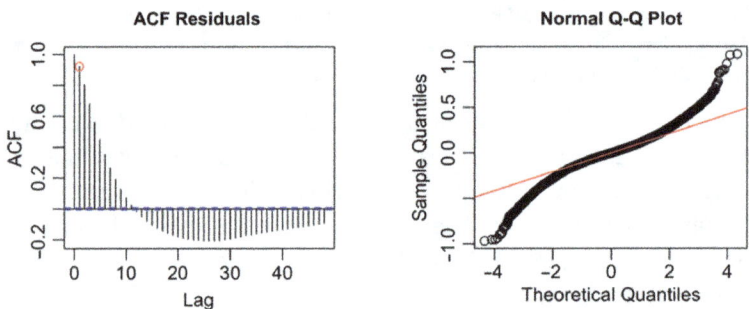

Figure 10: Residuals of the GAMM model for mouse tracking data. *Left panel:* Autocorrelation of residuals. The red circle marks the lag 1-value. *Right panel:* QQ-norm plot.

An ACF (autoregressive function) plot is used to diagnose the autocorrelation (left panel of Figure 10). On the X-axis of the plot the lag is represented, the number of trials back with which the correlation is calculated. The autocorrelation at lag 0 is necessarily 1, because this is the autocorrelation between all residuals and themselves. The autocorrelation at lag 1 (indicated with the red circle) is 0.94. So, the value of the residuals is 94% determined by the residual of the previous sample. The lag 2 value represents the autocorrelation between the residual and the residual of two samples backward. Ideally, the autocorrelation at the lags larger than 1 is as low as the blue dashed lines indicate. Autocorrelation can be described by an autoregressive model of order n, AR(n): $X_t = c + \sum_{i=1}^{n} \rho_i X_{t-i} + \varepsilon_t$, in which c is a constant, ρ_i is the amount of autocorrelation between the residuals and the residuals at lag *i*, and ϵ is noise.

Autocorrelation is generally associated with time course data, in which the samples are clearly related (e.g. van Rij et al. 2019), but also can show up in behavioral data, such as reaction times (e.g. Baayen and Milin 2010). Reaction times may show learning effects (gradually getting faster as the task becomes more familiar), fatigue, and concentration fluctuations. One of the causes of autocorrelation is correlation in the sampled data. The consequence of autocorrelation is that the model reports too much confidence in the estimates, because the model works with the assumption that all data points are independent. Thus, the model reports too small confidence bands and too low p-values, and the generalizability of the model is reduced. Note that autocorrelation is not a problem specific to GAMMs, but arises with every regression method that tries to fit time series data. When fitting linear regression models on time series data the autocorrelation may be more severe as the linear regression lines cannot capture non-linear trends over time (see Figure 9, Center panel). (The stronger autocorrelation in the residuals might be the reason why the LME polynomial model in this chapter reports significant differences for Accent and Congruency, even though these effects are not found to be significant with GAMMs.) A first step in analyzing time course data is reducing the sample size as far as possible so that the correlation between consecutive samples is reduced.

To inspect what causes the autocorrelation in the residuals of our mouse tracking data analysis, we visualize the fit of three randomly selected trials (Figure 11, Left panel). The gray lines are the raw data, the red lines the model fit (summed effects), and the gray shaded areas the residuals (difference between the data and the regression model). As time-series data by definition consist of sequences of strongly correlated measurements, the difference between the estimated regression lines and the data are strongly autocorrelated residuals. The model fits a unique line for each event, i.e., participant-trial combination, based on the *by-participant-condition* non-linear random smooth over Time and the *by-item-condition* non-linear random smooth over Time. The estimated effect is also adjusted with a random intercept for each unique event. Although the model captures the general trends of the three trials, it is not completely able to fit each individual mouse trajectory precisely. For a more precise model fit a *by-event* (unique participant-trial combination) non-linear random smooth needs to replace the current random effect structure. The Center panel of Figure 11 shows the much more precise model fit when by-event smooths are included: the residuals (gray shaded areas) are much smaller. However, autocorrelation is measured independently of the residual size: The Right panel of Figure 11 shows that the autocorrelation is reduced, but did not disappear completely. Nevertheless, smaller residuals will reduce the consequences of the autocorrelation in the residuals. Thus, it is very important to improve the model fit.

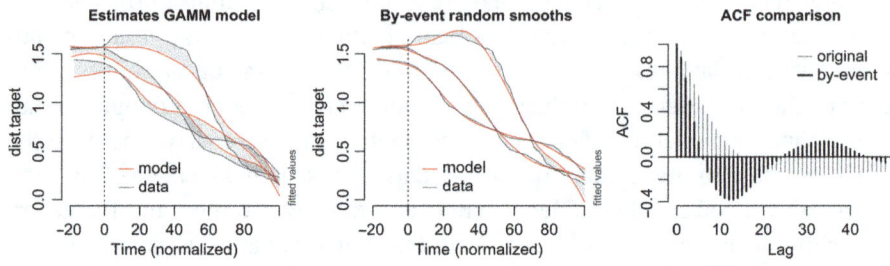

Figure 11: Data of three randomly sampled trials (black lines) compared with the model's estimates for the same trials (red lines) and the residuals (gray shaded areas). *Left panel:* fit of GAMM model discussed in Section 3c, *Center panel:* GAMM model with by-Event random non-linear smooths. The *Right panel* combines the ACF of the two models, the thin lines represent the original GAMM model, the thick lines represent the GAMM with by-Event random smooths.

Besides down sampling and improving the model fit, GAMMs as implemented in the R package *mgcv* (Wood 2011, 2017) provide another solution to account for the autocorrelation in the residuals. It is possible to include an AR(1) model (autoregressive model of order 1, as introduced above) for the residuals so that the GAMM model can take into account that the residuals are correlated while fitting the data. To include an AR(1) model, first the autocorrelation of lag 1 is estimated from a GAMM model that did not include an AR(1) model, and this value is provided to the new model as an autocorrelation measure. The model will adjust its confidence estimation accordingly. A model comparison procedure can be used to optimize the estimation of the autocorrelation parameter. Including an AR(1) model is a practical solution when the random effects structure that can be included is limited. However, the method is not perfect: an AR(1) model with the same autocorrelation parameter for all participants is often too simplistic and does not always sufficiently reduce the autocorrelation (Baayen et al. 2018; van Rij et al. 2019). Options to account for correlation in the residuals are also available in LME (package *nlme*, Pinheiro et al. 2017).

To summarize, for GAMMs analyses there are currently three solutions available to reduce the autocorrelation: (i) reducing the sample size, (ii) improving model fit by including by-event random smooths to capture individual time series, and (iii) including an AR(1) model so that the model takes into account the autocorrelation in the model fit by reducing its confidence in the observations.

5.3 Distribution of the residuals

The distribution of the residuals is generally investigated with a QQ-norm plot which plots the distribution of the model's residuals against a theoretical normal distribution with a similar standard deviation and mean (Right panel of Figure 10). Ideally, the residuals follow a straight line, which represents the normal distribution. However, for the GAMM model of mouse tracking data we see that the residuals deviate from a normal distribution, with the lowest residuals lower than expected for a normal distribution and with the highest residuals higher than expected. This pattern suggests that the data are following a t-distribution rather than a normal distribution, because the t-distribution has heavier tails than the normal distribution, i.e. higher probability for extreme high and low values than with normal distribution. This symmetrical deviation from normality is difficult to correct with transformations.

Residuals following a t-distribution are also regularly found in other biophysiological data, such as pupillometry measures or EEG data. GAMMs (the package *mgcv* version 1.8 or higher), but not LMEs, offer the possibility to fit a scaled t-distribution to the data. A disadvantage is that running the model under the assumption of a scaled t-distribution is still relatively slow (in mgcv version 1.8–17), so it is not possible to include non-linear random smooths for predictors with many levels when using this distribution. We advise comparing the model's estimates based on a Gaussian model and based on a scaled t-distribution to see whether and how the estimates change. As the autocorrelation in the residuals seem to affect the model estimates more severely, we generally focus on reducing the autocorrelation first.

5.4 Collinearity

In an ideal world, explanatory variables would be related to our dependent variables, while being unrelated to one another. Indeed, traditional experimental design can be thought of as an attempt to bring about just this situation. This would allow theorists to maximize explained variance in the dependent variable while simultaneously working toward the most comprehensive and accurate theoretical model.

We do not live in an ideal world, though. Many potential explanatory variables are related not only to our dependent variables but to one another, and sometimes strongly so. This is true both of stimulus characteristics such as frequency, length, and concreteness, and of participants characteristics such as age, education, and reading proficiency. This situation is referred to as *collinearity* (or sometimes *multicollinearity*). *Essential collinearity* refers to the underlying structure of a dataset, while *non-essential collinearity* simply depends on the particular scales on which the variables have been measured. *Essential collinearity* is the type that researchers care about most. We will return to this distinction below, when discussing the common suggestion that mean-centering improves collinearity. For now, we simply note that mean-centering does not improve essential collinearity in any way.

Collinearity can bring with it a set of problems for researchers. One is that, if a person is using significance testing, it is possible for a statistical model to explain a significant proportion of the variance in the dependent variable without a single one of the individual predictor variables being significant. This can occur because variance that can be explained by multiple explanatory variables is not assigned to any single one of them, although it is counted as explained variance in the evaluation of the overall model.

Perhaps more unsettling for researchers is the issue of *suppression*. Many different definitions of suppression have been used, but following Wurm and Fisicaro (2014), we use the term to refer to any case in which the sign of a predictor variable's zero-order correlation with the dependent variable (i.e. the bivariate correlation, controlling for no other variables) differs from its sign in a larger analysis with multiple explanatory variables.

Friedman and Wall (2005) showed that when there are only two predictor variables, it is easy to understand and predict what will happen to the signs of the regression coefficients as a function of the strength of the correlations. On the one hand, it is comforting to know that it will always be the weaker of the two predictors that will show the sign change. On the other hand, if the zero-order correlations between each predictor and the dependent variable are similar in size to one another, then in another data set (even using the same stimuli and task) their relative sizes might reverse. This would cause the sign of the previously-larger effect to be the one that now changes. In addition, such effects become harder to understand and predict with each explanatory variable added to the model.

The troubling effects of even slight changes in these "initial conditions" are what make some researchers mistakenly assert that there is computational instability in the models. Friedman and Wall (2005) say "multicollinearity does not affect standard errors of regression coefficients in ways previously taught"

(p. 127), and provide a very nice demonstration that any "instability" is not computational. It has to do with the underlying correlational structure of the dataset.

In the next section we will highlight some of the strengths and weaknesses of some of the potential solutions that have been offered.

Residualizing. Residualizing is a technique in which one predictor variable is regressed on one or more other predictor variables. The residuals (i.e. the unexplained portion of the variance) are retained and used in place of the original predictor variable. By definition this residualized variable will be uncorrelated with any variable on which it was residualized, so this method appears to offer a useful solution to collinearity. However, Wurm and Fisicaro (2014) present evidence from the literature that the risk of misinterpretation far outweighs anything that might be learned from such analyses, particularly because any information available from such analyses is also available from methods far less likely to be mischaracterized or misunderstood. In addition, for complex situations like those found in actual psycholinguistic studies, the likelihood increases that an analysis including residualized predictors cannot be meaningfully interpreted at all.

There is also a general interpretational problem that comes with residualization. This is illustrated nicely by Breaugh's (2006) example based on the strong correlation between the heights and weights of professional basketball players. He found that players' heights predicted their rebounding totals only if their weights were not controlled for. He questions, though, how one might interpret a height variable from which weight has been residualized. He says that " ... making subjunctive statements based upon a residual variable is inappropriate. Simply stated, there is no basis to assume that, if in reality height and weight were uncorrelated, height would not be related to rebounds. Given they are correlated, and highly so, we simply have no way of knowing" (p. 439). In the long run we are better off trying to understand why the predictors are correlated, which of course is easy for the present example.

Principal components. An alternative approach is to perform a principal components analysis on the set of predictor variables one wishes to use. Several methods exist, but in general the idea is that the number of predictors will be reduced to a small number of principal components that are orthogonal (i.e. uncorrelated with one another). The drawback is that the original predictor variables are now gone, and all we have left are mixtures of the predictors that cannot be analyzed back into their constituent parts. One can sometimes make statements such as "Principal Component #1 seems to be related to word frequency" by examining how individual predictors correlate with it, but in general that will not be sufficient for development or testing of a theoretical model.

Baayen, Wurm and Aycock (2007) used principal components analysis to capture sequential dependencies in a trial-by-trial analysis of lexical decision times. It was probably harmless to use in this situation, because they did not care about recovering the structure of the original predictors, but as Wurm and Fisicaro (2014) showed, if the only concern was in removing that extraneous variance (or "controlling for" it), then the approach bought them nothing.

Mean-centering. A number of researchers have suggested mean-centering (i.e. subtracting from each score the mean on that variable) as a way to reduce collinearity. Mean-centering addresses non-essential collinearity for the simple reason that it changes the scaling of the variables, but unfortunately it does nothing whatsoever to address the underlying structural relationships between the variables. Thus, essential collinearity is left unchanged by mean-centering. Worse still, mean-centering can mask some of the diagnostics used to assess collinearity (Belsley 1984; Pedhazur 1997), leading researchers to the mistaken belief that they have solved the problem. A number of authors, including Dalal and Zickar (2012), nevertheless recommend mean-centering because it can make the interpretation of regression coefficients easier and more immediately meaningful, but it does not in any way improve essential collinearity.

Other approaches include some that compute solutions over many different permutations and/or combinations of predictor variables. One example of this is random forests (Breiman 2001; Strobl, Malley and Tutz 2009), which assign a higher importance to a predictor variable if its original version predicts the dependent variable much better than a permuted version does. One practical concern is that even with current computing power, the analyses can take several hours to run (Tagliamonte and Baayen 2012). An additional question that has not been the topic of research so far as we are aware is the sensitivity of random forest computations to the "initial conditions" we spoke of above. That is, if predictor X_1 has a slightly stronger relationship to the dependent variable than predictor X_2 does, will it necessarily emerge as the more important predictor across the summary of the permuted analyses? If so, researchers are in the same worrisome situation of having to decide whether that initial ordering of the variables reflects reality, or whether it is perhaps something idiosyncratic about the particular dataset being analyzed.

Ridge regression. A final approach we will mention is called ridge regression (Hoerl 1962). It prevents error variance from increasing under conditions of high collinearity, and produces slightly conservative parameter estimates. The biggest drawback in our view is that it cannot be used with the kinds of designs most frequently employed by psycholinguists (repeated-measures designs, which are usually being analyzed with multilevel or mixed-effects models). It can, however, be used to analyze item sets.

We believe it worth emphasizing that all of these approaches will fail in one respect or another. Darlington (1990) wrote that it is a "misconception about collinearity ... that more advanced statistical methods might someday eliminate the problem. The problem is essentially that when two variables are highly correlated, it is harder to disentangle their effects than when the variables are independent. This is simply an unalterable fact of life" (Darlington 1990: 131; see also Darlington 1968; Pedhazur 1997).

Suggestions. Most textbooks on regression (e.g. Tabachnick and Fidell 2007) contain recommendations for what one might do to deal with high collinearity. Such suggestions include things like creating composite variables, omitting some predictors, and doing nothing. Indeed, if our goal for a particular set of predictor variables is simply to explain variance, then the best approach is to include any and all predictors that might have a relationship with the dependent variable. The same holds true if our goal is simply to be in a position to say that we have "controlled for" the effects of one or more variables. We can safely put them into our models and go about our business without any concern for what might have happened to their signs, or their p-values. In many cases, though, this won't do. No researcher is willing to maximize explained variance at the expense of parsimony and coherence in their theoretical model. If the goal is to have a good theoretical model, then we're back to having to decide what to do.

We would like to offer the suggestion that whatever approach is taken skirts the real issue. Statistical "control" (and everything that means: residualizing, principal components analysis, random forests, even the whole idea of multiple regression itself) is an attempt to "equate" or balance stimuli, which we talked about above in the context of traditional factorial designs. Meehl (1970: 385) spoke eloquently about the difficulties this poses: "When a social scientist of methodological bent tries to get clear about the meaning, proof, and truth of those counterfactuals that interpret statistical formalisms purporting to 'control the influence' of nuisance variables, he is disappointed to discover that the logicians are still in disagreement about just how to analyze counterfactuals" (see also Campbell, Converse and Rodgers 1976). Anderson (1963: 170) was more to the point a few years earlier: " ... one may well wonder exactly what it means to ask what the data would be like if they weren't what they are."

Darlington (1990: 155) says that "suppression rarely occurs in real data". Cohen et al. (2003) assert that it is more common in fields like economics than in the social sciences, because in those fields variables can sometimes have "equilibrium-promoting effects." We think it likely, though, that Darlington and Cohen et al. did not foresee the kind of statistical models being run in modern psycholinguistics, which can sometimes contain literally dozens of interrelated predictors.

Such models are probably indefensible anyway, and thus force us to confront the possibility that regression-based techniques are not up to the task we are asking of them. At some point a researcher must confront more directly what all of these intercorrelations mean, instead of hoping for a new, more creative analytic strategy to emerge. Why do these things co-vary? Which one might have temporal or theoretical priority? Which model is the most useful, not only in terms of explaining this dataset but in terms of making predictions about other datasets? Whatever approach or combination of approaches is used, we would urge researchers to use clear, precise, and proper language, and to include as much information as possible for those interested in replicating the analyses.

6 Discussion

In this chapter we have outlined three different analysis methods that could be used for analyzing psycholinguistic data. All three methods aim to account for the variability between participants and stimuli, which characterizes psycholinguistic data. However, the methods each have their own strengths and weaknesses.

6.1 Choosing a statistical method

Repeated-measures ANOVA is the oldest method and still most commonly used. The method provides robust results for balanced factorial designs without missing data, and with a dependent variable that is normally distributed and with the variance being homogeneous across conditions. Advantages of this method are that it is well-documented and that the results are easy to report. Disadvantages are that several analyses are required, i.e. F1 test, F2 test, and post-hoc tests for interpreting the results, and that the method is fairly limited in use. In practice, psycholinguistic data often contains covariates, such as frequency, time, or age, and missing data is a common problem with human participants or corpus data. The method is not suited for analyzing time series data, because it does not allow inspection of the time course directly, but rather requires collapsing over time windows.

Linear mixed-effects modeling (LME) is a well-established alternative analysis for repeated-measures ANOVA. The method is more robust than ANOVA with missing data and can handle unbalanced data and those that are not normally distributed, such as binomial data or count data. An advantage of the method is that the method allows direct analysis of sample data without the need to average. This reduces the number of analyses to perform. Other advantages are the possibility to include covariates, the flexibility of the method with missing data and unbalanced designs, and the interpretation of the results. The interpretation of the results is relatively easy in comparison with the other discussed methods, because the method provides the estimated coefficients. No additional post-hoc tests are required and the estimated variability between participants and items can be easily inspected. Disadvantages of the method are that it requires more time to run the analysis, and that the method is more vulnerable to anti-conservative estimates, i.e. over-fitting the data, when the random effect structure is too limited (Barr et al. 2013). It requires more effort to determine the structure of the random effects, because the maximal random effect structure (i.e. subjects and items vary in their sensitivity to all experimental manipulations), is not always possible (Baayen et al. 2017). Another disadvantage is that it cannot handle non-linear covariates very easily, as the shape of the non-linear pattern needs to be specified by the user. Finally, there are not many possibilities to account for the autocorrelation problem.

Generalized additive mixed modeling (GAMM) is a relatively new *non-linear* mixed-effects regression method that is particularly suited for analyzing non-linear data, such as time series data or data with non-linear covariates. It shares with LME that the method can handle unbalanced data and not normally distributed data, such as binomial data or count data, and allows direct analysis of sample data without the need to average. One of the main advantages of GAMMs is a better understanding of the data, because the method relies much more than the other methods on visualization of the estimates and results. Other advantages are the possibility to include non-linear effects and interaction surfaces, and non-linear random effects, and the possibility to account for autocorrelation in the residuals with an AR1 model. Disadvantages of GAMMs are that they can require a long time to run, and that the interpretation of the model takes more time, because the non-linear effects need to be visualized as coefficients are not provided. Another disadvantage of GAMMs is that finding the best-fitting model is less straightforward than with LME, as models are not strictly nested. A final disadvantage is that the results are less generalizable when autocorrelation plays a role, or when the model does not fit the data very well, for example when only limited random effects can be included. In these cases, one needs to be cautious with the interpretation of the results.

Thus, these three methods could be considered complementary: to analyze the data from a simple factorial balanced design, it may be valid to use a repeated-measures ANOVA although mixed-effects models are equally powerful alternatives (Baayen 2008: Chapter 7); but for unbalanced designs or data sets with linear covariates LME is a better choice, and when non-linear effects play a role GAMM is the preferred option. So instead of focusing on one single analysis method and letting that particular analysis method determine the design of our experiments, as often seem to be the underlying reason for factorial designs, the mixed-effects methods provide us a powerful tool to investigate different questions using more flexible designs. For example, when we only have ANOVA available as statistical method we need to carefully control the frequency of our stimuli in equally high and low frequency words for our different manipulations, dichotomizing frequency. However, GAMMs allow us to sample words with a range of frequencies and include frequency as continuous measure in our analysis. When we would like to use a GAMM analysis it is actually better to sample words with different frequencies from a *range* instead of selectively choosing the words with low and high frequency. In other words, the statistical methods that we have available for use will influence the choice of design. Moreover, the statistical method will also shape the questions we ask: for example, non-linear regression methods allow us to ask *at which moment* in the time course two conditions start to differ, instead of *whether* we detect early and/or late differences.

6.2 Implications for design

ANOVA compatible designs in reaction time studies have long dominated the analytic landscape in psycholinguistics as well as in other domains of inquiry (for a review, see Van Zandt 2002). Many did and still do believe that the only competent methodology is an experiment with a factorial design that allows for hypothesis testing and causal inference. By implication a study with a correlational design is necessarily inferior because it describes only an association. Assumptions like these motivate a common research practice in the domain of psycholinguistics that is to treat continuous measures dichotomously, by sampling at two points (ranges) along a continuum, and then matching the means of those groups on other relevant factors. Data generated in this framework are subject to several shortcomings, which include the consequences of (i) control by matching (ii) control by counterbalancing (iii) limitations of analyzing means and (iv) diminishing the richness of big data.

i) Control by matching. In the traditional design, it is typical to "manipulate" an independent variable or two of interest and then "match" words across the various levels of other potentially relevant measures. For example, it is typical to manipulate target frequency in a factorial manner (e.g. a range for high and a non-overlapping range for low treatment conditions) and control word length and number of words that differ from the target by one letter or phoneme (neighbors). Here, "control" entails dichotomizing a continuous variable and then matching means for each group along those other possible measures. One obvious problem with matching a measure of central tendency is that it does not make the distributions that they describe comparable. Parametric statistical analyses work best when distributions do not have long tails and outliers. Matching only on a measure of central tendency can violate this assumption. In part, the consequences of imposing a dichotomous structure on a continuous measure depend on the non-linearities in its behavior (see Baayen 2010).

When two independent variables are manipulated factorially, matching means across combinations of levels or treatment conditions gets even more tedious. The problem gets more complex when the measures to be matched are correlated, for example word length and frequency. Shorter words tend to be higher in frequency (*the*, *and*, *his*, *her*) and, because these covary, the set of words that are short but low in frequency (e.g., *awl*, *cob*, *ewe*) will, by definition tend to be statistically atypical. More realistically, clusters rather than pairs of measures tend to be related. For example, the many measures of frequency tend to be related not only to measures of length but also to measures of form similarity captured by neighbors. Therefore, manipulating frequency while matching on number of neighbors and length requires breaking a natural co-variation. One obvious implication is that words are not randomly selected to fill out a factorial design that includes measures that covary. The practical consequence is that matching in this way is likely to lead to selecting low frequency words that are atypically non-homogenous on related measures like number of neighbors or perhaps bigram structure. For example, whereas short words tend to have many neighbors, orthographic neighbors for *awl*, *cob*, *ewe* are 4, 28 and 5, respectively. The severity of the matching problem depends on the degree of correlation among measures. It is a general problem and applies not only to correlations of word frequency with form described above or of word frequency with semantic measures such as wordliness or semantic density (Keuleers and Marelli, this volume). The theoretical implication of reliable interactions such as these is that the conventional interpretation of frequency, tying it to activation of lexical entries without regard to their constituents may be flawed (Kuperman et al. 2009). This cannot be evaluated with factorial designs, however.

In this example, frequency, which is by its nature a continuous predictor, is treated dichotomously. Analyses of covariance provide a modest remedy when the focus is only a select number of measures and the correlation among them is not strong. Nonetheless, these analyses assume a linear relation between predictors. At least for frequency, linearity cannot be assumed without careful inspection of the dataset.

ii) Control by counterbalancing. In factorial designs, control is typically based on random assignment of participants and sometimes items to conditions along with changing the order in which items are presented or the location at which they appear on the screen. The underlying assumption is that counterbalancing assignment and order or location is sufficient to alleviate random differences between participants and between items. While in practice order effects such as training or fatigue are not always removed by aggregation, it is generally assumed that any effect worth studying should be robust to the noise associated with trial number or sequential order. Counterbalancing in this manner makes it basically impossible to track behavior that changes during the course of the experimental session as well as interactions that involve differences between participants or items. For example, with relevant controls, skilled readers tend to perform more consistently during the course of an experimental session than do less skilled readers. This cannot be detected easily when skill is treated dichotomously. Similarly, evidence that participants catch on or otherwise adjust to a property that differs among words (e.g. native or non-native accent) as they progress through the experimental session or trial would be missed. Finally, analyses include only correct trials therefore performance on prior trials is likewise treated as noise.

iii) The implications of aggregating over participants or items. Along with counterbalancing in this way is the convention of using means by participant by condition or of word by condition as the unit of analysis. For a period, it was conventional to report sets of analyses, one with subjects as the random effect and a second with items (Clark 1973). The rationale was to demonstrate that the findings generalize beyond the sample of participants and language materials that were tested. The fact that participants were nested within a particular combination of items and conditions was ignored (e.g. Raaijmakers et al. 1999). The fact that some participants perform more poorly than others and contribute fewer correct data points to their mean for a condition was also ignored when means are the unit of analysis. This practice becomes particularly problematic when missing data are meaningful as with clinical populations or studies that track acquisition (Keuleers and Marelli 2020, this volume).

iv) Diminishing the richness of big data. Large-scale datasets compiled from human behavioral measures (eye tracking, EEG), linguistic corpora (Nelson association norms, CELEX) or collected from digital social media provide data about individuals and about groups. New technologies have made salient many of the inadequacies of the factorial approach, especially with respect to changes in behavior over time and have inspired the adaptation of new quantitative analyses and measures in non-linguistic as well as linguistic domains. One now classical way to reduce the dimensionality of these data is by focusing on peaks and where they arise relative to the onset of an event. At its simplest, this technique assumes that one can identify a peak and distinguish it from a prolonged elevation and, that it is possible to define a peak globally rather than relative to a local baseline. With these constraints, it becomes more complex to detect a peak in conjunction with a general drift toward lower values or other types of artifacts. Of crucial importance with many of the technologies is appreciation of how behavior changes over time. There are multiple techniques of varying complexity to incorporate variability over time.

The simplest is to define bins or other fixed intervals and revert to computing means over smaller intervals. Decisions as to how many bins are often made on an ad hoc basis with little consideration of what makes one smoothing procedure preferable to another (e.g. detecting possible non-linear patterns). At the same time, choice of procedure can have dramatic consequences for the outcomes that emerge and the interpretation they warrant. For example, analyses of reaction time studies based on movement of a mouse to one of two designated locations on the computer screen depending on the decision on individual trials (audio and visual match, audio and visual mismatch) could restrict the dependent measure to time to execute the mouse trajectory from beginning to end. Alternatively, the analysis could divide the average trajectory into a number of smaller trajectories and then focus either on those means (x and y coordinates) or on how those means change over steps. Of course, one could also look at time to initiate the movement. Conditions could yield comparable total reaction times with different onsets to movement in which case we would know that, on average, participants who started later moved the mouse faster. Similarly, we could ask whether those who moved the mouse faster tended to have a more curved trajectory than those who moved it more slowly. Obviously, incorporating time steps into an analysis increases the number of dependent measures one can examine but restricting the analysis to means per time step dramatically diminishes the richness of the data.

6.3 Assessing significance

On the other hand, the analysis of more naturalistic but less balanced data will also reveal the limitations of the statistical techniques available. Problems such as limited sample sizes, non-normally distributed residuals, autocorrelation, and collinearity result in less reliable p-values, and less coherent model comparison procedures. Therefore, we strongly advise using different methods to test whether the experimental manipulations really explain variance in the data. Different methods that apply to all mixed-effects models are (i) a careful model comparison procedure to select the best-fitting model (this can be done manually, but there are also packages available that implement automatic comparison procedures), (ii) inspection of the model summaries and random effects, and (iii) visualization of the model's estimation of effects. Visualization of the model's estimates is traditionally not used so much in statistical analysis. However, the more complex the model the more important visualization is. The visualization of model estimates will quickly reveal problems with the model fit, for example by not capturing subject variability or by outliers that drive the significance of effects, and will aid the interpretation of the results.

If these three sources of information do not converge to the same conclusion, it is useful to investigate why this might be the case. The lack of convergence basically signals that the model's results are not stable, which could be due to one of the earlier described problems. In addition to these model selection methods, we strongly encourage investing time in model evaluation. Inspection of the residuals and testing the assumptions of regression models reveals critical information with respect to the generalizability and interpretation of the results.

In this chapter we have emphasized that the purpose of statistical analysis is not generating p-values, but to model the data to distinguish accidental patterns from replicable effects. We argue that when we want to take advantage of the recent experimental techniques to investigate online language processing such as eye tracking, EEG, articulography, or mouse tracking, we need to *understand* the patterns in the data instead of *reducing* and *simplifying* these patterns in order to derive a p-value. In this perspective, the limitations of the statistical model provide useful information that help us to understand the data.

6.4 Summary of results

In a repeated-measures ANOVA based on participant and item means for each condition, participants performed at chance level in recognizing the accent at study for words tested in an English accent. For the words in a Chinese accent, however, the participants' responses show a clear effect of study-test congruency. In all analyses target location (right versus left) was counterbalanced and differences due to location were treated as noise because they were not linguistically meaningful. LME analyses permitted the introduction of random slopes and intercepts and revealed that participants differed in overall performance (RT, accuracy) and in whether they treated match and mismatched study-test congruency trials in the same manner. GAMMs, a non-linear regression analysis allowed us to ask whether participants differed as they moved the mouse right or left during an experimental trial. It can account for hesitations and abrupt shifts in the mouse trajectory with the target distance measure and results can be interpreted as indices of uncertainty and changed decisions (Freeman, Dale and Farmer 2011; Freeman and Johnson 2016). Longer duration responses by mouse movements followed initially a more direct path than the short duration responses, but deviated in the mid portion of the trajectory – indicating uncertainty or revision of the response. More interestingly, some but not all participants used the additional time to produce a relatively straighter path. GAMMs are preferable to LME with polynomial curves because they specify the requisite polynomial and permit the inclusion of non-linear interaction surfaces. It is possible to determine at which moment the trajectories of different conditions start to differ. With respect to effects of test-study congruency, the GAMM model found no differences between an American and a Chinese accents.

References

Anderson, Norman H. 1963. Comparison of different populations: Resistance to extinction and transfer. *Psychological Review* 70(2), 162–179.
Baayen, R. Harald. 2008. *Analyzing linguistic data: A practical introduction to statistics using R*. Cambridge (UK): Cambridge University Press.
Baayen, R. Harald. 2010. A real experiment is a factorial experiment. *The Mental Lexicon* 5 (1) 149–157.
Baayen, R. Harald, Douglas J. Davidson, & Douglas M. Bates. 2008. Mixed-effects modeling with crossed random effects for subjects and items. *Journal of Memory and Language* 59 (4). 390–412.
Baayen, R. Harald, & Petar Milin. 2010. Analyzing reaction times. *International Journal of Psychological Research* 3 (2). 12–28.
Baayen, R. Harald, Jacolien van Rij, Cecile de Cat, & Simon N. Wood. 2018. Autocorrelated errors in experimental data in the language sciences: Some solutions offered by Generalized Additive Mixed Models. In Speelman, D., Heylen, K. and Geeraerts, D. (eds), *Mixed Effects Regression Models in Linguistics*, 49–69. Berlin, Springer.
Baayen, R. Harald, Shravan Vasishth, Reinhold Kliegl, & Douglas M. Bates. 2017. The cave of Shadows. Addressing the human factor with generalized additive mixed models. *Journal of Memory and Language* 94. 206–234.
Baayen, R. Harald, Lee H. Wurm, & Joanna Aycock. 2007. Lexical dynamics for low-frequency complex words: A regression study across tasks and modalities. *The Mental Lexicon* 2 (3). 419–463.
Barr, Dale J., Roger Levy, Christof Scheepers, & Harry Tily. 2013. Random effects structure for confirmatory hypothesis testing: Keep it maximal. *Journal of memory and language* 68 (3). 255–278.

Bates, Douglas, Martin Mächler, Ben Bolker, & Steve Walker. 2015. Fitting Linear Mixed-Effects Models Using lme4. *Journal of Statistical Software* 67 (1). 1–48.

Bates, Douglas, Reinhold Kliegl, Shravan Vasishth & R. Harald Baayen. 2015. Parsimonious mixed models. arXiv:1506.04967, 1–21.

Belsley, David A. 1984. Demeaning conditioning diagnostics through centering. *The American Statistician* 38. 73–77.

Breaugh, James A. 2006. Rethinking the control of nuisance variables in theory testing. *Journal of Business and Psychology* 20 (3). 429–443.

Breiman, Leo. 2001. Random forests. *Machine learning* 45 (1). 5–32.

Browne, Michael W. 2000. Cross-validation methods. *Journal of Mathematical Psychology* 44. 108–132.

Campbell, Angus, Philip E. Converse, & Willard L. Rodgers. 1976. *The quality of American life: Perceptions, evaluations, and satisfactions*. New York: Russell Sage Foundation.

Clark, Herbert H. 1973. The language-as-fixed-effect fallacy: A critique of language statistics in psychological research. *Journal of Verbal Learning and Verbal Behavior* 12 (1973). 335–359.

Cohen, Jacob, Patricia Cohen, Stephen G. West, & Leona S. Aiken. 2003. *Applied multiple regression/correlation analysis for the behavioral sciences* (3rd ed.). Mahwah, NJ: Lawrence Erlbaum Associates.

Dalal, Dev K., & Michael J. Zickar. 2012. Some common myths about centering predictor variables in moderated multiple regression and polynomial regression. *Organizational Research Methods* 15 (3). 339–362.

Darlington, Richard B. 1968. Multiple regression in psychological research and practice. *Psychological Bulletin* 69. 161–182.

Darlington, Richard B. 1990. *Regression and linear models*. New York: McGraw-Hill Publishing Company.

Fang, Yixin. 2011. Asymptotic Equivalence between Cross-Validations and Akaike Information Criteria in Mixed-Effects Models. *Journal of Data Science* 9. 15–21.

Freeman, Jonathan B., & Nalini Ambady. 2010. MouseTracker: Software for studying real-time mental processing using a computer mouse-tracking method. *Behavior Research Methods* 42. 226–241.

Freeman, Jonathan B., Rick Dale, & Thomas T. Farmer. 2011. Hand in motion reveals mind in motion. *Frontiers in Psychology* 2. https://www.frontiersin.org/articles/10.3389/fpsyg.2011.00059/full

Freeman, Jonathan B., & Kerri L. Johnson. 2016. More than meets the eye: split-second social perception. *Trends in cognitive sciences* 20 (5). 362–374.

Friedman, Lynn, & Melanie Wall. 2005. Graphical views of suppression and multicollinearity in multiple linear regression. *The American Statistician* 59 (2). 127–136.

Gelman, Andrew, & Jennifer Hill. 2007. *Data analysis using regression and multilevel hierarchical models*. Cambridge: Cambridge University Press.

Hoerl, Arthur E. 1962. Application of ridge analysis to regression problems. *Chemical Engineering Progress* 58. 54–59.

Hothorn, Torsten, Frank Bretz, & Peter Westfall. 2008. Simultaneous Inference in General Parametric Models. *Biometrical Journal* 50 (3). 346–363.

Keuleers, Emmanuel and Marco Marelli. 2020. Resources for mental lexicon research: A delicate ecosystem. In Vito Pirrelli, Ingo Plag & Wolfgang Dressler (eds.), Word

Knowledge and Word Usage: a Cross-disciplinary Guide to the Mental Lexicon, 164–184. De Gruyter.

Kuperman, Victor, Rob Schreuder, Raymond Bertram, & R. Harald Baayen. 2009. Reading of polymorphemic Dutch compounds: Towards a multiple route model of lexical processing. *Journal of Experimental Psychology: HPP* 35. 876–895.

Lawrence, Michael A. 2016. *ez: Easy Analysis and Visualization of Factorial Experiments*. R package version 4.4-0.https://CRAN.R-project.org/package=ez

Lin, Xihong, & Daowen Zhang. 1999. Inference in generalized additive mixed models by using smoothing splines. *Journal of the Royal Statistical Society (B)* 61 (2). 381–400.

Matuschek, Hannes, Reinhold Kliegl, Shravan Vasishth, R. Harald Baayen and Douglas Bates. 2017. Balancing Type I Error and Power in Linear Mixed Models. *Journal of Memory and Language* 94. 305–315.

Meehl, Paul E. 1970. Nuisance variables and the ex post facto design. In Michael Radner & Stephen Winokur (eds.), *Analyses of theories and methods of physics and psychology*, 373–402. Minneapolis: University of Minnesota Press.

Mirman, Daniel. 2014. *Growth Curve Analysis and Visualization Using R*. Boca Raton: Chapman and Hall.

Mirman, Daniel, James A. Dixon, & James S. Magnuson. 2008. Statistical and computational models of the visual world paradigm: Growth curves and individual differences. *Journal of Memory and Language* 59 (4). 475–494.

Pedhazur, Elazar J. 1997. *Multiple regression in behavioral research*. Fort Worth, TX: Harcourt Brace & Co.

Pinheiro, José, & Douglas Bates. 2000. *Mixed-effects models in S and S-Plus*. Springer, New York.

Pinheiro, José, Douglas Bates, Saikat DebRoy, Deepayan Sarkar, & R Core Team. 2017. *nlme: Linear and Nonlinear Mixed Effects Models*. R package version 3.1-131. https://CRAN.R-project.org/package=nlme

Raaijmakers, Jeroen G., Joseph M. C. Schrijnemakers, & Frans Gremmen. 1999. How to deal with "the language-as-fixed-effect fallacy": Common misconceptions and alternative solutions. *Journal of Memory and Language* 41 (3). 416–426.

Roberts, Seth, & Harold Pashler. 2000. How persuasive is a good fit? A comment on theory testing. *Psychological Review* 107. 358–367.

Strobl, Caroline, James Malley, & Gerhard Tutz. 2009. An introduction to recursive partitioning: Rationale, application, and characteristics of classification and regression trees, bagging, and random forests. *Psychological Methods* 14(4). 323–348.

Tabachnick, Barbara G., & Linda S. Fidell. 2007. *Using multivariate statistics* (5th ed.). Boston: Pearson Education, Inc.

Tagliamonte, Sali, & R. Harald Baayen. 2012. Models, forests and trees of York English: Was/were variation as a case study for statistical practice. *Language Variation and Change* 24. 135–178.

Vaci, Nemanja, Bartosz Gula, & Merim Bilalić. 2015. Is age really cruel to experts? Compensatory effects of activity. *Psychology and Aging* 30. 740–754.

van Rij, Jacolien, Petra Hendriks, Hedderik van Rijn, R. Harald Baayen, & Simon N. Wood. 2019. Analyzing the time course of pupillometric data. *Trends in Hearing Science* 23. 1–22.

van Rij, Jacolien, Martijn Wieling, R. Harald Baayen, & Hedderik van Rijn. 2017. *itsadug: Interpreting Time Series and Autocorrelated Data Using GAMMs*. R package version 2.3. https://CRAN.R-project.org/package=itsadug

Van Zandt, Trisha. 2002. Analysis of response time distributions. In John T. Wixted (Vol. Ed.) & Hal Pashler (Series Ed.) *Stevens' Handbook of Experimental Psychology (3rd Edition), Volume 4: Methodology in Experimental Psychology*, 461–516. New York: Wiley Press.

Wood, Simon N. 2011. Fast stable restricted maximum likelihood and marginal likelihood estimation of semiparametric generalized linear models. *Journal of the Royal Statistical Society (B)* 73(1). 3–36

Wood, Simon N. 2017. *Generalized additive models: An introduction with R*. Boca Raton: Chapman and Hall. Second Edition.

Wurm, Lee H., & Sebastiano A. Fisicaro. 2014. What residualizing predictors in regression analyses does (and what it does *not* do). *Journal of Memory and Language* 72. 37–48.

Paola Marangolo and Costanza Papagno
Neuroscientific protocols for exploring the mental lexicon: Evidence from aphasia

Abstract: Research over the past 30 years has developed several protocols to investigate the anatomo-functional architecture of the mental lexicon. The first is the neuropsychological approach, based on anatomo-clinical correlations in selected groups of brain-damaged patients and on single case studies, in which association and/or dissociation between a damaged brain area and a specific linguistic ability is deeply investigated: this approach has produced relevant insight in the organization of the semantic system. The instrumental approaches studying perfusion and metabolism, such as PET scan and fMRI, have supported these data extending our knowledge on the neural substrates of word comprehension and production. Results from studies using non invasive brain stimulation techniques, have contributed to confirm and refine previous data. Very recently, intraoperative direct electrical stimulation in patients with brain tumours has been proposed in order to make critical surgical decisions on which area can not be removed due to its crucial role in language processing. Right now, the most promising innovative approach suggests to combine different neuroimaging methods in order to overcome the limitations of each technique.

In the present chapter, we will present the main achievements obtained through these different approaches.

Keywords: neural correlates of word processing, word retrieval deficits, aphasia, neuroimaging methods, neuromodulation

1 Introduction

Disorders of language are a frequent consequence of stroke, and aphasia is one of the most socially disabling consequences (Rhode, Worrall, and Le Dorze 2013). Aphasia is an acquired language disorder, which occurs, in general, after a left hemispheric lesion (Basso, Forbes, and Boller 2013). The aphasic symptoms vary in terms of severity and degree of involvement across the modalities of language processing, including production and comprehension of speech, reading and writing. For example, a production deficit can range from the occasional inability to select the correct word to telegraphic and very limited speech output (Basso 2005).

The impact of this disorder on the person and its frequency of occurrence have led many researchers to explore the anatomical basis of the different aphasic symptoms in order to identify the neural mechanisms which support specific language functions.

It is well known that in aphasia word-finding difficulties are the most pervasive symptom of language breakdown and that naming disorders lead to a variety of errors because of damage to different stages of word processing. Generally, anomic difficulties arise from an inability to retrieve either the semantic word representation or the phonological word form (Levelt 1989; Levelt and Meyer 2000). Semantic impairments lead to difficulties in both word comprehension and production, whereas lexical phonological disturbances result in spoken word retrieval impairments with preserved word comprehension (Caramazza 1997; Lambon Ralph, Moriarty, and Sage 2002; Wilshire and Coslett 2000). Due to the frequency of anomic deficits, most of the research on the neural correlates of language has been focused in exploring how words are processed in the mental lexicon.

In this chapter, we will review the main neuroscientific approaches that have been applied for investigating the neural correlates of word processing. The first approach ever used is the anatomo-clinical correlation, first, in selected groups of brain-damaged patients and then on single case studies, in which associations but especially dissociations between symptoms and the damaged brain region were investigated. This approach has produced relevant insights in defining the architecture of the mental lexicon and the internal organization of its components. The instrumental approaches studying perfusion and metabolism, such as positron emission tomography (PET) and functional magnetic resonance imaging (fMRI), have supported these data, extending our knowledge on the neural substrates of word comprehension and production. Moreover, event-related brain potentials (ERPs) have further contributed to our understanding of the neural mechanisms underlying language processing. Recently, studies using neuromodulation techniques, such as transcranial magnetic stimulation (TMS) and transcranial direct current stimulation (tDCS), have confirmed and refined previous data. In addition, among the neurostimulation techniques, intraoperative direct electrical stimulation (DES) in patients with brain tumors has become a common clinical practice in order to assess the functional role of restricted brain regions, in order to maximize the extent of resection without provoking cognitive impairment, particularly of language.

Right now, the most promising innovative approach suggests combining different methods in order to overcome the limitations of each technique.

In the following pages, we will present the main results obtained in the study of the mental lexicon applying different methodological approaches.

2 The anatomo-clinical correlation approach and the group studies

Since Broca's discovery in 1861 and 1865, it has been established that damage to the foot of the left third frontal gyrus causes a dramatic deficit of speech production. Some years later, Wernicke (1874) pointed out that the areas of the brain anterior to the central sulcus are motor regions involved in speech production, while the posterior parts are sensory areas crucial for language comprehension. Indeed, lesions to Wernicke's area, corresponding to the third posterior part of the left superior temporal gyrus, impair comprehension (see Figure 1).

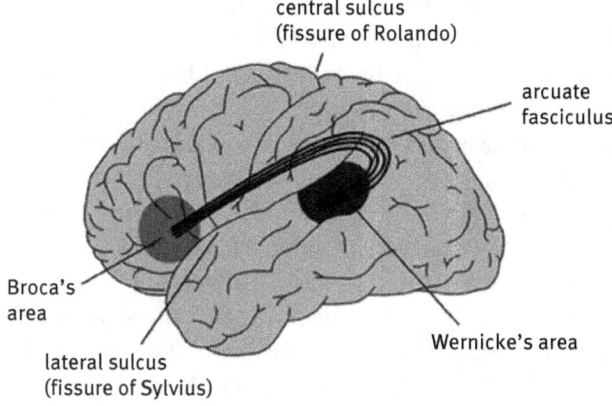

Figure 1: Localization of Broca's and Wernicke's area.

Wernicke assumed that since language is learned by imitating heard language, it is necessary for production to transfer information from the auditory receptive area to the anterior language motor area. Accordingly, patients with Wernicke's aphasia are impaired in understanding spoken or written language, and even though they can speak with an (almost) normal grammar, syntax, rate, and intonation, they do not produce a meaningful speech. Some years later in 1885, Wernicke suggested the existence of a third form of aphasia, namely conduction aphasia, due to the interruption of the white matter tracts connecting Wernicke's and Broca's areas, namely the arcuate fasciculus (Anderson et al. 1999). In conduction aphasia, a disconnection syndrome, the two language areas are preserved, but damage involves the association fibers causing a disorder of speech, which affects mainly repetition, with phonological errors, because the preserved Wernicke's area cannot control for phoneme selection. The patient, however, is aware of his/her errors and comprehension is preserved.

As Wernicke, many neurologists in the second half of the 19th century, took the view that language was a multi-componential function. The most influential was Lichtheim (1885), who added to the Wernicke's model the "concept center", where concepts are stored, and the center for the visual images of words and for the images of motor sequences involved in writing. In Lichtheim's view, the main language functions (speaking, understanding, reading and writing) are discrete entities, each related to a specific site in the brain. He argued that the concept area is not, in a strict sense, a center, but it is distributed in the brain. However, although Lichtheim's model still retained some anatomical basis, the anatomical site of its centers was mostly ignored. At that time there were three types of models: those based on the brain, where every center and connection pathway was localized in a definite cerebral structure (e.g., Wernicke's model); models not based on the brain in which there was no correspondence between centers and connections and brain structures (Kussmaul 1887, who assumed two centers for the images of words under the control of the concept center) and, finally, mixed models, such as the Lichtheim's one, in which parts of the model were psychological, but other maintained an anatomical basis. With respect to reading words, some years later, Dejerine (1891) distinguished two forms of alexic syndromes, alexia with agraphia and alexia without agraphia. Meanwhile, he clarified the neuroanatomical basis of reading and writing. Patients suffering alexia with agraphia had an acquired deficit in reading (alexia) and writing (agraphia) and this was associated with damage to the left angular gyrus. The left angular gyrus was, therefore, the center for the visual images of words. In contrast, alexia without agraphia, associated with lesions to the left occipital lobe and the posterior part of the corpus callosum, the splenium,[1] followed the disconnection of the left angular gyrus from the visual cortex (Dejerine 1891).

Although in the 19th century single case reports provided the main source of evidence on dissociated patterns of impairment due to different anatomical lesions, the qualitatively and non-systematic psychological analysis of the patient's pathological behavior, mostly confined to clinical observation, revealed

---

[1] The corpus callosum is the white matter bundle connecting the two cerebral hemispheres.

the weakness of this approach. An important source of data came from patients suffering traumatic injuries after World War II. Relying on the information acquired examining these subjects, Luria (1947, revised in 1970) published his relevant book Traumatic Aphasia, in which he attended to accommodate the localizationist approach with the idea of a functional system (an approach that, in some way, was later applied by the cognitive neuropsychologists, see Section 3). Many neuropsychologists from North America (Benton 1988; Geschwind 1965) took the view that standardized and quantitative methods had to be applied on groups of patients, in order to better define and classify the aphasic symptoms and their corresponding lesions and to replicate the results found on single cases. In describing the neoassociationist taxonomy of aphasic syndromes, which is very close to the Broca-Wernicke's classification, Geschwind (1965) used a neuroradiological approach. The typical procedure was to group neurological patients on the basis of the lesion side (left, right) and intra-hemispheric localization (anterior-frontal, posterior-temporal, etc). The performances on a standardized language examination of the different groups of patients were then compared with those of a group of normal controls, matched for demographic variables (i.e., age, educational level, time post-onset) and the corresponding patients' lesions were well-defined through validated methods. Indeed, the recent discovery of computerized tomography (CT) and of magnetic resonance imaging (MRI) allowed researchers to deeply investigate the neural correlates of the observed clinical symptoms. The aim was to establish anatomo-clinical correlations between damage to a specific left hemispheric area and the corresponding aphasic symptoms in the different modalities of language (i.e., production, reading, writing and/or comprehension) referring to the classic neurological models (e.g., Wernicke's model). Indeed, Geschwind (1965) resurrected the Wernicke-Lichtheim notion that certain areas of the left hemisphere have a strictly specialized function in language processing, and added a new form of aphasia, namely Anomic aphasia, characterized by word finding difficulties (i.e., anomia) in spontaneous speech and confrontation naming tasks in the context of preserved comprehension, repetition, reading and writing. As we will see in Section 3, this form of aphasia was the most thoroughly investigated type in the study of the mental lexicon.

Geschwind (1965)'s neoassociationist approach dominated aphasiology from the 1960s until the 1980s, and still has a significant influence. Wernicke's classification was repackaged as the Boston classification and became internationally known. Brain imaging was in its infancy, the main approaches being two: to collect patients on the basis of their symptoms and then assess the site of their lesion or, vice versa, to collect patients on the basis of their lesion and assess their language profile (e.g., Cappa et al. 1983). However, it was soon clear that patients with the same aphasic symptoms (e.g., anomia) can suffer an impairment at different levels of word production. Therefore, the advent of the cognitive approach and of new neuroimaging methods (see Section 3 and 4 below) gave new insights into language processing.

3 The cognitive approach: Single case studies

Although the classic anatomo-clinical approach provided knowledge about the relationships between a specific brain area and its function, during the 1970s, researchers began to investigate the nature of the cognitive mechanisms underlying language processing with less interest on brain localization. A novel neuropsychological approach to aphasia developed: the cognitive neuropsychological approach. The aim of this approach was to explore the functional architecture of normal language processes, through the investigation of brain-damaged patients' behavior (Caramazza 1984: 1986). According to the cognitive approach, the mental faculties, and language in particular, require a number of connected components with specific functional properties. The mind being a multi-component system with specific features and connections, a sub-component of the system (or the connections between two of them) can be selectively affected by a brain lesion. Brain-damaged patients, therefore, can be investigated with two objectives: (1) interpreting their impairment in terms of the defective function of one or more components or connections of the system; (2) increasing knowledge about the functional architecture of the language system (Caramazza 1986; Caramazza and Hillis 1993).

Indeed, in contrast with the classic anatomo-clinical method, cognitive neuropsychologists argued for a functional approach to the study of the mind explicitly independent from the study of the brain. The group study approach was strongly criticized and refused, since diagnostic criteria referring to classic aphasia categories would be too generic (Caramazza and McCloskey 1988).

In order to study the functional architecture of the language system, one type of neuropsychological finding, dissociation, was considered to have a special status (Caramazza 1986). A dissociation occurs when a group of patients (or a single patient) performs poorly on one task and at a normal level (or significantly better) on another task. This is a simple dissociation. One interpretation of the dissociation is that the two tasks are sub-served by two different functions, which explain why they are differently impaired. However, it might be possible that the two tasks are sub-served by the same mechanism but differ in the level of difficulty and the more difficult task shows greater impairment than the easier one, when the single sub-serving mechanism is impaired. According to Shallice (1988), the major attainment of single case studies has been the demonstration of the independence of specific subsystems by means of the double dissociation paradigm. A double dissociation occurs when patient A is impaired in task X and (nearly) unimpaired in task Y while patient B shows the reverse pattern.

By means of this approach, in the 1980s, the structure of the lexicon and how lexical representations interact was one of the most thoroughly investigated topics in cognitive neuropsychology.

The performance of brain-damaged patients with selective lexical-semantic disorders led researchers to decompose the normal language system into many interacting subcomponents and information processing models made up of boxes and arrows. A classic example is the word processing model proposed by Patterson & Shewell (1987), involving four different lexicons – the auditory input lexicon (corresponding to the auditory images of words), the orthographic input lexicon (corresponding to the visual images of words), the phonological output lexicon (corresponding to the motor images of words), and the orthographic output lexicon (corresponding to the motor images for writing) – plus a cognitive system, later identified as the semantic system.

This approach has provided several important insights in the lexicon architecture, thanks to the demonstration of selective deficits, such as the selective impairment of the semantic system, the dissociation between written and oral naming, the dissociation between nouns and verbs, the dissociation between abstract and concrete words and, inside concrete entities, the selective impairment of semantic categories.

For example, Caramazza and Hillis (1990) reported patient KE, who made semantically-related errors in reading, writing, naming and comprehension. The word *tiger*, for instance, was read "lion" and when the patient was presented with the picture of the tiger, he said "lion" and wrote <elephant>. In auditory- and written-word-picture matching tasks, he also made frequent semantic errors. The pervasiveness of the semantic errors and their similarity of occurrence across all modalities of input and output led the authors to hypothesize that the patient suffered damage to the semantic system.

Concerning the existence of two independent output lexicons, traditionally, it was proposed that successful writing requires a person to say the word to him/herself, translate the internally generated sounds into a string of letters, and finally write those letters ("phonic mediation theory" of writing) (Ellis and Young 1988). Recent advances in cognitive neuropsychology have, however, falsified this theory. First, patients have been reported who can still spell words whose spoken forms they were unable to retrieve form the phonological output lexicon (e.g., Bub and Kertesz 1982; Ellis, Miller, and Sin 1983). Secondly, single-case studies were provided with the opposite pattern: patients were reported who made errors in writing to dictation and written naming, but could still retrieve the phonological word forms in oral naming, reading and spontaneous speech (e.g., Hillis, Rapp, and Caramazza 1999).

One deeply investigated organization parameter of the lexicon was the grammatical category of words. Indeed, several studies were reported on patients showing word production deficits restricted to the noun or verb category suggesting that words belonging to different grammatical classes are independently represented in the lexicon (Shapiro, Shelton, and Caramazza 2000). Selective sparing of nouns relative to verbs has been frequently reported, usually in Broca's aphasia patients (Baxter, Dooren, and Warrington 1985; McCarthy, Rosaleen, and Warrington 1985; Miceli et al. 1984; 1988), while the opposite dissociation, namely, verbs relatively better preserved than nouns, has been less frequently documented but is not rare and is generally found in anomic patients (Miceli et al. 1984; 1988; Rapp and Caramazza 1998; Silveri and Betta 1997; Zingeser and Berndt 1990) and in semantic dementia (Papagno, Capasso, and Miceli 2009a). All these reports of selective dysfunction of nouns and verbs suggested that a dimension of lexical organization is the grammatical class of words.

The noun–verb dissociation observed in aphasic patients has been explained in several ways. According to Caramazza and colleagues (e.g., Rapp and Caramazza 2002), dissociated impairments may be caused by damage that selectively affects verbs or nouns at a late lexical stage (phonological or orthographic output lexicons); this is suggested by the fact that patients have been described with modality-specific deficits restricted principally (the first patient) or only (the second) to verbs either in oral or written production, respectively (Caramazza and Hillis 1991). Alternatively, Berndt et al. (1997) have claimed the existence of a lexical-syntactic representation of grammatical class at a more central lexical level (the lemma, see Levelt et al., 2000). Bird, Howard, and Franklin (2000), on the other hand, argued that noun-verb dissociation might be a semantic, rather than a lexical, phenomenon, and they also suggested that many dissociations might be generated by the fact that aphasic patients are more affected by imageability, which is lower for verbs (Paivio 1971).

Lexical representations specify more than information about the grammatical categories of words: they also include their possible morphological transformations. Disorders of morphological processing have been systematically observed in so-called agrammatic aphasia (e.g., Goodglass 1976). Indeed, difficulties with nominal, adjectival and verbal inflections are a common feature of agrammatic speech across different languages (e.g., Menn and Obler 1990). The reverse picture, apparent sparing of morphological endings associated with the production of neologistic root morphemes, has been reported in jargonaphasia (e.g., Buckingham and Kertesz 1976; Luzzatti, Mondini, and Semenza 2001; Marshall and Newcombe 1973; Semenza et al. 1990), but can be observed also in repetition (Kohn and Melvold 2000; Miceli, Capasso, and Caramazza 2004) and writing tasks (Badecker, Hillis, and Caramazza 1990). The errors made by these patients have led many authors to suggest that lexical information is represented in a morphologically decomposed form (Caramazza et al. 1985; Coltheart 1985), although not all authors agree with this view.

Further single case reports gave some suggestions regarding the internal organization of the semantic system. In an influential series of papers, Warrington and co-workers described patients with disorders that selectively affected abstract and concrete words (Warrington 1975, 1981), common and proper names (McKenna and Warrington 1978) and within the concrete entities, living and non-living things (McCarthy and Warrington 1990; Warrington and McCarthy 1983, 1987; Warrington and Shallice 1984).

Concerning the first issue, namely the double dissociation between concrete and abstract words, an advantage for concrete words as compared to abstract words was demonstrated in several psycholinguistic studies (see Paivio 1991 for a review). Neurologically unimpaired subjects fare better on concrete than on abstract words in free recall, cued recall, paired-associate learning and recognition memory; they are also faster at making lexical decisions to visually presented concrete than abstract words (James, 1975). This advantage is known as the concreteness effect. Aphasics frequently show an increased concreteness effect, since their performance is much better on concrete than abstract words in spontaneous speech (Howes and Geschwind 1964), reading (e.g., Coltheart, Patterson, and Marshall 1980), writing (e.g., Bub and Kertesz 1982), repetition (e.g., Martin and Saffran 1992), naming (e.g., Franklin, Howard, and Patterson 1995) and comprehension (e.g., Franklin, Howard, and Patterson 1994). Various hypotheses have been suggested to explain the concreteness effect, one possibility being that abstract words are represented entirely verbally, in the left hemisphere, whereas the representation of concrete words involves both verbal components in the left hemisphere and visuo-perceptual components in the right hemisphere (the so-called "dual-coding" theory; Paivio 1986). Alternatively, the concreteness effect has been attributed to a larger contextual support for concrete words ("context-availability" theory; Schwanenflugel and Shoben 1983). According to this account, concrete nouns are recognized faster because they activate richer associative information than abstract terms. Finally, an additional suggestion is that the concreteness effect stems from "ease-of-predication" (Jones 1985), as concrete words are supported by a larger number of semantic features than abstract words (see also Plaut and Shallice, 1991, 1993).

However, a reversal of the concreteness effect has been documented in a number of brain-damaged subjects (Bachoud-Lévy and Dupoux 2003; Breedin, Saffran, and Coslett 1994; Cipolotti and Warrington 1995; Macoir 2008; Marshall et al. 1996; Papagno, Capasso, and Miceli 2009a; Sirigu, Duhamel, and Poncet 1991; Warrington 1975, 1981; Warrington and Shallice 1984; Yi, Moore, and Grossman 2007), who demonstrate better performance on abstract as compared to concrete words. A reversed concreteness effect is incompatible with the three theories mentioned above, as these can accommodate the concreteness effect, but not its reversal. To explain the reversed concreteness effect, it has been proposed that abstract and concrete concepts are distinguished because they are acquired in a different way, and because of the relative weight of sensory-perceptual features in their representation (Breedin, Saffran, and Coslett 1994). Sensory experience would be crucial for the acquisition of concrete concepts, whereas abstract ones are acquired in the context of language, through exposure to multiple sentence contexts but without direct perceptual input. Since concrete words rely on visual/perceptual features more than abstract ones, loss of perceptual features would disproportionately impair concrete entities, producing a reversed concreteness effect. Crutch and Warrington (2005) have provided a different account: the primary organization of concrete concepts is categorical, whereas abstract concepts are predominantly represented by association to other items. In this framework, a reversed concreteness effect might result from selective damage to categorical information (which would selectively affect conceptual representations of concrete words).

A second repeatedly reported dissociation that has shed light on the architecture of the semantic system is the specific impairment of semantic categories. Warrington and Shallice (1984) proposed that the living/non-living distinction could be the by-product of a dichotomy, concerning the different weighting that visuo-perceptual and functional attributes have in the identification of members of living and non-living things, respectively. Identification of a given exemplar of a living category would rely upon visual features, such as color, size, shape, etc., whereas identification of a member of a non-living category (particularly of man-made artefacts) would crucially depend upon the different function of that object. Warrington and Shallice (1984) provided evidence from four patients (and not just one single case), but this dissociation has been repeatedly confirmed in additional single case reports, with the same pathology (herpes simplex encephalitis), or a form of dementia, called semantic dementia, in which there is a progressive impairment of the semantic system (Hodges et al. 1992).

Warrington and Shallice's (1984) 'differential weighting' account of the living/non-living distinction has been challenged by alternative models of category-specific disorders. On one hand, Caramazza and Shelton (1998) have argued that the dissociation between living and non-living entities does not depend on the sensory/functional dimension, but rather reflects the discrete organization in the brain of different 'domains of knowledge'. They suggest that evolutionary pressure may have resulted in the elaboration of dedicated neural mechanisms for the domains of 'animals' (potential predators), of 'plant life' (possible source of food and medicine or poison) and of man- made artefacts. Finally, some authors argued against this organization into modality-specific subsystems in favor of a unitary, amodal system of conceptual organization, one proposal being the Organized-Unitary-Content Hypothesis (OUCH; Caramazza et al., 1990). Extending this model, Gonnerman et al. (1997), Garrard et al. (1998, 2001), and Moss et al. (1998) have proposed that the dissociation between living and non-living things is more related to the different level of interconnections existing between sensory and functional attributes in these two categories than to the differential weighting of these attributes. According to this model, the semantic representations of living things are characterized by the congruity of perceptual and functional shared properties. For instance, the perceptual properties "having eyes" and "having ears" regularly co-occur with the functional attributes "can see" and "can hear", whereas artefacts have a greater proportion of distinctive properties that are less densely interconnected. This would explain why the number of patients with the opposite dissociation, namely a selective impairment of non-living things with sparing of living categories (Behrmann and Lieberthal 1989; Sacchett and Humphreys 1992; Warrington and McCarthy 1983, 1987) is limited.

Cognitive neuropsychologists were interested in functional processes involved in these dissociations, and not in the anatomical localizations of lesions. However, it was soon evident that these selective impairments were related to lesions in specific and different regions of the brain, giving therefore a new input to the study of the neural correlates of language and, in particular, of the mental lexicon.

4 Neuroimaging methods

As previously introduced, in the nineteenth and twentieth centuries, our understanding on how the human brain analyses and produces language was shaped by aphasiology. This approach helped to define a model of language architecture, in which Broca's and Wernicke's area were assigned the leading roles in language production and comprehension, respectively (Damasio and Geschwind 1980).

In the 1980s, the introduction of non-invasive functional brain imaging techniques, such as positron emission tomography (PET) and fMRI, causes a renewed interest for the study of the neural basis of language (Perani et al. 1999). The logic underlying this approach is complementary to that of the anatomo-clinical correlation method. In this case, the relevant correlation is between the localization of the variation (usually the increase) in the regional cerebral blood flow (rCBF) and the task performed by the subject, rather than between a defective performance and the site of the lesion. Practically, what is measured is the clearance of the tracer from different cerebral areas, which depends strictly on rCBF.

With both functional methods, the conclusion that a given task is associated with the activation of one or more cerebral areas is based on the comparison between the experimental condition and an appropriate control condition, which differs from the former only in the process or task under investigation. For example, the cerebral areas activated during listening to words may be revealed by subtracting from the rCBF activation values of this condition the activation pattern of the control condition in which subjects do not perform any task, but just look at a fixation point. Since the two conditions differ only in the auditory-verbal stimulation, their difference provides the activation pattern that is specific to word listening. However, one important limitation of these techniques is that they only suggest that a specific area is active when a given task is performed, but do not imply that this area is essential for the execution of the task (Menon and Kim 1999).

PET and fMRI have allowed the investigation of specific components of the mental lexicon (for example phonological vs. semantic) and its neural organization by means of specific experimental neurolinguistic paradigms. Phonological processing has been investigated in a number of fMRI studies using different tasks, which required the subjects to repeat syllables (Bookheimer et al. 2000; Wildgruber, Ackermann, and Grodd 2001); to read, listen, or attend to syllables or letters (Joanisse and Gati 2003; Paulesu et al. 2000; Poeppel et al. 2004); to read a pseudoword (constructed upon the orthographic rules of a given language but without meaning) or count the number of syllables it encompassed (Kotz et al. 2002; Meyer et al. 2002); to count the number of syllables in a word (Heim and Friederici 2003) or to discriminate whether a word ended with the same sound (Heim and Friederici 2003; Zatorre et al. 1996). A meta-analysis performed on these studies (Vigneau et al. 2006) revealed two main foci of activity: one mainly localized in the posterior part of the frontal lobe along the precentral gyrus and the second one in the temporal lobe along the superior temporal gyrus and the supramarginal gyrus. The authors proposed that these areas are organized into two neural components dedicated to speech sound perception and production: a frontotemporal auditory-motor network and a frontoparietal loop for phonological working memory (Vigneau et al. 2006) (see Figure 2).

With regard to semantic processing, the meta-analysis (Vigneau et al. 2006) included fMRI studies using different semantic tasks such as semantic retrieval

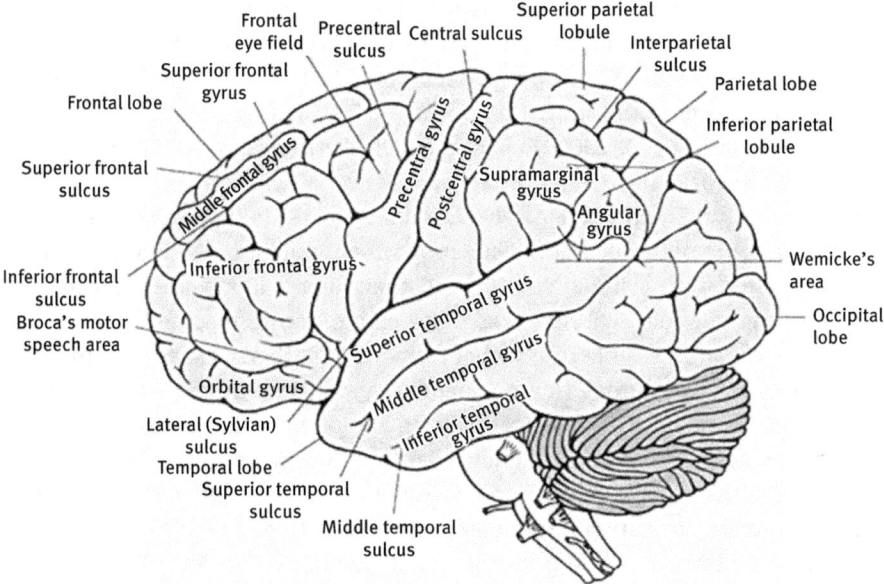

Figure 2: Representation of human cortical lobes and gyri on brain surface.

(James and Gauthier 2004; Heun et al. 2000); semantic selection (where semantic association activations with high or low competitors are compared) (Noppeney and Price 2004; Wise et al. 2001); or semantic priming tasks (Kotz et al. 2002; Wagner et al. 2000). Results showed that activations corresponding to semantic contrasts were mainly segregated into frontal and temporal regions distinct from the phonological network. The frontal operculum appeared to host semantic areas, while sub-parts of the pars triangularis of the inferior frontal gyrus (IFG) were differentially recruited: the dorsal part by the working memory component of phonology and the ventral part by semantic processing. These observations suggested a functional parcellation of the IFG for phonological and semantic processing (Vigneau et al. 2006). Another focus of activation was located in the orbital part of the IFG, a region that Demb et al. (1995) have proposed to be involved in online retrieval of semantic information. Indeed, this area is activated also during categorization tasks (Adams and Janata 2002; Binder et al. 2003; Braver and Bongiolatti 2002; Bright, Moss, and Tyler 2004; Jennings et al. 1998; Noesselt, Shah, and Jancke 2003; Noppeney and Price 2004; Perani et al. 1999; Poldrack et al. 1999), association (Booth et al. 2002; Damasio et al. 2001), and word generation tasks (Gurd et al. 2002; Martin et al. 1995) . The analysis of the semantic contrasts that elicit activation peaks in the temporal lobe revealed a clear functional organization, including a modality-specific verbal area in the superior temporal gyrus, a modality-independent verbal area in the middle temporal gyrus, and amodal conceptual areas in the angular and fusiform gyri. The superior temporal gyrus cluster was activated by semantic contrasts based on written words, such as reading words versus pseudowords (Fiebach et al. 2002; Fiez et al. 1999; Howard et al. 1992; Moore and Price 1999; Small et al., 1996), and categorization of written words (Chee et al. 2000; Heim, Opitz, and Friederici 2002; Jennings et al. 1998; Perani et al. 1999), leading to the hypothesis that the superior temporal area processes the graphemes converted into syllable sounds and maintained in working memory by means of the phonological networks that operate during reading; this processing makes them accessible in a verbal format for further syntactic (in the temporal lobe) or conceptual (in the angular gyrus and in the fusiform area) processing (Vigneau et al. 2006). Finally, the angular gyrus activation was considered involved in conceptual knowledge retrieval. This region, a high-order heteromodal association cortex, can be seen as a gateway, which coordinates reciprocal interactions between the sensory representation of words or objects and their meaning (Mesulam 2000; Vigneau et al. 2006). The fusiform area was supposed to be implicated in semantic processing of words and pictures (Binder et al. 1996, 1999; Bright, Moss, and Tyler 2004; Davis, Meunier, and Marslen-Wilson 2004; Vandenberghe et al. 1996). Vigneau et al. (2006) suggested that the angular and the fusiform gyri – the two amodal conceptual temporal areas devoted to meaning– and the temporal pole together with the inferior orbital frontal cluster constitute a temporo-frontal semantic network. This semantic network can be considered to construct an overall meaning on the basis of the association of integrated knowledge issued from the main domain of external (audition, vision) and internal (long-term memory, emotion) messages (Vigneau et al. 2006).

We have reported that the available evidence so far on single case studies suggests that different neural circuits are responsible for processing nouns and verbs, concrete and abstract concepts and different semantic categories.

In the case of verb-noun dissociation, neuroimaging studies in normal subjects, however, have provided only limited support to the lesion-based hypothesis. The discrepancies among studies were attributed to a number of factors, among which the fact that earlier studies investigating differences in noun and verb processing used nouns referring to objects and verbs referring to actions, therefore introducing a confound between the grammatical and the semantic class. In the imaging literature, this is the case not only in earlier studies using verb generation (Petersen et al. 1988, 1989; Martin et al. 1995; Warburton et al. 1996) but also in more recent ones using picture naming (Tranel et al. 2005).

Studies that attempted to lessen the semantic confound factor by using both concrete and abstract nouns and verbs provided mixed results. In an

Italian lexical decision study by Perani et al. (1999) using concrete and abstract nouns and verbs, verb-specific activations were reported in the left IFG but no noun-specific activations were observed. This finding was replicated in English in a semantic decision study using inflected nouns and verbs (Tyler et al. 2004) but not in a lexical decision study using uninflected words (Tyler et al. 2001). It was argued that greater left IFG activation for verbs than nouns in previous studies was not due to grammatical class differences but likely to morphosyntactic processes that may be more demanding for verbs than nouns (see Binder et al. 2004; Thompson-Schill et al. 1997; Vigliocco et al. 2006). It was also noted that most languages have more morphologically inflected verb than noun forms, so task performance on verbs may place greater demands on selection and decision processes attributed to the left IFG (Binder et al. 2004; Gold and Buckner 2002; Thompson-Schill et al. 1997). Accordingly, verb-specific activation may result from an interaction between grammatical class and task demands. Indeed, support to this hypothesis comes from a study by Longe et al. (2007), in which greater activations of the left IFG for verbs than nouns were observed when English speakers made semantic judgments on inflected words but not when they made judgments on the same uninflected words.

In an attempt to control for the semantic correlates of noun-verb differences, Shapiro, Moo, and Caramazza (2006) considered only areas of significant fMRI activations emerging both when speakers were producing phrases in response to real words (including abstract nouns and verbs) and when they were producing phrases in response to pseudowords. Moreover, in order to control for morphophonological correlates of grammatical class differences, only areas of significant activation when speakers were producing both regularly and irregularly inflected nouns and verbs were considered. Across three experiments, participants were presented with words (either a noun or a verb) or pseudowords (to be used in either a noun or verb context) and their task was to produce short phrases such as *many doors* or *he sweeps*. Significant greater activations for nouns across experiments were observed within the left fusiform gyrus, while significant greater activations for verbs were found in the left prefrontal cortex and left superior parietal cortex, suggesting that nouns and verbs were independently processed by different brain regions. In a PET study by Vigliocco et al. (2006) in Italian, only words referring to events, either nouns or inflected verbs, and referring to either sensation or motion were used. Participants were presented auditorily with blocks of sensory or motor nouns or verbs and asked to simply listen to the words. Whereas significant activation differences between sensory and motion words were found, no specific activations for nouns or verbs were observed.

More recently, Siri et al. (2008) performed an fMRI study presenting Italian speakers with pictures of events and asked participants to name them as (1) infinitive verb (e.g., *mangiare* 'to eat'); (2) inflected verb (e.g., *mangia* 'she/he eats'); and (3) action noun (e.g., *mangiata* 'the eating'). The authors did not find any verb-specific activation. However, reliable left IFG activations were found when contrasting the action noun with the infinitive verb condition. A second-level analysis indicated then that activation in the left IFG was the greatest for action nouns, intermediate for inflected verbs, and the least for infinitive verbs. The authors concluded that when all other factors are controlled (i.e., semantics, grammatical class), nouns and verbs are processed by a common neural system. Differences in the left IFG activation emerge only as a consequence of increased linguistic and/or general processing demands (Siri et al. 2008).

A similar result was obtained in a recent meta-analysis (Crepaldi et al. 2013) on the neuroimaging evidence concerning noun and verb processing: the results did not support the notion that verb processing is predominantly based in the left frontal cortex and noun processing on temporal regions, or that verb lexical-semantic representations rely on embodied information. Instead, this meta-analysis showed that the cerebral circuits for noun and verb processing are spatially close, relying on a wide network including frontal, parietal, and temporal regions (see also Piras and Marangolo 2007 for similar conclusions).

In conclusion, from the literature discussed above it seems likely that words belonging to different grammatical classes (nouns and verbs) are not actually represented in segregated neural networks. Rather, neural segregation emerges as the result of other differences between nouns and verbs. First, in previous patient and imaging studies, differences between nouns and verbs may have come about as a semantic difference between objects and actions. Indeed, in previous studies that did not suffer from this confound, and in which morphological processes were not highly engaged, no verb-specific activations in left IFG were found (Vigliocco et al. 2006). Moreover, as one controls for semantic differences (asking participants to name only events and more specifically the same events as either noun or verb) and manipulates the extent of morphological processing across the grammatical class of verbs and nouns, left IFG activations appear to be modulated by the complexity of the morphological processes rather than being associate to verb-specific processing (Siri et al. 2008). Thus, all of these results do call into question the view that grammatical class *per se* drives neural segregation, suggesting that both categories might rely on a common anatomical substrate, providing evidence for a more interactive system between the two classes of words.

Evidence from neuroimaging studies concerning the abstract-concrete dissociation is also controversial. The single case approach suggests that this dissociation appears in people with a pathology involving the anterior part of the left temporal lobe (such as in herpes simplex encephalitis or semantic dementia). Neuroimaging studies are sometimes difficult to evaluate, due to the extreme variability of the experimental paradigms, ranging from explicit semantic judgments to (auditory and/or visual) lexical decision tasks. In some cases, activations for concrete nouns were observed in left temporal regions usually affected as first areas by semantic dementia (Binder et al. 2005; Noppeney and Price 2004; Sabsevitz et al. 2005), but in other cases they occurred in regions not affected in earlier stages of semantic dementia, such as the left posterolateral temporal and prefrontal regions (Grossman et al. 2002b; Mellet et al. 1998) and the left superior temporal and inferior frontal regions (Sabsevitz et al. 2005). Interestingly, some investigations demonstrate significantly greater hemodynamic response to abstract than to concrete words in the right temporal pole (e.g., Kiehl et al. 1999; Perani et al. 1999), while no reports of greater activation for concrete than abstract words in the same region are described. In another study, activation to abstract terms was greater in the right than in the left temporal lobe (Whatmough et al. 2004). Finally, at least one study shows greater activation for concrete than abstract words in left temporal regions (Mellet et al. 1998).

As reported in the single case approach, one of the most studied topics in the neuroimaging literature is the dissociation between semantic categories. The single case approach suggested a correlation between the locus of lesion and the patterns of categorical impairment, which Gainotti (2000) summarized as it follows: (a) a bilateral injury to the antero-mesial and inferior parts of the temporal lobes in patients with a category-specific semantic impairment for living things; (b) a lesion of the infero-mesial parts of the temporo-occipital areas of the left hemisphere in patients showing a specific lexical impairment for members of the 'plants' category; (c) an extensive lesion of the areas lying on the dorso-lateral convexity of the left hemisphere in patients with a category specific semantic impairment for man-made artefacts. Taken together, these results seem to show that the category-specific disorder is crucially related to the kind of semantic information processed by the damaged areas, supporting the Warrington and Shallice's (1984) and Warrington and McCarthy's model (1987). Similarly, PET and fMRI studies have investigated whether there is evidence that different areas of the brain are differentially involved in processing/storing information corresponding to different categories of stimuli.

Chao, Haxby, and Martin (1999) observed that the medial aspect of the fusiform gyri differentially responded to pictures and/or words referring to tools (e.g., *hammer, saw*), whereas the lateral aspect of the fusiform gyri differentially responded to pictures of animals (e.g., *dog, horse*). Comparable segregation of activation has been observed in the lateral temporal cortex: items corresponding to animate categories (i.e., animals) differentially activated the superior temporal sulcus, whereas activation associated with inanimate categories (e.g., tools) activated more inferior regions on the left middle temporal gyrus. Furthermore, it has been observed that the superior temporal sulcus responds differentially to moving of animate entity (e.g., dog), whereas the left middle temporal gyrus differentially responds to moving of inanimate object. (e.g., a dot). This study seems to suggest that there is a neural differentiation by semantic category, at least between animate vs. inanimate categories.

In contrast, Devlin et al. (2002) in three different experiments failed to find functional segregation between animate vs. inanimate categories, suggesting that conceptual knowledge is represented in a unitary, distributed system undifferentiated by categories of knowledge.

5 Event-Related Potentials (ERPs)

The results of the neuroimaging studies described so far have revealed important correlation evidence for the involvement of several brain regions in word processing. However, neuroimaging methods do not provide the best temporal resolution available for studying cognitive functions. Indeed, fMRI does not directly measure neural activity, but instead relies on indirect changes in blood flow and volume triggered by modulation in neural activity (Kaan 2007). fMRI signals are much slower than neuronal activity, as the time course of hemodynamic signals is in the order of five seconds. As neurons work ten times faster (we can recognize an image in about 200 ms), the dynamics of fMRI signals are too slow to understand how the brain computes in real time (Kaan 2007). Since language processing occurs at an extremely fast rate to allow fully understanding of the stages involved and their timing, we need to apply a method with very good temporal resolution. Recording event-related brain potentials (ERPs) is such a technique. Electrical brain activity can be recorded by placing electrodes on a person's scalp. ERPs are obtained by presenting the participant with a given stimulus and recording the electrical potentials (brain waves) from the start of the stimulus or other events of interest. These potentials are then averaged over a large number of trials of the same type. Averaging will enhance the brain potentials that are related to the onset of the event and will reduce brain potentials that are not tied to the onset of the event and are assumed to be random (Kaan 2007). Several waveforms, such as the N1, P2, and N400, have been distinguished on the basis of their polarity, timing (latency) of the onset or the peak, their duration, and/ or distribution across the scalp, that is, at which position on the scalp a waveform is smallest or largest. Usually, the experiments include two or more conditions and investigate how ERP waveforms change as a function of the experimental manipulation.

ERPs provide several advantages for the study of language processing. First, ERPs allow researchers to collect a continuous stream of data with a temporal accuracy of a few milliseconds: the sampling rate is typically between 250 and 512 Hz (samples per second) in language-related experiments. This matches the fast rate of language comprehension, and, hence, represents an attractive feature for researchers wanting to track continuous online processing. A second, strong advantage of ERPs is that recording of ERPs is one of the few techniques that allow researchers to investigate online processing of spoken words and sentences (Kaan 2007).

In a seminal paper on ERPs and language, Kutas and Hillyard (1980) reported a negative component for words that are semantically anomalous given the preceding context (*he spread the warm bread with socks*), which they labelled the "N400" component. Since then, hundreds of experiments have replicated this result and investigated the cognitive and neural mechanisms underlying this component. The N400 is a negative component, peaking between 300 and 500 ms after onset of the critical stimulus (word or picture). The term "N400" is often used to refer to the component itself (all content words elicit an N400); the term "N400 effect" is used to refer to the difference in N400 amplitude in two conditions (e.g., semantically anomalous words vs. plausible words; or words preceded by an unrelated vs. a related word). Several neural sources have been proposed for the N400, among which are locations in the anterior temporal lobe (Nobre and McCarthy 1995; for more details see Van Petten and Luka 2006). The prevailing view of the N400 is that it reflects difficulty in semantically integrating the stimulus into the preceding context. This context can be a single word, sentence, discourse (Van Berkum, Hagoort, and Brown 1999), or a non-linguistic one, such as a picture sequence (West and Holcomb 2002). One argument in favor of the view that the N400 reflects semantic integration is that the N400 amplitude to content words (nouns, verbs and adjectives) decreases with each increasing linear word position in the sentence, that is, with a more strongly established semantic context (Van Petten 1993; Van Petten and Kutas 1990). Second, the N400 amplitude is affected by the expectancy of the word given the preceding context: if a word is highly expected given a preceding context, as in *the bill was due at the end of the month*, the N400 amplitude is smaller than when a word is unexpected, but still plausible, as in *the bill was due at the end of the hour* (Kutas and Hillyard 1984). The N400 has also been found to be sensitive to lexical properties, although this is somewhat controversial. Indeed, highly frequent content words elicit a smaller N400 than lower frequency words suggesting that the N400 might reflect the signature of lexical retrieval/access as well as word meaning integration in the learning of novel words (Van Petten 1993; Van Petten and Kutas 1990, 1991).

Studying overt language production with ERPs is difficult because mouth movements cause severe artifacts in the ERP signal. For this reason, researchers have used an indirect way to study production, namely by associating a particular (semantic, syntactic, phonological) aspect of the to-be-produced word to a particular manual response. Using the left and right scalp electrodes above the motor strip, one can record the activity related to hand movement preparation. The potential will be more negative at the electrode in the contralateral hemisphere to the response hand than in the hemisphere, ipsilaterally to the response hand. These recordings are time-locked to the onset of either the stimulus or the actual response. The potentials at the ipsilateral electrode are then subtracted from the potentials at the contralateral electrode and averaged over left and right response hand trials to cancel out activity not related to response hand selection. The resulting ERP is called "lateralized readiness potential", or LRP, which indexes response hand preparation. Word production paradigms using the LRP typically employ a two-choice go/no-go task. In such a task, the participant sees a series of pictures and is asked to respond with the right hand if, for example, a living object is depicted and with the left if an inanimate object is presented, but to respond only if, for example, the name of the object starts with an /s/ (go), and to withhold the response if the name starts with a /b/ (no-go) (Kaan 2007). Using such paradigms, investigators have tested in which order distinct sorts of information are accessed during word production (Levelt 1999) and the relative timing of these production stages. For instance, using a paradigm as the above and varying the type of information, the go/no-go decision based on semantic information was shown to precede the phonological information by 120 ms in production (Van Turennout, Hagoort, and Brown 1997), and the gender information to precede the phonological information by 40 ms (Van Turennout, Hagoort, and Brown 1998).

Although the use of ERPs is attractive to researchers investigating language processing, this technique also has limitations. First, many trials are needed to obtain ERPs with a good stimulus-to noise ratio. The number of trials depends on many factors, including the size of the effect and the number of participants. Typically, an experiment investigating word processing with 20 participants would require at least 40 stimulus tokens per condition, especially when the effect one is looking for is rather small. Presenting 40 or more items per condition (i.e., ambiguous vs. unambiguous word) in an experiment may lead to fatigue and processing strategies that are not intended by the investigator. A large number of items per condition is also required, because many trials will be lost due to artifacts. ERPs are sensitive to muscle tension and eye movements, which may confound the actual brain response. When dealing with healthy adult participants, trials with such artifacts are often rejected from the analysis. Participants are instructed to remain still and not to blink during designated times to minimize the number of artifacts. Such instructions, however, may affect the participant's attention to the stimuli. More importantly, although ERPs have a good temporal resolution, the pattern of activation recorded at the scalp is not very informative as to where in the brain the activity occurs (Kaan 2007).

6 Neuromodulation approach

In addition to the temporal limitation described so far regarding the fMRI technique, which might in part be overcome using ERPs, it should be noted that, although fMRI has been widely used for studying the neural correlates of language, it has a limited spatial resolution of about a cubic millimeter. In such a volume one can find 100,000 neurons. In other words, the 'fMRI microphone' cannot listen to individual cells, but to a whole stadium full of them. Therefore, this technique cannot unequivocally determine whether an active area is essential for a particular function or behavior (Price and Friston 1999).

In these last years, the progress of new technologies has made additional tools available. In the field of aphasia, the application of non-invasive stimulation methods, such as transcranial magnetic stimulation (TMS) and transcranial direct current stimulation (tDCS), has contributed to better define possible correlations between a specific brain region and its language function (Miniussi et al. 2008). In particular, TMS can be used to investigate the neural activity in a specific brain region avoiding the aforementioned criticism regarding the fMRI and ERPs methods. Indeed, the TMS-induced activity in the subpopulation of neurons located under the stimulating coil interacts effectively with any pattern of activity that is occurring at the time of stimulation (Walsh and Pascual-Leone 2003). In other words, unlike neuroimaging methods, which only indicate correlations between brain and behavior, TMS can be used to demonstrate causal brain-behavior relations.

More recent studies have also suggested to apply these techniques as adjuvant tools for planning new therapeutic interventions for language rehabilitation (Marangolo and Caltagirone 2014), and direct electrical stimulation (DES) in language areas has been used during intraoperative mapping to guide brain tumor surgery (see Papagno 2017).

In Section 6.1, the most recent neuroscientific evidence on the use of these stimulation techniques in investigating the neural correlates of word processing will be presented.

6.1 Transcranial magnetic stimulation (TMS)

The major potential contribution of TMS to our understanding of the lexicon organization consists in the transient disruption of focal cortical activity to establish the causal role and the timing of the contribution of a given cortical region in behavior. This effect allows empirically testing specific neuropsychological models and constructs. TMS produces either transient or enduring focal changes in patterns of brain activity (Miniussi et al. 2008). It employs the principle of electromagnetic induction and involves the generation of a rapid time-varying magnetic field in a coil of wire. When this coil is applied to the head of a subject, the magnetic field penetrates the scalp and skull and induces a small current parallel to the plane of the coil in the brain that is sufficient to depolarize neuronal membranes and generate action potentials.

There are several possible paradigms to study language by means of TMS. The first distinction is between offline and online paradigms: interference with cognitive processing when TMS is applied during performance of a task is called online TMS (Pascual-Leone, Walsh, and Rothwell 2000). In contrast, in the case of offline stimulation, TMS is applied for several minutes before the subject performs a given task.

The online approach transiently disrupts ongoing neural processing in the stimulated cortex while subjects perform a language task. This permits to infer causal relations with respect to the contribution of the stimulated area to a specific brain function (Hartwigsen 2015). Online TMS protocols consist in the application of single pulses, paired pulses and short high-frequency bursts of repetitive TMS (rTMS). While the majority of studies targeting language areas used rTMS to interfere with a specific language function (e.g., Papagno et al. 2009b, Sliwinska, Vitello, and Devlin 2014), some language studies also applied single, double, or triple pulse protocols in a chronometric fashion (e.g., Devlin, Matthews, and Rushworth 2003; Schuhmann et al. 2009, Sliwinska et al. 2012). This consists in delivering TMS at distinct time-points during a task to perturb intrinsic neural activity in the stimulated area. As a single TMS pulse interferes with ongoing neural activity for several tens of milliseconds, this approach provides high temporal resolution to identify the time period during which the stimulated region makes a critical contribution to that task. The effects of rTMS are often referred to as "virtual lesion" (Pascual-Leone, Walsh, and Rothwell

2000; Walsh and Cowey 2000). Generally, the experimental protocols in TMS studies have employed two different stimulation conditions: a real condition which allows to explore the effect of stimulation over the targeted area (i.e., Broca's area) on language processing and a "placebo" control condition (i.e., sham condition) in which the stimulator is turned- off after few seconds. This is performed in order to ensure that the behavioral changes are specifically attributable to stimulation (Marangolo and Caltagirone 2014).

Offline TMS is given continuously as long trains at a constant rate (i.e., continuous rTMS, often applied at a frequency of 1 Hz) or intermittently as repetitive bursts (i.e., intermittent or burst-like rTMS) to induce lasting functional effects in the stimulated area and connected sites (Siebner and Rothwell 2003). These protocols can modulate brain activation for a longer time period of about 30–45 min after the end of stimulation thus allowing for the induction of rapid functional reorganization in the stimulated area and in connected brain regions (Rossi and Rossini 2004). These "remote" effects may occur over large distances at interconnected sites. Usually, the applied rTMS protocol is "inhibitory" on motor cortical excitability, but the effects on cognitive functions may depend on the context.

A number of studies reported behavioral facilitation when single pulse TMS or high-frequency rTMS was given immediately before picture naming over left-hemispheric language areas (offline TMS) (e.g., Mottaghy et al. 1999; Mottaghy, Sparing, and Töpper 2006; Sparing et al. 2001; Töpper et al. 1998; Wassermann et al. 1999). For instance, in Töpper et al. (1998)'s study, TMS of the left motor cortex had no effect, while stimulation of Wernicke's area significantly decreased picture naming latencies. These data suggest that focal TMS facilitates lexical processes, likely inducing a general pre-activation of linguistic neural networks.

rTMS has been also used to investigate different classes of words (nouns and verbs). Response times following real stimulation over the left prefrontal cortex increased for verbs and pseudoverbs but were unaffected in the case of nouns and pseudonouns (Shapiro et al. 2001). Also, the issue concerning abstract/concrete nouns has been investigated using rTMS with a lexical decision paradigm (Papagno et al. 2009b). Interference with accuracy was found for abstract words when rTMS was applied over the left superior temporal gyrus, while for concrete words accuracy decreased when rTMS was applied over the right contralateral homologous site. Moreover, accuracy for abstract words, but not for concrete words, decreased after left IFG stimulation. These results suggest that abstract lexical entries are stored in the posterior part of the left temporal and possibly in the left frontal sites, while the regions involved in storing concrete items include the right temporal cortex. In contrast, other studies reported decreased behavioral accuracy when online rTMS bursts were applied during picture naming over frontal or temporal language areas (Flitman et al. 1998, Wassermann et al. 1999). These studies suggest that the type of task and the stimulation protocol strongly affect the results.

In sum, online and offline TMS represent complementary approaches that enable the researcher to investigate the functional relevance of the targeted brain area within a language network. The changes in neural activity evoked by TMS are generally measured as changes in reaction times and/or error rates. Effects of TMS on electrophysiological parameters or neural activation, on the other hand, can be assessed with ERPs or neuroimaging read-outs. However, risk of rTMS use should be assessed carefully and its dosage should generally be limited according to published safety guidelines (Wassermann 1998).

6.2 Transcranial Direct Current Stimulation (tDCS)

In more recent years, a new stimulation technique, namely transcranial direct current stimulation (tDCS), has been applied to the study of language. However, in comparison with TMS, whose focal activity allows inferring causal brain-behavior relation, tDCS, due to its large stimulation electrodes, is considerably less focal. Hence, tDCS is less suitable to investigate functional-anatomic subdivisions within the language system but it is mainly used for therapeutic purposes (e.g., in post-stroke rehabilitation, see Marangolo and Caltagirone 2014; Monti et al. 2013). Indeed, an important advantage of tDCS is the apparent absence of any significant unpleasant effects when using standard protocols. Specifically, tDCS has not been reported to provoke seizures, which is a frequent undesirable effect in brain-damaged subjects, since the delivered electrical current is well below the threshold of eliciting action potentials (Nitsche and Paulus 2011). Therefore, compared with the research on TMS discussed earlier, to date tDCS studies have not been performed for investigating possible correlations between a language task and its underlying neural representation but to understand whether this technique is a viable option for the recovery of language after stroke (Miniussi et al. 2008).

tDCS involves the application of small electrical currents (typically 1–2 mA) to the scalp through a pair of surface electrodes (5 x 7 cm large) over a long period, usually minutes (5–30 minutes), to achieve changes in cortical excitability by influencing spontaneous neural activity. Unlike TMS, which induces currents of sufficient magnitude to produce action potentials, the weak electrical currents employed in tDCS are thought to modulate the resting membrane potentials of neurons (Monte-Silva et al. 2013; Nitsche and Paulus

2011). The effect of tDCS depends on which electrode is applied to the scalp. Generally, the anode increases cortical excitability when applied over the region of interest, whereas the cathode decreases it limiting the resting membrane potential. These effects may last for minutes to hours depending on the intensity, polarity and duration of stimulation (Nitsche and Paulus, 2011). As TMS studies, tDCS experimental protocols make use of a crossover design, whereby each participant receives two different stimulation conditions: a real condition which allows researchers to explore the effect of stimulation over the targeted area (i.e., Broca's area) on the investigated function and a "placebo" control condition (i.e., sham condition) in which the stimulator is turned-off after a few seconds. This design has been implemented to ensure that the subject's behavioral changes are specifically attributable to the stimulation condition.

Like rTMS, most of the tDCS studies started with its application in the healthy population in order to investigate whether stimulation over the left language areas (i.e., Broca's or Wernicke's area) might facilitate language learning (Flöel et al. 2008), verbal fluency (Cattaneo, Pisoni, and Papagno 2011) and/or picture naming (Sparing et al. 2008). The results showed that it is possible to produce interaction between task execution and stimulation, thereby reducing or improving subject performance depending on the type of stimulation applied (anodal vs. cathodal). For instance, in a study by Flöel et al. (2008), tDCS was applied over the left Wernicke's area of 19 healthy individuals while they acquired 30 novel object names (nonwords). Each subject underwent one session of anodic tDCS, one session of cathodic tDCS, and one session of sham stimulation. The second electrode (reference electrode) was positioned over the contralateral supraorbital region. During stimulation, subjects were presented with a pair of stimuli (an auditory nonword matched with an object picture) they had to remember. In a subsequent phase, they had to judge whether the picture of the object and the novel word were the same as in the previously presented pair. Outcome measures were learning speed and learning success in acquiring the novel words. Results showed significant effects for both measures only during anodic stimulation of the left Wernicke's area. Similar results were obtained by Sparing et al. (2008) in a group of 15 healthy subjects who performed a picture naming task before and after stimulation of Wernicke's area. In their study, all subjects underwent four sessions of different stimulations: anodic, cathodic, and sham stimulation over the left Wernicke's area and anodic stimulation over the homologous right Wernicke's area. In all conditions the reference electrode was fixed contralaterally over the orbit. The authors found that the subjects responded significantly faster only following anodic tDCS over the left Wernicke's area. In a multimodal approach, Holland et al. (2011) investigated the effects of anodal tDCS over the left IFG (i.e., Broca's area) on behavioral performance and neural activity. Relative to sham tDCS, 2 mA of anodal tDCS significantly facilitated picture naming latencies. Behavioral improvements were accompanied by decreased task-related activity in the stimulated area during concurrent fMRI. Correlational analysis showed that faster naming responses were associated with decreased neural activity in the IFG. The decreased neural activation in this area was suggested to parallel effects of neural priming reported in previous behavioral studies. Accordingly, it was suggested that anodal tDCS during picture naming can facilitate behavioral responses via a regionally specific neural adaptation mechanism in the left IFG.

Given the facilitatory effects on language learning in the healthy population, as previously stated, most of current research in this area is devoted to assess whether tDCS might be used as an adjuvant strategy to language therapy in order to speed up language recovery in post-stroke aphasia. Indeed, a growing body of evidence has indicated that tDCS enhances language functions (Marangolo and Caltagirone 2014) and its use might be extended even in domains other than the treatment of word-finding difficulties (Baker, Rorden, and Fridrikson et al. 2010; Fiori et al. 2011; 2013), such as the recovery of articulatory deficits (Marangolo et al. 2011; 2013a) and speech production (Marangolo et al. 2013b; 2014).

To summarize, several possible mechanisms can account for the effects of TMS and tDCS on language performance. Both methods have given novel insights into the mechanisms of adaptive short/long term reorganization and plasticity in the undamaged and damaged language system.

6.3 Direct electrical stimulation (DES)

During brain surgery for tumor resection it is a common clinical practice to awaken patients in order to assess the functional role of restricted brain regions, so that the surgeon can maximize the extent of the exeresis without provoking cognitive impairment, particularly of language. This technique allows for localization of extremely small (1 cm^2) brain areas (Ojemann et al. 1989). Patients may be asked to perform a picture naming task while the surgeon inactivates restricted regions around the tumor by means of electrical stimulation. If the patient is unable to produce a response or produces an incorrect one, the surgeon refrains from removing the stimulated region. By cumulating performance over the areas stimulated and across subjects, a map can be constructed of the functional role of different brain regions (Papagno 2017). This neurophysiological procedure has allowed assessing the contribution of both cortical and subcortical structures, for example, in naming animate and inanimate objects (Papagno et al. 2011), nouns and verbs (Lubrano et al. 2014) and abstract and concrete words (Orena et al. 2019).

7 Conclusions and future directions

Over the past two decades, functional neuroimaging has dramatically increased our understanding of human brain functions and in particular of language. In earlier times, language could be studied only indirectly via neuropsychological tests administered to brain-damaged patients. Today, functional neuroimaging allows mostly non-invasive *in vivo* visualization of cerebral activity, although several limitations must be considered.

With regard to the study of the neural correlates of the mental lexicon, the findings summarized above might lead to the conclusion that there is considerable evidence that distinct cerebral areas process different classes of words (i.e., noun vs. verb; concrete vs. abstract; living vs. non-living stimuli). However, before drawing any definite conclusion it is necessary to consider that in language, more than in other cognitive domains, several uncontrolled variables could produce a misinterpretation of results. As previously discussed, the proposal that the difference between nouns and verbs cannot be reduced to a single factor but is actually based on a continuum of differences at the semantic, syntactic and phonological level has important implications. If we just think of the role of morphological factors, the presence of verb-specific suffixes in languages such as Italian might have played a role in the different experiments in which a verb-specific region was identified in Broca's area. Indeed, this area is also active during the detection of syntactic anomalies, suggesting that in some reported studies, the activation was related to grammatical specificity of the verb and not to the verb category *per se*. This fact underlines the need for a careful evaluation of all the variables before establishing a causal relationship between a language task and the activation of a specific brain region.

Moreover, when inferring brain functions using neuroimaging methods, it is important to recognize their limitations. The main limitation of fMRI is that it detects neural activity indirectly, through the associated hemodynamic variations. On the contrary, ERPs recordings can directly detect neural activity with optimal temporal resolution. Therefore, to date, there is a growing interest in combining the different techniques (i.e., simultaneous ERPs-fMRI recordings) for a better understanding of the brain dynamics involved in language processing.

Recently, there have been successful efforts to combine TMS with simultaneous ERP recording, in order to study the temporal and functional impact of TMS interference on cognitive processes (Fuggetta et al. 2009; Taylor, Nobre, and Rushworth 2007). The value of this combination lies in the fact that the fine temporal resolution of EEG allows one to make an on-line measure of the effects of TMS at different stages of processing (e.g., sensory and post-perceptual), within brain regions, which are anatomically remote from the area impaired by the TMS (Fuggetta et al. 2009). This technique has been used to gain insight into the neural basis of semantic systems and in particular to study the temporal and functional organization of object categorization processing.

The picture emerging from all these experiments that we have described suggests that word production is achieved by a network of regions which vary in their computational specificity. The challenge is connecting the brain science of language to formal models of linguistic representation. As underlined by Poeppel et al. (2012: 14130), "in the new neurobiology of language, the field is moving from coarse characterizations of language and largely correlational insights to fine-grained cognitive analyses".

References

Adams, Reginald B. & Petr Janata. 2002. A comparison of neural circuits underlying auditory and visual object categorization. *NeuroImage* 16. 361–377.
Anderson, Jeffrey, Robin Gilmore, Steven Roper, Bruce Crosson, Russell M. Bauer, Stephen Nadeau, David Q. Beversdorf, Jean Cibula, Miles Rogish, S. Kortencamp, John D. Hughes, Leslie J. Gonzalez-Rothi & Kenneth M. Heilman. 1999. Conduction Aphasia and the Arcuate Fasciculus: A Reexamination of the Wernicke-Geschwind Model. *Brain and Language* 70. 1–12.
Bachoud-Lévy, Anne. C. & Emmanuel Dupoux. 2003. An influence of syntactic and semantic variables on word form retrieval. *Cognitive Neuropsychology* 20, 163–188.
Badecker, William, Argye E. Hillis & Alfonso Caramazza. 1990. Lexical morphology and its role in the writing process: Evidence from a case of acquired dysgraphia. *Cognition* 35. 205–243.
Baker, Julie M., Chris Rorden & Julius Fridriksson. 2010. Using transcranial direct-current stimulation to treat stroke patients with aphasia. *Stroke* 41. 1229–1236.
Basso, Anna. 2005. *Aphasia Therapy*. Oxford University Press, England.
Basso, Anna, Margaret Forbes & François Boller. 2013. Rehabilitation of aphasia. *Handbook of Clinical Neurology* 110. 325–34.
Baxter, Doreen M. & Elizabeth K. Warrington. 1985. Category specific phonological dysgraphia. *Neuropsychologia* 23. 653–666.
Behrmann, Marlene & Terry Lieberthal. 1989. Category-specific treatment of a lexical-semantic deficit: a single case study of global aphasia. *British Journal of Disorders of Communication* 24. 281–299.

Benton, Arthur. 1988. Neuropsychology: Past, Present and Future. In François Boller & Jordan Grafman (eds.), *Handbook of Neuropsychology, Vol. 1.* 3–27. Amsterdam: Elsevier Science Publishers.

Berndt, Rita S., Charlotte Mitchum, Anne N. Haendiges & Jennifer Sandson. 1997. Verb retrieval in aphasia. Chracterizing single word impairments. *Brain and Language* 56. 68–106.

Binder, Jeffrey R., J. Albert Frost, Thomas A. Hammeke, Patrick S. Bellgowan, Stephen M. Rao & R.W. Cox. 1999. Conceptual processing during the conscious resting state: a functional MRI study.*Journal of Cognitive Neuroscience* 11. 80–93.

Binder, Jeffrey R., J. Albert Frost, Thomas A. Hammeke, Stephen M. Rao & R.W. Cox. 1996. Function of the left planum temporale in auditory and linguistic processing. *Brain* 119. 1239–1247.

Binder, Jeffrey R., Kristen A. McKiernan, Melanie E. Parsons, Chris F. Westbury, Edward T. Possing, Jacqueline N. Kaufman & Lori Buchanan. 2003. Neural correlates of lexical access during visual word recognition. *Journal of Cognitive Neuroscience* 15. 372–393.

Binder, Jeffrey R., Einat Liebenthal, Edward T. Possing, David A. Medler & B. Douglas Ward. 2004. Neural correlates of sensory and decision processes in auditory object identification. *Nature Neuroscience* 7. 295–301.

Binder, Jeffrey R., Chris Westbury, Kristen A. McKiernan, Edward T. Possing & David A. Medler. 2005. Distinct Brain Systems for Processing Concrete and Abstract Concepts. *Journal of Cognitive Neuroscience* 17. 905–17.

Bird, Helen, David Howard & Sue Franklin. 2000. Noun-Verb differences? A question of semantics: a response to Shapiro and Caramazza. *Brain and Language* 76. 213–22.

Bookheimer, Susan Y., Thomas A. Zeffiro, Teresa A. Blaxton, William Gaillard & William H. Theodore. 2000. Activation of language cortex with automatic speech tasks. *Neurology* 55. 1151–1157.

Booth, James R., D. D. Burman, Joel R. Meyer, Darren R. Gitelman, Todd B. Parrish & M. Marsel Mesulam. 2002. Modality independence of word comprehension. *Human Brain Mapping* 16. 251–261.

Braver, Todd S. & Susan R. Bongiolatti. 2002. The role of frontopolar cortex in subgoal processing during working memory. *NeuroImage* 15. 523–536.

Breedin, Sarah D., Eleanor M. Saffran & H. Branch Coslett. 1994. Reversal of the concreteness effect in a patient with semantic dementia. *Cognitive Neuropsychology* 11. 617–660.

Bright, Peter, Helene Moss & Lorraine K. Tyler. 2004. Unitary vs. multiple semantics: PET studies of word and picture processing. *Brain and Language* 89. 417–432.

Broca, Paul. 1861. Remarks on the locus of the faculty of articulated language, followed by an observation of aphemia (loss of speech). *Bulletin de la Société Anatomique de Paris* 6. 330–357.

Bub, Daniel & Andrew Kertesz. 1982. Evidence for lexicographic processing in a patient with preserved written over oral single word naming. *Brain* 105. 697–717.

Buckingham, Hugh W. & Andrew Kertesz. 1976. *Neologistic jargon aphasia.* Amsterdam: Swets & Zeitlinger.

Cappa, Stefano F., Giuseppina Cavallotti, Mario Guidotti, Costanza Papagno, Luigi A. Vignolo. 1983. Subcortical aphasia: two clinical-CT scan correlation studies. *Cortex* 19. 227–241.

Caramazza, Alfonso. 1984. The logic of neuropsychological research and the problem of patient classification in aphasia. *Brain and Language* 21. 9–20.

Caramazza, Alfonso. 1986. On drawing inferences about the structure of normal cognitive systems from the analysis of patterns of impaired performance: The case for single-patient studies. *Brain and Cognition* 5. 41–66.
Caramazza, Alfonso. 1997. How many level of processing are there in Lexical Access? *Cognitive Neuropsychology* 14. 177–208.
Caramazza, Alfonso & Argye Hillis. 1990. Where do semantic errors come from? *Cortex* 26. 95–122.
Caramazza, Alfonso & Argye E Hillis. 1991. Lexical organization of nouns and verbs in the brain. Nature 349, 788–790.
Caramazza, Alfonso & Argye Hillis. 1993. From a theory of remediation of cognitive deficits. *Neuropsychological Rehabilitation* 3. 217–234.
Caramazza, Alfonso & Michael McCloskey. 1988. The case for single-patient studies. *Cognitive Neuropsychology* 5. 517–28.
Caramazza, Alfonso, Gabriele Miceli, M. Caterina Silveri & Alessandro Laudanna. 1985. Reading mechanisms and the organization of the lexicon: Evidence from acquired dyslexia. *Cognitive Neuropsychology* 2. 81–l 14.
Caramazza A., Hillis A.E., Rapp BC and Romani C. (1990) The multiple semantics hypothesis: Multiple confusions? *Cognitive Neuropsychology*, vol 7, issue 3, 161–189.
Caramazza, Alfonso & Jennifer Shelton. 1998. Domain-specific knowledge systems in the brain: theanimate-inanimate distinction. *Journal of Cognitive Neuroscience* 10, 1–34.
Cattaneo, Zaira, Alberto Pisoni, Costanza Papagno. 2011. Transcranial direct current stimulation over Broca's region improves phonemic and semantic fluency in healthy individuals. *Neuroscience* 183. 64–70.
Chao, Linda L., James V. Haxby, Alex Martin. 1999. Attribute-based neural substrates in temporal cortex for perceiving and knowing about objects. *Nature Neuroscience* 2. 913–919.
Chee, Michael W. L., Brenda Weekes, Kok M. Lee, Chu S. Soon, Axel Schreiber, Jia J. Hoon & Marilyn Chee. 2000. Overlap and dissociation of semantic processing of Chinese characters, English words, and pictures: evidence from fMRI. *NeuroImage* 12. 392–403.
Cipolotti, Lisa & Elizabeth K. Warrington. 1995. Semantic memory and reading abilities: A case report. *Journal of the International Neuropsychological Society* 1. 104–110.
Coltheart, Mark, Karalyn E. Patterson & John C. Marshall. 1980. *Deep dyslexia*. London: Routledge.
Coltheart, Mark. 1985. Cognitive neuropsychology and the study of reading. *Attention and performance, XI*. Hillsdale, NJ: LEA.
Crepaldi, Davide, Manuela Berlingeri, Isabella Cattinelli, N. Alberto Borghese, Claudio Luzzatti & Eraldo Paulesu. 2013. Clustering the lexicon in the brain: a meta-analysis of the neurofunctional evidence on noun and verb processing. *Frontiers in Human Neuroscience* 7. 303.
Crutch, Sebastian J. & Eilzabeth K. Warrington. 2005. Abstract and concrete concepts have structurally different representational frameworks. *Brain* 128. 615–627.
Damasio, Antonio & Norman Geschwind. 1980. The neural basis of language. *Annual Revue of Neuroscience* 7. 127–47.
Damasio, Hanna, T.J. Grabowski, D. Tranel, R.D. Hichwa & A.R. Damasio, 2001. Neural correlates of naming actions and of naming spatial relations. *NeuroImage* 13. 1053–1064.

Davis, Matthew H., Fanny Meunier & William D. Marslen-Wilson. 2004. Neural responses to morphological, syntactic, and semantic properties of single words: an fMRI study. *Brain and Language* 89. 439–449.

Dejerine, Jules. 1891. Contribution to the study of subcortical motor aphasia and to the cerebral localization of the laryngeal centres (muscles of the vocal tract). *Mémoires de la Société de Biologie* 3. 155–162.

Demb, Jonathan B., John E. Desmond, Anthony D. Wagner, Chandan J. Vaidya, Gary H. Glover & John D. E. Gabrieli. 1995. Semantic encoding and retrieval in the left inferior prefrontal cortex: a functional MRI study of task difficulty and process specificity. *Journal of Neuroscience* 15, 5870–5878.

Devlin, Joseph T., Paul M. Matthews, Matthew F. Rushworth. 2003. Semantic processing in the left inferior prefrontal cortex: a combined functional magnetic resonance imaging and transcranial magnetic stimulation study. *Journal of Cognitive Neuroscience* 15. 71–84.

Devlin, Joseph T., Richard P. Russell, Matthew H. Davis, Cathy J. Price, Helen E. Moss, M. Jalal Fadili, Lorraine K. Tyler. 2002. Is there an anatomical basis for category-specificity? Semantic memory studies in PET and fMRI. *Neuropsychologia* 40. 54–75.

Ellis, Andrew W., Diane Miller & Gillian Sin. 1983. Wernicke's aphasia and normal language processing: A case study in cognitive neuropsychology. *Cognition* 15, 111–144.

Ellis, Andrew W. & Andrew W. Young. 1988. *Human Cognitive Neuropsychology*. Hove, UK: Lawrence Erlbaum Associates.

Fiebach, Christian J., Angela D. Friederici, Karsten Muller & D Yves von Cramon. 2002. fMRI evidence for dual routes to the mental lexicon in visual word recognition. *Journal of Cognitive Neuroscience* 14. 11–23.

Fiez, Julie A., David A. Balota, Marcus E. Raichle & Steven E. Petersen. 1999. Effects of lexicality, frequency, and spelling-to-sound consistency on the functional anatomy of reading. *Neuron* 24. 205–218.

Fiori Valentina, Susanna Cipollari, Margherita Di Paola, Carmelina Razzano, Carlo Caltagirone & Paola Marangolo. 2013. tDCS segregates words in the brain. *Frontiers Human Neurosci*ence 7.

Fiori, Valentina, Michela Coccia, Chiara V. Marinelli, Veronica Vecchi, Silvia Bonifazi, M. Gabriella Ceravolo, Leandro Provinciali, Francesco Tomaiuolo & Paola Marangolo. 2011. Transcranial Direct Current Stimulation (tDCS) improves word retrieval in healthy and nonfluent aphasic subjects. *Journal of Cognitive Neuroscience* 23, 2309–23.

Flitman, Stephen S., Jordan Grafman, Eric M. Wassermann, Victoria Cooper, Jerry O'Grady, Alvaro Pascual-Leone, Mark Hallett. 1998. Linguistic processing during repetitive transcranial magnetic stimulation. *Neurology* 50. 175–81.

Flöel, Agnes, Nina Rosser, Olesya Michka, Stefan Knecht & Caterina Breitenstein. 2008. Non invasive brain stimulation improves language learning. *Journal of Cognitive Neurosci*ence 8. 1415–1422.

Franklin, Susan, David Howard & Karalyn Patterson. 1994. Abstract word meaning deafness. *Cognitive Neuropsychology* 11. 1–34.

Franklin, Susan, David Howard & Karalyn Patterson. 1995. Abstract word anomia. *Cognitive Neuropsychology* 12. 549–566.

Fuggetta, Giorgio, Silvia Rizzo, Gorana Pobric, Michal Lavidor & Vincent Walsh. 2009. Functional Representation of Living and Nonliving Domains across the Cerebral

Hemispheres: A Combined Event-related Potential/Transcranial Magnetic Stimulation Study. *Journal of Cognitive Neuroscience* 21. 403–414.

Gainotti, Guido. 2000. What the locus of brain lesion tells us about the nature of the cognitive defect underlying category-specific disorders: a review. *Cortex* 36. 539–559.

Garrard, Peter, Matthew A. Lambon Ralph, Peter C. Watson, Jane Powis, Karalyn Patterson, John R. Hodges. 2001. Longitudinal profiles of semantic impairment for living and nonliving concepts in dementia of Alzheimer's type. *Journal of Cognitive Neuroscience* 13. 892–909.

Garrard, Peter, Karalyn Patterson, Peter C. Watson & John R. Hodges. 1998. Category specific semantic loss in dementia of Alzheimer's type. Functional-anatomical correlations from cross-sectional analyses. *Brain* 121. 633–646.

Geschwind, Norman. 1965. Disconnection syndromes in animals and man. *Brain* 88. 237–94.

Gold, Brian T. & Randy L. Buckner. 2002. Common prefrontal regions coactivate with dissociable posterior regions during controlled semantic and phenological tasks. *Neuron* 35. 803–812.

Goodglass, Harold. 1976. Agrammatism. In Haiganoosh Whitaker & Harry Whitaker (eds.), *Studies in neurolinguistics* (vol. 1). New York: Academic Press.

Gonnerman, Laura M., Elaine S. Andersen, Joseph T. Devlin, Daniel Kempler, Mark S. Seidenberg. 1997. Double dissociation of semantic categories in Alzheimer's disease. *Brain and Language* 57. 254–79.

Grossman, Murray, Phyllis Koenig, Chris DeVita, Giulia Glosser, David Alsop, John Detre & James Gee. 2002a. Neural representation of verb meaning: an fMRI study. *Human Brain Mapping* 15, 124–134.

Grossman, Murray, Phyllis Koenig, Chris DeVita, Giulia Glosser, David Alsop & John Detre. 2002b. The neural basis for category-specific knowledge: An fMRI study. *NeuroImage* 15. 936–948.

Gurd, Jennifer M., Katrin Amunts, Peter H. Weiss, Oliver Zafiris, Karl Zilles, John C. Marshall & Gereon R. Fink. 2002. Posterior parietal cortex is implicated in continuous switching between verbal fluency tasks: an fMRI study with clinical implications. *Brain* 125. 1024–1038.

Hartwigsen, Gesa. 2015. The neurophysiology of language: Insights from non-invasive brain stimulation in the healthy human brain. *Brain and Language* 148. 81–94.

Heim, Stefan, Bertram Opitz & Angela Friederici. 2002. Broca's area in the human brain is involved in the selection of grammatical gender for language production: evidence from event-related functional magnetic resonance imaging. *Neuroscience Letters* 328. 101–104.

Heun, Reiner, Frank Jessen, Uwe Klose, Michael Erb, Dirk Granath, Nikolaus Freymann & Wolfgang Grodd. 2000. Interindividual variation of cerebral activation during encoding and retrieval of words. *European Psychiatry* 15. 470–479.

Hillis, Argyle, Brenda Rapp & Alfonso Caramazza. 1999. When a rose is a rose in speech but a tulip in writing. *Cortex* 35. 337–356.

Hodges, John R., Karalyn Patterson, Susan Oxbury &, Elaine Funnell. 1992. Semantic dementia. Progressive fluent aphasia with temporal lobe atrophy. *Brain* 115. 1783–806.

Holland, Rachel, Alex P. Leff, Oliver Josephs, Joseph M. Galea, Mahalekshmi Desikan, Cathy J. Price, John C. Rothwell, Jennifer Crinion. 2011. Speech facilitation by left inferior frontal cortex stimulation. *Current Biology* 21, 1403–1407.

Howard, David, Karalyn Patterson, Richard Wise, R., W. Douglas Brown, Karl Friston, Cornelius Weiller & Richard Frackowiak. 1992. The cortical localization of the lexicons. Positron emission tomography evidence. *Brain* 115. 1769–1782.
Howes, Davis & Norman Geschwind. 1964. Quantitative studies of aphasic language. In D.M. Rioch & E. A. Wenstein (eds.), *Disorders of Communication*, 229–244. Baltimore: Williams and Wilkins.
James, Cariton T. 1975. The role of semantic information in lexical decisions. *Journal of Experimental Psychology: Human Perception and Performance* 1 (2). 130–136.
James, Thomas W. & Isabel Gauthier, 2004. Brain areas engaged during visual judgments by involuntary access to novel semantic information. *Vision Research* 44. 429–439.
Jennings, Janine M., Anthony R. McIntosh, Shitij Kapur, Robert B. Zipursky & Sylvain Houle. 1998. Functional network differences in schizophrenia: a rCBF study of semantic processing. *NeuroReport* 9. 1697–1700.
Joanisse, Marc F. & Joseph S. Gati, 2003. Overlapping neural regions for processing rapid temporal cues in speech and nonspeech signals. *NeuroImage* 19. 64–79.
Jones, Gregory V. 1985. Deep dyslexia, imageability, and ease of predication. *Brain and Language* 24. 1–19.
Kaan, Edith. 2007. Event-related potentials and language processing. *Language and Linguistics Compass* 1/6. 571–91.
Kiehl, Kent A., Peter F. Liddle, Andra M. Smith, Adrianna Mendrek, Bruce B. Forster & Robert D. Hare. 1999. Neural pathways involved in the processing of concrete and abstract words. *Human Brain Mapping* 7. 225–233.
Kohn, Susan E. & Janis Melvold. 2000. Effects of morphological complexity on phonological output deficits in fluent and nonfluent aphasia. *Brain and Language* 73. 323–346.
Kotz, Sonja A., Stefano Cappa, D. Yves von Cramon & Angela Friederici. 2002. Modulation of the lexical–semantic network by auditory semantic priming: an event-related functional MRI study. *NeuroImage* 17. 1761–1772.
Kussmaul, Adolf. 1887. Disturbances of speech: an attempt in the pathology of speech. In H.V. Ziemssen (ed.), *Encyclopedia of the Practice of Medicine*, vol. 14, New York: Wood.
Kutas, Martha & Steven A. Hillyard. 1980. Reading senseless sentences: brain potentials reflect semantic incongruity. *Science* 207. 203–05.
Kutas, Martha & Steven A. Hillyard. 1984. Brain potentials during reading reflect word expectancy and semantic association. *Nature* 307, 161–63.
Lambon Ralph, Mattew A., Lynne Moriarty & Karen Sage. 2002. Anomia is simply a reflection of semantic and phonological impairments: Evidence from a case-series study. *Aphasiology* 16. 56–82.
Levelt, Willem Johannes Maria. 1989. *Speaking from intention to articulation*. Cambridge, MA: The MIT Press.
Levelt, Willem Johannes Maria. 1999. Producing spoken language: a blueprint of the speaker. In Colin M. Brown & Peter Hagoort (eds), *The Neurocognition of Language* 83, 122, Oxford, UK: Oxford University Press.
Levelt, Willem Johannes Maria & Antje S. Meyer. 2000. Word for word: multiple lexical access in speech production. *European Journal of Cognitive Psychology* 12, 433–452.
Lichtheim, Ludwig. 1885. On aphasia. *Brain* VII. 433–84.
Longe, Olivia, Billy Randall, Emmanuel A. Stamatakis & Lorraine K. Tyler. 2007. Grammatical Categories in the Brain: The Role of Morphological Structure, *Cerebral Cortex* 17. 1812–1820.

Lubrano, Vincent, Thomas Filleron, Jean François Démonet & Franck-Emmanuel Roux. 2014. Anatomical correlates for category -specific naming of objects and actions: A brain stimulation mapping study. *Human Brain Mapping* 35. 429–443.

Luria, Aleksandr Romanovich. 1970. Traumatic aphasia: Its syndromes, psychology and treatment. Translated from the Russian by Douglas Bowen, with a foreword by MacDonald Critchley. *Janua Linguarum, series maior* 5, Mouton, The Hague.

Luzzatti, Claudio, Sara Mondini & Carlo Semenza. 2001. Lexical representation and processing of morphologically complex words: Evidence from the reading performance of an Italian agrammatic patient. *Brain and Language* 79, 345–359.

Macoir, Joël. 2008. Is a plum a memory problem? Longitudinal study of the reversal of concreteness effect in a patient with semantic dementia. *Neuropsychologia* 47, 518–35.

Marangolo, Paola & Carlo Caltagirone. 2014. Options to enhance recovery from aphasia by means of on-invasive stimulation and action observation therapy. *Expert Review of Neurotherapeutics* 14. 75–91.

Marangolo, Paola, Valentina Fiori, Maria Calpagnano, Serena Campana, Carmelina Razzano, Carlo Caltagirone, Andrea Marini. 2013b. tDCS over the left inferior frontal cortex improves speech production in aphasia. *Frontiers Human Neuroscience* 6, 7,539.

Marangolo, Paola, Valentina Fiori, Serena Campana, Maria Calpagnano, Carmelina Razzano, Carlo Caltagirone, Andrea Marini. 2014. Something to talk about: enhancement of linguistic cohesion through tDCS in chronic non fluent aphasia. *Neuropsychologia* 53. 246–56.

Marangolo, Paola, Valentina Fiori, Susanna Cipollari, Serena Campana, Carmelina Razzano, Margherita Di Paola, Giacomo Koch, Carlo Caltagirone. 2013a. Bihemispheric stimulation over left and right inferior frontal region enhances recovery from apraxia of speech in chronic aphasia. *European Journal of Neuroscience* 38, 3370–77.

Marangolo, Paola, Valeria Marinelli, Silvia Bonifazi, Valentina Fiori, Maria G. Ceravolo, Leandro Provinciali & Francesco Tomaiuolo. 2011. Electrical stimulation over the left inferior frontal gyrus (IFG) determines long-term effects in the recovery of speech apraxia in three chronic aphasics. *Behavioural and Brain Research* 225. 498–504.

Marshall, John C. & Freda Newcombe. 1973. Patterns of paralexia: A psycholinguistic approach. *Journal of Psycholinguistic Research* 2. 175–199.

Marshall, John C., Tim Pring, Shula Chiat, S & Jo Robson. 1996. Calling a salad a federation: An investigation of semantic jargon. Part 1. Nouns. *Journal of Neurolinguistics* 9. 237–250.

Martin, Alex, James V. Haxby, François M. Lalonde, Cheri L. Wiggs & Leslie G. Ungerleider. 1995. Discrete cortical regions associated with knowledge of color and knowledge of action. *Science* 270. 102–105.

Martin, Nadine & Eleanor M. Saffran. 1992. A computational account of deep dysphasia: Evidence from a single case study. *Brain and Language* 43. 240–274.

McCarthy, Rosaleen & Elizabeth K. Warrington. 1985. Category specificity in an agrammatic patient: The relative impairment of verb retrieval and comprehension. *Neuropsychologia*, 23. 709–727.

McCarthy, Rosaleen & Elizabeth K. Warrington. 1990. The dissolution of semantics. *Nature* 334. 428–430.

McKenna, Pat & Elizabeth K. Warrington. 1978. Category-specific naming preservation: a single case study. *Journal of Neurology, Neurosurgery, and Psychiatry* 41. 571–574.

Mellet, Emmanuel, Nathalie Tzourio-Mazoyer, Michel Denis & Bernard Mazoyer. 1998. Cortical anatomy of mental imagery of concrete nouns based on their dictionary definition. *NeuroReport* 9. 803–808.
Menn, Lise & Loraine K. Obler. 1990. Agrammatic aphasia. Philadelphia, PA: *John Benjamins Publishing Company* 3,117–178.
Menon, Ravi S. & Seong-Gi Kim. 1999. Spatial and temporal limits in cognitive neuroimaging with fMRI. *Trends in Cognitive Sciences* 3. 207–216.
Mesulam, Marsel. 2000. *Principles of Behavioral and Cognitive Neurology*. Oxford, UK: Oxford University Press.
Meyer, Martin, Kai Alter, Angela D. Friederici, Gabriele Lohmann & D. Yves von Cramon. 2002. FMRI reveals brain regions mediating slow prosodic modulations in spoken sentences. *Human Brain Mapping* 17. 73–88.
Miceli, Gabriele, Caterina Silveri, Giampiero Villa & Alfonso Caramazza. 1984. On the basis for agrammatics' difficulty in producing main verbs. *Cortex* 20. 207–20.
Miceli, Gabriele, Caterina Silveri, Ugo Nocentini & Alfonso Caramazza. 1988. Patterns of dissociation in comprehension and production of noun and verbs. *Aphasiology* 2. 351–58.
Miceli, Gabriele, Rita Capasso & Alfonso Caramazza. 2004. The relationships between morphological and phonological errors in aphasic speech: data from a word repetition task. *Neuropsychologia*, 42. 273–87.
Miniussi, Carlo, Stefano Cappa, Leonardo G. Cohen, Agnes Floel, Felipe Fregni, Michael A. Nitsche, Massimiliano Oliveri, Alvaro Pascual-Leone, Walter Paulus, Alberto Priori & Vincent Walsh. 2008. Efficacy of transcranial magnetic stimulation/transcranial direct current stimulation in cognitive neurorehabilitation. *Brain Stimulation* 1. 326–36.
Monte-Silva, Katia, Min-Fang Kuo, Silvia Hessenthaler, Shane Fresnoza, David Liebetanz, Walter Paulus & Michael A. Nitsche. 2013. Induction of late LTP-like plasticity in the human motor cortex by repeated non-invasive brain stimulation. *Brain Stimul*ation 6. 424–32.
Monti, Alessia, Roberta Ferrucci, Manuela Fumagalli, Franesca Mameli, Filippo Cogiamanian, Gianluca Ardolino & Alberto Priori. 2013. Transcranial direct current stimulation (tDCS) and language. *Journal of Neurology, Neurosurgery and Psychiatry* 84. 832–42.
Moore, Caroline J. & Cathy Price. 1999. Three distinct ventral occipitotemporal regions for reading and object naming. *NeuroImage* 10. 181–192.
Moss, Helen E., Lorraine K. Tyler, Mark Durrant-Peatfield & Elaine M. Bunn. 1998. 'Two eyes of a see-through': Impaired and intact semantic knowledge in a case of selective deficit for living things. *Neurocase* 4, 291–310.
Mottaghy, Felix M., Marcel Hungs, Marc Brügmann, Roland Sparing, Babak Boroojerdi, Henrik Foltys, Walter Huber & Rudolf Töpper. 1999. Facilitation of picture naming after repetitive transcranial magnetic stimulation. *Neurology* 53. 1806–1812.
Mottaghy, Felix M., Roland Sparing, Rudolf Töpper. 2006. Enhancing picture naming with transcranial magnetic stimulation. *Behavioural Neurology* 17. 177–186.
Nitsche, Michael & Walter Paulus. 2011. Transcranial direct current stimulation – update 2011. *Restoration Neurology and Neuroscience* 29, 463–92.
Nobre, Anna, & Gregory McCarthy. 1995. Language-related field potentials in the anteriormedial temporal lobe: II. Effects of word type and semantic priming. *Journal of Neuroscience* 15. 1090–99.

Noesselt, Tömme, Nadim J. Shah & Lutz Jäncke. 2003. Top–down and bottom– up modulation of language related areas – An fMRI study. *BMC Neuroscience* 4. 13.

Noppeney, Uta & Cathy Price. 2004. Retrieval of abstract semantics. *NeuroImage* 22. 164–170.

Ojemann, George, Jeff Ojemann, Ereegt Lettich & Mitchel Berger. 1989. Cortical language localization in left, dominant hemisphere: an electrical stimulation mapping investigation in 117 patients. *Neurosurgery* 71. 316–326.

Orena, Eleonora, Dario Caldiroli, Francesco Acerbi, Ilaria Barazzetta & Costanza Papagno. 2019. Investigating the functional neuroanatomy of concrete and abstract word processing through direct electric stimulation (DES) during awake surgery. *Cognitive Neuropsychology* 36, 167–177.

Paivio, Allan. 1971. *Imagery and verbal processes*. New York: Holt, Rinehart, and Winston.

Paivio, Allan. 1986. *Mental Representations: A Dual Coding Approach*. New York: Oxford University Press.

Paivio, Allan. 1991. *Images in mind: The evolution of a theory*. Sussex, U.K.: Harvester Wheatsheaf.

Papagno, Costanza. 2017. Studying cognitive functions by means of direct electrical stimulation. A review. *Neurological Science* 38, 2079–2087.

Papagno, Costanza, Rita Capasso & Gabriele Miceli. 2009a. Reversed of concreteness effect for nouns in a subject with semantic dementia. *Neuropsychologia* 47. 1138–1148.

Papagno, Costanza, Arianna Fogliata, Eleonora Catricalà & Carlo Miniussi. 2009b. The lexical processing of abstract and concrete nouns. *Brain Research* 1263. 78–86.

Papagno, Costanza, Marcello Gallucci, Alessandra Casarotti, Antonella Castellano, Andrea Falini, Giorgio Carrabba, Carlo Giussani, Encrica Fava, Lorenzo Bello & Alfonso Caramazza. 2011. Connectivity constraints on cortical reorganization of neural circuits involved in object naming. *Neuroimage* 55. 1306–1313.

Pascual-Leone, Alvaro, Vincent Walsh & John Rothwell. 2000. Transcranial magnetic stimulation in cognitive neuroscience- virtual lesion, chronometry, and functional connectivity. *Current Opinion in Neurobiology* 10. 232–237.

Patterson, Karalyn & Christina Shewell. 1987. Speak and spell: Dissociations and word class effect. In Max Coltheart, Giuseppe Sartori & Remo Job (eds.), *The cognitive neuropsychology of language*, 273–294. Hove, UK: Lawrence Erlbaum Associates

Paulesu, Eraldo, Eamon McCrory, Ferruccio Fazio, Lorena Menoncello, Nicola Brunswick, Stefano F. Cappa, Maria Cotelli, Giuseppe Cossu, Francesca Corte, M. Lorusso, Silvia Pesenti, A. Gallagher, Daniela Perani, Cathy Price, Chris D. Frith & Uta Frith. 2000. A cultural effect on brain function. *Nature Neuroscience* 3. 91–96.

Perani, Daniela, Stefano Cappa, Tatiana Schnur, Marco Tettamanti, Simona Collina, Mario M. Rosa & Ferruccio Fazio F. 1999. The neural correlates of verb and noun processing: A PET study. *Brain* 122. 2337–44.

Petersen, Steve E., Peter T. Fox, Michael I. Posner, Mark A. Mintun & Marcus E. Raichle. 1988. Positron emission tomographic studies of the cortical anatomy of single word processing. *Nature* 331. 585–589.

Petersen, Steve E., Peter T. Fox, Michael I. Posner, Mark Mintum & Marcus E. Raichle. 1989. Position emission tomographic studies of the processing of single words. *Journal of Cognitive Neuroscience* 5. 153–170.

Piras, Fabrizio & Paola Marangolo. 2007. Noun-Verb naming in aphasia: a voxel-based lesion-symptom mapping study. *Neuroreport* 18. 14–17.

Plaut, David C. & Tim Shallice. 1991. *Effects of word abstractness in a connectionist model of deep dyslexia*. In *Proceedings of the 13th Annual Meeting of the Cognitive Science Society*, 73–78. Chicago.

Plaut, David C. & Tim Shallice. 1993. Deep dyslexia: A case study of connectionist neuropsychology. *Cognitive Neuropsychology* 10. 377–500.

Poeppel, David, Karen Emmorey, Gregory Hickok & Liina Pylkkannen. 2012. Towards a new neurobiology of language. *The Journal of Neuroscience* 32. 14125–14131.

Poeppel, David, Andre Guillemin, Jennifer Thompson, Jonathan Fritz, Daphne Bavelier & Allen R. Braun. 2004. Auditory lexical decision, categorical perception, and FM direction discrimination differentially engage left and right auditory cortex. *Neuropsychologia* 42. 183–200.

Poldrack, Russell A., Anthony D. Wagner, Matthew W. Prull, John E. Desmond, Gary H. Glover & John D. Gabrieli. 1999. Functional specialization for semantic and phonological processing in the left inferior prefrontal cortex. *NeuroImage* 10. 15–35.

Price, Cathy & Karl J. Friston. 1999. Scanning patients with tasks they can perform. *Human Brain Mapping* 8, 102–108.

Rapp, Brenda & Alfonso Caramazza. 1998. A case of selective difficulty in writing verbs. *Neurocase*, 4. 127–140.

Rapp, Brenda & Alfonso Caramazza. 2002. A case of selective difficulty in writing verbs: A single case study. *Journal of Neurolinguistics* 15, 373–402.

Rhode, Alexia, Linda Worrall & Guylaine Le Dorze. 2013. Systematic review of the quality of clinical guidelines for aphasia in stroke management. *Journal of Evaluation of Clinical Practice* 1. 54–67.

Rossi, Simone & Paolo M. Rossini. 2004. TMS in cognitive plasticity and the potential for rehabilitation. *Trends in Cognitive Sciences* 8, 273–279.

Sabsevitz, David S., David A. Medler, Mark Seidenberg & Jeffrey R. Binder. 2005. Modulation of the semantic system by word imageability. *NeuroImage* 27. 188–200.

Sacchett, Carol & Glyn W. Humphreys. 1992. Calling a squirrel a squirrel but a canoe a wigwam: A category-specific deficit for artefactual objects and body parts. *Cognitive Neuropsychology* 9. 73–86.

Schuhmann, Teresa, Niels O. Schiller, Rainer Goebel & Alexander T. Sack. 2009. The temporal characteristics of functional activation in Broca's area during overt picture naming. *Cortex* 45. 1111–1116.

Schwanenflugel, Paula J. & Edward J. Shoben. 1983. Differential context effects in the comprehension of abstract and concrete verbal materials. *Journal of Experimental Psychology: Learning, Memory and Cognition* 9. 82–102.

Semenza, Carlo, Brian Butterworth, Marta Panzeri & Tiziana Ferreri. 1990. Word formation: Evidence from aphasia. *Neuropsychologia* 28. 499–502.

Shallice, Tim. 1988. *From neuropsychology to mental structure*. Cambridge: Cambridge University Press.

Shapiro, Kevin, Lauren R. Moo & Alfonso Caramazza. 2006. Cortical signatures of noun and verb production. *Protocol Natural Academy of Science USA* 103. 1644–1649.

Shapiro, Kevin, Alvaro Pascual-Leone, Felix Mottaghy & Massimo Gangitano. 2001. Grammatical distinctions in the left frontal cortex. *Journal of Cognitive Neuroscience* 13 (6). 713–720.

Shapiro, Kevin, Jennifer Shelton & Alfonso Caramazza. 2000. Grammatical class in lexical production and morhological processing: Evidence from a case of fluent aphasia. *Cognitive Neuropsychology* 17, 665–82.

Siebner, Hartwig R. & John Rothwell. 2003. Transcranial magnetic stimulation: new insights into representational cortical plasticity. *Experimental Brain Research* 148. 1–16.

Silveri, Caterina & Anna Maria Di Betta. 1997. Noun-verb dissociation in brain-damaged patients. Further Evidence. *Neurocase* 3. 477–88.

Siri, Simona, Marco Tettamanti, Stefano F. Cappa, Pasquale A. Della Rosa, Cristina M. Saccuman, Paola Scifo, Gabriella Vigliocco. 2008. The Neural Substrate of Naming Events: Effects of Processing Demands but not of Grammatical Class. *Cerebral Cortex* 18. 171–77.

Sirigu, Anna, Jean-René Duhamel & Michel Poncet. 1991. The role of sensorimotor experience in object recognition. *Brain* 114. 2555–2573.

Sliwinska, Magdalena W., Manali Khadilkar, Jonathon Campbell-Ratcliffe, Frances Quevenco & Joseph T. Devlin. 2012. Early and sustained supramarginal gyrus contributions to phonological processing. *Frontiers in Psychology* 3. 161.

Sliwinska, Magdalena W., Sylvia Vitello & Joseph T. Devlin. 2014. Transcranial magnetic stimulation for investigating causal brain-behavioral relationships and their time course. *Journal of Visualized Experiments* 89. e51735.

Small, Stephan, Douglas C. Noll, Charles A. Perfetti, Petr Hlustik, Robin Wellington & Walter Schneider. 1996. Localizing the lexicon for reading aloud: replication of a PET study using fMRI. *NeuroReport* 7. 961–965.

Sparing, Ronald, Manuel Dafotakis, Ingo G. Meister, Nivethida Thirugnanasambandam & Gereon R. Fink. 2008. Enhancing language performance with non-invasive brain stimulation – a transcranial direct current stimulation study in healthy humans. *Neuropsychologia* 46. 261–268.

Sparing, Ronald, Felix M. Mottaghy, Marcel Hungs, Marc Brügmann, Henrik Foltys, Walter Huber, Rudolf Töpper. 2001. Repetitive transcranial magnetic stimulation effects on language function depend on the stimulation parameters. *Journal of Clinical Neurophysiology* 18. 326–330.

Taylor, Paul, Anna C. Nobre, Matthew F. S. Rushworth. 2007. FEF TMS affects visual cortical activity. *Cerebral Cortex* 17. 391–399.

Thompson-Schill, Sharon L., Mark D'Esposito, Geoffrey K. Aguirre & Martha J. Farah. 1997. Role of left inferior prefrontal cortex in retrieval of semantic knowledge: a reevaluation. *Protocol of Natural Academy of Science USA* 23. 14792–14797.

Töpper, Rudolf Friedrich, Felix M. Mottaghy, Martin Brugmann, Johannes Noth & Walter Huber.1998. Facilitation of picture naming by focal transcranial magnetic stimulation of Wernicke's area. *Experimental Brain Research* 121. 371–378.

Tranel, Daniel, Coleman Martin, Hanna Damasio, Thomas J. Grabowski & Richard Hichwa. 2005. Effects of noun-verb homonymy on the neural correlates of naming concrete entities and actions. *Brain and Language* 92. 288–299.

Tyler, Lisa K., Peter Bright, Paul Fletcher & Emmanuel A. Stamatakis. 2004. Neural processing of nouns and verbs: the role of inflectional morphology. *Neuropsychologia* 42. 512–523.

Tyler, Lisa K., R. Russell, J. Fadili & H. E. Moss. 2001. The neural representation of nouns and verbs: PET studies. *Brain* 124. 1619–1634.

Van Berkum, Jos J.A, Peter Hagoort & Colin M. Brown. 1999. Semantic integration in sentences and discourse: evidence from the N400. *Journal of Cognitive Neuroscience* 11. 657–71.

Vandenberghe, Rik, Cathy Price, Richard Wise, Oliver Josephs & Richard S. J. Frackowiak.1996. Functional anatomy of a common semantic system for words and pictures. *Nature* 383. 254–256.
Van Petten, Cyma K. 1993. A comparison of lexical and sentence-level context effects and their temporal parameters. *Language and Cognitive Processes* 8. 485–532.
Van Petten, Cyma K. & Marta Kutas. 1991. Influences of semantic and syntactic context in open-and closed-class words. *Memory and Cognition* 19. 95–112.
Van Petten, Cyma K. & Marta Kutas. 1990. Interactions between sentence context and word frequency in event-related brain potentials. *Memory and Cognition* 18. 380–93.
Van Petten, Cyma K. & Barbara Luka. 2006. Neural localization of semantic context effects in electromagnetic and hemodynamic studies. *Brain and Language* 97, 279–93.
Van Turennout, Miranda, Peter Hagoort & Colin M. Brown. 1997. Electrophysiological evidence on the time course of semantic and phonological processes in speech production. *Journal of Experimental Psychology: Learning, Memory, and Cognition* 23. 787–806.
Van Turennout, Miranda, Peter Hagoort & Colin M. Brown. 1998. Brain activity during speaking: from syntax to phonology in 40 milliseconds. *Science* 280. 572–4.
Vigliocco, Gabriella, Jane Warren, Simona Siri, Joanne Arcuili, Sophie Scott & Richard Wise. 2006. The role of semantics and grammatical class in the neural representation of words. *Cerebral Cortex* 16. 1790–1796.
Vigneau, Mathieu, Virginie Beaucousin, Pierre-Yves Hervé, Hugues Duffau, Fabrice Crivello, Olivier Houdé, Bernard Mazoyer & Nathalie Tzourio-Mazoyer. 2006. Meta-analyzing left hemisphere language areas: Phonology, semantics and sentence processing. *NeuroImage* 30. 1414–32.
Warburton, Elizabeth, Richard J. Wise, Cathy J. Price, Cornelius Weiller, Uri Hadar, Stuart Ramsay & Richard Frackowiak. 1996. Noun and verb retrieval by normal subjects. Studies with PET. *Brain* 119. 1803–1817.
Wagner, Anthony D., Wilma Koutstaal, Anat Maril, Daniel L. Schacter & Randy L. Buckner. 2000. Task-specific repetition priming in left inferior prefrontal cortex. *Cerebral Cortex* 10. 1176–1184.
Walsh, Vincent & Alan Cowey. 2000. Transcranial magnetic stimulation and cognitive neuroscience. *Nature Review Neuroscience* 1. 73–9.
Walsh, Vincent & Alvaro Pascual-Leone. 2003. Transcranial magnetic stimulation: A neurochronometrics of mind. *Cambridge, Massachusetts*: Mit Press.
Warrington, Elisabeth K. 1975. The selective impairment of semantic memory. *The Quarterly Journal of Experimental Psychology* 27. 635–657.
Warrington, Elisabeth K. 1981. Concrete word dyslexia. *British Journal of Psychology* 72. 175–196.
Warrington, Elisabeth K. & Rosaleen McCarthy. 1983. Category specific access dysphasia. *Brain* 106. 859–878.
Warrington, Elisabeth K., Rosaleen McCarthy. 1987. Categories of knowledge. Further frationations and an attempted integration. *Brain* 110. 1273–1296.
Warrington, Elisabeth K. & Tim Shallice. 1984. Category specific semantic impairments. *Brain* 107. 829–854.
Wasserman, Eric M. 1998. Risk and safety of repetitive Transcranial Magnetic Stimulation: report and suggested guidelines from the International Workshop on the Safety of Repetitive Transcranial Magnetic Stimulation, June 5 –7,1996. *Electroencephalography and Clinical Neurophysiology* 108. 1–16.

Wassermann, Eric M., Teresa A. Blaxton, Elizabeth A. Hoffman, Cherisse D. Berry, H. Oletsky, Alvaro Pascual-Leone & William H. Theodore. 1999. Repetitive transcranial magnetic stimulation of the dominant hemisphere can disrupt visual naming in temporal lobe epilepsy patients. *Neuropsychologia* 37. 537–44.

Wernicke, Carl. 1874. *The aphasic symptom complex*. Breslau: Kohn und Weigert.

West, Caroline & Phillip J. Holcomb. 2002. Event-related potentials during discourse level semantic integration of complex pictures. *Cognitive Brain Research* 13. 363–75.

Whatmough, Christine, Louis Verret, Dion Fung, & Howard Cherktow. 2004. Common and contrasting areas of activation for abstract and concrete concepts: An H2 15O PET study. *Journal of Cognitive Neuroscience* 16. 1211–1226.

Wildgruber, Dirk, Hermann Ackermann & Wolfgang Grodd. 2001. Differential contributions of motor cortex, basal ganglia, and cerebellum to speech motor control: effects of syllable repetition rate evaluated by fMRI. *NeuroImage* 13. 101–109.

Wilshire, Carolyn E., H. Branch Coslett. 2000. Disorders of word retrieval in aphasia: Theories and potential applications. In Stephen E. Nadeau, Leslie J.G. Rothi & Bruce Crosson (eds.), *Aphasia and language: theory to practice*, 82–107. New York: Guillford Press.

Wise, Richard J.S., Sophie K. Scott, S. Catrin Blank, Cath J. Mummery, Kevin Murphy, Elizabeth A. Warburton. 2001. Separate neural subsystems within Wernicke's area. *Brain* 124. 83–95.

Yi, Hyon-Ah, Peachie Moore & Murray Grossman. 2007. Reversal of the concreteness effect for verbs in patients with semantic dementia. *Neuropsychology* 21. 9–19.

Zatorre, Robert J., Ernst Meyer, Albert Gjedde, Alan C. Evans. 1996. PET studies of phonetic processing of speech: review, replication, and reanalysis. *Cerebral Cortex* 6. 21–30.

Zingeser, Louise & Rita S. Berndt. 1990. Retrieval of nouns and verbs in agrammatism and anomia. *Brain and Language*, 39. 14–32.

Emmanuel Keuleers and Marco Marelli
Resources for mental lexicon research: A delicate ecosystem

Abstract: Resources are playing an ever-increasing role in current empirical investigations of the mental lexicon. Notwithstanding their diffusion and widespread application, lexical resources are often taken at face value, and there are limited efforts to better understand the dynamics and implications subtending resource developments, as well as the complex web of relations linking resources to each other. In the present chapter, we argue that describing these dynamics and relations is akin to investigating a complex and delicate ecosystem: resources are not independent and self-contained elements, but are rather the expression of a set of entangled components that span from our everyday language experience to the very scientific theories we develop to understand language.

Keywords: Megastudies, corpora, lexical database, crowdsourcing, linguistic intuition, ratings

1 Introduction

Knowledge about the nature and organization of the mental lexicon is strongly dependent on a large amount of resources which, at first sight, seem relatively independent from each other. A first group of resources provides researchers with objective information on the elements that make up the lexicon in its different linguistic and psycholinguistic interpretations. There are data reflecting properties such as word length, morphology, or pronunciation; data concerning distributional properties of words based on text corpora; lexicographic data with definitions and relations; and so forth. A second group of resources are derived from behavioral or neuropsychological investigation using the elements of the lexicon as stimuli: subjective expressions of single word properties or word relatedness;

Note: The authors would like to thank Dr. Paweł Mandera for many insightful comments on the topic of this paper.

Emmanuel Keuleers, Department of Cognitive Science and Artificial Intelligence, Tilburg University, Tilburg, The Netherlands
Marco Marelli, Department of Psychology, University of Milano-Bicocca, Milano, Italy

response latencies; eye movement trajectories; encephalographic activity; etc. Finally, there are resources which inform researchers about more abstract properties of the lexicon and its elements, such as linguistic grammars, cognitive theories and formalisms, algorithms for lexical analysis and word tagging, etc.

In this chapter, we will show that gaining a proper understanding of these resources requires seeing them as part of a complex dynamic system. Figure 1 illustrates this dynamic view on psycholinguistic resources. In Figure 1, ellipses represent resource "primitives", raw data that are used to develop the resources themselves. These primitives are restricted to language-associated human behavior. We conceive of these primitives as latent variables. They are not a directly accessible resource but instead they are the origin of the data we use. Every other linguistic or psycholinguistic resource can be considered a direct or indirect elaboration of these primitives. These general resource categories are represented as rectangles in Figure 1. The operation needed to derive a given resource type from another is represented by arrows. This schematic representation will serve as a guide throughout this chapter. We roughly divide our exposition in three parts. First, we will focus on the rightmost section of the Figure, highlighted in red. This part will deal with resources that are mostly related to psycholinguistics and cognitive linguistics, as it focuses on resources obtained through elicited behavior. Second, we will discuss resources that are mostly related to the collection of unelicited language behavior (leftmost part of the Figure, in blue), and that are often developed in the computational domain. Finally, we will briefly consider the center of our representation, and argue that

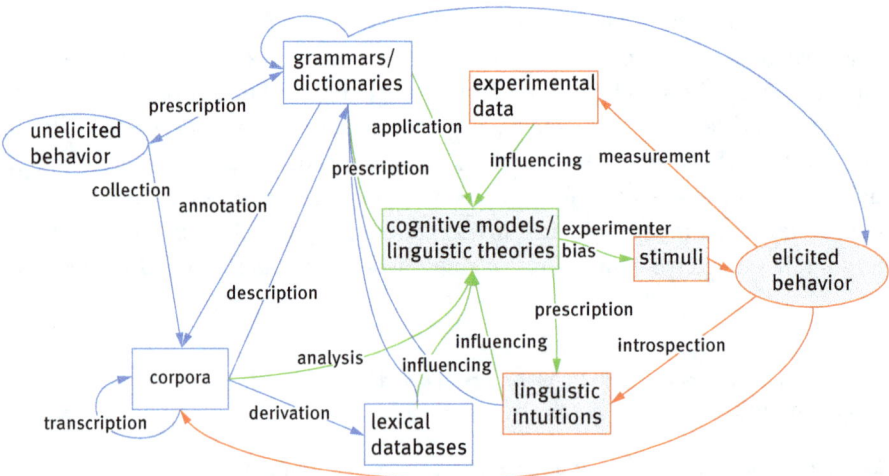

Figure 1: The resource ecosystem.

the very cognitive models and linguistic theories driving our research activity can be also considered resources that we use for investigating language. Note, however, that this subdivision is extremely rough. We have already mentioned that we believe that resources are not independent self-contained elements, but are rather the expression of a complex dynamic system that span from our everyday language experience to the very scientific theories we develop to understand language. This should be already evident by the deep entanglement between the elements we report in our figure: there is no isolated component, with most elements involved in ingoing and outgoing operations crucially binding them with each other. Indeed, given these considerations we believe that providing a complete taxonomy of resources is an impossible feat. The organization of this chapter has thus to be considered more of a working hypothesis, adopted for purely expository purposes.

2 From elicited behavior to experimental data and linguistic intuitions

In one way or another, human behavior underlies every form of linguistic data. In the present section we will focus on *elicited behavior*, or, in other words, behavior that is initiated at the researcher's input. In our schema (see Figure 1), the material that the researcher chooses to initiate a behavior is called *stimulus*. Depending on the researcher's intention, a stimulus will lead to *experimental data*, *linguistic intuitions*, or *corpora*. We will discuss the first two in this section, while corpora, which are most often not intentionally elicited, will be discussed in a later section on unelicited data.

It is important to note that *stimuli* are themselves a resource. Psycholinguistics has a long tradition in making data available to make it easier for researchers to select stimuli. An early example is found in Haagen (1949), who collected ratings for familiarity and vividness of imagery for more than 400 adjectives, in addition to ratings for synonymy and association of 440 adjective pairs. He specifically noted that the "study was undertaken to develop materials that might be used in studies of verbal learning" (Haagen 1949: 454). Similar efforts were conducted by Paivio, Yuille, and Madigan (1968) and by Nusbaum, Pisoni, and Davis (1984). The MRC database (Coltheart 1981) marks a radical change in the content of *stimulus* resources. While the purpose of the database remained unchanged – to serve as stimuli for psycholinguistic experiments – elicited ratings for words were merged with data from other resources containing information about syntactic class, formality of register, pronunciation, and word frequency. We find these latter resources scattered throughout our schema – a first indication of the dynamic nature of the resource system. Another class of *stimulus* resource are collections of pseudowords, which are essential to tap into the productive aspect of language. While the ARC database (Rastle, Harrington, and Coltheart 2002) still exhaustively lists pseudowords, subsequent efforts at building pseudoword resources, such as WordGen (Duyck et al. 2004), LiNGUA (Westbury, Hollis, and Shaoul 2007), and Wuggy (Keuleers and Brysbaert 2010) abandoned the listing approach in favor of algorithms that could dynamically generate pseudowords with certain properties. Following the theme that will pervade this chapter, these *stimulus* resources rely heavily on other resources, primarily on lists of existing words taken from *lexical databases*. While these resources are practical tools for researchers, the most frequent *stimulus* resources are probably lists of stimuli used in previous research and often appearing in the appendices of published papers, especially when it comes to the investigation of rare phenomena. In the domain of morphology, for example, lists of opaque words are often reused for the investigation of semantic processing. As noted above, *stimulus* resources are rarely limited to orthographic or phonetic strings. Most often they also merge estimates of different properties of these strings. In that respect, they have a certain degree of overlap with resources such as *dictionaries*, experimental *data*, and *frequency lists*. However, they crucially differ from these other resources in having a constrained use, namely to generate lists of stimuli for an experiment. Throughout the chapter, we will meet other examples of such apparent links, in which resources quite similar in substance are developed for and applied to different purposes, time after time illustrating an intertwined, dynamic, and complex system.

2.1 Experimental data

For the present purpose, we define *experimental data* as the result of measuring the response to stimuli using objective instruments. Measurements in psycholinguistics are usually chronometric or physiological. Chronometric measures are the result of recording elapsed time, for instance the measurement of reaction time in a word identification task or the measurement of fixation durations during reading. Physiological measures are the result of recording electrical (EEG) and magnetic (MEG) signals generated by the brain, recording the change in blood oxygenation level in grey matter (fMRI), or recording more peripheral activity, such as skin conductance, electrical activation in muscles, or pupil dilation.

Experimental data are often published in the normal course of research and are undeniably an exploitable resource. Meta-analysis can be used to combine data from several similar experiments to increase the strength of a statistical analysis; computational models can be validated by experimental data, etc. Unlike *stimulus* resources, experimental data are usually collected with the aim of testing specific hypotheses. Their use as a resource is mostly *secondary* and coincidental.

2.2 Megastudies

Megastudies are a category of experimental data whose *primary* purpose is to function as a resource. These data are collected specifically with the aim of maximizing utility and re-usability in the context of psycholinguistic research. In this aspect, they are similar to databases of ratings, but they differ firstly in the sense that what is being collected is measured via objective instruments and secondly in the sense that the collected measurements are usually considered to be *dependent* variables in experimental research. While experimental psychologists have long been committed to building and using resources of independent variables, such as the stimulus resources discussed above, they have been reluctant to build large collections of responses to those stimuli. In fact, the earliest collection of chronometric data that was designed specifically with re-use in mind (Balota et al. 2007) was published more than 60 years after Haagen's (1949) collection of stimulus ratings. Keuleers and Balota (2015) have tried to explain this time gap by a dogmatic adherence to strict temporality in the cycle of experimental research.

> In hindsight, one can ask why the psychologists who understood the benefit of collecting elicited ratings for a large number of words did not gather chronometric measures for recognition or classification of those words. One possibility is that the reuse of independent variables was considered safe but that recycling a dependent variable did not conform to the idea that formulating a hypothesis must always precede the collection of data in the cycle of scientific investigation. The fundamental idea behind that principle, however, is to prevent a hypothesis being generated based on data that are already collected. It is clear to see that a careless generalization of precedence in the scientific cycle to precedence in time is absurd, as it would imply that temporally earlier findings cannot be used to contest the validity of later findings. (Keuleers and Balota, 2015: 1459)

In line with this interpretation, it took some serendipity for psychologists to realize that objective dependent measures such as reaction times could be collected with reuse in mind. The events leading to this accidental insight started with Seidenberg and Waters (1989) who collected voice onset times for about 3,000 monosyllabic English words at McGill University. Their purpose was to compare the amount of variance in naming latency that could be explained by different theories of reading aloud. Seidenberg and Waters coined the term *megastudy* to refer to the – for that time – unusually large number of stimuli.

With an entirely different purpose, Treiman et al. (1995) re-used the McGill dataset to test hypotheses on the role of spelling consistency in reading aloud. In doing so, they implicitly acknowledged that an existing dataset could be used to examine a novel research question. However, they still seemed to consider the McGill dataset as merely a source of supporting evidence for results they had already obtained in their own experiments.

A few other studies followed, using more or less the same sets of items. Spieler and Balota (1997, 2000) collected naming times for both younger and older adults; Balota et al. (2004) did the same using lexical decision instead of naming.

The revolution in megastudy data came with the publication of the English Lexicon project (Balota et al. 2007), which provided both lexical decision and naming data for more than 40,000 words, collected at six different universities. The authors of the English Lexicon project were clear in their motivations: the database was to be used as a normative standard for lexical decision and naming in English. This would free researchers from the need to do a plethora of small factorial experiments in their laboratories, instead enabling them to look at the functional relationship between their variables of interest and visual word processing data.

The English Lexicon project was soon followed by the French Lexicon project (Ferrand et al. 2010), which collected lexical decision data for nearly 40,000 words, and some smaller efforts such as the Malay lexicon project (Yap et al.2010). Keuleers, Diependaele and Brysbaert (2010) made the process of collecting megastudy data much more efficient, by demonstrating that individual participants can yield reliable data for tens of thousands of trials. This approach resulted in the Dutch Lexicon project (Brysbaert et al.2016; Keuleers, Diependaele, and Brysbaert, 2010) and the British Lexicon project (Keuleers et al. 2012).

The megastudy approach was also quickly extended from simple visual word recognition to other, more complex paradigms at the word level, such as semantic priming (Hutchison et al., 2013), masked priming (Adelman et al. 2014), auditory lexical decision (Ernestus and Cutler 2015) and recognition memory (Cortese, Khanna, and Hacker 2010; Cortese, McCarty, and Shock 2015). More recently, large datasets of reading at the sentence level, such as the GECO eye-tracking corpus, have also become available (Cop et al. 2017).

Given the success of megastudy resources, researchers did not mind advancing knowledge from existing experimental data: megastudy data or the studies that were based on them data were not criticized because they violated the temporal precedence of hypothesis generation to data collection. Still, as Keuleers and Balota (2015) have pointed out, when data are available before the hypotheses are formulated, there is a real danger of data-driven hypothesis generation. Fortunately, researchers have started to address this problem by using methods such as bootstrapping (Kuperman 2015).

2.3 Clinical resources

Similar in concept to megastudies are resources that bundle experimental data from patients with language-related clinical symptoms. The Moss Aphasia Psycholinguistics Project Database (Mirman et al. 2010) contains picture naming and picture recognition data for 175 items from over 240 patients. For many of these patients, there are also demographic data, aphasia diagnostic tests, speech perception and recognition tests, and a variety of other language and memory tests. A more in-depth overview of large datasets in clinical research is provided by Faroqi-Shah (2016).

2.4 Crowdsourcing

While researchers are now mostly convinced that data collected on thousands of items can yield valid data for scientific investigation, another hurdle to overcome is the idea that reliable data can only be collected in controlled laboratory experiments. In the context of psycholinguistic research, crowdsourcing is used when elicited data (experimental data or intuitions) are collected outside laboratory settings from a large set of participants whose demographic characteristics are not known a priori. Recently, researchers have used crowdsourcing to create resources collected on very large and diverse samples. In the context of visual word recognition, Dufau et al. (2011) have started an effort using a specialized mobile app to generate lexical decision data in different languages. More recently, attention has shifted to collecting data by offering participants a game-like format to test their vocabulary. This has resulted in large resources containing data about word knowledge and word recognition times for over 50,000 Dutch words collected on several hundred thousand participants (Keuleers et al. 2015), for over 60,000 English words collected on over a million participants (Brysbaert et al. in press), and for over 45,000 Spanish words collected on over 160,000 participants (Aguasvivas et al., 2018).

An essential aspect of crowdsourcing in science is that part of the work of the scientist is transferred to laypersons, who each contribute a small part of the data. It could be argued that crowdsourcing has been an integral method in psycholinguistics from very early on because, unlike in other sciences where a skilled scientist who is familiar with an instrument can make better observations than a layperson, psychological observations are dependent on the naivety of the respondent, since involvement with the goals of the research would taint its results.

2.5 Linguistic intuitions

A critical aspect of experimental data is the involvement of objective measurement. However, behavior can also be elicited by a researcher with the aim of self examination. This is common in theoretical linguistics, for instance in the case of grammaticality judgements. The same approach is used in the compilation of psycholinguistic resources that rely on questionnaires asking participants about their intuition on certain aspects of linguistic experience, such as word age of acquisition (e.g. Kuperman, Stadthagen-Gonzalez, and Brysbaert 2012), valence, dominance, and arousal (Warriner, Brysbaert, and Kuperman 2013), concreteness (Brysbaert, Warriner, and Kuperman 2014), modality-specificity (Lynott and Connell 2013), or semantic features (McRae et al. 2005). The two critical differences between the results of the questionnaires that psycholinguists administer and the intuitions that theoretical linguists supply is that the data from questionnaires are *aggregated* over multiple participants and that the participants are *naive*. Thus, it is clear that when grammaticality ratings are collected on naive participants and aggregated (e.g., Bard, Robertson and Sorace 1996), there is no difference between the two.

The notion that a linguistic intuition is an (self-)elicited response simply means that theoretical linguists administer themselves examples of language usage *as stimuli* in order to produce the intuitions (*or responses)* that are at the center of their research. The terminology of stimulus-response is closely connected with behaviorism and therefore seems irreconcilable with the views espoused in generative grammar which use linguistic intuitions as a primary resource. It should be clear, however, that using a stimulus-response based research paradigm to gather data does not imply that the faculty of language operates on behaviorist principles. In the context of this work, the terminology allows us to consider both ratings and intuitions as closely related psycholinguistic resources.

Another important point is that elicited responses can result simultaneously in both experimental data and linguistic intuitions. For instance, in the lexical decision paradigm, the decision whether a stimulus is a word or not is an intuition or judgement (and indeed it is usually released in the context of related resources; e.g., Keuleers et al. 2015), whereas the time taken to make that decision is experimental data. To make the difference between these concepts even more clear: If we were to ask participants to estimate the time it would take them to recognize a stimulus word, we would consider it an intuition. Likewise, asking participants to rate a particular aspect of a linguistic stimulus on a numerical scale is not an objective measurement but the recording of an intuition.

In the context of stimulus resources we have already discussed collections of ratings. These are obviously collections of linguistic judgements, but their primary use is as *a resource* for selecting stimuli and to function as an independent variable. Secondarily, these ratings can also be treated, as described in the present section, as *dependent* variables providing inferential evidence for the development of cognitive models and linguistic theories.

3 From unelicited behavior to corpora and lexical statistics

Only an infinitesimal fraction of language production is elicited by scientists. Because language production is ephemeral, capturing it is notably difficult. Traditionally, language production was captured in field studies, providing direct access to language production. Still, even when there were direct means of recording the data, for instance through transcriptions, this was mostly limited to an extremely small fraction of the full range of language experiences. Cultural and historical changes have made this endeavor progressively more feasible. Increasing literacy in the general population, and the evolution of printing techniques first caused a massive growth in the production and availability of written language. Then, the development of audio and video recording made it possible to extend data collection to spoken data and gestures. Finally, the digital revolution had such an influence on the development of linguistic resources that nowadays we cannot imagine a non-digital corpus. Digital technologies are helping to collect and store progressively larger amount of language production data. Communication networks have also made the dissemination of the resources much faster. In addition, the digital world has become a source of peculiar language data and investigating the language used in social media and the web is now a central topic of study (e.g., Herdağdelen and Marelli, 2017; Schwartz et al., 2013).

While this progress has had an obvious impact on the development of various, large corpora, we should not forget that the evolution of grammar and lexicography is also a result of the technological innovations that make the examination of language possible independently of space and time. It is no exaggeration to say that these changes have revolutionized the way language science is done.

The present section will focus on the linguistic resources that are prominently based on unelicited behavior. Most notably, we will focus on corpora, lexical databases, and dictionaries and grammars.

3.1 Corpora

A corpus can be defined as a collection or sample of language events that are related to each other in one or more aspects. For example, the events can have the same source (e.g. newspaper writings, books, dialogue, etc.) or modality (e.g. written text, speech, gestures, video-recordings).

As mentioned earlier, corpus is now mostly used as synonym for digital corpus. However, this relatively recent trend can be traced back to the 1950s, with Padre Busa's "Index Thomisticus", an annotated and lemmatized corpus of the works by Thomas Aquinas. Another milestone in modern corpus linguistics came with the publication of "A Computational Analysis of Present-Day American English" (Kučera and Francis 1967), also known as the Brown corpus. This resource is still quite popular in many domains, notwithstanding its now well-known shortcomings (see below). Today, the size of these pioneering collections looks extremely limited. During the last two decades, we have seen a massive increase in the average corpus size, with modern corpora often containing billions of tokens. This rapid growth in the size of corpora is strictly related to the increasingly stronger association between computational linguistics and the web, that represents a massive, always-growing, and easy-to-harvest source of language data.

One result of this is that modern corpora will no longer be considered as static but as dynamic sources, where content is added on a real-time basis. One example of this is the NOW news corpus (Davies 2013), which currently contains 4.5 billion words and grows at a rate of nearly 6 million words each day. In other words, the modern conception of corpus as a very large digital collection of language material is bound to be superseded by the conception of a corpus as a stream.

The digital revolution also had profound repercussions on the treatment and processing of corpora. Not only has digitization made text processing much faster, it also has increased the synergy between corpus linguistics and resources from other domains. For instance, it has become trivial to annotate a text corpus with any information about a word found in dictionaries or other lexical databases, thanks to tools from natural language processing (e.g. Part-of-Speech taggers, lemmatizers, and parsers). However, while these resources have made corpus annotation easier, they have also brought with them an unavoidable imprecision in the annotation itself. No automatic annotation is perfect, and formal evaluation in this respect is only reliable to a certain extent: the state-of-the-art of a given method depends on a comparison with a gold standard which may have an obscure origin, or may not fit well the specific purpose of a researcher. The application of NLP tools in the development of the corpus can have a massive influence on the corpus itself and on the research that is being done using the corpus. This warning should not be forgotten or underestimated: the influence of computational methods on linguistic resources is so profound that it quickly becomes impossible to disentangle effects of resources from effects of computational methods. From the moment that the behavior in a corpus is annotated using an automated method, the corpus as a linguistic resource becomes tainted by previous linguistic resources and taints subsequent resources. And from the moment a computational method is trained using corpus data, the subsequent application of the method to other data becomes tainted by the initial corpus data. These loops of cross-fertilization characterize the picture of language resources that we are drawing in the present chapter.

Corpora represent an ideal case study for the complex dynamics in the resource ecosystem. There are mutual influences between different corpora and between corpora and other resource types. Modern corpora also lead to difficulties when trying to pigeonhole resources into strict taxonomies. Strictly speaking, a corpus is not necessarily a collection of samples of *unelicited behavior*. For instance, when behavior is recorded at the scientist's request, this request itself can influence the behavior, which should therefore be called partially elicited. While in its formal aspects the behavior looks like unelicited behavior (e.g. unrestricted speech), researchers need to be aware of the ways in which the behavior may conform to the participants' expectations of the requirements of their behavior. A typical example in this respect is the CHILDES project (MacWhinney 2000), which contains many records of spontaneous mother-child interactions in a controlled environment, at the researcher's request. Related to CHILDES is the TalkBank project (MacWhinney 2007), a varied collection of resources, ranging from structured elicitation to free discourse data from typical and disordered populations. In language research, many corpora walk the fine line between elicited and unelicited behavior.

3.2 Lexical databases

Entangled with corpora and computational methods in the resource ecosystem, we find lexical databases: collections of words that have been associated with one or more word properties. The properties are often derived from corpora, but can also be derived from experimental data, or other resources. Lexical databases can span from relatively simple resources, such as frequency norms, to data obtained through complex computational systems, such as automatically-obtained word meaning relations. In one of the typical loops of the resource ecosystem, lexical databases can also influence corpora, when they are used as a means for corpus annotation.

Frequency norms, or word occurrence counts, are the most typical example of a lexical database. Good frequency norms require high quality corpora, both in terms of size and source, and technologies to quickly process textual data. One of the first lexical databases containing word counts was developed as an educational resource. In the 1920s, Thorndike and Lorge started counting words occurring in magazines, newspapers and other contemporary sources with the express aim of providing a resource by which educators could select words for teaching materials. Their first publication was "A Teacher's word book of twenty thousand words" in 1931, followed by the thirty-thousand word version in 1944 (Thorndike and Lorge, 1944). This resource was almost immediately appropriated for scientific use most notably when Howes and Solomon (1951) published their seminal study on the effect of word frequency on word identification speed. Like the Thorndike-Lorge norms, many word frequency lists developed in the 20th century were distributed in book form. Although some older frequency resources are still available in book form, one of the consequences of larger corpora is that word frequency lists also grow. While it does not take more space to increase the counter for a word that has already been encountered, each new word that is discovered requires extra space. As a result, the adoption of better frequency norms based on larger corpora was crucially dependent on the adoption of a digital approach and today's massive corpora have led to word frequency resources that are only digitally available. Digital storage has also made it possible to distribute frequencies for *n-grams* (sequences of *n* successive words). Although a text of 1000 words has 1000 single words and 999 bigram tokens, the bigrams are far less likely to occur multiple times than single words and therefore lists of n-grams are much larger. For instance, the SUBTLEX-UK word frequency list (van Heuven et al. 2014) contains counts for nearly 350,000 word and nearly six times as many bigrams. Besides word frequencies, other simple count measures include document and page counts, that form the basis for measures of diversity or dispersion. More specialized or rarely-used count measures are often computed when needed, rather than disseminated with the lexical database.

The influence of frequency norms on other resources is remarkable, especially in the resources based on unelicited behavior. Count data is often used as information in lexicographic work. For instance, the decision whether to include a word in a dictionary can be based on its frequency in recent texts.

Likewise, the decision to remove a word from a practical rather than historical dictionary can be made on the basis a very low occurrence in contemporary word counts. Resources based on elicited behavior can also be affected by considerations related to lexical frequencies. In psycholinguistics, for instance, it is well known that word frequency has a large influence on language processing tasks. When resources such as stimulus lists are constructed, they often use frequency data as a guide to decide whether to include or exclude stimuli.

Counts can also act as the building block for more complex resources that aim at capturing higher-level linguistic information. For example, matrices that encode how often words are found together in a sentence or how often words are found in each document in a corpus form the basis of *vector space modelling*. These matrices, in which each word is represented by a series of numbers (vectors), can be processed through mathematical techniques in order to derive convenient data-driven representations of word meanings. This approach to semantics rests on the distributional hypothesis, stating that the meaning of a word can be approximated by the contexts in which that very word appears (Harris 1957), a general idea which traces back to philosophical proposals that are exemplified in Wittgenstein's works. The development of computational vector space modelling is relatively recent and makes use of such techniques as Latent Semantic Analysis (Landauer and Dumais 1997), Hyperspace Analogue to Language (Lund and Burgess 1996), and Latent Dirichlet Allocation (Blei et al. 2003). In such systems, semantic similarity is modelled in geometrical terms: since co-occurrence counts can be taken as coordinates in a high-dimensional space, the closer two vectors are, the more similar the corresponding word meanings will be. This is a direct consequence of the distributional hypothesis: words with similar meanings will often be found with the same surrounding words, leading to similar co-occurrence vectors. The approach was proven successful in capturing human intuitions concerning word meanings, and was then used as a way to automatically obtain semantic information in a number of domains, such as estimation of semantic relatedness and feature extraction. The approach is also used extensively in more applied natural language processing applications.

Psycholinguists often use the output of a distributional model as a resource for abstract semantic word representations. Two notably easy-to-access resources which, among other things, allow researchers to get distances between different semantic vectors are the LSA website (http://lsa.colorado.edu) and Snaut (Mandera, Keuleers, and Brysbaert 2017; available at http://meshugga.ugent.be/snaut/). More generally, there are a number of programming libraries available to build semantic vectors from a given corpus and to manipulate these semantic vector spaces, such as word2vec (Mikolov et al. 2013),

Dissect (Dinu, The Pham and Baroni 2013), Gensim (Řehůřek and Sojka 2011), and Tensorflow (Abadi et al. 2016).

While these techniques usually take unelicited behavior as their input, they are in fact completely agnostic to the origin of the co-occurrence data. For instance, Andrews, Vinson, and Vigliocco (2009) developed a multimodal distributional model that combines text-based data and human-generated experiential information, and De Deyne, Verheyen, and Storms (2015) have developed systems based on relatedness judgements. Moreover, in principle the techniques can work on any input modality, so that gesture-based models, sounds, and images can also be processed in similar ways.

It is however evident that quantitative representations for words, whether they are simple word frequencies or more complex estimates, are greatly influenced by the corpora that they are based on. In a very broad sense, the "world" that is captured by the corpus will also transpire in the measures induced from it: you can take the word out of the corpus but you can't take the corpus out of the word representation. Indeed, Louwerse and Zwaan (2009) have shown that the precision of text-based geographical estimates is associated with the physical distance between the text source and the considered place: the NY Times is better suited at estimating the location of East-Coast cities, and the LA Times is better suited at estimating the location of West-Coast cities. As a consequence, quantitative representations can not be regarded as unbiased samples of behavior, but should rather be always interpreted with their provenance in mind.

Lexical databases can also encode non-quantitative properties of words. A prominent example is WordNet (Miller et al. 1990), a large database that has been extremely influential in both cognitive science and computational linguistics. WordNet can serve as a collection of word senses, listing all possible meanings that a word can denote. In addition, WordNet provides information about synsets (groups of word that are pure synonyms), as well as different types of semantic relations between words (e.g. oak is a hyponym of tree). In the context of the resource ecosystem, Wordnet is a very strange beast. While it has all the characteristics of a lexical database, it is also extremely close to being a dictionary and a thesaurus (see below). Moreover, it is developed with an explicit reference to cognitive models of human semantic memory, making it a good candidate for what we called linguistic-intuition resources: in WordNet, words can be seen as self-administered stimuli for which experts provide their educated opinion. Additionally, even if such a claim was not advanced by its proponents, in computational linguistics WordNet is often considered an ontology, that is, a resource encoding the types, properties, and interrelationships of entities in the world.

WordNet can be taken as a further example of the entanglement between the components of the resource ecosystem. It results from the combination of several techniques used for resource development and illustrates the weak boundaries of different resource types when a rigid resource taxonomy is used. Practically, WordNet is often used as data source for techniques that are in turn at the basis of the development of other resources. Most notably, WordNet is a popular resource for the estimation of word meaning similarity, making it a primary influence on other lexical databases.

3.3 Dictionaries and grammars

The goal of recording vocabulary is very old. Dictionaries certainly predate the dramatic amounts of recorded language behavior that is available today. Lexicographic work is traditionally the result of observing *unelicited behavior*. However, the resource ecosystem reveals a more complex picture. An essential step in any lexicographic enterprise consists of listing words in a language, which may also be based on the examination of recorded behavior with the aim of discovering new word types. This means that, in the massively inter-influencing resource system, dictionaries and grammars are largely influenced by corpora. In the late 20th century, dictionary makers such as Collins started building corpora with the explicit aim of identifying new words and informing dictionary development (Sinclair 1987).

Development of dictionaries is almost always driven by other dictionaries and grammars, as they are almost never written without support from earlier resources of the same type. It can be argued that while *listing* the words is based mostly on unelicited behavior, every other aspect of lexicography mostly consists of self-elicited behavior equivalent to the linguistic intuitions we discussed earlier (for instance: definitions, lexical and ontological relationships), making the boundaries between dictionaries and other resources even fuzzier.

Dictionaries and other word lists are extremely influential as a linguistic resource. Because they are a reflection and a source of authority on the use and meaning of words, they modulate any type of human linguistic behavior, either elicited or unelicited. It could be said that of all linguistic resources, dictionaries influence language behavior the most. We could even ask the question whether language behavior influences dictionaries more than dictionaries influence the behavior itself.

Next to the recording of words, the recording of how words are used in different contexts and how they combine with each other in sentences (i.e. grammar) is one of the earliest linguistic endeavors. Rather than exhaustively listing, which is the goal of a dictionary, the goal of a descriptive grammar is to compress knowledge. Concepts like conjugation, inflection, syntactic classes, sentences and clauses allow for substituting lists of individual instances for a description of rules and exceptions. Like dictionaries, grammars influence behavior from the moment they exist and the more authority they receive, the more they influence the behavior.

For the reasons described above, relying on other resources for the construction of dictionaries and grammars leads to a cycle of self-reinforcement of prescriptive language behavior. This is not only the result of the obvious influence of pre-existing dictionaries, but also of the corpora themselves. It is in fact important to note that unelicited behavior is not equivalent to non-scripted behavior. Recorded behavior is very much biased to highly edited and scripted production. Written behavior is almost never captured before it has gone through several stages of editing (indeed, there are some specific corpora dealing with capturing the editing process itself, for instance in research on journalism). Spoken language production, especially the examples that can be found in corpora, is neither necessarily unscripted (e.g. films and tv programs in subtitle corpora). As a result, a large part of the language behavior considered in lexicography is already implicitly adherent to the prescriptive rules imposed by dictionaries and grammars.

This does not mean that all linguistic behavior is influenced by prescriptive resources. However, we should be aware that where editing and scripting are involved, the prescriptive influence is probably strong. This tendency becomes even more pronounced as the editing phase in language production becomes more and more driven by artificial software that directly interfaces with the resources. Consider how spellcheck and grammar check determine our online behavior in written production or how personalized dialogue systems (such as Apple Siri, Amazon Echo, or Google Home) recognize some commands while they do not recognize others. As a consequence, the connection between prescriptive sources and production get stronger with time, with technological innovation as its catalyst. On the other hand, it is also true that the massive availability of unelicited behavior makes the inclusion of new words or constructions more probable.

4 Cognitive models and linguistic theories: Feedback at the core

Up to this point, we have tried to frame resources in an atheoretical way. However, as Figure 1 reveals, theories and models are at the center of our formalization. They occupy the box with the largest number of connections, with outgoing arrows showing that theories heavily influence resource development and incoming arrows representing how theories are developed on the basis of the available resources.

This entanglement has far reaching implications for the epistemological status of resources and cognitive models or linguistic theories. It cannot be said that any of them are independent and contain an objective truth. The only exception to this would be the observation of unelicited behavior in a group of language users who have no concept of linguistic resources. In other words, when language is used in a context without any resource, its behavior can be regarded as unbiased. On the other extreme, there are such languages as modern English, where it has become impossible to disentangle the language behavior from the influence of the resources. Child language is no exception to this as it is completely contingent on the language of adults, which is itself a product of interaction between resources and behavior.

In this light, it is important to understand that any cognitive model or linguistic theory that is informed by such a *cultivated and resource-driven* language must acknowledge this fact and its consequences. One of the more important consequences is that certain aspects of language behavior may only arise in resource driven languages and not in language in its "ideal" pre-resource state. In other words, neither the language behavior nor the language faculty that we can observe today should be regarded as emerging from the simple interaction between humans endowed with the capacity for speech. Instead, we should always keep in mind that resources shape language, and that there is a constant feedback between language behavior and its resources. This relation will only become more pronounced as technological innovations become more related to the production of language. As a simple example, predictive text input, which is of course based on algorithms that interface with linguistic resources, influences language behavior at the exact moment it takes place. Technologies like grammar and spell-checking are also instances of the extreme entanglement between resources and language production.

The influence that linguistic theories have on resources derived from elicited behavior must also be acknowledged. However, this is perhaps less severe because it is epistemologically charted territory. It can suffice to classify this under experimenter bias and remedies to this bias are well known: responses should be elicited in double blind conditions so as to eliminate both experimenter bias and expectation bias. Scientists who wish to base their theories on their own intuitions should be aware of biases and strive to eliminate them or acknowledge that the subject under study is a language that is not only cultivated by prescriptive resources, but also by constraints on what the linguistic theory allows for.

References

Abadi, Martín, Paul Barham, Jianmin Chen, Zhifeng Chen, Andy Davis, Jeffrey Dean, Matthieu Devin, Sanjay Ghemawat, Geoffrey Irving & Michael Isard. 2016. Tensorflow: A system for large-scale machine learning. *12th USENIX Symposium on Operating Systems Design and Implementation (OSDI 16)*. 265–283.

Adelman, James S., Rebecca L. Johnson, Samantha F. McCormick, Meredith McKague, Sachiko Kinoshita, Jeffrey S. Bowers, Jason R. Perry, et al. 2014. A behavioral database for masked form priming. *Behavior Research Methods* 46 (4). 1052–1067. doi:10.3758/s13428-013-0442-y.

Aguasvivas, Jose Armando, Manuel Carreiras, Marc Brysbaert, Paweł Mandera, Emmanuel Keuleers & Jon Andoni Duñabeitia. 2018. SPALEX: A Spanish Lexical Decision Database From a Massive Online Data Collection. *Frontiers in Psychology* 9. doi:10.3389/fpsyg.2018.02156.

Andrews, Mark, Gabriella Vigliocco & David Vinson. 2009. Integrating experiential and distributional data to learn semantic representations. *Psychological Review* 116(3). 463–498.

Balota, David A., Andrew J. Aschenbrenner & Melvin J. Yap. 2013. Additive effects of word frequency and stimulus quality: The influence of trial history and data transformations. *Journal of Experimental Psychology: Learning, Memory, and Cognition* 39 (5). 1563–1571. doi:10.1037/a0032186.

Balota, David A., Michael J. Cortese, Susan D. Sergent-Marshall, Daniel H. Spieler & Melvin J. Yap. 2004. Visual Word Recognition of Single-Syllable Words. *Journal of Experimental Psychology: General* 133 (2). 283–316. doi:10.1037/0096-3445.133.2.283.

Balota, David A., Melvin J. Yap, Keith A. Hutchison, Michael J. Cortese, Brett Kessler, Bjorn Loftis, James H. Neely, Douglas L. Nelson, Greg B. Simpson & Rebecca Treiman. 2007. The English lexicon project. *Behavior Research Methods* 39(3). 445–459.

Bard, Ellen Gurman, Dan Robertson & Antonella Sorace. 1996. Magnitude estimation of linguistic acceptability. *Language* 72(1). 32–68.

Blei, David M., Andrew Y. Ng & Michael I. Jordan. 2003. Latent Dirichlet allocation. *Journal of Machine Learning Research* 3(Jan). 993–1022.

Brysbaert, Marc, Paweł Mandera, Samantha F. McCormick & Emmanuel Keuleers. In press. Word prevalence norms for 62,000 English lemmas. *Behavior Research Methods*.

Brysbaert, Marc, Michaël Stevens, Paweł Mandera & Emmanuel Keuleers. 2016. The impact of word prevalence on lexical decision times: Evidence from the Dutch Lexicon Project 2. *Journal of Experimental Psychology: Human Perception and Performance* 42 (3). 441–458. doi:10.1037/xhp0000159.

Brysbaert, Marc, Amy Beth Warriner & Victor Kuperman. 2014. Concreteness ratings for 40 thousand generally known English word lemmas. *Behavior Research Methods* 46(3). 904–911.

Coltheart, Max. 1981. The MRC psycholinguistic database. *The Quarterly Journal of Experimental Psychology Section A* 33(4). 497–505. doi:10.1080/14640748108400805.

Cop, Uschi, Nicolas Dirix, Denis Drieghe & Wouter Duyck. 2017. Presenting GECO: An eyetracking corpus of monolingual and bilingual sentence reading. *Behavior Research Methods* 49 (2). 602–615.

Cortese, Michael J., Maya M. Khanna & Sarah Hacker. 2010. Recognition memory for 2,578 monosyllabic words. *Memory* 18 (6). 595–609.

Cortese, Michael J., Daniel P. McCarty & Jocelyn Schock. 2015. A mega recognition memory study of 2897 disyllabic words. *The Quarterly Journal of Experimental Psychology* 68 (8). 1489–1501. doi:10.1080/17470218.2014.945096.

Davies, Mark. 2013. Corpus of News on the Web (NOW): 3+ billion words from 20 countries, updated every day. *URL* http://corpus.byu.edu/now.

De Deyne, Simon, Steven Verheyen & Gert Storms. 2015. The role of corpus size and syntax in deriving lexico-semantic representations for a wide range of concepts. *The Quarterly Journal of Experimental Psychology* 68 (8). 1643–1664. doi:10.1080/17470218.2014.994098.

Dinu, Georgiana, Nghia The Pham & Marco Baroni. 2013. DISSECT – DIStributional SEmantics Composition Toolkit. *Proceedings of the 51st Annual Meeting of the Association for Computational Linguistics: System Demonstrations*, 31–36.

Dufau, Stephane, Jon Andoni Duñabeitia, Carmen Moret-Tatay, Aileen McGonigal, David Peeters, F.-Xavier Alario, David A. Balota, et al. 2011. Smart Phone, Smart Science: How the Use of Smartphones Can Revolutionize Research in Cognitive Science. (Ed.) Kenji Hashimoto. *PLoS ONE* 6 (9).e24974. doi:10.1371/journal.pone.0024974.

Duyck, Wouter, Timothy Desmet, Lieven PC Verbeke & Marc Brysbaert. 2004. WordGen: A tool for word selection and nonword generation in Dutch, English, German, and French. *Behavior Research Methods, Instruments, & Computers* 36 (3). 488–499.

Ernestus, Mirjam & Anne Cutler. 2015. BALDEY: A database of auditory lexical decisions. *The Quarterly Journal of Experimental Psychology* 68(8). 1469–1488. doi:10.1080/17470218.2014.984730.

Faroqi-Shah, Yasmeen. 2016. The Rise of Big Data in Neurorehabilitation. *Seminars in Speech and Language* 37(01). 003–009. doi:10.1055/s-0036-1572385.

Ferrand, Ludovic, Boris New, Marc Brysbaert, Emmanuel Keuleers, Patrick Bonin, Alain Méot, Maria Augustinova & Christophe Pallier. 2010. The French Lexicon Project: Lexical decision data for 38,840 French words and 38,840 pseudowords. *Behavior Research Methods* 42(2). 488–496.

Haagen, C. Hess. 1949. Synonymity, vividness, familiarity, and association value ratings of 400 pairs of common adjectives. *Journal of Psychology* 27 (2). 453–463.

Harris, Zellig S. 1957. Co-occurrence and transformation in linguistic structure. *Language* 33 (3). 283–340.

Herdağdelen, Amaç & Marco Marelli. 2017. Social media and language processing: How Facebook and Twitter provide the best frequency estimates for studying word recognition. *Cognitive Science* 41 (4). 976–995.

Heuven, Walter J. B. van, Pawel Mandera, Emmanuel Keuleers & Marc Brysbaert. 2014. SUBTLEX-UK: A new and improved word frequency database for British English. *The Quarterly Journal of Experimental Psychology* 67 (6). 1176–1190. doi:10.1080/17470218.2013.850521.

Howes, Davis H. & Richard L. Solomon. 1951. Visual duration threshold as a function of word-probability. *Journal of Experimental Psychology* 41 (6). 401.

Hutchison, Keith A., David A. Balota, James H. Neely, Michael J. Cortese, Emily R. Cohen-Shikora, Chi-Shing Tse, Melvin J. Yap, Jesse J. Bengson, Dale Niemeyer & Erin Buchanan. 2013. The semantic priming project. *Behavior Research Methods* 45 (4). 1099–1114. doi:10.3758/s13428-012-0304-z.

Keuleers, Emmanuel & David A. Balota. 2015. Megastudies, crowdsourcing, and large datasets in psycholinguistics: An overview of recent developments. *The Quarterly Journal of Experimental Psychology* 68 (8). 1457–1468. doi:10.1080/17470218.2015.1051065.

Keuleers, Emmanuel & Marc Brysbaert. 2010. Wuggy: A multilingual pseudoword generator. *Behavior Research Methods* 42 (3). 627–633. doi:10.3758/BRM.42.3.627.

Keuleers, Emmanuel, Kevin Diependaele & Marc Brysbaert. 2010. Practice Effects in Large-Scale Visual Word Recognition Studies: A Lexical Decision Study on 14,000 Dutch Mono- and Disyllabic Words and Nonwords. *Frontiers in Psychology* 1. doi:10.3389/fpsyg.2010.00174.

Keuleers, Emmanuel, Paula Lacey, Kathleen Rastle & Marc Brysbaert. 2012. The British Lexicon Project: Lexical decision data for 28,730 monosyllabic and disyllabic English words. *Behavior Research Methods* 44 (1). 287–304. doi:10.3758/s13428-011-0118-4.

Keuleers, Emmanuel, Michaël Stevens, Paweł Mandera & Marc Brysbaert. 2015. Word knowledge in the crowd: Measuring vocabulary size and word prevalence in a massive online experiment. *The Quarterly Journal of Experimental Psychology* 68 (8). 1665–1692. doi:10.1080/17470218.2015.1022560.

Kučera, Henry & Nelson Francis. 1967. *Computational analysis of present-day American English*. Providence: R.I.: Brown University Press.

Kuperman, Victor. 2015. Virtual experiments in megastudies: A case study of language and emotion. *The Quarterly Journal of Experimental Psychology* 68 (8). 1693–1710. doi:10.1080/17470218.2014.989865.

Kuperman, Victor, Hans Stadthagen-Gonzalez & Marc Brysbaert. 2012. Age-of-acquisition ratings for 30,000 English words. *Behavior Research Methods* 44 (4). 978–990.

Landauer, Thomas K. & Susan T. Dumais. 1997. A solution to Plato's problem: The latent semantic analysis theory of acquisition, induction, and representation of knowledge. *Psychological Review* 104 (2). 211–240.

Louwerse, Max M. & Rolf A. Zwaan. 2009. Language encodes geographical information. *Cognitive Science* 33 (1). 51–73.

Lund, Kevin & Curt Burgess. 1996. Producing high-dimensional semantic spaces from lexical co-occurrence. *Behavior Research Methods, Instruments, & Computers* 28 (2). 203–208.

Lynott, Dermot & Louise Connell. 2009. Modality exclusivity norms for 423 object properties. *Behavior Research Methods* 41 (2). 558–564.

Lynott, Dermot & Louise Connell. 2013. Modality exclusivity norms for 400 nouns. The relationship between perceptual experience and surface word form. *Behavior research methods* 45 (2). 516–526. doi:10.3758/s13428-012-0267-0.

MacWhinney, Brian. 2000. *The CHILDES Project: The Database*. Vol. 2. Mahwah, NJ: Lawrence Erlbaum Associates.

MacWhinney, Brian. 2007. The Talkbank Project. In Joan C. Beal, Karen P. Corrigan & Hermann L. Moisl (eds.), *Creating and Digitizing Language Corpora*, 163–180. London: Palgrave Macmillan UK. doi:10.1057/9780230223936_7.

Mandera, Paweł, Emmanuel Keuleers & Marc Brysbaert. 2017. Explaining human performance in psycholinguistic tasks with models of semantic similarity based on prediction and counting: A review and empirical validation. *Journal of Memory and Language* 92. 57–78.

McRae, Ken, George S. Cree, Mark S. Seidenberg & Chris McNorgan. 2005. Semantic feature production norms for a large set of living and nonliving things. *Behavior Research Methods* 37 (4). 547–559.

Mikolov, Tomas, Kai Chen, Greg Corrado & Jeffrey Dean. 2013. Efficient estimation of word representations in vector space. *arXiv preprint arXiv:1301.3781*.

Miller, George A., Richard Beckwith, Christiane Fellbaum, Derek Gross & Katherine J. Miller. 1990. Introduction to WordNet: An on-line lexical database. *International Journal of Lexicography* 3 (4). 235–244.

Mirman, Daniel, Ted J. Strauss, Adelyn Brecher, Grant M. Walker, Paula Sobel, Gary S. Dell & Myrna F. Schwartz. 2010. A large, searchable, web-based database of aphasic performance on picture naming and other tests of cognitive function. *Cognitive Neuropsychology* 27 (6). 495–504. doi:10.1080/02643294.2011.574112.

Nusbaum, Howard C., David B. Pisoni & Christopher K. Davis. 1984. Sizing up the Hoosier mental lexicon: Measuring the familiarity of 20,000 words. *Research on Speech Perception Progress Report* 10 (10). 357–376.

Paivio, Allan, John C. Yuille & Stephen A. Madigan. 1968. Concreteness, imagery, and meaningfulness values for 925 nouns. *Journal of Experimental Psychology* 76 (1, part 2). 1–25.

Rastle, Kathleen, Jonathan Harrington & Max Coltheart. 2002. 358,534 nonwords: The ARC nonword database. *The Quarterly Journal of Experimental Psychology: Section A* 55 (4). 1339–1362.

Řehůřek, Radim & Petr Sojka. 2011. Gensim—Statistical Semantics in Python. http://www.fi.muni.cz/usr/sojka/posters/rehurek-sojka-scipy2011.pdf (30 May, 2017).

Schwartz, H. Andrew, Johannes C. Eichstaedt, Margaret L. Kern, Lukasz Dziurzynski, Stephanie M. Ramones, Megha Agrawal, Achal Shah, Michal Kosinski, David Stillwell & Martin EP Seligman. 2013. Personality, gender, and age in the language of social media: The open-vocabulary approach. *PloS One* 8 (9). e73791.

Seidenberg, Mark S. & G. S. Waters. 1989. Word recognition and naming: A mega study. *Bulletin of the Psychonomic Society* 27. 489.

Sinclair, John M. 1987. *Looking Up: An Account of the COBUILD Project in Lexical Computing and the Development of the Collins COBUILD English Language Dictionary*. London: Collins ELT.

Spieler, Daniel H. & David A. Balota. 1997. Bringing computational models of word naming down to the item level. *Psychological Science* 411–416.

Spieler, Daniel H. & David A. Balota. 2000. Factors influencing word naming in younger and older adults. *Psychology and Aging* 15 (2). 225–231. doi:10.1037//0882-7974.15.2.225.

Thorndike, Edward L. & Irving Lorge. 1931. *A teacher's word book of twenty thousand words*. New York: Teachers College, Columbia Unversity.

Thorndike, Edward L. & Irving Lorge. 1944. *The teacher's word book of 30,000 words*. New York: Teachers College Press.

Treiman, Rebecca, John Mullennix, Ranka Bijeljac-Babic & E. Daylene Richmond-Welty. 1995. The special role of rimes in the description, use, and acquisition of English orthography. *Journal of Experimental Psychology: General* 124 (2). 107.

Warriner, Amy Beth, Victor Kuperman & Marc Brysbaert. 2013. Norms of valence, arousal, and dominance for 13,915 English lemmas. *Behavior Research Methods* 45 (4). 1191–1207. doi:10.3758/s13428-012-0314-x.

Westbury, Chris, Geoff Hollis & Cyrus Shaoul. 2007. LINGUA: the language-independent neighbourhood generator of the University of Alberta. *The Mental Lexicon* 2 (2). 271–284.

Yap, Melvin J., Susan J. Rickard Liow, Sajlia Binte Jalil & Siti Syuhada Binte Faizal. 2010. The Malay Lexicon Project: A database of lexical statistics for 9,592 words. *Behavior Research Methods* 42 (4). 992–1003. doi:10.3758/BRM.42.4.992.

Part 2: **Topical issues**

Sabine Arndt-Lappe and Mirjam Ernestus
Morpho-phonological alternations: The role of lexical storage

Abstract: This chapter investigates how morphologically complex words contribute to our knowledge of what is stored in the mental lexicon. We first present the assumptions about lexical storage in the linguistic and psycholinguistic literature. We then discuss several morpho-phonological alternations, arguing that they contribute to the growing evidence for the storage of regular morphologically complex words, with more detail than is usually assumed to form the basis of traditional phonological rules. The key evidence comes from the productivity profiles of different kinds of alternations, from effects of the words' relative frequencies and of lexical neighborhoods, and from language change. We argue that the data can only be well accounted for by models that assign an important role to the storage of all words, with or without additional morpho-phonological rules, and discuss a variety of these models.

Keywords: morpho-phonology, sound alternations, lexical storage, lexical computation, (psycho-)linguistic models, lexical frequency, lexical neighbors

1 Introduction

One of the key questions of (psycho)linguistics concerns the contents of the mental lexicon: which words are stored in the mental lexicon, with what types of information? Chomsky and Halle (e.g. 1968) and early psycholinguistic models (e.g. Pinker 1991; Clahsen 1999; Taft 2004) assume that only those words and word forms are stored that cannot be computed on the basis of regular morphological, phonological, and semantic rules. The lexicon contains all monomorphemic words and all morphologically complex words that are irregular in their meaning, morphology, or phonology (cf. e.g. Di Sciullo and Williams' famous description of the lexicon as a "collection of the lawless", Di Sciullo and Williams 1987: 4). Words that are not stored in the mental lexicon are assumed to be computed every time they are processed by the language user. Some more recent linguistic and psycholinguistic work assumes, instead, that at least some regular morphologically complex words are lexically stored, with phonologically

---
Sabine Arndt-Lappe, Trier University
Mirjam Ernestus, Radboud University, Nijmegen

completely specified phonemes (e.g. Bybee 1988; Baayen, Dijkstra, and Schreuder 1997; Blevins 2003). This assumption finds some support in the results of psycholinguistic experiments, but the evidence does not seem conclusive.

The aim of this chapter is to discuss data from morpho-phonological alternations that bear on the issue of the storage of morphologically complex words. With the term morpho-phonological alternations, we refer to phonological differences between morphologically complex words and their bases, and between morphologically complex words sharing their affixes. In Lexical Phonology, these alternations are typically explained by phonological rules applying to the output of morphological rules. For example, English regular past-tense forms are created by affixation of /d/, which is followed by the phonological rules of voice assimilation and vowel epenthesis changing /d/ into [t] after voiceless obstruents (as in *walked*) or into [ɪd] after /t/ and /d/ (as in *wanted*). Conversely, morphological rules may also apply after phonological rules. A typical example is stress preservation in English derived words with so-called stress-preserving affixes. For example, main stress on the preantepenultimate syllable in a word like *móderately* can be explained if we assume that stress rules apply (assigning stress to the base adjective, *móderate*) before affixation of *-ly*. Stress of *móderate* is thus preserved in *móderately*. In addition to these sound alternations, which are accounted for by phonological rules in Lexical Phonology, we will consider alternations that are less productive and alternations where it is less clear what the phonological rule should look like (e.g. the irregular past tense in English). We will include these alternations as well because we do not want the phenomena of interest to be determined by a theory that is not accepted by all researchers. Moreover, we believe that also these alternations provide valuable insights into the processing of morpho-phonological alternations in general.

The question of whether or not regular complex words are stored is highly relevant for both theories of processing and theories of grammar: For processing, storage of regular complex words may mean that such words may not be computed every time they are processed by the language user. For both grammatical and processing theories, the possibility that regular complex words may be stored raises the question of whether and in how far stored forms bear on the grammatical rules producing morpho-phonological alternations.

This chapter contains four sections. We start with a description of what we know about the storage of morphologically complex forms, mostly from the psycholinguistic literature on morphological and phonological processing (Section 2). We discuss several morpho-phonological alternations and see what we can learn from these alternations about the storage of complex forms (Section 3). Both sections start from the simple assumption that morpho-phonological alternations just result from the interleaving of morphological and phonological processes (rules or constraints). In a final step, we will evaluate this simple assumption in the light of the evidence for storage and discuss a typology of contemporary models in the light of the evidence (Section 4). The chapter ends with our conclusions (Section 5).

2 Lexical storage in the linguistic and psycholinguistic literature

As mentioned above, Chomsky and Halle (e.g., 1968) and early psycholinguistic models (e.g. Clahsen 1999; Pinker 1991; Taft 2004) assume that only those words and word forms are stored that cannot be computed on the basis of regular morphological rules. These theories thus assume substantial differences between, for instance, irregularly inflected forms, which are lexically stored, and regularly inflected forms, which are not. This assumption is supported by several studies showing substantial differences in the brain regions involved in the processing of regular and irregular inflected forms (e.g. Beretta et al. 2003; Newman et al. 2007). Whether these differences arise from the presence versus absence of these forms in the mental lexicon or from some other substantial differences, for instance in meaning, between regular and irregular verbs, is, however, an open question. Work by Tabak, Schreuder, and Baayen (2005), for instance, showed that irregularly and regularly inflected forms differ in their semantic properties (e.g., the auxiliary verb for the past participle) and in the information structure of their inflectional paradigms (e.g., inflectional entropy).

The assumption that fully regular complex words are not lexically stored is especially challenged by psycholinguistic experiments showing that the ease with which a language user processes a complex word is co-determined by this word's frequency of occurrence (e.g., Baayen, Dijkstra, and Schreuder 1997; Bowden et al. 2010; Meunier and Segui 1999; see also Fábregas and Penke 2020, this volume). Stemberger and MacWhinney (1986), for instance, showed that participants in psycholinguistic experiments produce fewer errors for high frequency than for low frequency English inflected word forms. Baayen et al. (2003) showed that Dutch regular plural nouns are recognized more quickly if they are of a higher frequency of occurrence. The authors interpret these frequency effects as evidence for storage because they show that language users must have stored these frequencies, which makes it plausible that these word forms are stored themselves as well.

Note that especially the comprehension data cannot be explained with the alternative assumption that the frequencies of the complex forms are stored with the stems, with each frequency determining the ease of application of a morphological rule for the given stem (cf. Brand and Ernestus 2018). Suppose that

English stems are specified for how often they are subject to the rule of English regular past-tense formation. If a past-tense form has to be recognized, the past-tense suffix has to be stripped off, which reverses the past-tense formation rule. The resulting stem can then be looked up in the mental lexicon. Once the stem has been identified, the frequency information for the past-tense formation will become available. It is unclear how this information can affect the recognition process since it becomes available only after this process has been completed.[1]

The early literature showing frequency effects for high frequency regular complex words concludes that at least the high frequency words are lexically stored. Gordon and Alegre (1999) claim that a word is stored if it occurs more often than six times per million word tokens. This claim raises the question of how a language user knows whether a word's frequency of occurrence is higher than this threshold. The language user can only know this if the frequencies of all words are stored. It is therefore more probable that language users store all words of the language, which is in line with the work by de Vaan (e.g. de Vaan, Schreuder, and Baayen 2007; de Vaan, Ernestus, and Schreuder 2011), showing that language users form memory traces even for neologisms.

The question of which morphologically complex words are stored in the mental lexicon is still open, however. Frequency effects do not always seem to be present (e.g., Bowden et al. 2010). Some research suggests that the presence of frequency effects is influenced by the type of morphological process, by whether the affix has one or more morphological functions (like *-er* in English, which may turn an adjective in its comparative and a verb into an agent noun), and by the productivity of the affix (e.g. Bertram, Schreuder, and Baayen 2000, and references therein). More research is necessary for obtaining a clearer picture of which words are stored in the mental lexicon.

Another important question about the mental lexicon is which characteristics of words are stored. The minimal assumption is that only unpredictable characteristics are lexically stored. Thus, words with regular stress patterns are stored without this stress pattern (e.g. Peperkamp and Dupoux 2002) and phonemes are stored in the form of bundles of unpredictable phonological features (e.g. Lahiri and Reetz 2002, 2010). Other researchers (e.g. Frisch, Pierrehumbert, and Broe 2004; Mitterer 2011; Norris and McQueen 2008) assume that words are stored in the form of representations consisting of fully specified phonemes (or allophones) and prosodic information (including stress pattern, tone melody

---

[1] There is also an approach (e.g. Baayen et al. 2011) in which what is stored with the form is not frequency itself but some weight measure that reflects (a) linguistic experience (i.e. frequency of occurrence) and (b) discriminability within the lexical distribution.

in tone languages).² These representations may thus contain information that is redundant, for instance, results of place assimilation (e.g. English *thank* is represented as /θæŋk/, although the place of articulation of the nasal is redundant given the place of articulation of the following tautosyllabic stop) and regular stress pattern.

This controversy has also been addressed with psycholinguistic experiments. Lahiri (e.g. Lahiri and Marslen-Wilson 1991; Eulitz and Lahiri 2004) has argued on the basis of many experiments that predictable phonological features (e.g. the feature [coronal]) are not specified in the mental lexicon. To give an example, Eulitz and Lahiri (2004) conducted a mismatch negativity experiment where German participants listened to sequences of phonologically unmarked vowels (e.g. [ø], which is coronal, but which is not specified for this feature, since this feature is unmarked) interrupted by marked vowels (e.g. [o], which is specified for bilabial because this is a marked feature), or vice versa. The researchers observed more enhanced and earlier mismatch negativities (MMNs) when the vowels in the sequence were phonologically marked and the deviant vowel was underlyingly unmarked than vice versa. The authors argue that this data pattern supports the Featurally Underspecified Lexicon model because this model predicts that the conflict between surface coronal ([ø]) and underlyingly marked bilabial (/o/) is larger than between surface bilabial ([o]) and underlyingly unspecified place of articulation ([ø]).

Gaskell (2001), among other researchers, claims, in contrast, that their own experimental results present evidence against underspecification. They argue that, if phonemes are lexically underspecified, a marked sound (e.g. /m/, which is specified for place of articulation because it is [labial]) should always be ambiguous between an interpretation as a phoneme with the marked phonological feature (/m/ in the example) and the phoneme with the unmarked feature (/n/ in the example), which matches all realizations of the feature. This appears only to be the case if the marked sound occurs in a segmental context where it may result from assimilation. For instance, the [m] in *a quick rum picks you up* is typically interpreted as being ambiguous between the underlying /m/ of *rum* and the assimilated /n/ of *run*. In contrast, the [m] in *a quick rum does you good* is always interpreted as an underlying /m/, because the [m] cannot result from place articulation. This shows that the question about which characteristics of a word are lexically stored is still open.

---

2 Exemplar-based models assume that every word is mentally represented by a cloud of tokens of that word, which are acoustically fully detailed (e.g. Johnson, 2004, Goldinger 1998). We will not separately consider these models but consider them jointly with the models assuming that words are stored with fully specified phonemes and prosodic information.

Finally, Baayen et al. (2011; cf. Pirelli et al. 2020, this volume and Plag and Balling 2020, this volume for discussion) even cast doubt on the assumption that frequency effects imply storage of morphologically complex words. They show that in a model based on naïve discriminative learning (NDL), the frequency of the complex word needs not be stored with its form, but can also be stored in the form of connection weights between bigrams of the word and the combination of the stem meaning and the affix meaning. Because the connection weights connect form aspects to meaning, the word's formal aspects are distributed in the lexicon, unlike in more traditional models, but are still present. For the purpose of the present discussion, we consider this difference with more traditional models as irrelevant. Furthermore, note that since most current work in NDL is based on bigrams or trigrams, the theory does not (yet) specify the nature of phonological form representations. We will therefore not further discuss Baayen et al.'s account in this chapter.

In conclusion, we see that the questions of which words are stored in the mental lexicon and with which phonological information are still open. This calls for different types of data, including data from morpho-phonological alternations.

3 Evidence from morpho-phonological alternations on lexical storage

We now discuss how morpho-phonological alternations may bear on the issue of lexical storage. Some of the phenomena that we focus on have also been described in Plag (2014). We first discuss the productivity of some alternations (Section 3.1). If the alternations result from phonological rules that obligatorily follow morphological rules, the alternations should be fully productive. We then discuss the role of the word's frequency of occurrence relative to the frequency of occurrence of its base (Section 3.2). If alternations result from phonological rules, this relative frequency should not co-determine whether an alternation occurs or not. More evidence for the hypothesis that regular morphologically complex words may be stored comes from some data on language change, to be discussed in Section 3.3. Finally, lexical neighbors of complex words seem to be another factor influencing morpho-phonological alternations (Section 3.4), which is also unexpected if morpho-phonological alternations result from rules.

3.1 Productivity

If alternations result from the interplay of regular morphological, phonological and phonetic rules, their application should be completely predictable. That is, the alternation should be fully productive when the constraints of the different processes are fulfilled. This, however, is not always the case.

A case in point is the alternation resulting from speech reduction. Words are often pronounced with fewer phonemes in casual speech than in careful speech. Many of the reduction patterns can be accounted for with simple phonological rules. For instance, in Dutch, schwa is often absent next to continuants (e.g., *vorige* /vɔrəxə/ 'preceding' pronounced as [vɔrxə]), coda /r/ is often absent after schwa and low vowels (e.g., *waarschijnlijk* /ʋarsxɛɪnlək/ 'probably' pronounced as [ʋasxɛɪnlək]), and /t/ is often absent after /s/ (e.g. *winstmarge* /ʋɪnstmɑrʒə/ 'profit margin' pronounced as [ʋɪnsmɑrʒə]; e.g., Ernestus 2000). However, several studies have shown that the probability of an affixal segment to be absent (or reduced) may be word specific. Keune et al. (2005), for instance, studied Dutch words ending in the productive suffix -*lijk* /lək/ in a corpus of spontaneous Dutch, and noticed that these words differ in how frequently their suffix is produced without one of its consonants. Some words seldom show consonant reduction (i.e., tend to be pronounced with [lək] or [lk]), some words show all possible pronunciation variants of the suffix (ranging from [lək] to [k]), while other words only show either little reduction ([lək] or [lk]) or massive reduction ([k]). Which words show which variation seems unpredictable. This suggests that these morphologically complex words have to be stored in the mental lexicon, with information about their pronunciation variation.

Another study, also focussing on Dutch, investigated the probability that the past-participle prefix *ge-* /xə/ was pronounced without schwa in a sentence production study (Hanique, Ernestus, and Schuppler 2013). They found that the prefix was more likely to be absent in words in which the past-participle has a higher frequency of occurrence. This strongly suggests that these past-participles, although they are completely regular in their form and meaning, must be lexically stored. Note that, as explained in Section 2, this implies that all past-participles must be stored. The authors also claimed that the absence of schwa was often the result of a categorical process because schwa presence and schwa duration shared only few predictors (and schwa absence thus did not result from schwa shortening). This is another indication that the reduced past-participles are lexically stored and do not result from on-line phonetic processes.

Bybee (1988) investigated the productivity of a vowel alternation in Spanish verbal paradigms. In these verbs, the stem contains a mid vowel if unstressed and a diphthong if the vowel is stressed (e.g. *empiézo* 'I begin' versus *empezámos* 'we begin'; *cuénto* 'I count' versus *contámos* 'we count'). The alternation occurs in a large number of verbs, but not in all verbs. Two studies have investigated whether the alternation is (semi)productive. Kernan and Blount (1966) presented native speakers of Mexican Spanish with pseudowords functioning as third person indicatives (e.g. *suécha*) and asked them to use the verb in a preterite context, where the diphthong is not stressed. All participants created *suechó* with an unstressed diphthong, instead of *sochó*, which would have been the expected outcome if the morpho-phonological alternation was productive. Bybee and Brewer (1980) repeated the experiment but now presented participants not only with the third person indicative of each pseudoverb (e.g. *suécha*) but also with the infinitive (e.g., *sochár*), in which the stem vowel was unstressed. Together the two forms presented showed the morpho-phonological alternation. In approximately 75% of trials, participants produced the preterite form again with an unstressed diphthong, which shows that the morpho-phonological alternation is hardly productive, but restricted to a set of real verbs. In other words, these data suggest that the morpho-phonological alternation does not result from rule application but from the lexical storage of the forms (or at least of two pronunciation variants of the stems).

A morpho-phonological vowel alternation that is also constrained to a specific set of verbs but that nevertheless has been claimed to show some productivity is vowel alternation in irregular English verbs. Bybee and Moder (1983), Prasada and Pinker (1993), and Albright and Hayes (2003), for instance, famously showed that English native speakers produce irregular past tenses for pseudoverbs. However, they did not do so categorically – for example, the highest percentage of irregularly inflected nonce verbs in Prasada and Pinker's study was about 31%, among the group of nonce verbs that showed the highest degree of similarity to real irregularly inflecting verbs. Also, Bybee and Slobin (1982) showed that if native speakers irregularize real verbs, the resulting past-tense forms are other real words (in 91% of trials), often a verb (in 80% of trials). For instance, they produced *rose* as past tense for *raise*, *sat* for *seat*, and *sought* for *search*. This suggests, at best, that the morphologically conditioned vowel alternations are not very productive. Moreover, Bybee and Slobin's findings suggest that participants produce these alternations by retrieving the forms from the mental lexicon, and thus that all these forms are stored, rather than computed on the basis of (morpho)phonological rules. The question arises how common morpho-phonological alternations are that are not fully productive.

3.2 The frequency of the complex word relative to its base

We saw in Section 3.1 that the realization of an affix may be determined by the word's frequency of occurrence. Another important predictor of morpho-phonological alternations is the word's frequency of occurrence relative to the frequency of the base. This relative frequency can be interpreted as indicating how easily the word can be segmented in its base and affixes (Hay 2003): The higher a word's relative frequency, the less prominent its base is, and the more difficult it would be to segment the word.

One type of morpho-phonological alternation that shows an effect of this relative frequency concerns the positions of primary and secondary word stress in English derived words. As mentioned in Section 1, stress preservation (like the secondary stress in *originálity* from *original*) is assumed to be regular. Collie (Collie 2007, 2008), however, showed on the basis of dictionary data that stress preservation is not categorical but varies both within and across lexical types. For example, secondary stress in the word *accèlerátion* is invariably on the second syllable in Collie's data (2007, 2008), preserving the main stress of its base *accélerate* as a secondary stress. The word *règenerátion*, by contrast, does not preserve the stress of its base *regénerate*. Other words show variability between preserving and non-preserving stresses. Examples are *àntìcipátion ~ antìcipátion* (*antícipate*) and *pàrtìcipátion ~ partìcipátion* (*partícipate*). Crucially, this variation is not random, but correlates with the relative frequency of the derived word and its base: the more frequent the base as compared to the derived word, the higher the chances of stress preservation.

Relative frequency has also been reported to affect segment reduction. Hay (2003) noted that complex words with high relative frequencies (e.g. *exactly*) are more often reduced (produced without /t/) than complex words with low relative frequencies (e.g. *abstractly*). Following Hay, several studies have investigated the role of relative frequency on word and segment reduction, but only few found robust effects (see Hanique and Ernestus 2012 and Plag and Ben Hedia 2018 for overviews). In line with the mixed results reported in the literature, Plag and Ben Hedia found for two out of four English prefixes that the prefix is shorter the higher the word's relative frequency. Future research has to reveal when exactly a word's phonetic properties are affected by its relative frequency.

These relative frequency effects suggest that morphologically complex words are stored. First, these effects show that the frequencies of occurrence of the derived words must be stored, which makes it highly likely that the words themselves are stored as well. Second, the fact that exactly the complex words with the high relative frequencies show idiosyncratic behavior supports the storage account. Because these words are highly frequent, they are probably more often processed via their lexical representations, instead of via their stems, as their lexical representations are easily accessible due to their high frequencies.

3.3 Language change

If a morpho-phonological alternation results from the on-line application of morphological rules followed by phonological rules, the morpho-phonological alternation should disappear (or change) if the relevant phonological rule can no longer be applied (because the morphological rule has changed or because the phonological rule has disappeared). An example is Frisian breaking, where a falling diphthong in the singular stem alternates with a rising diphthong in the plural stem (e.g. *koal* [koəl] 'coal' versus *kwallen* [kwɑlən] 'coals'). In the innovative dialects, breaking no longer applies and both the singular and plural nouns have falling diphthongs (e.g. *koal* [koəl] 'coal' versus *koalen* [koələn] 'coal').

The plural nouns are not always adapted to the singulars. We discuss two examples, both also described by Booij (2012; and see also Booij 2009 for more examples). One example concerns umlaut in Old Germanic languages (e.g. Cercignani 1980; Wurzel 1980). This phonological rule changes back vowels into front vowels when the following (semi)vowel is /i/ or /j/. As a consequence, noun stems can have different vowels in the singular than in the plural if the plural suffix contains /i/ or /j/ (e.g. Old High German singular nominative *gast* 'guest' versus plural nominative *gesti* 'guests'). The plural affix has changed in most Modern Germanic languages such that it no longer contains /i/ or /j/ and the umlaut rule is no longer applicable. Nevertheless, many of the pertinent plural nouns still contain fronted vowels (e.g. Modern German *gast* /gast/ 'guest' versus *gäste* /gɛstə/ 'guests' with the plural suffix /ə/). In some singular-plural noun pairs, the fronted vowel is the only marker of plurality left (e.g. Modern German *Vater* /faːtɐ/ 'father' versus *Väter* /fɛːtɐ/ 'fathers'; English *foot* versus *feet*). The persistence of the vowel alternation can be accounted for with the assumption that the rule has changed and is now (partly) morphological in nature. This account implies that for some languages (e.g. English), a rule is assumed that applies to only a very restricted set of words and therefore touches upon the question of how many words have to show an alternation to support a (morpho)phonological rule. Another account postulates that both the singular and plural nouns were lexically stored and that the vowels of the plurals therefore did not change with the plural affix.

The storage account is supported by some Frisian nouns that showed the breaking pattern as described above. In contrast to the plurals of most nouns, which have been adapted to the corresponding singulars in innovative dialects, these words show the opposite pattern: the singulars have been adapted to the plurals, such that they both show falling diphthongs (e.g. *earm* [iərm] 'arm' versus *jermen* [jɛrmən] 'arms' has become *jerm* [jɛrm] 'arm' versus *jermen* [jɛrmən] 'arms'; Tiersma 1982). This opposite pattern is problematic for theoretical accounts that do not assume lexical storage of both the singular and plural nouns. They cannot easily explain why the result of the morpho-phonological rule is preserved while the underlying stored form is not. The pattern can be well explained with the assumption that both the singulars and plurals were lexically stored and that the change in pronunciation of the singulars results from paradigmatic leveling. Paradigmatic leveling then resulted in adaptation of the plural for most words and of the singular for some words. As noted by Booij (2012), the words showing adaptation of the singulars tend to occur in pairs (*jerm* 'arm') or in groups (*toarn* 'thorns', *trien* 'tears') and their plurals are therefore of higher frequencies of occurrence than their singulars. The lexical representations of these plurals are therefore probably stronger than of their corresponding singulars.

3.4 Lexical neighbors

The probability of a given word to show a certain morpho-phonological pattern may be influenced by the behavior of the lexical neighbors. Take, for instance, the Spanish vowel alternation already discussed in Section 3.1: The diphthong-monophtong alternation in verbs is not fully productive. This also holds for alternations among derived words and their bases: some of these derived words obey the alternation pattern, others do not. Moreover, for many forms there are alternatives, with and without diphthongs (cf. *cal*[je]*ntito* vs. *cal*[e]-*ntito* 'warm/cozy' derived from *cal*[jé]*nte* 'hot', Carlson and Gerfen 2011: 512). On the basis of corpus data, Carlson and Gerfen (2011) show that the number of types with diphthongs varies with the derivational suffix. Crucially, however, the variation is probabilistic – it is not the case that, depending on the morphological category, derivatives exhibit or fail to exhibit diphthongs categorically. Carlson and Gerfen also found that the probability of diphthongs appearing in the stem is correlated with the number of hapax legomena with the derivational suffix, and with the frequency of the derivative. Among derivational categories with few hapaxes, the higher the frequency of the derivative, the lower the probability of diphthongs. In terms of storage, Carlson and Gerfen's study suggests that derivatives, at least of low-productivity derivational categories, are stored with their phonological forms. Also, it seems that speakers keep a statistical record of the probability with which diphthongization occurs within a morphological category. This presupposes storage of derived words, including their morphological structure.

Also compound stress in English shows effects of lexical neighborhoods. English noun-noun compounds exhibit two different prominence patterns. Main prominence can be on the left (= first) constituent (e.g. *chéese cake*) or on the right (= second) constituent (e.g. *apple píe*). Stress assignment is categorical in some compounds (e.g. *apple píe*, always right-stressed) and variable in others (e.g. *políce helmet ~ police hélmet*, Bell 2015). One important predictor for whether a compound has primary stress on the first or on the second constituent are the constituent families of both the first and the second constituent (Arndt-Lappe 2011; Bell 2013; Plag 2010; Plag et al. 2008). Compounds tend to be stressed in the same way as compounds that have the same left or right constituent (i.e. that are members of their constituent families). Famous examples are street and road name compounds: For example, street names ending in *Street* are invariably stressed on the first constituent (e.g. *Óxford Street*, *Chúrch Street*, *Thómson Street*); road names ending in *Road* are invariably stressed on the second constituent (e.g. *Abbey Róad*). The phenomenon is, however, by no means restricted to street and road names, and it encompasses both first and second constituents. For compounds that exhibit variable stress (of the type *políce helmet ~ police hélmet*), Bell (2015) has demonstrated that within-type variability occurs exactly in those cases in which the constituent families of the first and the second constituents call for different stress patterns.

Another example of a morpho-phonological alternation where the word's lexical neighborhood plays a role is the regular past-tense formation in Dutch. Dutch regular past tenses are created by adding the allomorph -/tə/ *-te* to stems underlyingly ending in voiceless obstruents and the allomorph -/də/ *-de* to all other stems. For instance, the past tense of *sto*/p/ 'stop' is *stopte*, while the past tense of *schro*/b/ 'scrub' is *schrobde*. This alternation has been assumed to be exceptionless (e.g. Booij 1995: 61; the irregular Dutch past tenses show vowel alternation, rather than suffixation). Note that the affix is added before final devoicing: it is the underlying voicing of the stem-final segment that determines the past-tense allomorph, rather than the voicing of this segment when the stem is pronounced in isolation.

Although the alternation is completely regular, native speakers may choose the inappropriate allomorph for certain verbs (e.g., Ernestus and Baayen 2004). Several studies have shown that native speakers make errors especially for those verbs that need a different allomorph than the verbs ending in a similar vowel and an obstruent of the same place and manner of articulation (e.g., Ernestus 2006; Ernestus and Baayen 2003, 2004). For instance, native speakers often produce errors for *schrobben* (with the stem *schro*/b/), which has as its phonological neighbors many verbs ending in a short vowel and /p/ (e.g. *sto*/p/, *klo*/p/, *ha*/p/, *kla*/p/, *sta*/p/, *me*/p/, *ste*/p/, *di*/p/, *ni*/p/), but only few verbs ending in a short vowel and /b/ (*to*/b/, *sli*/b/, and *kra*/b/). Vice versa, they make very few errors for *stoppen*, because this verb takes the majority allomorph in its phonological neighborhood. If speakers do not make errors and produce the correct forms for verbs that deviate from the majority of verbs in the phonological neighborhoods, they need more time to produce these forms, as shown in experiments in which they are auditorily presented with the infinitives and requested to choose between the past-tense affixes *-te* and *-de*. These findings are unexpected for a morpho-phonological alternation that has always been claimed to be regular.

4 Which models can account for the evidence?

After we have looked at what we know about storage, we will now address the question what exactly the implications are for (psycho)linguistic models of morphology-phonology interaction in both speech production and comprehension. Section 3 presented evidence that there is storage of morpho-phonological alternants. Current models of morphology-phonology interaction have generally taken notice of this type of evidence. These models differ in the way in which they incorporate this evidence, and in the importance that they attribute to it. In what follows, we will broadly group models along the storage–computation continuum (see Table 1 in Fábregas & Penke this volume, which specifies for several individual models their assumptions about storage and computation). We will start with models that focus on computation (Section 4.1). Section 4.2 will discuss models that incorporate storage as a second mechanism, alongside a computational rule mechanism. Finally, Section 4.3 will focus on models that minimize computational mechanisms and focus on storage.

4.1 Only computation

Maximization of the computational mechanism is an underlying assumption in many current discussions of morpho-phonological alternations and in speech production models based on the one developed by Levelt (1989). For example, Inkelas (2014) provides a comprehensive overview of many ways in which phonological structure can be influenced by morphological structure. The emphasis is always on providing a computational (constraint-based) mechanism that would be able to predict alternations, and that assumes minimal structure in the inputs to computation. There is little discussion of the possibility, and the potential consequences of the possibility, that outputs of morpho-phonological rules could be stored. Similarly, the focus on maximizing computation can be seen in current theoretical work. For example, in their introductory article to a special issue on exponence in *Lingue e Linguaggio*, Fábregas, Krämer, and McFadden (2014) describe the central problem of the division of labor between storage and computation in the mental lexicon, in view of the presence of alternations, as follows: "If we think of a child acquiring Navajo, how much information will she *have to* memorize and store in a list and how much information will she *be able to* derive from what she has stored, given productive and to a great extent predictable rules in her language?" (Fábregas, Krämer, and McFadden 2014: 3; emphasis added). The choice of words here indicates the focus in theorizing: the computational mechanism is to be maximally explanatory; storage, by contrast, is minimized.

The main rationale behind the computability assumption is that grammatical theory aims at explaining productive grammatical patterns. Productive grammatical patterns are patterns that (a) are regularly extended to novel words, and that (b) have a high type frequency in the language, i.e. are seen in many different words. Storage is often used in computational approaches to explain the existence of forms in a language that do not have these two properties, and that, therefore, form exceptions. Another common, albeit often tacit, assumption about storage is that, even if regular complex forms are stored, this is not relevant to productive computation. This is because productive computation is conceptualized as a (relatively) closed system, in which a rule or constraint mechanism operates on abstract, symbolic representations. It is irrelevant to the system itself whether or not outputs of such computation are stored, as there is no direct pathway in which stored items can influence productive computation. Such influence is, instead, restricted to situations in which the system is acquired, in language acquisition and diachronic transmission (cf. e.g. Salmons and Honeybone 2015 for an interesting discussion, focusing on the structuralist heritage of recent approaches to sound change).

Phenomena like the ones described in Section 3 provide a threefold challenge to this rationale. First, they provide evidence that storage is not always minimal, which calls into question the alleged negative correlation of storage and productivity. Second, some of the evidence suggests that stored forms are relevant to productive computation, which provides a challenge to models which assume that storage and computation coexist without influencing each other. Finally, phenomena like the ones described in Section 3 raise questions about the general nature of constraints on morpho-phonological alternations.

The clearest case in point here showing how storage can be relevant to computation are effects of lexical neighbors in productive morphological processes. For example, we saw in Section 3.4 that stress assignment in English noun-noun compounds and the selection of the past-tense allomorph for Dutch regular verbs is systematically sensitive to the characteristics of the lexical neighbors sharing the same constituents (e.g., Dutch *schro*/b/ is often erroneously suffixed with -/tə/, following the neighbors ending in a short vowel and /p/; and there is a systematic difference in the position of stress in compounds for street names ending in *Street* and those ending in *Road*: *Óxford Street* vs. *Oxford Róad*). Similarly, all phenomena discussed in Section 3 in which the application of a regular alternation is dependent on the frequency of individual words or on lexical neighborhood shows that storage may be grammatically relevant, and is difficult to reconcile with a purely computational account. This is true especially of the affixal reduction patterns cited, but also of the intricacies involved in the directionality of paradigm leveling in the Frisian umlauting pattern.

One traditional strategy of dealing with narrow-scope or word-specific patterns in computational models is to assume that forms which fail to undergo a morpho-phonological rule are exceptions. Exceptions are stored forms that may be retrieved holistically (cf. e.g. Zuraw 2010 for a proposal within a computational model). The data presented in Section 3, however, raise the question of how to define the scope of 'exceptional', and how to delimit exceptional forms from regular ones. In particular, they show that the assumption that 'exceptional' means 'narrow-scope' does not always hold. For example, the influence of lexical neighbors on stress assignment in English compounds is not restricted to a small set of lexical exceptions, but seems the predominant determinant of compound stress in the majority of the data (Arndt-Lappe 2011; Plag 2010). Also word-specific reduction and deletion patterns as described in Section 3.1 are difficult to account for. First of all, this approach would force us to decide whether application or non-application of the phonological rule (i.e. a reduction rule) is exceptional. Secondly, again, it is not true that word-specific behavior is rare, as would be expected if this was the exception.

A key argument in computational models for the distinction between regular and exceptional patterns is that exceptional patterns are not productive. The simplest version of this is that alternations which are seen only in exceptional forms are not productive, i.e. do not appear in many words, and, more importantly, do not appear in novel words. Conversely, regular alternations are productive. Indeed, in the phenomena that we discussed in Section 3, productivity is an important correlate of whether or not a morpho-phonological alternation occurs. For example, the Spanish dipthong-monophthong alternation is only marginally extended to novel words (Bybee 1988), and is observed to occur particularly frequently with affixes that are not very productive in the language (Carlson and Gerfen 2011). Similarly, vowel alternations in English past tense forms (traditionally considered 'irregular') show semi-productivity, in that they are only rarely extended to novel forms (e.g. Bybee and Slobin 1982, and see Ramscar 2002 for the role of semantics). However, the connection between morpho-phonological alternations and productivity is that both productivity and exceptionality are not dichotomous, but gradient notions.

Computational models have taken different routes in how they explain this type of gradience. One common assumption is that morpho-phonological rules themselves can apply in a probabilistic fashion. This is assumed, for example, in accounts that are based on rule or constraint induction, such as the Minimal Generalization Learner (MGL, Albright 2002; Albright and Hayes 2003) and the stochastic Optimality Theory tradition (OT, Boersma 1998; Boersma and Hayes 2001 et seq.).

In the Minimal Generalization Learning approach, symbolic rules are induced from the lexicon. These rules are symbolic in the sense that they operate on traditional phonological features and specified, abstract contexts. Unlike rules in other approaches, however, they operate on different levels of generality and are in competition with each other. The Minimal Generalization Learner has successfully been applied to model the semi-productive behavior of the irregular past tense in English (Albright and Hayes 2003) discussed in Section 3.1. The main reason for the success of the model is that the irregular pattern is particularly productive among words that are highly similar. During the model's learning phase in which rules are induced from the lexicon, these phonological neighborhoods will lead to the emergence of relatively specific morpho-phonological rules producing the irregular alternation. Crucially, these rules will operate on a low level of generality, which means that they apply only to very narrow phonological contexts. For novel words that match the context of these low-level rules, these rules will compete with more general rules calling for the regular alternation. It is then a matter of probabilities which of the rules applies to a given novel form. The surface result is variation. On a general level, the Minimal Generalization Approach seems ideally suited to modeling semi-productive behavior in which semi-productivity emerges in relatively tight phonological neighborhoods. It is less clear how the model will deal with word-specific morpho-phonological variation, as described in Section 3.1. One basic assumption made by the model is that all generalizations can be represented in terms of traditional phonological rules, making recourse to phonological feature representations and standard contextual information (cf. Albright 2009 for extensive discussion). Another basic assumption is that, once the learning phase is over, the system is static and hard-wired. Stored forms therefore influence computation only in the learning phase.

Stochastic OT (Boersma 1998; Boersma and Hayes 2001 et seq.) works in a similar fashion. It assumes phonological constraints which, if they are ranked similarly high in the hierarchy, sometimes swap positions, resulting in variation. Stochastic OT can both model speech production and comprehension. The rankings of constraints are learned by means of the Gradual Learning Algorithm. Phonetic learning can occur continuously, for instance, when the system hears a sound that does not match the sound of the word as stored in the mental lexicon, which results in the adjustment of the relevant constraints.

Stochastic OT has been tested, for instance, on regular past-tense formation for pseudoverbs in Dutch (Ernestus and Baayen 2003). As explained above, the Dutch past-tense affix depends on the underlying voice specification of the verb stem-final segment: it is -/tə/ -*te* if the segment is underlyingly voiceless, otherwise it is -/də/ -*de*. Because stem-final obstruents are devoiced in Dutch in word-final position, speakers cannot know the underlying voice specification for the final segment of pseudoverb stems produced in isolation and therefore should not be able to produce the past-tense forms for these pseudoverbs. Nevertheless, Dutch speakers are very consistent in their choice for -*te* or -*de* for some pseudoverbs encountered in isolation while they show more variation for other pseudoverbs. They appear to be more likely to chose -*te* if there are more real verbs that take -*te* and that sound similar to the pseudoverb stem as its sounds in isolation. For instance, most participants (75%) choose -*te* for [dɑp], which corresponds to the fact that most Dutch verbs ending in a short vowel and a biliabial stop are affixed with -*te*. We see here the direct phonological neighborhood at work, which also affects the formation of past-tense forms for real verbs, as explained in Section 3.4. Stochastic OT can well account for this gradience with 20 phonological constraints that express the possibilities that a word-final obstruent can be both voiced or voiceless, based on its place of articulation or based on the preceding phoneme (e.g., the constraints 'bilabial stops are underlyingly voiced'; 'bilabial stops are underlyingly voiceless'; 'obstruents preceded by other obstruents are voiced'; 'obstruents preceded by other obstruents are voiceless'). All verbs are thus subject to opposite constraints (some stating that the obstruent should be voiced and others that the obstruent should be voiceless). If the opposite constraints are assigned similar positions in the constraint hierarchy, they may sometimes swap positions, which explains the variation among participants. By means of Boersma's Gradual Learning Algorithm implemented in *Praat* (Boersma and Weenik 2018), the constraints can be assigned positions on the basis of the real verbs in Dutch (the training set). The resulting hierarchy can simulate participants' gradient preferences for -*de* or -*te* for pseudoverbs in past-tense production experiments (the test sets).

Both the Minimal Generalization Learner and the Stochastic OT tradition make a distinction between a training phase and a test phase. Thus, the link between stored elements and the grammatical system is only an indirect one. Stored elements can lead to an update of the grammatical system in the training phase. Approaches differ in whether they assume such updating to happen only in language acquisition or throughout life. Other theoretical models have taken a different route to explaining the gradient relation between productivity and regularity or exceptionality in morpho-phonological alternations. They recognize both storage and computation to be influences on grammar, and, thus, do not restrict the influence of stored forms to a learning phase. It is to these models that we now turn.

4.2 Computation and storage

We now turn to models that assume that complex words can be processed both by directly accessing the lexical representations of these words or by computation. We will see that the data presented in Section 3 are better accounted for in such models than in purely computational models. We will also see, however, that these models face challenges as well.

Most models of morphological processing suppose that all complex words can be processed both via access of the lexical representations of the words or via parsing of the words from (in production) or into (in comprehension) their parts. The models differ in how the labor is divided between storage and computation. For instance, in the Augmented Addressed Morphology Model, proposed by Caramazza, Laudanna, and Romani (1988), morphologically complex words are only decomposed if they cannot be processed via lexical representations (e.g., because they do not have lexical representations as they have not been encountered before). In the Parallel Dual Route model (e.g. Baayen, Dijkstra, and Schreuder 1997), in contrast, morphologically complex words are simultaneously processed via morphological parsing and access of lexical representations, and the output of the fastest route determines language behaviour.

In what follows we will first look at our data in Section 3 in terms of how they can be accounted for by these architectures. The storage of morphologically complex words can account for the data presented in Section 3 as far as frequency effects on real words are concerned. As we discussed in Section 3.1, high-frequency words may not conform to regular reduction patterns. Because highly frequent words are often used, articulation may be faster and weaker, leading to reduction during articulation. If these reduced word pronunciation variants are lexically stored, they may form the starting points of articulation of the next occurrences of the words, which, during the articulation process, may be even more reduced. As a consequence, high frequency words may show more substantial reduction than low frequency words. This phenomenon is difficult to explain without lexical storage. Note that an account with frequency-sensitive rules may account for production data but, as explained above, cannot account for the effect of word variant frequency in comprehension data.

Section 3.1 also showed that at least some of the morpho-phonological patterns (e.g., vowel alternation in Spanish verbal paradigms and vowel alternation in English irregular verbs) are not as productive as would be expected under the assumption that they result from a set of rules. The low productivity of these patterns suggests that the alternations rather reflect lexical storage of the pertinent verb forms. The alternations may originally result from morpho-phonological rules, which are no longer productive, and their outputs are lexically stored. Note, however, that this assumption makes it difficult to explain the semi-productivity displayed by these patterns.

Section 3.2 reported research showing that the pronunciation of morphologically complex words is affected by the relative frequencies of their full forms and their bases: words with relatively high frequency forms tend to show idiosyncratic behavior. This can be especially well explained by models assuming that both lexical storage and computation may play a role in the processing of regular complex words, like the Parallel Dual Route Model (e.g., Baayen, Dijkstra, and Schreuder 1997). The most influential idea here is that the likelihood of decomposition is a function of a complex word's formal and semantic segmentability, which in turn is correlated with the relative frequency of the derived word and its base word (Hay 2001, 2003; Hay and Baayen 2002). For a word whose full form frequency is higher than that of the base word, the route involving the lexical representation of the full form (often called the 'whole-word route') is likely to be faster than the parsing route (often called 'decomposition route'), which involves the lexical representation of the base. Hence, in such case the whole-word route is more influential. As a consequence, these words may start behaving like mono-morphemic words, for instance, with respect to stress. Furthermore, since words with high relative frequencies tend to have high absolute frequencies as well, they are more prone to reduction, and their reduced variants may be lexically stored (as explained above).

Section 3.3 described phenomena of language change forming support for the hypothesis that also regular morphologically complex words are lexically stored. Models assuming that these forms can both be processed via direct access to their full form lexical representations and via computation can easily account for these phenomena.

The neighborhood effects described in Section 3.4 cannot be explained as resulting from the competition between whole-word access and decomposition. The same is true for semi-productive alternations like the irregular past tense pattern in English (cf. Section 3.1). Instead, what is required here is a mechanism by which stored words can affect the processing of other words.

This is possible in the approach proposed by Stephen Pinker, and others, in the 1990s (especially Prasada and Pinker 1993; Pinker and Prince 1994; Marcus et al. 1995; Pinker 1999), who assume that the computational route is based on rule mechanisms while analogical mechanisms, based on a single word or a very restricted set of words, can play a role in the lexical route. Both types of mechanisms can give rise to novel forms. Regular formations emerge from the grammatical rule system. Semi-productive and semi-regular formations emerge from the analogical mechanisms in the lexicon that creates novel forms on the basis of analogies with real, stored items. Crucially, and unlike other analogy-based approaches to morpho-phonological alternations, which we will discuss in Section 4.3 below, the analogical mechanisms are assumed to be fundamentally different in nature and status from the grammatical rule mechanisms. As a consequence, there is a qualitative difference between the way in which irregular patterns are productive and the way in which regular patterns are productive (Prasada and Pinker 1993: 43). Irregular patterns are not fully productive, and, in order for them to be applied to a novel form, a very high degree of similarity is required. Regular patterns, by contrast, are highly productive (but may be blocked by real irregular forms), and their extendability is not influenced by the degree to which a novel item is similar to real items. The analogical patterns are captured in terms of a probabilistic, associative mechanism; the regular patterns are captured in terms of a deterministic rule mechanism.

In sum, we see that models assuming both computation and storage and assuming that storage may influence the online processing of complex words come a long way towards accounting for the type of morpho-phonological alternations introduced in Section 3. These approaches, however, leave some questions unresolved. For models like the Parallel Dual Route model, an important question is how it is determined which of the two routes is fastest for a given complex word or morphological category. Another question, which has so far attracted not so much attention in the literature, is how exactly decomposition works. This is particularly true for the details about how the phonological form of complex words may be decomposed. Cf. Fábregas & Penke (this volume) for a discussion of different approaches to decomposition within morphological theory, which are concerned with the relation between formal and morphosyntactic complexity.

Yet another challenge for these models is the assumption that the two mechanisms for processing complex words (via direct access of the whole form representation or via decomposition) are qualitatively distinct. These models therefore seem to have little to say about morpho-phonological alternations in which similarity-based generalizations are not semi-productive, but highly productive. The neighborhood effects described in Section 3.4 are a case in point. Neither in English compound stress nor in the Dutch past tense do lexical neighborhood effects seem confined to small sets of pertinent words. Still, they are clearly similarity-based. In other words, it seems that any type of gradience between the behavior of productive and unproductive patterns seems problematic, as the models rest on a categorical divide between regular and exceptional behavior.

A very different type of model assuming that both lexical storage and computation may play a role in the processing of complex words is the version of the Stratal Phonology model proposed by Ricardo Bermúdez-Otero (2012, 2018). The approach builds on the basic assumption that the lexicon is organized into strata (stem level vs. word level, following traditional ideas in Lexical Phonology and Morphology), and that there may be storage on both strata. The latter assumption follows the proposal laid out by Jackendoff (1975) and others that lexical rules (such as morpho-phonological rules) are essentially redundancy rules, i.e. derivational rules that exist alongside stored outputs of such rules. One basic assumption that the Stratal Phonology approach shares with Pinker's model is that there are two computational mechanisms, a grammatical rule mechanism and an analogical pattern-associator mechanism. What is new in the Stratal Phonology approach is the assumption that there are two types of storage of complex words. Stem-level derivatives are always stored, and stored properties include detailed surface realizations ('detail' comprises, e.g., stress, foot structure, and allophonic variants). Word-level derivatives, by contrast, are not always stored; if they are stored, their representations make the morphological segmentation visible to the phonological system. As a consequence, independent of whether or not a word-level derivative is stored, the grammatical mechanism always applies to constituent morphemes, and storage is irrelevant to the grammatical system. For stem-level derivatives, in contrast, the grammatical mechanism competes with processing via the full stored forms very much in the way envisaged in the models discussed above (e.g., the Parallel Dual Route model). This is where variation among surface realizations can arise. The distinction between stem-level and word-level derivation largely corresponds to the traditional distinction between Level I and Level II affixation made in Lexical Phonology and Morphology. Unlike other dual mechanism theories, the Stratal Phonology approach is specific about what the grammatical mechanism is like: The grammatical mechanism is the set of phonological rules that also apply to monomorphemic words.

The basic assumptions made by the Stratal Phonology approach can be illustrated well with how this approach accounts for variable secondary stress in English words like *antìcipátion ~ ànticipátion* (derived from *antícipate*, Collie 2007, 2008; Bermúdez-Otero 2012, cf. Section 3.2). The morphological process in which the variation is found is a stem-level process. The fact that preservation is variable both within and between word types provides evidence for competition between whole-word and decomposed processing. Which of the two types of processing is more likely depends on the frequency of the derivative relative to the frequency of its base (as in models like the Parallel Dual Route model, see above). The interaction in the Stratal Phonology approach, however, is not trivial. Secondary stress preservation (e.g. in *antìcipátion*) may be a result of both decomposed access (*antícipate* + *-ion*) or whole-word access (*antìcipátion*). Secondary stress on the first syllable (e.g. in *ànticipátion*) can be a result of whole-word access (*àntìcipátion*) or of the application of the default phonological rule to the whole word, which assigns secondary stress to the first syllable also in monomorphemic items. Non-preserving first-syllable stress, thus, can only arise if the word has been stored with that pattern, or if it is processed like a monomorphemic word. These are predictions that, to our knowledge, await further testing.

One question that does not find an immediate answer in the model is how the system knows whether a given derivative is a stem-level or a word-level derivative. Also, the approach predicts variation in morpho-phonological alternations to occur among stem-level derivatives, but not among word-level derivatives. For example, it is unclear how the model would account for the language change phenomena described in Section 3.5, which indicate that word-level forms can be lexically stored. The Stratal Phonology approach would in these cases not predict that competition between decomposition and direct access to stored forms may lead to output variation.

In conclusion, models assuming that complex words can be processed both via the stored whole-word representations or by means of computation can explain many more language phenomena than the models discussed in Section 4.1, which assume that lexical representations of complex words play no important role in language processing. However, the two strictly distinct processing routes imply clearly distinct morphological patterns, which do not match the data. This raises the question to what extent models that assign a major role to storage and analogical processing can explain the data. We will turn to this question now.

4.3 Only storage

A group of theories that have abandoned the grammar-lexicon dichotomy assume extensive storage and base the processing of both real and novel words on the patterns in the lexicon. We will use 'storage models' as a label to refer to this group of theories. Processing in storage models involves comparison of the input (in comprehension and production) with patterns present in the stored representations. Among pertinent approaches, there is a vivid debate about the exact nature of lexical representations and about the nature of the computational processing mechanism.

With regard to the nature of lexical representations, the main question is what information exactly is stored. The morpho-phonological alternations that we introduced in Section 3 of this chapter all provide evidence that morpho-phonological alternants, both regular and semi-regular, may be stored. Storage is not maximally economic, that is, abstract, as stored components encompass aspects of pronunciation that would also fall in the realm of traditional grammatical rules (e.g. vowel reduction, umlauting, stress assignment).

Our data can well be accounted for by Construction models, which assume storage in terms of schemata on different levels of abstractness, organized in terms of inheritance hierarchies and covering a continuum from very detailed representations of concrete pronunciations to abstract representations resembling feature representations (Booij 2010, 2018).

The most compelling evidence for abstract representations comes from non-concatenative morphology. For example, Dawdy-Hesterberg and Pierrehumbert (2014) argue that abstract consonant-vowel (CV) skeletal representations are an essential prerequisite to guarantee learnability of broken plural patterns in Arabic in a storage model (the computational implementation they use is the Generalized Context Model, GCM; Nakisa, Plunkett, and Hahn 2001; Nosofsky 1986). Davis and Tsujimura (2018) is a recent discussion of the role of abstract, prosodic templates in a Construction Morphology account of Arabic nonconcatenative morphology.

Recent work suggests that more detailed phonetic characteristics may be part of lexical representations as well. Several studies report differences in the exact articulation of phonemes as a function of their morphological status. For example, Plag, Homann, and Kunter (2017) show that homonymous word-final -s in English differs in phonetic detail depending on whether it is part of a monomorphemic word, an affix, or a clitic. Similarly, Strycharczuk and Scobbie (2016, 2017) show that fronting of /u/ and /ʊ/ as well as velarization of /l/ differ in phonetic detail between morphologically simplex and complex words in Southern British English. Since the generalizations involve abstract morphological categories, abstract lexical representations containing some phonetic detail may suffice to account for these data.

The findings can also easily be explained in classic exemplar models, which assume that each token of each word is stored with all its fine phonetic detail, without any abstraction (e.g., Goldinger 1996; Johnson 1997; Pierrehumbert 2002; cf. Gahl and Yu 2006 for an overview). Many studies within the field of word comprehension have investigated this possibility of fully detailed representations. Moreover, this possibility is supported by word-specific pronunciations of alternants like those of the Dutch suffix /lək/ (Section 3.1). Some researchers, however, wonder whether these representations are part of the mental lexicon (neocortex) or of episodic memory (hippocampus). If they are part of episodic memory, they may only play a minor role in everyday language processing (e.g., Hanique, Aalders, and Ernestus 2013a; Nijveld, ten Bosch, and Ernestus 2015).

For models that do not assume high levels of abstraction like Construction models, an important question is how a novel complex form is computed on the basis of the stored word forms. Unlike in neogrammarian style analogies, in which there is usually only one single model form that forms the basis of its analogue, most contemporary models assume that it is sets of similar forms that are relevant ('gangs', e.g. Bybee 2001). Models that implement such mechanisms are commonly referred to as 'analogical models'. How exactly stored word forms interact to account for the productivity and semi-productivity of the patterns described in Section 3 is conceptualized in different ways among analogical approaches.

The three most well-known computationally implemented models are Analogical Modeling (AM(L), Skousen 1989; Skousen, Lonsdale, and Parkinson 2002), the Tilburg Memory-Based Learner (TiMBL, Daelemans and van den Bosch 2005), and the Generalized Context Model (GCM, Nosofsky 1986). All three models have been shown to be very successful in modeling phenomena which are subject to neighborhood effects and phenomena which exhibit semi-productivity. They are in principle agnostic to the exact nature of lexical representations, including the degree of abstraction involved (cf. above). They differ in terms of how they define relevant similar word forms (from now on 'exemplars') for a given classification task; this particularly concerns the degree of similarity and the properties of an exemplar which are used to measure similarity.

AM is the model that most radically implements the idea that linguistic generalizations do not have an independent status (as pre-wired configurations) but are emergent in the course of a specific language processing task. Thus, in AM the question of which exemplars are relevant for a given task is answered for each occurrence of an item on an individual basis and crucially depends on the distribution of overlapping properties in the lexicon at the very moment the task has to be performed. Starting from the most similar exemplar, the algorithm checks all property combinations and considers those exemplars to be relevant which it can include without weakening the certainty of the prediction (cf. especially Skousen 2002a; 2002b for explanation). This procedure obviously comes at a high computational cost, a problem which has been argued to challenge the psychological plausibility of the model (Baayen, Hendrix, and Ramscar 2013).

TiMBL implements a set of memory-based learning techniques that are known as 'k Nearest Neighbor' ('k-NN') models. The different options that are available essentially formulate computational rules according to which the algorithm decides which exemplars are relevant for a given task, and how these exemplars are weighted. These rules pertain to the degree of similarity of given items (the parameter 'k') and the relative importance of properties of exemplars, which is determined for the whole dataset on the basis of a variety of information-theoretic measures. Unlike in AM, there is a training phase and a test phase in TiMBL. Rules about the relative importance of properties are learned in the training phase and then applied to novel items in the test phase. TiMBL implementations are therefore less costly than those with AM, computationally, but the theoretical status of the computational rules often remains unclear. They also differ from the AM computational rules in that, once formulated in the training phase, they are invariable and continuously available in the test phase and thus lexically stored.

In the GCM, a measure for the strength of association of a novel item with a particular output category (e.g. a morpho-phonological alternant) is computed on the basis of the novel item's similarity with all exemplars sharing that output category, weighted by the number of those exemplars. Like in TiMBL, additional computational rules can be formulated that further constrain which exemplars are relevant (cf. e.g. Albright and Hayes 2003; Dawdy-Hesterberg and Pierrehumbert 2014 for an implementation). These rules are then applied to all items in the same way. Also these rules are continuously available and thus stored in the lexicon.

Several studies have directly compared the performance of several computational models on the basis of the same dataset. One example is Ernestus and Baayen (2003) on the creation of regular past-tense forms for Dutch nonce verbs (cf. Section 3.4). Dutch speakers base their choice between the affixes -*de* and -*te* not so much on their interpretation of the underlying voicing of the stem-final obstruent (as they should according to the morpho-phonological rule) but on the phonological similarity of the final rhyme of the stem. Ernestus and Baayen first determined which phonological features were relevant by means of TiMBL simulations of the real verb data. They then modeled their experimental data of nonce verbs by means of Stochastic OT (Boersma 1998) with 10 or 20 constraints, two types of statistical models (generalized linear modeling, which is often used in the field of sociolinguistics to account for variation, and classification and regression trees), and two analogical models (an analogical Spreading Activation model, Schreuder and Baayen 1995, and AM). The Stochastic OT account with 20 constraints, classification and regression trees, and the two analogical models performed well in predicting both the participants' majority choice and the variation among participants.

Although the Stochastic OT approach accounts well for the data, there are several reasons not to favor this approach. First, the modeling requires a high number of parameters (20), which may lead to overfitting of the data, and the model may not extend to new participants, which is undesirable. Second, the account within

Stochastic OT has to assume both natural constraints and their unnatural counterparts. Finally, unlike the analogical models, the Stochastic OT approach cannot be extended to the data on real verb forms (Ernestus and Baayen 2004). It cannot explain why the variation among participants and among a single participant's answers to phonologically similar verbs correlates with the processing times of these verbs: why speakers need more time to correctly produce a real past tense form if there are more verbs in its phonological neighborhood taking the other allomorph (personal communication; Ernestus 2006). The data on regular past-tense formation in Dutch would therefore favor analogical models.

Albright and Hayes (2003) directly compared the three types of approaches that we distinguished in this chapter: a strictly computational account with stochastic rules (the Minimal Generalization Learner, discussed in Section 4.1 above), a dual-route model (discussed in Section 4.2), and a purely analogical account (the Generalized Context Model). As a testbed, they conducted an experiment in which participants heard English nonce verbs and were asked to provide the past tenses. Other researchers used the same data to compare the Minimal Generalization Learner with the Tilburg Memory-Based Learner (Keuleers 2008) and the Analogical Model of Language (Chandler 2010). The participants produced regular and irregular past tenses and showed high agreement for some verbs and more variation for other verbs. The data cannot be explained with a simple dual route model (without analogical mechanisms) since this model cannot explain the (semi-)productivity of the irregulars. Moreover, the model cannot easily explain the variation in the data. Both MGL and the three analogical models (GCM, TiMBL, AM) reached similarly high accuracy scores in predicting participants' behavior (cf. Keuleers 2008: 130f. on a scaling issue in Albright and Hayes' original GCM model, which had seemed to put MGL at an advantage).

Regarding the question of how well analogical models are suited to accounting for morpho-phonological alternations, we see several important issues emerging from existing studies. Like the types of models discussed in Sections 4.1 and 4.2, the analogical models, too, leave some questions open. Thus, the high accuracy scores of pertinent implementations are not sufficient as a basis for evaluating models. Instead, we need to know more about how these accuracy scores are achieved, and we need to be able to determine how appropriate they are on the basis of what we know about language processing (cf. e.g. Arndt-Lappe 2018 for discussion). The issues stand out particularly clearly for the English past tense (and, to some extent, for Spanish diphthongization, cf. e.g. Albright 2009 discussed in Section 3.1) because these phenomena have attracted so many pertinent studies in the past.

One issue that requires further research is how similarity is computed in analogical models. Albright and Hayes (2003) and Albright (2009) point out that their version of the analogical model used what they call 'variegated' similarity (i.e. similarity based on any feature of the word), and argued that the use of variegated similarity constitutes a disadvantage for the model. For example, the set of exemplars on the basis of which Albright and Hayes' GCM predicted the past tense of the nonce word *scoil* contained words which are similar to *scoil* in different ways, such as, for example *spoil* and *scawl*. Such exemplars tend not to be the most relevant exemplars, and implementations of analogical models differ in the constraints they impose on the inclusion of such exemplars (in order to base the model on what Albright and Hayes called 'structured' similarity). What we can learn from this issue is that analogical models need mechanisms to avoid unlikely similarity relations to apply frequently.

The second aspect of analogical models that deserves closer investigation is the role of the density of the analogical gangs determining how a word is processed. As is well-known, lexical neighborhoods differ in density – there are densely populated and more sparsely populated areas (e.g. Luce and Pisoni 1998; cf. e.g. Dąbrowska 2008 on the relevance of similarity structure for morphological productivity). This means that some words have many neighbors that are highly similar to that word, whereas others do not. The structure of the similarity space has been shown to be relevant for an analogical account of English past tense alternants. Irregular alternants of the English past tense are well-known to concentrate in densely populated clusters of highly similar exemplars (termed 'Islands of Reliability' in Albright 2002; Albright and Hayes 2003). Regular past tense forms, by contrast, are known to be less similar to each other, globally. Keuleers (2008) discusses a large series of TiMBL models, for which he shows that, as a tendency, irregulars are better predicted if the similarity space considered (the parameter 'k' in TiMBL) is more narrow; by contrast, regular forms tend to be better predicted with larger values of k. For AM, which is more flexible with regard to the similarity space considered, this would mean that classification of verbs as regular may be based on more distant exemplars than is the case for classification of irregulars. More research is needed to explore the relation between analogical mechanisms and the similarity structure of the lexicon on which such predictions are based.

A third aspect concerns the question of how an analogical model can account for regular alternations of the English past tense, as most pertinent work has focused on modeling the interaction of regular vs. irregular alternations. By 'regular' alternation we mean the alternation between [t], [d] and [ɪd] as in *walk*[t], *wav*[d], and *hunt*[ɪd]. We use the label 'regular' here although, in an analogical model, there is no principled difference between 'regular' and 'irregular' alternations in the traditional sense. The main modeling challenge for analogical models with regard to regular alternants is (a) that selection of one alternant is mandatory once a lexical item has been identified as 'regular' e.g. by the speaker (i.e. there is no or little variation between alternants), and (b) that the alternation interacts with general constraints on sound patterns in the language (e.g. that a verbal form like *hun*[tt], with the [t] alternant as a past tense marker, is not possible because word-final [tt] sequences are not possible elsewhere in the language). Keuleers (2008) is to our knowledge the only study that discusses the issue in detail. He presents a range of TiMBL simulations in which both regular and irregular alternants are predicted, showing that competing unattested regular alternants receive little support if the model is restricted to taking into account only a narrow similarity space. This again raises the question what constraints analogical models should impose on the range of exemplars that are considered for comparison.

A final question with respect to models that assign an important role to lexical storage is whether all words that occur in the language are stored in the mental lexicon and can play a role in the analogical generalizations. This may be the case for languages like English, with relatively low numbers of derivational and inflectional forms for a single base. It is an open question whether this also holds for inflectional languages like Finnish. Note that the answer to the question which form is lexically stored cannot depend on the frequency of occurrence of the form: in order to know whether a form is more or less frequent than the frequency threshold, the form's frequency has to be stored and therefore the form itself as well.

In sum, the storage models are promising in that they can account for more data than those discussed in Sections 4.1 and 4.2. Like the types of models discussed in Sections 4.1. and 4.2., however, the storage models, too, leave some questions open. These especially concern the issue of which stored words exert which influence on a given word.

5 Conclusions

In the present chapter, we looked at the relation between morpho-phonological alternations and word storage and discussed the implications of this relation for theories of language processing and linguistic generalization. Section 2 discussed the growing psycholinguistic evidence for the storage of regular and irregular morphologically complex words. Even though the question of what aspects of complex words are stored is still unresolved in many respects, it seems clear that storage is ubiquitous, and that stored representations include more detail than is usually assumed to form the basis of traditional phonological rules. In Section 3 we discussed morpho-phonological alternations that show traits of lexical storage, in the sense that these alternations can only be explained if we assume lexical storage of at least some alternants. Several critical issues for an account of these alternations emerged from these phenomena.

Productivity
Morpho-phonological alternations are not always fully productive. Instead, there appears to be a continuum from word pairs whose alternation does not generalize to other word pairs to highly productive alternation processes. These data point to a single type of cognitive mechanism that allows alternation patterns to differ in their productivity depending on their support in the lexicon. The fact that the productivity of alternations forms a continuum also makes it difficult to partition the range of alternation phenomena into traditional oppositions like 'natural' – 'unnatural', 'phonologically conditioned' – 'lexically conditioned' or 'regular' – 'irregular'. For example, among the phenomena discussed in Section 3.1, both deletion of [ə] in the Dutch prefix /xə/ and monophthongization of diphthongs in unstressed positions of Spanish verbs can be described as 'phonologically natural' weakening processes; this is harder for the vowel alternations encountered in English 'irregular' verbs. However, all processes show very similar effects of storage.

Relative frequency of a complex word and its base
Relative frequency effects suggest that pronunciations of complex words and their bases may be stored, and that morphological complexity (i.e. the transparency of the relation between a complex word and its base) comes in different degrees. The likelihood of a morpho-phonological alternation to occur is correlated with the degree of complexity of a complex word: Complex words with lower relative frequencies tend to be less likely to undergo an alternation (i.e. pronunciations that differ from the pronunciations of their bases) than words with higher relative frequencies. These data point to an architecture that allows access to both stored pronunciations of regular complex words and the computation of a new pronunciation on the basis of the pronunciation of paradigmatically related words (which is the base word in all reported cases). The data also suggest that, rather than being, as is often assumed, evidence for the application of productive phonological rules, alternations might be effects typically encountered in stored word pairs. It is an open question to what extent this observation bears out beyond the group of reported cases showing relative frequency effects.

Language change
Variability in the application of leveling phenomena provides yet another type of evidence that morpho-phonological alternants may be stored. The Frisian case reported in Section 3.3 shows that the directionality of change does not always correspond to the directionality of phonological rules, and that again relative frequency plays an important role This suggests an architecture in which pronunciations are determined by the strength of stored representations of alternants.

Lexical neighbors
Lexical neighborhood effects present clear evidence that the influence of stored pronunciation alternants on language production and comprehension is not limited to mere access to and retrieval of those pronunciations. Instead, there are morpho-phonological alternations that can only be explained by means of analogical processes with stored pronunciations of lexical neighbors, like those discussed in Section 3.4. The data point to a cognitive mechanism that integrates stored representations of alternants in the production and comprehension of both real and novel complex words.

Theoretical models that incorporate storage differ in when the words in the lexicon come into play. While some models assume that the lexicon is continuously checked, others assume that the information in the lexicon is stored separately, for instance in the form of alternation rules, and that these rules are responsible for the productivity of a lexical pattern. Computationally implemented models have been developed within the different theoretical frameworks to enable researchers to test model predictions against data, most of which have been experimentally elicited data. This holds in particular for variants of models we have labeled 'computational models' (Section 4.1) and 'analogical models' (Section 4.3). Both types of model have been shown to be highly successful in modeling critical phenomena like those discussed in this chapter.

Several studies have directly compared approaches with the help of algorithms implementing computational and analogical models. The results, however, are not very clear, and comparisons have often been restricted to a comparison of predictive accuracy for a given dataset and theoretical arguments based on single examples. In addition, it is sometimes very hard to define conceptual differences between models that are independent of their technical implementations. Moreover, much of the debate between frameworks has also made reference to arguments that have so far resisted systematic testing. For example, Stochastic OT has been argued to face problems concerning naturalness and learnability. Analogical models, by contrast, have been argued to be computationally implausible or unconstrained.

The question thus arises how to tease apart these two groups of models. Comparisons based on more datasets, at least as far as morpho-phonological alternations are concerned, are necessary. In addition, pertinent datasets should represent phenomena that differ in their (semi-)productivity from the phenomena that have been investigated so far (such as, e.g., irregular past tenses in English or diphthongization in Spanish). Teasing apart the models seems important given that the two groups of models come from research traditions that make fundamentally different assumptions about the nature of language processing. On the other hand, the two groups of models share the underlying assumption that linguistic generalization starts 'bottom up', in the lexicon; from that perspective, differences between models seem to be more subtle.

Finally, future work will need to combine the mechanisms that have been devised to implement computational and analogical approaches with explicit theories about the nature of representations and lexical distributions. This will enable researchers to eventually develop testable hypotheses of how different degrees of productivity of morpho-phonological alternations can emerge from distributions of stored pronunciations in a single-mechanism model. Needless to say, this is an interdisciplinary endeavor.

References

Albright, Adam. 2002. Islands of reliability for regular morphology: evidence from Italian. *Language* 78 (4). 684–709.

Albright, Adam. 2009. Modeling analogy as probabilistic grammar. In James P. Blevins & Juliette Blevins (eds.), *Analogy in Grammar*, 185–213. Oxford: OUP.

Albright, Adam & Bruce Hayes. 2003. Rules vs. analogy in English past tenses: a computational/experimental study. *Cognition* 90. 119–161.

Arndt-Lappe, Sabine. 2011. Towards an exemplar-based model of stress in English noun–noun compounds. *Journal of Linguistics* 47 (11). 549–585.

Arndt-Lappe, Sabine. 2018. Emergent generalisation in an analogy-based model of word formation: two case studies. In Christoph Haase & Anne Schröder (eds.), *Analogy, Copy, and Representation*, 23–36. Bielefeld: Aisthesis.

Baayen, R. Harald, Ton Dijkstra & Robert Schreuder. 1997. Singulars and plurals in Dutch: evidence for a Parallel Dual-Route Model. *Journal of Memory and Language* 37 (1). 94–117.

Baayen, R. Harald, James M. McQueen, Tom Dijkstra & Rob Schreuder. 2003. Frequency effects in regular inflectional morphology: revisiting Dutch plurals. In Harald R. Baayen & Robert Schreuder (eds.), *Morphological Structure in Language Processing*, 355–390. Berlin: Mouton de Gruyter.

Baayen, R. Harald, Peter Hendrix & Michael Ramscar. 2013. Sidestepping the combinatorial explosion: An explanation of n-gram frequency effects based on naive discriminative learning. *Language and Speech* 56. 329–347.

Baayen, R. Harald, Petar Milin, Dusica Filipović Durdević, Peter Hendrix & Marco Marelli. 2011. An amorphous model for morphological processing in visual comprehension based on naive discriminative learning. *Psychological Review* 118. 438–482.

Bell, Melanie. 2013. *The English Noun Noun Construct: Its Prosody and Structure*. Ph. D. dissertation, University of Cambridge.

Bell, Melanie. 2015. Inter-speaker variation in compound prominence. *Lingue e Linguaggio* 14 (1). 61–78.

Beretta, Alan, Carrie Campbell, Thomas H. Carr, Jie Huang, Lothar M. Schmitt, Kiel Christianson & Yue Cao. 2003. An ER-fMRI investigation of morphological inflection in German reveals that the brain makes a distinction between regular and irregular forms. *Brain and Language* 85 (1). 67–92.

Bermúdez-Otero, Ricardo. 2012. The architecture of grammar and the division of labour in exponence. In Jochen Trommer (ed.), *The Phonology and Morphology of Exponence – the State of the Art*, 8–83. Oxford: OUP.

Bermúdez-Otero, Ricardo. 2018. Stratal Phonology. In S. J. Hannahs & Anna R. K. Bosch (eds.), *The Routledge Handbook of Phonological Theory*, 100–134. Abingdon, OX: Routledge.

Bertram, Raymond, Robert Schreuder & R.Harald Baayen. 2000. The balance of storage and computation in morphological processing: The role of word formation type, affixal homonymy, and productivity. *Journal of Experimental Psychology: Learning, Memory, and Cognition* 26 (2). 489–511.

Blevins, James P. 2003. Stems and paradigms. *Language* 79 (4). 737–767.

Boersma, Paul. 1998. *Functional Phonology: Formalizing the interactions between Articulatory and Perceptual Drives*. The Hague: Holland Academic Graphics.

Boersma, Paul & Bruce Hayes. 2001. Empirical tests of the Gradual Learning Algorithm. *Linguistic Inquiry* 32. 45–86.

Boersma, Paul & David J. M. Weenik. 2018. *PRAAT: Doing Phonetics by Computer*.

Booij, Geert. 1995. *The Phonology of Dutch*. Oxford: OUP.

Booij, Geert. 2009. Lexical storage and phonological change. In Kristin Hanson & Sharon Inkelas (eds.), *The Nature of the Word: Studies in Honor of Paul Kiparsky*, 487–506. Cambridge, MA: MIT Press.

Booij, Geert. 2010. *Construction Morphology*. Oxford: OUP.

Booij, Geert. 2012. *The Grammar of Words. Third Edition*. Oxford: OUP.

Booij, Geert (ed.). 2018. *The Construction of Words: Advances in Construction Morphology* (Studies in Morphology 4). Cham: Springer.

Bowden, Harriet W., Matthew P. Gelfand, Cristina Sanz & Michael T. Ullman. 2010. Verbal inflectional morphology in L1 and L2 Spanish: a frequency effects study examining storage versus composition. *Language Learning* 60 (1). 44–87.

Brand, Sophie & Mirjam Ernestus. 2018. Listeners' processing of a given reduced word pronunciation variant directly reflects their exposure to this variant: evidence from native listeners and learners of French. *Quarterly Journal of Experimental Psychology* 71 (5). 1240–1259.

Bybee, Joan. 1988. Morphology as lexical organization. In Michael Hammond & Michael Noonan (eds.), *Theoretical Morphology: Approaches in Modern Linguistics*, 119–141. San Diego: Academic Press.

Bybee, Joan. 2001. *Phonology and Language Use*. Cambridge: CUP.

Bybee, Joan & Carol L. Moder. 1983. Morphological classes as natural categories. *Language* (59). 251–270.

Bybee, Joan L. & Mary A. Brewer. 1980. Explanation in morphophonemics: changes in Provençal and Spanish preterite forms. *Lingua* 52 (3–4). 201–242.

Bybee, Joan L. & Dan I. Slobin. 1982. Rules and schemas in the development and use of the English past tense. *Language* 58 (2). 265.

Caramazza, Alfonso, Alessandro Laudanna & Cristina Romani. 1988. Lexical access and inflectional morphology. *Cognition* 28 (3). 297–332.

Carlson, Matthew T. & Chip Gerfen. 2011. Productivity is the key: morpho-phonology and the riddle of alternating diphthongs in Spanish. *Language* 87 (3). 510–538.

Cercignani, Fausto. 1980. Early 'umlaut' phenomena in the Germanic languages. *Language* 56 (1). 126–136.

Chandler, Steve. 2010. The English past tense: analogy redux. *Cognitive Linguistics* 21 (3). 371–417.

Chomsky, Noam & Morris Halle. 1968. *The Sound Pattern of English*. New York: Harper & Row.

Clahsen, Harald. 1999. Lexical entries and rules of language: A multidisciplinary study of German inflection. *Behavioral and Brain Sciences* 22. 991–1060.

Collie, Sarah. 2007. *English Stress Preservation: A Case for Stratal Optimality Theory*: PhD dissertation, University of Edinburgh.

Collie, Sarah. 2008. English stress preservation: the case for 'fake cyclicity'. *English Language and Linguistics* 12 (3). 505–532.

Dąbrowska, Ewa. 2008. The effects of frequency and neighbourhood density on adult speakers' productivity with Polish case inflections: an empirical test of usage-based approaches to morphology. *Journal of Memory and Language* 58 (4). 931–951.

Daelemans, Walter & Antal van den Bosch. 2005. *Memory-Based Language Processing*. Cambridge: CUP.

Davis, Stuart & Natsuko Tsujimura. 2018. Arabic nonconcatenative morphology in Construction Morphology. In Geert Booij (ed.), *The Construction of Words: Advances in Construction Morphology* (Studies in Morphology 4), 315–339. Cham: Springer.

Dawdy-Hesterberg, Lisa G. & Janet B. Pierrehumbert. 2014. Learnability and generalisation of Arabic broken plural nouns. *Language, Cognition and Neuroscience* 29 (10). 1268–1282.

de Vaan, Laura, Mirjam Ernestus & Robert Schreuder. 2011. The lifespan of lexical traces for novel morphologically complex words. *The Mental Lexicon* 6 (3). 374–392.

de Vaan, Laura, Robert Schreuder & R.Harald Baayen. 2007. Regular morphologically complex neologisms leave detectable traces in the mental lexicon. *The Mental Lexicon* 2 (1). 1–23.

Di Sciullo, Anna-Maria & Edwin Williams. 1987. *On the Definition of the Word*. Cambridge, MA: MIT Press.

Ernestus, Mirjam. 2000. *Voice Assimilation and Segment Reduction in Casual Dutch: A Corpus-Based Study of the Phonology-Phonetics Interface*. Utrecht: LOT.

Ernestus, Mirjam. 2006. Statistically gradient generalizations for contrastive phonological features. *The Linguistic Review* 23 (3). 4.

Ernestus, Mirjam & R. Harald Baayen. 2003. Predicting the unpredictable: Interpreting neutralized segments in Dutch. *Language* 79 (1). 5–38.

Ernestus, Mirjam & R.Harald Baayen. 2004. Analogical effects in regular past tense production in Dutch. *Linguistics* 42 (5). 873–903.

Eulitz, Carsten & Aditi Lahiri. 2004. Neurobiological evidence for abstract phonological representations in the mental lexicon during speech recognition. *Journal of Cognitive Neuroscience* 16 (4). 577–583.

Fábregas, Antonio, Martin Krämer & Thomas McFadden. 2014. On the representation and selection of exponents. *Lingue e Linguaggio* XII (1). 3–22.

Fábregas, Antonio & Martina Penke. this volume. Word storage and computation. In Vito Pirrelli, Ingo Plag & Wolfgang Dressler (eds.), *Word Knowledge and Word Usage: a Cross-disciplinary Guide to the Mental Lexicon*, 444–494. Berlin/Boston: De Gruyter.

Frisch, Stefan A., Janet B. Pierrehumbert & Michael B. Broe. 2004. Similarity avoidance and the OCP. *Natural Language & Linguistic Theory* 22 (1). 179–228.

Gahl, Susanne & Alan C. L. Yu. 2006. Introduction to the special issue on exemplar-based models in linguistics. In Susanne Gahl & Alan C. L. Yu (eds.), *The Linguistic Review* (Special Issue on Exemplar-based Models in Linguistics) 23. 213–216.

Gaskell, M. G. 2001. Phonological variation and its consequences for the word recognition system. *Language and Cognitive Processes* 16 (5–6). 723–729.

Goldinger, Stephan D. 1996. Words and voices: Episodic traces in spoken word identification and recognition memory. *Journal of Experimental Psychology. Learning, Memory, and Cognition* 22 (5). 1166–1183.

Goldinger, Stephen D. 1998. Echoes of echoes? An episodic theory of lexical access. *Psychological Review* 105 (2). 251–279.

Gordon, Peter & Maria Alegre. 1999. Is there a dual system for regular inflections? *Brain and Language* 68(1–2). 212–217.

Hanique, Iris, Ellen Aalders & Mirjam Ernestus. 2013. How robust are exemplar effects? *The Mental Lexicon* 8. 269–294.

Hanique, Iris & Mirjam Ernestus. 2012. The role of morphology in acoustic reduction. *Lingue e Linguaggio* XI (2). 147–164.

Hanique, Iris, Mirjam Ernestus & Barbara Schuppler. 2013. Informal speech processes can be categorical in nature, even if they affect many different words. *Journal of the Acoustical Society of America* 133 (3). 1644–1655.

Hay, Jennifer. 2001. Lexical frequency in morphology: Is everything relative? *Linguistics* 39 (6). 1041–1070.

Hay, Jennifer. 2003. *Causes and Consequences of Word Structure*. London: Routledge.

Hay, Jennifer & R. Harald Baayen. 2002. Parsing and productivity. In Geert Booij & Jaap van Marle (eds.), *Yearbook of Morphology 2001*, 203–235. Dordrecht: Kluwer.

Inkelas, Sharon. 2014. *The interplay of morphology and phonology* (Oxford surveys in syntax and morphology 8). Oxford: OUP.

Jackendoff, Ray. 1975. Morphological and semantic regularities in the lexicon. *Language* 51 (3). 639–671.

Johnson, Keith. 1997. Speech perception without speaker normalization: An exemplar model. In Keith Johnson & John Mullenix (eds.), *Talker Variability in Speech Processing*, 145–166. San Diego: Academic Press.

Johnson, Keith. 2004. Massive reduction in conversational American English. In: *Spontaneous speech: Data and analysis. Proceedings of the 1st session of the 10th international symposium*. p. 29–54.

Kernan, Keith T. & Bertram G. Blount. 1966. The acquisition of Spanish grammar by Mexican children. *Anthropological Linguistics* 8 (9). 1–14.

Keuleers, Emmanuel. 2008. *Memory-Based Learning of Inflectional Morphology*. PhD. dissertation, University of Antwerp.

Keune, Karen, Mirjam Ernestus, Roeland van Hout & R. Harald Baayen. 2005. Variation in Dutch: from written MOGELIJK to spoken MOK. *Corpus Linguistics and Linguistic Theory* 1 (2). 183–223.

Lahiri, Aditi & William Marslen-Wilson. 1991. The mental representation of lexical form: a phonological approach to the recognition lexicon. *Cognition* 38 (3). 245–294.

Lahiri, Aditi & Henning Reetz. 2002. Underspecified recognition. In Carlos Gussenhoven & Natasha Warner (eds.), *Laboratory Phonology 7*, 637–675. Berlin: Mouton de Gruyter.

Lahiri, Aditi & Henning Reetz. 2010. Distinctive features: phonological underspecification in representation and processing. *Journal of Phonetics* 38 (1). 44–59.

Levelt, Willem J. M. 1989. *Speaking: from Intention to Articulation*. Cambrdige, MA: MIT Press.

Luce, Paul A. & David B. Pisoni. 1998. Recognizing spoken words: the neighbourhood activation model. *Ear and Hearing* 19. 1–36.

Marcus, Gary F., Ursula Brinkmann, Harald Clahsen, Richard Wiese & Stephen Pinker. 1995. German inflection: the exception that proves the rule. *Cognitive Psychology* 29. 189–256.

Meunier, Fanny & Juan Segui. 1999. Morphological priming effect: the role of surface frequency. *Brain and Language* 68 (1–2). 54–60.

Mitterer, Holger. 2011. The mental lexicon is fully specified: evidence from eye-tracking. *Journal of Experimental Psychology. Human Perception and Performance* 37 (2). 496–513.

Nakisa, Ramin, Kim Plunkett & Ulrike Hahn. 2001. Single and dual route models of inflectional morphology. In Peter Broeder & Jaap M. J. Murre (eds.), *Models of Language Acquisition. Inductive and Deductive Approaches*, 201–222. Oxford: OUP.

Newman, Aaron J., Michael T. Ullman, Roumyana Pancheva, Diane L. Waligura & Helen J. Neville. 2007. An ERP study of regular and irregular English past tense inflection. *NeuroImage* 34 (1). 435–445.

Nijveld, Annika, Louis ten Bosch & Mirjam Ernestus. 2015. Exemplar effects arise in a lexical decision task, but only under adverse listening conditions. In Scottish consortium for ICPhS, Marie Wolters, Judy Livingstone, Bernie Beattie, Rachel Smith, Mike MacMahon, Jane Stuart-Smith, James M. Scobbie (eds.), *Proceedings of the 18th International Congress of Phonetic Sciences (ICPhS 2015)*. Glasgow: University of Glasgow.

Norris, Dennis & James M. McQueen. 2008. Shortlist B: A Bayesian model of continuous speech recognition. *Psychological Review* 115 (2). 357–395.

Nosofsky, Robert M. 1986. Attention, similarity, and the identification-categorization relationship. *Journal of Experimental Psychology: General* 115. 39–57.

Peperkamp, Sharon & Emmanuel Dupoux. 2002. A typological study of stress 'deafness'. In Carlos Gussenhoven & Natasha Warner (eds.), *Laboratory Phonology 7*, 203–240. Berlin: Mouton de Gruyter.

Pierrehumbert, Janet. 2002. Word-specific phonetics. In Carlos Gussenhoven & Natasha Warner (eds.), *Laboratory Phonology 7*, 101–140. Berlin: Mouton de Gruyter.

Pinker, Stephen. 1991. Rules of language. *Science* 253. 530–535.

Pinker, Stephen. 1999. *Words and Rules: The Ingredients of Language*. New York: Harper Collins.

Pinker, Steven & Alan Prince. 1994. Regular and irregular morphology and the status of psychological rules in grammar. In Susan D. Lima, Roberta Corrigan & Gregory K. Iverson (eds.), *The Reality of Linguistic Rules*, 321–351. Amsterdam / Philadelphia: John Benjamins.

Pirrelli, Vito, Claudia Marzi, Marcello Ferro, Franco Alberto Cardillo, Harald R. Baayen & Petar Milin. this volume. Psycho-computational modelling of the mental lexicon. In Vito Pirrelli,

Ingo Plag & Wolfgang Dressler (eds.), *Word Knowledge and Word Usage: a Cross-disciplinaryGuide to the Mental Lexicon*, 21-80. Berlin/Boston: De Gruyter.

Plag, Ingo. 2010. Compound stress assignment by analogy: the constituent family bias. *Zeitschrift für Sprachwissenschaft* 29 (2). 243-282.

Plag, Ingo. 2014. Phonological and phonetic variability in complex words: An uncharted territory. *Italian Journal of Linguistics / Rivista di Linguistica* 26 (2). 209-228.

Plag, Ingo & Sonia Ben Hedia. 2018. The phonetics of newly derived words: testing the effect of morphological segmentability on affix duration. In Sabine Arndt-Lappe, Angelika Braun, Claudine Moulin & Esme Winter-Froemel (eds), *Expanding the Lexicon: Linguistic Innovation, Morphological Productivity and Ludicity*, 93-116. Berlin/Boston: de Gruyter.

Plag, Ingo, Julia Homann & Gero Kunter. 2017. Homophony and morphology: the acoustics of word-final S in English. *Journal of Linguistics* 53 (01). 181-216.

Plag, Ingo, Gero Kunter, Sabine Lappe & Maria Braun. 2008. The role of semantics, argument structure, and lexicalization in compound stress assignment in English. *Language* 84 (4). 760-794.

Plag, Ingo & Laura Winther Balling. this volume. Derivational morphology: An integrative perspective on some fundamental questions. In Vito Pirrelli, Ingo Plag & Wolfgang Dressler (eds.), *Word Knowledge and Word Usage: a Cross-disciplinary Guide to the Mental Lexicon*, 288-328. Berlin/Boston: De Gruyter.

Prasada, Sandeep & Stephen Pinker. 1993. Generalization of regular and irregular morphological patterns. *Language and Cognitive Processes* 8. 1-56.

Ramscar, Michael. 2002. The role of meaning in inflection: why the past tense does not require a rule. *Cognitive Psychology* 45 (1). 45-94.

Salmons, Joseph & Patrick Honeybone. 2015. Structuralist historical phonology: systems in segmental change. In Patrick Honeybone & Joseph Salmons (eds.), *The Oxford Handbook of Historical Phonology (Oxford Handbooks in Linguistics)*, 32-46. Oxford: OUP.

Schreuder, Robert & R. Harald Baayen. 1995. Modeling morphological processing. In Laurie B. Feldman (ed.), *Morphological Aspects of Language Processing*, 131-154. Hillsdale, New Jersey: Lawrence Erlbaum.

Skousen, Royal. 1989. *Analogical Modeling of Language*. Dordrecht: Kluwer.

Skousen, Royal. 2002a. An overview of Analogical Modeling. In Royal Skousen, Deryle Lonsdale & Dilworth B. Parkinson (eds.), *Analogical Modeling*, 11-26. Amsterdam / Philadelphia: John Benjamins.

Skousen, Royal. 2002b. Issues in Analogical Modeling. In Royal Skousen, Deryle Lonsdale & Dilworth B. Parkinson (eds.), *Analogical Modeling*, 27-48. Amsterdam / Philadelphia: John Benjamins.

Skousen, Royal, Deryle Lonsdale & Dilworth B. Parkinson (eds.). 2002. *Analogical Modeling*. Amsterdam / Philadelphia: John Benjamins.

Stemberger, Joseph P. & Brian MacWhinney. 1986. Frequency and the lexical storage of regularly inflected forms. *Memory & Cognition* 14 (1). 17-26.

Strycharczuk, Patrycja & James M. Scobbie. 2016. Gradual or abrupt?: the phonetic path to morphologisation. *Journal of Phonetics* 59. 76-91.

Strycharczuk, Patrycja & James M. Scobbie. 2017. Whence the fuzziness?: morphological effects in interacting sound changes in Southern British English. *Laboratory Phonology* 8 (1). 131.

Tabak, Wieke M., Robert Schreuder & R. Harald Baayen. 2005. Lexical statistics and lexical processing: semantic density, information complexity, sex, and irregularity in Dutch. In

Stephen Kepser & Marga Reis (eds.), *Linguistic Evidence: Empirical, Theoretical, and Computational Perspectives*, 529–555. Berlin: Mouton de Gruyter.
Taft, Marcus. 2004. Morphological decomposition and the reverse base frequency effect. *The Quarterly Journal of Experimental Psychology* 57A (4). 745–765.
Tiersma, Peter M. 1982. Local and general markedness. *Language* 58(4). 832–849.
Wurzel, Wolfgang U. 1980. Ways of morphologizing phonological rules. In Jacek Fisiak (ed.), *Historical Morphology*, 443–462. The Hague: Mouton.
Zuraw, Kie. 2010. A model of lexical variation and the grammar with application to Tagalog nasal substitution. *Natural Language & Linguistic Theory* 28 (2). 417–472.

Claudia Marzi, James P. Blevins, Geert Booij and Vito Pirrelli
Inflection at the morphology-syntax interface

Abstract: What is inflection? Is it part of language morphology, syntax or both? What are the basic units of inflection and how do speakers acquire and process them? How do they vary across languages? Are some inflection systems somewhat more complex than others, and does inflectional complexity affect the way speakers process words? This chapter addresses these and other related issues from an interdisciplinary perspective. Our main goal is to map out the place of inflection in our current understanding of the grammar architecture. In doing that, we will embark on an interdisciplinary tour, which will touch upon theoretical, psychological, typological, historical and computational issues in morphology, with a view to looking for points of methodological and substantial convergence from a rather heterogeneous array of scientific approaches and theoretical perspectives. The main upshot is that we can learn more from this than just an additive medley of domain-specific results. In the end, a cross-domain survey can help us look at traditional issues in a surprisingly novel light.

Keywords: Inflection, paradigmatic relations, word processing, word learning, inflectional complexity, family size, entropy

1 The problem of inflection

Inflection is the morphological marking of morphosyntactic and morphosemantic information like case, number, person, tense and aspect (among others) on words. For instance, a word may be specified as singular for the grammatical category of number, i.e. it has a certain value for the feature 'number'. The feature 'number' has two values in English: singular and plural. The choice of specific values for such features may depend on syntactic context or semantic context.

Claudia Marzi, Vito Pirrelli, Italian National Research Council (CNR), Institute for Computational Linguistics, Pisa, Italy
James P. Blevins, George Mason University, College of Humanities and Social Sciences, Fairfax, USA
Geert Booij, Leiden University, Leiden University Centre of Linguistics, Leiden, Netherlands

 Open Access. © 2020 Claudia Marzi et al., published by De Gruyter. This work is licensed under a Creative Commons Attribution-NonCommercial-NoDerivatives 4.0 International License.
https://doi.org/10.1515/9783110440577-007

Morphosyntactic features are inflectional features that play a role in syntax. That is, they play an essential role in the interface between morphology and syntax. For instance, the syntax of languages often requires that words in specific syntactic contexts agree with respect to the value for certain features of other, syntactically related words. An example is subject-verb agreement in English: the finite form of a verb has to agree in the values for person and number with those of the subject. Another well-known type of agreement is gender agreement: in many languages determiners and modifying adjectives have to agree in gender with their head noun.

Besides agreement, there is a second type of syntactically driven feature value selection, traditionally referred to as government: a word or syntactic construction is said to govern the choice of a feature value for another word. For instance, in many languages nouns have to be marked for case, depending on the syntactic or semantic role of that noun (subject, object, agent, etc.). The grammatical or semantic role of an NP then governs the case marking of its head noun.

Morphosemantic features are features that are not required by a syntactic context, and their choice is primarily motivated semantically. For example, all finite forms of English have a tense property such as present or past. Their choice is not governed by syntactic context, but by what content the speaker wants to convey. Yet, the choice is obligatory, as a specific tense property has to be chosen. In this respect, inflection differs from derivation, which is not obligatory. However, context may play a role in the choice of morphosemantic features as well. For instance, in a sentence such as *Yesterday I went to the movies* the past tense form *went* is normally required because of the presence of the adverb *yesterday*.

Inflection may be divided into two subtypes: *inherent inflection* and *contextual inflection* (Booij 1993, 1996; Kibort 2010). Inherent inflection is primarily determined by what the speaker wants to express, and is therefore a matter of choice. The speaker determines, for example, the choice between present tense and past tense of verb forms, and the choice of number (singular or plural) for nouns. Contextual inflection is the kind of inflection that is required by syntactic context. This is the case for the choice of person and number values for finite verbs in English, which is a matter of agreement. Hence, in English the feature 'number' is inherent for nouns, but contextual for verbs. Case marking on nouns may function as contextual inflection in a language like German, where subject nouns and object nouns have to be marked as having nominative and accusative case respectively. That is, this instance of case marking is required by syntax. These are the so-called structural cases, and stand in contrast with semantic case marking, which is a case of inherent inflection. For instance, in Latin we can express the instrumental use of a knife by means of marking the noun with ablative case: *cultr-o* 'with a knife'. This is a semantically governed case, and hence a matter of inherent inflection. Adjectives in German agree in case marking with their head nouns, and, therefore, case marking is contextual. A survey of the different types of inflectional features is given in Kibort (2010).

An example that illustrates what can be expressed by inflection is the following sentence of the language Maale, a North Omotic language spoken in South Ethiopia (Amha 2001: 72):

(1) bayí-ské-nn-ó   tá   zag-é-ne
     cow-INDF-F-ABS   1SG.NOM   see-PRF-AFF.DECL
     'I saw a cow (which I did not know before)'

The word for *cow* has morphological markers for indefiniteness, feminine gender, and absolutive case, and the verb is marked for aspect (Perfect) and for the sentence being affirmative (AFF) and declarative (DECL) in meaning. The ending -*ne* is the cumulative exponence of the two sentence modalities Affirmative and Declarative. The pronoun for 'I' is the nominative form, but there is no separate case marker. This example illustrates some of the formal complications in the expression of inflectional categories, and in particular that there may be no one-to-one mapping of form and meaning in inflection. Inflection may thus considerably increase the formal complexity (discussed in Section 8) of a language system.

A third type of traditional inflectional features are purely morphological features such as inflectional classes for nouns and verbs. In Latin, case marking on nouns is performed in five different ways, and hence it is conventional to distinguish five different inflectional classes (declensions) for nouns. Individual nouns are then marked for the inflectional class they belong to by means of a feature. These features are purely morphological because they tend to have no role in syntax or semantics. Similarly, Latin is associated with a number of inflectional classes for verbs, the conjugations. The patterns described in terms of inflectional classes add substantially to the complexity of a language, and raise the question how children acquire such morphological systems.

In many languages the gender of nouns is marked on related words. For instance, in Dutch nouns have either common or neuter gender, and this manifests itself in agreement phenomena: determiner and adjective have to agree in gender and number with the head noun. However, the nouns themselves do not carry a morphological marker for gender. Thus, one can only discover the gender of Dutch nouns indirectly, by looking at agreement data. This is another challenge for the language learner.

Two interacting but logically distinct issues lie at the core of any linguistic or psycholinguistic account of inflection:

A. the issue of what syntactic contexts require morphosyntactic and/or morpho-semantic word marking and for what lexical/grammatical units;
B. the issue of how morphosyntactic and morpho-semantic information is overtly realized on lexical/grammatical units.

In this chapter we mainly focus on the second issue, the ways in which morphosyntactic and morphosemantic information is morphologically marked. It must be observed that there is no one-to-one relationship between inflectional features and units of form ('morphs') in inflected words, as we will see in Section 2: one morph may express more than one inflectional property (cumulative exponence), and one inflectional property may be expressed by more than one feature (extended exponence). Moreover, the same inflectional property may be expressed in a number of different ways. The patterns of interdependent choices are expressed by inflectional classes. A simple example from English is that the past tense forms of verbs may be formed either by means of suffixation of the stem with -*ed*, or by means of various types of apophony (Ablaut), i.e. vowel change in the stem, usually with consequences for the form of participles. It does not make any difference for the role of the feature value 'Past' in syntax and semantics by which formal means it is expressed. This issue is broached in more detail in Section 2.

Given the lack of a one-to-one mapping of form and meaning in the domain of inflection, it is useful to introduce paradigms, systematically structured sets of inflectional forms of words, in order to make the right generalizations and the proper computations (discussed in Section 5). The nature and structure of inflectional paradigms are discussed in Section 3.

The inflectional paradigms of words may also contain word combinations. For instance, in Germanic and Romance languages various inflectional forms can be treated as consisting of an auxiliary and a non-finite form of a verb. This is referred to as periphrasis (Section 4).

After this brief sketch of the nature of inflectional systems, we will discuss in more detail the way inflection is acquired, how machines can learn it, how it can be modeled computationally and how morphological complexity can be computed (Sections 5–8). Section 9 will summarize our findings.

2 Inflectional syntagmatics

The inflectional features of a morphological system determine observable patterns of variation in shape and distribution. In turn, observable patterns of variation cue features. Yet the relations between features and patterns of variation are often intricate, typically involving complex interactions between syntagmatic arrangements and paradigmatic classes.

2.1 Morphemes and inflection

Post-Bloomfieldian models seek to establish a tight connection between inflectional features and morphotactic units by bundling features and forms into inflectional 'morphemes'. In the immediate constituent analyses developed by Bloomfield's successors, inflectional formatives were included among the terminal elements of a syntactic representation, along with bound stems and free forms. The idea of treating inflectional sub-word units as syntactic elements was taken over by generative accounts, leading to the notion of 'functional categories' and to a general conception of morphology as the 'syntax of words'.

These inflectional sub-word 'units' have long presented some of the most stubbornly recalcitrant challenges for morphemic analysis. Initial attempts to align individual inflectional features with morphotactic units created analytical conundrums in languages as inflectionally impoverished as English. Harris (1942: 113) and Hockett (1947: 240) struggled with the task of segmenting English *children* into morphemic units, due to uncertainty about the synchronic status of the historical strong (*-r*) and weak (*-en*) plural markers. Cognate patterns in other West Germanic languages raise similar problems. For example, some nouns in Modern German distinguish singulars and plurals by an ending, as illustrated by *Tag~Tage* 'day(s)'. Other nouns mark the contrast by a medial vowel alternation as in *Garten~Gärten* 'garden(s)'. In other nouns, the contrast is marked both by an ending and vowel alternation, as in *Fuchs~Füchse* 'fox(es)'. In yet other nouns, such as *Kabel* 'cable(s)' there is no variation between the singular and plural. A biunique correspondence cannot be established in a uniform manner between the feature 'plural' and a 'unit of form' in these cases without assigning more abstract analyses to the surface forms.

Various technical strategies have been explored for assigning morphemic analyses to these and other seemingly non-biunique patterns of inflectional marking. One type of proposal generalizes the notion of 'form'. Among the initial generalizations were different varieties of 'special morphs', such as the 'process morphs' that bundled pairs of alternating vowels into 'units'. Modern descendants include morphophonemic 'readjustment rules' (Halle and Marantz 1993), which intervene between morphemic analyses and surface forms. An alternative strategy involves reclassifying patterns of surface variation, so that some markers can be discounted in determining morphemic biuniqueness (Noyer 1992).

Contemporary interest in exploring these types of technical refinements tends to be concentrated in communities with an overarching commitment to a syntacticocentric conception of morphology. From a morphological perspective, the core problems of morphemic analysis derive from an excessively narrow view of morphological structure and, as such, do not seem amenable to purely technical solutions. Instead, as argued in Matthews (1972, 1991), biunique relations are best understood as limiting cases of generally many-to-many relations between inflectional features and units of form. The extended discussion of Latin conjugational patterns in Matthews (1972) traces the problems of segmentation and interpretation created by coercing a morphemic analysis onto languages that do not conform to an agglutinative ideal. Many-to-many relations between features and forms are so endemic to Latin and Ancient Greek that they are robustly exhibited by regular and even exemplary items. To illustrate this point, Matthews (1991: 174) considers the Ancient Greek form *elelýkete* (e-le-ly-k-e-te) 'you had unfastened', which, as he notes, does not show "any crucial irregularity" and "is in fact the first that generations of schoolchildren used to commit to memory":

> But categories and formatives are in nothing like a one-to-one relation. That the word is Perfective is in part identified by the reduplication *le-* but also by the suffix *-k-*. At the same time, *-k-* is one of the formatives that help to identify the word as Active; another is *-te* which, however, also marks it as '2nd Plural'. (Matthews 1991: 173)

The deeper problem, as Matthews emphasizes, is not just that 'flectional' languages like Latin or Greek appear to exhibit morphemic indeterminacy, but that the indeterminacy is the artifact of a method. By foisting an agglutinative analysis onto flectional languages, a morphemic approach creates problems for which it can provide no principled solution. The attempt to address these problems through technical refinements of a morphemic model seems futile; at least some languages falsify the assumptions of the model:

> One motive for the post-Bloomfieldian model consisted, that is to say, in a genuinely factual assertion about language: namely, that there is some sort of matching between minimal 'sames' of 'form' (morphs) and 'meaning' (morphemes). Qua factual assertion this has subsequently proved false: for certain languages, such as Latin, the correspondence which was envisaged apparently does not exist ... One is bound to suspect, in the light of such a conclusion, that the model is in some sense wrong. (Matthews 1972: 124)

Subsequent studies have provided further confirmation that inflectional features and units of form are, in the general case, related by many-to-many 'exponence' relations. One strand of this research has even explored relations that are more 'exuberantly' many-to-many than the patterns exhibited by classical languages (Harris 2009; Caballero and Harris 2010). A pair of related conclusions can be drawn from this work. The first is that, when applied to all but the most uniformly agglutinative structures, morphemic models create problems of analysis while also obscuring the organization and function of form variation. The second is that morphemes cannot provide the basis for inflectional description and that even descriptive conventions like 'morpheme glosses' harbor untenable idealizations.

2.2 Varieties of exponence

Although exponence relations do not share the descriptive shortcomings of morphemes, they exhibit their own characteristic limitations. What unites the diverse exponence relations investigated in the realizational literature is a fundamentally negative property: the relations all involve non-biunique feature-form associations. The realizational tradition offers no positive characterization of these relations, and contains almost no discussion of what functions, if any, might be associated with different patterns of exponence.

A model that recognizes many-to-many feature-form relations sacrifices the attractively simple compositional semiotics of a morphemic model, in which complex forms and complex meanings are built up in parallel from atomic form-meaning pairs. As expressed by the 'Separation Hypothesis' (Beard 1995), realizational accounts treat feature bundles as 'minimum meaningful units' and assign no meaning or function to variation in the 'spell-out' of bundles. In effect, realizational models move from one extreme to another, replacing individually meaningful morphemes with collectively meaningless exponents.

Both of these extremes reflect a set of limiting assumptions about the nature of inflectional functions and meanings. Three assumptions are of particular importance. The first is that meanings are exclusively 'extramorphological' and do not encode information about the shape or distribution of related forms, or other properties of the morphological system. The second is that discrete meanings are associated statically with forms, not determined dynamically within a network of contrasts. The third is that analyses and interpretations are taken to be assignable to forms in isolation from the systems in which they function.

By incorporating these assumptions, realizational approaches close off any inquiry into the meaning or function of different patterns of inflectional exponence. The adoption of other, equally conservative, assumptions imposes similarly severe constraints. Whereas the role of paradigmatic structure has been a matter of dispute for most of the modern period, the relevance of morphotactic structure has remained almost unquestioned. However, in even the best-studied languages, there have been no systematic attempts to provide cognitive motivation for the morphotactic structures assigned in standard descriptions. It is sometimes believed that a shift from orthographic to phonemic representation places analyses on a firmer foundation. But it is well-known that inflectional contrasts may be cued by sub-phonemic contrasts (Baayen et al. 2003; Kemps et al. 2005). Moreover, the crude procedures of distributional analysis used to determine morphotactic structure have no provision for distinguishing sequences that function as units in the synchronic system from those that are diachronic relics of the processes of morphologization that produced the system.

2.3 Synchronic vs diachronic structure

The confound between synchronically active structure and diachronic residue derives ultimately from the general conflation of synchronic and diachronic dimensions in the post-Bloomfieldian tradition. To a large extent, this tradition is guided by the goal of exploring the descriptive potential of recasting diachronic analyses in synchronic terms. Underlying representations are transparent synchronic proxies for the 'least common ancestors' of a set of surface forms. Due to the regularity of sound changes, these ancestors will tend to be definable in terms of a minimum edit distance from their descendants. The serial structure of derivations likewise mirrors the temporal order of the sound changes that occur in the history of a language. The agglutinative bias of a morphemic model (termed 'The Great Agglutinative Fraud' by Hockett (1987: 83)) also reflects an essentially historical perspective. A perfectly agglutinative system is one in which the waves of grammaticalization that build up complex forms preserve the discrete meaning and morphotactic separability of the morphologized parts, while maintaining a link between their meaning and form.

However, the shift from a diachronic to a synchronic perspective is as disruptive to the interpretation of a post-Bloomfieldian model as the move from biuniqueness to many-to-many exponence relations is for the semiotics of a realizational approach. Morphotactic structure is often a useful guide to the historical processes that applied to produce the inflected forms of a language. Yet knowledge of the historical origins of forms can distort analyses of their current status and function. This problem arises in an acute form in the 'templatic' analyses assigned to languages of the Algonquian and Athapaskan families. One tradition of analysis, illustrated in the Navajo grammar of Young and Morgan (1987), associates verbs with morphotactic 'templates' consisting of sequences of 'slots', each containing a substitution class of formatives. An intricate overlay of distributional and interpretative dependencies holds between the 'choices' at different points in the template. Not all slots need be 'filled' in with a surface form and, typically, many are empty. As a result, there is a vast contrast between the complexity of the 'underlying' templatic structure and the morphotactics of surface forms. In effect, the dimensions of variation in the templatic descriptions provide a record of the history of the derivation of the modern forms. The apparent 'choices' are no longer independent in the modern languages but have been encapsulated in larger recurrent sequences, as represented in the type of bipartite structure proposed by McDonough (2000).

In sum, despite the appeal of a uniform approach to syntactic and inflectional patterns, the models developed within the broad post-Bloomfieldian tradition incorporate biases and assumptions that have mostly impeded attempts to understand the structure and organization of inflectional systems. The analytical assumptions incorporated in approaches that were developed expressly to model inflectional patterns offer a usefully different perspective.

3 Paradigmatic distribution and interpretation

As their name suggests, classical 'Word and Paradigm' (WP) models shift the fundamental part-whole relation in an inflectional system onto the relation between individual words and inflectional paradigms. This shift does not deny the significance of sub-word variation but instead interprets variation in a larger paradigmatic context. The context is defined by the interaction of two main relational dimensions. The first dimension is **discriminative**, implicit in the etymological origin of the term 'inflection', which, as Matthews (1991: 190) notes, derives "from a Latin Verb whose basic meaning was 'to bend' or 'to modify'". Patterns of form variation serve to distinguish larger 'free forms' with an independent distribution that can communicate meaning or function within a system. In contrast to morphemic models, variants are not individually meaningful; in contrast to realizational models, they are not collectively meaningless. The variants that discriminate a form determine its place in a similarity space defined by the inflectional contrasts exhibited by a language.

The second dimension is **implicational** or **predictive**, expressed by "the ... general insight ... that one inflection tends to predict another" (Matthews 1991: 197). Patterns of variation within an inflectional system tend to be interdependent in ways that allow speakers to predict novel forms on the basis of forms that they have encountered. The predictive patterns that hold between forms determine the place of a form within implicational networks.

Discriminative and implicational relations are particularly relevant to the organization of inflectional systems, which exhibit highly uniform patterns of contrast and predictability. The inflected variants of an open-class item typically define a closed, uniform feature space and a largely transparent semantic space. For an item of a given word class or inflection class, it is possible to specify the features that are distinctive for that item. This degree of uniformity and item-independence is what permits the strict separation of features and form in a realizational model. From even partial exposure to an inflectional system, speakers can arrive at reliable expectations about the number of forms of an item, assign interpretations to these forms, and even predict the shape of not yet encountered and potential variants.

The discriminative and implicational organization of inflectional systems is saliently reflected in the ways that these systems are described. The notion of a 'morphological gap' tends to be applied to cases in which predictable inflected forms are either missing or occur less frequently than expected (compared with the frequency of corresponding forms of other items of the same class). Unattested derivational formations are more rarely described as 'gaps', since a derivational system is not conceptualized as a closed, fully populated, space of forms. The notions 'suppletion', and even 'syncretism', also apply almost exclusively to inflected forms. Suppletion reflects unmet expectations about predictability and syncretism violates assumptions of discriminability. In the derivational domain, both patterns are usually treated as cases of ambiguity. Conversely, whereas derivational formations are often described as 'established', this term is rarely applied to individual inflected forms.

3.1 Words

The role of words and paradigms is a distinctive characteristic of classical WP descriptions of inflectional patterns. The use of word forms to exhibit variation accords with the view that "[t]he word is a more stable and solid focus of grammatical relations than the component morpheme by itself" (Robins 1959: 128). In support of this claim, paradigmatic approaches present individual case studies but no systematic attempt to explain **why** words provide a useful basis for inflectional description. Instead, word-based analyses of inflectional systems exploit the generally positive correlation between unit size and grammatical determinacy. In part, this correlation derives from the monotonic nature of determinacy. A fully determinate form may be composed of individually indeterminate parts. To take a simple example, the indeterminacy associated with an element such as English *-er*, which may mark comparative forms of adjectives or agentive nominals, is resolved in the word form *spammer*. In contrast, a set of fully determinate parts cannot be arranged into an indeterminate whole without contradicting the original assumption that they are determinate.

The modern development of a quantitative and cognitively-grounded discriminative approach offers a further perspective on this issue. As 'free forms' in the sense of Bloomfield (1933), words are the smallest units with an independently statable range of distributions and uses. As such, words are the smallest units with the kinds of individual 'conditioning histories' that are approximated by semantic vectors in models of distributional semantics such as Marelli and Baroni (2015). Correlating with these distributional and functional properties are measures of the uncertainty at word boundaries and the 'informativeness' of these boundaries, as operationalized by effects on compressability (Gertzen et al. 2016).

The interpretive determinacy of words also underlies the 'morphological information' that they express, i.e. information about the shape and distribution of other forms in a system. A form in isolation is of limited diagnostic value, reflecting the fact that such 'pure' forms are ecologically invalid abstractions. Speakers encounter forms in syntagmatic and paradigmatic contexts that guide their interpretation and support reliable inferences about related forms. The Paradigm Structure Constraints of Wurzel (1970) represent an early attempt to model this structure in terms of logical implication. Subsequent approaches, exploiting insights from the morphological processing tradition represented by Kostić et al. (2003) and Moscoso del Prado Martín et al. (2004), develop more robust information-theoretic measures of implicational structure. This approach has offered a useful perspective on questions concerning the structure and 'complexity' of patterns and classes, the nature of defectiveness and other properties of inflectional systems. Overall, the approach lends support to the traditional view that the inflectional component is not an unstructured inventory but, rather, a system, in which patterns of interdependency facilitate predictions about the whole system from a subset of its forms. Patterns of predictability also contribute to an understanding of the learnability of complex inflectional systems, and help to clarify the degree of variation in the complexity of descriptions of inflectional systems. In at least some cases, this variation reflects the intrinsic difficulty of describing systems as assemblages of independent items that are composed of recurrent parts. Although this may provide a reasonable basis for enumerating the patterns attested in a language by means of a written grammar, it is not a plausible model of acquisition or use. Much of the extreme cross-linguistic variation in grammars and typological accounts appears to be an artefact of descriptive tasks that never arise for speakers and hence are not subject to pressures that ensure learnability.

3.2 Paradigms

In descriptions of inflection class morphology, the variation exhibited by a class system is typically illustrated by full paradigms of 'exemplary' items, together with diagnostic 'principal parts' for non-exemplary items. There has been a tendency for this descriptive practice to be overinterpreted, by advocates as well as by opponents of paradigmatic approaches.

Reflecting the pedagogical origins of the classical tradition, exemplary paradigm and principal part descriptions are designed to provide a description of inflectional patterns that is maximally transparent for learners. There is neither cognitive nor empirical motivation for assuming that this pedagogical organization mirrors the format in which speakers represent knowledge about inflectional patterns. This observation can be traced at least to Hockett (1967), in speculations about the divergence between pedagogical and cognitively-plausible models of paradigmatic structure, and morphological description in general:

> in his analogizing ... [t]he native user of the language ... operates in terms of all sorts of internally stored paradigms, many of them doubtless only partial; and he may first encounter a new basic verb in any of its inflected forms. (Hockett 1967: 221)

The intervening half century has seen the development of methodologies for probing speakers' morphological knowledge, though the most robust measures, such as morphological family size (de Jong et al. 2000; Mulder et al. 2014), apply to derivational families. In parallel, large-scale corpora and other lexical resources have provided detailed information about the composition and structure of the forms 'in circulation' within a speech community. It is well established that forms exhibit a Zipfian distribution (Zipf 1935), in which the frequency of a word is (approximately) inversely proportional to its rank in a frequency table. There are two particularly significant consequences for the learning of inflectional systems. First, roughly half of the forms that a speaker encounters will be occurrences of a small number of high frequency items (*the*, *of*, etc., in English). Second, almost half of the items of a language will be hapax legomena, i.e., forms that occur exactly once in a corpus, irrespective of its size, and thus are unlikely to be encountered multiple times by speakers.

These distributional biases support Hockett's conjecture about the nature of the input that a speaker encounters. They also argue against a naive pedagogically-influenced conception of paradigmatic structure and against any version of the 'Full Listing Hypothesis' (Hankamer 1989) on which speakers would be assumed to memorize the inflected forms of a language. Speakers appear to encounter only a small proportion of the forms of open-class items; for up to half of the lexicon, they may encounter just a single form. Nevertheless, speakers appear to be able to 'pool' the variation exhibited by partial paradigms and extend attested patterns to new forms. The format of this knowledge and the mechanisms that speakers use to amalgamate and extrapolate patterns are not yet well understood. However, there is evidence to suggest that speakers exploit lexical neighborhoods to define an analogical base that can bootstrap the process (Blevins et al. 2017).

The morphological processing literature has also investigated a range of effects in which paradigmatic structure appears to play a significant role. Among the most striking of these is the **relative entropy** effects first reported in Milin et al. (2009a, 2009b). These studies found that speakers in a lexical decision task were sensitive to the divergence between the frequency distribution of an item's inflectional paradigm and that of its inflection class. To take a specific example, the more closely the distribution of the forms of the Serbian noun *planina* 'mountain' matches the distribution of the 'feminine' declension in Serbian, the faster and more accurately speakers recognize forms of *planina*. This finding has been confirmed in follow-up studies including Baayen et al. (2011) and Milin et al. (2017).

3.3 Syntagmatic/paradigmatic integration

The interpretation of syntagmatic variation as, in part, a marker of paradigmatic relations also clarifies the motivation for the representational agnosticism of Neogrammarians such as Paul (1920). On the type of 'constructive' (Blevins 2006) interpretation of structure adopted in Post-Bloomfieldian models, forms are composed of a determinate sequence of atomic elements. On a more agnostic 'abstractive' interpretation, structure emerges from patterns exhibited by sets of forms. Multiple form classes are potentially relevant for the purposes of discriminating forms and deducing implications. Hence, the determination of syntagmatic structure, like the enumeration of inflection classes, is task-dependent. The structure exhibited by forms, like the number of classes contained by a language, depends on the purposes for which one is assigning structure or counting classes.

Current approaches to the modelling of inflectional patterns address a broad range of other issues. Network architectures, particularly 'wide learning' networks (Baayen and Hendrix 2017) provide a representation of paradigmatic structure that avoids the 'combinatorial explosion' (Baayen et al. 2013) associated with lists of forms, particularly if surface variants are encoded by exemplars. Models of vector semantics provide a way of grounding the interpretation of forms in an observable dimension of variation, i.e. distribution. The other observable dimension, variation in shape, is described by discriminable contrasts. Taken together, these dimensions offer an interpretation of the features employed in the description of inflectional systems, without assigning a 'meaning' to the features themselves.

4 Periphrasis and grammaticalization

We have to do with periphrasis if for certain cells of an inflectional paradigm no synthetic morphological form is available. Instead, a combination of words, an analytic or periphrastic form has to be used. For instance, Latin has no synthetic forms for the perfective passive of verbs, as illustrated here for the 3SG forms of the verb *laudāre* 'to praise':

Table 1: Imperfective and perfective 3SG forms of laudāre.

Imperfective	Active	Passive
PRESENT	*laudat*	*laudātur*
PAST	*laudābat*	*laudābātur*
FUTURE	*laudābit*	*laudābitur*

Perfective	Active	Passive
PRESENT	*laudāvit*	*laudātus/a/um est*
PAST	*laudāverat*	*laudātus/a/um erat*
FUTURE	*laudāverit*	*laudātus/a/um erit*

The cells for the perfective passive are a combination of the passive participle (that, like adjectives, agrees with the subject of the clause with respect to case, gender and number) and a form of the verb *esse* 'to be'. If these word combinations were not considered part of the verbal paradigm, Latin verbs would have a paradigm with a gap for the perfective passive forms. These periphrastic forms receive a perfect interpretation, although the forms of the verb *esse* 'to be' are that of the imperfect tense.

An additional argument for considering these word combinations as filling paradigm cells is the following. Latin has a number of so-called deponent verbs, verbs with a passive form but an active meaning. For instance, the verb *loquor* 'speak' is such a deponent verb. The crucial observation is that a word-sequence such as *locutus est* receives an active interpretation as well, and means 'he has spoken'. This parallelism in interpretation as active meanings is to be expected if these analytic forms belong to the inflectional paradigm of verbs (Börjars et al. 1997).

This means that phrasal constructions may express inflectional properties, just like morphological constructions (Ackerman and Stump 2004; Börjars et al. 1997; Sadler and Spencer 2001). Moreover, they cannot be analyzed as regular syntactic combinations because the morphosyntactic features of these constructions cannot always be determined on the basis of those of their word components (Ackerman and Stump 2004; Popova 2010). This can be illustrated by the periphrastic constructions for perfect tense in Dutch. These are combinations of the verbs *hebben* 'have' or *zijn* 'be' with the past participles of verbs, as in:

(2) *Jan   heef-t   het   boek ge-lez-en*
    John have-3S   DET   book PTCP-read-PTCP
    'John has read the book'

(3) *Het   meisje is   ge-vall-en*
    DET   girl   be.3S   PTCP-fall-PTCP
    'The girl has fallen'

These two verbs are called auxiliaries, as they do not have their regular meaning in periphrasis, but instead express perfect aspect. The auxiliaries in these sentences have a present tense form. The past participles do not carry the perfective meaning either, as they can also be used with an imperfect meaning in passive sentences. Hence, the perfect meaning is the holistic property of the word combination as a whole. This is why we speak of periphrastic constructions, because constructions are form-meaning combinations with possibly holistic properties that cannot be deduced from properties of their constituents.

Periphrastic constructions require a formal analysis which does justice to these holistic properties. One model is that of Paradigm Function Morphology. In this model phrasal combinations can function as the realization of the set of morphosyntactic and/or morphosemantic features of a lexeme. For instance, *heeft gelezen* in example (2) is treated as the realization of the lexeme *lezen* 'to read' with the feature values [3.sg.perf] (Popova 2010).

In the framework of Construction Morphology, periphrastic constructions are accounted for by means of the notion of 'constructional idiom' (Booij 2010). In English, for instance, the perfect tense form of verbs is a complex verbal predicate that consists of a form of the verb *have* with a past participle. This specific pattern expresses the perfect meaning, which cannot be derived from the meaning of one of the constituent words: neither the verb *have*, nor the participle itself is the carrier of the perfect meaning. The following constructional idiom may be assumed for the English perfect tense construction:

(4)   [[have]$_{Vi}$ [past participle]$_{Vj}$]$_{Vk}$ ↔ [PERF [SEM$_j$]]$_{SEMk}$

where PERF stands for the meaning 'perfect tense', and SEM for the meaning of the relevant indexed constituent.

The use of auxiliaries for periphrastic constructions is a case of grammaticalization, i.e. the process by which words with an original lexical meaning acquire a more grammatical meaning (Hopper and Traugott 1993). For instance, English *have* has the lexical meaning of 'possess' but this is not the relevant meaning in the periphrastic tense forms. Dutch has two auxiliaries for perfect tense, reflecting two different historical sources of these constructions, a possessive construction and a predicative one. In English the predicative construction was the source of the use of the auxiliary *be*, as in older English *He is fallen* 'He is in a situation of fallen-ness', which is now replaced in present-day English by *He has fallen*. This illustrates that English *have* is even more grammaticalized than its Dutch counterpart.

5 Lexicon and inflection in computational morphology

In computational terms, many aspects of the theoretical debate dealt with in the previous sections boil down to the problem of dealing with cases of many-to-many surface relations between form and function at the word level. Consider the representations in (5) and (6), where the Italian verb forms *tengo* '(I) hold' (present indicative, 1st person singular) and *tieni* '(you) hold' (present indicative, 2nd person singular) – from the verb TENERE 'hold' – are segmented into their surface constituents.

(5)   [[*teng*] $_{HOLD}$ + [*o*] $_{pres\ ind\ 1s}$] $_{HOLD\ pres\ ind\ 1s}$

(6)   [[*tien*] $_{HOLD}$ + [*i*] $_{pres\ ind\ 2s}$] $_{HOLD\ pres\ ind\ 2s}$

The same word forms are split into more abstract sub-lexical constituents in (7) and (8):

(7)   [[*ten*] $_{HOLD}$ + [*o*] $_{pres\ ind\ 1s}$] $_{HOLD\ pres\ ind\ 1s}$

(8)   [[*ten*] $_{HOLD}$ + [*i*] $_{pres\ ind\ 2s}$] $_{HOLD\ pres\ ind\ 2s}$

Representations in (7) and (8) define a sign-based (biunique) relationship between the stem *ten* and its lexeme HOLD. This is blurred in (5) and (6), where lexical formatives are not identical, leaving us with the problem of classifying *teng* and *tien* as stem allomorphs of the same verb. In the generative linguistic literature, shorter lexicons are generally preferred over more verbose ones, under the standard generative assumption that what can be computed should not be stored. However, for a fully-inflected form to be produced from the representation in (7), some adjustment rules have to be added to the grammar (e.g. a velar insertion rule before back vowels in the case at hand). In the Italian conjugation, many of these rules do not apply across the board, but obtain for particular lexemes in specific contexts only (Pirrelli and Battista 2000). So the question of descriptive economy cannot really be confined to the lexicon, since a compact lexicon may call for a rather profligate set of *ad hoc* rules. Information theory provides a means to address these empirical issues on a principled basis. In an information-theoretic adaptation of Harris' ideas (1951), Goldsmith (2001, 2006) models the task of morphological induction as a data compression (or Minimum Description Length, MDL) problem: "find the battery of inflectional markers forming the shortest grammar that best fits the empirical evidence" (Rissanen 1989). The grammar is a set of paradigms, and the empirical evidence a reference corpus, where each form occurs with a specific frequency distribution. In this framework, MDL penalizes two descriptive extremes. First, it disfavors an extremely redundant grammar, where each word form is part of a singleton paradigm that has that form as its only member. This in fact amounts to a repository of fully listed words, where each form is assigned the probability with which it occurs in the corpus. At the opposite end, a very compact grammar contains one overall paradigm only, where any verb stem can freely combine with any affix. This is a very short and redundancy-free grammar, but it overgenerates wildly, thus providing a poor approximation of the distributional evidence of the forms attested in the corpus. In what follows, we consider a rather more classical computational approach to this issue, using Finite State Transducers.

5.1 Finite State Transducers

A Finite State Transducer (FST) is an abstract computational device that turns an input string into an output string. Figure 1 depicts an FST for the present indicative stems of the Italian verb TENERE 'hold': namely *ten-*, *tien-* and *teng-*. In the graph, nodes (circles) are memory states, and directed arcs (arrows) represent transitions from one state to another. Each arc is decorated with either a single symbol, or a pair of symbols separated by a colon. The colon is a mapping operator and reads: "the symbol on the left (or lexical symbol) is mapped onto the symbol on the right (either a surface symbol or a gloss)". If only one symbol appears on the arc, this means that the symbol is mapped onto itself, i.e. lexical and surface symbols are identical. Lower-case characters in the Latin alphabet represent simple letters; 'ϵ' is a meta-symbol representing the null character; and 'Σ' is a variable ranging over any input symbol. Finally, upper-case Latin characters are linguistic glosses that express morphosyntactic features (e.g. 'PAST' or '3S'), stem indexes (e.g. 'B_1') and lexical content ('TENERE').

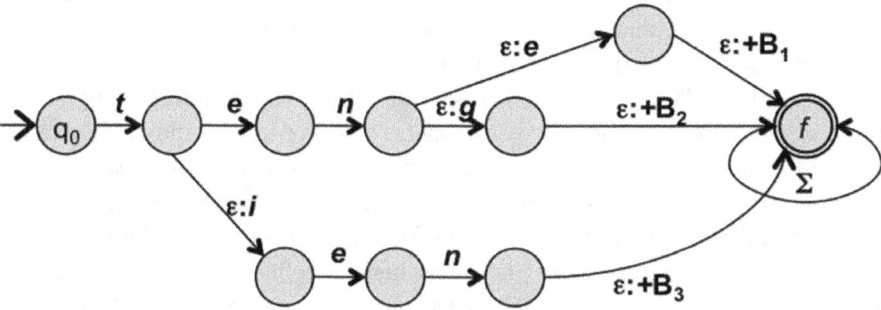

Figure 1: A Finite State Transducer for the present indicative stem allomorphs of Italian TENERE 'hold'.

Starting from the initial state q_0, the FST reads one input symbol at a time from left to right, until it consumes the whole input string. Upon reading a symbol (e.g. 't' in *teng-*) in a particular state, the transducer looks for a state-leaving arc that is labelled with the same input symbol. If such an arc exists, it is traversed, and the mapping operation annotated on the arc is carried out. An input string is successfully processed if the FST finds itself in the final state *f* after reading the final letter of the input string. Note that all branches of the FST in Figure 1 end up with a stem index (B_i) being inserted: e.g. 'ϵ: + B_2'. The index enforces the constraint that the just read off stem allomorph is followed by an inflectional ending selecting the appropriate index.[1]

---

[1] Stem indexing (Stump 2001) enforces a relationship between a verb stem and a set of cells in the verb paradigm. Although stem indexes and stem formation processes are often mutually implied (as illustrated by the FST in Figure 1), they might occasionally be independent (Pirrelli & Battista 2000).

For example, in the present indicative, *teng-* can be followed only by the first singular and third plural ending.

A number of properties make FSTs theoretically interesting devices. FSTs are not classical rewrite rules. They enforce a correspondence relation between two distinct *levels* of representation. The relation is declarative, parallel and bi-directional. We can easily swap input and output symbols and use, for word generation, the same transducer designed for word parsing. This means that we can understand the *teng-ten* relation in either of the following ways: (i) *g* is trailed after *ten-* to incrementally (in Stump's 2001 terms) add B_2 to the resulting representation; (ii) *teng is* the result of applying to *ten* a specific paradigm function that realizes the appropriately indexed allomorph B_2. In the former case B_2 adds some (disjunctive) morphological content. In the latter case, it is only the indexed trace of a realizational process.

Secondly, FSTs represent lexical items as a union set of intersecting automata. Since automata define processing operations over lexical and surface representations, the whole finite state machinery amounts to a two-level word graph incorporating lexical information, morphotactic constraints and context-sensitive formal changes, all cast into a uniform format. FSTs thus blur the distinction between lexical representations and rule schemata defined over lexical representations. This makes them extremely powerful processing devices, capturing morphological generalizations at fine-grained levels of generality, ranging from sweeping, exceptionless phonological processes to lexically-conditioned surface adjustments. The overall emerging view is closer to the idea of a large, integrated repository of both specific and general information, than to the classical notion of a generative grammar consisting of a lexical repository and a set of rules.

On a less positive note, the high expressive power of FSTs can get a major liability. For a lexicon of average inflectional complexity, it soon becomes extremely cumbersome to craft by hand the whole range of fine-grained mapping relations that are needed for recognition/production. And this can be uselessly laborious. For example, since every stem must be associated with a specific cell index, transitions to cell-specific indexes must also be stipulated for the singleton stem of a regular paradigm. We thus miss the obvious generalization that only irregular paradigms require explicit stipulation of the transitions from stem alternants to specific subsets of paradigm cells. The DATR formalism (Evans and Gazdar 1996) provides an effective framework for implementing default statements through inheritance relations in the lexicon, and can be used to enforce both high- and low-order constraints on stem allomorphy.

5.2 Hierarchical lexicons

A DATR lexicon is an inheritance network of nodes, each consisting of a set of morphologically related forms, ranging from major inflection classes (Table 2, columns 1 and 2), to regular (Table 2, column 3) and subregular paradigms (Table 2, column 4). An inflected form like, e.g., *tengo* is obtained from the abstract lexical schema 'X + o' by assigning 'X' an appropriate stem.

Each entry node is defined by a "name" (the unique identifier in bold ended by a colon), followed by a few "statements", each taking one line in Table 2, with the following general format: "attribute == value" (where '==' is an assignment operator). An attribute is surrounded by angle brackets. It can consist of a single label (e.g. "<B>", in Table 2), or by a sequence of blank-separated labels, defining an increasingly specific attribute (e.g. "<B 2>"). The empty label '<>' denotes the most general or unspecified attribute. Any label added to '<>' defines a branching node in the hierarchy: the further down we go in the hierarchy, the more specific the attribute. Accordingly, '<pres ind 3S>' is more specific than '<pres ind>', which is in turn more specific than '<pres>'. A value can be a constant string (e.g. *tem* in column 3, Table 2), or another attribute, either simple or complex.

Table 2: DATR lexical entries for Second Conjugation (2C) Italian verbs.

1	2	3	4
Morpholex-paradigm-0: <B>== "<root>".	**2C_VERB:** <>== Morpholex-paradigm-0 <pres ind 1S>== "<B 2>" o <pres ind 2S>== "<B 3>" i <pres ind 3S>== "<B 3>" e <pres ind 1P>== "<B 4>" i a m o <pres ind 2P>== "<B>" e t e <pres ind 3P>== "<B 2>" o n o.	**TEMERE:** <>== 2C_VERB <root>== t e m.	**TENERE:** <>== 2C_VERB <B 2>== t e n g <B 3>== t i e n <root>== t e n.

Hierarchies of specificity play a crucial role in DATR information flow. General information, defined by attributes higher up in the hierarchy, tends by default to percolate to lower (more specific) attributes, unless the latter explicitly contain overriding information. For example, the node 'Morpholex-paradigm-0' (column 1, Table 2) states that the index 'B' is assigned whatever string is assigned to the 'root'. This information is inherited by the node '2C_VERB' (short for "second conjugation verb": column 2, Table 2) through the statement "<>== Morpholex_paradigm_0", which reads: "whatever information is in Morpholex_paradigm_0 is copied here". This statement boils down to adding all statements in 'Morpholex_paradigm_0' to '2C_VERB'. At this level, however, 'root' is assigned no surface string. This is done in the node 'TEMERE' (column 3, Table 2), which stipulates that all statements of '2C_VERB' ("<>== 2C_VERB") are inherited locally: here, the attribute 'root' is instantiated with the string *tem*. In turn, 'B' is assigned the local value of 'root' (<B>= "<root>"). At the same time, more specific 'B' attributes ('B 2', 'B 3', and 'B 4') inherit the string *tem* as their value, for want of more specific information being assigned locally. Inheritance thus captures the general statement that, in regular verbs, the basic stem 'B' is assigned by default to all present indicative cells. Conversely, in an irregular verb like 'TENERE' (column 4, Table 2), stem indexes ('B 2' and 'B 3') are explicitly assigned specific allomorphs (respectively *teng* and *tien*), thereby overriding the default distribution of the string *ten* canonically assigned to 'root'.

Thanks to default inheritance, DATR can describe fragments of comparatively complex inflectional systems like the Italian conjugation in a compact and elegant way (Pirrelli and Battista 2003). Note that fully-specified paradigms and abstract paradigmatic schemata are represented with the same toolkit of formal tools, in line with the view that they are statements of the same kind, which differ only in coverage. These statements are expressed in terms of paradigmatic relations between stem indexes, and bear witness to the theoretical usefulness of word paradigms as descriptive formal devices (Pirrelli 2000; Blevins 2003, 2006, 2016). We will return to issues of inter-cell predictability later in this chapter (Section 8), in connection with the problem of measuring the inflectional complexity of a language in information theoretic terms (e.g. Ackerman and Malouf 2013).

DATR offers a handy computational framework for modelling Jackendoff's (2002) idea of the lexicon as containing entries whose information may range from very general (i.e. obtaining for an entire class of verbs) to very specific (i.e. holding for one verb lemma or one verb form only). In DATR, the lexicon is not just a list of stored units, but defines the linguistic domain where morphological processes apply, thus coming very close to a rigorous computational framework for testing the Lexicalist hypothesis (Halle 1973; Jackendoff 1975; Aronoff 1976; Scalise 1984; Lieber 1992). Someone may keep considering it useful and conceptually desirable to draw a line between pieces of lexical information that are actually listed (and thus form the lexicon in a strict sense) from those which are computed on-line through general morphological statements. Nonetheless it soon gets very difficult to comply with this principled distinction, especially when it comes to the description of inflectional systems of average complexity (see Corbett and Fraser 1993 for another example with Russian inflection).

Upon reflection, this is not just an issue of descriptive accuracy. In fact, it boils down to the deeper, explanatory question of how children can come up with the relevant knowledge needed to optimally process inflected forms. According to this learning-based view, redundant patterns are predominantly statistical, and even irregularities appear to be motivated by their frequency distribution in the system and the general-purpose learning strategies of the human language processor. All of this can admittedly be very different in character from the formal constraints on units, representations or rule systems proposed within theoretical and computational models. Nonetheless, it represents, in our view, an extremely insightful entry point to the grand issue of language architecture. In the following section we shortly consider some implications of the regular vs. irregular distinction from a developmental perspective, to then move on to the computational modelling of inflection acquisition (see Ravid, Keuleers and Dressler 2020, this volume, for a more comprehensive overview of morphology acquisition).

6 Acquiring inflection

6.1 The logical problem of acquiring inflection

According to a classic account (Berwick 1985; Pinker 1989, 1984), the task of a child attempting to learn how verbs and nouns are inflected can be described as involving grammar hypothesis testing. This is not too dissimilar from the MDL grammar evaluation framework illustrated in the previous section. Children need to arrive at a grammar hypothesis H that includes all well-formed inflected forms of the input language, while excluding ill-formed ones. An important logical problem with this account is represented by the case when the child's grammar is a superset of the target grammar (Pinker 1989): the child masters all correctly inflected forms, but nonetheless also produces some ungrammatical forms (e.g. (s)he says *went* and **goed* interchangeably). How can children recover from these errors?

In the acquisitional literature, the question of whether children can correct themselves on the basis of received explicit negative evidence (e.g. negative correction by their care-givers) has been highly debated. Some scholars suggest there is little reason to believe that children are supervised in this way (Bruck and Ceci 1999; Taatgen and Anderson 2002; but see Chouinard and Clark 2003 for a different view). Even when they are corrected (which is neither frequent nor systematic), they may take little notice of correction. In contrast with this position, other scholars (Kilani-Schoch et al. 2009; Xanthos et al. 2011) emphasize the impact on child's morphology learning of both explicit and implicit, positive and negative feedback by parents, thereby questioning speculative claims (of direct or indirect Chomskyan inspiration) of poor and noisy input evidence in child-directed speech.

Proponents of lack of corrective feedback in child's input have hypothesized that possibly innate mechanisms for self-correction are in place. For example, according to Marcus et al. (1992), a *blocking mechanism* may suppress *ed*-verb past formation in English **goed*, due to the stored representation of irregular *went* being entrenched in the lexicon by repeated exposure. This is in line with Pinker and Ullman's (2002) 'Words and Rules' theory, according to which only irregularly inflected forms are stored in full. Regulars are either combined online from their stems and affixes in word generation, or are split into stems and affixes in recognition under the assumption that their access units are sublexical. In producing an inflected form, the lexicon is accessed first, and on-line assembly is pre-empted if the target (irregular) form is found there. Otherwise, a regular form is produced by using combinatorial rules.

However logically elegant and simple, lexical blocking seems to make rather unrealistic assumptions about how children come up with a regular vs. irregular distinction while being exposed to inflectional systems of average complexity. For example, Pinker and Ullman (2002) suggest that there is only one default regular pattern in the inflection of any language, and that the decision is dichotomous: the child considerably constrains the hypothesis space, as only one inflectional process can be held as a "regular" candidate for any specific paradigm function. This assumption, however, appears to seriously underestimate the systemic complexity of highly-inflecting languages. For example, the verb conjugations of Italian and Modern Greek show a graded hierarchy of regularity-by-transparency effects of morphological processing: many verbs present phonologically predictable adjustments that obscure the stem-ending boundary; some others keep the transparency of the stem-ending boundary at the price of introducing formally unpredictable fillers like thematic vowels, etc. Thus, the central question is how children can possibly home in on the decision of storing an irregular form as an unsegmented access unit, and a regular form as consisting of at least two distinct access units. We know that, for some models of lexical access, the decision does not have to be yes-or-no. For example, so-called "race models" (Schreuder and Baayen 1995; Baayen et al. 1997) assume that words can possibly be stored as both whole forms and sublexical access units, thus providing two parallel access routes that are concurrently activated and adjudicated on the basis of frequency and task-based effects. However, the same models leave the issue of word segmentation seriously underspecified: how does the child segment a morphologically complex word that is taken to be regular? How and when does perception of sublexical structure develop in child lexical competence to trigger lexical self-organization?

In a comprehensive comparison of the developmental stages in the acquisition of verb inflection in nearly two dozen languages (the Indo-European, Ugro-Finnic and Semitic families plus Turkish), Bittner, Dressler and Kilani-Schoch (2003) observe that the transition from rote lexical storage to morphological processing is the result of a process of active knowledge construction by the child, crucially conditioned by typological factors such as richness, uniformity and transparency of inflectional paradigms (Dressler 2010). Nevertheless, scholars widely differ in the way they conceptualize this process.

In the framework of Natural Morphology (Dressler 2010, 2005), an increase in children's inflectional productivity follows the establishment of the first "miniparadigms": i.e. non-isolated mini-sets of minimally three phonologically unambiguous and distinct inflected forms of the same lemma. Miniparadigms thus mark the turning point between a "premorphological" and a "protomorphological" phase in child acquisition of inflection. The onset of this transition phase can vary considerably, depending on type and token frequency, lexicon size, phonological salience, regularity and transparency of the morphological system.

Legate and Yang (2007) model child acquisition of English inflection as a maturation period during which the child starts entertaining a grammar hypothesis compatible with a language that does not manifest tense marking (e.g. Chinese), to eventually eliminate it. The crucial observation here is that elimination of this hypothesis is a gradual process. The frequency of inflectionally unmarked usages by the child goes down incrementally, mostly over a 2–3-year span (Haegeman 1995; Phillips 1995). More interestingly for our present concerns, the length of such a maturational period and the frequency of inflectionally unmarked usages are influenced by the richness and complexity of the inflection system being acquired. Based on distributional evidence in the child-directed portion of the Brown's (1973) Harvard Studies, the Leveille corpus and the Geneva corpus in the CHILDES database (MacWhinney 1995), Legate and Yang observe that the percentage difference between clauses with overt tense morphology (e.g. *I walked to school*) and clauses with no tense morphology (e.g. *I make him run*) is nearly 6% in English, 40% in French, and 60% in Spanish. Accordingly, they make the prediction that the maturational period for a child to acquire contextually appropriate tense marking will be longer for English and shorter for Spanish. This is borne out by developmental data. The greater balance of inflectional contrast in the Spanish verb system shows an inverse correlation with the lower percentage of unmarked usages observed in Spanish children (17%), compared with German children (58%) and English children (87%) (data form the CHILDES corpus, reported in Freudenthal et al. 2010).

In a series of influential papers on discriminative language learning, Ramscar and colleagues (Ramscar and Yarlett 2007, Ramscar and Dye 2011) focus on the logical problem of acquisition of English noun inflection to show that children can in fact recover from superset inflection grammars by learning probabilistically-cued responses, according to the Rescorla-Wagner model of classical conditioning (Rescorla and Wagner 1972). Early in training, children go through a transitional phase where more forms like – say – *mouses and mice are produced interchangeably. Due to the high number of -s plural nouns, compared with the relatively small frequency of mice, the pressure for mice to be replaced by the over-regularized *mouses is strong and dominates competition. In the end, however, children's over-regularized response is surpassed by the "imitation" signal, i.e. by the increasing strength of the imitative response mice when its performance curve reaches asymptote.

The discriminative account dispenses with both innate blocking mechanisms and parameterized grammar hypotheses. In the acquisition of verb inflection, input evidence of tense-marked forms like walked, ate and sang strengthens the association with the implicit morpho-semantic notion of [+Past] and the referential content of the three forms (namely WALK, EAT and SING). Root infinitives of the same verbs, on the other hand, will in turn reinforce associative links with [−Past], and, over again, with WALK, EAT and SING. Thus, at early stages of English acquisition, the lexical semantics of each verb is more likely to be associated with verb forms that are unmarked for tense than with tensed forms (in line with Legate and Yang's distributional evidence). This intra-paradigmatic competition (i.e. competition between finite and nonfinite forms belonging to the same verb paradigm) turns out to be more balanced in a richer and more complex inflection system, like Spanish or Italian conjugation, where paradigm cells are, in the vast majority of cases, associated with formally distinct, fully contrastive verb forms.

6.2 Paradigms and entropy

It is useful to see how word competition is related to the entropy $H(P)$ of the distribution of phonologically distinct members in the verb paradigm P, or "contrastive" paradigm entropy, defined in equation (1):

$$H(P) = - \sum_{f_i \in P} p(f_i) log_2(p(f_i)) \quad (1)$$

where f_i ranges over all formally distinct inflected forms of P, and the probability $p(f_i)$ is estimated by the ratio between the token frequency $t(f_i)$ and P cumulative frequency $\sum_{f_i \in P} t(f_i)$.

Table 3 shows a (fictitious) distribution of inflected verb forms in three present indicative (sub)paradigms for English *sing*, German *singen* 'sing', and Spanish *cantar* 'sing', under the simplifying assumption that distributions do not vary across languages, but only depend on lexical information (the verb being inflected) and morphosyntactic information (the selected paradigm-cell). When we calculate the entropy of each present indicative paradigm based on its distinct inflected forms, we are assessing how uniformly distributed the formal contrast is within the paradigm. Even if we assume that frequency distributions do not vary across languages, the comparative complexity[2] of the inflection system in each language appears to affect the amount of intra-paradigmatic formal competition: the more discriminable the inflected forms are, the more entropic (i.e. the more balanced) their competition will be. When more cells are assigned the same form, cumulative frequency by form winnows down contrastive paradigm entropy, prompting a greater bias for fewer forms. Accordingly, the English bare form *sing* is largely dominant in its own present indicative paradigm.[3]

Table 3: Frequency distributions of verb forms in the present indicative paradigms of English, Spanish and German; $p(pc|s)$ is the conditional probability of a paradigm cell pc given a verb stem s.

pres ind	English			Spanish			German		
p-cell	sing	freq	p(pc|s)	cantar	freq	p(pc|s)	singen	freq	p(pc|s)
1S	sing	5	0.14	canto	5	0.14	singe	5	0.14
2S	sing	2	0.06	cantas	2	0.06	singst	2	0.06
3S	sings	10	0.29	canta	10	0.29	singt	10	0.29
1P	sing	4	0.11	cantamos	4	0.11	singen	4	0.11
2P	sing	2	0.06	cantáis	2	0.06	singt	2	0.06
3P	sing	12	0.34	cantan	12	0.34	singen	12	0.34
	Σ	35	1	Σ	35	1	Σ	35	1

---

2 The term "complexity" is used here in the intuitive sense of "formal variety/richness". We will provide a more rigorous definition in Section 8 of this chapter.
3 In the case of the *sing* present indicative subparadigm, contrastive entropy is calculated as follows:

$-p(sing) \cdot \log_2(p(sing)) - p(sings) \cdot \log_2(p(sings)) = 0.87$,

where $p(sing)$ and $p(sings)$ are estimated as the ratio between their respective token frequencies in the subparadigm (25 and 10), and their cumulative token frequency (35). For the German and Spanish subparadigms, the same formula yields higher entropy values, respectively 1.68 and 2.28.

An important difference between Legate-Yang's model and the naive discriminative approach of Ramscar and colleagues is that, unlike the latter, the former makes the finite vs. non-finite competition hardly sensitive to lexical patterning in the data: any usage of finite marking in the child's input will reward a [+Tense] grammar *across the board*, lending support to any prospective tense-marking usage, irrespective of whether it involves an auxiliary, a copula or a lexical verb. Legate and Yang's model assumes that children are not learning how to inflect words, but how to reject a particular grammar hypothesis (or parameter setting). Contrariwise, a discriminative model makes any further usage of tense marking contingent upon the amount of contrastive competition *within* a specific paradigm.

The prediction that paradigm-specific distributions of finite and nonfinite forms play a role in determining the time course of inflection development is supported by the pattern of results reported in four quantitative analyses of early child language (Hamann and Plunkett 1998; Krajewski et al. 2012; Pine et al. 2008; Wilson 2003). In particular, by counting the number of times three classes of inflected verb forms (1SG and 3SG copula BE, 1SG and 3SG auxiliary BE, and 3SG -s) are overtly realized by English speaking children in obligatory contexts relative to all such contexts (or production rate), a few key findings are reported. First, there are significant differences in the rate at which typically developing children produce copula BE (e.g. *It's good*), auxiliary BE (e.g. *I'm eating*) and third person singular present forms (e.g. *He runs*), as indicated by the following ranking: *cop BE > aux BE > 3SG*. The second finding is that *is* is produced at a higher rate with pronominal subjects than with lexical subjects. Thirdly, both copula and auxiliary *is* are produced at a significantly higher rate than *am*; among all instances of *is*, those preceded by *it* are realized significantly more often than those preceded by *he*.

6.3 Form and distribution effects

Discriminative learning paves the way to a coherent operationalization of inflection acquisition in terms of learning contrasts within and across the two observable dimensions of variation in an inflectional system (Blevins 2016): form classes and frequency distribution classes. The discovery of phonological and semantic sublexical invariants (e.g. stems in lexical paradigms, or inflectional endings in conjugation classes), has often been invoked as a mechanism accounting for the acquisition of inflectional morphology (Bybee 1988, 1995; Peters 1997; Penke 2012). Furthermore, an explanatory mechanism that crucially rests on the amount of competing sources of discriminative information in the input can naturally be extended beyond the word level. To illustrate, the following nuclear sentences form a sort of *multi-word* or *syntactic paradigm*,[4] defined as a set of *constructions* in complementary distribution and mutual competition.

(9) She walks to school
    She drinks cola
    She's walking to school
    Does she drink cola?

From this perspective, "[g]rammatical features, properties and categories can likewise be interpreted as proxies for form classes, distribution classes or some combination of the two. In this way, morphological terminology that misleadingly implies an associated semantics can be reduced to robustly observable dimensions of form variation" (Blevins 2016: 249). *Prima facie* sign-based relationships between form and content like 3SG -*s* in English verb conjugation are derived from the relation between a morphological marker and its embedding syntactic context. From this perspective, inflectional paradigms are descriptively useful shorthands for construction-based paradigms, where discriminative relations are expressed between fully spelled-out lexical forms and grammatical forms, rather than between word forms and abstract paradigm cells.

The idea is in line with Harris's (1968) distributional approach to word segmentation and morpheme segmentation, where structural boundaries are identified at the points of likelihood discontinuity between adjacent symbols. We will consider these issues in more detail in Section 7.2.2. Note that a distributional, discriminative approach to inflection in fact conflates the two interlocked issues of how inflection is marked and in what contexts (see Section 1 above). Both aspects appear to capture distributional relations, and can be viewed as the same linguistic phenomenon looked at on different time scales. The distributional constraints that require verb marking, or agreement between two co-occurring units, are captured within a relatively large temporal window. Realizational effects are perceived on a shorter time scale. Contexts, as well as complex words, are split at their "joints" by contrasting "minimal" pairs of neighbors. Accordingly, paradigmatic relations emerge as contrastive points in a multidimensional space where shared lexical units (e.g. *she* WALK*s* vs. *he* WALK*ed*) or shared grammatical units (e.g. SHE IS walk*ING* vs. SHE IS sing*ING*) are observed to occur in complementary distribution.

---

[4] We can trace back the first formulation of this idea to P.H. Matthews' *Syntax* (1981: 265–291), where a prescient construction-based interpretation of Chomskyan transformational rules is offered.

This view is supported by evidence that children acquire inflected forms by binding them to larger unanalyzed word "chunks" (Cazden 1968; MacWhinney 1976). Further support comes from evidence of children with Specific Language Impairment[5] (SLI), who have difficulty with the interpretation of a complex sentence like *The cow sees the horse eating* (Leonard and Deevy 2011; Leonard et al. 2013). In addition, Purdy et al. (2014) show that older children with a history of SLI present a P600[6] for subject-verb agreement violations as in **Every night they talkS on the phone*, but not for violations as in **He makes the quiet boy talkS a little louder*. If the children fail to grasp the structural dependencies between *He makes* and the clause that followed, no error would be detected, because the sequence *the quiet boy talks a little louder* would seem grammatical.

This data makes an interesting connection with the most significant processing limitations observed in children with SLI: slow processing speed (Stark and Montgomery 1995; Kail and Leonard 1986; Wulfeck and Bates 1995, among others) and limited phonological working memory capacity (Briscoe et al. 2001; Farmer 2000; Montgomery 2004, among others). In particular, if children with SLI are weak in retaining the phonological representation of a new word (for long enough for it to be stored in long term memory), this may result in a limited lexicon and a limited grammar. Development in the processing and production of complex sentences may also be delayed as a consequence of an impoverished lexicon, since complex sentences often involve verbs subcategorizing for sentential arguments. A more direct consequence of a limited working memory capacity in children with SLI is the difficulty to retain distant dependency relations in context, which explains their apparent insensitivity to violations as in **He makes the quiet boy talkS a little louder*.

To sum up, inflection appears to develop in children as a highly interactive system, interfacing formal and functional features on different time scales. A rich, contrastive morphological system is helpful to acquire syntactic dependencies. At the same time, full mastery of inflection is contingent upon the intake of larger and larger syntactic contexts, where functional dependencies are realized as extended, multi-word exponents. Such a two-way implication is hardly

---

[5] Specific Language Impairment is a significant deficit in language ability that cannot be attributed to hearing loss, low non-verbal intelligence, or neurological damage (Leonard 2014; Montgomery & Leonard 1998; Rice et al. 2000).

[6] P600 is a peak in electrical brain activity that is measured with electroencephalography around 600 milliseconds after the stimulus that elicits it. P600 is commonly associated with hearing or reading grammatical (in particular, syntactic) errors (see Marangolo & Papagno 2020, this volume).

surprising upon reflection, since different forms of the same verb paradigm are less functional if no verb arguments are yet expressed in context (Gillis 2003).

We emphasized the largely distributional character of inflectional paradigms, whose cells define grammatical abstractions over a multi-dimensional network of formal contrasts in syntactic and pragmatic contexts. Nonetheless, paradigms acquire an autonomous relevance in word processing: they stake out the linguistic space where lexical forms get co-activated and compete in word recognition and production through contrastive formal oppositions.

Contrastive paradigm entropy correlates with inflection rates in child production, and marks an important typological difference between inflecting languages like Spanish or Italian and languages of the nearly isolating type such as English. Finally, as we will see in more detail in the ensuing sections, issues of intra-paradigmatic formal contrast are also relevant for understanding the communicative function of the opposition between regularly and irregularly inflected words.

7 Machine learning of inflection

The task of modelling, with a computer, the dynamic process whereby a child gets to acquire her/his full morphological competence is reminiscent of Zellig Harris' empiricist goal of developing linguistic analyses on the basis of purely formal, algorithmic manipulations of raw input data: so called "discovery procedures" (Harris 1951). Absence of classificatory information (e.g. morphosyntactic or lexical information) in the training data qualifies the discovery algorithm as *unsupervised*. Conversely, when input word forms are associated with output information of some kind, then discovery is said to be *supervised*, and the task is modelled as a classification problem.

7.1 Constructive vs. abstractive approaches

Borrowing Blevins' (2006) terminology, a useful distinction can be made here between *constructive* and *abstractive* algorithms for word learning. Constructive algorithms assume that classificatory information is morpheme-based. Word forms are segmented into morphemes for training, and a classifier must learn to apply morpheme segmentation to novel forms after training. An abstractive learning algorithm, on the other hand, sees morphological structure as emerging from full forms, be they annotated with classificatory information (supervised mode) or not (unsupervised mode). From this perspective, training data consist of unsegmented word forms (strings of either letters or sounds), possibly coupled with their lexical and morphosyntactic content. Accordingly, morphological learning boils down to acquiring knowledge from lexical representations in training, to generalize it to unknown forms. In this process, word-internal constituents can possibly emerge, either as a result of the formal redundancy of raw input data (unsupervised mode), or as a by-product of form-content mappings (supervised mode).

In fact, for too many languages, morpheme segmentation is not a well-defined task, due to the notorious problems with the Bloomfieldian, sign-based notion of morpheme, and the non-segmental processes of introflexive (i.e. root and pattern), tonal and apophony-based morphologies. So, the assumption that any word form can uniquely and consistently be segmented into morpheme-like constituents is at best dubious, and cannot be entertained as a general bootstrapping hypothesis for morphology learning.

In some abstractive algorithms, discovery procedures for morphological structure are constrained by a-priori assumptions about the morphology of the language to be learned. For example, knowledge that the target language morphology is concatenative biases the algorithm hypothesis search for stem-ending patterns. Thus, although no explicit morpheme segmentation is provided in training, the way word forms are tentatively split into internal constituents presupposes considerable information about boundary relations between such constituents (e.g. Goldsmith 2001). In some other algorithms, an alignment between morphologically related forms is enforced by either (i) using fixed-length positional templates (e.g. Keuleers and Daelemans 2007; Plunkett and Juola 1999), or (ii) tying individual symbols (letters or sounds) to specific positions in the input representation (so-called "conjunctive" coding: Coltheart et al. 2001; Harm and Seidenberg 1999; McClelland and Rumelhart 1981; Perry et al. 2007; Plaut et al. 1996), or (iii) resorting to some language-specific alignment algorithms (Albright 2002) or head-and-tail splitting procedures (Pirrelli and Yvon 1999). However, the ability to recognize position-independent patterns in symbolic time series, like the word *book* in *handbook*, or the Arabic verb root shared by *kataba* 'he wrote' and *yaktubu* 'he writes', appears to lie at the heart of human learning of inflection. Hence, a principled algorithm for morphological bootstrapping should be endowed with a capacity to adapt itself to the morphological structure of the target language, rather than with a language-specific bias.

In "features and classes" approaches (De Pauw and Wagacha 2007; McNamee and Mayfield 2007), a word form is represented as a set of redundantly specified n-grams, i.e. possibly overlapping substrings of n characters making up the input string: for example, '*wa*', '*al*', and '*lk*' for the string *walk*. N-grams have no internal structure and may be order-independent. The algorithm may start with the hypothesis that each word form is in a class of its own, and uses a stochastic classifier to calculate the conditional probability of having a certain class (a word form) given the set of distributed n-grams associated with the class. N-grams that occur in many words will be poorly discriminative, whereas features that happen to be repeatedly associated with a few word forms only will be given a morphologically meaningful interpretation.

Discriminative approaches to learning such as "features and classes" have a lot to offer. First, they are able to deal with the problem of learning "a-morphous" morphologies on a principled basis, addressing traditional conundrums in the morpheme-based literature such as morphemes with no meanings ("empty morphemes"), meanings with no morphemes ("zero morphemes"), bracketing paradoxes, etc. Secondly, they seem to exploit the time-honored linguistic *principle of contrast* (Clark 1987, 1990), according to which *any* formal opposition can be used to mark a grammatical or lexical opposition. Thirdly, they bring word learning down to more general mathematical models of classical conditioning (Rescorla and Wagner 1972) in behavioral psychology, according to which cues are constantly in competition for their predictive value for a given outcome. In what follows we will focus on abstractive, discriminative approaches to word learning and explore their implications for models of inflection. Such approaches see inflectional morphologies as **complex adaptive systems**, whose internal organization is the dynamic, continuously changing outcome of the interaction of distributional properties of input data, levels of lexical representation, and innate learning and processing constraints.

7.2 Associative vs. discriminative approaches

It is useful to describe discriminative learning by contrasting it with classical models of associative learning. The *gradient descent* training of connections from input nodes to output nodes in a two-layer perceptron for word production is a well-known example of associative learning. In learning inflection, the task is to map an input representation (say "*go* PAST") onto the corresponding output representation (*went*). With PDP connectionist networks (Rumelhart and McClelland 1986), input representations are "wired in" on the input layer through dedicated nodes. A letter string like #go# (where '#' marks the start and the end of the string) is simultaneously input through context-sensitive, conjunctive encoding of each symbol together with its embedding context. Accordingly, the input *g* in #go# is encoded as a #_g_o node. Output representations are learned by adjusting connection weights through *back-propagation* of the error feedback. Back-propagation consists in altering the weights of connections emanating from the activated input node(s), for the level of activation of output nodes to be attuned to the expected output. According to the "delta rule" (equation (2)), connections between the jth input node and the ith output node are in fact changed in proportion to the difference between the target activation value $\hat{h}_i$ of the ith output node and the actually observed output value h_i:

$$\Delta w_{i,j} = \gamma \cdot \left(\hat{h}_i - h_i\right) \cdot x_j \qquad (2)$$

where $w_{i,j}$ is the weight on the connection from the jth input node to the ith output node, γ is the network learning rate, and x_j is the activation of the jth input node. Note that, for $x_j = 0$, the resulting $\Delta w_{i,j}$ is null. In other words, nothing changes in the connections emanating from an input node if that node is not activated.

The "delta rule" in equation (2) is primarily *associative*. Learning proceeds by increasingly associating co-occurring cues (input nodes) and outcomes (output nodes), or by dissociating them when explicit evidence to the contrary is provided by means of correction. Activation of an output node in the absence of an activated input node does not affect the connection from the latter to the former, and nothing is learned about their cue-response relationship. Interposition of a hidden layer of nodes mediating input and output nodes makes the relationship between input and output representations non-linear, but does not make it up for lack of explicit negative evidence. In the end, learning is based on the fundamental assumption that the network is systematically "corrected", i.e. it is told that an input-output connection is right or wrong.

A more realistic connectionist approach to language learning is offered by Recurrent Neural Networks (hereafter RNNs), which provide a principled solution to the problem of learning words with no external feedback (Elman 1990; Jordan 1997). RNNs are multi-layer perceptrons equipped with a first layer of hidden nodes interposed between the input layer and the output layer, and an extra layer of hidden nodes containing a copy of the activation state of the hidden layer at the previous time tick. In RNNs, a string is input as a time series of symbols (not as a synchronous activation pattern), with each symbol being presented at a discrete time tick. Furthermore, word learning is conceptualized as a prediction-driven task. Upon presentation of an individual symbol on the input layer, an RNN must guess the upcoming symbol on the output layer. In a nutshell, the network learns to predict sequences of symbols based on its past experience. This is fairly ecological: prediction is known to be heavily involved in human language processing (Altmann and Kamide 2007; DeLong, Urbach, and Kutas 2005; Pickering and Garrod 2007). In addition, it provides a natural answer to the lack-of-feedback problem. Everything the network has to do is to wait for an upcoming symbol to show up. If the symbol does not match the current network prediction, connection weights are adjusted for the current input symbol to be the most likely network's response when a similar sequence is presented over again.

Simple RNNs are serial memories. They can improve on sequence prediction by keeping memory of the immediately preceding context through patterns of re-entrant connections in the hidden layer. At the same time, they plausibly address the problem of context-sensitive encoding of input symbols. The way a symbol is internally encoded by a *RNN* crucially depends on the network's memory of embedding sequences where the symbol was found. Different training data will yield different internal representations. There is no need for pre-wired input nodes encoding specific symbols in specific contexts. In principle, a *RNN* trained on strings from one language, can be trained on strings from another language, gradually adjusting its input nodes for them to be able to capture different serial dependencies in the way symbols are distributed.

Simple *RNNs* are trained with the same delta rule used for simple perceptrons. They learn to make context-dependent predictions that approximate the conditional probabilities of ensuing elements. To illustrate, the conditional probability of having 'b' immediately following 'a' (or $p(b|a)$) is estimated by $p(a,b)/p(a)$. Since the connection between an input node representing 'a' and an output node representing 'b' is strengthened by equation 2 in proportion to how often the bigram *ab* is found in input (and the learning rate γ), the network's prediction of 'b' given 'a' will be a direct function of $p(a,b)$. However, due to equation (2), the network learns nothing about – say – $p(c,b)$ or $p(a,c)$, from the distribution of *ab*'s. The assumption is in line with a purely associative view of error-driven learning and is supported by the intuitive observation that serial predictions can rely on already processed symbols only.

Discriminative learning couples equation (2) with the idea that multiple cues are constantly in competition for their predictive value for a given outcome. Accordingly, learning proceeds not by simply *associating* co-occurring cues and outcomes, but by *discriminating* between multiple cues. In Rescorla-Wagner's (1972) equations, the associative step is complemented with a competition-driven step, which forces the associative strength to take a step down when the outcome is present and the cue is not. Recent applications of Rescorla-Wagner equations to modelling a number of language tasks (see Pirrelli et al. 2020, this volume) are based on estimating the connection weights between two levels of representation: one for raw strings, based on n-gram encoding, the other one for the symbolic encoding of morpho-lexical and morphosyntactic units.

Temporal Self-Organizing Maps (*TSOMs*) have recently been proposed to memorize symbolic time-series as chains of specialized processing nodes, that selectively fire when specific symbols are input in specific temporal contexts (Ferro et al. 2011; Marzi et al. 2014; Pirrelli et al. 2015). *TSOMs* consist of:
1. one layer of input nodes (where an input stimulus is encoded),
2. a bidimensional grid of processing nodes (the map proper),
3. two levels of independently trainable connections:
    a. input connections
    b. temporal connections.

Through the level of input connections, information flows from the input layer to all map nodes (one-way input connections). A second level of connectivity goes from each map node to any other node on the map (including itself), forming a pool of re-entrant temporal connections that update each map node with the state of activation of the map at the previous time tick (one-time delay). Like with *RNNs*, a word is input to a *TSOM* as a time series of symbols, one symbol at a time. At each time tick, activation spreads through both input and temporal connections to yield an overall state of node activation, or Map Activation Pattern, at time *t*. In particular we use $MAP_t(s)$ to refer to the Map Activation Pattern relative to the current stimulus *s*. The node with the top-most activation level in $MAP_t(s)$ is referred to as Best Matching Unit, or $BMU_t(s)$. Finally, a time series of sequentially activated *BMUs*, namely <$BMU_1(s_1)$, ..., $BMU_t(s_t)$> is called a *BMU* chain.

A full description of the *TSOM* architecture and learning equations can be found in Pirrelli et al. 2020, this volume. Suffice it to say here that the learning algorithm modulates weights on re-entrant temporal connections for *BMU* chains to optimally process the most likely input strings. In particular, for any input bigram '*ab*', the connection strength between $BMU_{t-1}(a)$ and $BMU_t(b)$ will:
(i) increase every time '*a*' precedes '*b*' in training (entrenchment)
(ii) decrease every time '*b*' is preceded by a symbol other than '*a*' (competition and inhibition).

Steps (i) and (ii) incrementally enforce node specialization. The map tends to allocate maximally distinct nodes for the processing of (sub)strings, as a function of their frequency in training. To illustrate the effects of node specialization vs. sharing on the representation of inflected forms of the same paradigm, Figure 2 sketches two possible end states in the allocation of *BMU* chains responding to four German forms of *beginnen* 'begin': *BEGINNEN* (infinitive, 1p and 3p present indicative), *BEGINNT* (3s and 2p present indicative), *BEGANNT* (2p preterite) and *BEGONNEN* (past participle). In the left panel, *BMUs* are arranged in a word tree. At any node n_i, one can always retrace backwards the nodes activated to arrive at n_i. The right panel of Figure 2, on the other hand, offers a compressed representation for the three words, with letters shared by the three forms activating identical *BMUs*. As a result, when the shared node '*N*' is activated, one loses information of which node was activated at the previous time tick.

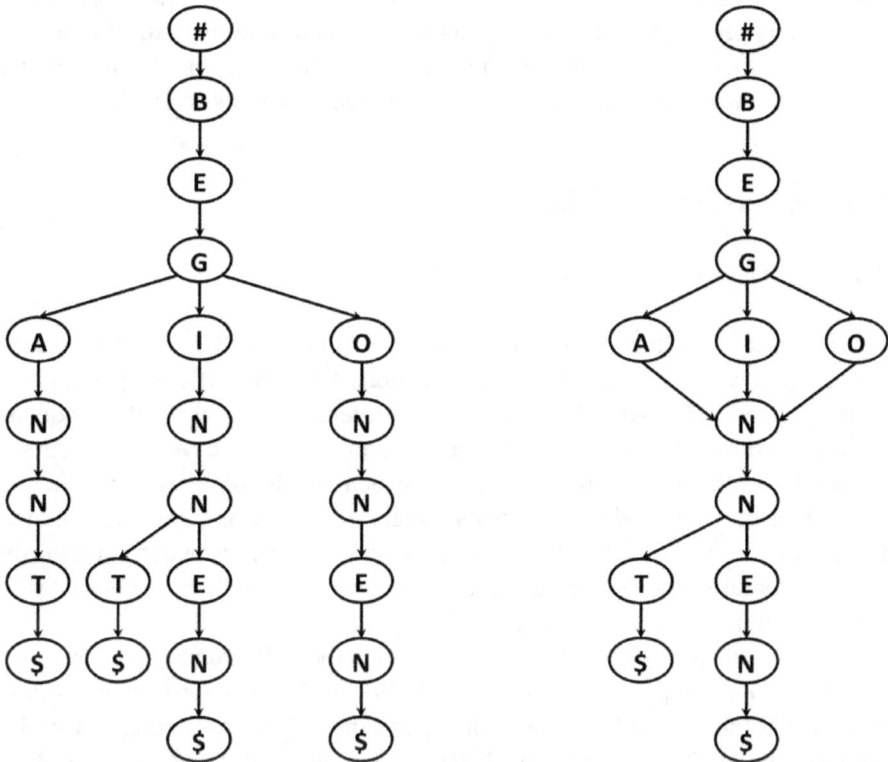

Figure 2: A word node tree (a) and a word node graph (b) representing German '#BEGINNEN$', 'BEGINNT$', 'BEGANNT$' and '#BEGONNEN$'. Vertices are specialized nodes and arcs stand for weighted connections. '#' and '$' are, respectively, the start-of-word and the end-of-word symbol.

Let us briefly consider the implications of the two *BMU* structures for word processing. In the word-tree (left), *BEGINNEN*, *BEGINNT*, *BEGANNT* and *BEGONNEN* are perceived by the map as distinct forms at the earliest branching point in the hierarchy (the '*G*' node). From that point onwards, the four words activate three distinct node paths, which further bifurcate into a fourth path at the point where *BEGINNEN* and *BEGINNT* become distinct. Clearly, whenever a node has one outgoing connection only, the TSOM has no uncertainty about the ensuing step to take, and can anticipate the upcoming input symbol with certainty. In the word-graph on the right, on the other hand, branching paths converge to the same node as soon as the four input forms share an input symbol. Having more branches that converge to a common node increases the processing uncertainty by the map. The node keeps memory of many preceding contexts, and its possible continuation paths are multiplied accordingly. As we will see in the following section, this dynamic plays a key role in word acquisition and paradigm organization with TSOMs.

7.3 Processing inflection

7.3.1 The pace of acquisition

Token frequency is known to pace the acquisition of content words (i.e. excluding function words such as articles, prepositions and conjunctions), particularly at early stages of language development (Huttenlocher et al. 1991; Goodman et al. 2008; Rowe 2012). It is widely accepted that speakers have fairly accurate knowledge of the relative frequencies with which individual verbs appear in different tenses, or with different combinations of person and number features (Ellis 2002). Even if it is clear that speakers do not actively engage in consciously counting features, they nevertheless are very good at estimating frequency distributions and their central tendencies.

Early acquisition of frequent words is generally understood to be a memory effect: the more frequently a word is input, the more deeply entrenched its storage trace in the speaker's mental lexicon, and the quicker its access. In TSOMs, word processing is intimately tuned to word storage. Nodes that are repeatedly activated by an input string, become increasingly specialized for processing that string. At the same time, they are the memory nodes used for its long-term representation. The reason why frequent words are acquired at earlier stages can be better understood in terms of this processing-storage dynamic.

To investigate how word frequency distributions affect the acquisition of inflected words in a discriminative recurrent neural network, Marzi and colleagues (Marzi et al. 2014, 2016, 2018) ran a series of experiments where the inflectional systems of various languages (English, German, Italian, Modern Greek, Spanish, Standard Modern Arabic) are acquired by a TSOM trained on different frequency distributions of the same data. In the experiments, the acquisition of each input word form is timed by the epoch when the word is recalled correctly from its memory trace on the map.[7]

As an example, Figure 3 shows the pace of acquisition of verb forms from three German paradigms: a regular one (*brauchen* 'need'), a moderately irregular one (*wollen* 'want'), and a highly irregular one (*sein* 'be'). In the plots, circles represent word forms, ranked on the *y*-axis by increasing frequency values, and plotted on the *x*-axis by their epoch of acquisition. Each panel shows the outcome of two training regimes: white circles correspond to forms that are presented to a TSOM 5 times each (uniform training regime); black circles correspond to the same forms when they are presented to a TSOM with their (scaled) frequency distributions in a reference corpus (realistic training regime). Acquisition times are averaged over 5 repetitions of the same experimental condition in the two training regimes.

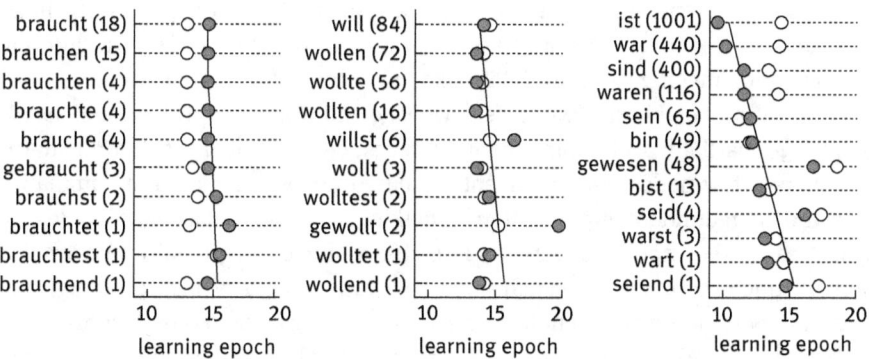

Figure 3: TSOMs' learning epochs for *brauchen* 'need', *wollen* 'want', *sein* 'be' with uniform (white circles) and realistic (dark circles) training conditions. For each form, frequencies are given in brackets.

We observe a significant interaction between the pace of word acquisition in the two training regimes and the degree of inflectional (ir)regularity of a paradigm. In a regular paradigm like *brauchen* (Figure 3, left panel) word forms are acquired by a TSOM at about the same epoch: between epoch 13 and 15 in a

---

7 Intuitively, a word memory trace in a TSOM is the "synchronous" union set of the map activation patterns (*MAPs*) for all symbols making up the word, or Integrated Activation Pattern (*IAP*). For a sequence of symbols to be recalled accurately from a memory trace, each *BMU* must contain detailed information about each symbol and its position in the target word. If either information is wrong, the sequence is wrongly recalled.

uniform training regime (white circles), and between epoch 14 and 17 in a realistic training regime (black circles). Note that, on average, words are learned earlier when they are uniformly distributed. The latter effect is perceivably reduced in *wollen* (Figure 3, center panel), and reversed in *sein* (Figure 3, right panel), where realistically distributed items (black circles) tend to be learned more quickly than when the same items are presented five times each (white circles). Furthermore, the time span between the first and the last acquired form in the same paradigm is fairly short in *brauchen*, longer in *wollen*, and even longer in *sein*.

Prima facie, these results are compatible with a dual-route account of regular and irregular inflection (e.g. Pinker and Ullman 2002). One could argue that the short time span taken to acquire regular forms supports the nearly instantaneous application of a general rule to the paradigm, following the acquisition of its stem. Likewise, the prolonged time span taken for the acquisition of an irregular paradigm is evidence that irregular forms are memorized in a piecemeal, itemized fashion. However, since no rule learning is in place in a TSOM, a different generalization mechanism must be invoked to account for this evidence.

In a TSOM, neighboring words (e.g. *walking* and *walked*, or *walking* and *speaking*), trigger partially overlapping memory traces, i.e. integrated activation patterns that share a few nodes. Entrenchment of shared nodes benefits from cumulative exposure to redundant input patterns, making a TSOM sensitive to sublexical structures in the input. Conversely, non-shared nodes in partially overlapping memory traces compete for synchronous activation primacy in processing, and play an important role in extending inflection analogically across paradigms.

To understand how inter-paradigmatic analogical extension takes place, suppose that the (regularly) inflected form *walking* is presented to a TSOM for the first time. Its overall integrated activation pattern takes advantage of full activation of the stem *walk-* from – say – the already known *walks*, and the activation of *ing*-nodes trained on other forms like *speaking* or *making*. Note that *ing*-nodes will compete with the *s*-node of *walks*, prospectively activated by the forward temporal connections emanating from *walk*-nodes. A successful generalization ultimately depends on the final outcome of this competition, based on the synchronous activation of map nodes by the two different layers of TSOM connectivity: the input layer and the temporal layer. The comparatively faster process of acquisition of the inflected forms in a regular paradigm takes place when all inflectional endings are repeatedly seen across several paradigms,[8] and the paradigm-specific stem is

---

[8] We discuss processing effects of the frequency distribution of forms sharing the same inflectional ending (or inflectional entropy) in Section 7.3.2.

already acquired. This generalization step is markedly more difficult within irregular paradigms, where more stem allomorphs are available and compete with one another for activation primacy (e.g. *sings, sang, sung*). This is a gradient irregularity effect: the more stem allomorphs are found in a paradigm, the longer the time needed to acquire and associate them all with their endings.

Note finally the important difference in the pace of acquisition between the two distributions of *sein*, in sharp contrast with the strong correlation between the two distributions of *brauchen*. Despite the difference in the order of magnitude between the two distributions, the comparative insensitivity of regulars to frequency effects is reminiscent of a regularity-by-frequency interaction (Ellis and Schmidt 1998). In inflection, being more regular means being repeatedly attested in large classes of verb paradigms, and, within each paradigm, across all paradigm cells. This is not the case for irregular inflection. A radically suppletive paradigm like *sein* makes it hardly possible to infer an unattested form from other members of the same paradigm. The majority of *sein* forms are acquired one by one, as an inverse function of their own frequency distribution (and length): high-frequency items are learned earlier (Figure 3, black circles in the top left corner of the rightmost panel), and low-frequency items tend to be learned later. Conversely, in a paradigm like *brauchen*, the cumulative token frequency of the invariant stem *brauch-* compensates for the varying rate at which individual forms are shown in input. This is also true of affix allomorphs. The frequency of regular affixation is multiplicatively affected by an increase in the number of lexemes in training. A doubling in the number of verb entries in training results (if we ignore phonological adjustments) in doubling the number of affixes they select. With irregular verbs, this is hardly the case, as affix allomorphs thinly spread across irregulars, clustering in small subclasses, and incrementing their frequency rather unevenly. Thus, the pace of acquisition of regular paradigms will be less sensitive to token frequency effects of single forms, since it can benefit from the cumulative boost in frequency of other forms in the same paradigm (for stems) and other forms of other paradigms (for affixes).

All these competition effects point to the important role that paradigm entropy plays in word processing/learning. We already mentioned paradigmatic entropy in connection with child acquisition of inflection (Section 6.2).

7.3.2 Inflectional regularity: A processing-oriented notion

How degrees of inflectional regularity affect processing strategies has been recently evaluated cross-linguistically by looking at the way a TSOM predicts an upcoming input form in word recognition (Marzi et al. 2018; Marzi, Ferro and Pirrelli 2019).

The panels in Figure 4 illustrate the dynamic of word access for verb sets of 6 languages: Standard Modern Arabic, English, German, Modern Greek, Italian and Spanish, which offer evidence of graded levels of morphological (ir)regularities and complexity. For each language, they plot how easily regularly vs. irregularly inflected verb forms are predicted by a TSOM trained on 50 high-frequency sub-paradigms, each containing 15 uniformly distributed forms. Symbol prediction is graphed by the distance of each symbol to the morpheme boundary between the word stem and its inflectional ending (centered on the first symbol of the ending: $x = 0$). Each plot shows, on the y-axis, how well a symbol is predicted by the map on the basis of its preceding context. Symbol prediction in regular forms is plotted by green dashed lines, and symbol prediction in irregular forms by red solid lines.

In all tested languages, the stem prediction rate increases more steadily in regulars than irregulars (negative values on the x-axis, p-value <.001). The trend reflects the reduction in uncertainty that the map experiences when serial information is received (like in spoken word recognition). As the signal unfolds, the set of possible competing sequences that are compatible with the signal narrows down, until the point is reached when only one candidate can match the incoming signal (so-called "uniqueness point" in Marslen-Wilson's cohort model, 1990). For sure, not all stem allomorphs of a paradigm are equally likely to be compatible with an incoming signal at any given point in time. Competition among available candidates is modulated by frequency, with more frequent allomorphs being more entrenched and so more likely to win over their competitors. The result is that the map is slower to recognize low frequency allomorphs with high-frequency competitors, as the latter are harder to eliminate (Lively, Pisoni and Goldinger 1994; Luce 1986; Luce and Pisoni 1998).

Turning back to Figure 4, another significant cross-linguistic effect is the drop in the prediction rate at the morpheme boundaries ($x = 0$), in both regularly and irregularly inflected forms. We take such a level of discontinuity at the morpheme boundary to reflect the map's sensitivity to syntagmatic word structure. Harris' *Mathematical Structures of language* (1968) describes how sublexical structures can be segmented out of a continuous string of symbols using the sequential likelihood between adjacent symbols. This work provided the foundations for much of later information-theoretic work on the bootstrapping of linguistic knowledge from unsupervised data (Brent 1999; Christiansen et al. 1998; Juola 1998). Our evidence is in keeping with this work. Since our training data contain no information about morphological structure, word structure emerges as an effect of specialization of processing nodes through learning. By being repeatedly exposed to input sequences, *BMUs* develop a context-sensitive representation of input symbols through incoming temporal connections, while developing at the same time strong expectations for symbols yet to come, through

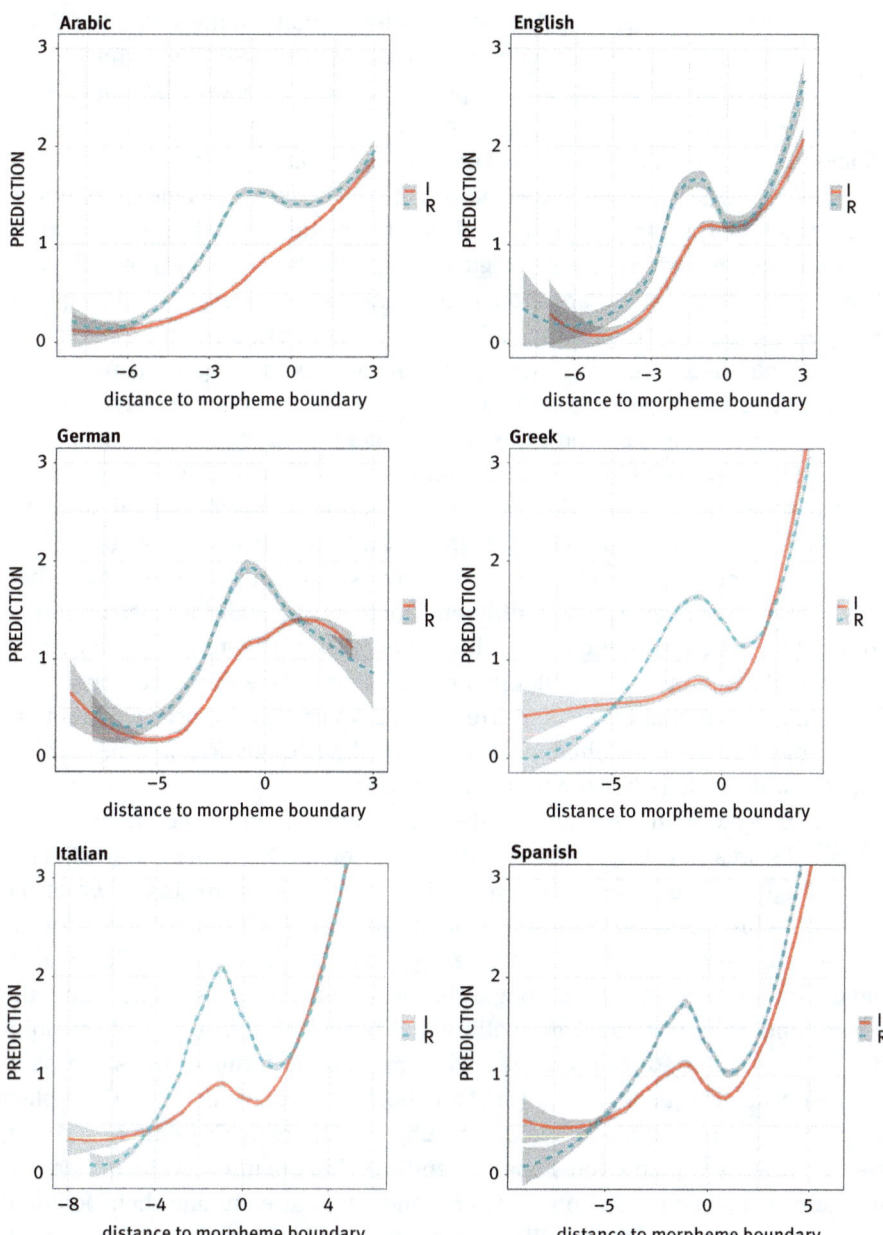

Figure 4: For each language set, regression plots of interaction effects between morphological (ir)regularity and distance to morpheme boundary, in non-linear models (GAMs) fitting the number of symbols predicted by TSOMs. Categorical fixed effect is regularity (green dashed lines) vs. irregularity (red solid lines).

outgoing temporal connections. In the end, discontinuity in the strength of local temporal connections correlate with (graded) levels of sublexical structure.

The drop of prediction rates at morpheme boundaries tends to be more prominent for regular stems than for irregular ones. This is a clear paradigm effect. Stem allomorphs are found in a few paradigm cells only, and select a subset of the inflectional endings available in their paradigm. This reduces the amount of uncertainty at the morpheme boundary, as shown by the difference in prediction drop between regulars and irregulars in Figure 4. In particular, in Arabic irregular paradigms, inflectional endings are strongly predicted as a consequence of being cued by inflecting prefixes. Interestingly, from a cross-linguistic perspective, it can be observed that discontinuous patterns, typically attested in irregular paradigms of concatenative languages and systematically attested in non-concatenative morphologies such as Arabic, tend to require a higher processing cost of stems, and a lower cost in processing inflectional endings (Hahn and Bailey 2005).

These results provide evidence that perception of morphological structure crucially interacts with formal transparency and regularity in all languages. As a general trend, sublexical constituents are perceptually more salient when they remain *unchanged* across different contexts. In addition, perception of structural discontinuity increases with *the number* of different contexts where constituents are found. In regular paradigms, stems and endings combine more freely than stems and endings in irregular paradigms do. Hence regulars tend to exhibit a clearer morphological structure than irregulars, which, in turn, tend to induce a more holistic processing strategy.

As observed with stems, also inflectional endings tend to be predicted better by a *TSOM* as more symbols are input. Once more, this is mainly an effect of increasingly reduced processing uncertainty due to the narrowing down of the set of possible inflectional endings compatible with the input sequence. In the end, a uniqueness point is reached, i.e. a processing point where only one candidate inflectional ending is compatible with the unfolding signal, and the whole input form is recognized. Balling and Baayen (2008, 2012) call the point at which an inflected form can be told from all other forms of the same paradigm *Complex Uniqueness Point* (*CUP* for short). They show that late *CUPs* elicit longer processing responses by human subjects than early *CUPs* do. As a result, we expect steeper prediction slopes for endings that are uniquely identified earlier, and less steep prediction slopes for endings that eliminate their potential competitors at a later stage. What we observe by looking at our data is that, most often, the facilitative effect of regularity on stem processing is partially reversed with inflectional endings. Endings that are selected by irregular stems tend to be predicted more easily than endings of regular stems. In fact, irregular stems are more discriminative for the class of endings they can possibly select, and this speeds up processing of ensuing endings, since they exhibit earlier *CUPs* than regulars do.

8 Measuring inflectional complexity

It makes a lot of intuitive sense to claim that some languages are inflectionally more complex than others. Everybody would agree that the English conjugation system is simpler than the German system, which is, in turn, simpler than the verb system of Modern Standard Arabic. However, when we try to motivate these deceptively trivial judgements, we are faced with a number of difficulties.

Descriptive linguists have often approached the issue through comprehensive catalogues of the morphological markers and patterns attested in a given language (Bickel and Nichols 2005; McWorther 2001; Shosted 2006). According to such approaches, the complexity of an inflectional system is assessed by enumerating the category values instantiated in the system and the range of available markers for their realization. The utility of such "enumerative" complexity or *E-complexity* (Ackerman and Malouf 2013) is however dubious on many counts.

As already shown in Section 6, researchers from diverse theoretical perspectives observe that rich inflection in fact facilitates early morphological production. In competition-based (Bates and MacWhinney 1987), as well as functional (Slobin 1982, 1985) and cue-response discriminative perspectives (Baayen et al. 2011), non-ambiguous morphological paradigms such as those of Italian conjugation are argued to provide better syntactic cues to sentence interpretation, as compared, for example, to the impoverished inflectional system of English verb agreement. Biuniqueness form-meaning relationships make inflectional markers more transparent, more compositional and in the end easier to be acquired than the one-to-many mappings of morphological forms to syntactic features that are found in English, Swedish and Dutch (Phillips 1995, 1996; Dressler 2010). Some researchers (e.g. Blom and Wijnen 2006; Crago and Allen 2001; Legate and Yang 2007) have focused on the amount of finite verbs that children receive from the adult input, to observe that the high percentage of overtly inflected forms correlates with the early production of finite forms by children. In the framework of Natural Morphology, Dressler and colleagues (Bittner et al. 2003) claimed that a richer inflection makes children more aware of morphological structure, so that they begin to develop intra-paradigmatic relations sooner than children prompted by simpler systems do (as confirmed by the quantitative results in Xanthos et al. 2011).

Another argument emphasizes that the logical problem of acquiring an inflection system consists in learning not just the full range of formal markers, but the set of implicative relations between fully-inflected forms, which allow novel forms to be deduced from known forms (or the cell-filling problem, Ackerman and Malouf 2013; Ackerman, Blevins, Malouf 2009). To illustrate, suppose we have two hypothetical inflection systems, each with two categories only (say, singular and plural) and three different endings for each category: A, B, C for singular, and D, E and F for plural. In one system, paradigms are found to present three possible pairs of endings only: <A, D>, <B, E>, <C, F>, corresponding to three different inflection classes. In the second system, any combination is attested. Clearly, the latter system would be more difficult to learn than the former, as it makes it harder to infer the plural form of a word from its singular form, or vice versa. In the former system, on the other hand, exposure to one form only, no matter whether in the singular or plural, would make the speaker certain about the other form. Nonetheless, both systems present the same degree of *E-complexity*.

A number of information theoretic approaches have been proposed to model inflectional complexity in terms of either Kolmogorov complexity (Kolmogorov 1965), or Shannon entropy (Shannon 1948). The idea behind Kolmogorov complexity is to measure a dataset of inflected forms with the shortest possible grammar needed to describe them, in line with the Minimum Description Length principle (Rissanen 1989) we illustrated in connection with Goldsmith's (2001) grammar evaluation metric. The approach, however, typically (but not always, see Juola 1998) implies that a definition of morphological complexity is heavily dependent on the grammar formalism adopted (Bane 2008; Sagot and Walther 2011; Sagot 2018). To obviate this, Ackerman, Blevins and Malouf (2009), and Ackerman and Malouf (2013) use Shannon's information entropy to quantify prediction of an inflected form as a paradigm-based change in the speaker's uncertainty. They conjecture that inflectional systems tend to minimize the average conditional entropy of predicting each form in a paradigm on the basis of any other form of the same paradigm (Low Conditional Entropy Conjecture or LCEC). This is measured by looking at the distribution of inflectional markers across inflection classes in the morphological system of a language.

More recently, Bonami and Beniami (2017) propose to generalize affix-to-affix inference to inference of intra-paradigmatic form-to-form alternation patterns, along the lines of Pirrelli and Yvon (1999), Albright (2002) and Bonami and Boyé (2014). The approach offers several advantages. It avoids the need for theoretically-loaded segmentation of inflected forms into stems and affixes in the first place. Secondly, it models implicative relations between stem allomorphs (or stem-stem predictability), thereby providing a principled way to discover so-called "principal parts", i.e. a minimal set of selected forms in a paradigm from which all other paradigm members can be deduced with certainty (Finkel and Stump 2007, among others). Finally, it emphasizes the role of joint prediction, i.e. the use of set of forms to predict one missing form of the same paradigm, as a convenient strategy to reduce the speaker's uncertainty in the cell filling problem.

To sum up, entropic scores provide extremely valuable insights into the organization of static, synchronic paradigms. Nonetheless, measuring entropic complexity is heavily dependent on the algorithmic procedures we use for producing sets of alternation patterns, and establishing what counts as a partition of paradigm cells selecting the same stem alternant. Although speakers are very good at finding redundant patterns in paradigmatically related forms, it is not clear how their "discovery procedures" can be implemented in a typologically unbiased way. Besides, there are crucial complementary questions about how such patterns are processed and acquired that have so far been relatively neglected by the linguistic literature. We contend that inflectional complexity is an inherently multi-factorial and dynamic notion, which depends on the distributions of both stem and affix allomorphy, and on their interaction in the processing of larger syntactic constructions. Most of the quantitative metrics reviewed so far appear to focus on one or two specific factors only.

We see two principled hurdles in any attempt to identify a single, overall figure of merit for morphological complexity. First, it is exceedingly difficult, if possible at all, to integrate many distribution scores into a single overall figure, approximating a comprehensive level of inflectional complexity. Secondly, it remains to be explained how such a global score can in fact govern local inference steps, such as those taken by speakers learning an inflection system, and how it can ultimately be derived from them. We suggest that data-driven computational modelling provides a unique chance to empirically evaluate to what extent systemic complexity spontaneously emerges from acquisition of concrete examples of usage of an inflection system. Using cognitively-inspired computational models of morphology learning, we can investigate the interaction of different factors by controlling these factors within independent training regimes, and by running different instantiations of our models on each such regime. Dynamic analysis of the way the performance of our learning systems is affected across training regimes can help us understand more of factor interaction. Methodologically, this is not too far from what is done in experimental psycholinguistics, with the important qualification that computational and psycholinguistic approaches assign different epistemological roles to behavioral data and underlying neurocognitive mechanisms (see Pirrelli et al. 2020, this volume; Marzi, Ferro and Pirrelli 2019). Nonetheless, in spite of some methodological differences, computer simulations of theoretically-posited but unobservable processes offer a sound way to overcome the problem of investigating factor interaction, and provide a window on mechanisms and representations that cannot be observed directly in human subjects.

To illustrate, let us turn back to the cross-linguistic evidence in Section 7.3.2. Figure 5 plots, for each of our sample languages, a regression model for the rate of symbol prediction in serial word processing. Languages exhibit a similar trend, though with significantly different slopes (p-values <.001), with Greek forms being arguably the slowest to process (less steep slope), and English forms the quickest ones (steeper slope). Our evidence is in line with LCEC (Ackerman and Malouf 2013). The overall processing ease of considerably different inflectional systems appears to oscillate within a fairly limited range of variation. In our language sample, the upper bound (low processing costs) and lower bound (high processing costs) of this range are marked by English and Modern Greek respectively. When we do not consider word length as a co-variate, our space of processing ease is staked out by Spanish (upper bound) and Standard Modern Arabic (lower bound) respectively.[9]

Overall, conjugations present marginal differences in the processing overhead they require, in spite of their typological diversity. Interestingly enough, their diversity is reflected by the different processing profiles exhibited by sublexical constituents in the different languages (Figure 5). Unsurprisingly, Italian and Spanish show a very similar syntagmatic profile, with growing prediction rates for endings (whose x values are >0). Since they typically exhibit very long suffixes with the infixation of a thematic vowel, the more symbols of inflectional endings are input, the easier for a TSOM to predict the symbols to come. This is mainly the effect of an increasingly reduced processing uncertainty due to the narrowing down of the set of possible inflectional endings compatible with the input sequence.

TSOM **discriminative access** can considerably benefit from a smaller selection of inflectional endings being available at the stem-ending boundary. In Arabic imperfective forms, for example, prefixation conveys person features, thus making selection of inflectional endings highly predictable, given the stem. Conversely, Arabic stems are significantly more difficult to predict, as confirmed by the smaller coefficients for both intercept and slope (p-value <.001) in our generalized additive model. Unlike Arabic and English, all other languages in our test sample exhibit a wider selection of inflectional endings available at the

---

[9] Prediction across input words is calculated by incrementally assigning each correctly predicted symbol a 1-point score, i.e. the prediction score of the preceding symbol incremented by 1. Otherwise, for unpredicted symbols the score is 0. Therefore, the longer the input word, the more likely it is to be predicted. In our set of data, Spanish verb forms tend to be longer than any others.

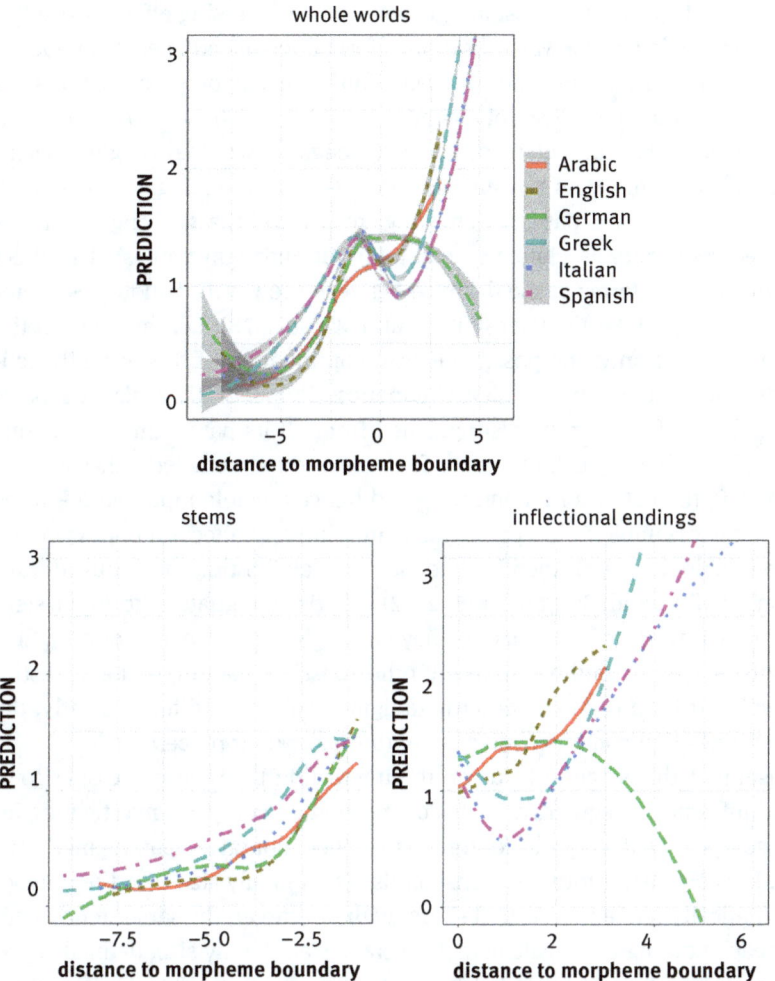

Figure 5: Regression plot of interaction effects between languages and distance to morpheme boundary, in a GAM fitting the number of symbols predicted by TSOMs for input words (Top panel, adapted from Marzi et al. 2018), and for stems (left panel) and inflectional endings (right panel) separately.

morpheme boundary. Nonetheless, language-specific processing effects are better understood by looking at the way inflection is formally realized in each language.

In particular, German inflection presents fairly systematic processes of stem alternation, followed by a full set of embedded endings such as *-e, -en, -end* (e.g. *beginn-e, beginn-en, beginn-end*, respectively '(I) begin', '(we, they) begin', 'beginning' (present participle)). As a result, German stems and endings are predicted according to two reversed patterns, showing, respectively, a growing and a decreasing prediction rate, as plotted in Figure 5 (left and right panels). The effect can be understood in terms of the distance between the word's Uniqueness Point (UP, Marslen-Wilson 1984; Marslen-Wilson and Welsh 1978), i.e. the point in the input where there is only one possible lexical continuation of the currently activated node chain, and the Complex Uniqueness Point, or CUP, i.e. the point where an inflected form can be distinguished from all its paradigm companions (see §7.22). The earlier the UP, the easier for a stem to be predicted. Likewise, the earlier the CUP, the better for an ending – and hence a whole input word – to be accessed. These disambiguation points have an inhibitory effect on both word access and prediction, as confirmed by evidence on reaction times in acoustic word recognition (Balling and Baayen 2008, 2012). UP disambiguates the input stem from other onset-overlapping stems (be they paradigmatically-related or not). CUP distinguishes a specific ending from any other possible candidate, i.e. it distinguishes the input form from any other paradigmatically related form. Clearly, the fewer the endings that combine with a stem, the easier their processing.

It is useful at this stage to focus on the interaction between processing complexity and inflectional regularity. In this connection, we propose investigating inflectional complexity through a continuous, graded notion of paradigmatic (ir)regularity. For each target form, we consider its "stem-family size", i.e. the number of paradigmatically-related forms that share, with our target, the same stem. In addition, for each paradigm, we calculate its average stem-family size, defined as the average size of the stem families belonging to the paradigm. This average score provides a quantifiable, graded notion of "paradigm regularity" that can be used in place of the traditional, dichotomous classification of inflected forms as either regular or irregular.

Figure 6 shows how the two measures affect symbol prediction by a TSOM in the serial processing of fully inflected forms (top panels), as well as their stems and inflectional endings separately (respectively, left and right panels). Note that there is a clear, facilitative effect of the family size on the processing of stems only: the greater the number of forms sharing the same stem, the easier their processing (i.e. the greater the number of predicted symbols). Conversely, when we consider full-forms and endings, there is an inhibitory effect of the family size: the more inflected forms share the same stems, the greater the processing uncertainty due to

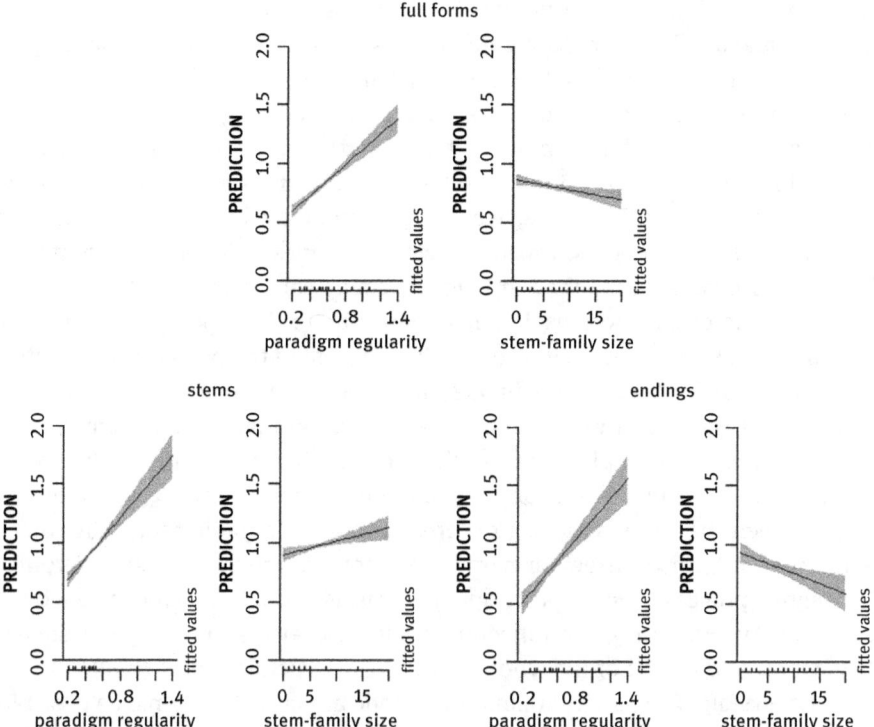

Figure 6: GAMs predicting for our set of languages (as categorical fixed effect) the number of symbols predicted by TSOMs: fixed effects are plotted separately as paradigm regularity and stem-family size for full-forms (top panels), stems (left panels), endings (right panels). In addition to these covariates, the three GAM models include as smooth effect the corresponding length: word length for the full-form model, stem and suffix length respectively for the stem and ending models.

the larger set of possible inflectional endings compatible with the input sequence. Interestingly, a graded notion of paradigm regularity, ranging from idiosyncratic to regular paradigms, going through intermediate levels of (ir)regularity, positively correlates with our task. The upshot is that regularity favors entrenchment of stems, with an average facilitative effect on processing. Paradigm entrenchment, however, has a structural price to pay, with more complex (larger) inflection systems being more difficult to process than simpler ones.

In a functional perspective, the evidence offered here can be interpreted as the result of a balancing act between two potentially competing communicative requirements: (i) a recognition-driven tendency for a maximally contrastive system, where all inflected forms, both within and across paradigms, present the earliest possible uniqueness points (UP and CUP); and (ii) a learning-driven bias for a maximally generalizable inflection system, where, for each paradigm, all forms in the paradigm can be deduced from any one of its forms, or from the smallest possible set of known forms. Clearly, a maximally contrastive system would take the least effort to process, but would require full storage of all (unpredictable) items, thus turning out to be slow to learn. A maximally generalizable system, on the other hand, would be comparatively easier to learn, but rather inefficient to process, especially when it comes to low-frequency items. What we observe is that, although languages may vary in the way they distribute processing costs across each single word due to the typological variety of the inflectional processes they resort to, if we measure the per-word processing cost as a linear function approximately interpolating prediction scores for the start-of-word and end-of-word symbols, we get values that are fairly similar.

This observation is also compatible with another clear pattern shown by the data presented in this section. In each of our sample languages, the difference between the processing cost of forms in regular paradigms and the processing cost of forms in irregular paradigms shows a structure-sensitive profile. The higher processing cost of irregular stems is partially compensated by a lower cost in processing the inflectional endings selected by irregular stems. Once more, at the level of the whole word, these structural effects make the inflectional system, from an information theoretic angle, as functional as possible to possibly contrasting processing requirements.

It should nonetheless be appreciated that the facilitative effect of fully contrastive paradigms is the result of the interaction of more factors, including complexity of the paradigm, word length and frequency distribution. Comparatively small differences have mostly been observed between languages that exhibit the same (or a comparable) number of morphosyntactic oppositions, which require the same (or a comparable) amount of syntactic contexts to be checked and interpreted. When these conditions are not controlled, acquiring an inflection system with a larger number of contrasting forms may turn out to be harder than acquiring a simpler inflection system. For example, Basque verb agreement marks an inflected verb form with affixes for subject, direct object and indirect object case. The system is agglutinative, and the number of possible distinct affix combinations for ditransitive verbs soon gets very large (up to 102 different forms in the present indicative of the auxiliary). Quantitative evidence from child language inflection shows that production of root infinitive is more frequent and prolonged in Basque than it is in a less inflectionally rich language like Spanish (Austin 2010, 2012). In fact, this may be a consequence of several concomitant factors. Basque paradigms have a much larger number of cells than Spanish paradigms have. Furthermore, the amount of syntactic context that must be processed for a child to check case assignment on the main verb form, is considerably larger than what is needed for Spanish. Once more, it is not one factor only, but the concomitant interaction of a number of factors that may be responsible for a more complex system, and account for slower inflection acquisition.

Far from dealing with the full complexity of inflectional systems across languages, we suggested here a departure from traditional approaches based on either the stocktaking of features and their markers, or a full grammatical description of an inflection system, which all seem to require a lot of knowledge about lexical/grammatical units as well as rules/processes for their recombination/merging. Computer simulations of (discriminative) inflection learning offer a novel perspective on these issues, since they do not require that formal representations are already established. Our evidence naturally prompts the view that the overall complexity of an inflectional system is the resulting equilibrium state of a number of conflicting processing requirements and adaptive responses to task-dependent pressures (see also Marzi, Ferro and Pirrelli 2019).

9 Concluding remarks

Inflection is a fundamental area of word inquiry that lies at the interface between morphology proper, i.e. knowledge of how words are shaped and internally structured, and syntax, i.e. knowledge of what syntactic contexts make certain lexical shapes obligatory. The two dimensions are logically distinct and, in principle, independent. Nothing, in the specific way words are arranged syntagmatically, impinges on the way the same words are inflectionally marked. The great variety of formal means by which identical clusters of inflectional features are marked in morphology, both cross-linguistically and within the same language, bears witness to this autonomy, and lends itself reluctantly to being cast into combinatorial patterns of morpheme arrangement. In this chapter, we mainly focused on aspects of word realization, i.e. on knowledge of the way words are inflected, and on what factors influence speakers' acquisition of this knowledge. Here, we recap a few take-home points.

Of late, the time-honored idea that word forms are organized through paradigmatic families has proved to be extremely fruitful in accounting for important effects of lexical organization and processing. Paradigms appear to organize word forms in a network of items in complementary distribution (or, as Saussure put it, *in absentia*). This network is controlled by two functionally-motivated, interacting principles. The first principle is discriminative: formal variants must be able to mark the entire space of inflectional contrasts exhibited by a language. From this perspective, the more dissimilar an inflected form is from its paradigm companions, the more effectively it is associated with its cluster of inflectional features (or paradigm cell). However, if paradigmatically related forms were all arbitrarily different, a speaker would be in no position to interpret or produce novel forms. The second principle counterbalances this effect. It is implicational or predictive: patterns of variation tend to be interdependent in ways that allow speakers to predict novel forms on the basis of encountered forms. This is a hallmark of regular inflection. Nevertheless, even the most suppletive or least predictable paradigms in a language typically present a few implicational patterns of formal redundancy.

A discriminative/implicational account of the paradigm dimension sheds light on the graded nature of (ir)regularity and structure in inflectional systems. Morphological irregularity is not dysfunctional, but responds to a maximally contrastive function in both word recognition and production. Since irregularly inflected forms are typically isolated, and are acquired by being committed to memory, it is only to be expected that irregularity strongly correlates with token frequency. Regularly inflected forms, on the other hand, can benefit from repeated patterns of intra-paradigmatic formal redundancy and are, therefore, also sensitive to family size (or type frequency) effects.

Any inflectional system of average complexity typically presents a whole range of gradation along this continuum. Models that postulate a dichotomous classification of inflected forms between regulars and irregulars can only account for somewhat ideal cases of particularly simple inflectional systems. Both morphological theory and computational morphology have laid considerable emphasis on graded patterns of inflectional generalization governed by lexical information. For decades, this has been one of the cornerstones of Lexicalist Morphology and has guided important computational work on inheritance lexical networks such as DATR. The idea that both general and irregular inflectional patterns can be cast into formally uniform statements ultimately blurs the distinction between rules and lexical entries. In DATR, so-called lexical rules are expressed as statements containing free variables, which are bound to constant, local values within individual, idiosyncratic lexical entries.

The idea of measuring the complexity of an inflectional system in terms of inferential uncertainty (or information entropy) represents an important recent development in paradigm-based approaches to inflection. For any given verb stem s, one can estimate how easily an unknown stem-affix combination s-a_j can be predicted on the basis of an already encountered stem-affix combination s-a_k for the same verb. In addition, we can also estimate how much reduction in uncertainty we get in guessing s-a_j, when we know more stem-affix combinations for the same paradigm. Overall, formal irregularity is not randomly scattered across paradigm cells. An inflectional system tends to reduce the amount of uncertainty in mastering it. Besides, however complex and irregular, an inflectional system tends to be organized in such a way that less predictable forms are usually more frequent than more predictable forms.[10] It is such an implicatively organized system of patterns and subpatterns that effectively addresses learnability issues, by constraining an otherwise unrestricted set of combinatorial options. Such a global functional property of inflectional systems is significantly missed by purely realizational models of inflection.

A further step in the same direction is made by moving from inheritance networks to recurrent neural networks (RNNs), where the paradigmatic organization of lexical forms is responsible for coactivation and competition of concurrently stored items in word recognition and production. The step has far reaching consequences on the way we look at word knowledge, as it shifts the research focus from what speakers know when they know inflection, to how speakers develop knowledge of inflection through input exposure. According to a learning-based perspective, redundant patterns are predominantly statistical, and even irregularities appear to be motivated by their frequency distribution in the system and the general-purpose learning strategies of the human language processor. All these issues are very different in character from the formal constraints on units, representations or rule systems proposed within theoretical and computational models. Nonetheless, they offer an insightful perspective on language architecture, and shed novel light on issues of inflectional complexity.

The most influential legacy of connectionism for models of lexical processing is probably the idea that storage and processing are not segregated in functionally independent modules of the language architecture, but are better conceived of as two interlocked dynamics of the same underlying process. In processing an input stimulus, nodes respond with a short-term activation. Due to reinforcement and competitive specialization, specific nodes are trained to respond more and more strongly to a specific class of stimuli only, forming a long-term memory trace for that class. Nodes that are repeatedly fired at short time delays by the same time series of stimuli give rise to a long-term chain of nodes specialized for processing that series. To put it in terms of Hebb's law of neural plasticity, nodes used together wire together. Once more, nodes that get repeatedly activated in a

---

10 This is in fact connected with language usage and its functional relation to language change. One can hypothesise that high-frequency items are used more frequently and are thus more prone to being phonetically reduced (e.g. Bybee 2000; Jurafsky et al. 2002; Pluymaekers et al. 2005). Alternatively, it can be argued that high frequency be a consequence of the grammaticalization of a lexical item, and its resulting light functional load (Hopper & Traugott 1993). Nevertheless, common currency in language usage can play a role in protecting high-frequency irregular forms from analogical levelling (Milizia 2015).

processing routine for a specific input word, are the same units that are used for the stored representation of that word. This relatively straightforward mechanism provides a causal link between input word frequency, degrees of entrenchment of lexical representations and processing effects.

In line with neuro-anatomical evidence (Wilson 2001; D'Esposito 2007; Ma et al. 2014), RNNs model lexical working memory as the transient activation of long-term memory structures. From this perspective, word family relations are long term memory effects, based on concurrent storage of full forms. But there is more to it than just a memory effect. The two fundamental classes of redundant inflectional patterns, stems and affixes, give rise to different, interacting word families (namely, paradigms and inflectional classes), which appear to play an important role in the way individual forms are processed and perceived by the speakers.

Focusing on paradigms first, when one member of a paradigm (say *walks*) is input to an RNN, other non-target memory chains such as *walk*, *walked* and *walking* are synchronously activated, due to the shared nodes associated with the common stem. The more regular the paradigm, the fewer its stem allomorphs, and the more entrenched, on average, their corresponding memory chains. Co-activation, however, raises uncertainty at the stem boundary, where many outgoing connections project their expectations for different upcoming endings. Such a degree of uncertainty can be taken to be an information-theoretic correlate of morphological structure at the level of network connectivity. High entropy paradigms increase uncertainty at the stem boundary, and make their internal structure more salient. Conversely, low entropy families develop more holistic word chains. This explains why forms in regular paradigms are perceived more compositionally than irregular ones are. Unlike irregular paradigms, where each allomorph can appear in a subset of paradigm cells only, regular stems appear throughout their paradigms.

Competition between paradigmatically unrelated forms, on the other hand, takes place with forms sharing the same inflectional ending (e.g. all *ing*-forms). In self-organizing RNNs, the strength of the connection linking – say – *speak*- and *walk*- to *ing* is controlled by the conditional probability of *speak*- and *walk*- given -*ing*. A high entropy distribution of *ing*-forms, corresponding to a more uniform distribution, favors a more balanced allocation of weights on connections at the stem boundary. Conversely, high frequency *ing*-forms tend to proportionally strengthen their connections to -*ing* nodes, weakening the corresponding connections from their low frequency competitors.

There is a clear relationship between high levels of uncertainty at the stem boundary and word processing effects. Other factors being equal, uniformly distributed members of (high entropy) inflectional families will take equal or comparable time for processing. Conversely, an unbalanced competition, with few family members occurring much more frequently than others, results in the RNN being slower to recognize low frequency forms with high frequency competitors, as the latter are harder to eliminate (Lively et al. 1994; Luce 1986; Luce and Pisoni 1998). This explains why higher entropy families are processed more easily (Baayen et al. 2011; Bertram et al. 2000; Moscoso et al. 2004; Kuperman et al. 2010).

In realistic input conditions, inflectional endings are not distributed uniformly (Blevins et al. 2017). Hence, for any paradigm, the most balanced distribution of its members is the one where inflected forms with high frequency endings are seen more often than inflected forms with low frequency endings. In fact, this distribution strengthens the inflected forms that appear with competitive (high frequency) endings, while weakening those that select weaker endings, and this explains the role of inflectional entropy on processing (Milin et al. 2009a, 2009b).

Complex processing dynamics offer a novel perspective on assessment of complexity issues in typologically diverse inflection systems. Nowadays, computer simulations and non-linear models of data regression offer the opportunity to visualize time-bound effects of structure complexity on word processing at a considerable level of detail. One can thus inspect the non-linear trend of the processing cost of forms in both regular and irregular paradigms, as well as differential processing patterns in typologically different languages. Although languages may considerably vary in the way processing costs are apportioned within specific inflection systems, when processing costs are measured as a linear function interpolating processing ease from the start of the word to its end, linear slopes for different inflection systems are fairly comparable, suggesting that inflection systems are, ultimately, the result of a balancing act among a number of potentially conflicting requirements and adaptive responses to task-dependent pressures.

However logically independent, the paradigmatic and syntagmatic dimensions of inflection must functionally interact during language acquisition. A distributional, discriminative approach to learning appears to conflate the issues of *how* inflection is marked, and in *what contexts* marking applies. We already mentioned evidence that children learn words in chunks (MacWhinney 1976; Wilson 2003). Upon hearing contexts where the same verb is found in different morphosyntactic contexts (as in "SHE walkS" and "THEY walk"), the child is in a position to use information of the pronominal subject and the verb suffix to discriminate third person singular contexts from non-third person singular contexts, thereby discovering the relationship between S-inflection and SHE in pre-verbal position. Paradigmatic word relations are ultimately associated with contrastive points along the syntagmatic dimension. Likewise, paradigm cells can be viewed as grammatical abstractions over this multi-dimensional space of systematic distributional contrasts in context. Clearly, this requires that longer stretches of words be concurrently committed to memory and organized through superpositional memory chains.

There is mounting evidence that this must be true. The human brain is understood to "contain" not only morphologically simple words, but also inflected and derived forms, compounds, light verb constructions, collocations, idioms, proverbs, social routine clichés and pre-compiled routinized chunks maximizing processing opportunities (Jackendoff 2002). Recognition of idiomatic expressions and multi-word units provides strong evidence of a processing system that uses all available pieces of information as soon as possible to constrain memory search and speed up processing of the most highly expected input (Grimm et al. 2017; McCauley and Christiansen 2017; Vespignani et al. 2010). Likewise, deficits in the working memory span (e.g. in children with SLD) explain difficulties in the acquisition of inflection, especially for large embedding contexts. The formal and structural similarity between periphrastic inflection and idiomatic expressions (Booij 2010; Bonami 2015) bears witness to the functional interaction between concurrent, redundant storage of multi-word chunks and inflectional marking in language acquisition. We still know comparatively little about the way this is implemented in the brain. Nevertheless, recent empirical and experimental evidence suggests that the brain might make use of relatively unlimited long-term memory resources to compensate for the relatively limited capacity of working memory (Tremblay and Baayen 2010). By storing a number of frequently needed/used multi-word units as holistic chunks, the human processor can augment its capacity by filling working memory slots with word chunks rather than individual words. More recent neuro-functional models of working memory as a limited attentional resource distributed flexibly among all items to be maintained during processing (Ma et al. 2014) can also take advantage of pre-compiled long memory chunks. In fact, since the latter are retrieved through long-term temporal connections, working memory resources can be more efficiently used to maintain inter-chunk connections. We believe that dynamic memory models such as those suggested by Ma and colleagues, which are based on the functional integration between working memory and long-term memory resources, will shift the theoretical debate away from the traditional dichotomy between word-centred vs. syntactically-oriented accounts of inflection. Future research will likely focus on scale-free mechanisms for concurrent memorization of time-series of symbols of different length, as well as scale-dependent effects of their concurrent, hierarchical organization in the human brain.

References

Ackerman, Farrell, James P. Blevins, & Robert Malouf. 2009. Parts and wholes: Implicative patterns in inflectional paradigms. In James P. Blevins & Juliette Blevins (eds.), *Analogy in grammar: Form and acquisition*, 54–82. Oxford: Oxford University Press.

Ackerman, Farrell & Robert Malouf. 2013. Morphological organization: The low conditional entropy conjecture. *Language* 89 (3). 429–464.

Ackerman, Farrell & Gregory Stump. 2004. Paradigms and periphrastic expressions. In Louisa Sadler & Andrew Spencer (eds.), *Projecting morphology*, 11–54. Stanford: CSLI Publications.

Albright, Adam. 2002. Islands of reliability for regular morphology: Evidence from Italian. *Language* 78. 684–709.

Altmann, Gerry T. M. & Yuki Kamide. 2007. The real-time mediation of visual attention by language and world knowledge: Linking anticipatory (and other) eye movements to linguistic processing. *Journal of Memory and Language* 57 (4). 502–518.

Amha, Azeb. 2001. *The Maale language*. Dissertation University of Leiden.

Aronoff, Mark. 1976. *Word formation in generative grammar*. Cambridge: the MIT Press.

Austin, Jennifer. 2010. Rich inflection and the production of finite verbs in child language. *Morphology* 20 (1). 41–69.

Austin, Jennifer. 2012. The case-agreement hierarchy in acquisition: Evidence from children learning Basque. *Lingua* 122 (3). 289–302.

Baayen, R. Harald, Tom Dijkstra & Robert Schreuder. 1997. Singulars and plurals in Dutch: Evidence for a parallel dual-route model. *Journal of Memory and Language* 37 (1). 94–117.

Baayen, R. Harald & Peter Hendrix. 2017. Two-layer networks, non-linear separation, and human learning. In Martijn Wieling, Martin Kroon, Gertjan van Noord (eds.), *From Semantics to Dialectometry. Festschrift in honor of John Nerbonne*, 13–22. London, College Publications.

Baayen, R. Harald, Peter Hendrix & Michael Ramscar. 2013. Sidestepping the combinatorial explosion: Towards a processing model based on discriminative learning. *Language and Speech* 56. 329–347.

Baayen, R. Harald, Petar Milin, Dušica Filipović Đurđević, Peter Hendrix, Marco Marelli. 2011. An amorphous model for morphological processing in visual comprehension based on naive discriminative learning. *Psychological Review* 118 (3). 438–481.

Baayen, R. Harald, James M. McQueen, Tom Dijkstra & Robert Schreuder. 2003. Frequency effects in regular inflectional morphology: Revisiting Dutch plurals. In R. Harald Baayen & Robert Schreuder (eds.), *Morphological structure in language processing*, 355–390. Berlin: De Gruyter Mouton.

Balling, Laura W. & R. Harald Baayen. 2008. Morphological effects in auditory word recognition: Evidence from Danish. *Language and Cognitive processes* 23 (7–8). 1159–1190.

Balling, Laura W. & R. Harald Baayen. 2012. Probability and surprisal in auditory comprehension of morphologically complex words. *Cognition* 125 (1). 80–106.

Bane, Max. 2008. Quantifying and measuring morphological complexity. In *Proceedings of the 26th West Coast Conference on Formal Linguistics*. 69–76.

Bates, Elizabeth & Brian MacWhinney. 1987. Competition, variation and language learning. In B. MacWhinney (ed.), *Mechanisms of language acquisition*, 157–163, Hillsdale, NJ: Lawrence Erlbaum Associates.

Beard, Robert. 1995. *Lexeme-Morpheme Base Morphology: A General Theory of Inflection and Word Formation*. Cambridge: SUNY Press.
Bertram, Raymond, R. Harald Baayen & Robert Schreuder. 2000. Effects of family size for complex words. *Journal of Memory and Language* 42. 390–405
Berwick, Robert C. 1985. *The acquisition of syntactic knowledge*. Cambridge, MA: MIT Press.
Bickel, Balthasar & Johanna Nichols. 2005. Inflectional synthesis of the verb. Martin Haspelmath, Matthew S. Dryer, David Gil & Bernard Comrie (eds.), *The World Atlas of Language Structures*, 94–97. Oxford: Oxford University Press
Bittner, Dagmar, Wolfgang U. Dressler & Marianne Kilani-Schoch (eds.). 2003. *Development of verb inflection in first language acquisition: A cross-linguistic perspective*. Berlin/New York: Mouton de Gruyter.
Blevins, James P. 2003. Stems and paradigms. *Language* 79 (2). 737–767.
Blevins, James P. 2006. Word-based morphology. *Journal of Linguistics* 42 (3). 531–573.
Blevins, James P. 2016. *Word and paradigm morphology*. Oxford: Oxford University Press.
Blevins, James P., Petar Milin & Michael Ramscar. 2017. The Zipfian paradigm cell filling problem. Ferenc Kiefer, James P. Blevins & Huba Bartos (eds.), *Perspectives on morphological organization: data and analyses*, 139–158. Leiden: Brill.
Blom, Elma & Frank Wijnen. 2006. Development need not be embarrassing: The demise of the root infinitive and related changes in Dutch child language. Manuscript, University of Amsterdam/Utrecht University.
Bloomfield, Leonard. 1933. *Language*. University of Chicago Press, Chicago.
Bonami, Olivier. 2015. Periphrasis as collocation. *Morphology* 25, 63–110.
Bonami, Olivier & Sarah Beniami. 2017. Joint predictiveness in inflectional paradigms. *Word Structure* 9 (2). 156–182.
Bonami, Olivier & Gilles Boyé. 2014. De formes en thèmes. In Florence Villoing, Sarah Leroy & Sophie David (eds.), *Foisonnements morphologiques. Etudes en hommage à Françoise Kerleroux*, 17–45. Presses Universitaires de Paris Ouest.
Booij, Geert. 1993. Against split morphology. In Geert Booij & Jaap van Marle (eds.), *Yearbook of Morphology 1993*. 27–49. Dordrecht: Kluwer.
Booij, Geert. 1996. Inherent versus contextual inflection and the split morphology hypothesis. In Geert Booij & Jaap van Marle (eds.), *Yearbook of Morphology 1995*. 1–16. Dordrecht: Kluwer.
Booij, Geert. 2010. *Construction morphology*. Oxford: Oxford University Press.
Börjars, K., Nigel Vincent & Carol Chapman. 1997. Paradigms, periphrases, and pronominal inflection: a feature-based account. In Geert Booij & Jaap van Marle (eds.), *Yearbook of Morphology 1996*, 155–180. Dordrecht: Kluwer.
Brent, Michael R. 1999. Speech segmentation and word discovery: A computational perspective. *Trends in Cognitive Sciences* 3. 294–301.
Briscoe, Josie, Dorothy V.M. Bishop & Courtenay F. Norbury. 2001. Phonological processing, language, and literacy: A comparison of children with mild-to-moderate sensorineural hearing loss and those with specific language impairment. *Journal of Child Psychology and Psychiatry, and Allied Disciplines* 42. 329–340.
Brown, Roger. 1973. *A first language: early stages*. Cambridge, MA: Harvard University Press.
Bruck, Maggie & Stephen J. Ceci. 1999. The suggestibility of children's memory. *Annual review of psychology* 50 (1). 419–439.
Bybee, Joan. 1988. Morphology as lexical organization. *Theoretical morphology* 119–141.
Bybee, Joan. 1995. Regular Morphology and the Lexicon. *Language and Cognitive Processes* 10(5). 425–455.

Bybee, Joan. 2000. Lexicalization of sound change and alternating environments. In Michael B. Broe & Janet M. Pierrehumbert (eds.), *Laboratory Phonology V: Acquisition and the Lexicon*, 250–268. Cambridge: Cambridge University Press.

Caballero, Gabriela & Alice C. Harris. 2010. A Working Typology of Multiple Exponence. In Ferenc Kiefer, Mária Ladányi & Péter Siptár (eds.), *Current issues in morphological theory: (ir)regularity, analogy and frequency. Selected papers from the 14th International Morphology Meeting, Budapest, May 13–16*, 163–188. John Benjamins.

Cazden, Courtney B. 1968. The acquisition of noun and verb inflections. *Child development* 39 (2). 433–448.

Chouinard, Michelle M. & Eve Clark. 2003. Adult reformulations of child errors as negative evidence. *Journal of Child Language* 30. 637–669.

Christiansen, Morten H., Joseph Allen & Mark S. Seidenberg. 1998. Learning to segment speech using multiple cues: A connectionist model. *Language and Cognitive Processes* 13. 221–268.

Clark, Eve V. 1987. The principle of contrast: A constraint on language. In Brian MacWhinney (ed.), *Mechanisms of language aquisition*. 1–33. Hillsdale, NJ: Lawrence Erlbaum Associates.

Clark, Eve V. 1990. On the pragmatics of contrast. *Journal of child language* 17(2). 417–431.

Coltheart, Max, Kathleen Rastle, Conrad Perry, Robyn Langdon & Johannes Ziegler. 2001. DRC: A Dual Route Cascaded model of visual word recognition and reading aloud. *Psychological Review* 108. 204–256.

Corbett, Greville G. & Norman M. Fraser. 1993. Network Morphology: A DATR account of Russian nominal inflection. *Journal of Linguistics* 29. 113–142.

Crago, Martha B. & Shanley Allen. 2001. Early finiteness in Inuktitut: The role of language structure and input. *Language Acquisition* 9 (1). 59–111.

D'Esposito, Mark. 2007. From cognitive to neural models of working memory. *Philosophical Transactions of the Royal Society of London B: Biological Sciences 362* (1481). 761–772.

de Jong, Nivja H., Laurie B. Feldman, Robert Schreuder, Matthew Pastizzo & R. Harald Baayen. 2002. The processing and representation of Dutch and English compounds: Peripheral morphological and central orthographic effects. *Brain and Language* 81 (1). 555–567.

De Pauw, Guy & Peter W. Wagacha. 2007. Bootstrapping morphological analysis of Gĩkũyũ using maximum entropy learning. *Proceedings of the 8th Annual Conference of the International Speech Communication Association* (INTERSPEECH 2007), Antwerp. 1517–1520.

DeLong, Katherine A., Thomas P. Urbach & Marta Kutas. 2005. Probabilistic word pre-activation during language comprehension inferred from electrical brain activity. *Nature Neuroscience* 8 (8). 1117–1121.

Dressler, Wolfgang U. 2005. Word-formation in natural morphology. In Pavol Štekauer & Rochelle Lieber (eds.), *Handbook of word-formation*, 267–284. Dordrecht: Springer

Dressler, Wolfgang U. 2010. A typological approach to first language acquisition. In Michèle Kail & Maya Hickmann (eds.), *Language acquisition across linguistic and cognitive systems*, 109–124.

Ellis, Nick C. 2002. Reflections on frequency effects in language processing. *Studies in second language acquisition* 24(2). 297–339.

Ellis, Nick C., & Richard Schmidt. 1998. Rules or associations in the acquisition of morphology? The frequency by regularity interaction in human and PDP learning of morphosyntax. *Language and cognitive processes* 13 (2–3). 307–336.

Elman, Jeffrey L. 1990. Finding Structure in Time. *Cognitive Science* 14(2). 179–211.
Evans, Roger & Gerald Gazdar. 1996. DATR: A language for lexical knowledge representation. *Computational Linguistics* 22 (2). 167–216.
Farmer, Marion. 2000. Language and social cognition in children with specific language impairment. *Journal of Child Psychology and Psychiatry, and Allied Disciplines* 41. 627–636.
Ferro, Marcello, Claudia Marzi & Vito Pirrelli. 2011. A self-organizing model of word storage and processing: implications for morphology learning. *Lingue e Linguaggio* X(2). 209–226.
Finkel, Raphael & Gregory Stump. 2007. Principal parts and morphological typology. *Morphology* 17. 39–75.
Freudenthal, Daniel, Julian Pine & Fernand Gobet. 2010. Explaining quantitative variation in the rate of Optional Infinitive errors across languages: a comparison of MOSAIC and the Variational Learning Model. *Journal of child language* 37(3). 643–669.
Geertzen, Jeroen, James P. Blevins & Petar Milin. 2016. The informativeness of linguistic unit boundaries. *Italian Journal of Linguistics* 28(2). 1–24.
Gillis, Steven. 2003. A case study of the early acquisition of verbs in Dutch. In Dagmar Bittner, Wolfgang U. Dressler & Marianne Kilani-Schoch (eds.), *Development of verb inflection in first language acquisition: A cross-linguistic perspective*, 171–203. Berlin/New York: Mouton de Gruyter.
Goldsmith, John. 2001. Unsupervised learning of the morphology of a natural language. *Computational Linguistics* 27(2). 153–198.
Goldsmith, John. 2006. An algorithm for the unsupervised learning of morphology. *Natural Language Engineering* 12. 1–19.
Goodman, Judith C., Philip L. Dale & Ping Li. 2008. Does frequency count? Parental input and the acquisition of vocabulary. *Journal of Child Language* 35. 515–531.
Grimm, Robert, Giovanni Cassani, Steven Gillis & Walter Daelemans. 2017. Facilitatory effects of muli-word units in lexical processing and word learning: a computational investigation. *frontiers in psychology* 8. https://www.frontiersin.org/articles/10.3389/fpsyg.2017.00555/full (accessed 10 August 2019).
Haegeman, Liliane. 1995. Root infinitives, tense, and truncated structures. *Language Acquisition* 4. 205–255.
Hahn, Ulrike & Todd M. Bailey. 2005. What makes words sound similar? *Cognition* 97. 227–267.
Halle, Morris. 1973. Prolegomena to a theory of word formation. *Linguistic Inquiry* 4. 451–464.
Halle, Morris & Alec Marantz. 1993. Distributed morphology and the pieces of inflection. In Hale, K. & SJ Keyser (eds.), *The View from Building 20*. Cambridge, Mass: MIT Press.
Hamann, Cornelia & Kim Plunkett. 1998. Subjectless sentences in child Danish. *Cognition* 69 (1). 35–72.
Hankamer, Jorge. 1989. Morphological parsing and the lexicon. In William Marslen-Wilson (ed.), *Lexical representation and process*, 392–408. The MIT Press.
Harm, Michael W. & Mark S. Seidenberg. 1999. Phonology, reading acquisition and dyslexia: insights from connectionist models. *Psychological Review* 106(3). 491–528.
Harris, Alice C. 2009. Exuberant exponence in Batsbi. *Natural Language and Linguistic Theory* 27. 267–303.

Harris, Zellig S. 1942. Morpheme alternants in linguistic analysis. *Language* 18. 109–115. Reprinted in Joos (1957), 109–115.
Harris, Zellig S. 1951. *Methods in Structural Linguistics*. University of Chicago Press, Chicago.
Harris, Zellig S. 1968. *Mathematical structures of language*. New York: Wileyand Sons.
Hockett, Charles F. 1947. Problems of morphemic analysis. *Language* 23. 321–343. Reprinted in Joos (1957), 229–242.
Hockett, Charles F. 1967. The Yawelmani basic verb. *Language* 43. 208–222.
Hockett, Charles F. 1987. *refurbishing our foundations: elementary linguistics from an advanced point of view*. John Benjamins, Amsterdam.
Hopper, Paul & Elizabeth Traugott. 1993. *Grammaticalization*. Cambridge: Cambridge University Press [2003^2].
Huttenlocher, Janellen, Wendy Haight, Anthony Bryk, Michael Seltzer & Thomas Lyons, T. 1991. Early vocabulary growth: Relation to language input and gender. *Developmental psychology* 27(2), 236.
Jackendoff, Ray. 1975. Morphological and semantic regularities in the lexicon. *Language* 51. 639–671.
Jackendoff, Ray. 2002. *Foundations of language: Brain, meaning, grammar, evolution*. Oxford University Press; Oxford.
Jordan, Michael. 1997. Serial order: a parallel distributed processing approach. *Advances in Psychology* 121. 471–495.
Juola, Patrick. 1998. Measuring linguistic complexity: The morphological tier. *Journal of Quantitative Linguistics* 3(5). 206–213.
Jurafsky, Daniel, Alan Bell & Cynthia Girand. 2002. The role of the lemma in form variation. Papers in laboratory phonology VII. 4–34.
Jurafsky, David, Alan Bell, Michelle Gregory & William D. Raymond. 2001. Probabilistic relations between words: Evidence from reduction in lexical production. In Joan L. Bybee & Paul Hopper (eds.), *Frequency and the Emergence of Linguistic Structure*, 229–254. Amsterdam: Benjamins.
Kail, Robert & Laurence L. Leonard. 1986. Word-finding abilities in children with specific language impairment. *Monographs of the American Speech-Language-Hearing Association* 25.
Kemps, Rachèl J.J.K., Mirjam Ernestus, Robert Schreuder & R.Harald Baayen. 2005. Prosodic cues for morphological complexity: The case of Dutch plural nouns. *Memory & Cognition* 33 (3). 430–446.
Keuleers, Emmanuel & Walter Daelemans. 2007. Memory-based learning models of inflectional morphology: A methodological case-study. *Lingue e Linguaggio* 6(2). 151–174.
Kibort, Anna. 2010. Towards a typology of grammatical features. In Anna Kibort & Greville G. Corbett (eds.), *Features. Perspectives on a key notion in linguistics*, 64–106. Oxford: Oxford University Press.
Kilani-Schoch, Marianne, Ingrida Balciuniene, Katharina Korecky-Kröll, Sabine Laaha & Wolfgang U. Dressler. 2009. On the role of pragmatics in child-directed speech for the acquisition of verb morphology. *Journal of Pragmatics* 41(2). 219–239.
Kolmogorov, Andrej N. 1965. Three approaches to the quantitative definition of information. *Problems of information transmission* 1(1). 1–7.
Kostić, Aleksandar, Tanja Marković & Aleksandar Baucal. 2003. Inflectional morphology and word meaning: Orthogonal or co-implicative domains? In R. Harald Baayen & Robert

Schreuder (eds.), *Morphological Structure in Language Processing*, 1–44. Mouton de Gruyter, Berlin.

Krajewski, Grzegorz, Lieven, Elena V.M. & Anna L. Theakston. 2012. Productivity of a Polish child's inflectional noun morphology: A naturalistic study. *Morphology* 22 (1). 9–34.

Kuperman, Victor, Raymond Bertram & R.Harald Baayen. 2010. Processing trade-offs in the reading of Dutch derived words. *Journal of Memory and Language* 62 (2). 83–97.

Legate, Julie A. & Charles Yang. 2007. Morphosyntactic learning and the development of tense. *Language Acquisition* 14 (3). 315–344.

Leonard, Laurence. 2014. *Children with Specific Language Impairment*. The MIT Press.

Leonard, Laurence & Patricia Deevy. 2011. Input distribution influences degree of auxiliary use by children with specific language impairment. *Cognitive Linguistics* 22. 247–273.

Leonard, Laurence, Patricia Deevy, Patricia Fey & Shelley Bredin-Oja. 2013. Sentence comprehension in specific language impairment: A task designed to distinguish between cognitive capacity and syntactic complexity. *Journal of Speech, Language, and Hearing Research* 56. 577–589.

Lieber, Rochelle. 1992. *Deconstructing morphology*. Chicago: Chicago University Press.

Lively, Scott E., David B. Pisoni & Stephen D. Goldinger. 1994. Spoken word recognition: Research and theory. In Morton A. Gernsbacher (ed.), *Handbook of psycholinguistics*, 265–301. San Diego, CA: Academic Press.

Luce, Paul A. 1986. A computational analysis of uniqueness points in auditory word recognition. *Perception and Psychophysics* 39. 155–158.

Luce, Paul A. & David B. Pisoni. 1998. Recognizing spoken words: The neighborhood activation model. *Ear and hearing* 19 (1). 1–36.

Ma, Wei J., Masud Husain & Paul M. Bays. 2014. Changing concepts of working memory. *Nature Neuroscience* 17 (3). 347–356.

MacWhinney, Brian. 1976. Hungarian research on the acquisition of morphology and syntax. *Journal of Child Language* 3. 397–410.

MacWhinney, Brian. 1995. *The CHILDES Project: Tools for analyzing talk*. Lawrence Erlbaum, Mahwah, NJ.

Marangolo, Paola & Costanza Papagno. 2020. Neuroscientific protocols for exploring the mental lexicon: evidence from aphasia. In Vito Pirrelli, Ingo Plag & Wolfgang U. Dressler (eds.), *Word knowledge and word usage: a cross-disciplinary guide to the mental lexicon*, 124–163. De Gruyter.

Marcus, Gary F., Steven Pinker, Michael Ullman, Michelle Hollander, T. John Rosen, Fei Xu & Harald Clahsen. 1992. Overregularization in language acquisition. *Monographs of the Society for Research in Child Development* 57(4, Serial No. 228).

Marelli, Marco & Marco Baroni. 2015. Affixation in semantic space: Modeling morpheme meanings with compositional distributional semantics. *Psychological Review* 122 (3). 485–515.

Marslen-Wilson, William D. 1984. Function and process in spoken word recognition: A tutorial overview. In Herman Bouma & Don G. Bouwhuis (eds.), *Attention and performance X: Control of language processes*, 125–150. Hillsdale: Erlbaum.

Marslen-Wilson, William D. 1987. Functional parallelism in spoken word-recognition. *Cognition* 25 (1–2). 71–102.

Marslen-Wilson, William D. & Alan Welsh. 1978. Processing interactions and lexical access during word recognition in continuous speech. *Cognitive Psychology* 10. 29–63.

Marzi, Claudia, Marcello Ferro, Franco Alberto Cardillo & Vito Pirrelli. 2016. Effects of frequency and regularity in an integrative model of word storage and processing. *Italian Journal of Linguistics* 28 (1). 79–114.

Marzi, Claudia, Marcello Ferro, Ouafae Nahli, Patrizia Belik, Stavros Bompolas & Vito Pirrelli. 2018. Evaluating Inflectional Complexity Crosslinguistically: a Processing Perspective. In *Proceedings of 11th LREC 2018*, Miyazaki, Japan. Paper 745.

Marzi, Claudia, Marcello Ferro & Vito Pirrelli. 2014. Morphological structure through lexical parsability. *Lingue e Linguaggio* XIII(2). 263–290.

Marzi, Claudia, Marcello Ferro & Vito Pirrelli. 2019. A processing-oriented investigation of inflectional complexity. *Frontiers in Communication* 4. 48, 1–23. https://doi.org/10.3389/fcomm.2019.00048

Matthews, Peter H. 1972. *Inflectional Morphology: a theoretical study based on aspects of latin verb conjugation*. Cambridge University Press, Cambridge.

Matthews, Peter H. 1991. *Morphology: an introduction to the theory of word-structure*. Second Edition. Cambridge University Press, Cambridge.

McCauley, Stewart M. & Morten H. Christiansen. 2017. Computational investigations of multiword chunks in language learning. *Topics in Cognitive Science* 9 (3). 637–652.

McClelland, James L. & David E. Rumelhart. 1981. An interactive activation model of context effects in letter perception: Part 1. An account of Basic Findings. *Psychological Review* 88. 375–407.

McDonough, Joyce. 2000. On the bipartite model of the Athabaskan verb. In Theodor Fernald & Paul Platero (eds.), *The Athabaskan Languages: Perspectives on a Native American Language Family*, 139–166. Oxford: Oxford University Press.

McNamee, Paul & James Mayfield. 2007. N-gram morphemes for retrieval. *Working Notes for the CLEF 2007 Workshop*, Budapest.

McWorther, John. 2001. The world's simplest grammars are creole grammars. *Linguistic Typology* (5). 125–166.

Milin, Petar, Laurie B. Feldman, Michael Ramscar, Peter Hendrix & R. Harald Baayen. 2017. Discrimination in lexical decision. *PloS one* 12 (2). e0171935.

Milin, Petar, Dušica Filipović Đurđević & Fermín Moscoso del Prado Martín. 2009a. The simultaneous effects of inflectional paradigms and classes on lexical recognition: Evidence from Serbian. *Journal of Memory and Language* 60 (1). 50–64.

Milin, Petar, Victor Kuperman, Aleksandar Kostić & R. Harald Baayen. 2009b. Words and paradigms bit by bit: An information theoretic approach to the processing of paradigmatic structure in inflection and derivation. In James P. Blevins & Juliette Blevins (eds.), *Analogy in grammar: Form and acquisition*, 214–252. Oxford University Press.

Milizia, Paolo. 2015. Patterns of syncretism and paradigm complexity: The case of old and middle Indic declension. In Matthew Baerman, Dunstan Brown & Greville G. Corbett (eds.), *Understanding and Measuring morphological complexity*, 167–184. Oxford: Oxford University Press.

Montgomery, James W. 2004. Sentence comprehension in children with specific language impairment: Effects of input rate and phonological working memory. *International Journal of Language & Communication Disorders* 39. 115–133.

Montgomery, James W. & Laurence B. Leonard. 1998. Real-time inflectional processing by children with specific language impairment: Effects of phonetic substance. *Journal of Speech, Language, and Hearing Research* 41. 1432–1443.

Moscoso del Prado Martín, Fermín, Aleksandar Kostić & R. Harald Baayen. 2004. Putting the bits together: An information theoretical perspective on morphological processing. *Cognition* 94 (1). 1–18.

Mulder, Kimberley, Ton Dijkstra, Robert Schreuder & R.Harald Baayen. 2014. Effects of primary and secondary morphological family size in monolingual and bilingual word processing. *Journal of Memory and Language* 72. 59–84.

Noyer, Rolf. 1992. *Features, positions and affixes in autonomous morphological structure.* Ph.D. thesis, MIT.

Paul, Hermann. 1920. *Prinzipien der Sprachgeschichte.* Max Niemayer Verlag, Tübingen.

Perry, Conrad, Johannes C. Ziegler & Marco Zorzi. 2007. Nested incremental modeling in the development of computational theories: the CDP+ model of reading aloud. *Psychological review* 114(2). 273–315.

Penke, Martina. 2012. The dual-mechanism debate. In Markus Werning, Wolfram Hinzen & Edouard Machery (eds.), *The Oxford handbook of compositionality*, 574–595. Oxford: Oxford University Press.

Peters, Ann M. 1997. Language typology, prosody, and the acquisition of grammatical morphemes. *The crosslinguistic study of language acquisition* 5. 135–197.

Phillips, Colin. 1995. Syntax at two: Cross-linguistic differences. In Carson Schuetze, Jennifer Ganger & Kevin Broihier (eds.), *Papers on language processing and acquisition*, 225–282. Cambridge, MA: MIT.

Phillips, Colin 1996. Root infinitives are finite. In Andy Stringfellow, Dalia Cahana-Amitay, Elizabeth Hughes & Andrea Zukowski (eds.), *Proceedings of the 20th annual Boston University conference on language development*, 588–599. Somerville, MA: Cascadilla Press.

Pickering, Martin J. & Simon Garrod. 2007. Do people use language production to make predictions during comprehension? *Trends in Cognitive Sciences* 11 (3). 105–110.

Pine, Julian M., Gina Conti-Ramsden, Kate Joseph, Elena V.M. Lieven & Ludovica Serratrice. 2008. Tense over time: Testing the Agreement/Tense Omission Model as an account of the pattern of tense-marking provision in early child English. *Journal of Child Language* 35. 55–75.

Pinker, Steven. 1984. *Language learnability and language development.* Cambridge, MA: Harvard University Press.

Pinker, Steven. 1989. *Learnability and cognition. The acquisition of argument structure.* Cambridge, MA: MIT Press.

Pinker, Steven & Michael T. Ullman. 2002. The past and future of the past tense. *Trends in cognitive sciences* 6 (11). 456–463.

Pirrelli, Vito. 2000. *Paradigmi in morfologia. Un approccio interdisciplinare alla flessione verbale dell'italiano.* Pisa-Roma: IEPI.

Pirrelli, Vito & Marco Battista. 2000. The paradigmatic dimension of stem allomorphy in Italian verb inflection. *Italian Journal of Linguistics* 12 (2). 307–380.

Pirrelli, Vito & Marco Battista. 2003. Syntagmatic and paradigmatic issues in computational morphology. *Linguistica Computazionale* XVIII–XIX. 679–702.

Pirrelli, Vito, Marcello Ferro & Claudia Marzi. 2015. Computational complexity of abstractive morphology. In Matthew Baerman, Dunstan Brown & Greville G. Corbett (eds.), *Understanding and measuring morphological complexity*, 141–166. Oxford: Oxford University Press.

Pirrelli, Vito, Claudia Marzi, Marcello Ferro, Franco Alberto Cardillo, Harald R. Baayen & Petar Milin. 2020. Psycho-computational modelling of the mental lexicon: a discriminative learning perspective. In Vito Pirrelli, Ingo Plag & Wolfgang U. Dressler (eds.), *Word knowledge and word usage: a cross-disciplinary guide to the mental lexicon*, 21–80. De Gruyter.

Pirrelli, Vito & François Yvon. 1999. The hidden dimension: a paradigmatic view of data-driven NLP. *Journal of Experimental and Theoretical Artificial Intelligence* 11. 391–408.

Plaut, David C., James L. McClelland, Mark S. Seidenberg & Karalyn Patterson. 1996. Understanding normal and impaired word reading: Computational principles in quasi-regular domains. *Psychological Review* 103, 56–115.

Plunkett, Kim & Patrick Juola. 1999. A connectionist model of English past tense and plural morphology. *Cognitive Science* 23 (4), 463–490.

Pluymaekers, Mark, Mirjam Ernestus & R. Harald Baayen. 2005. Articulatory planning is continuous and sensitive to informational redundancy. *Phonetica* 62. 146–159.

Popova, Gergana. 2010. Features in periphrastic constructions. In Anna Kibort & Greville G. Corbett (eds.), *Features. Perspectives on a key notion in linguistics*. Oxford: Oxford University Press, 166–184.

Purdy, John D., Laurence B. Leonard, Christine Weber-Fox & Natalya Kaganovich. 2014. Decreased sensitivity to long-distance dependencies in children with a history of Specific Language Impairment: Electrophysiological evidence. *Journal of Speech, Language, and Hearing Research* 57 (3). 1040–1059.

Ramscar, Michael & Melody Dye. 2011. Learning language from the input: Why innate constraints can't explain noun compounding. *Cognitive Psychology* 62 (1). 1–40.

Ramscar, Michael & Daniel Yarlett. 2007. Linguistic self-correction in the absence of feedback: a new approach to the logical problem of language acquisition. *Cognitive Science* 31 (6). 927–960.

Ravid, Dorit, Emmanuel Keuleers and Wolfgang U. Dressler. 2020. Word storage and computation. In Vito Pirrelli, Ingo Plag & Wolfgang U. Dressler (eds.), *Word knowledge and word usage: a cross-disciplinary guide to the mental lexicon*, 582–622. De Gruyter.

Rescorla, Robert A. & Allan R. Wagner. 1972. A theory of Pavlovian conditioning: Variations in the effectiveness of reinforcement and nonreinforcement. *Classical conditioning II: Current research and theory* 2. 64–99.

Rice, Mabel L., Kenneth Wexler, Janet Marquis & Scott Hershberger. 2000. Acquisition of irregular past tense by children with specific language impairment. *Journal of speech, language, and hearing research* 43(5). 1126–1144.

Rissanen, Jorma. 1989. *Stochastic complexity in statistical inquiry*. World Scientific Series in Computer Science. Singapore: World Scientific.

Robins, Robert H. 1959. In defence of WP. *Transactions of the Philological Society* 58, 116–144. Reprinted in *Transactions of the Philological Society* 99. 116–144.

Rowe, Meredith. 2012. A longitudinal investigation of the role of quantity and quality of child-directed speech in vocabulary development. *Child Development* 83. 1762–1774.

Rumelhart, David & James McClelland. 1986. On learning the past tense of English verbs. In Rumelhart, D.E, McClelland J. & the PDP Research Group (eds.), *Parallel distributed processing: Explorations in the microstructure of cognition*. Vol. 1. 216–271, The MIT Press.

Sadler, Louisa & Andrew Spencer. 2001. Syntax as an exponent of morphological features. In Geert Booij & Jaap van Marle (eds.), *Yearbook of Morphology 2000*, 71–96. Dordrecht: Kluwer.

Sagot, Benoît. 2018. *Informatiser le lexique: Modélisation, développement et utilisation de lexiques morphologiques, syntaxiques et sémantiques*. Habilitation, Université Paris-Sorbonne.

Sagot, Benoît, & Geraldine Walther. 2011. Non-canonical inflection: data, formalisation and complexity measures. In *International Workshop on Systems and Frameworks for Computational Morphology*. 23–45. Springer, Berlin, Heidelberg.

Scalise, Sergio. 1984. *Generative morphology*. Dordrecht: Foris.

Schreuder, Robert & R. Harald Baayen. 1995. Modeling morphological processing. In Laurie B. Feldman (ed.), *Morphological aspects of language processing*, 131–156. Erlbaum.

Shannon, Claude E. 1948. A mathematical theory of communication. *Bell System Technical Journal* 27. 379–423.

Shosted, Ryan. 2006. Correlating complexity: a typological approach. *Linguistic Typology* (10). 1–40.

Slobin, Dan I. 1982. Universal and particular in the acquisition of language. In Eric Wanner & Lila Gleitman (eds.), *Language acquisition: The state of the art*, 128–172. Cambridge: Cambridge University Press.

Slobin, Dan I. (ed.). 1985. *The crosslinguistic study of language acquisition*. Hillsdale, NJ: Lawrence Erlbaum.

Stark, Rachel & James Montgomery. 1995. Sentence processing in language-impaired children under conditions of filtering and time compression. *Applied Psycholinguistics* 16. 137–154.

Stump, Gregory. 2001. *Inflectional morphology: a theory of paradigm structure*. Cambridge (UK): Cambridge University Press.

Taatgen, Niels A. & John R. Anderson. 2002. Why do children learn to say "broke"? A model of learning the past tense without feedback. *Cognition* 86(2). 123–155.

Tremblay, Antoine & R. Harald Baayen. 2010. Holistic processing of regular four-word sequences: A behavioral and erp study of the effects of structure, frequency, and probability on immediate free recall. In David Wood (ed.), *Perspectives on formulaic language: Acquisition and communication*, 151–173. Bloomsbury Publishing.

Vespignani, Francesco, Paolo Canal, Nicola Molinaro, Sergio Fonda & Cristina Cacciari. 2010. Predictive Mechanisms in Idiom Comprehension. *Journal of Cognitive Neuroscience* 22 (8). 1682–1700.

Wilson, Margaret. 2001. The case for sensorimotor coding in working memory. *Psychonomic Bulletin & Review*, 8 (1). 44–57.

Wilson, Stephen. 2003. Lexically specific constructions in the acquisition of inflection in English. *Journal of Child Language* 30. 75–115.

Wulfeck, Beverly & Elizabeth Bates. 1995. Grammatical sensitivity in children with language impairment. *Technical Report CND-9512*. San Diego: Center for Research in Language, University of California at San Diego.

Wurzel, Wolfgang U. 1970. *Studien zur deutschen Lautstruktur*. Berlin: Akademie-Verlag.

Xanthos, Aris, Sabine Laaha, Steven Gillis, Ursula Stephany, Ayhan Aksu-Koç, Anastasia Christofidou, Natalia Gagarina, Gordana Hrzica, F. Nihan Ketrez, F., Marianne Kilani-Schoch, Katharina Korecky-Kröll, Melita Kovac̆evic´, Klaus Laalo, Marijan Palmovic´, Barbara Pfeiler, Maria D. Voeikova & Wolfgang U. Dressler. 2011. On the role of morphological richness in the early development of noun and verb inflection. *First Language* 31(4), 461–479.

Young, Robert & William Morgan. 1987. *The Navajo Language*. University of New Mexico, Albuquerque.

Zipf, George K. 1935. *The psychobiology of language*. Houghton-Mifflin.

Ingo Plag and Laura Winther Balling
Derivational morphology: An integrative perspective on some fundamental questions

Abstract: This chapter tries to answer some central questions in the study of derivational morphology: What are the units of analysis? What are the mechanisms that underlie the creation, as well as the syntagmatic and paradigmatic relationships, of derived words? For each of these questions we discuss a wide variety of approaches in different subdisciplines of linguistics (phonetic, theoretical-linguistic, psycholinguistic, neurolinguistic and computational-linguistic), and see what evidence the diverse approaches have brought forward to support their ideas.

Keywords: Derivational morphology, morpheme, Discriminative learning, Computational modeling, Evidence in morphology, Psycholinguistics, Priming

1 Introduction: What is derivational morphology?

Derivational morphology (or 'derivation' for short) belongs to the realm of word-formation and is usually defined negatively as the kind of word-formation that is not compounding. Compounding is widely understood as the formation of words by concatenating two or more lexemes or bases. Thus, derivation is concerned with the ways in which morphologically complex lexemes are related to, or derived from, other lexemes by affixational or non-affixational means, but not by combination with other lexemes.

This definition of derivation leaves us with a problem of demarcation between compounding and derivation, which hinges on the question of what we understand by 'lexeme' or 'base' as against 'affix'. Additionally, since there is the basic distinction between word-formation and inflection, there is the problem of demarcation of derivation (as part of word-formation) vis-à-vis inflection. Both demarcation problems have been amply discussed in the literature (more recently, for example, by Lieber and Stekauer 2009, ten Hacken 2014),

---

Ingo Plag, Institut für Anglistik und Amerikanistik, English Language and Linguistics, Heinrich-Heine-Universität Düsseldorf, Düsseldorf, Germany
Laura Winther Balling, Widex A/S, Nymøllevej, Lynge, Denmark

Open Access. © 2020 Ingo Plag and Laura Winther Balling, published by De Gruyter. This work is licensed under a Creative Commons Attribution-NonCommercial-NoDerivatives 4.0 International License.
https://doi.org/10.1515/9783110440577-008

and we will briefly summarize from that literature only what is relevant for the present chapter. We start with inflection vs. derivation.

Traditionally, inflection is considered to be concerned with the encoding of syntactic information, while derivation encodes lexical information. But what do we mean by 'syntactic' and 'lexical'? The definition of these terms is, obviously, theory-dependent but there seems to be a growing consensus that the two notions refer to endpoints on a scale rather than to a clear-cut categorical opposition (see, for example, Dressler et al. 2014). The idea of a cline is, for example, found in the distinctions between contextual inflection, inherent inflection and derivation (Booij 1993, and Chapter 7, Marzi et al. 2020, this volume). Contextual inflection such as agreement morphology is uncontroversially syntactic in nature, while inherent inflection such as plural or tense marking is more ambiguous and may encode categories that in some languages can be taken to be derivational.

The literature on the topic usually puts forward a number of criteria to distinguish between inflection and derivation, such as position (inflection is more peripheral), productivity (inflection is more productive), semantics (inflection encodes grammatical meaning) or transparency (inflection is more transparent). These criteria lead to satisfactory classifications in many cases but borderline cases remain, and this has led some people to reject the distinction altogether. Certain theories (e.g. Beard 1995) dispose of the distinction because it is deemed unnecessary in their framework. We will leave these issues open since to a large extent the debate is irrelevant for the present treatment. Nothing we say below hinges on whether we assume that derivation and inflection need to be separated or not. We simply look at phenomena that are standardly classified as derivational in nature. The reader may feel free to assign these phenomena to the morphological compartment they think appropriate.

With regard to the delimitation of derivation and compounding several problems can be discerned. One frequently discussed problem is how to determine whether a given form should be classified as a base or an affix. If a base, the complex word would be a compound, if an affix, the complex word would be a derived word. Borderline cases are well-known and again there seems to be a cline rather than a dichotomy. If we include non-affixational word-formation processes such as reduplication or blending, we may suspect that these might be processes that involve the concatenation of bases and could thus be regarded as compounding processes. And indeed, blending in English has been explicitly argued to be a kind of compounding (accompanied by the loss of phonological material, Bauer et al. 2013, Arndt-Lappe and Plag 2013). Reduplication, on the other hand and by its very nature, never involves different bases, which is probably the reason why it is generally regarded as a kind of derivation (but see Štekauer et al. 2012, who treat full reduplication as compounding).

Obviously, derivational morphology is a vast field. The list of formal processes or relationships occurring in derivation is long and poses many challenges, both empirical and theoretical, for the analyst: prefixation, suffixation, infixation, circumfixation, transfixation, conversion, reduplication, truncation, back-formation, templatic derivation, etc. In the present chapter we therefore need to be very selective on our coverage, and will focus on very few, but rather fundamental, questions in the study of derivation, approaching these from an interdisciplinary perspective that combines insights from phonetics, theoretical linguistics, psycholinguistics, neurolinguistics and computational linguistics.

In particular we will deal with two long-standing, central issues.[1] The first is what units of analysis we need to assume (Section 2), the second is what kinds of mechanisms manipulate these units (Section 3). An integrative approach allows us to take a fresh look at these issues in order to reassess the debates and open up new research perspectives.

2 What are the units?

There has been a fierce debate in theoretical linguistics about the nature of morphological knowledge and its organization in syntax or lexicon. Numerous theories have been proposed and depending on which theory one looks at, a different unit may be taken as central for an understanding of word structure, while other units are claimed to be non-existing or epiphenomenal. Prominent approaches in this debate have been grouped under the names of 'word-and-paradigm', 'item-and-arrangement' or 'item-and-process'. For example, while word-and-paradigm morphologists believe in the central importance of the word and reject morphemes as independent units, item-and-arrangement theorists may hold the opposite to be true. We will not review all existing approaches here but try to scrutinize commonly proposed units for their usefulness and for the cross-disciplinary evidence that can be put forward for their existence.

---

1 With regard to other issues, the reader is referred to other chapters of this volume, e.g. Chapter 6 on morpho-phonology (Arndt-Lappe and Ernestus 2020, this volume), Chapter 10 on morpho-pragmatics (Merlini Barbaresi and Dressler 2020, this volume), or Chapter 14 on acquisition (Ravid, Keuleers, and Dressler 2020, this volume).

2.1 The word

The central unit in word-formation is the word. However, although this notion is used without hesitation by most researchers, attempts at defining it have shown that it is a rather problematic notion, even if restricted to its morphological aspects. Ultimately, a language-independent definition seems impossible (see the discussion in Haspelmath 2011), and even language-dependent criteria at various levels of description (phonological, morphological, semantic, syntactic etc.) often run into problems by being either hard to apply or yielding contradictory results. It should be noted, however, that computational models of unsupervised word segmentation can reach surprisingly high levels of accuracy (e.g. Synnaeve et al. 2014), which shows that the concept may not be as elusive as some might think.

In spite of these issues, the daily practice in linguistic theory of all flavors and in computational linguistics is to use the word as a basic unit of analysis, which, from a practical point of view, makes a lot of sense, given the many useful insights linguists have arrived at by employing this notion.

But is there any evidence for its reality apart from distributional or theoretical arguments? Research in psycholinguistics and neurolinguistics has basically also followed this traditional strategy, using words as experimental stimuli to test all kinds of theories and hypotheses. Thus, most studies using key methods such as lexical decision, priming, picture naming or self-paced reading are based on the word as a unit of analysis, and by extension, of representation and processing. A partial exception to this otherwise dominant tendency is the study of multi-word units, including both idioms and those units known as 'lexical bundles', i.e. sequences of words that frequently occur together but do not have an idiomatic meaning. When such sequences show frequency effects (e.g. Tremblay et al. 2011), it may indicate that levels higher than the word are represented and processed as lexical (rather than syntactic) units.

However, though such studies show evidence of higher-level units, they do not fundamentally question the psychological reality of the word, and in fact, to our knowledge, there is no study explicitly addressing the question whether the word exists in the minds of the speakers or not. Instead, word-based experiments, although not testing explicitly the existence of words, have provided ample indirect evidence for the psychological or neurological reality of the word as a unit of representation and processing – and one that participants in such experiments accept intuitively when for instance asked to decide whether a string is a word or not. It has to be noted, however, that for languages for which the notion of word seems especially problematic, for example polysynthetic languages, behavioral or neurological evidence is very scarce. Additionally, it seems that the centrality of the notion of word may be overestimated due to the effect of literacy, but experiments and linguistic theories are so overwhelmingly based on behavior of literate language users that it is difficult to say anything meaningful about the status of the word in a non-literate language.

The fact that the word is so widely accepted as a linguistic unit may be interpreted as good news for approaches in which the word is the central, or indeed the only, unit of analysis, as, for example, in what Blevins (2006) calls 'abstractive' word-based approaches. In such approaches, word forms are the basic units of the system, and recurrent parts are abstractions over these full forms. Crucially, recurrent minimal parts are not listed as independent units. This makes different empirical predictions than a model that assumes that minimal parts are the building blocks for the creation of words (see Blevins 2006: 537ff for more detailed discussion of this point).

In an abstractive word-based system, derivational morphology is thus conceived of as the relation between complex words, and not, for example, between affixes and their bases. Early proponents of modern word-based derivational morphology are Aronoff (1976) and Booij (1977), and Construction Morphology (e.g. Booij 2010, see Section 3.3) is a modern descendent of this approach.

2.2 The morpheme as a minimal sign

Traditionally, the morpheme constitutes a minimal sign, combining a form and a meaning. Roots and affixes are classical instances of morphemes, but so-called 'prosodic templates' as found in Semitic languages have also been subsumed under that notion. In these languages root morphemes are comprised of non-contiguous segments with interleaving elements. Depending on which vowels surface in the interleaving slots, different meanings emerge, for the Arabic root *k-t-b* for instance the words *kitaab* 'book' versus *kataba* 'he wrote' versus *kaatib* 'writer' (Ryding 2005: 46).

The most pervasive problem of the notion of morpheme is the relation of form and meaning itself. There are a number of problems that arise if one tries to identify minimal signs inside words. First, there is the problem of what Hockett named 'total accountability' (Hockett 1947). Thus, every word should exhaustively be analyzable into morphemes. This brings up a number of problems. First, there is the problem of zero morphs, that is meaning without phonological realization, such as the plurals of nouns like *sheep* in English, or *Segel* 'sail' in German, in which plural is not overtly marked. In the realm of derivation, conversion would be a case in point, where for example a verb such as *cook* comes to serve also as a noun, without any morphological marking. Second, there is phonological material (sometimes called 'empty morphs') that has no meaning, for example -*n*- in *plato-n-ic* or -*in*- in *attitud-in-al* (alternatively, such forms are treated as part of stem allomorphs). Third, there is multifunctionality, by which a single morpheme can have different meanings, for example -*er* in English, which can express an agentive meaning (*writer*), but can also derive inhabitant nouns (e.g. *Londoner*).

Sometimes it is not even clear whether there is a clear meaning associated with a particular form. Consider (1):

(1)   a. submit, permit, remit, admit
       b. infer, confer, prefer, refer, transfer

In (1-a) and (1-b), -*mit* and -*fer* are clearly recurrent elements at the level of form, but their meanings are essentially unclear (see, e.g., Plag 2018 for detailed discussion).

Another problem for the mapping of form and meaning with morphemes are most cases of non-concatenative morphology. In conversion, for instance, no (change in) form corresponds to some (change in) meaning. Other cases in point are vowel alternations (as in English *rise* – causative *raise*, Arabic *Maryam* – diminutive *Maryuum*), or phonological truncation (as in English *celeb* – *celebrity*). With such derivatives it is very hard to say what form is being mapped on the given meaning.

Another, related, problem is that the notion of morpheme rests on the assumption that there are clear boundaries that separate from each other the different morphemes that a word is made up of. Even adherents of the morpheme concede that these boundaries may vary in strength, as in *Sound Pattern of English* (Chomsky and Halle 1968) or *Lexical Phonology and Morphology* (Kiparsky 1982), which posit two or more kinds of boundary. More recent research, especially on affix ordering (Hay and Plag 2004; Plag and Baayen 2009), has demonstrated, however, that morphological segmentability is in fact gradient, and that there are no clear cut-off points for positing only two or three degrees of boundary strength.

The idea of discrete and categorical boundaries is also challenged by work on semantic transparency. While syntax and inflection have a strong tendency to exhibit full semantic compositionality in the sense of Frege (1892), derivational morphology often shows semantic opacity, i.e. forms where the semantics of the derived word is not the sum of its parts (see, among many treatments, Ronneberger-Sibold 2003 for illustration and discussion). There is a consensus that semantic opacity is a gradient phenomenon (e.g. Gonnerman and Anderson 2001, Pastizzo and Feldman 2001), and both the existence and the gradience of semantic opacity is a challenge to the notion of morpheme.

According to Hay (2001, 2003) morphological segmentability is also influenced by the frequential properties of base and derivative, which in turn often go together with gradient phonological and semantic opacity. Consider *government* vs. *discernment*. The derived word *government* is far more frequent than its base govern (the opposite is true for the pair *discern–discernment*). Notably, *government* is also somewhat opaque in its meaning ('body that governs', rather than 'action of governing') and phonologically considerably reduced. All three properties contribute to its being less easily segmentable than, say, *discernment* (see Plag 2018 for an introduction to the notion of variable morphological segmentability). Another example is the English nominalizing suffix *-th*, which is much less easily separable from its base (e.g. *depth*) than *-ness* (e.g. *soundness*), and even the same affix can be more or less separable in different words (e.g. *soundness* vs. *business*). The evidence for the gradience of boundaries is hard to reconcile with the idea of the morpheme as a discrete unit.

What is more, phonetic studies have shown that adding an affix to a base also affects the acoustic properties of the base, such that a base occurring on its own systematically differs acoustically from its realization as part of a derived word, for example in duration and pitch. For example, the base *help* without a suffix is generally shorter when it occurs in *helper* than if it occurs as a free morpheme (Lehiste 1972, Kemps et al. 2005, Frazier 2006, Blazej and Cohen-Goldberg 2015).

Importantly, two of these studies (i.e. Blazej and Cohen-Goldberg 2015; Kemps et al. 2005) have also shown that the sub-phonemic acoustic information is in fact used by listeners in lexical processing. In Blazej and Cohen-Goldberg's (2015) perception experiment, for example, listeners were able to distinguish between (segmentally identical) free and bound forms (e.g. *clue* as in *clue*, versus *clue* as in *clueless*) without hearing the suffix. Complex words thus do not behave as mere concatenations of distinct units, but significantly blur the alleged separate identity of the morphemes.

While such results may be seen as further evidence that the morpheme as a separable unit is untenable, there is also phonetic evidence that seems to speak in favor of the morpheme. Thus, Plag et al. (2015) have shown, albeit for inflection, that the different suffixal S morphemes in English (and indeed non-morphemic S) have systematically distinct durations. While such findings seem inexplicable for traditional models of the morpheme (which only allow for phonemic formal representations), the differences in duration could nevertheless be taken as indicating different morphs belonging to different morphemes. However, Plag et al. (2015) did not look at the acoustic properties of the stems to which the different S morphemes attached, so that it is still unclear whether the differences between the distinct Ss are accompanied by differences in the stems. If so, this would tie in with the results by Kemps et al. (2005) and Blazej and Cohen-Goldberg (2015).

The insights from perception described above align nicely with other results from psycholinguistics that have been produced in the context of the debate about the nature of lexical storage and retrieval. Large parts of the literature on morphological processing are concerned with the question of whether complex words are segmented into their constituent morphemes or are instead treated holistically, and which mechanism might be responsible for the assumed differences in processing. This volume devotes a whole chapter to this debate (see Chapter 12, Fábregas and Penke 2020, this volume) and we only briefly summarize it here, restricting ourselves mostly to derivational morphology.

We start, however, with inflection, since the debate about morphemes vs. whole words as units for lexical processing and representation has focused mostly on inflection, with three theoretical positions. Firstly, all inflectional forms may be stored as morphemes and then combined based on rules during production or comprehension. Secondly, all morphologically complex words may be processed associatively, with no rule-based combination of morphemes. Thirdly, rule-based processing may apply to regular words and associative processing to irregular ones. In fact, the first position, usually associated with Generative Phonology (Chomsky and Halle 1968), is not psycholinguistically tenable. Instead, the so-called past-tense debate occurs between the second and the third position.

The Dual-Mechanism or Declarative-Procedural model (Ullman 2001, 2004, Pinker and Ullman 2002) posits two fundamentally distinct cognitive processing systems, one based on rules, which applies to regular inflected words as well as syntax and other supposedly symbolic domains, while the other, based on associative mechanisms, applies to irregular complex words. In opposition to this, various associative models, which are often but not necessarily connectionist, hold that all words, whether simple or complex, regular or irregular, are processed in fundamentally the same way (e.g. Seidenberg and McClelland 1989, Joanisse and Seidenberg 1999). In such models, morphological effects arise not as the result of morphemic representations, but due to the relationships in form and meaning that morphological structure codes.

For derivational morphology, the picture is more complex, because forms that are entirely regular in form and meaning are rarer for derivation than for inflection; in fact, full formal and semantic regularity tends to be seen as a characteristic of inflection as a morphological operation, while derivation is characterized by many-to-many mappings, more gradience and semantic and phonological irregularity. However, some of the same diagnostics of rule vs. analogy are used both in the past-tense debate, which focuses on inflection, and in the broader word recognition literature, which includes derived words as well as other morphologically complex words.

The most important diagnostic, since (at least) Taft (1979), is probably frequency effects. This is based on the rationale that units for which we observe frequency effects are also units of representation in the mental lexicon. Thus, so runs the logic, if for morphologically complex words, we see that faster recognition of words with higher base frequency, then the base must be the unit on which the processing of such words is based. If for instance the high base-frequency *own-er* is processed faster than the lower base-frequency *send-er*, this would traditionally be evidence of morpheme-based recognition of these words. If, instead, effects of the frequency of whole complex words are observed, the unit of processing for such words is traditionally taken to be the whole word rather than the morphemes.

Countless studies have investigated the effect of base vs. whole-word frequency, usually in factorial designs where the frequencies are manipulated categorically, comparing words with high and low values on base or whole-word frequency. Whole-word frequency effects are the largest and most pervasively found, across a range of languages (e.g. Taft 1979 for English, Baayen et al. 1997 for Dutch, Lehtonen et al. 2006 for Swedish, Balling and Baayen 2012 for Danish, Meunier and Segui 1999 for French, Moscoso del Prado Martín et al. 2004 for Finnish and Moscoso del Prado Martín et al. 2005 for Hebrew), but base frequency effects are also found in a number of studies (Baayen et al. 1997; New et al. 2004; Taft 1979; Vannest et al. 2002). The relevance of the two types of different frequency effects is hypothesized to vary depending on a range of factors, most prominently formal and semantic regularity, with stronger base frequency effects for regular and transparent words and stronger whole-word frequency effects for more irregular and opaque words.

More recently, experiments employing regression designs, where it is possible to investigate graded effects of different frequency measures, have shown more complex patterns of co-existing and sometimes interacting whole-word and morpheme frequency effects (e.g. Baayen et al. 2007; Balling and Baayen 2008; Kuperman et al. 2008; Plag 2009). In addition to these complexities, the case has been made by Baayen et al. (2007) that base frequency may in fact not be a good indicator of morphemic processing, i.e. processing in which the morpheme is the basic unit of representation. The argument is based on the fact that the frequency of a base as an independent word is not really informative about the relevance of that base in the context of a specific complex word. This interpretation is supported by the relative weakness of base frequency effects, even in the presence of other morphemic effects. Conversely, whole-word frequency may in turn not solely indicate word-based processing of complex words; instead, it may also be understood as the combinatorial probability of the constituent morphemes co-occurring and thus a measure of morphemic processing. Such an understanding is supported by the strength and pervasiveness of whole-word frequency effects, by their early occurrence as measured by eye-tracking of compound reading (Kuperman et al. 2008), and by the interactions between different frequencies referenced above.

The literature on morphological processing is predominantly focused on (visual) word recognition, but evidence from word production does exist and uses similar experimental manipulations. Thus, manipulations of morpheme vs. whole-word frequency are also used in the production literature as a diagnostic of morphemic vs. whole-word representations for complex words. The evidence from this research is mixed, with some studies showing whole-word frequency effects for complex words (e.g. Chen and Chen 2006; Janssen et al. 2008) and others showing morpheme frequency effects for similar words (e.g. Bien et al. 2005; Roelofs 1996).

Despite the similarity in the use of frequency manipulations, the literature on word production deviates in (at least) two ways from that on word recognition: firstly, the stimuli are often compound words rather than derived, at least partly for the practical reason that compound words are easier to depict and thus elicit from participants. Secondly, a central concern for the studies mentioned above (as well as those cited in Section 2.3 below) is the level of the production process at which morphological information becomes relevant; an aspect that we have to ignore here to avoid straying too far from the fundamental questions of derivational morphology. However, an important similarity remains across processing directions, namely that there is evidence of both morphemic and whole-word frequency effects, and that the interpretation of these frequency effects, as we saw above, may not be as clear-cut as has been previously assumed.

The processing literature thus shows a complex picture. However, it seems clear that processing cannot to any pervasive extent be based on combinatorial processing of morphemic representations. There is a growing consensus that all sorts of information is used during processing, cf. for instance Libben's (2006) notion of maximization of opportunity. The types of information used relate both to whole complex words and to the morphological structures of such words, but importantly, this does not necessarily entail morphemic representations.

In conclusion, theories that restrict their inventory of units to morphemes must either stretch this notion to such an extent that it becomes unrecognizable, or they simply ignore important evidence that morphemes are not the neat discrete units that these theories are working with.

2.3 The morpheme as a phonological spell-out: The separation of form and meaning

Both word-based and morpheme-based approaches to morphology can be characterized as sign-based for they assume units of form and meaning. There are, however, also approaches that separate form and meaning in morphology. Proponents of such an approach are Beard (1995), Don (1993), Gussmann (1987a), Szymanek (1985). Distributed Morphology (Halle and Marantz 1993) also adopts a separationist view. We will restrict the following discussion of separationism to aspects that are of special relevance to derivational morphology.

Separationism proposes a radical solution to address the problem of many-to-many relations between form and meaning in morphology: What is traditionally called a morpheme is taken to be merely a phonological spell-out (a 'vocabulary item' in Distributed Morphology lingo) of a grammatical or semantic category. This dissociation of meaning and phonological spell-out supposedly "accounts for asymmetries of affixal sound and meaning such as polysemy, synonymy, zero and empty morphology, which plague other approaches" (Beard 1990: 103).

Unfortunately, there are hardly any studies available on derivational morphology that systematically compare the merits and problems of sign-based vs. separationist accounts of the same derivational phenomenon. Plag (1999), however, provides a comprehensive formal and semantic analysis of derivation into verbs in English and discusses in detail the implications for the two kinds of morphological theory. Existing separationist accounts of English verbal derivation (Gussmann 1987b, Beard 1995) assume that the different productive processes (-*ize*, -*ify*, -*ate* and conversion) are all spell-out operations on only two underlying semantic operations. The semantic analysis in Plag (1999) shows, however, that each of the four verb-deriving processes comes with its own intricate polysemy (see also Bauer et al. 2013; Lieber 1998, 2004) and that the separationists' crucial assumption of absolute synonymy (Beard 1995: 78) of all pertinent forms is wrong.

Synonymy and polysemy thus seem to constitute an interesting difference between inflection and derivation. While in inflection, the assumption of absolute synonymy of different affixes ('spell-outs') is uncontroversial at least for contextual inflection (such as structural case marking or agreement), absolute synonymy of different derivational affixes seems very unusual. The latter point is supported by large-scale empirical evidence across many derivational processes as gleaned by Bauer et al. (2013) in their recent survey of English morphology. Furthermore, polysemy is absent from, at least, contextual inflection (or else goes under the name of syncretism and is viewed as homonymy rather than polysemy).

Given that the major claim of separationist morphology is the lack of morphological signs it is unclear what kind of independent neurological or behavioral evidence could prove this assumption (see Chapter 4, Marangolo and Papagno 2020, this volume, and Chapter 12, Fábregas & Penke 2020, this volume, for discussion). After all, it is hard to prove the non-existence of something. However, two related lines of behavioral research address the separationist rejection of morphemic units.

Firstly, there is a whole literature comparing formal (mainly orthographic), semantic and morphological priming effects and their time courses, i.e. the facilitation of the reading of a target word depending on whether it has been preceded by a word that is orthographically (*twin-twinkle*), semantically (*idea-notion*) or morphologically (*government-govern*) related compared to an unrelated prime word (*idea-tin*). If morphological priming effects can be shown to be the sum of semantic and formal overlap, it would provide evidence against an independent role for morphology in word recognition.

However, such priming studies show that morphological priming effects tend to be stronger and more consistent across different types of priming (subliminal, immediate and delayed) than both semantic and formal priming effects (e.g. Feldman 2000; Marslen-Wilson et al. 1994; Rastle et al. 2000). In fact, purely formal priming effects are surprisingly elusive and, if found, tend to be inhibitory (e.g. Gonnerman et al. 2007; Longtin et al. 2003; Marslen-Wilson and Zhou 1999). This does not entirely rule out that morphological effects are epiphenomenal, arising from interacting effects of semantic and formal relatedness, but it clearly does not support that idea.

The second line of research concerns the question of whether morphological effects are graded depending on semantic and formal overlap between a complex word and its morphological relatives, specifically its base. Although the majority of studies in this area are again priming studies, there are exceptions to this, which is an advantage given the way especially subliminal priming relies on misleading the processing system, by briefly presenting a word that may or may not be related to that target word that participants are asked to focus on.

Starting with the priming literature, the seminal study of Marslen-Wilson et al. (1994) showed morphological priming effects that were the same irrespective of whether the formal relation between the word pairs was transparent, e.g. *punishment-punish*, or more opaque, e.g. *vanity-vain, elusive-elude*. By contrast, morphological priming does seem to vary depending on the degree of semantic transparency (Longtin et al. 2003; Marslen-Wilson et al. 1994; Rastle et al. 2000), though there is some debate as to whether this also holds for very early priming effects (Feldman et al. 2015; Rastle and Davis 2008).

Also word recognition studies that do not employ priming show effects of semantic transparency on recognition, with word recognition becoming faster the more transparent the combination of base and affix (Baayen et al. 2007; Balling and Baayen 2008; Wurm 1997). Such graded morphological effects are potentially problematic for models relying on morphemes as units of representation, though some level of morphemic representation may still be postulated if it is posited that whole-word and morpheme representations interact during processing.

Again, the word production literature uses similar manipulations, but, as we saw above, with a skew towards compound words as stimuli. Nonetheless, a brief review of the findings is relevant due to the similarity of manipulations. The picture-word interference paradigm resembles the priming paradigms used to study word recognition. In picture-word interference, a written or spoken context word – essentially a prime – is presented before a picture that the participants are requested to name. Effects of the relation between the context word and the target picture are taken as evidence of relations or overlap between representations in the mental lexicon. The results of these studies show that, also in this domain, morphological effects seem to be qualitatively different from semantic and formal effects: while a semantic relation between context word and target results in interference, at least for categorically related words (Costa et al. 2005; Schriefers et al. 1990), morphological relatedness produces shorter naming latencies for the target, i.e. facilitation (Dohmes et al. 2004; Zwitserlood et al. 2000, 2002). This holds whether or not the morphologically complex context word is semantically transparent or not, and with both immediate and delayed presentation of the target relative to the prime (Dohmes et al. 2004). Facilitation is even observed with morphologically complex pseudo-word primes (Bölte et al. 2013). Formal priming effects are again more elusive than both semantic and morphological effects.

2.4 Phonaesthemes

One particularly problematic potential unit of morphological analysis is the so-called 'phonaestheme'. The debate has centered around the question whether phonaesthemes should be regarded as kinds of morphemes. Phonaesthemes are defined as subparts of roots that show a recurrent sound-meaning pairing, and thus resemble morphemes, but are different from morphemes in at least two important respects. First, their semantics is rather vague and not very consistent (e.g. 'light emitted from a source', as in, for example, *glimmer, glow, gleam, glare* as opposed to *glove, glue, glum*). Second, once separated out, the morphological status of the residue is unclear (what is, for example, *-immer* or *-ow* in *glimmer* and *glow*, morphologically speaking?). Here, the problem of total accountability raises its ugly head again.

Theoretical linguists have struggled with the problems posed by phonaesthemes but have not reached a consensus. In a most recent attempt, Kwon and Round (2015) develop a catalogue of seven criteria and systematically compare roots and affixes with phonaesthemes using these criteria. Only one criterion, the presence of a non-recurrent residue is the sole clear difference between phonaesthemes and other derivational entities that are considered morphemic in nature. In view of this result, theories can choose whether they would extend the notion of morpheme to such entities.

However, there is still the question of whether phonaesthemes have any relevance for the speakers of a language. Bergen (2004) conducted a priming experiment which showed that phonaesthemically related primes facilitate processing, with semantic priming and orthographic priming each yielding quantifiably different priming effects from phonaesthemic priming. This is very similar to the priming effects found with morphemes, discussed above, and ties in with earlier psycholinguistic work on phonaesthetic neologisms (e.g. Abelin 1999; Hutchins 1998; Magnus 2000). In a broader perspective this means that language users unconsciously and generally pick up all sorts of recurrent form-meaning pairings and make use of these pairings even when they are not clearly compositional or categorical (see also Pastizzo and Feldman 2009).

2.5 None of the above

All of the morphological building blocks discussed so far try to approach the crucial problem of form-meaning mappings by segmentation. Language is either segmented into units of finer or coarser grain size that carry meaning (phonaesthemes, morphemes, words), or it is segmented into separate units of phonology, and units of semantics that are then mapped onto each other via complex mapping rules.

A radically different approach is taken in network models in which, crucially, morphological effects are emergent from association processes between certain kinds of formal representation and certain kinds of conceptual units. There are two main types of models: distributed connectionist models (e.g. Gonnerman et al. 2007; Harm and Seidenberg 2004; McClelland and Elman 1986; Norris 1994) on the one hand, and Naive Discriminative Learning (NDL) models on the other hand (e.g. Baayen et al. 2011, 2015, see also Chapter 2, Pirrelli et al. 2020 this volume). These two main types differ more in the processing mechanisms than in the representational units they use. These units ultimately do not seem to have a particular theoretical status apart from the idea that the building blocks are decidedly non-morphemic.

Both types of architecture operate with input and output layers, in NDL known as cues and outcomes, with weighted connections between them determining the degree of activation of a given outcome based on a given input pattern. In connectionist models of language processing, the representational units may be individual letters or phonemes defined by values on a number of binary features (e.g. Joanisse and Seidenberg 1999). The output layer is typically a semantic representation of some sort, which may be distributed such that a word's meaning is represented by its pattern of activation of different semantic features (e.g. Plaut and Gonnerman 2000), or localist with one unit per word meaning (e.g. Joanisse and Seidenberg 1999).

In NDL, the input units are n-grams of varying sizes, pairs (bigrams) or triplets (tri-grams) of letters or phonemes. Crucially, the n-grams have no independent theoretical status. For illustration, consider the phrase *in its context*, which, under a trigram approach, would consist of the trigrams /ɪnɪ/, /nɪt/, /ɪts/, /tsk/ and so on. These trigrams stand for triphones, which in turn simply represent contrasts in the speech signal that are not directly linked to units of meaning (for example, /ɪnɪ/ does not 'carry' any meaning). Rather, the trigrams are used by the learning system as continuously incoming cues for establishing relationships between sound and other experiences. The relationships are not encoded in the form of words, morphemes or anything of that sort, but as weights of the association between cues and outcomes. The choice of triphones as against diphones (or single sounds) as input units is ultimately driven by practical considerations, and it is acknowledged that these n-grams are ultimately not fine-grained enough to capture all subtleties of the phonetic input (see Baayen et al. 2015: 2 for more discussion).

In terms of the outcome units, most recent work in NDL has come up with so-called 'lexomes'. These are defined as an arguably somewhat intangible

> theoretical construct at the interface of language and a world that is in constant flux with the flow of experience. Lexomes are the lexical dimensions in the system of knowledge that an individual acquires and constantly modifies as the outcome of discriminatively learning from experience within a culture. Because lexomic contrasts serve as communicative counterparts to the specific experiences individuals and cultures discriminate for practical and communicative purposes, they can be evoked in context either by language use or real world experience. Accordingly, the more that a lexome is activated in a given context, the greater the degree of confidence that the cues that culturally discriminate it from other outcomes are present in the external world. (Baayen et al. 2015: 5)

Since the theoretical import of these associative models is mainly in their processing mechanism, we discuss them in more detail in Section 3.5, focusing on NDL.

2.6 Synthesis: What does the evidence say?

There is a long tradition in theoretical linguistics to view morphology either as the combination of minimal signs (see Section 2.2.), as the formal-semantic relationship between words (Section 2.1), or as the combination of phonological elements with semantic-functional elements (as described in Section 2.3). While the theoretical debates seem to have reached a dead end with beliefs rather than evidence dominating the individual researcher's concept of morphological units, the evidence from psycholinguistics points towards a solution.

Both strictly morphemic and separationist models are seriously challenged by the empirical evidence. It seems that a gradient view of morphology in which speakers and listeners make use of all sorts of sound-meaning pairings can better account for the intricate experimental results. These results suggest a continuum of variable association strengths between sound patterns and meaning. At one end of the continuum we find the constellation of strong and clear associations that is traditionally referred to as 'morpheme', while towards the other end of the continuum association between meaning and form becomes less and less strong and consistent. There are weaker and stronger multifaceted associations along both the paradigmatic and the syntagmatic dimensions, and these associations structure the lexicon and guide the processing of words.

Such a gradient view is further supported when one looks at the structural and cognitive mechanisms that have been proposed in order to understand derivational morphology. This will be the topic of the next section.

3 What are the mechanisms?

3.1 Lexical or syntactic?

In theoretical discussions of derivational morphology the question looms large whether morphology should be seen as an independent module of grammar, as part of the lexicon, or as simply non-existing as an independent module because it is part of syntax. Much of this debate focuses on the mechanisms, rather than on the units, that are taken to be instantiated in morphology. For example, proponents of a syntactic view of morphology assume that word-internally the same mechanisms are at work as above the level of the word, i.e. in phrases, clauses and sentences, only with units that happen to be smaller than the word. Although a lot of ink has been spent to decide the issue, no consensus has been reached, and it is unclear what kind of evidence or killing theoretical argument might be able to solve the issue. The problem of the lexicon-syntax divide is intertwined with the problem of what kinds of particular mechanisms play a role in derivation. In the following we will review the different mechanisms proposed by various theories, sometimes also making reference to the more general question of whether morphology exists or not.

3.2 Rules

One of the most pervasive mechanisms, and one that has been used in different frameworks, is that of the 'rule'. Most approaches conceive of rules as input-output devices that either add structure to given representations or manipulate symbolic representations. Rules have been designed to generate new words in a deterministic fashion, or to formalize generalizations over existing forms. The former have usually been depicted as unidirectional rules, the latter as bidirectional rules (also known as 'redundancy rules', e.g. Jackendoff 1975).

Both morpheme-based and word-based morphology have used rules to account for derivation. Example (2-a) gives a syntactic phrase structure rule and (2-b) illustrates a similar kind of rule for the structure of words.

(2)   a. Phrase structure rules
         NP   →   (article) (adjective) noun
         PP   →   preposition NP
   b. Syntactic rules below the word level
         word → root (suffix)
         word → root (suffix)

Figure 1 illustrates a word-based rule in the spirit of, for example, Aronoff (1976).

In rule-based frameworks, word-formation rules are accompanied by morpho-phonological adjustment rules which handle allomorphy or morpho-phonological alternations such as stress shift, assimilation or deletion. Word forms that do not conform to the rules are taken to be idiosyncratic exceptions (or unsystematic analogical formations) that need to be listed in the lexicon, while regular forms are not listed.

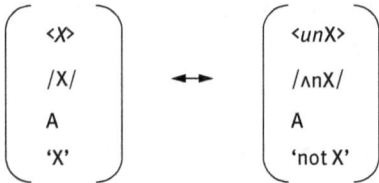

Figure 1: A word-based word-formation rule (from Plag 2018: 182, 'A' stands for 'Adjective').

There are at least three major problems with such deterministic rules. First, the dichotomy between rule and list is a fallacy. Numerous studies have shown that even derived words of the lowest frequency leave traces in memory and show frequency effects that would be impossible if these words were not part of the language user's mental lexicon (e.g. de Vaan et al. 2007; Baayen et al. 2007). Thus, any model that does not take into account the massive storage capacities of our mental lexicon is unconvincing.

Second, the amount of variation is often so large and internally structured that it cannot be satisfactorily accounted for by referring to the notions of rule and exception. For example, Collie (2008) demonstrates that a considerable proportion of the forms in her sample do not show the stress preservation that should regularly result from the pertinent rule (e.g. English *decónsecrate – dèconsecrátion* instead of predicted *decònsecrátion*). (Bauer et al. 2013; Chapter 9, Libben, Gagné and Dressler 2020, this volume) discuss numerous morpho-phonological alternations that show much more variation than previously assumed.

Similarly, affixes are often assumed to attach to a well-defined set of syntactically or semantically defined base categories, for example to verbal bases in the case of English *-able*. However, in reality one often finds minority patterns that can hardly be dismissed as mere exceptions. For example, we find a considerable number of *-able* forms based on nouns whose meaning is very similar to that of the deverbal forms (Plag 2004). Another such case is English *-ee*, which also attaches primarily to verbs but has a significant minority of denominal formations, too (Barker 1998; Mühleisen 2010; Plag 2004). In such cases the problem cannot be solved by simply adding the minority category to the rule as this would lead to massive overgeneration.

Third, rules are usually defined with a particular input being related to a particular output. It has been shown, however, that many morphological patterns are much better accounted for in an output-oriented fashion instead of an input–output relation (see, for example, Bauer et al. (2013: Chapter 9) on phonological aspects, and Plag (2004) on semantic aspects of output-orientedness).

Psycholinguistic and neurolinguistic evidence for the existence of rules in derivational morphology is scarce. In fact, the focus in the psycholinguistic literature has been almost exclusively on whether or not morphemic units are relevant for processing (as reviewed in Section 2 above), rather than on the mechanisms by which they may be combined for interpretation in language comprehension, an issue which is notoriously difficult for derived words whose interpretation is frequently characterized by some level of opacity. The way the combination problem is usually handled is by postulating whole-word representations in addition to any morphemic representations, and avoiding the need for rules by assuming that the meaning of the combination is part of the whole-word representations. The whole-word representations may be on a later level of processing than the morphemic ones as in the model of Taft (1994), or vice versa as in the Supralexical model of Giraudo and Grainger (2001); alternatively, the two types of units may be on the same level in dual-route competition models (e.g. Frauenfelder and Schreuder 1992).

3.3 Schemas and inheritance

One important alternative to traditional rule-based approaches in derivation is Construction Morphology, as developed by Booij (2010). Although using a different notation, Construction Morphology is very similar to earlier HPSG-inspired approaches, which also used multiple inheritance hierarchies and special types of lexical rules to come up with a system of lexeme formation (see Bonami and Crysmann 2016 for a summary). We will focus on Construction Morphology for practical reasons as this framework uses a less technical formal notation and is more widely known.

In Construction Morphology derivational phenomena are formalized using so-called 'schemas'. A schema expresses a generalization about the form, meaning and syntax of derived words in the lexicon,+ and can serve as the basis for new coinages. The idea that word-formation patterns are abstractions over sets of related words in the lexicon has a long tradition (from Paul 1880 to Bybee 1995, to mention only two prominent thinkers). Example (3) (taken from Booij 2010: 80) illustrates Booij's approach with the Dutch deverbal nominal suffix *-er*. To the left of the double arrow we find a morphological pattern, in this case a word with a base V and the suffix *-er*. To the right of the double arrow we find the semantic interpretation of this pattern, with the subscript indices indicating cross-reference relations with the respective entities to the left of the double arrow. The notation 'SEM' stands for the semantic representation of the subscripted base.

(3) $[V_i\text{ -er}]_j \leftrightarrow [\text{entity involved in SEM}_i]_j$

Schemas can be related to subschemas in hierarchies of schemas via inheritance. For example, the polysemy of the suffix -er can be captured by positing a more general schema, given in (4a), which dominates pertinent subschemas given in (4b) through (4f). The different kinds of syntactic categories that can be inserted for 'X' in (4a) are given in parentheses. The subschemas inherit the properties of the dominant schema and specify a particular semantic pattern among the -er-derivatives. An example with English translation is given below each schema. Schema (4d) is a subschema of (4c), as it inherits all properties from (4c), but makes the notion 'person' more specific ('inhabitant'). Example (5) illustrates the inheritance hierarchy for the schemas in (4).

(4) a. $[X_i\text{ -er}]_j \leftrightarrow [\text{entity with some relation R to SEM}_i]_j$ (X = V, N, QN, Num)
     b. $[V_i\text{ -er}]_j \leftrightarrow [\text{entity involved in SEM}_i]_j$
         klopp-er 'knocker'
     c. $[N_i\text{ -er}]_j \leftrightarrow [\text{ person with some relation R to SEM}_i]_j$
         VVD-er 'member of VVD'
     d. $[N_i\text{ -er}]_j \leftrightarrow [\text{ inhabitant of SEM}_i]_j$
         Amsterdamm-er 'inhabitant of Amsterdam'
     e. $[QN_i\text{ -er}]_j \leftrightarrow [\text{ object with property SEM}_i]_j$
         tienponder 'ten-pounder'
     f. $[Num_i\text{ -er}]_j \leftrightarrow [\text{ entity with some relation R to SEM}_i]_j$
         twintig-er 'person in his twenties'

(5)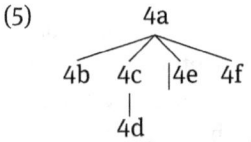

Paradigmatic relationships between formation patterns can be formalized by relating schemas to schemas. For example, the fact that all English nouns in -ist have a related form in -ism is captured in (6).

(6) $< [X\text{-ism}]_{Ni} \leftrightarrow \text{SEM}_i > \approx$
     $< [X\text{-ist}]_{Nj} \leftrightarrow [\text{person with property Y related to SEM}_i]_j >$

In order to coin new words, speakers may use schemas by simply unifying a particular base word ('X') with a schema. As the schemas differ in their degree of abstractness, the coinage of forms can happen at all levels. There is, however, no explicit mechanism that would predict which schemas are productive and which ones are not, and psycholinguistic evidence for the existence of schemas is also absent.

Booij concedes that it is also possible to coin a word in analogy to a single existing word, sometimes referred to as 'local analogy' (Booij 2010: 88–93) or 'surface analogy' (Motsch 1981), but it remains somewhat unclear how such local analogies can be integrated into the schema-based model. In fact, there are analogical models on the market in which local analogies and wide-ranging generalizations emerge from a single analogical algorithm, which seems to make the postulation of constructional schemas unnecessary. We will discuss such models in the next section.

3.4 Analogy

Analogy is a very old concept in philosophy and linguistics, and one that has attracted a plethora of interpretations and definitions (see Arndt-Lappe 2015 for an overview and discussion of linguistic aspects). We will discuss analogy as a general mechanism by which words can be derived on the basis of similarities to existing words in the lexicon. The relevant sets of similar words (called sets of 'neighbors' or 'analogical sets') that form the basis for the analogical process may be very large or may be as small as one word. The crucial point is that the analogies are based on those exemplars in the lexicon that are informative with respect to the given task. What counts as informative is determined by the model, which also means that, in contrast to traditional applications of the notion of analogy, computational algorithms make testable predictions, and their performance can be compared to that of alternative models, for example rule systems. Work using computational analogical algorithms such as TiMBL ('Tilburg Memory-based Learner', Daelemans et al. 2007) or AM ('Analogical Model of Language', Skousen and Stanford 2007), has shown that many properties of morphological systems can be modeled quite successfully in this way.

Krott and colleagues (Krott et al. 2001, 2004a, 2004b), for example, showed that the notorious variability in the use of linking morphemes in Dutch and German compounds can be accounted for by analogy. In a nutshell, a given compound chooses the linking morphemes that other compounds with the same first or second constituent have. Similarly, English noun-noun constructs vary in their stress pattern, with roughly one third of these compounds in running speech being right-stressed and two thirds left-stressed. As demonstrated by Plag (2010) and Arndt-Lappe (2011), the prominence pattern of a given compound can be successfully predicted on the basis of analogy.

In the realm of derivational morphology, such models have only been sparsely used so far. Eddington (2002), for example, investigated Spanish diminutive allomorphy, Chapman and Skousen (2005) dealt with the competition between different negative prefixes in English and Arndt-Lappe (2014) was concerned with the rivalry between the English nominalizing suffixes -*ness* and -*ity*. Notably, all of these papers focus on phenomena of rival affixation in which there is a kind of variation that does not lend itself easily to a rule-based deterministic analysis. And indeed, the analogical models can deal with this variation quite well and achieve very satisfactory accuracy rates.

What is more, however, is that an analogical algorithm can not only model the behavior of isolated idiosyncratic formations and semi-regular behavior. Quite strikingly, the models are also able to come up with decisions that look categorical for certain, well-defined sets of words. This fact can be seen as the main advantage over rule-based deterministic models, which are characterized by the presence of at least two kinds of mechanisms, the rule and the exception.

But how does the algorithm do its job? We will roughly explain the procedure for AM. Let us assume that there is a candidate word for which we want to predict a certain behavior, for example, whether it will take -*ity* or -*ness* as an affix. First, the model must create an analogical set for the given candidate. To include a word in the analogical set a certain degree of similarity with the candidate is necessary. The similarity is computed over formal, syntactic, or semantic features coded for each word in the lexicon. AM decides this for each candidate individually on the basis of the degree of overlap in its features with the words in the lexicon. The model will always include maximally similar words into the analogical set, and words with lower degrees of similarity will be incorporated only if this does not lead to greater uncertainty with respect to the classification task.

On the basis of the analogical set, the model computes a probability of a particular choice based on the distribution of the two suffixes in the analogical set. In calculating these probabilities, AM takes into account the degree of similarity between the words in the analogical set and the candidate, as well as the number of words with a particular set of features. The more similar a word is to the candidate, the more weight it receives. And the more words share a particular set of features, the greater the weight assigned to each of these words. For the distribution of the rival nominalizing suffixes, the model cannot only reach high levels of general accuracy. What is more interesting from a theoretical point of view is that the model can also account for the different degurss of productivity in different subsets of the data. Differences in the degrees of specificity of the domains for -*ity* and -*ness* translate into differences between more local and more general analogies. The analogical sets are generally quite small (for example between 10 and 16 words for candidates ending in -*able*, -*ous* or -*y*, with an overall lexicon of

545 pertinent words). Nevertheless, the default status of *-ness* emerges from the fact that analogies predicting *-ness* are based on a lesser degree of similarity than those predicting *-ity* (Arndt-Lappe 2014: 541).

Given that variability phenomena are a kind of home turf for analogical algorithms it is not surprising that the few studies of derivational morphology that have implemented such models have also been occupied with diachronic research questions. The standard procedure of such studies is to predict the distribution of forms in one time period (e.g. the 19th century) on the basis of a lexicon from the preceding time period (e.g. the 18th century). The results of such exercises are again quite impressive. For example, in Arndt-Lappe (2014) 85 percent of the predictions are correct if we want to predict the behavior of 20th century neologisms on the basis of the 19th century lexicon.

While analogical algorithms perform well with cases of affixal rivalry, it remains to be seen whether analogical modeling can be extended to other problems, such as predicting the semantic interpretation of a new derivative based on the semantics of the affix involved and the semantics of its base, a rather challenging issue to model given the elusiveness of semantic features.

3.5 Association of cues and outcomes: Naive Discriminative Learning

The subsequent discussion of associative models will focus on NDL. This is done not only because NDL is the more recent, and perhaps more provocative, addition to the language processing literature. What makes this approach especially interesting is the fact that it is based on an explicit theory of learning that is well established in cognitive psychology (e.g Rescorla 1988a, Pearce and Bouton 2001). The general cognitive mechanisms assumed in this theory have been shown to be able to model a number of important effects observed in animal learning and human learning, for example the blocking effect (Kamin 1968) and the feature-label ordering effect (Ramscar et al. 2010). The approach has recently been extended to language learning and language usage, and has been implemented by Harald Baayen and colleagues to model many different kinds of morphological and syntactic phenomena (e.g. Arnon and Ramscar 2012; Baayen et al. 2011, 2013, 2015; Baayen and Ramscar 2015; Blevins et al. 2015; Ramscar et al. 2010, 2013).

The central idea of associative learning theory is that learning results from exposure to informative relations among events in the environment. These relations, or associations, are used to build an overall representation of the world. Organisms adjust their representations based on new, informative experiences.

Technically, the events which an organism is exposed to, and between which associations are established are conceived as 'cues' and 'outcomes'.

The crucial question already hinted at in Section 2.5 above is how this association process can be conceptualized and modeled. In NDL the association is achieved by using the so-called Rescorla-Wagner equations (Rescorla and Wagner 1972, Rescorla 1988b). The reasoning underlying these equations goes as follows. Cues may be absent or present, and outcomes may be present or absent, which means that a particular cue may co-occur with a particular outcome, or it may not. The association strength or 'weight' of an outcome increases with every time that the cue and the outcome co-occur and decreases whenever the cue occurs without the outcome. The changes of these weights over time are modeled by the Rescorla-Wagner equations such that the weight of a cue to some outcome at time point t+1 equals its weight at point t plus some change (as specified mathematically in the equations).[2]

At the end of the learning process a stable state is reached in which each outcome is associated with its final association strength. This final association strength is conceived as the activation for this outcome on the basis of the training with all cues and can be computed as the sum of all changes in the weights during learning.

Let us see how this works. We start with a set of words, i.e. a toy lexicon, some of them complex, some of them simplex, and we want to know whether the NDL model arrives at something that looks like a sensible morphological analysis without positing any morphological unit or operation.

Our data set is given in Table 1. It contains eight words, given in the column 'Words'. The column 'Cues' contains for each word a sequence of bigrams, i.e. orthographic digraphs (with hash marks representing word boundaries). Each bigram functions as a cue in the modeling process.[3] The column 'Outcomes' lists the meanings (or 'lexomes') corresponding to the words in the first column. These meanings are represented in a very simplified manner by simply listing the orthographic form of the word in inverted commas. For words with

---

[2] We spare the reader the mathematical details, as they are not important for our discussion. The reader is referred to the original literature (e.g. Rescorla and Wagner 1972), or to Baayen et al. (2011), who introduce and discuss in more detail Rescorla-Wagner equations using linguistic examples.

[3] We use digraphs as bigrams as if we were modeling reading comprehension. For modeling auditory comprehension, bigram cues could be represented by phoneme pairs, for example. For the purpose of our exercise nothing hinges on the choice of digrams instead of unigrams or trigrams.

Table 1: Toy lexicon (Frequencies are taken from the SUBTLEX-US corpus, Brysbaert and New 2009).

Words	Cues	Outcomes	Frequency
baptize	#b, ba, ap, pt, ti, iz, ze, e#	'baptize'	37
chance	#c, ch, ha, an, nc, ce, e#	'chance'	12303
extreme	#e, ex, xt, tr, re, em, me, e#	'extreme'	558
modernize	#m, mo, od, de, er, rn, ni, iz, ze, e#	'modern', 'make'	6
optimal	#o, op, pt, ti, im, ma, al, l#	'optimal'	15
optimize	#o, op, pt, ti, im, mi, iz, ze, e#	'optimal', 'make'	5
sand	#s, sa, an, nd, d#	'sand'	1035
size	#s, si, iz, ze, e#	'size'	2353

more than one clearly discernible meaning component, each meaning is separated from the other by a comma.

As the reader may notice when checking the table, the morphological phenomenon to be investigated here is the expression of causative meaning (paraphrased here as 'make'). Note that we have three words ending in what morphologists would call the suffix -*ize*, with one of the words being rather opaque, *baptize*, which is paraphrased by the OED as '[t]o immerse in water, or pour ... water upon, ... in token of initiation into a religious society, especially into the Christian Church'. The word thus does not straightforwardly combine the meaning of 'make' with the meaning of the base (which would generate something like 'make bapt', whatever 'bapt' might mean). Though somewhat opaque from a syntagmatic perspective, the word *baptize* may nevertheless be argued to be morphologically complex due to its relation to *baptism* and due to the fact that it is a verb, a predictable property if one assumes that the word ends in the suffix -*ize*. The meanings of *modernize* and *optimize*, in contrast, clearly involve two meaning components, as nicely illustrated by the OED paraphrases 'to make modern' and 'to render optimal'.

For each of the 40 different cues, e.g. for each of the bigrams in column 2, the model will compute association strengths with each of the outcomes, i.e. the nine different meanings. Overall, there are 360 connections for which the model arrives at an association weight. A subset of the network of cues and outcomes (with only four bigrams, four meanings and 16 connections) is shown in Figure 2, illustrating all connections but not the respective association weights.

Before turning to the overall results of our modeling exercise let us look at possible association weights between cues and outcomes with the help of Figure 2. As can be easily imagined, the bigram <nd> should be an excellent cue for the

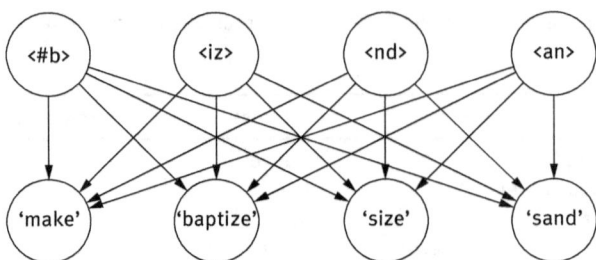

Figure 2: Association from cues to outcomes.

meaning 'sand' because this bigram only co-occurs (with a frequency of 1035) with the meaning 'sand'. In the model we should therefore expect a rather high association weight between this bigram and the meaning 'sand'. We also expect the bigram <an> to be a good cue for the meaning 'sand', but since this cue also co-occurs with one other meaning ('chance'), its association weight with 'sand' should be smaller than that of <nd>. The bigram <#b> should be a very good cue for 'baptize', but should not be a good cue for 'size'. In fact, we would even expect to see a negative association weight here, since its presence at the beginning of a word is likely to be a good cue that the meaning of the word will not be something like 'size'.

Using the ndl package (Arppe et al. 2014) for R (R Core Team 2014) we can compute the association weights after learning has reached a stable state (the R code to reproduce our model is given in the appendix). The result is a matrix which gives the association weight of each cue to each outcome. Four lines of this matrix (corresponding to the network shown in Figure 2) are given for illustration in Table 2.

Table 2: Weight matrix for four bigrams.

	'baptize'	'chance'	'extreme'	'make'	'modern'	'optimal'	'sand'	'size'
#b	0.213	−0.007	−0.004	−0.110	−0.016	−0.089	0.014	−0.062
iz	0.041	−0.032	−0.030	0.106	0.034	0.017	−0.019	0.128
nd	0.014	−0.030	0.006	0.036	0.012	0.006	0.220	−0.069
an	0.007	0.124	−0.009	0.017	0.006	0.003	0.190	−0.076

The weights range from 0.220 to -0.76. We can see that at the end of the learning process <#b> is positively associated with 'baptize' (with a rather high weight of 0.213) and negatively with most other meanings. <iz> is positively associated with the meanings 'baptize', 'make', 'modern', 'optimal' and 'size'. Of these connections the association with 'make' is strongest (0.106). As expected above, the bigrams <an> and <nd> are excellent cues to the meaning 'sand', with <nd> reaching the highest weight (0.220).

The sum of the association weights of a particular word form can now be conceptualized as the degree of activation of a particular meaning by the string of bigrams corresponding to the word form in question. Full activation amounts to a value of 1. For example, if we take the string of bigrams #b_ba_ap_pt_ti_iz_ze_e#, we can add up the weights of these bigrams for the meaning 'baptize' to arrive at the activation of this meaning by this word form, as shown in Table 3.

Table 3: Activation weights of bigrams for the meaning 'baptize'.

#b	ba	ap	pt	ti	iz	ze	e#	sum of weights
0.213	0.213	0.213	0.125	0.125	0.041	0.041	0.029	1

Table 4 shows a part of the weight matrix, giving the activation of meanings for four selected bigram strings. The weight sums are mostly extremely small, which means that there is no activation of the respective meaning by the cue. Some of the activation sums reach unity (the latter are given in bold), which means that these meanings are activated by the respective cues. For illustration, consider the joint activation of the meaning of 'chance' by the bigrams #b_ba_ap_pt_ti_iz_ze_e#, which is vanishingly small. In contrast, the activation of the meaning 'baptize' by the same string is maximal. This is a welcome result.

Table 4: Activations of meanings by bigram strings.

	baptize	chance	make	modern	optimal
#b_ba_ap_pt_ti_iz_ze_e#	**1.00**	2.57e-16	0.00	9.71e-17	6.56e-16
#c_ch_ha_an_nc_ce_e#	−3.82e-17	**1.00**	1.18e-16	1.70e-16	3.56e-17
#m_mo_od_de_er_rn_ni_iz_ze_e#	4.09e-16	2.91e-16	**1.00**	**1.00**	−5.38e-16
#o_op_pt_ti_im_mi_iz_ze_e#	−3.82e-16	1.32e-16	**1.00**	−4.30e-16	**1.00**

From a morphological perspective the most important result is that the two strings #m_mo_od_de_er_rn_ni_iz_ze_e# and #o_op_pt_ti_im_mi_iz_ze_e# (and only those two strings) activate the meaning 'make', as well as the meanings 'modern' and 'optimal'. This result mirrors a classical morphological analysis, but crucially the model has arrived at this analysis without having posited or used any morphological parsing or structure. The model thus captures morphological patterns, but morphology actually remains implicit.

Our modeling exercise was meant to illustrate how an NDL approach can achieve morphologically interpretable results without assuming any morphological units, and without assuming any operations that are defined by making use of such units. Whether such a radical approach to word structure is feasible on a larger scale has been tested for some problems of derivational morphology in Baayen et al. (2011). In that paper, Baayen and colleagues model a wide range of inflectional, syntactic and word-formation phenomena, and we will concentrate here on two issues relating to derivational morphology. The first is the processing costs of derived words, the second the problem of phonaesthemes.

Traditionally, a number of diagnostic lexical measures are assumed to reflect morphological processes, and these measures crucially refer to entities that are taken to be morphologically relevant. Among these are, for example, frequency of the derived word, frequency of the base, morphological family size of the derivative,[4] morphological family size of the base, and the frequency of the letter bigram straddling the morpheme boundary between base and affix. In many experiments it has been shown that these measures can account for the distribution of behavioral measures in experimental tasks, such as reaction times (see again Section 2 for discussion).

The general question for us now is whether an NDL model can simulate the results observed in behavioral experiments correctly even though this model has no access to the morphological entities that underlie the traditional diagnostic measures. This question can be answered by relating reaction times to the activation weights derived in NDL models. Large positive activation weights can be taken to negatively correlate with reaction times since higher activation goes together with shorter reaction times.[5]

Using different data sets, Baayen et al. (2011) show that the simulated reaction times generated by the NDL model nicely correlate with the reaction times observed in experiments. NDL models thus closely approximate the effects of the lexical-morphological variables without assuming the morphological entities and morphology-based measures that underlie such variables.

---

[4] Morphological family size is a type count of the number of morphologically related forms of a base (see, for example, Schreuder and Baayen 1997).
[5] Depending on the properties of the data set at hand, and to achieve a better fit, it may be necessary to mathematically transform the association weights. See Baayen et al. (2011: 451) for discussion.

With regard to morphological productivity in derivation, NDL makes interesting and quite realistic predictions. Thus, in their study of processing and productivity Baayen et al. (2011) investigate the activation levels of the productive nominalizing suffix -*ness* (as in *randomness*) and the unproductive suffix -*th* (as in *truth*). While the activation for the productive suffix is higher, the activation for -*th* is not zero. This suggests two things. First, the model correctly predicts reduced processing costs for neologisms with productive suffixes. Second, new formations in -*th* might occasionally occur, which is also correct (cf. *strongth, slowth, firmth,* and *oldth,* all from the Urban Dictionary, http://www.urbandictionary.com).

To see how NDL can deal with phonaesthemes, Baayen et al. (2011) used data from the priming study by Bergen (2004), discussed in Section 2.4 above. The NDL model was able to simulate reaction times which strongly correlated with the reaction times in Bergen's experiment. This shows that priming effects also emerge under the conditions of discriminative learning, and they do so again in the absence of any morphologically defined unit.

To summarize, we can say that in NDL effects emerge that run under the name of 'morpheme' or 'phonaestheme' in other models, but without the need of assuming the existence of such units. The fact that NDL implements an established theory of learning makes this approach especially attractive. There are, however, also some problems. The first concerns the cues and outcomes. The ontological nature of the outcomes as "symbolic focal points mediating between linguistic form and experience of the world" (Baayen and Ramscar 2015: 9) is not quite clear. There must be some abstraction going on with regard to establishing 'symbolic' focal points that is not built into the system. Similarly, on the cue level, it is left open how the n-grams themselves are learned. Baayen and colleagues are aware of these problems and work around them by assuming that these elements are "simply available to the learner" (Baayen and Ramscar 2015: 9).

Another reason for worry is that an NDL approach ultimately seems to lead to the abandonment of what is commonly known as the 'mental lexicon', and it is unclear how an NDL model could capture the many different insights that people have gained under this perspective.

3.6 Summary

We have seen in this section that researchers have come up with a wide range of mechanisms to account for the mapping of sound and meaning in derived words. In view of the results emerging from empirical studies and computational implementations, it appears that widely established concepts such as 'rule', or even 'mental lexicon' are somewhat simplistic and in need of an overhaul. Especially the variation found in the data is a matter of concern that future research must address.

4 Where are we going?

Answering the question 'where are we going from here?' is hardly an easy one in any research field. For derivational morphology, several of the issues that we have discussed in this chapter have become matters of conviction in addition to being research questions, which does not make the task easier. Nonetheless, we shall try to sketch some key issues and avenues of research as we perceive them.

In general, it can be said that the findings from different subfields can hardly be reconciled with the reductionist views of most current theories. These views are reductionist in the sense that they try to reduce the often complex and gradient mappings of form and meaning to a manageable, even if simplistic, set of units and necessary mechanisms of combination. Formal modeling is one avenue for exploring how the multitude of effects arise and co-exist, sometimes in interactions. Here, we have focused on Naive Discriminative Learning, which has the advantage of being an application to language of a well-known learning model that has been used to account for a range of other phenomena in cognitive psychology. However, interesting and testable predictions may also be derived from other algorithms.

One important future challenge is to ensure that the models proposed are sufficiently able to account for different processing circumstances and a wide range of linguistic phenomena. Typically, linguists have been guilty of ignoring processing-related issues, while psychologists and psycholinguists have ignored the complexity of the linguistic system. A case in point of the former is the emphasis on problems of zero morphs and empty morphs (outlined in Sections 2.2 and 2.3), which are very much theory-internal linguistic problems without major implications for processing. An example of psycholinguists ignoring the complexity of the system is the focus of much experimental work on whether or not morphemes are relevant units of processing, with little attention paid to how such morphemes might then be combined to produce whole-word meaning, no trivial issue in derivation.

Another challenge is the fact that the psycholinguistic study of derivational morphology, and inevitably to some extent also this chapter, has often focused to a large extent on the visual recognition of morphologically complex words, with auditory comprehension and both spoken and written word production being confined to secondary roles. This is in noteworthy contrast to theoretical morphology, which often focuses on word 'formation' and thus implicitly on word production. The ideal must surely be models that account for both auditory and visual processing in both comprehension and production with a certain degree of systematicity and consistency. A related concern is the interaction between visual and auditory modalities and the impact of literacy not only on the processing that we study in our experiments but also on our definitions of words and morphemes, and our very thinking about morphology.

Finally, derivational morphology and morphological processing of course do not exist in a vacuum, but in the context of many other linguistic and extralinguistic influences, which should ideally be accounted for in the same integrated model. Some such influences are speaker and register variability. It has been shown, for example, that age plays a significant role in shaping the lexicon over time. Not only does age of acquisition have an important effect on long-term representation of words (e.g. Brysbaert et al. 2000), there are also significant changes in the size of the lexicon over time, with important consequences for, among other things, processing time (e.g. Ramscar et al. 2014). Morphological knowledge itself seems to vary across speakers as a function of education, and may interact with differences in orthographic knowledge or register. Plag et al. (1999), for example, show that productive derivation is very restricted in spoken registers, unlike in written registers.

Obviously, we are still far away from devising models that can cope with all sources of variation and calling for such models moves beyond the optimistic into downright daydreaming. However, whether daydream or not, it is an ideal that should be kept in mind to avoid getting lost in the complexity and minute details of derivational morphology.

Acknowledgments: We are very grateful for comments on earlier versions of this paper by Marios Andreou, Sonia Ben Hedia, Olivier Bonami, Wolfgang U. Dressler, Antonio Fábregas, Lea Kawaletz and Julia Zimmermann. Parts of this paper were written during a research stay of the first author at Université Paris-Diderot in the fall of 2015. The financial support by LABEX that enabled this stay is gratefully acknowledged.

Appendix: R code for NDL example

```
> install.packages("ndl")
> library(ndl)
```

```
> Word <- c("baptize", "chance", "extreme", "modernize", "optimal",
"optimize", "sand", "size")
> Outcomes <- c("baptize", "chance", "extreme", "modern make", "optimal",
"optimal make", "sand", "size")
> Frequency <- c(37, 12303, 558, 6, 15, 5, 1035, 2353)
> ize <- data.frame(Word, Outcomes, Frequency)
> ize$Cues <- orthoCoding(ize$Word, grams=2)
> ize
```

Word	Outcomes	Frequency	Cues
baptize	baptize	37	#b_ba_ap_pt_ti_iz_ze_e#
chance	chance	12303	#c_ch_ha_an_nc_ce_e#
extreme	extreme	558	#e_ex_xt_tr_re_em_me_e#
modernize	modernize	6	#m_mo_od_de_er_rn_ni_iz_ze_e#
optimal	optimal	15	#o_op_pt_ti_im_ma_al_l#
optimize	optimize	5	#o_op_pt_ti_im_mi_iz_ze_e#
sand	Sand	1035	#s_sa_an_nd_d#
size	Size	2353	#s_si_iz_ze_e#

```
> ize.w = estimateWeights(ize)
> round(ize.w, 3)
```

	baptize	chance	extreme	make	modern	optimal	sand	size
#b	0.213	-0.007	-0.004	-0.110	-0.016	-0.089	0.014	-0.062
#c	-0.007	0.154	-0.015	-0.019	-0.006	-0.003	-0.030	-0.006
#e	-0.004	-0.015	0.131	-0.011	-0.003	-0.002	0.006	-0.015
#m	-0.016	-0.006	-0.003	0.102	0.130	-0.007	0.012	-0.052
#o	-0.089	-0.003	-0.002	0.131	-0.007	0.199	0.006	-0.026
#s	-0.048	-0.036	-0.009	-0.126	-0.040	-0.020	0.150	0.284
al	0.006	0.010	0.006	-0.145	0.021	0.061	-0.019	0.084
an	0.007	0.124	-0.009	0.017	0.006	0.003	0.190	-0.076
ap	0.213	-0.007	-0.004	-0.110	-0.016	-0.089	0.014	-0.062
ba	0.213	-0.007	-0.004	-0.110	-0.016	-0.089	0.014	-0.062
ce	-0.007	0.154	-0.015	-0.019	-0.006	-0.003	-0.030	-0.006
ch	-0.007	0.154	-0.015	-0.019	-0.006	-0.003	-0.030	-0.006
d#	0.014	-0.030	0.006	0.036	0.012	0.006	0.220	-0.069
de	-0.016	-0.006	-0.003	0.102	0.130	-0.007	0.012	-0.052

(continued)

	baptize	chance	extreme	make	modern	optimal	sand	size
e#	0.029	0.106	0.085	0.076	0.024	0.012	-0.043	0.107
em	-0.004	-0.015	0.131	-0.011	-0.003	-0.002	0.006	-0.015
er	-0.016	-0.006	-0.003	0.102	0.130	-0.007	0.012	-0.052
ex	-0.004	-0.015	0.131	-0.011	-0.003	-0.002	0.006	-0.015
ha	-0.007	0.154	-0.015	-0.019	-0.006	-0.003	-0.030	-0.006
im	-0.089	-0.003	-0.002	0.131	-0.007	0.199	0.006	-0.026
iz	0.041	-0.032	-0.030	0.106	0.034	0.017	-0.019	0.128
l#	0.006	0.010	0.006	-0.145	0.021	0.061	-0.019	0.084
ma	0.006	0.010	0.006	-0.145	0.021	0.061	-0.019	0.084
me	-0.004	-0.015	0.131	-0.011	-0.003	-0.002	0.006	-0.015
mi	-0.094	-0.013	-0.007	0.276	-0.028	0.138	0.025	-0.110
mo	-0.016	-0.006	-0.003	0.102	0.130	-0.007	0.012	-0.052
nc	-0.007	0.154	-0.015	-0.019	-0.006	-0.003	-0.030	-0.006
nd	0.014	-0.030	0.006	0.036	0.012	0.006	0.220	-0.069
ni	-0.016	-0.006	-0.003	0.102	0.130	-0.007	0.012	-0.052
od	-0.016	-0.006	-0.003	0.102	0.130	-0.007	0.012	-0.052
op	-0.089	-0.003	-0.002	0.131	-0.007	0.199	0.006	-0.026
pt	0.125	-0.010	-0.006	0.021	-0.022	0.110	0.020	-0.088
re	-0.004	-0.015	0.131	-0.011	-0.003	-0.002	0.006	-0.015
rn	-0.016	-0.006	-0.003	0.102	0.130	-0.007	0.012	-0.052
sa	0.014	-0.030	0.006	0.036	0.012	0.006	0.220	-0.069
si	-0.062	-0.006	-0.015	-0.162	-0.052	-0.026	-0.069	0.353
ti	0.125	-0.010	-0.006	0.021	-0.022	0.110	0.020	-0.088
tr	-0.004	-0.015	0.131	-0.011	-0.003	-0.002	0.006	-0.015
xt	-0.004	-0.015	0.131	-0.011	-0.003	-0.002	0.006	-0.015
ze	0.041	-0.032	-0.030	0.106	0.034	0.017	-0.019	0.128

References

Abelin, Asa. 1999. *Studies in sound symbolism*. Göteborg University Dissertation.
Arndt-Lappe, Sabine. 2011. Towards an exemplar-based model of stress in English noun-noun compounds. *Journal of Linguistics* 47 (11). 549–585.
Arndt-Lappe, Sabine. 2014. Analogy in suffix rivalry: the case of English -ity and -ness. *English Language and Linguistics* 18 (3). 497–548. doi:10.1017/S136067431400015X.
Arndt-Lappe, Sabine. 2015. Word-formation and analogy. In Peter O. Müller, Ingeborg Ohnheiser, Susan Olsen & Franz Rainer (eds.), *Word-Formation: An International Handbook of the Languages of Europe*, 822–841. Berlin: de Gruyter Mouton.

Arndt-Lappe, Sabine & Mirjam Ernestus. 2019. Morpho-phonological alternations: the role of lexical storage. In Vito Pirrelli, Ingo Plag & Wolfgang Dressler (eds.), *Word Knowledge and Word Usage: a Cross-disciplinary Guide to the Mental Lexicon*, 185–220. De Gruyter.

Arndt-Lappe, Sabine & Ingo Plag. 2013. The role of prosodic structure in the formation of blends. *English Language and Linguistics* 17. 537–563.

Arnon, Inbal & Michael Ramscar. 2012. Granularity and the acquisition of grammatical gender: How order-of-acquisition affects what gets learned. *Cognition* 122 (3). 292–305.

Aronoff, Mark. 1976. *Word Formation in Generative Grammar*. Cambridge, Mass: MIT Press.

Arppe, Antti, Peter Hendrix, Petar Milin, Harald R. Baayen & Cyrus Shaoul. 2014. ndl: Naive Discriminative Learning. http://CRAN.R-project.org/package=ndl.

Baayen, R. Harald, Ton Dijkstra & Robert Schreuder. 1997. Singulars and Plurals in Dutch: Evidence for a Parallel Dual-Route Model. *Journal of Memory and Language* 37. 94–117.

Baayen, R. Harald., Peter Hendrix & Michael Ramscar. 2013. Sidestepping the Combinatorial Explosion: An Explanation of n-gram Frequency Effects Based on Naive Discriminative Learning. *Language and Speech* 56 (3). 329–347. doi:10.1177/0023830913484896.

Baayen, R. Harald, Petar Milin, Dusica Filipovic Durdevic, Peter Hendrix & Marco Marelli. 2011. An amorphous model for morphological processing in visual comprehension based on naive discriminative learning. *Psychological Review* 118 (3). 438–481.

Baayen, R. Harald & Michael Ramscar. 2015. Abstraction, storage and naive discriminative learning. In Ewa Dabrowska & Dagmar Divjak (eds.), *Handbook of Cognitive Linguistics*, vol. 39, 100–120. Walter de Gruyter GmbH & Co KG.

Baayen, R. Harald, Shaoul C. J. Willits, Jon Willits & Michael Ramscar. 2015. Comprehension without segmentation: A proof of concept with naive discrimination learning. *Language, Cognition, and Neuroscience* 31 (1). 106–128.

Baayen, R. Harald, Lee H. Wurm & Joanna Aycock. 2007. Lexical Dynamics for Low-Frequency Complex Words: A Regression Study Across Tasks and Modalities. *The Mental Lexicon* 2. 419–463.

Balling, Laura Winther & R. Harald Baayen. 2008. Morphological effects in auditory word recognition: Evidence from Danish. *Language and Cognitive Processes* 23. 1159–1190.

Balling, Laura W. & R. Harald Baayen. 2012. Probability and surprisal in auditory comprehension of morphologically complex words. *Cognition* 125. 80–106.

Barker, Chris. 1998. Episodic *-ee* in English: A thematic role constraint on a new word formation. *Language* 74 (4). 695–727.

Bauer, Laurie, Rochelle Lieber & Ingo Plag. 2013. *The Oxford reference guide to English morphology*. Oxford: Oxford University Press.

Beard, Robert. 1990. The nature and origins of derivational polysemy. *Lingua* 81. 101–140.

Beard, Robert. 1995. *Lexeme-morpheme base morphology: a general theory of inflection and word formation*. Albany, NY: State University of New York Press.

Bergen, Benjamin K. 2004. The psychological reality of phonaesthemes. *Language* 80. 290–311.

Bien, Heidrun, Willem M. J. Levelt & R. Harald Baayen. 2005. Frequency effects in compound production. *Proceedings of the National Academy of Sciences of the USA* 102. 17876–17881.

Blazej, Laura J. & Ariel M. Cohen-Goldberg. 2015. Can we hear morphological complexity before words are complex? *Journal of Experimental Psychology: Human Perception and Performance* 41 (1). 50–68.

Blevins, James P. 2006. Word-based morphology. *Journal of Linguistics* 42 (3). 531–573.
Blevins, James P., Farrell Ackerman & Robert Malouf. 2015. Morphology as an adaptive discriminative system. In Heidi Harley & Daniel Siddiqi (eds.), *Morphological metatheory*, 271–302. Amsterdam and Philadelphia: John Benjamins.
Bölte, Jens, Petra Dohmes & Pienie Zwitserlood. 2013. Interference and Facilitation in Spoken Word Production: Effects of Morphologically and Semantically Related Context Stimuli on Picture Naming. *Journal of Psycholinguistic Research* 42. 255–280.
Bonami, Olivier & Berthold Crysmann. 2016. The role of morphology in constraint-based lexicalist grammars. In Andrew Hippisley & Gregory T. Stump (eds.), *Cambridge Handbook of Morphology*, 609–656. Cambridge: Cambridge University Press.
Booij, Geert E. 1977. *Dutch Morphology. A Study of Word Formation in Generative Grammar.* Dordrecht: Foris.
Booij, Geert E. 1993. Against split morphology. In Geert E. Booij & Jaap van Marle (eds.), *Yearbook of Morphology 1993*, 27–50. Dordrecht: Kluwer Academic Publishers.
Booij, Geert E. 2010. *Construction Morphology*. Oxford: Oxford University Press.
Brysbaert, Marc, Marielle Lange & Ilse van Wijnendaele. 2000. The effects of age-of-acquisition and frequency-of-occurence in visual word recognition: Further evidence from the Dutch language. *European Journal of Cognitive Psychology* 12. 65–85.
Brysbaert, Marc & Boris New. 2009. Moving beyond Kučera and Francis: A critical evaluation of current word frequency norms and the introduction of a new and improved word frequency measure for American English. *Behavior research methods* 41 (4). 977–990.
Bybee, Joan L. 1995. Regular morphology and the lexicon. *Language and Cognitive Processes* 10. 425–455.
Chapman, Don & Royal Skousen. 2005. Analogical modeling and morphological change: the case of the adjectival negative prefix in English. *English Language and Linguistics* 9 (2). 333–357.
Chen, Train-Min. & Jenn Yeu. Chen. 2006. Morphological encoding in the production of compound words in Mandarin Chinese. *Journal of Memory and Language* 54. 491–514.
Chomsky, Noam & Morris Halle. 1968. *The Sound Pattern of English*. New York: Harper and Row.
Collie, Sara. 2008. English stress preservation: The case for 'fake cyclicity'. *English Language and Linguistics* 12 (3). 505–532.
Costa, Alberto, F.-Xavier Alario & Alfonso Caramazza. 2005. On the categorical nature of the semantic interference effect in the picture-word interference paradigm. *Psychonomic Bulletin and Review* 12. 125–131.
Daelemans, Walter, Jakub Zavrel, Ko van der Sloot & Antal van den Bosch. 2007. TiMBL: Tilburg Memory Based Learner, version 6.0, *Reference Guide: LK Technical Report 04-02*. Tilburg: ILK. available from http://ilk.uvt.nl/timbl.
Dohmes, Petra, Pienie Zwitserlood & Jens Bölte. 2004. The impact of semantic transparency of morphologically complex words on picture naming. *Brain and Language* 90. 203–212.
Don, Jan. 1993. *Morphological Conversion*. Utrecht: OTS, Rijksuniversiteit.
Dressler, Wolfgang, Gary Libben & Katharina Korecky-Kröll. 2014. Conflicting vs. convergent vs. interdependent motivations in morphology. In Brian MacWhinney, Andrej Malchukov & Edith Moravcsik (eds.), *Competing Motivations in Grammar and Usage*, 181–196. Oxford: Oxford University Press.
Eddington, David. 2002. Spanish diminutive formation without rules or constraints. *Linguistics* 40. 395–419.

Fábregas, Antonio & Martina Penke. 2019. Word storage and computation. In Vito Pirrelli, Ingo Plag & Wolfgang Dressler (eds.), Word Knowledge and Word Usage: a Cross-disciplinary Guide to the Mental Lexicon, 444–494. Berlin/Boston: De Gruyter.
Feldman, Laurie Beth. 2000. Are morphological effects distinguishable from the effects of shared meaning and shared form? *Journal of Experimental Psychology: Learning, Memory, and Cognition* 26 (6). 1431–1444.
Feldman, Laurie Beth, Petar Milin, Kit W. Cho, Fermín Moscoso del Prado Martín & Patrick O'Connor. 2015. Must analysis of meaning follow analysis of form? A time course analysis. *Frontiers of Human Neuroscience* 9. 111. doi: 10.3389/fnhum.2015.00111.
Frauenfelder, Ulrich H. & Robert Schreuder. 1992. Constraining Psycholinguistic Models of Morphological Processing and Representation: The Role of Productivity. In Geert E. Booij & Jaap van Marle (eds.), *Yearbook of Morphology 1991*, 165–183. Dordrecht: Kluwer Academic Publishers.
Frazier, Melissa. 2006. Output-output faithfulness to moraic structure: Evidence from American English. In *Proceedings of NELS*, vol. 36, 1.
Frege, Gottlob. 1892. Über Sinn und Bedeutung. *Zeitschrift für Philosophie und philosophische Kritik* 100. 25–50.
Giraudo, Hélène & Jonathan Grainger. 2001. Priming complex words: Evidence for supralexical representation of morphology. *Psychonomic Bulletin and Review* 8. 127–131.
Gonnerman, Laura M. & Elaine S. Anderson. 2001. Graded semantic and phonological similarity effects in morphologically complex words. In Sabrina Bendjaballah, Wolfgang U. Dressler, Oskar E. Pfeiffer & Maria D. Voeikova (eds.), *Morphology 2000: Selected papers from the 9th Morphology meeting*, 137–148. Amsterdam: John Benjamins.
Gonnerman, Laura M., Mark S. Seidenberg & Elaine S. Anderson. 2007. Graded Semantic and Phonological Similarity Effects in Priming: Evidence for a Distributed Connectionist Approach to Morphology. *Journal of Experimental Psychology: General* 136. 323–345.
Gussmann, Edmund (ed.). 1987a. *Rules and the Lexicon*. Lublin: Catholic University of Lublin.
Gussmann, Edmund. 1987b. The lexicon of English de-adjectival verbs. In Edmund Gussmann (ed.), *Rules and the Lexicon*, 79–101. Lublin: Catholic University of Lublin.
ten Hacken, Pius. 2014. Delineating derivation and inflection. In Rochelle Lieber & Pavol Štekauer (eds.), *The Oxford handbook of derivational morphology*. Oxford Handbooks in linguistics, 10–25. Oxford: Oxford University Press.
Halle, Morris & Alec Marantz. 1993. Distributed morphology and the pieces of inflection. In Kenneth Hale & Samuel J. Keyser (eds.), *The View from Building 20: Essays in Linguistics in Honor of Sylvain Bromberger*, vol. 24 Current Studies in Linguistics, 111–176. Cambridge and Mass: MIT Press.
Harm, Michael W. & Mark S. Seidenberg. 2004. Computing the meanings of words in reading: Cooperative division of labor between visual and phonological processes. *Psychological Review* 111. 662–720.
Haspelmath, Martin. 2011. The indeterminacy of word segmentation and the nature of morphology and syntax. *Folia Linguistica* 45 (1). 31–80.
Hay, Jennifer. 2001. Lexical frequency in morphology: is everything relative? *Linguistics* 39 (6). 1041–1070.
Hay, Jennifer B. 2003. *Causes and Consequences of Word Structure*. New York and London: Routledge.

Hay, Jennifer & Ingo Plag. 2004. What constrains possible suffix combinations? On the interaction of grammatical and processing restrictions in derivational morphology. *Natural Language & Linguistic Theory* 22 (3). 565–596.

Hockett, Charles F. 1947. Problems of Morphemic Analysis. *Language* 23 (4). 321–343. http://www.jstor.org/stable/410295.

Hutchins, Sharon Suzanne. 1998. *The psychological reality, variability, and compositionality of English phonesthemes*. Atlanta: Emory University Dissertation.

Jackendoff, Ray. 1975. Morphological and semantic regularities in the lexicon. *Language* 51 (3). 639–671.

Janssen, Niels, Yanchao Bi & Alfonso Caramazza. 2008. A tale of two frequencies: Determining the speed of lexical access for Mandarin Chinese and English compounds. *Language and Cognitive Processes* 23. 1191–1223.

Joanisse, Mark F. & Mark S. Seidenberg. 1999. Impairments in verb morphology after brain injury: a connectionist model. *Proceedings of the National Academy of Science* 96. 7592–7597.

Kamin, Leon J. 1968. Attention-like processes in classical conditioning. In M. R. Jones (ed.), *Miami symposium on the prediction of behavior*, 9–31. Miami: Miami University Press.

Kemps, Rachèl J. J. K, Lee H. Wurm, Mirjam Ernestus, Robert Schreuder & R. Harald Baayen. 2005. Prosodic cues for morphological complexity in Dutch and English. *Language and Cognitive Processes* 20 (1–2). 43–73.

Kiparsky, Paul. 1982. Lexical morphology and phonology. In In-Seok Yang (ed.) *Linguistics in the Morning Calm: Selected Papers from SICOL*, 3–91. Seoul: Hanshin.

Krott, Andrea, R. Harald Baayen & Robert Schreuder. 2001. Analogy in morphology: Modeling the choice of linking morphemes in Dutch. *Linguistics* 39. 51–93.

Krott, Andrea, Peter Hagoort & R. Harald Baayen. 2004a. Sublexical units and supralexical combinatorics in the processing of interfixed Dutch compounds. *Language and Cognitive Processes* 19. 453–471.

Krott, Andrea, Gary Libben, Gonia Jarema, Wolfgang U. Dressler, Robert Schreuder & R. Harald Baayen. 2004b. Probability in the grammar of German and Dutch: Inter-fixation in tri-constituent compounds. *Language and Speech* 47. 83–106.

Kuperman, Victor, Raymond Bertram & R. Harald Baayen. 2008. Morphological Dynamics in Compound Processing. *Language and Cognitive Processing* 23. 1089–1132.

Kwon, Nahyun & Erich R. Round. 2015. Phonaesthemes in morphological theory. *Morphology* 25 (1). 1–27. doi:10.1007/s11525-014-9250-z.

Lehiste, Ilse. 1972. *Suprasegmentals*. Cambridge and Mass: MIT Press.

Lehtonen, Minna, Helga Niska, Erling Wande, Jussi Niemi & Matti Laine. 2006. Recognition of Inflected Words in a Morphologically Limited Language: Frequency Effects in Monolinguals and Bilinguals. *Journal of Psycholinguistic Research* 35. 121–146.

Libben, Gary. 2006. Why study compound processing? In Gary Libben & Gonia Jarema (eds.), *The representation and processing of compound words*, 1–22. Oxford: Oxford University Press.

Libben, Gary, Christina Gagné & Wolfgang U. Dressler. 2019. The representation and processing of compounds words. In Vito Pirrelli, Ingo Plag & Wolfgang U. Dressler (eds.), *Word Knowledge and Word Usage: a Cross-disciplinary Guide to the MentalLexicon*, 329–345. Berlin/Boston: De Gruyter.

Lieber, Rochelle. 1998. The suffix -*ize* in English: Implications for morphology. In Steven Lapointe, Diane Brentari & Patrick Farrell (eds.), *Morphology and its Relation to Phonology and Syntax*, 12–34. CSLI publications.

Lieber, Rochelle. 2004. *Morphology and lexical semantics*. Cambridge: Cambridge University Press.
Lieber, Rochelle & Pavol Štekauer. 2009. Introduction: Status and definition of compounding. In Rochelle Lieber & Pavol Stekauer (eds.), *The Oxford handbook of compounding Oxford Handbooks in linguistics*, 3–18. Oxford, New York: Oxford University Press.
Longtin, Catherine-Marie, Juan Segui & Pierre A. Hallé. 2003. Morphological priming without morphological relationship. *Language and Cognitive Processes* 18. 313–334.
Magnus, Margaret. 2000. *What's in a Word? Evidence for Phonosemantics*. Trondheim: University of Trondheim Dissertation.
Marangolo, Paola & Costanza Papagno. 2020. Neuroscientific protocols for exploring the mental lexicon: evidence from aphasia. In Vito Pirrelli, Ingo Plag & Wolfgang U. Dressler (eds.), *Word Knowledge and Word Usage: a Cross-disciplinary Guide to the Mental Lexicon*, 124–163. Berlin/Boston: De Gruyter.
Marslen-Wilson, William, Lorraine K. Tyler, Rachelle Waksler & Lianne Older. 1994. Morphology and Meaning in the English Mental Lexicon. *Psychological Review* 191. 3–33.
Marslen-Wilson, William & Xiaolin Zhou. 1999. Abstractness, Allomorphy, and Lexical Architecture. *Language and Cognitive Processes* 14. 321–352.
Marzi, Claudia, James P. Blevins, Geert Booij & Vito Pirrelli. 2020. Inflection at the morphology-syntax interface. In Vito Pirrelli, Ingo Plag & Wolfgang U. Dressler (eds.), *Word Knowledge and Word Usage: a Cross-disciplinary Guide to the Mental Lexicon*, 221–287. Berlin/Boston: De Gruyter.
McClelland, James L. & Jeffrey L. Elman. 1986. The TRACE model of speech perception. *Cognitive Psychology* 18. 1–86.
Merlini Barbaresi, Lavinia & Wolfgang U. Dressler. 2020. Pragmatic Explanations in Morphology. In Vito Pirrelli, Ingo Plag & Wolfgang U. Dressler (eds.), *Word Knowledge and Word Usage: a Cross-disciplinary Guide to the Mental Lexicon*, 397–443. Berlin/Boston: De Gruyter.
Meunier, Fanny & Juan Segui. 1999. Frequency Effects in Auditory Word Recognition: The Case of Suffixed Words. *Journal of Memory and Language* 41. 327–344.
Moscoso del Prado Martín, Fermín, Raymond Bertram, Tuomo Häikiö, Robert Schreuder & R. Harald Baayen. 2004. Morphological Family Size in a Morphologically Rich Language: The Case of Finnish Compared With Dutch and Hebrew. *Journal of Experimental Psychology: Learning, Memory, and Cognition* 30. 1271–1278.
Moscoso del Prado Martín, Fermín, Avital Deutsch, Ram Frost, Robert Schreuder, Nivja H. de Jong & R. Harald Baayen. 2005. Changing places: A cross-language perspective on frequency and family size in Hebrew and Dutch. *Journal of Memory and Language* 53. 496–512.
Motsch, Wolfgang. 1981. Der kreative Aspekt in der Wortbildung. In Leonhard Lipka (ed.), *Wortbildung*, 94–118. Darmstadt: Wissenschaftliche Buchgesellschaft.
Mühleisen, Susanne. 2010. *Heterogeneity in word-formation patterns*. Amsterdam / Philadelphia: John Benjamins.
New, Boris, Marc Brysbaert, Juan Segui, Ludovic Ferrand & Kathleen Rastle. 2004. The Processing of singular and plural nouns in French and English. *Journal of Memory and Language* 51. 568–585.
Norris, Dennis G. 1994. Shortlist: A connectionist model of continuous speech recognition. *Cognition* 52. 189–234.
OED. 2013. *The Oxford English Dictionary online*. Oxford: Oxford University Press.

Pastizzo, Matthew John & Laurie Beth Feldman. 2001. Discrepancies between orthographic and unrelated baselines in masked priming undermine a decompositional account of morphological facilitation. *Journal of Experimental Psychology: Learning, Memory and Cognition* 28. 244–249.

Pastizzo, Matthew John & Laurie Beth Feldman. 2009. Multiple dimensions of relatedness among words: Conjoint effects of form and meaning in word recognition. *The Mental Lexicon* 4 (1). 1–25. doi:10.1075/ml.4.1.01pas.

Paul, Herrmann. 1880. *Prinzipien der Sprachgeschichte*. Halle: Max Niemeyer.

Pearce, John M. & Mark E. Bouton. 2001. Theories of associative learning in animals. *Annual review of psychology* 52 (1). 111–139.

Pinker, Steven & Michael T. Ullman. 2002. The past and future of the past tense. *Trends in Cognitive Sciences* 6. 456–463.

Pirrelli, Vito, Claudia Marzi, Marcello Ferro, R. Harald Baayen & Petar Milin. 2020. Psycho-computational modelling of the mental lexicon. A discriminative learning perspective. In Vito Pirrelli, Ingo Plag & Wolfgang U. Dressler (eds.), *Word Knowledge and Word Usage: a Cross-disciplinary Guide to the Mental Lexicon*, 21–80. Berlin/Boston: De Gruyter.

Plag, Ingo. 1999. More on infinitives in creole. The nature of Sranan fu and its complements. In Pauline Christie, Barbara Lalla, Velma Pollard & Lawrence Carrington (eds.), Studies in Caribbean Language II. *Papers from the Ninth Biennial Conference of the Society for Caribbean Linguistics, 1992*, 250–264. St. Augustine: Society for Caribbean Linguistics.

Plag, Ingo. 2004. Review of Carlin, Eithne B. and Jacques Arends. (eds.): *Atlas of the Languages of Suriname*. Leiden: KITLV Press 2000. Zeitschrift f¨ur Sprachwissenschaft 23. 144–145.

Plag, Ingo. 2010. Compound stress assignment by analogy: the constituent family bias. *Zeitschrift für Sprachwissenschaft* 29 (2). 243–282.

Plag, Ingo. 2018. *Word-formation in English*. 2nd ed. Cambridge: Cambridge University Press.

Plag, Ingo & Harald Baayen. 2009. Suffix ordering and morphological processing. *Language* 85 (1). 109–152.

Plag, Ingo, Christiane Dalton-Puffer & R. Harald Baayen. 1999. Morphological productivity across speech and writing. *English Language and Linguistics* 3 (2). 209–228.

Plag, Ingo, Julia Homann & Gero Kunter. 2015. Homophony and morphology: The acoustics of word-final S in English. *Journal of Linguistics* 53 (1). 181–216. (doi:10.1017/S0022226715000183).

Plaut, David C. & Laura M. Gonnerman. 2000. Are non-semantic morphological effects incompatible with a distributed connectionist approach to lexical processing? *Language and Cognitive Processes* 15 (4/5). 445–485.

R Core Team. 2014. R: *A Language and Environment for Statistical Computing*. http://www.R-project.org/.

Ramscar, Michael, Melody Dye & Stewart M. McCauley. 2013. Error and expectation in language learning: The curious absence of mouses in adult speech. *Language* 89 (4). 760–793.

Ramscar, Michael, Peter Hendrix, Cyrus Shaoul, Petar Milin & R. Harald Baayen. 2014. The myth of cognitive decline: Non-linear dynamics of lifelong learning. *Topics in cognitive science* 6 (1). 5–42.

Ramscar, Michael, Daniel Yarlett, Melody Dye, Katie Denny & Kirsten Thorpe. 2010. The effects of feature-label-order and their implications for symbolic learning. *Cognitive Science* 34 (6). 909–957.

Rastle, Kathleen & Matthew H. Davis. 2008. Morphological decomposition based on the analysis of orthography. *Language and Cognitive Processes* 23. 942–971.

Rastle, Kathleen, Matthew H. Davis, William D. Marslen-Wilson & Lorraine K. Tyler. 2000. Morphological and semantic effects in visual word recognition: A time-course study. *Language and Cognitive Processes* 15. 507–537.

Ravid, Dorit, Emmanuel Keuleers & Wolfgang U. Dressler. 2020. Emergence and early development of lexicon and morphology. In Vito Pirrelli, Ingo Plag & Wolfgang U. Dressler (eds.), *Word Knowledge and Word Usage: a Cross-disciplinary Guide to the Mental Lexicon*, 582-622. Berlin/Boston: De Gruyter.

Rescorla, Robert A. 1988a. Behavioral studies of Pavlovian conditioning. *Annual Review of Neuroscience* 11 (1). 329–352.

Rescorla, Robert A. 1988b. Pavlovian conditioning: It's not what you think it is. *American Psychologist* 43 (3). 151–160.

Rescorla, Robert A. & Allan R. Wagner. 1972. A theory of Pavlovian conditioning: Variations in the effectiveness of reinforcement and nonreinforcement. In Abraham H. Black & William F. Prokasy (eds.), *Classical conditioning II: Current research and theory*, 64–99. New York: Appleton-Century-Crofts.

Roelofs, Ardi. 1996. Serial order in planning the production of successive morphemes of a word. *Journal of Memory and Language* 35. 854–876.

Ronneberger-Sibold, Elke. 2003. On useful darkness. Loss and destruction of transparency by linguistic change, borrowing, and word creation. In Jaap van Marle & Geeert E. Booij (eds.), *Yearbook of Morphology 2002*, 81–104. Dordrecht: Kluwer Academic Publishers.

Ryding, Karin C. 2005. *A reference grammar of modern standard Arabic*. Cambridge University Press.

Schreuder, Robert & R. Harald Baayen. 1997. How complex simplex words can be. *Journal of Memory and Language* 37. 118–139.

Schriefers, Herbert, Antje S. Meyer & Willem J. M. Levelt. 1990. Exploring the time course of lexical access in production: Picture-word interference studies. *Journal of Memory and Language* 29. 86–102.

Seidenberg, Mark S. & James L. McClelland. 1989. A distributed, developmental model of word recognition and naming. *Psychological Review* 96. 523–568.

Skousen, Royal & Thereon Stanford. 2007. AM:: Parallel. available from http://humanities.byu.edu/am/.

Štekauer, Pavol, Salvador Valera & Livia Kortvélyessy. 2012. *Word-formation in the world's languages: a typological survey*. Cambridge: Cambridge University Press.

Synnaeve, Gabriel, Isabelle Dautriche, Benjamin Börschinger, Mark Johnson, Emmanuel Dupoux et al. 2014. Unsupervised word segmentation in context. In *25th International Conference on Computational Linguistics: Technical Papers*, Dublin: Dublin City University and Association for Computational Linguistics.

Szymanek, Bogdan. 1985. *English and Polish adjectives. A study in lexicalist word-formation*. Lublin: Catholic University of Lublin.

Taft, Marcus. 1979. Lexical Access via an Orthographic Code: The Basic Orthographic Syllabic Structure (BOSS). *Journal of Verbal Learning and Verbal Behavior* 18. 21–39.

Taft, Marcus. 1994. Interactive-activation as a Framework for Understanding Morphological Processing. *Language and Cognitive Processes* 9. 271–294.

Tremblay, Antoine, Bruce Derwing, Gary Libben & Chris Westbury. 2011. Processing advantages of lexical bundles: Evidence from self-paced reading and sentence recall tasks. *Language Learning* 61 (2). 569–613.
Ullman, Michael T. 2001. The declarative/procedural model of lexicon and grammar. *Journal of Psycholinguistic Research* 30. 37–69.
Ullman, Michael T. 2004. Contributions of memory circuits to language: the declarative/procedural model. *Cognition* 92. 231–270.
de Vaan, Laura, Robert Schreuder & R. Harald Baayen. 2007. Regular morphologically complex neologisms leave detectable traces in the mental lexicon. *The Mental Lexicon* 2. 1–23.
Vannest, Jennifer, Raymond Bertram, Juhani Järvikivi & Jussi Niemi. 2002. Counterintuitive Cross-Linguistic Differences: More Morphological Computation in English than in Finnish. *Journal of Psycholinguistic Research* 31. 83–106.
Wurm, Lee H. 1997. Auditory Processing of Prefixed English Words is Both Continuous and Decompositional. *Journal of Memory and Language* 37. 438–461.
Zwitserlood, Pinie, Jens Bölte & Petra Dohmes. 2000. Morphological effects on speech production: evidence from picture naming. *Language and Cognitive Processes* 15. 563–591.
Zwitserlood, Pinie, Jens Bölte & Petra Dohmes. 2002. Where and how morphologically complex words interplay with naming pictures. *Brain and Language* 81. 358–367.

Gary Libben, Christina L. Gagné and Wolfgang U. Dressler
The representation and processing of compounds words

Abstract: Compound words may be the language structures that are most fundamental to human linguistic ability and most revealing of its dynamics. We review evidence to date on the representation and processing of compound words in the mind and highlight the implications that they have for the broader understanding of language functioning and lexical knowledge. Our examination of the nature of compounds focuses on their deceptive simplicity as well as their dual nature as words and lexical combinations. Compound processing appears to be advantaged when compounds belong to morphologically productive families and when they are both formally and semantically transparent. We also claim that current findings offer converging evidence that compound word processing is characterized by both whole word and constituent activation for compound types.

Keywords: morphology, compounding, compound words, processing, psycholinguistics, semantic transparency, compositionality, productivity

1 Introduction and overview

Perhaps the most fascinating thing about language is that, through apparently simple acts of creating and combining words, human beings are able to develop the extraordinary richness and suppleness of communication that characterizes our species. In this chapter, we focus on compound words, which may constitute the language structure that is most fundamental to the human ability to create new language entities from existing ones. In this way, compounding offers special insight into the representation and processing of multimorphemic words across languages. Compounds are prevalent across languages, they often play an important role in the creation of new words within a language, and the major constituents of compound words are typically easily identified by native speakers. These properties make compounding an ideal candidate for the cross-

Gary Libben, Brock University
Christina L. Gagné, University of Alberta
Wolfgang U. Dressler, University of Vienna; Austrian Academy of Sciences

linguistic investigation of the effects of positional, morphological, and semantic factors in lexical representation and processing.

In the sections below, we examine these factors through an integrated lens with which we strive to bring together linguistic and psycholinguistic insights into the role of compounding in lexical ability and the organization of the mental lexicon. We begin in Section 2 below with perspectives on the overall nature of compounding. In Section 3, we discuss semantic issues, focusing on transparency. This is followed by a discussion of more formal aspects of compound constituency (Sections 4, 5, 6) and, in Section 7, the effects of productivity in representation and processing. We discuss the acquisition of compounding in Section 8 and conclude with a summary statement concerning the evidence to date on the representation and processing of compound words in the mind.

2 The nature of compounding

2.1 Deceptive simplicity

Compounding is perhaps the simplest of morphological phenomena. Yet, it is often the things that appear to be the simplest that turn out to be the most revealing. A compound such as *boxcar* seems exceedingly straightforward. We know that it is a type of car, not a type of box. We are perfectly comfortable that it is a type of railway carriage, not a type of automobile. We feel that it is well-named (being box-shaped). Yet, *tramcar*, *sidecar*, and *stockcar* feel equally well-named. From the simple compound *boxcar,* larger compounds are easily constructed. These would include three-constituent compounds such as *boxcar wheel,* four-constituent compounds such as *railway boxcar* and, potentially, considerably larger constructions (e.g., *railway boxcar inspection facility*) that are linguistically quite complex, but not particularly difficult to process.

As the examples above indicate, compounds in a language such as English exhibit headedness, incorporate a variety of semantic relations between constituents, and exhibit recursion. In English, the head of the compound, the element which typically determines the lexical category of the compound, is always the last element of a compound. Thus, *boxcar* is a noun because *car* is a noun. However, this consistency of lexical category leaves open many semantic possibilities for the ways in which the head of a compound be related to modifying elements. For example, a *boxcar* has a *box*, but a *tramcar* does not have a *tram* – it is rather the other way around.

2.2 Distinguishing between compound words and other morphologically complex structures

One would expect that even an idealized native speaker of English (in the Chomskyan sense of someone who has perfect knowledge of the language) would struggle to classify English suffixed words (e.g., *warmed, warming, warmly, warmth, warmer*) as being examples of either inflectional or derivational morphology (or indeed know what that distinction refers to). However, compound words such as *skateboard, chessboard,* or *billboard,* seem to be an entirely different matter. Native speakers of English typically know what they are and typically have no difficulty appreciating their word-internal structure. This ease of identification seems to be a linguistic phenomenon. The real-world objects to which these words correspond have very little in common in terms of their physical structure – a *skateboard* has wheels, *a chessboard* does not. A *chessboard* is typically small and horizontal, a *billboard* is typically large and vertical. Yet, virtually all native speakers of English would recognize these words as having a common linguistic structure. They are all composed of two word-like elements, of which the second is the element *board*.

This simple initial observation highlights the dual nature that makes compound words so revealing of fundamental aspects of language representation and processing. On the one hand, compound words typically contain very recognizable sub-elements. On the other hand, they are used as integrated structures with specific whole-word meanings. This dual nature is the theme to which we will return throughout this chapter.

2.3 The dual nature of compound words: Can a word contain more than one word?

The dual nature of compound words has captured the attention of language theorists from the time of antiquity. Aristotle was perhaps the first to address the matter (in the Poetics), mainly because he recognized that the dual nature of compounds was problematic for an atomic theory of word meaning. The word *hard* has an atomic meaning. The words *hardness, hardship* and *harden* are clearly related to *hard*, but they too can be described as having an atomic meaning. In contrast, the compound words *hardhat, hardwood* and *blowhard* seem clearly to be composed of elements which themselves have lexical meaning. That was Aristotle's problem and he solved it by claiming that words within compounds lose their individual meaning to the meaning of the whole.

Jackendoff (2002, 2010) has also focused on what compounds can tell us about language evolution and the consequences that the role of compounding in human history can have for our understanding of compound semantics and more broadly, for the placement of compounding in a taxonomy of language structures. Jackendoff points out similarities between his perspective and that of Fanselow (1985) who characterizes compounding as a relic of a simpler human language system. Under this view, compounding can be linked to the kinds of (reduced) syntactic analyses seen among persons with Broca's aphasia and deep dyslexia. Jackendoff (2010) claims that the links between contemporary compounding and our linguistic history as a species explains the differences between properties of compounding and those of other morphological structure. He states that compounding is not a grammatical phenomenon, but, rather, a protogrammatical one (Jackendoff 2010: 422).

In the discussion that follows, we will treat compound words as those words that are built upon two or more lexical elements (i.e, roots, stems, or words). In doing this, we acknowledge the paradoxical situation in which the term compound words seems to be quite easy for dictionaries to define (e.g., Cambridge Dictionary: "A word that combines two or more different words"; Mirriam Webster: "A word consisting of components that are words"; Oxford: "A word made up of two or more existing words"). Morphologists have had a rather more difficult time arriving at a characterization of compound words that is adequate typologically and theoretically (see, for example Anderson 1992: 294–305; Lieber and Stekauer 2009).

It should be noted that definitions of compound construction (even those in the *A-morphous* tradition) typically begin with the assumption that compound constituents, when they are free-standing elements (e.g., *box* and *car* in English) will be non-distinct from their forms as words. This assumption has been challenged by Libben (2014) in which it is claimed that the activities of compound word production and comprehension creates new lexical forms that acquire specific morphological properties as compound heads (e.g., *-car*) or modifiers (e.g. *box-*) that are related to, but distinct, from the free standing words from which they come. Libben (2017) has argued that *duality* is a central property of compound words (and indeed all morphological structures). Under this perspective no multimorphemic construction can be assigned a univocal morphological structure. Rather, as cognitive processes, multimorphemic words exist as morphological superstates, which have the 'potential' to assume a variety of actual morphological states, depending on situational and processing demands.

3 Matters of meaning: Semantic transparency and compositionality

For compound words, the term semantic transparency is much debated in linguistic theory (see Acquaviva 2017; Rainer et al.2014). It most often refers to the extent to which the constituents of compounds maintain their whole word meaning within the compound structure. The term semantic transparency is related to, but not identical to the notion of semantic compositionality (Gagné, Spalding, and Nisbet 2016), which addresses the extent to which the meaning of a compound is a function of the meanings of its constituents and the manner in which they are put together syntactically (see Pelletier 2016).

To be sure, some compound words are more semantically transparent than others. At the extremes are very transparent forms such as *mountaintop*, which seems to mean nothing more or less than "the top of a mountain". At the other extreme are words such as *humbug*, whose meaning ('something designed to mislead or deceive') seems to have nothing to do with either *hum* or *bug*. It seems, however, that these examples are quite atypical. The vast majority of compounds have semantic properties that are similar to the examples with which we began this chapter: *skateboard*, *chessboard*, and *billboard*. In all these cases, a language user may appreciate the contribution of each lexical element to the meaning of the compound word as a whole, but it is also the case that if a language user did not previously know the meaning of the whole compound word, it would be very difficult to figure it out on the basis of the meanings of the constituent elements alone.

The theoretical construct of semantic transparency has been defined in various ways in psycholinguistic research. Semantic transparency has been discussed from the perspective of the compound, but also from the perspective of each constituent. For example, it has been defined in terms of the degree to which the meaning of the compound is predictable from the constituents, but it has also been defined in terms of the degree to which the meaning of each constituent is retained. Finally, semantic transparency has also been equated with the degree of association and semantic similarity between the meanings of a compound and each of its constituents. These various theoretical ways of construing semantic transparency have resulted in different ways of operationalizing this variable in psycholinguistic experiments and there are three primary ways of measuring semantic transparency. First, semantic transparency of compound constituents have been classified categorically as either transparent or opaque (e.g., Libben 2010, Sandra 1990, Smolka and Libben 2017). In Libben (1998, 2010), this approach was used to create the following 2 X 2 classification for bi-constituent compounds: transparent-transparent, opaque-transparent, transparent-opaque, opaque-opaque. A still finer gradation has been proposed by Mattiello and Dressler (2018).

A second way to measure semantic transparency has been to use participant ratings on a scale ranging from very opaque to very transparent (e.g., Fiorentino and Fund-Reznicek 2009; Libben et al. 2003). The specific aspect that is rated varies but the two most common ones are the degree to which the meaning of the compound is predictable from the constituents and the degree to which each of the constituents retain their meaning in the compound. A third way of operationalizing transparency is by using estimates of semantic distance based on patterns of co-occurrence of words, such as latent semantic analysis (e.g., Kuperman 2013). Semantic distance is an indication of the degree of association between two words. These various ways of operationalizing semantic transparency have been shown to reflect different aspects of semantic transparency (e.g., Gagné, Spalding, and Nisbet 2016).

Semantic transparency has played an important role in evaluating theories of morphological processing because it has been shown to influence processing in both comprehension and production tasks. In general, compounds with opaque constituents are more difficult to process than compounds with transparent constituents. For example, lexical decision latencies were shorter for compounds with a semantically transparent head than for compounds with an opaque head (e.g., Libben, et al. 2003). Similarly, in an eye-tracking study, gaze durations were longer for opaque compounds than for transparent compounds (Underwood, Petley, and Clews 1990). Typing the initial letter of a word took longer for compounds with opaque first constituents than for compounds with transparent first constituents (Gagné and Spalding 2014a). In terms of priming experiments, both transparent and opaque compounds show evidence of repetition priming, i.e., they both benefit from exposure to one of the constituents. However, only transparent compounds benefit from exposure to a word that is semantically related to one of the constituents (e.g., Sandra 1990). The locus of the difference in processing difficulty for transparent and opaque compounds appears to arise from the degree of competition or conflict between aspects of the whole-word and the constituents. For example, manipulations that aid parsing of the compound and the identification of the constituents (such as presenting the constituents in different colors or inserting a space between the constituents) benefitted the processing of transparent compounds but slowed the processing of opaque compounds (Ji et al. 2011). Studies measuring typing latencies (e.g., Libben and Weber 2014) found that there is an increase in latency for the first letter of the second constituent relative to the last letter of the first constituent and that this delay is smaller for fully opaque compounds than for fully transparent or partially-opaque compounds. Although coming from a variety of tasks, these findings are similar in that they suggest that compound processing involves not only access of the entire word, but also access of the constituents.

Given that the constituents of a compound appear to be available during processing, this raises questions concerning the role of those constituents. In particular, are the constituents used to access the whole word recognition via conjunctive activation or are they actively involved in some sort of meaning construction process, as is the case during conceptual combination for novel combination (Gagné and Spalding 2009)? Central to this issue is the notion of compositionality (cf. Acquaviva 2017; Rainer et al. 2014). Is it the case that compounds are fully compositional in that their entire meaning can be derived solely from the constituents? Probably not. There are always aspects that are not directly known from the parts alone but are known only via the combination of those parts. However, in this sense, the same can be said of other constructions such as noun phrases. To take an example dating back to early work on conceptual combination, the knowledge that a *wooden spoon* is made of wood and that a *metal spoon* is made of metal can be determined from the linguistic construction and knowledge of the constituent concepts. However, the knowledge that wooden spoons are larger than metal spoons and are more likely to be used for cooking than for eating is not directly inherited from each constituent directly but is something that is inferred based on the combination, as well as from world knowledge. Thus, the lack of full predictability in terms of meaning does not necessarily entail that compounds are not compositional. On the contrary, even partial compositionality provides some aspects of a compound's meaning. For example, people can determine that a raspberry is some type of berry even though they are not entirely sure what the "rasp" contributes to it. Indeed, knowledge of the constituents does allow for the creation of a gist-based interpretation and the ease of construction of this interpretation influences ease of processing (e.g., Gagné and Spalding 2014b; Schmidtke et al. 2016).

4 Compound heads and compound modifiers

Relations among compound words and their constituents offer a special opportunity to understand how word and constituent meanings interact in lexical representation and processing. Moreover, it creates comparable opportunities across languages. As Dressler (2006) has noted, compounding is a near ubiquitous feature of word formation across languages. And, the fact that compound words, by definition, are composed of two or more lexical elements, makes them an ideal word type with which to examine cross-linguistic similarities and differences. For example, in English, as in all Germanic languages, all compounds are "head-final" – the last element of the compound carries its grammatical features and typically signifies its semantic category. Thus, whereas a *skateboard* is a type of *board* (because *board* is the final element, a *boardroom* could never be a type of *board*. It must be a type of *room*. There are languages for which this order is reversed. In Hebrew, for example, all compounds are head initial so that the word *chessboard* has the form *board-checkmate* (*lu'ach shachmat*). French, like other Romance languages has both head-initial and head-final compounding, with a preference for the head-initial variation. Thus, in French, the compound *skateboard* is a compound with board as its initial element (*planche à roulette*).[1]

5 Non-lexical elements within compounds

As the French example above illustrates, not all languages represent compound words as simple concatenations of lexical elements. The compound *planche à roulette*, for example contains the preposition *à*, (meaning *to* in English). The presence of such grammatical elements is not at all uncommon and can also be seen in some (rare) English forms such as *man-of-war*. Although prepositions within compounds seem to signal the semantic relation between the lexical elements of a compound, it is not clear that they are used by language users during lexical comprehension or that they add comprehensibility. The word for *potato* in French is the compound *pomme de terre* (apple of the earth), which contains the preposition *de* (meaning *of*). The words for *apple* in Dutch and Austrian German contain the same lexical elements, with no preposition (*ardappel, Erdapfel,* respectively) and, of course, have the exact same meaning. In Hebrew and in Persian it has the same lexical elements (*earth* and *apple*), but, again, no intervening prepositional element.

---

1 The compounds we cite as examples can be described as endocentric (see Bisetto & Scalise 2005). These are typically words for which the compound is a hyponym of its head element (e.g., *housecat* is a type of *cat*, *boxcar* is a type of *car*). Exocentric compounds (e.g. *egghead, scarecrow*) are less common and show a much less straightforward relation between the final element and the whole compound (e.g., An *egghead* is not a type of *head*, but rather a type of person; a *scarecrow* is not a type of *crow*, but rather a figure of a man placed in a field in order to scare crows away).

In addition to overt prepositions, compounds can contain internal elements, most often referred to as interfixes. A very common type of interfix is the vowel 'o', which can be seen in the English word *gasometer* and *thermometer* (Dressler and Barbaresi 1991). This particular interfix can be traced back to a thematic vowel in Latin and Ancient Greek. It is widespread in Romance languages and Modern Greek, e.g. Italian *sessu-o-fobo* 'sex-o-phobic', Greek. *xart-o-péktis* 'card player' (< *xartí* 'card' and *péktis* 'player', Ralli 1992: 152), as well as in Slavic languages, e.g. Polish *kraj-o-znawstwo* (literally 'country science', meaning the study of national customs). Germanic languages such as Dutch commonly also show interfixes, as does German, which has a very complex system of interfixation in which compound words can have no interfix or the interfixes 'e', en', 'n', 's', and 'er', as in the word *Kindergarten*, which is composed of the elements *kind+er+garten*, meaning *child* + interfix + *garden*. Although it seems that, in principle, the presence of such interfixes could serve as constituent boundary markers that aid in the on-line processing of compound words, current evidence suggests that compounds with interfixes are processed more slowly than those without interfixes (Dressler et al. 2001).

6 Compound words across writing systems

As the French example above illustrates, not all languages represent compound words in their orthography as single words. German, as a language, is famous in the popular literature for having extremely long compounds. However, as shown in our examples of *boxcar wheel* and *railway boxcar* above, the presence of three constituent and four constituent compounds is not unusual in English either. The difference, of course is that German compounds are written without spaces between constituents whereas, in English, compounds with more than two constituents are written with at least one space at the point of the major constituent boundary. The result, from a processing perspective, is that a person reading a German compound is faced with the challenge of finding the constituent morphemes. At the other extreme are writing systems for Chinese (and Japanese Kanji) in which the reader has the opposite challenge. In Chinese, which also has a great deal of compounding, the reader needs to correctly group characters so that constituent morphemes are joined into compound structures because the constituent morphemes are represented as single characters surrounded by spaces (see Miwa, Libben, and Yu 2017).

It is not always the case that compounds are represented in a consistent form in a language's writing system. In English, whether a compound is written as two words, as a hyphenated word, or as a single word is generally related to the extent to which it is lexicalized. There are, however, many exceptions (e.g., *ice cream*) in which a high frequency compound is written as two words, or in different ways, depending on context (e.g., *ice cream* vs. *ice-cream cone*). As reported by Bertram (2012), Finnish has shown a tendency to use hyphenation to increase reading transparency. Bertram et al.(2011) have also reported the development of within-experiment processing advantages when hyphens are inserted into Dutch and Finnish compounds that are normally written as one word. These apparent examples of hyphenation advantages in the processing of existing compounds points to the conclusion that facilitating constituent access has processing advantages and thus that such constituent access is integral to normal compound word processing.

7 Productivity

Productivity of word formation is a multifaceted linguistic construct (see Bauer 2001; Dal and Namer 2017; Plag 1999) that basically refers to the potential to form new words to express a concept with a given pattern or word-formation rule.

As we noted at the outset of this chapter, compounding, particularly in languages such as English and German is extremely productive. New words will often be coined through compounding. Because the meanings of newly coined compounds are scaffolded by the meanings of the words to which their constituents are related, they are much easier to understand than monomorphemic neologisms would be. For example, the 2017 additions to the Mirriam Webster English dictionary include the compounds *abandonware*, *binge-watch*, *photobomb*, and *humblebrag*. It is testimony to the productivity of compounding as a word formation process in English that the reader will not be terribly surprised to learn that *humblebrag* means 'to make a seemingly modest, self-critical, or casual statement or reference that is meant to draw attention to one's admirable or impressive qualities or achievements'.

It is noteworthy that *humblebrag* is easily understood despite the fact that neither the constituents *humble* nor *brag* commonly participate in English compounding. The effects of compound productivity are yet stronger when there is a known pattern. For example, given the pattern *Brazil nut*, *peanut*, *pine nut*, and *hazelnut*, a new compound (e.g., *orange nut*) is easily incorporated into the morphological family.

Productive patterns differ among languages along a number of dimensions, including obligatoriness. In Slavic languages, for example, the medial insertion of the interfix –e- or –o- is obligatory (e.g. Russian *zemlʹ+e+trˋasenie* 'earthquake', where the interfix –e- replaces the feminine nominative singular stem ending -a of *zemlʹa* 'earth').

More productive patterns produce more new words than less productive patterns. This relates to the profitability of a pattern in both type and token frequency. However profitability may also be restricted by grammatical restrictions, for example in the above-mentioned Russian pattern, where after a root-final palatalized consonant, such as *lʹ*, an -e-interfix has to be inserted, whereas it is an -o-interfix that must be inserted after a root-final non-palatalized consonant. An additional consideration is that pragmatics may have an impact on frequency, e.g. which pattern is deemed to be fashionable.

Dressler (2007) has argued that the most productive patterns apply to new foreign words whose shape is thereby adapted to conditions holding for earlier existing words. An example is the German compound *Firm+en+gruppe* 'group of firms', where the -en- interfix replaces the final stem vowel of *Firma*. Less productive rules may have more restricted application, so that they apply to native words, but not to foreign words. The reason for this is that creating a new word on the basis of a new foreign word violates existing lexical norms more than creating a new word on the basis of a well-established existing word.

Productivity is clearly a scalar concept ranging from fully productive patterns to unproductive ones. No new words are created non-intentionally or subconsciously, i.e. with little language awareness via an unproductive pattern (see Dal and Namer 2017: 71–73). But poets (and, similarly, advertisers) may use unproductive patterns in creating occasionalisms for a poetic function at a specific place in a text. For example, in his novel *Der Tod des Vergil* 'The Death of Vergil', the Austrian poet Hermann created many 'occasional' compounds, such as *Tod und Aber+tod* 'deaths and deaths again' with the isolated first member *aber*, which recurs only in the unproductive compound *aber+mals* 'again' and in the unproductive pattern restricted to high numbers, such as *hunderte und aber+hunderte* 'hundreds upon hundreds of'.

Although the notion of productivity refers to potential words that can be created through a word formation pattern, when that potential is realized, it shapes the patterns of actual words in the language. Thus, the richness of compounding in a language is very much related to the number of productive compounding patterns that the language possesses.

8 The acquisition of compound knowledge

Productivity is also important for language acquisition: In languages with rich and productive compounding, the degree of richness of compounding in child-directed speech is predictive for the age at which compounds become productive in child speech. As reported in Dressler, Ketrez, and Kilani-Schoch (2017), this occurs earlier in children acquiring Danish, German, Estonian, Finnish and Saami than in acquiring French, Greek, Russian and Hebrew, where compounding is less productive (cf. Berman 2009; Dressler, Lettner, and Korecky-Kröll 2010 and the chapter by Keuleers, Ravid, and Dressler 2020, in this volume).

Productive use of compounding by children is demonstrated in the frequency of compound types and the co-occurrence of at least a small family size of their compound members either in the same position in a compound and/or by being produced as autonomous words. This is most often followed by children's creative formation of novel words, such as Danish *bamse+hund* 'teddy bear dog', *hunde+mann* 'dog man' (both produced at age 2;4, Kjærbæk and Basbøll 2017). All such neologisms produced by children are morphosemantically transparent, which is not the case for adults (Mattiello and Dressler 2018), who often form new morphosemantically opaque compounds by analogy to already existing morphosemantically opaque compounds as in *babymoon* created in analogy to *honeymoon*. This difference points to a view in which compounding may begin with spontaneous productivity from which later analogical patterns develop.

Early emergence of compounding is facilitated by morphotactic (or phonological) transparency, which in turn facilitates morphological decomposition of complex words and word forms (cf. Aksu-Koç and Slobin 1985; Dressler, Ketrez, and Kilani-Schoch 2017). Thus, in German, compounding that involves the simple concatenation of words (e.g. *Polizei+auto* 'police car') emerges earlier than any compounding patterns that insert an interfix (or linking morpheme) between the two words (e.g. *-n*-interfix in *Orange+n+zuckerl* 'orange candy'). Productivity and transparency enable children acquiring agglutinating languages, such as Finnish and Saami, to produce compounds precociously. Furthermore, exocentric compounds (e.g. *hot-head*) are more opaque than endocentric ones, because they only have a covert head, i.e. the head must be reconstructed. This explains their rarity in adult languages and especially in child-speech.

The approach of Lexical Typology, which compares in an onomasiological way whether complex concepts are expressed by compounds, derivations, multilexical words, phrases or simplex words in various languages, allows us to characterize the relative prominence of compounding in these languages and also to predict the prominence of compounding in child language (Dressler, Ketrez, and Kilani-Schoch 2017), both in terms of early emergence and in type and token frequency, provided that the prominence in child-directed speech does not differ much from prominence, as found in corpora, dictionaries and grammars.

Since compounded nouns are the most diffused types of compounds, probably due to a certain noun bias of many languages, it is no wonder that compounded nouns are often the first to emerge in child speech. Moreover, both child-directed and child speech show in most languages of the sample studied in Dressler, Ketrez, and Kilani-Schoch (2017) a clear preference for a noun in the non-head position. In some of them noun-noun compounds are the only ones produced in early child speech.

9 Conclusions and implications for the mental representation and processing of compound words

Our discussion of compound words began with the claim that compounding may be the oldest of human morphological processes. As the considerations above suggest, it may also be the best. Because the morphological components of compounds are relatively unconstrained positionally (e.g. a noun such as *board* can be both the modifier in a compound noun such as *boardroom* and the head in a compound noun such as *surfboard*), a large number of compounds can be created from a small number of lexical constituents. The development of compound families may serve to organize lexical knowledge in the mind so that conceptual associations are scaffolded by lexical overlap.

An important feature of compounding is its transparency of structure. As we have noted above, native speakers of a language can easily identify compounds as words that contain lexical subunits. Thus, at the conscious level and in the automatic processes of online lexical processing, compounds have constituent structure.

It seems that this dual nature has substantial processing advantages. It maximizes the opportunity for meaning creation, it maximizes the opportunity for linkage within the mental lexicon, and it provides both the means and motivation for lexical expansion across the lifespan and within a language community. Compound constituents play a role not only in word creation, but also routinely during language comprehension and production. If this were not the case, it would be difficult to explain why the semantic transparency of known compound words would play a role in lexical recognition and production. Indeed, numerous studies have demonstrated that when a compound word such as *boxcar* is encountered its processing by native speakers of a language includes the activation of *box* and *car* as distinct units (Gagné 2017; Libben 2014). At present, it is less clear whether constituent activation effects are present when compound words are read in connected text and the extent to which the effects seen in visual word recognition are as evident in auditory processing or in language production, for which there has thus far been considerably less experimental evidence. Nevertheless, it seems to be the case that a summary statement concerning evidence to date on the representation and processing of compound words in the mind might be as follows.

Compound words that are easiest to process are those that belong to productive patterns, are morphologically simple (without interfixation), and are semantically transparent. Evidence thus far obtained in studies of online compound processing suggests that both whole word representations and constituents of compound words are activated. This activation is present whether or not compound words are semantically transparent and whether or not they are written with spaces, without spaces, or with hyphens. Thus, compound words are both greater than the sum of their parts and greater than the division of their wholes.

References

Acquaviva, Paolo. 2017. Morphological semantics. In Andrew Hippisley & Gregory Stump (eds.), *The Cambridge Handbook of Morphology*, 117–148. Cambridge: Cambridge University Press.

Aksu-Koç, Ayhan & Dan I. Slobin. 1985. The acquisition of Turkish. In Dan I. Slobin (ed.), *The Crosslinguistic Study of Language Acquisition*, Hillsdale, NJ: Lawrence Erlbaum, 839–878.

Anderson, Stephen 1992. *A-Morphous Morphology*. Cambridge: Cambridge University Press.

Aristotle. *Poetics*. (E.M. Edgehill, Translation), retrieved from http://classics.mit.edu//Aristotle/poetics.html April 5, 2013.

Bauer, Laurie. 2001. *Morphological Productivity*. Cambridge: Cambridge University Press.

Berman, Ruth A. 2009. Acquisition of compound constructions. In Pavol Štekauer & Rochelle Lieber (eds.), *Handbook of Compounding*, 298–322. Oxford: Oxford University Press, 298–322.

Bertram, Raymond. 2012. Eye movements and morphological processing in reading. In Gary Libben, Gonia Jarema & Chris Westbury (eds.), *Methodological and analytic frontiers in lexical research*, 279–305. John Benjamins.

Bertram, Raymond, Victor Kuperman, R. Harald Baayen & Jukka Hyönä. 2011. The hyphen as a segmentation cue in triconstituent compound processing: It's getting better all the time. *Scandinavian Journal of Psychology* 52. 530–544.

Bisetto, Antonietta & Sergio Scalise. 2005. The classification of compounds. *Lingue e Linguaggio*, IV (2), 319–332.

Dal, Georgette & Fiammetta Namer. (2017). Productivity. In Andrew Hippisley & Gregory Stump (eds.) *The Cambridge Handbook of Morphology*, 70–89. Cambridge: Cambridge University Press.

Dressler, Wolfgang U. 2006. Compound types. In Gary Libben & Gonia Jarema (eds.), *The representation and processing of compound words*, 23–44. Oxford University Press.

Dressler, Wolfgang U. (2007). Productivity in word formation. In Gonia Jarema & Gary Libben (eds.), *The Mental Lexicon: Core Perspectives*, 159–183. Amsterdam: Elsevier.

Dressler, Wolfgang U., F. Nihan Ketrez & Marianne Kilani-Schoch (eds.). 2017. *Nominal Compound Acquisition*. Amsterdam: Benjamins.

Dressler, Wolfgang U., Laura E. Lettner & Katharina E. Korecky-Kröll. 2010. First language acquisition of compounds: with special emphasis on early German child language. In: Sergio Scalise & Irene Vogel (eds.), *Cross-disciplinary issues in compounding*, 323–344. Amsterdam: Benjamins.

Dressler, Wolfgang U., Gary Libben, Jacqueline Stark, C. Pons & Gonia Jarema. 2001. The processing of interfixed German compounds. In Geert Booij and Jap van Marle (eds.), *Yearbook of Morphology*, 185–220. Dordrecht: Kluwer Academic.

Dressler, Wolfgang U. & Lavinia Merlini Barbaresi. 1991. Elements of morphopragmatics. In Jef Verschueren (ed.), *Levels of linguistic adaptation*, 33–51. John Benjamins. doi: 10.1075/pbns.6.2.04dre

Fanselow, Gisbert. 1985. Die Stellung der Wortbildung im System kognitiver Module. *Linguistische Berichte* 96. 91–126.

Fiorentino, Robert & Ella Fund-Reznicek. 2009. Masked morphological priming of compound constituents. *The Mental Lexicon* 4(2). 159–193.

Gagné, Christina L. 2017. Psycholinguistic Approaches to Morphology. In Mark Aronoff (ed.), *Oxford Research Encyclopedia of Linguistics*. Oxford: Oxford University Press. doi: 10.1093/acrefore/9780199384655.013.258

Gagné, Christina L., & Thomas L. Spalding. 2009. Constituent integration during the processing of compound words: Does it involve the use of relational structures? *Journal of Memory and Language*, 60, 20–35. doi:10.1016/j.jml.2008.07.003

Gagné, C. L. & Thomas L. Spalding. 2014a. Adaptation effects in lexical processing. *Suvremena Lingvistika* (Contemporary Linguistics) 40. 127–149.

Gagné, Christina L., & Thomas L. Spalding. 2014b. Conceptual composition: The role of relational competition in the comprehension of modifier-noun phrases and noun-noun compounds. In Brian H. Ross (ed.), *The psychology of learning and motivation*, 97–130. New York: Elsevier. doi:10.1016/B978-0-12-407187-2.00003-4

Gagné, Christina L., Thomas L. Spalding & Kelly A. Nisbet. 2016. Processing English compounds: Investigating semantic transparency. *SKASE Journal of Theoretical Linguistics* 13(2). 2–22.

Ji, H., Gagné, C. L., & Spalding, T. L. (2011). Benefits and costs of lexical decomposition and semantic integration during the processing of transparent and opaque English compounds. *Journal of Memory & Language*, 65, 406–430.

Jackendoff, Ray. 2002. *Foundations of Language: Brain, Meaning, Grammar, and Evolution*. Oxford: Oxford University Press.

Jackendoff, R. (2010). *Meaning and the lexicon: the parallel architecture*. New York: Oxford University Press.

Kjærbæk, Laila & Hans Basbøll. 2017. *Compound Nouns in Danish child language.* In Wolfgang U. Dressler, W. U., F. Nihan Ketrez & Marianne Kilani-Schoch (eds.), *Nominal Compound Acquisition*, 39–62. Amsterdam: Benjamins.

Kuperman, Victor. 2013. Accentuate the positive: Semantic access in English compounds. *Frontiers in Psychology* 4(203),1–10. https://www.frontiersin.org/article/10.3389/fpsyg.2013.00203 (accessed 5 August 2019)

Lieber, Rochelle & Pavol Štekauer. 2009. Introduction: status and definition of compounding. In Rochelle Lieber & Pavol Štekauer (eds), *The Oxford handbook of compounding*, 3–18. Oxford: Oxford University Press.

Libben, Gary. 1998. Semantic transparency in the processing of compounds: Consequences for representation, processing, and impairment. *Brain and Language* 61. 30–44.

Libben, Gary. 2010. Compound words, semantic transparency, and morphological transcendence. In Susan Olsen (ed.), *New impulses in word-formation*, 317–330. Hamburg: Buske.

Libben, Gary. 2014. The nature of compounds: a psychocentric perspective. *Cognitive Neuropsychology* 31. 8–25. doi:10.1080/02643294.2013.874994

Libben, Gary. 2017. The quantum metaphor and the organization of words in the mind. *Cultural Cognitive Science* 1. 49–55. doi:10.1007/s41809-017-0003-5

Libben, Gary, Martha Gibson, M., Yeo Bom Yoon & Dominiek Sandra. 2003. Compound fracture: The role of semantic transparency and morphological headedness. *Brain and Language* 84. 50–64.

Libben, Gary & Silke Weber. 2014. Semantic transparency, compounding, and the nature of independent variables. In Franz Rainer, Francesco Gardani, Hans Christian Luschützky & Wolfgang U. Dressler (eds.), *Morphology and meaning*, 205–222.Amsterdam: Benjamins.

Mattiello, Elisa & Wolfgang U. Dressler. 2018. The Morphosemantic Transparency/Opacity of Novel English Analogical Compounds and Compound Families. *Studia Anglica Posnaniensia* 53. 67–114. doi: 10.2478/stap-2018-0004.

Miwa, Koji, Gary Libben & Ikemoto Yu. 2017. Visual trimorphemic compound recognition in a morphographic script. *Language, Cognition and Neuroscience* 32 (1). 1–20. doi:10.1080/23273798.2016.1205204

Pelletier, Francis J. 2016. Semantic Compositionality. *Oxford Research Encyclopedia of Linguistics*. http://linguistics.oxfordre.com/view/10.1093/acrefore/9780199384655.001.0001/acrefore-9780199384655-e-42 (Accessed 29 Oct. 2017).

Plag, Ingo. 1999. *Morphological Productivity: Structural Constraints in English Derivation*. Mouton de Gruyter.

Rainer, Franz, Wolfgang U. Dressler, Francesco Gardani & Hans Christian Luschützky. 2014. Morphology and meaning: An overview. In Franz Rainer, Francesco Gardani, Hans Christian Luschützky & Wolfgang U. Dressler (eds), *Morphology and Meaning*, 4–46. Amsterdam: Benjamins.

Ralli, Angela. 1992. Compounds in Modern Greek. *Rivista di Linguistica* 4(1). 143–173.

Sandra, Dominiek. 1990. On the representation and processing of compound words: automatic access to constituent morphemes does not occur. *Quarterly Journal of Experimental Psychology* 42. 529–567.

Schmidtke, Daniel, Victor Kuperman, Christina L. Gagné & Thomas L. Spalding. 2016. Competition between conceptual relations affects compound recognition: The role of entropy. *Psychonomic Bulletin & Review* 23(2). 556–570.

Smolka, Eva & Gary Libben. 2017. 'Can you wash off the hogwash?' – semantic transparency of first and second constituents in the processing of German compounds and compounding. *Language, Cognition and Neuroscience* 32(4). 514–531.

Underwood, Geoffrey, Kate Petley & Susan Clews. 1990. Searching for information during sentence comprehension. In Rudolf Gruner, Géry d'Ydewalle & Ruth Parham (eds.), *From eye to mind: Information acquisition in perception*, 191–203. Amsterdam: North Holland.

Paolo Acquaviva, Alessandro Lenci, Carita Paradis and
Ida Raffaelli
Models of lexical meaning

Abstract: Lexical semantics is concerned with modeling the meaning of lexical items. Its leading questions are how forms and meanings combine, what they mean, how they are used, and of course also how they change. The answers to these five questions make up the fundamental theoretical assumptions and commitments which underlie different theories of lexical semantics, and they form the basis for their various methodological choices. In this chapter, we discuss four main models of lexical meaning: relational, symbolic, conceptual and distributional. The aim is to investigate their historical background, their specific differences, the methodological and theoretical assumptions that lie behind those differences, the main strengths and the main challenges of each perspective.

Keywords: relational approach, symbolic approach, cognitive semantics, distributional semantics, lexical meaning, polysemy, color terms, semantic coercion, structuralist semantics

1 Introduction

While we might say that the first stages of lexical semantics originated already in the first decades of the 19th century, its orientation during the first 100 years was historical and its main concern was diachronic lexical change (Geeraerts 2010). Lexical semantics as we see it today is concerned with modeling the meaning of lexical items. Its leading questions are how forms and meanings combine, what they mean, how they are used, and of course also how they change. These aspects are challenging, since language is dynamic and word meanings are not easily placed in neat little boxes. Meaning definition, description and explanation are hard nuts for all semanticists, irrespective of theoretical affiliation and

---

Paolo Acquaviva, University College Dublin, School of Languages, Cultures and Linguistics, Dublin 4, Ireland
Alessandro Lenci, Università di Pisa, Dipartimento di Filologia, Letteratura e Linguistica, Pisa, Italy
Carita Paradis, Lund University, Centre for Languages and Literature, Lund, Sweden
Ida Raffaelli, Faculty of Humanities and Social Sciences, University of Zagreb, Department of Linguistics, Zagreb, Croatia

∂ Open Access. © 2020 Paolo Acquaviva et al., published by De Gruyter. This work is licensed under a Creative Commons Attribution-NonCommercial-NoDerivatives 4.0 International License.
https://doi.org/10.1515/9783110440577-010

scientific priorities. If the priority is to describe the empirical domain of meanings in real language in a sufficiently fine-grained way, to be able to explain the mappings of concepts to forms, to account for how meanings of lexical items are learned and how meanings change, then a methodology must be selected that meets those requirements. If, on the other hand, concerns of economy and explicit formalization take priority over the need to consider language use in all its guises, then another type of methodology is called for. In other words, our research questions, our scope and priorities govern our methods.

Paradis (2012) establishes five questions that are of key importance to any theory of lexical semantics which makes claims to be a coherent framework within which lexical meanings can be described and explained:
– What is the nature of meaning in language?
– What is the relation between words and their meanings?
– How are meanings of words learned and stored?
– How are meanings of words communicated and understood by language users?
– How and why do meanings of words change?

The answers to these five questions make up the fundamental theoretical assumptions and commitments which underlie different theories of lexical semantics, and they form the basis for their various methodological choices. Related to the research questions and the basic assumptions of meaning in language is the question of how meaning representations can and should be modeled, how meanings relate to world knowledge and at what level of granularity. Four main approaches emerge as important, each with its own merits and limitations: relational, symbolic, conceptual and distributional.

The *relational approach* is mainly associated with paradigms that view lexical meaning as a network of mutually influencing intralinguistic relations. The structuralist paradigm (one of the most prominent relational approaches), conceived foremost by Saussure, argues for a twofold understanding of the nature of lexical meaning. The first one is that meaning is realized as an interrelation between the sound-image and the concept (the signifier and the signified) and that it is bidirectional, each evoking the other. This conception was later elaborated by Ullmann (1969) in his semantic triangle as one of the main principles of the communication process, as a model of how lexical meaning is realized between the speaker and the listener. The second one includes the notion of the *value* that is in the core of language as a system. Language is a system of interdependent terms in which the value of each term results solely from the simultaneous presence of the others (Saussure 1986: 114). The value influences the meaning of the lexical item, but it is external to it. Its content is fixed by the association of everything that exists outside it. Being part of a system, the lexical item is endowed not only with a meaning but also with a value that determines the position of the lexical item with respect to other units in the language system (Saussure 1986: 116). The structuralist paradigm has a clear stance about how lexical meaning changes. Coseriu (1973) makes a clear distinction between innovations that are driven by individuals in language use, on the one hand, and meaning change that amounts to an innovation that has become an element of the language system, thus influencing other (lexical) meanings within the system. The structuralist approach was well aware of language use as a source of meaning change. However, its research focus was oriented towards the interdependency of one lexical meaning to another. This is the main reason why lexical-semantic relations such as synonymy and antonymy are considered as the most prominent types of relations that the structuralist paradigm deals with. On the other hand, polysemy, which clearly shows that the distinction between usage and the system is not clear-cut, was neglected by many structuralist scholars.

Next, the *symbolic approach* to meaning-making in languages is employed by the generativist school of thought as well as by formalists more generally. Meanings are represented by symbols and processed through symbol manipulation following explicit rules. The content of a sentence equals the beliefs or thoughts, which are connected to each other via inferential relations. In other words, language is modeled as a string of symbols that are parsed in the computation according to a set of grammatical rules. The computational system operates on the syntactic structures in the derivation. The nodes of the structure are filled with semantic features which eventually interact with general cognitive and motor abilities. The language faculty is distinct from the latter systems but interfaces with them, which makes inferencing and verbal use of natural language possible. While the interpretation of an expression is relative to a context, the way symbols are manipulated is independent of the environment, that is, of factors like the communicative situation, the speakers, or the type of discourse. The advantages of such an approach are that some very general aspects of language structure can be captured and described. Its limitations emerge when it comes to modeling rich meaning representations, and it has not much to say when it comes to explanations for concept acquisition, variation, language shifts and change, metaphorization and language use in different discourses (Eckardt 2006).

The third approach to the modeling of representations, the *conceptual approach*, embraces all kinds of meanings, not only formalizable meanings, and takes an interest in the psychological side of language understanding and the richness of lexical knowledge. This approach provides the tools for the investigation of concept formation based on spatial structures, shifts in meaning and motivations for polysemies such as metonymization, metaphorization and constructionalization (Croft and Cruse 2004, Paradis 2011, Traugott and Trousdale 2013), which represent significant challenges for the structuralist and the symbolic approach. The approach to the analysis of meaning in language is usage-based and as a consequence it takes an interest in the description and explanation of language use in all its structural and cultural complexity. This approach is represented by the Cognitive Linguistics school of thought, which relies on dynamic and spatial structures, variously referred to as image schemas (Langacker 1987, Lakoff 1987, Talmy 2000), configurations and construals (Paradis 2005, 2015) and conceptual spaces or the geometry of meaning (Croft, 2012, Gärdenfors 2014). These are all theoretical entities that are used to describe, predict and explain the phenomena in language use that the research focusses on.

The fourth model of semantic representation, the *distributional approach*, is grounded on the assumption that lexical meaning depends on the contexts in which lexemes are used. At least parts of a word content can be characterized by its contextual representation, to be defined as an abstraction over the linguistic contexts in which a word is encountered (Miller and Charles 1991). In distributional approaches, semantic similarity of lexical items is treated as a dependent variable of the contexts in which they are used, that is a function of their contextual representations. Distributional semantics is not only an assumption about meaning representations, but it is also a computational framework to learn them from linguistic distributions automatically extracted from corpora. Lexemes are in fact represented with real-valued vectors encoding their co-occurrence statistics with linguistic contexts. Semantic similarity among lexemes is then modeled by measuring their vector similarity. Methods for computational analysis of word distributional properties have been developed both in computational linguistics and in psychology (Lenci 2008, 2018). In the cognitive sciences, many researchers have strongly argued for the psychological validity of distributional representations as models of semantic memory (Landauer and Dumais 1997, Jones, Willits, and Dennis 2015). For instance, corpus-derived measures of semantic similarity have been assessed in a variety of psychological tasks ranging from similarity judgments to modeling of semantic and associative priming, categorization, and predicate-argument thematic fit. Innovative applications of distributional semantics are also being explored in linguistics, for instance in the study of semantic change (Sagi, Kaufmann, and Clark 2009) and lexical variation (Peirsman and Speelman 2009), to provide the notion of synonymy with a more robust empirical foundation (Geeraerts 2010), and for the diachronic investigation of construction productivity (Perek 2016).

In Section 2, we review the main properties of the four models of lexical meaning we have sketched above. In Section 3, we consider two specific empirical domains and the challenges that they pose to these models, namely color terms and semantic flexibility in context.

2 Perspectives on lexical meaning

This section overviews various perspectives on lexical meaning emerging from different theoretical approaches: grouping large families of analyses under broad labels, we review first structuralist approaches, then approaches that share a formal and symbolic orientation, then the Cognitive Linguistics approach, and finally the recent development of structuralist approaches known as distributional semantics. As will be seen, fundamentally different theoretical choices lead to analyses that highlight different aspects of the phenomena, and in many respects complement each other.

2.1 The structuralist perspective

One of the main properties of the structuralist paradigm is its diversity of approaches and models. Although it is a relationally-oriented paradigm, focused on investigating lexical meaning from an intralinguistic perspective, the structuralist paradigm embraces a diversity of models and approaches that showcase a close relation to some contemporary models. This is especially relevant for what is known as the field theory elaborated by Trier (1931). In Trier's terms lexical fields differ from conceptual fields. A lexical field covers the extension of a conceptual field. All lexemes are of equal importance in structuring a field. A lexical field is composed of paradigmatically related lexemes, frequently parasynonyms, with a shared unique conceptual base. The main idea of field theory is that lexical items do not exist in isolation. Being members of a field, lexemes are an integrative part of the language system, sharing with other members of the field the same conceptual, that is to say, semantic area. Trier's model is often regarded as the most prominent field model within the structuralist paradigm. The idea of clear-cut boundaries between lexemes within a field and between fields has been strongly criticized, especially by cognitive linguists.

However, it should be pointed out that there are some field models within the structuralist paradigm that are clearly distinguished from Trier's model, although sharing some main features with it. Most notably, these are Guiraud's model of morphosemantic fields (1967) and Baldinger's model of onomasiological fields (1984). They both share with Trier's model the idea of lexemes interrelated in sense. They differ with respect to the way they see the organization of lexemes within the field. The structure of morphosemantic fields, as well as onomasiological fields, broadly corresponds to the principles of prototype organization of categories and lexical structures. In other words, lexemes do not have an identical role in structuring the field (as they do according to Trier): one of them is the center or the core of the field, and others, depending on their characteristics, are positioned closer to it or further away from it. Therefore, morphosemantic and onomasiological fields are heterogeneous, as opposed to Trier's fields which are homogeneous.

Morphosemantic and onomasiological fields differ in their structure. Both are organized around a central lexeme, which is related to other lexemes by derivational and semantic processes (for morphosemantic fields) or by their semantic structure (for ononomasiological fields). The difference lies in the nature of the relation between the central element and the others. In a morphosemantic field, the center is a lexeme that is the morphological and semantic basis for all the derivationally motivated lexemes. Thus, the Croatian adjective *jasan* 'clear' is the core lexeme of the field composed of lexemes formed from this adjective like *pojasniti* 'to clear', *objasniti* 'to explain', *izjasniti se* 'to declare oneself', and so on. The core of the onomasiological field is a lexeme that is most frequently used in the variety of senses largely corresponding to the conceptual background of the field. For example the Croatian verb *željeti* 'to wish' is the core of its onomasiological field since it is the verb most frequently used when talking about wishing something. It has the most general meaning and can appear in a variety of contexts, whereas *žudjeti* 'to long for' has a more specific meaning, and is used less frequently, and thus cannot be the center of the field. The usage of particular lexemes and their semantic structures are crucial for the internal organization of onomasiological fields, a fact which shows that lexical relations within the field are due to properties of individual lexemes. The model of onomasiological fields is an excellent example of the correlation between language use and language system that was not embraced by all models within the structuralist paradigm. It should be pointed out that Trier's field theory is regarded as a dominant structuralist model in the context of lexical field analysis. Cognitive Linguistics often criticizes Trier's conception of homogenous fields, claiming that they are better analyzed as heterogeneous and centered around a prototypical lexeme, with all other lexemes at various distances from it. Even such a brief overview, then, is enough to show that the structuralist conceptions of morphosemantic and onomasiological fields are distinct but parallel notions. It also evidences that the models for lexical description developed by the structuralist paradigm were more varied than is generally acknowledged. Thus, the structuralist paradigm should not be regarded in opposition to some of the Cognitive Linguistic tenets, but rather as its predecessor in some aspects.

Linguistic approaches and traditions differ in how they view the impact of use on the semantic structure of a lexeme. Broadly speaking, one of the most prominent models of lexical semantic analysis within the structuralist framework, namely componential analysis, has in all its versions ignored the impact of context and, in general, language use. Moreover, the components encoded by a lexical item have been defined as mirroring the main properties of referents.

These properties are considered as necessary and sufficient conditions, and thus as objective elements that form lexical meaning. Componential analysis detaches considerations of use from its description of lexical meaning, which is regarded as a stable and fixed structure that enters different types of intralinguistic relations. Therefore, as stated by Lakoff (1987: 157–184), componential analysis is considered as being part of the objectivist paradigm that describes meaning structure as a (logical) combination of components that are the primitive building blocks out of which complex categories (semantic structures) are constructed. Within the objectivist paradigm, the semantic structure is a product of a set of atomic concepts (Lyons 1993: 321) that describe it exhaustively.

Although it could be argued that the critique of componential analysis mainly comes from post-structuralist approaches, foremost Cognitive Linguistics, it has to be pointed out that even some of the most prominent structuralist scholars, like André Martinet or Georges Kleiber, were strict opponents to this model of meaning description. Kleiber (1978) claims that components, which correspond to the properties of entities in the real world, do not mirror any kind of contextual or syntagmatic constraints imposed on the lexical items. In other words, nothing in the componential analysis approach indicates the nature of contextual or syntagmatic constructions that determine the usage of a lexical item. Therefore, according to the componential analysis approach an utterance such as *The seat is ringing* would be unproblematic since there is no constituent that describes the semantic structure of the noun *seat* that would indicate that such a usage is not in accordance with our world knowledge that seats cannot ring, whereas telephones can.

André Martinet (1989) was also was also critical of componential analysis, considering it as a model that has not captured the main features of how lexical meaning is constructed (or construed). Martinet (1989) claims that for an in-depth analysis of lexical meaning it is necessary to know all the contexts in which a lexical item can appear. Thus, the only path to describe the meaning of a lexeme is through the analysis of contexts, that is the different usages of a lexical item. For Martinet, lexical meaning is a concrete realization of the lexical item in language use. To corroborate his claim, he gives examples of lexical items referring to abstract domains, such as *democracy, love,* or *government*. The meaning of these lexemes cannot be learned by ostension, like meanings of nouns referring to concrete domains like *chair, dog,* or *head*. Meanings of lexemes referring to abstract concepts can be learned only through their usage, that is, through the repetition of lexical items in certain contexts. Within the structuralist paradigm, such view of how lexical meaning is constructed, especially in Martinet's perspective, posits lexical meaning as an extralinguistic phenomenon that does not necessarily have an impact on the intralinguistic relations that constitute the language system.

For example, Coseriu (2000) argues that lexical meaning has to be described only with respect to intralinguistic relations. Contextual realizations of lexical items are rather *ad hoc* categorizations that have no impact on the language system. These stances are not completely in accordance with Baldinger's approach to onomasiological fields, as was previously indicated.

It was already pointed out by Saussure (1986) that language cannot be separated from language use or, in Saussurian terms, speaking. Language is a product that is passively assimilated by the individual. Speaking, on the other hand, is an individual act. It is deliberate and intellectual, and allows the speaker to use the language code to express his own thoughts. The liaison between language and speaking is clearly defined by Saussure and has become one of the backbones of modern linguistics. Language and speaking are interdependent. Language is necessary if speaking is to be intelligible and produce all its effects; but speaking is necessary for the establishment of language, and historically its actuality always comes first. Speaking is what causes language to evolve: impressions gathered from listening to others modify our linguistic habits (Saussure 1986: 18–19). However, Saussure is very clear about the object of modern linguistics. It is the language and language only and it cannot be confused with speaking. The boundaries between language and speaking should not be erased.

Although the claim about the clear boundaries between language and speaking was one of the principal tenets of structuralism, some linguists like Roman Jakobson thought that an important goal was to identify how certain aspects of lexical meaning, while realized in a context, acquire a decontextualized, context-invariant quality. A very clear definition of decontextualization as a process related to linguistic acquisition is given by Langacker (1987:63). According to him, decontextualization is an important process in acquiring a linguistic unit or a sense. If a property is constant across contexts the property may survive the decontextualization process and remain a semantic specification of the resulting unit. Decontextualization lies at the origin of every new sense that becomes an element of the semantic structure of a lexical item. Although Cognitive Linguistics in many of its approaches focuses on decontextualization as one of the major processes in acquisition of lexical meanings, it should be pointed out that this phenomenon was already analyzed by structuralists and can be traced back to the pre-structuralist linguistics as well.

Within the structuralist framework this phenomenon was explored in detail by Stephen Ullmann (1983) as shifts of applications. For example, the Croatian verb *skinuti* 'to take off (clothes or books from the shelf)' occurs often in contexts such as *skinuti nečije pokrete* 'to take off someone's gestures', *skinuti nečiji izraz lica* 'to take off someone's facial expression'. In these contexts, the verb *skinuti* realizes the sense 'to imitate'. Since such usage has recently become frequent, we could argue that the verb has developed a new sense that first appeared as a shift in application of the lexical item in a specific context, but it has become decontextualized over time. Both Jakobson and Ullmann see this phenomenon as one of the main sources of polysemy. This is quite similar to the Cognitive Linguistic point of view on polysemy as motivated by context and language use. Polysemy is one of the major topics in Cognitive Linguistics (Lakoff 1987; Langacker 1987; Paradis 2000, 2001; Taylor 2003, among others), since it reflects the impact language use has on the language system, that is, language knowledge. Differently from the structuralist paradigm, Cognitive Linguistics does not argue for clear boundaries between the two. What makes it partly similar to the structuralist paradigm is the view of language knowledge (i.e., system) and language use (i.e., speaking) as interrelated and at a high degree of correlation.

Frequency of usage has a huge impact on the change of lexical items, both at the formal and the semantic levels. The co-occurrence of two or more words that regularly and frequently appear together in different contexts was already identified by Antoine Meillet (1958) as one of the major sources of lexical and semantic changes. Although he was Saussure's disciple, Meillet's views on lexical semantics and semantic change are by and large rooted in a pre-structuralist interpretive framework. One of the most remarkable examples used already by Meillet is the origin of the French analytic negation system. In French there is a number of words that originally refer to concrete entities such as *personne* 'person', *pas* 'step', *point* 'dot', *rien* (Latin *res/rem* 'thing'). All these words acquired a new, negative sense because of their frequent usage with the adverbe *ne*. In French, *ne . . . .pas/point/person/rien* is an obligatory negative construction in which the words are used in their new senses, which were driven by the frequent and regular co-occurrence with the conjunction *ne*. Moreover, the noun *personne* means 'nobody' in the utterance such as *Qui as-tu vu? Personne.* 'Whom did you see? Nobody.' The origin of the French negation system is also an excellent example of syntactically or construction driven semantic change. The lexical items *pas* or *personne* have preserved both senses in modern French, which are realized in very different syntactic constructions. However, lexical meanings (very often the etymological ones) can disappear over time (see Geeraerts 1997). As shown in Raffaelli (2009), frequent usage of a lexical item in certain contexts could lead to the loss of the original sense of a certain lexical item. This is the case of the Croatian adjective *trudan* 'pregnant' whose original sense was 'hard', 'tired'. The utterance of the adjective in contexts related to pregnancy led to the semantic change of the adjective *trudan* which is nowadays used exclusively in the sense 'pregnant'. However, it is also an excellent example of the fact that language diversity (the existence of different dialects) has to be taken into account when some statements about language changes are given. The adjective *trudan* 'pregnant' has preserved its original sense in one of the Croatian dialects – the Čakavian dialect.

Language use is at the origin of language evolution, language acquisition and language organization, and the question of how language is used cannot be considered separated from the question of what language is. Although it is generally thought that the structuralist paradigm was primarily a relation-oriented approach mostly focused on intralinguistic relations, this brief discussion has illustrated some of the main ideas shared by structuralist and post-structuralist paradigms (especially Cognitive Linguistics) having their origins back in pre-structuralist approaches to lexical semantics (as shown with Meillet's examples). Thus, the structuralist paradigm should be regarded in correlation and not in opposition to what came before and what followed it.

2.2 Formal and symbolic approaches

Recent controversies like that involving Adger (2015a,b), Behme and Evans (2015), and Evans (2014) give the impression that much recent research stands opposed to an older paradigm, deductive, based on introspection, inattentive to the wealth of empirical phenomena uncovered by typological and quantitative approaches, entirely based on syntax, and revolving around the work of Noam Chomsky. In fact, this is by and large a strawman, as critics of so-called "formalist" (or, less aptly, "generative") models typically focus narrowly on certain methodological aspects of Minimalist syntax and of frameworks directly related to it (like Distributed Morphology), disregarding the enormous diversity of theoretical positions which can be termed (strictly or loosely) "Chomskyan", and the wealth of empirical evidence and falsifiable predictions contained in them. In fact, there is no coherent family of theories which could be meaningfully grouped under the label of "formal", especially from the perspective of their approach to semantics and, what is relevant here, lexical semantics. Instead of trying to outline a non-existent "formalist" view on the mental lexicon, it is instructive to consider how a specific set of assumptions about language and the mind can shape our research questions on the mental lexicon, and what distinctive contributions they have made and can make.

2.2.1 Meaning and lexical meaning

The claim of linguistic nativism is logically distinct from the claim that language can be modeled by means of symbolic representations involving specific formal tools (generative grammars). In principle, an innate language capacity could be characterized in different, non-formalized terms; for example, it might be framed as a description of the typological variation space based on non-categorical primitives (as "relative pronoun" or "purposive clause" or "agentivity" could be) and specifying a range of potentially language-specific combinatorial patterns. Conversely, a formal symbolic representation can aim at modeling just any information system, not just innate knowledge. The claim that linguistic behavior is best explained by reference to an innate linguistic capacity, and the claim that this capacity is best modeled by means of a formal generative grammar, are both substantive theoretical choices; but it is the second that more directly concerns the definition of lexical items and their content.

A very large family of approaches embraces a representational theory of the mind, and views language as tacit knowledge of a system. A theory of language in this perspective aims to model the content of this knowledge through rules and principles. Language is thus viewed as a mind-internal reality, with a precise psychological and neurological basis; however, most approaches aim to model the structure of the *content* of this knowledge, not directly of the mind states of speakers. Grammar thus models a knowledge that is bio-physically instantiated in the brain, but analyzes it at a level of abstraction. In the words of Adger (2015b):

> Generative grammar takes the right level of abstraction to be one at which a particular computable function can be specified, as this is the level at which an explanation can be given of a basic property of human beings: our capacity to systematically pair sound and meaning over an unbounded domain by using discrete symbolic resources. The explanation given by generative grammar is that the human mind implements a particular computable function that creates an unbounded set of hierarchically structured objects that interface in particular ways with the systems of sound and meaning.

From this perspective, lexical meaning, and linguistic meaning in general, is fundamentally a mind-internal construct, insofar as the theory models a mind-internal competence. This internalist stance, however, can be more or less prominent. The work of Noam Chomsky has consistently asserted the mind-internal nature of linguistic meaning, and denied the usefulness of world-determined reference. However, these considerations have little direct impact on his technical contributions, which mostly concern themselves with the combinatorial apparatus (a fully developed and original argument that addresses the notion of truth from a Minimalist perspective can instead be found in the work of Hinzen 2007). In contrast to this radically internalist stance, which minimizes the role of the relation between linguistic meaning and mind-external reality, classic model-theoretic semantics based on truth conditions is predicated of an externalist approach. The point has some significance, because semantic frameworks deriving from Montague semantics have historically evolved alongside Chomskyan models of syntax (Government-Binding and then Minimalism), often presupposing each other despite the sharply different philosophical assumptions. What is significant, and instructive, is that this contiguity has allowed formal syntax and semantics to develop as closely related subdisciplines sharing a large body of results.

Beside semantic internalism, "generative" models typically also subscribe to the view that language is a specific cognitive ability irreducible to non-linguistic ones. Linguistic knowledge, in this view, certainly interfaces with non-linguistic knowledge; but it is not subsumed by it, and in particular it is not based on mind-external properties of the body (as opposed to a strict interpretation of the thesis of embodied cognition). An influence of the human body in linguistically relevant categories can be compatible with this position, but not the idea that the mental lexicon, as a part of the theory of language, is shaped by mind-external factors.

Concerning specifically *lexical* meaning, what deserves to be highlighted is the theoretical sharpening of the notion of lexical item, and the vast body of generalizations and predictions that has resulted from approaches as different as syntax-based lexical decomposition (in several different varieties: von Stechow 1995, Hale and Keyser 2002, Ramchand 2008, Harley 2012, 2014, Borer 2013), Pustejovsky's Generative Lexicon framework (Pustejovsky 1995), Rothstein's (2004, 2010) semantic analyses of verbal and nominal predicates, and the decompositions into semantic primitives proposed by Lieber (2004), Jackendoff (1990, 2010, 2011), and above all Levin and Rappaport Hovav (Rappaport Hovav and Levin 1998, Levin and Rappaport Hovav 2011).

In all these approaches, and in others less directly related to lexical decomposition, the central role accorded to the combinatory principles underlying symbolic structures makes it imperative to specify the basic elements of these structures, their formal properties, how these properties relate to those of complex structural objects, and to what extent they can be equated with "words". As we will see in more detail in Section 2.2.2 below, it is often less than straightforward to precisely determine what linguistic element counts as a lexical item for semantic purposes, in part because a lexical item is often fully specified only in a given context. The content of lexical words, then, must be characterized in the larger semantic context above word level – lexical semantics is part of semantics. Besides, a satisfactory characterization should be framed in terms that can be applied to the typologically most diverse systems (including for instance polysynthetic languages, where the traditional notion of word is quite problematic), while guaranteeing predictivity and falsifiability: there are boundaries to the contents that can be lexicalized, as well as significant generalizations concerning the relation between the morphological make-up of a word and what it can mean. The "formal" theories that address these challenges attempt to elucidate lexical knowledge by means of representations that aspire to explicitness, and which aim to capture significant generalizations about what can and above all cannot be encapsulated in a word's meaning.

While the content of a concept can show gradience and prototype effects suggestive of a radial category, the theoretical terms used to model them in this type of approach are categorical, as items of a meta-language well distinct from any object natural language. Features, lexical categories, semantic categories, and similar formal tools do not have the function to model what speakers "have in mind" when they use language, but to provide the terms for what aims to be part of a theory of grammar as tacit knowledge. Thus, characterizations such as "negative", "nominal", "mass", or "imperfective", are typically reconstructed in formal terms using logical notions such as "monotone-decreasing" or "cumulative", or non-logical terms that define, for example, categories like nouns or verbs as clusters of features, or structural configurations (as in Distributed Morphology, or in Borer's Exoskeletal framework). Evidently it is an open question, and one that can be decided (at least in part) empirically, to what extent such formal tools can provide a satisfactory account for both lexical and supralexical semantic phenomena.

A crucial aspect of the use of formal categories in symbolic representations is that it allows the value of complex expressions to be rigorously computed as a function of the value of their parts and of their structural relation with each other. Compositionality is best seen as an empirical hypothesis: assuming that structures are interpreted compositionally, we can account for the ease to learn, formulate, and understand semantically contentful complex structures. The hypothesis is certainly a powerful and very plausible one – as long as it corresponds to the interpretive properties of structured expressions. For phrases and sentences, a strictly compositional account must contend with the context-dependence of important aspects of the interpretation, where certain senses are activated as a consequence of the linguistic and extra-linguistic context. For lexical items, the question whether lexical content should be modeled as a structured representation (rather than an atom) intersects the question whether such representations can effectively be analyzed compositionally (see Gerner 2014 for a recent study of non-compositionally interpreted complex words). The peculiarities that distinguish lexically encapsulated meaning (like kill or unpopular) from the meaning of complex phrases (like cause to die or not popular) are well known since the debate surrounding generative semantics in the early 1970s, and have been central to much linguistic theorizing since then. Even restricting our attention to formal semantic or to syntactic approaches, many proposals have been advanced, which differ along multiple dimensions: the distinction between "lexical" and "grammatical" information, the distinction (if any) between linguistic and non-linguistic content, the identification of semantic primitives, and of course the details of structural representations (beyond the overview by Engelberg 2011, see Dowty 1979, Wunderlich 1997, von Stechow 1995, Levin and Rappaport Hovav 1998, 2011, Rothstein 2004, Hale and Keyser 2002, Borer 2005, 2013, among many). The issues at stake are, in fact, very broad because they concern at the same time semantics (not just lexical), syntax, morphology, and the representation of conceptual content. In this broad context, the semantic compositionality of the posited representations is a more or less explicit assumption, most prominent in formal truth-conditional semantics; in addition, it surfaces explicitly where a lexical semantic core is associated with a local structural domain for idiosyncratic, non-compositional interpretation distinct from its "regularly" interpreted grammatical context (Marantz 1997, Arad 2003, Harley 2014), rather than with an atomic semantic "root" (Levin and Rappaport Hovav 1998, 2011) or with a conceptual content that does not directly feature in the grammatical representation (Schwarze and Schepping 1995, Borer 2013).

All work in the various approaches discussed in this section privileges a view of linguistic knowledge as internalized representation, and consequently is not directly concerned with mind-external and social aspects. However, this does not mean that such aspects are irrelevant, or problematic. Larson and Segal (1994) briefly consider the challenges posed by interpersonal and historical factors on a notion of internalized knowledge of meaning, and argue that an internalist perspective is compatible with a notion of S(ocial)-meaning (socially determined) as opposed to the I(nternal)-meaning that the theory attempts to model directly. The two notions can be posited side by side, and both have a role to play in a global account of a community's lexical conventions, even though the knowledge of (lexical) semantic facts is by assumption internalized knowledge of an individual. While the specific properties of this inter-individual aspect of lexical knowledge have not been very significant in the study of the mental lexicon (as opposed to diachronic analyses; see Ouhalla 2012 for an example), the issue is anything but irrelevant in itself. In fact, a better understanding of the manifestations of shared lexical knowledge is arguably a desideratum, made all the more urgent by the development of quantitative and distributional approaches (see Section 2.4), which foreground statistical patterns of usage.

2.2.2 Words and word pieces in the mental lexicon

A mind-internal perspective sits comfortably with the analysis of the lexicon as *mental* lexicon. It would seem straightforward, then, to equate the basic symbols of formal representations (at least those that do not clearly have a grammatical or syncategorematic function) with lexical items, understood as items of the mental lexicon. In fact, this amounts to a serious oversimplification. On the psychological side, what is stored in memory and retrieved as a unit can correspond to a lexical stem shorn of grammatical specifications, or to a grammatical word, or to a semantically identified "lemma". But the ubiquity of polysemy, the difficulty in distinguishing "senses" on objective grounds, and the fact that each "sense" has a different network of associations and is differently related to non-linguistic knowledge, mean that the precise content of a semantic lemma is not usually self-evident. This conclusion was already clear from the discussion of "lexical units", "lexemes", and "sense spectra" in Cruse (1986); it has been reinforced by Murphy's (2002) important observation that 'a word does not simplistically relate to a concept (no matter how represented), but to a network of interrelated and overlapping distinct "senses", related to background world-knowledge' (2002: 441). On the linguistic side, the relation between lexical stems and "items in the mental lexicon" is first of all blurred by compounds (including seemingly transparent ones like *bedroom*; see Libben and Weber 2014), to which we should add blends (*infotainment*), clippings (*exam, vet*); more significant are cases like particle verbs or other separable verbs, where the two elements do not form a syntactic unit. In a broader typological perspective, the boundary between inflectional realization and the derivation of a distinct lexical item is not always clear in languages that form nouns by joining a stem to a classifier or to a noun class prefix, nor is it always self-evident whether what counts as a single lexical item is the complex or the stem alone. Similar considerations apply to so-called ideophones, free morphemes that in languages like Korean or Japanese modulate a verb's lexical meaning (see Tsujimura 2014). Finally, even superficially unremarkable complexes like adjective + noun can in fact be sharply distinct for semantic purposes, between "regular" modification structures (like *strong tea*) and cases where the modifier has syntactically the same status but in fact identifies a distinct entity (like *green tea*, which does not denote the same substance as *tea* but rather a sub-kind). In all these cases, the "lexical items" whose content is available in the mental lexicon are not revealed by simple inspection, but must be identified on the basis of empirically motivated theoretical choices; see Svenonius (2008) for an example that distinguishes various types of classifiers and modifiers on a structural basis (for much broader typological studies of classifier structures, see Senft 2000 and Aikhenvald 2002).

As can be seen, the questions that arise when asking more precisely what linguistic entity correlates with a semantically-identified "lexical item", are typically brought into focus by examining how morphology relates to semantics. This should not surprise us, as morphology is centrally concerned with discriminating on principled grounds between operations on lexical items and operations that create new ones. A morphosemantic perspective is therefore central to the study of the mental lexicon.

The need to make explicit what exactly counts as a "lexical item" for semantics, and to do so in relation to morphology and syntax, leads therefore to a number of questions, which require precise theoretical choices. In fact, this brings out the problematic nature of the notion of lexical item itself – clearly a major issue for the study of the mental lexicon. Positions vary greatly on this fundamental point, and this is not the place to attempt a review of them. Still, it is important to note that the opposition between "lexicalist" and "non-lexicalist" theories is about the lexicon as part of linguistic competence, not about the existence of (something like) the mental lexicon. If only lexicalist approaches envisage a lexicon as a distinct linguistic component, this does not mean that non-lexicalist approaches (like Borer 2005a, b, 2013; or Harley 2012) give up on a semantic notion of lexical item. On the contrary, they explicitly assert the existence of such semantic listemes, but not as part of the linguistic knowledge that determines what words are and can be. This is different from claiming, for instance, that the semantic side of a lexical item is an emergent notion, resulting from a stable network of associations, and ultimately reducible to a set of uses. Words, however defined or "distributed", have a semantic content which is not just an epiphenomenon. This content either determines (for lexicalists) or is correlated to (for non-lexicalists) a cluster of linguistic properties. From the former camp, Levin (2011) makes this point explicit, as she distinguishes the mass of information (stated or implied) associated with the use of a verb in context from the semantic properties that are necessarily present across all uses of a verb, regardless of context; these alone constitute the verb's lexicalized meaning. A non-lexicalist perspective likewise recognizes this cluster of linguistic properties, but analyzes them in the same way as it analyzes non-listed linguistic objects like phrases and sentences, viewing "lexicality" as a matter of association with knowledge of a different kind: about listed forms, about morphological properties, and, crucially for the present purposes, about a conceptual content (this is obviously a simplified generalization; Fábregas and Scalise 2012 offer a more detailed overview, especially on pp. 4–6; and Borer 2013 is the most developed exposition of a non-lexicalist approach, with a detailed account of the relation between grammar and encyclopaedic content).

2.2.3 Variation in the empirical domain

For all approaches, the goal is to systematize as precisely as possible the context-invariant information associated with lexical items (revolving around argument structure and event structure for verbs, and countability and individuation for nouns), and to do so in a way that can predict significant generalizations across typologically different languages. The empirical domain of lexical semantic phenomena to explain is vast, including for instance the role of verb *Aktionsart* on deverbal nominalizations (see Alexiadou and Rathert 2010), restrictions on causative readings and on denominal verbalizations (like the impossibility of a reading "to make laugh" in **the clown laughed the children*, and the fact that "they put salt in the box" can be expressed as *they boxed the salt* but not as **they salted the box*; Hale and Keyser 2002), crosslinguistically stable differences between the morphological complexity of adjectives expressing basic states like *loose* and event-derived states like *broken* (Koontz-Garboden 2005), the fact that simple verbs can express the manner of an event, like *swim*, or its result, like *clean*, but not both (Rappaport Hovav and Levin. 2010). A central place in this domain of explananda is occupied by so-called "lexicalization patterns" (the term from Talmy 1985), typologically representative alternations in the way languages encapsulate information lexically.

Typology and the crosslinguistic dimension are a key aspect of this type of investigation, and in this connection the contributions by Gennaro Chierchia (Chierchia 1998, 2010) stand out. They propose a broad-ranging semantic parametrization of the interpretation of nouns across natural languages, as fundamentally denoting kind-level entities or predicates. The analysis is couched in rigorous formal semantic terms, but at the same time it has direct consequences – and predictions – for morphology and syntax, correlating with important typological properties such as the obligatoriness of classifiers or the presence of an inflectional plural.

The debate inspired by these contributions has promoted a significant advance in comparative lexical semantics (Chung 2000, Longobardi 2001, Wilhelm 2008, to name only a few); in turn this has fruitfully interacted with syntactic and morphological approaches (especially Borer 2005a, b, and much work inspired by it) to provide a similar impulse on comparative research on countability and individuation (see Massam 2012 and literature cited there). This is clearly a strand of research that has a particular relevance for the study of the mental lexicon, as it addresses on empirical bases the perennial question of the tension between a presumably universal cognitive apparatus and the very diverse linguistic encapsulations of meaning.

2.2.4 Lexical knowledge and concepts

The study of the mental lexicon is where the theme of universality and crosslinguistic variation in lexical semantics intersects the question of semantics and conceptual content. Most proposals about the decomposition of lexical items have generally identified semantic content with conceptual content; the exchange between Fodor and Lepore (1999) and Hale and Keyser (1999) illustrates some of the arguments, limited to one particular syntactic approach. However, it is far from obvious that the structures posited by lexical decomposition accounts (which are hypothesized as *linguistic* objects) should directly reflect *conceptual* structure. A brief review will give an idea of the various positions defended in the literature.

Some theorists have explicitly equated semantic and conceptual knowledge; for instance Jackendoff (1990, 2002) analyzed the building blocks of lexical semantics as elements of a *conceptual* representation, so that primitives like GO or TO are conceptual in nature and not strictly language-internal (even though they are invoked to account for the linguistic properties of words). On the other hand, the "Two-Level Model" of Bierwisch and Schreuder (1992) (see also Kaufmann 1995 and Wunderlich 1997) distinguish two distinct levels, a conceptual one and a semantic one from which grammatically relevant aspects of meaning are calculated. As shown in the useful critical discussion of Dölling and Heyde-Zybatow (2007), a distinction between grammatically represented information which is structurally represented, and "pure" conceptual content without grammatical relevance, is quite common, both in lexicalist accounts (Rappaport Hovav and Levin 1998) and in non-lexicalist ones (Goldberg 1995; Borer 2005a,b, 2013; Ramchand 2008). It is certainly understandable that linguistic semantics should focus predominantly on the former dimension; however, this has arguably limited the contribution of lexical semantics to the study of the mental lexicon. Consider the simple observation that languages differ in the way they cut up a range of perceptual experiences: Borer (2005a: 12) notes that in English bees "sting" but mosquitoes "bite", like dogs and snakes; by contrast, in Hebrew the attacks of bees and mosquitoes are described by the same verb (*'aqac*), while those of dogs and snakes are described by two more distinct verbs (*našax* and *hikiš* respectively). Surely, the different ranges of applicability point to different boundaries in the "conceptual content" of these terms. But in Borer's words "it would be unfortunate to conclude from this that Hebrew speakers live in a different conceptual (or, for that matter, physical) world from that occupied by English speakers." (Borer 2005a: 12). If, say, $BITE_1$ and $BITE_2$ are distinct but commensurable (Borer suggests "bundles of features, plausibly hierarchically arranged"), then their conceptual content must be elucidated in a way that accounts for this (presumed) overlap, and makes clear what empirical evidence can be brought to bear on the matter. Crucially, this would go beyond a lexical semantic analysis. Just as crucially, though, it would *relate* semantics to the psychological investigation of concepts; and this is needed to avoid the unenlightening situation where a "lexical concept" is defined as the conceptual content of a lexical item, and a lexical item, circularly, as the linguistic encapsulation of a concept (see Acquaviva and Panagiotidis 2012 for a critical discussion).

The question of how lexical semantic explanation can be related to psychologically plausible models of mental representation has indeed acquired a certain degree of urgency, as shown in the important contributions of Riemer (2013, 2016); especially so since many psychological accounts of the representation of verbal meaning no longer support the classic notion of modality-independent, discrete, stable "concepts". In order to contribute to a theory of the mental lexicon, therefore, lexical semantics can no longer rely on some assumed psychological notion of "conceptual content", but should itself strive to validate its results in ways that are psychologically plausible.

An interesting development in this connection is represented by those investigations that seek to shed light on the psychological representation of polysemy. Several studies (see Brown 2008 for a critical review, as well as Murphy 2007, both cited by Rainer 2014) have attempted to establish on experimental grounds whether the distinct senses that can be activated by a single form like *paper* (substance or daily publication) are stored, accessed, and represented as subentries of a larger item, or rather as independent entries, as distinct from each other as homonyms. Apart from their intrinsic importance as contributions to the understanding of the mental lexicon, such studies can be particularly useful in bridging the gap between the use of "linguistic" analysis (using language-internal evidence) and the use of psychological and neurological evidence; see in particular Pylkkänen, Llinás and Murphy (2006) in this connection.

2.3 The cognitive perspective

In this section we give a presentation of the foundational ideas of Cognitive Linguistics and relate them to the views in Generativist and Structuralist approaches. The section starts with the basic assumptions and proceeds to take a closer look at some core lexical semantic concepts in the literature, and how they are treated within this framework. As we have seen in Sections 2.1 and 2.2, the assumptions differ across theoretical accounts. Cognitive Linguistics takes a pragmatically enriched view of meaning modeling where natural language use is of key importance (Cruse and Croft 2004, Paradis 2005, Fillmore 2006, Goldberg 2006, Geeraerts 2010, Gärdenfors 2014). Lexical items do not have stable meanings, rather they evoke meanings when they are used in discourse. Discursive meanings of lexical items are viewed as construals of specific meanings in specific contexts (Paradis 2015). Meaning creation in context is both dynamic and constrained by encyclopaedic factors and conventionalization patterns. The way people use and understand language is related to the world around us. Language is dependent on our sensory and cognitive system, on the one hand, and on our role as members of different cultures on the other. The way we experience the world is decisive for how we understand it and how we portray it in human communication. The focus of interest is different from the symbolic approach in that researchers in this field take an interest in how language is used in all its richness and in different contexts (for a comparison between the generative and the cognitive commitments, see also Paradis 2003). Language and concept formation has socio-psychological grounding. Category membership is primarily a matter of more or less, rather than either-or, which is an idea launched by Wittgenstein (1968). His notion of family resemblance and gradience for membership of the category of game influenced prototype theorists' work (Rosch 1973, 1975), sociolinguists such as Labov and subsequently the Cognitivist movement (Taylor 2003, for a discussion of gradience and categoriality, see Aarts 2004).

According to the Cognitivist approach, meaning in language is encyclopaedic in the sense that there is no specific point along a linguistic-encyclopaedic continuum where we can say that linguistic knowledge ends and encyclopaedic knowledge starts. This does not mean that all aspects of meaning are considered to be of exactly the same type (Langacker 1987: 158–161, Paradis 2003, Croft and Cruse 2004). The major dividing line between the two is rather whether it is at all possible to distinguish between linguistic knowledge and encyclopaedic knowledge. The reason for this difference between the approaches hinges on the stand for or against language as a separate module in the brain. To illustrate the problems with the exclusion of encyclopedic lexical knowledge for the description and motivations of meaning variability of lexical items, Paradis (2003) gives examples of words in the English language, arguing that knowing the meaning of *open, fast* and *newspaper* in different contexts always involves knowing about the kinds of activities, properties and things involved. In order to understand the meaning of *open* we need to know what kind of activities we perform when we open things such as boxes, debates, pubs, computers or books. Similarly, we need to know what entities can be fast and in what way or whether newspaper refers to an artefact, a company or people working there.

Language is considered to be shaped by the two main functions it serves: the *semiological function* and the *interactive function* (Langacker 1998: 1). The semiological function is the mapping of meanings (conceptualizations) to linguistic forms in speech and writing. These structures are often referred to as form-meaning pairings or constructions (Fillmore and Kay 1995; Goldberg 1995). The interactive function, on the other hand, concerns the communicative side of language use as a social phenomenon including aspects such as the function of providing information as well as expressing the speaker's subjective stance and intersubjective awareness (Verhagen 2005, Gärdenfors 2014; Paradis 2015). Both the semiological and the interactive functions are important for the guiding idea that language use must be explained with reference to the underlying mental processes as well as with reference to the social and situational context. At the core of the Cognitive approach is the meaningful functioning of language in all its guises and all its uses in text and discourse. It is a usage-based framework with two different applications, one ontological and one methodological, both of which are central to the framework. In the first application of the term usage-based, meanings of words are acquired, develop and change through their use in social communication (Traugott and Dasher 2001, Tomasello 2003, 2008 Paradis 2008, 2011). The other application of the term usage-based refers to the fact that naturally occurring text-based data are important as behavioral data sources to gain insight into the nature of meaning in "real" language use (Gonzalez-Marquez et al. 2007).

The Cognitive approach to meaning does not only contrast to formal approaches, but also to the Structuralist approach which sees language as an autonomous intralinguistic system of relations between lexical items, organized on the basis of lexical fields (Lehrer 1974, Cruse 1986). According to that view, meanings of lexical items are not substantial, but relational and defined in terms of what they are not. For instance, *weak* gets its meaning from its relation to *strong. Strong* means what it does because it does not mean "weak". Paradigmatic relations like these hold between lexical items which can felicitously fill the same slot in an expression or a sentence (Lyons 1977). The same applies to synonyms such as *mother* and *mum* in *my mother is tall; my mum is tall,* or hyponyms such as *horse* and *animal* in *the horse is in the stables; the animal is in the stables*. This paradigmatic approach to meaning does not make much sense in the Cognitive framework, as we will see below. There was however also another line of research within Structuralism within which the scholars instead stressed the importance of the syntagm for lexical meaning, i.e. linear relations formed between lexical items in a sentences Cruse (1986: 16). Through these syntagmatic structuralist ideas and through the development of machine-readable corpora, collocations and co-occurrence patterns became important theoretical notions (Firth 1957, Sinclair 1987). The approach to lexical meaning endorsed by the syntagmatic structuralists assumes that a lexical item gets its meaning from the totality of its uses or, put differently, a lexical item gets its meaning from the company it keeps in language use. In this respect, the syntagmatic approach paved the way for new trends in linguistics, namely for usage-based approaches to lexical semantics where contextual factors and real language in use are prime research objectives for the description of meanings. This includes Cognitive Linguistics approaches and computational approaches to lexical meaning (Pustejovsky 1995, Jackendoff 2002, Lenci and Sahlgren, to appear).

Following up on the notion of the syntagm within the Cognitive perspective, we point to the the contribution of lexical items to the syntagmatic context at the level of sentence or utterance as well as the contribution of the syntagmatic contexts to the interpretation of the lexical item. As concrete examples of topics and their treatments within Cognitive Linguistics, the notions *polysemy, homonymy, synonymy, hyperonymy* and *hyponymy* and *antonymy* and the relations they may form due to contextual factors at the syntagmatic level are selected for a brief discussion. Like meanings in general, relational variants are viewed as construals of meanings and may be grouped into three main types.

- Polysemes are lexical items that have the same form. They evoke different but related meanings in their syntagmatic strings. Homonyms also share the same form, but their meanings are not at all related.
- Synonyms have different forms. They evoke meanings that are similar to some degree but are instantiated in different domain matrices or frames. Similarly, hyperonyms and hyponyms do not share forms but evoke related meanings at different levels of generality, i.e. more general or less general.
- Antonyms have different forms. They evoke opposite properties of the same meaning. Following Jones et al. (2012), the term is used as a cover term for all different types of opposites in language.

Let us consider a pair of lexical items from the first category, where the items share form but both differ and share aspects of meaning. Consider (1) from an interview with Woody Allen.[1]

(1) *As I've said many times, rather than* live on *in the hearts and minds of my fellow man, I would rather live on in my apartment* [emphasis added].

(2) *The pen is mightier than the sword.*

The two uses of *live on* in (1) are polysemes. The explanation for our interpretation of the two expressions is that they share aspects of meaning but occur in two different syntagmatic contexts and totally different meaning domains support those contexts. The first use of *live on* is instantiated in a mental domain by *in the hearts and minds of my fellow man*, while the second use of *live on* is couched in a concrete place, namely *in my apartment*. Polysemous lexical items such as *live on* are related by way of comparison, more precisely through metaphorization. A state in the domain of apartment is compared to a state in the mental domain. The two states share properties, but are instantiated in different domains (e.g., Lakoff and Johnson 1980, Gibbs 1994, Giora 2003, Hanks and Giora 2011, Paradis 2015).

Pen and *sword* in (2) do not refer to the objects as such but to what these objects are used for and to their users. The meanings are metonymically construed through the affordances of the conceptual structure of PEN and SWORD respectively, that is, what they are used for and by whom. That part of the conceptual structure is made salient through zooming in on the most relevant aspect. The lexical items can be seen as shortcuts to the relevant areas in conceptual space (Paradis 2004, Panther and Thornburg 2003, Benczes, Barcelona and Ruiz de Mendoza Ibáñes 2011). If we regard them as construals of usage, we are able to explain classical philosophical problems such as whether a fake gun is a gun or as in (2) where pen and sword are both hyponyms of weapon. In this context, *mightier* links *pen* and *sword*. The interpretation of *pen* is metonymically related to how the pen is used and so is the interpretation of sword (Paradis 2004). In this particular syntagm, neither is used to refer to the artefacts *per se* but to their use that communication is a more effective tool that violence or military force and thereby a hyponymic relation is construed.

---

[1] Paris Review. The art of humour no1 http://www.theparisreview.org/interviews/1550/the-art-of-humor-no-1-woody-allen. (7 October 2015)

Both types of polysemes are motivated variants in the sense that they evoke meanings which are related through a construal of comparison and resemblance (metaphorization), or through a contingent relation and a part-whole construal of salience (metonymization) (Croft and Cruse 2004, Paradis 2004, 2005, 2015). In contrast, homonyms such as *sole* (the bottom part of a shoe) and *soul* (the spirit) are arbitrary variants with the same form but with unrelated meanings. Homonyms just happen to sound and/or look the same in contemporary speech or writing.

Secondly, synonyms are lexical items that share core aspects of meaning, but differ with respect to the patterning and ranking of the meaning domains on the basis of which they are profiled.

(3) They are *rich/prosperous/loaded*.

(4) The twins are *ambidextrous/both-handed*.

In (3) *rich/prosperous/loaded* all refer to wealth, but in slightly different ways and contexts, where *rich* is more neutral with respect to usage while *prosperous* is formal and *loaded* is not. It is well-known that there are no absolute synonyms in language use. There is a gradient of conceptual and communicative similarity (Cruse 2011: 142–145, Divjak 2010, Storjohann, 2010). From a conceptual point of view synonymy can be described as the opposite of polysemy. Synonyms share core conceptual structures which are expressed through different word forms. Metaphorical polysemes and homonyms, on the other hand, are instantiated in different conceptual domains, under the constraint of invariant configurations (Lakoff 1990, Paradis 2012, 2015), while expressed by the same lexical item, and metonymical variants are instantiated in the same domain. The conventional meaning of the lexical item and the discursive meaning are in a part-whole relationship created through a construal of salience that zooms in or zooms out (Paradis 2004).

Furthermore, hypernyms and hyponyms are also synonyms in the sense that they share core meanings but differ with respect to specificity or generality as in (5) and (6). Synonyms are construable as a bi-directional coupling, as in if you are rich you are also prosperous or loaded, and if somebody is ambidextrous he or she is also both-handed and vice versa. In the case of hypernyms and hyponyms the bi-directionality does not hold. The meaning construal is unidirectional as seen in (5) and (6).

(5) *Mumbling is talking but talking is not necessarily mumbling.*

(6) *A dagger is a knife but a knife is not necessarily a dagger.*

Finally, antonymy is a binary construal of opposition that holds between two different lexical items in discourse. It is a relation of difference in similarity. Antonyms always evoke opposite properties of one and the same conceptual dimension (Paradis and Willners 2011, Jones et al. 2012). For instance, *good* and *bad* may be used as antonyms along the dimension of MERIT and *good* and *evil* along the dimension of BENEVOLENCE. Interestingly, antonymic lexical items are in fact used in the same semantic contexts also when they are not used to express opposition (Paradis et al. 2015). Contrary to what one may think in the first place, this means that antonymy differs from synonymy in that it thrives on similarity and the members form pairs along one dimension. Given *long*, *short* comes to mind immediately. For this reason, the question "What is the opposite of X?" is easy to answer, while it is hard to find an answer to "What is the synonym of X?". In contrast to the other relations, antonymy is a truly fundamental relation in the sense that it appears to be the most readily apprehended by speakers of a language.

Contrast in perception and bipolar organization in cognition are the underpinnings of antonymy in language. Most speakers have strong intuitions about how antonyms are used and that some antonyms are perceived to be better exemplars than others. Research using different observational techniques has established that there are a number of opposable word pairs that have special status as canonical antonyms (Murphy et al. 2009; Paradis et al. 2009, Paradis and Willners 2011, van de Weijer et al. 2012, van de Weijer et al. 2014). The strength of antonym couplings is determined by factors such as the degree of conventionalization as form-meaning pairs in discourse, the degree of entrenchment as antonymous words in memory, and the salience of the dimensional domain they express, e.g. LUMINOSITY *dark-light*, STRENGTH *weak-strong*, SIZE *small-large*, WIDTH *narrow-wide*. It has been argued that it is the meaning dimension that is the cause of the strength of the lexical relation rather than the effect of the high frequency of these words in language (Murphy and Andrew 1993; van de Weijer et al. 2012). The contentful meaning structures, e.g. LUMINOSITY or STRENGTH, of the dimensions that form the base of canonical antonyms, coincide with the core of semantic types that are central to all human activities, as noted by Dixon (2009).

2.4 The distributional perspective

Distributional semantics is a rich family of computational models assuming that the statistical distribution of words in linguistic context plays a key role in characterizing their semantic behavior. The theoretical foundation of distributional semantics is what has become known as the Distributional Hypothesis: *Lexemes with similar distributional properties have similar meanings*. Distributional semantics has been attracting a growing interest especially in the last twenty years, but its roots are much older. They lie in linguistic and philosophical traditions that, despite being substantially different, share the common assumption that *the meaning of words must be described by looking at how they are used in language*.

Zellig Harris is usually referred to as the theoretical and methodological source of research in distributional semantics: "If we consider words or morphemes A and B to be more different in meaning than A and C, then we will often find that the distributions of A and B are more different than the distributions of A and C. In other words, difference of meaning correlates with difference of distribution." (Harris, 1954: 156). In his later works, Harris characterizes linguistic distributions in terms of syntactic dependencies involving relations between a word acting as *operator* and a word acting as its *argument*. The "selection" (that is, the distribution) of a word is the set of operators and arguments with which it co-occurs with a statistically significant frequency, and is strongly correlated to its meaning. According to Harris, meaning "is a concept of no clear definition" (Harris 1991: 321), but distributional analysis can turn it into a measurable, objective and therefore, scientific notion: "Selection is objectively investigable and explicitly statable and subdividable in a way that is not possible for meanings – whether as extension and referents or as sense and definition." (Harris 1991: 329). The goal of Harris' distributional programme is therefore not to exclude meaning from the study of language, but rather to provide a scientific foundation for its investigation.

Distributional semantics is a direct product of American structuralism, but it is also strongly indebted to European structural linguistics. The (semantic) relation between two words or morphemes is defined differentially, based on their distributional behavior. Like for De Saussure, words have meaning only within a linguistic system, in which they are used and entertain various relations with other expressions. Jakobson (1959) calls the knowledge of such relations "linguistic acquaintance", whose importance supersedes the role of the "direct acquaintance" with the entities words refer to. The latter may even be lacking (for instance, we can use *ambrosia* correctly even without direct experience of its referent), while linguistic acquaintance is an essential condition to understand the meaning of any lexeme. Structural semantics proceeded independently from distributionalism, but the latter was often adopted as a method to define paradigms in terms of syntagmatic relations. The Distributional Hypothesis can indeed be reformulated in stricter structuralist terms (Sahlgren 2006): *Lexemes that share syntagmatic contexts have similar paradigmatic properties*. For instance, Apresjan (1966) referred to Harris' distributional methodology as a way to provide more objectivity to the investigation of semantic fields by grounding it on linguistic evidence. Apresjan carried out a distributional analysis of adjectives in terms of their frequency of co-occurrence with various syntactic contexts. The interplay between syntagmatic and paradigmatic dimensions is also central for Cruse (1986): The greater the paradigmatic "affinity" of lexical items, the more congruent their patterns of syntagmatic relations.

The idea that distributional analysis is the key to understand word meaning has also flourished within the linguistic tradition stemming from John Firth. In fact, corpus linguistics represents another important root of distributional semantics. Firth's contextual theory of meaning was based on the assumption that meaning is a very complex, and multifaceted reality, inherently related to language use in contexts (e.g., social setting, discourse, etc.). One of the key "modes" of meaning of a word is what he calls "meaning by collocation" (Firth 1951), determined by the context of surrounding words. The study of collocations has kept on growing as an independent line of research, but its theoretical assumptions and methods are deeply intertwined with distributional semantics. Finally, another crucial philosophical reference for distributional semantics is represented by the usage-based view of meaning developed by Ludwig Wittgenstein in his later writings. In the *Philosophical Investigations*, Wittgenstein urges us not to assume a general and fixed meaning of words. Instead, we should look at *how* the words are being used, because "the meaning of a word is its use in the language." (Wittgenstein 1953).

2.4.1 Distributional semantic models

The Distributional Hypothesis is a general assumption on the relationship between meaning and linguistic distributions, and states that the semantic similarity of lexical items is a function of their distribution in linguistic contexts. Distributional Semantic Models are computational methods that turn this hypothesis into a scientific framework for semantic analysis. Distributional Semantic Models are also commonly referred to as *word space models, semantic space models, (semantic/distributional) vector space models, geometrical (semantic) models, context-theoretic semantic models, statistical semantic models* or *corpus-based semantic models*. These names emphasize different aspects of the way Distributional Semantic Models learn and represent the semantic content of lexical items. Distributional Semantic Models form a vast multifarious family of computational methods often developed within very different research traditions and for diverse purposes (e.g., information retrieval, natural language processing, cognitive modeling), but they all share the following principles: words are represented as vectors built from their distribution in the contexts extracted from corpora, and similarity between words is approximated in terms of geometric distance between their vectors.

The standard organization of Distributional Semantic Models is usually described as a four-step method (Turney and Pantel 2010):

1. for each target word, contexts are first collected from a (usually large) corpus and counted to build a *co-occurrence matrix*. The matrix rows correspond to the target lexemes and its columns to the contexts;
2. raw frequencies are then transformed into significance scores (e.g., positive pointwise mutual information) that are more suitable to reflect the importance of the contexts to characterize the target lexemes;
3. the resulting matrix tends to be very large and sparse, requiring techniques to limit the number of dimensions, such as Singular Value Decomposition or Principal Component Analysis.
4. finally, a similarity score is computed between the vector rows, using various vector similarity measures, the most common one being the cosine.

Distributional Semantic Models have many design options, due to the variety of parameters that can be set up at each step of the process and may affect the results and performances of the system. The definition of context is surely a crucial parameter in the implementation of the models. Three types of linguistic environments have been considered: in *document-based models*, as in *Latent Semantic Analysis* (Landauer and Dumais, 1997), words are similar if they appear in the same documents or in the same paragraphs; *word-based models* consider a linear window of collocates around the target words (Lund and Burgess, 1996; Sahlgren, 2006); *syntax-based models* are closer to Harris' approach as they compare words on the basis of their dependency relations (Curran, 2003; Padó and Lapata, 2007; Baroni and Lenci, 2010). Word-based models have an additional parameter represented by the window size (from a few words to an entire paragraph), while syntax-based models need to specify the type of dependency relations that are selected as contexts. Some experiments suggest that syntax-based models tend to identify distributional neighbors that are taxonomically related, mainly co-hyponyms, whereas word-based models are more oriented towards identifying associative relations (Van de Cruys, 2008; Peirsman *et al.*, 2007; Levy and Goldberg, 2014). However, the question whether syntactic contexts provide a real advantage over linear models is still open. On the other hand, a more dramatic difference exists with respect to document-based models, which are strongly oriented towards neighbors belonging to loosely defined semantic topics or domains (Sahlgren, 2006).

Recently, a new family of Distributional Semantic Models have emerged, which take a radically different approach to learn distributional vectors. They are based on neural network algorithms and are called *predict models,* because, instead of building a co-occurrence matrix by counting word distributions in corpora, they directly create low-dimensional distributional representations by learning to optimally predict the contexts of a target word. These representations are also commonly referred to as *(neural) word embeddings.* The most popular neural Distributional Semantic Model is the one implemented in the *word2vec* library (Mikolov et al. 2013).

Because of its history and different roots, distributional semantics is a manifold program for semantic analysis, which is pursued in disciplines as different as computational linguistics and psychology. The goals of Distributional Semantic Models are equally various: thesaurus construction, word-sense disambiguation, cognitively plausible models for language acquisition and processing, etc. Within this broad range of applications, we can distinguish between a weak and a strong version of the Distributional Hypothesis (Lenci 2008).

The *Weak Distributional Hypothesis* is essentially a method for semantic analysis. The starting assumption is that lexical meaning (whatever this might be) determines the distribution of words in contexts, and the semantic properties of lexical items act as constraints governing their syntagmatic behavior. Consequently, by inspecting a relevant number of distributional contexts, we can identify those aspects of meaning that are shared by lexemes with similar linguistic distributions. The Weak Distributional Hypothesis assumes the existence of a *correlation* between semantic content and linguistic distributions, and exploits such correlation to investigate the semantic behavior of lexical items. It does not entail that word distributions are themselves constitutive of the semantic properties of lexical items at a cognitive level, but rather that meaning is a kind of "hidden variable" responsible for the distributions we observe, which we try to uncover by analyzing such distributions.

The *Strong Distributional Hypothesis* is instead a cognitive assumption about the form and origin of semantic representations. Repeated encounters with lexemes in language use eventually lead to the formation of a distributional representation as an abstract characterization of the most significant contexts with which the word co-occurs. Crucially, the Strong Distributional Hypothesis entails that word distributions in context have a specific *causal role* in the formation of the semantic representation for that word. Under this version, the distributional behavior of a lexeme is not just regarded as a way to describe its semantic properties, but rather as a way to explain them at the cognitive level.

The strong and weak versions of the Distributional Hypothesis set very different constraints and goals for computational models. Most of the Distributional Semantic Models in computational linguistics usually content themselves with the weak version, and conceive of distributional semantics as a method to endow natural language processing systems with semantic information automatically acquired from corpora. On the other hand, Distributional Semantic Models in cognitive research confront themselves with the potentialities as well the problems raised by the Strong Distributional Hypothesis, which must therefore face the tribunal of the cognitive evidence about semantic representations. In any case, the success of the Distributional Hypothesis, either as a descriptive method for semantic analysis or as an explanatory model of meaning, must be evaluated on the grounds of the semantic facts that it is actually able to explain.

2.4.2 Distributional representations as semantic representations

The main characters of distributional semantics can be summarized as follows:
- the theoretical foundation of distributional semantics is the Distributional Hypothesis. This is primarily a conjecture about semantic similarity, which is modeled as a function of distributional similarity: *semantic similarity* is therefore the core notion of distributional semantics;
- the Distributional Hypothesis is primarily a conjecture about *lexical meaning*, so that the main focus of distributional semantics is on the lexicon, specifically on content words (i.e., nouns, verbs, adjectives, and adverbs);
- distributional semantics is based on a *holistic* and *relational* view of meaning. The content of lexical items is defined in terms of their (dis)similarity with other lexemes;
- distributional semantics is based on a *contextual* and *usage-based view of meaning*. The content of lexical items is determined by their use in contexts.
- the Distributional Hypothesis is implemented by Distributional Semantic Models These are computational methods that learn distributional representations of lexical item from corpus data. The distributional representation of a lexeme is a *distributional vector* recording its statistical distribution in linguistic contexts;
- semantic similarity is measured with distributional vector similarity.

What are then the main features of distributional vectors as semantic representations? How do they differ from other types of representations of lexical meaning? As noted above, distributional semantics is strictly and naturally related to the structuralist view of meaning. This follows not only from the history itself of distributional semantics, but also from its relational view of meaning. Like structuralist approaches, distributional semantics considers the meaning of a lexical item as dependent on its relations with the other lexemes in the semantic space. A close "family resemblance" also exists with cognitive models, with which distributional semantics share a usage-based view of meaning.

Stronger differences instead divide distributional semantics from approaches to meaning adopting semantic representations in terms of symbolic structures. In symbolic models, lexical items are mapped onto formal structures of symbols that represent and make explicit their semantic properties. What varies is the formal metalanguage used to build semantic representations (for example, networks, frames, semantic features, recursive feature structures, and so on). Symbolic semantic representations are *qualitative*, *discrete*, and *categorical*. Semantic explanations only refer to the structure of semantic symbols with which lexical meanings are represented. For instance, in a semantic network like WordNet (Fellbaum 1998), the hypernym hierarchy of *car* explains that *John bought a car* entails that *John bought a vehicle*. Semantic similarity is also defined over the lexical symbolic structures, for instance by measuring the overlap between feature lists (Tversky 1977) or the distance in semantic networks (Budanitsky and Hirst 2006).

The characters of distributional semantics also make it quite different from theories of meaning that are not grounded on the Distributional Hypothesis, most notably formal (model-theoretic) semantics. Formal semantics is itself a rich and variegated family of semantic models that share a referential (denotational) view of meaning, based on the assumption that meaning is essentially a relation between the symbols of languages and entities external to language, and that the goal of semantics is to characterize the truth conditions of sentences as a function of the reference (denotation) of their parts. In fact, the core notions of Frege's programme for formal semantics – truth, reference, and logical form – are as different as possible from those of Harris' program for distributional semantics – linguistic contexts, use, and distributional vectors. The distance between these two semantic paradigms can be best appreciated by considering the contrast between their main philosophical references: the early Wittgenstein of the *Tractatus Logico-Philosophicus* (Wittgenstein 1922) for formal semantics, and the later Wittgenstein of the *Philosophical Investigations* for distributional semantics. Therefore, it is no surprise that formal and distributional semantics, as the heirs of these two radically different views on meaning, have proceeded virtually ignoring each other, focussing on totally different semantic phenomena. As a matter of fact, a whole range of issues in the agenda of formal semantics, such as semantic compositionality, quantification, inference, anaphora, modality, or tense, have remained beyond the main horizon of distributional semantics.

Distributional vectors are very different from semantic representations adopted in symbolic and formal models of meaning. Distributional representations are *quantitative*, *continuous*, *gradable* and *distributed*. These properties directly stem from the fact that distributional representations are not symbolic structures, but real-valued vectors. Quantitative and gradable semantic representations are commonly adopted in cognitive science to account for key properties of concepts such as graded category membership, typicality and vagueness (Hampton 2007). Concepts are thus represented with vectors of features, weighted according to their importance for a concept (Smith and Medin 1981, McRae et al. 1997). Vector dimensions are typically derived from semantic feature norms (McRae et al. 2005a), which are collected by asking native speakers to generate properties they consider important to describe the meaning of a word. The number of subjects that listed a certain feature for a concept is then used as feature weight.

The quantitative and gradable character of distributional representations makes them very similar to the way information is represented in artificial neural networks. Connectionist models use non-symbolic distributed representations formed by real-valued vectors such that "each entity is represented by a pattern of activity distributed over many computing elements, and each computing element is involved in representing many different entities" (Hinton et al. 1986: 77). Distributional representations are also distributed because the semantic properties of lexical items emerge from comparisons between their n-dimensional vectors, for example by measuring their similarity in distributional vector space. The semantic content of a word therefore lies in its global distributional history encoded in the vector, rather than in some specific set of semantic features or relations. Neural networks are general algorithms that encode information with vectors of neural unit activations and learn high-order representations from co-occurrence statistics across stimulus events in the environment. Connectionism is fully consistent with the distributional hypothesis, since linguistic co-occurrences are just a particular type of stimuli that can be learnt by neural networks. A natural convergence thus exists between research on neural networks and distributional semantics. In distributional approaches to meaning, lexical representations emerge from co-occurrences with linguistic contexts. Moreover, distributional semantic spaces are built with computational models – including neural networks – that use domain-independent learning algorithms recording the distributional statistics in the linguistic input. Nowadays, neural networks in fact represent one particular family of computational models in distributional semantics (cf. Section 2.4.1).

The notions of distributed and distributional representations are closely related but need to be kept well distinguished. In fact, the former concerns the *way* semantic information is represented with vectors, while the latter concerns the *source* of the information used to build the vectors. The term "distributional" specifically refers to the property of vectors to encode the statistical distribution of lexemes in linguistic contexts. *All distributional representations are distributed, but not all distributed representations are distributional.* It is indeed possible to represent words with distributed semantic representations that are not distributional. Vector space representations of meaning are in fact common in cognitive science (Markman 1999). Osgood (1952) and Osgood, Suci and Tannenbaum (1957) are among the first models of concepts in terms of n-dimensional semantic spaces. However, the dimensions of Osgood's semantic spaces are not distributional, but are built according to the method of "semantic differential": subjects are asked to locate the meaning of a word along different scales between two polar adjectives (e.g., *happy – sad, slow – fast, hard – soft*, etc.), and their ratings are used to determine its position in the semantic space, which mainly capture connotative aspects of meaning. Rogers and McClelland (2004) use a neural network to learn distributed representations with vector dimensions encoding specific semantic properties (e.g., *has_wings, flies, is_a_plant*, etc.), and computational simulations with distributed representations derived from feature norms are proposed by Cree, McRae and McNorgan (1999) and Vigliocco (2004). Gärdenfors (2000, 2014) represents concepts and lexical meanings with regions in "conceptual spaces". These are defined as vector spaces whose dimensions are "qualities" of objects, corresponding to the different ways stimuli are judged to be similar or different, such as weight, temperature, height, etc. In Gärdenfors' classical example, colors are characterized by a three-dimensional vector space defined by hue, brightness, and saturation. The meaning of a color term like *red* is then identified with a region in this color space, and color similarities are defined via the distance of the corresponding regions in space. The geometrical representation of concepts proposed by Gärdenfors indeed closely resembles vector-based representations adopted in distributional semantics, but the dimensions of conceptual spaces correspond to attributes of objects, rather than to linguistic contexts.

3 Empirical challenges: Two illustrations

In the introduction, we identified five questions that are crucial for all treatments of meaning in language. In relation to lexical semantics, they concern the nature of lexical meaning, what the relation between words and their meanings is, how meanings are learned, stored, communicated and understood, and how they change. Section 2 has broadly followed these as guiding questions in reviewing and comparing the main approaches to lexical semantics. In this concluding section, we will invert the perspective and consider two specific empirical domains and the challenges that they pose, namely color terms and semantic flexibility in context. The two are viewed from different perspectives, which foreground respectively the need for extensive and carefully constructed data sets, and the need for a clear delineation (theoretical as well as empirical) of what counts as "lexical item" and how it is modeled, for any data-driven conclusion about the mental lexicon and generally about the role of language in cognition.

3.1 Color terms

What all approaches have in common is the need for empirically-based observation in one form or another, be they textual or experimental. In much of today's research on lexical meaning we often see a combination of methods facilitated by the rapid development of technical knowledge when it comes to theoretical computational advances as well as when it comes to technical equipment for data storage and analysis. For all approaches, we also see the need for proper integration with mental processes related to the cognitive system (categorization and reasoning), to the perceptive and affective systems, and to the role of communication, that is, how human beings make use of language to make themselves understood and to obtain responses to what they are saying.

The color domain has been one of the most investigated, as well as one of the most "popular" areas within the realm of lexical semantics. The study that changed the investigation of color terms is the famous Berlin and Kay's (1969) study of color terms in various languages. It has become a backbone for other types of research of color terms and it has been further developed since its publication. As pointed out by Majid, Jordan and Dunn (2015), the methodology given by Berlin and Kay was refined in the World Color Survey (Kay et al., 2009) – the largest ever empirical study of semantics, featuring 110 languages spoken primarily by small-scale, preliterate, non-industrialized communities. The World Color

Survey enabled researchers to show cross-linguistic differences in color naming that reflect cognitive principles and to point to differences in boundaries that languages impose onto the color spectrum. As emphasized by Majid, Jordan and Dunn (2015), Berlin and Kay's work has been an inspiration for many types of research, but it has been also criticized for over-sampling or under-sampling Indo-European color terms. Research on color terms was conducted with regard to some Indo-European sub-families, like Slavic (Comrie and Corbett 1993), but no large-scale investigation has been undertaken. Therefore, there was room for a more integrative study that would take into account data from a large number of Indo-European languages. Such an endeavor was a project called Evolution of Semantic Systems (EOSS). The project was conducted at the Max Planck Institute for Psycholinguistics (Nijmegen) from 2011 to 2014 and included research on 50 Indo-European languages. The project was grounded on linguistic, psychological and anthropological theoretical frameworks. One of the basic goals of the project was to investigate color terms speaker use in the partition of the color spectrum. Research on color terms within the EOSS project consisted of several different trials with adult participants. The empirically-based results from the project enabled further investigation of lexicalization patterns speakers use in color naming and thus conveying different meanings. First, it enabled a cross-linguistic analysis of genetically related languages. For example, a cross-linguistic analysis of lexicalization patterns used in color naming in Croatian, Polish and Czech (Raffaelli, Kopecka, Chromý, 2019) showed a high degree of correlation between word-formation processes and the meanings that are conveyed by particular color terms. Thus, for example all the three languages use suffixes like -*kast* (Croatian), -*aw* (Polish) or -*av* (Czech) to convey the meaning 'ish' like *zelenkast* 'greenish', or -*ast* (Croatian), -*ow* (Polish) or -*ov* (Czech) with the meaning 'N-like' like *narančast* 'orange-like'. However, Polish and Czech have some additional suffixes with meanings that do not appear in Croatian like -*sk-*/-*ck-* 'typical of' (Czech) or -*n-* 'made of' (Polish). Second, results from psycholinguistic research (based on the frequency data of the terms used in the partition of the color spectrum) enabled comparison to the data collected via other empirically-based methods. For example, the EOSS data for Croatian were compared to the frequency data from the Croatian n-gram system (based on the Web as Corpus approach) consisting of 1.72 billion tokens (Dembitz et al., 2014). The 165 different Croatian color terms (types) from the EOSS project were checked in the Croatian n-gram system in order to provide evidence about their attestation in a large language resource. Moreover, the combination of two different methods shed light on the correlation between the strategies speakers use in color-naming, and the degree of conventionalization based on the corpus data. The frequency data from the Croatian n-gram system show that basic color terms are significantly the most frequent ones, and are thus highly conventionalized. The data also show that compounding is a more pervasive process in the formation of color terms in Croatian than derivation (which is usually more productive in the formation of new lexemes). This means that compounding allows for a more fine-grained naming of the color spectrum and allows for greater creativity in color naming than derivation does. There is also a high degree of frequency correlation between the most frequent compound terms in the two data sets. The compound *zeleno-plava* 'green-blue' and *plavo-zelena* 'blue-green' are the most frequent compound terms. These terms cover the central and the largest part of the color spectrum (typical for all the Indo-European languages) and according to the corpus data refer to phenomena in nature like, see, water, different types of plants, etc. The combination of the two methods also showed the continuum of more and less conventionalized terms and their cognitive entrenchment. Terms less frequently used by speakers in the process of color naming are also the less frequent terms in the corpus. The combination of the two empirically based methods could have impact on future research of the correlation between perception and cognition as universal human capacities and the constraints imposed by cultural differences and typological differences of languages on the formation of lexical items.

Interesting evidence on the interplay between language and perception comes from the study of congenital blind subjects, who show a close similarity with sighted subjects in the use and understanding of color terms. In a multidimensional scaling analysis performed by Marmor (1978) with similarity judgments about color terms, the similarity space of the congenital blind subjects closely approximates Newton's color wheel and the judgments by sighted control participants. Therefore, she concludes that knowledge of color relations can be acquired without first-hand sensory experience. The congenital blind child studied by Landau and Gleitman (1985), Kelli, was indeed able to acquire impressive knowledge about color terms, including the constraints governing their correct application to concrete nouns, without overextending them to abstract or event nouns. The common interpretation of these data is that congenital blind people possess substantial knowledge about the visual world derived through linguistic input. Language-derived information either comes in the form of "supervised" verbal instructions (e.g., teaching that cherries are red) or in the form of "unsupervised" distributional analysis of linguistic contexts. Language, in fact, contains expressions such as *yellow banana* or *red cherry* that can be used to learn information about color-noun associations, as well as the general constraints concerning the applicability of color adjectives or visual verbs only to particular noun classes.

On the other hand, the similarities between color spaces in congenital and blind subjects are not fully uncontroversial. For instance, Shepard and Cooper (1992) find important differences between the color spaces of sighted and congenital blind subjects, differently from Marmor (1978). Connolly et al. (2007) also show that the lack of visual experience of colors indeed has significant effects on the conceptual organization in blind subjects. They collect implicit similarity judgments in an odd-man-out task about two categories of concepts, "fruits and vegetables" and "household items". Cluster analysis of the similarity judgments reveals a major overlap between the blind and sighted similarity spaces, but significant differences for clusters of the "fruit and vegetables" category for which color is a "diagnostic" property (i.e., critical to identify the exemplars of that category, such as being yellow for a banana). Even for blind subjects with good knowledge of the stimulus color, this is not relevant to organize the similarity space. The hypothesis by Connolly et al. is that such contrast stems from the different origin of color knowledge in the two groups. In the congenital blind, color knowledge is "merely stipulated", because it comes from observing the way color terms are used in everyday speech, while in the sighted it is an immediate form of knowledge derived from direct sensory experience, and used to categorize new exemplars. Similar differences have been found in the feature norming study by Lenci et al. (2013): Congenital blind subjects in fact produced significantly less color terms when describing concrete objects than sighted control subjects (Lenci, Baroni and Cazzolli 2013). These contrasting pieces of evidence show that, on the one hand, distributional information is rich enough to allow the organization of the color space to be derived from the linguistic input, while on the other hand the lack of direct perceptual experience may result in critical differences in the role of and use of color information.

The role of linguistic and perceptual information as sources of semantic representation is still a puzzle with many missing pieces. New technologies that enable new experiments, precisely calculated results and data collected via different methods should be considered as the methodological backbone of contemporary research in lexical semantics, and as the only way to fill these gaps. Experientially-based approaches to lexical semantics can provide evidence about how word meanings are construed, to what extent they are conventionalized and how much they are influenced by perception and cognition or by cultural diversity and different typological properties. The examples given above are just an illustration of an attempt to integrate traditional and theoretically well elaborated topics with empirically-based methods.

3.2 Coercion and semantic flexibility in context

It is a simple fact that words assume different meanings in different contexts. If this plasticity had no bounds, any word could mean anything, given an appropriate context. Since that is not the case, a notion of lexical content distinct from that determined by context of use is justified; but it is a content that is at least partly shaped by its context. For this reason, investigating the boundaries of context-determined flexibility is and has been a central task of research in lexical semantics (see already Cruse 1986). This traditional topic, extensively addressed in structural and cognitive approaches, acquires a particular prominence also in "formal" models with the advent of analyses that decompose lexical items into complex formal structures (syntactic or otherwise). In rough general terms, if lexical content is modeled as a linguistically represented structure, embedded in a larger structure, the question of what constrains lexical semantic flexibility in context is resolved into the question of how lexical meaning can and cannot be structurally decomposed. Among the large number of phenomena and competing approaches, we can concentrate here specifically on the phenomenon of coercion, whereby a context enforces an interpretation on a lexical item that lacks it in any other contexts. The typical illustrations involve entity-denoting nominals coerced into a different interpretation by predicates that take eventualities as arguments:

(7) a. *Syd grabbed the book / cigar / bottle of wine.*
 b. *Syd enjoyed the book / cigar / bottle of wine.*

Asher (2011: 16) observes that what drives this adaptation cannot be the semantics of the nominal object, because the same effect is replicated when this is a non-existent word like *zibzab*:

(8) *Syd enjoyed the zibzab.*

Not every predicate can freely impose its requirements, however. Still following Asher (2011: 215), we can observe that the modifier *slow* qualifies a processual notion licensed by the head noun in *a slow person* ("slow in understanding") or *a slow animal* ("slow in moving"), but not in the semantically anomalous *a slow tree*, although world knowledge could in principle license the reading "a slow-growing tree". Likewise, we can *enjoy an apple* or *finish an apple*, but not really *end an apple*; and the previous mention of a relevant discourse entity allows us to interpret *start with the kitchen* as 'start *painting* the kitchen' in (9b), but not in (9c) (adapted from Asher 2011: 19–20):

(9) a. ? *Yesterday, Sabrina started with the kitchen.*
b. *Yesterday, Sabrina painted her house. She started with the kitchen.*
c. ? *Last month, Sabrina painted her cousin's house. Then today, she started with the kitchen.*

Positing articulated structures for the content of lexical items with different properties (like *end* and *finish*), and providing explicit constraints on how these meanings combine in context, is one way to approach these phenomena. By this move, "coercion is not really a problem about meaning change in the lexicon; it's a problem about compositionality – about how lexically given meanings combine together in the right sort of way" (Asher 2011: 18). This aspect assumes particular prominence in syntactic decomposition approaches, which analyze lexical content in terms of the same types of formal objects (structures, primitives, combinatorial principles) as those that define linguistic contexts. Crucially, when decompositional analyses are sufficiently precise, their empirical value can be compared across different models and frameworks. Asher (2011: 252–255) presents some empirical arguments against the generalized use of abstract verbs for "locative" or "possessive" functions (Harley 2004, Cable 2011, among others), but he also notes that structures like *want a beer* effectively seem to motivate one extra verbal predicate represented in the syntactic structure, not just as a lexical inference; this is what licenses *rapidly* in (10a) but not (10b), as a modifier of an abstract "have" predicate in a subordinate clause:

(10) a. *John wanted his stitches out rapidly.*
b. ? *The dog enjoyed his food rapidly.*

More recently, Larson (2011) provided additional independent evidence for a hidden clausal structure as a uniform complement of *want* (and other intensionality-inducing verbs). Importantly, the clausal analysis that Larson argues for derives from a hypothesis on the *semantics* of verbs like *want*; it therefore predicts (successfully) the existence of similar phenomena also in other languages, insofar as volitional predicates can be identified. It should be noted that Larson's syntactic analysis (like Cable's) does not incorporate all the assumptions of Harley's original Distributed-Morphological account.

At least for certain verbal predicates, then, a decompositional analysis is empirically well established and, more importantly, not limited to any one technical framework. If a notion of "lexical item" is revealed as oversimplistic for at least those cases, on language-internal grounds, it is at least a reasonable hope to see these results subjected to critical assessment on experimental grounds, by psycho- and neurolinguistic approaches to the mental lexicon. A failure to take them into account leads to attributing properties (content, priming potential, ease of retrieval) to assumed "lexical items" whose existence is in fact not motivated outside of the morphological or phonological level.

Beside this general point, which is enough to cast doubt on naive approaches to lexical semantics that simplistically assume "words", interdisciplinary perspectives arise more specifically in connection with coercion. This label groups together various phenomena of polysemy in context, which evidently have a great importance for a proper understanding of lexical knowledge as a psychological phenomenon and its neurological grounding. If linguistic data can shed light on the way lexical knowledge is structured and distributed over formal representations (say, with the morphosyntactic representation *want [a cigar]* mapped to an abstract clausal structure WANT [HAVE CIGAR]), psycholinguistic investigations are indispensable for understanding the dynamic aspect of this phenomenon: what distinct sense components are activated in processing, for instance, and how do they relate to non-linguistic background knowledge (if a clear divide can be drawn)? The very fact that, for instance, *end* and *finish* have different coercion properties shows that contextual flexibility varies lexically and does not entirely reduce to encyclopedic inferences; at the same time, however, we need to know how much of the information that goes into activating different senses is a function of linguistic knowledge, and how much of it derives from non-linguistic knowledge – if the two can be discriminated, something which grammatical theory alone cannot verify. Similarly, it is well known that languages with a clear mass-count opposition in nominals differ in how easily they allow nouns to be coerced into a non-favored interpretation (as in *there is still a lot of car to paint*), a fact which highlights the language- and grammar-dependent nature of this type of coercion. A traditional approach would take for granted that synonyms like *car* and *voiture* are also directly comparable in terms of the conceptual content they express (and so, differences in flexibility must depend on grammar). But there is no clearcut divide between "grammar" and "lexical item" in most decompositional accounts; the asymmetry in linguistic flexibility derives from properties of the grammatical representation which are directly reflected in the conceptual content of these nouns. It would be extremely instructive to complement this theoretical stance with observable evidence suggestive of asymmetries in conceptual representation, or in the possibility to activate certain senses in a given context of use.

The flexibility of word interpretations in contexts has been extensively investigated in distributional semantics. Erk and Padó (2008) use a Distributional Semantic Model to address a crucial aspect of compositionality, namely the fact that when words are composed, they tend to affect each other's meanings. This phenomenon is related to what Pustejovky (1995) refers to as "co-compositionality". For instance, the meaning of *run* in *The horse runs* is different from its meaning in *The water runs* (Kintsch 2001). Erk and Padó (2008) claim that words are associated with various types of expectations (e.g., typical events for nouns, and typical arguments for verbs) that influence each other when words compose, thereby altering their meaning (McRae et al. 2005b). They model this context-sensitive compositionality by distinguishing the lemma vector of a word w_1 (i.e., its out-of-context representation), from its vector in the context of another word w_2. The vector-in-context for w_1 is obtained by combining the lemma vector of w_1 with the lemma vectors of the expectations activated by w_2. For instance, the vector-in-context assigned to *run* in *The horse runs* is obtained by combining the lemma vector of *run* with the lemma vectors of the most typical verbs in which *horse* appears as a subject (e.g. *gallop*, *trot*, etc.). Like in Mitchell and Lapata (2010), various functions to build vectors in contexts are tested. Erk and Padó (2008) evaluate their model for context-sensitive vector representation to predict verb similarity in context (for instance *slump* in the context of *shoulder* is more similar to *slouch* than to *decline*) and to rank paraphrases.

Distributional analyses have also been proposed for cases of coercion like (7b) and (9) (Lapata and Lascarides 2003; Zarcone et al. 2013; Chersoni et al. 2017). Such models assume that the retrieved event (like "reading" in *The man began the book*) is the event most compatible with corpus-derived knowledge about typical events and their participants. This is in contrast to traditional accounts of coercion (Pustejovsky 1995) which ascribe covert event retrieval to complex lexical entries associating entities with events corresponding to their typical function or creation mode (e.g., qualia roles). Distributional semantics can thus provide a more economical and general explanation of phenomena like coercion that challenge formal models of compositionality. Moreover, the advantage of distributional approaches to coercion is that they can account for psycholinguistic evidence showing the influence of context on the interpretation of coercion sentences (Zarcone et al. 2014). For example, given *baker* and *child* as subjects of *finish the icing*, *baker* will cue *spread* as a covert event, while *child* will cue *eat* (even though it is perfectly possible that bakers eat icing or that children spread it).

Generally speaking, hypotheses framed in the terms of grammatical theories tend to lack independent evidence when it comes to deciding not how to model linguistic information, but whether some information is part of linguistic knowledge or not. The very notion of "sense" could be brought into sharper focus by crossing the results of formal linguistic and experimental investigations, so that what counts as a meaning "component" for grammatical analysis is at the same time independently validated on psycholinguistic grounds, and vice versa. In turn, an independently validated delineation of senses would prove useful in solving the central question whether speakers represent them as a continuum, or whether they are grouped together under a general category corresponding to a semantic item of the mental lexicon – and in that case, whether this is stored and assessed as a listeme, and to what extent its content coincides with what is posited on purely language-internal grounds.

These are, as is clear, just a few suggestions on how a closer synergy between linguistic, psycholinguistic, and neurolinguistic approaches to lexical semantic coercion could contribute to a better understanding of the mental lexicon.

4 Conclusion

The positions outlined in this chapter illustrate different, quite often incompatible perspectives on lexical semantics. In this they reflect the considerable diversity that characterizes linguistics as a whole. The chapter has reviewed the four key approaches that have emerged in the study of lexical semantics, with the goal of clarifying their historical background, their specific differences, the methodological and theoretical assumptions that lie behind those differences, and the main strengths and the main challenges of each perspective.

A certain degree of complementarity is inevitable in such a diverse theoretical landscape. It should be noted that behind each of the main perspectives lies a vast number of studies and often quite divergent priorities. When we move away from fundamental assumptions and programmatic goals, it becomes clear that the various perspectives prove anything but equivalent in their ability to successfully deal with the various aspects of lexical knowledge such as synonymy and antonymy, attested ranges of lexicalization patterns, compositionality of meaning in complex words, paradigmatic patterns across related lexical items, family-resemblance effects, context-induced malleability, flexibility of meaning in use and context-invariant patterns. The questions that arise in the study of the mental lexicon and of lexical structures bring this complementarity into sharp focus. Over and above the requirements of a linguistic theory of lexical knowledge, the various approaches must provide an analytical framework that can be naturally compared, and preferably reconciled, with the results of psycholinguistic and neurolinguistic investigation.

It would be wrong, however, to see linguistic theories of lexical meaning as inevitably incomplete rival models, in need of validation from mind and brain sciences. Psychological and neurological methods of analysis cannot lead to useful results about the relation between cognition and language, and specifically of lexical knowledge, without assuming a model of what lexical knowledge consists of: how it is organized, what its semantic building blocks are, what a 'lexical item' is precisely, what the role of context and of non-linguistic knowledge is, and how these aspects relate to background assumptions about linguistic meaning. The models of lexical meaning we have reviewed articulate different answers to this type of question, and in their ongoing development they have amassed a wealth of results and partial conclusions that deserve to be integrated (and challenged) by any investigation of the nature of lexical meaning.

References

Aarts, Bas. 2004. Modelling linguistics gradience. *Studies in language* 28 (1). 1–49.
Acquaviva, Paolo, & Phoevos Panagiotidis 2012. Lexical decomposition meets conceptual atomism. *Lingue e Linguaggio* XI (2). 165–180.
Apresjan, Jurij D. 1966. Analyse distributionnelle des significations et champs sémantiques structurés. *Langages* 1 (1). 44–74.
Adger, David. 2015a. Mythical myths: Comments on Vyvyan Evans' "The Language Myth". *Lingua* 158. 76–80.
Adger, David. 2015b. More misrepresentation: A response to Behme and Evans 2015. *Lingua* 162. 160–166.
Aikhenvald, Alexandra. 2002. *Classifiers*. Cambridge: Cambridge University Press.
Alexiadou, Artemis & Monika Rathert (eds.). 2010. *The syntax of nominalizations across languages and frameworks*. Berlin & New York: De Gruyter.
Arad, Maya. 2003. Locality constraints on the interpretation of roots: the case of Hebrew denominal verbs. *Natural Language and Linguistic Theory* 21. 737–778.
Asher, Nicholas. 2011. *Lexical meaning in context*. Cambridge: Cambridge University Press.
Baldinger, Kurt. 1984. *Vers une sémantique moderne*. Paris: Klincksieck.
Baroni, Marco & Alessandro Lenci. 2010. Distributional Memory: A General Framework for Corpus-Based Semantics. *Computational Linguistics* 36 (4). 673–721.
Behme, Christina & Vyvyan Evans. 2015. Leaving the myth behind: A reply to Adger (2015). *Lingua* 162. 149–159.
Benczes, Reka, Antonio Barcelona & Francisco Ruiz de Mendoza Ibáñez (eds.). 2011. *Defining metonymy in Cognitive linguistics: Towards a consensus view*. Amsterdam: John Benjamins.
Bierwisch, Manfred & Robert Schreuder. 1992. From concepts to lexical items. *Cognition* 42. 23–60.
Booij, Geert. 2010. *Construction Morphology*. Oxford: Oxford University Press.
Borer, Hagit. 2005a. *In Name Only*. Oxford: Oxford University Press.
Borer, Hagit. 2005b. *The normal course of events*. Oxford: Oxford University Press.
Borer, Hagit. 2013. *Taking form*. Oxford: Oxford University Press.
Berlin, Brent & Paul Kay. 1969. *Basic Color Terms: Their Universality and Evolution*. Berkeley, CA: University of California Press.
Brown, Susan Windisch. 2008. Polysemy and the mental lexicon. *Colorado Research in Linguistics* 21. 1–12.
Budanitsky, Alexander & Graeme Hirst. 2006. Evaluating WordNet-based measures of lexical semantic relatedness. *Computational Linguistics* 32. 13–47.

Cable, Set. 2011. A New Argument for Lexical Decomposition: Transparent Readings of Verbs. *Linguistic Inquiry* 42. 131–138.
Chersoni, Emmanuele, Alessandro Lenci & Philippe Blache. 2017. Logical Metonymy in a Distributional Model of Sentence Comprehension. In *Proceedings of the 6th Joint Conference on Lexical and Computational Semantics* (*SEM 2017). 168–177.
Chierchia, Gennaro. 1998. Reference to Kinds across Languages. *Natural Language Semantics* 6. 339–405.
Chierchia, Gennaro. 2010. Mass nouns, vagueness and semantic variation. *Synthese* 174. 99–149.
Chung, Sandra. 2000. On reference to kinds in Indonesian. *Natural Language Semantics* 8 (2). 157–171.
Conklin, Harold C. 1973. Color categorization. *American Anthropologist* 75. 931–942.
Comrie, Bernard & Greville G. Corbett (eds.). 1993. *The Slavonic Languages*. London: Routledge.
Connolly, Andrew C., Lila R Gleitman & Sharon L. Thompson-Schill. 2007. Effect of congenital blindness on the semantic representation of some everyday concepts. *Proceedings of the National Academy of Sciences of the United States of America* 104 (20). 8241–8246.
Coseriu, Eugenio. 1973. *Sincronía, Diacronía e Historia – El problema del cambio lingüístico*. Madrid: Editorial Gredos, S.A.
Coseriu, Eugenio. 2000. Structural semantics and "cognitive" semantics. *Logos and Language* 1–1. 19–42.
Cree, George S., Ken McRae & Chris McNorgan. 1999. An attractor model of lexical conceptual processing: simulating semantic priming. *Cognitive Science* 23 (3). 371–414.
Croft, William & D. Alan Cruse. 2004. *Cognitive Linguistics*. Cambridge: Cambridge University Press.
Croft, William. 2012. *Verbs: aspect and causal structure*. Oxford: Oxford University Press.
Cruse, D. Alan. 1986. *Lexical semantics*. Cambridge: Cambridge University Press.
Cruse, Alan. D. 2011. *Meaning in Language*. Oxford: Oxford University Press.
Curran, James R. 2003. *From Distributional to Semantic Similarity*. PhD thesis, University of Edinburgh.
Dembitz, Šandor, Gordan Gledec & Mladen Sokele. 2014. An economic approach to big data in a minority language. *Procedia Computer Science* 35. 427–436.
Divjak, Dagmar. 2010. *Structuring the Lexicon: a Clustered Model for Near-Synonymy*. Berlin: De Gruyter
Dixon, R. M. W. & Alexandra Y. Aikhenvald. 2009. *Adjective classes: A cross-linguistic typology*. Oxford: Oxford University Press.
Dölling, Johannes & Tatjana Heyde-Zybatow. 2007. Verb Meaning: How much Semantics is in the Lexicon? In Andreas Späth (ed.), *Interface and interface Conditions*, 33–76. Berlin: de Gruyter.
Dowty, David. 1979. *Word meaning and Montague grammar*. Dordrecht: Kluwer.
Eckardt, Regine. 2006. *Meaning change in grammaticalization: An inquiry into semantic reanalysis*. Oxford: Oxford University Press.
Engelberg, Stefan. 2011. Frameworks of lexical decomposition of verbs. In Claudia Maienborn, Klaus von Heusinger & Paul Portner (eds.), *Semantics: An international handbook of natural language meaning*, Vol. 1, 358–399. Berlin: Mouton de Gruyter.
Erk, Katrin & Sebastian Padó 2008. A structured vector space model for word meaning in context. In *Proceedings of EMNLP 08*. 897–906.

Evans, Vyvyan. 2014. *The language myth: Why language is not an instinct*. Cambridge: Cambridge University Press.
Fábregas, Antonio & Sergio Scalise. 2012. *Morphology. From data to theories*. Edinburgh: Edinburgh University Press.
Fellbaum, Christiane (ed). 1998. WordNet: *An Electronic Lexical Database*. Cambridge, MA: MIT Press.
Fillmore, Charles J. & Paul Kay. 1995. *Construction grammar*. Berkeley: Ms., University of California, Berkeley.
Fillmore, Charles. 2006. Frame semantics. In Dirk Geeraerts (ed.), *Cognitive Linguistics: basic readings*, 373–400. Berlin: Mouton de Gruyter.
Firth, John R. 1951. Modes of meaning. In John R. Firth (ed.), *Essays and Studies* [Reprinted in *Papers in Linguistics 1934–1951*], 190–215. London: Oxford University Press.
Firth, J. R. 1957. A synopsis of linguistic theory, 1930–1955. *Studies in linguistic analysis*, 1–32. Oxford: Philological Society.
Fodor, Jerry & Ernie Lepore. 1999. Impossible words? *Linguistic Inquiry* 30. 445–453.
Gärdenfors, Peter. 2000. *Conceptual Spaces: On the Geometry of Thought*. Cambridge, MA: MIT Press.
Gärdenfors, Peter. 2014. *The geometry of meaning: semantics based on conceptual spaces*. Cambridge, MA: MIT Press.
Geeraerts, Dirk. 1997. *Diachronic Prototype Semantics – A Contribution to Historical Lexicology*. Oxford: Clarendon Press.
Geeraerts, Dirk. 2010. *Theories of lexical semantics*. Oxford: Oxford University Press.
Gerner, Matthisa. 2014. Noncompositional scopal morphology in Yi. *Morphology* 24. 1–24.
Gibbs, Raymond. 1994. *The poetics of mind. Figurative thought, language, and understanding*. New York: Cambridge University Press.
Giora, Rachel. 2003. *On our mind: salience, context and figurative language*. New York: Oxford University Press.
Landau, Barbara & Lila R. Gleitman. 1985. *Language and experience. Evidence from the Blind Child*. Cambridge, MA: Harvard University Press.
Goldberg, Adele. 1995. *Constructions: A construction grammar approach to argument structure*. Chicago: University of Chicago Press.
Goldberg, Adele. 2006. *Constructions at work: The nature of generalization in language*. Oxford: Oxford University Press.
Gonzalez-Marquez, Monica, Irene Mittelberg, Seana Coulson & Michael, J. Spivey. 2007. *Methods in Cognitive Linguistics*. Amsterdam: John Benjamins.
Guiraud, Pierre. 1967. *Structures étymologiques du lexique français*. Paris: Larousse
Hale, Kenneth & Samuel Jay Keyser. 1999. A response to Fodor and Lepore, "Impossible words?". *Linguistic Inquiry* 30. 453–466.
Hale, Kenneth & Samuel Jay Keyser. 2002. *Prolegomenon to a theory of argument structure*. Cambridge, MA: MIT Press.
Hale, Kenneth & Samuel Jay Keyser. 2005. Aspect and the syntax of argument structure. In Nomi Erteschik-Shir and Tova Rapoport (eds.), *The Syntax of Aspect*, 11–41. Oxford: Oxford University Press.
Hampton, James A. 2007. Typicality, graded membership, and vagueness. *Cognitive Science*, 31, 355–383.
Hanks, Patrick & Rachel Giora. 2011. *Metaphor and figurative language*. London: Routledge

Harley, Heidi. 2004. Wanting, Having, and Getting: A Note on Fodor and Lepore 1998. *Linguistic Inquiry* 35. 255–267.
Harley, Heidi. 2012. Semantics in Distributed Morphology. In Claudia Maienborn, Klaus von Heusinger & Paul Portner (eds.), *Semantics: An international handbook of natural language meaning*, volume 3 (HSK 33.3), 2151–2172. Berlin: Mouton de Gruyter.
Harley, Heidi. 2014. On the identity of roots. *Theoretical Linguistics* 40 (3/4). 225–276.
Harris, Zellig S. 1954. Distributional structure. *Word* 10 (2–3). 146–162.
Harris, Zellig S. 1991. *A Theory of* Language *and Information: A Mathematical Approach*. Oxford: Clarendon Press.
Hinton, Geoffrey E., James L. McClelland & David E. Rumelhart. 1986. Distributed representations. In David E. Rumelhart & James L. McClelland (eds), *Parallel Distributed Processing: Explorations in the Microstructure of Cognition. Volume 1: Foundations*, 77–109. Cambridge, MA: MIT Press.
Hinzen, Wolfram. 2007. *An essay on names and truth*. Oxford: Oxford University Press.
Jackendoff, Ray. 2010. *Meaning and the lexicon: The parallel architecture 1975–2010*. Oxford: Oxford University Press.
Jackendoff, Ray. 1990. *Semantic structures*. Cambridge, MA: MIT Press.
Jackendoff, Ray. 2002. *Foundations of language*. Oxford: Oxford University Press.
Jackendoff, Ray. 2011. Conceptual semantics. In Klaus von Heusinger, Claudia Maienborn, & Paul Portner (eds.), *Semantics: An onternational handbook of natural language meaning*, volume 1, 688–709. Berlin: Mouton de Gruyter.
Jakobson, Roman. 1959. On linguistic aspects of translation. In Reuben A. Brower (ed.), *On Translation*, 232–239. Cambridge, MA: Harvard University Press.
Jones, Michael N., Jon A. Willits & Simon Dennis. 2015. Models of Semantic Memory. In Jerome R. Busemeyer, Zeng Whang, James T. Townsend & Ami Eidels (eds.), *Oxford Handbook of Mathematical and Computational Psychology*, 232–254. Oxford: Oxford University Press.
Jones, Steven, M. Lynne Murphy, Carita Paradis & Caroline Willners. 2012. *Antonyms in English: construals, constructions and canonicity*. Cambridge: Cambridge University Press.
Kaufmann, Ingrid. 1995. What is an (im)possible verb? Restrictions on semantic form and their consequences for argument structure. *Folia Linguistica* 29. 67–103.
Kay, Paul, Brent Berlin, Luisa Maffi, William R. Merrifield & Richard Cook. 2009. *The World Colour Survey*. Stanford: CSLI Publications
Kintsch, Walter. 2001. Predication. *Cognitive Science* 25 (2). 173–202.
Kleiber, Georges. 1978. *Le mot "ire" en ancien français (XIe-XIIe siècles) – Essai d'analyse sémantique*. Paris: Klincksieck.
Klein, Devorah & Gregory Murphy. 2001. The Representation of Polysemous Words. *Journal of Memory and Language* 45. 259–282.
Koontz-Garboden 2005, On the typology of state/change of state alternations. *Yearbook of Morphology 2005*, 83–117. Dordrecht: Springer.
Lakoff, George & Mark Johnson. 1980. *Metaphors we live by*. Chicago: Chicago University Press.
Lakoff, George. 1987. *Women, fire and dangerous things*. Chicago: Chicago University Press.
Lakoff, George. 1990. The invariance hypothesis. *Cognitive Linguistics*, 1(1). 39–74.
Landauer, Thomas K. & Susan Dumais. 1997. A solution to Plato's problem: The latent semantic analysis theory of acquisition, induction, and representation of knowledge. *Psychological Review* 104 (2). 211–240.
Langacker, Ronald. 1987. *Foundations of cognitive grammar*. Stanford: Stanford University Press.

Langacker, Ronald. 1998. Conceptualization, Symbolization, and Grammar. In Michael Tomasello (ed.), *The New Psychology of Language: Cognitive and Functional Approaches to Language Structure*, 1–39. Mahwah, NJ and London : Erlbaum.

Lapata, Mirella & Alex Lascarides. 2003. A probabilistic account of logical metonymy. *Computational Linguistics* 29 (2). 263–317.

Larson, Richard. 2011. Clauses, propositions and phases. In Anna-Maria DiSciullo & Cedric Boeckx (eds.). *The biolinguistic rnterprise: New perspectives on the evolution and nature of the human language faculty*, 366–391. Oxford: Oxford University Press.

Larson, Richard, & Gabriel Segal. 1994. *Knowledge of meaning*. Cambridge, MA: MIT Press.

Lehrer, Adrienne. 1974. *Semantic fields and lexical structure*. Amsterdam: North Holland.

Lenci, Alessandro. 2008. Distributional approaches in linguistic and cognitive research. *Italian Journal of Linguistics* 20 (1). 1–31

Lenci, Alessandro. 2018. Distributional models of word meaning. *Annual Review of Linguistics* 4. 151–171.

Lenci, Alessandro, Marco Baroni & Giulia Cazzolli. 2013. Una prima analisi delle norme semantiche BLIND. In Giovanna Marotta, Linda Meini & Margherita Donati (eds.), *Parlare senza vedere: Rappresentazioni semantiche nei non vedenti*, 83–93. Pisa, ETS.

Lenci, Alessandro, Marco Baroni, Giulia Cazzolli & Giovanna Marotta. 2013. BLIND: a set of semantic feature norms from the congenitally blind. *Behavior Research Methods* 45(4). 1218–1233.

Levin, Beth. 2011. Conceptual categories and linguistic categories I: Introduction. http://web.stanford.edu/~bclevin/lsa11intro.pdf (Accessed on 29/4/2019).

Levin, Beth & Malka Rappaport Hovav. 2011. Lexical conceptual structure. In Klaus von Heusinger, Claudia Maienborn, & Paul Portner (eds.), *Semantics: An international handbook of natural language meaning*, volume 1, 418–438. Berlin: Mouton de Gruyter.

Levy, Omer & Yoav Goldberg. 2014. Linguistic regularities in sparse and explicit word representations. In *Proceedings of the Eighteenth Conference on Computational Language Learning*. 171–180.

Libben, Gary & Silke Weber. 2014. Semantic transparency, compounding, and the nature of independent variables. In Franz Rainer, Francesco Gardani, Hans Christian Luschütsky & Wolfgang U. Dressler (eds.), *Morphology and meaning*, 205–222. Amsterdam & Philadelphia: John Benjamins.

Lieber, Rochelle. 2004. *Morphology and Lexical Semantics*. Cambridge: Cambridge University Press.

Longobardi, Giuseppe. 2001. How comparative is semantics? A unified parametric theory of bare nouns and proper names. *Natural Language Semantics* 9/4. 335–369.

Lucy, John. A. 1997. The linguistics of "color." In Clyde Laurence Hardin & Luisa Maffin (eds.), *Color categories in thought and language*, 320–346. Cambridge: Cambridge University Press.

Lund, Kevin & Curt Burgess. 1996. Producing high-dimensional semantic spaces from lexical co-occurrence. *Behavior Research Methods, Instruments, & Computers* 28. 203–208.

Lyons, John. 1977/1993. *Semantics*. Cambridge: Cambridge University Press.

Majid, Asifa, Fiona Jordan & Michael Dunn. 2015. Semantic systems in closely related languages. *Language Sciences* 49 (1). 1–18.

Majid, Asifa & Stephen C. Levinson. 2007. The language of vision I: Colour. In Asifa Majid (ed.), *Field manual*, vol. 10, 22–25. Nijmegen: Max Planck Institute for Psycholinguistics.

Malt, Barbara C. & Asifa Majid. 2013. How thoughts is mapped into words. *WIREs Cognitive Science* 4 (6). 583–597.
Marantz, Alec. 1997. No Escape from syntax: Don't try morphological analysis in the privacy of your own lexicon. In Alexis Dimitriadis, Laura Siegel, Clarissa Surek-Clark & Alexander Williams (eds.), *Proceedings of the 21st Annual Penn Linguistics Colloquium: Penn Working Papers in Linguistics 4.2*, 201–225.
Markman, Arthur B. 1999. *Knowledge Representation*, Mahwah, NJ: Lawrence Erlbaum Associates.
Marmor, Gloria S. 1978. Age at onset of blindness and the development of the semantics of color names. *Journal of Experimental Child Psychology* 25 (2). 267–278.
Martinet, André. 1989. Reflexions sur la signification. *La linguistique – Sens et signification* 25. 43–51
Massam, Diane (ed.). 2012. *Count and mass across languages*. Oxford: Oxford University Press.
McRae, Ken, Virginia R. de Sa & Mark S. Seidenberg. 1997. On the nature and scope of featural representations of word meaning. *Journal of Experimental Psychology: General* 126 (2). 99–130.
McRae, Ken, Mary Hare, Jeffrey L. Elman & Todd Ferretti. 2005b. A basis for generating expectancies for verbs from nouns. *Memory & Cognition* 33 (7). 1174–1184.
McRae, Ken, George S. Cree, Mark S. Seidenberg & Chris McNorgan. 2005a. Semantic feature production norms for a large set of living and nonliving things. *Behavior Research Methods* 37 (4). 547–559
Meillet, Antoine. 1958. Comment les mots changent de sens. *Linguistique historique et linguistique générale* 1. 230–271.
Mikolov, Tomas, Kai Chen, Greg Corrado & Jeffrey Dean. (2013). Efficient Estimation of Word Representations in Vector Space. In *Proceedings of the International Conference on Learning Representations*. 1–12.
Miller, George & Walter Charles. 1991. Contextual correlates of semantic similarity. *Language and Cognitive Processes* 6 (1). 1–28.
Mitchell, Jeff & Mirella Lapata. 2010. Composition in distributional models of semantics. *Cognitive Science* 34(8). 1388–1429.
Murphy, Gregory & Jane Andrew. 1993. The conceptual basis of antonymy and synonymy in adjectives. *Journal of Memory and Language*, 32. 301–319.
Murphy, Gregory. 2002. *The big book of concepts*. Cambridge, MA: MIT Press.
Murphy, Gregory. 2007. Parsimony and the psychological representation of polysemous words. In Marina Rakova, Gergely Pethő, & Csilla Rakosi (eds.), *The cognitive bases of polysemy: New sources of rvidence for theories of word meaning*, 47–70. Frankfurt: Peter Lang.
Murphy, M. Lynne. 2003. *Semantic relations and the lexicon*. Cambridge: Cambridge University Press.
Murphy, M. Lynne, Paradis, Carita, & Caroline Willners. 2009. Discourse functions of antonymy: a cross-linguistic investigation of Swedish and English. *Journal of pragmatics*, 41(11). 2159–2184.
Osgood, Charles E. 1952. The nature and measurement of meaning. *Psychological Bulletin* 49. 197–237.
Osgood, Charles E., George J. Suci & and Percy H. Tannenbaum. 1957. *The Measurement of Meaning*. Urbana, IL: University of Illinois Press.

Ouhalla, Jamal 2012. Lexical change and the architecture of the lexicon. In Esther Torrego (ed), *Of Grammar, Words, and Verses. In Honor of Carlos Piera*, 41–66. Amsterdam: John Benjamins.
Padó, Sebastian & Mirella Lapata. 2007. Dependency-based construction of semantic space models. *Computational Linguistics* 33 (2). 161–199.
Panther, Klaus-Uwe & Linda Thornburg. 2003. *Metonymy and pragmatic inferencing*. Amsterdam: John Benjamins.
Paradis, Carita. 2000. Reinforcing Adjectives: A cognitive semantic perspective on grammaticalization. In Ricardo Bermúdez-Otero, David Denison, Richard M. Hogg & Christopher B. McCully (eds.), *Generative Theory and Corpus Studies*, 233–258. Berlin/ New York: Mouton de Gruyter.
Paradis, Carita. 2001. Adjectives and boundedness. *Cognitive Linguistics* 12 (1). 47–65.
Paradis, Carita. 2003. Is the notion of linguistic competence relevant in Cognitive Linguistics? *Annual Review of Cognitive Linguistics* 1. 207–231.
Paradis, Carita. 2004. Where does metonymy stop? Senses, facets and active zones. *Metaphor and symbol*, 19 (4) 245–264.
Paradis, Carita. 2005. Ontologies and construals in lexical semantics. *Axiomathes* 15. 541–573.
Paradis, Carita 2008. Configurations, construals and change: expressions of degree. *English Language and Linguistics* 12 (2). 317–343.
Paradis, Carita. 2011. Metonymization: key mechanism in language change. In Reka Benczes, Antonio Barcelona & Fransisco Ruiz de Mendoza Ibáñez (eds.). *Defining metonymy in Cognitive Linguistics: Towards a Consensus View*, 61–88. Amsterdam: John Benjamins.
Paradis, Carita. 2012. Lexical semantics. In Carol A. Chapelle (ed.), *The encyclopedia of applied linguistics*, 690–697. Oxford: Wiley-Blackwell.
Paradis, Carita. 2015. Meanings of words: Theory and application. In Ulrike Hass & Petra Storjohann (eds.) *Handbuch Wort und Wortschatz (Handbücher Sprachwissen-HSW Band 3)*, 274–294. Berlin: Mouton de Gruyter, Berlin.
Paradis, Carita, Caroline Willners & Steven Jones. 2009. Good and bad opposites: using textual and psycholinguistic techniques to measure antonym canonicity. *The Mental Lexicon*, 4(3). 380–429.
Peirsman Yves, Kris Heylen & Dirk Speelman. 2007. Finding semantically related words in Dutch. Cooccurrences versus syntactic contexts. In Marco Baroni, Alessandro Lenci and Magnus Sahlgren (eds.), *Proceedings of the 2007 Workshop on Contextual Information in Semantic Space Models: Beyond Words and Documents*, 9–16.
Peirsman, Yves & Dirk Speelman. 2009. Word space models of lexical variation. In Roberto Basili & Marco Pennacchiotti (eds.), *Proceedings of the EACL GEMS Workshop*, 9–16.
Perek, Florient. 2016. Using distributional semantics to study syntactic productivity in diachrony: A case study. *Linguistics* 54 (1). 149–188.
Pustejovsky, James. 1995. *The generative lexicon*. Cambridge, MA: MIT Press.
Pylkkänen, Liina, Rodolfo Llinás & Gregory Murphy. 2006. The representation of polysemy: MEG evidence. *Journal of Cognitive Neuroscience* 18. 97–109.
Raffaelli, Ida. 2009. *Značenje kroz vrijeme: poglavlja iz dijakronijske semantike*. [Meaning through time: chapters in diachronic semantics] Zagreb: Disput.
Raffaelli, Ida, Jan Chromý, Anetta Kopecka. 2019. Lexicalization patterns in color naming in Croatian, Czech and Polish. In Raffaelli, Ida, Daniela Katunar & Barbara Kerovec (eds.), *Lexicalization patterns in color naming: a cross-linguistic perspective*. Amsterdam: John Benjamins

Rainer, Franz. 2014. Polysemy on derivation. In Rochelle Lieber & Pavol Štekauer (eds.), *The Oxford handbook of derivational morphology*, 338–353. Oxford: Oxford University Press.

Ramchand, Gillian. 2008. *Verb meaning and the lexicon: A first-phase syntax*. Cambridge: Cambridge University Press.

Rappaport Hovav, Malka & Beth Levin. 1998. Building verb meanings. In Miriam Butt & Willi Geuder (eds.), *The Projection of arguments: Lexical and compositional factors*, 97–134. Stanford, Ca: CSLI Publications.

Rappaport Hovav, Malka & Beth Levin. 2010. Reflections on manner/result complementarity. In Edit Doron, Malka Rappaport Hovav & Ivy Sichel (eds.), *Syntax, lexical semantics, and event structure*, 21–38. Oxford: Oxford University Press.

Rieger, Terry, Paul Kay & Naveen Ketharpal. 2007. Color naming reflects optimal partitions of color space. *Proceedings of the National Academy of Sciences of the United States of America* 104(4). 1436–1441.

Riemer, Nick. 2013. Conceptualist semantics: explanatory power, scope and uniqueness. *Language Sciences* 35. 1–19.

Riemer, Nick. 2016. Internalist semantics: meaning, conceptualization and expression. In Nick Riemer (ed.), *The Routledge handbook of semantics*, 30–47. London: Routledge.

Rogers, Timothy T. & James L. McClelland. 2004. *Semantic Cognition: A Parallel Distributed Processing Approach*. Cambridge MA: MIT Press.

Rosch, Eleanor. 1973. Natural categories. *Cognitive psychology* 4. 328–350.

Rosch, Eleanor. 1975. Cognitive representations of semantic categories. *Journal of Experimental Psychology: General* 104. 192–233.

Rothstein, Susan. 2004. *Structuring events: A study in the semantics of lexical aspect*. Oxford: Blackwell.

Rothstein, Susan. 2010. Counting and the mass-count distinction. *Journal of Semantics* 27. 343–397.

Sagi, Eyal, Stefan Kaufmann & Brady Clark. 2009. Semantic density analysis: Comparing word meaning across time and phonetic space. In *Proceedings of the EACL GEMS Workshop*. 104–111.

Sahlgren, Magnus. 2006. *The Word-Space Model. Using Distributional Analysis to Represent Syntagmatic and Paradigmatic Relations between Words in High- Dimensional Vector Spaces*. PhD thesis, Stockholm University.

Saussure, Ferdinand de. 1959/1986. *Course in general linguistics*. London: Peter Owen.

Schwarze, Christoph & Marie-Therese Schepping. 1995. Polysemy in a two-level semantics. In Urs Egli, Peter E. Pause, Christoph Schwarze, Arnim von Stechow & Götz Wienold (eds.), *Lexical knowledge and the organization of the language*, 275–300. Amsterdam: John Benjamins.

Senft, Gunter (ed.). 2000. *Systems of Nominal Classification*. Cambridge: Cambridge University Press.

Shepard, Roger N. & Lynn A. Cooper. 1992. Representation of Colors in the Blind, Color-Blind, and Normally Sighted. *Psychological Science*, 3(2), 97–104.

Sinclair, John. 1987. *Looking up: an account of the COBUILD project in lexical computing and the development of the Collins COBUILD English Language Dictionary*. London: Harper Collins.

Smith, Edward E. & Douglas L. Medin. 1981. *Categories and Concepts*. Cambridge, MA: Harvard University Press.

Storjohann, Petra. 2010. Synonyms in corpus texts: Conceptualisation and construction. In: Petra Storjohann (ed.), *Lexical-Semantic Relations: Theoretical and Practical Perspectives*, 69–94 Amsterdam: John Benjamins.
Svenonius, Peter. 2008. The position of adjectives and other phrasal modifiers in the decomposition of DP. In Louise McNally & Chris Kennedy (eds.), *Adjectives and adverbs: Syntax, semantics, and discourse*, 16–42. Oxford: Oxford University Press.
Talmy, Leonard. 1985. Lexicalization patterns. In Timothy Shopen (ed.), *Language typology and syntactic description*, volume 3, 57–149. Cambridge: Cambridge University Press.
Talmy, Leonard. 2000. *Toward a cognitive semantics*. Cambridge, MA: MIT Press.
Taylor, John. 2003. *Linguistic Categorization*. Oxford: Oxford University Press.
Tomasello, Michael. 2003. *Constructing a language: a usage-based theory of language acquisition*. Cambridge, MA: Harvard University Press.
Tomasello, Michael. 2008. *Origins of human communication*. Cambridge, MA: MIT Press.
Traugott, Elisabeth & Richard B. Dasher. 2001. *Regularity in semantic change*. Cambridge: Cambridge University Press.
Traugott, Elizabeth & Graeme Trousdale. 2013. *Constructionalization and Constructional Changes*. Oxford: Oxford University Press.
Trier, Jost. 1931. *Der deutsche Wortschatz in Sinnezirk der Verstandes: Die Geschihte eines sprachlichen Feldes, I von den Anfängen bis zum Beginn des 13Jh*. Heidelberg: Winter
Tsujimura, Natsuko. 2014. Mimetic verbs and meaning. In Franz Rainer, Francesco. Gardani, Hans Christian Luschütsky & Wolfgang U. Dressler (eds.), *Morphology and meaning*, 303–314. Amsterdam & Philadelphia: John Benjamins.
Turney, Peter D. & Patrick Pantel. 2010. From frequency to meaning: Vector space models of semantics. *Journal of Artificial Intelligence Research* 37. 141–188.
Tversky, Amos. 1977. Features of similarity. *Psychological Review* 84(4). 327–352.
Ullmann, Stephen. 1969. *Précis de sémantique française*. Bern: A. Francke.
Ullmann, Stephen. 1973. *Meaning and Style*. Oxford: Basil Blackwell.
Ullmann, Stephen. 1983. *Semantics – An Introduction to the Science of Meaning*, Oxford: B. Blackwell.
van de Cruys, Tim. 2008. A comparison of bag of words and syntax-based approaches for word categorization, *Proceedings of the ESSLLI Workshop on Distributional Lexical Semantics*. 47–54.
van de Weijer, Joost, Carita Paradis, Caroline Willners & Magnus Lindgren. 2012. As lexical as it gets: the role of co-occurrence of antonyms in a visual lexical decision experiment. In Dagmar Divjak & Staphan Th. Gries (eds.), *Frequency effects in language: linguistic representations*, 255–279. Berlin: Mouton de Gruyter.
van de Weijer, Joost, Carita Paradis, Caroline Willners & Magnus Lindgren. 2014. Antonym canonicity: temporal and contextual manipulations. *Brain & Language*, 128(1) 1–8.
Verhagen, Arie. 2005. *Constructions of intersubjectivity: discourse, syntax and cogntion*. Oxford: Oxford University Press.
von Stechow, Arnim. 1995. Lexical decomposition in syntax. In Urs Egli, Peter E. Pause, Christoph Schwarze, Arnim von Stechow & Götz Wienold (eds.), *Lexical knowledge and the organization of the language*, 81–118. Amsterdam & Philadelphia: John Benjamins.
Vigliocco, Gabriella & David P. Vinson. 2007. Semantic representation. In Gaskell, Gareth (ed.), *The Oxford Handbook of Psycholinguistics*, 195–215. Oxford: Oxford University Press.

Vigliocco, Gabriella, David P. Vinson, William Lewis & Merrill F. Garrett. 2004. Representing the meanings of object and action words: The featural and unitary semantic space hypothesis. *Cognitive Psychology* 48. 422–488.

Wilhelm, Andrea. 2008. Bare nouns and number in Dëne Sųłiné. *Natural Language Semantics* 16 (1). 39–68.

Wittgenstein, Ludwig. 1922. *Tractatus Logico-Philosophicus*. London: Routledge & Kegan Paul. Translated by C.K. Ogden.

Wittgenstein, Ludwig. 1968. *Philosophical investigations* (translated by G.E.M. Anscombe). Oxford: Blackwell.

Wunderlich, Dieter. 1997. Cause and the structure of verbs. *Linguistic Inquiry* 28. 27–68.

Zarcone, Alessandra, Alessandro Lenci, Sebastian Padó & Jason Utt. 2013. Fitting, Not Clashing! A Distributional Semantic Model of Logical Metonymy. In *Proceedings of IWCS 2013*. 404–410.

Zarcone, Alessandra, Sebastian Padó & Alessandro Lenci. 2014. Logical Metonymy Resolution in a Words-as-Cues Framework: Evidence From Self-Paced Reading and Probe Recognition. *Cognitive Science* 38. 973–996.

Lavinia Merlini Barbaresi and Wolfgang U. Dressler
Pragmatic explanations in morphology

Abstract: This chapter focuses on new perspectives and the recent history of pragmatic explanations in morphology, both on morphopragmatic issues where pragmatics is of primary importance, such as in diminutives, and where pragmatic interpretations are clearly secondary to semantic meanings as in most pragmatic aspects of inflectional morphology. The main categories dealt with are evaluatives, extragrammatical and grammatical reduplication, honorifics, but there is a survey of many others as well. The discussion also includes emotional, sociopragmatic and psycholinguistic argumentations (especially from language development). The outlook urges for more consideration of morphopragmatic issues in areas of cognitive science.

Keywords: Morphopragmatics, pragmatics, diminutives, reduplication, evaluatives

1 Introduction

This focus of this chapter is on the importance of the interaction between pragmatics and morphology against a background of competing approaches and neighboring disciplines whose main difference lies in the nature of the interaction between semantic and pragmatic meanings. We are opposed to those who assume only a secondary interaction between morphosemantics and morphopragmatics, i.e. who take morphosemantics as always primary, and only secondarily exploited pragmatically. This view is compatible with a Fodorian view of modularity (Fodor 1983), where only after the encapsulated course of derivation of the morphotactics and morphosemantics of a pertinent morphological category, interaction with pragmatics is possible. In contrast, our view (since Dressler and Merlini Barbaresi 1994a) assumes the possibility of a basic pragmatic meaning of a morphological category or a pertinent language-specific morphological rule, although it does not exclude a secondary interaction with pragmatics for a corresponding rule in other languages, or for different morphological categories. This will give us the opportunity to provide a detailed, updated map of a largely uncharted territory, and to revive our complaint

Lavinia Merlini Barbaresi, University of Pisa, Italy
Wolfgang U. Dressler, University of Vienna, Department of Linguistics, Vienna, Austria

against the persisting neglect of pragmatic motivations in morphology and against the presentation of pragmatic meanings as semantic ones.

We argue that the explanatory power of pragmatics is not sufficiently exploited to account for the complex meanings and effects conveyed by certain morphological operations, mainly exemplified in the domain of evaluative word formations, such as diminutives. Morphopragmatics precisely covers the area of the general pragmatic meanings generated by morphological rules.

To give an example, in the expressive Italian speech act

(1) *Come vorrei essere nel mio lett+ino!*
'How I'd love to be in my bed-DIM',

the diminutive can be easily substituted with the augmentative *lett+one*, and used in the same context to refer to the same bed. Thus, the semantic meanings of small size (diminutive) and big size (augmentative) cannot be the primary reason for using them. It is rather the emotional coloring of the speech act, which drives the imagination of the desired bed.

A discussion on the state of the art in this and similar areas of research gives us the scope for a fresh outlook on morphopragmatics, and new evidence for re-proposing and elaborating on some crucial points of our theory of morphopragmatics (Dressler and Merlini Barbaresi 1994a) and for widening the topic area of morphopragmatic investigations.

In a pragmatic perspective, language is viewed as action, or, more precisely, as social interaction arising among participants when jointly producing speech act sequences in a speech situation (after Austin 1962, Eco 1987:704, Kempson et al. 2016, Vernant 2003). A large part of this chapter is intended to show how patterns of word-formation (be it derivational morphology or compounding) and of inflection may either have a basic pragmatic meaning (e.g. hypocoristics and diminutives), or at least obtain regular pragmatic effects triggered secondarily on the basis of a semantic meaning and reference, whose interpretation is strictly conditioned by contextual factors, as is the case, for instance, with pronouns, plurals and the categories of aspect and mood (Binnick 2009). The approach is mainly synchronic, but some diachronic argumentations will be included. Other disciplines, as, for example, psycholinguistics and corpus linguistics, will become relevant whenever they can give helpful hints.

After a brief introduction into the history or research on the morphology-pragmatics interface (§ 2) and on the impact of emotion (§ 3) we present our extended and interdisciplinary view on morphopragmatics (§ 4), deal with related studies (§ 5), competing approaches (§ 6), especially Daniel Juravsky on evaluatives (§ 7), the objects of our analysis (§ 8), especially diminutives and related evaluatives (§ 9), then with honorifics (§ 10), morphopragmatics in inflectional morphology (§ 11), and reduplication (§ 12) plus extragrammatical English reduplication (§ 13). The brief conclusion (§ 14), after the references, by an appendix of utterances illustrating the various pragmatic uses of diminutives.

2 Early studies in morphology interfacing with pragmatics

Important precursors to the theory of morphopragmatics are found in early studies on diminutives: De Amicis (1905) gave an ample pre-theoretical description of their pragmatic effects in Italian, more complete than Staverman's (1953) for Dutch.

Spitzer (1921) pioneered the important notion whereby the pragmatic scope of the diminutive is the whole utterance and not just the diminutivized word (cf. Dressler and Merlini Barbaresi's 1994a: 218 elaboration of the concept). For example, diminutivization of the speech act of the Italian invocations

(2) a. *Madonna santa!*
       'Oh holy virgin!'
    b. *Dio buono!*
       'Good Lord!'

results in *Madonn+ina santa!*, which could be conceivably interpreted as being a simple diminutivization of the head noun. However, since *Dio* 'God' cannot be diminutivized in Italian (in contrast to Spanish *Dios+ito* and German *Ach Gott+chen* in exclamations), the attributive adjective is diminutivized in *Dio buon+ino!*, clearly not meaning that the goodness of God is diminutivized. Rather the expression of inner states may be downgraded in the speech situation of restrained complaints and mild commiserations or, conversely, upgraded when pleading. Note also the substitution of Italian *lett+ino* by *lett+one* in (1).

In this connection, also Alonso (1933/1961) must be mentioned because he was the first scholar who systematically related the emotional values of diminutives to context, participants' attitudes and, ante litteram, to types of speech acts, as is the case of the examples just mentioned.

3 Emotion

Within linguistics, the subsequent stream of studies on diminutives (for example, Dardano 1978, Klimaszewska 1983, Volek 1987, Wierzbicka 1984, 1991) all contributed to downgrading the denotative meaning of smallness in favor of emotional values, whose meanings and effects depend on the motivating context, interacting participants, speech acts and discourse register.

A natural connection between emotions and the pragmatics of social actions is also a major tenet in recent psychological and philosophical theories. For example, Wüschner (2015) explores the idea that emotions in social contexts and their intentionality may be conceived of as pragmatic or epistemic actions, i.e. not only as inner states. This applies directly to the down- and upgrading in the invocations mentioned in (2). Moreover, Slaby and Wüschner (2014) conceptualize emotions as unfolding in relational and dialogical acts. As such, they are to be seen less as mental states and more as one's behavior in and towards the world. They observe (see Slaby and Wüschner 2014: § 3) that in recent studies emotions are variously described, for example as 'felt evaluatives' (Helm 2001), 'feelings towards' (Goldie 2000), 'affective perceptions' (Döring 2007), or 'felt evaluative attitudes' (Deonna and Teroni 2012) What is especially interesting for us here is the recognition of an evaluative attitude inherent in the interactants' dialogical acts.

A more indirect contribution to the emotionalist line of research is found in studies on politeness (Brown and Levinson 1983, Leech 1983 and 2014, Haverkate 1990, Sifianou 1992, Watts 2003), where various interfaces between morphology/grammar and pragmatics are assumed. In Leech (2014), the interface of pragmatics and linguistic form ('pragmalinguistics') and that between pragmatics and society ('sociopragmatics') are the basis of his renovated approach to politeness. Leech (2014: ix and Ch.9) asks two important questions that can be generalized and become pertinent to all investigations concerning pragmatics: (1) how do we know about the pragmatics of politeness? (2) what kind of observational or experimental evidence can be brought to bear?

Morphopragmatics tries to answer such questions empirically by isolating, through the analysis of various discourse types and tokens, those linguistic (morphological) elements that are capable of systematically contributing stable pragmatic effects. Evidence of a correct pragmatic interpretation rests not only on the complex inferential work of the interpreter (cf. the notion of 'contextually drawn plausible inferences' in Ariel 2007:1) aimed at recognizing such effects, but especially on objectifying contextual and co-textual motivations and perlocutionary reactions, by recognizing relevant linguistic cues and indices (cf. Bazzanella 2004), i.e. in linking the interpretation of morphopragmatic elements to the co-text and/or context. Only in this way can we interpret the function of diminutivization in the invocations of (2) as either downgrading or upgrading. When used in pleading, the speaker wants to increase, i.e. to upgrade, the addressee's readiness to fulfil the speaker's direct or indirect request (i.e. the intended perlocutionary sequel). In contrast, when complaining, the speaker wants to downgrade, the addressee's possible negative reactions. Such interpretations by an analyst must be confirmed by other coherent cues in the situational context or in the preceding or following co-text.

The scope of influence of the morphological elements is the utterance, as said above, but the pragmatic effects obtained may actually extend to the entire text (cf. Watts' 2003:142 discourse-oriented perspective in relation to politeness). The speech act and speech act sequence have proved to be too narrow a target for a safe pragmatic evaluation (Leech 2014). Conversational discourse can give a better account of the dynamically changing behaviors of the individuals involved. An example is the ludic character of diminutives in pastoral poetry of the 18th century and in Mozart's opera *Così fan tutte*.

Of relevance is the concept of pragmatic act (Mey 2001), whereby the focus of the analysis has shifted from the speech act to the situation of utterance for its understanding. The issue of analysis beyond utterances has also been on the agenda of dialogue studies (e.g. Weigand 2000, 2010a, 2010b; Carbaugh 2013; Cooren 2010). A broader scope is actually implied in the computational notion of dialogue act (DA) (Bunt 1979, 2000, 2011, Bunt et al. 2017 and the connected area of research). DAs can be thought of as a tag set that classifies utterances according to a combination of pragmatic, semantic, and syntactic criteria. Kecskes (2016) speculates on the interfacing of DAs with pragmatics. See the interesting elaboration of various concepts and modalities of computational pragmatics in Jurafsky (2006), which, for him, is also a starting point for revisiting the problem of speech act interpretation.

4 Morphology and pragmatics

In Dressler and Merlini Barbaresi's Morphopragmatics (1986, 1987, 1989, 1994a and continued by both authors together or separately), the mutual relation between the two areas of morphology and pragmatics is amply and systematically described, i.e. morphological rules and elements are analyzed in their interaction with pragmatic conditions. More precisely, morphopragmatics deals with grammatical morphological operations that autonomously (cf. Potts's 2007 notion of 'independence') assign pragmatic meanings to the utterance, i.e. obtain regular pragmatic changes when moving from the input to the output of a morphological operation, both within word formation and inflection. The authors' theoretical position actually rests on a major premise: they view semantics as a specialized subpart of pragmatics in general (Morris 1938). But elsewhere in this chapter we use pragmatics, as in general usage, only as pragmatics from which the specialized subpart of semantics has been subtracted.

Morphopragmatics can be paralleled with, but distinguished from, other well-established sub-areas of research, like morphosemantics, lexical semantics of morphology (Lieber 2004), lexical pragmatics of morphology, sociopragmatics and pragmatics of syntactic patterns and textual strategies (for a more detailed account, cf. Dressler and Merlini Barbaresi 1994a:55 and Merlini Barbaresi 2015b). But some extra observations on these disciplines are in order here, because of their close relevance to our general discussion.

Lexical pragmatics of morphology is the area where most often uncertainty can arise concerning the boundaries of a morphological operation. It deals with the pragmatic meanings idiosyncratically acquired by single complex words, like, for example, lexicalized *starl-et*, somewhat derogatory due to connotations acquired by use over time, or *bunn-y* 'rabbit', a diminutive of Scottish dialectal *bun*, pet name for *rabbit*, selecting a child environment and obtaining a pragmatic meaning of endearment, or, more recently, a sexist environment in connection with its use in the Playboy magazine. The pragmatic meanings/effects belong to the word itself and its circumstances of use, and not to the word-formation operation. The majority of the early studies aiming at a pragmatic account of word-formation belong here. The pragmatic meaning of a morphological rule is unfortunately often conflated with that of the individual lexical item.

What is neglected in this latter approach is a focus on the capacity of the morphological operation involved in the construction of the complex word to obtain similar effects regularly, given certain sets of contextual conditions (for diminutive formation, for example, typically, child-centered speech situations and the emotionality involved, ludic character of playfulness among intimates, familiarity and informality in general), and given certain regulating factors (typically, sympathy and empathy, but also understatement, euphemism, false modesty, irony and sarcasm).

The area must be restricted and specified with respect to current general theories of Lexical Pragmatics (LP) within cognitive linguistics, which investigates the processes by which literal meanings of words are modified in use, basically through the pragmatic operations of narrowing (meaning restricted to the specific case) or broadening (approximation or category extension), which correspond to the two types of lexical pragmatic processes that take place during comprehension. The linguistic meaning of a word in an utterance only provides a point of departure for an inferential process of meaning construction (Rebollar 2013); see also Blutner (1998) and Wilson and Carston (2007). Of course, within this type of studies, the focus is again on the word in use (whether simplex or complex) and not on word-formation mechanisms and their effects.

Experimental Pragmatics is another area of research that tangentially touches upon morphopragmatics. Experimental approaches draw on formal semantics and pragmatics with perspectives from psychology and cognitive science, and concentrate on the actual mental processes involved in language comprehension (Schwarz 2014: 2). More specifically, they investigate to what extent the overall message conveyed by a certain utterance is actually covered by the literal meaning of the sentence uttered. In doing that, they foreshadow various possible enrichments of the literal meaning that are clearly pragmatically-based as crucially related to the context of the utterance. Within this area, some aspects of non-literal meaning are investigated that are also keypoints in a morphopragmatic investigation: namely irony, sarcasm, metonymy, and metaphor (see also Potts 2006 and Potts et al. 2015). An example amply discussed in Dressler and Merlini Barbaresi (1994a: 370–372) is the episode of an Italian professor misunderstanding as sarcastic the literal semantic meaning of diminution in the phrase *quel libr+etto* 'that rather small book', uttered by a student in referring to an objectively small book written by the same professor. In considering the larger context less superficially, the professor could have acknowledged the student's attempts to understate modestly his amount of preparation for the ongoing exam.

A recent theoretical approach by Bara (2011) based in 'cognitive pragmatics', provides extra validation to the approach above. On an interactive perspective, cognitive pragmatics focuses on the mental states (emotional and cognitive) of the participants in a conversation, in their developing along the conversation time. The analysis of the mental processes of human communication is based on three fundamental concepts: cooperation, sharedness, and communicative intention (not dissimilar from the principles proposed by Grice 1975). Shared beliefs and knowledge ('common ground' in Clark 1996) are of special significance for us, as it accounts for the possibility of comprehending non-standard communication such as humorous talk, irony, jokes, deceit and figurative language, which are often the target of a morphopragmatic investigation. Bara (2011: 457) also observes that studies in intercultural communication (Piller 2010, Spencer-Oatey and Franklin 2009) have shown that the culture dimension may be responsible for differences in the pragmatic possibilities of realizing interactional communication, also due to the impact of cross-cultural psychology (Berry and Poortinga 2011). An example is the above-mentioned episode of the misunderstanding of the Italian student's diminutive *libr+etto*, because according to our experience students from some other nations would not choose such a strategy of modesty when taking an exam.

This approach has weakened the thesis of universality in favor of a greater attention to be paid to an ethnocentric dimension, which also points to the need to carry out pragmatic interpretations with great attention to specific interpreters and contextual sets. But this is a bias, of course, against the universal validity of many current models of linguistic analysis (see problems of universalism vs. relativism in Ronga et al. 2014). Expectedly, cognitive pragmatics and cognitive sociolinguistics (see Kristiansen and Dirven 2008) have much to contribute to overcome such limitations. A similar earlier but much simpler approach to diminutives, which still lacks this interdisciplinary perspective, can be found in Dressler and Merlini Barbaresi (1994a: 410–414).

It is also relevant to mention Schmid (2012), dealing with the construal of non-explicit and non-literal meaning-in-context and Kempson and al.'s (2016) concept of a psycholinguistically motivated model of analysis that includes in its definition of 'context' the various processing paths that unfold for each participant in the course of the interaction (see also Duranti and Goodwin 1992).

The area of sociopragmatics (relative to morphological rules) also deserves attention, because it actually may overlap with that of the pragmatics of morphology in various ways. In agreement with one main point in our general discussion, Körtvélyessy and Štekauer (2014) complain about the neglect reserved to the social aspects of derivational morphology by social studies (in comparison to the massive contributions of psychological studies), in particular to the factors that affect the formation and interpretation of complex words. Prieto (2015, see also Prieto 2005), in reference to Spanish, confirms this result. Unlike numerous sociolinguistic studies dealing with phonological and syntactic aspects of language, there are just very few publications addressing the issues of morphology. Prieto underlines the fact that evaluative suffixes have sociolinguistic effects, as they mark the language of social groups as well as the context (especially informal speech situation).

Expectedly, sociopragmatics would seem more than entitled to answer questions concerning word-formation rules and their interpreters, contextual and indexical factors and variables of their use, as well as factors regulating interactant rapport. Examples may be social preferences in the use of specific word-formation mechanisms (e.g. evaluatives), as regulated by genre, sex, age, diastratic and diatopic varieties, channel of communication, formal vs. informal situations. A notion of adaptability (Verschueren 1999), in the social-interactive sense and in terms of language being adaptive to the process of communication, is especially relevant. Various restrictions on the pragmatic use of diminutives, for example, are regulated by such concepts. A pragmatic foundation is also at the basis of the sociopragmatic norms regulating the use of honorifics (more in § 9). A study centered on the sociopragmatics of diminutives is De Marco (1998).

From a morphopragmatic perspective, a mutual relevance of the two disciplines can be found, for example, in the use of polite or strategic diminutives in discourse, as in Italian *solo un minut+ino* 'just a sec, lit. 'only a minute+DIM'; Mexican Spanish *ahor+ita* 'immediately, lit. 'now+DIM', or in mitigated requests, as Italian *Mi fai un piacer+ino?* "can you do me a little favor (lit. a favor+DIM)?", as well as in the use of honorifics and polite pronouns.

5 Morphopragmatic and related studies

The morphopragmatic approach attracted other scholars, who applied the model to different speech situations or other languages or other categories. For example, Kilani-Schoch and Dressler (1999) elaborated and specified the model on the French *-o* suffix, Crocco Galéas (1992) on the pragmatic difference between learned and usual Italian ethnics, Laalo (2001) on the pragmatics of Finnish diminutives, Biscetti (2001) on diminutives in technical terminology, Merlini Barbaresi (2001) on the English *-y/ie* suffix, Merlini-Barberesi (2014) on the English *-let* suffix, Mattiello (2009) on the morphopragmatics of English and Italian negative prefixes, and Appah and Amfo (2012) on the morphopragmatics of the diminutive suffix (*-ba/-wa*) in Akan.

With somewhat different applications, Cantero (2003) studies the Spanish morphopragmatic elements and Badarneh (2010) the pragmatics of diminutives in Jordanian Arabic. Pertinent observations on the pragmatic roles of diminutives and other morphological elements are already present in Bazzanella, Caffi, and Sbisà (1991).

Other related studies show divergent interpretations, such as Kiefer (2004) on Hungarian diminutives (and excessives), who derives the pragmatic effects of diminutives from their semantic meanings, i.e. from semantic diminution, according to his principle (p. 327) "morphopragmatics entails semantics". In his Hungarian example:

(3)   *a konyak+ocska helyèben*
      'in place of the little brandy',

Kiefer (2004: 338) derives the pragmatic meaning from the thereby eliminated semantic meaning of smallness, from the intimate relationships between the adult interactants in casual conversation, and from the suggestion that the speaker "is on good terms with alcoholic drinks".

This conflicts with a basic tenet of the theory pioneered by Dressler and Merlini Barbaresi, who, advocate priority of pragmatics over semantics for diminutives in the languages investigated, except English (see Dressler and Merlini Barbaresi 2001: 43 onwards. Another exception is French, see Fradin 2003, Dressler 2010).

Various scholars, who include pragmatic explanations in their analyses of evaluatives' meanings, do not necessarily theorize about their semantic vs. pragmatic status: see for example Böhmerová's (2011) extended study on Slovak diminutives and augmentatives, Bardaneh's (2010) on Jordanian Arabic, Reynoso Noveròn (2005) on Mexican Spanish, Pakendorf (2017) on Even (a Tungusic language spoken in Siberia) diminutive suffixes, of which only a part has clear pragmatic meanings. More radically, Meibauer (2014: 117) observes that recent important theorists in morphology do not even feel the need for an interface between morphology and pragmatics (for example Lieber 2004). Not dissimilarly, a pragmaticist like Ariel (2010) amply theorizes on pragmatics but with no allusion to morphology. We find no mention of morphology, either, in The Oxford Handbook of Pragmatics (Horn and Ward 2006), although a specific section is devoted to pragmatics and its interfaces.

A whole line of theoretical studies, dealing with diminutives or more broadly evaluatives, neglect reference to pragmatics. This is the case of Scalise (1984, 1994), whose theoretical proposal for locating evaluatives and only evaluatives in a 'third morphology' between inflectional and derivational morphology, has had the merit of attracting greater attention to evaluatives. There are other important studies where the pragmatics of evaluatives is discussed as a matter of semantics, although without necessarily assuming the same boundaries between semantics and pragmatics. First of all we have to refer to the extended studies by Grandi (2002, 2011, 2015, 2017, cf. Carstin 2017 about boundaries between pragmatics and semantics in general), but also note, for example, Bosanac et al. (2009), exploring the semantic background of Croatian diminutives. Even Schneider (2003), in his important study on English diminutives, in spite of his pragmatic program, actually conceives of an attitudinal meaning, identified as affection and emotion, as a feature of the diminutive suffix semantics, which he represents as nice/sweet+small.

Scalises's (1984, 1994) idea of a "third morphology" in addition to inflection and derivation, is correct only insofar as evaluatives combine formal properties of prototypical inflection and prototypical derivation, as conceptualized by Dressler (Dressler 1989, Dressler and Merlini Barbaresi 1994a, b, Dressler et al. 2014). However, if this is the only reason for Scalise to propose a "third morphology", it should be observed that such a mixture of prototypical properties of inflection and derivation is not restricted to evaluatives alone. There exist many other morphological categories that share characteristics of both prototypical inflection and prototypical derivation, such as infinitives, participles, and noun plurals, with language-specific variations of how many properties of inflection and derivation they have.

Diminutives in the European languages represent a case of non-prototypical derivation, i.e. they are closer to prototypical derivation than to prototypical inflection, whereas Bantu diminutives represent a case of non-prototypical inflection, being closer to prototypical inflection. For example, in Shona (Déchaine et al. 2015: 504), they do not change word class, have inflectional agreement and systematically peripheral position (i.e. outside derivational suffixes). In what follows, we provide a few examples for the non-prototypical properties of diminutives in European and many other languages.

Prototypical derivational suffixes are heads and thus determine word class and gender of the derived complex word. This property is shared by German diminutives, as in *dumm* 'stupid, dumb' → Austrian German neuter noun *das Dumm+erl* 'the dumb person', *die Mutter* 'the mother (fem.)' → neuter DIM *das Mütter+chen/-lein/-l*, but feminine gender is maintained in the variant *die Mutt+i*. Romance and Slavic diminutive suffixes most of the time do not change word class or gender, whereas this is prototypically the case when a derivational suffix is attached. Modern Greek *-áki* transforms a masculine or feminine word into a neuter, whereas competing Greek diminutive suffixes preserve word class and gender.

Prototypically derivational suffixes precede inflectional ones, which holds in most languages also for diminutive suffixes. Exceptions, though, occur in several languages (Derzhanski 2005), for example in German *Kind+er+chen* 'childr+en+DIM', or in Johann Sebastian Bach's sarcastic *Lied+er++chen* 'song+s+DIM' about a rival composer, an occasionalism which sounds nearly acceptable to native speakers today. However, as noted, belonging to non-prototypical derivational or inflectional morphology does not as such justify establishing a "third morphology" for evaluatives only. What is specific for diminutives, however, and presumably for other morphopragmatic categories, is the lack of lexical and pattern blocking, when they have a (at least predominantly) pragmatic meaning. For example, from recent English loanwords, the following Italian diminutives have been derived:

(4)   *vipp+ino/+etto/+ar+ello/+uccio, manager+ino/+etto/+ello/+uccio*

(and 14 more such diminutive sets derived from other bases in Dressler et al. 2019). Comparable Polish diminutive competitions have been reported by Malicka-Kleparska (1985). Although competing word derivations exist also in prototypical derivational morphology (Plag 1999; Bauer, Lieber and Plag 2013), such massive competition between suffixations for one and the same base without a difference in semantic meaning does not seem to have been observed so far in the area of prototypical derivational morphology

There are other recent studies whose theoretical approaches underestimate the explanatory power of pragmatics in finding the right interpretation of evaluatives in their context. For instance, Fortin (2011) intends to cover what he considers as underdeterminacy with his notion of 'multidimensional semantics' of evaluatives. On a comparative line, in the majority of the contributions contained in the extended work edited by Grandi and Körtvélyessy (2015), specific reference to pragmatics is amply disregarded.

As illustrated in Körtvélyessy (2014), also evaluative morphology is not universal, it is language-specific. Through her analysis of 203 languages of the world, Körtvélyessy also suggests that the most productive morphological process in the field of evaluative morphology is suffixation. However, the process of reduplication (§ 12, but also prefixation) relative to a large number of world languages challenges such primacy, as shown in the constellation of studies concerning the 60, not yet or hardly documented languages described in Grandi and Körtvélyessy (2015). The descriptions of the morphological processes of affixation and reduplication in these extra-European languages greatly enlarge the picture of the phenomenon of evaluatives and of their theoretical issues.

Among the studies on language-specific evaluatives in Europe, we mention Stefanescu (1992), Rainer (1993), Napoli and Reynolds 1995, Dal (1997), De Marco (1998), Mutz (2000), Gracía and Turón (2000), Nekula (2003), Fradin et al.(2003), Merlini Barbaresi (2004, 2014), Prieto (2005), often with no or rare reference to pragmatic uses.

Grandi (2002, 2011, 2015, 2017) deserves special attention in the panorama of studies on evaluatives for his vastness of topics, centered on the formal and semantic aspects of evaluatives in many languages, or dealing with their historical origin and development, also from a typological perspective. His theoretical model is based on viewing the linguistic evaluative strategy as the realization of four semantic primitives, the values BIG, SMALL, GOOD and BAD, of which the first two are descriptive, the second two are said to be qualitative, all four, though, being strictly semantic.

6 Morphopragmatics and its competitors

This bibliographic discussion is concluded here by contrasting Dressler and Merlini Barbaresi's model of Morphopragmatics (1994a) with competitors and afterwards (§ 7) with another important and widely accepted model, that of Jurafsky (1996).

6.1 Evaluatives

According to Dressler and Merlini Barbaresi's theory of morphopragmatics, a large number of meanings obtained by evaluatives (especially diminutives and augmentatives), such as downgrading and upgrading of illocutionary force, sympathy and empathy, understatement, euphemism, false modesty, irony and sarcasm can be explained only via a pragmatic interpretation (referring at least to European languages). This is in line with their conception of a priority of pragmatics over, or at least independence of, semantics. Both categories of evaluatives exhibit great polysemy, often paradoxically contradictory (a diminutive like Italian *cas+ina* 'house-DIM' can be nice and cosy or, in other contexts, poorly small and unattractive, or the augmentative Italian *occhi+oni* 'eyes-AUG' conveys a meaning of beauty, whereas *gamb+one* 'huge legs', conveys the reverse). Moreover, in spite of their semantic polarity, diminutives and augmentatives, in some cases, are felt as indistinguishable, as shown, for example in translation, e.g. of Italian into English, a language lacking the category of augmentatives: Italian AUG *biond+one* is translated into English as DIM *blond+ie*, similarly Italian *grass+one* is translated as *fatt+y*. This choice can only be explained if we conceive of a dominant pragmatic meaning and advocate its autonomy from semantics (more in Dressler and Merlini Barbaresi 2001 and Merlini Barbaresi 2014).

These authors claim for both diminutives and augmentatives a complex meaning structure which cannot be exhaustively described in terms of morphosemantic denotation and connotations plus some type of contextual pragmatics. Rather, they envisage a global concept having both semantic and pragmatic invariant features. That is, the complex meaning structure of evaluatives is definable in terms of a morphosemantic denotation (dimensional smallness vs. bigness), morphosemantic connotations (positive and negative) and morphopragmatic meanings characterized by a subjective, fictive evaluation and a context of lowered formality, both implying a state of non-seriousness. In particular, word connotations, intended as stable meanings picked up from contextual uses over time, are often misinterpreted as pragmatic in nature, but they are instead part of the complex semantics of the word and are not obtained through synchronic morphological operations.

A priority of the present approach is to demonstrate the autonomous capacity of morphological rules of conveying pragmatic meanings and therefore to recognize a clear separation between their semantics and pragmatics.

6.2 Fictiveness

The authors advocate a thesis whereby the denotative meaning is attributed to morphosemantics and the remainder of the meaning components to morphopragmatics. In addition to the basic semantic meaning [small], with its allosemes [unimportant] and [young] for diminutives, and [big] plus its allosemes [important] and [exaggerate] for augmentatives, the authors propose for both an invariant, non-semantic, still more basic pragmatic feature [fictive], which implies reference to the speaker's attitude in the speech event and which naturally conforms to the fuzziness of subjective evaluations.

6.3 Non-seriousness

The invariant morphopragmatic feature [fictive] is further specified as a character [non-serious], which frames the majority of the diminutive meanings in discourse, for example, imprecision, attenuation, euphemism, but also irony, meiosis, ludic attitude, and others (cf. Schneider's 2013: 144 interesting notion of sub-normality, and some principles current in politeness, such as modesty, opinion reticence and low assertiveness, as in Leech 1983).

This is confirmed by the corpus-linguistic analysis of the competition between the Standard German suffix *-chen* and the Austrian German *-erl* in different genres (Schwaiger et al. 2019): in the electronic Austrian Media Corpus, the ratio between the two types of diminutives is 2.5 *X+chen* to 1 *X+erl*, but in our corpus of early Viennese child speech, the corresponding ratio is 1 to 2.8, because the Austrian variant is for small children more intimate and ludic. However, in the tweet corpus of the Academiae Corpora of the Austrian Academy of Sciences the ratio is 1 *X+chen* to 270 *X+erl*, because twittering is considered as a rather ludic and non-serious form of communication. Similar confirmation comes from the contrast carried out in Dressler and Merlini (1994a) between the two different iconic renderings of love in the Mozart libretti of diminutive-rich *Così fan tutte*, where love is treated as non-serious (like in earlier pastoral poetry), and diminutive-poor *Don Giovanni*, where love is presented as dramatic and demoniac.

In general, the great prominence of diminutives also in (especially early) child speech and child-directed speech can be explained, within our framework, by characterizing the speech situation as often ludic and including a participant who is considered, also legally, as a non-serious participant when compared to adults. This fits to the general finding that the earliest meanings of diminutives in child speech, that analysts can identify, are pragmatic and that children first express smallness analytically by adjectives meaning "small". As to pragmatic effects, directly recoverable pragmatic meanings are acquired much earlier than inferential meanings (Savickiene and Dressler 2007, Dressler and Korecky-Kröll. 2015, Kilani-Schoch et al. 2011).

The speaker evaluates the speech act and the speech situation as non-serious, in the sense of non-formal, non-demanding, non-binding. An evaluative diminutive suffix appears to conform to the speaker's evaluation of non-socially dangerous contextual premises, naturally exemplified by speech situations centered on children and intimates, or, conversely, to the speaker's evaluation of a socially-dangerous situation that needs some hedging, illustrated, for example, by threatening speech acts, like requests, critical assertions, etc. In general, the diminutive suffix indexes the speaker's lowered responsibility and entails lower distance between speaker and addressee.

Also augmentatives, albeit more rarely, can induce contextual non-seriousness (e.g. a comical effect due to exaggeration), and can serve, via different routes, the same mitigation strategy. For example, an augmentative can downgrade the weight of requests, as in Italian:

(5) *Raga[zzi], qualcuno me lo fa un piacer+one?*
"Hey, buddies, can somebody do me a (big) favor-AUG ?"

(6) *Sono una sfacciat+ona, ma vorrei chiederti un piacer+one*
'I am an impertinent-AUG, but I'd like to ask you a favor-AUG'
'I know this might sound really cheeky but I must ask you a big favor, can I?'

Or, in critical assertions, the exaggeration expressed by the augmentative confers a ludic character to the offence, actually mitigating it, as in Italian:

(7) *Sai cosa ti dico, spiritos+one?*
'You know what I tell you, witty-AUG'
'You know what, funny guy?'

6.4 Evaluation act

(8) *Well, speak to your little wife+let, your little bunn+y, for God's sake*
(from Albee's "Who's afraid of Virginia Woolf?" mentioned in Schneider 2013)

The evaluation in the example above is implicit and indirect, it is pragmatically obtained in the course of the interaction but rests on a sort of prior personal prejudice which remains unexpressed. What is made explicit is some type of contextual conditions which semiotically stand for something else. Through the speaker's sarcasm, we can easily reconstruct the state of his disapproval of the addressee's wife or of wives in general and of their silly influence on their husbands. The specific contextual factor is pragmatically determined by the type of interaction (and interactants) and favors the use of linguistic elements capable of a shift from a semantic to a pragmatic dimension. Even a single textual element such as a diminutive, in fact, may obtain such a shift and, as seen above, may allow the speaker to express an evaluation, i.e. a judgement 'as to value' (not 'as to fact') (Dressler and Merlini-Barbaresi 1994a), although implicitly and indirectly.

A 'judgement as to value' is a mental operation assessing the value of an object or event, as more or less desirable and important in the interpreter's views and involves an explicit or implicit act of approval or disapproval. The act of evaluation stems from an audience-directed intention (in the sense of Strawson 1964: 459), both communicative and persuasive, and comes in successive steps. First, it is self-directed and refers to the speaker's affective and attitudinal dispositions. These consist of continua of implied personal feelings, like interest / disinterest, pleasure / displeasure, attachment / detachment, approval / disapproval, whose different degrees and combinations regulate the evaluative orientation, both axiologically and in terms of affective intensity of the utterance. A second step of the speaker's evaluation is directed at the social context of use and its relevant properties. These will regulate the terms and the forms of the evaluation in accordance with contextual variables, such as, for example, degree of formality, participant closeness, purpose or other specific circumstances. It is at this point that the speaker will judge contextual conditions asmore or less favorable for the use of evaluative affixes or other morphological mechanisms.

At this phase, the evaluative process is still a private act, based on the speaker's perception of the object (cf. Fradin's 2003 notion of referent's pole) and on his/her personal intentions, perspectives and standards of evaluation (Fradin's locutor's pole). It acquires social relevance when it is translated into a speech act involving an addressee (Fradin's interlocutor's pole). The evaluation, then, becomes a social act that may trigger perlocutionary reactions. The addressee may or may not recognize the favorable conditions and share or reject (various degrees of intensity of) the speaker's evaluative attitude.

A consequence of the wide scope of the evaluative process is also the pragmatic relevance of diminutives for the whole speech act rather than just for the diminutivized word (as already mentioned in § 1 and 2), although a diminutive suffix needs a specific landing-site on a specific word (Dressler and Merlini Barbaresi, 1994a: 218–228). The choice of the landing-site may depend on specific grammatical and lexical conditions of a language.

An example is the sarcastic speech act of the rhetorical question at the beginning of Figaro's aria in Mozart's "Le nozze di Figaro" I, 3:

(9) *Se vuol ballare signor cont+ino?*
 'if he wants dance Sir count-DIM'
 'Would his lordship, that dumb count, care to dance with me?'

In German, the prefixed title 'Sir/Lordship' and 'count' is not a legal landing-site for a diminutive suffix, because such prefixed titles cannot be diminutivized. In the most popular German translation

(9a) *Will der Herr Graf ein Tänz+chen nun wagen?*
 'wants the Sir count a dance-DIM now dare?'

neither of the two nouns 'Lordship' and 'count' is a possible landing-site, therefore the noun 'dance' is diminutivized. And this pragmatic attitude sets the tone for the whole aria to follow.

7 Jurafsky

Jurafsky (1996: 563) challenges Dressler and Merlini Barbaresi's core argument relative to the feature [non-serious] (see Dressler and Merlini Barbaresi 2001 for a general critical rebuttal), which he (following Wierzbicka 1984) proposes to replace with 'child' and its meaning [small], as a semantic prototype that he postulates to be at the center of a universal radial category (Lakoff 1987) of diminutive meanings (Vanhove and Hamid Ahmed 2016: 4 oppose this conception). He considers these multiple meanings as the result of recurrent semantic processes in both a synchronic and a diachronic perspective. As a synchronic object, the radial category motivates the sense relations of a polysemous category, but as a diachronic object, it gives account of the meaning changes from the more physical, central sense of 'child' to the more general, abstract and qualitative meanings (e.g. pragmatic) of the edge. Jurafsky's major asset is his universalistic cognitive approach, i.e. he explores 60 languages, and identifies a synchronic complex network of meanings, all diachronically postulated as emanating from the central meaning [small], of which each language instantiates at least a portion coherently connected with the center.

Prieto (2015) fills a big lacuna in Jurafsky's work by extending his radial system to augmentatives, but providing no opposite analogue to the core concept [child] of diminutives. Matisoff (1992), in his study of diminutives and augmentatives in some languages of Southeast Asia, maintains that the origin of augmentative markers is the word for 'mother', but, according to Vanhove and Hamid Ahmed (2016), this is not proved and in any case far from being universal.

Dressler and Merlini Barbaresi (2001: 45) and Mutz (2015:144) challenge the possibility to use a unique model to represent both synchronic and diachronic variation. Both studies oppose Jurafsky's assumption of a universal unidirectionality of the meaning 'child' to cover all the meaning variations synchronically represented, for example in the Indo-European languages, where many diminutive suffixes have developed from derivational suffixes (e.g. creating denominal relational adjectives), unconnected with the meaning 'small'.

To the universalistic quality of Jurafsky's semantic model, so vastly applicable and actually applied in evaluative analyses, morphopragmatics opposes a more dynamic capacity to generate pragmatic meanings, thanks to the invariant feature [fictive], inherent in evaluatives, which is immediately capable of both building a favorable set of situational circumstances, including co-text (non-serious, personalized and subjective), and creating pragmatic meanings (attenuation, euphemism, ludic attitude, contempt, etc.) suited to the speech act sequences involved (cf. Biscetti and Dressler 2002). Compare the following utterances A and B: the simple adding of a diminutive in B invites a complex pragmatic interpretation (mitigated non-offensive criticism or hedged request), which would be inadequate for A utterances:

(10) a. Il tuo ragazzo è grasso!
      'your boyfriend is fat!'
   b. Il tuo ragazzo è grass+ott+ello! 'fat-DIM_1.DIM_2'
      'your boyfriend is a bit plump'

(11) a. Non potresti darmi un aiuto?
 'couldn't you give me a help?'
 b. Non potresti darmi un aiut+ino? 'help-DIM'
 'what would you say to a bit of help?'

The advantage of a morphopragmatic approach compared to others also rests on its capability to accommodate major problems connected with a synchronic analysis of diminutives (and augmentatives), namely their seemingly irregular and unpredictable polysemy, and on its capability to systematize and explain their variety of forms and functions.

In this regard, and to resume our general criticism concerning the vast neglect of pragmatics, we like to mention Simon and Wiese (2011: 21–22), as reported in Grandi (2017), who confirm our point and criteria and view "the possibility of directly involving pragmatic aspects in morphology" in order to explain some of the seemingly contradictory properties of diminutives and augmentatives, whose "erratic behaviour" – they say – "turns out to be more systematic when viewed from a morphopragmatic perspective". Consider also Fortin's (2011: 1) reply to Stump (1993): "Stump's definition of evaluation semantics as "diminution, augmentation, endearment and contempt" is too limited. As is well known, evaluative affixes have many other uses, e.g., non-seriousness/informality, intensification, exactness, attenuation, approximation, and illocutionary mitigation, among others (see, e.g, Dressler and Merlini-Barbaresi 1994a; Jurafsky 1996)".

8 Objects of analysis

On a world-wide perspective, the expression of evaluative meanings can be approached onomasiologically through different linguistic means, singularly or in various combinations: for example, at the level of phonology, with consonant, vowel or tone alternations and expressive palatalization; at the level of morphology, with suffixes, prefixes, semi-prefixes, interfixes and more rarely infixes, often accompanied by gender and number changes (cf. Grandi and Körtvélyessy 2015, where more than 50 world languages have been analyzed). Also what Dressler and Merlini Barbaresi (1994a, Doleschal and Thornton 2000, Mattiello 2013) call extra-grammatical mechanisms, may be involved, like clipping, blending and echo-word formation (cf. Bauer, Lieber and Plag 2013 for different interpretations). More rarely, compounding, particles and clitics may have an evaluative function. Lexical constructions with evaluative adjectives, nouns or adverbs may add to or interfere with evaluations obtained by single constituents of the text. Let us summarize the most important morphological mechanisms employed in the European languages discussed here.

As anticipated above, among the best candidates for a morphopragmatic description are evaluative suffixes, such as diminutives and augmentatives (more rarely pejoratives), on which Dressler and Merlini-Barberesi based their main demonstration (mostly with reference to Italian, German, English and other European languages), but also elatives, (e.g. Italian *-issimo*), patterns of reduplication, excessives, and, within inflection, personal pronouns of address and honorifics, whose basic characters equally allow for a morphopragmatic analysis, to be discussed later (see § 10, 11). Extra-grammatical phenomena were not included in the 1994 model, but they are mentioned here, especially because they configure a context of intimate, informal discourse, where pragmatic meanings are expectable.

Examples are mainly drawn from languages of the European area (from corpora, web, personal collections), contextualized examples from various languages (see Appendix).

Below we group a sample of the morphological devices whose meanings seem to be primarily located in pragmatics and thus most likely to be involved in exemplary morphopragmatic operations. The list includes evaluatives, already partly illustrated above but worth of a more specialized treatment:

a) evaluative/alterative affixes (diminutives, augmentatives, pejoratives) (examples from Italian, German, English, Spanish, French), including ante-suffixal interfixes, as in various Romance languages (e.g. Italian ludicrous *top+**ol**+one* vs. serious *top+one* 'sewer rat-AUG'), more in § 8 and in the Appendix. On hypocoristics see § 9.1.

b) clipped forms, blends or portmanteaus (e.g. French *intell+o* ← *intellectuel* 'intellectual', Australian contemptuous *win-o*, "an alcoholic", *comm-o* for communist, Spanish *telebobela* 'silly soap opera' ← *telenovela* 'soap opera' and *boba* 'silly'. These formations are implicitly evaluative and often restricted in speech situations and relations between interactants (Kilani-Schoch and Dressler 1999, Scullen 1997, Antoine 2000).

c) Italian elative *-issimo* as a pragmatic intensifier in rebuttals to assertions or questions (Dressler and Merlini Barberesi 1994a, Merlini Barbaresi 2004: 449)

d) The use of some formatives, prefixoids and suffixoids derived from negatively connoted words (e.g. Italian *-poli* ← *Tangent+o+poli* 'bribing system' in *vallett+o+poli* 'irregular recruitment of TV starlets'; English *-gate* ← *Watergate* in *Enron-gate,* English *-holic* in *work+a+holic, shop+a+holic*), which have pragmatic meanings at least in the early stages of their

productivity, whereas later some of them may have become normal suffixes or combining forms.
e) The English disdainful analytic form *little* reduced and unstressed (cf. Schneider 2013), as in

(12) *I can't stand your little tricks*;
compare

(13) *Estoy harto de tus brom+ita-s*
'I'm fed up with your nasty little jokes';

Fr. *petit* reduced to the prefix *ti-*, diminutive in French Creoles (Avram 1998), hypocoristic in Québec, expressing tenderness, as in *ti-Jean* 'Johnny'.
f) Feminine motional suffixes. Through the procedure of motion between genders, feminine nouns can be obtained from the masculine ones, as well as masculine nouns from the feminine ones, by adding motional suffixes or substituting the appropriate gender marker (e.g. in Italian, the feminine marker *-a* replaces the masculine *-o* in such new words as *sindac-a* 'mayor-FEM', *magistrat-a* 'magistrate/judge-FEM', *ministr-a* 'minister-FEM'). The advent of feminist movements has led to a highly increased profitability of feminine motional suffixes in many languages (Doleschal 2005). The situation is pragmatically complex. For example, when referring to a plurality of female and male teachers, traditionalists and antifeminists use the (traditionally also generic) zero plural of the masculine deverbal agent noun *Lehrer*. One official egalitarian written correspondent is *Leh-rer-Inn-en* 'teacher-FEM. Motion-Pl' with an internal capital letter I. Its normative pronunciation requires the insertion of a glottal stop before this internal /i/. But most often the glottal stop is not pronounced, which renders this generic plural identical with that of the feminine agent noun *Lehrerinnen*. Therefore, many speakers replace such plurals with paraphrases such as *Lehrerinnen und Lehrer*. Thus, this motion suffix has become an object of morphopragmatics.
g) Metaphorical compounds, often exploited pragmatically, to express exaggeration, tenderness, irony, e.g. English *giant-killer, baby-dolphin, baby-trees, pico-brain, uber-brain*, Italian literary *pietre-bambine*, i.e. *pietr-uzze* 'stone-DIM-PL' (in D'Arrigo's novel Horcynus Orca), *pargoletta mano* 'child-DIM hand', metaphor for "little hand" (in Carducci's poem "Pianto Antico") are often pragmatically exploited, e.g. tenderness in *baby-dolphin, pargoletta mano*, exaggeration and irony in *pico-brain, uber-brain*. (Merlini Barbaresi 2015a). Phrasal compounds have also been described as being created for expressive reasons (Meibauer 2007, 2015, Trips 2012, 2014).

h) German intensifying compounds. This is another type of pragmatically exploited compounds. While *blút+arm* 'lit. blood-poor' means 'anaemic', the prosodically different *blút+árm* means "poor as a church-mouse". Compounds with such double stress express an intensifying evaluation and cannot be used in formal speech situations (Schmitt 1998; Klara 2009).
i) Honorifics, for example the Japanese suffix *-masu*. These are devices grammaticalizing politeness (more in § 10).
j) Some inflectional categories having a pragmatic foundation: (1) personal pronouns (cf. Dressler and Merlini Barbaresi 1994a: 60–72); (2) English present perfect, whose meanings Žic Fuchs (2009) considers to be the result of conventionalized pragmatic inferences about the currently relevant state; pragmatic uses of plural forms (more in § 11.1); (3) excessives (more in § 11.2); (4) evidentials as morphologizing source of information and surprise, as in Turkish, Bulgarian, Albanian, Korean, etc. (cf. Cornillie and Marín Arrese 2015); (5) affective demonstratives, such as English *this* (Potts and Schwarz 2010, Halm 2018); (6) Pragmatics has also a role in the well-known specific and context-sensitive uses of other inflectional categories such as historical presents and infinitives, and infinitives used for giving orders as well as past participles for giving warnings.
k) reduplication and echo forms in extra-European languages (Austronesian Muna contemptuous affixed *ka-guru-guru* 'poorly performing teacher', affectionate affixed *ka-lima-lima* 'little hands'), vs. reduplicatives in the European area (e.g. English *Lizzy-wizzy, easy peasy, teensy-weensy*, French *joujou* "toy", *Zizou* for Zidane, *sousoupe* "soup" (Merlini Barbaresi 2008). See also Yiddish *shm*-reduplicatives (echo words) indicating irony, derision or scepticism, as in "He's just a baby! Baby-*shmaby*. He's already 5 years old!'

Only some of the devices mentioned above will have a more detailed account.

9 Evaluatives

Evaluative diminutive and augmentative suffixes are capable of modifying the denotative semantic meaning of their bases in terms of dimension or in terms of quality (pejoratives) and in addition, they may confer to their bases and to the entire utterance, a vast array of pragmatic meanings, which co-vary with contextual and discursive variables. It would be impossible to derive such variations from morphosemantic meanings. Diminutives may be totally responsible for the added utterance meanings, with the word-base being either neutral (*book-let*) or contributory (*dear+ie*, Italian *piccol+ino* "small-DIM") or even contrary (Spanish fem. *gord+ita* or Italian *gross+ina* "big-DIM") to the effect pursued. With Italian augmentatives, the word-base meaning can hardly be contradictory because augmentatives always retain some of their denotation of bigness even when especially engaged in conveying pragmatic, non-denotational meanings (cf. Italian *piccol+ona* " small-AUG") (Merlini Barbaresi 2004).

Due to non-seriousness, pragmatic meanings are especially consonant with informal interactional discourse (in-group or intimate), in which participants' attitudes, emotions, and beliefs are foregrounded. Their type and intensity is regulated by the participants' epistemic commitment and evaluative judgements.

9.1 Diminutives

Among evaluatives, diminutives (e.g. English *kitchen+ette*, Spanish *hasta+lueg+ito* 'bye-bye-DIM', Austrian German *Papp+erl* 'meal-DIM', Italian *dormit+ina* 'a nap-DIM', cf. § 5–7) are the morphological mechanism that best exemplifies the variety of morphopragmatic meanings/effects. They are the unmarked evaluative category, i.e. the presence in a language of a productive category of augmentatives, by implication, also means the presence of diminutives (cf. Grandi 2011). Apparently, though, in Australian Warlpiri (Bowler 2015: 439), augmentatives are more common than diminutives. In Berber, Grandi (2015: 453) discusses the systematic and intricate relationship between feminine gender and diminutives and between masculine and augmentatives, which may greatly confound the picture.

Moreover, diminutives are almost universally represented cross-linguistically. At least all languages possess the pragmatically-connected category of hypocoristics, which may share with diminutives specialized contexts of use, namely, child-directed, pet-directed, and lover-directed discourse types. And, in their being strongly conditioned by an interpersonal dimension, hypocoristics appear essentially pragmatic in nature and function.

9.1.1 Hypocoristics

Although in many languages there is a large overlap between markers of hypocoristics (and appellatives) and of diminutives, each category may have access to its own variety of means or even combine means of the two categories. For example, in Italian, together with a large use of diminutive markers (appellatives *picc+ol+ino*, *om+etto* and *Cicc+ina*, *Pepp+ino*), we find reduplicatives as appellatives/hypocoristics for babies, like *puffo puffo, iccio-ciccio*, echo word, like *Gino-pino, kiki*, (see mothers' web blogs), or in English, abbreviations and reduplicatives, as *hun* for *honey*, *babe* for *baby*, or *luv* for *love*, *Lizz+y-wizz+y*, etc., but also combinations of different markers, like Italian *puff+etto-puff+etto)*, *kik+ina* (reduplicative plus DIM) or English *lov+ie-dov+ie, sweet+ie* (< *sweetheart*).

In some languages, we can still formally distinguish hypocoristics and proper (non-hypocoristic) diminutives. For example, in German, the adjective *lieb* 'dear' can give rise, to both the gendered hypocoristic nominalization *der/die Lieb+i* 'the dear one' (referring only to the speaker's boy/girl-friend), and to the neuter diminutive *das Lieb+chen* 'the beloved girl/woman'. In general, it seems to be the case that the existence of pragmatic diminutives in a language implies the co-existence of hypocoristics. Moreover, in hypocoristics, the dominance of the pragmatic character over the semantic one is even greater and clearer than in diminutives.

9.2 Augmentatives and pejoratives

These evaluative types are much less widespread cross-linguistically (Dahl 2006, Grandi 2011) and in terms of pragmatic effects less efficient than diminutives. Their markedness does not only show in their cross-linguistic implicational relation to diminutives, but also in the fact that, if they occur in the same language, then the paradigm of diminutives is richer than the paradigms of augmentatives and pejoratives (type frequency) and that diminutives are used more often than augmentatives and pejoratives (token frequency). Moreover, there seem to exist always more competing rules of diminutives (e.g. Italian productive suffixations in *–ino, -etto, -uccio, -uzzo, -olo, -onzolo*, plus several unproductives) than of productive augmentatives (It. *-one*) and pejoratives (It. *-accio, -astro*), see Merlini Barbaresi (2004). Their pertinence to pragmatics is less direct and exclusive, because, as said above, at most, they confer to their bases a combination of semantic and pragmatic meaning. When pragmatics is predominant, both augmentatives and pejoratives may be very close to diminutives in their effects, i.e. they may actually be alternative marks for signaling morphopragmatic meanings. In Italian, for example, augmentatives or pejoratives can convey, in addition to their semantic meanings [big] and [bad], respectively, tenderness and jocular closeness, as in: *Il mio fratell+one/ino!* 'My brother-AUG/DIM!' or in a famous epithet pronounced by the comedian Roberto Benigni *Ah, Wojtył+accio* "Oh, (pope) Wojtyła-PEJ", or, current in

Tuscany, *Gin+ett+accio*, 'Gino-DIM-PEJ' referred to Gino Bartali, which combines Tuscan ludic irreverence with affection.

Arguments for the primacy of the pragmatic meaning of evaluatives (especially of diminutives) have been given before, including evidence from acquisition and corpus-linguistic analysis of genres (§ 6.3). Here we want to add the diachronic comparative argument of the development of corresponding Romance diminutives and augmentatives from Latin sources (cf. Hasselrot 1957; Mutz 2000, 2015): one finds the etymologically identical suffix in Italian *cavall+one* = Spanish *cabal+ón* 'horse-AUG' and French *aigl+on* 'eagle-DIM' (also hypocoristic of Napoleon's son). Similarly, Spanish *libr+ote* 'book-AUG' corresponds to French *îl+ot* 'island-DIM', *vieill+ot* 'old-DIM', hypocoristic *Pierr+ot*. In Italian, the semantic meaning of the correspondent suffix is rather imprecise: for example, the size of a *tazz+otta* 'cup-DIM' lies in between the sizes of a *tazz+ina* 'cup-DIM' and a *tazz+ona* 'cup-AUG'. Diachronic jumps from "small" to "big" or the reverse would be surprising, whereas the primacy of a common pragmatic meaning renders secondary semantic meaning changes easier to understand.

10 Honorifics

Honorifics represent a main means of grammaticalizing politeness (Haase 2000). The most frequently described cases are various Japanese honorifics, starting with personal pronouns. There is a scale even for the first person singular, starting with *tin*, which can be used only by the Japanese emperor, but came into disuse after the death of emperor Hirohito. His successor Akihito preferred, instead, the most formal normal variant *watakusi* over the less formal variant *watasi*.

Much more pragmatically relevant is the verbal humbling suffix *-masu*, which, among the various means of honorification, is the only grammatical suffix, whose use is restricted to pragmatic meanings (Harada 1976, Ide 2003, Fukada and Asato 2004).

We exemplify the pragmatic features of the speech situation with the following pair of statements (both meaning "here is a book"):

(14) Koko ni hon ga ari- *masu*
 Koko ni hon ga aru
 'Here PARTICLE book PARTICLE there'

where the more polite or humble form with *-masu* is used instead of the simple form by:

(a) female rather than male speakers, (b) higher educated speakers with more prestigious professions than lower educated ones, (c) towards addressees that belong to a ratified out-group (vs. in-group) rather than towards bystanders, (d) towards strangers. Also authority relations play a role: if addressees have authority over the speakers, these must use *-masu* when speaking to them. There is also the conventional impact of the occasion and topic of interaction. In contrast to evaluatives, speech act intensification or mitigation is expressed by other devices than *-masu*.

What is much more common in many languages are honorifics attached to names or human subjects in general (Haase 2000, Shibatani 2006). This is also not foreign to Japanese: for example, the suffix *-chan* is limited to addressing very familiar interactants and children in an affectionate way. A very special honorific system exists in Lhasa Tibetan (Simon and Hill 2015: 387–388), where compounds used for honorific evaluation consist of a honorific first and a non-honorific second constituent; if the second constituent is already a lexical honorific, the first constituent "is replaced by an honorific categoriser morpheme" (Simon and Hill 2015: 387).

11 Morphopragmatic inflection

Although morphopragmatics plays a smaller role in inflection than in word formation (as already noticed in the greater proximity of diminutives to derivation than to inflection) we have already mentioned pragmatic foundations of inflectional categories in § 8. and inflectional properties of honorifics in § 9. Here we are going to briefly discuss pragmatic uses of plurals (§11.1) and excessives (§ 11.2).

11.1 Pragmatic uses of plurals

Well-known instances of secondary metaphoric or indexical uses of the plural are the pluralis maiestatis employed by emperors, kings or other secular or ecclesiastic authorities or the defocusing devices (cf. Shibatani 1990: 364) of the pluralis modestiae of the authorial plural.

Much less studied (but see Dressler and Mörth 2012) are pragmatic differences which exist, at least optionally, between German plural doublets such as *Rikscha+s* vs. *Riksch+en* from singular *die Rikscha* 'rikshaw' (< Japanese *jinrikisha*), *Datscha+s* vs. *Datsch+en* from singular *die Datscha* 'dacha' (< Russ. *dača*), *Schmock+s* vs. *Schmöck+e* from Singular *der Schmock* 'shmock, hack writer'.

The respective -s plural variants can have a connotation of strangeness, either of foreignness or of connoting pejoratively an out-group, as in the use of *Schmock+s* used by antisemites and particularly Nazis against Jews. In contrast, *Riksch+en* is used in Germany predominantly for rikshaws in Germany, *Rikscha+s* for those in Asia. As to *Datsch+en,* due to Russian influence, it was used predominantly in East Germany, whereas *Datsch+as* was used in West Germany.

11.2 Excessives

The excessive is the highest degree of adjective (and adverb) gradation in Dutch, German, North Germanic languages, Hungarian and Finnish. It represents an absolute intensification of the superlative (Dressler and Kiefer 1990, Dressler and Merlini Barbaresi 1994a: 558–573), on which it is also formally built. In the above-mentioned Germanic languages it is formed with the prefix *aller-* 'of all', in Hungarian by a repetition of the superlative suffix (coordinated by 'and'), and in Finnish in two analytic ways (Raun 1960). The pragmatic conditions for its use can be of two kinds:

(a) when there is a pragmatic insistence on the absolute poles of a hierarchy, as in reference to an absolute monarch or to God, as in: Danish *den aller+hellig+ste Fader* = German *der aller+heilig+ste Vater* 'the Holy Father', (b) when addressing a monarch in German up to the 19th century (in Danish up to the 18th century), as in *Aller+gnädig+ster Herr!* = Danish *aller+naadig+ste Herre!* 'most gracious Lord!', paralleled by a sign of humbleness, as in a letter signed with German *aller+untertänig+st* = Danish *aller+underdanig+st* 'most devout/submissive'.

(b) when, in accordance with the Jakobsonian principle of equivalence, the very last threshold on a paradigmatic scale of intensification is projected syntagmatically into the very last instance of a succession of instances, within a coherent chunk of text or discourse. This is exemplified in the exaggerated sequence in Heinrich Böll's novel *Der Lorbeer ist immer noch bitter*:

(15) *diese immer wieder verzögerten Abschiede, von denen jeder der **letzte** zu sein schien, bis dann doch noch der **aller+letzte** und der **aller+aller+letzte** kam*
'these again and again delayed farewells, of which each seemed to be the last one, until still the very last and the very, very last came'

12 Reduplication

According to Haspelmath's (2003: 274) definition, reduplication is a morphological process which repeats the morphological base entirely or only partially. Restricting the phenomenon to morphology, though, is perhaps an unduly limitation. In fact, reduplication can be better described as a borderline case between morphology, phonology and the lexicon, which lends itself to being treated from diverse perspectives and theoretical approaches. For our purposes, though, the notions of morphological process and lexical reduplicate form are the most relevant ones and sufficient.

On reduplication, there is an abundance of studies and of research projects (Hurch 2007), Kouwenberg and La Charité (2003) both enlarging its phenomenology and promoting novel research paradigms. As observed by Hurch (2007), reduplication lends itself perfectly as a test field for theories that opt for a non-segmental organization of phonology and morphology. It is relevant here because it may be alternative or complementary to suffixation in obtaining evaluative meanings in many languages of the world.

Reduplicative morphological constructions are indeed the second-best candidates for a morphopragmatic analysis. Like evaluative affixes, they seem to be an ideal test area for theories capable of accounting for a plurality of forms, of semantic meanings, often underdetermined and even contradictory, for a large variety of functional properties and, importantly, for motivations and explanations which often appear basically rooted in pragmatics.

In a recent publication (Grandi and Körtvélyessy 2015), a large number of extra-European languages, not yet investigated in terms of evaluative morphology, are described to give a fairly representative picture of the phenomenon worldwide. In these languages, reduplicative strategies appear to be an important alternative option for expressing meaning modifications comparable to those achieved by evaluative affixation.

12.1 Grammatical vs. extragrammatical reduplications

Reduplication is amply productive in many areas of the world, but not in the contemporary languages of Western Europe, except for the area of English, which greatly deviates from the rest of Europe both in terms of productivity and of type and token frequency.

A preliminary observation is in order: reduplication (often combined with affixes or particles) across the majority of the extra-European languages, although difficult to describe systematically, is mostly a grammatical (regular) phenomenon, engaged in fairly transparent (the reduplicative formation is always recognizable in spite of various base modifications), non-arbitrary operations, capable of regular strategies of grammar (plurality, feminine gender, imperfective aspect, distributive, iterative) and of encoding well-defined meanings (diminutive, augmentative, among others, mostly tinged with emotionality). Their formation rules and output data are, in other words, generally predictable and stable, even when they seem contradictory in meaning.

Many patterns of reduplication are in fact recognized and described by scholars as evaluative in nature, for example, in Austronesian Muna (van den Berg 2015: 367), reduplication can express diminution and tenderness (e.g. *lima* "hands' > affixed *ka-lima-lima* 'little hands'), contempt (*guru* 'teacher' > affixed *ka-guru-guru* 'poorly performing teacher'), approximation (*lolu* "stupid" > affixed *no-ka-lolu-lolu* 'rather stupid'), attenuation (*linda* 'to dance' > affixed *no-poka-linda-linda* 'dance a little, just for fun') and intensification (*ai* 'younger sibling' > *ai-ai* 'youngest sibling'). In Bikol (Mattes 2014), full reduplication may be used to express diminutives and augmentatives as well as plurals and intensives. In Taiwanese Hakka, they convey attenuation/approximation, as in *giang giang* 'somewhat afraid' vs. *giang* 'afraid' (Lai 2006:491, reported in Arcodia 2015).

In contrast, in the so-called Western area, reduplication is mostly an extragrammatical morphological formation (Dressler and Merlini Barbaresi 1994a, Dressler 2000, Doleschal and Thornton 2000, Mattiello 2013) mostly not rulebound, morphotactically unstable and fuzzy in the meanings obtained. At variance with the type described above, it more clearly partakes of the nature of word-formation, in that it is capable of enriching the lexicon of a language, if not with synonyms at least with connoted variants, e.g. English noun and verb *hush-hush* 'secret', noun and adjective *goody-goody* 'ostentatiously virtuous person', adjective *gaga* 'senile', adjective *go-go* 'aggressive', noun (echo word) *knick-knack* "a small worthless object."

All types are pertinent to this discussion because they may be alternative or complementary to affixation in obtaining evaluative meanings and hypocorism.

Moreover, reduplicative constructions can raise comparative or contrastive theoretical issues that can help clarify the picture of evaluatives in general and of their pragmatic motivations.

12.2 Iconicity

A great practical and theoretical gap between evaluative affixation and reduplication, though, lies in the semantic disequilibrium which arises from the fact that evaluative affixes have a meaning of their own, interfering and combining with that of the base, whereas a reduplication mechanism obtains meaning effects which seem regulated by very basic semiotic principles, like, for example, the time-honored iconic maxim "more of the same form equals more of the same meaning" (Lakoff and Johnson, 1980:128, see Kouwenberg and LaCharite 2003, on Caribbean creole languages), which is pertinent to plurality (e.g. Indonesian *orang* "person" *orang orang* "many people"), intensification (Thai-Cadai *dii* 'good', *díi-dii* 'very good', Chinese *hóng* 'red', *hóng hóng* 'dark red'. See Moravcsik (1978: 316) for a much less optimistic view on such predictability of meanings (in connection with reduplication or any other expression).

12.3 Evaluation meanings

A more sophisticated iconic principle may also be at work and is needed to explain opposite meanings also obtained, namely diminution, attenuation, imitation, etcetera, which some scholars consider instead as non- or anti-iconic (Regier 1998). This principle refers to a more general motivation which, in order to be explanatory, requires a complex cognitive elaboration: a change of quantity, whatever direction is intended, may diagram either intensification or diminution, but the path to reach the actual meaning pole may be much more tortuous and indirect. For example, more spots of color on a surface may result in lower intensity as in Jamaican Creole *yelo-yelo* 'yellow-spotted, yellowish', or a repetitive, intermittent action appears attenuated, less effective than a continuous action (see the above-mentioned Muna *linda* 'to' dance' vs. affixed (*no-poka*)-*linda-linda* 'dance a little, just for fun'), which is not dissimilar from Italian *salt+ell+are* 'jump-DIM-ending' < *saltare* 'jump' and *dorm+icchi+-are* 'sleep-DIM-ending, sleep intermittently' or *bago* 'new' > *bagu-bato* 'rather new, newish'.

An object may acquire lower importance (cf. the notion of "non-seriousness" in morphopragmatics), for example in Tagalog *bahay* 'house' > *bahay bahayan* 'toy house', *tao* 'person' > *tau-tauhan* 'puppet'. Also in Bikol, full reduplication may be used to express diminutives as well as plural and intensive, as in *mahal* 'expensive', *mahal-mahal* is both "rather expensive" and "very expensive". See Mattes on Bikol (2014) for an extensive treatment of this iconic evaluative principle and of the ambiguity involved and its possible solutions (also in Yami, a Philippine language, reduplicative *ara-rako* means both 'all big' and 'biggish'). Unfortunately the data reported in Grandi and Körtvélyessy (2015) as well as in other specialized studies are hardly or not at all contextualized, which renders interpretation difficult, but can we perhaps envisage some type of meiosis similar to that encountered in Italian or English (see APPENDIX). *Mahal-mahal* in its attenuated meaning, for example, seems to compare with euphemistic and understated assertions, like Italian *E' costos+etto* 'it's quite costly' with the intended meaning 'very costly'. An interesting case of diminutivum modestum is found in Sɛlɛɛ, a Niger-Congo language (Agbetsoamedo and Di Garbo 2015: 493), in an offer context, but it is a case of analytical diminutive with *pìtìpìtì* "little". In Sɛlɛɛ, the pragmatic meaning of the diminutive marker, *bi* can be intensified by lengthening the vowel or reduplicating it, as in *biibii*.

In Somali (Lampitelli 2015: 507), reduplication is very productive and is largely employed to express approximation, attenuation, reduction (with adjectives), pluractionality (Bertinetto and Lenci 2012) with verbs, *bood* 'to jump' > *bood-bood* 'to jump repeatedly, in small jumps'.

In Zulu (van der Spuy and Mjiyako 2015:519), partial and full reduplication is a complex system and an important way of marking evaluative meanings with nouns, adjectives and verbs. With verbs, it normally means 'do X a little' (Doke 1973), but also 'do X repeatedly' or 'do X without much skill'. This last meaning is primarily pragmatic, precisely self-deprecating, as in *ngi-ya-cul-a-cula* "I'm just singing a bit' (cf. Italian *cant+icchi+-are* with a diminutive suffix). In Zulu, reduplicatives often codify negative evaluations (e.g. *a-rang* 's/he does', but *a-rang a-rang* 's/he boasts, shows off'). The analysts here try an interesting explanation, which implies a complex cognitive path. They suggest that in Zulu culture, the insistent repetition of the same action can be interpretable as a 'performance' and therefore as a way for somebody to show off, even with a suspicion of evil intentions.

The data examined above provide just a sketchy picture of the great number of languages where evaluation is expressed by morphological means, be it affixes or reduplicatives: what is amazing is the pervasiveness and persistence of the same meaning effects (sometimes with further specifications) obtained cross-linguistically. Is this indicative of a universal semantics or of a shared pragmatics?

13 Extragrammatical English reduplication

As compared to the types discussed above, the Western-European reduplicatives are much less predictable, and this is mainly due to the large numbers of patterns available, their rule-unboundedness, low internal regularity, fuzzy meanings and even the mystery that often characterizes the modalities of their formation, i.e. the hardly or non-discernible path from input to output data. Still, these morphological formations (also called echo words), unlike the reduplicatives examined in § 12, have in their weaknesses – irregular grammar, non-componential semantics, often unrecognizable bases, un-headedness – a key to becoming established items in the lexicon. Some of the English reduplicatives, in fact, have been there for centuries (e.g. see the so-called copy reduplicatives, i.e. based on identical member repetition – as in *ha-ha* – which are recorded in some Old English documents dating back to the year 1000, or Shakespearian *skimble-skamble* 'senseless' and *hurly-burly* 'confusion'). This is expectable, because their mechanism of formation is not always identifiable or easily repeatable. They are created often analogically (cf. the notion of 'analogy via schema' Mattiello 2017), mainly in harmony with a well-established sound pattern. If they come to cover some useful areas of meaning, over time, they become lexicalized and enter mainstream usage, as for example late 16th century *helter-skelter* 'disorder', while others may fall into relative disuse. Their spelling or even their meaning is unstable, though, and may vary a lot in the course of use. In the extra-European languages seen above, by contrast, very rare lexicalizations are reported in connection with reduplication (for example, Rubino 2005: 12, mentions Llocano *bánga* "pot" > *banga bánga* 'skull').

For a detailed account of reduplicatives, centered on or including European ones, after Jespersen (1942), Marchand (1960) and Thun (1963), see Marantz (1982), Minkova (2002), Inkelas and Zoll (2005), Nadarajan (2006), Merlini Barbaresi (2008), Mattiello (2013), Kallergi (2015) and the publications connected with the above mentioned Graz project and web-site (Hurch 2007).

13.1 Evaluation meanings

The meaning of reduplication seems to be close to the meaning of diminutives (or augmentative and pejoratives) in several European languages (Dressler and Merlini Barbaresi 1994a, Merlini Barbaresi 2008) but especially in English. Like evaluatives, it can express empathy, endearment in child/lover/pet-centered situations but also be derogatory in other situations. For example,

(16) *Don't be silly-billy!*
   has the same type of *jocularity* and mild criticism as Italian

(17) *Non fare la sciocch-ina!*
   'Don't make the silly-DIM' .

(18) E. *Who's my boobsy-woobsy?*

said by a tender *mother* to her child parallels

(19) It: *Chi è il mio bimb-ol-ino piccol-ino?*
'Who is my baby-INTERFIX-DIM little-DIM'.(see APPENDIX).

Unlike other Western European languages, English, widely and productively exploits extragrammatical reduplication also as a word formation mechanism for enriching the lexicon. But, as seen above, reduplicatives can also cover areas of morphopragmatic use that in other languages are normally covered by evaluative suffixes. Moreover, they suit similar contexts of use, namely informal, familiar, even slangy speech.

13.2 Exragrammatical character

Although difficult to describe in terms of rules, and for that reason marginalized by grammarians, English reduplicatives are by no means neglectable: they are lively, expressive and widespread (Merlini Barbaresi 2008). We distinguish various patterns: (1) apophonic reduplicatives (also called echo words), exhibiting a systematic alternation of the stressed vowel, such as *chit-chat, dilly-dally, flip-flop, knick-knack, see-saw, zigzag, ping pong;* (2) rhyming reduplicatives, exhibiting rhyming constituents and apophony of the initial consonant, as in *boogie-woogie, bow-wow, fuzzy-wuzzy;* (3) rhyming compounds, in which both bases are meaningful, for example, *artsy-craftsy, fag-hag, willy-nilly, walkie-talkie, nit-wit;* 4) copy reduplicatives, in which the second member is the exact copy of the first, as in *bye-bye, gale-gale, go-go, ga-ga*. All types have morphopragmatic applications. For example, rhyming reduplicatives are especially used for hypocoristics and appellatives, as in *Georgie-Porgie, Humpty-Dumpty, Lizzy-Wizzy* and Ruskin's (letters to his mother) *grammie-wammie-mammie, Poos-Moos, Poosky-Woosky, Puss-Moss*, where he also affectionately refers to an allegorical figure of 'Logic' in a painting as *Lodgie-Podgie*. In a large majority of cases, the mechanism of reduplication also involves the adding of the evaluative/familiarizing/nursery suffix *-y/ie*, which contributes to the same pragmatic meaning.

Reduplicatives are confined to extra-grammatical morphology, together with other phenomena (called "oddities" by Aronoff, in Bauer 1984: 232), like abbreviations, blends, hypocoristics, backformation, acronyms and initialisms (Mattiello 2013), because they exhibit various violations of basic properties of morphological grammar. For example, (a) whereas rules of canonical derivation and compounding are predictable in meaning and form change (*read-able, book-cover*), reduplicatives at most show some very general similarity of form; (b) whereas word formation rules form new words (as in *grave > gravity*), reduplication more often obtains connoted variants (*dinner* > *din-din, marry* > *marry-schm-arry*), only capable of morphopragmatic effects; (c) whereas canonical formations rely on existing stem or word bases, reduplicatives often have no meaningful bases, hardly recognizable as pre-existent morphemes (*riff-raff, zig-zag*), or they are modified before reduplication and made less recognizable (*teeny-weeny* < *tiny*). In the onomatopoeic type (*tip-top*), the two constituents form a phonetic unit and no independent word bases are identifiable, since there is no semantic connection to the homophonous words *tip, top*; (d) morphosemantic headedness is only very rarely assignable.

Extragrammatical reduplications do not appear to form a homogeneous set. This is in line with their great interspeaker variation and their preferential use in areas where audacious formations are currently created, e.g. poetry, advertising, slang, fancy denominations (as trade names). Even among native speakers, their collocation in the language proves difficult. For example, the long lists continuously created in the web, mainly by the contribution of ordinary users, do not distinguish among canonical compounds and rhyming reduplicatives (*cook-books, flower-power, snail-mail* vs. *nitty-gritty, super-duper, teenie-weenie*).

Their rhyming sound pattern is the most apparent characteristic and its expressive force is so motivating that, sometimes, word-bases undergo major modifications to allow rhyme, e.g. in *cell-yell* (referred to noisy cellular phones), *Anglo-banglo* (a person of mixed English and Bengali descent).

13.3 Gamut of meanings

In general, the semantics exhibited by extragrammatical reduplicatives is restricted to a very limited range of meanings, more often pejorative: each area of meaning is shared by more reduplicatives, which is evidence of their indeterminacy and vagueness. Some of the represented meaning areas are:

(a) pretentiousness, as in *artsy-fartsy, culture-vulture;* (b) smallness, as in *itty-bitty, bitsy-witsy*; (c) indecision, as in *dilly-dally, shilly-shally*; (d) confusion, carelessness and disorder, as in *higgledy-piggledy, hitty-missy*; (e) trickery and secrecy, as in *hokey-pokey, hugger-mugger, jiggery-pokery*; (f) foolishness or inferior quality, as in *nitwit, silly-billy*; (g) fussiness, as in *fuddy-duddy, worry-wart*.

Not all English reduplicatives, of course, but the majority of them can be accommodated in these areas. In each of the sets, meaning is very fluid, often crossing areas and in fact many of the items could be listed elsewhere. Their indeterminacy is one of the reasons why reduplicatives are marginalized as 'non-serious', non-legitimate lexemes, more expressive than cognitive, indexical of the speaker's feelings rather than thoughts. Pragmatic meanings, of course, are rooted in this quality.

14 Conclusions

In this chapter we revised our morphopragmatic model (Dressler and Merlini 1994a) by connecting it with further areas of pragmatics, by contrasting it with competing views and by adding external evidence from acquisition and diachrony. We have confirmed that morphopragmatics is more directly present in word formation than in inflection. The reason seems to be that pragmatics is most pertinent for the level of the lexicon (to which word formation is subordinate due to its lexical function) on the one hand and for the discourse level on the other hand. Inflectional morphology is subordinated to syntax due to its syntactic function and thus only indirectly connected with the pragmatic use of syntactic constructions. The importance of pragmatics at the discourse level appears in the broad scope of the evaluative act and the pragmatic relevance of morphopragmatic elements beyond the meaning of the complex word where it is morphologically manifest. The avoidance of semantic (including connotational) synonymy leads to frequent lexical blocking, which is not the case for competition among pragmatic diminutives (Dressler et al. 2019).There is also no lexical blocking in the competition among German intensifying adjectival compounds, such as *stock+dumm* 'utterly stupid, lit. stupid like a stick' = *sau+/blitz+/kreuz+/boden+/vieh+dumm* 'lit. stupid like a sow/lightning/cross/ground/lifestock'. An impact of lack of blocking on processing may be the reason for the lack of priming effects of the Italian diminutive suffix *–etto*, in contrast to non-evaluative suffixes (Giraudo and Dal Maso 2016).

Morphopragmatics is absent in vast areas of cognitive science. One reason is the difficulty of testing morphopragmatic elements in formal psycholinguistic tests. Thus, we failed in testing pragmatic aspects of diminutives with aphasics, in contrast to semantic ones (Dressler et al. 1996, Franceschet et al. 2013). A second reason is that corpus-linguistic investigation of morphopragmatic elements requires very time-consuming manual control of contexts. Thus, we were unable to find any relevant publication written within the new approach of corpus pragmatics.

In cognitive science there exists the long-standing, but controversial and overly simplistic claim (see Stemmer 1999b; Perkins 2007) that right-handers process grammar in the left hemisphere of the brain and pragmatics in the right hemisphere. Since our model assumes a direct connection between morphological grammar and pragmatics, it clearly does not support the assumed dichotomy between the two hemispheres.

References

Agbetsoamedo, Yvonne. & Francesca Di Garbo, 2015. Sɛlɛɛ. In Nicola Grandi & Livia Körtvélyessy (eds.), *Edinburgh Handbook of Evaluative Morphology*, 487–495. Edinburgh University Presss.

Alonso, Amado. 1961. Nociòn, emociòn, acciòn y fantasia en los diminutivos. *Estudios linguisticos: Temas españoles*, 161–189. Madrid: Gredos.

Antoine, Fabrice. 2000. Dictionnaire français-anglais des mots tronqués. Louvain: Peeters.

Appah, Clement K.I. & Nana A. Amfo. 2012. The morphopragmatics of the diminutive morpheme (-ba/-wa) in Akan. In Livia Körtvélyessy & Pavol Stekauer (eds.), *Lexis 6: Diminutives and Augmentatives in the Languages of the World*, 85–103. http://lexis.univ.-lyon3.fr/IMG/pdf/Lexis_6.pdf.

Arcodia, Giorgio F. 2015. Chinese. In Nicola Grandi & Livia Körtvélyessy (eds.), *Edinburgh Handbook of Evaluative Morphology*, 352–360. Edinburgh: Edinburgh University Press.

Ariel, Mira. 2007. *Relational and independent strategies in interpreting and conjunction.* Unpublished ms. Tel Aviv University.

Ariel, Mira. 2010. *Defining Pragmatics*. New York: Cambridge University Press.

Austin, John L. 1962. *How to do things with words: The William James lectures delivered at Harvard University in 1955*. Oxford: Clarendon Press.

Avram, Andrei A. 1998. The diminutive noun prefix *ti-* in the French Creoles: Substrate influence or grammaticalization. *Revue Roumaine de Linguistique* 43. 135–154.

Bardaneh, Muhammad A. 2010. The pragmatics of diminutives in colloquial Jordanian Arabic. *Journal of Pragmatics* 42 (1). 153–167.

Bara, Bruno G. 2011. Cognitive pragmatics: The mental processes of communication. *Intercultural Pragmatics* 8. 443–485.

Bauer, Laurie. 1984. Perspectives on words. In *Views of English 3*, Wellington: VUW English Department.

Bauer, Laurie, Rochelle Lieber, & Ingo Plag. 2013. *The Oxford Reference Guide to English Morphology*. Oxford: Oxford University Press.

Bazzanella, Carla. 2004. Emotions, Language, and Context. In Edda Weigand (ed.), *Emotion in Dialogic Interaction*, 55–72. Amsterdam, Benjamins.

Bazzanella, Carla, Claudia Caffi & Marina Sbisà. 1991. Scalar dimensions of illocutionary force, In Igor Žagar (ed.), *Speech acts: Fiction or reality?*, paper 7. Ljubljana: Institute for Social Sciences.

Berry, John W. & Ype H. Poortinga. 2011. *Cross-cultural psychology: Research and applications* (3rd ed.). Cambridge: Cambridge University Press.

Bertinetto, Pier Marco & Alessandro Lenci 2012. Pluractionality, habituality and gnomic imperfectivity. In Robert I. Binnick (ed.), *Oxford Handbook of Tense and Aspect*, 852–880. Oxford: Oxford University Press.

Binnick, Robert I. 2009. Tense and aspect. In Frank Brisard, Jan-Ola Östman & Jef Verscheuren (eds.), *Grammar, meaning, and pragmatics*, 268–288. Amsterdam: Benjamins.

Biscetti, Stefania. 2001. A contrastive morphopragmatic study of Italian and English diminutives in technical terminology. In Enikő Németh (ed.), *Pragmatics in 2000: Selected papers from the 7th International Pragmatics Conference*, vol.2. 81–91 Antwerp: International Pragmatics Association.

Biscetti, Stefania & Wolfgang U. Dressler 2002. Funzioni testuali degli alterativi. In Roland Bauer & Hans Goebl (eds.), *Parallela 9*, 53–68. Wilhelmsfeld: Egert.

Blutner, Reynhard. 1998. Lexical Pragmatics. *Journal of Semantics* 15: 115–162.

Böhmerová, Ada. 2011. Suffixal diminutives and augmentatives in Slovak: a systemic view with some cross-linguistic considerations. In Livia Körtvélyessy & Pavol Stekauer (eds.), *Diminutives and Augmentatives in the Languages of the World*, 59–84. http://lexis.univ.-lyon3,fr/MG/psf/Lexis_6.pdf.

Bosanac, Siniša, Dora Lukin & Petra Mikolić. 2009. *A Cognitive Approach to the Study of Diminutives: The Semantic Background of Croatian Diminutives*. Zagreb: Sveučilište u Zagrebu.

Bowler, Margit. 2015. Walrlpiri. In Nicola Grandi & Livia Körtvélyessy (eds.), *Edinburgh Handbook of Evaluative Morphology*, 438–447. Edinburgh: Edinburgh University Press.

Brown, Penelope & Stephen C. Levinson. 1983. *Politeness*. Cambridge: Cambridge University Press.

Bunt, Harry. 1979. Conversational principles in question-answer dialogues. In D. Kallmann & G. Stickel (eds), *Zur Theorie der Frage*, 119–141. Tübingen: Narr Verlag.

Bunt, Harry. 2000. Dynamic interpretation and dialogue theory. In Martin Taylor, Françoise Néel, and Don Bouwhuis (eds.), *The structure of multimodal dialogue* II, 139–166. Amsterdam: Benjamins.

Bunt, Harry. 2011. The Semantics of Dialogue Acts. *Proceedings 9th International Conference on Computational Semantics* (IWCS 2011), Oxford, 1–14.

Bunt, Harry, Volha Petukhova & Alex Fang. 2017. Revisiting the ISO standard for dialogue act annotation. *Proceedings 13th Joint ISO – ACL Workshop on Interoperable Semantic Annotation* (isa-13) September 19, 2017 Montpellier, France.

Cantero, Monica. 2003. *La morfopragmatica del español*. München: Lincom Europa.

Carbaugh, Donal. 2013. On Dialogue Studies. *Journal of Dialogue Studies* 1. 9–28.

Carstin, Robyn. 2017. Pragmatics and semantics. In Yan Huang (ed.), *The Oxford Handbook in Pragmatics*, 453–472. Oxford: Oxford University Press.

Clark, Herbert H. 1996. Communities, commonalities, and communication. In John Gumperz & Stephen Levinson (eds.). *Rethinking linguistic relativity*, 324–355. Cambridge: Cambridge University Press.

Cooren, François. 2010. *Action and Agency in Dialogue: Passion, incarnation and ventriloquism*. Amsterdam: Benjamins.

Cornillie, B. & J.I. Marín Arrese (eds.). 2015. Evidentiality and the Semantics-Pragmatics Interface. *Belgian Journal of Linguistics 29*.

Crocco Galéas, Grazia. 1992. Morfopragmatica e pragmatica lessicale degli etnici italiani. In Giovanni Gobber (ed.), *La linguistica pragmatica*, 61–71. Roma: Bulzoni.

Dal, Georgette. 1997. *Grammaire du suffixe -et(te)*. Paris: Didier Érudition.

Dahl, Östen. 2006. Diminutives and Augmentatives. In Keith Brown (ed.), *Encyclopedia of Language and Linguistics*, Vol. 3, 594–595. Oxford: Elsevier.

Dardano, Maurizio. 1978. *La formazione delle parole nell'italiano di oggi*. Roma: Bulzoni.

De Amicis, Edmondo. 1905. *L'idioma gentile*. Milano: Treves.

Déchaine, Rose Marie, Raphaël Girard, Calisto Mudzingwa & Martina Wiltschko. 2015. Shona. In Nicola Grandi & Livia Körtvélyessy (eds.), *Edinburgh Handbook of Evaluative Morphology*, 496–506.
De Marco, Anna. 1998. *Sociopragmatica dei diminutivi in italiano*. Rende: Centro Editoriale e Librario, Università degli Studi di Calabria.
Deonna, Julien A. & Fabrice Teroni. 2012. *The Emotions. A Philosophical Introduction*. New York: Routledge.
Derzhanski, Ivan A. 2005. On Diminutive Plurals and Plural Diminutives. In Geet Booij, Emiliano Guevara, Angela Ralli, Salvatore Sgroi & Sergio Scalise (eds). *Morphology and Linguistic Typology: On-line Proceedings of the Fourth Mediterranean Morphology Meeting*, 73–90, Università degli Studi di Bologna.
Doke, Clement M. 1973. *Textbook of Zulu grammar*. Cape Town: Longman.
Doleschal, Ursula. 2005. Genus und Geschlecht. Die Repräsentation der Geschlechter in der Grammatik. In Tina Bahovec (ed.), *Frauen Männer*, 314–324. Klagenfurt: Drava.
Doleschal, Ursula & Anna M. Thornton (eds.). 2000. *Extragrammatical and marginal morphology*. München: Lincom Europa.
Döring, Sabine A. 2007. Seeing What to Do: Affective Perception and Rational Motivation. *Dialectica* 61. 363–394.
Dressler, Wolfgang U. 1989. Prototypical Differences between Inflection and Derivation. *Zeitschrift für Phonetik, Sprachwissenschaft und Kommunikationsforschung* 42. 3–10.
Dressler, Wolfgang. U. 2000. Extragrammatical vs. marginal morphology. In Ursula Doleschal & Anna M. Thornton (eds), *Extragrammatical and marginal morphology*, 1–10.
Dressler, Wolfgang U. 2010. Morphologie dynamique et statique des diminutifs. *Mémoires de la Société de Linguistique de Paris* 17. 141–154. Leuven: Peeters.
Dressler, Wolfgang U. & Ferenc Kiefer 1990. Austro-Hungarian morphopragmatics. In Wolfgang U. Dressler, Hans Luschützky, Oskar Pfeiffer & John Rennison (Eds.), *Contemporary Morphology*, 69–77. Berlin, de Gruyter.
Dressler, Wolfgang U. & Katharina Korecky-Kröll. 2015. Evaluative morphology and language acquisition. In Nicola Grandi & Livia Körtvélyessy (eds.), *Edinburgh Handbook of Evaluative Morphology*, 134–141. Edinburgh University Press.
Dressler, Wolfgang, Gary Libben & Katharina Korecky-Kröll. 2014. Conflicting vs. convergent vs. interdependent motivations in morphology. In Brian MacWhinney, Andreï Malchukov & Edith Moravcsik (eds.). *Competing Motivations in Grammar and Usage*, 181–196. Oxford: Oxford University Press.
Dressler, Wolfgang. U. & Lavinia Merlini Barbaresi. 1986. How to fix interfixes? *Acta Linguistica Hungarica* 36: 53–68.
Dressler, Wolfgang. U. & Lavinia Merlini Barbaresi. 1987. *Elements of morphopragmatics*. Duisburg: LAUD A 194 [now also in Jef Verschueren (ed.), *Levels of linguistic adaptation. Selected papers of the International Pragmatic Conference. Antwerp. II*, 33–51. Amsterdam: Benjamins].
Dressler, Wolfgang. U. & Lavinia Merlini Barbaresi. 1989. Interfissi e non-interfissi autosuffissali nell'italiano, spagnolo e inglese. In Fabio Foresti, Elena Rizzi, & Paola Benedini (eds.), *L'italiano tra le lingue romanze*. Atti del XX Congresso della Società di Linguistica Italiana, 243–252. Roma: Bulzoni.
Dressler, Wolfgang U. & Lavinia Merlini Barbaresi. 1994a. *Morphopragmatics: Diminutives and Intensifiers in Italian, German and other Languages*. Berlin: Mouton de Gruyter.

Dressler, Wolfgang & Lavinia Merlini Barbaresi. 1994b. Italian diminutives as non-prototypical word formation. In Livia Tonelli & Wolfgang U. Dressler (eds.). *Natural Morphology: Perspectives for the Nineties*, 21–29. Padova: Unipress.

Dressler, Wolfgang U. & Lavinia Merlini Barbaresi. 2001. Morphopragmatics of diminutives and augmentatives: on the priority of pragmatics over semantics. In István Kenesei & Robert M. Harnish (eds.) *Perspectives on Semantics, Pragmatics and Discourse*, 43–58. Amsterdam: Benjamins.

Dressler, Wolfgang. U., Lavinia Merlini Barbaresi, Sonja Schwaiger, Jutta. Ransmayr & Katharina Korecky-Kröll. 2019. Rivalry and coexistence among Italian and German diminutives. In Franz Rainer, Francesco Gardani, Hans C. Luschützky & Wolfgang U. Dressler (eds.) *Competition in Morphology. Selected Papers from the 17th International Morphology Meeting*, 123–144. Berlin: Springer.

Dressler, Wolfgang U. & Karlheinz Mörth 2012. Produktive und weniger produktive Komposition in ihrer Rolle im Text an Hand der Beziehungen zwischen Titel und Text. In Livio Gaeta & Barbara Schlücker (eds.), *Das Deutsche als kompositionsfreudige Sprache*, 219–233. Berlin: de Gruyter.

Dressler, Wolfgang, Jacqueline Stark, Christiane Pons, Ferenc Kiefer, Katalin Kiss & Eva Mészáros. 1996. *Cross Language Analysis of German- and Hungarian-Speaking Broca's Aphasics' Processing of Selected Morphonological and Morphological Features: a pilot study*. Research Institute for Linguistics, Hungarian Academy of Sciences, Working Papers in the Theory of Grammar, Vol.3, No.1.

Duranti, Alessandro & Charles Goodwin. 1992. *Rethinking Context: an Introduction*. Cambridge: Cambridge University Press.

Eco, Umberto. 1987. Semantics, pragmatics, and text semiotics. In Jef Verschueren & Marcella Bertuccelli-Papi (eds.), *The pragmatic perspective. Selected papers from the 1985 International Pragmatics Conference*, 695–714. Amsterdam: Benjamins.

Fodor, Jerry. 1983. *The modularity of Mind*. Cambridge: MIT Press.

Fortin, Antonio. 2011. *The Morphology and Semantics of Expressive Affixes*. PhD thesis, University of Oxford. URL: ling.auf.net/lingbuzz/001365/v1.pdf.

Fradin, Bernard. 2003. Le traitement de la suffixation en –ET. *Langages* 152. 51–77.

Fradin, Bernard, Nabil Hathout & Fanny Meunier. 2003. La suffixation en -ET et la question de la productivité. *Langue Française* 140. 56–78.

Franceschet, Roberta, Davide Bertocci, Serena De Pellegrin, Wolfgang U. Dressler, Carlo Semenza. (2013). Diminutivization in patients with aphasia and children. *Procedia – Social and Behavioral Sciences* 94. 103–104.

Fukada, Atsushi & Noriko Asato. 2004. Universal politeness theory: application to the use of Japanese honorifics. *Journal of Pragmatics* 36. 1991–2002.

Giraudo, Hélène & Serena dal Maso. 2016. Suffix perceptual salience in morphological masked priming. *Lingue e Linguaggio* 15. 85–106.

Goldie, Peter. 2000. *The Emotions: A Philosophical Exploration*. Oxford: Oxford University Press.

Gracía, Luisa & Lidia Turón. 2000. On Appreciative Suffixes. *Acta Linguistica Hungarica* 47. 231–234.

Grandi, Nicola. 2002. *Morfologie in contatto. Le costruzioni valutative nelle lingue del Mediterraneo*. Milano: Franco Angeli.

Grandi, Nicola. 2011. Renewal and innovation in the emergence of Indo-European evaluative morphology. *Lexis 6: Diminutives and Augmentatives in the Languages of the World* (6). 5–26.

Grandi, Nicola. 2015. The Place of Evaluation within Morphology. In Nicola Grandi & Livia Körtvélyessy (eds.), *Edinburgh Handbook of Evaluative Morphology*, 74–90. Edinburgh: Edinburgh University Press.

Grandi, Nicola. 2017. Evaluatives in Morphology. In *Oxford Research Encyclopedia of Linguistics*.

Grandi, Nicola & Livia Körtvélyessy (eds.). 2015. *Edinburgh Handbook of Evaluative Morphology*. Edinburgh: Edinburgh University Press.

Grice, Herbert P. 1975. Logic and Conversation. In Peter Cole & Jerry L. Morgan (eds.). *Syntax and Semantics*, Vol. 3, *Speech Acts*, 41–58. New York: Academic Press.

Haase, Martin 2000. *Die Grammatikalisierung von Höflichkeit*. München: Lincom Europa.

Halm, Tamás. 1018. From possessive suffix to affective demonstrative suffix in Hungarian: a grammaticalization analysis. International Morphology Meeting 18, Budapest, 10.5.2018.

Harada, Shin'ichi. 1976. Honorifics. In Masayoshi Shibatani (ed.). *Japanese Generative Grammar*, 499–561. New York: Academic Press.

Haspelmath, Martin. 2003. The geometry of grammatical meaning : Semantic maps and crosslinguistic comparison. In Michael Tomasello (ed.), *The new psychology of language*. Vol.2, 211–242. Mahwah: Erlbaum.

Hasselrot, Bengt. 1957. *Etudes sur la formation diminutive dans les langues romanes*. Wiesbaden: Harrassowitz.

Haverkate, Henk. 1990. A speech act analysis of irony. *Journal of Pragmatics* 14. 77–109.

Helm, Bennet W. 2001. Emotions and Practical Reason: Rethinking Evaluation and Motivation. *Noûs* 35. 190–213.

Horn, Laurence R. & Gregory Ward (eds.). 2006. *Handbook of Pragmatics*. Oxford: Blackwell.

Hurch, Bernhard (ed.). 2007. *Studies on Reduplication*. Berlin: De Gruyter.

Ide, Sachiko. 2003.The speaker's viewpoint and indexicality in a high context culture. In K. Kataoka & Sachiko Ide (eds.). *Culture, Interaction, and Language*, 3–20. Tokyo: Hituzisyobo.

Inkelas, Sharon & Cheryl Zoll. 2005. *Reduplication: Doubling in Morphology*. Cambridge: Cambridge University Press.

Jespersen, Otto. 1942. *A modern English grammar*, Part VI, Morphology, Copenhagen: JES.

Jurafsky, Daniel. 1996. Universal tendencies in the semantics of the diminutive. *Language* 72. 533–578.

Jurafsky, Daniel. 2006. Pragmatics and Computational Linguistics. In Laurence R. Horn & Gregory Ward (eds.), *Handbook of Pragmatics*, 578–604. Oxford: Blackwell.

Kallergi, Haritini. 2015. *Reduplication at the Word Level. The Greek Facts in Typological Perspective*. Studia Typologica 17. Berlin: De Gruyter.

Kecskes, Istvan. 2016. A Dialogic Approach to Pragmatics. *Russian Journal of Linguistics* 20. 26–42.

Kempson, Ruth, Ronnie Cann, Eleni Gregoromichelaki & Stergios Chatzikyriakidis. 2016. *Language as Mechanisms for Interaction*. (draft 2016).

Kiefer, Ferenc. 2004. Morphopragmatic phenomena in Hungarian. *Acta Linguistica Hungarica* 51. 325–349.

Kilani-Schoch, Marianne & Wolfgang U. Dressler. 1999. Perspective morphopragmatique sur les formations en –o du français branché. In Igor Mel'čuk (ed), *Dictionnaire explicatif et combinatoire du français contemporain. Recherches lexico-sémantiques IV*, 55–66. Montréal: Les Presses de l'Université de Montréal.

Kilani-Schoch, Marianne, Fernando Sánchez Miret & Wolfgang U. Dressler. 2011. Towards naturalness scales of pragmatic complexity. *Papers and Studies in Contemporary Linguistics* 47. 237–263.

Klara, Ludmila. 2009. Ist steinreich auch steinreich? Adjektivische Steigerungskomposita des Gegenwartsdeutschen und ihre Akzentuierung. PhD thesis, München: Ludwig-Maximilians-Universität.

Klimaszewska, Zofia. 1983. *Diminutive and augmentative Ausdrucksmöglichkeiten des Niederländischen, Deutschen und Polnischen: Eine konfrontative Darstellung*. Wrocław: Wydawnictwo Polskiej Akademii Nauk.

Körtvélyessy, Livia. 2014. Evaluative Derivation. In Rochelle Lieber & Pavol Štekauer (eds.), *The Oxford Handbook of Derivational Morphology*, 296–316. Oxford: Oxford University Press.

Körtvélyessy, Livia. 2015. *Evaluative Morphology from a Cross-Linguistic Perspective*. Cambridge: Cambridge Scholars Publishing.

Körtvélyessy Livia & Pavol Štekauer. 2014. Derivation in a Social Context. In Rochelle Lieber & Pavol Štekauer (eds.), *The Oxford Handbook of Derivational Morphology*, 407–423. Oxford: Oxford University Press.

Kouwenberg, Silvia & Darlene La Charité. 2003. More of the same: Iconicity in reduplication and the evidence for substrate transfer in the genesis of Caribbean Creole languages. In Silvia Kouwenberg (ed.), *Twice as Meaningful. Reduplication in Pidgins, Creoles and Other Contact Languages*. London: Battlebridge.

Kristiansen, Gitte & René Dirven (eds.). 2008. Cognitive sociolinguistics: Language variation, cultural models, social systems. Berlin: Walter de Gruyter.

Laalo, Klaus. 2001. Diminutives in Finnish child-directed and child speech: Morphopragmatic and morphophonemic aspects. *Psychology of Language and Communication* 5. 72–80.

Lai, Hwei-Ling. 2006. Iconic coding of conceptualization: Hakka reduplicative construction. *Language and Linguistics* 7. 483–499.

Lakoff, George. 1987. *Women, Fire, and Dangerous Things: What Categories reveal About The Mind*. Chicago: University of Chicago Press.

Lakoff, George. & Mark Johnson. 1980. *Metaphors We Live By*. Chicago: University of Chicago Press.

Lampitelli, Nicola. 2015. La flexion nominale en Somali de Djibouti: Constatations empiriques et implications théoriques. Paper presented at Xuska 40 guurada farsoomaliida [Celebration for the 40th anniversary of Somali writing], Université de Djibouti, Sjibouti, 17–22 december.

Leech, Geoffrey N. 1983. *Principles of pragmatics*. London: Longman.

Leech, Geoffrey N. 2014. *The Pragmatics of Politeness*. Oxford: Oxford University Press.

Lieber, Rochelle. 2004. *Morphology and Lexical Semantics*. Cambridge: Cambridge University Press.

Malicka-Kleparska, Anna. 1985. Parallel derivation and lexicalist morphology: the case of Polish diminutivization. In Edmund Gussmann (ed.), *Phono-Morphology. Studies in the Interaction of Phonology and Morphology*, 95–112. Lublin: Katolicki Uniwersytet Lubelski.

Marchand, Hans. 1960. *The Categories and Types of Present-Day English Word-Formation: A Synchronic-Diachronic Approach*. Wiesbaden: Harrassowitz.

Marantz, Alec. 1982. Re-duplication. *Linguistic Inquiry* 13. 483–545.

Matisoff, James A. 1992. The mother of all morphemes. Augmentatives and diminutives in areal and universal perspective. In Martha Ratliff (ed.), *Papers from the first annual meeting of the Southeast Asian Society 1991*, 293–349. Tempe: Arizona State University.

Mattes, Veronika. 2014. *Types of reduplication. A case study of Bikol*. Berlin: Mouton de Gruyter.

Mattiello, Elisa. A morphopragmatic analysis of English and Italian negative prefixes. *Studi e Saggi Linguistici* 47. 125–156.

Mattiello, Elisa. 2013. *Extra-grammatical morphology in English. Abbreviations, blends, reduplicatives and related phenomena*. Berlin: Mouton De Gruyter.

Mattiello, Elisa. 2017. *Analogy in Word-formation. A Study of English Neologisms and Occasionalisms*. Berlin: Mouton De Gruyter.

Meibauer, Jörg. 2007. How marginal are phrasal compounds. Generalized insertion, expressivity, and I/Q-interaction. *Morphology* 17. 233–259.

Meibauer, Jörg. 2014. Word-Formation and Contextualism. *International Review of Pragmatics* 6. 103–126

Meibauer, Jörg. 2015. On \R" in phrasal compounds – a contextualist approach. In Trips, C. and Kornfilt, J. (eds*.) Phrasal compounds from a theoretical and typological perspective, Language Typology and Universals* 68, 241–261.

Merlini Barbaresi, Lavinia. 2001. The pragmatics of the "diminutive" y/e suffix in English. In Chris Schaner-Wolles, John Rennison & Friedrich Neubarth (eds.). *Naturally!* 315–326. Torino: Rosenberg & Sellier.

Merlini Barbaresi, Lavinia. 2004. Alterazione (pp. 264–292) and Aggettivi deaggettivali (pp. 442–449). In Maria Grossmann & Franz Rainer (eds.), *La formazione delle parole in italiano*. Tübingen: Niemeyer.

Merlini Barbaresi, Lavinia. 2008. Extra-grammatical morphology. English Reduplicatives. In John Douthwaite & Domenico Pezzini (eds.), *Words in Action: Diachronic and Synchronic Approaches to English Discourse*, 228–241. Genova: ECIG

Merlini Barbaresi, Lavinia. 2014. English Evaluative Suffixes: A Preference for Pragmatics over Semantics. In Alison Duguid, Anna Marchi, Alan Partington & Charlotte Taylor (eds.), *Gentle Obsession. Literature, Linguistcs, and Learning in honour of John Morley*, 33–44. Roma: Editoriale Artemide.

Merlini Barbaresi, Lavinia. 2015a. The Pragmatics of word-formation. In Peter O. Müller, Ingeborg Ohnheiser, Susan Olsen & Franz Rainer (eds.), *Word Formation. An International Handbook of the Languages of Europe*, 1128–1142 (Vol. 2). Berlin: Mouton De Gruyter,

Merlini Barbaresi, Lavinia. 2015b. Evaluative morphology and pragmatics. In Nicola Grandi & Livia. Körtvélyessy (eds.), *Edinburgh Handbook of Evaluative Morphology*, 32–42. Edinburgh University Press.

Mey, Jacob L. 2001. *Pragmatics: An Introduction*. Oxford: Wiley-Blackwell.

Minkova, Donka. 2002. Ablaut reduplication in English: The criss-crossing of prosody and verbal art. *English Language and Linguistics* 6. 133–169

Moravcsik, Edith. 1978. Reduplicative constructions. In J. H. Greenberg (ed.). *Universals of human language: Word structure* 3, 297–334. Stanford: Stanford University Press

Morris, Charles W. 1938. *Foundations of the theory of signs*. Chicago: Chicago University Press.

Mutz, Katrin. 2000. *Die italienischen Modifikationssuffixe*. Frankfurt/Main: Lang.

Mutz, Katrin. 2015. Evaluative Morphology in a diachronic perspective. In Nicola Grandi & Livia Körtvélyessy (eds.), *Edinburgh Handbook of Evaluative Morphology*, 142–154. Edinburgh University Press.

Nadarajan, Shanthi. 2006. A crosslinguustic study of reduplication. Arizona Working Papers. *SLAT* 13. 39–53.
Napoli, Donna Jo & Bill Reynolds. 1995. Evaluatice Affixes in Italian, *Morphology Yearbook* 1994. 151–178,
Nekula, Marek. 2003. System und Funktionen der Diminutive: Kontrastiver Vergleich des Deutschen und Tschechischen. *Brücken* 11. 145–188.
Nieuwenhuis, Paul. 1985 *Diminutives*. Unpublished PhD thesis, University of Edinburgh.
Pakendorf, Brigitte. 2017. Lamunkhin Even evaluative morphology in cross-linguistic comparison. *Morphology* 27. 123–158.
Perkins, Michael R. 2007. *Pragmatic Impairment*. Cambridge: Cambridge University Press.
Piller, Ingrid. 2010. *Intercultural communication: A Critical Introduction*. Edinburgh: Edinburgh University Press.
Plag, Ingo. 1999. *Morphological Productivity. Structural Constraints in English Derivation*. Berlin: Mouton de Gruyter.
Potts, Christopher. 2006. How far can pragmatic mechanisms take us? *Theoretical Linguistics* 32. 307–320.
Potts, Christopher. 2007. The Expressive Dimension. *Theoretical Linguistics* 33. 165–198.
Potts, Christopher, Daniel Lassiter, Roger Levy & Michael C. Frank. 2015. Embedded implicatures as pragmatic inferences under compositional lexical uncertainty. *Journal of Semantics* 33. 755–802.
Potts, Christopher & Florian Schwarz. 2010. Affective 'this'. *Linguistic Issues in Language Technology* 3 (5). 1–30.
Prieto, Victor. M. 2005. *Spanish evaluative morphology: Pragmatic, sociolinguistic, and semantic issues*. Doctoral dissert. University of Florida.
Prieto, Victor M. 2015. The semantics of evaluative morphology. In Nicola Grandi & Livia Körtvélyessy (eds.), *Edinburgh Handbook of Evaluative Morphology* 21–31. Edinburgh University Press.
Rainer, Franz. 1993. *Spanische Wortbildungslehre*. Tübingen: Niemeyer.
Raun, Alo. 1960. The equivalents of English "than" in Finno-Ugric. *American Studies in Uralic Linguistics* 1: 149–247.
Rebollar, Bárbara E. 2013. *Lexical pragmatics and the nature of word meaning*. RODIN, Universidad de Cádiz. http://hdl.handle.net/10498/17171.
Regier, Terry. 1998. Reduplication and the arbitrariness of the sign. In Morton A. Gernsbacher & Sharon J. Derry (eds.), *Proceedings of the Twentieth Annual Conference of the Cognitive Science Society*, 887–892. Mahwah, NJ: Lawrence Erlbaum.
Reynoso Noveròn, Jeanett. 2005. Procesos de gramaticalización por subjetivazión: el uso del diminutivo en español. In David Ellington (ed.), *Selected Proceedings of the 7th Hispanic Linguistics Symposium*, 79–86. Somerville: Cascadilla Proceedings Project.
Ronga Irene, Carla Bazzanella, Erling Strudsholm & Luisa Salvati. 2014. Black as night or as a chimney sweep? *Intercultural pragmatics* 11. 485–520.
Rubino, Carl. 2005. Reduplication: Form, function and distribution. In Bernhard Hurch (ed.) *Studies on Reduplication*, 11–29. Berlin: Mouton de Gruyter.
Savickiene, Ineta & Wolfgang U. Dressler (eds.). 2007. *The Acquisition of Diminutives: a crosslinguistic perspective*. Amsterdam: Benjamins.
Scalise, Sergio. 1984. *Generative morphology*. Dordrecht: Foris.
Scalise, Sergio. 1994. *Morfologia*. Bologna: Il Mulino.
Schmid, Hans-Jörg. 2012. *Cognitive Pragmatics*. Berlin: Mouton De Gruyter.

Schmitt, Christian. 1998. Zur Gradation mittels Präfixoiden. In Udo Figge, Franz-Josef Klein & Annette Moreno (eds.), *Grammatische Strukturen und grammatischer Wandel im Französischen*, 425–449. Bonn: Romanistischer Verlag.

Schneider, Klaus P. 2003. *Diminutives in English*. Tübingen: Niemeyer.

Schneider, Klaus P. 2013. The truth about diminutives, and how we can find it: some theoretical and methodological considerations. *SKASE Journal of Theoretical Linguistics* 10 (1). http://www.skase.sk/Volumes/JTL22/pdf_doc/08.pdf.

Schwaiger, Sonja, Adrien Barbaresi, Katharina Korecky-Kröll, Jutta Ransmayr & Wolfgang U. Dressler. 2019. Variation between diminutives in Austrian electronic corpora. In Lars Bülow, Ann Kathrin. Fischer, Kristina Herbert (eds.), *Dimensions of Linguistic Space: Variation, Multilingualism, Conceptualisations* [*Dimensionen des sprachlichen Raums: Variation, Mehrsprachigkeit, Konzeptualisierung*], https://doi.org/10.3726/b15250 (accessed 5 August 2019). Frankfurt: Peter Lang.

Schwarz, Florian. 2014. *Experimental Perspectives on Presuppositions*. London: Palgrave Macmillan.

Scullen, M. E. 1997. *French Prosodic Morphology, A Unified Account*. Bloomington: Indiana University Linguistics Club.

Shibatani, Masayoshi. 1990. *The Languages of Japan*. Cambridge: Cambridge University Press.

Shibatani, Masayoshi. 2006. Honorifics. *Encyclopedia of Languages and Linguistics*. Amsterdam: Elsevier.

Sifianou, Maria. 1992. The use of diminutives in expressing politeness. Modern Greek versus English. *Journal of Pragmatics* 17. 155–173.

Simon, Camille & Nathan W. Hill. 2015. Tibetan. In Nicola Grandi & Livia Körtvélyessy (eds.), *Edinburgh Handbook of Evaluative Morphology*, 381–388. Edinburgh: Edinburgh University Press.

Simon, Horst. J., & Heike Wiese. 2011. What are exceptions? And what can be done about them? In Horst J. Simon & Heike Wiese (eds.) *Expecting the unexpected: Exceptions in grammar*, 3–31. Berlin: Mouton De Gruyter.

Slaby, Jan, & Philipp Wüschner. 2014. Emotion and agency. In Sabine Roeser & Cain Todd (eds.), *Emotion and Value*, 212–228. Oxford: Oxford University Press.

Spencer-Oatey, Helen & Peter Franklin. 2009. *Intercultural Interaction. A Multidisciplinary Approach to Intercultural Communication*. Basingstoke: Palgrave Macmillan,

Spitzer, Leo. 1921. Das Suffix –*one* im Romanischen. In Ernst Gamillscheg & Leo Spitzer (eds.), *Beiträge zur Romanischen Wortbildungslehre*, 183–205. Genève: Olschki.

Staverman, W.H. 1953. Diminutivitis Neerlandica [Dutch diminutive sickness]. *De Gids* 116. 407–419.

Stefanescu, Ioana. 1992. On diminutive suffixes. *Folia Linguistica* 26. 339–356.

Stemmer, Brigitte (ed.). 1999. Pragmatics: Theoretical and Clinical Issues. *Brain and Language* 68 (3). Amsterdam: Elsevier.

Strawson, Peter F. 1964. Intention and convention in speech acts. *Philosophical Review* 73 (4). 439–460.

Stump, Gregory. T. 1993. How peculiar is evaluative morphology? *Journal of Linguistics* 29. 1–36.

Thun, Nils. 1963. *Reduplicative Words in English: A Study of Formation of the Types* Tick-tick, Hurly-burly *and* Shilly-shally. Uppsala: Bloms.

Trips, Carola. 2012. Empirical and theoretical aspects of phrasal compounds: Against the 'syntax explains it all' attitude. In Angela Ralli, Geert Booij, Sergio Scalise & Athanasios

Karasimos (eds.), *Online Proceedings of the eighth Mediterranean Morphology Meeting*, 322–346. University of Patras.

Trips, Carola. 2014. How to account for the expressive nature of phrasal compounds in a conceptual-semantic framework. *SKASE Journal of Theoretical Linguistics* 11:33–61.

Vanhove, Martine & Mohamed-Tahir Hamid Ahmed. 2016. Diminutives and augmentatives in Beja (North-Cushitic). <halshs-01485949>

van den Berg, René. 2015. *Muna*. In Nicola Grandi & Livia Körtvélyessy (eds.), *Edinburgh Handbook of Evaluative Morphology*, 367–374. Edinburgh: Edinburgh University Press.

Van der Spuy, Andrew & Lwazi Mjiyako. 2015. Evaluative morphology in Zulu. In Nicola Grandi & Livia Körtvélyessy (eds.), *Edinburgh Handbook of Evaluative Morphology*, 515–522. Edinburgh: Edinburgh University Press.

Vernant, Denis. 2003. The classification of speech acts revisited: a dialogical and actional perspective. In Jean Caelen, Daniel Vanderveken & Denis Vernant (eds.), *Logic and dialogue*, 45–68. Dordrecht: Kluwer.

Verschueren, Jef. 1999. *Understanding Pragmatics*. Oxford: Oxford University Press.

Volek, Bronislava. 1987. *Emotive signs in language and semantic functioning of derived nouns in Russian*. Amsterdam: Benjamins.

Watts, Richard. 2003. *Politeness*. Cambridge: Cambridge University Press.

Weigand, Edda. 2000. The Dialogic Action Game. In Malcolm Coulthard, Janet Cotterill & Frances Rock (eds.), *Dialogue Analysis VII: Working with Dialogue: Selected Papers from the 7th IADA conference, Birmingham 1999–2000*, 1–18. Tübingen: Niemeyer.

Weigand, Edda. 2010a. Linguists and their speakers. *Language Sciences* 32. 536–544.

Weigand, Edda. 2010b. Language as Dialogue. *Intercultural Pragmatics* 7. 505–515.

Wierzbicka, Anna. 1984. Diminutives and depreciatives: semantic representation for derivational categories. *Quaderni di Semantica* 5. 123–130.

Wierzbicka, Anna. 1991. *Cross-cultural pragmatics: The semantics of human interaction*. Berlin: Mouton de Gruyter.

Wilson, Deirdre & Robyn Carston. 2007. A unitary approach to lexical pragmatics: relevance, inference and *ad hoc* concepts. In Noël Burton-Roberts (ed.), *Pragmatics*, 230–260. Basingstoke: Palgrave Macmillan.

Wüschner, Philipp. 2015. Emotion and Agency. In Sabine Roeser & Cain Todd (eds.), *Emotion and Value*. Oxford: Oxford University Press.

Žic Fuchs, Milena. 2009. *Kognitivna lingvistika i jezične strukture: engleski present perfect* [Cognitive Linguistics and Language Structures: the English Present Perfect]. Zagreb: Nakladni zavod Globus.

Appendix

1. *Emotion, tenderness* (a mother to a child):
E. Who's my lovely little girl*ie*? b) Who's my *boobsy-woobsy*? (personally heard)
   Ge. Wer komm-*erl*-t denn da? "who come-DIM-s PART here?" "what cute boy is coming here?" (personally reported)

Lithuanian: *mama,* statyk, statyk, mam*yte* "mother, build it, build it, mother-Dim" (from Ineta Dabašinskienė 2009 *Intimacy. Familiarity and formality*)

2. *Playful irony*
It. Il confronto è tra le Sarkoz*ettes* e le Berlusconette "the comparison is between (the fem.Pl.) Sarkoz(y)-DIMs and Berluscon(i)-DIMs" (Corriere della Sera Magazine 24-4-08)

3. *Derogatory irony*
E. He's got a wife and a couple of wif*ies* (girl-friends) (from Nieuwenhuis 1985).

4. *Euphemism*
Ge. Er hat ein Glä*schen* über den Durst getrunken "He has just drunk one little glass too many" (he is totally drunk). (often cited)

5. *False modesty*
It. Avrei anch'io una mia teori*etta* "I'd have me too a theory-DIM" (a little theory of my own) (heard at a Conference in Italy).

6. *Ironical understatement*
E. There is just a *teeny-weeny* drawback*ette*. (from Nieuwenhuis 1985)

7. *Emotion, pleasure*
Fr. Gentil papa veut bien ramener bonne *sou-soupe*? "Do you think that big daddy can bring ome more *soupy-woupy*?" (Reverso Context).

8. *Pleading*
Sp. Deme un peda*cito* de pan! 'Give me a piece-DIM of bread!' (personally reported)
  Lithuanian: Ar galėčiau gauti kavyt*ės*? "Could I have (some) coffee-DIM?" (from Ineta Dabašinskienė 2009 *Intimacy. Familiarity and Formality*)

9. *Hedged request, jocularity*
It. Ci sarebbe anche da tenere il San Bernard*uccio*, il cagn*etto* 'there should also have to take care of the Saint Bernard-DIM, the doggie'(you should also take care of ...) (TV Spot 2014)
  E. Could I leave here my *doggy-woggy* [a big dog, in fact] for just half an hour? (heard from English friends)

10. *Contempt*
E. Larry Sabato, a well-respected political analyst, sent out an email last week trying to debunk the Hillary *boom-let* (Times, Sunday Times 2005).

11. *Sarcasm* (political TV talk)
It. Cosa fate voi nei vostri salott-*ar-elli* ? "what do you do in your drawing room-Interfix-DIMs?" (silly little parties?).

12. *Sarcasm* (a police inspector to a thief)
It. Il suo è un mestier*ino* che rende! "yours is a job-DIM which rewards" (a quite rewarding job)

13. *Ironic understatement*
E. There' s also *the bijou snag(g)-ette* that administrators and the finance sector actually need to work together a lot of the time (http://old.qi.com/talk).

14. *Anger* or *sarcasm*
E. Not looking too good for you, *fat-s-o* (Merriam Webster online Dictionary).

15. *Mitigation*
E. We must enable nonverbal *aut-ie-s* (clipped *autistic* + *-ie-s*) to communicate by independent typing or devices that talk for them (Jerry Newport, *Your Life is Not a Label*)

Part 3: **Words in usage**

Antonio Fábregas and Martina Penke
Word storage and computation

Abstract: The goal of this chapter is to assess some representative morphological theories with respect to their compatibility with results coming from psycholinguistic experiments. We will concentrate mainly on the question of whether inflected words are computationally built by the addition of discrete units, called 'morphemes', or have to be treated as undecomposable wholes which relate to each other through connections with other words. The issue is complicated by two problems: the nature of morphemes as abstract units that anchor phonological and semantic information or symbolic Saussurean units, and the problem of whether inflected forms are decomposable at some level of analysis or must be stored as fully built forms.

Keywords: word storage, computation, morphological theory, lexical decision, frequency effect, morphological priming

1 Introduction

It is uncontroversial that a part of knowing a natural language involves learning an idiosyncratic set of stored units that are associated with three sets of information that cannot be derived by any rule, and hence are idiosyncratic: a set of formal features (standardly assumed to include entities like N, V, A, Tense, Plural number, etc.), a phonological representation and a semantic representation. The competence of a speaker is furthermore assumed to include a part that is stored and a part that is computed, which involves building complex structures from the stored units. This is, however, all that is uncontroversial, and virtually any aspect of the specific form in which the association happens, the way the units are combined and the richness with which these levels are represented in the lexicon is subject to a lively debate across morphological theories.

The immediate goal of this paper is to assess a number of influential theories in morphology with respect to the adequacy of the predictions they make with respect to storage and computation, as far as those predictions can be tested with the available tools established in the field of psycholinguistics.

Antonio Fábregas, Universitet i Tromsø, Institutt for Språk og Kultur
Martina Penke, Universität zu Köln, Department für Heilpädagogik und Rehabilitation

͏ Open Access. © 2020 Antonio Fábregas and Martina Penke, published by De Gruyter. This work is licensed under a Creative Commons Attribution-NonCommercial-NoDerivatives 4.0 International License.
https://doi.org/10.1515/9783110440577-012

There are a number of problems that we face when assessing a morphological theory with experimental psycholinguistic tools. Morphological theories tend to stress the aspects of language known since Chomsky (1957) as 'competence', that is they aim to capture the abstract language capacity of an idealized speaker/hearer and to arrive at a generalization of morphology that is valid across languages, morphological systems and individual speakers. In contrast, they rarely introduce questions related to 'performance', i.e. the processing and parsing of speech in production and perception, that are central in psycholinguistic research. Also, morphological theories are normally designed from a speaker's perspective, and are much more explicit and clear when it comes to answering the question of how a speaker produces new words or the right form of the word given a context, than they are on the issue how the hearer or reader reconstructs, from the sequence that is received, the right grammatical and semantic properties that the word stands for. In contrast, much psycholinguistic research on the processing of inflected words has focused on data from single-word reading and hence on the reader perspective. Related to this issue is the problem that morphological theories might not be specific enough to derive precise predictions that would be testable in a psycholinguistic experiment – a problem we will see exemplified in some of the morphological theories discussed in this chapter. While morphological theories might pose some challenges for the psycholinguist eager to test them, morphological theorists often refrain from using data obtained in a psycholinguistic experiment as evidence for or against specific theoretical assumptions. Instead, theoretical considerations are generally based on intuitive insights or grammaticality judgements (cf. Penke and Rosenbach 2007 for discussion). In fact, psycholinguistic data, as all data, are 'noisy' as behavior in an experimental setting is not only influenced by the linguistic issues at stake but is potentially influenced by a number of factors relating to the subject, the experimental setting, or the environment in which the experiment takes place. How successful the influence of such interfering factors can be reduced is largely dependent on the experimenter's aptitude. Whether or not experimental data can be considered a solid piece of evidence or whether it is flawed by factors not sufficiently controlled in the experimental setting might be difficult to assess for theoreticians unfamiliar with experimental procedures and data. The aim of our paper is to bridge this gap by showing how morphological theories can be tested by psycholinguistic data and which type of evidence would bear on theoretical assumptions.

In our exposition of storage and computation in morphological theory and psycholinguistic experimentation, we will focus on inflection rather than derivation. One main reason for this is that we consider the status of inflection to be less controversial, and hence better suited for an overview: its obligatoriness of application makes inflection a likely candidate for computation. In contrast, when the divide between storage and computation is assessed in derivational morphology, it is less evident what one should be looking for, as there are degrees of productivity as well as abundant gaps and cases of affix rivalry dependent on fine-grained semantic or grammatical differences between affixes that are roughly synonymous.

Before moving to the overview of the relevant theories that we have singled out in this chapter, a couple of caveats are in order.

1.1 What are the units?

This chapter deals with the divide between storage and computation, so we must start by providing cursory definitions of the two concepts, which will be developed later (see in particular Section 1.2, where we will see that what is considered 'computation' is subject to a lot of debate).
a) A form is stored if it is listed as a unit (with or without internal structure).
b) A form is computed if it is the output of some operation that takes units as its input.

This divide, thus, crucially depends on whether something is a stored unit; therefore, the first question becomes to determine what the units are.

The answer is not trivial. A central concern is whether the minimal units are words, something bigger than the word or something smaller than the word. The main question is whether a form like (1) has to be taken as one single unit or two.

(1)   boys

If (1) is one single unit, that unit has been called, for lack of a better term, 'word', with well-known complications that question whether (1) is a unit only at a phonological level or whether its atomicity extends also to other components of grammar. For instance, it is quite clear that (1) is not an atom from a semantic perspective, as it denotes at least two notions: plurality (roughly 'more than one') and a particular class of animate entities defined through age and biological sex. It is more controversial whether (1) is also an atom from a syntactic perspective (see Julien 2007; Williams 2007 and Embick and Noyer 2007 for different views).

Example (1) has also been analyzed as (at least) two units, in which case the term 'morpheme' is used: an inflectional marker for 'Number' (-s) and a base categorized as a noun (*boy*). If one follows that route, the conclusion is that, *ceteris paribus*, the minimal units that are stored are smaller than words. Words, understood as (structured) sets of morphemes, might be stored when the semantic or phonological information associated with them is not identical to those associated with their individual morphemes, as in (2), where the meaning of the word would be claimed to be underivable from the meaning of its composing morphemes: this is known as Demotivation of Meaning, Lexicalization or Non-Compositionality.

(2) understand (≠ stand under something)

Another situation where theories that accept morphemes as minimal units could allow for a storage of a full form is irregular forms.[1] Consider (3). Here, the morphophonology of the form does not allow for a straightforward segmentation into two units, each corresponding to a different morpheme.

(3) a. went (go)
     b. wrote (write)
     c. came (come)
     d. slept (sleep)

Finally, other theories have suggested that the stored units might be bigger than words. Baayen, Milin, Durdevic, Hendrix, and Marelli (2011) have argued that the meaning of words or morphemes is crucially dependent on the linguistic context,

---

[1] Note that in theoretical approaches, generally different subsets of irregular forms receive a different treatment. One crucial divide in approaches that concentrate on the way in which sets of morphosyntactic features are identified with morphophonological exponents is the one that is found between forms like *feet* and forms like *children*, to give two examples of English plural marking. In the second case it is still possible to segment two exponents (*child*, albeit with a phonological change in its vowel, and *-ren*); in the first case, in contrast, in most analyses there is only one exponent that expresses plural through a change in the vowel of the root. Ignoring analyses where plural is expressed in this case as a floating feature (e.g., [front]), only one synthetic form would in such cases correspond to what presumably are two distinct morphosyntactic units. In many approaches each of these two cases are analyzed differently: the *feet*-cases as one exponent corresponding to two morphosyntactic units, unified in one single position of exponence through fusion (Halle and Marantz 1993), spanning (Ramchand 2008), phrasal spell out (Caha 2009; Fábregas 2014a) or conflation (Hale and Keyser 2002), and the *children*-cases essentially as cases where one exponent selects a marked exponent for plural when the two exponents are immediately adjacent to each other (therefore, when there is no additional exponent between the two of them), and thus as a case of morphologically-conditioned allomorphy (Embick 2010). Note, however, that both cases have the same status from the perspective that we are adopting here: in both cases, the speaker producing the form will be facing a situation where the general rule does not apply and the special status of the root has to be taken into account in order to produce a non-general marking of the plural. Similarly, in both cases the child acquiring the language would have to get direct evidence from the input that the general plural rule is not applied to a subset of roots that include *foot* and *child*, and the frequency with which these irregular forms are found in the input will be crucial (cf. Penke 2006; Marcus et al. 1992: 55ff.).

even ignoring idiomatic cases; if one goal of storage is to associate a phonological (or orthographic) representation to an idiosyncratic meaning, then it follows that at least at some stage any word or morpheme has to be stored with some context in order to register its meaning. Without going to that extreme, DiSciullo and Williams (1987) already noted that syntactic phrases need to be stored in the lexicon whenever they have an idiomatic meaning (4).

(4) to lose one's head

The problem of identifying the minimal units of storage, as can be seen already from this cursory overview, which will be expanded throughout the chapter, is severe. But it gets worse. As the astute reader might have already noticed, the question of whether the forms in (3) are in principle decomposable cannot be answered unless one has decided what counts as a 'morpheme', and more specifically, how abstract a morpheme representation has to be.

There is one intuitive sense in which 'morphemes' correspond to minimal Saussurean signs, Janus-like objects with two sides: a phonological representation and a meaning. This is the traditional view of the morpheme as the minimal sign (cf. Hockett 1947, 1954; Jespersen 1933). In such case one expects, assuming a naive phonological component, that none of the forms in (3) are decomposable; if our system contains a more sophisticated phonological component, allowing floating features, subsegmental representations and readjustment rules (Chomsky and Halle 1968), (3b), (3c) and (3d) could be decomposable. In this kind of 'grounded' view of morphemes, they could be represented as (5).

(5)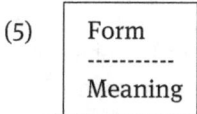

It is well-known, however, that this sign-definition of morpheme runs into problems (see Anderson 1992: Chapter 3; Aronoff 1976 and Stump 1998, 2001: Chapter 1 for overviews). The classical notion of a morpheme as a Saussurean sign was questioned very early in the morphological tradition. The discussion is typically traced back to a controversy between Hockett (1947) and Nida (1948). Inside a structuralist framework, the main point of contention between these two authors had to do with the status that non-segmentable morphological marking should have in the theory. Non-segmentable morphological marking involves, roughly, all cases where it is impossible to find definite boundaries inside a complex word such that a morpheme is isolated to the right, and another one to the left. (6) is a case of segmentable morphology:

(6) eat-s

Cases of non-segmentable marking are quite varied. They include, but are not restricted to, cases where morphological complexity is expressed through a segmental or suprasegmental alternation in the base, i.e. replacive morphology, as in (7a), with suppletion being the most extreme case of this, as in (7b).

(7) a. wât ~ wàt [Shilluk, Nilotic]
         house.SG house.PL
     b. go ~ went

In fact, a good deal of the debate refers to how (7b) should be analyzed. Hockett (1947), who argued for a traditional view of morphemes, proposed an analysis that Nida (1948) considered counterintuitive: the past tense information is expressed through a zero morph (a morpheme without phonological information). Once this morpheme is present in the word, it selects a marked allomorph of the root:

(8) go-ø > went-ø

Nida criticizes, explicitly, that this analysis forces a paradoxical conclusion: the alternation that we can see on the surface (*go ~ went*) does not directly encode any grammatical distinction, while the grammatical contrast between present and past is not overtly marked.[2] Nida (1948) concludes, then, that, if we do not want to fall into this kind of paradox, the inescapable conclusion should be that morphosyntactic alternations are submorphemic. The consequences of what Nida intended to say[3] are less clear than what the branch of analyses that derived from Nida's observations have actually said, which involves denying the reality of morphemes as stored, Saussurean signs. Thus, theories that side with Nida in this respect have denied that 'morphemes' have the status of units of morphological analysis. These approaches claim that the smallest units of morphological analysis are words, and

---

[2] Note that Chomsky and Halle's (1968) analysis of suppletion as phonological change from one single underlying abstract representation is in essence an offspring of Hockett's account. See Bermúdez-Otero (2012) for a criticism of approaches to the lexicon where hyperabstract representations and rules are proposed: they make acquisition essentially impossible.

[3] Surprisingly, the essence of what Nida said is compatible with some in principle remote approaches, such as some versions of Generative Semantics (see specifically McCawley 1968), where it is proposed that single morphemes are tree structures whose nodes codify different (semantic) pieces of information. Modern Nanosyntax (Starke 2009) also shares this conception of morphemes as complex objects (phrases), which lets contrasts emerge as submorphemic alternations between heads.

then the question is whether 'morphemes' have reality at some non-morphological level. Some (Anderson 1992; Aronoff 1976) admit that 'morphemes' can be units at a phonological level, while some do not even recognize them as units of this sort (Word and Paradigm approaches; Stump 1993, 2001). However, they agree that proper symbolic decomposition should not be applied below the word level. For instance, Aronoff (1976) drew attention to examples like (9), where a naive decomposition of the words into a prefix and a verbal stem would face the challenge of assigning some concrete, consistent meaning to each morpheme.

(9) re-stitute, pro-stitute, in-stitute, con-stitute

Aronoff's conclusion, further developed in Aronoff (1994), is that morphemes have to be viewed as abstract objects, not traditional signs.

Not all researchers feel that the above-mentioned facts necessarily mean that morphemes cannot be used as units. In order to account for the mismatches between marking, meaning and function at the word level, Beard (1995), Halle and Marantz (1993) or Ackema (1995) argued for the Separation Hypothesis. Separationist theories do not treat morphemes as signs, but as some sort of abstract placeholders where phonological and semantic information is anchored. Instead of the representation in (5), the schematic view of the morpheme could be represented as (10).

(10) Form ⟶ MORPHEME ⟵ Meaning

This, as we will see, has potentially crucial consequences: the same morpheme can be associated with different meanings and forms (e.g., 'plural', in an abstract sense, will not always mean 'more than one', as in *to have the brains*), and it will open the door to treating all forms in (3) as decomposable at some abstract level, with additional operations making the decomposition not evident from the surface. Thus, the nature of the minimal units that one assumes to be stored is inseparable from the question of how abstract these units are; we will get back to this issue in Section 1.3.

1.2 What is stored and what is computed?

With respect to the second issue, the division of labor between storage and computation, it can be interpreted in two different ways. First, the division can be interpreted as whether complex words are composed out of morphemes or not. This treats the division between 'regular' and 'irregular' as meaning 'decomposable' and 'non-decomposable', essentially. This conception of computation as regularity is typical for theories where the units are morphemes. For instance, in Wunderlich's (1997) Minimalist Morphology framework (henceforth, MM), regular words such as *classified* are computed by combining morphemes following a restricted set of rules, and irregular words such as *went* are stored as unanalyzed units. We will see that, in this sense, a theory that does not treat morphemes as units, such as Anderson's (1992) A-morphous Morphology, would be classified as a theory where every word is stored, irrespective of whether it is regular or irregular.

Theories where words (but not morphemes) are units also can involve computation, but in a second sense. In this second interpretation, it refers to whether a word needs to be stored as a lexical entry or not. Take A-morphous Morphology (Anderson 1992): in this theory the form of a regular word would be a predictable effect of the application of a rule to a base, because the rule comes with a description of the kind of phonological change that it triggers on the base. Hence, full regular forms are not listed inside lexical entries, even if no morphemes are segmented inside them. It is crucial to differentiate this notion of computation from the previous one, where it equals 'segmentability'. In the A-morphous Morphology proposal, an 'irregular' form is a form listed as (part of) a lexical entry, like in the previous approach to storage, but computation does not amount to segmentability.

The issue whether being regular implies being decomposed or computed already shows that the assessment of the adequacy of theories through psycholinguistic methods is not trivial: each field has given a different amount of attention to this debate, and the ways of interpreting the divide lead to different classifications of theories.

1.3 The abstractness problem: Unitary and separationist theories

There is a third complication to the task that we undertake in this chapter. As we saw in Section 1.1, some of the theories that acknowledge the existence of morphemes adhere to the Separation Hypothesis. The initial motivation for Separationism is to be able to treat the surface mismatches between marking, meaning and function without giving up the notion of 'morpheme' as the relevant unit of analysis. This comes at the cost of dissociating the morphosyntactic side of the morpheme (the formal grammatical features they encode) from its morphophonological side (the kind of phonological marking, if any, that they trigger on the base). Several principles have been proposed that present this hypothesis: Beard (1995), who uses Separation; the Feature Disjointness Hypothesis in Embick (2000), and the Separationist Hypothesis in Ackema and Neeleman (2004). These approaches share one property: they explicitly propose that the level that deals with the way in which grammatical and semantic properties are defined is distinct from the level that determines how these properties are going to be spelled out by segments with (possible) phonological information. Thus they all would agree that, in some way, grammar has to distinguish between two kinds of objects, in practice 'distributing' lexical entries across modules of the grammar:

(11) a. [plural], [past], [noun], [imperfective], [feminine]...
     b. -s, -ed, -ation, -ing, -ess...

These two lists of units represent separate sides of what traditionally was considered a morpheme, and grammar must have some procedure whereby the units in one level are associated with the units in the other level, sometimes not in a one-to-one fashion. In Embick's Feature Disjointness Hypothesis, formulated inside Distributed Morphology (Halle and Marantz 1993), the modules are ordered with respect to each other and each one of the two lists in (11) are accessed at different times, with the structural properties of the word being defined at an early level, and the abstract units getting spelled out later (a procedure known as Late Insertion, cf. Bonet 1991; Noyer 1992). In this proposal, this spell-out level is where 'morphemes' are defined:
a. specific items, like *-ed*, *went* or *-s* are introduced in morphosyntactic environments that match the features to which they are associated;
b. these items can carry with them idiosyncratic morphological properties (e.g., the conjugation class of a verb, or the declension class of a noun) and idiosyncratic, non-predictable semantic information (e.g., that *cat* refers to a particular animal, while *dog* refers to another one);
c. the phonological and semantic computation takes into account these idiosyncratic properties and their phonological information.

Separationist theories present one problem for the goals of this chapter: what can be decomposed at one level might be not decomposed at another one. In a separationist model, there is a divorce between the structural properties of the word at an abstract level, and their surface realization. In irregular verbs, for instance, a separationist model proposes that the underlying structure of the form is identical in a regular and in an irregular verb, and the difference emerges at spell out. Thus, at one level (the abstract representation) one should not expect differences between regulars and irregulars; at the other level (the surface materialization) one expects differences between the two classes of verbs, because the regular form will spell out with more than one morpheme, while the irregular will be spelled out by one single synthetic morpheme. The problem is this: the experimental predictions are less clear unless one can guarantee that the experimental design targets only morphophonological or morphosyntactic representations. At present, however, it is unclear whether the experimental methods currently employed in psycholinguistic research allow for selectively targeting storage or computation of inflected words at the level of morphophonological or morphosyntactic representations.

'Unitary' morphological theories, in contrast, do not incorporate the Separation Theory. In these theories, morphemes (or words) are signs, and there is only one list of stored items with entries that already contain information about grammatical, phonological and semantic properties. Good examples of these theories are Halle (1973) or Wunderlich's MM (Wunderlich 1997).

Let us now move to a closer examination of the existing theories.

2 Theoretical approaches to morphological decomposition

In this section we will introduce the positions that have been advocated in morphological theories with respect to the issue whether at least some inflected forms are decomposed into smaller units. If that is the case, the next question is whether this decomposition is identifying morphemes or some other units of analysis, such as the exponent.

In order to carry out the comparison of the relevant theories, we will concentrate on four questions:

a. What is stored in theory X?
b. Is the storage divided in one single list (unitary) or in several (separationist)? (that is, is all stored information kept in the same place, or is it distributed across different modules, each one accessed at distinct points?)
c. What is computed?
d. What kind of computation is relevant?

2.1 Radical decomposition

A proposal that accepts the Separation Hypothesis and Late Insertion can claim that all words that are morphosyntactically complex are decomposed at an abstract level. This includes cases that are irregular in a traditional sense. When such approaches argue that both words and phrases are generated by the same component of grammar, they are labeled 'Neo-constructionist approaches'.

In a Neo-constructionist model, the main idea is that – if one considers only the morphosyntactic side of the word – any inflected word is decomposable. In fact, this model gives primacy to the morpheme above the word: morphemes, as morphophonological objects that spell out syntactic heads, are the units that compete with each other, and no independent object 'word', distinct from 'phrase' at a morphosyntactic level, is accepted. Said more clearly: no word would be stored as a unit at the relevant level.[4] In summary:
a. Regular and irregular forms share the same morphosyntactic representation.
b. Regular and irregular forms are differentiated only by the nature of the spell-out procedure they receive.
c. The units of analysis are syntactic heads, spelled out as single morphemes.
d. Heads/morphemes are combined through syntactic merge.

Distributed Morphology (DM) is an example of this kind of theory. In this clearly separationist approach, at least two kinds of units have to be distinguished: abstract sets of features (morphosyntax) and exponents (morphophonology). Computation here is syntactic and morphophonological: the sets of features are merged together by syntax, and how they are spelled out is determined by different kinds of rules. In DM there is one single generative component of grammar – syntax – that puts together syntactic heads, which at this point only contain abstract features like those in (12).

(12) [v], [T^{past}], [√]

Syntax combines these heads through binary merge, producing a tree structure like (13).

(13)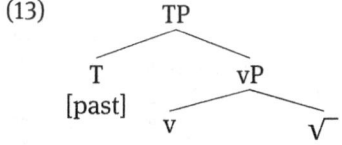

A past tense like *wrote* and a past tense like *classified* would be identical at this level: both regular and irregular words are, thus, computed in syntax. The

---
4 Lexical Integrity effects are treated as epiphenomena following from the phonological properties of the morpheme, or some semantic factors; see Lieber 1992; Embick and Noyer 2007.

differences emerge in the next level, when these heads are reinterpreted as positions of insertion for exponents, which introduce (among other idiosyncratic properties) specific morphophonological information. At that later level, lexical entries like those in (14) are accessed. These entries read the abstract features in (13) and check what exponent is associated with them. (14) represents the exponents involved in the regular form *classified*.

(14) a. *-ed* <--> [T^{past}]
　　 b. *-ify* <--> [v]
　　 c. *class-* <--> [√]

Thus, (13) becomes (15) after Late Insertion of the exponents.[5]

(15)
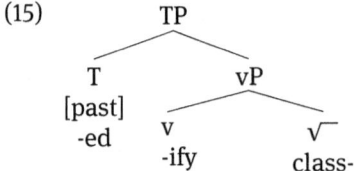

DM claims that there is an additional level mediating between the syntactic and the phonological representation where several operations have to take place, and an extra level of readjustment rules taking place after the insertion of the exponents, where some other operations can happen. These two levels following or preceding the insertion of vocabulary items are responsible for irregular forms. Schematically, the order of levels is given in (16):

---

[5] Note that we gloss over a potentially significant factor here: how deterministic the insertion of exponents is. If we look at (14), it is clear that there should be a very high number of exponents that in principle can be inserted in the root position: here insertion is not obviously deterministic (although see Borer 2013, who proposes that already in the syntax, roots are distinguished by a phonological index which determines later if the spell out will be done through one or another exponent). In contrast, presumably the only English exponent that can spell out the node T[past] alone will be *-ed*, so in this case insertion will be deterministic: only one exponent will correspond to the feature representation T[past]. The exponent corresponding to v is in an intermediate position: not any element can be introduced here, but there is a set of at least three items (*-ify, -ise, -en*) that can be used to verbalize a root. For this distinction between different kinds of exponents and the different conditions of insertion that affect them, see Harley and Noyer 1998.

(16) Abstract hierarchical structure
 |
 Morphological operations
 |
 Insertion of exponents
 |
 Readjustment rules

Consider first an irregular form like *wrote* (cf. Halle and Marantz 1993). DM treats this irregular form as the result of the application of a readjustment rule along the lines of (17), that is, a (morphophonological) operation that manipulates the morphophonological representation of an exponent in a particular context. Thus, there is a second computation at this level, where stored units (now exponents) are subject to an operation. Technical decisions aside, what is of relevance for us here is that this means that these irregular forms are derived by rule, involving therefore computation and not storage.[6]

(17) /aɪ/ --> /ou/ / X__Y [past]
 For X = √write

There are only two differences between regular and irregular inflected forms, then, both becoming relevant after the exponents are inserted: the form needs a readjustment rule that a form like *classify* does not need to undergo and the verbal exponents that undergo the rule must be marked somehow in the exponent lexical list.

A more controversial issue is the less frequent suppletive alternations like *go* ~ *went*, which seem to be difficult to formalize as a mere morphophonological readjustment. For some time, it has been assumed in DM and similar approaches that a root element cannot vary so radically in its phonological content across spell out contexts (e.g., Borer 2013). For this reason, the standard analysis of these forms did not use readjustment rules of any kind. This kind of irregularity was treated as the result of an operation in the morphological component

---

6 In fact, see Embick and Halle 2005, where it is claimed that readjustment rules do not block the insertion of other exponents: consider *tol-d*, where *tell* has both undergone a readjustment rule and the past morpheme is overtly introduced.

followed by insertion of an exponent that cumulatively spells out Past and Verb (Halle and Marantz 1993: 129):

(18)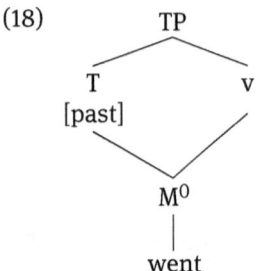

Thus, in this account the suppletive exponent has a separate lexical entry, even though at the morphosyntactic level it is still decomposed. In order to arrive at the morphological representation that allows the two syntactic heads T and v to be spelled out by one single form, the morphological component has to fuse these two heads in one single position of exponence. One aspect of this account that has been criticized is that it involves a certain degree of looking forward: the operation that fuses the two heads into one morpheme is triggered by the existence of a single exponent for the set T+v, even though that exponent has not yet been introduced. Needless to say, this account would expect a distinction between suppletive verbs and other irregular verbs, which still are derived by rules.

However, recently, Harley (2014), discussing data from Hiaki, has convincingly argued that suppletion can involve a root node. This step has the immediate consequence that the situation of suppletion in DM is unclear now, and could be implemented through readjustment rules. In such case, which is subject to debate still, all irregular verbs would be derived by rule.

2.2 No morphological decomposition

Other morphological theories (e.g., Anderson 1992; Aronoff 1976) have actually made the point that morphemes are simply convenient labels to talk about sets of segments inside words that we perceive as complex. They have no psychological reality and they have no place in a linguistic theory as primitives at a morphological level.[7]

---

[7] But see Marantz 2013 for a different interpretation of Anderson 1992.

The common property of these theories is the proposal that the lexicon does not store morphemes. The minimal objects that can be stored in this component are words, which then, by definition, are presented without any kind of internal morphological structure. Whatever morphological information might be relevant for word external phenomena has to be specified in a morphosyntactic signature of the word.

Both Aronoff (1976) and Anderson's (1992) A-morphous Morphology accept that 'morphemes' can be phonologically segmented, but deny that they have the status of morphological primitives. Computation in A-morphous Morphology involves rules that take words as input and produce new words: this is restricted only to regular formations, while irregular forms still have their own stored lexical entry.

In Anderson, regular inflection is performed through the application of rules that take a base and apply some change to it, which can affect its semantics, grammatical distribution and phonological shape. What seems to be a 'morpheme' in the classical sense is part of the description of the base: precisely the kind of phonological change that the rule triggers in the base. Take (19) as a simplified illustration of this kind of rules.

(19) Word formation rule for regular past tense, English
$$\begin{bmatrix} V \\ Past \end{bmatrix}$$

/X/ -> /Xed/

Specifically, Anderson proposes that inflection is performed through Inflectional Word Formation Rules (Anderson 1992: 122–123):

> [A] set of inflectional Word Formation Rules form part of the grammar, and operate to map lexical words (actually, lexical stems) onto fully inflected surface words. Such an inflectional Word Formation Rule takes as its input a pair {P, M}; this consists of a phonologically specified stem P from the lexicon [...] and the morphosyntactic representation M of some position in a Phrase Marker. [...] Each individual Word Formation Rule operates on the stem P so as to form a new stem P' that reflects the phonological stem (such as the addition of affixal material) associated with a part of the word's productive inflection. [...] Each rule may be regarded as a sort of generalization of the notion of 'morpheme', whose form (or signifiant) corresponds to the rule's Structural Change, and whose content (or signifié) corresponds to its Structural Description.

Let us stop here for a moment to ponder the consequences of this, and focus on the problem we advanced in Section 1.2 in respect of the two senses of 'stored' in theoretical morphology. First, this system might have something that could be abstractly interpreted as a 'morpheme', but its shape is not the one of a sign, that is, it would not make any sense to talk about a lexical entry /ed/ associated with a past tense meaning. However, Anderson's system is still symbolic at another level: it produces regular forms through a rule, which codifies a set of possible phonological changes and associates these changes with a more or less specific grammatical and semantic change. In consequence, even though there are no stored entries for any morpheme, regular inflectional forms do not have an entry of their own, and in that sense they are not stored, but computed through a rule. If we restrict the notion of storage to the question of whether morphemes have separate entries and regular forms are computed by combining those morphemes, Anderson's theory is, however, a clearly non-decompositional theory where words are the only objects that can be stored.[8] Note also that, as has been pointed out in other works (Williams 2007), Anderson's theory is to some extent separationist as it divides quite radically the syntactic aspect of the rule from its phonological effect.

What would be an example of a fully stored word in Anderson? It would be an irregular inflected word, such as the plural *oxen* instead of *oxes (Anderson 1992: 132–134), or, by extension, *wrote* instead of *writed. Anderson's proposal is that such irregular forms must be listed as stems inside the lexical entry of the base, and already associated with the maximal set of features that explains their distribution: *oxen* would be specified already as [+Noun, +Plural], as opposed to *ox*, which would lack the [+Plural] specification. A further principle of blocking of less specific forms by more specific forms would prevent the redundant *oxens from being produced. Anderson further allows that the output of a rule (computed forms) becomes opaque over time if some unpredictable idiosyncrasies are associated with it. In that case, after some time the form would be stored as a stem with its own lexical entry. Grammatical change, then, can turn a computed form into a stored one.

---

8 In fact, being regular is, for Anderson (1992), just an illusion produced by the tendency to correlate common sets of segments that recurrently appear in words that share one piece of information with the expression of that piece of information. In other words, if speakers see that a segment /xy/ appears frequently in words that share the information [A], there is a psychological tendency to identify /xy/ as the way to denote (symbolically) [A]. But, as Anderson points out, this psychological tendency does not mean necessarily that grammar identifies /xy/ with [A]. In fact, he continues, this is anyways what would happen with phonaesthemes, that is, phonological segments that convey or suggest some concept (typically, 'small' and 'big') and tend to appear in words expressing that concept, such as high front vowels in words denoting smallness (*tiny, little, bit, kitten* …). And yet, with these segments, no reasonable morphologist, even if they advocate that morphemes are units, would attempt to segment the high front vowels and associate them to an abstract representation [small].

Anderson's theory illustrates the fact that in some theories the terms 'decomposable' and 'computed' are independent: regular inflectional forms are computed, not stored, but they are not decomposable at a morphological level. Thus, Anderson (1992) is not a pure example of a non-symbolic theory for word formation.

In contrast, Rumelhardt and McClelland's (1986) Distributed Connectionist approach is a perfect example of a purely non-decompositional, non-symbolic approach where words are never decomposed at a morphological level: both regular and irregular forms are stored, and no rule is used to relate two word forms. Distributed Connectionism, as a program to study cognitive phenomena, proposes that production and recognition of forms is performed through an architecture of simple processing units – which are general information-processing devices – associated with each other through weighted connections of different strengths. Their view of how forms are related to each other is a pattern associator network (Kohonen 1977), which relates through connections a pool of basic forms (root forms in English) with a pool of output patterns related to past tense: the pattern associator contains a set of connections relating, with different strengths, input and output forms, until an optimal performance is reached and the strength of the connections becomes relatively fixed. In this system, there are typically three layers: the input layer, the hidden layer that intermediates between input and output by defining an internal representation, and the output layer that produces the appropriate behavior in the context. Note in (20), which is a feed-forward structure, that each unit is connected to each unit of the next layer; these connections are not of equal strength, though, but any cognitive process involves the parallel activation of several of these connections, in a cooperative fashion (see also Marzi et al. 2020, this volume and Pirrelli et al. 2020, this volume).

(20)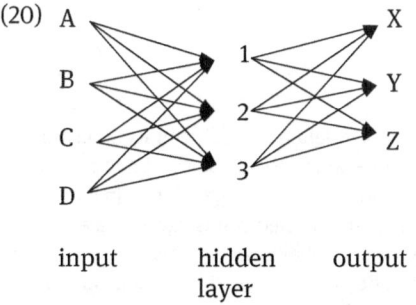

        input   hidden   output
                    layer

Simplifying matters now, in a connectionist model all words are stored, without internal segmentation, and related to each other through associative connections (as in 21). No different representation is assumed for regular and irregular forms, and learning implies (a) learning new stored forms, such as *classified, cars, wrote* or *went* and, crucially, (b) manipulating the strength of the connection between two or more of these entries, so that one is registered as the past of the other, etc. Simplifying the claim to just pairs of words, the learner becomes trained in associating one form with the other, and each with its right meaning and distribution.[9]

(21)

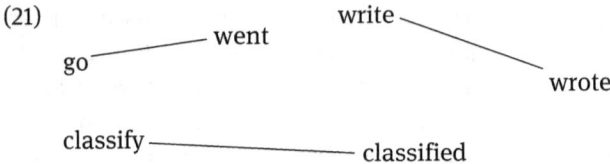

2.3 Mixed approaches

There are also approaches that in one sense or the other claim that decomposition and absence of decomposition are both (simultaneously or alternatively) attested in the lexicon.

One early example where some complex words are stored as wholes and some are decomposed into morphemes, which have their own entry, is Halle (1973), where he sets the basis for what after him became the development of generative morphology (Lieber 1980; Scalise 1984; Siegel 1974, among many others). What is crucial for us in this approach is that Halle proposed a system where words are in principle put together compositionally through the addition of morphemes, but at a later level the result is compared to a list of full words, stored as units that might block the output of the rules that combine morphemes. Schematically (Halle 1973: 8), the sequence looks like this:

---

[9] Building up on the original work of Rumelhart and McClelland (1986), connectionist modellers have set out to construct a multitude of different network models that claim to adequately simulate the different behavior observed for regular and irregular inflected forms in experimental research, although both regular as well as irregular inflected forms are represented and processed in a single associative network by identical mechanisms (see Marcus 2001 for an overview of such models). Recent developments include, for instance, the Naive Discriminative Learning (NDL) model (Baayen et al. 2011; see Plag and Balling 2020, this volume) and constructivist networks (cf. Penke and Westermann 2006). However, the literature is much too extensive and too specific to discuss the different models even cursorily. Interested readers are referred to Marcus 2001; Penke 2012a and Plag and Balling 2020, this volume.

(22) List   -->   Rules   --> Filter   -->   Dictionary
      of   of   of words
      morphemes   word formation

The list of morphemes, paired with grammatical information about their properties, feeds the rules of word formation, which contain sets of rules dictating how those morphemes need to be combined. But of capital importance to Halle is the fact that individual words have idiosyncratic characteristics: next to 'regular' words like *arrival* ('the action of arriving'), other words of seemingly the same structure, [V + *al*]$_N$, have a special meaning, such as *transmittal*, restricted to transmitting official documents and not any kind of transmission. The role of the filter is to add these pieces of idiosyncratic information to the words productively generated by the rules, and even, sometimes, to mark some of the potential words as not subject to insertion in a tree structure (e.g., *derival), that is, as not actual words. The dictionary, the final step in the sequence, contains the list of all words that actually exist in the language.

We mention Halle in this context because his theory has one crucial property of a mixed model: words can be generated (computed) and listed (stored). However, the contrast between regular and irregular does not coincide with computed vs. stored in Halle (1973). For instance, some irregularities – understood as idiosyncrasies that cannot be accounted for by word formation rules – would not be dealt with in the dictionary of words through the storage of the whole form, but would be accounted for by the filter component through a readjustment rule. Such is the case in (23), where the final [t] of some bases becomes spirantized in a specific morphological context (see, for instance, Siegel 1974).

(23) president > presidential

Moreover, in Halle (1973) the dictionary contains fully inflected words, that is, not just stems like *eat*, but actually whole paradigms like {*eat, eats, ate, eaten, eating*}. This brings up a question: if complex words are taken directly from the dictionary, how do we know that they are stored as segmentable, internally complex units, and not just as full, atomic representations? Halle is in fact fully aware of the problem, and mentions it (Halle 1973: 16).

> I have proposed above that the syntactic component has direct access to the dictionary; i.e., that the lexical insertion transformations take items from the dictionary rather than from the list of morphemes. Although the content of the dictionary is entirely determined by the content of the list of morphemes, the rules of word formation and the exception filter, there is no need to assume that these components are always fully

involved in every speech act. Instead it is possible to suppose that a large part of the dictionary is stored in the speaker's permanent memory and that he needs to invoke the word formation component only when he hears an unfamiliar word or uses a word freely invented. While this is by no means an exceptional occurrence, its frequency is quite low.

Interestingly, Halle is not explicit with respect to whether the storage in the dictionary is segmented or not. It is not implausible to think, however, that once the word is stored, and given that the list of morphemes is not accessed directly, the word should be stored as one atomic unit, and thus, without internal boundaries.

Thus, in Halle's proposal a word could be viewed as segmentable from one perspective, but as not segmentable from another one, depending on whether we are talking about words as members of the dictionary (which is closest to a lexical representation) or as the output of the word formation rules. This, again, shows that the question of storage can be seen in different ways inside a morphological theory.

If Halle's model is mixed because it allows both for computation and storage of the same word, other models are mixed in a simpler way, which allows one to establish more direct predictions with respect to the experimental results. These models claim that the list of exponents of a language contains both individual morphemes and whole words, with the second class being restricted to irregular forms like *wrote* or *went*.

Wunderlich's Minimalist Morphology (Wunderlich 1997) is an example of this kind of mixed model where regular forms like *spied* are computed by combining morphemes, while irregulars like *ran* have their own lexical entries as unanalyzed units. Morphemes are understood as signs, which means that in this system there is only one lexical list (as opposed to Distributed Morphology, for instance). Morphology is a generative component of grammar that takes individual entries and combines them, prototypically in a concatenative and compositional way that produces regular forms. Irregular forms, in contrast, are not built by any kind of computation, but are simply taken from the lexicon, where all their features are specified – as there is no separation hypothesis in MM. Once the word projects in a syntactic tree, all the features contained in the form will be checked against the relevant heads in syntax. Assume, for the sake of the argument, that *ran* has the features specified in (24):

(24) [Past, +external argument, verb]

This means that the inflected form, which in this case is stored as an undecomposed lexical entry, will have to license these features in syntax with the heads that carry these pieces of information. These heads presumably would be V (lexical verb), v (responsible for defining the external argument) and Tense. In the case of forms like *wrote*, where DM used readjustment rules, MM uses a non-symbolic generalization, an inheritance tree associated with the lexical entry of the irregular verb, as in (25) which is a generalization aimed at capturing the vocalic changes in irregular strong verbs in German (Wunderlich 1992, 1996).

(25)
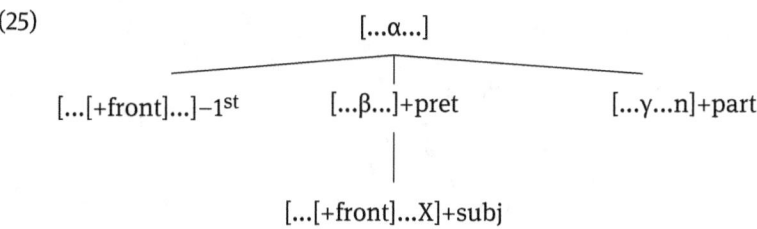

This captures, for instance, that in the paradigm of *werfen* 'throw', we predict *werf-* for a first person present indicative, *wirf-* for the present of the second person, *warf* for the past, *würfe* for the subjunctive and *-worfen* for the participle. Thus, in this theory there is a very clear cut between irregularity (stored in the lexical entry, non-symbolic) and regularity (computed through combination of morphemes via symbolic generalisations).

Finally, Nanosyntax is a Neo-constructionist framework that however falls into the mixed approaches to the extent that the exponent list contains entries for single morphemes, allowing decomposition of a complex word, but systematically also entries that correspond to a whole irregular word (Caha 2009; Dékány 2012; Fábregas 2007a, 2007b, 2009, 2014a, 2014b; Lundquist 2009; Muriungi 2008; Ramchand 2008; Ramchand and Svenonius 2014; Starke 2002, 2009, 2014a, 2014b, among others). In contrast to DM, however, the main proposal in Nanosyntax is that exponents are not necessarily introduced in heads – terminal nodes – but can actually correspond to the spell out of whole phrases. By assumption, each syntactic head in Nanosyntax contains only one (interpretable) feature. What this means is that, in contrast to DM, it is unnecessary to propose a list of stored elements for morphosyntax: those heads are not expected to be subject to variation in terms of their feature endowment, as they only carry one feature each. Thus, this approach only needs to assume one single idiosyncratic list, which contains exponents pairing the syntactic heads with phonological and conceptual-semantic content, essentially defining which and how many heads each morpheme identifies. The representation of a verb in the past tense in this framework could roughly correspond to (26).[10]

(26)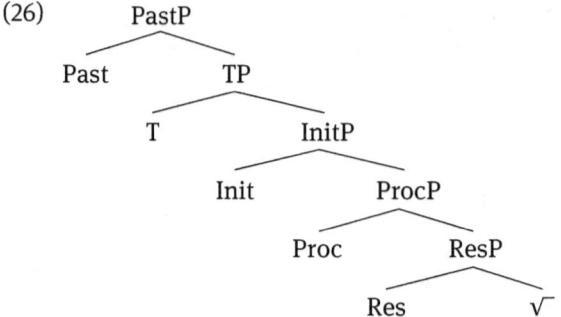

Notice that here we have divided the head v into three heads: Init, Proc and Res (Ramchand 2008). This illustrates nicely the consequences in Nanosyntax of the claim that an abstract head can have one interpretable feature at most. The reason for decomposing the verb into these three heads is that the aspectual information associated with the event expressed by *go* consists of more than one interpretable property. When someone goes somewhere, we are expressing three subevents: there is a process whereby an entity moves (ProcessP, or ProcP); there is an initial phase where the entity initiates some movement presumably using its own locomotive capacity (InitiationP, or InitP), and if the event is completed, there is a result state where the entity is now in a different location (ResultP, or ResP). Second, notice that tense has also been divided into two heads: one that denotes tense in itself, as a deictic category that places the eventuality with respect to the utterance, and another one that specifically gives the past value to that deictic orientation, denoting that the event is placed before the utterance time.

If we now look to the case of *classified*, it becomes apparent that – in contrast to Distributed Morphology – the exponents that spell out the structure are not just introduced in the head position, as there are only three exponents for 6 heads. Nanosyntax claims that exponents typically correspond to phrasal constituents, that is, that what looks like a single morpheme on the surface corresponds to an in principle unbounded set of heads, as roughly represented in (27):

---

10 It is controversial whether roots, as category-less units, are allowed in Nanosyntax or not. Nothing in our exposition crucially depends on this fact.

(27)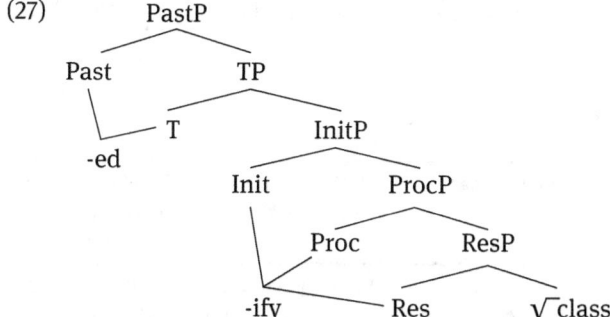

However, the regular word would still be decomposed in a number of surface exponents. In contrast, an irregular form will be stored as a different unanalyzed exponent in the list: while the underlying structure of both verb classes could be identical, the difference emerges only at the level where the exponents have to be introduced.

(28) went <-->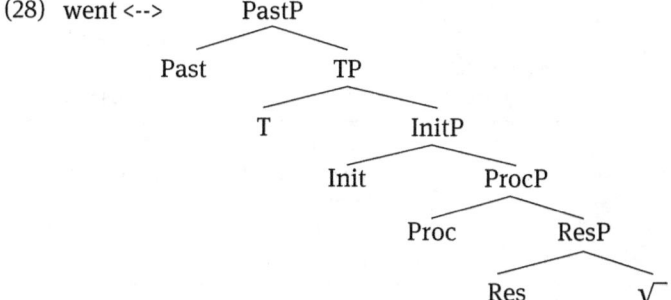

To wrap up this section, here are the crucial points made by the authors discussed here, with the exception of Halle (1973), where there is no real division between regulars and irregulars.
a. Words can have internal morphological structure; in fact, regular words are decomposed in morphemes
b. Irregular words, involving substitution of segments and not addition of new morphemes, are listed as atoms.

2.4 Wrap up

In Table 1, we summarize the main properties of the theories discussed here, for them to be connected in a principled way with their potential psycholinguistic predictions. We summarize here our four criteria: (a) what is stored, (b) whether storage uses one single list or several, (c) what is computed and (d) what kind of computation is proposed.

Table 1: Key features of discussed theoretical models.

	(a) What is stored?	(b) How many lists?	(c) What is computed?	(d) What kind of computation is relevant?
Distributed Morphology (Halle and Marantz 1993)	Syntactic heads and exponents that spell them out; no word is stored	At least two: one for morphosyntax and one for morphophonology	Both regular and irregular forms are computed by syntactic rules and can be decomposed morphologically	Spell out, including readjustment rules, following a non-trivial set of post-syntactic operations
A-morphous morphology (Anderson 1992)	Only words (no morphemes are stored)	Arguably two: the phonological and the grammatical side of a rule do not match one-to-one	Any form derived from another word	Rule-based: words are taken as their inputs and produce other words as their outputs
Distributed Connectionism (Rumelhardt and McClelland 1986)	Regular and irregular words	Only one	All word relations are expressed through non-symbolic association	Strength of connections between forms
Halle (1973)	Morphemes in the lexicon; actual words in the dictionary	Only one	All words	Combination of morphemes through word formation rules
Minimalist Morphology (Wunderlich 1992)	Morphemes and irregular words	Only one	Only regular forms	Affixation
Nanosyntax (Starke 2002)	Morphemes and irregular words	Arguably one: a list of exponents directly spelling out tree structures	Syntactically, both; morphologically, only regular forms	Insertion in (non-terminal) nodes

We now move on to an evaluation of how the psycholinguistic evidence supports some of these approaches, or at least some aspects of them, but before doing so we will introduce the psycholinguistic research methods that are employed to investigate storage and computation of inflected words.

3 Psycholinguistic tools

The rationale behind psycholinguistic research is that a specific and established experimental effect is used to test the predictions derived from theoretical approaches. A number of different experimental effects such as the *frequency effect*, the *priming effect* or the *ungrammaticality effect* have been identified in psycholinguistic research over the last decades. The presence, absence, or strength of the tested effect in the experimental data is interpreted as evidence for or against a given theoretical model. Here we introduce the two most relevant experimental effects that have been used to explore representations and mechanisms involved in inflectional morphology: the frequency effect and the priming effect.

3.1 The frequency effect: The lexical-decision task as a window to lexical storage

An experimental effect that is used to establish whether an element of interest is stored in the mental lexicon is the frequency effect. The frequency effect is typically measured in a lexical-decision experiment.

To understand the meaning of a spoken or written word we have to build up a graphemic or phonetic representation that allows us to activate the word's entry in the mental lexicon. Activation of the lexical entry gives us access to the word's meaning. The frequency effect captures the observation that the more often we encounter a specific word, the quicker we are to activate the word's lexical entry, as memory traces get stronger with each exposure. The time we take to activate a lexical entry can be measured with a lexical-decision task where subjects have to decide as quickly and accurately as possible whether a presented item is an existing word or not by pressing a 'yes' or 'no' button on a keyboard. The reaction time required to carry out this word-nonword discrimination task is measured from the presentation of the item up to the pressing of the response button (see Figure 1 for an example of the set-up of a lexical-decision experiment). To test for a frequency effect, reaction times for frequently and infrequently occurring lexical units are compared. A frequency effect is stated if subjects take significantly less time to decide that frequent items (such as the

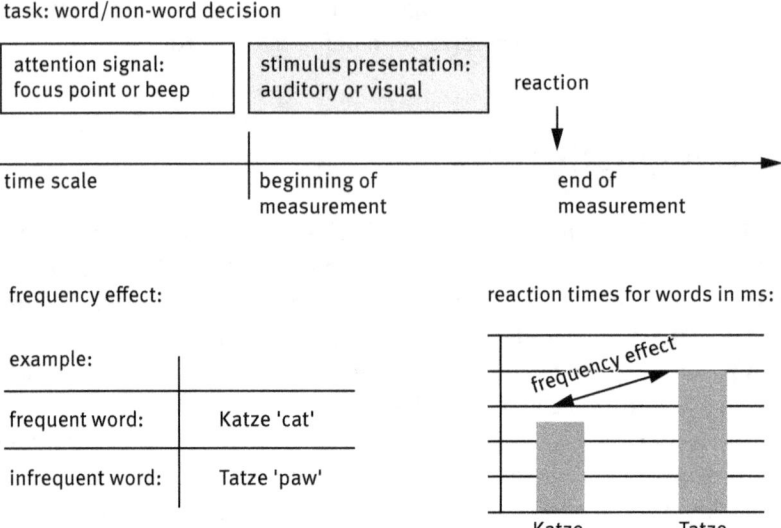

Figure 1: Frequency effect in a lexical-decision experiment.

German word *Katze* 'cat' in Figure 1) are existing words than they take for infrequent items (such as the phonologically similar word *Tatze* 'paw'). In contrast, items not stored in the mental lexicon will not display a frequency effect in a lexical-decision experiment since there are no memory traces that could be influenced by frequency of activation. The frequency effect can thus be used as a diagnostic tool to investigate which entities are stored in the mental lexicon. While it is uncontroversial that roots and stems are stored in the mental lexicon and should hence be affected by frequency of activation, the issue whether inflected word forms or inflectional affixes are also stored in the mental lexicon is disputed both in theoretical and psycholinguistic research (cf. for instance Penke 2006).

Lexical-decision times are, however, not only influenced by how frequently we have encountered a specific element. Other factors, not related to frequency, will also influence reaction times and interfere with the frequency effect. Thus, reaction times to longer words (e.g. *crystallize*) are longer compared to shorter words (e.g. *cure*). Also the type of non-word displayed might influence reaction times. Non-words are presented to provide subjects with a meaningful task (word/non-word discrimination) ensuring that they actually read (or listen) to the stimuli presented. If, however, non-words only consist of unpronounceable letter strings (e.g. *cccc*), the word/non-word discrimination can be done on visual characteristics of the stimuli alone, without the need to actually read the words. In this case reaction times to words might not reflect the time taken to activate a lexical entry. All factors that might potentially affect reaction times have to be carefully controlled in a lexical-decision experiment to ensure that it is only the frequency of occurrence of the tested lexical items that influence decision times (see Balota 1994; Cortese and Balota 2012 for a more thorough discussion of factors influencing visual word recognition).

3.2 The priming effect: Cross-modal priming yields evidence for morphological decomposition

The lexical-decision task can also be used to test for another effect important in psycholinguistic research: the priming effect. The priming effect captures the observation that subjects are quicker to respond to a word in a lexical-decision task if they have already encountered the very same word shortly before in the experiment. This priming of the target word by a prior presentation of this word (the prime) is most likely due to the fact that the activation threshold for the target's lexical entry is still lowered from the first activation of this lexical entry by the prime. This lexical entry can hence be activated more easily when the word is encountered again (cf. e.g. Balota 1994; Cortese and Balota 2012; Foster 1999).

In a priming experiment we compare two conditions, a primed and an unprimed condition that are typically distributed over two subject groups. Consider Figure 2 for explanation. In both subject groups the lexical-decision times for the target element (e.g. *chair*) are measured. For subject group A, this target word is primed since subjects have encountered this word before. This first presentation of the element is called the prime. In group B, in contrast, the target (e.g. *chair*) is not primed by a prior presentation of this word. A comparison of the lexical-decision times to the target element (e.g. *chair*) taken by the two subject groups will yield a priming effect, i.e. reaction times to the target will be significantly shorter in subject group A, for which the target has been primed, compared to reaction times of group B, for which the target has not been primed.

A number of different priming methodologies are employed in psycholinguistic research. The one that is considered most relevant for the issue of storage and computation in the mental lexicon is the cross-modal priming paradigm (cf. e.g. Marslen-Wilson 2007). In a cross-modal priming task the reaction times to a visually presented target word are evaluated in relation to an auditorily presented prime word. In the priming condition the auditorily presented prime word and the visually presented target word are identical. In the

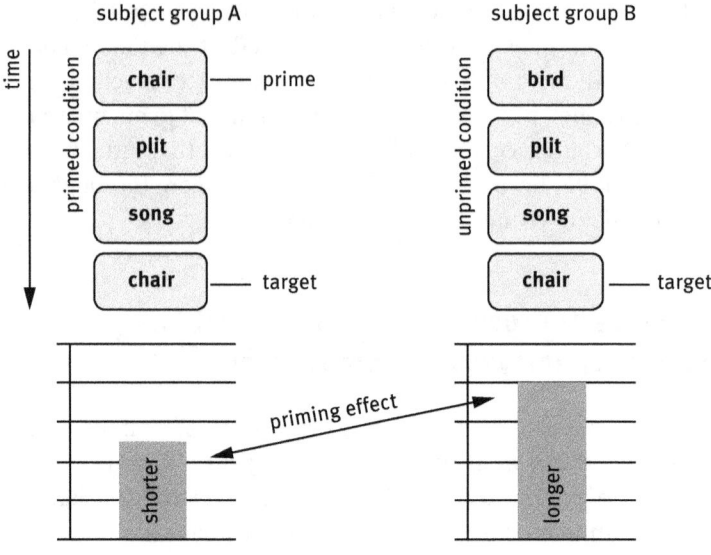

Figure 2: The priming effect in a lexical-decision task (identity priming).

unprimed condition, the auditorily presented word is semantically, morphologically and phonologically unrelated to the visually presented target word (see Figure 3 for an example of the set-up of a cross-modal priming experiment). The cross-modal presentation of prime and target ensures that shorter reaction times in the primed condition are not due to the perception of surface visual or

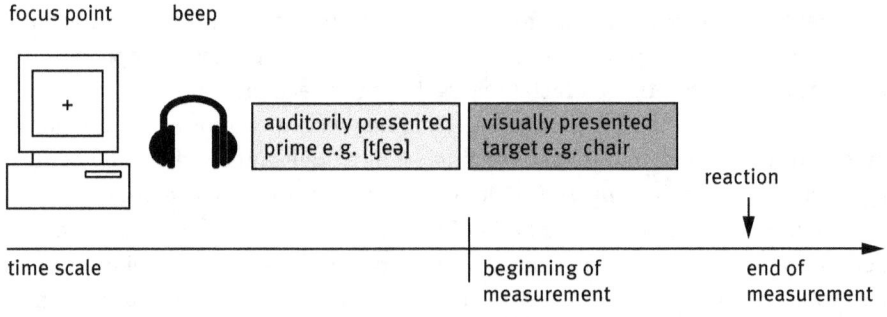

Figure 3: Exemplary set-up for a cross-modal priming experiment.

sound similarities between prime and target, as would be possible if both elements were presented auditorily or visually. With a cross-modal presentation, we ensure that the priming effect is due to the activation of the lexical entry by prime and target word.

The priming effect can be used to investigate whether complex word forms are composed out of constituent morphemes. In morphological priming a morphologically related word such as *sings* is presented as prime for the target base form *sing*. Morphological priming is evaluated against an identity condition where prime (e.g. *sing*) and target (e.g. *sing*) are identical. The identity condition serves as a baseline to explore whether an inflected prime such as *sings* will prime a target *sing* as effectively as the word *sing* itself. The rationale behind the morphological priming effect is the following: When an inflected prime such as *sings* is encountered, it is decomposed into its constituent parts, the stem *sing-* and the affix *-s*. The stem then activates its entry in the mental lexicon. Due to this activation, the activation threshold for this entry is lowered. When the target *sing* is presented subsequently, the stem *sing* has already been activated before and its activation threshold has been lowered. The access to this stem's entry is now faster – a priming effect occurs. If, in contrast, inflected forms are not decomposed into stem and affix but are stored as whole word forms in the mental lexicon, the inflected prime (i.e. *sings*) will not be decomposed and hence, the stem's lexical entry will not be directly activated by the prime. Subsequent presentation of the target (i.e. *sing*) will then not lead to a priming effect comparable to the identity condition (prime *sing*, target *sing*), since the stem *sing* has not been directly activated by the inflected prime *sings* presented before. Thus, an inflected word form that is morphologically related to a target word will only fully prime this target if the inflected form is decomposed into its constituent morphemes. The priming effect is hence used to explore whether or not inflected word forms are decomposed into constituent morphemes.[11]

---

[11] The same rationale applies to investigations focusing on the issue whether compounds or derived words are decomposed. As morphologically related words are generally similar in form (orthography or phonology) and meaning, experiments testing morphological priming have to make sure that the priming effect is not simply due to an overlap in form and/or meaning between prime and target. This can, for instance, be achieved by comparing morphological priming conditions to experimental conditions addressing overlap in form (e.g. prime *ring*, target *sing*) or in meaning (e.g. prime *tune*, target *sing*) (cf. e.g. Frost et al. 2000).

4 Psycholinguistic evidence

Let us now consider what the psycholinguistic evidence testing for storage or computation has to say regarding the discussed theoretical frameworks. Before starting, we would like to make some cautionary remarks. For one, it is not possible to discuss every relevant experiment that has been conducted in the field. Rather, our exposition will focus on showing what type of evidence can be used in principle in addressing the issue of storage and computation in the mental lexicon. Second, as already indicated above, all experimental research is in danger to be flawed by factors not sufficiently controlled in the experimental set-up (see Cutler 1981). As the field develops, factors that were not considered vital at the time the experiment was run might turn out to be important in the future, thus leading to a different evaluation of the experimental findings. Most research related to the issue of storage and computation of inflected forms has focused on the English past tense (cf. e.g. Pinker 1999 for an overview). English, however, is not ideally suited to investigate regular and irregular inflected forms. In English, regular inflected forms have an overt suffix (e.g. *-ed* in *laugh – laughed,* or *-s* in *chair – chairs*), whereas irregular inflected forms often only display a change of the stem vowel (e.g. *sing – sang, tooth – teeth*) and there are no endings that always appear on irregular inflected forms. Hence, the regularity or irregularity of inflected forms is confounded with the presence or absence of a separable inflectional ending in English. This confound might affect experimental research. For instance, due to the suffix, regular inflected forms are often longer than irregular inflected forms that only show stem changes. Also experiments making use of a different priming technique, i.e. masked priming, have found a very early, presumably prelexical effect in processing visually presented words in which potential affixes are stripped on the basis of morpho-orthographical cues alone (cf. Rastle and Davis 2008). Such an operation would apply to regular verbs but not to irregular verbs without a separable ending (e.g. *sang*) (but see Crepaldi, Rastle, Coltheart, and Nickels 2010). A difference between regular and irregular inflected forms that shows up in an experiment might, hence, be due to the presence of a separable ending rather than to the issue whether the inflection is regular or irregular. Given this potential confound, we will concentrate our exposition mainly on data from German – a language where irregular inflected forms have separable endings too and where the issue of storage and computation of inflected forms has been thoroughly investigated over the last 20 years (cf. Clahsen 1999; Penke 2006 for an overview).

4.1 Testing for storage

The frequency effect has been used to investigate which entities are stored in the mental lexicon. If an inflected form is stored in the mental lexicon, we should observe a frequency effect, i.e. reaction times to frequently occurring inflected word forms should be quicker compared to more infrequently occurring inflected word forms. As an example, consider a lexical-decision experiment that was investigating whether German past participle forms are stored in the mental lexicon (Clahsen, Eisenbeiss, and Sonnenstuhl 1997).

Regular inflected past participles are built with the suffix -*t* that is attached to the verb's base. Hence, regular inflected past participles do not show stem changes in the participle form, as in (29a) and (29b). In contrast, irregular inflected past participles often show a modification of the stem vowel in the participle form and take the ending /n/, as in (29c).[12] Neither the stem vowel nor the phonological shape of the verb's base predict whether a verb is regularly or irregularly inflected. Consider for example the verbs *blinken* 'flash' and *trinken* 'drink': Whereas *trinken* in (29c) has the irregular participle form *getrunken*, the verb *blinken* in (29b) has the regular participle form *geblinkt*. The prefix *ge-* is phonologically conditioned and occurs on regular and irregular past participle forms.

(29)   *Infinitive*   *Participle*   *Gloss*
    a. tanz-en   ge-tanz-t   'dance'
    b. blink-en   ge-blink-t   'flash'
    c. trink-en   ge-trunk-en   'drink'

In their lexical-decision task Clahsen, Eisenbeiss, and Sonnenstuhl (1997) presented infrequently and frequently occurring German regular and irregular participles and measured how long it took their subjects to decide whether the presented participle was a German word or not. Consider two irregular participles such as *gegraben* (from the verb *graben* 'dig') and *geschlagen* (from the verb *schlagen* 'hit'). While the German CELEX corpus (Baayen, Piepenbrock, and van Rijn 1993) yields 34 occurrences of the participle *gegraben* in its database of 6 million words, the participle *geschlagen* is much more common and occurs 644 times in this corpus. If these irregular participle forms are stored in the mental lexicon, we should expect a frequency effect in lexical-decision times. Thus, it should take subjects longer to decide that *gegraben* is a German

---

[12] In spoken language the ending is usually only realized as /n/. The ending is, however, written as <en>.

word compared to the more frequent *geschlagen*. Clahsen, Eisenbeiss, and Sonnenstuhl obtained lexical-decision times for 9 infrequent (mean participle frequency 81) and 9 frequent irregular participles (mean participle frequency 364) from 26 adult native speakers of German and found a clear and significant frequency effect for irregular inflected participles. Whereas their subjects took 652 ms (mean reaction time) to decide that an infrequent irregular participle was an existing word, the mean reaction time for frequent irregular participles was only 593 ms (see Figure 4, part a). This frequency effect indicates that irregular inflected participle forms are stored.

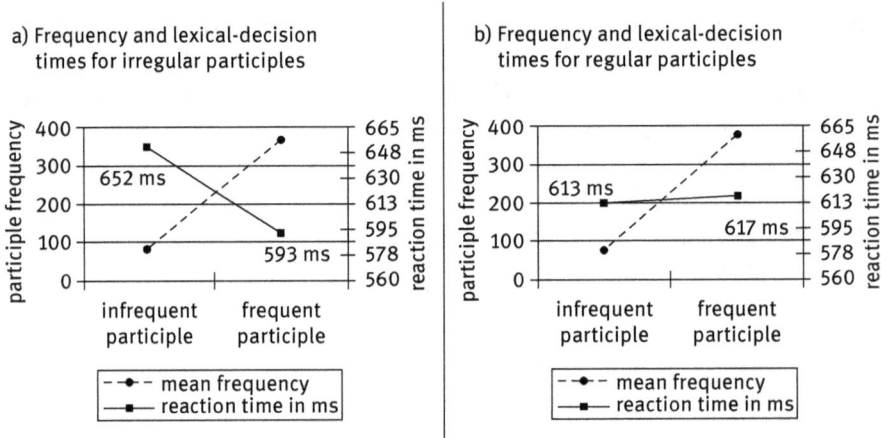

Figure 4: Lexical-decision times for regular and irregular German participles according to Clahsen, Eisenbeiss, and Sonnenstuhl (1997).

In the same experiment, Clahsen, Eisenbeiss, and Sonnenstuhl also tested lexical-decision times to 9 infrequent regular participles, such as *gepflanzt* 'plant' (frequency 27, mean frequency of 9 infrequent regular participles 78) and to 9 frequent regular participles such as *gespielt* 'play' (frequency 348, mean frequency of 9 frequent regular participles 379). If regular inflected participle forms are stored like irregular participle forms in the mental lexicon, we should observe a frequency effect, with longer lexical-decision times for infrequent regular participles compared to frequent ones. However, no such frequency effect occurred. The mean decision times for infrequent (613 ms) and frequent (617 ms) regular participles did not differ significantly, despite the fact that frequent and infrequent regular participles were matched in frequency to frequent and infrequent irregular participles (see Figure 4, part b). The lack of a frequency effect for regular participles indicates that these regular inflected forms are not stored in the mental lexicon.

To ensure that differences between regular and irregular participle forms were only due to the regularity of the inflectional marking, Clahsen, Eisenbeiss, and Sonnenstuhl matched the participle forms in the regular and irregular condition for frequency and made sure that the chosen irregular participle forms did not show any ablaut in the verb stem and only differed with respect to their participle ending /t/ or /n/. A replication of this study made use of a slightly modified set of items also controlled for word length and the frequency of the verb's stem between regular and irregular participles. This study confirmed the findings of Clahsen, Eisenbeiss, and Sonnenstuhl for another group of 30 participants (Neubauer and Clahsen 2009). A frequency effect for irregular inflected forms and a lack of a frequency effect for matched regular inflected forms have also been observed for a different set of participle forms including irregular participles that have an ablauting participle stem (Clahsen, Eisenbeiss, and Sonnenstuhl 1997) and for German noun plurals that display a similar difference between regular and irregular forms (Penke and Krause 2002).

While the above mentioned studies compared lexical-decision times to regular and irregular inflected forms carefully matched to each other, a number of studies have focused on regular inflected forms only. Lexical-decision studies on highly inflecting languages such as Finnish have confirmed that regular inflected forms are associated with longer reaction-times compared to monomorphemic words matched in word length. This processing cost for regular inflected forms suggests that the form is decomposed into its constituent morphemes – a process that involves additional operations and hence more time compared to monomorphemic words (e.g. Laine Vainio, and Hyönä 1999; Lehtonen et al. 2007).

Studies focusing on the processing of regular inflected forms have identified a number of conditions and factors within an individual speaker or a given language and inflectional system that will lead an individual to store at least some regular inflected forms (e.g. Alegre and Gordon 1999; Bertram et al. 2000; Bertram, Schreuder, and Baayen 2000; Lehtonen and Laine 2003).

Consider for example language acquisition. From an acquisitional perspective, a number of regular inflected forms have to be stored by the child before she would be able to generalize a productive means to produce regular inflected forms from these stored forms (see e.g. Weyerts and Clahsen 1994; Penke 2006, 2012b). Even after a rule or affix entry for the regular inflection has been derived by the child, the once stored regular inflected forms might remain in the mental lexicon.

Also, it might be the case that accessing a frequently occurring stored form in the mental lexicon is quicker than decomposing this form into constituent morphemes before access (e.g. compare the reaction times for frequent regular (617 ms) and frequent irregular participles (593 ms) in the experiment described above).[13] Thus, it might be advantageous to store those regular participle forms an individual often encounters. In fact, Alegre and Gordon (1999) observed a frequency effect within a group of frequently occurring regular English past tense forms, indicating that these very frequent regular forms are stored. For a group of regular past tense forms with a lower frequency of occurrence a frequency effect was, however, not observed by Alegre and Gordon, suggesting that less commonly occurring regular past tense forms are not stored (see also Lehtonen and Laine 2003 for similar findings on Finnish).

Bertram and colleagues have suggested affix homonymy as another factor that might lead to regular inflected forms being stored in the mental lexicon (Bertram et al. 2000; Bertram, Schreuder, and Baayen 2000). Based on investigations of homonymous affixes in Finnish and Dutch Bertram and colleagues suggested conditions under which regular inflected forms might be stored to speed-up performance. They, for instance, suggested that regular inflected forms are stored if homonymous affixes occur with comparable frequency (Bertram et al. 2000; Bertram, Schreuder, and Baayen 2000). Also, Baayen, Dijkstra, and Schreuder (1997) reported a frequency effect for nouns inflected with the Dutch regular plural suffix *-en*, but no frequency effect for verbs inflected with the verbal plural affix *-en* and suggested that regular inflected noun plurals might be stored because the noun affix *-en* occurs with considerable less frequency than the homonymous regular verbal suffix *-en*. Note, however, that this finding could not be replicated for German where a similar homonymy between a regular noun plural suffix *-en* and a regular verbal ending *-en* exists (Penke and Krause 2002), suggesting that the storage of homonymous regular inflected forms is dependent on language-specific factors.

Last but not least, gender and age of acquisition have also been suggested to influence storage of regular inflected forms (Ullman 2005). Neubauer and Clahsen (2009), for example, conducted a modified version of the Clahsen,

---

13 Note, however, that the reverse seems to hold for speech production. In a production experiment on English regular and irregular past tense forms Cohen-Shikora and Balota (2013) reported that the production of regular past tense forms was significantly faster than the production of irregular past tense forms matched for frequency, word length, phonological and orthographical complexity. Thus, it might be the case that advantages associated with storage or computation of inflected forms differ for speakers and hearers/readers.

Eisenbeiss, and Sonnenstuhl (1997) study presented above with a group of native German speakers and a group of advanced adult Polish learners of German. While their native German subjects displayed no frequency effect for the regular inflected participles, the results for the second-language learners of German showed a strong frequency effect for regular as well as irregular inflected participles. Based on these results Neubauer and Clahsen concluded that adult second-language learners rely more on memorization of inflected forms than native speakers. Ullman (2005) has suggested that the stronger reliance on memorization might be due to increasing levels of estrogen during adolescence that inhibit the procedural memory system subserving grammatical computations and enhance the declarative memory system that underlies the mental lexicon. Hence, second-language learners that start learning after a certain critical age as well as women for whom estrogen levels are higher than in men tend to store regular inflected forms instead of computing them.

As this short discussion has exemplified, the issue whether or not regular inflected forms are stored in the mental lexicon has led to a number of experimental studies that yielded divergent results with respect to frequency effects for regular inflected forms. Nevertheless, the following summary of the available literature is justified:

a. Whereas studies have disputed whether and which regular inflected forms display frequency effects in lexical-decision experiments, the finding that such effects can reliably be found for irregular inflected forms is not controversial.
b. Lexical-decision tasks where reaction-times for carefully matched regular and irregular inflected forms are directly compared quite consistently report different performance patterns for regular and irregular inflected forms: whereas irregular inflected forms yield a frequency effect, no frequency effect is observed for regular inflected forms, indicating that regular inflected forms are generally not stored as fully inflected forms.
c. Studies focussing on regular inflected forms only, have identified certain factors that might nevertheless lead to the storage of regular inflected forms. These studies have provided important insights on how individual speakers organize their mental lexicon to cope with the requirements of speedy speech production and comprehension given the language they speak and the inflectional system at stake. However, one could argue that the aim of theoretical models as discussed above is a different one. The issue is not to highlight conditions under which it might be advantageous for an individual to store a regular inflected form given the time pressures of speech production and comprehension, but the aim is to provide a generalization of the representation of inflectional morphology that is valid

across languages, inflectional systems and individuals. To achieve this goal and to gain a deeper understanding of the principles governing the system under investigation morphological theories generally abstract away from individual findings and concrete experimental data, a procedure that has been advocated by Chomsky as the Galilean style of rational inquiry in linguistic research (e.g. Chomsky 2002; see Penke and Rosenbach 2007). Given this perspective of theoretical models, the currently available evidence suggests that, notwithstanding specific parsing requirements favoring storage of regular inflected forms under certain conditions, regular inflected forms do not have to be stored but are in general computed.

4.2 Testing for decomposition

The cross-modal priming paradigm has been used in psycholinguistic research to investigate whether regular and irregular inflected forms are decomposed and activate their constituent morphemes in the mental lexicon. Sonnenstuhl, Eisenbeiss, and Clahsen (1999) used the cross-modal priming paradigm to investigate the processing of regular and irregular inflected German participles. They compared lexical-decision times for regular inflected first person singular forms such as *plane* 'plan' in three conditions: (a) in the identity condition the target first person singular form (e.g. *plane*) was preceded by an identical verb form as prime (prime *plane*, target *plane*); (b) in the morphological condition the target first person singular form (e.g. *plane*) was preceded by a participle form as prime (prime *geplant* 'planned', target *plane*); and (c) in the control condition the target was preceded by a prime not phonologically, morphologically, or semantically related to the target (prime *öffne* 'open', target *plane*) (cf. Table 2, part A).

The rationale behind this experimental set-up is the following: when a subject encounters the regular inflected first person singular form (e.g. *plane*), this form is decomposed into the verb stem *plan* and the inflectional suffix *-e*. As the verb stem is identical to the verb's base (e.g. *plan* 'plan'), this base entry is activated. In the identity condition, the same regular inflected form is presented twice, as auditory prime and as visual target for lexical decision. By encountering the target, the form is again decomposed, and the verb's base is activated. Since the base has already been activated by parsing the prime, subjects are now quicker to activate the base entry again and are hence quicker to decide that the presented target form (e.g. *plane*) is an existing German word, compared to the control condition where the target (e.g. *plane*) is not related to the prime (e.g. *öffne*). The identity condition is then used as a baseline to establish whether a priming effect will also occur in the morphological test condition where subjects encounter a participle form such as *geplant* as prime before the target first person singular form (e.g. *plane*).

Table 2: Priming effects for regular and irregular inflected German participles according to Sonnenstuhl, Eisenbeiss, and Clahsen (1999).

A. Priming with regular inflected participles			
	(i) identity condition	(ii) morphological condition	(iii) control condition
prime (auditory)	*plane* ('plan$_{1.Sg.}$')	*geplant* ('planned.')	*öffne* ('open$_{1.Sg.}$')
target (visual)	*plane* ('plan$_{1.Sg.}$')	*plane* ('plan$_{1.Sg.}$')	*plane* ('plan$_{1.Sg.}$')
lexical-decision time for target	581 ms	581 ms	611 ms

☞ no significant difference in reaction-time between identity and morphological condition

B. Priming with irregular inflected participles			
	(i) identity condition	(ii) morphological condition	(iii) control condition
prime (auditory)	*schlafe* ('sleep$_{.Sg.}$')	*geschlafen* ('slept.')	*beuge* ('bow$_{.Sg.}$')
target (visual)	*schlafe* ('sleep$_{.Sg.}$')	*schlafe* ('sleep$_{.Sg.}$')	*schlafe* ('sleep$_{.Sg.}$')
lexical-decision time for target	563 ms	595 ms	620 ms

☞ Significant diffference in reaction-time between identity and morphological condition

When subjects heard a regular inflected participle form such as *geplant* in the morphological condition, the mean reaction time for the target form (e.g. *plane*) (581 ms) was not different from the identity condition where the form *plane* was presented twice (581 ms) (cf. Table 2, part A). This observation indicates that a regular participle form such as *geplant* is as good a prime for the inflected form *plane* as is the form *plane* itself. The explanation for the observed morphological priming effect is the following: when a subject encounters a regular inflected participle such as *geplant* as prime, this form is decomposed into its constituent parts, the stem *plan* and the participle affix *-t*, during lexical access. As the stem *plan* is identical to the verb's base entry (e.g. *plan*), this base entry is activated in the mental lexicon. Due to this activation, the activation threshold for this entry is lowered. When the regularly inflected form *plane* is presented subsequently as target for lexical decision, this form, too, is decomposed into the stem *plan* and the first person singular affix *-e*. The stem will then activate the verb's base entry (e.g. *plan*). Since this base entry has already been activated before by the prime word and since its activation threshold has therefore been lowered, the access to this base entry is now faster – a morphological priming effect occurs.

What if an irregular participle such as *geschlafen* ('slept') precedes its regular inflected first person singular form (e.g. *schlafe*)? In this case, the mean lexical-decision time for the target form (e.g. *schlafe*) (595 ms) is significantly longer compared to the identity condition where *schlafe* is presented twice (563 ms) (cf. Table 2, part B). This result shows that an irregular participle such as *geschlafen* does not prime the inflected form *schlafe* as effectively as a regular participle such as *geplant* primes the inflected form *plane*. Why not? Sonnenstuhl, Eisenbeiss, and Clahsen (1999) have suggested that irregular inflected participles such as *geschlafen* are not decomposed into stem and affix since they are stored as whole word forms in the mental lexicon. Thus, the presentation of the irregular participle *geschlafen* does not lead to a direct activation of the verb's base entry *schlaf*. When the regular inflected target form *schlafe* is subsequently presented as target, this form is decomposed into stem *schlaf* and affix *-e* and the verb's base entry *schlaf* is activated. However, since the base entry *schlaf* has not been directly activated by the participle prime presented before, there is no priming effect comparable to the identity condition where the form *schlafe* is presented as prime and target.[14]

Summarizing, the priming data from Sonnenstuhl, Eisenbeiss, and Clahsen (1999) suggest that irregular participles do not prime regular inflected forms as effectively as regular participles. The priming effect observed for regular participles indicates that regular inflected forms are decomposed into stem and affix constituents. The finding that irregular participles do not display a similar priming effect, in contrast, suggests that irregular inflected forms are not composed out of stem and affix, but are stored as whole word forms in the mental lexicon.

A critical issue in evaluating differential priming effects of regular and irregular inflected forms is whether differences in priming can be related to

---

[14] Note, however, that compared to the control condition (620 ms) the morphological condition (595 ms) yields a partial priming effect. This partial priming can be accounted for by the assumption that irregular inflected forms are associated with the verb's base entry in the mental lexicon (see also Allen and Badecker 2002). Thus, although the irregular inflected form is not decomposed into stem and affix and is thus not able to directly activate the verb's base entry, it is nevertheless able to lower the activation threshold for the base entry via the associative connections between the inflected form and its base.

differences in regularity alone or whether items in the regular and irregular condition also differ with respect to other dimensions. Regular and irregular inflected forms may, for example, differ in how much they overlap in phonological form with the morphologically related target form. Thus a regular inflected English past tense form such as *walked* is more similar to a target *walk* than the irregular inflected form *taught* is to *teach*. However, the different morphological priming effects observed for regular and irregular inflected German participles by Sonnenstuhl, Eisenbeiss, and Clahsen (1999) cannot be explained by differences with respect to form or meaning overlap between regular and irregular inflected forms, by differences in word length, or by differences in the frequency distribution of the regular and irregular inflected participle forms. Specifically, regular and irregular inflected participles were equally similar to their base forms (*geschlafen – schlaf* vs. *geplant – plan*) because only irregular participles without stem changes were tested. Also differences between the regular and the irregular experimental condition cannot be due to differences in meaning overlap between the two conditions since the same inflected verb forms (first person singular forms and participles) were tested in the regular and the irregular conditions. Thus, Sonnenstuhl, Eisenbeiss, and Clahsen suggest that the difference in priming effects observed for regular and irregular inflected participles is related to the regularity of the inflectional marking alone.

Differential priming effects for regular and irregular inflected forms have been confirmed in cross-modal priming experiments across inflectional systems and languages. Sonnenstuhl, Eisenbeiss, and Clahsen (1999) confirmed their finding of full-priming with regularly inflected morphological primes and the lack of a full-priming effect with irregular inflected morphologically related primes in a second experiment, where they tested regular and irregular inflected German noun plurals (see also Sonnenstuhl and Huth 2002). A priming asymmetry with full-priming for regular inflected forms and partial or no priming for irregular inflected forms was also found in English where *walked* primes *walk* as effectively as *walk* primes *walk,* whereas *gave* will not prime *give* (cf. e.g. Marslen-Wilson, Hare, and Older 1993; Stanners et al. 1979).[15] A comparable priming asymmetry has also been reported for Greek (Tsapkini, Jarema, and Kehayia 2004).

In contrast, to the studies mentioned above, some studies have claimed a comparable facilitation in morphological priming conditions for regular and irregular inflected forms. Such differences in outcome might be related to

---

15 See Allen and Badecker (2002) for an explanation for why irregular inflected English past tense forms have been associated with partial priming or no priming in previous studies.

differences in experimental design. Thus, studies that do not include an identity condition, for instance, do not allow for identifying whether reported priming effects are full (i.e. comparable to identity priming) or partial (e.g. Feldman et al. 2010; Orsolini and Marslen-Wilson 1997; Smolka, Zwitserlood, and Rösler 2007). Also, different evaluations of what constitutes a regular or irregular inflected form will lead to different interpretations of the data. Feldman et al. (2010) for example refer to a study on French inflected verbs by Meunier and Marslen-Wilson (2004) as supporting their finding of a comparable priming effect for regular and irregular inflected forms. Indeed, Meunier and Marslen-Wilson found no difference between the four different French verb classes tested in their priming study, but they only tested forms inflected with regular affixes in all four verb classes. Hence, no differences with respect to decomposition were to be expected for these forms – as Meunier and Marslen-Wilson note themselves.

Summarizing, while controversies in the field focus on the issue whether irregular inflected forms do or do not display priming effects comparable to the effects observed for regular inflected forms, it is not disputed that regular inflected forms yield full morphological priming effects, indicating that these forms are decomposed into constituent morphemes.

4.3 Evaluating the evidence

Let us now evaluate how the morphological theories discussed in Section 3 fare vis-à-vis the evidence discussed. We will focus here on those findings that are relatively uncontroversial in the field of psycholinguistics.

4.3.1 Irregular inflected forms display frequency effects

It is uncontroversial in psycholinguistic research that irregular inflected forms display frequency effects in a lexical-decision task: reaction times to infrequent inflected forms are significantly longer compared to frequent inflected forms. Controversies focus on the issue whether regular inflected forms display frequency effects too.

As described above, the frequency effect observed for irregular inflected forms is evidence that these inflected forms are stored in the mental lexicon. Hence, all morphological theories that do not assume storage of irregular inflected forms would not be compatible with the available psycholinguistic evidence. This would be problematic for Distributed Morphology (see Section 3.1), that argues that irregular inflected forms are computed through readjustment rules. Although the verb bases that undergo a specific readjustment rule have to be stored in the input conditions of this rule (see 17), the resulting irregular form is not stored, as there is a rule that derives it. Hence the observed frequency effects for irregular inflected forms cannot be straightforwardly explained in this framework. A frequency effect for irregular verbs might result from different frequencies of the readjustment rules necessary to derive irregular inflected forms, i.e. a less frequently applied rule might take more time for activation or computation compared to a more frequently applied readjustment rule. Note, however, that in the experiment of Clahsen, Eisenbeiss, and Sonnenstuhl (1997) described above all irregular participles had to undergo the same readjustment rule (30). When the same readjustment rule applies for all items in the irregular test condition, no frequency effect should occur according to Distributed Morphology, contrary to findings. This explanation of the observed frequency effect for irregular inflected forms can thus be ruled out.

(30) /V/ --> /V/ / X__Yn [participle]
      For X = √grab, schlaf, lauf, ...

Another potential explanation for a frequency effect in irregular inflected forms that would be compatible with Distributed Morphology is that such a frequency effect is not due to different frequencies of the inflected forms but to different frequencies of the base forms. Recall that it takes longer to activate a less frequently occurring base compared to a frequently occurring base. Base frequencies did, however, not differ between regular and irregular test conditions in the study of Clahsen, Eisenbeiss, and Sonnenstuhl-Henning (1997), and can thus not account for the observation that a frequency effect was only observed for irregular but not for regular forms. A similar critique can be made of Halle's (1973) model, to the extent that in his model all words, regularly or irregularly inflected, are computed at some level in the lexicon.

In contrast, the finding of a frequency effect for irregular inflected forms is compatible with all theories that assume that these forms are stored in the mental lexicon in one way or another: MM, A-morphous Morphology, Nanosyntax and Distributed Connectionist models.

4.3.2 Regular inflected forms are decomposed

The finding that regular inflected verbs display a full morphological priming effect is not disputed in psycholinguistic research either. Controversies concern the question whether similar priming effects can be obtained for irregular inflected verbs. The observation that a regular inflected form such as *sings* primes a target *sing* as effectively as an uninflected prime *sing* suggests that regular inflected forms are decomposed into constituent morphemes (*sing-*, *-s*). On a principled view then, morphological accounts that assume that inflected forms are not decomposed into constituent morphemes (see Section 3.2.) are not compatible with this finding. This would, in principle, cause problems for Anderson's (1992) A-morphous Morphology and for Distributed Connectionist models.

Is it possible to reconcile these accounts with the available experimental evidence? With respect to A-morphous Morphology much of the answer hinges on the issue how a hearer or reader would parse a regular inflected form according to this theory, which is in fact formulated from a speaker's perspective. Can an inflectional rule be reversed so that the base can be derived from the inflected form, in practice undoing the job that the rule does? If so, the fact that the base is primed by the inflected regular form might not in itself be a counter-argument to Anderson's (1992) proposal.

A priming effect might also be reconciled with connectionist approaches and result from the phonological overlap between inflected form (*sings*) and base (*sing*). Note, however, that in the priming experiment by Sonnenstuhl, Eisenbeiss, and Clahsen (1999) described above the amount of phonological overlap was controlled for regular and irregular inflected forms (compare regular *geplant – plane* and irregular *geschlafen – schlafe*). Despite a similar phonological overlap between inflected forms and base forms in regular and irregular inflected forms, a full priming effect was only observed for the regular inflected forms. This renders it unlikely that a priming effect can be based on phonological overlap alone, which is a problem for connectionist approaches.

The finding should also be problematic for Halle's (1973) account. Halle proposes that word forms are stored in the dictionary while the word formation component would only be put to use when encountering an unfamiliar word or when using an invented word. Hence, regular and irregular inflected forms would be equally stored in the dictionary according to his proposal and could be parsed and understood without recourse to the word formation component. A full priming effect for existing regular inflected forms that is indicative of morphological decomposition would thus not be predicted by Halle's account.

The finding that regular inflected forms are decomposed into constituent morphemes is, however, fully compatible with those approaches that assume that regular inflected forms are composed out of constituent morphemes, i.e. Distributed Morphology, MM and Nanosyntax.

4.3.3 Regular and irregular inflected forms are different

A consistent finding of experiments that have directly compared the reactions to carefully controlled regular and irregular inflected forms is that regular and irregular inflected forms are associated with different performance patterns in these experiments. In the experiments described above regular and irregular inflected forms differ with respect to frequency effects as well as with respect to priming effects. This would be hard to reconcile with theoretical approaches that do not assume differences between regular and irregular inflected forms with respect to storage or computation, specifically Distributed Morphology, where all forms are computed, and Distributed Connectionist models, as well as Halle's (1973) theory, where all words are or can be stored.

At a closer look, however, things are not as easy. While Distributed Morphology assumes that all inflected forms are computed in the morphosyntactic component, regular and irregular inflected forms do differ as only the latter undergo a readjustment rule – a difference that in principle could account for different performance patterns in psycholinguistic experiments. In connectionist models, different performance patterns between regular and irregular inflected forms might be based on differences in the input data the network receives and computes. Thus, for instance in English past tense inflection, regular inflected forms by far outnumber irregular inflected forms with regard to type and token frequency, i.e. the number of regular inflected verbs as well as the frequency of their past tense forms by far exceed those of irregular inflected verbs (cf. Clahsen 1999 for discussion). While this difference might underlie the different performance pattern observed in psycholinguistic testings on English regular and irregular morphology (cf. e.g. Gonnerman, Seidenberg, and Andersen 2007), the frequency distribution of regular and irregular inflected forms (participles and noun plurals) is different in German, where, for instance, the regular -s Plural is in fact quite infrequent (cf. Clahsen 1999). Despite differences in the frequency distribution of regular and irregular inflected forms in English and German, psycholinguistic experiments have yielded comparable findings, for instance with respect to morphological priming (e.g. Stanners et al. 1979; Marlsen-Wilson, Hare, and Older 1993). This observation casts doubt on the assumption that differences between regular and irregular inflected forms can solely be based on differences in the frequency distributions of regular and irregular forms.

It would seem that the finding of different performance patterns for regular and irregular inflected forms would be particularly problematic for Halle's (1973) account. Recall that Halle's theory cross-cuts the distinction between regular and irregular inflected forms. Regular and irregular inflected forms familiar to an individual will be stored in the dictionary, else they will be derived by word formation rules. While a regular or irregular inflected form might be stored or derived by rule, there is no principled difference between the operations and representations involved in regular and irregular inflected forms in his account. How different performance patterns could result from the processing of regular and irregular inflected forms matched for frequency and hence (un)familiarity for the experimental subjects remains a challenge for this account.

The different performance patterns associated with regular and irregular inflected forms might also pose a challenge to separationist theories such as Distributed Morphology and Nanosyntax, which assume that regular and irregular inflected forms have the same representation at the morphosyntactic level and only differ at spell out. While one could argue that the different performance patterns observed in psycholinguistic experiments originate at the morphophonological level, where regular and irregular inflected forms differ according to separationist theories, we cannot at this point exclude the possibility that the tested effects address the morphosyntactic level, where both types of inflected forms display the same type of representation. To clarify this issue, experimental effects have to be found that selectively target morphosyntactic and morphophonological representations.

In contrast to the discussed theories, Minimalist Morphology – a unitarist theory that draws a distinction between regular and irregular inflected forms in terms of computation – and A-morphous Morphology (where there are rules relating regular forms, but irregulars are stored) are compatible with the evidence regarding different performance patterns for regular and irregular inflected forms.

4.3.4 Controversial findings

In contrast to the three findings discussed above, the following two findings are debated in psycholinguistic research, as discussed in Sections 4.1 and 4.2:

a. Regular inflected forms do not show a frequency effect.
b. Irregular inflected forms do not show full priming.

Most studies that have directly compared regular and irregular inflected forms conclude that regular inflected forms are not subject to frequency effects, whereas irregular inflected forms are. The lack of a frequency effect for regular inflected forms can be interpreted as these forms not being stored. This finding would run against models where regular forms are stored, i.e. connectionist models and Halle's (1973) model, which assumes that the dictionary stores familiar regular forms. Also, priming experiments have shown that irregular inflected forms do not prime their base as effectively as regular inflected forms, suggesting that irregular forms are not subject to decomposition, and thus that they are not computed by aggregation of different pieces. This finding might go against the proposal in Distributed Morphology, where irregulars are derived through readjustment rules. Note, however, that the absence of an effect in a given experiment does not provide strong evidence that the effect is absent on principled grounds. The inability to find an effect might also be due to the experimenter's inability to find the effect. Thus, for instance large variances in the data might prohibit finding a statistically significant difference in reaction times to frequent and infrequent regular inflected forms. Carefully chosen stimuli as well as replications of the experimental results across subject groups, inflectional systems and languages would, of course, strengthen the assumption that the lack to find an effect is not an accident. With respect to the evaluation of the discussed morphological theories there is, however, no need to rely on these two negative findings, as they provide no new evidence regarding the discussed morphological theories.

The following Table 3 summarizes how each one of the theories discussed here fares with respect to the experimental results according to our assessment.

Table 3: Summary of the psycholinguistic evaluation of the discussed theoretical models.

finding compatible with	Irregulars display frequency effect (thus, are stored)	Regulars are decomposed (thus, they are computed)	Distinct nature of regulars and irregulars (thus, both cannot be stored, both cannot be computed)
Distributed Morphology	No	Yes	Perhaps
A-morphous Morphology	Yes	Perhaps	Perhaps
Distributed Connectionism	Yes	No	No
Halle (1973)	No	No	No
MM	Yes	Yes	Yes
Nanosyntax	Yes	Yes	Perhaps

The conclusion is that out of the theories discussed here, those that seem to fit better with the available psycholinguistic evidence are, in our opinion, MM and Nanosyntax, and possibly A-morphous Morphology.

5 Conclusions

To conclude, in this chapter we have reviewed which aspects of morphology are computed and stored in a number of different theories that we believe are representative of different theoretical standpoints in the field. We have confronted the predictions of these theories to the currently available experimental psycholinguistic evidence, in an attempt to connect two sides of the debate that tend not to be combined. From this overview, several conclusions can be drawn.

An interesting outcome of this overview is that the theories that we think fare better with respect to the psycholinguistic evidence cut across the two dimensions that arguably are the most prominent ones in theoretical debates: (i) lexicalism vs. neo-constructionism and (ii) Item-and-Arrangement vs. Item-and-Process. Two of them are lexicalist theories (MM and A-morphous Morphology), while the third is neo-contructionist (Nanosyntax); one of them is clearly Item-and-Process (A-morphous Morphology) while the other two argue that morphemes are segmentable units (MM and Nanosyntax). This fact is not trivial and suggests to us that the debate about storage vs. computation is deeper and has more consequences than the other two analytical oppositions just mentioned.

Second, we have also seen that not all theories allow for psycholinguistic tests to the same extent. Specifically, approaches with a grounded notion of morpheme as a unitary object make clearer predictions with respect to priming and frequency effects than separationist approaches where morphophonological aspects are in principle independent of the abstract morphosyntactic representation. Testability is presumably a legitimate factor to evaluate theories, and this would imply that a theory like MM is in principle better suited than, for instance, Nanosyntax to set the grounds for a more stable collaboration between psycholinguists and theoretical morphologists. However, psycholinguistic techniques, making fine-grained distinctions between morphophonology and morphosyntax, might be developed in order to test the more fine-grained predictions of separationist theories. Another issue is whether a theory allows for explicit predictions regarding the processing of inflected words by a hearer or reader. As morphological theories are typically designed from a speaker's perspective, such predictions are not always easily derived and – as in the case of Item-and-Process theories – require some principled thoughts on the reversibility of morphological rules.

Finally, several properties have emerged that have to be met by a morphological theory in order to be compatible with the experimental evidence about storage vs. computation. In such a theory, regular and irregular morphology must be treated differently in a principled matter, with evidence strongly suggesting that the first is computed while the second is stored. Presumably, the dictionary component, if there is any in the theory, cannot simply be a place where complex words are listed as soon as they are learned. That theory has to be explicit with respect to what the allowed computational operations are and what the limits are of what can be stored.

There are many open issues still, but we hope that in writing this chapter we have encouraged other scholars to consider seriously how psycholinguistics and theoretical morphology can collaborate in order to produce an account of storage and computation that is both theoretically sound and compatible with the experimental evidence available.

References

Ackema, Peter. 1995. *Syntax below Zero*. Doctoral dissertation, OTS, Utrecht University.
Ackema, Peter & Ad Neeleman. 2004. *Beyond Morphology: Interface Conditions on Word Formation. Oxford Studies in Theoretical Linguistics: Vol.6*. Oxford University Press: Oxford, UK.
Alegre, María & Peter Gordon. 1999. Frequency effects and the representational status of regular inflections. *Journal of Memory and Language* 40 (1). 41–61.
Allen, Mark & William Badecker. 2002. Inflectional regularity: Probing the nature of lexical representation in a cross-modal priming task. *Journal of Memory and Language* 46 (4). 705–722.
Anderson, Stephen. 1992. *A-morphous Morphology*. Cambridge: Cambridge University Press.
Aronoff, Mark. 1976. *Word Formation in Generative Grammar*. Cambridge, MA.: MIT Press.
Aronoff, Mark. 1994. *Morphology by Itself: Stems and Inflectional Classes*. Cambridge, MA.: MIT Press.
Baayen, R. Harald, Petar Milin, Dušica Filipović Đurđević, Peter Hendrix, & Marco Marelli. 2011. An amorphous model for morphological processing in visual comprehension based on naive discriminative learning. *Psychological Review* 118. 438–481
Baayen, R. Harald, Ton Dijkstra, & Robert Schreuder. 1997. Singulars and plurals in Dutch: Evidence for a parallel dual-route model. *Journal of Memory and Language* 37 (1). 94–117.
Baayen, R.Harald, Richard Piepenbrock, & Hedderick van Rijn. 1993. *The CELEX Lexical Database* (CD-ROM). Philadelphia: Linguistic Data Consortium.
Balota, David. 1994. Visual word recognition: The journey from features to meaning. In Morton Gernsbacher (ed.), *Handbook of Psycholinguistics*, 303–358. San Diego: Academic Press.
Beard, Robert. 1995. *Lexeme-Morpheme Base Morphology: A General Theory of Inflection and Word Formation*. New York: SUNY.
Bermúdez-Otero, Ricardo. 2012. The architecture of grammar and the division of labour in exponence. In Jochen Trommer (ed.), *The Morphology and Phonology of Exponence*, 8–84. Oxford: Oxford University Press.
Bertram, Raymond, Matti Laine, Harald Baayen, Robert Schreuder, & Jukka Hyönä. 2000. Affixal homonymy triggers full-form storage, even with inflected words, even in a morphologically rich language. *Cognition* 74 (2). B13–B25.
Bertram, Raymond, Robert Schreuder, & R. Harald Baayen. 2000. The balance of storage and computation in morphological processing: The role of word formation type, affixal

homonymy, and productivity. *Journal of Experimental Psychology: Learning, Memory, and Cognition* 26 (2). 489–511.
Bonet, Eulàlia. 1991. *Morphology after Syntax*, Doctoral dissertation, Cambridge, MA., MIT.
Borer, Hagit. 2013. *Taking Form. Vol. 3 of the Exoskeletal Trilogy*. Oxford: Oxford University Press.
Caha, Pavel. 2009. *The Nanosyntax of Case*. Ph.D. dissertation. CASTL, University of Tromsø.
Chomsky, Noam. 1957. *Syntactic Structures*. Berlin: De Gruyter.
Chomsky, Noam. 2002. *On Nature and Language*. Cambridge: Cambridge University Press.
Chomsky, Noam & Morris Halle. 1968. *The Sound Pattern of English*. Cambridge, MA.: MIT Press.
Clahsen, Harald. 1999. Lexical entries and rules of language: A multidisciplinary study of German inflection. *Behavioral and Brain sciences* 22 (6). 991–1013.
Clahsen, Harald, Sonja Eisenbeiss, & Ingrid Sonnenstuhl-Henning. 1997. Morphological structure and the processing of inflected words. *Theoretical Linguistics* 23 (3). 201–249.
Cohen-Shikora, Emily R., & David A. Balota. 2013. Past tense route priming. *Cognition* 126 (3). 397–404.
Cortese, Michael J. & David A Balota. 2012. Visual word recognition in skilled adult readers. In Michael Spivey, Ken McRae, & Marc F. Joanisse (eds.), *The Cambridge Handbook of Psycholinguistics*, 159–185. Cambridge: Cambridge University Press.
Crepaldi, Davide, Kathleen Rastle, Max Coltheart, & Lindsay Nickels. 2010. 'Fell'primes 'fall', but does 'bell'prime 'ball'? Masked priming with irregularly-inflected primes. *Journal of Memory and Language* 63 (1). 83–99.
Cutler, Anne. 1981. Making up materials is a confounded nuisance: or Will we be able to run any psycholinguistic experiments at all in 1990? *Cognition* 10. 65–70.
Dékány, Eva. 2012. *A profile of the Hungarian DP*. Ph.D. dissertation, CASTL, University of Tromsø.
DiSciullo, Anna-Maria & Edwin Williams. 1987. *On the Definition of Word*. Cambridge, MA.: MIT Press.
Embick, David. 2000. Features, syntax and categories in the Latin perfect. *Linguistic Inquiry* 31. 185–230.
Embick, David. 2010. *Globalism vs. Localism in Morphology and Phonology*. Cambridge, MA.: MIT Press.
Embick, David & Morris Halle. 2005. On the status of stems in morphological theory. In Twan Geerts, Ivo Van Ginneken, & Haike Jacobs (eds.), *Proceedings of Going Romance 2003*, 59–88. Amsterdam: John Benjamins.
Embick, David & Rolf Noyer. 2007. Distributed Morphology and the syntax-morphology interface. In Gillian Ramchand & Charles Reiss (eds.), *The Oxford Handbook of Linguistic Interfaces*, 289–325. Oxford: Oxford University Press.
Fábregas, Antonio. 2007a. (Axial) Parts and wholes. *Nordlyd* 34. 1–32.
Fábregas, Antonio. 2007b. The Exhaustive Lexicalisation Principle. *Nordlyd* 34. 165–199.
Fábregas, Antonio. 2009. An argument for phrasal spell out: Indefinites and interrogatives in Spanish. *Nordlyd* 36. 129–168.
Fábregas, Antonio. 2014a. Phrasal spell out: An argument for haplology. *Linguistic Analysis* 39. 83–125.
Fábregas, Antonio. 2014b. Argument structure and morphologically underived nouns in Spanish and English. *Lingua* 141. 97–120.
Feldman, Laurie B., Aleksandar Kostić, Dana M. Basnight-Brown, Dušica Filipović Đurđević, & Matthew John Pastizzo. 2010. Morphological facilitation for regular and irregular verb formations in native and non-native speakers: Little evidence for two distinct mechanisms. *Bilingualism: Language and Cognition* 13 (2). 119–135.

Forster, Kenneth I. 1999. The microgenesis of priming effects in lexical access. *Brain and Language* 68 (1). 5–15.
Frost, Ram, Avital Deutsch, Orna Gilboa, Michal Tannenbaum, & William Marslen-Wilson. 2000. Morphological priming: Dissociation of phonological, semantic, and morphological factors. *Memory & Cognition* 28(8). 1277–1288.
Gonnerman, Laura, Mark S. Seidenberg, & Elaine S. Andersen. 2007. Graded semantic and phonological similarity effects in priming: Evidence for a distributed connectionist approach to morphology. *Journal of Experimental Psychology: General* 136 (2). 323–345.
Hale, Kenneth & Samuel J. Keyser. 2002. *Prolegomenon to a Theory of Argument Structure*. Cambridge, MA.: MIT Press.
Halle, Morris. 1973. Prolegomena to a theory of word formation. *Linguistic Inquiry* 4. 451–464.
Halle, Morris & Alec Marantz. 1993. Distributed Morphology and the pieces of inflection. In Kenneth Hale & Samuel J. Keyser (eds.), *The View from Building 20*, 111–176. Cambridge, MA.: MIT Press.
Harley, Heidi. 2014. On the identity of roots. *Theoretical Linguistics* 40, 225–276.
Harley, Heidi & Rolf Noyer. 1998. Licensing in the non-lexicalist lexicon: Nominalizations, vocabulary items and the encyclopaedia. In Heidi Harley & Rolf Noyer (eds.), *Papers from the MIT / Upenn Roundtable on Argument Structure and Aspect*, 119–137. Cambridge, MA., MIT Linguistics.
Hockett, Charles F. 1947. Problems of morphemic analysis. *Language* 23. 321–343.
Hockett, Charles F. 1954. Two models of grammatical description. *Word* 10. 210–231.
Jackendoff, Ray. 1975. Morphological and semantic regularities in the lexicon. *Language* 51. 639–671.
Jespersen, Otto. 1933. *Essentials of English Grammar*. London: George Allen, Turnbull and Spears.
Julien, Marit. 2007. On the relation between morphology and syntax. In Gillian Ramchand & Charles Reiss (eds.), *The Oxford Handbook of Linguistic Interfaces*, 209–238. Oxford: Oxford University Press.
Kohonen, Teuvo. 1977. *Associative Memory: A System-Theoretical Approach*. New York: Springer.
Laine, Matti, Seppo Vainio, & Jukka Hyönä. 1999. Lexical access routes to nouns in a morphologically rich language. *Journal of Memory and Language* 40(1). 109–135.
Lehtonen, Minna, Toni Cunillera, Antoni Rodríguez-Fornells, Annika Hultén, Jyrki Tuomainen, & Matti Laine. 2007. Recognition of morphologically complex words in Finnish: Evidence from event-related potentials. *Brain Research* 1148. 123–137.
Lehtonen, Minna & Matti Laine. 2003. How word frequency affects morphological processing in monolinguals and bilinguals. *Bilingualism: Language and Cognition* 6(03). 213–225.
Lieber, Rochelle. 1980. *On the Organization of the Lexicon*, Doctoral dissertation, University of New Hampshire.
Lieber, Rochelle. 1992. *Deconstructing Morphology*. Chicago: Chicago University Press.
Lundquist, Björn. 2009. *Nominalizations and Participles in Swedish*. Ph.D. dissertation, CASTL, University of Tromsø.
Marantz, Alec. 2013. No escape from morphemes in morphological processing. *Language and Cognitive Processes* 28(7). 905–916.
Marcus, Gary, F. 2001. *The Algebraic Mind: Integrating Connectionism and Cognitive Science*. Cambridge, MA.: MIT Press.
Marcus, Gary F., Steven Pinker, Michael Ullman, Michelle Hollander, T. J. Rosen, & F. Xu. 1992. *Overregularization in Language Acquisition*. Chicago: University of Chicago Press.

Marslen-Wilson, William D. 2007. Morphological processes in language comprehension. In M. Gareth Gaskell (ed.), *The Oxford Handbook of Psycholinguistics*, 175–191. Oxford: Oxford University Press.

Marslen-Wilson, William, M. Hare, L., & Older. 1993. Inflectional morphology and phonological regularity in the English mental lexicon. In *Proceedings of the 15th Annual Meeting of the Cognitive Science Society*. 693–698.

Marzi, Claudia, James P. Blevins, Geet Booij, & Vito Pirrelli. 2020. Inflection at the morphology-syntax interface. In Vito Pirrelli, Ingo Plag, & Wolfgang U. Dressler (eds.), *Word Knowledge and Word Usage: a Cross-disciplinary Guide to the Mental Lexicon*, 221–287. Berlin: De Gruyter.

McCawley, James. 1968. Lexical insertion in a grammar without deep structure. In B. Darden, C. Bailey, & A. Davison (eds.), *CLS 4. Papers from the Fourth Meeting of the Chicago Linguistic Society*, 71–80. Chicago, Chicago Linguistic Society.

Meunier, Fanny & William Marslen-Wilson. 2004. Regularity and irregularity in French verbal inflection. *Language and Cognitive Processes* 19(4). 561–580.

Muriungi, Peter. 2008. *Phrasal Movement in the Bantu Verb*. Ph.D. dissertation, CASTL, University of Tromsø.

Neubauer, Kathleen & Harald Clahsen. 2009. Decomposition of inflected words in a second language. *Studies in Second Language Acquisition* 31(03). 403–435.

Nida, Eugene. 1948. The identification of morphemes. *Language* 24. 414–441.

Noyer, Rolf. 1992. *Features, Positions and Affixes in Autonomous Morphological Structure*. Doctoral dissertation, Cambridge, MA., MIT.

Orsolini, Margherita, & William Marslen-Wilson. 1997. Universals in morphological representation: Evidence from Italian. *Language and Cognitive Processes* 12(1). 1–47.

Penke, Martina. 2006. *Flexion im mentalen Lexikon*. Berlin: Walter de Gruyter.

Penke, Martina. 2012a. The Dual-Mechanism Debate. In Markus Werning, Wolfram Hinzen, & Edouard Machery (eds.): *The Oxford Handbook of Compositionality*, 574–595. Oxford: Oxford University Press.

Penke, Martina 2012b. *The acquisition of inflectional morphology*. Working paper, University of Cologne. DOI: 10.13140/RG.2.2.21194.06085.

Penke, Martina & Marion Krause. 2002. German noun plurals: A challenge to the dual-mechanism model. *Brain and Language* 81(1). 303–311.

Penke, Martina & Anette Rosenbach. 2007. What counts as evidence in linguistics? An Introduction. In Martina Penke & Anette Rosenbach (eds.), *What Counts as Evidence in Linguistics – the Case of Innateness*, 1–50. Amsterdam: John Benjamins.

Penke, Martina & Gert Westermann. 2006. Broca's area and inflectional morphology: Evidence from Broca's aphasia and computer modeling. *Cortex* 42(4). 563–576.

Pinker, Steven. 1999. *Words and Rules: The Ingredients of Language*. New York: Basic Books.

Pirrelli, Vito, Claudia Marzi, Marcello Ferro, R. Harald Baayen, & Petar Milin. 2020. Psycho-computational modelling of the mental lexicon. A discriminative learning perspective. In Vito Pirrelli, Ingo Plag, & Wolfgang U. Dressler (eds.), *Word Knowledge and Word Usage: a Cross-disciplinary Guide to the Mental Lexicon*, 21–80. Berlin: De Gruyter.

Ramchand, Gillian. 2008. *First Phase Syntax*. Cambridge: Cambridge University Press.

Ramchand, Gillian & Peter Svenonius. 2014. Deriving the functional hierarchy. *Language Sciences* 46. 152–174.

Rastle, Kathleen & Matthew H. Davis. 2008. Morphological decomposition based on the analysis of orthography, *Language and Cognitive Processes* 23 (7–8). 942–971.

Rumelhart, David E. & James L. McClelland. 1986. *Parallel Distributed Processing: Explorations in the Microstructure of Cognition*. Cambridge, MA.: MIT Press.
Scalise, Sergio. 1984. *Generative Morphology*. Dordrecht: Foris.
Selkirk, Elizabeth. 1982. *The Syntax of Words*. Cambridge, MA.: MIT Press.
Siegel, Dorothy. 1974. *Topics in English Morphology*, Ph. D. dissertation, Cambridge, MA., MIT Press.
Smolka, Eva, Pienie Zwitserlood, & Frank Rösler. 2007. Stem access in regular and irregular inflection: Evidence from German participles. *Journal of Memory and Language* 57(3). 325–347.
Sonnenstuhl, Ingrid, Sonja Eisenbeiss, & Harald Clahsen. 1999. Morphological priming in the German mental lexicon. *Cognition* 72 (3). 203–236.
Sonnenstuhl, Ingrid & Axel Huth. 2002. Processing and representation of German-n plurals: A dual mechanism approach. *Brain and Language* 81 (1). 276–290.
Stanners, Robert F., James J. Neiser, William P. Hernon, & Roger Hall. 1979. Memory representation for morphologically related words. *Journal of Verbal Learning and Verbal Behavior* 18 (4). 399–412.
Starke, Michal. 2002. *Nanosyntax. Lecture notes*. University of Tromsø.
Starke, Michal. 2009. Nanosyntax: a short primer to a new approach to language. *Nordlyd* 36. 1–6.
Starke, Michal. 2014a. Cleaning up the lexicon. *Linguistic Analysis* 39. 245–257.
Starke, Michal. 2014b. Towards elegant parameters: Linguistic variation reduces to the size of lexically-stored trees. In Carme Picallo (ed.), *Linguistic Variation in the Minimalist Framework*, 140–155. Oxford: Oxford University Press.
Stump, Gregory T. 1993. On rules of referral. *Language* 69. 449–479.
Stump, Gregory T. 1998. Inflection. In Andrew Spencer & Arnold M. Zwicky (eds.), *The Handbook of Morphology*, 13–43. Oxford: Blackwell.
Stump, Gregory T. 2001. *Inflectional Morphology: A Theory of Paradigm Structure*. Cambridge: Cambridge University Press.
Tsapkini, Kirana, Gonia Jarema, & Eva Kehayia. 2004. Regularity re-revisited: Modality matters. *Brain and Language* 89 (3). 611–616.
Ullman, Michael T. 2005. A cognitive neuroscience perspective on second language acquisition: The declarative/procedural model. In C. Sanz (ed.), *Mind and Context in Adult Second Language Acquisition* 141–178. Washington: Georgetown University Press.
Weyerts, Helga & Harald Clahsen. 1994. Netzwerke und symbolische Regeln im Spracherwerb: Experimentelle Ergebnisse zur Entwicklung der Flexionsmorphologie. *Linguistische Berichte* 154. 430–460.
Williams, Edwin. 2007. Dumping lexicalism. In Gillian Ramchand & Charles Reiss (eds.), *The Oxford Handbook of Linguistic Interfaces*, 353–383. Oxford: Oxford University Press.
Wunderlich, Dieter. 1992. A minimalist analysis of German verb morphology. *Working Papers SFB 282, Theorie des Lexikons 21*. Düsseldorf: University of Düsseldorf.
Wunderlich, Dieter. 1996. Minimalist Morphology: The role of paradigms. In Geert Booij & Jaap van Marle (eds.), *Yearbook of Morphology 1995*, 93–114. Dordrecht: Kluwer.
Wunderlich, Dieter. 1997. A minimalist model of inflectional morphology. In Chris Wilder, Hans-Martin Gärtner, & Manfred Bierwisch (eds.), *The Role of Economy Principles in Linguistic Theory*, 267–298. Berlin: Akademie Verlag.

Madeleine Voga, Francesco Gardani and Hélène Giraudo
Multilingualism and the Mental Lexicon

Insights from language processing, diachrony,
and language contact

Abstract: The way in which the bilingual's two languages can co-exist and interact with each other is crucial for the study of language coactivation. This question has been tackled from the perspective of experimental psycholinguistics and that of language contact which can be brought together in the light of different, yet concomitant evidence related to multiple interactions between words from the two languages. Most of these interactions can be accounted for in terms of common and/or parallel morphological representations between the two languages. The two masked priming experiments using cross-script materials reported in this chapter corroborate and extend this hypothesis by showing that different 'levels' of morphological and/or etymological relatedness underlie different priming effects. The morphological priming pattern reflects an organisation of the lexicon based on 'cross-language derivational families', whereby morphologically complex L1 words automatically activate their base word in L2. Evidence that the opposite is not true suggests the existence of a looser link between L2 words and representations at the semantic-conceptual level, while still being compatible with evidence that translation primes induce significant effects in both L2-to-L1 and L1-to-L2 directions. Evidence from language contact supports the idea that the two languages do not behave in a strictly symmetric way. The more tenuous link between L2 vocabulary and a morphological/conceptual level is mirrored by the morphological integration of loan words into a matrix language, as a significant, preliminary step in the direction of a full conceptual integration. Further data from morphological integration in accordance with the cross-language priming data point to a view of the bilingual lexicon as a unified lexico-semantic architecture.

Keywords: bilingualism, lexical access, cognate effect, word family effect, co-morphologies, language contact

---

Madeleine Voga, University Paul-Valéry Montpellier III, Montpellier, France
Francesco Gardani, University of Zurich, Zurich, Switzerland
Hélène Giraudo, CLLE, University Toulouse, CNRS, Toulouse, France

 Open Access. © 2020 Madeleine Voga et al., published by De Gruyter. [CC BY-NC-ND] This work is licensed under a Creative Commons Attribution-NonCommercial-NoDerivatives 4.0 International License.
https://doi.org/10.1515/9783110440577-013

1 Introduction

The ability of bilinguals to master multiple languages is remarkable. An important question related to bilingual performance, with various implications for online processing, concerns the ways two language systems can in fact co-exist in a synergistic relationship and co-activate each other, while preventing, at the same time, their interaction from seriously disrupting daily verbal communication. As we know, language switches can be quite frequent in appropriate circumstances; however, it is a fact that bilinguals (or multilinguals) are good at preventing interferences between two (or more) languages (see Esposito et al. 2013; Marian et al. 2017) and can effectively function on either of them. The main focus of the present chapter will be on understanding how this is possible, and what the multifarious outcomes are of the dualistic dynamic of co-activation/competition between co-existing language systems. As we shall see in more detail in the following pages, speakers are very sensitive to word family effects, and these effects may effortlessly involve words of different languages in a highly integrated word knowledge system. The consequences of these effects on language performance can nonetheless be diverging and somewhat apparently contradictory, depending on as diverse factors as the nature of the specific language task speakers are engaged in, its illocutionary force, or its intended perlocutionary effects.

In order to describe the structure of the lexicon as well as the mechanisms responsible for processing words coming from two languages, we have to define the extent to which words from the languages of the bilingual are linked. There are four theoretical options to describe bilingual lexical representation, by combining four variables: separate lexica vs. unified lexicon and selective vs. non-selective access. In the present chapter, we explore the connections between related, albeit not necessarily converging research fields, such as experimental psycholinguistics and historical linguistics, by focusing on the role of morphological factors in influencing both human processing and mental representation of cognates.

The chapter is structured as follows. Section 1.1 discusses research on selective to non-selective access in the bilingual lexicon; Section 1.2 focuses on the definition of the cognate relation and on morphological transfer; Section 1.3 is concerned with cognate and non-cognate effects in cross-language processing; and Section 1.4 with indirect ways to study the issue of unified lexicon vs. separate lexica and the role of morphology. Section 2 presents two masked priming experiments with cross-script cognates. The psycholinguistic results are discussed in Section 3. Section 4 presents data on morphological integration (4.1) and co-morphologies (4.2) and shows how these support claims based on the psycholinguistic evidence. Section 5 closes up the chapter.

1.1 From selective to non-selective access in the bilingual lexicon

A well-known fact about bilingualism is that both languages of the bilingual are simultaneously activated, even when one of the two languages seems to be out of play (i.e., the non-target language). Many recent studies refer to language co-activation (e.g., van Hell and Dijkstra 2002; van Hell and Tanner 2012), which relates to the fact that access to the bilingual lexicon is profoundly non-selective with respect to languages (see below). Given this non-selective access, part of the research focuses on the examination of effects related to cross-language interaction. This interaction can be positive (as with the cross-language effect of the Morphological Family Size, e.g., Mulder et al. 2014) or negative, i.e. it creates interferences. Although language switches can be quite frequent in appropriate circumstances, bilinguals easily manage to prevent interferences, which may never surface in the performance of the speaker. In addition, the positive interactions *across* languages are not directly observable in natural speech, which is why psycholinguistics provide protocols, mainly behavioral, and, more recently, neuropsychological (e.g., Schwartz and Kroll 2006; van Heuven et al. 2008) aiming to unravel the organization and architecture of the bilingual lexicon. This interaction is not restricted to languages presenting formal and systematic similarities, but can be observed in bilinguals for whom the two languages belong to different systems (e.g., Hoshino and Kroll 2008, for Japanese-English bilinguals). The resulting cross-language activation and competition can be seen in brain activity in fMRI studies of proficient bilinguals (e.g., van Heuven et al. 2008).

The specification of the bilingual lexicon is based on two components: a structural aspect, relative to the organization of the two languages, and a processing one. As far as the structural component is concerned, a distinction obtains between lexical storage independent of the language and lexical storage depending on the language. A lexical storage independent of the language implies that the bilingual possesses a unified lexicon encompassing the two languages (integrated lexica hypothesis). Language-dependent storage implies the existence of two different lexica, one for each language (e.g., as in Kroll and Stewart's (1994) Revised Hierarchical Model, see Section 1.4.1). With regard to online processing, a distinction is made between selective vs. non-selective access. Given that all contemporary models of visual word recognition assume multiple matching between an input representation and a lexical representation in memory, the question of selective vs. non-selective access involves determining whether words from the two languages are simultaneously contacted/accessed during visual word recognition or if only the target language is activated. As van Heuven, Dijkstra and Grainger (1998) observe, four theoretical options can be found in the literature:

a) The first option involves selective access, combined with two independent lexica on the structural level. In this type of model, a research mechanism would have to first search the representations of the first lexicon and those of the second lexicon afterwards, in order to find the representation matching the input.
b) The second option postulates a selective access with a unified (integrated) lexicon, in which there is one node[1] for the first language (L1) and another for the second language (L2). Given that words from the non-target language are never activated (van Heuven et al. 1998), this theoretical option would be functionally equivalent to the first one: words from one language cannot have any influence, i.e. they cannot activate or inhibit processing of words in the other language.
c) The third option postulates a non-selective access with independent lexica: words from the two languages are activated in parallel (not in a serial manner), in such a way that all words that are partially compatible with the stimulus will be activated. Given that this option is based on independent lexica, the activation takes place via a mechanism that will search among the words of each language, separately from the other language. In an interactive activation model like the one presented by McClelland and Rumelhart (1981), the separate lexica hypothesis implies the existence of inhibitory connections within each lexicon.
d) The fourth option combines a non-selective access with an integrated (unified) lexicon, which is independent of language. Words from both languages will be activated in parallel and all words partially compatible with the stimulus will be activated at the same time, depending on criteria such as their frequency in the language. In an interactive activation perspective (McClelland and Rumelhart 1981) the unified lexicon hypothesis postulates the existence of inhibitory connections between the words of the *different* languages. As we shall see in Section 1.3, the distinction between parallel non-selective access with separate lexica vs. integrated lexicon is quite difficult to demonstrate empirically. All we can have is indirect evidence, mainly related to the various interactions between the two lexica, i.e. cross-language effects in which variables characterizing one language influence processing of the other (e.g., van Heuven, Dijkstra, and Grainger 1998, with orthographic neighbors, or cross-language Morphological Family Size effects, e.g., Mulder et al. 2014; Mulder, Dijkstra, and Baayen 2015).

---

[1] See the architecture of the Interactive Activation Model (McClelland and Rumelhart 1981, 1988).

As far as selective vs. non-selective access is concerned, a first group of studies on bilingual[2] lexical access (Gerard and Scarborough 1989; Scarborough, Gerard, and Cortese 1984) put forward data in favor of selective access. Gerard and Scarborough (1989) used interlexical homographs (or false cognates), i.e., words that are written the same in the two languages, in the specific case, English and Spanish, but do not mean the same thing, e.g., *red* 'color' in English and 'clean' in Spanish. These interlexical homographs do not have the same frequency in the two languages (the English word is more frequent, in our example). The task was a monolingual lexical decision task and the results showed that only the target language frequency was relevant to predict the reaction times for the identification of the stimuli. In other words, even though *red* is very frequent in English, bilinguals were not quicker than Spanish monolinguals in recognizing the word, when the target language was Spanish. This was taken as evidence in favor of a selective access, in which the language processing system chooses to follow the path of one of the two languages, as if the other one did not exist.

While the very beginning of bilingual research is characterized by a consensus on selective access, which led the authors of the first model of bilingual production (Kroll and Stewart's 1994 Revised Hierarchical Model as well as its early version, the Word Association Model) to assume a selective access with separate lexica, during the 1990s, this position has been revised. One of the first studies to mark this revision is Altenberg and Cairns (1984). In an English lexical decision experiment with English-German bilinguals, the authors used non-words containing letter sequences that did not conform to the phonotactic properties of English, but conformed to those of German (e.g., PFLOK). Results demonstrated that bilingual subjects needed more time than monolinguals to reject these words, which is interpreted as evidence that the bilingual is unable to supress one of his two languages, even if the context of the task is strictly monolingual. Many subsequent studies explored experimental situations where the words of the different languages were intermixed or where the L2 was the target language. Results show that bilinguals activate words from their two languages when they make lexical decisions in the non-dominant language (L2), as well as when words from their L1 are present in the experiment. These L1 words can either be distractors (De Groot,

---

2 As Kroll and Stewart (1994: 151 fn1) stress, the term bilingual in the literature related to bilingual perception and production, refers to "individuals who acquired L2 in late childhood or early adulthood in a context where L1 was already clearly established, and for the most part, after any biologically sensitive or critical period in development had occurred. One difference between adult and child bilinguals is that for adults most new L2 words correspond to concepts that have already been acquired".

Delmaar, and Lupker 2000, exp. 3; Dijkstra, Van Jaarsveld, and Ten Brinke 1998, exp. 2), target words (van Heuven, Dijkstra, and Grainger 1998), or primes in masked priming experiments (Gollan, Forster, and Frost 1997), as we shall see in more detail in Section 2. Evidence for non-selective access comes from a multitude of tasks and languages: from simple naming (e.g., Jared and Kroll 2001, with English-French and French-English participants) and association tasks (e.g., Van Hell and De Groot 1998, Dutch-English bilinguals), to progressive demasking (e.g., van Heuven, Dijkstra, and Grainger 1998; Dijkstra, Grainger, and van Heuven 1999, both with Dutch-English bilinguals) and masked priming with cognate and non-cognate words (e.g., De Groot and Nas 1991, with English-Dutch bilinguals; Gollan, Forster, and Frost 1997, with Hebrew-English bilinguals; Voga and Grainger 2007, with Greek-French bilinguals). All these data support the non-selective hypothesis.

Among these studies published in the last 25 years dealing with the separate vs. integrated lexica issue, many use cognate materials such as *palace – palacio* in English-Spanish, *pyramid – pyramida* in English-Hebrew, or πόρτα /'porta/ – *porte* 'door' in Greek-French. The cognate effect, which in processing terms is the fact that a cognate word (e.g., *palacio*) will significantly facilitate the recognition of its translation in the other language (e.g., *palace* in English) is one of the best-studied and most robust bilingual effects. This cognate effect is found not only when both prime and target words are written in the same alphabet, but also when they are written in different scripts (cross-script priming task):[3] e.g., κέντρο /'kendro/ – *centre* in Greek-French (Voga and Grainger 2007; see also Gollan, Forster, and Frost 1997, Hebrew-English). This effect also provides the basis for several applications in second language learning, especially related to vocabulary in a second language. For example, Sheng et al. (2016) with children from 4 to 7 (English-Spanish and Mandarin-English) demonstrated that cross-linguistic similarities at the phonological level allow bootstrapping of vocabulary learning.

The next section focuses on the definition of the cognate relation, which may differ according to the type of protocol used, e.g., lexical access (word recognition) vs. word production protocols, or according to the languages being studied, i.e., more or less diachronically related and morphologically or formally overlapping. As we will see in Section 1.2, the way in which *cognateness*

---

[3] The fact that psycholinguistic research on bilingualism tends to create categories on the basis of formal factors, (e.g., same-script, cross-script) may seem inappropriate and difficult to understand from a linguistic point of view. However, from a psycholinguistic point of view, formal factors can completely change the nature of the processes the experiment taps into. This is especially true for visual protocols, such as the one we use here (Section 2).

is defined depends on the discipline considered. One of the aims of this chapter is to explore the connections between related, albeit not necessarily converging research fields, such as historical linguistics and psycholinguistics, by focusing on the role of morphological factors in influencing both human processing and mental representation of cognates.

1.2 Cognate definition and morphological transfer

The term 'cognate' is used in different ways in psycholinguistics and historical linguistics. In historical linguistics, cognates are words that are etymologically linked. The etymological link can be either directly inherited from a common ancestor or borrowed via language contact. By way of example, the numerals English *ten*, Dutch *tien*, and German *zehn* are cognates via inheritance, as they stem directly from reconstructed Germanic **tehun*, which itself is related to Tocharian A *śäk*, Ancient Greek *déka*, Latin *decem*, Old Church Slavonic *desętĭ* and so forth; and all of them descend from reconstructed Indo-European **dek̂m̥*. According to an etymological approach, Spanish *diez* and English *ten* are cognates. Also English *curtain* and German *Gardine* are cognates; however, not via inheritance but via language contact because they were both borrowed from French *courtine*. In psycholinguistics, the notion of cognate is based on the criterion of perceptual recognizability, which requires formal similarity under the exact conditions of a given experiment, as we shall illustrate in the next section through a brief data review. In a visual masked priming experiment, for instance, it is crucial that the orthographic overlap is measured in an objective way, and kept stable throughout the experiment. A consequence of the psycholinguistic logic and experimental constraints is that two words which match each other formally are considered as cognates, irrespective of any etymological relation of inheritance or borrowing between them. Formal match is conceived in terms of acoustic (i.e., phonetic) or visual (i.e., orthographic) overlap, which is why 'cognateness' can be a matter of degree in psycholinguistics. Consequently, while Spanish *diez* and English *ten* are considered cognates by historical linguists, they are hardly viewed as such by psycholinguists; on the other hand, lexical borrowings such as English *curtain* and German *Gardine* are cognates according to both approaches: they are etymologically related words, and they bear both acoustic and visual similarities.

Admittedly, historical linguists and psycholinguists have different aims by vocation. The former want to understand how language change comes along and why languages develop the way they do. The latter study language processing through standardized protocols in order to specify the way in which words are represented in the mental lexicon, and, when it comes to morphology, how constructed words are represented and processed by the language processing system. In historical linguistics, the study of the transfer of single morphological formatives has proved a fruitful heuristic tool in investigations of the genealogical relatedness of languages or language groups, such as in the studies by Whaley (2012), Mithun (2013), Law (2014) and Robbeets (2015) (but see Grant 2008: 166, with the proviso that the so-called *Ludolf's rule*, that is, the idea that morphology is a more reliable source for historical reconstruction than phonology or basic vocabulary, might lead to wrong analyses).

Under specific sociological conditions, including intense bilingualism and socio-economic dominance, morphological formatives can be transferred from a Source Language (SL) to a Recipient Language (RL). Prototypically, morphological borrowing occurs when SL formatives apply to native lexemes of an RL (Gardani 2008, 2012, 2018). As a case in point, consider the following instance in Bolivian Quechua, which has borrowed the plural formative *-s* from the contact language, Spanish, and compulsorily uses it to mark plural on all Quechua nouns ending in a vowel (Bolivian Quechua data from Muysken 2012: 33–34, based on Urioste 1964).

(1)   Quechua   Bolivian Quechua   Spanish
    a. *wasi*   b. *algu*   c. *perro*
       'house'   'dog'   'dog'
       wasikuna   *algus*   *perros*
       'houses'   'dogs'   'dogs'

The example in (1b) shows that a Spanish formative (1c) is used in Bolivian Quechua to mark nominal plural, in spite of the existence in Quechua of a nominal plural formative *-kuna* (1a). Clearly, such a process of mixing presupposes high bilingual competence, at least in some phases of the change process.

One of the mechanisms commonly regarded as leading to stabilized change is codeswitching, also with respect to morphology. For example, research in codeswitching has shown that some morpheme types, precisely plural formatives, are often maintained in bilinguals during codeswitching (Myers-Scotton 2013). The hypothesis is that the insertion of plural forms of an embedded language (corresponding to SL) into a matrix language (corresponding to RL) acts as an anchoring of such morphemes and paves the way for their later spreading to lexemes belonging to the native stock of the matrix language. Data on idiolectal use from the conversational *Siarad corpus* of Welsh-English bilinguals (ESRC Centre for Research on Bilingualism in Theory and Practice 2011) seems to support this claim. In (2a-d), we see four Welsh nouns, all belonging to the native Celtic lexical stratum, which mark the plural by means of a formative *-s* (and its allomorph -/is/ in (2d)), which is clearly borrowed from English. In the parallel data set in (2a'-d';), the same nouns have different forms as they mark the plural by native inflectional formatives and patterns.

(2)   Welsh (idiolectal)   Welsh (standard)
     a. *taids*   a'. *teidiau*
          'grandfathers'
     b. *crancs*   b'. *crancod*
          'crabs'
     c. *annwyds*   c'. *anwydau*
          'colds'
     d. *enfysys*   d'. *enfysau*
          'rainbows'

The data presented in (1) and (2) show that there are multiple interactions between the different language systems mastered by bilingual speakers. In his macro-ecological approach to language evolution, Mufwene (2001, 2008) understands interaction in terms of feature competition and selection. The competition of grammatical patterns which may lead to processes of linguistic diversification is amplified in situations of language contact: all languages involved in the contact setting make concurrent contributions to a pool of features which the speakers exploit in order to create their idiolect. Also, the use of different grammatical systems can relate to the need to serve different communicative purposes or depend on different pragmatic contexts. For example, from the viewpoint of his 'activity-oriented' approach, Matras (2015: 76) argues that inflection is indicative of the language choice made by the bilingual speaker and related to their identity, and so "the purpose of borrowed inflectional morphology is to re-draw social boundaries".

In what follows, our theoretical starting point will be the hypothesis that most of these interactions presuppose mental representations that are based on morphological knowledge, effectively emerging from the self-organization and interaction of possibly diverse language systems (Bybee 1988, 1995, 2006, 2007, 2010). In the 'emergent lexicon' approach proposed by Joan Bybee (2007: 280), the lexicon reflects the speakers' linguistic experience, and lexical storage is highly affected by language use. Bybee (1985, 1995, 2007) uses the notion of *lexical strength* to illustrate the fact that "memory for linguistic units is superpositional: "[...] every time a word or a larger linguistic unit (a phrase or idiom) is processed, it is mapped onto, or superimposed on, some existing mental representation" (Bybee 1995: 232). Following this approach, there is no real separation of lexicon and grammar, in the sense that the 'knowledge' underlying the fluent use of language is procedural knowledge based on memorized 'chunks' of linguistic experience much larger than the analytic units of morphemes or even words. These chunks give rise to emergent grammatical patterns, which can possibly be based on competing grammatical systems if the speaker is exposed to more than one language. In what follows, we will focus on the empirical import of this hypothesis by looking at data from language contact and change, as well as what we know about speakers' morphological knowledge, as it can be elicited by means of experimental protocols tapping into bilingual competence.

1.3 Cognate and non-cognate effects in cross-language processing: Focus on cross-script studies

As already mentioned above, for most psycholinguists, cognates are translation equivalents sharing significant formal overlap. In a full bottom-up approach to bilingual lexical access, written word recognition starts at the level of visual features (letters) and activation spreads up to the lexical level (e.g., in the Bilingual Interactive Model, BIA, of Dijkstra, van Heuven, and Grainger 1998). In bottom-up protocols, maximal formal overlap is crucial, as it constitutes the necessary condition in order to attribute the cognate status to a pair of words. For instance, *hotel* or *sport* in English, French and Dutch (e.g., Dijkstra et al. 1999), or *gat-gato* 'cat', in Catalan-Spanish (Costa, Caramazza, and Sebastien-Gales 2000) are considered as cognates,[4] whereas other pairs of words, though morphologically and historically related, are not always given the same status. For instance, Dijkstra et al. (1999) suggest that the term 'semi-cognate' would be preferable for pairs such as *height – hoogte* or *rain – regen* in English-Dutch. In our opinion, this reluctance to attribute the cognate status to pairs of items sharing medium or reduced formal overlap (especially orthographic) reflects the overreliance, at least until recently, on formal/visual factors and a

---

[4] One may wonder whether the studies using cognate pairs, especially those with maximal orthographic overlap, really assess the semantic level of processing or whether they simply report formal overlap effects: this objection, however, runs contrary to evidence that these effects do not occur for monolinguals (Garcia-Albea et al. 1985) and that proficiency level seems to play an important role (de Groot et al. 2002). However, the role of formal overlap is acknowledged to be important, especially in visual masked priming protocols (e.g., Forster 1999; Forster, Mohan, and Hector 2003). We will come back to this question further.

comparative neglect of factors related to the core levels of lexical processing, i.e., those implying meaning. The fact that certain aspects of the form-meaning relation that undoubtedly form the basis for cross-language effects have been neglected (i.e. such as those observed with cognates and non-cognates) can be seen as a side-effect of different approaches adopted in word-recognition vs. word-production studies (cf. Section 1.4.1).

Contrary to the strict definition of the cognate relation we saw above, experimental data showed that even word pairs with low formal similarity induce robust cognate effects. In many studies, very often published by the proponents of Kroll and Stewart's (1994) Revised Hierarchical Model (as well as its early version, the Word Association Model), a more flexible definition of the cognate relation is used, and pairs of words such as *height – hoogte* are found to induce cognate effects of large amplitude, comparable to those sharing maximal formal overlap. For example, de Groot and Nas (1991), under masked conditions, obtain robust facilitatory cognate effects (exp. 2: 58ms from L1 to L2 and 39ms from L2 to L1, with Dutch-English bilinguals; see also Dufour and Kroll 1995; Van Hell and de Groot 1998, for similar effects).

Additionally, results from cross-script studies reinforce this looser conception of cognateness, given that under these conditions and in the visual modality (masked priming), formal overlap is discarded because of the difference between the alphabet of the prime and that of the target. Although cross-script cognate priming is not automatic, as shown by the lack of facilitation found in the Arabic-French study by Bowers, Mimouni, and Arguin (2000), in most of the experimental situations tested, cross-script cognate effects are observed. In Gollan, Forster, and Frost 1997, for example, with the masked priming technique and a 50ms Stimulus-Onset Asynchrony (henceforth SOA), Hebrew-English bilinguals exhibit a 53ms effect for cognates in exp. 1 (and a 36ms effect for non-cognates),[5] with pairs of words such as *television – televizya* in English-Hebrew. This cognate effect, independent of visual overlap, is found for other pairs of languages, sharing more or less dissimilar writing systems, e.g., Chinese-English (e.g., Jiang 1999; Jiang and Forster 2001), or alphabets, e.g., Greek-French (e.g., Voga and Grainger 2007). In Voga and Grainger's study, the cognate effect induced by the

---

5 This is an important finding, given that in many of the previously published studies non-cognates either induce no effect (e.g., Sanchez-Casas, Davis, and Garcia-Albea 1992), either induce effects of smaller amplitude (de Groot and Nas 1991). Non-cognate effects can only result from shared semantic representations, given that they share no orthographic or phonological overlap (e.g., λάθος /'laθos/ – *erreur* 'error') in Greek-French. Some recent studies on language co-activation report on non-cognate effects (e.g., Dimitropoulou, Duñabeitia, and Carreiras 2011a; 2011b).

L1 Greek prime κύκλος /'kyklos/ 'cycle' on the L2 French target *cycle* 'cycle', under conditions very similar to those of Gollan, Forster, and Frost (1997), induces a 36ms facilitation (exp. 1). It is noteworthy that this robust cross-script cognate effect is found relative to a phonological control baseline, and not an unrelated one, as in most of the published studies. Experiment 2 goes further, controlling the role of phonological similarity of cognates, given that orthographic overlap is greatly reduced: the effect induced by two types of cognates, high-overlap ones, such as *μετρό* (/me'tro:/) – *metro* 'subway', and low-overlap ones, such as *κέντρο* (/'kendro/) – *centre* 'center' is assessed relatively to two types of controls. Results show that both categories of cognates induce significant priming compared both to the unrelated (55 and 45ms respectively) and to the phonological control (38 and 46ms respectively). The classic interpretation of the cognate effect attributes a part of the facilitation to the semantic priming component, which is common to all translations, and another part on the form-priming component, which is specific to cognate translations. What the above results demonstrate is that even in these very early stages of processing, it is mainly the semantic component of the cognate relation that underpins the effect. The fact that significant non-cognate effects are found in the same study, and within the same experiment, also advocates in favor of this interpretation, thus assigning an important role to semantics during the early stages of cross-language lexical processing. Using translation equivalents (non-cognates)[6] such as *λάθος* /'laθos/ – *erreur* 'error', in exp. 2, Voga and Grainger (2007) obtain a 36ms effect (relative to a phonological control) and a 23ms effect (relative to an unrelated control); in exp. 3, with different stimuli, such as *δώρο* /'ðoro/ – *cadeau* 'gift', they obtain 27 and 22ms of translation priming effect. These effects

---

[6] The term 'non-cognates' here means exactly the same as 'translation equivalents', traditionally used to designate words that do not bear any formal relation (orthographic and/or phonological) but have the same meaning. Here, we chose to use this term instead of 'translation equivalents', following other works (Dimitropoulou, Duñabeitia, and Carreiras 2011b; Peeters, Dijkstra, and Grainger 2013; but contrary to Dimitropoulou, Duñabeitia, and Carreiras 2011a). Additionally, it is clear from Section 1.3 that the term 'cognate' takes various definitions in the psycholinguistic literature. In the light of the cross-script perspective of our experiments and of a considerable amount of data, we consider that words presenting formal differences but sharing a common etymology (e.g., κέντρο /'kendro/ 'center' in Greek-English) should be considered as cognates, exactly as *sport – sport*, to which recent literature refers as 'orthographically identical cognates' (e.g., Peeters et al. 2013). We thus call all these words 'cognates', without using the term 'semi-cognates', which is rather scarce in the psycholinguistic literature. The issue of the different mappings, mainly of morphological nature, between Greek and French words, and their cognate or cognate-like effects in processing protocols, is specifically addressed in Voga and Anastassiadis-Symeonidis (2018).

are roughly of the same amplitude as the non-cognate effects found in the Gollan, Forster, and Frost (1997) study, and they should be interpreted as evidence in favor of an early participation of factors related to lexical meaning.

It should be noted at this point that the compatibility between the Greek-French and the Hebrew-English data stressed above, should not overshadow the fact that the two pairs of languages are not equivalent with respect to the orthographic overlap they share. We could even hypothesise that given the alphabetic nature of French and Greek, as well as the fact that 14 out of 24 (uppercase) letters of the Greek alphabet are common to letters of the Latin alphabet[7] (and 12 out of 24 for lowercase letters), some kind of letter-to-letter correspondence does exist between the Latin and the Greek alphabet, attested for instance by the fact that a Greek speaker can easily spell a French/English word to another Greek speaker using exclusively Greek letters (with some exceptions). Obviously, this is not the case between Hebrew and English, where not only the consonants representing Hebrew roots are graphically different from Latin characters, but also the morphological structure of the two languages differs considerably, since Hebrew has a non-linear morphology. It is thus possible that cross-language effects (L1 to L2 or L2 to L1) such as those we are presenting in Section 2 with Greek-French materials may not be replicable with language pairs sharing reduced orthographic overlap.

To sum up, the implications of cross-script cross-language priming results for the questions above (selective vs. non-selective access, independent lexica vs. integrated lexicon, 'prerequisites' of maximal formal overlap for the cognate relation) are quite straightforward. First, the non-target language, at least when it is L1 (as in Gollan, Forster, and Frost 1997, as well as Voga and Grainger 2007) cannot be suppressed[8] and exerts its influence, even when the duration of the prime is below the conscious perception threshold. Second, this transfer of activation from one language to another, shown here by the abundant evidence of the cognate effect, can survive also in cases of null orthographic

---

7 Clearly, a mapping at the level of letters does not imply a mapping at the level of phonemes. For instance, the Greek grapheme Ρ/ρ corresponds to French grapheme R/r, but Greek [r] is different from French [R].

8 Recall that in the masked priming technique, participants respond to stimuli in the target language and are completely unaware of the existence of the prime in the other language (see also the 'procedure' section of the present study), for example the L1 Greek subject in Voga and Grainger (2007), is not aware that L1 primes, e.g., κύκλος, appear in the screen before the French target, e.g., *cycle*, he thus thinks that he is responding to a 'French' experiment, using exclusively French stimuli. The cross-language masked priming protocol is thus bilingual in nature (two languages implied), even if participants cannot consciously process, or even perceive, the stimuli presented as primes.

overlap, as illustrated by evidence of Hebrew-English or Chinese-English bilinguals, at least if there is a certain amount of phonological overlap (e.g., *television – televizya*). Moreover, the cognate effect can also survive reduced phonological overlap combined with largely reduced orthographic overlap, as demonstrated in the case of Greek-French cognates (*κέντρο* /ˈkendro/ – *centre*).[9] In such an experimental situation, the cognate and non-cognate effects occur relative to phonological controls (Voga and Grainger 2007). Non-cognate effects occur relatively easily under certain circumstances, namely cross-script conditions (e.g., Gollan, Forster, and Frost 1997 for Hebrew-English; Voga (in press) and Voga and Grainger 2007 for Greek-French), i.e., in the presence of an orthographic cue. The orthographic cue is thought to orient the language processing system towards the appropriate lexicon, therefore rendering processing of the prime more efficient and enabling thus the contact to the semantic representation of the target. This is found to be the case even for long and less familiar non-cognate words (Voga 2017, e.g. αποκλειστικός /apoklistiˈkos/ 'exclusive', 40ms of translation effect and 40ms of morphological effect in the L1 to L2 direction).[10]

A possible objection to the summary above, is that masked priming was initially developed to study form-related factors in lexical access (for a review, see Forster, Mohan, and Hector 2003), that is sensitive to perceptual similarity between primes and targets and, finally, that priming effects can be task-specific, e.g., present in a lexical decision task but absent in a same-different task (Kinoshita and Lupker 2003; Norris and Kinoshita 2008; see also Baayen 2014). As far as bilingual data are concerned, the fact that effects with translation equivalents, which are effects based on a common semantic representation, appear under masked priming conditions, i.e., under conditions where the conscious perception of the prime is not possible (usually SOAs around 50 milliseconds), indicates that lexical access includes a semantic component, not only a formal one. Additionally, the fact that cross-script cognate words manage to prime each other in both directions (L1 to L2 and L2 to L1)[11] even when the effects are estimated relative to phonological controls (and not only unrelated controls), argues in favor of a semantic participation in cross-language priming effects. These facts

---

9 The two cross-script situations (Hebrew-English and Greek-French) differ not only with respect to orthographic overlap, but also historically: words such as κέντρο and *centre* bear a diachronic relationship, leading to a rich morphological family in the 'other' language, here, French.
10 These words bear, however, similar morphological structure. For a review of priming results of different morphological mappings on Greek-French words, cf. Voga and Anastassiadis-Symeonidis (2018).
11 The L2 to L1 direction gives somehow mixed results, as we will see in Section 1.4.2.

suggest an early involvement of semantics in cross-language processing, an aspect that should not be neglected. The interaction of the meaning component with (more or less) shared form should be studied more precisely. In other words, in accordance with the definition of cognate in historical linguistics, the cognate effect should be studied with respect to the 'larger chain of morphological relations' (Mulder et al. 2014). The experimental results presented in Section 2 explore this interaction between meaning and form through cross-language morphological effects.

1.4 Indirect ways to study the issue of *unified lexicon vs. separate lexica* and the role of morphology

1.4.1 Word-recognition vs. word-production perspectives

The Revised Hierarchical Model (RHM, Kroll and Stewart 1994; for a critical review, see Kroll et al. 2010) is one of the very first models of bilingual processing, and for this reason it is quite influenced by data in favor of selective access. It operates a distinction between the lexical and the conceptual level. At the lexical level, the two lexica are distinguished, one for the words of the mother tongue (L1) and another one for the words of the other language (L2). These two lexica are connected through a shared conceptual system which contains the meanings of the words.

As shown in Figure 1, the model assumes that both lexical and conceptual links are bidirectional, but that they differ in strength. The lexical link from L2 to L1 is assumed to be stronger than the lexical link from L1 to L2, because L2 words were initially associated to L1, and in this sense, the model is hierarchical. Likewise, the link from L1 to conceptual memory is assumed to be stronger than the link from L2 to conceptual memory (Kroll and Stewart 1994: 158). It should be noted that this model was designed to make predictions about translation effects from L1 to L2 and vice versa, especially for production protocols. Consequently, semantic and conceptual aspects are of particular relevance, and this is one of the main reasons why its authors assume different strength of connections between the lexical and the conceptual level for the two languages.

This is not the case with word recognition models, such as the equally influential BIA Model (Dijkstra, van Heuven, and Grainger 1998; van Heuven, Dijkstra, and Grainger 1998), focusing on perception effects. Initially, this model was an extension of the Interactive Activation Model of visual word recognition, first proposed by McClelland and Rumelhart (1981), and as such, did not deal with

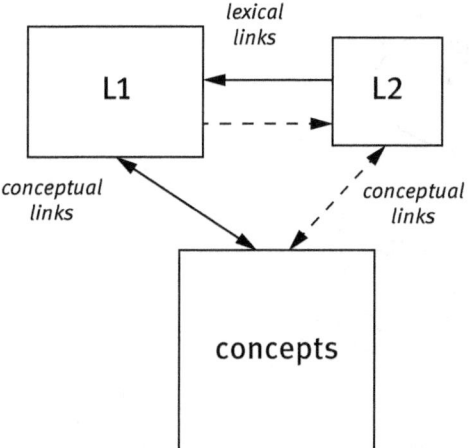

Figure 1: Revised Hierarchical Model of lexical and conceptual representation in bilingual memory (Kroll and Stewart 1994).

semantics (cf. Figure 2). Semantics were introduced in the BIA+ Model (cf. Figure 3), along with phonological information, in order to capture cross-script effects (like those we saw in Section 1.2), as well as a task schema, designed to capture the fact that bilingual word identification also has to reflect the task context (e.g., the fact that participants are responding to a monolingual or bilingual task).

We can observe that quite often in the recent literature, the still very influential RHM is taken to be a model based on independent, separate lexica (see, e.g., Brysbaert and Duyck 2010: 360). This fact, along with others, reflects the strict dichotomy between lexical access – perception (bottom-up) models and production (top-down) models. Recently, psycholinguistic research has started emphasizing the need for a unified account, based not on a separation between production and perception, but on an integrative approach (Pickering and Garrod 2013), and empirical evidence supporting integrative theories is beginning to emerge (Silbert et al. 2014).

As mentioned above, the issue of empirically distinguishing between parallel non-selective access with separate lexica vs. parallel access with an integrated, unified lexicon, is a very difficult one. We can only have indirect evidence coming from various kinds of interaction between the two languages. For much of the 'word recognition' research, this issue has been addressed through the study of interferences between word-forms of the two languages: for instance, van Heuven, Dijkstra, and Grainger (1998) show that the number of L1 (Dutch) orthographic neighbors influences processing when identifying L2 (English) words. This piece of evidence, while being among the first ones proving that

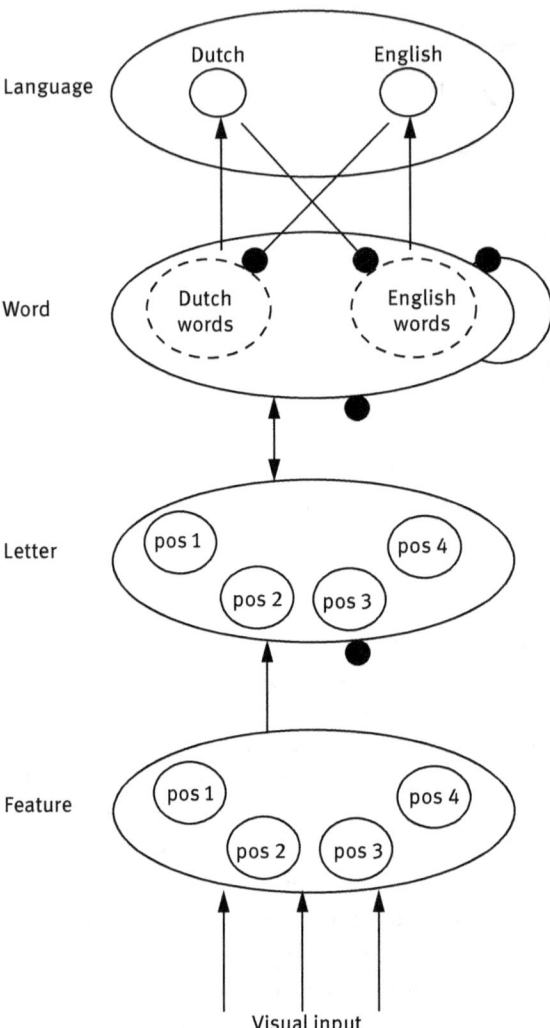

Figure 2: The Bilingual Interactive Activation Model of Visual Word Processing (van Heuven, Dijkstra, and Grainger 1998).

the two lexica (or words from the unified lexicon) do interact, focuses, following the logic of bottom-up models, on orthographic factors, which do not tell us the whole story. One of the merits of the RHM is that it attempted to address, mainly from a word production, top-down perspective, the interactions between the various components on a more central level ('core' level) than most bottom-up studies, by investigating the connections from the L1 lexicon

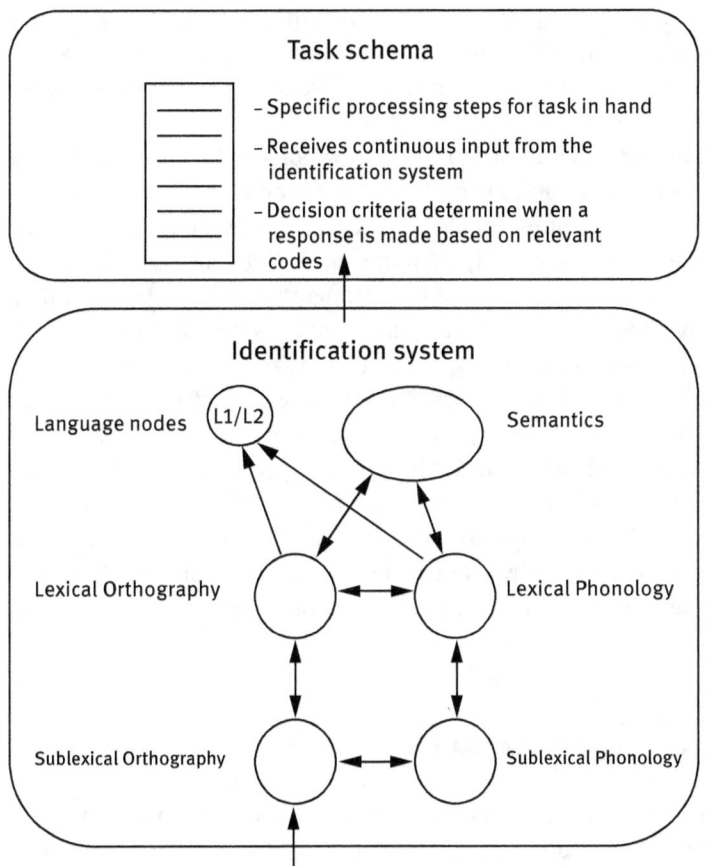

Figure 3: The BIA+ Model (Dijkstra and van Heuven 2002).

to the conceptual level, from the conceptual level to the L2 lexicon, etc. This kind of approach is of particular interest, not only locally for the study of cognates, but also, more generally, in order to answer the question as to whether the connection between the two lexica (or the words from the unified lexicon) is morphological in nature.

Indeed, if the cognate effect arises from the combined interaction of shared meaning and shared form, attributing the effect to morphological factors seems a natural step to take. The first researchers who have expressed this idea are Bybee (1985, 1988), on more theoretical grounds, and Kirsner (1986) based on experimental work. Bybee describes the monolingual lexicon as consisting of lexical paradigms (or 'clusters'), formed by a base-word and its derivatives: an organization transcending languages. While this approach, tested mainly through long-term priming in several studies (e.g., Kirsner, Lalor, and Hird 1993) is attractive, it nevertheless loses some of its appeal when it has to face two types of data. The first type of data concerns the priming asymmetries presented in some detail below (Section 1.4.2). The second type of evidence concerns the existence of non-cognate effects, such as those reviewed in Section 1.3, since non-cognates cannot belong to the same lexical paradigm, and hence should not produce priming effects. As we have seen in Section 1.3, non-cognate effects are found systematically under cross-script conditions, i.e., more easily than in same-script conditions. However, we have to concede that the influence of the orthographic cue is, by definition, related to a purely 'bottom-up-word-recognition' perspective. Consequently, it would be a little bit far-fetched to disregard entirely the role of morphology in bilingual processing, because of the existence of non-cognate effects, and despite the existence of robust cross-language morphological effects, both same-script and cross-script (e.g., Duñabeitia et al. 2013; Voga 2014, 2017; Sánchez-Casas and García-Albea 2005; Voga and Anastassiadis-Symeonidis 2018). Moreover, it would be an oversight if we did not attempt to exploit the opportunity given by the orthographic cue, in order to specifically address the role of morphological factors in bilingual processing and to examine the strength of morphological mappings across languages.

1.4.2 The question of priming asymmetries

A piece of evidence that, at first glance, seems at odds with an organization of the bilingual lexicon based upon morphological principles, is the asymmetry between the two priming directions. If words from the (separate or integrated) lexica belonged to the same 'lexical cluster' (following Bybee 1985, 1988) or to a kind of 'cross-language morphological family' (e.g., Mulder et al. 2014; Mulder, Dijkstra, and Baayen 2015), cross-language facilitation should be found in both priming directions, and not only in the L1 to L2 direction.

One of the first studies to show an asymmetry between the two priming directions is Keatley, Spinks, and de Gelder (1994), where the L2 to L1 direction does not induce significant cognate priming, neither for Chinese-English nor for French-English bilinguals. In their classic study with Hebrew-English bilinguals, Gollan, Forster, and Frost (1997) obtained a 53ms cognate priming effect in the L1 to L2 direction, but a non-significant effect in the opposite direction (9ms). This asymmetry is found in other studies (e.g., for Chinese-English: Jiang and Forster 2001; Chen et al. 2014; Allen, Conklin, and van Heuven 2015, for Japanese-English cognates).

However, there are studies that do not report asymmetrical effects (e.g., Duyck and Warlop 2009, for Dutch-French non-cognates), as well as studies in which an asymmetry is found for one type of cognate stimuli but not for the other. Data from Greek-French bilinguals (Voga 2014), having lived for several years in the L2 country, show that for cognates of Greek etymology, e.g., ιδέα /i'ðea/ – *idée* 'idea', the priming direction L1 to L2 gives a 56ms cognate effect and the opposite direction gives a 24ms significant effect,[12] which is not a clear asymmetry. On the other hand, the etymologically French (Latin) cognates, e.g., *role* – ρόλος /'rolos/ 'role' or *cuisine* – κουζίνα /ku'zina/ 'kitchen' fail to induce any significant effect in the L2 to L1 direction, despite the fact that they manage to prime in the L1 to L2 direction (34ms for cognate and 28ms for morphological priming),[13] and in spite of the fact that participants were living in the L2 country, i.e., they represented the type of bilingual who has the greatest chances to exhibit L2 to L1 priming effects (Finkbeiner et al. 2004; Grainger and Frenck-Mestre 1998). In Voga (2014), the etymologically L2 cognates, contrary to their L1 counterparts, confirm the asymmetrical pattern between the two priming directions and behave similarly to the non-cognates tested with low-proficiency Greek learners of Spanish (Dimitropoulou, Duñabeitia, and Carreiras 2011a).

The aforementioned findings do not constitute an exhaustive review on priming asymmetries. They nevertheless clearly illustrate the fact that these asymmetries can diverge according to several factors.

i) The nature of the task, i.e., tasks explicitly relying on the semantic component such as semantic categorization, vs. those in which perceptual factors are more implied, such as the lexical decision task (Finkbeiner et al. 2004, with non-cognates);

ii) Participants' level of proficiency. As it is acknowledged, low-proficient bilinguals perform worse than more proficient bilinguals in tasks requiring lexico-semantic activation of L2 items (for a review, see Kroll et al. 2010);

iii) Language environment (e.g., Finkbeiner et al. 2004);

---

12 A 56ms effect is certainly not equivalent to a 24ms one, but the latter still constitutes a real, significant effect, especially if we consider the fact that participants are faster when they respond to L1 than L2 stimuli, a trend inversely proportional to their L2 proficiency. This behavioral fact, which can potentially function as a bias, is not sufficiently discussed in the majority of published studies reporting priming asymmetries.

13 It should be noted that, as far as morphological priming is concerned, the two types of morphological primes, etymologically Greek cognate derivatives, as well as their Latin-French counterparts, are equally decomposable in terms of morphemes (base + suffix).

iv) The types of materials used, cognates in Voga (2014) vs. non-cognates[14] in Dimitropoulou, Duñabeitia, and Carreiras (2011a), or features of the materials, e.g., cognates of L1 vs. L2 etymology (Voga 2014). This last factor suggests that the question of priming asymmetries could be related to the morphological organization of the bilingual lexicon and that the reliance of historical linguistics on factors such as etymology can have a psychological reality.

2 Etymology and Morphological Family Size in the bilingual lexicon: Evidence from cross-script cognates

In order to describe the structure of the lexicon as well as the mechanisms responsible for processing words coming from two languages, we have to define the extent to which words from the languages of the bilingual are linked. Another related question is whether this connection takes place at a syntagmatic level, inside the boundaries of the word to be recogniszd, or at a paradigmatic level, i.e. extending beyond the limits of the lexical unit presented as a target in the experiment. The study we report here aims to provide experimental evidence on this question by manipulating a paradigmatic variable, the Morphological Family Size (MFS, de Jong, Schreuder, and Baayen 2000; Schreuder and Baayen 1997). The MFS has been found to influence bilingual processing (Dijkstra et al. 2005, on English-Dutch interlingual homographs; Mulder et al. 2014; Mulder, Dijkstra, and Baayen 2015, both with Dutch-English cognates and the lexical decision task). The role of MFS will be examined along with the etymological origin of the cognates, since simultaneous manipulation of these variables will inform us about the asymmetries between the two languages of the bilingual. It can also reveal the effect of the network of paradigmatic relations lying behind an individual word-form. This issue is strongly related to the other question of whether bilinguals have separate or unified lexica. From this perspective, Greek-French bilingualism constitutes a particularly interesting ground, since it is characterized by an important proportion of cognate words, originating from both etymologies

---

[14] In fact, priming asymmetries have been studied more often through non-cognate rather than cognate materials. This may look surprising; however, from an experimental point of view, it is undoubtedly easier to find balanced materials among non-cognate translation equivalents than among cognates.

(Anastassiadis-Symeonidis 1994, 2007) as a result of intense borrowing in both directions, through different historical periods.

The experiments below are based on a non-selective access approach, according to which the possible interactions between two languages constitute evidence in favour of the integrated lexica hypothesis. Given that cross-script protocols (e.g., Greek-French), albeit bottom-up (i.e., masked priming), exhibit particular sensitivity to 'core' factors, one of the most informative ways to test the morphological account of the bilingual lexicon would be through a cross-script protocol using materials that can be distinguished on the basis of a morphological variable, i.e., the MFS. In the experiments reported below, the MFS is controlled along with the etymological origin of our materials. Importantly, the cross-script nature of the experiment limits the participation of low-level form factors and enables the orthographic cue to immediately 'channel' the activation induced by the prime in the appropriate direction (i.e., towards the appropriate node of the unified lexicon).

2.1 Participants, stimuli and design

The experimental task was primed lexical decision, tested in two directions: Greek to French priming (exp. 1a) and French to Greek priming (exp. 1b). The 42 participants were Greek native speakers who had been studying and/or living in France for 4 to 8 years.[15] All of them responded to both experiments (1a and 1b) with the appropriate design. 192 targets were used overall, 96 words and 96 pseudowords. The 96 targets were all Greek-French cognates, nouns or adjectives and their frequency was assessed via the Lexique database (New et al. 2001). The 96 word stimuli were divided in four categories (see Table 1 for examples):

i) 24 cognates of Greek etymology and large MFS (GrMFS+)
ii) 24 cognates of Greek etymology and small MFS (GrMFS−)
iii) 24 cognates of French-Latin etymology and large MFS (FrMFS+)
iv) 24 cognates of French-Latin etymology and small MFS (FrMFS−)

The MFS count was based on the Modern Greek Dictionnary (2003) and the Reverse Modern Greek Dictionary (Anastassiadis-Symeonidis 2002, and its digital version). To illustrate, a lexical unit such as αθλητής /aθli'tis/ 'athlete' is part of a

---

15 Prior to experiments, participants were asked to fill in a short questionnaire on their study/work experiences, and were tested for their French naming skills (following the naming test of Jared and Kroll, 2001).

rich morphological family including: αθλητισμός /aθlitiz'mos/ 'athletism', αθλητικός /aθliti'kos/ 'athletic', άθληση /'aθlisi/ 'sport', αντιαθλητικός /andi aθliti'kos/ 'antiathletic', έπαθλο /'epaθlo/ 'trophy', δίαθλο /'ðiaθlo/ 'diathlon', τρίαθλο /'triaθlo/ 'triathlon', πένταθλο /'pendaθlo/ 'pentathlon', πολυαθλητής /poliaθli'tis/ 'polyathlete', δεκαθλητής /ðecaθli'tis/ 'decathlete', συναθλητής /sinaθli'tis/ 'sports partner', συνάθληση /si'naθlisi/ 'sports partnership', υπεραθλητής /iperaθli'tis/ 'super-athlete', αθλώ /a'θlo/ 'train', αθλούμαι /a'θlume/ 'train oneself', and has thus an MFS of 15. On the other hand, a lexical unit such as στομάχι /sto'maxi/ 'stomach' has a very small MFS, formed by 3 lexical units στομαχάκι /stoma'xaki/ 'stomach$_{DIM}$', στόμαχος /'stomaxos/ 'stomach' in medical terminology, and στομαχιάζω /stoma'xjazo/ 'to have a difficult digestion').[16]

Every target could be preceded by one of the three following types of prime, which constitute the three priming conditions:

i) the prime was the translation of the cognate in the other language, e.g., for the prime *αθλητής* /aθli'tis/ in Greek, the target was *athlète* in French. Primes were always presented in the nominative singular for Greek and in the singular for French;

ii) the prime had a morphological relation to the target, e.g., for the target *crème* (in the L1 to the L2 direction), the prime was *κρεμούλα* /kre'mula/ 'cream$_{DIM}$'. As Table 1 shows, the derivations used in this condition were diminutives, augmentatives as well as some adjectives;

iii) the last type of prime is the unrelated one, on the basis of which the results were estimated. In the experiments reported here, the unrelated prime is a word from the other language without any grapho-phonological or etymological relation to the target.

The 96 pseudowords were created in such a way that they respected the phonotactic constraints of each language (French and Greek) and were preceded by pseudo-primes mimicking primes of real words. The materials (words and pseudowords) were distributed in three experimental lists. The stimuli were distributed in the three lists according to a Latin square design.

As Table 1 shows, stimuli sample (number of letters and lexical frequency) and orthographic and phonological overlap for the 12 experimental conditions (3 priming conditions × 4 types of target). In exp. 1a, where the priming direction is from the L1 to the L2, the prime is *αθλητής* /aθli'tis/ and the target is

---

[16] Following De Jong, Schreuder, and Baayen (2000), neither inflected verb forms nor compounds were included in the count. Although the calculation of MFS was based on Greek, and not on French, special care was taken in order to avoid cognates that had a large MFS in one language and a much smaller one in the other.

Table 1: (exp. 1a and 1b, here the L1→ to L2 direction is showed).

			Primes			
	Targets	translation	Phon. overlap	Orth. overlap	morphological	Unrelated
Cognates of Greek etym. MFS+	athlète 6.5 lett. 39 occ/m.	αθλητής 'athlete'	76%	31%	αθλητικός 'athletic'	μάγουλο 'cheek'
Cognates of Greek etym. MFS–	estomac 6.1 lett. 15.4 occ/m.	στομάχι 'stomach'	77%	33%	στομαχικός 'of the stomach'	κατσίκα 'goat'
Cognates of French etym. MFS+	cuisine 6 lett. 61.4 occ/m.	κουζίνα 'kitchen'	85%	36%	κουζινίτσα 'kitchen$_{DIM}$'	στέμμα 'crown'
Cognates of French etym. MFS–	crème 5.5 lett. 43.7 occ/m.	κρέμα 'cream'	87%	35%	κρεμώδης 'creamy'	ευρύς 'broad'

athlète 'athlete', while in exp. 1b, where the priming direction is from the L2 to the L1, the prime is *athlète* and the target is *αθλητής* /aθli'tis/. This design, i.e., primes and targets changing following the priming direction, is the same for all the conditions, translation, morphological and unrelated.

2.2 Procedure and apparatus

The experiment was conducted on a PC computer using the DMDX software (Forster and Forster 2003). Each trial consisted of three visual events. The first was a forward mask consisting of a row of ten hash marks that appeared for 500ms. The mask was immediately followed by the prime. The prime was in turn immediately followed by the target word which remained on the screen until participants responded. The prime duration used in this experiment was 50ms. All stimuli appeared in the middle of the screen presented in lowercase characters[17] in order to preserve stress markers over the appropriate vowels. In

---

[17] It should be noted that for the application of the masked priming technique in Modern Greek, and, contrary to what is generally applied for other languages, e.g., English, targets as well as primes are presented in lowercase letters (and not in uppercase letters for the target and lowercase letters for the prime). This adjustment aims to avoid disguising the

order to prevent orthographic overlap being confounded with visual overlap, the size of the font was manipulated (Times New Roman 16 point for targets and Arial 12 point for primes; for a similar presentation see Frost, Forster, and Deutsch 1997). Participants were seated 50 cm from the computer screen. They were requested to make lexical decisions (YES, it is a word; NO, it isn't) on the targets as quickly and as accurately as possible, by pressing the appropriate button of the keyboard.

2.3 Results

The analysis of results was conducted on the reaction times (RTs) of correct answers after exclusion of errors[18] as well as outliers (RT> 1500ms and RT< 350msec, less than 3% of the overall data). Three items were excluded from the statistical analysis because of high error rates. The results for words are presented in graphic below, and in a more detailed way in Tables 2 and 3 in the Appendices. The details of the statistical analysis (ANOVA) are given in the Appendices 1a and 1b.

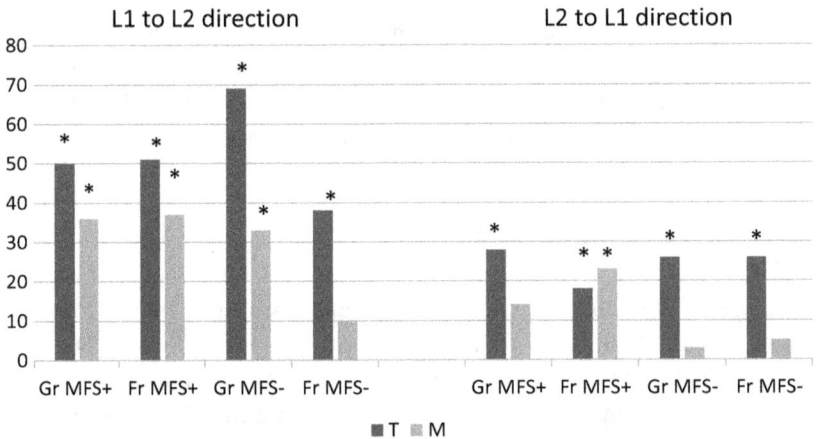

Graph 1: Translation (T) and morphological (M) net priming effects (in milliseconds) for the four types of cognate (etym. Greek MFS+, etym. French MFS+, etym. Greek MFS- and etym. French MFS-) in the two priming directions. Significant priming effects (translation and morphological) are denoted by an asterisk.

---

phonological identity of the stimulus, given that lexical stress, always marked on words of more than one syllable, serves also to disambiguate lexemes.
18 The ANOVA on the errors as well as the analysis for pseudowords will not be presented here.

2.4 Discussion of the results (exp. 1a and exp. 1b)

Summarizing the above results, we have demonstrated that:
i) With respect to the main effect of the MFS variable, the results show that it is significant for the L2 to L1 priming direction. In other words, when participants are making lexical decisions on targets in their L1 (κουζίνα, /ku'zina/, 'kitchen'), their RTs are influenced by the MFS of the L2 (since the prime was in L2, e.g., *cuisinière*, 'cooker'). This suggests an interaction between words from the two lexica, or inside the integrated lexicon.
ii) In the L1 to L2 direction, the main effect of the MFS factor is not found to be significant, but the MFS x etymology interaction can also be interpreted in the same terms: MFS interacts with etymology of the prime (κουζίνα /ku'zina/ 'kitchen'), and this influences RTs for lexical decisions in the other language (L2). This also provides evidence in favor of an integrated lexicon. If the words of the two languages belonged to different lexica, it would be difficult to have this type of influence on the participants' RTs, i.e., the global effect of the MFS (L1 to L2 direction) or the MFS x etymology interaction.
iii) What our results also show is that etymology, i.e., whether the cognate comes from the L1 or the L2, also plays a role, since this factor is significant in both directions of priming. This illustrates the fact that the words from the two languages do not behave in a strictly equivalent way, as we can see in the results of the planned comparisons (see Appendices 1a and 1b).
iv) As far as priming effects are concerned, it is clear that cognates manage to induce translation priming in both directions (L1 to L2 as well as L2 to L1). While the results are not of the same amplitude (52ms on average for the L1 to L2 direction and 24,5ms in average in the opposite direction), they do not exhibit the clear asymmetry found in other studies.
v) Both types of cognates, etymologically Greek and French ones, induce significant translation priming, though its amplitude is not strictly equivalent, particularly in the L1 to L2 direction. In this direction, etymologically Greek cognates induce on average 60ms of facilitation, whereas French cognates induce on average 44.5ms. Once again, we cannot talk about an asymmetry related to the etymological origin of our stimuli. We observe however that words of L1 etymology do not behave exactly in the same way as words of L2 etymology, even when these words are presented in the L2.
vi) Regarding the pattern of effects in the L1 to L2 direction, i.e., statistically equivalent translation and morphological effects for MFS+ stimuli, combined to morphological priming effects for three out of four types of cognates, we observe that morphological effects occur more broadly in the L1 to L2 direction than in the opposite one. In the L2 to L1 priming direction, only one category

of items, French MFS+ cognates, manages to induce morphological effect. Moreover, in the L1 to L2 priming direction, the morphological effect occurs *simultaneously* to the translation effect for the three out of four conditions. This result suggests that the strength of morphological connections is *greater* among etymologically L1 words (as well as etymologically L2 MFS+ words) than among etymologically L2 words (especially MFS- ones). This difference in the strength of connections is a result predicted by the RHM, as we shall see below (Section 3.2). The results of the L2 to the L1 direction point to the same type of interpretation: while all L2 translation primes are connected to their L1 cognate target word, and no asymmetry is found for the cognate effect, only L2 morphologically complex words from big families (e.g., *cuisinière*) have strong enough connections with the representation of the target (e.g., κουζίνα 'kitchen') to induce morphological cross-language priming effects.

However, before interpreting the differences between the two directions as being related to the organization of the bilingual lexicon, we have to acknowledge that the reaction times on the whole are slower when participants respond to L2 stimuli rather than when they respond to L1 ones (e.g., for the morphological condition of etymologically Greek cognates, 615ms in the L2 to L1 direction vs. 662ms in the opposite one). This is normal, given that our participants are proficient yet unbalanced bilinguals, who learned French as a foreign language. This pattern of RTs[19] is not an exception, it is related to language dominance and characterizes a majority of studies with unbalanced bilinguals and L2 learners. Therefore, there is the possibility that some effects, in this direction (L2 to L1), e.g., morphological, did not have the time to emerge during the 50ms time-window of our experiments. We can therefore make the assumption that the bilingual processing system was able to directly recognize the L1 target, thanks to the presence of the orthographic cue, but by doing so, no time was left for the morphological effect to emerge. In order to test this assumption other SOAs should be tested, and particularly the 66ms SOA.[20]

---

19 As well as of errors, much more frequent in the L1 to L2 direction than when participants respond to stimuli of their mother tongue.
20 The 66ms SOA is the following SOA, given that the prime duration depends on screen refreshing times (usually around 16ms). This prime duration has been shown to be sensitive to morphological effects.

3 Interpretation of the psycholinguistic data

One of the main interests of the psycholinguistic study presented above is that Greek and French scripts present a somewhat intermediate orthographic overlap, i.e. much greater than Hebrew and English scripts, or Chinese and English scripts. This is of special interest, given that the Greek-French combination still is cross-script, and Greek is a morphologically rich language. Although some recent studies focus on this language combination, for instance Dimitropoulou et al. (2011a), who study priming asymmetries with non-cognate words and low-proficiency ESL speakers, the number of studies involving it still remains limited. Despite reduced orthographic overlap, Greek and French (or English) share a significant number of lexical units. This renders the creation of the linguistic materials needed to test the kind of hypothesis we entertain here much easier. It also proves that combining variables such as the MFS, which is realized synchronically through the connections that constructed words share, with a variable of a diachronic nature such as etymology, is possible, in a psycholinguistic experimental setting.

3.1 Language co-activation in the 'unified lexico-semantic architecture'

The linguistic (Section 1.2) and psycholinguistic data (Section 2) discussed above point to the question of how bilinguals manage to prevent interferences between their two languages, presented in the introduction through the distinction between the storage component (separate lexica vs. unified/integrated lexicon), and selective vs. non-selective access. From this point of view, the psycholinguistic data we present here call for an interpretation in terms of a 'unified lexico-semantic architecture' (with non-selective access, which is a well-established assumption). In the experiment above, despite the reduced orthographic overlap between Greek and French, all four types of cognate, etymologically Greek or French-Latin, coming from large or small morphological families, induced significant cross-language translation priming in both directions. The asymmetry between the two directions of priming, found in some studies (e.g., Allen, Conklin, and van Heuven 2015; Chen et al. 2014; Gollan, Forster, and Frost 1997) but not in others (e.g., Duyck and Warlop 2009; Voga 2014) is not really found in our data. While cognate translation effects are of lesser amplitude in the L2 to L1 direction, they are nevertheless significant and cannot be interpreted as 'weak' (compared to the L1 to L2 direction) especially given that RTs, on the whole, are faster in the L2 to L1 direction. Our results thus constitute another demonstration of the well-known fact that, even in the context of the L2 to L1 priming direction, our proficient yet unbalanced bilinguals show themselves unable to 'suppress' their L2 when responding to L1 targets.

Our study demonstrates for the first time that this 'impossibility to deactivate' the L2 is observed not only when processing targets belonging etymologically to the L2 (e.g., κρέμα /'krema/ 'cream'), but also when processing targets belonging to L1 (presented in the L1 language and alphabet, e.g., αθλητής /aθli'tis/ 'athlete'). In the case of etymologically L1 words (presented in the L1 alphabet), we could have hypothesized a reduced participation of the L2 'part of the lexicon', since these words have nothing to do with the L2. If words from the two languages were represented separately in the bilingual lexicon of our Greek (L1) participants, we would expect a word such as αθλητής /aθli'tis/ 'athlete' to be recognized without any, or with a minimal participation of its French translation athlète, especially in the light of several studies showing asymmetrical effects between the two priming directions (e.g., Allen, Conklin, and van Heuven 2015; Chen et al. 2014; Gollan, Forster, and Frost 1997). This does not seem to be the case, however, since we observe robust translation effects induced by L2 primes on L1 targets (28ms, in the MFS+ etymologically Greek condition), which provides evidence for a unified lexicon with parallel access, at least for participants having reached a certain level of proficiency. The fact that the L1 target αθλητής /aθli'tis/ 'athlete' benefits from the L2 prime athlète, in the same way (same amplitude) as the etymologically L2 target κρέμα /'krema/ 'cream' benefits from its L2 prime crème, suggests that these two effects have little chance of coming from functionally separate lexica, as certain accounts assume (mainly the RHM, e.g., Schwartz, Kroll, and Diaz 2007). Therefore, these effects should be interpreted in favor of what Schoonbaert et al. (2009) call a 'unified lexico-semantic architecture'.

It is useful to appreciate that this co-activation, while it is enhanced through variables of orthographic nature (here the orthographic cue, see also Dimitropoulou, Duñabeitia, and Carreiras 2011a, 2011b) does not restrict itself to the low levels of processing, neither does it depend on any kind of decomposition into morphemes (e.g., Crepaldi et al. 2010; Rastle and Davis 2008) as the above results clearly show. It extends to the more central levels ('core levels'), at which the content of lexical units is represented (de Jong et al. 2000; Dijkstra et al. 2005; Mulder, Dijkstra, and Baayen 2015; Mulder et al. 2014) and which seem to be organized paradigmatically.

3.2 Implications for models of bilingual processing

If we assume that the bilingual processing system has to activate some kind of semantic/conceptual representation in order to pass from the L2 prime to the L1 target[21] (or the other way round), cognate translation priming effects provide strong evidence that L2 semantic representations are related to those of the L1. In the L1 to L2 direction, the fact that the cognate and morphological effects do not differ in amplitude or time-course (at least for the MFS+ words) provides evidence in favor of a paradigmatic or paradigm-like organization of the cognate words contained in the bilingual unified lexicon. This organization can be described in terms of a 'cross-language derivational family' in which morphologically complex L1 words containing salient suffixes (Giraudo and Dal Maso 2016), for instance κρεμούλα 'cream$_{DIM}$' or αθλητικός 'athletic' will automatically activate the base word in the other language (*crème, athlète*). In other words, presentation of an L1 morphologically complex word as a prime to the processing system will automatically activate the L2 representation of the words morphologically related to it (target).

However, the same is not true for the L2 to L1 priming direction. In our data, the fact that L2 primes have not managed, on the whole, to induce morphological facilitation on the L1 target, could be interpreted in terms of a looser link between L2 words and the semantic-conceptual level, compared to the link between L1 words and the corresponding concepts, exactly as the RHM assumes (Kroll et al. 2010; Kroll and Stewart 1994). Though the RHM assumes functionally distinct lexicons for L1 and L2 words, it posits a common semantic/conceptual store to which words from both languages are linked: during progress in L2 proficiency, links between L2 words and their corresponding concepts are strengthened in such a way that lexical and semantic connections of L2 words become comparable to those of L1 words. According to this model, in word production, translation from L2 to L1 can be accomplished lexically, without semantic access, if the L2 word enabled lexically mediated retrieval of the translation. In contrast, L1 to L2 (forward) translation would be semantically mediated because of the strong L1 link to meaning. Our general pattern of morphological results in the L2 to L1 direction is compatible with such an approach, given the absence of morphological effects for three out of four types of cognates, suggesting lexically rather than semantically mediated processing. This

---

[21] The alternative hypothesis here would be to assume that the effects described above are nothing more than form effects. However, this is unlikely, given the very limited (and stable, see Table 1) orthographic overlap combined with stable phonological overlap through the cross-script experiments reported here.

does not mean however, that morphology is absent from L2, as certain accounts assume on the basis of L2-L2 morphological priming data (e.g., Clahsen et al. 2010; Silva and Clahsen 2008; but see Dal Maso and Giraudo 2014; Voga, Anastassiadis-Symeonidis, and Giraudo 2014). The data of exp. 1b (L2 to L1) show robust morphological priming for stimuli from big morphological families (Graph 1, FrMFS+).

The fact that both translation and morphological L2 primes produce less facilitation when processing the L1 targets (cf. Graph 1) can also be interpreted in an interactive activation perspective (IA, McClelland and Rumelhart 1981) with a unified lexicon, in which words which are partially compatible with the stimulus will be activated at the same time, as a function of criteria such as their frequency in the language(s). If we assume that L2 words have a lower lexical frequency, the direct consequence would be that resting levels of activation are very different for L1 and for L2 cognates: L1 cognates whose resting level of activation is higher are accessed more rapidly than L2 cognates which are characterized by lower resting levels of activation. When an L1 cognate is presented as the prime, its word representation is instantly active and this activation will rapidly flow to the semantic level, whereas more time (and/or more activation) may be needed for an L2 cognate which will not be able to activate the semantic level quickly enough (Voga and Giraudo, 2017 for a similar explanation in inflectional processing). While the presence of the orthographic cue (i.e., due to cross-script conditions) manages to neutralize the effect of inhibitory connections between words from the two languages (see option (d) in the introduction) thus rendering cognate translation effects possible, this activation remains weaker in the L2 to L1 direction than in the opposite one. Consequently, this weaker activation does not manage to reach the semantic level, at least not in a way that would be able to induce morphological facilitation (as in the L1 to L2 priming direction). In such an interpretation of our effects, the fact that one category of morphological primes still manages to induce facilitation (i.e., the MFS+ etymologically French primes) should be interpreted in terms of the positive action of the rich morphological family that managed to reinforce activation of the L1 target.

4 Interpretation of the language change data

Aiming at describing the structure of the bilingual lexicon, we wanted to define the extent to which words from the languages of a bilingual individual are linked. As we have seen in Section 2.4, the results of the exp. 1a and exp. 1b show that etymology, i.e., whether the cognate comes from an L1 or an L2, plays a role in priming. Words from the two languages, therefore, do not behave in a strictly symmetric way. Is this asymmetry related to the morphological organization of the lexicon? Evidence from language contact seems to support this view: the tenuous link between L2 vocabulary and a morphological/conceptual level of organization is mirrored by morphological integration of loan words into a matrix language, as this can represent significant steps in the direction of a full conceptual integration (Section 4.1). Other data drawn from research in language contact, concerning the existence, in one and the same language, of parallel morphological systems in settings characterized by balanced high proficiency bilingualism, provide supporting evidence for a unified lexicon with parallel access (Section 4.2).

4.1 Evidence from morphological integration

When loans enter a recipient language, they can be fitted morphologically in order to serve the specific morphosyntactic requirements of the recipient language. Morphological integration is a matter of degree, so that 'full integration' occurs when loanwords are treated as if they were native items, for example, the Ancient Greek noun *lampás* (feminine; genitive singular *lampádos*) 'torch' was integrated into Latin as *lampada* (feminine; genitive singular *lampadae*) (Gardani 2013: 48). In other cases, however, loanwords are not assigned any paradigmatic pattern, they are, as it were, undigested, to use Mifsud's (1995: *passim*) terminology. An example of such a case is found in the Tūrōyo dialect of New Aramaic (spoken in the village Mīdin, south-eastern Turkey, and in the diaspora). Here, the Kurdish (i.e., Indo-European) adjectival feminine ending -*e* has remained confined to one Kurdish-borrowed adjective, *rāṣt* 'right' (data from Jastrow 1985: 238).

(3) Tūrōyo New Aramaic
 ʔídi ʔi-rāṣṭe
 hand DET.SG.F-right
 'the right hand'

Given that the formative -*e* has not spread to native lexemes of the recipient language and is not found on other Kurdish-origin adjectives, one can argue that this form has not been perceived as a morphological entity by the speakers of the recipient language.

However, we know that the borrowing agents can be sensitive to morphological formatives. Let us consider the case of Arvanítika, a variety of Tosk Albanian which has been involved in intense and four centuries long language contact with dominant Greek. When Greek nouns ending in [a] are borrowed into Arvanítika, the segment [a] is automatically replaced by [ə] because speakers perceive and reanalyse [a] as the Albanian postposed definite feminine article (Tsitsipis 1998: 22). Thus, given a Green noun velóna 'needle', the resulting Arvanítika base form is velónë, and velóna is the definite form; see example (4a), where the forms are contrasted with their standard Albanian counterparts (4b).

(4)   Arvanítika   Albanian
     a. *velónë*   b. *gjilpërë*
        'needle'   'needle'
        velón-a   *gjilpër-a*
        needle-DET   needle-DET
        'the needle'   'the needle'

An even more impressive case of morphological awareness is provided by the adaptation of loan-nouns in the Romani varieties of Bugurdzi Romani and Romungro Romani. The data in (5), from Elšík (2000: 21), show a systematic coincidence of the morphotactic boundaries of the stems in the SLs and in the respective RLs, in spite of the paradigmatic allomorphy in the SLs, as is visible by comparing the stems with the base forms (i.e., nominative singular) of the SLs.

(5)   SL   base form in SL   stem in SL   base form in Romani (RL)
     a. Serbo-Croatian *orao* 'eagle'   *orl-*   *orl-os* (Bugurdzi)
     b. Albanian   *ahër* 'stable'   *ahr-*   *ahr-i* (Bugurdzi)
     c. Hungarian   *majom* 'monkey' *majm-*   *majm-o* (Romungro)

Noticeably, the Romani forms are based on the stem without the epenthetic second vowel /a/, e.g., *orl-*, which recurs in most of the paradigm, while the purely phonological epenthesis occurs only in the nominative singular, *orao*. Thus the (often much) higher type and token frequency of the paradigm slots lacks this vowel (6). This clearly points to the fact that the higher type and token frequency of the paradigm cells lacking this vowel plays a major role in processing and consequently in morphological integration.

(6) Serbo-Croatian

	singular	plural
nominative	òrao	òrlovi
genitive	òrla	orlova
dative	orlu	orlovima
accusative	orla	orlove
vocative	orle	orlovi
locative	orlu	orlovima
instrumental	orlom	orlovima

Both the Arvanítika and the Romani cases unambiguously demonstrate that bilingual speakers have access to the morphological structure of complex forms of different source languages and are able to manipulate meaningful or compositional strings.

4.2 Evidence from co-morphologies

In Section 1.2, we have discussed cases in which morphological material of an SL spreads to RL-native bases. We have also referred to codeswitching studies showing that often plural forms of an embedded language are maintained into the matrix language. We have evidence that this process can not only go beyond individual codeswitching practices but also involve large sets of formatives. The stock example is the English paradigm *alumnus alumni*,[22] borrowed *tout court* in its orthographic format from Latin, by retaining the Latin paradigmatic inflections that are relevant to English morphosyntax, that is, those realizing the number values of singular and plural. A more notable manifestation of the phenomenon can be illustrated by the use of Latin genitives in Church holiday names (7a) and formulae (7b) in German (see Gardani 2018: 2–3).

(7) German
    a. *Christi*   *Himmelfahrt*
        Christ.GEN.SG   ascension
        'The ascension of Jesus'
    b. *Geburt*   *Mariae*
        birth   Mary.GEN.SG
        'Nativity of Mary'

---

[22] See also the English pair *lexicon lexica*, from Ancient Greek, which occurs so frequently in our chapter.

Still, such cases are a marginal phenomenon in English and German, not only in quantitative but also in qualitative terms. For example, it is questionable whether speakers of German are generally able to analyse *Christi* and *Mariae* as complex forms containing the inflectional formatives *-i* and *-ae*, respectively. Most likely, cases such as the German ones qualify as fossilized forms belonging to inactive morphology.

The situation is different in languages with elaborated paradigms, where this type of transfer can reach more prominent levels. In a study mainly focusing on Berber, Kossmann (2008, 2010) has labeled the phenomenon *parallel system borrowing* because it is a process whereby loanwords retain (parts of) their original paradigms and, in this way, come to establish themselves as inflectional systems that are parallel to the native paradigms of the RL. Kossmann stresses that "different morphologies occur in different etymological strata" (Kossmann 2008: 18).

The idea that a language can have different grammars is not new. A great deal of research taking this perspective has focused on phonology (e.g., Itô and Mester 1999; Inkelas and Zoll 2007; Calabrese and Wetzels 2009; Mansfield 2015), prosody (Kubozono 2006; Kang 2010; Davis, Tsujimura, and Tu 2012), syntax (Pintzuk 1996) and also on morphology (e.g., Kiparsky 1982a, 1982b). With respect to the selectional restrictions on the occurrence of non-inherited material in an RL, Matras (2002: 193) speaks of 'compartmentalized grammar', based on the observation that in some languages (contextually, Romani) "different sets of grammatical markers are employed with different parts of the vocabulary" (see also Elšík and Matras 2006: 324–333; Friedman 2013; Matras 2015: 66–75). We shall illustrate etymon-based 'morphological compartmentalization' (Matras 2015: 66–75) with data from Romani. Here, there exist distinct inflectional classes which occur either with native vocabulary or with borrowed vocabulary (see Adamou 2012; Bakker 1997; Boretzky 1989; Boretzky 1994; Boretzky and Igla 1991; Boretzky and Igla 1999; Elšík 2000; Elšík and Matras 2006; Friedman 2013; Igla 1996; Matras 2002). In (8), the present paradigm of the native Indo-Aryan verb *astaráv* 'hold' is compared with that of the Turkish-borrowed verb *beklérim* 'wait'. While *astaráv* inflects according to native Indo-Aryan morphology, *beklérim* is morphologically identical to the Turkish original (data from Igla 1996: 61). Crucially, the Turkish inflections occur exclusively with lexemes borrowed from Turkish.

(8) Ajia Varvara Romani (Igla 1996: 61)

	Present	Turkish	Romani: Turkish morphology	Romani: Indo-Aryan morphology
	1sg	bekle-r-im	beklé-rim	astar-áv
	2sg	bekle-r-sin	beklé-rsin	astar-és

3sg	bekle-r	beklé-r	astar-él
1pl	bekle-r-iz	beklé-ris	astar-ás
2pl	bekle-r-siniz	beklé-rsinis	astar-én
3pl	bekle-r-lar	beklé-rlár	astar-én
	'wait'	'wait'	'hold'

In the same language, we find a less strict instantiation of compartmentalization. Ajia Varvara Romani has borrowed the participle *-(i)mé* from the Greek passive participle *-ménos*. The formative *-(i)mé* does not occur on inherited Indo-Aryan verbs; however, despite its Greek origin, it applies not only to the Greek lexical stratum but also to other European loans. The following examples of loanwords from Greek (9a), Romanian (9b), Slavic (9c) and Turkish (9d) (Igla 1996: 73) illustrate this point nicely.

(9) Ajia Varvara Romani
  a. *xolamé*   *xolá(v)ol*
     'angered'   'to get angry'
  b. *logodimé*   *logodisá(v)ol*
     'engaged'   'to affiance'
  c. *ožonimé*   *ožonisá(v)ol*
     'married'   'to marry'
  d. *sastimé*   *sastú*
     'wondered' 'he wondered (3.SG.PST)'

Of course, one could argue that the Romani data just mirror the geo-political circumstances and the several historical stages in which lexical borrowing occurred, but the fact that the borrowed formatives have not been extended to the inherited Indo-Aryan lexicon seems to point to the speakers' reactivity to the existence in their lexicon of different etymological strata, in the sense of networks of cognates, and of different morphological systems which come to co-exist under one roof. The data presented in this section confirm the view of a unified lexicon with parallel access emerging from the experimental evidence.

5 Conclusion

In this paper, we have explored the connections between related, albeit not necessarily converging research fields, such as psycholinguistics and historical linguistics, by focusing on the role of morphological factors in influencing both human processing and mental representation of cognates. We have presented two masked priming experiments conducted on Greek native speakers who had French as L2, in which we tested two variables (Morphological Family Size and etymology) related to the cognate 'advantage' in processing and production. We found (a) evidence in favor of language co-activation, whereby words from the two lexica interact, irrespective of the language they belong to; (b) the strength of morphological connections is greater among etymologically L1 words than among etymologically L2 words; (c) it is 'impossible to deactivate' the L2, not only with processing targets belonging etymologically to the L2, but also with processing targets belonging to L1. The results of the experiment square well with data from loanword integration and coexisting morphological systems. The morphological integration of loan words into a matrix language confirms that the link between the L2 vocabulary and a morphological level of organization is tenuous and that there is an asymmetry between L1 words and L2 words. Other set of data on compartmentalized morphological systems in one and the same language supports evidence for a view of bilingual lexical representation as a unified lexicon with parallel access.

References

Adamou, Evangelia. 2012. Verb morphologies in contact: Evidence from the Balkan area. In Martine Vanhove, Thomas Stolz, Aina Urdze & Hitomi Otsuka (eds.), *Morphologies in contact*, 143–162. Berlin: Akademie Verlag.

Allen, David, Kathy Conklin & Walter J.B. van Heuven. 2015. Making sense of the Sense Model: Translation priming with Japanese-English bilinguals. *The Mental Lexicon* 10. 32–55.

Altenberg Evelyn P. & Helen Smith Cairns. 1984. The effects of phonotactic constraints on lexical processing in bilingual and monolingual subjects. *Journal of Verbal Learning and Verbal Behavior* 22. 174–188.

Anastassiadis-Symeonidis, Anna. 1994. *Neological borrowing in Modern Greek. Direct loans from French and Anglo-American: A morpho-phonological analysis*. Thessaloniki: Aristotle University. [Νεολογικός δανεισμός της νεοελληνικής. Άμεσα δάνεια από τη γαλλική και αγγλοαμερικανική. Μορφοφωνολογική ανάλυση.]

Anastassiadis-Symeonidis, Anna. 2002/2008. Reverse Modern Greek Dictionnary. Aristotle University of Thessaloniki: Manolis Triantafyllidis Institute. [Αντίστροφο λεξικό της Νέας Ελληνικής. Αριστοτέλειο Πανεπιστήμιο Θεσσαλονίκης : Ινστιτούτο Νεοελληνικών Σπουδών Ίδρυμα Μανόλη Τριανταφυλλίδη].
http://www.greek-language.gr/greekLang/modern_greek/tools/lexica/reverse/index.html

Anastassiadis-Symeonidis, Anna. 2007. L'emprunt du grec moderne au français. In Jean Pruvost (éd.), *Les journées des dictionnaires 2007-Dictionnaires et mots voyageurs-Les 40 ans du Petit Robert de Paul Robert à Alain Rey*, 137–152. Paris: Éditions de Silves.

Baayen, R. Harald. 2014. Experimental and psycholinguistic approaches to studying derivation. In Rochelle Lieber & Pavol Štekauer (eds.), *The Oxford handbook of derivational morphology*, 95–117. Oxford University Press.
Bakker, Peter. 1997. Athematic morphology in Romani: The borrowing of a borrowing pattern. In Yaron Matras, Peter Bakker & Hristo Kyuchukov (eds.), *The typology and dialectology of Romani* (Current Issues in Linguistic Theory 156), 1–21. Amsterdan & Philadelphia: John Benjamins.
Basnight-Brown, Dana M. & Jeanette Altarriba. 2007. Differences in semantic and translation priming across languages: the role of language direction and language dominance. *Memory and Cognition* 355. 953–65.
Boretzky, Norbert & Birgit Igla. 1991. *Morphologische Entlehnung in den Romani-Dialekten*. Essen: Universität GH Essen: Universität GH Essen.
Boretzky, Norbert & Birgit Igla. 1999. Balkanische (südosteuropäische) Einflüsse im Romani. In Uwe Hinrichs (ed.), *Handbuch der Südosteuropa-Linguistik*, 709–731. Wiesbaden: Harrassowitz.
Boretzky, Norbert. 1989. Zum Interferenzverhalten des Romani. *Zeitschrift für Phonetik, Sprachwissenschaft und Kommunikationsforschung* 42 (3). 357–374.
Boretzky, Norbert. 1994. *Romani: Grammatik des Kalderaš-Dialekts mit Texten und Glossar* (Balkanologische Veröffentlichungen 24). Wiesbaden: Harrassowitz.
Bowers, Jeffery S., Zohra Mimouni & Martin Arguin. 2000. Orthography plays a critical role in cognate priming: Evidence from French/English and Arabic/French cognates. *Memory & Cognition* 28. 1289–1296.
Brysbaert, Maarc & Wouter Duyck. 2010. Is it time to leave behind the Revised Hierarchical Model of bilingual language processing after fifteen years of service? *Bilingualism: Language & Cognition* 133. 359–371.
Bybee, Joan L. 1985. *Morphology: A study of the relation between meaning and form*. Amsterdam: John Benjamins.
Bybee, Joan L. 1988. Morphology as lexical organisation. In Michael Hammond & Michael Noonan (eds.), *Theoretical morphology. Approaches to modern linguistics*, 119–142. San Diego: Academic Press.
Bybee, Joan L. 1995a. Regular morphology and the lexicon. *Language and Cognitive Processes* 10 (5). 425–455.
Bybee, Joan L. 1995b. Diachronic and typological properties of morphology and their implications for representation. In Laurie B. Feldman (ed.), *Morphological aspects of language processing*, 225–246. Hillsdale NJ: Lawrence Erlbaum Associates Inc.
Bybee, Joan L. 2006. From usage to grammar: The mind's response to repetition. *Language* 82 (4). 711–733.
Bybee, Joan L. 2007. *Frequency of use and the organization of language*. Oxford & New York: Oxford University Press.
Bybee, Joan L. 2010. *Language, usage and cognition*. Cambridge & New York: Cambridge University Press.
Calabrese, Andrea & Leo W. Wetzels (eds.). 2009. *Loan phonology* (Current Issues in Linguistic Theory 307). Amsterdam & Philadelphia: John Benjamins.
Chen, Baoguo, Huixia Zhou, Yiwen Gao & Susan Dunlap. 2014. Cross-language translation priming asymmetry: A test of the Sense model. *Journal of Psycholinguistic Research* 433. 225–40.

Clahsen, Harald, Claudia Felsen, Kathleen Neubauer, Mikako Sato & Renita Silva. 2010. Morphological structure in native and non-native language processing. *Language Learning* 60. 21–43.

Costa, Albert, Alfonso Caramazza & Nuria Sebastian-Galles. 2000. The cognate facilitation effect: implications for models of lexical access. *Journal of Experimental Psychology: Learning Memory and Cognition* 26. 1283–1296

Crepaldi, Davide, Kathleen Rastle, Max Coltheart & Lindsey Nickels. 2010. Fell primes fall but does bell prime ball? Masked priming with irregularly-inflected primes. *Journal of Memory and Language* 631. 83–99.

Dal Maso, Serena & Hélène Giraudo. 2014. Masked morphological priming in Italian L2: Evidence from masked priming. *Linguisticae Investigationes* 37 (2). 322–337.

Davis, Stuart, Natsuko Tsujimura & Jung-yueh Tu. 2012. Toward a taxonomy of loanword prosody. *Catalan Journal of Linguistics* 11. 13–39.

de Groot, Annette M. B. & Jerard L. J. Nas. 1991. Lexical representation of cognates and noncognates in compound bilinguals. *Journal of Memory and Language* 30. 90–123.

de Groot, Annette M. B., Susanne Borgwaldt, Mieke Bos & Ellen van den Eijnden. 2002. Lexical decision and word naming in bilinguals: Language effects and task effects. *Journal of Memory and Language* 47. 91–124.

de Groot, Annette M. B., Philip Delmaar & Stephen Lupker. 2000. The processing of interlexical homographs in translation recognition and lexical decision: Support for nonselective access to bilingual memory. *Quarterly Journal of Experimental Psychology* 53A. 397–428.

de Jong, Nivja H., Robert Schreuder & R. Harald Baayen. 2000. The morphological size effect and morphology. *Language and Cognitive Processes* 15. 329–365.

de Jong, Nivja H., Robert Schreuder & R. Harald Baayen. 2003. Morphological resonance in the mental lexicon. In R.H. Baayen and R. Schreuder (eds.), *Morphological structure in Language processing*, 65–88. Berlin: Mouton de Gruyter.

Dijkstra, Ton, Jonathan Grainger & Walter J. B. van Heuven. 1999. Recognition of cognates and interlingual homographs: The neglected role of phonology. *Journal of Memory and Language* 41. 496–518.

Dijkstra, Ton, Fermín Moscoso del Prado Martín, Béryl Schulpen, Robert Schreuder & R. Harald Baayen. 2005. A roommate in cream: Morphological family size effects on interlingual homograph recognition. *Language and Cognitive Processes* 20. 7–41.

Dijkstra, Ton & Walter J.B. van Heuven. 2002. The architecture of the bilingual word recognition system: From identification to decision. *Bilingualism: Language and Cognition* 5. 175–197.

Dijkstra, Ton, Henk Van Jaarsveld & Sjoerd Ten Brinke. 1998. Interlingual homograph recognition: Effects of task demands and language intermixing. *Bilingualism: Language and Cognition* 1. 51–66.

Dimitropoulou, Maria, Jon Andoni Duñabeitia & Manuel Carreiras. 2011a. Masked translation priming effects with low proficient bilinguals. *Memory & Cognition* 392. 260–275.

Dimitropoulou, Maria, Jon Andoni Duñabeitia & Manuel Carreiras. 2011b. Two words, one meaning: evidence for automatic co-activation of translation equivalents. *Frontiers in Psychology* 2. doi:10.3389/fpsyg.2011.00188.

Dufour, Robert & Judith F. Kroll. 1995. Matching words to concepts in two languages: A test of the concept mediation model of bilingual representations. *Memory and Cognition* 23. 166–180.

Duñabeitia, Jon Andoni, Maria Dimitropoulou, Joanna Morris & Kevin Diependaele. 2013. The role of form in morphological priming: Evidence from bilinguals. *Language and Cognitive Processes* 287. 967–987.

Duyck, Wouter & Nele Warlop. 2009. Translation priming between the native language and a second language: new evidence from Dutch-french bilinguals. *Experimental Psychology* 563. 173–9.

Elšík, Viktor & Yaron Matras. 2006. *Markedness and language change: The Romani sample* (Empirical Approaches to Language Typology 32). Berlin: Mouton de Gruyter.

Elšík, Viktor. 2000. Romani nominal paradigms: Their structure, diversity, and development. In Viktor Elšík & Yaron Matras (eds.), *Grammatical relations in Romani: The noun phrase* (Current Issues in Linguistic Theory 211), 9–30. Amsterdam & Philadelphia: John Benjamins.

Esposito, Alena G., Lynne Baker-Ward & Shane Mueller. 2013. Interference suppression vs. response inhibition: An explanation for the absence of a bilingual advantage in preschoolers' stroop task performance. *Cognitive Development* 28 (4). 354–363.

ESRC Centre for Research on Bilingualism in Theory and Practice. 2011. The Siarad corpus. http://siarad.org.uk/speakers.php?c=siarad.

Finkbeiner, Matthew, Kenneth Forster, Janet Nicol & Kumiko Nakamura. 2004. The role of polysemy in masked semantic and translation priming. *Journal of Memory and Language* 511. 1–22.

Forster, Kenneth I. & Jonathan C. Forster. 2003. DMDX: A Windows display program with millisecond accuracy. *Behavioral Research Methods: Instruments & Computers* 35. 116–124.

Forster, Kenneth I., Kathleen Mohan & Jo Hector. 2003. The mechanics of masked priming. In S. Kinoshita & S. J. Lupker (eds.), *Masked priming: State of the art*, 3–37. Hove: Psychology Press.

Forster, Kenneth I. 1999. The microgenesis of priming effects in lexical access. *Brain and Language* 68. 5–15.

Friedman, Victor A. 2013. Compartmentalized grammar: The variable (non)-integration of Turkish verbal conjugation in Romani dialects. *Romani Studies* 23 (1). 107–120.

Frost, Ram, Kenneth I. Forster & Avital Deutsch. 1997. What can we learn from the morphology of Hebrew? A masked priming investigation of morphological representation. *Journal of Experimental Psychology: Learning, Memory and Cognition*, 23. 829–856.

Gardani, Francesco. 2008. *Borrowing of inflectional morphemes in language contact*. Frankfurt am Main: Peter Lang.

Gardani, Francesco. 2012. Plural across inflection and derivation, fusion and agglutination. In Lars Johanson & Martine I. Robbeets (eds.), *Copies versus cognates in bound morphology*, 71–97. Leiden & Boston: Brill.

Gardani, Francesco. 2013. *Dynamics of morphological productivity: The evolution of noun classes from Latin to Italian* (Empirical Approaches to Linguistic Theory 4). Leiden & Boston: Brill.

Gardani, Francesco. 2018. On morphological borrowing. *Language and Linguistics Compass* 12(10). 1–17.

Gerard, Linda D. & Don L. Scarborough. 1989. Language-specific lexical access of homographs by bilinguals. *Journal of Experimental Psychology: Learning, Memory, and Cognition* 15 (2). 305–315.

Giraudo, Hélène & Serena Dal Maso. 2016. The salience of complex words and their parts: Which comes first? *Frontiers in Psychology* 7. 1778.

Giraudo, Hélène & Jonathan Grainger. 2000. Effects of prime word frequency and cumulative root frequency in masked morphological priming. *Language and Cognitive Processes* 15. 421–444.

Giraudo, Hélène & Jonathan Grainger. 2001. Priming complex words: Evidence for supralexical representation of morphology. *Psychonomic Bulletin and Review* 81. 127–131.

Gollan, Tamar, Kenneth I. Forster & Ram Frost. 1997. Translation priming with different scripts: Masked priming with cognates and noncognates in Hebrew-English bilinguals. *Journal of Experimental Psychology: Learning Memory and Cognition* 23. 1122–1139.

Grainger, Jonathan & Cheryl Frenck-Mestre 1998. Masked priming by translation equivalents in proficient bilinguals. *Language and Cognitive Processes* 13 (6). 601–623.

Grant, Anthony. 2008. Contact-induced change and the openness of 'closed' morphological systems: Some cases from Native America. *Journal of Language Contact* 2 (1). 165–186.

Hoshino, Noriko & Judith F. Kroll. 2008. Cognate effects in picture naming: Does cross-language activation survive a change of script? *Cognition* 106(1). 501–511.

Igla, Birgit. 1996. *Das Romani von Ajia Varvara: Deskriptive und historisch-vergleichende Darstellung eines Zigeunerdialekts*. Wiesbaden: Harrassowitz.

Inkelas, Sharon & Cheryl Zoll. 2007. Is grammar dependence real? A comparison between cophonological and indexed constraint approaches to morphologically conditioned phonology. *Linguistics* 45 (1). 133–171.

Itô, Junko & Armin Mester. 1999. The phonological lexicon. In Natsuko Tsujimura (ed.), *The handbook of Japanese linguistics*, 62–100. Malden, Mass: Blackwell.

Jared, Debra & Judith F. Kroll. 2001. Do bilinguals activate phonological representations in one or both of their languages when naming words? *Journal of Memory and Language* 44. 2–31.

Jastrow, Otto. 1985. *Laut- und Formenlehre des neuaramäischen Dialekts von Mīdin im Tūr 'Abdīn*, 3rd edn. Wiesbaden: Harrassowitz.

Jiang, Nan & Kenneth I. Forster. 2001. Cross-language priming asymmetries in lexical decision and episodic recognition. *Journal of Memory and Language* 44. 32–51.

Jiang, Nan 1999. Testing processing explanations for the asymmetry in masked cross-language priming. *Bilingualism: Language and Cognition* 21. 59–75.

Kang, Yoonjung. 2010. Tutorial overview: Suprasegmental adaptation in loanwords. *Lingua* 120 (9). 2295–2310.

Keatley, Catharine W., John A. Spinks & Beatrice de Gelder. 1994. Asymmetrical cross-language priming effects. *Memory & Cognition* 22 (1). 70–84.

Kinoshita, Sachiko & Stephen Lupker. 2003. *Masked priming: the state of the art*. New York & Hove: Psychology Press.

Kiparsky, Paul. 1982a. From cyclic phonology to lexical phonology. In Harry van der Hulst & Norval Smith (eds.), *The structure of phonological representations*, 131–175. Dordrecht: Foris.

Kiparsky, Paul. 1982b. Lexical morphology and phonology. In The Linguistic Society of Korea (ed.), *Linguistics in the morning calm: Selected papers from SICOL-1981*, 3–91. Seoul: Hanshin.

Kirsner, Kim 1986. Lexical representation: Is a bilingual account necessary? In Jyotsna Vaid (ed.), *Language processing in bilinguals: Psycholinguistic and neuropsychological perspectives*, 21–46. Hillsdale NJ: Erlbaum.

Kirsner, Kim, Erin Lalor & Kathryn Hird. 1993. The bilingual lexicon: Exercise meaning and morphology. In Robert Schreuder & B. Weltens (eds.), *The bilingual lexicon*, 215–248. Amsterdam: John Benjamins.

Kossmann, Maarten. 2008. On the nature of borrowing in Cypriot Arabic. *Zeitschrift für arabische Linguistik* 49. 5–24.

Kossmann, Maarten. 2010. Parallel System Borrowing: Parallel morphological systems due to the borrowing of paradigms. *Diachronica* 27 (3). 459–487.

Kroll, Judith F. & Erika Stewart. 1994. Category interference in translation and picture naming: Evidence for asymmetric connections between bilingual memory representations. *Journal of Memory and Language* 33. 149–174.

Kroll, Judith F., Janet G. van Hell, Natasha Tokowicz & David W. Green. 2010. The Revised Hierarchical Model: A critical review and assessment. *Bilingualism: Language & Cognition* 133. 373–381.

Kubozono, Haruo. 2006. Where does loanword prosody come from? A case study of Japanese loanword accent. *Lingua* 116 (7). 1140–1170.

Law, Danny. 2014. *Language contact, inherited similarity and social difference: The story of linguistic interaction in the Maya lowlands*. Amsterdam & Philadelphia: John Benjamins.

Mansfield, John. 2015. Loan phonology in Murrinhpatha. In Mark Harvey & Alexis Antonia (eds.), *The 45th Australian Linguistic Society Conference Proceedings – 2014*, 153–172: University of Newcastle.

Marian, Viorica, James Bartolotti, Sirada Rochanavibhata, Kailyn Bradley & Arturo E. Hernandez. 2017. Bilingual cortical control of between- and within-language competition. *Scientific Reports* 7 (1). 11763.

Marslen-Wilson, William D. 1987. Functional parallelism in spoken word-recognition. *Cognition* 25 (1–2). 71–102.

Matras, Yaron. 2002. *Romani: A linguistic introduction*. Cambridge: Cambridge University Press.

Matras, Yaron. 2015. Why is the borrowing of inflectional morphology dispreferred? In Francesco Gardani, Peter Arkadiev & Nino Amiridze (eds.), *Borrowed morphology* (Language Contact and Bilingualism 8), 47–80. Berlin, Boston & Munich: De Gruyter Mouton.

McClelland, James L. & David E. Rumelhart. 1981. An interactive activation model of context effects in letter perception: Part 1. An account of basic findings. *Psychological Review* 88. 375–407.

McClelland, James L. & David E. Rumelhart. 1988. *Computational models of cognition and perception. Explorations in parallel distributed processing: A handbook of models, programs, and exercises*. Cambridge, MA: The MIT Press.

Mifsud, Manwel. 1995. *Loan verbs in Maltese: A descriptive and comparative study*. Leiden: Brill.

Mithun, Marianne. 2013. Challenges and benefits of contact among relatives: Morphological copying. *Journal of Language Contact* 6 (2). 243–270.

Modern Greek Dictionary. 2003. Aristotle University of Thessaloniki: Manolis Triantafyllidis Foundation.

Mufwene, Salikoko S. 2001. *The ecology of language evolution* (Cambridge Approaches to Language Contact). Cambridge & New York: Cambridge University Press.

Mufwene, Salikoko S. 2008. *Language evolution: Contact, competition and change*. London: Continuum.

Mulder, Kimberley, Ton Dijkstra & R. Harald Baayen. 2015. Cross-language activation of morphological relatives in cognates: The role of orthographic overlap and task-related processing. *Frontiers in Human Neuroscience 9* (16).

Mulder, Kimberley, Ton Dijkstra, Robert Schreuder & R. Harald Baayen. 2014. Effects of primary and secondary morphological family size in monolingual and bilingual word processing. *Journal of Memory and Language* 72. 59–84.

Muysken, Pieter. 2012. Root/affix asymmetries in contact and transfer: Case studies from the Andes. *International Journal of Bilingualism* 16 (1). 22–36.

Myers-Scotton, Carol. 2013. Paying attention to morpheme types: Making borrowability more precise. In Carol de Féral (ed.), *In and out of Africa. Languages in question. In honour of Robert Nicolaï. Volume 1: Language contact and epistemological issues* (Bibliothèque des Cahiers de l'Institut de Linguistique de Louvain (BCILL) 130), 31–42. Leuven: Peeters.

New, Boris, Christophe Pallier, Ludovic Ferrand & Rafael Matos. 2001. Une base de données lexicales du français contemporain sur Internet: Lexique. *L'Année Psychologique* 101. 447–462.

Norris, Dennis & Sachiko Kinoshita. 2008. Perception as evidence accumulation and Bayesian inference: Insights from masked priming. *Journal of Experimental Psychology: General* 1373. 434–455.

Peeters, David, Ton Dijkstra & Jonathan Grainger. 2013. The representation and processing of identical cognates by late bilinguals: RT and ERP effects. *Journal of Memory and Language* 68. 315–332.

Pickering, Martin J. & Simon Garrod. 2013. An integrated theory of language production and comprehension. *Behavioral and Brain Sciences* 36 (4). 329–347.

Pintzuk, Susan. 1996. Old English verb-complement word order and the change from OV to VO. *York Papers in Linguistics* 17. 241–264.

Rastle, Kathleen & Matthew H. Davis. 2008. Morphological decomposition based on the analysis of orthography. *Language and Cognitive Processes* 23. 942–971.

Robbeets, Martine. 2015. *Diachrony of verb morphology: Japanese and the Transeurasian Languages* (Trends in Linguistics. Studies and Monographs 291). Berlin & Boston: De Gruyter Mouton.

Sánchez-Casas, Rosa & José E. García-Albea. 2005. The representation of cognate and noncognate words on bilingual memory: Can cognate status be characterized as a special kind of morphological relation? In Judith F. Kroll & Annette M. B. De Groot (eds.), *Handbook of Bilingualism: Psycholinguistic Approaches*, 226–250. New York: Oxford University Press.

Sanchez-Casas, Rosa, José E. García-Albea & Christopher W. Davis. 1992. Bilingual lexical processing: Exploring the cognate/non cognate distinction. *European Journal of Cognitive psychology* 4. 293–310.

Scarborough, Don L., Linda Gerard & Charles Cortese. 1984. Independence of lexical access in bilingual word recognition. *Journal of Verbal Learning and Verbal Behavior* 23. 84–99.

Schoonbaert, Sofie, Wouter Duyck, Marc Brysbaert & Robert J. Hartsuiker. (2009). Semantic and translation priming from a first language to a second and back: Making sense of the findings, *Memory and Cognition* 37(5). 569–586.

Schreuder, Robert & R. Harald Baayen. 1997. How complex simplex words can be. *Journal of Memory and Language* 37. 118–139.

Schwartz, Ana I. & Judith F. Kroll. 2006. Bilingual lexical activation in sentence context. *Journal of Memory and Language* 55(2). 197–212.

Schwartz, Ana I., Judith F. Kroll & Michele Diaz. 2007. Reading words in Spanish and English: Mapping orthography to phonology in two languages. *Language and Cognitive Processes* 22. 106–129.

Sheng, Li, Boji Pak Wing Lam, Diana Cruz & Aislynn Fulton. 2016. A robust demonstration of the cognate facilitation effect in first-language and second-language naming. *Journal of Experimental Child Psychology* 141. 229–238.

Silbert, Lauren J., Christopher J. Honey, Erez Simony, David Poeppel & Url Hasson. 2014. Couple Neural Systems Underlie the Production and Comprehension of Naturalistic

Narrative Speech. *Proceedings of the National Academy of Sciences of the United States of America*, 111 (43). E4687–E4696.
Silva, Renita & Harald Clahsen. 2008. Morphologically complex words in L1 and L2 processing: Evidence from masked priming experiments in English. *Bilingualism: Language and Cognition* 11. 245–260.
Tsitsipis, Lukas D. 1998. *A linguistic anthropology of praxis and language shift: Arvanítika (Albanian) and Greek in contact* (Oxford Studies in Language Contact). Oxford & New York: Clarendon Press (Oxford University Press).
Urioste, Jorge L. 1964. *Transcripciones quechuas I–VII*. La Paz: Instituto de Cultura Indígena.
van Hell, Janet G. & Annette M. B. De Groot. 1998. Conceptual representation in bilingual memory: Effects of cognateness and cognate status in word association. *Bilingualism: Language and Cognition* 1. 193–211.
van Hell, Janet G. & Ton Dijkstra. 2002. Foreign language knowledge can influence native language performance in exclusively native contexts. *Psychonomic Bulletin & Review* 9. 780–789.
Van Hell, Janet & Darren Tanner 2012. Second Language Proficiency and Cross-Language Lexical Activation. *Language Learning* 62. 148–171.
van Heuven, Walter J. B., Ton Dijkstra & Jonathan Grainger 1998. Orthographic neighbourhood effects in bilingual word recognition. *Journal of Memory and Language* 39. 458–483.
van Heuven, Walter J. B., Herbert Schriefers, Ton Dijkstra & Peter Hagoort. 2008. Language conflict in the bilingual brain. *Cerebral Cortex* 18. 2706–2716.
Voga, Madeleine & Anna Anastassiadis-Symeonidis. 2018. Connecting lexica in bilingual cross-script morphological processing: Base and series effects in language co-activation. *Lexique* 23. 160–184.
Voga, Madeleine, Anna Anastassiadis-Symeonidis & Hélène Giraudo. 2014. Does morphology play a role in L2 processing? Two masked priming experiments with Greek speakers of ESL. *Lingvisticæ Investigationes* 37 (2). 338–352.
Voga, Madeleine & Hélène Giraudo. 2017. Word and beyond-word issues in morphological processing. *Word Structure*, 10 (2). 235–254.
Voga, Madeleine & Jonathan Grainger. 2007. Cognate status and cross-script translation priming. *Memory and Cognition* 35. 938–952.
Voga, Madeleine. 2014. Διαγλωσσική ομοτυπία και μεταφραστική προτεραιοποίηση: ο ρόλος του ορθογραφικού δείκτη και της ετυμολογίας μέσα από δύο ελληνο-γαλλικά πειράματα [Cognateness and masked priming: the role of the orthographic cue and etymology through two Greek-French experiments]. *Studies in Greek Linguistics* 34. 104–125.
Voga, Madeleine. 2017. Μορφή, μορφολογική δομή και αναπαράσταση στο δίγλωσσο νοητικό λεξικό: Μεταφραστική προτεραιοποίηση με ελληνογαλλικά μεταφραστικά αντίστοιχα [Form, morphological structure and representation in the bilingual mental lexicon: Masked priming with Greek-French cognates and non-cognates]. *Studies in Greek Linguistics* 37. 129–152.
Voga, Madeleine. in press. Lexical co-activation with prefixed cognates and non-cognates: evidence from cross-script masked priming. In Marcel Schlechtweg (ed.), *The learnability of complex constructions from a cross-linguistic perspective*. Trends in Linguistics: Studies and Monographs. Berlin: Mouton De Gruyter.
Whaley, Lindsay. 2012. Deriving insights about Tungusic classification from derivational morphology. In Lars Johanson & Martine I. Robbeets (eds.), *Copies versus cognates in bound morphology*, 395–409. Leiden & Boston: Brill.

Abbreviations

DET	determiner
F	feminine
GEN	genitive
PL	plural
PST	past/preterit
RL	recipient language
SG	singular
SL	source language

Appendices

Appendix 1a: Results and statistical analysis for the L1 to L2 priming direction

Table 2 (exp. 1a): Reaction Times (RTs, in milliseconds) and percentages of errors for lexical decisions in the twelve experimental conditions, translation (T), morphological (M) and unrelated (Unr.) for the four types of target in the L1 to L2 priming direction. Net priming effects are assessed relative to the unrelated condition. The asterisk means that the effect is statistically significant.

Words	Translation (T)		Morphological (M)		Unlreated (Unr)		Net priming effect	
	RT	Error	RT	Error	RT	Error	Unr – T	Unr – M
Cognates of Greek etym. MFS+	632	2,67	646	1,78	682	1,48	50*	36*
Cognates of Greek etym. MFS–	643	3,57	679	2,67	712	2,97	69*	33*
Cognates of French etym. MFS+	664	3,27	678	6,54	715	5,05	51*	37*
Cognates of French etym. MFS–	645	2,67	673	3,86	683	4,16	38*	10

Main factors: the effect of prime condition is significant, $F1(2, 82) = 37.41$, $p<.0001$, $F2(2, 178) = 25.73$, $p<.0001$; the main effect of *etymology* is significant in the analysis by subjects, $F1(1, 41) = 5.95$, $p<.05$, $F2<1$. The MFS factor is not significant (both $Fs<1$), but the interaction between etymology and MFS is significant, $F1(1, 41) = 17.36$, $p<.001$, $F2(1, 89) = 4.64$, $p<.05$.

Planned comparisons were conducted in order to assess the statistical significance of the differences in RTs related to our hypotheses: the differences between the unrelated and the translation conditions (facilitation due to the cognate prime) are significant for all the types of cognates: for cognates of Greek etymology MFS+ (50 ms of effect), $F1(1, 41) = 23.61$, $p<.001$, $F2(1, 23) = 12.81$, $p<.001$; for cognates of Greek etymology MFS– (69 ms of effect), $F1(1, 41) = 43.88$, $p<.001$, $F2(1, 23) = 15.18$, $p<.001$; for cognates of French etymology MFS+ (51 ms), $F1(1, 41) = 15.56$, $p<.001$, $F2(1, 21) = 15.64$, $p<.001$, and, finally, for etymologically MFS– French cognates (38 ms), $F1(1, 41) = 16.8$, $p<.001$, $F2(1, 23) = 6.91$, $p<.05$.

The differences between the unrelated and the morphological conditions (facilitation induced by the Greek derivation on the French target) were statistically significant for the three first types of cognates, for etymologically Greek MFS+ cognates (36 ms), $F1(1, 41) = 6.71$, $p<.05$, $F2(1, 23) = 6.29$, $p<.05$; for etymologically Greek MFS– cognates (33 ms), $F1(1, 41) = 5.43$, $p<.05$ $F2(1, 21) = 8.20$, $p<.01$; for etymologically French MFS+ cognates (37 ms) the difference was significant for subjects $F1(1, 41) = 10.37$, $p<.01$, and marginally significant for items $F2(1, 22)$ $3.53, p<.06$. For etymologically French MFS– cognates the morphological effect (10 ms) was not significant, $F1(1, 41) = 1.24$, $F2<1$.

The difference between translation and morphological conditions was not significant for MFS+ cognates, neither for those of Greek etymology, $F1(1, 41) = 1.79$, $F2(1, 23) = 1.30$, nor for those of French etymology (both $Fs<1$), but it was for MFS– cognates, of Greek etymology, $F1(1, 41) = 10.96$, $p<.01$, $F2(1, 22) = 7.06$, $p<.05$, as well as of French etymology, $F1(1, 41) = 8.54$, $p<.01$, $F2(1, 23) = 5.30$, $p<.05$.

Appendix 1b: Results and statistical analysis for the L2 to L1 priming direction

Table 3 (exp. 1b): Reaction Times (RTs, in milliseconds) and percentages of errors for lexical decisions in the 12 experimental conditions, translation (T), morphological (M) and unrelated (Unr.) for the four types of target, in the L2 to L1 direction. Net priming effects are accessed relative to the unrelated condition. The asterisk means that the effect is statistically significant.

Words	Translation (T)		Morphological (M)		Unrelated (Unr)		Net priming effect	
	RT	Error	RT	Error	RT	Error	Unr– T	Unr – M
Cognates of Greek etym. MFS+	587	0,005	601	0,005	615	0,01	28*	14

Table 3 (exp. 1b) (continued)

Words	Translation (T)		Morphological (M)		Unrelated (Unr)		Net priming effect	
	RT	Error	RT	Error	RT	Error	Unr– T	Unr – M
Cognates of Greek etym. MFS–	607	0,01	630	0,01	633	0,01	26*	3
Cognates of French etym. MFS+	617	0,005	612	0,01	635	0,002	18*	23*
Cognates of French etym. MFS–	609	0,002	630	0,008	635	0,03	26*	5

Main effects: the effect of prime condition is significant, $F1(2, 82) = 16.73$, $p<.001$, $F2(2, 178) = 18.34$, $p<.001$; the main effect of etymology is significant only in the analysis by subjects, $F1(1, 41) = 13.83$, $p<.0001$, $F2(1, 89) = 2.16$, as well as the effect of the MFS factor, significant only by subjects, $F1(2, 41) = 11.92$, $p<.001$, but close to significance in the analysis by items, $F2(1, 89) = 3.37$ [$\alpha<.05$, $F(1, 89)$ ≤ 3.94]. The interaction between etymology and MFS is significant by subjects, $F1(1, 41) = 11.99$, $p<.001$, $F2<1$.

Planned comparisons: all types of cognates induce significant translation effects, etymologically Greek MFS+ cognates (28 ms), $F1(1, 41) = 13.83$, $p<.001$, $F2(1, 23) = 16.27$, $p<.001$; etymologically Greek MFS- cognates (26 ms), $F1(1, 41) = 9.45$, $p<.01$, $F2(1, 23) = 6.55$, $p<.05$; etymologically French MFS+ cognates (18 ms), $F1(1, 41) = 4.33$, $p<.05$, $F2(1, 21) = 5.38$, $p<.05$, as well as etymologically French MFS– cognates (26 ms), $F1(1, 41) = 11.33$, $p<.001$, $F2(1, 23) = 30.49$, $p<.001$.

The only significant difference (23 ms) between the morphological and the unrelated conditions is found for French MFS+ cognates, $F1(1, 41) = 5.63$, $p<.05$, $F2(1, 21) = 6.30$, $p<.05$. For the other types of cognates, the morphological conditions do not induce any facilitation, for Greek MFS+ cognates, $F1(1, 41) = 2.80$, $F2(1, 23) = 2.80$, for Greek as well as French MFS- cognates both $Fs<1$.

Translation prime conditions statistically differ from morphological ones, except for those of etymologically French MFS+ cognates (both $Fs<1$). For the other types of cognates, facilitation induced from translation primes differs from the morphological effect: for Greek MFS+ cognates (14 ms of difference), $F1(1, 41) = 5.02$, $p<.05$, $F2(1, 23) = 8.75$, $p<.01$; for Greek MFS– cognates (23 ms of difference), $F1(1, 41) = 5.29$, $p<.05$, $F2(1, 22) = 4.05$, $p<.06$; for French MFS– cognates (21 ms difference), $F1(1, 41) = 6.58$, $p<.05$, $F2(1, 23) = 6.99$, $p<.05$.

Marco Marelli, Daniela Traficante and Cristina Burani
Reading morphologically complex words: Experimental evidence and learning models

Abstract: The study of complex word processing has been centered on the notion of morpheme as a processing unit. Evidence from psycholinguistics and cognitive neuropsychology has been taken as suggestive of symbolic morphemic representations at the lexical level, on a par with words. However, several phenomena observed in morphological processing suggest a more complex picture. The crucial role played in reading by the distributional properties of both the complex word and its morphemic constituents (e.g., family size, morphological entropy, orthography-semantics consistency) highlights the limits of the 'morpheme-as-unit' assumption. Moreover, results from the developmental literature show that morphology is an age-related emergent aspect of written word processing, exploited to overcome reading challenges for both typically developing readers and children with dyslexia. A unitary account for this complex scenario may be offered by learning models that focus on form-to-meaning mapping.

Keywords: lexical morphology, word processing, reading acquisition, learning models

1 Introduction

In its most traditional definition, morphemes are characterized as the minimal meaning-associated units in a language (Bloomfield 1933). This definition, although maybe simplistic and descriptive (Blevins 2016), makes it immediately clear why the topic has attracted so much attention in the psycholinguistic community. As information-carrying elements, morphemes are potentially very helpful in language processing, providing useful cues about the meaning of a given word. As a consequence, the question as to whether and how morphological information plays a role at the cognitive level has been central in psycholinguistic research, especially the one focusing on word processing. In this

---

Marco Marelli, Department of Psychology, University of Milano-Bicocca, (Italy)
Daniela Traficante, Department of Psychology, Catholic University of Milan, (Italy)
Cristina Burani, Institute of Cognitive Sciences and Technologies, National Research Council, Rome, (Italy); Department of Life Sciences, University of Trieste, (Italy)

Open Access. © 2020 Marco Marelli et al., published by De Gruyter. This work is licensed under a Creative Commons Attribution-NonCommercial-NoDerivatives 4.0 International License.
https://doi.org/10.1515/9783110440577-014

chapter we will discuss the achievements of this research field, by stressing to what extent the theoretical view on the role of morphology in word reading has changed (and it is still changing). Our main focus will be on results from written word reading, as main source of evidence in the literature. Throughout the chapter we will consider evidence drawn from two main tasks, i.e., visual lexical decision (participants decide whether a printed stimulus is a word or not) and word naming (participants read aloud as fast as possible a given letter string, be it a word or a non-word). The two tasks tap into partially different components of the reading process, thus they may highlight different roles for morphemes and morphological processing, depending on the involved processing components. Data from adult readers, brain-damaged patients, and children with and without reading deficits will be discussed.

2 A role for morphemes

Most of the studies on the morphological processing of adult readers has been guided, more or less explicitly, by the hypothesis that morphemes and/or complex words are stored as representational units within the cognitive system. Researchers mostly assumed that morphologically complex words could, in principle, activate representations in the reader's mind (or her/his mental lexicon) that are univocally associated to some linguistic concept (the ideas of morpheme and/or word). This "representational view" characterized the morphological processing research, especially in its early history. In fact, one of the most persistent experimental questions wondered whether morphemes are accessed in visual word recognition.

2.1 Listing models and parsing models

In early debates, two main views on the issue were considered. Either morphologically complex words were segmented during reading, and hence morphemes were represented and accessed in the cognitive system, or the mental lexicon was populated by whole words, and hence alleged morphological effects in word processing were to be considered a by-product of the relations between independent representation units.

The former position, represented by *full-parsing* theories, is ideally exemplified by the model proposed by Taft and Forster (1975). In this perspective, words are accessed through the representations of the morphemes that form them, implying that an early procedure is first applied to segment the complex word in its constituents, that are in turn used to compute the whole-word representation. In the original proposal by Taft and Forster, which dealt with the processing of prefixed stimuli, the procedure was accomplished by a *prefix-stripping* operation that is able to parse a word on the basis of the prefix, consequently isolating the constituent morphemes (for an alternative architecture, see Taft 1994). The parsing-and-recombination procedure is traditionally considered to be costly (in terms of cognitive resources), but constituted a reasonable proposal in so far (i) said procedure is necessary to understand the meaning of novel words (we easily understand the meaning of *windowless*, even if we have never heard the word before) and (ii) through its explicit representations, it accounts for the morphological awareness that even uneducated speakers can manifest.

The latter position opposes to full-parsing theories the *full-listing* proposals (or *whole-word* approaches; e.g., Butterworth 1983), that posit an explicit representation for any complex form, being it derived, inflected, or compound. For example, in this perspective separate units for *run, running, runs, runner, homerun*, etc. will be included in the mental lexicon. In this model morphology would not emerge as a direct consequence of explicit morpheme access, rather depending on reliable and stable (*paradigmatic*, even) relations between independent lexical units. The processing of *runner* will not be characterized by morphological effects because the -*er* affix is stripped from its stem; rather, these will depend on the orthographical, phonological, and semantic overlap between *runner* and *run*.

A third position has also emerged, proposing middle-ground views between either extreme proposals described above. In the *mixed* or *dual-route* models, both morphological segmentation and whole-word access are possible, with the efficiency of either operations depending on many possible factors. Examples of this position are the Augmented Addressed Morphology (AAM) model (Burani and Caramazza 1987; Caramazza, Laudanna, and Romani 1988) and parallel dual-route models by Schreuder and Baayen (1995; Baayen, Dijkstra, and Schreuder 1997) and Grainger and Ziegler (2011). In these perspectives, word processing would proceed both in a morpheme-based fashion and by means of a direct access to the word representation. The two procedures will always be in place at the same time, although in some cases a given route will be more efficient than its counterpart (e.g., the parsing route for novel words, the direct route for high-frequency words). The mechanisms underlying the interplay between the two routes vary, with some approaches assuming a completely parallel, horse-race architecture, and other positing interacting procedures. Indeed, one of the more recent models of this family, the multi-route account by Kuperman et al. (2009), is characterized by massively interacting multiple procedures that maximize the efficiency in word processing by exploiting all available cues to access word meaning.

2.2 Empirical evidence for morphological effects

It must be noted that, in "representational" approaches such as the ones just described, it is difficult to completely get rid of the morpheme role. Certainly, even whole-word approaches do not completely exclude morpheme-based processes, rather relegating them to limited, infrequent contexts able to trigger these "special" operations (e.g., the first time a novel complex word is encountered). And indeed, empirical results seem to be in line with the morphological assumption. In the remaining of the present section, we will describe pieces of evidence that make morpheme representations fundamental for models of written word recognition. We will focus on (i) effects of morphological structure in word reading, (ii) morphological priming effects, (iii) letter transposition effects, and (iv) morpheme frequency effects.

Morphological structure is known to influence word processing, even in non-lexical orthographic strings. In their pioneering lexical-decision study, Taft and Forster (1975) found that non-words made of an existing prefix paired with an existing stem (*de+juvenate*) take longer to be rejected than combinations of existing prefixes and non-existing stems (*de+pertoire*). That is, when asked to decide, as fast as possible, whether a given string is an existing word or not, participants find more difficult to evaluate *dejuvenate* than *depertoire*. The effect holds for inflectionally suffixed non-words, as shown by Caramazza, Laudanna, and Romani (1988) in Italian, and is confirmed when combinations of existing stems and non-existing suffixes are compared with combinations of existing stems+derivational suffixes (*vetralle* vs. *vetrezza*; e.g., Burani et al. 1997). Even when a difference in response times does not emerge (e.g., Burani, Marcolini, and Stella 2002), an effect on the responses can still be observed, with items composed of morphemes accepted as "words" more often than items not including any morpheme. Recently, Crepaldi, Rastle, and Davis (2010; see also Crepaldi et al. 2013) have shown that the effect is not only determined by the lexical status of the constituent morphemes, but also by their position. That is, a suffix is expected to be found at the end of a word, hence *shootment* is slower to be rejected than *shootmant*, whereas no difference is observed between *mentshoot* and *mantshoot*. The evidence provided by this "morpheme interference" paradigm has reliably shown that a string having an acceptable morphological structure is taken as a possible word more than a string lacking this property. Readers are particularly sensitive to this structure, and find it harder to consider corresponding items as non-existing. It is worth noting that the "morpheme interference" effect applies also to languages with a non-concatenated morphological structure such as Hebrew, in which root letters are interleaved with pattern letters. For Hebrew morphologically complex non-words, the magnitude of the costs due to root extraction (on both response latencies and accuracy) was found to be much stronger than in English (Yablonski and Ben-Shachar 2016), suggesting that the morphemic interference effect might be correlated to the richness in morphology of a given language more than to the linearity of its structure. Implicitly, all these results provide strong support to the hypothesis that morphemes play a role in written word processing. Certainly, how this role is expressed is not necessarily straightforward – most studies tend to adopt a lexical interpretation, in which the activation of morpheme representations associated with items like *shootment* makes it more difficult to reject them in a lexical decision task. However, also a semantic interpretation is possible: since legal morpheme combinations are potentially *novel* words (e.g., Marelli and Baroni 2015), participants may take more time rejecting them because they cannot help but computing the corresponding novel meanings. Indeed, we may find it difficult to consider *windowless* a non-word, even if we have never heard it before, because the associated meaning is so easy to compute that seems familiar to us. Consistently with this view, Burani et al. (1999) showed that lexical decision to pseudo-words made up of a root and a derivational suffix is affected by the semantic interpretability of the root-suffix combination (although not by its grammatical appropriateness): non-existent root-suffix combinations took longer to be rejected and resulted in more false alarms when they had been rated as highly interpretable than when they had a lower interpretability. It must be noted that computation of meaning was found to be task-dependent: in the same study, the degree of interpretability of new root-suffix combinations did not affect naming performance. However, and irrespective of differences in interpretability, pseudo-words made up of two morphemes were named faster and more accurately than pseudo-words with no morphological constituency (see also Burani, Marcolini, and Stella 2002). The high sensitivity to semantic variables of lexical decision and the insensitivity to semantics of word naming was confirmed by Baayen, Wurm, and Aycock (2007) for morphologically complex words. The latter two studies, while showing the centrality of the semantic component in the licensing process involved in lexical decision on complex stimuli, also indicate the dissociability of meaning from the activation of morphological structure in word naming, thus suggesting the possibility of morpho-lexical non-semantic word naming. Whatever the interpretation (purely lexical or semantics-oriented), the results obtained from both lexical decision and naming show the importance of morphology in visual word recognition.

Further evidence for the crucial role of morphemes has been provided by lexical decision experiments which adopted the priming technique. In this paradigm, typically, a *prime* word (e.g., *cat*) is presented before the key, *target* item (e.g., *dog*), on which a response is requested to the participants. If participants are faster at answering in the above setting as opposed to a corresponding, control condition (e.g., *dog* preceded by the prime *sad*), it will follow that the association between *dog* and *cat* is somehow relevant at cognitive level. This very paradigm has been applied to the morphological domain by introducing complex words (as targets or, more often, primes) in place of the monomorphemic examples above, with a priming effect reliably emerging in this condition too (pairs like *follower-follow* elicit faster response times than paired control conditions). The phenomenon is present both in cross-modal (auditory prime and visual target) contiguous priming (e.g., Marslen-Wilson et al. 1994) and in intra-modal contiguous and long-term visual priming (e.g., Drews and Zwitzerlood 1995; Feldman and Soltano 1999; Rueckl and Aicher 2008). However, in all these variants of the paradigm, morphological priming is most evident for semantically transparent primes (e.g., *punishment-punish*), and it is usually not observed when semantically opaque primes (e.g., *department-depart*) are considered. In other words, when the association between the complex prime and its stem target is not also sustained by semantic similarity, morphological priming effects do not typically emerge (see, however, the next section for a more thorough discussion of the issue). Nevertheless, the effect cannot be discarded as a simple by-product of semantic similarity: as Feldman (2000) demonstrated, morphological priming effects are significantly larger (and more long-lasting) than the sum of effects observed in purely semantic (*pledge-vow*) and orthographic (*vowel-vow*) conditions (see also Drews and Zwitzerlood 1995). This supports the hypothesis that morphological relatedness is distinct from the composite effects of semantic and orthographic similarity, further sustaining the idea of representational units for morphemes in the mental lexicon.

Often in conjunction with a priming paradigm, the transposed letter effect (Forster et al. 1987) has been also applied to the study of morphology. This effect is observed when imprecisions in the position of word letters are tolerated so that a non-word is identified as its lexical counterpart (*jugde* read as *judge*). Christianson, Johnson, and Rayner (2005) showed that primes containing letter transpositions within morphemes (e.g., *baoster-boaster*) facilitate word naming as much as correctly spelled primes, whereas the same advantage is not found for primes having letter transpositions across morpheme boundaries (e.g., *boasetr-boaster*). This pattern of results was also found in Basque and Spanish using a lexical decision task (Duñabeitia, Perea, and

Carreiras 2007). Again, these pieces of evidence support the morpheme-as-unit position: jumbling letters is not particularly disruptive when morpheme boundaries are respected, suggesting that word access proceeds on the basis of its constituent morphemes.

Finally, lexical processing is influenced by the *frequency* of the word morphemes. Lexical frequency is a measure of how often a given lexical unit appears in a language vocabulary and it is simply estimated by counting word occurrences in a large collection of texts. The frequency effect is one of the oldest and most studied effects in psycholinguistics: the higher the frequency of a word, the faster a reader will process it (in terms of, e.g., response times or eye-fixation durations; Solomon and Howes 1951). It is usually considered diagnostic of word representation: if a frequency effect can be observed for a given lexical category, the member of that category should be represented in the cognitive system (and accessed during language processing). Indeed, over and above the effect of word frequency, an effect of morpheme frequency is also observed in many languages (e.g., English: Taft 1979, Hay 2001; Dutch: Baayen, Dijkstra, and Schreuder 1997; Italian: Burani and Caramazza 1987; Burani, Salmaso, and Caramazza 1984), suggesting that morpheme representations are routinely accessed when reading a morphologically complex word. However, a reader is not only influenced by the frequency of morphemes, but also by the frequency of the complex word as a whole, indicating that the representation of the complex form is retrieved as well (and leading to the development of the dual-route models described above). The specific interplay between the involved representations is still not clear at the moment, and there is evidence indicating that the scenario is probably more complex than the one described in dual-route systems. For example, Baayen, Dijkstra, and Schreuder (2007) showed that lexical decision latencies are characterized by an interaction between stem and derived-word frequencies, with inhibitory stem effects for high-frequency words and facilitatory stem effects for low-frequency words. Burani and Thornton (2003) found an interaction between stem and suffix frequency effects, with the former crucially determining the emergence of the latter. Conversely, Ford, Davis, and Marslen-Wilson (2010) showed that stem frequency facilitated responses but only to productively suffixed derived words.

In conclusion, even if some results are not completely straightforward, and possibly more complex scenarios are suggested, the evidence reviewed indicates that morphological information plays a role in word processing. The dominant view on how these morphological effects are expressed at the cognitive level has been connoted in representational terms: explicit, symbolic units for morphemes are stored in the mental lexicon, and are activated during the processing of a complex word.

3 Morpheme representations: From IF to HOW

Having established the importance of morphological information in word reading, more recent psycholinguistic literature has investigated how this information unfolds when a complex word is processed. In this perspective, the morphological-processing literature has progressively moved its focus from the question "Are morphemes represented in the mental lexicon?" to the question "How and when are morpheme representations accessed in word processing?", generating one of the most heated debate in the field, that has dominated the literature during the last ten years.

3.1 The early processing of morphemes

The main controversy concerned how early morpheme representations come into play during word reading, and in particular whether morphemes are accessed before or after lexical access. Initially, the literature has seen two opposing approaches, usually labelled as *sub-lexical* and *supra-lexical* (or morpheme-based vs. lexeme-based, Aronoff 1994). The former position (Rastle, Davis, and New 2004; Taft 2004) ideally follows from the traditional full-parsing models (Taft and Forster 1975), positing that complex words are automatically parsed and the resulting morpheme representations lead to lexical access (either through recombination or via spreading activation). The latter perspective (e.g., Giraudo and Grainger 2000) sees morphological access as a consequence of word activation, and dependent on an abstract representation level at which *lexemes* are organized in morphological families. Within a hybrid account (Diependaele, Sandra, and Grainger 2009), the parallel access to whole-word representations and morpho-orthographic units should maximize the probability of successful word recognition, at least for morphologically simple languages such as English (Beyersmann, Coltheart, and Castles 2012).

The focus on early processing is still evident in the present literature – the review by Amenta and Crepaldi (2012) on morphological processing discussed early effects as crucial for model adjudication – and has led to new trends in the adopted methodology. Given the central role of *timing* in current research on morphology, techniques that have good temporal resolutions have become progressively more important. Results from eye-tracking studies have been used to investigate what happens when a word is fixated for the first time – namely, during the first 150–250 ms of processing (e.g., Kuperman, Bertram, and Baayen 2010). Event-Related Potentials (ERP) permit to capture how brain activation (in terms of electric signal on the scalp) unfolds when reading a complex word, and are now quite widespread in the investigation of morphological processing (e.g., Lavric, Clapp, and Rastle 2007; Morris, Grainger, and Holcomb 2008). However, probably the most popular technique used to address the "early processing" issue has been the *masked priming* paradigm (Forster and Davis 1984).

This technique is very similar to the traditional priming approaches, with the crucial difference being how the prime stimulus is treated. In masked priming, the prime is presented very briefly (usually less than 50ms) and squeezed between a forward mask (e.g., a string of hash marks) and the target item itself. Under these conditions, the prime is virtually invisible, ensuring that the resulting priming effect will not be influenced by the conscious appreciation of the prime-target relation. Over and above this desirable aspect, masked priming is usually taken as a way to isolate early cognitive processes. The assumption is that the masking condition limits the processing of the prime, so that any observable effect on the target would depend on information that is extracted from the prime during its very short presentation; as a consequence if, for example, a morphological priming is observed under these conditions, it will follow that morphemes are accessed during the first 50ms of processing. Although this interpretation is not granted, and different positions concerning the paradigm exist (see, e.g., Tzur and Frost 2007, for a perceptual explanation, or Norris and Kinoshita 2008, for a task-dependent theory), it is the most common one in morphological processing literature. In these terms, the very evidence from masked priming strongly supports sub-lexical models of word access, with morphological effects clearly emerging from the paradigm: prime-target pairs in which the prime is a complex word (e.g., *killer-kill*) elicit larger priming effects than orthographic control pairs, that are similar in form but not morphologically related (e.g., *scandal-scan*). This was taken as evidence that words are automatically parsed into their morphemes early, which are in turn activated before word access (Rastle et al. 2000).

Interestingly, masked priming effects interpretable as morphological parsing can be observed for both semantically transparent derived words (e.g., *killer*) and opaque words whose morphological complexity is only apparent (e.g., *corner*).[1] That is, larger priming effects are found for both *killer-kill* and

---

[1] Most often, the word recognition literature does not distinguish between genuine morphologically complex words whose meaning cannot be fully derived compositionally (semantically opaque words like *courteous*) and words that are apparently complex because of a sheer orthographic chance (pseudo-complex words like *corner*). In fact, empirical evaluations found no difference in behavioral responses between either case, at least when masked priming is applied (e.g., Longtin, Segui, and Halle 2003). Following this tradition, in the present chapter

corner-corn pairs, as opposed to *scandal-scan*, even if there is no real relation (semantic or morphological) between *corner* and *corn*. The reliability of these results, replicated in masked priming studies in a number of languages (e.g., French: Longtin, Segui, and Halle 2003; English: Rastle, Davis, and New 2004; Russian: Kazanina et al. 2008; Italian: Marelli et al. 2013), led to the hypothesis that early morphological parsing proceeds in a semantically blind, form-based fashion. In other words, early parsing is *morpho-orthographic*: words that are, form-wise, morphologically complex will be automatically parsed into their constituent morphemes irrespective of any high-level consideration about their meanings. Indeed, this procedure will not even be influenced by the lexicality of the complex form: priming effects are found also when using novel derived words as primes (e.g., *quickify*; Meunier and Longtin 2007).

3.2 Semantic modulation of morpheme access

However, positing that there is no role for semantics in early word *decomposition* does not necessarily mean excluding semantic influence completely. In fact, how meaning can modulate morphological effects at early levels remains the center of a heated debate (Rastle and Davis 2008). On the one hand, *form-then-meaning* accounts (Rastle, Davis, and New 2004) assume very early morpho-orthographic parsing, with semantics entering in the picture only at later stages (where, indeed, no priming effect can be found for semantically opaque pairs; Rueckl and Aicher 2008). On the other hand, *form-with-meaning* accounts (Feldman, O'Connor, and Moscoso del Prado Martín 2009) point to an early involvement of word and morpheme meanings, with semantics influencing the ease of morpheme processing. Divergent predictions concerning priming patterns are quite straightforward: whereas the latter explanation implies a significant difference in masked-priming effects for transparent as opposed to semantically opaque item pairs (that is, larger priming effects for *killer-kill* than *corner-corn*), the former does not predict such a difference. The debate is far from being settled, also considering that it is difficult to empirically sustain a null effect. And if many studies have failed in finding such semantic effect (e.g., Beyersmann et al. 2015b; Kazanina et al. 2008; Longtin, Segui, and Halle 2003; Rastle, Davis, and New 2004), there are also a number of experiments in which the semantic effect significantly emerges (e.g., Feldman et al. 2012; Feldman, O'Connor, and Moscoso

---

we will use the terms "opaque" and "opaqueness" to define both cases like *courteous* and cases like *corner*.

del Prado Martín 2009; Järvikivi and Pyykkönen 2011; Kazanina 2011; Marelli et al. 2013). Certainly, even when statistically significant, the semantic effect seems to be small.

Recent evidence suggests that both explanations may be founded on simplistic assumptions, as early morpho-semantic effects are more complex than expected. Marelli et al. (2013), for example, have shown that evidence of morpho-orthographic decomposition is crucially dependent on the lexical-decision paradigm. In fact, if, in place of performing a lexical decision on a primed target, participants are asked questions concerning the semantic category of the target (e.g., "does the word denote an animal?"), eye fixation times reveal priming effect in the transparent condition only (i.e., significant facilitation for *killer-kill* but not for either *corner-corn* or *scandal-scan*). Said facilitation is already evident on first-fixation durations on the word, indicating that the semantic contribution emerges early during processing. Such task-dependent effects are problematic for accounts based on *obligatory* morphological decomposition. Moreover, Tsang and Chen (2014), in experiments on Chinese, have found significant priming effects for pairs like *butterfly-milk* in masked conditions. That is, even if there is automatic morpheme-access in semantically opaque compounds, the semantic features of the morphemes are nevertheless activated (see also Tsang and Chen 2013). In other words, the segmentation process may be semantically-blind, but the morpheme activation is semantically connoted. Further evidence in this regard has been provided by Amenta, Marelli, and Crepaldi (2015) in Italian, in natural language-processing situations: the very same semantically opaque words (e.g., *gallone* – 'gallon', lit. *big-rooster*) are characterized by inhibitory stem-frequency effects on reading times when presented in sentences prompting their opaque meaning (*gallone* as *gallon*), as opposed to facilitatory stem-frequency effects when embedded in sentences prompting the potential transparent meaning (*gallone* as *big rooster*). A corresponding example in English would be *summer,* which primarily denotes a season but, in the right context, can indicate *someone who sums* ("I am not good at math, but I am a good summer"). In this perspective, morphologically complex words are parsed irrespective of their semantic transparency, but morpheme meanings are accessed straight away, even if their semantic contribution is not helpful for computing the complex word meaning (as it happens to be the case for semantically opaque words; see also Marelli and Luzzatti, 2012).

According to the model by Marelli and Baroni (2015), a compositional perspective would be crucial to understand these pieces of evidence and, more in general, the role of meaning in morphological processing. In this perspective, a priming effect would emerge also for semantically opaque words at early processing stages not because semantics is not important, but because an erroneous, "transparent", alternative meaning is automatically computed. That is, masked priming would limit information uptake so that no explicit lexical knowledge about the whole-word meaning could be accessed; as a consequence, morphemes would be automatically combined in a productive, synchronic fashion, generating a whole-word meaning that will be semantically related to its stem even for semantically opaque words (e.g., *summer* as *someone who sums*, *irony* as *made of iron*, etc.). In other words, Marelli and Baroni (2015) moved the research focus from the "form vs. meaning" debate to the understanding of which type of semantics influences morphological effects at different processing levels. Hopefully, this change in perspective may help solving the deadlock that seemingly has characterized recent literature on early morphological effects.

4 The contribution of cognitive neuropsychology

Cognitive neuropsychology is the study of the mechanisms of the mind through the assessment of brain-damaged individuals. By examining the behavior of such individuals, in principle, it is possible to establish relations between cognitive functions and brain structure, as well as to individuate specific cognitive *module*s (as in the Fodor's definition; Fodor 1983). For example, if a certain patient exhibits the behavior A and not the behavior B, and in a different patient the behavior B is spared whereas the behavior A is impaired, this *double dissociation* will indicate that the two behaviors are the expressions of specific and separate mind components. Not surprisingly, methods from cognitive neuropsychology have been also applied to the investigation of morphological processing, with the aims of isolating the processing of morphologically complex words, or finding evidence for the representations of morphemes in the mental lexicon.

Most results in favor of a morphological level of analysis in the language system come from the assessment of people with acquired reading disorders. Following a brain injury, patients can manifest an impairment when processing written materials, a problem that is evident in their language productions. For example, a patient could read the word *thing* as *think* (*visual error*), the word *bottle* as *cup* (*semantic error*), or the word *speak* as *speaker* (*morphological error*). This error pattern (along with the inability of reading unfamiliar and novel words) is the typical manifestation of *deep dyslexia* (Coltheart, Patterson, and Marshall 1980). The morphological manifestation of the disorder has been considered indicative of a representation level that is specific to lexical morphology (Patterson 1980; Job and Sartori 1984). In morphological errors, morphemes (stems or affixes) can be deleted (*speaker* read as *speak*), inserted (*speak* read as *speaker*), or substituted (*speaker* read as *speaking*). This phenomenon has been taken as evidence of word processing being morpheme-based: morphemes are the building blocks of word processing, and are hence the most affected by the lexical impairment characterizing deep dyslexia. Although these errors may be at times difficult to distinguish from visual and semantic ones (since morphological relatives are also visually and semantically related, Badecker and Caramazza 1987; Funnell 1987), more recent evidence indicates that morphological manifestations in neuropsychological patients cannot be reduced to a by-product of either semantic or orthographic similarity. For example, in the production of DE, the patient described by Rastle, Tyler, and Marslen-Wilson (2006), morphological errors were more often observed in actual derived words (*killer*) as opposed to pseudo-suffixed (*irony*) or non-complex words with embedded lexical strings (*cornea*), thus ruling out an explanation in terms of visual errors. Also, a semantic explanation is very unlikely – errors were mostly novel words generated by the substitution of the affix, whereas semantic errors can occur only between words with a proper semantic representation (see also Castles et al. 1996; Marelli et al. 2011). Moreover, Badecker (1997) has described the case of a patient, FM, committing morphological errors also when presented with irregular verbs (*began* read as *begin*, as well as *passed* read as *pass*). This evidence suggests that morphological representations would be situated (also) at the morpho-syntactic level, representing functional relations between lexical elements irrespective of their morphological parsability.

Further research has provided a better understanding of the role of lexical frequency in morphological processing, and how patients' performance can be modulated by the frequency of the complex word and its constituent morphemes. For example, Luzzatti, Mondini, and Semenza (2001) showed that the patient MB was better at reading singular forms as opposed to plural forms, but the effect disappeared when considering plural-dominant words (i.e., words whose plural form is more frequent than its singular one: *stars*, *eyes*, etc.). That is, the patient's errors affected more less-marked forms (in line with Badecker 1997), but his performance was also modulated by the frequency of the specific inflectional alternatives considered. The authors considered this evidence as supporting dual-route models of word processing (Schreuder and Baayen 1995), in which representations of complex words can also be accessed directly, in a whole-word manner, especially in case of very familiar (i.e., very frequent) forms. MB's impairment affected the morpheme-based route more seriously, leaving the whole-word procedure relatively spared (see also Biedermann et al. 2012). Further evidence in these regards emerges from the study of neglect dyslexia, a peripheral reading disorder specifically affecting the leftmost part of the presented materials: patients suffering from neglect dyslexia may read *wedding* as *ding*. Neglect dyslexia was employed as experimental model to study the processing of stems in suffixed words. Arduino, Burani, and Vallar (2002) found that patients affected by neglect dyslexia are better at reading derived words with high-frequency stems than derived words with low-frequency stems. This was taken as an indication that morpheme plays a role in word reading, with more familiar morphemes being more salient, and hence more capable to pierce through the patients' disorder and activate the corresponding representations. Moreover, a better performance was observed for existing derived words, as opposed to novel derived words, thus speaking for the parallel role of whole-word representations.

In conclusion, neuropsychological studies closely follow the psycholinguistic tradition in supporting the hypothesis that morphemes are represented in the mental lexicon, and play an important role in word processing (e.g., Job and Sartori 1984). In line with results on unimpaired participants, these studies do not exclude a parallel role of a whole-word procedure, mostly determined by the familiarity of the complex form (e.g., Luzzatti, Mondini, and Semenza 2001). The neuropsychological tradition has also highlighted an aspect that was mostly overlooked by the previously discussed studies, namely, the importance of a morphosyntactic level of analysis. Results as the ones reported by Badecker (1997) indicate that morphemes are also linked at more abstracts level of representations, where paradigmatic relations are prominent (see also Marelli et al., 2012).

5 Outside the morphological-representation comfort zone

The literature reviewed so far is mostly in line with a morphemes-as-units view on the role of morphology in word processing. This is the case at both the level of empirical evidence, and the level of theoretical assumptions. On the one hand, results of experiments are quite consistent with the idea that morphemes play an important role in word reading. On the other hand, this very premise has been taken as a central assumption of most cognitive models, and was conveniently adopted as a working hypothesis when running empirical research. As a consequence, one may claim that psycholinguistic studies have found evidence for morphological units because they were designed to look for that evidence. Indeed, studies that have attempted to move outside the "comfort zone" of the morpheme-representation assumption, have provided results pointing to more complex scenarios.

5.1 Unexpected results in masked priming

We have already discussed results that do not conveniently fit the dominant assumption of morphemes as form representations, devoid of meaning and function, that serve as intermediate step to whole-word lexical and/or semantic representations. The studies by Marelli et al. (2013), Tsang and Chen (2014), and Amenta, Marelli, and Crepaldi (2015) have shown that morpheme access is not purely form-based, rather reflecting complex semantic operations. Moreover, the results by Badecker (1997) indicate that morphological information is (also) represented at a higher level, providing evidence of functional links between morphologically-related elements that are not morpheme-mediated (e.g., *bring-brought*; see also Kelliher and Henderson 1990; Smolka, Zwitserlood, and Rösler 2007, for German).

The limits of the hypothesis of a purely form-based early decomposition are also highlighted by other works employing the masked priming paradigm. Consistently with Badecker's (1997) results, Crepaldi et al. (2010) found, in a masked priming paradigm, significant priming effects for pairs including an irregular past verb and its base form (e.g., *fell-fall*), whereas the same priming effect did not emerge for orthographic control pairs (e.g., *bell-ball*). In other words, the priming effect is elicited by a paradigmatic relation and does not require a parsing procedure of the inflected form (as in the case of regular inflection: *played* as *play* plus *-ed*), and cannot be explained in terms of form similarity. This effect is difficult to account for in the framework of a simple morpho-orthographic decomposition, even if this process is restricted to early processing stages: paradigmatic relations, although not morpheme-mediated, emerge very early as an important factor in word processing. Other studies have shown that early morphological effects are not strictly dependent on the full parsability of the complex word – that is, the prime does not need to be clearly decomposable in constituent morphemes to elicit a masked priming effect. In fact, the results by McCormick, Rastle, and Davis (2008) indicate that morphological priming in masked conditions is robust to orthographic alterations frequently found in complex words (e.g., missing final *e*: *adorable-adore*; shared final *e*: *lover-love*; duplicated final consonant: *dropper-drop*). Priming effects emerge irrespective of the semantic relations between prime and target (e.g., significant priming effect for *badger-badge*; McCormick, Rastle, and Davis 2008) and the lexicality of the prime (e.g., significant priming effect for *adorly-adore*; McCormick, Rastle, and Davis 2009).

In conclusion, studies on masked priming indicate that early morphological processing is more flexible than predicted by a strict morpho-orthographic assumption, both on the syntactic (Crepaldi et al. 2010) and the orthographic side (McCormick, Rastle, and Davis 2008). Relations between different morphological forms play an early role in word access irrespective of their surface properties. It is worth noting that the effects discussed (i.e., priming irrespective of full-parsability in morphemes of the complex prime word, and irrespective of a semantic relation between prime and target) are usually not found in developing readers. The emergence of purely morphological effects devoid of orthographic and semantic similarity between prime and target is the result of literacy acquisition. These issues will be discussed in the next section.

5.2 Paradigmatic effects in morphological processing

The importance of paradigmatic aspects is also evident in the effects of morphological entropy in word reading. Literature on entropy effects has explicitly refuted the decompositional interpretation, rather redefining morphology in an information-theoretical framework (Milin et al. 2009). The basic assumption of this approach is that words are organized in paradigms, and morphology is reflected in this very organization. Entropy provides a convenient way to measure the information carried by a given paradigm, quantifying the amount of predictability of the system. The less predictable a paradigm, the more the carried information, the larger the associated entropy. Entropy increases with the number of members in the paradigm, and when the probabilities of the members are more similar (with maximal entropy in the case of uniform distributions).

Baayen, Wurm, and Aycock (2007) showed that both *inflectional entropy* (i.e., entropy computed on the set of possible inflected forms with a given stem) and *derivational entropy* (i.e., entropy computed on the set of possible derived forms with a given stem) have facilitatory effects in lexical decision: the more informative the associated paradigm, the faster the responses to the target word. Milin, Filipović Đurđević, and Moscoso Del Prado Martín (2009) employed entropy measures for describing paradigmatic effects in the context of complex paradigm classes (Serbian nominal paradigms). They computed the typical probability distribution of the frequency of use among the forms of an inflectional class (e.g., for feminine nouns belonging to the 3rd class, the -*e* form is associated to a probability of about .40) and the distribution of the inflectional paradigm of a specific stem (e.g., the -*e* form of the stem *knjiga*, 'book', is associated to a probability of about .40, whereas the -*e* form of the stem *pučina*, 'open sea', is associated to a probability of about .20). Once these two probability distributions are obtained, the *relative entropy* of a stem simply captures the degree of divergence between them. And response times were shown to be positively associated with the new measure: the larger the relative entropy (i.e., the more deviant the paradigm of a given noun), the longer the response times. Baayen et al. (2011) further showed that relative entropy modulates priming effects in masked conditions. Finally, also aphasic patients were shown to be sensitive to morphological entropy (Van Ewijk and Avrutin 2011; Marelli et al. 2012b; note however that patients were not tested on word reading in these studies). Altogether, results on the effects of entropy measures propose a different view of the morphological effects on word reading, namely one that focuses more on the idea of paradigms than that of morpheme units. Approaches positing morphemes to be represented as independent representation entries have clearly a hard time explaining paradigmatic effects.

Conceptually related to these paradigm effects, family size also constitutes an important predictor of the processing of written words. Family size is defined as the type count of the morphological relatives of a given word. For example, the family size of *run* is the number of complex words including *run* as constituent morpheme (e.g., *runner, running, homerun, runaway*, etc.). Family size is a reliable predictor of response times in word reading: the larger the family size, the faster the processing. Effects of family size are observed for both simple (Schreuder and Baayen 1997) and complex words (Bertram, Baayen, and Schreuder 2000). However, family size is believed not to be strictly morphologically-connoted, rather capturing semantic and syntactic aspects of the considered word. In fact, it provides better predictions in terms of response times if semantically opaque forms are excluded from the count (Bertram, Baayen, and Schreuder 2000; Moscoso del Prado Martín et al. 2004). Conversely, irregular relatives must be included, irrespective of the lack of morpheme-based association with the target word (De Jong, Schreuder, and Baayen 2000). Moreover, and most surprisingly, family size is predictive of monolinguals' lexical decision latencies across unrelated languages (Moscoso Del Prado Martín et al. 2005), indicating that family size is not simply associated to morphological forms, rather capturing cross-language similarities in semantic space. Although alternative explanations for these effects are possible (e.g., De Jong, Schreuder, and Baayen 2003; Grainger and Jacobs 1996), it seems that also family size is best characterized in an information-theory framework (Moscoso del Prado Martín, Kostić, and Baayen 2004), in line with the paradigmatic effect described above.

5.3 The impact of non-morphological form-meaning associations

The interpretation of morphemes as fundamental units between form and meaning is also jeopardized by the impact of non-morphological form-meaning relations to word reading. Let's consider *phonaesthemes*. These are phonological/

orthographic chunks that reliably connote aspects of the correspondent word meanings, without being characterized in morphological terms. For example, most English words beginning with *sn-* have meanings related to nose and mouth (*snore, snack, sniff, snarl, sneeze, snort*) and most words beginning with *gl-* have meanings related to light and vision (*glimmer, glisten, glitter, gleam, glow, glint*), even if none of these words is morphologically complex (i.e., it cannot be parsed in morpheme constituents). Crucially, these form-meaning associations have an effect on word reading (Bergen 2004): prime-target pairs having a phonaestheme in common (e.g., *snort-sniff*) elicit larger priming effects than semantic (e.g., *cord-rope*) and orthographic (e.g., *flour-flag*) control pairs. Not only, priming effects for phonaestheme pairs are also larger than priming effects for word pairs with overlapping forms *and* meanings, if this association is not frequently observed throughout the whole lexicon (e.g., *skipper-skiff*). That is, phonaesthemes seem to play a role in word processing that goes beyond both morphology and simple form-meaning associations, speaking for the importance of distributional aspects in these effects: orthographic-semantic patterns have to be reliably present in language usage in order to play a role in language processing.

In line with this interpretation, Marelli, Amenta, and Crepaldi (2015) have shown that lexical recognition is influenced by the orthography-semantics consistency (OSC) of the considered word. The study was inspired by a curious side effect in morphological priming experiments: stems from transparent sets elicit faster responses than stems from opaque sets, irrespective of the prime preceding them, and even if the item sets are carefully matched for a number of variables. This effect is explained in terms of OSC: stems from transparent sets (e.g., *widow*) are orthographic strings that only appear in words that are related to the correspondent meaning (e.g., *widower, widowed, widowhood*), whereas stems from opaque sets (e.g., *whisk*) are orthographic strings appearing also in words unrelated to the correspondent meaning (e.g., *whisker, whiskey, whisky*). In this perspective, the former words are, throughout the whole lexicon, reliable orthographic cues for their own meanings, whereas the latter provide unreliable information in these regards. In other words, the former are better *symbols* than the latter. OSC, computed as the frequency-weighted average semantic-similarity between a word and its orthographic relatives, provides an efficient estimate of this reliability-as-symbol, and represents a new example as to how distributionally based form-meaning associations, over and above morphological considerations, are central to word reading. Given these pieces of evidence, it is sensible to ask ourselves whether morphological effects really need dedicated modules/representations to be explained, or may be rather accounted for by more general-purpose mechanisms that capture statistically strong form-meaning patterns.

In the present section, we have presented a series of phenomena that deviate from those expected by approaches taking morphemes as fundamental processing units in word reading. This is not to say that said approaches are necessarily unable to explain the described effects. Rather, predictions in these regards do not emerge naturally in these frameworks, and corresponding models must be adjusted with *ad-hoc* solutions (e.g., dedicated modules, additional processing steps). Conversely, architectures in which said effects automatically follow from their basic assumptions will provide more general and epistemologically valid interpretative frameworks for the complex pattern of results we presented.

6 The emergence of morphology in reading acquisition

In the present section, we will discuss evidence for the role of morphology in reading acquisition. Also in this domain the dominant view of morphemes as crucial processing units seems to fit uncomfortably with many of the obtained results, which rather depict morphology as a by-product system emerging from language learning.

The relation between orthographic patterns and morphemic units seems to be grasped by children before formal teaching is provided to them. Byrne (1996), in research on the hypotheses developed by pre-literate children on the relationship between print and spoken language, noted that pre-literate children tend to grasp the grapheme-to-morpheme transcription (e.g., the plural /s/ in *cats*) more easily than the grapheme-to-phoneme correspondence (e.g., the phonemic /s/ in *bus*). These data show that children are able to map the English orthography onto the morphemes learnt during language acquisition. Children often encounter new complex words as far as they proceed through school grades, and the opportunity of recognizing known morphemes embedded in strings of letters can help them to read and understand the meaning of the derived or compound words they come across (Bertram, Laine, and Virkkala 2000).

6.1 Morphological awareness and literacy acquisition

Morphological awareness can be defined as the awareness of the morphemic structure of words in oral language, and the ability to reflect on and manipulate that structure (see Carlisle 1995; Deacon, Tong, and Mimeau 2019). It is typically described as a late emerging ability closely connected to orthographic skills (Ehri 2005), and it plays an important role not only in decoding skills, but also in text comprehension.

The role of morphemic structure in reading acquisition has been shown by Mann and Singson (2003). These authors found that in early school grades, phonological awareness failed to reach significance level in predicting reading skills beyond third grade, whereas morphological awareness increased its role from fourth grade (when also the number of new complex words in the texts increases). In particular, children decoded derived words with a low frequency stem less correctly than derived words with a high frequency stem, and this data suggests that children refer to stems, at least by the third grade. It is also worth noting that about 20% of the errors made by children consisted in attaching the correct suffix to a wrong stem (e.g., *careful* was read as **creeful*), while errors involving the suffix were made less frequently (about 4% of errors were of the kind *methodical* read as *method*; 5% of errors were like *imaginable* read as *imagination*). This pattern of errors suggests that the suffix is "the best (and perhaps the only) place to look for hints as to how to decode the word" (Mann and Singson 2003: 19), when a new complex word has to be read. Evidence for the role of morphological structure in word naming comes also from Carlisle and Stones (2005), who found that both lower elementary readers (second and third grade) and upper elementary students (fifth and sixth grade) were more accurate in reading derived words with transparent structure than simple words, matched by length and frequency. However, only younger readers, in front of a derived word, were faster too.

The ability to parse words into morphemes has been studied in relation to morphological awareness also by Deacon, Kieffer, and Laroche (2014). In a longitudinal study through third to fourth grades, they found both a direct effect of morphological awareness on reading comprehension and an indirect effect via word reading skills. These data are consistent with other studies on the early years of primary school (Jarmulowics et al. 2008), but are different from the results of studies carried out with children in the sixth grade, where only a direct effect of morphological awareness on reading comprehension has been found (Kieffer and Lesaux 2012), irrespective of decoding skills. This pattern of results suggests a developmental shift, from early literacy to a mastery phase: at the beginning, morphological awareness has an important role in gaining accuracy and fluency in decoding and, as a consequence, in driving reading comprehension. In skilled readers morphological awareness can help in connecting different parts of the text and in making inferences, but does not influence accuracy and fluency of decoding anymore. In children with dyslexia, there is evidence that morphological and semantic processing might offer compensation mechanisms of phonological deficits (Elbrö and Arnbak 1996; Casalis, Colé, and Sopo 2004; Catts, Adlof, and Ellis Weismer 2006). However, further research is required to better explain the reliability and the direction of the effects involving morphological awareness, comprehension and decoding skills. In fact, there is also evidence for a reciprocal influence of reading comprehension and morphological awareness: third and fourth grade children with good skills in text comprehension might apply the understanding of the meaning to detect morphemic parts of novel words (Deacon, Kieffer, and Laroche 2014).

6.2 Morphological effects in different languages

The attitude of children to use morphemic units in processing complex words has been observed in English (e.g., Deacon, Whalen, and Kirby 2011), and in several other languages (see, e.g., Verhoeven and Perfetti 2011). Overall, the opportunity of recognizing morphemic units increases accuracy and/or reduces latency in reading. However, Casalis, Quémart and Duncan (2015), through a direct comparison of English and French, proposed that morphological effects may vary according to the consistency of grapheme-to-phoneme correspondence and morphological richness of the language. These authors found that, in a lexical-decision task, the recognition of a stem within a complex word led French fourth-grade children to faster responses in comparison to simple words. However, the presence of a stem in the complex word tended to inhibit whole-word recognition in English speaking children matched by grade with their French peers, a finding easily interpretable as the result of lexical competition. In English morphologically complex words, the stem corresponds to the base word (e.g., *farm-er*), which might cause lexical interference rather than a facilitation effect. However, in both languages, children were slower and less accurate in rejecting pseudo-words in which there was a stem and/or a suffix, thus replicating for opaque orthographies the morpheme interference effect obtained on the lexical-decision accuracy of third and fifth grade Italian children (Burani, Marcolini, and Stella 2002), similarly to adults of different languages.

Interestingly, when naming was used as an experimental paradigm in transparent orthographies, the morphemic effect resulted in a strong facilitation, not inhibition, of response to pseudo-words containing real morphemes. Italian children of different ages have been repeatedly shown to gain advantage in both latency and accuracy from the presence of a stem when naming pseudo-words (Burani et al. 2008; Burani, Marcolini, and Stella 2002; Traficante et al. 2011), irrespective of its being combined with either a suffix or a non-suffix (e.g., *bagn-ezza*, '*bath-ness'; *bagn-ezzo, '*bath-noss'; Traficante et al. 2011). However, the presence of a suffix (e.g., *bagn-ezza, '*bath-ness'; *bogn-ezza, '*bith-ness') had a positive effect on accuracy, as compared to matched pseudo-words that did not include any morpheme (e.g., *bogn-ezzo, '*bith-noss'; Traficante et al. 2011). Even more interestingly, the morphological benefit on reading performance was found to be particularly strong in children with dyslexia (Burani et al. 2008; Traficante et al. 2011). The advantage due to stem-suffix composition in word naming has been reported also for low-frequency words: these were read faster and more accurately than simple words matched by frequency (Marcolini et al. 2011; see also Deacon and Whalen 2011). However, it is worth noting that children with dyslexia showed such an advantage also for high frequency words (Marcolini et al. 2011). This evidence suggests that the use of reading units (morphemes), larger than the single grapheme but shorter than the word, can be particularly useful for children who are struggling in processing the word as a whole-unit (De Luca et al. 2010), irrespective of word frequency. Similar results were found by Suárez-Coalla and Cuetos (2013) for Spanish children with dyslexia, who showed shorter latencies in reading both words and pseudo-words composed of morphemes than simple stimuli.

All these cross-linguistic data suggest that, during literacy acquisition, children learn to detect and exploit frequent and stable chunks of letters corresponding to morphemes, shared by several words. In this way they optimize fluency and accuracy in decoding new and unfamiliar words, but the gain they get from morphemic structure may vary according to the characteristics of their language, the frequency of morphologically complex stimuli, and their reading ability (for reviews, see Burani 2010; Deacon, Tong, and Mimeau 2019). The orthographies of languages like Italian, Spanish and German present quite consistent grapheme-to-phoneme correspondences, that allow children to reach a good level of accuracy using small grain-size units in decoding new words (as suggested by the *grain-size theory* by Ziegler and Goswami 2005). However, the opportunity of detecting morphemic units (stems and affixes) that are larger than single graphemes, can allow them avoiding the time-consuming grapheme-to-phoneme reading procedure, gaining in fluency, and this morpheme-based reading behavior is particularly useful for children with dyslexia (Burani et al. 2008; Marcolini et al. 2011; Suárez-Coalla and Cuetos 2013; Traficante 2012). Moreover, readers of morphologically rich languages are used to encounter long complex words, whose stem can be combined with several different affixes (both inflectional and derivational), and the higher the number of words that share the same stem is, the higher the probability for that stem to become a useful chunk for decoding (Traficante and Burani 2003; Traficante et al. 2014). Thus, for children exposed to a language with rich morphology the presence of a stem may improve both fluency and accuracy in word recognition and naming.

In English, the opacity of the orthography does not allow the reader to rely on small grain-size units, thus children must memorize the association between whole-word orthographic and phonological representations as soon as possible to reach a good level of accuracy. It is worth noting that most English words are simple and quite short (mono- or disyllabic), the affixes have a key-role in stress assignment and are recognized as useful chunks early in learning to read (Mann and Singson 2003); finally, in the case of semantically transparent derived words, the stem corresponds to the base word. For all these reasons, in processing a long complex word, a good strategy for English-speaking children should be to strip affixes away to isolate the stem. In this way the probability of a correct pronunciation, if the stem is a known word, increases in comparison to the strategy of reading through smaller units.

6.3 What drives morphemic parsing in young readers?

A final issue is when, during development, morphological relationships are established in the mental lexicon as autonomous from orthographic and semantic similarity. In the preceding sections, we have presented evidence for morphological priming effects on adult word recognition irrespective of full parsability in morphemes of the complex prime word, and irrespective of a semantic relation between prime and target. As anticipated, such effects are usually not found in developing readers. A first set of studies showed that children do not always gain advantage of the morphemic structure of complex words, but only when they can easily detect the stem embedded in the complex word, without orthographic modifications. In Hebrew, despite its rich morphology, Schiff, Raveh, and Kahta (2008) reported that third and seventh graders, in a masked priming paradigm, showed morphological priming only when the root prime had the same three- or two- consonantal letter root representation as the target (e.g., *NGŠ* primed *mtNGŠ*, 'bump into'; *GŠ* primed *hGŠh*, 'handing over'), but not when prime and target had allomorphic root representations (*NGŠ* did not prime *hGŠh*, 'handing over'). This finding is not consistent with adults' performance (McCormick, Rastle and Davis 2008; Schiff, Raveh, and Kahta 2008; Velan et al. 2005) to conclude that in the mental lexicon of Hebrew children both types of root representations (three- and two- letters roots) are present, but the allomorphic forms are not connected yet.

These results are consistent with those of Quémart and Casalis (2014) on French, who showed that children's visual word recognition was a function of the phonological and orthographic relationships between derived words and their stems. Quèmart and Casalis (2014) submitted third, fourth and fifth grade typically developing children and adults to a lexical decision task in which a base word was preceded by a derived word prime in different conditions of orthographic-phonological prime-target relationship. At the shortest (60ms) prime duration the authors reported significant priming effects in children only when prime and target shared a morphological relationship without any form shift in the stem (as in *nuageux-NUAGE*, '*cloudy-cloud*'). With longer (250 ms) prime exposure, significant priming effects were found in all conditions of morphological relatedness, irrespective of orthographic-phonological alterations (i.e., priming effects were found also when the morphological relationship involved a phonological although not orthographic modification of the stem, as in *bergerie-BERGER*, '*sheepfold-shepherd*', and when the relationship between stem and derived word involved an alteration that was both phonological and orthographic, as in *soigneux-SOIN*, '*careful-care*'). In contrast, adults showed significant priming for all the morphological conditions at all prime exposure times. Thus allomorphic variations may prevent lexical activation of stems at the fastest word exposures in children but not in adults. According to the authors, children need more time to activate a stem in the case of a phonological or an orthographic shift because activation of the allomorphic stems is not automatized yet.

The results obtained using the priming technique find a correspondence with other results drawn from unprimed lexical decision and naming experiments. Carlisle, Stone and Katz (2001) studied two groups of English-speaking young readers, with and without reading difficulties (with ages ranging from 10.75 years to 15.75 years) and a group of adults who performed both tasks. Participants were presented with stable words (in which no phonological alteration occurred between base and derived words, as in *cultural*), shift words (in which a phonological alteration occurred, as in *majority*) and foils. Results showed an effect of phonological transparency in all groups, confirming that it takes longer to respond to complex words with a phonological alteration in the base than to complex words without a phonological alteration. Finally, Lázaro, García, and Burani (2015) submitted Spanish third and fourth graders, with and without reading deficits, to a lexical decision task. They found that, irrespective of reading ability, all children gained more advantage from stem frequency in words in which the stem had no orthographic alteration with respect to the base word (e.g., *colorista* from *color*, '*colorful*' from '*color*') than in words with modified stem (e.g., *dentista* from *diente*, '*dentist*' from '*tooth*'). All these studies, carried out in several languages with different orthographies show that, contrary to what was found by McCormick, Rastle, and Davis (2008) in adults, orthographic-phonological alterations of the stem make it more difficult for children to benefit from access to the base word in performing visual tasks on derived words.

6.4 Children's sensitivity to form-meaning association in accessing morphemic structure

As mentioned in the preceding sections, the masked priming paradigm in lexical decision has been adopted in adults to assess whether the detection of morphemic units is driven by semantic information (Longtin, Segui, and Halle 2003; Rastle, Davis, and New 2004). Recently, this paradigm has been used with children and a complex pattern of results emerged, with age of children and language features influencing the size of priming effects (Beyersmann, Castles, and Coltheart 2012; Quémart and Casalis 2015; Quémart, Casalis, and Colé 2011; Shiff, Raveh, and Fighel 2012). Beyersmann, Castles, and Coltheart (2012) presented English-speaking third and fifth graders with morphologically (e.g., *golden-GOLD*), pseudo-morphologically (e.g., *mother-MOTH*) related pairs and control condition. With 50ms prime exposure, a priming effect was found only with truly suffixed primes. These data have been interpreted as evidence that the ability of children in using the morphemic structure of complex words is based on activation of the meaning shared by different words with the same stem.

A different pattern of results came from French. Quémart Casalis, and Colé (2011) presented French third, fifth and seventh graders with a masked primed paradigm, using three different degrees of stimulus-onset-asynchrony (SOA) (60ms, 250ms, 800ms) between prime and target, to assess the relation between level of processing of the letter string and type of information used in word recognition. The true morphological relationship (e.g., *tablette-TABLE*, 'little table-table') was associated to reliable priming at any SOA, while the pseudo-derivation condition (e.g., *baguette-BAGUE*, 'French stick-ring') produced a priming similar to the morphological one at 60ms, but lower than that condition at 250ms prime exposure. With the longest SOA (800ms) the pseudo-derivation priming effect disappeared, suggesting that with long prime duration morphemic parsing is based only on the activation of semantic properties of morphemes. In order to interpret this inconsistent pattern of results with children reading different languages, the authors proposed that the richness of French morphology might lead young readers to be more competent in detecting morpho-orthographic units than their English-speaking peers.

As for the inconsistency between English-speaking children's and adults' data, a developmental trend has been hypothesized, suggesting that in early literacy levels the form-meaning relationship would be the main dimension that drives morphemic parsing, while in skilled reading the morpho-orthographic dimension would be prevalent. In other words, purely morpho-orthographic decomposition would be a late-occurring milestone in reading acquisition (Beyersmann, Castles, and Coltheart 2012). To assess the relationship between reading proficiency and morpho-orthographic decomposition ability, Beyersmann et al. (2015a) presented French primary school children through second to fifth grade with a masked primed lexical decision task, and took into account not only performance to the task, but also children's literacy skills. It was expected that effects of morpho-orthographic priming should increase with increasing reading proficiency, as suggested by the difference between English speaking children and adults. To avoid any idiosyncratic relationship between stem and suffix in the pseudo-derived condition (see criticisms made by Baayen et al. 2011 to the results by Rastle, Davis, and New 2004), the experimental primes other than in true morphological relation (e.g., *tristesse-TRISTE*, 'sadness-sad'), were all pseudowords, with different relations with targets. There were a suffixed non-word prime condition (e.g., **tristerie-TRISTE*, '*sadery-sad*'), a non-suffixed non-word condition (e.g., **tristald-TRISTE*, '*sadald-sad*'), and an unrelated prime control condition (e.g., *direction-TRISTE*, '*direction-sad*'). Results showed a reliable priming effect for suffixed words, larger than the priming effects of other suffixed and non-suffixed non-word conditions, confirming that the segmentation of the string of letter in stem + suffix units is driven by semantic interpretability of the combination. The two non-word conditions (suffixed and non-suffixed) produced priming of a similar size, suggesting that French children (irrespective of grade) are able to detect and use the stem unit. The advantage gained from the stem embedded in a non-word prime was positively correlated with literacy skill: the higher the skill, the larger the obtained priming effect. In other words, skilled readers are more likely to exploit a known stem in a string of letters, than low-proficiency readers.

These results are consistent with those of a previous study (Quémart and Casalis 2015), in which French children with dyslexia showed a reliable priming effect for morphological condition (e.g., *tablette-TABLE*, 'little table-table'), but not for pseudo-derived condition (e.g., *baguette-BAGUE*, 'French stick-ring') and orthographic control (e.g., *abricot-ABRI*, 'apricot-shelter'). In Hebrew, Schiff, Raveh and Fighel (2012), studying the role of semantic consistency in parsing derived words, found a reliable morphological priming effect when prime and target were morphologically and semantically related (e.g., prime: *hNHGh*, 'leadership'; target: *mNHiG*, 'leader'), irrespective of reading skill. However, differences between 4th graders and 7th graders were observed for semantically inconsistent prime-target couples. For younger readers, semantically inconsistent condition (e.g., prime:

NHiGh, '*driving*'; target: mNHiG, '*leader*') did not produce any priming effect, whereas for older children the priming effect of the semantically inconsistent condition approached significance, as found in adult readers (Bentin and Feldman 1990; Frost, Forster, and Deutsch 1997). The authors interpreted these data as evidence that the higher the reading skills are, the more abstract and independent from semantic properties the morphological representations within the mental lexicon.

To summarize, data from developmental studies on visual word recognition indicate that, in children, the meaning of the morphemic units is subliminally activated, irrespective of reading skills. Thus, semantics is likely to be the early dimension on which the ability of using morphemic structure develops, whereas the sensitivity to purely morpho-orthographic relations seems to be a late acquisition, as data from young skilled readers (Beyersmann et al. 2015a) and adults (Rastle and Davis 2008) show. So, it is possible to draw a developmental trajectory in the ability of detecting morphemic units in letter strings that originates from the semantic dimension of morphemes and leads to morpho-orthographic representations, supporting the view of morphology as a by-product system that develops according to general language learning mechanisms. Overall, the reviewed studies suggest that morphological representations may become more and more abstract with increasing reading ability and word exposure. In the early stages of reading development, readers heavily rely on the orthographic and semantic consistency of a stem to successfully identify the derived word, and in later stages, with increased exposure to written language and increased reading ability, a certain level of generalization develops in the mental lexicon.

7 Data-driven computational models: A solution to the conundrum?

In the present chapter, we have first presented the most popular idea underlying the study of morphological effects in word reading, namely that morphemes are represented in the cognitive system, and these representational units are activated when processing a morphologically complex word. This assumption has been profitably applied to psycholinguistic studies for nearly four decades. However, recent results seem to draw a more complex scenario in which, on the one side, form-meaning associations that are not morpheme-mediated have a role to play (e.g., Bergen 2004; Marelli, Amenta, and Crepaldi 2015) and, on the other side, paradigmatic effects modulate the influence of morphology in word recognition (Milin, Filipović Đurđević and Moscoso del Prado Martín 2009; Moscoso del Prado Martín et al. 2004). Although these pieces of evidence do not necessarily invalidate models assuming morphemes as explicit representations, they do not seem to be directly predicted by such systems either. Moreover, the developmental literature converges on characterizing morphology as an emerging phenomenon, with morphological awareness becoming progressively more important in language development (Deacon, Kieffer, and Laroche 2014; Jarmulowicz et al. 2008). Indeed, morphological complexity seems to help word processing in early readers, thus suggesting that morphemes may act as distributional cues that can be efficiently exploited to facilitate reading (Burani 2010; Burani et al. 2008; Carlisle and Stone 2005; Deacon, Tong, and Mimeau 2019; Mann and Singson 2003; Traficante et al. 2011). To capture these phenomena in a modelling perspective it is crucial to consider learning-oriented processes, often lacking in traditional models of morphological processing. In conclusion, it may be the case that different views on morphology would provide a more efficient way to account for such a diverse pattern of effects.

7.1 Morphology as consistent associations within the language system

In these terms, a promising approach could characterize morphology as an epiphenomenon of more general-purpose learning mechanisms that exploit consistencies in the language system. This notion is certainly not new. In embryo, it can be found in the full-listing proposals (e.g., Butterworth 1983), since they typically see morphology as a by-product of form and meaning similarity between independent representations. More formally, it has been an important theoretical assumption of models from the *connectionist* tradition (see Seidenberg and McClelland 1989). In these systems there are no explicit, symbolic representations for morphemes and/or words. Rather, connectionist architectures are populated by simple elements (graphemes, phonemes, semantic features), organized in different layers. Typically, a set of non-symbolic nodes (the *hidden layer*) is implemented between these, and morphology (as well as lexicality) naturally unfolds by means of consistent patterns of activation within the links connecting the different layers (Plaut and Gonnerman 2000; Rueckl and Raveh 1999). In other words, in these models the morphological status of *-er* is not captured through an explicit representation unit for the suffix, rather emerging as strong connection links between the graphemic units (*e* and *r* at word endings) and the corresponding semantics (abstract nodes indicating *instrumental* or *agentive* traits). Crucially, connection weights are estimated through an iterative learning process that builds on examples of "correct" form-meaning associations. In other words, during the learning phase weights are continuously updated with the purpose to progressively minimize the error in the system output (through various learning rules, e.g., the widely used *delta rule*). By means of hidden units, the learning procedure ends up extracting a high-order structure from patterns of low-level features (i.e., graphemic and semantic nodes), which guarantees high generalization power and the capability of exhibiting morphological effects that cannot be reduced to simple orthographic and/or semantic similarity (Plaut and Gonnerman 2000).

From a theoretical point of view, the connectionist models offer an ideal interpretative framework to address the sensitive aspects we discussed in previous sections. On the one hand, the connectionist approach defines morphology as a specific expression of a more general cognitive ability to capture form-meaning patterns, hence providing a natural explanation for the distributional, graded effects reviewed above. On the other hand, it considers morphology as the result of a learning procedure, in line with the evidence from reading acquisition. In this regard the connectionist approach has provided interesting simulations of how morphological effects may depend on the degree of morphological connectivity of a language, with morphologically rich languages as Italian and Hebrew more likely to show morphological effects in the absence of semantic relations (Plaut and Gonnermann 2000; see also Bentin and Feldman 1990). The approach has been very successful also on the empirical side. Connectionist simulations work well in reproducing priming patterns and their graded effects according to the degree of morphological connectivity of the language (e.g., Plaut and Gonnerman 2000), the acquisition of morphological chunks in learning (e.g., Moscoso del Prado Martin, Schreuder, and Baayen 2004), and morphological errors in neuropsychological patients (e.g., Joanisse and Seidenberg 1999; Plaut and Shallice 1993).

7.2 Evidence from large-scale models

Still, most traditional connectionist networks are based on toy models for specific tasks, with input and training data de-facto hand-coded, and are thus limited in their explanatory power. More recent computational proposals have exploited large collections of texts (*corpora*) as sources of training data, hence basing their models on examples of natural language usage. For example, the *Naïve Discriminative Reader* (NDR), a model proposed by Baayen et al. (2011) to account for morphological effects in word processing, was trained on the

British National Corpus (http://www.natcorp.ox.ac.uk/). NDR architecture is similar to those proposed in the connectionist paradigm: an input layer (populated by orthographic unigrams and bigrams) is directly connected to a semantic layer (populated by symbolic word meanings); connections between layers are learnt by means of the Rescorla-Wagner equations (Rescorla and Wagner 1972), which are strictly related to the connectionist delta rule. Indeed, NDR is equivalent to a connectionist network without hidden layers, namely a *perceptron* (Rosenblatt 1958).

Despite its simplicity, NDR provides a unique account for a wide range of morphological effects, ranging from family size (Schreuder and Baayen 1997), to inflectional entropy (Milin, Filipović Đurđević, and Moscoso del Prado Martín 2009), to priming (Rastle, Davis, and New 2004), again suggesting that morphology may simply reflect a cognitive sensitivity to systematic relations between forms and meanings. Indeed, distributional phenomena emerge naturally from the NDR perspective, which also predicted new surprising effects, crucially depending on word usage in context; namely, the effect of *relative prepositional entropy* indicates that the processing of isolated word is influenced by the way those words are paired with prepositions within the whole corpus (Baayen et al. 2011). Similarly, effects related to phonaesthemes (Bergen 2004) and, potentially, OSC (Marelli, Amenta, and Crepaldi 2015) follow naturally from the NDR premises.

Over and above the larger scale (in comparison to traditional connectionist proposals), NDR also offered a novel perspective from the theoretical point of view. On the one hand, it moved the interpretative focus from *association* to *discrimination* (Ramscar et al. 2010): in the NDR framework, "learn" is equivalent to "learn to distinguish". Morphemes are an epiphenomenon of simple discriminative cues, namely chunks of graphemic symbols that help distinguish between different meanings. On the other hand, NDR takes a psychologically plausible, biologically grounded stance on learning. In fact, Rescorla-Wagner equations (Rescorla and Wagner 1972) are inspired by classical conditioning (Pavlov 1927; Rescorla 1988), defining an approach in which the connection that is formed between graphemic symbols and semantic units is comparable to that emerging between conditioned and unconditioned stimuli. In conclusion, NDR provides a morphological model that does not rely on explicit morpheme representations, focuses on form-meaning statistical patterns that emerge in word distributions, and is centered on a psychologically plausible learning mechanism. Although it is not uncontroversial (for example in relation to masked-priming data; Beyersmann et al. 2015b), its explanatory power is certainly remarkable, and constitutes a profitable interpretative framework for the understanding of morphological effects in reading.

If NDR models morphology by assuming a relatively underspecified semantic system, other computational approaches have specifically looked at how morphology can inform word meanings. The system proposed by Marelli and Baroni (2015) models morphological derivation in distributional semantics (Turney and Pantel 2010). This theory is based on the assumption that similar words appear in similar contexts; as a consequence, a word meaning can be represented through the contexts the given word appears in (Landauer and Dumais 1997) or, in more formal terms, through a *vector* encoding the co-occurrence counts between the target word and other words in the lexicon. In Marelli and Baroni's (2015) proposal, if word meanings can be approximated by vectors, affix meanings can be modelled as *functions* (i.e., *matrices*) mapping the meaning of the stem into the meaning of the derived form (*FRACSS*: Functional Representation for Affixes in Compositional Semantic Space). FRACSSs are learned through examples of stems and corresponding derived forms (similarly to NDR, the model is trained on a large natural-language corpus), and define a flexible system that is able to account for a range of semantic effects associated to morphology: semantic transparency effects in lexical decision and priming paradigms, explicit intuitions on complex word meanings, the immediate understanding of the meaning of novel words, the possibility of transparent readings of semantically opaque words. Although a high-level description of the FRACSS system fits a representational account of morphology (each stem and affix has its own distributed representation), the way morphemes are computationally characterized is quite different from the symbolic units so popular in the psycholinguistic tradition. On the one hand, stems are modelled as distributed patterns of activation across a set of sub-symbolic nodes. On the other hand, affixes are closer to *processes* than representation units: following the functional assumption, FRACSS can indeed be seen as a contextual update (cued by the affix orthographic signs) of a core meaning (expressed through the stem).

To summarize, the architectures described in the present section represent a powerful tool for the investigation of morphological effects in reading. Indeed, they provide a convincing scenario to naturally frame the graded, paradigmatic, and learning effects we presented in the previous sections (which uncomfortably fit a strict representational view on morphemes). Notwithstanding the many differences, all these systems have a focus on data-driven methods that can extract statistically reliable patterns from examples of real language usage. These patterns emerged as crucial not only at the interplay between form and meaning (Baayen et al. 2011), but also within the orthographic (Moscoso del Prado Martín, Schreuder, and Baayen 2004) or semantic systems themselves (Marelli and Baroni, 2015). The success of these computational approaches crucially highlights the importance of two (closely related) components when it comes to investigate morphology: on the one hand, the distributional characterization of the elements under investigation on the basis of real language usage; on the other hand, the definition of a learning system that is able to extract information from these very distributions. Future research should accord the proper weight to these aspects, if we aim to achieve a unified explanation of the many and diverse effects emerging in complex-word reading.

References

Amenta, Simona & Davide Crepaldi. 2012. Morphological processing as we know it: An analytical review of morphological effects in visual word identification. *Frontiers in Psychology* 3 (232). https://doi.org/10.3389/fpsyg.2012.00232.

Amenta, Simona, Marco Marelli & Davide Crepaldi. 2015. The fruitless effort of growing a fruitless tree: Early morpho-orthographic and morpho-semantic effects in sentence reading. *Journal of Experimental Psychology: Learning, Memory & Cognition* 41 (5). 1587–1596.

Arduino, Lisa S., Cristina Burani & Giuseppe Vallar. 2002. Lexical effects in left neglect dyslexia: A study in Italian patients. *Cognitive Neuropsychology* 19 (5). 421–444.

Aronoff, Mark. 1994. Morphology by itself: Stems and inflectional classes. Cambridge, MA: MIT press.

Baayen, R. Harald, Ton T. Dijkstra & Robert Schreuder. 1997. Singulars and plurals in Dutch: Evidence for a parallel dual-route model. *Journal of Memory and Language* 37 (1). 94–117.

Baayen, R. Harald, Petar Milin, Dusica Filipović Đurđević, Peter Hendrix & Marco Marelli. 2011. An amorphous model for morphological processing in visual comprehension based on naive discriminative learning. *Psychological review* 118 (3). 438–481.

Baayen, R. Harald, Lee H. Wurm & Joanna Aycock. 2007. Lexical dynamics for low-frequency complex words: A regression study across tasks and modalities. *The Mental Lexicon* 2 (3). 419–463.

Badecker, William. 1997. Levels of morphological deficit: Indications from inflectional regularity. *Brain and Language* 60 (3). 360–380.

Badecker, William & Alfonso Caramazza. 1987. The analysis of morphological errors in a case of acquired dyslexia. *Brain and Language* 32 (2). 278–305.

Bentin, Shlomo & Laurie B. Feldman. 1990. The contribution of morphological and semantic relatedness to repetition priming at short and long lags: Evidence from Hebrew. *The Quarterly Journal of Experimental Psychology* 42 (4). 693–711.

Bergen, Benjamin K. 2004. The psychological reality of phonaesthemes. *Language* 80 (2). 290–311.

Bertram, Raymond, R. Harald Baayen & Robert Schreuder. 2000. Effects of family size for complex words. *Journal of Memory and Language* 42 (3). 390–405.

Bertram, Raymond, Jukka Hyönä & Matti Laine. 2000. The role of context in morphological processing: Evidence from Finnish. *Language and Cognitive Processes* 15 (4–5). 367–388.

Bertram, Raymond, Matti Laine, R. Harald Baayen, Robert Schreuder & Jukka Hyönä. 2000. Affixal homonym triggers full-form storage, even with inflected words, even in a morphologically rich language. *Cognition* 74 (2). B13–B25.
Bertram, Raymond, Matti Laine & Minna Maria Virkkala. 2000. The role of derivational morphology in vocabulary acquisition: Get by with little help from my morpheme friends. *Scandinavian Journal of Psychology* 41 (4). 287–296.
Beyersmann, Elisabeth, Anne Castles & Max Coltheart. 2012. Morphological processing during visual word recognition in developing readers: Evidence from masked priming. *The Quarterly Journal of Experimental Psychology* 65 (7). 1306–1326.
Beyersmann, Elisabeth, Max Coltheart & Anne Castles. 2012. Parallel processing of whole words and morphemes in visual word recognition. *The Quarterly Journal of Experimental Psychology* 65 (9). 1798–1819.
Beyersmann, Elisabeth, Jonathan Grainger, Séverine Casalis & Johannes C. Ziegler. 2015a. Effects of reading proficiency on embedded stem priming in primary school children. *Journal of Experimental Child Psychology* 139 (11). 115–126.
Beyersmann, Elisabeth, Johannes C. Ziegler, Anne Castles, Max Coltheart, Yvette Kezilas & Jonathan Grainger. 2015b. Morpho-orthographic segmentation without semantics. *Psychonomic Bulletin & Review* 23 (2). 533–539.
Biedermann, Britta, Antje Lorenz, Elisabeth Beyersmann & Lyndsay Nickels. 2012. The influence of plural dominance in aphasic word production. *Aphasiology* 26 (8). 985–1004.
Blevins, James P. 2016. The minimal sign. In Gregory T. Stump & Andrew Hippisley (eds.), *The Cambridge Handbook of Morphology*, 102–137. Cambridge: Cambridge University Press.
Bloomfield, Leonard. 1933. *Language*. New York: Holt.
Burani, Cristina. 2010. Word morphology enhances reading fluency in children with developmental dyslexia. *Lingue e Linguaggio* IX (2). 177–198.
Burani, Cristina & Alfonso Caramazza.1987. Representation and processing of derived words. *Language and Cognitive Processes* 2 (3–4). 217–227.
Burani, Cristina, Francesca M. Dovetto, Alberto Spuntarelli & Anna M. Thornton. 1999. Morpho-lexical access and naming: The semantic interpretability of new root-suffix combinations. *Brain and Language* 68 (1–2), 333–339.
Burani, Cristina, Francesca M. Dovetto, Anna M. Thornton & Alessandro Laudanna. 1997. Accessing and naming suffixed pseudo-words. In Geert E. Booij & Jap van Marle (eds.), *Yearbook of Morphology 1996*, 55–72. Dordrecht: Kluwer Academic Publishers.
Burani, Cristina, Stefania Marcolini, Maria De Luca & Pierluigi Zoccolotti. 2008. Morpheme-based reading aloud: Evidence from dyslexic and skilled Italian readers. *Cognition* 108 (1). 243–262.
Burani, Cristina, Stefania Marcolini & Giacomo Stella. 2002. How early does morpholexical reading develop in readers of a shallow orthography? *Brain and language* 81 (1–3). 568–586.
Burani, Cristina, Dario Salmaso & Alfonso Caramazza. 1984. Morphological structure and lexical access. *Visible Language* 18 (4). 342–352.
Burani, Cristina & Anna M. Thornton. 2003. The interplay of root, suffix and whole-word frequency in processing derived words. In R. Harald Baayen & Robert Schreuder (eds.), *Morphological Structure in Language Processing*, 157–208. Berlin: Mouton de Gruyter.
Butterworth, Brian. 1983. Lexical representation. In Brian Butterworth (ed.), *Language production* (Vol. 2), 257–294. London: Academic Press.

Byrne, Brian. 1996. The learnability of the alphabetic principle: Children's initial hypotheses about how print represents spoken language. *Applied Psycholinguistics* 17(4), 401–426.

Caramazza, Alfonso, Alessandro Laudanna & Cristina Romani. 1988. Lexical access and inflectional morphology. *Cognition* 28(3). 297–332.

Carlisle, Joanne F. 1995. Morphological awareness and early reading achievement. In Laurie B. Feldman (ed.), *Morphological aspects of language processing*, 189–209. Hillsdale, N.J: LEA.

Carlisle, Joanne F. & C. Addison Stone. 2005. Exploring the role of morphemes in word reading. *Reading Research Quarterly* 40 (4). 428–449.

Carlisle, Joanne F., C. Addison Stone & Lauren A. Katz. 2001. The effect of morphological transparency on reading complex words. *Annals of Dyslexia* 51 (1), 249–274.

Casalis, Séverine., Pascale Colé & Delphine Sopo. 2004. Morphological awareness in developmental dyslexia. *Annals of Dyslexia* 54 (1). 114–138.

Casalis, Séverine, Pauline Quémart & Lynne G. Duncan. 2015. How language affects children's use of derivational morphology in visual word and pseudoword processing: Evidence from a cross-language study. *Frontiers in Psychology* 6 (452). https://doi.org/10.3389/fpsyg.2015.00452.

Castles, Anne, Max Coltheart, Greg Savage, Andree Bates & Lauren Reid. 1996. Morphological processing and visual word recognition: Evidence from acquired dyslexia. *Cognitive Neuropsychology* 13 (7). 1041–1057.

Catts, Hugh W., Suzanne M. Adlof & Susan Ellis Weismer. 2006. Language deficits in poor comprehenders: A case for the simple view of reading. *Journal of Speech, Language & Hearing Research* 49 (2). 278–293.

Christianson, Kiel, Rebecca L. Johnson & Keith Rayner. 2005. Letter transpositions within and across morphemes. *Journal of Experimental Psychology: Learning, Memory & Cognition* 31 (6). 1327–1339.

Coltheart, Max, Karalyn Patterson & John C. Marshall. 1980. *Deep dyslexia*. London: Routhledge & Kegan Paul.

Crepaldi, Davide, Kathleen Rastle, Max Coltheart & Lyndey Nickels. 2010. 'Fell' primes 'fall', but does 'bell' prime 'ball'? Masked priming with irregularly-inflected primes. *Journal of Memory and Language* 63 (1). 83–99.

Crepaldi, Davide, Kathleen Rastle & Colin J. Davis. 2010. Morphemes in their place: Evidence for position-specific identification of suffixes. *Memory & cognition* 38 (3). 312–321.

Crepaldi, Davide, Kathleen Rastle, Colin J. Davis & Stephen J. Lupker. 2013. Seeing stems everywhere: Position-independent identification of stem morphemes. *Journal of Experimental Psychology: Human Perception and Performance* 39 (2). 510–525.

Deacon, S. Hélène, Michael J. Kieffer & Annie Laroche. 2014. The relation between morphological awareness and reading comprehension: Evidence from mediation and longitudinal models. *Scientific Studies of Reading* 18 (6). 432–451.

Deacon, S. Hélène, Xiuli Tong & Catherine Mimeau. 2019. Morphological and semantic processing in developmental dyslexia across languages: A theoretical and empirical review. In Ludo Verhoeven, Charles Perfetti & Kenneth Pugh (eds.), *Developmental dyslexia across languages and writing systems*, 327–349. Cambridge: Cambridge University Press.

Deacon, S. Hélène, Rachel Whalen, & John R. Kirby. 2011. Do children see the danger in dangerous? Grade 4, 6, and 8 children's reading of morphologically complex words. *Applied Psycholinguistics* 32 (3). 467–481.

De Jong, Nivja H., Robert Schreuder & R. Harald Baayen. 2000. The morphological family size effect and morphology. *Language and Cognitive Processes* 15 (4–5). 329–365.

De Jong, Nivja H., Robert Schreuder & R. Harald Baayen. 2003. Morphological resonance in the mental lexicon. In R. Harald Baayen & Robert Schreuder (eds.), *Morphological structure in language processing*, 65–88. Berlin: Mouton de Gruyter.

De Luca, Maria, Cristina Burani, Despina Paizi, Donatella Spinelli & Pierluigi Zoccolotti. 2010. Letter and letter-string processing in developmental dyslexia. *Cortex* 46 (10). 1272–1283.

Diependaele, Kevin, Dominiek Sandra & Jonathan Grainger. 2009. Semantic transparency and masked morphological priming: The case of prefixed words. *Memory & cognition* 37 (6). 895–908.

Drews, Etta & Pienie Zwitserlood. 1995. Morphological and orthographic similarity in visual word recognition. *Journal of Experimental Psychology: Human Perception and Performance* 21 (5). 1098–1116.

Duñabeitia, Jon Andoni, Manuel Perea & Manuel Carreiras. 2007. Do transposed-letter similarity effects occur at a morpheme level? Evidence for morpho-orthographic decomposition. *Cognition* 105 (3). 691–703.

Ehri, Linnea C. 2005. Learning to read words: Theory, findings and issues. *Scientific Studies of Reading*, 9 (2), 167–188.

Elbro, Carsten & Elisabeth Arnbak. 1996. The role of morpheme recognition and morphological awareness in dyslexia. *Annals of Dyslexia* 46 (1). 209–240.

Feldman, Laurie B. 2000. Are morphological effects distinguishable from the effects of shared meaning and shared form? *Journal of Experimental Psychology: Learning, Memory & Cognition* 26 (6). 1431–1444.

Feldman, Laurie B., Aleksandar Kostić, Vasilije Gvozdenović, Patrick A. O'Connor & Fermín Moscoso del Prado Martín. 2012. Semantic similarity influences early morphological priming in serbian: A challenge to form-then-meaning accounts of word recognition. *Psychonomic bulletin & review* 19 (4). 668–676.

Feldman, Laurie B., Patrick A. O'Connor & Fermín Moscoso del Prado Martín. 2009. Early morphological processing is morphosemantic and not simply morpho-orthographic: A violation of form-then-meaning accounts of word recognition. *Psychonomic bulletin & review* 16 (4). 684–691.

Feldman, Laurie B., & Emily G. Soltano. 1999. Morphological priming: The role of prime duration, semantic transparency and affix position. *Brain and Language* 68 (1–2). 33–39.

Fodor, Jerry A. (1983). *The modularity of mind: An essay on faculty psychology*. Cambridge, MA: The MIT press.

Ford, Michael A., Matthew H. Davis & William Marslen-Wilson. 2010. Derivational morphology and base morpheme frequency. *Journal of Memory and Language* 63 (1), 117–130.

Forster, Kenneth I. & Chris Davis. 1984. Repetition priming and frequency attenuation in lexical access. *Journal of Experimental Psychology: Learning, Memory & Cognition* 10 (4). 680–698.

Forster, Kenneth I., Chris Davis, Colin Schoknecht & Ronald Carter. 1987. Masked priming with graphemically related forms: Repetition or partial activation? *The Quarterly Journal of Experimental Psychology* 39 (2). 211–251.

Frost, Ram, Kenneth I. Forster & Avital Deutsch. 1997. What can we learn from the morphology of Hebrew? A masked-priming investigation of morphological representation. *Journal of Experimental Psychology: Learning, Memory & Cognition* 23 (4). 829–856.

Funnell, Elaine. 1987. Morphological errors in acquired dyslexia: A case of mistaken identity. *The Quarterly Journal of Experimental Psychology A: Human Experimental Psychology* 39 (3). 497–539.

Giraudo, Hélène, & Jonathan Grainger. 2000. Effects of prime word frequency and cumulative root frequency in masked morphological priming. *Language and Cognitive Processes* 15 (4–5). 421–444.

Grainger, Jonathan & Arthur M. Jacobs. 1996. Orthographic processing in visual word recognition: a multiple read-out model. *Psychological Review* 103 (3), 518–565.

Grainger, Jonathan & Johannes C. Ziegler. 2011. A dual-route approach to orthographic processing. *Frontiers in Psychology* 2 (54). https://doi.org/10.3389/fpsyg.2011.00054

Hay, Jennifer. 2001. Lexical frequency in morphology: Is everything relative? *Linguistics* 39 (6). 1041–1070.

Howes, Davis H. & Richard L. Solomon. 1951. Visual duration threshold as a function of word-probability. *Journal of Experimental Psychology* 41 (6). 401–410.

Jarmulowicz, Linda, Sarah E. Hay, Valentina L. Taran & Corinna A. Ethington. 2008. Fitting English derivational morphophonology into a developmental model of reading. *Reading and Writing: An Interdisciplinary Journal* 21 (3). 275–297.

Järvikivi, Juhani & Pyykkönen Pirita. 2011. Sub-and supralexical information in early phases of lexical access. *Frontiers in Psychology* 2 (282). https://doi.org/10.3389/fpsyg.2011.00282.

Joanisse, Marc F. & Mark S. Seidenberg. 1999. Impairments in verb morphology after brain injury: A connectionist model. *Proceedings of the National Academy of Sciences* 96 (13). 7592–7597.

Job, Remo & Giuseppe Sartori. 1984. Morphological decomposition: Evidence from crossed phonological dyslexia. *The Quarterly Journal of Experimental Psychology* 36 (3). 435–458.

Kazanina, Nina. 2011. Decomposition of prefixed words in Russian. *Journal of Experimental Psychology: Learning, Memory & Cognition* 37 (6). 1371–1390.

Kazanina, Nina, Galina Dukova-Zheleva, Dana Geber, Viktor Kharlamov & Keren Tonciulescu. 2008. Decomposition into multiple morphemes during lexical access: A masked priming study of Russian nouns. *Language and Cognitive Processes* 23 (6). 800–823.

Kelliher, Susan & Leslie Henderson. 1990. Morphologically based frequency effects in the recognition of irregularly inflected verbs. *British Journal of Psychology* 81 (4). 527–539.

Kieffer, Michael J. & Nonie K. Lesaux. 2012. Direct and indirect roles of morphological awareness in the english reading comprehension of native English, Spanish, Filipino & Vietnamese speakers. *Language Learning* 62 (4). 1170–1204,

Kuperman, Victor, Raymond Bertram & R. Harald Baayen. 2008. Morphological dynamics in compound processing. *Language and Cognitive Processes* 23 (7–8). 1089–1132.

Kuperman, Victor, Raymond Bertram & R. Harald Baayen. 2010. Processing trade-offs in the reading of dutch derived words. *Journal of Memory and Language* 62 (2). 83–97.

Kuperman, Victor, Robert Schreuder, Raymond Bertram & R. Harald Baayen. 2009. Reading polymorphemic Dutch compounds: toward a multiple route model of lexical processing. *Journal of Experimental Psychology: Human Perception and Performance* 35 (3). 876–895.

Landauer, Thomas K. & Susan T. Dumais. 1997. A solution to Plato's problem: The latent semantic analysis theory of acquisition, induction & representation of knowledge. *Psychological Review* 104 (2). 211–240.

Lavric, Aureliu, Amanda Clapp & Kathleen Rastle. 2007. ERP evidence of morphological analysis from orthography: A masked priming study. *Journal of cognitive neuroscience* 19 (5). 866–877.

Lázaro, Miguel, Laura García & Cristina Burani. 2015. How orthographic transparency affects morphological processing in young readers with and without reading disability. *Scandinavian Journal of Psychology* 56 (5). 498–507.

Longtin, Catherine-Marie, Juan Segui & Pierre A. Halle. 2003. Morphological priming without morphological relationship. *Language and Cognitive Processes* 18 (3). 313–334.

Luzzatti, Claudio, Sara Mondini & Carlo Semenza. 2001. Lexical representation and processing of morphologically complex words: Evidence from the reading performance of an italian agrammatic patient. *Brain and language* 79 (3). 345–359.

Mann, Virginia A. & Maria Singson. 2003. Linking morphological knowledge to English decoding ability: large effects of little suffixes. In Egbert M.H. Assink & Dominiek Sandra (eds.), *Reading complex words: Cross-language studies*, 1–25. Amsterdam: Kluwer Academic.

Marcolini, Stefania, Daniela Traficante, Pierluigi Zoccolotti & Cristina Burani. 2011. Word frequency modulates morpheme-based reading in poor and skilled italian readers. *Applied Psycholinguistics* 32 (3). 513–532.

Marelli, Marco, Silvia Aggujaro, Franco Molteni & Claudio Luzzatti. 2012a. The multiple-lemma representation of Italian compound nouns: A single case study of deep dyslexia. *Neuropsychologia* 50 (5). 852–861.

Marelli, Marco, Simona Amenta & Davide Crepaldi. 2015. Semantic transparency in free stems: The effect of Orthography-Semantics Consistency on word recognition. *The Quarterly Journal of Experimental Psychology* 68 (8). 1571–1583.

Marelli, Marco, Simona Amenta, Elena A. Morone & Davide Crepaldi. 2013. Meaning is in the beholder's eye: Morpho-semantic effects in masked priming. *Psychonomic bulletin & review* 20 (3). 534–541.

Marelli, Marco, Elena Barbieri, Giusy Zonca & Claudio Luzzatti (2012b). Grammatical Class, Inflectional Entropy and Imageability Effects in Picture Naming: A Multiple Single-case Study on Italian Aphasic Patients. *Procedia-Social and Behavioral Sciences* 61. 214–215.

Marelli, Marco & Marco Baroni. 2015. Affixation in semantic space: Modeling morpheme meanings with compositional distributional semantics. *Psychological Review* 122 (3). 485–515.

Marelli, Marco & Claudio Luzzatti. 2012. Frequency effects in the processing of Italian nominal compounds: Modulation of headedness and semantic transparency. *Journal of Memory and Language* 66 (4). 644–664.

Marelli, Marco, Daniela Traficante, Silvia Aggujaro, Franco Molteni & Claudio Luzzatti. 2011. Grammatical and semantic effects in reading derived nouns: A study of deep dyslexia. *Procedia: Social and Behavioral Sciences* 23. 69–70.

Marslen-Wilson, William, Lorraine K. Tyler, Rachelle Waksler & Lianne Older. 1994. Morphology and meaning in the English mental lexicon. *Psychological Review* 101 (1). 3–33.

McCormick, Samantha F., Kathleen Rastle & Matthew H. Davis. 2008. Is there a 'fete' in 'fetish'? Effects of orthographic opacity on morpho-orthographic segmentation in visual word recognition. *Journal of Memory and Language* 58 (2). 307–326.

McCormick, Samantha F., Kathleen Rastle & Matthew H. Davis. 2009. Adore-able not adorable? orthographic underspecification studied with masked repetition priming. *European Journal of Cognitive Psychology* 21 (6). 813–836.

Meunier, Fanny, & Catherine-Marie Longtin. 2007. Morphological decomposition and semantic integration in word processing. *Journal of Memory and Language* 56 (4), 457–471.

Milin, Petar, Dusica Filipović Đurđević & Fermín Moscoso del Prado Martín. 2009. The simultaneous effects of inflectional paradigms and classes on lexical recognition: Evidence from Serbian. *Journal of Memory and Language* 60 (1). 50–64.

Milin, Petar, Victor Kuperman, Aleksander Kostić & R. Harald Baayen. 2009. Paradigms bit by bit: An information theoretic approach to the processing of paradigmatic structure in inflection and derivation. In: James P. Blevins & Juliette Blevins (eds.), *Analogy in Grammar: Form and Acquisition*, 214–252. Oxford: Oxford University Press.

Morris, Joanna, Jonathan Grainger & Philip J. Holcomb. 2008. An electrophysiological investigation of early effects of masked morphological priming. *Language and Cognitive Processes* 23 (7–8). 1021–1056.

Moscoso del Prado Martín, Fermín, Raymond Bertram, Tuomo Häikiö, Robert Schreuder, & R. Harald Baayen. 2004. Morphological family size in a morphologically rich language: the case of Finnish compared with Dutch and Hebrew. *Journal of Experimental Psychology: Learning, Memory & Cognition* 30 (6). 1271–1278.

Moscoso del Prado Martín, Fermín, Avital Deutsch, Ram Frost, Robert Schreuder, Nivja H. De Jong & R. Harald Baayen. 2005. Changing places: A cross-language perspective on frequency and family size in Dutch and Hebrew. *Journal of Memory and Language* 53 (4). 496–512.

Moscoso del Prado Martín, Fermín, Aleksander Kostić & R. Harald Baayen. 2004. Putting the bits together: An information theoretical perspective on morphological processing. *Cognition* 94 (1). 1–18.

Moscoso del Prado Martín, Fermín, Robert Schreuder & R. Harald Baayen. 2004. Using the structure found in time: Building real-scale orthographic and phonetic representations by accumulation of expectations. In Howard Bowman & Christophe Labiouse(eds.), *Connectionist models of cognition, perception and emotion: Proceedings of the Eighth Neural Computation and Psychology Workshop*, 263–272. Singapore: World Scientific.

Norris, Dennis & Sachiko Kinoshita. 2008. Perception as evidence accumulation and Bayesian inference: insights from masked priming. *Journal of Experimental Psychology: General* 137 (3). 434–455.

Patterson, Karalyn. 1980. Derivational errors. In Max Coltheart, Karalyn Patterson, & John C. Marshall (eds.), *Deep Dyslexia*, 286–306. London: Routledge & Kegan.

Pavlov, Ivan P. 1927. *Conditional Reflexes*. New York: Dover Publications.

Plaut, David C. & Laura M. Gonnerman. 2000. Are non-semantic morphological effects incompatible with a distributed connectionist approach to lexical processing? *Language and Cognitive Processes* 15 (4–5). 445–485.

Plaut, David C. & Tim Shallice. 1993. Deep dyslexia: A case study of connectionist neuropsychology. *Cognitive Neuropsychology* 10 (5). 377–500.

Quémart, Pauline & Séverine Casalis. 2014. Effects of phonological and orthographic shifts on children's processing of written morphology: A time-course study. *Scientific Studies of Reading* 18 (5). 363–382.

Quémart, Pauline & Séverine Casalis. 2015. Visual processing of derivational morphology in children with developmental dyslexia: Insights from masked priming. *Applied Psycholinguistics* 36 (2). 345–376.

Quémart, Pauline, Séverine Casalis & Pascale Colé. 2011. The role of form and meaning in the processing of written morphology: A priming study in french developing readers. *Journal of experimental child psychology* 109 (4). 478–496.

Ramscar, Michael, Daniel Yarlett, Melody Dye, Katie Denny & Kirsten Thorpe. 2010. The effects of feature-label-order and their implications for symbolic learning. *Cognitive Science* 34 (6). 909–957.

Rastle, Kathleen & Matthew H. Davis. 2008. Morphological decomposition based on the analysis of orthography. *Language and Cognitive Processes* 23 (7–8). 942–971.

Rastle, Kathleen, Matt H. Davis, William Marslen-Wilson & Lorraine K. Tyler. 2000. Morphological and semantic effects in visual word recognition: A time-course study. *Language and Cognitive Processes* 15(4–5). 507–537.

Rastle, Kathleen, Matthew H. Davis & Boris New. 2004. The broth in my brother's brothel: Morpho-orthographic segmentation in visual word recognition. *Psychonomic bulletin & review* 11 (6). 1090–1098.

Rastle, Kathleen, Lorraine K. Tyler & William Marslen-Wilson. 2006. New evidence for morphological errors in deep dyslexia. *Brain and language* 97 (2). 189–199.

Rescorla, Robert A. 1988. Pavlovian conditioning it's not what you think it is. *American Psychologist* 43 (3). 151–160.

Rescorla, Robert A., & Allan R. Wagner. 1972. A theory of Pavlovian conditioning: Variations in the effectiveness of reinforcement and nonreinforcement. In Abraham H. Black & William F. Prokasy (eds.), *Classical conditioning: Current research and theory II*, 64–99. New York: Appleton-Century-Crofts.

Rosenblatt, Frank. 1958. *The perceptron: A theory of statistical separability in cognitive systems (Project Para)*. Buffalo, New.York: Cornell Aeronautical Laboratory.

Rueckl, Jay G. & Karen A. Aicher. 2008. Are CORNER and BROTHER morphologically complex? Not in the long term. *Language and Cognitive Processes* 23 (7–8). 972–1001.

Rueckl, Jay G. & Michael Raveh. 1999. The influence of morphological regularities on the dynamics of a connectionist network. *Brain and Language* 68 (1). 110–117.

Schiff, Rachel, Michal Raveh & Avital Fighel. 2012. The development of the hebrew mental lexicon: When morphological representations become devoid of their meaning. *Scientific Studies of Reading* 16(5). 383–403.

Schiff, Rachel, Michal Raveh & Shani Kahta. 2008. The developing mental lexicon: Evidence from morphological priming of irregular hebrew forms. *Reading and Writing: An Interdisciplinary Journal* 21 (7). 719–743.

Schreuder, Robert & R. Harald Baayen. 1995. Modeling morphological processing. In Laurie B. Feldman (ed.), *Morphological Aspects of Language Processing*, 131–154. Hillsdale, New Jersey: Lawrence Erlbaum.

Schreuder, Robert & R. Harald Baayen. 1997. How complex simplex words can be. *Journal of Memory and Language* 37 (1). 118–139.

Seidenberg, Mark S. & James L. McClelland. 1989. A distributed, developmental model of word recognition and naming. *Psychological Review* 96 (4). 523–568.

Smolka, Eva, Pienie Zwitserlood & Frank Rösler. 2007. Stem access in regular and irregular inflection: Evidence from German participles. *Journal of Memory and Language* 57 (3), 325–347.

Solomon, Richard and Davis, H. Howes. 1951. Word frequency, personal values, and visual duration thresholds. *Psychological Review* 58 (4). 256.

Suárez-Coalla, Paz & Fernando Cuetos. 2013. The role of morphology in reading in Spanish-speaking children with dyslexia. *Spanish Journal of Psychology* 16 (e51). 1–7.

Taft, Marcus. 1979. Recognition of affixed words and the word frequency effect. *Memory & Cognition* 7 (4). 263–272.

Taft, Marcus. 1994. Interactive-activation as a framework for understanding morphological processing. *Language and Cognitive Processes* 9(3). 271–294.

Taft, Marcus. 2004. Morphological decomposition and the reverse base frequency effect. *The Quarterly Journal of Experimental Psychology A: Human Experimental Psychology* 57A (4). 745–765.

Taft, Marcus & Kenneth I. Forster. 1975. Lexical storage and retrieval of prefixed words. *Journal of Verbal Learning and Verbal Behavior* 14 (6). 638–647.

Traficante, Daniela. 2012. From graphemes to morphemes: An alternative way to improve skills in children with dyslexia. *Revista de investigación en Logopedia* 2 (2). 163–185.

Traficante, Daniela & Cristina Burani. 2003. Visual processing of Italian verbs and adjectives: The role of inflectional family size. In R. Harald Baayen & Robert Schreuder (eds.), *Morphological Structure in Language Processing*, 45–64. Berlin: Mouton de Gruyter.

Traficante, Daniela, Stefania Marcolini, Alessandra Luci, Pierluigi Zoccolotti & Cristina Burani. 2011. How do roots and suffixes influence reading of pseudowords: A study of young Italian readers with and without dyslexia. *Language and Cognitive Processes* 26 (4). 777–793.

Traficante, Daniela, Marco Marelli, Claudio Luzzatti & Cristina Burani. 2014. Influence of verb and noun bases on reading aloud derived nouns: Evidence from children with good and poor reading skills. *Reading and Writing* 27 (7). 1303–1326.

Tsang, Yiu-Kei & Hsuan-Chih Chen. 2013. Early morphological processing is sensitive to morphemic meanings: Evidence from processing ambiguous morphemes. *Journal of Memory and Language* 68 (3). 223–239.

Tsang, Yiu-Kei & Hsuan-Chih Chen. 2014. Activation of morphemic meanings in processing opaque words. *Psychonomic bulletin & review* 21 (5). 1281–1286.

Turney, Peter D. & Patrick Pantel. 2010. From frequency to meaning: Vector space models of semantics. *Journal of Artificial Intelligence Research* 37 (1). 141–188.

Tzur, Boaz & Ram Frost. 2007. SOA does not reveal the absolute time course of cognitive processing in fast priming experiments. *Journal of Memory and Language* 56 (3). 321–335.

Van Ewijk, Lizet & Sergey Avrutin. 2011. Verb retrieval in non-fluent aphasia: An information-theoretic approach. *Procedia: Social and Behavioral Sciences* 23. 104–105.

Velan, Hadas, Ram Frost, Avital Deutsch & David C. Plaut. 2005. The processing of root morphemes in Hebrew: Contrasting localist and distributed accounts. *Language and Cognitive Processes* 20 (1–2). 169–206.

Verhoeven, Ludo & Charles A. Perfetti. 2011. Morphological processing in reading acquisition: A cross-linguistic perspective. *Applied Psycholinguistics* 32 (3). 457–466.

Yablonski, Maya & Michal Ben-Shachar. 2016. The morpheme-interference effect in Hebrew: A generalization across the verbal and nominal domains. *The Mental Lexicon* 11 (2). 277–307.

Ziegler, Johannes C. & Usha Goswami. 2005. Reading acquisition, developmental dyslexia and skilled reading across languages: A psycholinguistic grain size theory. *Psychological Bulletin* 131 (1), 3–29.

Dorit Ravid, Emmanuel Keuleers and Wolfgang U. Dressler
Emergence and early development of lexicon and morphology

Abstract: This chapter examines the emergence and development of lexicon and morphology in children's first three years of life. It provides a novel perspective on this dynamic and intense period of language learning by integrating different viewpoints on children's cognitive development with insights from empirical studies and theoretical properties of learning systems. The chapter is organized around seven focal points, which discuss the following: the limitations of linguistic terminology in the study of child language development; the relation between word learning and concept learning; typological influences on morpho-lexical development; the role of context; the co-development of lexicon and grammar; the importance of word class; and finally, the central role of development. Throughout the chapter, discussion of the focal points is supported by existing and novel empirical evidence from Hebrew and other languages.

Keywords: morpho-lexicon, early language acquisition, dynamic systems, typology, developmental processes, lexicon in context

1 Introduction

The examination of morpho-lexical acquisition and development in this chapter focuses on the well-researched period of the first three years of life. This is because most researchers would agree that children growing up in a monolingual environment have access to the vast majority of morphological and syntactic structures of their language before they reach school age. But questions about the nature and processes of morpho-lexical development are particularly relevant for the first three years of life as the most dynamic and intense period of language learning, which constitutes the basis for adult processing (Bonin et al. 2004; Johnston and Barry 2006). This is when the links between concepts and thought are first forged (Arunachalam and Waxman 2010a; Ferguson and Waxman 2017; Imai and Gentner

---

Dorit Ravid, School of Education, Tel Aviv University
Emmanuel Keuleers, Department of Cognitive Science and Artificial Intelligence, Tilburg University, Warandelaan Tilburg, The Netherlands
Wolfgang U. Dressler, Department of Linguistics, Universität Wien, Porzellangasse, Wien

Open Access. © 2020 Dorit Ravid et al., published by De Gruyter. This work is licensed under a Creative Commons Attribution-NonCommercial-NoDerivatives 4.0 International License.
https://doi.org/10.1515/9783110440577-015

1997), and when the foundations of lexicon and grammar are laid (Devescovi et al. 2005; Trudeau and Sutton 2011; Noble et al. 2016) and are put to use in early conversation (Abbot-Smith et al. 2016; Graf and Davies 2014). Moreover, the young lexicon reflects and in fact magnifies the core morphological and lexical features of the language being learned (Ravid et al. 2008), so that any foray into early lexical learning can teach us much about lexical development in general.

For an overall perspective on the path of early lexical development, consider the account presented in Caselli, Casadio and Bates (2001). While we do not necessarily adhere to this model in our presentation of morpho-lexical acquisition, it can provide readers who are not acquainted with the developmental psycholinguistic literature with a top-down picture of the growth of the lexicon in young children. The Caselli, Casadio and Bates account starts with a *Routine and Word Games* phase with a small (1–50 words) vocabulary, consisting mostly of communicative/social words (sound effects, social routines, onomatopoeic words, and names of favorite people) (Dromi 1987; Fenson et al. 1994; Kauschke and Hofmeister 2002). This phase is followed by a *Reference* phase (50–200 words), when the majority of words in the lexicon are nominals; when the core lexicon reaches about 100 words, it evolves into the third phase of *Predication*, characterized by increasing numbers of verbs, followed by adjectives, coinciding with first word combinations, and involving the ability to encode relational meanings (Thibaut and Witt 2015). Finally, when lexical size reaches about 300–500 words, the fourth phase of *Grammar* kicks in, correlated with indices of grammatical productivity such as MLU (mean length of utterance) and MSP (mean size of paradigm) (Xanthos et al. 2011). At this time, the lexicon contains a considerable number of function words in addition to content words. This is the arena our chapter aims to characterize and explain.

2 Focal assumptions

Seven focal assumptions provide the narrative and organizational framework of this chapter. They are as follows:
- Linguistic terminology must be contextualized
- Development is key
- Word learning is conceptual learning
- Language typology affects word learning
- Words are learned in context
- Lexicon and grammar co-develop
- Lexical learning is paced by word class.

2.1 Linguistic terminology must be contextualized

The literature on child language development uses formal linguistic terminology as a matter of course. When we read that children have a lexicon or that children acquire morphology, we can easily get the impression that the way language is structured in a child's mind is accurately reflected by the structure of language assumed by formal linguistics. However, the linguistic terminology used in the field of child language acquisition long predates the development of the field itself.

Therefore, in writing this chapter about the emergence and development of lexicon and morphology, we found it important to point out that the linguistic terminology we use should be seen as a convention rather than as a reflection of a child's mind. We think that in studying how children gain command of communication in their language, the usage of linguistic terminology should be contextualized. We will therefore briefly discuss three core linguistic concepts used throughout this chapter: language acquisition, lexicon and morphology.

The term *language acquisition* represents a linguistics-centered view on how children learn to communicate. It presupposes an abstract goal, *language*, that the child is unaware of, and that must be *acquired*. Young language learners, however, cannot be described as algorithms attempting to discover the structures and functions that linguists have defined. Rather, children are motivated to understand their environment, to express their desires and needs, and to achieve their goals. One way in which a child can do this is by observing communication and attempting to communicate with others. Successful communication is the standard by which a child learns the shared conventions used by people in her environment.

Like other linguistic terminology, the notions of *lexicon* and *morphology* do not originate in the study of children's communicative development. The term *lexicon* is rooted in the philological interpretation of Greek poetic texts, where it is generally used to refer to a list of words that a writer uses or, more generally, an exhaustive compilation of word usage. The term *morphology* originated with Goethe, who used it in the context of biological taxonomy, which in turn inspired its use in linguistics.

In the second half of the 20th century, in the wake of the cognitive revolution (Miller 2003), scholars started to draw direct parallels between linguistic terms and mental constructs, with Chomsky (1957) explicitly claiming grammar to be a cognitive faculty and later giving the lexicon a place in his theory (Chomsky 1965). In the literature, the term *mental lexicon* became used in reference to Chomsky's concept of lexicon (e.g., Lieberman 1969), finding its way into mainstream textbooks on psycholinguistics (Clark and Clark 1977; Foss and Hakes

1978). Around the same time, Taft and Forster (1975) started to draw parallels between linguistic morphology and the mental processing of morphologically complex words. Later, Pinker (1998, 1999) popularized the idea that the linguistic distinction between regular and irregular morphology corresponds with distinct cognitive processing systems.

In studying the development of children's communicative abilities, attributing a mental status to the linguistic notions of lexicon and morphology seems attractive. However, the systematic ways in which linguists use lexicon and morphology do not imply that children's knowledge or performance rely on a similar systematic organization. We must be aware that these concepts do not reside in the child; rather, they should be seen as conventions according to which scholars describe and classify children's communicative abilities, taking their description of adult lexicon and morphology as model. But older children, adolescents and adults reanalyze young children's acquisition outcomes. When we say that children *know* certain words or that their lexicon *contains* certain words, we do so according to a given linguistic definition of what a word is and according to a list of words matching this definition. Similarly, when we say that children have certain morphological abilities, we do so according to a pre-defined notion of morphology and of morphological categories. Likewise, these pre-defined linguistic concepts are used to construct stimuli for experimental tasks in which children's responses are elicited. The terminology we use also constrains what is considered relevant to observation and how observations are classified. For example, when we say that children have *correctly* acquired a word or a morphological category, the judgement of correctness is based on what is in the adult inventory instead of what constitutes communicative success.

Therefore, studying children's communicative development within a linguistic framework is useful because it allows us to describe part of children's linguistic development in a conventional way. However, we should also be aware that many aspects of child language are difficult to grasp or even misconstrued in using these conventions.

2.2 Development is key

From a linguist or language teacher's bird's eye perspective, morphological systems may be hugely complex and often opaque in terms of both meaning and structure, with immense variations across languages (Ackerman and Malouf 2013). The same question can be asked regarding the path to acquisition of the rich lexical semantics of words in adult language. For example, when Hebrew-acquiring children in their third year of life were asked (in the context of a music lesson) *le-histovev ba-xéder* 'to-wander in (=around)-the-room', many of them instead started turning around and around, following a basic interpretation of this instruction. Innate, abstract knowledge and universal maturational constraints have been invoked (Chomsky 1988) to explain the discrepancy between complex, rich and automatic morpho-lexical usage in adults, on the one hand, and children's limited cognitive abilities and the purported absence of negative evidence in language learning, on the other. One of the main problems with this view is that it conceives of morpho-lexical development as a straight line. Children must incessantly acquire more words and more morphological processes on their road to become ideal language users. However, any type of learning that progresses only in one way is doomed to fail in a noisy environment, as is illustrated by the classical hill climbing problem. Mountain climbers can use a strategy in which they start climbing and keep on going until there is no more up. Unless the mountain has a straight one-way slope, this strategy will almost surely fail. The climber must be able to backtrack from a local peak to be able to find the top of the mountain. A mountain with one straight slope to the top corresponds to a non-noisy environment. However, the situations in which language learning occurs are definitely noisy. Children are confronted with mountains of data and must make temporary assumptions about how to communicate successfully. The ability to let go of those assumptions, i.e., *non-monotonic learning*, eventually leads to a more successful way of communication.

Straight-line conceptions of language acquisition do not account for non-monotonic learning. On the other hand, there are models in which learning is central (see, for instance, Section 2.5.1). Because these models are constantly driven by the data, they are non-monotonic by design. Several strands of research on lexical and grammatical acquisition show that dynamic non-monotonic learning is key for morpho-lexical development. There is mounting evidence that children do require, receive and make use of efficacious positive and negative, direct and indirect feedback on their language productions over a long period of time (Chouinard and Clark 2003; Clark 2010; MacWhinney 2004; Moerk 1991). Elman (2003) formulated the idea that development in naturally noisy environments is the driving force in language learning, drawing attention to the important notion of "starting small" (Elman 1993), which means that young children are aided rather than hindered by limited cognitive resources. They start out with limited memory resources that only gradually improve and are at first exposed to only a limited number of frequent core examples of a language category. More complex but less representative sub-categories and items join in to construct categories over time.

We thus assume that morpho-lexical development occurs under constant pressure from the changing nature of the language input and the ability to predict relationships based on current stochastic knowledge. Knowledge structures emerge as a result of increased discrimination caused by learning over many different events. And morpho-lexical development is a gradual, uneven developmental process in which learners integrate different pieces of evidence to establish more and more relationships and regularities. Two studies illustrate this generalization. A study of Spanish acquisition (Mariscal 2009) showed that children construct abstract agreement categories based on a dynamically changing confluence of sources in the input, such as noun phonology and the shape of determiners, pronouns, and adjectives. A study on Lithuanian agreement (Savickienė, Kempe and Brooks 2009) found that children make use of the mediating factor of diminutive morphology in learning to mark adjective agreement and to ease acquisition of number and case in general (Savickienė and Dressler 2007). Both studies interpreted their results as showing that children store representations of units of various sizes and form generalizations at differing degrees of abstraction – rather than applying a rule to all members of a symbolic category. The same seems to be true of adult second language learners (Brooks, Kempe and Donachie 2011, on Russian).

To illustrate this path, take the example of Hebrew monosyllabic masculine nouns patterned as *CeC* (with Cs standing for root consonants) such as *ec* 'tree', *ken* 'nest', *cel* 'shadow', or *lev* 'heart'. Learning how to pluralize such nouns is a study in the work of frequency, transparency, regularity, and consistency. Young children tend to attach the regular masculine *-im* suffix to a non-changed stem, yielding correct *ecim* 'trees' but incorrect *kenim* 'nests', *celim* 'shadows' or *levim* 'hearts'. Gaining morpho-lexical experience about the distributions of categories of Hebrew plurals from encounters with numerous singular and plural nouns (Ravid and Schiff 2009) will result in a set of different, and more specific, expectations regarding *CeC* nouns. They tend to change their vowels as in *ken/kinim* 'nest/s' or to reveal a "double" root, as in, *cel/clalim* 'shadow/s'. Moreover, final voiced consonants tend to attract the irregular *-ot* on masculine nouns (Ravid and Schiff 2012), and hence, *lev/levavot* 'heart/s'. The property that *CeC* nouns share with other plural categories – changing vowels in the stem and irregular suffix – will emerge first, whereas greater exposure to more monosyllabic nouns will result in doubling consonants. Increased success on pluralizing nouns will reflect emerging generalizations based on type and token frequency and consistency of plural forms.

Another example of an uneven non-monotonic developmental process, which has been called a blind-alley development (Bittner, Dressler and Kilani-Schoch 2003), is characterized by children constructing, for a short transitional period, patterns which present a developmental direction away from adult targets. A case in point is, in the German compound development of two Viennese children, the over-generalization of a schwa (written -e-) at the end of the first compound constituent which represents descriptively both the overgeneralization of an -e- interfix and the lack of having an -n- interfix after a stem-final schwa. For example, from 2;2 onwards, Lena produced, for a few months, more incorrect than correct -e- interfixes, e.g. *Kinnesette* for *Kind+er+kassette* 'child-cassette', *Ralewasser* for *Mineral+wasser* 'mineral water', while omitting the -n- interfix in *Plattespieler* for *Platte+n+spieler* 'record-player'. The insertion of an -n- interfix in German *Platte+n+spieler* 'record-player' renders the identification of the first compound member *Platte* more difficult and thus diminishes morphotactic (also called: phonological) transparency of the compound. This obstacle for acquisition can explain why German children acquire interfixed compounding later than purely concatenative, i.e. interfixless compounding, as exemplified by *Polizei+auto* 'police car' (Dressler et al. 2010), although both patterns are productive and very frequent in ADS (adult directed speech) and CDS (child directed speech).

2.3 Word learning is conceptual learning

Cognitive science regards the human brain as the most powerful learning device shaped by evolution (Griffiths et al. 2010). A major task carried out by the human brain is mapping out the external and internal world in terms of objects, people, places, states, properties, ideas, actions, events, and processes (Sperber and Wilson 1998). These are encoded across an array of forms, from overt lexical units to periphrastic constructions (Goldberg, 1995). Our interest in the current context lies in the crossroads of language and conceptual development at a time when the foundations of individual human knowledge are established (Tooby, Cosmides and Barrett 2005; Wellman and Gelman 1998). We adopt here Evans' (2009) notion of *lexical concepts* as sense units inferred from the ambient language and stored as part of language knowledge, providing access to encyclopaedic knowledge structures, often encapsulating complex and informationally diffuse ideas (Langacker 1987). Importantly, Evans regards lexical concepts as knowledge structures specialized for symbolic representation.

Children begin linguistic acquisition with strong conceptual capacities and a tendency to encode lexical concepts in linguistic units (Clark 2004; Mandler 2000; Spelke 2000). Early on, infants are able to distinguish between different people, objects and events by noticing their perceptual properties, the ways they move and interact, and the changes they undergo (Arunachalan and Waxman 2010b; Clark and Lindsey 2015; Gentner and Boroditsky 2001). Across the learning years, children sharpen these abilities, enhanced by their socio-cognitive and linguistic development, by the emergence of categories from items used, learned and repeated, by the changing linguistic and communicative contexts in which they occur, and by feedback extracted from the ambient language – from both older and more experienced language users, as well as from the children themselves (Blackwell 2005; Clark 2015; Houston-Price, Plunkett and Duffy 2006). Following the ultimate achievement of exhaustive categorization in infants – discovering that every object can be named (Booth and Waxman 2002; Nazzi and Bertoncini 2003) – children obtain an increasing lexicon of words guided by principles such as Conventionality (well established words have conventional meanings) and Contrast (words differ in meaning[1]) (Clark 1993). Words breed concepts, and concepts lay the ground for new words (Waxman and Leddon 2011).

Based on these abilities, children's vocabulary will grow and diversify in both breadth and depth in tandem with the increase in the range of situations, events, states and relationships encountered (Evans 2009), with a focus on literacy contexts and events (Anglin 1993; Ravid 2005; Ravid and Tolchinsky 2002). Later Language Development across the school years ushers in written language, forming the basis for the literate lexicon, which is embedded in academic fields and disciplines (Olson 1996). Thus, new lexical items, more meanings and word knowledge in general will come to reflect the conceptual knowledge of adult language users and their construal of the world. Against the backdrop of initial lexical learning and the long developmental route to the mature lexicon, the acquisition window adopted in the current chapter focuses on the core mental lexicon of children as a faithful reflection of their knowledge base about the world prior to the onset of written language (Berman 1997).

2.4 Language typology affects word learning

Much about the course of lexical learning is universal. Symbolic play, communicative gestures and word comprehension start in infants around their first birthday (Barbieri et al. 2009; Fasolo and D'Odorico 2012), platformed by shared cognitive and socio-cognitive skills (Tomasello 2003). Moreover, the semantic-pragmatic contents of children's early lexicons are strikingly similar across different languages and cultures, based on perceptual salience, frequency and

---

1 But that does not hold for pragmatically used diminutives and hypocoristics. Thus, in Italian, diminutives from English *vip* do not block each other: *vipp-ino*, *vipp-etto*, *vipp-uccio* + three others, plus 24 more examples of diminutive suffixation rivalry, more in Dressler et al. 2019.

communicative relevance (Clark 1993; Golinkoff and Hirsh-Pasek 2008; Pruden et al. 2006; Slobin 1985). However, languages differ dramatically in how semantic concepts such as space, number or time are formally encoded (Bowerman and Choi 2001; Lucy and Gaskins 2001). The typological impact of morphological richness is especially compelling in the course of lexical learning. This is because comparable lexical meaning can be expressed with varying degrees of morphological complexity in different languages (Koptjevskaja-Tamm 2012). For example, verb semantics follows verb morphology, taking into account the meaning of each derivational component, so that an unanalyzed form correlates with a simple meaning, while a complex, derived form correlates with a likewise complex meaning (Kibrik 2012; Talmy 2007).

This means that in acquiring a vocabulary, children learning a morphology-rich language will have to pay particular attention to the internal structure of words in order to learn to extract and express meaning. The literature indeed shows that the role of morphology in lexical acquisition varies with its richness and prominence in the language. Morphological development is faster when the input language is morphologically richer (Dressler 2007; Xanthos et al. 2011). Thus, Turkish children acquire their very rich inflectional morphology earlier than English children acquire their relatively morphologically poor one (Dressler 2010). In languages with a rich morphology, lexical growth interfaces with morphology earlier on and in more ways (Ravid 2012) in both typically developing and disordered populations (Bavin 1998; Dromi, Leonard and Shteiman 1993; Levie, Ben-Zvi and Ravid 2017). For example, for Hebrew- and Arabic-speaking children, verb learning is necessarily bound with learning the two non-linear morphological components of Semitic root and pattern. Thus, young Hebrew-speaking children rely on tri-consonantal roots as the most accessible option in their lexical innovations (Berman 1985; Clark 1993). Children as young as three years of age are able to interpret novel root-based nouns, indicating their ability to extract the root from the given test item. By age four, they are able to coin semantically appropriate novel verbs from other verbs in a form consistent with the structural stipulations of their grammar (Berman 1990; Berman 1999; Clark and Berman 1984). In fact, non-linear root-and-pattern affixation precedes linear suffixation in the acquisition of Hebrew adjectives (Berman 1994; Berman 1997; Ravid, Bar-On, et al. 2016; Ravid and Nir 2000). Likewise, children acquiring spoken Palestinian Arabic are able to manipulate "broken" root-and-pattern noun plurals such as *shubba:k/shabbabi:k* 'window/s', as early as age three-four years (Ravid and Hayek 2003; Ravid and Farah 1999; Saiegh-Haddad, Hadieh and Ravid 2012).

2.5 Words are learned in context

The linguistic literature has long recognized that words are creatures of their communicative environments (Medina et al. 2011). Lexical meaning is generally derived directly from how language is actually used (Clark and Wong 2002; Croft 2000; Langacker 2000), consistent with Wittgenstein's dictum that "For a *large* class of cases – though not for all – in which we employ the word 'meaning' it can be defined thus: the meaning of a word is its use in the language" (Wittgenstein 1953, 43).

The syntactic, discursive, pragmatic and environmental contexts in which words are encountered are not merely helpful in lexical acquisition and processing, they are in fact inherent to determining the nature of a word's meaning, including context-specific shifts in senses (Evans 2009; Pustejovsky 1995). To gain the breadth and depth of word knowledge, words must be experienced frequently in their contexts (Ambridge et al. 2015; Hulme et al. 1997; Sandoval and Gómez 2013). That is, numerous, variegated encounters with words are critical for them to be interpreted, organized into categories (Ferguson and Waxman 2017) and learned, including the creation of long-range relationships between similar environments to sustain new-word acquisition (Clark, 2016; Landauer and Dumais, 1997).

This insight promotes the examination of children's productions in their natural context. Cross-sectional testing, a long tradition in child language investigation, is somewhat problematic as it overlooks the different developmental paths of different children, based on formal tests that often use adult-directed adult language as a yardstick instead of the input of the investigated children, and probe children's metalinguistic knowledge instead of their spontaneous usage in natural interactions. While we do not debate the importance of cross-sectional investigations, some of which providing evidence in the current study, this underscores the importance of collecting and analyzing longitudinal corpora of children's spontaneous interactions with care-takers and their environment (Bittner et al. 2003; Dressler et al. 2017; Savickienė and Dressler 2007; Slobin 1985; Stephany and Voeikova 2009).

2.5.1 Frequency, information, and learning

To fully understand the contextual learning of words, it is necessary to understand how mere frequency influences word learning. Frequency, or the number of occurrences of a word in the environment, is one of the most important factors in adult lexical processing, so that the speed with which adults can identify words is sensitive to minute differences in frequency of occurrence of those words (Keuleers, Brysbaert and Diependaele 2010). When considering the role of frequency in acquisition, a first thing to note is that encounters with words are, first and foremost, opportunities for lexical learning. All else being equal, the frequency of a word in CDS is proportional to learning opportunity. A second fact worth underscoring is that the role of a word's frequency before it has been learned is different from its role after it has been learned. While greater frequency initially corresponds to greater opportunity for learning, once a word has been acquired, greater frequency reinforces its acquisition by easing processing and serving to bootstrap the learning of other words.

A simple but naive view of acquisition would suggest that words that are more frequent are also acquired earlier. However, if the child were indeed to develop her lexicon based on frequency distributions alone, she would start by learning some very frequent function words and pronouns. Morphemes, especially affixes, which are also very frequent in speech, would also be acquired very early. But this is not the case: Lexical learning starts with referential rather than grammatical elements. There are several reasons why the relation between frequency and acquisition is not so straightforward. First, frequent words are often not related to things that are salient, that is, of importance to the child. Second, frequent words such as articles, and function words are often irrelevant in achieving communicative success, especially early on. Moreover, they are usually very abstract, representing relations rather than objects, people and events. Finally, words that are used often and across contexts are not informative about a particular situation, and therefore they are less likely to draw a child's attention (cf. Section 2.5.2).

Information theory (Shannon and Weaver 1949) offers a mathematical basis for understanding the learning of words in context. Consider a situation in which a parent and child are playing with a ball while suddenly a cat walks in. Let's assume that the child hears a few sentences in which *the ball* occurs, while in one situation it hears *the cat*. Frequency information only tells us that the word *the* has been encountered 5 times, the word *ball* has been encountered 4 times and the word *cat* just once. Therefore, we would expect the child to learn the word *the* before it learns the words *ball* and *cat* – which is never the case. Information theory allows us to go beyond this simple frequency information by evaluating how informative each word is. First, we need to establish that a word that occurs with equal frequency in any situation is not informative about any of those situations in particular. On the other end of a spectrum, a word that occurs in a single situation is probably informative about that situation. Information theory calls the unpredictability of an event its *entropy*. The lower the entropy of a word, the more informative a word is about a particular situation. Entropy can be computed according to the formula:

$$H = - \sum_i p_i log_2(p_i)$$

In our example, this gives the following results:

$$H_{the} = -5 \times 0.2 log_2(0.2) = 2.32$$

$$H_{ball} = -4 \times 0.25 log_2(0.25) + 1 \times 0 log_2(0) = 2.00$$

$$H_{cat} = -1 \times 1 log_2(1) + 4 \times 0 log_2(0) = 0$$

Thus, while *the* occurs often, it is not predictive of any situation. The entropy of *ball* is slightly lower, and therefore it is more informative about the situations *ball* occurs in. Finally, there is no uncertainty about the situation that *cat* occurred in. Although the frequency of *cat* is just one, its absence in other situations means that it was almost certainly relevant to the situation it occurred in. Information theory therefore shows that while each occurrence of a word presents a child with learning opportunities, the distribution of those learning opportunities across contexts also plays an important role in acquisition.

The intuitions that information theory provides about learning occurring against a background of contextual events are also present in the discriminative learning model (Rescorla and Wagner 1972) which has been successfully applied to language learning tasks. The Rescorla-Wagner model is a general learning model that can be applied to any task where the occurrence of a certain type of events happens in connection with another type of events. In the context of language acquisition, the model has been applied to word learning (Ramscar, Dye and Klein 2013), showing that when learning new words, children's judgements about what is most informative about those words is predicted by their co-occurrence with objects and events in the environment, relative to how well other words match those objects and events. A central feature of the model is that it attends to whether events occur together (positive evidence) as well as whether they do not occur together (negative evidence). In this view, also called *discriminative learning*, children can work out the meaning of words by calculating whether the positive evidence for a word is larger than the negative evidence. For instance, if a child hears the phrase *the ball* three times accompanied by a picture of a ball, and *the cat* two times, associated with a picture of a cat, it will be clear that there is positive evidence for an association between the word *cat* and something in the picture of the cat and for an association between the word *ball* and something in the picture of the ball. However, the set of events would also have provided information to discriminate between the parts of the pictures tied to the words *cat* and *ball*, because positive evidence for one was also negative evidence for the other. Second, there has been absolutely no learning of the word *the* as there was only positive evidence connecting it to every outcome.

2.5.2 Parental input and word learning

In child language, the connection between how often a word occurs in the environment and the time at which it is learned can be elusive, so that care should be taken to use valid measures. Word frequency in corpora correlates with age of acquisition (AoA) when these corpora consist of CDS or children's own output, Child Speech (CS) (Ashkenazi, Ravid and Gillis 2016; Kidd, Lieven and Tomasello 2010; Matthews et al. 2005), but not when this frequency is derived from written language (Goodman, Dale and Li 2008; Hansen 2017). Child lexical development is thus highly reliant on the quantity and quality of the ambient language and while later on in development peer input becomes more important (Labov 2014; Ravid, Olshtain and Ze'elon 2003), early child lexical development depends most notably on the linguistic input provided by parents.

The study of the relation between CDS and CS has long been absent from the scientific inquiry into language acquisition, largely due to nativistic assumptions and to the excessive reliance on experimental results where CDS has not been available. But this study has gained momentum in the last decades under datadriven, usage-based accounts, as reviewed in Behrens (2006). Studies indicate that CDS is the main source available to the child regarding the patterning of words and morphemes in her language (Hoff-Ginsberg 1985; Maslen et al. 2004), presenting children with the core, most frequent and consistent aspects of linguistic systems (Ravid et al., 2008; Ravid, Ashkenazi, et al. 2016). CDS moreover mediates word learning by presenting words in short utterances (Bergeson, Miller and McCune 2006) and at a slower rate of speech when children start using words and combining them (Ko 2012). Mediated language input enables young learners to analyze the distributional properties of the speech they hear and induce linguistic categories based on distributional and frequency information through pattern detection (Tomasello 2006). Child-adult conversations allow word learning to take place in situations characterized by mutual attention and responsiveness, in constant interaction with adults' corrections, reformulations and expansions and children's own uptake and imitations (Clark 2007; Clark and Bernicot 2008; Veneziano and Parisse 2010). To take a specific example, in languages with rich and variegated compounding devices, the degree of richness of compounding in CDS is a predictor for the age of compounds becoming productive in CS. As shown in Dressler et al. (2017), this takes place earlier in children acquiring Danish, Estonian, Finnish, German and Saami (before two years of age) than in children acquiring French, Greek, Hebrew and Russian, where compounding is a less prevalent device (Berman 2009; Clark and Berman 1984; Ravid and Zilberbuch 2003).

The relationship between children's ambient language and their own speech has been demonstrated using different research methods such as computer simulations, artificial language learning, naturalistic corpus analysis, and elicitation procedures for all aspects of native language learning (Behrens, 2008). Particularly relevant to the topic at hand, these relations impact lexical learning: higher frequency words in CDS are acquired earlier on in CS (Hansen 2017; Huttenlocher et al. 1991; Kidd, Lieven and Tomasello 2010). Moreover, children's production of specific structures has been shown to correlate highly with parents' frequent and variegated usage of these structures (Brodsky, Waterfall and Edelman 2007; Naigles and Hoff-Ginsberg 1998). It is not only token frequency that drives lexical learning, as high type frequency of a certain category will lead to earlier productivity of this category in the child's speech (Bybee 2001, 2006; Lieven 2010; Maslen, Theakston and Tomasello 2004). As type frequency increases, a category is formed, which can be deployed to produce and understand items that were not present in the input (Borovsky and Elman 2006; Boyd and Goldberg 2009). Note, however, that while acknowledging these strong relationships, the input is not a direct representation of the child's actual intake and the output is not a direct representation of the uptake. Prosodically and positionally more salient structures have a higher chance of being perceived and thus taken in by children than less salient structures; and what children attend to and take up is a black box for the observer, who has to reconstruct children's uptake by a close study of input-output relations (Goldschneider and DeKeyser 2001; Harris 1992; Stemberger and Chávez-Peón 2014).

2.5.3 Hebrew verb roots: A case study in the CDS-CS relation

A recent study of Hebrew verb development (Ashkenazi 2015; Ashkenazi et al. 2016) demonstrates CDS – CS relations, focusing on the Semitic roots of verbs, a critical morpho-lexical component in Hebrew (Ben Zvi and Levie 2016; Berman 1985; Ravid 1995). Most Hebrew words participate in morphological families based on a single root and varying in the non-linear vocalic patterns that shape different words (Berman 1987; Bolozky 1999; Ravid 1990; Schwarzwald 2002). For example, the morphological family related by root *m-s-r* 'deliver, convey' contains the verbs *masar* 'deliver', *nimsar* 'be delivered', *hitmaser* 'devote oneself', the adjective *masur* 'devoted', and the nouns *mesira* 'delivery', *hitmasrut* 'dedication', *mesirut* 'devotion', *méser* 'message', *mimsar* 'relay', *tamsir* 'handout', *timsóret* 'transmission', and *misron* 'text message'. Abundant evidence points to the Semitic root as the most accessible Hebrew morpheme across different age groups and populations (Levie, Ben Zvi and Ravid 2017; Ravid 2003). Root-and-pattern structure organizes lexical processing and learning in Hebrew speech, reading and writing (Bar-On and Ravid 2011; Frost 2012; Frost, Deutsch and Forster 2000; Gillis and Ravid 2006; Ravid 2001, 2005, 2012; Ravid and Bar-On 2005; Ravid and Schiff 2006a; Velan et al. 2005). Hebrew verbs constitute the prototypical habitat of this non-linear structure as an early-acquired content-word class composed solely of roots and patterns in both derivation and temporal inflection (Berman, 1994; Ravid et al. 2016a). Thus, verb acquisition is highly dependent on learning to identify relations among verbs sharing the same root, that is, sharing similar basic lexical content, with different vocalic patterns (termed *binyanim* lit. 'buildings') encoding transitivity and Aktionsart relations. For example, *nirdam/hirdim* 'fall asleep/put to sleep' or *lavash/hilbish/hitlabesh* 'wear/dress someone/dress oneself' share roots *r-d-m* 'sleep' and *l-b-š* 'wear' respectively in verbs with different vocalic patterns.

Ashkenazi (2015) showed that verb and root types produced by the two children (aged 1;8–2;2) in her densely recorded database (Table 1) were a subset of their parents' usage. That is, the children did not produce any verb form or verb root that did not appear in their parents' recorded usage, although they were evidently exposed to a larger set of language by them and by other caregivers. This finding illustrates the critical influence lexical input exerts on lexical uptake and output, and in a wider perspective, points to a core lexical inventory that is probably shared across caregivers and children. She also showed that parental verb types and tokens and children's verb types and tokens were highly correlated: Not only was each parent's root inventory and

Table 1: Words, verbs and roots in Ashkenazi (2015).

Numbers	CHILD SPEECH (CS)			CHILD DIRECTED SPEECH (CDS)		
	Total	Girl	Boy	Total	To Girl	To Boy
Word tokens	72,086	39,717	32,369	299,461	158,679	140,782
Verb tokens	7711	4610	3101	55,109	31,279	23,830
Verb types	259	204	172	684	531	503
Root types	224	204	172	534	437	426

total root input highly correlated with the child's root inventory and total root input, the root productions of the parents of the different children were highly correlated in types, structural (regular and irregular) root categories, and tokens. Likewise, the root productions of the different children were highly correlated; and the root productions of the first set of parents were highly correlated with the root productions of the toddler of the other parents. As roots are the basic lexical unit in Hebrew verbs, this indicates that the structure of the core verb lexicon in parents and children is highly similar (Ashkenazi, Gillis and Ravid 2019).

2.5.4 SES and maternal input profoundly influence morpho-lexical abilities

The robust relationship between parents' and children's lexicons leads to the question whether poor lexical input can deprive children of maximizing their language abilities. Differences in Socio-Economic Status (SES) have been linked to linguistic domains critical to early language learning, including sensitivity to the phonetic structure of words, morpho-phonology, and Theory of Mind (Blachman et al. 1999; Cutting and Dunn 1999; Korecky-Kröll and Dressler 2015; Nittrouer, 1996; Shatz et al. 2003; Ravid 1995). Lexical development is particularly affected by SES background (Arriaga et al. 1998; Qi et al. 2006). From infancy, the lexical repertoire of low-SES children lags behind that of more advantaged peers (Black, Peppé and Gibbon, 2008), with slower growth of both oral and written vocabulary (Farkas and Beron 2004; Walker et al. 1994). These SES-related effects on language abilities emerge early on (Betancourt, Brodsky and Hurt 2015; Fernald, Marchman and Weisleder 2013; Fish and Pinkerman 2003), involving the development of crucial brain regions (Kishiyama et al. 2009; Noble, Norman and Farah 2005), and important cognitive functions (D'Angiulli et al. 2008; Engel, Santos and Gathercole 2008; Farah et al. 2006; Fazio 1997).

To demonstrate the impact of SES on morpho-lexical knowledge in school age, Ravid and Schiff (2006b) compared high-SES and low-SES Hebrew-speaking grade school children on their ability to analyze roots and patterns in morphologically complex written words. This was a task that required the completion of an analogy problem by picking the correct noun out of five alternatives. Out of the four distractors, three were morphological – two of them root-related and one pattern-related; the fourth distractor bore a semantic, but non-morphological relationship to the target noun.

Figure 1 shows that the low-SES children consistently lagged two years behind their high-SES peers in range of correct responses, indicating a lesser ability to analyze words into their root and pattern components – a skill that is

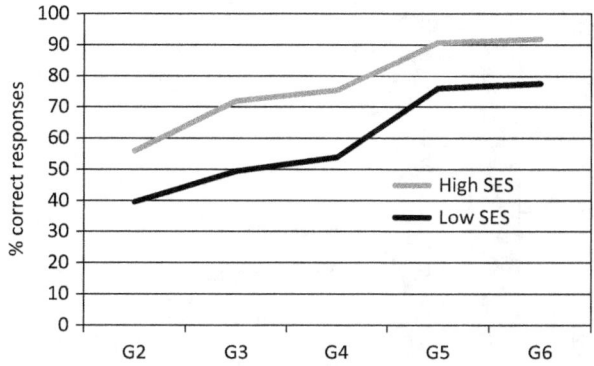

Figure 1: Correct responses on the Analogy Task in Hebrew-speaking grade schoolers from high- and low-SES backgrounds (Ravid & Schiff, 2006b).

both reliant on and supportive of lexical knowledge (Anglin 1993; Carlisle 2000).

Figures 2 and 3 indicate that the difference was not only quantitative. When high-SES children made an error, they overwhelmingly chose the Semitic root distractor in all age groups. In contrast, low-SES children in second grade chose other distractors more often, including non-morphological semantic distractors; in older age groups, they chose the root distractor more often. In a morphologically rich language such as Hebrew, where lexical learning is dependent on extracting structural and semantic connections between words,

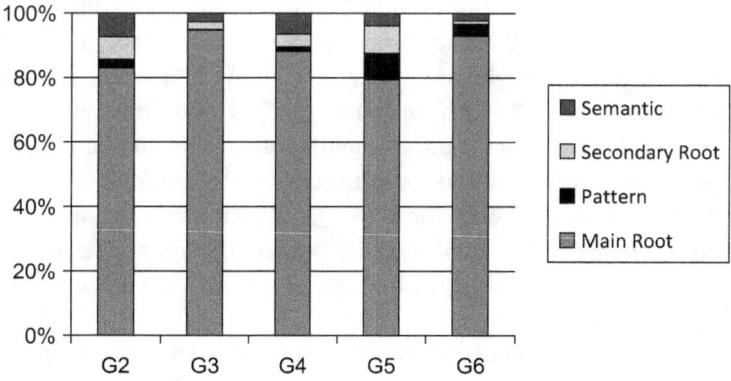

Figure 2: Erroneous responses based on types of distractors in the Analogy Task, high-SES grade schoolers (Ravid & Schiff, 2006b).

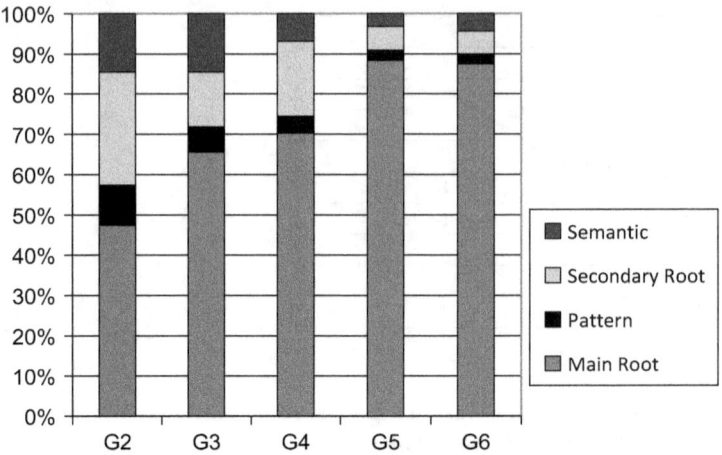

Figure 3: Erroneous responses based on types of distractors in the Analogy Task, low-SES grade schoolers (Ravid & Schiff, 2006b).

these discrepancies raise concerns regarding a reduced ability to understand and learn new words. Several other studies have shown that school-aged children from low SES struggle in relating words via their inflectional and derivational morphemes (Berman, Nayditz and Ravid 2011; Schiff and Lotem 2011; Schiff and Ravid 2012), with disturbing similarities to children with linguistic impairment (Levie, Ben-Zvi and Ravid 2017).

One major source of SES-related differences in schoolchildren is parental input and interaction in early childhood, with maternal education as a differentiating factor (Prevoo et al. 2014; Suizzo and Stapleton 2007). The literature shows that children from low-SES background are provided with less linguistic input, less scaffolding and fewer elaboration and commentary on their spoken production (Hart and Risley 1995; Hoff and Tian 2005). These differences are related to maternal sensitivity and cognitive stimulation, on the one hand, and to maternal speech and linguistic input to children, on the other (Hoff 2003; Hoff and Naigles 2002; Weizman and Snow 2001), with maternal engagement and parenting style mediating the relationship between SES and maternal language (Raviv, Kessenich and Morrison 2004; Song, Spier and Tamis-Lemonda 2014; Vernon-Feagans et al. 2008).

A recent study comparing the CDS of two native Hebrew-speaking mothers of toddler girls aged 1;6, one from high- and another from low-SES background, is a case in point (Ravid and Zimmerman 2017). This study found that at a time known for accelerated language development and subsequent increasing complexity in CDS in many children and parents (Foursha-Stevenson et al. 2017; Lieven 2008; Ravid et al. 2008; Snow 1995), linguistic input to the toddler from low SES was scarcer based on all measures used. She experienced less speech input, mostly directive and non-elaborative, with a lower density and diversity of lexicon and morpho-syntax, and almost no object and activity naming. There was constant background noise accompanying the highly repetitive, sometimes incomprehensible input. Little linguistic interaction took place between mother and child, and the mother often did not follow up her daughter's interest in her surroundings.

A second study compared input from native Hebrew-speaking mothers of different SES backgrounds to two respective infants at 3, 6, 9 and 12 months of age (Peleg 2013). Across the study, there was more verbal input to the high-SES infant at all time points. The high-SES mother's speech was more variegated, and her pragmatic categories were fine-tuned to the child. In the recordings, she repeats, refers, elaborates, informs, encourages, names, and introduces new vocabulary at appropriate ages. Her speech was encouraging, and contained more nouns, more verbs, and more adjective types than in the low-SES mother. The latter talked much less, was less pragmatically tuned to the child, exhibited more vagueness, prohibited more, provided fewer opportunities for learning, and had a more restricted lexicon.

Two figures demonstrate these effects by comparing the numbers of words (tokens and types) and utterances (Figure 4), and the content word lexicon (tokens, inflected word types and lemmas of nouns, verbs and adjectives) the infants heard at 9 and 12 months by the high-SES mother and the low-SES mother respectively (Figure 5). The two findings demonstrated in these figures repeatedly echoed across this study. One, the consistent discrepancy in the number of linguistic units offered by the high-SES mother as compared to the mother from low SES in same-length recordings. And two, the fact that this number increased in the high-SES mother towards the first year of life, when children are in need of rich and variegated lexical input, whereas in the low-SES mother it actually declined. These findings join many other studies in linking the amount and quality of linguistic input addressed to children with SES background of parents in general and mothers in particular (Black, Peppé, and Gibbon 2008; Hoff 2003; Rowe 2008), with scarcer input resulting in children's slower and less effective rate of language acquisition (Ginsborg 2006; Korecky-Kröll et al. 2017). Again and again, this linkage proved to be a major stumbling block in low-SES children's linguistic and cognitive development (Rowe, Raudenbush and Goldin-Meadow 2012).

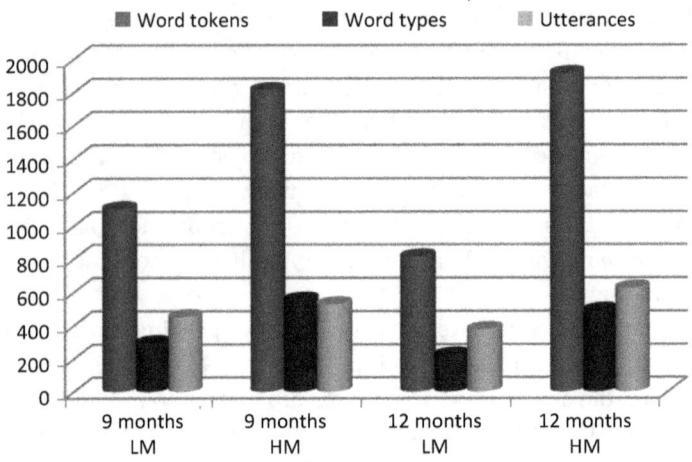

Figure 4: Numbers of word tokens, word types, and utterances in CDS by low SES and high SES mothers (respectively) to infants aged 9 and 12 months (Peleg, 2013).

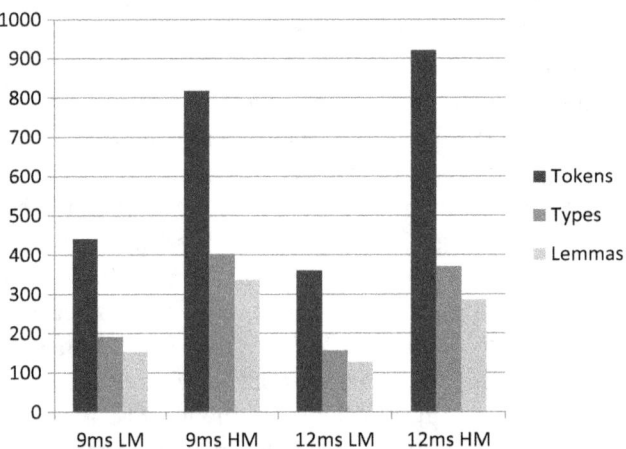

Figure 5: Numbers of content-word tokens, types, and lemmas in CDS by low-SES and high-SES mothers (respectively) to infants aged 9 and 12 months (Peleg, 2013).

2.6 Lexicon and grammar co-develop

The generative tradition views lexicon and grammar as essentially separate cognitive capacities (e.g., Clahsen and Veríssimo 2016; Pinker 1998), which would also suggest different temporal development. However, the acquisition literature supports the view that children's grammatical development emerges in tandem with their lexical growth (Ashkenazi et al., 2019). One facet of this relationship is the close affinity between lexical frequency and the formation of grammatical generalizations (Ambridge et al. 2008; Borovsky, Elman and Fernald 2012; Matthews et al. 2005). Across languages, vocabulary size has been found to be the single most powerful predictor of children's grammatical development (Caselli et al. 2001; Devescovi et al. 2005). This makes sense, as content words fill designated syntactic positions in clauses and phrases, constitute the heads of syntactic phrases, and provide the stems for morphological inflection. The development of skills which allow children to organize words into morphological families and to form new words in word formation (derivation and compounding), and to express syntactic and pragmatic relations (inflection) are sustained and fed by the emergence and consolidation of syntactic abilities (Arnon and Clark 2011; Borovsky et al. 2016).

The inherent relationship between lexical and grammatical development is demonstrated in a study that investigated the growth of Hebrew temporal semantics, the structure of the Hebrew verb paradigm, and the emergence of communicative competence in conversation in mental verbs produced in the conversation of preschool children (Egoz-Liebstein 2010). Mental verbs, designating psychological events, states and concepts of desire, belief, and intention (e.g., *know, forget, lie, understand, plan*), occupy an important place in the construal of behavior and thus on the understanding of self and interpersonal relations (Montgomery 2002). Tables 2 and 3 and Figures 6 and 7 tell a developmental story that connects morphology, lexicon and semantics in a compelling way. From a distributional perspective, the sheer volume of mental verbs (in verb lemmas) increases across the preschool and early school years, with a prominent increase in new mental verb lemmas in the two oldest groups. An analysis of these lemmas (Table 2 and 3) indicates that the numbers of the *binyan* patterns that mental verbs take increase as children grow older; and that these verbs diversified in content and abstractness from toddlerhood to later childhood – from modal *want*

Table 2: Numbers and names of different *binyan* verb patterns of mental verb in children's Hebrew peer talk (Egoz-Liebstein 2010).

2-year olds	2;6-year olds	3-year olds	4-year olds	5-year olds	7-year olds
Qal	Qal, Hif'il, Hitpa'el	Qal, Hif'il, Pi'el	Qal, Nif'al, Hif'il, Hitpa'el	Qal, Nif'al, Hif'il, Pi'el, Hitpa'el	Qal, Nif'al, Hif'il, Pi'el, Hitpa'el

Table 3: New mental verb lemmas in each age group, baselined on the youngest group (Egoz-Liebstein 2010).

2-year olds	2;6-year olds	3-year olds	4-year olds	5-year olds	7-year olds
be able	think	upset	worry	choose	dream
love	be afraid	hope	remember	be chosen	investigate
want	forget	calm down,Tr	be angry	hate	feel concern
know	understand		be sure	be offended	mistake
	scare		enjoy	calm down,Int	be right
	interrupt		change	confuse	be happy
	allow		bore	give up	swear
	feel shame		believe	teach	interest
			decide	cheat	lie
			offend	terrify	plan
			get confused	invent	be willing
				agree	disgust
				feel	
				mean	
				insist	

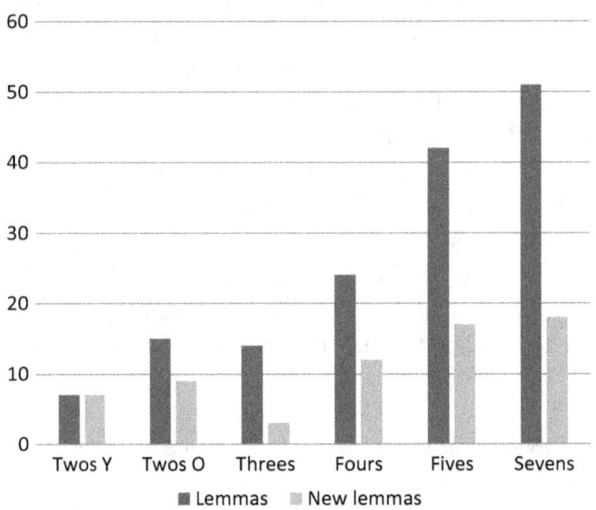

Figure 6: Increase in numbers of mental verb lemmas and new mental verb lemmas in children's peer talk (Egoz-Liebstein 2010). Children's age groups are, respectively 2;0, 2;6, 3, 4, 5 and 7.

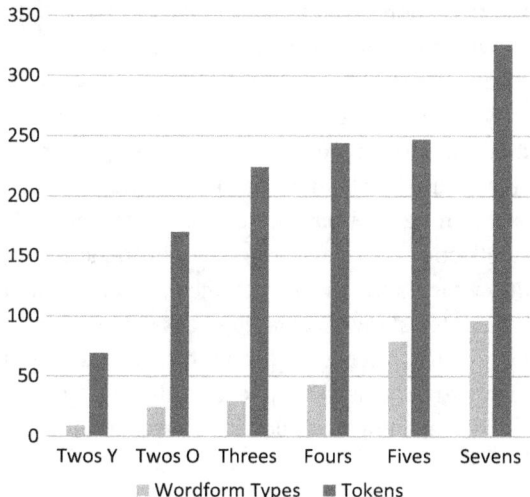

Figure 7: Increase in numbers of mental verb tokens and inflected mental verb types in children's peer talk (Egoz-Liebstein 2010). Children's age groups are, respectively 2;0, 2;6, 3, 4, 5 and 7.

and *be able*, the canonical cognitive *know* and canonical emotive *love* in the youngest age group, through basic concepts like *think* and *understand* in 2;6-year-olds, to mentalistic states and events like *worry, remember, confuse* and *mistake* and verbs involved in interpersonal "mind reading" such as *offend, agree* and *lie* in the older age groups. This is one basis for children's narrative abilities and hypothetical mental and interactional transactions.

Derivational morphology (Table 2) clearly supports this growth with a concurrent increase in the different *binyan* verb patterns of mental verbs, indicating the emergence of robust morphological abilities (Ravid, Ashkenazi, et al. 2016). While all mental verbs in the youngest group of toddlers were in *Qal*, the most basic and prevalent verb pattern in Modern Hebrew, 2;6- and three-year transcripts showed mental verbs in three different verb patterns, increasing to four in four-year-olds, and finally all five non-passive *binyan* verb patterns in the two oldest groups. Thus, both lexical frequency (in terms of verb lemmas and new lemmas) and lexical diversity (in terms of number of *binyan* verb patterns) increased in mental verbs in childhood.

Inflectional morphology (tense and mood, number, gender and person agreement) consolidated across the same period, especially towards school age, with a parallel growth of lexical and grammatical morphology supporting discursive abilities. In toddlers, the extremely limited expression of mental verbs also focused on self in present tense, with no person inflections. The sheer volume of mental talk in tokens leaped in three-year-olds, with the emergence of person inflections and reference to past mental actions/states coming at the same time. The growing command of inflectional verb morphology and temporality promoted less concrete and immediate conversational foci in children by asking questions, addressing interlocutors with inquiries regarding others' mental states and processes, and narrative talk. The growth of this mental lexicon in verb lemmas in four- and five-year-olds was accompanied by diversifying inflections, underscoring the consolidation of verb paradigm and verb temporality, which support maintenance of conversation topic. Finally, second-grade seven-year-olds showed a great increase in word form types with all person, number and gender inflections, evenly distributed across tense and mood categories, with many large same-verb inflection clusters, accompanying the emergence of 'mental state reasoning' in children's conversations.

2.7 Lexical learning is paced by word class

The last point in our presentation of lexical and morphological development is that the semantics, syntax, and morpho-phonology of different word classes affect their accessibility to children as well as the rate of their uptake. Thus, for example, adjectives are the smallest (often absent) and most diverse lexical category in many languages (Dixon and Aikhenvald 2006; Schachter and Shopen 2007). As relational terms, adjectives show up later on in child speech than nouns and verbs (Salerni et al. 2007), and they constitute a low-frequency class compared to other content words in children's early lexicons (Tribushinina et al. 2015; Sandhofer, Smith, and Luo 2000). A full array of adjectival categories is far from present even in six-year-olds (Blackwell 2005; Blodgett and Cooper 1988), suggesting it coincides with the consolidation of a literate lexicon and its cognitive correlates (Dockrell and Messer 2004; Ravid, Bar-On et al. 2016). The size and makeup of the adjective category can therefore be taken as a yardstick for language development and proficiency across development (Ravid and Levie 2010).

Data from an unpublished doctoral dissertation (Herzberg 2010) on the lexical development of three typically-developing native Hebrew-speaking children from mid-high-SES background provide an illustration of the development of word classes across the second and third year of life. Herzberg (2010) examined the changing distributions of three classes of word tokens in the early lexicon – communicative/social words (including childish inventions and unintelligible communications), content words and function words. These distributions were examined longitudinally from two perspectives – based on children's chronological

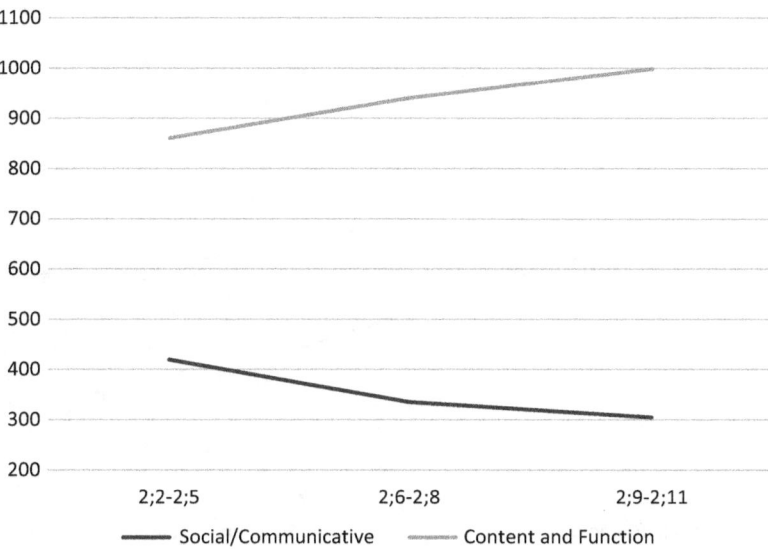

Figure 8: Median tokens of social/communicative and referential (content/function) words in three typically-developing Hebrew-speaking children, by chronological age (Herzberg, 2010).

age and on their MLU. Figure 8 shows the increase in the median tokens of referential (content/function words) versus the decline in social/communicative words across three time points in the third year of life. Figure 9 shows the same findings in medians across two MLU data points – at point 1, with speech samples ranging from 1–2 words per utterance, and at point 2 (MLU 2–3 words per utterance). Clearly, when children's speech became more syntactically organized towards age 3, their lexicons started to resemble those of older children, adolescents and adults in having mainly content and function words, the building blocks of syntactic units and the expressors of referential and relational meanings.

The analyses of the token distributions of the three major content word categories in Hebrew – nouns, verb, and adjectives – illustrate the impact of lexical class in terms of children's ages and their MLU. Figures 10 and 11 show that from both perspectives, the number of nouns declined, while the number of verbs increased. Adjectives, as well-known from the literature, were the smallest class in the lexicon, but it too increased with age and with the advent of syntactic constructions. Thus, when assessing the linguistic development of children, one cannot ignore the importance of different word classes.

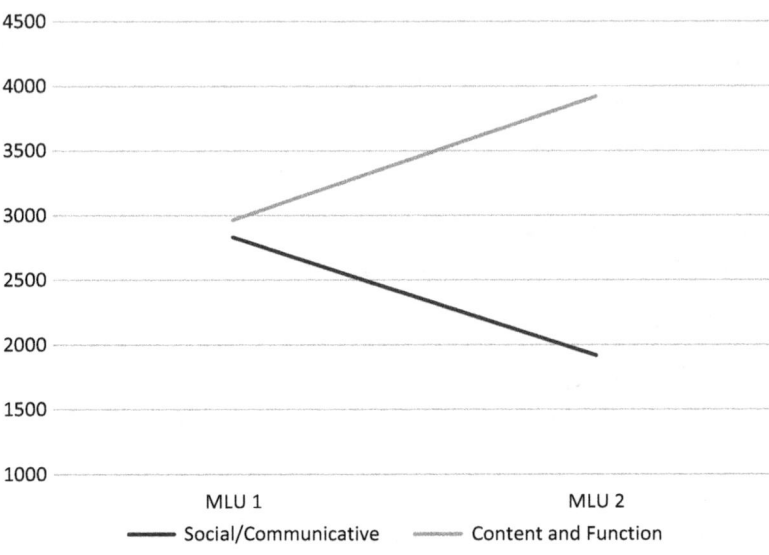

Figure 9: Median tokens of social / communicative and referential (content / function) words in three typically-developing Hebrew-speaking children, by MLU periods (Herzberg, 2010).

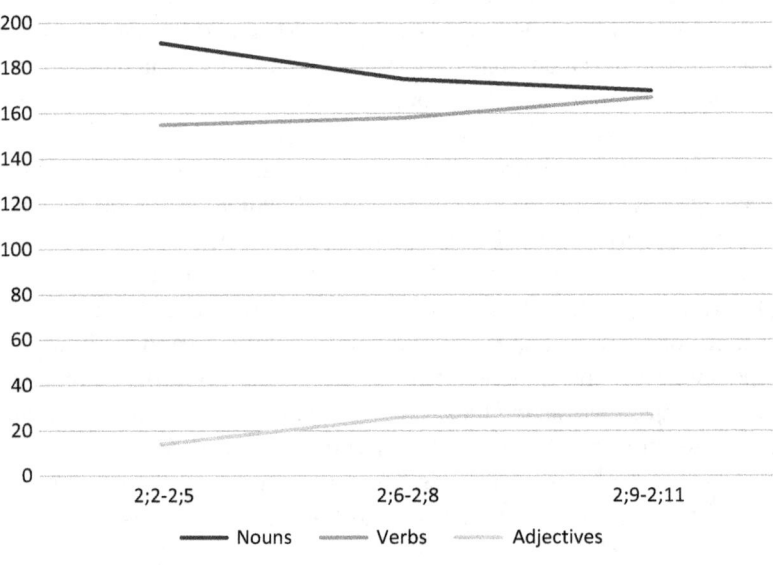

Figure 10: Median tokens of nouns, verbs and adjectives in three typically-developing Hebrew-speaking children, by chronological age (Herzberg, 2010).

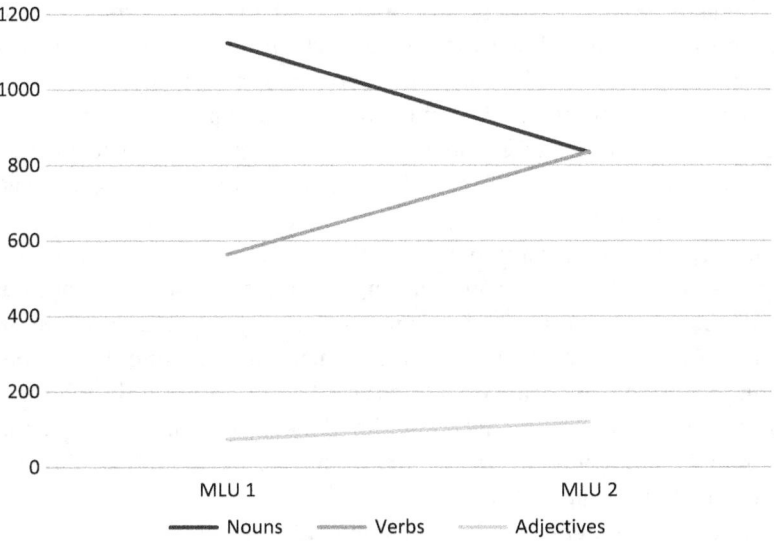

Figure 11: Median tokens of nouns, verbs and adjectives in three typically-developing Hebrew-speaking children, by MLU periods (Herzberg, 2010).

3 Conclusion

This chapter aimed at providing a broad perspective on morpho-lexical development during children's first three years of life. The chapter started by pointing out that linguistic terminology only provides descriptive conventions for structuring certain aspects of this development, but that the development process itself should not be understood simply as acquisition of linguistic structure. Instead, we formulated our examination of morpho-lexical development as a linguistic vantage point on a complex and dynamical development process.

Regarding the development process as central inevitably leads to understanding acquisition of morphology and lexicon in terms of dynamical learning systems that are data-driven, non-monotonic, and capable of operating in noisy environments. It further implies that the acquisition of morphology and lexicon cannot be isolated from learning in general. Instead, it is inseparable from the learning of concepts, categories, and relations. This interdependence is also reflected in the evidence that shows that lexical learning is paced by word class: adjectives are learned later than nouns and verbs and command of function words comes much later than their individual frequency would predict.

Although the semantic-pragmatic contents of children's lexicons are similar across languages and cultures, morpho-lexical development in typologically different languages offers us insight on the relation between information and acquisition. Specifically, morphology is learned early on in environments where crucial information is expressed through morphology. For instance, Arabic and Hebrew speaking children acquire the ability to understand and use complicated root patterns early on. On the other hand, children struggle with the acquisition of morphological relics that carry little information, such as the irregular past tense and plural in English.

The pervasive role of information in lexical development is further addressed by the perspective that word learning is essentially context learning. Empirical evidence shows that children must frequently experience words in their context before they are acquired. Both information theory and discriminative learning are approaches that can address contextual learning. In the same vein, distributional semantics models (e.g., Landauer and Dumais 1997; Lund and Burgess 1996; Mikolov et al. 2013) address the way in which lexical representations can be built from context.

The context in which children learn also includes the social environment. Specifically, parents have an important impact on the development process, leading to high correlations between the contents and structure of child-speech and the corresponding parental child-directed speech. But parents are not only a source of input; they also actively mediate in children's morpho-lexical development, facilitating learning through feedback and through modulation of their own language.

Parents' profound impact on children's morpho-lexical development process is further substantiated by studies that examine the influence of parental SES. Parents' linguistic proficiency is linked with their SES and this transfers to their children, leading to lags of up to two years in morpho-lexical development in children with a low-SES background compared to children with a high-SES background.

Studying the development of lexicon and morphology involves taking a linguistic perspective on children's general development process. Complex and dynamical learning systems that are able to capture the amount and variety of information children are exposed to can be useful in understanding linguistic development within the general development process. While existing frameworks such as information theory and discriminative learning offer us ways to model certain aspects of dynamical learning processes, they are also limited if they address children's environment as a monolithic source of information. The enormous influence of parental input and SES on the morpho-lexical development process means that, going forward, it will be very important to understand and model children's larger environment as a dynamical system, composed of many different actors and information sources.

References

Abbot-Smith, Kirsten, Erika Nurmsoo, Rebecca Croll, Heather Ferguson & Michael Forrester. 2016. How children aged 2; 6 tailor verbal expressions to interlocutor informational needs. *Journal of Child Language* 43(6). 1277–1291.
Ackerman, Farrell & Robert Malouf. 2013. Morphological organization: The low conditional entropy conjecture. *Language* 89 (3). 429–464.
Ambridge, Ben, Evan Kidd, Caroline F. Rowland & Anna L. Theakston. 2015. The ubiquity of frequency effects in first language acquisition. *Journal of Child Language* 42 (2). 239–273.
Ambridge, Ben, Julian M. Pine, Caroline F. Rowland & Chris R. Young. 2008. The effect of verb semantic class and verb frequency (entrenchment) on children's and adults' graded judgements of argument-structure overgeneralization errors. *Cognition* 106 (1). 87–129.
Anglin, Jeremy M. 1993. Vocabulary development: A morphological analysis. *Monographs of the society for research in child development*.
Arnon, Inbal & Eve V. Clark. 2011. Why brush your teeth is better than teeth–Children's word production is facilitated in familiar sentence-frames. *Language Learning and Development* 7 (2). 107–129.
Arriaga, Rose I., Larry Fenson, Terry Cronan & Stephen J. Pethick. 1998. Scores on the MacArthur Communicative Development Inventory of children from low and middle-income families. *Applied Psycholinguistics* 19 (2). 209–223.
Arunachalam, Sudha & Sandra R. Waxman. 2010a. Language and conceptual development. *Wiley Interdisciplinary Reviews: Cognitive Science* 1 (4). 548–558.
Arunachalam, Sudha & Sandra R. Waxman. 2010b. Meaning from syntax: Evidence from 2-year-olds. *Cognition* 114 (3). 442–446.
Ashkenazi, Orit. 2015. *Input-output relations in the early acquisition of Hebrew verbs*. Tel Aviv: The Jaime and Joan Constantiner School of Education, Tel Aviv University PhD Dissertation.
Ashkenazi, Orit, Dorit Ravid & Steven Gillis. 2016. Breaking into the Hebrew verb system: A learning problem. *First language* 36 (5). 505–524.
Ashkenazi, Orit, Gillis, Steven, and Ravid, Dorit. 2019. input-output relations in the early acquisition of Hebrew verbs. Journal of Child Language. DOI: https://doi.org/10.1017/S0305000919000540.
Ateş-Şen, A. Beyza & Aylin C. Küntay. 2015. Children's sensitivity to caregiver cues and the role of adult feedback in the development of referential communication. In Ludovica Serratrice & Shanley M. Allen (eds.), *The acquisition of reference* (Trends in Language Acquisition 15), 241–262. Amsterdam & Philadelphia: John Benjamins Publishing Company.
Barbieri, Filippo, Antimo Buonocore, Riccardo Dalla Volta & Maurizio Gentilucci. 2009. How symbolic gestures and words interact with each other. *Brain and language* 110 (1). 1–11.
Bar-On, Amalia & Dorit Ravid. 2011. Morphological analysis in learning to read pseudowords in Hebrew. *Applied Psycholinguistics* 32 (3). 553–581.
Bassano, Dominique. 2000. Early development of nouns and verbs in French: Exploring the interface between lexicon and grammar. *Journal of Child Language* 27 (3). 521–559.
Bavin, Edith L. 1998. Factors of typology on language acquisition: Some examples from Warlpiri. In Anna Siewirska & Jae Jung Song (eds.), *Case, typology and grammar: In honor of Barry J. Blake* (Typological Studies in Language 38), 37–56. Amsterdam & Philadelphia: John Benjamins Publishing Company.

Behrens, Heike. 2006. The input–output relationship in first language acquisition. *Language and Cognitive Processes* 21 (1–3). 2–24.

Behrens, Heike (ed.). 2008. *Corpora in language acquisition research: History, methods, perspectives* (Trends in Language Acquisition Research 6). Amsterdam & Philadelphia: John Benjamins Publishing Company.

Ben-Zvi, Galit & Ronit Levie. 2016. Development of Hebrew derivational morphology from preschool to adolescence. In Ruth Berman (ed.), *Acquisition and development of Hebrew: From infancy to adolescence*, 135–173. John Benjamins.

Bergeson, Tonya R., Rachel J. Miller & Kasi McCune. 2006. Mothers' speech to hearing-impaired infants and children with cochlear implants. *Infancy* 10 (3). 221–240.

Berman, Ruth A. 1985. Crosslinguistic evidence for the language-making capacity. In Dan Isaac Slobin (ed.), *The crosslinguistic study of language acquisition*, vol. 1, 255–371. Hillsdale, N.J.: Lawrence Erlbaum Associates.

Berman, Ruth A. 1987. A developmental route: Learning about the form and use of complex nominals in Hebrew. *Linguistics* 25 (6). 1057–1086.

Berman, Ruth A. 1990. On acquiring an (S) VO language: Subjectless sentences in children's Hebrew. *Linguistics* 28 (6). 1135–1166.

Berman, Ruth A. 1994. Developmental perspectives on transitivity: A confluence of cues. In Yonata Levy (ed.), *Other children, other languages: Issues in the theory of language acquisition*, 189–241. Psychology Press.

Berman, Ruth A. 1997. Early acquisition of syntax and discourse in Hebrew. In Y Shimron (ed.), *Psycholinguistic studies in Israel: Language acquisition, reading, and writing*, 57–100.

Berman, Ruth A. 1999. Children's innovative verbs versus nouns: Structured elicitations and spontaneous coinages. In Lise Menn & Nan Bernstein Ratner (eds.), *Methods for studying language production*, 75–98. Psychology Press.

Berman, Ruth A. 2004. Between emergence and mastery: The long developmental route of language acquisition. In Ruth A. Berman (ed.), *Language development across childhood and adolescence* (Trends in Language Acquisition Research 3), 9–34. Amsterdam & Philadelphia: John Benjamins Publishing Company.

Berman, Ruth A. 2009. Acquisition of compound constructions. In Rochelle Lieber & Pavol Štekauer (eds.), *The Oxford Handbook of Compounding*, 298–322. Oxford: Oxford University Press.

Berman, Ruth, Ronit Nayditz & Dorit Ravid. 2011. Linguistic diagnostics of written texts in two school-age populations. *Written Language & Literacy* 14 (2). 161–187.

Betancourt, Laura M., Nancy L. Brodsky & Hallam Hurt. 2015. Socioeconomic (SES) differences in language are evident in female infants at 7months of age. *Early Human Development* 91 (12). 719–724. doi:10.1016/j.earlhumdev.2015.08.002.

Bittner, Dagmar. 2003. The emergence of verb inflection in two German speaking children. In Dagmar Bittner, Wolfgang U. Dressler & Marianne Kilani-Schoch (eds.), *Development of verb inflection in first language acquisition: A cross-linguistic perspective*, 53–88. Walter de Gruyter.

Bittner, Dagmar, Wolfgang U. Dressler & Marianne Kilani-Schoch. 2003. Introduction. In Dagmar Bittner, Wolfgang U. Dressler & Marianne Kilani-Schoch (eds.), *Development of verb inflection in first language acquisition: A cross-linguistic perspective*, vii–xxxviii. Walter de Gruyter.

Blachman, Benita A., Darlene M. Tangel, Eileen Wynne Ball, Rochella Black & Collen K. McGraw. 1999. Developing phonological awareness and word recognition skills: A two-year intervention with low-income, inner-city children. *Reading and Writing* 11 (3). 239–273.

Black, Esther, Sue Peppé & Fiona Gibbon. 2008. The relationship between socio-economic status and lexical development. *Clinical Linguistics & Phonetics* 22 (4–5). 259–265.

Blackwell, Aleka Akoyunoglou. 2005. Acquiring the English adjective lexicon: relationships with input properties and adjectival semantic typology. *Journal of Child Language* 32 (3). 535–562.

Blodgett, Elizabeth G. & Eugene B. Cooper. 1988. Talking about it and doing it: Metalinguistic capacity and prosodic control in three to seven year olds. *Journal of Fluency Disorders* 13 (4). 283–290.

Bloom, Paul. 2000. *How children learn the meanings of words*. Cambridge, MA: The MIT press.

Bolozky, Shmuel. 1999. *Measuring productivity in word formation: The case of Israeli Hebrew*. Leiden: Brill.

Bonin, Patrick, Christopher Barry, Alain Méot & Marylène Chalard. 2004. The influence of age of acquisition in word reading and other tasks: A never ending story? *Journal of Memory and Language* 50 (4). 456–476.

Booth, Amy E. & Sandra R. Waxman. 2002. Word learning is "smart": evidence that conceptual information affects preschoolers' extension of novel words. *Cognition* 84 (1). B11–B22. doi:10.1016/S0010-0277(02)00015-X.

Borovsky, Arielle, Erica M. Ellis, Julia L. Evans & Jeffrey L. Elman. 2016. Semantic structure in vocabulary knowledge interacts with lexical and sentence processing in infancy. *Child Development* 87 (6). 1893–1908.

Borovsky, Arielle & Jeffrey L. Elman. 2006. Language input and semantic categories: A relation between cognition and early word learning. *Journal of Child Language* 33 (4). 759–790.

Borovsky, Arielle, Jeffrey L. Elman & Anne Fernald. 2012. Knowing a lot for one's age: Vocabulary skill and not age is associated with anticipatory incremental sentence interpretation in children and adults. *Journal of Experimental Child Psychology* 112 (4). 417–436.

Bowerman, Melissa & Soonja Choi. 2001. Shaping meanings for language: universal and language-specific in the acquisition of semantic categories. In Melissa Bowerman & Stephen Levinson (eds.), *Language acquisition and conceptual development*, 475–511. Cambridge: Cambridge University Press.

Boyd, Jeremy K. & Adele E. Goldberg. 2009. Input effects within a constructionist framework. *The Modern Language Journal* 93 (3). 418–429.

Brodsky, Peter & Heidi Waterfall. 2007. Characterizing motherese: On the computational structure of child-directed language. *Proceedings of the Annual Meeting of the Cognitive Science Society*, vol. 29. 833–838.

Brooks, Patricia J., Vera Kempe & Annemarie Donachie. 2011. Second language learning benefits from similarity in word endings: Evidence from Russian. *Language Learning* 61 (4). 1142–1172.

Bybee, Joan. 2001. Frequency effects on French liaison. *Typological Studies in Language* 45. 337–360.

Bybee, Joan. 2006. From usage to grammar: The mind's response to repetition. *Language* 82 (4). 711–733.

Candan, Ayşe, Aylin C. Küntay, Ya-ching Yeh, Hintat Cheung, Laura Wagner & Letitia R. Naigles. 2012. Language and age effects in children's processing of word order. *Cognitive Development* 27 (3). 205–221.

Carlisle, Joanne F. 2000. Awareness of the structure and meaning of morphologically complex words: Impact on reading. *Reading and Writing* 12 (3). 169–190.

Caselli, Maria C., Paola Casadio & Elizabeth Bates. 2001. Lexical development in English and Italian. In Michael Tomasello & Elizabeth Bates (eds.), *Language development: The essential readings*, 76–110. Malden, MA: Blackwell.

Chomsky, Noam. 1957. *Syntactic structures*. The Hague: Mouton.

Chomsky, Noam. 1965. *Aspects of the theory of syntax*. Cambridge, MA: M.I.T. Press.

Chomsky, Noam. 1988. *Language and problems of knowledge: The Managua lectures*. Cambridge, MA: The MIT Press.

Chouinard, Michelle M. & Eve V. Clark. 2003. Adult reformulations of child errors as negative evidence. *Journal of Child Language* 30 (3). 637–669.

Clahsen, Harald & João Veríssimo. 2016. Dual Morphology in the mental lexicon: Experimental evidence from the acquisition and processing of Greek and Portuguese. In M Guijarro-Fuentes, M Juan-Garau & P Larrañaga (eds.), *Acquisition of Romance languages: Old acquisition challenges and new explanations from a generative perspective*, 41–64. De Gruyter Mouton.

Clark, Eve V. 1993. *The lexicon in acquisition* (Cambridge Studies in Linguistics 65). Cambridge: Cambridge University Press.

Clark, Eve V. 2004. How language acquisition builds on cognitive development. *Trends in Cognitive Sciences* 8(10). 472–478.

Clark, Eve V. 2007. Young children's uptake of new words in conversation. *Language in Society* 36 (2). 157–182.

Clark, Eve V. 2010. Adult offer, word-class, and child uptake in early lexical acquisition. *First Language* 30 (3–4). 250–269.

Clark, Eve V. 2015. Lexical meaning. In Edith L. Bavin & Letitia R. Naigles (eds.), *The Cambridge Handbook of Child Language* (Cambridge Handbooks in Language and Linguistics), 351–368. 2nd edn. Cambridge: Cambridge University Press.

Clark, Eve V. 2016. *Language in Children*. New York: Routledge

Clark, Eve V. & Ruth A. Berman. 1984. Structure and use in the acquisition of word formation. *Language* 60 (3). 542–590.

Clark, Eve V. & Josie Bernicot. 2008. Repetition as ratification: How parents and children place information in common ground. *Journal of Child Language* 35 (2). 349–371.

Clark, Eve V. & Kate L. Lindsey. 2015. Turn-taking: a case study of early gesture and word use in answering WHERE and WHICH questions. *Frontiers in Psychology* 6. 890.

Clark, Eve V. & Andrew D. W. Wong. 2002. Pragmatic directions about language use: Offers of words and relations. *Language in Society* 31 (2). 181–212. doi:10.1017/S0047404501020152.

Clark, Herbert H. & Eve V. Clark. 1977. *Psychology and language: An introduction to psycholinguistics*. New York: Harcourt Brace Jovanovich.

Croft, William. 2000. *Explaining language change: An evolutionary approach*. Harlow: Pearson Education.

Cutting, Alexandra L. & Judy Dunn. 1999. Theory of mind, emotion understanding, language, and family background: Individual differences and interrelations. *Child Development* 70 (4). 853–865.

D'Angiulli, Amedeo, Anthony Herdman, David Stapells & Clyde Hertzman. 2008. Children's event-related potentials of auditory selective attention vary with their socioeconomic status. *Neuropsychology* 22 (3). 293.

Devescovi, Antonella, Maria Cristina Caselli, Daniela Marchione, Patrizio Pasqualetti, Judy Reilly & Elizabeth Bates. 2005. A crosslinguistic study of the relationship between grammar and lexical development. *Journal of Child Language* 32 (4). 759–786.
Dixon, Robert M. W & Alexandra Y Aikhenvald. 2006. *Adjective classes: A cross-linguistic typology*. Oxford: Oxford University Press.
Dockrell, Julie E. & David Messer. 2004. Lexical acquisition in the early school years. In Ruth A. Berman (ed.), *Language development across childhood and adolescence* (Trends in Language Acquisition 3), 35–52. Amsterdam: John Benjamins.
Dressler, Wolfgang U. 2007. Introduction. In Sabine Laaha & Steven Gillis (eds.), *Typological perspectives on the acquisition of noun and verb morphology* (Antwerp Papers in Linguistics 112), 3–10.
Dressler, Wolfgang U. 2010. A typological approach to first language acquisition. In Michèle Kail & Maya Hickmann (eds.), *Language acquisition across linguistic and cognitive systems*, vol. 52, 109–124. Amsterdam: John Benjamins.
Dressler, Wolfgang U., F. Nihan Ketrez & Marianne Kilani-Schoch. 2017. Discussion and outlook. In Wolfgang U. Dressler, F. Nihan Ketrez & Marianne Kilani-Schoch (eds.), *Nominal Compound Acquisition* (Language Acquisition and Language Disorders), vol. 61, 287–305. Amsterdam: John Benjamins.
Dressler, Wolfgang U., Laura E. Lettner & Katharina Korecky-Kröll. 2010. First language acquisition of compounds: With special emphasis on early German child language. In Sergio Scalise & Irene Vogel (eds.), *Cross-disciplinary issues in compounding*, 323–344. Amsterdam: John Benjamins.
Dressler, Wolfgang U., Lavinia Merlini Barbaresi, Sonja Schwaiger, Jutta Ransmayr, Sabine Sommer-Lolei & Katharina Korecky-Kröll. 2019. Rivalry and lack of blocking among Italian and German diminutives in adult and child language. In Franz Rainer, Francesco Gardani, Wolfgang U. Dressler & Hans Christian Luschützky (eds.), *Competition in inflection and word-formation*. Berlin: Springer.
Dromi, Esther. 1987. *Early lexical development*. Cambridge: Cambridge University Press.
Dromi, Esther, Laurence B. Leonard & Michal Shteiman. 1993. The grammatical morphology of Hebrew-speaking children with specific language impairment: Some competing hypotheses. *Journal of Speech, Language, and Hearing Research* 36 (4). 760–771.
Egoz-Liebstein, Topaz. 2010. *Mental verbs in Hebrew preschool peer talk*. Tel Aviv: Tel Aviv University MA Thesis.
Elman, Jeffrey L. 1993. Learning and development in neural networks: The importance of starting small. *Cognition* 48 (1). 71–99.
Elman, Jeffrey L. 2003. Development: It's about time. *Developmental Science* 6 (4). 430–433.
Engel, Pascale Marguerite Josiane, Flávia Heloísa Santos & Susan Elizabeth Gathercole. 2008. Are working memory measures free of socioeconomic influence? *Journal of Speech, Language, and Hearing Research* 51 (6). 1580–1587.
Evans, Vyvyan. 2009. *How words mean: Lexical concepts, cognitive models, and meaning construction*. Oxford: Oxford University Press.
Farah, Martha J., David M. Shera, Jessica H. Savage, Laura Betancourt, Joan M. Giannetta, Nancy L. Brodsky, Elsa K. Malmud & Hallam Hurt. 2006. Childhood poverty: Specific associations with neurocognitive development. *Brain Research* 1110 (1). 166–174.
Farkas, George & Kurt Beron. 2004. The detailed age trajectory of oral vocabulary knowledge: Differences by class and race. *Social Science Research* 33 (3). 464–497.

Fasolo, Mirco & Laura D'Odorico. 2012. Gesture-plus-word combinations, transitional forms, and language development. *Gesture* 12 (1). 1–15.

Fazio, Barbara B. 1997. Memory for rote linguistic routines and sensitivity to rhyme: A comparison of low-income children with and without specific language impairment. *Applied Psycholinguistics* 18 (3). 345–372.

Fenson, Larry, Philip S. Dale, J. Steven Reznick, Elizabeth Bates, Donna J. Thal, Stephen J. Pethick, Michael Tomasello, Carolyn B. Mervis & Joan Stiles. 1994. Variability in early communicative development. *Monographs of the Society for Research in Child Development* 59 (5).

Ferguson, Brock & Sandra Waxman. 2017. Linking language and categorization in infancy. *Journal of Child Language* 44 (3). 527–552.

Fernald, Anne, Virginia A. Marchman & Adriana Weisleder. 2013. SES differences in language processing skill and vocabulary are evident at 18 months. *Developmental Science* 16 (2). 234–248.

Fish, Margaret & Brenda Pinkerman. 2003. Language skills in low-SES rural Appalachian children: Normative development and individual differences, infancy to preschool. *Journal of Applied Developmental Psychology* 23 (5). 539–565.

Foss, Donald J. & David T. Hakes. 1978. *Psycholinguistics: An introduction to the psychology of language*. Englewood Cliffs, NJ: Prentice-Hall.

Foursha-Stevenson, Cassandra, Taylor Schembri, Elena Nicoladis & Cody Eriksen. 2017. The influence of child-directed speech on word learning and comprehension. *Journal of Psycholinguistic Research* 46 (2). 329–343.

Frost, Ram. 2012. A universal approach to modeling visual word recognition and reading: Not only possible, but also inevitable. *Behavioral and Brain Sciences* 35 (5). 310–329.

Frost, Ram, Avital Deutsch & Kenneth I. Forster. 2000. Decomposing morphologically complex words in a nonlinear morphology. *Journal of Experimental Psychology: Learning, Memory, and Cognition* 26 (3). 751.

Gentner, Dedre & Lera Boroditsky. 2001. Individuation, relativity, and early word learning. In Melissa Bowerman & Stephen Levinson (eds.), *Language acquisition and conceptual development*, vol. 3, 215–256. Cambridge: Cambridge University Press.

Gillis, Steven & Dorit Ravid. 2006. Typological effects on spelling development: A crosslinguistic study of Hebrew and Dutch. *Journal of Child Language* 33 (3). 621–659.

Ginsborg, Jane. 2006. The effects of socio-economic status on children's language acquisition and use. In Judy Clegg & Jane Ginsborg (eds.), *Language and social disadvantage: Theory into practice*, 9–27. Chichester: John Wiley & Sons.

Goldberg, Adele E. 1995. *Constructions: A construction grammar approach to argument structure*. Chicago: University of Chicago Press.

Goldschneider, Jennifer M. & Robert M. DeKeyser. 2001. Explaining the "natural order of L2 morpheme acquisition" in English: a meta-analysis of multiple determinants. *Language Learning* 51 (1). 1–50.

Golinkoff, Roberta Michnick & Kathy Hirsh-Pasek. 2008. How toddlers begin to learn verbs. *Trends in Cognitive Sciences* 12 (10). 397–403.

Goodman, Judith C., Philip S. Dale & Ping Li. 2008. Does frequency count? Parental input and the acquisition of vocabulary. *Journal of Child Language* 35 (3). 515–531.

Graf, Eileen & Catherine Davies. 2014. The production and comprehension of referring expressions. In Danielle Matthews (ed.), *Pragmatic Development in First Language Acquisition*, 161–181. Amsterdam & Philadelphia: John Benjamins Publishing Company.

Griffiths, Thomas L., Nick Chater, Charles Kemp, Amy Perfors & Joshua B. Tenenbaum. 2010. Probabilistic models of cognition: Exploring representations and inductive biases. *Trends in Cognitive Sciences* 14 (8). 357–364.

Hansen, Pernille. 2017. What makes a word easy to acquire? The effects of word class, frequency, imageability and phonological neighbourhood density on lexical development. *First Language* 37 (2). 205–225.

Harris, Margaret. 1992. *Language experience and early language development: From input to uptake*. Hove: Psychology Press.

Harris, Paul L. 1992. From simulation to folk psychology: The case for development. *Mind & Language* 7 (1–2). 120–144.

Hart, Betty & Todd R. Risley. 1995. *Meaningful differences in the everyday experience of young American children*. Baltimore, MD: Paul H. Brookes.

Herzberg, Orly. 2010. *Lexical development in Hebrew-speaking toddlers with and without hearing impairment*. Tel Aviv: Tel Aviv University Doctoral dissertation.

Hoff, Erika. 2003. The specificity of environmental influence: Socioeconomic status affects early vocabulary development via maternal speech. *Child Development* 74 (5). 1368–1378.

Hoff, Erika & Letitia Naigles. 2002. How children use input to acquire a lexicon. *Child Development* 73 (2). 418–433.

Hoff, Erika & Chunyan Tian. 2005. Socioeconomic status and cultural influences on language. *Journal of Communication Disorders* 38 (4). 271–278.

Hoff-Ginsberg, Erika. 1985. Some contributions of mothers' speech to their children's syntactic growth. *Journal of Child Language* 12 (2). 367–385.

Houston-Price, Carmel, Kim Plunkett & Hester Duffy. 2006. The use of social and salience cues in early word learning. *Journal of Experimental Child Psychology* 95 (1). 27–55. doi:10.1016/j.jecp.2006.03.006.

Hulme, Charles, Steven Roodenrys, Richard Schweickert, Gordon D.A. Brown, Sarah Martin & George Stuart. 1997. Word-frequency effects on short-term memory tasks: Evidence for a redintegration process in immediate serial recall. *Journal of Experimental Psychology: Learning, Memory, and Cognition* 23 (5). 1217–1232.

Huttenlocher, Janellen, Wendy Haight, Anthony Bryk, Michael Seltzer & Thomas Lyons. 1991. Early vocabulary growth: Relation to language input and gender. *Developmental Psychology* 27 (2). 236–248.

Imai, Mutsumi & Dedre Gentner. 1997. A cross-linguistic study of early word meaning: Universal ontology and linguistic influence. *Cognition* 62 (2). 169–200.

Johnston, Robert A. & Christopher Barry. 2006. Age of acquisition and lexical processing. *Visual Cognition* 13 (7–8). 789–845.

Jones, Susan S., Linda B. Smith & Barbara Landau. 1991. Object properties and knowledge in early lexical learning. *Child Development* 62 (3). 499–516.

Kauschke, Christina & Christoph Hofmeister. 2002. Early lexical development in German: A study on vocabulary growth and vocabulary composition during the second and third year of life. *Journal of Child Language* 29 (4). 735–757.

Keuleers, Emmanuel, Kevin Diependaele & Marc Brysbaert. 2010. Practice Effects in Large-Scale Visual Word Recognition Studies: A Lexical Decision Study on 14,000 Dutch Mono- and Disyllabic Words and Nonwords. *Frontiers in Psychology* 1. doi:10.3389/fpsyg.2010.00174. http://journal.frontiersin.org/article/10.3389/fpsyg.2010.00174/abstract.

Kibrik, Andrej A. 2012. What's in the head of head-marking languages. In Pirkko Suihkonen, Bernard Comrie & Valery Solovyev (eds.), *Argument structure and grammatical relations: A cross-linguistic typology*, 211–240. Amsterdam & Philadelphia: John Benjamins Publishing Company.

Kidd, Evan, Elena V. M. Lieven & Michael Tomasello. 2010. Lexical frequency and exemplar-based learning effects in language acquisition: Evidence from sentential complements. *Language Sciences* 32 (1). 132–142.

Kishiyama, Mark M., W. Thomas Boyce, Amy M. Jimenez, Lee M. Perry & Robert T. Knight. 2009. Socioeconomic disparities affect prefrontal function in children. *Journal of Cognitive Neuroscience* 21 (6). 1106–1115.

Ko, Eon-Suk. 2012. Nonlinear development of speaking rate in child-directed speech. *Lingua* 122 (8). 841–857.

Koptjevskaja-Tamm, Maria. 2012. New directions in lexical typology. *Linguistics* 50 (3). 373–394.

Korecky-Kröll, Katharina & Wolfgang U. Dressler. 2015. Rajendra Singh: In memoriam. Papers from a special commemorative session at the 44th Poznán Linguistic Meeting. In Katarzyna Dziubalska-Kołaczyk & Jarosław Weckwerth (eds.), *(Mor)phonotactics in high vs. low SES children*, 25–40. Poznán: Adam Mickiewicz University Press.

Korecky-Kröll, Katharina, Kumru Uzunkaya-Sharma & Wolfgang U. Dressler. 2017. Requests in Turkish and German child-directed and child speech. In F. Nihan Ketrez, Aylin C. Küntay, Şeyda Özçalışkan & Aslı Özyürek (eds.), *Social environment and cognition in language development: Studies in honor of Ayhan Aksu-Koç* (Trends in Language Acquisition 21), 53–68. Amsterdam & Philadelphia: John Benjamins Publishing Company.

Labov, William. 2014. The sociophonetic orientation of the language learner. In Chiara Celata & Silvia Calamai (eds.), *Advances in sociophonetics*, vol. 15, 17–29. Amsterdam & Philadelphia: John Benjamins Publishing Company.

Landauer, Thomas K. & Susan T. Dumais. 1997. A solution to Plato's problem: The latent semantic analysis theory of acquisition, induction, and representation of knowledge. *Psychological Review* 104 (2). 211–240.

Langacker, Ronald W. 1987. *Foundations of Cognitive Grammar: Theoretical prerequisites*. Stanford, CA: Stanford University Press.

Langacker, Ronald W. 2000. A Dynamic Usage-Based Model. In Michael Barlow & Suzanne Kemmer (eds.), *Usage-Based Models of Language*, 1–63. Cambridge: Cambridge University Press.

Levie, Ronit, Galit Ben-Zvi & Dorit Ravid. 2017. Morpho-lexical development in language impaired and typically developing Hebrew-speaking children from two SES backgrounds. *Reading and Writing* 30 (5). 1035–1064.

Libben, Gary & Gonia Jarema (eds.). 2006. *The representation and processing of compound words*. Oxford: Oxford University Press.

Lieberman, Marcia R. 1969. The New Linguistics and the New Poetics. *College English* 30 (7). 527. doi:10.2307/374001.

Lieven, Elena. 2008. Building language competence in first language acquisition. *European Review* 16 (4). 445–456.

Lieven, Elena. 2010. Input and first language acquisition: Evaluating the role of frequency. *Lingua* 120 (11). 2546–2556.

Lucy, John A. & Suzanne Gaskins. 2001. Grammatical categories and the development of classification preferences: A comparative approach. In Melissa Bowerman & Stephen

Levinson (eds.), *Language acquisition and conceptual development*, 257–283. Cambridge: Cambridge University Press.

Lund, Kevin & Curt Burgess. 1996. Producing high-dimensional semantic spaces from lexical co-occurrence. *Behavior Research Methods, Instruments, & Computers* 28 (2). 203–208.

MacWhinney, Brian. 2004. A multiple process solution to the logical problem of language acquisition. *Journal of Child Language* 31 (4). 883–914.

Mandler, Jean M. 2000. Perceptual and conceptual processes in infancy. *Journal of Cognition and Development* 1 (1). 3–36.

Mariscal, Sonia. 2009. Early acquisition of gender agreement in the Spanish noun phrase: starting small. *Journal of Child Language* 36 (1). 143–171.

Maslen, Robert JC, Anna L. Theakston, Elena VM Lieven & Michael Tomasello. 2004. A dense corpus study of past tense and plural overregularization in English. *Journal of Speech, Language, and Hearing Research* 47 (6). 1319–1333.

Matthews, Danielle, Elena Lieven, Anna Theakston & Michael Tomasello. 2005. The role of frequency in the acquisition of English word order. *Cognitive Development* 20 (1). 121–136.

Medina, Tamara Nicol, Jesse Snedeker, John C. Trueswell & Lila R. Gleitman. 2011. How words can and cannot be learned by observation. *Proceedings of the National Academy of Sciences* 108 (22). 9014–9019.

Mikolov, Tomas, Ilya Sutskever, Kai Chen, Greg S. Corrado & Jeff Dean. 2013. Distributed representations of words and phrases and their compositionality. *Advances in Neural Information Processing Systems 26 (NIPS 2013)*, 3111–3119.

Miller, George A. 2003. The cognitive revolution: a historical perspective. *Trends in Cognitive Sciences* 7 (3). 141–144. doi:10.1016/S1364-6613(03)00029-9.

Moerk, Ernst L. 1991. Positive evidence for negative evidence. *First Language* 11 (32). 219–251.

Montgomery, Derek E. 2002. Mental verbs and semantic development. *Journal of Cognition and Development* 3 (4). 357–384.

Naigles, Letitia R. & Erika Hoff-Ginsberg. 1998. Why are some verbs learned before other verbs? Effects of input frequency and structure on children's early verb use. *Journal of Child Language* 25 (1). 95–120.

Nazzi, Thierry & Josiane Bertoncini. 2003. Before and after the vocabulary spurt: Two modes of word acquisition? *Developmental Science* 6 (2). 136–142.

Nittrouer, Susan. 1996. The relation between speech perception and phonemic awareness: Evidence from low-SES children and children with chronic OM. *Journal of Speech, Language, and Hearing Research* 39 (5). 1059–1070.

Noble, Claire, Faria Iqbal, Elena Lieven & Anna Theakston. 2016. Converging and competing cues in the acquisition of syntactic structures: the conjoined agent intransitive. *Journal of Child Language* 43 (4). 811–842.

Noble, Kimberly G., M. Frank Norman & Martha J. Farah. 2005. Neurocognitive correlates of socioeconomic status in kindergarten children. *Developmental Science* 8 (1). 74–87.

Olson, David R. 1996. *The world on paper: The conceptual and cognitive implications of writing and reading*. Cambridge: Cambridge University Press.

Peleg, Shany. 2013. *Maternal input in mothers from different SES background in the first year of life*. Tel Aviv: Tel Aviv University MA Thesis.

Pinker, Steven. 1998. Words and rules. *Lingua* 106 (1). 219–242.

Prevoo, Mariëlle JL, Maike Malda, Judi Mesman, Rosanneke AG Emmen, Nihal Yeniad, Marinus H. van Ijzendoorn & Mariëlle Linting. 2014. Predicting ethnic minority children's vocabulary from socioeconomic status, maternal language and home reading input: different pathways for host and ethnic language. *Journal of Child Language* 41 (5). 963–984.

Pruden, Shannon M., Kathy Hirsh-Pasek, Roberta Michnick Golinkoff & Elizabeth A. Hennon. 2006. The birth of words: Ten-month-olds learn words through perceptual salience. *Child Development* 77 (2). 266–280.

Pustejovsky, James. 1995. *The generative lexicon*. Cambridge, MA: MIT press.

Qi, Cathy Huaqing, Ann P. Kaiser, Stephanie Milan & Terry Hancock. 2006. Language performance of low-income African American and European American preschool children on the PPVT–III. *Language, Speech, and Hearing Services in Schools* 37 (1). 5–16.

Ramscar, Michael, Melody Dye & Joseph Klein. 2013. Children Value Informativity Over Logic in Word Learning. *Psychological Science* 24 (6). 1017–1023. doi:10.1177/0956797612460691.

Ravid, Dorit. 1990. Internal structure constraints on new-word formation devices in Modern Hebrew. *Folia Linguistica* 24 (3–4). 289–348.

Ravid, Dorit. 1995. *Language change in child and adult Hebrew: A psycholinguistic perspective*. Oxford: Oxford University Press.

Ravid, Dorit. 2001. Learning to spell in Hebrew: Phonological and morphological factors. *Reading and Writing* 14 (5). 459–485.

Ravid, Dorit. 2003. A developmental perspective on root perception in Hebrew and Palestinian Arabic. In Joseph Shimron (ed.), *Language processing and acquisition in languages of Semitic, root-based morphology*, vol. 28, 293–320. Amsterdam & Philadelphia: John Benjamins Publishing Company.

Ravid, Dorit. 2005. Hebrew orthography and literacy. In R Malatesha Joshi & P.G. Aaron (eds.), *Handbook of orthography and literacy*, 339–363. London: Routledge.

Ravid, Dorit. 2012. *Spelling morphology* (Literacy Studies). Vol. 3. Boston, MA: Springer.

Ravid, Dorit, Orit Ashkenazi, Ronit Levie, Galit Ben Zadok, Tehila Grunwald, Ron Bratslavsky & Steven Gillis. 2016. Foundations of the early root category. In Ruth A. Berman (ed.), *Acquisition and development of Hebrew: From infancy to adolescence*, vol. 19, 95–134. Amsterdam & Philadelphia: John Benjamins Publishing Company.

Ravid, Dorit & Amalia Bar-On. 2005. Manipulating written Hebrew roots across development: The interface of semantic, phonological and orthographic factors. *Reading and Writing* 18 (3). 231–256.

Ravid, Dorit, Amalia Bar-On, Ronit Levie & Odelia Douani. 2016. Hebrew adjective lexicons in developmental perspective. *The Mental Lexicon* 11 (3). 401–428.

Ravid, Dorit, Wolfgang U. Dressler, Bracha Nir-Sagiv, Katharina Korecky-Kröll, Agnita Souman, Katja Rehfeldt, Sabine Laaha, Johannes Bertl, Hans Basbøll & Steven Gillis. 2008. Core morphology in child directed speech: Crosslinguistic corpus analyses of noun plurals. In Heike Behrens (ed.), *Corpora in language acquisition research*, 25–60. Amsterdam & Philadelphia: John Benjamins Publishing Company.

Ravid, Dorit & Rola Farah. 1999. Learning about noun plurals in early Palestinian Arabic. *First Language* 19 (56). 187–206.

Ravid, Dorit & Lubna Hayek. 2003. Learning about different ways of expressing number in the development of Palestinian Arabic. *First Language* 23 (1). 41–63.

Ravid, Dorit & Ronit Levie. 2010. Hebrew adjectives in later language text production. *First Language* 30 (1). 27–55.

Ravid, Dorit & Michal Nir. 2000. On the development of the category of adjective in Hebrew. In M Beers, B van den Bogaerde, G Bol, J de Jong & C Rooijmans (eds.), *From sound to*

sentence: Studies on first language acquisition, 113–124. Groningen: Centre for Language and Cognition.
Ravid, Dorit, Elite Olshtain & Rachel Ze'elon. 2003. Gradeschoolers' linguistic and pragmatic speech adaptation to native and non-native interlocution. *Journal of Pragmatics* 35 (1). 71–99.
Ravid, Dorit & Rachel Schiff. 2006a. Morphological abilities in Hebrew-speaking gradeschoolers from two socioeconomic backgrounds: An analogy task. *First Language* 26 (4). 381–402.
Ravid, Dorit & Rachel Schiff. 2006b. Roots and patterns in Hebrew language development: evidence from written morphological analogies. *Reading and Writing* 19(8). 789–818. doi:10.1007/s11145-006-9004-3.
Ravid, Dorit & Rachel Schiff. 2009. Morphophonological categories of noun plurals in Hebrew: a developmental study. *Linguistics* 47 (1). 45–63.
Ravid, Dorit & Liliana Tolchinsky. 2002. Developing linguistic literacy: A comprehensive model. *Journal of Child Language* 29 (2). 417–447.
Ravid, Dorit & Shoshana Zilberbuch. 2003. Morphosyntactic constructs in the development of spoken and written Hebrew text production. *Journal of Child Language* 30 (2). 395–418.
Ravid, Dorit & Anael Zimmerman. 2017. Maternal input at 1;6: A comparison of two mothers from different SES backgrounds. In F. Nihan Ketrez, Aylin C. Küntay, Şeyda Özçalışkan & Aslı Özyürek (eds.), *Social environment and cognition in language development: Studies in honor of Ayhan Aksu-Koç* (Trends in Language Acquisition 21), 35–52. Amsterdam & Philadelphia: John Benjamins Publishing Company.
Raviv, Tali, Maureen Kessenich & Frederick J. Morrison. 2004. A mediational model of the association between socioeconomic status and three-year-old language abilities: The role of parenting factors. *Early Childhood Research Quarterly* 19 (4). 528–547.
Rescorla, Robert A. & Allan R. Wagner. 1972. A theory of Pavlovian conditioning: Variations in the effectiveness of reinforcement and nonreinforcement. In Abraham H. Black & William F. Prokasy (eds.), *Classical conditioning: current research and theory*, vol. 2, 64–99. New York: Appleton-Century-Crofts.
Rowe, Meredith L. 2008. Child-directed speech: relation to socioeconomic status, knowledge of child development and child vocabulary skill. *Journal of Child Language* 35 (1). 185–205.
Rowe, Meredith L., Stephen W. Raudenbush & Susan Goldin-Meadow. 2012. The pace of vocabulary growth helps predict later vocabulary skill. *Child Development* 83 (2). 508–525.
Saiegh-Haddad, Elinor, Areen Hadieh & Dorit Ravid. 2012. Acquiring noun plurals in Palestinian Arabic: Morphology, familiarity, and pattern frequency. *Language Learning* 62 (4). 1079–1109.
Salerni, Nicoletta, Alessandra Assanelli, Laura D'Odorico & Germano Rossi. 2007. Qualitative aspects of productive vocabulary at the 200-and 500-word stages: A comparison between spontaneous speech and parental report data. *First Language* 27 (1). 75–87.
Sandhofer, Catherine M., Linda B. Smith & Jun Luo. 2000. Counting nouns and verbs in the input: differential frequencies, different kinds of learning? *Journal of Child Language* 27 (3). 561–585.
Sandoval, Michelle & Rebecca L. Gomez. 2013. The development of nonadjacent dependency learning in natural and artificial languages. *Wiley Interdisciplinary Reviews: Cognitive Science* 4 (5). 511–522.
Savickienė, Ineta & Wolfgang U. Dressler. 2007. Introduction. In Ineta Savickienė & Wolfgang U. Dressler (eds.), *The Acquisition of Diminutives: A cross-linguistic perspective*, 1–12. Amsterdam & Philadelphia: John Benjamins Publishing.

Savickienė, Ineta, Vera Kempe & Patricia J. Brooks. 2009. Acquisition of gender agreement in Lithuanian: Exploring the effect of diminutive usage in an elicited production task. *Journal of Child Language* 36 (3). 477–494.

Scalise, Sergio & Irene Vogel. 2010. *Cross-disciplinary issues in compounding*. John Benjamins Publishing.

Schachter, Paul & Timothy Shopen. 2007. Parts-of-speech systems. In Timothy Shopen (ed.), *Language typology and syntactic description*, vol. 1, 1–60. 2nd edn. Cambridge: Cambridge University Press.

Schiff, Rachel & Einav Lotem. 2011. Effects of phonological and morphological awareness on children's word reading development from two socioeconomic backgrounds. *First Language* 31 (2). 139–163.

Schiff, Rachel & Dorit Ravid. 2012. Linguistic processing in Hebrew-speaking children from low and high SES backgrounds. *Reading and Writing* 25 (6). 1427–1448.

Schwarzwald, Ora R. 2002. *Modern Hebrew morphology*. Tel Aviv: Open University.

Shannon, Claude E & Warren Weaver. 1949. *The mathematical theory of communication*. Urbana, IL: University of Illinois Press.

Shatz, Marilyn, Gil Diesendruck, Ivelisse Martinez-Beck & Didar Akar. 2003. The influence of language and socioeconomic status on children's understanding of false belief. *Developmental Psychology* 39 (4). 717.

Slobin, Dan Isaac. 1985. Crosslinguistic evidence for the language-making capacity. In Dan Isaac Slobin (ed.), *The crosslinguistic study of language acquisition*, vol. 2, 1157–1256. Hillsdale, N.J.: Lawrence Erlbaum Associates.

Snow, Catherine E. 1995. Issues in the study of input: Finetuning, universality, individual and developmental differences, and necessary causes. In Paul Fletcher & Brian MacWhinney (eds.), *The handbook of child language*, 179–193. Malden, MA: Blackwell Publishing.

Song, Lulu, Elizabeth T. Spier & Catherine S. Tamis-Lemonda. 2014. Reciprocal influences between maternal language and children's language and cognitive development in low-income families. *Journal of Child Language* 41 (2). 305–326.

Sperber, D., & Wilson, D. (1998). The mapping between the mental and the public lexicon. Language and thought: Interdisciplinary themes. In P. Carruthers & J. Boucher (Eds). *Thought and language* (p. 184–200). Cambridge, UK: CUP.

Spelke, Elizabeth S. 2000. Core knowledge. *American Psychologist* 55 (11). 1233.

Stemberger, Joseph Paul & Mario E. Chávez-Peón. 2014. Overgeneralization in the processing of complex forms in Valley Zapotec child language. *The Mental Lexicon* 9 (1). 107–130.

Stephany, Ursula & Maria D. Voeikova. 2009. Introduction. In Ursula Stephany & Maria D. Voeikova (eds.), *Development of nominal inflection in first language acquisition: A cross-linguistic perspective* (Studies on Language Acquisition), vol. 30, 1–14. Berlin: Mouton de Gruyter.

Suizzo, Marie-Anne & Laura M. Stapleton. 2007. Home-based parental involvement in young Children's education: Examining the effects of maternal education across US ethnic groups. *Educational Psychology* 27 (4). 533–556.

Taft, Marcus & Kenneth I. Forster. 1975. Lexical storage and retrieval of prefixed words. *Journal of Verbal Learning and Verbal Behavior* 14 (6). 638–647. doi:10.1016/S0022-5371(75)80051-X.

Talmy, Leonard. 2007. Lexical Typologies. In Timothy Shopen (ed.), *Language Typology and Syntactic Description: Volume 3, Grammatical Categories and the Lexicon*. Cambridge: Cambridge University Press.

Thibaut, Jean-Pierre & Arnaud Witt. 2015. Young children's learning of relational categories: multiple comparisons and their cognitive constraints. *Frontiers in Psychology* 6. 643.

Tomasello, Michael. 2003. *Constructing a language: A usage-based theory of language acquisition*. Cambridge, MA: Harvard University Press.

Tomasello, Michael. 2006. Acquiring linguistic constructions. In R Siegler & D Kuhn (eds.), *Handbook of child psychology*, 256–293. New York, NY: John Wiley.

Tooby, John, Leda Cosmides & H. Clark Barrett. 2005. Resolving the debate on innate ideas. In Peter Carruthers, Stephen Laurence & Stephen Stitch (eds.), *The innate mind: Structure and content*, 305–337. Oxford: Oxford University Press.

Tribushinina, Elena, Maria D. Voeikova & Sabrina Noccetti. 2015. Adjective Acquisition Across Languages. In Elena Tribushinina, Maria D. Voeikova & Sabrina Noccetti (eds.), *Semantics and morphology of early adjectives in first language acquisition*, 1–22. Newcastle upon Tyne, UK: Cambridge Scholars Publishing.

Trudeau, Natacha & Ann Sutton. 2011. Expressive vocabulary and early grammar of 16-to 30-month-old children acquiring Quebec French. *First Language* 31 (4). 480–507.

Velan, Hadas, Ram Frost, Avital Deutsch & David C. Plaut. 2005. The processing of root morphemes in Hebrew: Contrasting localist and distributed accounts. *Language and Cognitive Processes* 20 (1–2). 169–206.

Veneziano, Edy & Christophe Parisse. 2010. The acquisition of early verbs in French: Assessing the role of conversation and of child-directed speech. *First Language* 30 (3–4). 287–311.

Vernon-Feagans, Lynne, Nadya Pancsofar, Mike Willoughby, Erica Odom, Alison Quade, Martha Cox & Family Life Key Investigators. 2008. Predictors of maternal language to infants during a picture book task in the home: Family SES, child characteristics and the parenting environment. *Journal of Applied Developmental Psychology* 29 (3). 213–226.

Walker, Dale, Charles Greenwood, Betty Hart & Judith Carta. 1994. Prediction of school outcomes based on early language production and socioeconomic factors. *Child Development* 65 (2). 606–621.

Waxman, Sandra R. & Erin M. Leddon. 2011. Early word learning and conceptual development: Everything had a name, and each name gave birth to a new thought. In Usha Goswami (ed.), *Blackwell handbook of childhood cognitive development*, 180–208. 2nd edn. Malden, MA: Wiley-Blackwell.

Weizman, Zehava Oz & Catherine E. Snow. 2001. Lexical output as related to children's vocabulary acquisition: Effects of sophisticated exposure and support for meaning. *Developmental Psychology* 37 (2). 265.

Wellman, Henry M. & Susan A. Gelman. 1998. Knowledge acquisition in foundational domains. In Deanna Kuhn & Robert Siegler (eds.), *Handbook of Child Psychology*, vol. 2, 523–573. 5th edn. Hoboken, NJ: John Wiley & Sons.

Wittgenstein, Ludwig. 1953. *Philosophische Untersuchungen* [Philosophical investigations]. (Trans.) Gertrude E.M. Anscombe. Oxford: Basil Blackwell.

Xanthos, Aris, Sabine Laaha, Steven Gillis, Ursula Stephany, Ayhan Aksu-Koç, Anastasia Christofidou, Natalia Gagarina, Gordana Hrzica, F. Nihan Ketrez, Marianne Kilani-Schoch, Katharina Korecky-Kröll, Melita Kovačević, Klaus Laalo, Marijan Palmović, Barbara Pfeiler, Maria D. Voeikova & Wolfgang U. Dressler. 2011. On the role of morphological richness in the early development of noun and verb inflection. *First Language* 31 (4). 461–479.

Thomas Berg
Morphological slips of the tongue

Abstract: This chapter presents an overview of naturally occurring morphological slips of the tongue. The empirical focus is on German speech errors, but data from other languages are also considered. A classification scheme is devised along five dimensions. In addition to the traditional division of morphology into compounding, derivation, and inflection and the distinction between free and bound morphemes as well as that between prefixes and suffixes, the contrast between contextual and non-contextual influences and the morphological nature of the words in which the error morphemes are embedded take center stage. These five dimensions are shown to affect error rates. In line with linguistic analyses, the distinction between inflection and derivation is not sharply drawn in language processing. Productivity facilitates the occurrence of non-contextual errors. Morphological and phonological processing display significant differences. Whereas phonological processing is mainly a sequencing problem, morphological processing grapples more strongly with issues of selection. Additionally, the selection problem is more acute in inflectional than in derivational morphology.

Keywords: morphologial processing, error classification, derivation-inflection continuum, selection vs. sequencing, German, productivity

1 Introduction

Speech errors, ordinarily defined as deviations from the speaker's intention, constitute interdisciplinary evidence *par excellence*. They are the result of a processing breakdown, i.e., the output of a production system which has gone awry. Inevitably, these disruptions involve linguistic elements and thereby tap into a representational system which makes available the information to be processed. Thus, speech errors derive their interdisciplinary status from the fact that they owe their psychological nature to the generative system which gives rise to them, and their linguistic nature to the "raw material" which they operate on.

Acknowledgements: I acknowledge with gratitude Cristina Burani's, Wolfgang Dressler's and Vito Pirrelli's comments on an earlier version as well as Frauke Gebauer's help with the Finnish data.

Thomas Berg, Department of English, University of Hamburg, Überseering 35, 22297, Hamburg, Germany

๏ Open Access. © 2020 Thomas Berg, published by De Gruyter. [cc) BY-NC-ND] This work is licensed under a Creative Commons Attribution-NonCommercial-NoDerivatives 4.0 International License.
https://doi.org/10.1515/9783110440577-016

It stands to reason that the units suffering a malfunction can be identified as the units contained in the mental lexicon. This assumption is based on the hypothesis that the representational system accords a place to certain units but not to others or, couched in a probabilistic framework, gives more prominence to some units rather than others. The argument is then that the more support a given unit receives from the psycholinguistic system, the more prone it is to error. Duly interpreted, error rates may consequently serve as a window on the content of the representational system, which is standardly considered to consist of units and levels.

On this logic, morphological slips of the tongue attest to the reality of a morphological processing level. By the same token, the occurrence of affix slips attests to the psychological reality of affixes. The same argument applies at a fine-grained level. An error on the prefix *pre-* or the stem *nuptial* in *prenuptial* would lend credence to the reality of a morphological boundary between the two constituent morphemes.[1] This argument capitalizes on the fact that speech errors are local phenomena. They tend to involve single rather than double or multiple units. That is to say, they break off one unit at a subordinate level from a unit at a superordinate level while leaving other subordinate-level units untouched. For example, the single morpheme *pre-* is broken off from *prenuptial*, or the single word *prenuptial* is broken off from *prenuptial agreement*.

Note that the units in the mental lexicon need not be identical to those postulated by linguists. This is because of a lack of consensus between linguists and psycholinguists on both research objectives and methodology. Generally speaking, linguistic investigations conceive of language as a product whereas the psycholinguistic view of language is in processual terms. While the gold standard in psycholinguistics is the search for psychological reality, theoretical linguists do not consider themselves bound by any extrinsic evaluation metric. Of course, it is highly unlikely that the units posited by linguists and those in the mental lexicon form non-overlapping sets. However, this does not by any means justify taking their identity for granted.

One of the most basic dichotomies in the study of language is Saussure's distinction between the syntagmatic and the associative (paradigmatic) dimension of language. In speech error research, these terms are often replaced by the more transparent labels "contextual" and "non-contextual", and this practice is followed here. We begin by exemplifying these two error types.

---

[1] We will not go deeply into the question of how many errors of one type are required to support the psychological reality of a particular unit. Singleton occurrences can be no more than illustrative. Reliable claims have to demonstrate that the rate of a particular error type exceeds chance levels.

(1) This longish woodish – longish wooden object (from Stemberger 1998: 437)

(2) You have chown – chewed on ice. (from Stemberger 1985a: 178)

Case (1) illustrates a suffix substitution slip (*-en* > *-ish*). It is assigned to the class of contextual errors because the error unit has in all likelihood been "borrowed" from the adjacent word *longish*. Case (2) highlights a temporary processing difficulty during the formation of the past participle of *to chew*. Although as a regular verb it requires the suffix *-ed*, it was inflected like an irregular verb and underwent ablaut and irregular suffixing. As there is no "external" motivation for this error, it is classified as non-contextual.

Roughly speaking, contextual errors reveal a sequencing problem while non-contextual errors reveal a selection problem. Essentially, contextual slips arise from the early or late intrusion of units which should have occurred, or actually occurred, elsewhere in an utterance. Thus, the units as such were correctly selected but inserted at the wrong place (or time). By contrast, in non-contextual slips, a wrong element was selected at the right place (or time). Selection may be envisioned as a process where a pool of candidate items is available to the language user, where only one of these items can be produced at any one time and where therefore a decision has to be made for one unit and against all others.

Contextual and non-contextual errors shed light on different aspects of the morphological system. Non-contextual slips grant insight into the degree of competition among the members of a paradigm, as illustrated in (2), where the irregular past participle competes with the regular one. The higher the error rate, the stronger the competition in the paradigm. However, competition in contextual slips is of a different nature. It is not brought about by structural alternatives offered by a particular language in an effort to express a certain intention or satisfy certain syntactic constraints, but rather by a more or less accidental co-occurrence of morphologically complex words in the linear representation of speech. Contextual errors provide evidence of the cohesiveness of morphologically complex words. The higher the error rate, the lower the degree of cohesion. The logic is simple enough. The more strongly a given morpheme is tied to another, the less easy it is for this morpheme to break free and undergo misordering. Thus, contextual slips of the tongue reveal the salience of the morphological representation, i.e. the extent to which morphemes "stick out" in words. For instance, the error in (1) highlights a morphological boundary in *wood-en* as well as in *long-ish*.[2]

---

[2] A single dash in the orthographic representation indicates a morpheme boundary.

It is worth emphasizing that, in line with recent developments in experimental morphology (see Hay and Baayen 2005), all central notions used in this chapter, in particular competition, salience and boundary, are of a gradient rather than categorical nature. While this is unremarkable for concepts such as competition, it represents a radical break with tradition when it comes to linguistic structure. A given word is traditionally regarded as either monomorphemic or polymorphemic. It either contains a morpheme boundary or it does not. In contradistinction to the received view, the notion of salience embodies the idea that the constituent morphemes of a word may have a variable representational strength. Similarly, the binary notion of a linguistic boundary is re-interpreted in terms of gradient boundary strength.

In this conceptual framework, there is a certain independence between contextual and non-contextual morphology. The size of paradigms and the relationship of the elements within them may be somewhat independent of the cohesiveness of morphemes in words. The factors that lead to the formation of paradigms are unlikely to be identical to those which determine the cohesiveness of morphologically complex words. However, this is not to say that these factors are completely different. Both contextual and non-contextual slips crucially rely on morphological structure. It may very well be that a vibrant paradigmatic morphology invigorates syntagmatic morphology.

The hypothesis of relative independence can be empirically tested by comparing the rates of contextual and non-contextual tongue slips across languages. It is also worthwhile examining the frequency of contextual and non-contextual errors from a language-specific perspective. It is known from the analysis of phonological slips of the tongue in many languages that contextual slips dwarf non-contextual ones (e.g. Stemberger 1989 on English; Berg 2003 on German; Wan 2007 on Mandarin Chinese; Pérezet et al. on Spanish 2007; Liu 2013 on Min). It is not known, however, whether this strong asymmetry can be replicated at the morphological level.

Given that inflection is generally more productive than derivation and that productivity implies heightened availability, inflectional errors may be less dependent on contextual triggers than derivational errors. Hence, non-contextual slips may be expected to have a higher share among inflectional than derivational errors.

The paradigmatic axis stands or falls on the notion of paradigms. In linguistics, paradigms are standardly understood to be comprised of elements of the same category. Typical examples include the case paradigm of nouns and the person paradigm of verbs. These paradigms are categorical in nature. It is an open question whether the psycholinguistic notion of paradigm has the same content as the linguistic notion. While the linguistic definition builds on alternative options which are all well-formed in certain contexts, it has not as yet been investigated whether the psycholinguistic conception is similarly constrained. Depending on the extent to which slips of the tongue exceed the limits of well-formedness, it might be that the processing system operates on a looser conception of paradigm than the one that prevails in linguistic theory.

The nature of paradigms raises major issues in the organization of the basic morphological components. Numerous studies have argued for a non-categorical boundary between derivation and inflection (e.g. Dressler 1989, Bertram, Schreuder, and Baayen 2000; Dressler 1989; González Torres 2010). This hypothesis allows one to predict that interactions between inflectional and derivational morphemes should not be ruled out in slips of the tongue.

Bybee (1985) went a step further by including lexical morphemes. She proposed a lexicon-grammar continuum and arranged lexical morphemes towards the lexical end, inflectional morphemes towards the grammatical end and derivational morphemes in-between the two. Such a continuum entails far-reaching predictions for tongue slips. Whatever the speech error patterns may be, they are expected to form a monotonic increase or decrease on the lexicon-grammar cline. By way of example, suppose there is a decrease in contextual substitution slips from lexical to derivational morphemes. We would then predict an even lower rate of contextual substitutions involving inflectional morphemes. When the rate of lexical slips is higher than that of grammatical slips, we will speak of a *lexicalness bias*.[3] Inversely, when the rate of grammatical slips outweighs that of lexical slips, we will speak of a *grammaticalness bias*.

This opening section raises more questions than this paper can possibly answer. The major aim of this chapter is to present a survey of the types of morphological errors that occur and to document certain influences to which these errors are subject. This tour will take us to the three major morphological components, viz. compounding, derivation and inflection. The empirical focus is on speech error data from German. The principal reason for this choice is that German is highly productive of compounding and derivational slips – two important error classes on which English scores rather low (see Stemberger 1998 on compounding and Melinger 2003 on derivation). Further motivation for this decision derives from the fact that no comprehensive analysis of morphological slips of the tongue has so far been undertaken. However, other languages will not be completely ignored. Besides English, slips from half a dozen additional languages will be

---

3 We introduce the label "lexicalness bias" here to avoid confusion with the simpler term "lexical bias", which is used in speech error research to describe an effect in phonological slips whereby the likelihood of a phonological error is heightened if the higher-level unit is a real word in the language (e.g. Hartsuiker et al. 2006).

discussed, however cursorily. This more inclusive perspective allows us to transcend the limitations imposed by the analysis of a single language.

The present chapter concentrates on the speech of linguistically competent adults using their native language – or rather their derailments. The empirical evidence on which it draws mainly comes from a corpus of more than 6000 slips of the tongue I collected over a four-year period by noting down what I judged to be a deviation from the speaker's intention. I recorded as much context as I could accurately remember and as I deemed necessary for adequate categorization. The errors were gleaned from natural communicative situations in which I took part or from radio and television broadcasts (see Berg 1988 for further details). Given the focus of this study on naturalistic data, only passing reference is made to the experimental literature. All of the data presented in this study come from oral production. Written production appears to generate too few genuinely morphological slips for a detailed examination (Ellis 1979). While morphological errors occur in perception, they are in the vast majority of cases the result of phonological misperceptions (Bond 1999) and therefore largely unsuitable for morphological analysis. In this study, the terms "speech error" and "slip of the tongue" are used interchangeably.

2 An analysis of morphological slips of the tongue

It is only natural for an examination of morphological errors to respect the tripartite distinction between compounding, derivation and inflection. A further relevant distinction is that between free and bound morphemes, i.e. stems and affixes. In slips of the tongue, these two dimensions interact in ways which do not play a prominent role in theoretical morphology. In particular, stems in derived words do not behave like stems in inflected words in speech errors. It is therefore necessary to consider stems in derivational and inflectional morphology separately. More generally put, the behavior of lower-level units depends on the nature of the higher-level unit of which they are a part. This is why the headings of the following three subsections reflect the perspective of the superordinate unit, to wit: the word.

The error analysis will begin with compounding, proceed to derivation and then turn to inflection. All three subsections distinguish between contextual and non-contextual errors. Possible interactions between derivational and inflectional affixes will be subsequently examined. Finally, the roles of selection and sequencing will be considered.

2.1 Errors in compound words

A key issue in compound research is the level at which compounds are represented. Are they lexical objects and as such holistically represented or morphological objects and as such analytically represented?[4] These alternatives invite disparate predictions regarding the cohesiveness of compounds in speech errors. As lexical objects, they are expected to be cohesive, i.e. to act as units; however, as morphological objects, they are expected to fall apart, i.e. the preferred error locus would be the individual morpheme.

To arbitrate between these options, all tongue slips involving a nominal compound were subjected to scrutiny. German (G.) has a strong propensity for nominal compounding (Berg 2017) and thus generates this error type in sufficiently large numbers. There are 71 contextual and 66 non-contextual items in my database. Let us begin with the former set.

2.1.1 Contextual slips

The most insightful tongue slips are those in which the structure of the utterance imposes the least bias on the error outcome. This requirement is met by the co-occurrence of two compounds in a linear string, with both of these being involved in the malfunction. The main question is whether the compound as a whole or one of its constituent morphemes undergoes misordering (in this connection, see also Chapter 9, Libben, Gagné and Dressler 2020, this volume). There are 9 relevant cases in my data two of which are given in (3) and (4). The first line provides the error as it occurred, the second line the interlinear gloss and the third line the translation into English. The critical parts are set in bold for easy identification. A dash marks the abortion of the utterance following error detection. The corrected utterance occurs to the right of the dash.

(3) G. Gestern   hat die chemische Industrie auf der
    yesterday has the chemical   industry at the
    Pressekonferenz– auf der **Hannovermesse** eine
    press conference   at   the Hanover fair   a

---

[4] That they can also be phonological objects was experimentally shown by Jacobs & Dell (2014).

Pressekonferenz gegeben
press conference given
'Yesterday the chemical industry gave a press conference at the Hanover Fair.'

(4) G. Wir haben morgen Elter**nabend** vom Kinder**abend**–
we have tomorrow parent evening of.the children's evening
vom Kinder**garten**.
of.the nursery school
'Tomorrow we'll have a parent-teacher meeting at the nursery school.'

Example (3) documents the interaction of two compounds at the word level. The compound *Presse-konferenz* 'press conference' ousts the compound *Hannover-messe* 'Hanover Fair'. In (4), by contrast, single morphemes are implicated. The second morpheme in *Eltern-abend* 'parent-teacher meeting' supplants the second morpheme in *Kinder-garten* 'nursery school'. There are 4 cases where it cannot be determined whether the entire compound or one of its constituents is involved in the malfunction. Eliminating these ambiguous cases brings down the number to 5 slips. Of these, one leaves the compounds intact while the compounds are broken up in the other 4 cases.

In the light of the low number of pertinent errors, the following conclusions should be regarded as tentative. Compounds are processed and represented at both the lexical and the morphological level. Thus, the issue is not whether they are lexical *or* morphological objects. In fact, they are both. This duality can be made more precise by considering error rates. The higher number of single-morpheme slips suggests that compounds fall apart rather easily. That is to say, they exhibit a relatively low degree of cohesiveness.

This conclusion is confirmed by a look at the next error type, in which a nominal compound interacts with a non-compound noun. Logically, there are three possibilities: (i) the compound may replace the simple noun, (ii) the simple noun may replace the compound noun, and (iii) the simple noun may replace one part of the compound. The first two options argue for a holistic representation, the third option for an analytic representation of compounds. Here are two relevant cases.

(5) G. Die **Schiedsrichter**– die **Zuschauer** sind nicht so zufrieden
the referee(s) the spectators are not so happy

mit **Schiedsrichter** Robert Welz.
with referee (proper noun)
'The spectators are not really happy about referee Robert Welz.'

(6) G. Man hat vor'm Zahn**arzt** schon **Arzt– Angst**.
one has of.the dentist even doctor fear
'Some people are even afraid of the dentist.'

The two errors show how a compound may intrude upon a non-compound noun. In (5), the compound *Schieds-richter* 'referee' replaces the non-compound noun *Zuschauer* 'spectators' in full whereas the target word *Angst* 'fear' in (6) is replaced by the second morpheme in *Zahn-arzt* 'dentist'. There are 49 anticipatory and perseveratory errors of this type in my collection. Subtracting 23 ambiguous slips leaves us with 26 critical cases of which 9 evince cohesive and 17 incohesive behavior.

This distribution tallies nicely with the previous results. Compounds can act both cohesively and incohesively. However, these two options are not equiprobable. Compounds are more on the incohesive than on the cohesive side.

The constellation of a compound and a simple noun also generates exchanges, i.e. bipositional errors. Again, we witness both holistic and analytic behavior, as exemplified by (7) and (8), respectively.

(7) G. mit dem **Bus** im **Kinderwagen**. *for:* mit dem
with the bus in.the pram with the
Kinderwagen im **Bus**.
pram in.the bus
'with the pram on the bus'

(8) G. **Bürger Bremer**meister– **Bremer** **Bürger**meister
(adjectival name of town) mayor
'the mayor of Bremen'

The entire compound *Kinder-wagen* 'pram' trades places with the simple noun *Bus* 'bus' in (7). In contrast, the compound *Bürger-meister* 'mayor' is split in (8). Its first morpheme switches position with the adjective *Bremer* 'of Bremen', which can also be a noun referring to a citizen of the town of Bremen. There are 3 cohesive and 3 incohesive exchanges involving compounds in my data, which is largely in harmony with the findings reported above.

A further difference between (7) and (8) is worth mentioning. While the interacting elements are adjacent in (8), they are separated by the complex preposition *im* 'in the' in (7). These two tongue slips may give us a clue as to when a compound is processed holistically or analytically. It may be speculated that the larger the linear distance between the interacting elements, i.e. the larger the processing window, the more likely the compound is to act as a unit. Inversely, a smaller processing window may be claimed to support analytic behavior. Actually, there are too few errors in my corpus to make this hypothesis anything more than suggestive.

The remaining 7 contextual slips allow one to catch a glimpse of the internal structure of compounds. They demonstrate that the linear order of the constituents of compounds has to be computed online even though it may be supposed to be lexically fixed. As linear order is generated anew in each production of a compound, morphological ordering errors such as (9) and (10) may see the light of day.[5]

(9) G. Dann machen wir uns   'n **Quarkobst–**
    then make   we ourselves a   cream.cheese.fruit
    Obstquark.
    fruit.cream.cheese
    'We'll prepare cream cheese with fruit later.'

(10) G. **Bezirksregierung– Regierungsbezirk** Lüneburg   ist es
     district.government   government.district (name of town) is it
     ja.
     PARTICLE
     'This area is administered by the local government of the town of Lüneburg.'

In both (9) and (10), the internal morpheme order was reversed in the compounds. The resulting compound *Quark-obst* in (9) is not lexicalized while *Bezirks-regierung* 'local government' in (10) is impeccable. These ordering errors lend additional support to the claim that the morphemes inside compounds are rather loosely connected and that, by implication, compounds are relatively incohesive objects.

---

[5] Kindred errors were reported for English by Stemberger (1985a). Note as well that similar sequencing errors have been observed in language acquisition (e.g. Rainer 2010: 35) and aphasia (e.g. Badecker 2001).

2.1.2 Non-contextual slips

The non-contextual slips by and large replicate the patterns in contextual slips. The following logical possibilities exist: (i) a bipartite compound noun (AB) is replaced by a different compound noun (CD), (ii) an entire compound (AB) replaces, or is replaced by, a non-compound noun (C), and (iii) one constituent of a compound (A in AB) is replaced by a single lexeme (C) whereas the other constituent (B) is left untouched. While options (i) and (ii) argue for a holistic representation, option (iii) supports an analytic representation.

In contrast to the contextual tongue slips, option (ii) is not attested in my database. Because such an error type presupposes a high degree of cohesion within compounds, the absence of this error class is compatible with the claim that nominal compounds are of limited cohesiveness. Note that this error type is further discouraged by the unequal morphological status of a compound and a non-compound word. Option (i) is exemplified in (11), option (iii) in (12) and (13).

(11) G. Habt ihr mal   'n **Strohhalm**– **Streichholz**?
     have you PARTICLE a straw.blade   match
     'Have you got a straw – a match?'

(12) G. Nächsten Montag müssen wir unsere Baukonstruktions**zeitung**–
     next   Monday must   we our   construction.newspaper
     zeichnung abgeben.
     draft   hand in
     'We have to hand in our construction newspaper – draft next Monday.'

(13) G. Das sind Streikkosten, die   wir bei Beginn   des
     that are strike.costs   which we at beginning of.the
     Arbeits**amt**es–   Arbeits**kampf**es kalkuliert hatten.
     employment.office–   labor.dispute   calculated had
     'These are strike costs which we counted at the beginning of the labor dispute.'

The intended compound *Streich-holz* 'match' is supplanted by the non-intended compound *Stroh-halm* 'straw' in (11). In (12), by contrast, the final constituent of the compound *Baukonstruktions-zeichnung* 'construction draft' is ousted by the similar-sounding lexeme *Zeitung* 'newspaper'. The fact that the resultant compound *Baukonstruktions-zeitung* is a possible, albeit unlikely word provides strong support for the hypothesis that the malfunction arose at the morphological rather than the lexical level. However, determining the error locus proves more difficult in (13). This slip is ambiguous between the interaction of two entire compounds or the interaction of the final constituents of the two compounds. The fact that the word *Arbeits-amt* used to be the ordinary German word for 'employment office' argues for the former possibility. On the other hand, the observation that compounds as units are seldom involved in errors argues for the latter possibility. Ultimately, it may be wrong to conceive of this classification problem in strictly binary terms. A more adequate analysis may hold that the error occurred at the morphological level but that it was facilitated by the item *Arbeitsamt* in the mental lexicon – a lexical bias effect at the morphological level (see footnote 3). In this spirit, it was decided to classify cases like (13) for example as single-morpheme slips.

Leaving aside 1 blend error and 3 ambiguous cases, we count 62 non-contextual slips of which 6 are whole-word errors and 56 single-morpheme errors. This strong predominance of the latter error type further strengthens our earlier hypothesis that the constituents of nominal compounds do not stick together well.

The standard analysis of hierarchical (or determinative) compounds is in terms of the head-modifier distinction. What role does this distinction play in slips of the tongue? By definition, heads are more important constituents than modifiers because they provide a semantic frame for the interpretation of modifiers and because they pass on their formal properties to the entire compound. Transposing this difference into the world of psycholinguistics, we may expect heads to be more powerful, that is, more strongly activated in the processing network. Since tongue slips result from excessive competition, i.e. too small a difference in the activation levels of competing units, a larger number of errors may be predicted to occur on heads than on modifiers. A modifier slip is shown in (14), a head slip in (15) (see also (12)).

(14) G. Sie wollte **Reaktion**slehrerin– **Religion**slehrerin werden.
 she wanted.to reaction.teacher religion.teacher become
 'She was going to be a religion teacher.'

(15) G. Der Pass ist aus Sicherheits**gurte**n gesperrt. *for:* aus
 the pass is for safety.belts blocked for
 Sicherheits**günde**n.
 safety.reasons
 'The pass has been blocked for safety belts.' intended: 'for safety reasons'

The modifier *Religion* 'religion' in *Religion-s-lehrerin* 'religion teacher' was substituted for by the phonologically similar lexeme *Reaktion* 'reaction' in (14). In (15), however, the head *Gründe(n)* 'reasons' in *Sicherheit-s-gründen* 'safety reasons' made way for the lexeme *Gurte* 'belts', possibly with some lexical support from the lexicalized compound *Sicherheit-s-gurt* 'safety belt' (in addition to the phonological similarity between *Gurt* [gurt] and *Grund* [grunt]).

The 56 single-morpheme errors divide into 22 modifier and 34 head slips. The ratio of one-third to two-thirds is statistically significant (binomial, $p < 0.03$). Thus, the above prediction is confirmed: heads are psycholinguistically more active than modifiers. A related asymmetry emerges in contextual errors although the number of relevant slips is much lower. It is worthy of note that the naturalistic speech error data replicate the head-modifier asymmetry observed in experimental studies (e.g. Isel, Gunter, and Friederici 2003; Juhasz, Starr, Inhoff, and Placke 2003; Marelli, Crepaldi, and Luzzatti 2009).

To conclude, the error evidence shows that compounds straddle the boundary between the lexical and the morphological level. They are represented at both and therefore behave as units or fall apart, as the case may be. The fact that the latter behavior predominates suggests that nominal compounds are relatively incohesive objects in German. In other words, the constituents of compounds are separated by a distinct morphological boundary. Even though nominal compounds were treated indiscriminately in the foregoing, it is not claimed here that they form a totally homogeneous group. In fact, it is most likely that the strength of the morphological boundary is compound-specific.

2.2 Errors in derived words

The distinction between non-contextual and contextual slips is not identical to the contrast between derivational errors proper (e.g. *philosophist* for *philosopher*; Stemberger 1985a) and stem or affix errors unrelated to word-formation processes (e.g. *dealsman* < *dealer* x *salesman*; Fromkin 1973). While, as noted previously, errors of word formation are non-contextual in nature, this is not the only non-contextual error type. In particular, blend errors, which are not identical to word-formation processes as conventionally understood, are of the non-contextual kind. Note also that whereas (non-contextual) derivational word formation is restricted to affixing, contextual slips may involve both free and bound morphemes.

2.2.1 Contextual slips

Let us begin with stem errors in derived words. It is notable that stems in derived words undergo misordering rather easily. In (16), the two interacting stems are adjoined to derivational affixes. Error (17) shows the interaction of two stems of which one is integrated into a derived word while the other is not.

(16) G. **leer**ende **Gähn**e. *for:* **gähn**ende **Leer**e
– – yawning emptiness
'gaping void'

(17) G. Es war albern von de Gaulle, mit der **Droh**ung– mit der
it was stupid of de Gaulle with the threat with the
Spaltung zu **droh**en.
splitting to threaten
'It was a stupid idea of de Gaulle's to threaten to effect a splitting.'

Example (16) involves the bimorphemic noun *Leer-e* 'emptiness' and the trimorphemic adjective *gähn-end-e* 'yawning', where the inflectional suffix *-e* may be put to the side. The error documents an exchange of the two stems *leer* 'empty' and *gähn* 'yawn'. The stem *leer* attaches to the participial/adjectival suffix *-end*, which stays in its original location. The stem *gähn* attaches to the nominal suffix *-e*, which is also stranded. The reversal of the two stems yields the nonce adjective *leerend* and the nonce noun *Gähne*. Thus, both *gähn-end* and *Leer-e* have been broken up into their constituent morphemes. Case (17) involves the bimorphemic noun *Spalt-ung* 'splitting' and the bimorphemic verb *droh-en*, 'to threaten'. The verbal stem *droh* 'threaten' intrudes upon the nominal stem of *Spalt-ung* to yield *Droh-ung* 'threat'. This error, then, relies on a morphological analysis of *Spalt-ung* into a stem and a suffix.

In order to determine the cohesiveness of derived words, it is necessary to compare the rate of stem errors in derived words to the rate of whole-word errors where the stem and the derivational affix are misordered in tandem. The higher the ratio of the former to the latter error type, the lower the degree of cohesion of derived words. The following tongue slips may serve as exemplification. Case (18) illustrates a prefix-stem structure, (19) a stem-suffix structure.

(18) G. Er wird diesen **Vorschlag**– diese Ankündigung vor
he will this proposal this announcement prior.to
seinem Rücktritt verbinden mit dem **Vorschlag**...
his resignation combine with the proposal
'Prior to his resignation, he will combine this annoucement with the proposal...'

(19) G. die **Mutter** meiner **Freundin**– die **Freundin** meiner **Mutter**
 the mother of.my female.friend the female.friend of.my mother
 'my mother's friend'

In (18), the prefix-stem sequence *Vor-schlag* 'proposal' is dislocated as a unit.⁶ So is the noun *Freund-in* 'female friend', which consists of the stem *Freund* and the feminine suffix *-in* in (19). Some measure of association between stems and derivational affixes has to be reckoned with.

The following count is based on all contextual substitutions in which the error word is morphologically complex (while the target word need not be). There are 27 whole-word slips and 50 stem slips in my error collection. The proportion of 35% to 65% suggests that derived words form moderately incohesive units. Clearly, an intermediate level of cohesion has to be acknowledged. As far as their cohesiveness is concerned, derived words and compounds appear to pattern similarly.

We proceed to the analysis of affix errors, which are quite common in German. The anticipatory addition of a prefix is illustrated in (20), that of a suffix in (21).

(20) G. Ich habe mich für Rollen-**ent**-spiel **ent**schieden. *for:*
 I have myself for role-PREFIX-play decided
 Rollenspiel
 role play
 'I have decided on role play.'

(21) G. Da müsste man mal genauer in die
 PARTICLE would.have.to you PARTICLE more.closely in the
 Klatschspalt**ung**en der Zeit**ung**en schauen. *for:*
 gossip.splittings of.the newspapers look
 Klatschspalten
 gossip.columns
 'You would have to take a closer look at the gossip columns of the newspapers.'

In (20), the prefix *ent-* in *ent-scheiden* 'to decide' was copied into the compound *Rollen-spiel* 'role play' to produce the non-word *Rollen-ent-spiel*. Similarly, the nominal suffix *-ung* in *Zeit-ung* 'newspaper' was inserted between the stem *Spalte*

---

6 It is unlikely that the preposition *vor* as a free-standing closed class item played a major role in bringing about this speech error.

'column' and the plural marker /n/ in (21). While the local error word *Spalt-ung-en* 'splittings' is lexicalized, the compound *Klatsch-spaltungen* is nonsensical.

The error rates disclose a significant contrast. A total of 165 contextual prefix slips accompany 53 contextual suffix slips in my sample (76%–24%). This is a surprising result. Berg (2016) reports that the token frequency of suffixes is almost twice as high as that of prefixes in the CELEX database. General language usage would therefore lead us to expect more suffix than prefix errors. This contrast cements the validity of the prefix-suffix asymmetry in the error data.

The lower number of suffix slips compared to prefix slips suggests that stem-suffix sequences form a more tightly knit unit than prefix-stem sequences. Put another way, there are different morphological linkages at work: a weaker link between prefixes and stems and a stronger link between stems and suffixes. This weaker link grants prefixes a certain independence from stems, which allows prefixes to be rather freely involved in errors. Suffixes, by contrast, are so intimately connected to their stems that they have difficulty in disconnecting. This asymmetry lends credence to a right-branching analysis of prefix-stem-suffix structures such as *unthinkable* (Berg 2012). There is a functional difference between prefixes and suffixes which may explain their differential involvement in slips of the tongue. On the basis of English and German data, Berg (2015) argued that prefixes are more lexical and suffixes more grammatical in nature. This disparity leads us back to the lexicalness bias, which states that the higher the lexicalness of a unit, the more often it is involved in errors. Because prefixes are more lexical than suffixes, there are far more prefix slips than suffix slips.

The English (E.) error patterns resemble the German data closely. Let us highlight the category of exchanges. While stem exchange errors do occur, affix exchanges are almost non-existent. I spotted a single case (22) in Fromkin's entire (unpublished) corpus and another singleton case (23) in Jaeger's (2005: 400) error collection.

(22) E. He is not very forc**y** and push**ful**. *for:* force**ful** and push**y**.

(23) E. The seemingly insecure professor is actually a witt**ing** and charm**y** – witt**y** and charm**ing** conversationalist.

The suffixes *-ful* and *-y* are reversed in (22), the suffixes *-y* and *-ing* in (23). It is probably no coincidence that the words in which the malfunction occurred are both adjectives in (22) and (23). This word-class identity is a likely facilitator of the attachment of the suffixes to the inappropriate stems.

As in compounds (see Section 2.2.1), ordering problems may arise inside derived words. According to the like-with-like constraint, prefixes interact with other prefixes and suffixes with other suffixes. This constraint thus presupposes prefix (or suffix) sequences in language structure for prefix (or suffix) misorderings to occur. Because stems may be preceded by two derivational prefixes, the theoretical possibility of prefix misorderings exists in German. And in fact, errors like (24) for example have found their way into my corpus.

(24) G. Das kann uns auch noch **vorbe**stehen– **bevor**stehen.
      that may us also still   –   lie ahead
      'The worst may still be to come.'

The target word *be-vor-stehen* 'to lie ahead' consists of the two prefixes *be-* and *vor-* and the stem *stehen*. The two prefixes reverse their order in (24). The suprasegmental level is also implicated. The stressed prefix *vor-* takes its stress value along, thereby yielding a different rhythmic structure (from amphibrachic to dactyl in the phonological representation). It is worth noting that suffix misorderings are not attested in my data although suffix sequences do occur in the language. This disparity is congruent with the lexicalness bias.

The previous analysis relied on the notion of word classes and thus was predicated on the tacit assumption that word-class information is available at the level at which morpheme slips arise. This is an important assumption which touches on the richness of the morphological representation. Are morphological errors really sensitive to word class? Opinions are divided on this issue. Whereas MacKay (1979) claims that stem slips are almost always of the same word class as the target, Garrett (1980) argues that there is no such sensitivity. In Garrett's corpus, slips of the tongue involving different word classes occur slightly more often than those involving the same word class. As Garrett does not calculate a null hypothesis, this empirical difference is difficult to evaluate. He assigns morphological errors to a processing level at which word class is not represented and thereby implicitly denies a word-class effect.

Stemberger (1985b) objects to Garrett's conclusions, arguing that it is necessary to distinguish between errors involving inflected words and errors involving derived words. His data reveal no difference in word-class sensitivity between uninflected and inflected words. Both sets of errors are highly sensitive to word class. This finding is consistent with the view that word class is part of the representation of lexical morphemes.

Note that the issue of a general word-class sensitivity cannot be easily settled for English because English lexemes are notorious for their word-class ambiguity. This problem brings us back to German where word class can usually be determined unambiguously. We consider stem substitution errors which may involve the same word class, as in (25), or different word classes, as in (26).

(25) G. Ich kenne **Schüler– Kinder**, die zur **Schule** gehen.
　　　　I　know　pupils–　children who to.the school　go
　　　'I know pupils – children who attend school.'

(26) G. Finde ich gar　　　nicht gut,　dass er　noch
　　　　find　I　certainly not　good that　he PARTICLE
　　　Feiertag–　　**Vater**tag　　**feier**t.
　　　bank.holiday–　father's.day　celebrates
　　　'I really don't like him celebrating bank holiday – father's day.'

While the interacting units *Kinder* 'children' and *Schule* 'school' in (25) are both nouns, the verb *feiern* 'to celebrate' ousts the noun *Vater* 'father' in (26).

An analysis of all stem substitution errors in my German collection brings forth a majority of word-class-identical interactions. A total of 310 slips divide into 194 word-class-identical and 116 word-class-divergent cases (62.6%–37.4%). The null hypothesis was derived by perusing 33 pages (pp. 221–253) of Steger et al.'s (1971) compilation of samples of spoken German and extracting all theoretical possibilities of stem interaction. An attempt was made to respect real error characteristics such as the distance between error and source as faithfully as possible. In this set of 79 potential interactions, only 20 (25%) were found to involve word-class-identical elements. The actual error patterns are significantly different from chance (binomial, $p < 0.001$). It may thus be concluded, in keeping with Stemberger's results for English, that stems in German are subject to a word-class constraint at the moment that they undergo misordering.

Up to now, the analysis has been exclusively based on languages with a concatenative morphology. It is highly remarkable that basically the same error patterns emerge in languages with a non-concatenative morphology such as Arabic. In this language, all morphology is bound. Oversimplifying somewhat, lexical morphemes take the shape of discontinuous strings of consonants while grammatical morphemes take the shape of discontinuous strings of vowels. For example, the word *ʃaraba* 'to drink/he drank' consists of the lexical morpheme *ʃ-r-b* 'drink' and the third person singular past tense marker *a-a-a*. A lexical-morpheme error would accordingly involve the consonantal skeleton and leave the vowel pattern unscathed. In point of fact, such cases occur quite commonly in a corpus of Jordanian Arabic (A.) speech errors collected by Hassan Abd-El-Jawad. Two of these cases are reported in (27) and (28).

(27) A. **faaðu baali**.　*for:* **baalu　faaði**.
　　　–　　head.my　　head.his　empty
　　　'His head is empty.'

(28) A. il-*ḥ*asas il-**wattaar**.   *for:* il-watar   il-*ḥ*assaas.
     –   the-tendon   the-tendon vulnerable
'The tendon is vulnerable.'

Case (27) involves biconsonantal, (28) triconsonantal roots undergoing a reversal. To be specific, the roots *b-l* 'head' and *f-ð* 'empty' switch places in (27) and the roots *w-t-r* 'tendon' and *ḥ-s-s* 'vulnerable' do likewise in (28). The gemination of the word-internal consonant in *ḥassaas* 'vulnerable' behaves like the vowels in that it stays put in its original location. The minimum conclusion which can be drawn from these and kindred slips is that a morphological level is created irrespective of whether the phonemes making up morphemes are continuous or discontinuous. A stronger claim would be that morphological processing is not radically different in languages with a concatenative morphology and those with a non-concatenative morphology.

In their dataset, Abd-El-Jawad and Abu-Salim (1987) find slightly more reversals of consonantal roots than of whole words.[7] It would be interesting to know whether (lexical) morphemes are more error-prone in languages with a concatenative morphology than in those with a non-concatenative morphology. One reason why this might be so is that morphemes are more highly integrated into the word structure in Arabic than in English and hence may be expected to break loose less easily in the former than the latter language. To test this claim, a fairly elaborate argument would be required because the two languages do not easily compare.

This subsection will be rounded off with a look at an attendant error process known as accommodation. This intriguing phenomenon comes in two types (Berg 1987). The typical instance of a syntagmatic slip involves the movement of a particular error unit from position A to position B. During this process of relocation, the integrity of the error unit is generally preserved. However, this is not always so. The moving unit may undergo a change because its new position imposes certain formal constraints which did not exist in the old position. If the error unit respects these constraints, accommodation takes place, as in (29); if, however, the error unit ignores these constraints, accommodation fails, as in (30).

---

[7] This pattern is not replicated in Hamrouni's (2010) experimental study of Tunesian Arabic speech errors in which whole-word slips predominate. As she concedes herself, methodological shortcomings might be responsible for this result.

(29) G. dass sie die Augen**schüsse**– die Augen**zeugen** einfach
that they the eye.shots the eye.witnesses simply
niederge**schoss**en haben.
down.shot have
'that they just shot the eye witnesses.'

(30) G. Auswärts ge**tor**ene **Schoss**e– ge**schoss**ene **Tor**e zählen doppelt.
away – – kicked goals count twice
'Goals scored in an away match count twice.'

This pair of examples has been selected with special care. It presents a rare case of the same unit being involved in different errors (and in different ways at that). This unit is the verb *schieß-en* 'to shoot/to kick' with its past participle *ge-schoss-en*. The corresponding noun is *Schuss* 'shot/kick' in the singular and *Schüsse* 'shots/kicks' in the plural. The tonic vowels /iː/, /ɔ/, /u/ and /y/ are therefore indicative of word class (and more specific features).

In (29), the verbal stem *schoss* intrudes upon the second constituent of the nominal compound *Augen-zeuge-n* 'eye witnesses'. The "outgoing" noun *Zeuge* 'witness' imposes its nominal nature on the "incoming" verbal stem and therefore changes the vowel from /ɔ/ to /y/. The resulting word is the lexicalized plural noun *Schüsse* 'shots'. The entire compound *Augenschüsse* is not an established word. This is a clear case of morphophonological accommodation.

In (30), the past participle *ge-schoss-en* 'kicked', which functions as an adjective, trades places with the noun *Tor* 'goal'. As the stem of this adjective enters a nominal slot, it might be expected to adopt nominal properties, as was the case in (29). However, this does not happen. The tonic vowel /ɔ/ of *geschossen* does not turn into /u/ or /y/. This is thus an instance of a failure to accommodate. The conditions under which accommodation does or does not take place await a more detailed investigation.

Accommodation does not only involve the segmental but also the suprasegmental level. Ferreira and Humphreys (2001) and Wardlow Lane and Ferreira (2010) capitalized on a notable interaction between word class and stress placement in English. For example, the lexeme *record* is initially stressed as a noun but finally stressed as a verb. The authors experimentally elicited stem exchanges on VPs such as *taped the record*. They found that when the target VP was mispronounced as *recorded the tape*, the lexeme *record* typically underwent a stress shift. This is another case of word-class-specific accommodation.

The second type of accommodation induces a change on a neighbor of the error unit, not on the error itself. Due to syntagmatic constraints, a conflict may arise between the error unit in its new location and the "old" context. If the processing system manages to resolve this conflict, accommodation takes place; if it does not, accommodation fails. Curiously enough, I did not find any such accommodation failures in my error sample. Three cases of accommodation are provided below, with (31) from German and (32) and (33) from English.

(31) G. Dann haben sie   Schwierigkeiten, die **Formulierung**en– die
     then have   they difficulties   the formulations   the
     Schwierigkeiten   zu   **formulier**en.
     difficulties   to   formulate
     'Then they have difficulties putting the difficulties into words.'

(32) E. I think it's **careful** to measure with **reason**. for: **reasonable** to measure with **care**. (from Fromkin 1973)

(33) E. People still see Libya as a **national danger** – as a **dangerous nation**. (from Pfau 2009: 246)

Example (31) testifies to the intrusion of the verbal stem *formulier* 'formulate' on the noun *Formulierungen* 'formulations'. The critical feature of this tongue slip is the alternative ways of nominalization. The suffix *-keit* nominalizes the adjective *schwierig* 'difficult' whereas the suffix *-ung* nominalizes the verbal stem *formulier* 'formulate'. As can be seen in (31), the intruding stem selects the appropriate suffix *-ung* and thereby does away with the suffix *-keit*.

The two English slips attest to the interaction of a denominal adjective and a noun. In (32), the noun *care* enters the *X-able* slot. There is no phonological obstacle to *care-able*, given the orthodoxy of such forms as *bear-able*. Also the morphological rules of English do not ban *care-able*. This stem-suffix combination is just unusual and certainly much less frequent than *care-ful*. The change from *-able* to *-ful* may thus be understood as a way of generating an output which is lexically unobjectionable. The accommodation in (33) seems to be governed by similar principles. The non-accommodated hypothethical output *nation-ous* creates neither a phonological nor a morphological anomaly, given the existence of cases such as *cavern-ous* and *fam-ous*.

2.2.2 Non-contextual slips

Before we consider errors of word formation, it is fitting to discuss blend errors in which two stem-affix sequences are blended into one, i.e. $stem_1$-$affix_1$ x $stem_2$-

affix₂ -> stem₁-affix₂ or stem₂-affix₁. A prefix-stem blend is given in (34), a blend involving a suffix in (35).

(34) G. Das ist ein häufiger **Vor**wand– **Ein**wand gegen die
that is a common excuse objection against the
Reiseunternehmen.
tourist companies
'That is an excuse – an objection which is commonly levelled against tourist companies.'

(35) G. Bemerke– Bemerk**ung**en
– comments

Example (34) illustrates a blend of the semantically related words *Ein-wand* 'objection' and *Vor-wurf* 'reproach' which share the morphological structure of prefix + stem. The error word *Vor-wand* preserves this structure by combining the prefix of *Vor-wurf* with the stem of *Ein-wand*. The fact that the error word *Vor-wand* 'excuse' is a real word may have facilitated this processing failure. Case (35) is an uncommon blend of two plural words with a different morphological structure, to wit: the prefix-stem word *Ver-merke* 'notes' and the prefix-stem-suffix word *Be-merk-ung-en* 'comments'. In view of the fact that *Bemerkungen* was the intended item, the error word *Bemerke* may be interpreted as involving the deletion of the nominalizing suffix *-ung*. This loss may be understood as an interference of the suffixlessness of *Vermerk* 'note'.

The quantitative patterns in blends confirm the asymmetry between prefixes and suffixes observed in contextual slips. In fact, this asymmetry is even more pronounced in blends. There are 69 clear and 44 ambiguous prefix blends but hardly any suffix blends in my error corpus. Case (35) is the only pertinent case and singleton cases are almost always open to alternative analyses.

We move on to word formation proper. Word-formation errors provide evidence of the competition between alternative strategies of deriving words, strategies which are appropriate in one particular context, though not in another. The greater the similarity, both formal and semantic, among these options, the stronger the competition and hence, the higher the probability of a malfunction. Such a conflict is nicely illustrated in English by the choice between the Germanic negative prefix *un-* and the Romance negative prefix *il-*, as in *unlawful* and *il-legal*. It is therefore no wonder that errors involving negative prefixes figure prominently in Fromkin's corpus. Here are two relevant cases.

(36) E. I'm **in**able to walk – I'm **un**able to walk.

(37) E. I'm physically **dis**comfortable. for: **un**comfortable.

Both slips illustrate the confusion between negative prefixes. The prefix *un-* is substituted for by *in-* in (36) and by *dis-* in (37). It is likely that the occurrence of these two slips was promoted by the related nouns *inability* and *discomfort*, respectively. In fact, the same stem (i.e. *able* and *comfort*) is expanded by different prefixes in different word classes.

These word-formation errors raise the intriguing issue of how similar they are to blend errors such as (34) above. Is it even possible to argue that word-formation errors actually are blend errors? For instance, is *inable* the outcome of blending *unable* and *inability* together? A provisional answer is that the two error types are similar, though not identical. Empirically, the two error types pattern differently. While true blends almost invariably involve interacting units from the same word class, word-formation errors are less constrained. As can be seen in (36) and (37), they may show an interference from a different word class. Furthermore, somewhat disparate mechanisms appear to underlie the two error types. Whereas genuine blends require the activation of all four morphemes (i.e. $affix_1$, $stem_1$, $affix_2$, $stem_2$), word-formation errors make do with the activation of the intended $affix_1$ and $stem_1$ as well as the inadvertent $affix_2$. The strong activation of a particular unintentional stem may not be necessary although it is quite possible that the weak activation of a number of inadvertent stems (a so-called gang effect) plays a role in this game.

There is some evidence that the patterns of word-formation errors are asymmetrical. There are more errors in which a less regular form is replaced by a more regular form than vice versa. One measure of irregularity is the extent of morphophonological adjustment attendant upon affixation. Thus, the more regular suffix *-ment* intrudes upon its rival *-ity* more often than vice versa. Cases such as (38) are accordingly more frequent than cases such as (39) (both from the Fromkin corpus). Similar slips were experimentally induced by MacKay (1978).

(38) E. His sincereness is unquestionable. *for:* his sincerity.

(39) E. comfortability. *for:* comfortableness.

Word-formation errors can be found in corpora from several other languages including German (Berg), Spanish (del Viso, Igoa, and García-Albea 1987) and French (Rossi and Peter-Defare 1998). Rather than documenting these cases in any detail, we will pick out a word-formation process which involves a stem-internal change as a concomitant of affixation, as in (38) above. In German, suffixing may be accompanied by a vowel change named umlaut.[8] The issue is how reliably this vowel change is implemented in speech errors. The notable answer is "not very". Here are two pertinent examples.

(40) G. sauberlich–   säuberlich.
      –   'neat'

(41) G. ohnmachtig– ohnmächtig.
      –   'unconscious'

As can be seen from these errors, suffixing may operate smoothly while umlauting may fail. In (40), the adjective *sauber* 'clean' takes the suffix *–lich*. The attendant vowel change from /aʊ/ to /ɔɪ/ does not, however, take place. The same problem can be observed in (41) where the vowel /a/ is not umlauted to /e/ following the attachment of the suffix *–ig* to the noun *Ohnmacht* 'fainting'.

These slips demonstrate that suffixing and umlaut are two distinct processes. Umlaut is rather independent of suffixing. The probable reason that makes umlaut so vulnerable is the inherent processing difficulty involved in stem-internal changes. On the assumption that the base is drawn on for the generation of the morphologically complex word, the umlaut vowel competes with the non-umlauted vowel. If the latter is strong, the former may have a hard time asserting itself. In (40), for example, the base *sauber* 'clean' is far more frequent than the derived word *säuberlich* 'neat'. On the assumption that high lexical frequency strengthens the phonological representation (e.g. Dell 1990), it is to be expected that the umlaut vowel may occasionally lose to the vowel of the base.

2.3 Errors in inflected words

The categories that are relevant to the study of inflected words are similar, though not identical to those relevant to the description of derived words. In particular, there are no blends of the type stem$_1$-affix$_1$ x stem$_2$-affix$_2$ > stem$_1$-affix$_2$ or stem$_2$-affix$_1$ in inflectional morphology. This is very different from what was observed in derivational morphology. The reason for this non-occurrence

---

[8] The term "umlaut" is used here mainly for convenience. It is not intended to describe an orthographic device. As slips of the tongue are by definition spoken-language phenomena, the term refers to a morphologically conditioned vowel change in the stem.

lies in the low semantic content in inflectional affixes. This prevents the competition between words with different stems and different inflectional suffixes. Thus, the critical precondition for blending is not fulfilled.

2.3.1 Contextual slips

The major behavioral difference between stems in inflected and stems in derived words is that the former are more autonomous vis-à-vis their bound morphemes than the latter. Hence, stem slips occur more frequently in inflected than in derived words. In all probability, two related effects combine to boost the rate of stem slips. For one thing, the low degree of cohesion in inflected words grants stems their independence; for another, the grammatical nature of inflectional morphemes makes them reluctant to undergo misordering. As a result, the typical error in inflected words is a stem slip which leaves inflectional material behind. The frequency of this error type is impressive. It is well represented in large and small corpora from diverse languages. Following is a cross-section of tongue slips from English, German, Norwegian (N.), Spanish (S.) and Italian (I.).

(42) E. Make it so the **apple** has less **tree**s. *for:* so the **tree** has less **apple**s. (from Garrett 1975: 159)

(43) G. Bill Haley, der **Rock** des **König**s– der **König** des **Rock**s.
Bill Haley the rock of.the king– the king of.the rock
'Bill Haley, the king of rock'

(44) N. ikke ei **sol** for **sky**a. *for:* ikke ei **sky** for
not a sun in.front.of cloud-the not a cloud in.front.of
sola. (from Foldvik 1979: 119)
sun.the
'not a sun in front of the cloud' for: 'not a cloud in front of the sun'

(45) S. Lo que pasa es que, hoy en día, una **cuer**a
it what happens is that nowadays a –
de **suel**o– una **suel**a de **cuer**o
of floor– a sole of leather
(from del Viso, Igoa, and García-Albea 1987: 96)
'Nowadays, a leather sole...'

(46) I. I **parol**e di **error**a. *for:* gli **error**i di
    the.PL speech.PL of.the error.SG   the.PL error.PL of.the
    parola
    speech.SG
    (from Magno Caldognetto, Tonelli, and Pinton 1987)
    'speech errors'

All five errors exemplify the reversal of nominal stems. The inflectional material which stays put is quite diversified. The plural suffix is stranded in (42), the case marker in (43), the definiteness marker in (44), the gender (or inflectional class) marker in (45) and again the number marker in (46). There is a noteworthy difference between the slips from the Germanic and those from the Romance languages. Roughly speaking, the former language group has a word-based morphology whereas the latter group has a stem-based morphology. While the suffixes are attached to free-standing words in English and Norwegian, they are epoxied to bound stems in Spanish and Italian. On the face of it, this disparity does not seem to play a major part in error generation. However, whether the morphological status of the stem has an effect on the incidence of stem slips (and suffix slips, for that matter) remains to be ascertained. An informed guess would be that, *ceteris paribus*, the rate of stem slips is higher in a word-based than in a stem-based morphology because bound stem + suffix sequences are probably more cohesive than free stem + suffix sequences.

Errors involving inflectional suffixes display an amazing variety of functions. Among the many features that may be misordered are case, person, number, tense, finiteness and comparison.[9] In point of fact, no grammatical category appears to be immune to malfunction. Two examples from German are provided in (47) and (48).

(47) G. Grock**en**– Grog trink**en** nie 12 (Personen).
    –   grog drink never 12 (people)
    'There will never be 12 people drinking grog.'

(48) G. Du möchst', dass ich schön **geriecht**– **riech**e und **ge**pflegt bin.
    you like.to that I nicely –   smell and neat   am
    'You like me to smell good and be neat.'

---

[9] Linking elements inside compounds (e.g. *Arbeit-s-zeit* 'working time') may also be involved in errors. However, they are not considered here because they have mostly lost their morphological status (see e.g. Nübling & Szczepaniak 2013).

The third person plural suffix *-en* is anticipated in (47) while the past participle marker is anticipated in (48). More specifically, the suffix /-ən/ (phonetically a syllabic nasal) of the verb form *trink-en* '(they) drink' is inadvertently attached to the noun *Grog* 'grog' in (47). The error word *Grocken*, in which the devoicing of final <g> is preserved, is a non-word. Case (48) shows the intrusion of the past participle circumfix *ge_t* of *ge-pfleg-t* 'neat' upon the first person singular form *riech-e* '(I) smell'. This slip leads to the ungrammatical form *ge-riech-t* 'smelt', which would be the regular formation of the past participle of *riech-en* 'to smell'. However, *riechen* is an ablaut verb and as such requires a vowel change in non-present tenses (and a different suffix in the past participle). There is a notable parallel here between this misordering error and errors of word formation in which an irregular verb form is replaced with a regular one (see below).

Exchanges involving inflectional suffixes are quite rare, thus paralleling the behavior of derivational affixes. There is not a single such error in my German sample. Two relevant cases, one from Spanish and the other from Finnish (F.) are reproduced below. It is probably no coincidence that Hokkanen's (2001) Finnish corpus contains a few such items as Finnish makes heavy use of inflections. Example (50) has been slightly shortened. (INE = inessive; ELA = elative)

(49) S. He   cantado líne**o**   y   bing**a**. *for:* líne**a**   y   bing**o**. (from Igoa,
        I.have   cried   –   and –   line   and   bingo
        García-Albea and Sánchez-Casas 1999: 179)
        'I cried line and bingo.'

(50) F. mukana ... on ... (ihmiset) ... eri
        in.it   are   (people)   various
        ryhmi**ssä**   kertoma**sta**   näkemyksiään.   *for:* ryhmi**stä**
        group.PL.INE   tell.3rdINF.ELA   view.PL.their   group.PL.ELA
        kertoma**ssa**. (from Hokkanen 2001: 98–99)
        tell.3rdINF.INE
        'In the debate, there are people from various groups who are expressing their views.'

The two gender (or noun class) markers *-o* for masculine and *-a* for feminine trade places in (49). This slip compares in an interesting way to (45) above in which the stems were reversed and the gender markers stayed put. The same structures may give rise to stem or suffix slips. It is not known which factors decide for the one and against the other error type. The Finnish tongue slip illustrates a reversal of two case markers. (The concomitant vowel harmonic changes need not concern us here.) The elative suffix -*stä* 'from' swaps places with the inessive suffix -*ssa*, which codes durational aspect on the verb. Not surprisingly, this reversal creates an ungrammatical utterance.

Slips of the tongue raise an interesting issue pertaining to error localization. Compare the two plural errors in (51) and (52).

(51) G. ein Song, den Sie sicherlich kennen als Tanznummer**n**–
a song which you certainly know as dance.numbers–
Tanznummer auf Parties und auf Fete**n**.
dance number at parties and at parties
'(This is) a song which you know as dance music played at parties.'

(52) G. Klaus Schlappner, der V**ä**ter– Vater der Erfolg**e** der
(proper noun) the fathers father of.the successes of.the
Waldhöfer.
(proper noun)
'Klaus Schlappner, the man to whom the Waldhof team owe their success'

In (51), the plural suffix /n/ of *Feten* 'parties' appears on the head of the compound *Tanznummer* 'dance music'. Because both constituents take the same plural allomorph, the allomorph /n/ may be argued to be involved in the error. However, such an analysis is not available for the plural error in (52). The two nouns *Vater* 'father' and *Erfolg* 'success' select quite different allomorphs. The noun *Vater* is pluralized by umlaut alone while the noun *Erfolg* is pluralized by suffixing a schwa. If schwa had been tacked onto *Vater*, the nonce word *Vater-e* would have been outputted. What happened instead is that the abstract plural morpheme was anticipated. So *Vater* was pluralized by means of umlaut and the correct form *Väter* saw the light of day.

A similar phenomenon can be observed in verbs. Contrast (53) to (54).

(53) G. ... ins 3 zu 2 ummünd**e**ten. Und daraus machte**te**–
to 3 to 2 changed. and from.that –
machte dann Dieter Zimmer wenigstens noch das 3 zu 3.
made then (proper noun) at.least PARTICLE the 3 to 3.
'... changed the score to 3 – 2. Dieter Zimmer finally turned this score into 3 – 3.'

(54) G. Und wir damit auch anfingen, Jazzelemente zu **mocht**en–
and we with.it also began jazz.elements to –
*mög*en.
like
'And so we began to like jazz elements.'

The two interacting verbs *ummünd-en* 'to change' and *mach-en* 'to make' in (53) form their regular past tenses by adding the suffix *-te*. This suffix could therefore be easily added to the error verb. What makes this slip remarkable is that the suffix is added to the past tense form *mach-te*, thereby creating double past tense marking. However, the main point in the present context is that the same allomorph appears on the two interacting verbs. This is not so in (54), which also involves past tense marking. While the verb *anfang-en* 'to begin' is an ablaut verb, the verb *mög-en* 'to like' is completely irregular and has the suppletive past tense form *mochte* 'liked'. What happened in (54) is that the past tense of *anfang*-en intruded upon the infinitive *mög-en* and thereby distorted it to *mochten*.[10]

Structural linguistics offers a straightforward account of the contrast between (51) and (53) on the one hand and (52) and (54) on the other: the former error pair originates at the allomorphic level whereas the latter originates at the morphemic level. This view nicely accommodates the impression that the former error pair arises at a more concrete and the latter at a more abstract processing level. While this account seems to make good sense, it is not obvious that it is the correct one. It could also be argued that all four slips arise at the same processing level. This would be the more abstract rather than the more concrete one. The morphemic account adopts a different take on the concrete errors and claims that they look as if they occurred at the concrete level but actually do not. The seemingly concrete errors are also compatible with the view that they arise at the morpheme level although no morphophonological changes are needed. It is an open question whether two error loci are required to account for the full spectrum of slips or whether a single error locus suffices.

Little is known about the vulnerability of individual grammatical categories. The null hypothesis would be that they are all equally error-prone, but this is unlikely to be true. One alternative hypothesis is that the error rate increases with increasing lexicalness of a grammatical category. Igoa, García-Albea, and Sánchez-Casas (1999) report that there are more number than gender reversals

---

10 Note as an aside that German infinitives are not inflected for past tense.

in their Spanish corpus of tongue slips.[11] Unfortunately, they do not report whether the same asymmetry emerges in other error categories. As no frequency information is provided on the occurrence of gender and number suffixes in general language usage, this result is at best suggestive.

2.3.2 Non-contextual slips

Inflectional errors tend to be asymmetrical. There are usually more substitutions from A to B than from B to A. In some domains, omissions outnumber additions. This has to do with the unequal status of the elements in the paradigm. Stronger inflections replace weaker inflections rather than vice versa. Strength is determined by regularity and by the ratio of formally marked to formally unmarked forms. The higher this ratio, the higher the number of additions; the lower this ratio, the higher the number of omissions.

The processing problems besetting inflected words are quite similar for nouns, verbs and adjectives. The focus of the analysis will be on verbs, which allow for the greatest inflectional range and which therefore provide more insight than other word classes. However, nouns will be briefly touched on.

Probably the best known asymmetry is that between regularly and irregularly inflected verbs. Past tense formation may serve as an illustration. As in English, German verbs may form their past tenses by adding a suffix or by changing the stem vowel. The former strategy is standardly described as a regular, the latter as an irregular process. A regularization error is reported in (55), an irregularization error in (56).

(55) G. Er pfeif**te**– er pf**i**ff.
　　　he –　　　　'he whistled'

(56) G. weil　　sie　so　richtig　　auf stur　　**schielt**.
　　　because she so completely to obstinate –
　　　for: schalte**te**
　　　　　　switched
　　　'because she was being utterly obstinate'

---

[11] This is consistent with Burani's (1992) experimental study of Italian, in which gender was found to constrain errors more strongly than number. Gender is more closely associated with its noun than number and hence, gender markers break free less easily in malfunctions than number markers.

In (55), the ablaut verb *pfeif-en* 'to whistle' was inflected as if it was a regular verb. It is notable that the regular past tense form (i.e. the error) does not sound wide of the mark, thus possibly foreshadowing incipient language change. Inversely, the regular verb *schalt-en* 'to switch' underwent an ablaut change from /a/ to /i:/ in (56). Such a vowel change is certainly not unmotivated in the morphology of German. Several verbs including *halten* 'to hold' and *schlafen* 'to sleep' have an /i:/ in their past tense forms. It may be assumed that the irregularity of these verbs exerts pressure on the regularity of the target verb. A malfunction occurs when the competitor verbs are momentarily more highly activated than the target verb. The larger number of regularization slips relative to irregularization slips ensues from the higher type frequency of regular than irregular verbs.[12]

In the creation of past tense forms, regular morphology competes with irregular morphology. If this competition leads to an error, the resultant error type is necessarily a substitution. However, this is not the only possible error type. If past tenses are derived from base forms, it is to be expected that the process of past tense formation may occasionally fail to occur. This happened in (57). Because this error type is missing from both Meringer's (1908) and my data set, an example from English was chosen. Of course, omission errors are not confined to verbal morphology. As shown in (58), plural formation on German nouns is subject to the same error process (called no-marking by Stemberger and MacWhinney 1986).

(57) E. Boy, that dr**aw** him out – dr**ew** him out (from Stemberger and MacWhinney 1986: 20)

(58) G. Sie meinen, dass die Muse**um**– Muse**en** die Werbung
you believe that the.PL museum museums the advertising
entdeckt haben.
discovered have
'So you believe that the museums have discovered advertising for themselves.'

The context of both slips leaves no doubt that an overtly inflected form was intended. The form *draw* in (57) is ungrammatical without the third person singular marker. The definite article *die* in (58) is unambiguously plural and hence

---

[12] On the basis of English experimental data, Stemberger & Middleton (2003) argue that phonological asymmetries contribute to shaping morphological error patterns.

incompatible with the following singular noun *Museum* 'museum'. In my corpus, all no-marking slips involving plural occurred on nouns with highly irregular plural formation. In German, there are a few nouns which form the plural by a stem-final change from [-um] to [-en], as in (58). This strongly suggests an interaction between irregularity and error-proneness. The higher the irregularity of a particular form, the higher the risk of faulty production.

The opposite of an omission is an addition error, i.e. the addition of material to a position where it is inappropriate. Such errors are found in English and German verbs, as illustrated in (59) and (60), respectively.

(59) E. They behave**s** in a certain way. *for:* behave. (from Stemberger 1985c: 251)

(60) G. Weißt du, warum ich das gut fant**e**? *for:* gut fand?
     know you why I that good – good found
     'Do you know why I liked it?'

Example (59) shows the addition of the morpheme /z/, which functions as the third person singular marker on present tense verbs. Addition errors presuppose a paradigm structure where some cells are filled (i.e. explicit marking) and others are empty (no marking). This is the case in present tense verb inflection in English where the third person singular is marked while the other persons are not. The German error shows the addition of the first person singular suffix /-ə/ to the past tense form of the ablaut verb *finden* 'to find'. Even though the subject *ich* 'I' indeed requires a first person singular verb form, past tenses of ablaut verbs do not mark the first person singular. There is thus a gap in the paradigm of past tense verbs (though not in present tense verbs), which may be erroneously filled, as in (60).[13]

Ablaut verb forms may not only be replaced with suffixed verb forms, as in (55), one ablaut pattern may also be supplanted by another. This possibility typically arises from the fact that a given verb may have more than one ablaut

---

13 A sideways glance at the phonological level is appropriate here. The erroneous addition of the vocalic person suffix shifted the stop in the verb form from word-final (*fand*) to word-medial position. This shift is of some theoretical interest in the phonology of German. If, as is standardly assumed, the stop is underlyingly voiced and undergoes devoicing in word- or syllable-final sites, it would be expected to be pronounced voiced (i.e. *fande*). However, it was pronounced voiceless (i.e. *fante*) in (60) (see error (47) above, which shows a similar effect). That is, it preserved its voiceless quality from the time before the error happened. This casts doubt on the claim that it was ever underlyingly voiced.

vowel in its paradigm, as in English *to write, wrote, written*. However, this is not a necessary condition. Refer to (61) and (62).

(61) G. als   es um   Formsachen g*a*ng. for: g*i*ng
     when it about formalities   –   went
     'when formalities were at issue'

(62) G. als   die uns einl*ied*– einl*u*d.
     when she us   –   invited
     'when she invited us'

The verb *geh-en* 'to go' has an /ɪ/ in the past tense and an /a/ in the past participle form. The substitution of /ɪ/ by /a/ in (61) probably reflects the intrusion from this alternative ablaut vowel. Remarkably, there is no form with /i:/ in the paradigm of the ablaut verb *einlad-en* 'to invite' which could account for the vowel change from /u:/ to /i:/ in (62). It is therefore likely that this slip was caused by other verbs. In fact, such an account was proposed for error (56) above. Other verbs such as *bleib-en* 'to stay' and *lauf-en* 'to run' make /i:/ a highly available past tense vowel, which may occasionally interfere with the target vowel of an ablaut verb which does not have /i:/ in its past tense form.[14]

The next type of verb error reveals a further asymmetry. If, as is generally held, inflected verbs are formed on the basis of infinitival stems, there is a certain dependence of ablaut vowels on base vowels in ablaut verbs. From this dependence we may derive the prediction that the vowel of the infinitive will replace the vowel of the finite form more frequently than vice versa. This prediction is borne out by the error data. While the vowel of the infinitive is largely immune to malfunction, inflected forms often contain the vowel of the infinitive, as can be seen in (63) and (64).

(63) G. Ähnliches   g*e*lt– g*i*lt   hier.
     something.similar –   applies here
     'Something similar applies here.'

---

[14] There is one minor complication to be noted. The prefix part of the circumfix is subject to an independent error bias which facilitates the loss of word-initial unstressed prefixes. As the prefix part of the circumfix is formally identical to a genuine prefix, the former behaves like the latter. However, this does not undermine the empirical claim that the components of circumfixes act in unison because both may be argued to have been generated together before the deletion error on the prefix took place.

(64) G. Die spring– sprang auf den Teppich.
    she –   jumped on the carpet
    'She jumped onto the carpet.'

The infinitive *gelt-en* 'to apply' requires a change from /e/ to /ɪ/ in the third person singular present tense form *gilt* '(it) applies'. This change fails to materialize in (63). Similarly, the verb *spring-en* 'to jump' requires a change from /ɪ/ to /a/ in all past tense forms. The erroneous form *spring* in (64) also preserved the vowel of the infinitive.

To make the case for this asymmetry convincing, it has to be shown that the direction of influence from inflected forms to infinitives is appreciably weaker than from infinitives to inflected forms. In fact, this is so. There is only a single such case in my database, which is reproduced below.

(65) G. Das kann man noch nicht weissen– wissen.
    that can one yet not   –   know
    'We cannot know beforehand.'

The ablaut verb *wiss-en* 'to know' has the diphthong /aɪ/ in its present tense singular forms. This diphthong blotted out the monophthong /ɪ/ of the infinitival stem. Coupled with the relative frequency of errors such as (63) and (64), the extreme uncommonness of slips like (65) for example lends strong support to the claim that inflected verb forms are not directly retrieved from the mental lexicon but generated with the aid of the infinitive.

Ablaut verb forms undergo two kinds of change. A verb may not only undergo a vowel change but also receive a suffix which marks person and number (or a circumfix in past participles). The necessity of two changes allows us to study the relationship between these changes. Are these implemented independently of each other or are these part of the same underlying process? In the latter case, we would expect malfunctions to implicate both parts simultaneously. In the former case, the malfunction may affect one part but leave the other intact. If the two processing operations are independent of each other, the possibility of an asymmetry arises. One part may be more error-prone than the other. Such an asymmetry is illustrated in (66) and (67). No. (66) involves present tense, (67) past participle formation.

(66) G. Der leest– liest da.
    he   – reads there
    'He is reading over there.'

(67) G. wenn ich was   getrinken habe. for: getrunken habe.
       when I something –   have   drunk   have
       'when I have had a drink'

Third person singular verb forms are marked by the suffix /-t/. In order to generate the intended form *liest* '(he) reads' in (66), the infinitival stem *les* 'read' has to undergo ablauting and suffixing. What we actually observe is the selection of the correct suffix but the misselection of the vowel. A similar pattern can be seen in (67). The past participle circumfix *ge_en* was correctly produced while the production of the correct ablaut vowel /u/ failed.

These two slips are entirely typical. Whenever two operations have to be carried out and one of them fails, the one involving affixes succeeds whereas the one involving ablaut does not. This is not to say that affixing is immune to error. It may of course be misapplied, but when this happens, it occurs independently of ablaut processing. We may therefore conclude that the different changes involved in the creation of finite forms are independently effected (see also MacKay 1976) and thoroughly asymmetrical. The correct production of the ablaut vowel entails the correct production of the affix. However, the correct production of the affix does not predict the correct production of the ablaut vowel.

How can this asymmetry be accounted for? The answer is not entirely clear. Errors are known to result from competition. The general explanation would accordingly be that ablaut vowels face more serious competition than affixes do. This is certainly true of English, where affixes compete with "nothing" (no marking, as in present tense verb inflection) and hence "have nothing to fear". In German, by contrast, most regular verb forms require inflectional marking. Thus, inflectional suffixes have a large number of competitors, which would lead us to expect strong competition. There are two possible solutions to this problem. Contra Bybee and Newman (1995), ablaut may be *inherently* more difficult to process than affixing. As their name suggests, ablaut vowels have a strong phonological component which appears to be weaker in affixes. If phonological units are more error-prone than morphological units, we would have an explanation for the differential behavior of ablaut and affixes. Alternatively, affixes may be hypothesized to have competitors which are largely innocuous. It is conceivable that syntax constrains the replacement of, let us say, one person affix by another and thereby renders affix errors unlikely. As no such constraints apply to ablaut, ablaut is more vulnerable than affixing.

The preceding analysis, which uncovered a certain independence between affixing and vowel alternation, raises the more general issue of whether any two modifications of a base form are carried out independently of each other.

Let us go back to (67). Circumfixes provide an intriguing test case to which the affix-ablaut asymmetry may be compared. By definition, circumfixes consist of two parts of which one precedes and the other follows the stem. If the two components are processed independently of each other, we would expect to find slips of the tongue in which one component is correctly produced whereas the production of the other goes wrong; if, by contrast, there is no processing independence between the two components, such errors would be impossible. In actual fact, neither my own nor Meringer's German corpus includes a single pertinent item. The non-attestation of this error type strongly suggests that the two operations involved in circumfixing are tightly integrated into a single processing routine and hence do not run independently.

Why do we observe symmetrical processing of the two parts of circumfixes but asymmetrical processing between affixes and ablaut vowels? The answer to this question is complementary to the account previously proffered of the asymmetry between affixing and ablaut. Attaching a circumfix is a symmetrical procedure which involves the addition of a prefix and that of a suffix. Both the prefix and the suffix compete with nothing, so the two processing operations can be performed with equal accuracy. These near-identical processing constraints on the prefix part and the suffix part are responsible for the non-independent generation of the prefix and the suffix and hence the non-occurrence of tongue slips in which only one of these units is uttered. Note that this account does not categorically rule out such errors. It merely claims that these slips have an extremely low probability of materializing.

The above analysis of circumfixing has shown that the absence of certain slips can be as theoretically illuminating as their actual occurrence. As we turn to phonologically conditioned allomorphy, we are struck by the extreme uncommonness of allomorphic errors. Apparently, people hardly ever err on the selection of the appropriate allomorph. There are no such errors in my German corpus, but Stemberger (1998: 436), while noting the unusualness of this error type, reports the following case.

(68) E. Queen Elizabeth'**es** – Queen Elizabeth'**s** mother

Although the dental fricative /θ/ requires a non-syllabic allomorph, the syllabic possession marker /ɪz/ was selected. Phonotactic constraints may be partly responsible for the rarity of such cases, but only partly so because we do not observe the misselection of the voiceless allomorph /-s/ in the third person singular form of verbs ending in sonorants even though such clusters would be phonotactically legal (as in *else* and *fence*).

The rarity of allomorphy errors stands in marked contrast to the relative commonness of (ir)regularization errors in (55) and (56) above. Of course, regularizations are also allomorphic errors in that the irregular past tense allomorph is replaced with the regular one. The difference between the two types of allomorphy is that the possessive and the third person singular inflection in English are phonologically conditioned whereas the decision between regular and irregular past tense formation in German and English is lexically conditioned. We thus come across a striking processing disparity between phonologically and lexically motivated allomorphy. The former is largely immune while the latter is prone to error.

A possible explanation of the extraordinary accuracy with which phonologically determined allomorphy is processed is its high degree of automaticity. Tongue slips involving phonemes which serve as input to allomorphic processes are a powerful demonstration of this claim. Consider (69).

(69) E. The infant tuck**s** – touch**es** the nipple (from Stemberger 1985b: 176)

Example (69) exemplifies the non-contextual substitution of morpheme-final /tʃ/ by /k/. What makes this slip remarkable is that the target and the error phoneme require different third person singular allomorphs. As can be seen, the allomorph which is appropriate to the error context is chosen. Given that such an accommodation is the rule, it allows one to argue that phonologically conditioned allomorph selection is a highly automatized process and as such largely invulnerable to malfunction. In contrast, lexically conditioned allomorphy is less automatized. By definition, it involves a decision which is particular to each verb and where phonology is of little help. Highly similar phonological structures may support regular or irregular verbs, as in English *to mend* versus *to send*. This similarity may be argued to increase competition between the two verb classes. Thus, the selection of lexically determined allomorphs involves a certain processing effort and is therefore more error-prone than phonologically determined allomorphy.

The preceding analysis was simplified by the fact that morphological processes tend to leave the stem unruffled (putting umlaut to the side). However, there are also more complex cases where the selection of stems and affixes is interdependent. Such interaction is rife in Finnish. Two pertinent cases, taken from Hokkanen (2001: 103), are shown in (70) and (71).

(70) F. **tämä**-llä.   for:**tä**-llä
      this-ADE   this-ADE
      'with this'

(71) F. **tarkempi**-n. for: **tarkemmi**-n
accurate.COMPARATIVE-ADV accurate.COMPARATIVE-ADV
'with greater accuracy'

When the demonstrative pronoun *tämä* 'this' in (70) is uninflected, it is disyllabic. However, when combined with suffixes such as inessive *-llä*, the second syllable of *tämä* disappears. This did not happen in (70). Case (71) is a stem selection error. Finnish stems may distinguish between a strong and a weak form. In the case at hand, *tarkempi* (from *tarka* 'accurate' and *empi* 'more') is the strong form and *tarkemmi* the weak form. The adverbializing suffix /-n/ requires the weak form. What went wrong in (71) is that the strong form was selected instead of the weak form.

3 On the interaction of derivational and inflectional morphemes

It has repeatedly been claimed that speech errors respect linguistic categories. For instance, consonants do not interact with vowels in phonology and prefixes do not interact with suffixes in morphology (e.g. Wells-Jensen 2007, but see Meijer 1997). If derivation and inflection constitute strictly separated processing components, the interaction of derivational and inflectional morphemes is categorically ruled out. Of course, a non-categorical framework makes the opposite prediction, provided certain structural requirements are met. In particular, both types of morphemes should be admitted to the same morphological position and be allowed to occur in the same morphological context. German fulfils these requirements perfectly and thus offers an ideal opportunity to study the relationship between inflection and derivation.

As in the previous section, it is fitting to distinguish between contextual and non-contextual slips. As a matter of fact, non-contextual slips respect the boundary between inflection and derivation. However, contextual slips crossing this boundary do occur in my corpus. The following two errors are paired in that the same prefixes with opposite directionality are implicated.

(72) G. Hätt' ich mich darauf **ge**lassen– **ver**lassen, was die anderen
had I myself on.it let relied what the others
gesagt haben.
said have
'If I had relied on what the others told me'

(73) G. Das **ver**schiebt sich ja; guck mal, wie die
that displaces itself PARTICLE; look PARTICLE how it
verdrückt– **ge**drückt ist.
– compressed is
'It gets displaced, you see; look how compressed it is.'

The two tongue slips involve the same prefixes *ge-* and *ver-*. The first intrudes upon the second in (72) and the second upon the first in (73). Hence, the interaction is both ways. The prefix *ge-* is the initial part of the past participle circumfix (see Section 2.3.2) and as such indubitably of an inflectional nature. By contrast, the prefix *ver-* is part of the complex verb *(sich) ver-lass-en* 'to rely' in (72) and *(sich) ver-schieb-en* 'to displace' in (73) and as such unquestionably of a derivational nature. As the errors demonstrate, the differing status of these prefixes does not preclude their interaction.

Fromkin's English corpus contains the following suffix exchange.

(74) E. cold**y** and wind**er**. for: cold**er** and wind**y**

The comparative marker *-er* is clearly inflectional while the adjectival suffix *-y* is clearly derivational. Again, this difference does not stop the two suffixes from interacting. Such slips can only occur if inflectional and derivational morphemes represent partially overlapping processing vocabularies. This hypothesis finds a natural place in a conceptual frame which locates inflection and derivation along a continuum.

By the same logic, there would be no reason to categorically rule out the interaction of stems and affixes. One such error is found in my data. It is given in (75).

(75) G. Ein**sal**– Ein*s*icht in das Schick**sal**.
– insight into the fate
'the acceptance of fate'

Example (75) involves the prefix-stem word *Ein-sicht* 'insight' and the stem-suffix word *Schick-sal* 'fate'. The (unproductive) suffix *-sal* in *Schick-sal* supplants the stem *Sicht* 'sight' in *Ein-sicht*, yielding the nonsensical word *Ein-sal*, which supposedly consists of a prefix and a suffix (and nothing but). Since this is a solitary error, it would be unwise to base a far-reaching argument on it. What it does suggest, however tentatively, is that also the distinction between lexical and derivational morphemes is a fuzzy one. This would be in keeping with Bybee's (1985) proposal of a lexicon-grammar continuum.

On the other hand, the fact that non-contextual slips do not allow "crosstalk" between lexical, derivational and inflectional morphemes suggests that a lexicon-grammar continuum may be too simplistic a model of the mental lexicon. There is more structure than is captured by a continuum. The critical question is how to reconcile the notion of continuum with the notion of paradigm. In any event, paradigms have a clear psycholinguistic analogue in that they may be held responsible for the absence of non-contextual cross-talk errors.

4 Putting some of the pieces together

After the separate analysis of the three major morphological components, it is appropriate to take a bird's-eye perspective and put together some of the parts of the puzzle. Our focus will be on the rate of contextual and non-contextual slips in the three morphological components. Refer to Table 1, which excludes deletions because contextual and non-contextual deletions do not compare easily.

Table 1: Rate of contextual and non-contextual slips (including blends) as a function of morphological component.

morphological process	error type	contextual	non-contextual	(blend)	total
compounding		72 (51.8%)	67 (48.2%)	(1)	139
derivation		268 (59.2%)	185 (40.8%)	(143)	453
inflection		74 (45.1%)	90 (54.9%)	(0)	164
total		414 (54.8%)	342 (45.2%)	(144)	756

The first observation to make about Table 1 is that blend errors distribute extremely unevenly across the different morphological structures. Whereas they almost never occur in compound and inflected words, they abound in derived words. In the light of this unevenness, it was decided to neglect them in the following discussion. Note, however, that the conclusions would not be different if blends had been included. The totals and the percentages in Table 1 also ignore this error category.

As can be seen, contextual slips are in the majority, although non-contextual slips are fairly well represented. This share is much higher than what is observed at the phonological level where non-contextual slips form a small minority (see Section 1). While the ratio of contextual to non-contextual slips does not vary excessively from one morphological component to another, the rate of non-contextual errors is significantly higher in inflection than in derivation ($\chi^2(1) = 9.7$, $p < 0.01$). This is as was predicted in the beginning section. There is thus a decline in the incidence of non-contextual slips as we go from inflectional to derivational morphology to phonology.

The two differences, viz. that between morphology and phonology as well as that between inflection and derivation, can probably be accounted for in a similar fashion. Non-contextual inflectional slips are boosted by two factors – the conflict between paradigmatic options such as regular and irregular past tense formation and the conflict between the base and inflected words such as the infinitive and the present tense forms. Both conflicts create competition, which is especially strong when the base has to be changed to form an inflected word (by ablaut, for example). As argued above, adding an affix creates less competition. It is claimed here that inflection makes heavier use of highly competitive morphological processes than derivation. As a result, non-contextual inflectional slips outnumber non-contextual derivational slips.

There is probably an additional factor which amplifies the disparity between non-contextual inflectional and derivational slips. As widely agreed upon, derived words display a higher degree of lexicalization than inflected words do. This difference implies that there is less competition between the base and a derived form than between the base and an inflected form because a morphologically complex word is more autonomous vis-à-vis its base in derivation than in inflection.

The behavior of derived and inflected words may also be approached from the perspective of productivity. A link may be postulated between non-contextuality and productivity. The higher the productivity of a component, the higher the rate of non-contextual slips. It is generally agreed that inflection is more productive than derivation. It is also uncontroversial that segmental phonology is a largely unproductive system. This hierarchy is reflected in the diminishing rate of non-contextual slips from inflectional to derivational morphology to phonology.

Why does productivity boost non-contextuality? Productivity may be argued to accord a given unit or process an elevated resting level of activation, thereby granting it a certain autonomy and increasing its availability. This heightened availability allows the inadvertent intrusion of such a unit at relatively low noise levels, hence its relatively frequent involvement in slips of the tongue.

As was pointed out in Section 1, contextual errors are an index of a sequencing problem whereas non-contextual errors highlight a selection problem. The larger number of non-contextual slips in morphology than in phonology suggests that selection is only a minor issue in phonology but more of an issue in morphology. How can this difference be accounted for? I maintain that paradigms vary in their internal structure, with more paradigmatic pressure in morphological than in phonological paradigms. For instance, there is more competition between regular and irregular verbs than between the phonemes /p/ and /b/. This explanation can be straightforwardly extended to the difference between inflection and derivation. Because derivational paradigms are uncommon, selection errors are also uncommon in derived words. And because paradigms are typically found in inflectional morphology, selection errors are rather more frequent in inflected words.

It is not clear whether sequencing presents the same challenge in morphology and phonology. It may be that the lower number of units to be serialized per time unit in morphology than in phonology makes morphological ordering a less difficult task than phonological ordering.

To conclude, there is a stronger link between morphological processes and non-contextual slips than between morphological processes and contextual slips. Errors of productive morphology are generally of the non-contextual type. The fact that they do not require contextual support attests to the high availability of morphological processes. In contrast, contextual slips do not depend that strongly on morphological processes. All that they require is morphological structure.

5 Conclusion

The predominance of phonologically oriented analyses of speech errors has led to a certain neglect of morphological slips of the tongue. Notwithstanding Stemberger's highly significant speech error work on English, the impoverished morphology of English renders it a less than ideal language to study. In fact, hardly any in-depth studies of morphological slips from languages other than English have been performed. The present contribution was written with the aim of developing a classification scheme which provides an insightful organization of the multitude of major error types. If this attempt is accepted, it may serve as a point of departure for more detailed analyses.

If little is known about morphological processing in languages other than English (and German), even less is known about cross-linguistic differences between morphological slips of the tongue. It is highly likely that the rates of error types are strongly language-specific. As long as this is a simple spin-off of different language structures and different language use, this may not come as much of a surprise. However, when the cross-linguistic error patterns are not a trivial spin-off of language-specific opportunities, they gain theoretical significance.

A cross-linguistic comparison might discover that some error types are present in one language but (virtually) absent from another (see the discussion of addition and deletion errors in verbs in Section 2.3.2). For obvious reasons, attention has hitherto been focused on attested error types. However, it is likely that the absence of a given error type is also theoretically significant. Only a cross-linguistic investigation can sharpen our awareness of what to expect and thereby direct our attention to error types which do not occur even though they might.

References

Abd-El-Jawad, Hassan & Issam Abu-Salim. 1987. Slips of the tongue in Arabic and their theoretical implications. *Language Sciences* 9. 145–171.

Badecker, William. 2001. Lexical composition and the production of compounds: Evidence from errors in naming. *Language and Cognitive Processes* 16. 337–366.

Berg, Thomas. 1987. The case against accommodation: Evidence from German speech error data. *Journal of Memory and Language* 26. 277–300.

Berg, Thomas. 1988. *Die Abbildung des Sprachproduktionsprozesses in einem Aktivationsflussmodell: Untersuchungen an deutschen und englischen Versprechern.* Tübingen: Niemeyer.

Berg, Thomas. 2003. Die Analyse von Versprechern. In: Theo Herrmann & Joachim Grabowski (eds.), *Enzyklopädie der Psychologie: Sprachproduktion*, 247–264. Göttingen: Hogrefe.

Berg, Thomas. 2012. *Structure in language. A dynamic perspective.* New York: Routledge.

Berg, Thomas. 2015. Locating affixes on the lexicon-grammar continuum. *Cognitive Linguistic Studies* 2. 150–180.

Berg, Thomas. 2016. The multiplanar nature of frequency. *Glottotheory* 7, 1–19.

Berg, Thomas. 2017. Compounding in German and English: A quantitative translation study. *Languages in Contrast* 17. 43–68.

Bertram, Raymond, Robert Schreuder & R. Harald Baayen. 2000. The balance between storage and computation in morphological processing: The role of word formation type, affixal homonymy, and productivity. *Journal of Experimental Psychology: Learning, Memory, and Cognition* 26. 489–511.

Bond, Zinny S. 1999. Morphological errors in casual conversation. *Brain and Language* 68. 144–150.

Burani, Cristina. 1992. Patterns of inflectional errors with reference to the Italian adjectival system. *Rivista di Linguistica* 4. 255–272.
Bybee, Joan L. 1985. *Morphology. A study of the relation between meaning and form*. Amsterdam: John Benjamins.
Bybee, Joan L. & Jean E. Newman. 1995. Are stem changes as natural as affixes? *Linguistics* 33. 633–654.
del Viso, Susana, José M. Igoa & José E. García-Albea. 1987. Corpus of spontaneous slips of the tongue in Spanish. Oviedo: Universidad de Oviedo.
Dell, Gary S. 1990. Effects of frequency and vocabulary type on phonological speech errors. *Language and Cognitive Processes* 5, 313–349.
Dressler, Wolfgang U. 1989. Prototypical differences between inflection and derivation. *Zeitschrift für Phonetik, Sprachwissenschaft und Kommunikationsforschung* 42. 3–10.
Ellis, Andrew W. 1979. Slips of the pen. *Visible Language* 13. 265–282.
Ferreira, Victor S. & Karin R. Humphreys. 2001. Syntactic influences on lexical and morphological processing in language production. *Journal of Memory and Language* 44. 52–80.
Foldvik, Arne Kjell. 1979. Norwegian speech error data – A source of evidence for linguistic performance models. *Nordic Journal of Linguistics* 2. 113–122.
Fromkin, Victoria A. 1973. *Speech errors as linguistic evidence*. The Hague: Mouton.
Garrett, Merrill F. 1975. The analysis of sentence production. In Gordon H. Bower (ed.), *The psychology of learning and motivation. Vol. 9*, 133–177. New York: Academic Press.
Garrett, Merrill F. 1980. Levels of processing in sentence production. In Brian Butterworth (ed.), *Language production. Vol. 1*, 177–220. London: Academic Press.
González Torres, Elisa. 2010. The inflection-derivation continuum and the Old English suffixes *-a, -e, -o, -u*. *Atlantis. Journal of the Spanish Association of Anglo-American Studies* 32. 103–122.
Hamrouni, Nadia. 2010. Structure and processing in Tunesian Arabic: Speech error data. Unpublished Ph.D. thesis, University of Arizona.
Hartsuiker, Robert J., Inés Antón-Méndez, Bjorn Roelstraete & Albert Costa. 2006. Spoonish spanerisms: A lexical bias effect in Spanish. *Journal of Experimental Psychology: Learning, Memory, and Cognition* 32. 949–953.
Hay, Jennifer B. & R. Harald Baayen. 2005. Shifting paradigms: gradient structure in morphology. *Trends in Cognitive Science* 9. 344–348.
Hokkanen, Tapio. 2001. *Slips of the tongue. Errors, repairs, and a model*. Helsinki: Finnish Literature Society.
Igoa, José M., José E. García-Albea & Rosa Sánchez-Casas. 1999. Gender-number dissociations in sentence production in Spanish. *Rivista di Linguistica* 11. 163–196.
Isel, Frédéric, Thomas C. Gunter & Angela D. Friederici. 2003. Prosody-assisted head-driven access to spoken German compounds. *Journal of Experimental Psychology: Learning, Memory, and Cognition* 29. 277–288.
Jacobs, Cassandra L. & Gary S. Dell. 2014. 'hotdog', not 'hot dog': the phonological planning of compound words. *Language, Cognition and Neuroscience* 29. 512–523.
Jaeger, Jeri J. 2005. *Kid's slips*. Mahwah, N.J.: Lawrence Erlbaum.
Juhasz, Barbara J., Matthew S. Starr, Albrecht W. Inhoff & Lars Placke. 2003. The effects of morphology on the processing of compound words: Evidence from naming, lexical decisions and eye fixations. *British Journal of Psychology* 94. 223–244.

Libben, Gary, Christina Gagné & Wolfgang U. Dressler. this volume. The representation and processing of compounds words. In Vito Pirrelli, Ingo Plag & Wolfgang U. Dressler (eds.), *Word Knowledge and Word Usage: a Cross-disciplinary Guide to the Mental Lexicon*, 336–352. De Gruyter.
Liu, Joyce H.C. 2013. The effects of contextual availability and phonetic similarity on speech errors. *Concentric: Studies in Linguistics* 39. 1–21.
MacKay, Donald G. 1976. On the retrieval and lexical structure of verbs. *Journal of Verbal Learning and Verbal Behavior* 15. 169–182.
MacKay, Donald G. 1978. Derivational rules and the internal lexicon. *Journal of Verbal Learning and Verbal Behavior* 17. 61–71.
MacKay, Donald G. 1979. Lexical insertion, inflection, and derivation: Creative processes in word production. *Journal of Psycholinguistic Research* 8. 477–498.
Magno Caldognetto, Emanuela, Livia Tonelli & A. Pinton. 1987. I morphemi radicali nella produzione della parola. *Acta Phoniatrica Latina* 9. 373–380.
Marelli, Marco, Davide Crepaldi & Claudio Luzzatti. 2009. Head position and the mental representation of nominal compounds. *The Mental Lexicon* 4. 430–454.
Meijer, Paul J.A. 1997. What speech errors can tell us about word-form generation: The roles of constraint and opportunity. *Journal of Psycholinguistic Research* 26. 141–158.
Melinger, Alissa. 2003. Morphological structure in the lexical representation of prefixed words: Evidence from speech errors. *Language and Cognitive Processes* 18. 335–362.
Meringer, Rudolf. 1908. *Aus dem Leben der Sprache. Versprechen, Kindersprache, Nachahmungstrieb*. Berlin: Behrs.
Nübling, Damaris & Renata Szczepaniak. 2013. Linking elements in German: Origin, change, functionalization. *Morphology* 23. 67–89.
Pérez, Elvira, Julio Santiago & Alfonso Palma. 2007. Perceptual bias in speech error data collection: Insights from Spanish speech errors. *Journal of Psycholinguistic Research* 36. 207–235.
Pfau, Roland. 2009. *Grammar as processor*. Amsterdam: John Benjamins.
Rainer, Franz. 2010. *Carmens Erwerb der deutschen Wortbildung*. Wien: Österreichische Akademie der Wissenschaften.
Rossi, Mario & Evelyne Peter-Defare. 1998. *Les lapsus*. Paris: Presses Universitaires de France.
Steger, Hugo, Ulrich Engel & Hugo Moser. 1971. *Texte gesprochener deutscher Standardsprache. Band 1*. Munich: Hueber.
Stemberger, Joseph P. 1985a. *The lexicon in a model of language production*. New York: Garland.
Stemberger, Joseph P. 1985b. An interactive activation model of language production. In Andrew W. Ellis (ed.), *Progress in the psychology of language. Vol 1*, 143–186. London: Lawrence Erlbaum.
Stemberger, Joseph P. 1985c. Bound morpheme loss errors in normal and agrammatic speech: One mechanism or two? *Brain and Language* 25. 246–256.
Stemberger, Joseph P. 1989. Speech errors in early child language production. *Journal of Memory and Language* 28. 164–188.
Stemberger, Joseph P. 1998. Morphology in language production with special reference to connectionism. In Andrew Spencer & Arnold M. Zwicky (eds.), *The handbook of morphology*, 428–452. Oxford: Blackwell.
Stemberger, Joseph P. & Brian MacWhinney. 1986. Frequency and the lexical storage of regularly inflected forms. *Memory & Cognition* 14. 17–26.

Stemberger Joseph P. & Christine S. Middleton. 2003. Vowel dominance and morphological processing. *Language and Cognitive Processes* 18. 369–404.

Wan, I.-Ping. 2007. Mandarin speech errors into phonological patterns. *Journal of Chinese Linguistics* 35. 185–224.

Wardlow Lane, Liane & Victor S. Ferreira. 2010. Abstract syntax in sentence production: Evidence from stem-exchange errors. *Journal of Memory and Language* 62. 151–165.

Wells-Jensen, Sheri. 2007. A cross-linguistic speech error investigation of functional complexity. *Journal of Psycholinguistic Research* 36. 107–157.

Mila Vulchanova, David Saldaña and Giosué Baggio
Word structure and word processing in developmental disorders

Abstract: Developmental disorders offer a rare view into properties of language that might go unnoticed in typically developing individuals. Quite often such cases are used to demonstrate dissociations between language and the rest of cognition. Yet, detailed recent research suggests that the picture is more complex and nuanced. For instance, in high-functioning autism, we find a dissociation between vocabulary skills and the acquisition and processing of figurative expressions, suggesting that bigger-size lexical units (such as non-transparent idioms or conventional metaphors) are probably stored and processed differently than word-size items. Other populations, such as children with language impairment, have problems with units of a smaller size, namely morphemes, and how they are used to indicate relations of agreement in grammar. Children suffering from dyslexia experience problems in cracking the orthographic code and how it maps onto the sound structure of oral language. Finally, some children will only experience problems in understanding text and what individual words in a given text mean, but not in decoding itself. This chapter provides an overview of developmental deficits that affect language, with a focus on how lexical items are acquired, stored and processed in atypical populations.

Keywords: word knowledge, word learning, language impairment, Williams syndrome, autism, reading deficits, poor comprehenders

1 Introduction

On the view of the mental lexicon reflected in the current volume, word knowledge is best conceived as an interface between multiple levels of representation. Lexical items are multiple linking rules between phonology (the sound segment),

---

Mila Vulchanova, Giosué Baggio, Norwegian University of Science & Technology (NTNU), Language Acquisition & Language Processing Lab, Department of Language & Literature, Trondheim, Norway
David Saldaña, Universidad de Sevilla, Laboratorio de Diversidad, Cognición y Lenguaje, Individual Differences, Language and Cognition Lab, Departamento de Psicología Evolutiva y de la Educación, Sevilla Spain

Open Access. © 2020 Mila Vulchanova et al., published by De Gruyter. This work is licensed under a Creative Commons Attribution-NonCommercial-NoDerivatives 4.0 International License.
https://doi.org/10.1515/9783110440577-017

grammar information (features that indicate how the word can be used in larger linguistic contexts, e.g. phrases and sentences), and semantics (the meaning associated with the sound segment) (Jackendoff 2002). For languages with an orthographic tradition, the form part of the word also includes the word's orthography (Levelt 1989). When words are acquired in infancy, children form stable associations between sound and meaning, which are necessary for the word to become part of the speaker's lexical inventory. Word learning has been shown to depend on multiple instances of exposure to the word, in varied contexts. Perfetti and Hart (2002) and Perfetti (2007) suggest that multiple encounters with the word ensure the creation of a common core (lexical) representation, which is a nexus of phonological, orthographic and semantic information. Fast and efficient retrieval of a word relies exactly on the quality of all the features which form part of the word representation. Furthermore, recent longitudinal research suggests that individual word mastery (comprehension and production) is characterized by specific spatio-temporal signatures, and does not rely solely on the word's frequency in the infant's environment (Roy et al. 2015).

Word knowledge develops early in infancy and successful comprehension and production of words is an important milestone in early language acquisition. A crucial step along the path of acquiring words is the infant's ability to associate a phonological form with its referent. Word learning depends on a number of mechanisms, such as mutual exclusivity, which is the ability of the child to map a novel label, rather than an already known one, to a new referent. The syntactic context of a new word has also been suggested to contribute to establishing its meaning (a mechanism known as "syntactic bootstrapping"). Other factors of crucial importance in word learning are speech perception and speech processing (Swingley and Aslin 2007). In fact, Swingley and Aslin suggest that speech processing can impose limitations on early word learning. They show that lexical competition (inhibitory interaction among words in speech comprehension) can prevent children from using their full phonological sensitivity in learning new words. However, other research highlights that semantic and syntactic information can attenuate the inhibitory effect of phonological similarity (Dautriche, Swinlgley and Christophe 2015).

An important individual factor in word learning is phonological memory and the ability to store and retrieve information about (new) words. Mani and Plunkett (2010) provided evidence of the relevance of phonological similarity for word access (retrieval) as early as 18 months. In that study infants saw images of objects (*cat*) followed by an image of an object, whose label had the same onset as the previously shown object (*cup*) alongside an unrelated distractor image. Infants displayed significantly stronger preference (proportion of looks) for the phonologically related item (*cup*) when they heard the word, compared to the unrelated object. This and other studies reflect the nature of the infant lexicon and provide evidence of priming from early on in the developing lexicon (Mani and Plunkett 2010).

Two important steps characterize new word learning. The first step is consolidation, which obtains initially from encountering the word to storing it in long term memory. The second, equally important stage is the word's integration in the already existing lexicon, whereby it becomes part of a network of lexical representations. These processes have been documented in both adult (Dumay and Gaskell 2007; Gaskell and Dumay 2003) and child (Henderson et al. 2014) word learning research. In these studies integration was tested based on the strength and time course of phonological competition. Phonological competition is one of the best documented processes which tap lexical knowledge and the nature of the mental lexicon. Adult proficient speakers of a language, upon hearing a word (e.g., *candle*) have been shown to activate phonological neighbors in parallel to the word they are hearing (words with the same onset, e.g., *candy*). Phonological competition is very fast (typically in the first 200 ms.) and is characterized by fast decay (Tanenhaus, Spivey-Knowlton, Eberhard and Sedivy 1995). Lexical competition of this type has been shown to last longer for children, and, unlike adults, children are more likely to yield to phonological competition by selecting a non-target referent (Huang and Snedeker 2011).

Typically, word knowledge is assessed on the basis of vocabulary size (breadth) and vocabulary depth (associations with other words in the lexicon; semantic networks). Both measures reflect a child's lexical skills and competence. It is important to observe that the causal link between vocabulary status and some of the meschanisms that underlie word learning is bi-directional. Thus, while early word learning relies on memory capacity, vocabulary knowledge itself contributes to phonological and short-term memory later in development.

Given this complexity and multiplicity of factors that impact on word learning and processing, as well as the environmental influences on word acquisition, an important question is how words are acquired and processed in developmental deficits. What aspects of word knowledge are compromised and what challenges do impaired individuals experience in understanding and using words? Responding to these questions could also shed light on the nature of word learning, its relation to the acquisition and development of other dimensions of language, and the dichotomy between language and other cognitive processes.

2 Developmental disorders

Developmental disorders are a variety of conditions characterized by impairment of specific aspects of cognitive functioning, including language. Evidence from current research suggests that they are biologically conditioned. However, their etiology remains largely undetermined, and many genes have been implicated in causing disruption of the structures that support language learning and use. The most common and well-studied language-related deficits include language impairment (LI), reading and writing difficulties (dyslexia), and autism spectrum disorder (ASD). Each of these deficits is characterized by a (unique) phenotype representing the cluster of features and impairments at the cognitive level which define the condition. A serious problem with most deficits, however, is the great amount of commonly observed co-morbid overlap of the impairments in the phenotype between conditions. Autism, for example, frequently appears together with language impairment, and language impairment and dyslexia are also frequently co-morbid.

2.1 Language Impairment

Language impairment (LI), currently also labelled developmental language disorder (DLD), is a developmental disorder that selectively compromises language competencies and skills in affected children. Depending on cut-off points, the deficit is estimated to affect the language development of around 7% of children (van der Lely 2005; Norbury et al. 2016). Children with LI cannot keep up with age peers in their language development and manifest problems in core domains of grammar (syntax and morphology), phonology, as well as oral language comprehension and the lexicon (Rice 2007; Leonard 1998). The accepted definitions of language impairment rest on both exclusionary and inclusionary criteria. The main inclusionary criterion is the observed systematic underperformance in core domains of language relative to age expectations. Among exclusionary criteria, the most important ones are the absence of any obvious language-independent cause for the condition, such as hearing loss or intellectual disability (or overall delayed development). Like many other developmental deficits, LI is characterized by heterogeneity, leading to disagreement concerning whether a core deficit can be identified and how to define the phenotype (Bishop 2004; Leonard 1998; Marshall and van der Lely 2007; van der Lely 2003). Attempts have been made to suggest sub-groups including children with similar profiles of language strengths and weaknesses. At the same time, it is possible to assume that these are just variable manifestations of the same language deficit (Bishop 1997; see Marshall and van der Lely 2007 for a discussion). Studies using MRI and brain morphometry seem to support the idea of a common core language problem. They have shown that core areas of perisylvian language networks, such as the pars triangularis (adjacent to classical Broca's area) of the left inferior frontal gyrus, are smaller in children with language impairment compared to age-matched controls, and the normal leftward asymmetry in the same networks (left larger than right) is reversed: these structural abnormalities were predictive of language disability in the atypical sample (Gauger et al. 1997).

The majority of children with LI could be included in a group often labelled Grammatical-LI – G-(S)LI – which is characterized by specific problems in the domain of morphology and grammar (formal aspects of words and word structure), and to a lesser extent in the domain of the lexicon (lexical knowledge and meaning), with vocabulary knowledge considered a relative strength (e.g., Spaulding, Hosmer and Schechtman 2013). Problems that are widely reported in the research literature include omissions of tense forms of regular verbs in obligatory contexts and frequent substitutions of inflected forms with either bare/root forms (e.g. infinitives), where the language allows a bare form to be used (e.g., English) or other inflected default forms, when it does not (e.g., Italian; Penke 2008). Interestingly, a dissociation can be observed between clear problems in the domain of inflectional morphology contra relatively intact use of derivational morphology and spared lexical knowledge. Furthermore, less problems have been reported for irregular verbs in English (van der Lely and Ullman 2001). This may suggest that for such children the deficit manifests itself in problems with word structure, and the way it encodes grammar information, but not with lexical meaning. However, these findings have not been replicated for other languages with irregular verbal paradigms, such as German, Dutch, Italian and Spanish (Kornilov et al. 2012).

Despite the robust findings of primarily verb inflection problems in English-speaking environments, research on LI in other languages suggests that the manifestation of the deficit is subject to variation, much in the same way as the systematic grammar variation across languages. Thus, Spanish-speaking children with LI, when compared to age-matched peers and younger children matched on Mean Length of Utterance (MLU), demonstrate problems specific to Spanish grammar, namely related to the relatively richer paradigm of nouns, such as adjective agreement inflections, as well as limitations in the use of direct object clitics, which are typical of Spanish syntax and are characterized by dedicated placement in the structure of the sentence (Bedore and Leonard 2001). Also the errors made by Spanish children with LI primarily consist of substitutions of the required form by a neighboring form in the same paradigm and one which shares most grammatical features with the target form, except for one (e.g., target tense and number, but wrong person). Similar problems in noun-related morphology and object clitics have been reported for LI in French and Greek (Bedore and Leonard 2001). It has also been shown that the size of the inflectional paradigm affects the rate of substitution errors, and richer paradigms with more forms lead to higher substitution rates (Dromi et al. 1999).

There exist multiple accounts of what is causing the disorder. While some accounts view the deficit as primarily morphosyntactic in nature (Clahsen 1989; Clahsen et al. 1997; Gopnik 1999), other accounts attribute the morphology (inflection) deficit to a phonological problem seen in the inability to represent adequately the inflection which is in a weak phonological position at the end of the word. It will appear then that the problem is not a difficulty in suffixation/inflection as such, but rather in the phonological context of the suffix, which places the acquisition and use of that morpheme at risk (Joanisse and Seidenberg 1998, 2003; McClelland and Patterson 2002). A related account links the observed problems to perception and processing problems, which eventually compromise morphosyntax (Joanisse 2004; Leonard 1998). These accounts seem consistent with studies demonstrating a selective auditory perceptual deficit in children with language impairment for brief, but not for long tones in some (non-linguistic) sound contexts (Wright et al. 1997), and with neuroscience research showing smaller volumes or no leftward asymmetry in the planum temporal, adjacent to or comprising the primary auditory cortex, in language-impaired children (Gauger et al. 1997). Other approaches explain the grammar deficit as immaturity of the feature system (e.g, the marking of finiteness) and view the condition as a disruption in the language growth of children with LI (Rice 2007; Rice et al. 1995). Marshall and van der Lely (2007) offer an alternative account motivated by the complexity of language structure. In their computational grammatical complexity (CGC) hypothesis, they attribute the specific deficits found in children with LI to a deficit in representing language complexity at the three levels most relevant for grammar: phonology, morphology, and syntax. While processing accounts face the problem that perceptual deficits are not commonly found in LI children (Bishop et al. 1999; van der Lely et al. 2004), a valid argument in support of such an approach is the robust evidence of a phonological memory and a phonological processing deficit in LI children, also reflected in poor performance on non-word repetition (Bishop et al. 1996; Coady and Evans 2008; Conti-Ramsden 2003; Conti-Ramsden et al. 2001; Conti-Ramsden and Hesketh 2003; Dollaghan and Campbell 1998; Ellis Weismer et al. 2000; Gray 2003).

What is apparent in most approaches, however, is the awareness that morphology (word structure) and syntax are intimately linked to, and interface richly with, phonology, the latter mediating language form at the level of sound. Languages express form and meaning distinctions by means of phonology, and inflection paradigms reflect similarity in phonological form. Thus, word roots which pattern together tend to inflect similarly by belonging to the same inflection class (paradigm). Sensitivity to this similarity rests on the intersection between phonology and morphology. Supportive evidence of the importance of the phonology/morphology interface comes from a study by Marshall and van der Lely (2007), where they found that consonantal clusters that arise by adding an inflectional suffix/ending were the most likely environment to prevent the production of regular past tenses in English for LI children in a past-tense elicitation task. Furthermore, morphological distinctions encode features of importance for sentence structure (syntax), such as tense, person and number. Thus, compromised sensitivity to any of these interfaces or representations may lead to the core deficits observed in grammar in children with LI.

An interesting finding concerning how words are retrieved in this population is an observed difference between LI children who show a consistent frequency effect for both regular and irregular verbs alike, and control typically developing children who only show this effect for irregular verbs, as would be expected (van der Lely and Ullman 2001). This suggests that in LI, regularly inflected items are stored in the mental lexicon very much like irregular forms. Thus, it may be the case that children with language impairment attempt to retrieve regular forms from the lexicon rather than compute them online. The absence of such a dissociation between regular and irregular morphology, which has been shown in typical populations, has interesting consequences for Pinker's (1998) dual processing hypothesis. The main assumption in this approach is that the default mechanism first attempts to retrieve the (irregular) form from the lexicon, only then to proceed to apply the grammar rule, if no such form can be retrieved. It is then puzzling why language impaired children are not successful in producing the correct regular form, if they tend to store it along with irregular forms.

It deserves notice that some studies also report semantic problems in LI children. A broad range of semantic difficulties have been reported, ranging from problems with the acquisition of novel words, to the storage and organization of already acquired words, to lexical access/retrieval (Brackenbury and Pye 2005). Regrettably, most studies are confined to assessing receptive and expressive vocabulary size, but not so much accompanying semantic difficulties. A study by Gray (2004) documents that existing lexical knowledge, as measured by the Peabody Vocabulary Test (PPVT-III), and fast-mapping ability can identify poor word-learners among a group of LI children, and that problems were specifically related to word production in that group. A study based on a large sample (N=519) evaluated longitudinal vocabulary growth in affected and non-affected children (Rice and Hoffman 2015). Children with LI showed lower levels of vocabulary at all assessment time points, and the gap between them and their age peers never closed with time. This study, however, documents that individual variation in both groups was explained by non-verbal IQ and maternal education level. In addition, in both groups, vocabulary acquisition slowed down around age 12 years, suggesting that children with LI follow an otherwise similar developmental trajectory, despite the receptive vocabulary deficit. Research using ERPs has found that children with language impairment show reduced N400 amplitudes (Sabisch et al. 2006), consistent with weaker lexical representations in this population (for a review, see Friederici 2006). There is also recent evidence that the very process of word acquisition may be compromised. Collisson et al. (2015) found that pre-school children with language impairment were on average significantly worse than typical children on visual paired-associate learning and that the language-impaired children did not demonstrate the expected shape bias in object label learning. Furthermore, individual variation in language outcomes was significantly predicted by visual paired-associate learning skills, but not by other non-verbal or verbal measures, in both the language-impaired children and their age-matched controls.

Lexical processing in language impairment is a relatively new topic in research on this population. Dollaghan (1998) has shown that children with LI need more acoustic information to identify spoken words compared to age-matched peers. In an ERP study Kornilov et al. (2015) document reduced negativity amplitudes (N400) in a group of LI children for phonological competitor words of visually presented targets, as well as for words that were not semantically or phonologically related to the pictured object. There was also a depressed phonological mapping negativity in an early time window, indicative of a deficit in phonological processing or early lexical access. The authors interpret this evidence as support for a multi-dimensional view of the deficit, and explain the pattern of performance in light of a neuroplasticity account of neurodevelopmental disorders, whose deviant response patterns can be explained as the result of impaired language development, which, in turn, alters the brain circuits that support language growth and use (Bishop 2013).

Indeed, children with LI have been shown to experience problems in the very process of word learning. They seem to have difficulties in word consolidation (Kan and Windsor 2010). Furthermore, their vocabularies appear to be characterized by greater instability and increased lexical uncertainty, most likely as a result of increased competition effects and fast lexical decay of the target word (McMurray, Samuelson, Lee and Tomblin 2010; McMurray, Munson and Tomblin 2014). For a recent comprehensive review of lexical learning and processing in developmental language impairment, see Nation (2014).

From the concise review above it becomes evident that children with LI manifest problems in both the acquisition of word structure and detecting and using word structure in grammar (e.g., applying inflectional rules). In accounting for the insight into language structure and its biological basis offered by grammatical impairment, van der Lely and Pinker (2014) suggest that a distinction can be made between "extended" and "basic" morphology/phonology/syntax. On this distinction, children with LI demonstrate relatively spared abilities in the basic domains, e.g., perception of individual sounds, storage of morphemes (roots) and lexical items, but display compromised skills in the "extended" domains, which require the online computation of complex forms. However, emerging evidence suggests also deficits in the storage and organization of lexical knowledge (e.g., semantic skills), and in the access and retrieval of words (Nation, 2014). Such problems, are also more prevalent in a group labelled "poor comprehenders", which will be addressed below.

2.2 Williams Syndrome

Williams Syndrome (WS) is a rare developmental disorder characterized by relatively spared language abilities and compromised spatial cognition and motor skills (Bartke and Siegmüller 2004; Lukács 2005). Traditionally, WS has been seen as diametrically opposed to language impairment when comparing their contrasting cognitive and language profiles. Thus, together LI and WS are often used to argue for a double dissociation between language and the rest of cognition. Detailed studies, however, suggest that aspects of language may also be affected in WS. Of interest for the current chapter is the attested strength in domains of vocabulary knowledge where individuals with WS show superior performance compared to controls (Bellugi et al. 1990). Studies that have documented this strength have used semantic fluency tasks (e.g. subjects are asked to provide as many examples as they can of a given semantic category, such as animals). The interesting observation is that children with WS displayed atypical responses in those first studies. Subsequent research has failed to show any group differences between participants with WS and typical controls concerning response typicality or frequency (Jarrold et al. 2000; Levy and Bechar 2003; Scott et al. 1995).

Individuals with WS have also been shown to process homonyms/homographs atypically. In a task that involved pairing a homonymous word with one of its possible readings, children with WS failed to associate the word with its more frequent sense (Rossen et al. 1996). However, these results are open to interpretation and are possibly related to the nature of the task.

One study documents increased semantic priming, as judged from increased late positivity in WS participants in response to auditorily presented stimuli, only in the sentence-final condition where words were congruent with the preceding sentence. For the anomalous words condition, however, responses in the WS group were comparable to those of controls (Neville, Mills and Bellugi 1994). These results are, however, challenged by a later study, which shows normal semantic priming effects in WS (Tyler et al. 1997).

Thus, the picture that emerges concerning semantic skills in Williams Syndrome is controversial. On the one hand, specific strengths in vocabulary knowledge have been reported, while on the other, there is recent evidence that vocabulary acquisition in that population is not typical, and, quite likely, children with WS rely on different mechanisms compared to typical children (Brock 2007). One conclusion is that, with development, the advantage at receptive vocabulary skills is apparently enhanced, and this is what has probably given rise to the original reports of an unusual vocabulary strength.

2.3 Autism

Autism is a neurodevelopmental disorder characterized by deficits in social reciprocity and communication and by repetitive and restricted patterns of behavior (Lord et al. 2000; DSM-5). Autism spectrum disorder offers vast heterogeneity, not in the least regarding the language profiles of individuals on the spectrum, ranging from highly verbal on the higher end, to non-verbal on the lower end (Rapin et al. 2009; Kjelgaard and Tager-Flusberg 2001). For this reason, and due to the similarity with the profile that defines language impairment, recent accounts consider the co-occurrence of language problems with autistic symptomatology as an instance of co-morbidity with language impairment (the ASD + LI group) (Kjelgaard and Tager-Flusberg 2001).

Individuals in the high-functioning autism (HFA) group, which includes persons with Asperger's syndrome, are characterized by largely intact structural language, including adequate grammar and vocabulary size. Another current label for this part of the spectrum is highly verbal individuals with autism. Even though no problems have been reported in core grammar domains (morphology and syntax) in that group, subtle dissociations within these domains have been observed. Thus, a study of Finnish adolescents with Asperger's syndrome documents a significant difference from controls on the comprehension of instructions (Saalasti et al. 2008). This is surprising in view of the otherwise intact syntax competence in such participants (e.g. knowledge of imperatives). However, a possible explanation for this result may be the communicative value of instructions as requests for action and a possible failure by participants to read the intentions of the speaker.

Some studies attest a specific strength in highly verbal participants with autism in the domain of morphology. These strengths manifest specifically in aspects of word form and in the ability to detect grammar patterns and the regularity in inflectional paradigms (Smith and Tsimpli 1995; Vulchanova et al. 2012a, 2012b; Walenski et al. 2014). This strength is further corroborated by a talent for learning the grammars of second languages found even in individuals on the lower end of the spectrum (Smith and Tsimpli 1995). The specific advantage in regular morphology evident in the HFA profile applies to the detection and production in required context of regular and sub-regular tense forms, as well as plural forms of nouns. Vulchanova et al. (2012b) document a significantly superior performance by a highly verbal adolescent with autism in comparison with a group of age-matched controls, particularly for sub-regular past tense forms of verbs. These findings are consistent with the results in Walenski et al. (2014), where a group of highly verbal participants with autism displayed smaller latencies on producing regular verb forms in English compared to similarly aged controls. The authors explain faster responses by the ASD participants in terms of a deficit in inhibition. This is couched within the dual processing hypothesis (Pinker 1998) and the procedural deficit hypothesis (Ullman 2004; Mostofsky et al. 2000), where the first step in producing the correct form involves an attempt to retrieve a stored form, as applicable to irregular verbs. If retrieval of this form fails (e.g., if no such form has been stored), then a regular form can be computed online. Thus, it seems that individuals with HFA are too fast to proceed to the second stage by-passing the retrieval stage, or rather, failing to inhibit direct generation of a regular form. This tendency is further explained in terms of a deficit in frontal/basal ganglia circuits that underlie grammar (for converging evidence on the role of basal ganglia anomalies in autism, see Sears et al. 1999; Qiu et al. 2010; Estes et al. 2011). An alternative explanatory account, however, is offered by the weak central coherence hypothesis (Frith and Happe 1994; Happe and Frith 2006), where the local processing bias in autism can confer a strength at pattern detection of the type necessary for regular and, possibly, sub-regular, grammar inflection (Vulchanova et al. 2012b).

Given the social and communication impairment in autism, an interesting question is whether it affects the way such children learn words. Vocabulary size and word knowledge have been systematically found to be a strength in autism. Furthermore, children with autism typically do not manifest problems in word learning and can use mutual exclusivity as a mechanism in word-learning similarly to typically developing children (Rescorla and Safyer, 2013; Marchena et al. 2011; Eigsti et al. 2007). Still, an interesting difference in word learning has been observed between children with autism and typically developing children. On the assumption that word learning involves the successful association between phonological pattern and meaning mediated by social cues provided by the context, Norbury et al. (2010) tested how these aspects of words affect the process of novel word learning in verbal children with autism compared to typical controls. While the typical children were more attentive to the social cues in the context, the children with autism were more sensitive to the formal (phonological) aspects of words, suggesting a deviant pattern of word learning. They were also less successful than the controls in vocabulary consolidation reflected in acquisition of both phonological and semantic information four weeks after the learning session. These results suggest a specific advantage in the formal aspects of words (phonological pattern), as well as in perceptual processes (e.g., imagery) associated with semantic decisions (Gaffrey et al. 2007), and a deficit in semantics (word meaning). As such they are consistent with the advantage at acquiring and using regular and sub-regular inflectional morphology and a sensitivity to the formal patterns of language. They are also consistent with findings in research of poor multisensory temporal integration in autism, reflected in the way information from multiple modality sources (e.g., auditory and visual perception) is integrated, which may affect the way sound patterns and meaning are associated in word-learning (Stevenson et al. 2014). Previous research has also established superior orthographic processing in autism regardless of language status, with a significant overlap between the group of precocious readers (hyperlexia) and autism traits (Nation 1999). This provides further support for the advantage at formal aspects of words contra word semantics, and a dissociation between these two in the autistic profile. Such dissociations in clinical populations have inspired the independent lexical access model proposed by Caramazza (1997).

The advantage at formal aspects of words, however, can also have adverse effects on word learning. A study by Henderson, Powell, Gaskell and Norbury (2014) aimed to estabslish whether individual differences in vocabulary knowledge in ASD might be explained by problems in the consolidation, and especially the integration of newly learned words with already existing vocabulary. The group with autism demonstrated similar success at novel spoken word recognition and identification 24 hours after training, suggesting adequate initial consolidation. However, the participants with autism only showed immediate phonological competition for the novel words, but unlike the typical participants, did not display competition effects 24 hours after training. These results suggest problems in the process of word learning, especially regarding subsequent lexical integration. Also, the presence of immediate phonological competition may be potentially problematic for the storage of lexical items. This is reminiscent of the findings from typically developing, albeit much younger, children (Swingley and Alsin, 2007).

Knowledge of highly idiosyncratic and specialized vocabulary has been reported in autism (Volden and Lord, 1991; Rouhizadeh et al., 2014). Often discrepancies are found between receptive and expressive measures, with receptive competence and comprehension being more affected (Lord and Paul 1997). However, such findings are contradictory, with some studies showing no such discrepancy (Kjelgaard and Tager-Flusberg 2001). Still, the latter study documents great heterogeneity in performance on a comprehensive battery of language tests (receptive vocabulary – PPVT, expressive vocabulary – EVT, receptive and expressive grammar – CELF), thus establishing three sub-groups of children: those with no language impairment, a borderline group and a group with language impairment.

Despite the overall vocabulary strength, a commonly observed phenomenon is a deficit in interpreting word meaning, especially in context (Frith and Snowling 1983; Happé 1997). These findings are based on studies of ambiguity due to the existence of homographs in language. Thus, younger children with autism showed a tendency to read the frequent pronunciations of homograph words regardless of context. In a similar way, Joliffe and Baron-Cohen (1999) found a deficit in the integration of sentence information for the purpose of identifying the correct reading of the homograph. However, other studies have shown that competence at making use of context depends on language status, and children with higher verbal age can perform at the level of controls (Snowling and Frith 1986). Success in that group may also depend on the exact position of the homograph in the sentence. Lopez and Leekam (2003) found that even though children with ASD performed worse than controls, they were more successful with homographs occurring later in the sentence (middle or end), suggesting sensitivity to context also in that group. A study by Brock et al. (2008) showed that participants with autism display a tendency similar to controls to use predictions based on the meaning of the lexical verb, as reflected in an increase in looks to a picture matching the object of the verb. At the same time both groups were less likely to be distracted by a phonological competitor of the object word. This tendency, however, was mediated by language status in the autism group. In that study, context was restricted to the level of the sentence, with a focus on the information encoded in the lexical verb and the ability to use that information to successfully orient to the possible object.

The notion of context has been questioned itself. It appears that highly verbal individuals with autism are capable of employing minimal local context, e.g. the phrase or even the sentence (Vulchanova et al. 2012a, 2012b). It seems that it is not the size of the processing domain which is problematic, but rather the number of operations that are needed to arrive at the correct interpretation. Quite likely, the problems reside in integrating grammar and semantic information, which is distributed and expressed at different loci in the sentence, such as inflections marking tense, aspect, or syntactic function (subject, object), thus taxing the processing system.

Against the problems with word meaning, an often observed strength in the ASD population is a tendency for superior word decoding. Children with autism frequently constitute the greater part of the group of early precocious readers, a condition also known as hyperlexia (Nation 1999; Nation et al. 2006).

The advantage in decoding the formal aspects of words, such as orthography for example, is also evident in studies that address the extent to which highly verbal children with autism can monitor their own reading process. A study by Micai, Vulchanova and Saldana (2019) documents that ASD children perform equally well on detecting spelling errors in a text when explicitly instructed to do so, but fail to detect semantic errors, despite explicit instruction. The same study revealed an atypical gaze pattern in performing the error detection task in comparison to age-, IQ- and comprehension-matched controls.

A consistent problem reported in autism is difficulties with the comprehension of figurative language. Research in this domain documents subtle dissociations between the ability to understand literal expressions and the comprehension of nonliteral (figurative) language. For instance, high-functioning individuals with autism with intact structural language skills often fail to understand the meaning of jokes, irony, and idiomatic language (Chahboun et al. 2016a, 2016b; Gold and Faust 2010; Vulchanova et al. 2012a, 2012b; Vulchanova et al. 2015).

Such dissociations between structural language skills and extended uses of language (e.g., figurative language) raise interesting questions concerning theories of the nature and processing of idiomatic expressions. Some theories assume that idioms (which are one instance of figurative language) need to be stored (Bobrow and Bell 1973; Swinney and Cutler 1979). Other accounts highlight idiom decomposability and suggest that idiom interpretation depends on identifying the individual constituents, because most idioms are decomposable (Hamblin and Gibbs 1999). Thus, the idea is that compositional (literal) interpretation proceeds up until a point when a key word is encountered, which provides an indication (the key) of the figurative nature of the expression (Titone and Connine 1999). It is thus suggested that processing and understanding idioms cannot be reduced to lexical access or lexical retrieval only (Cacciari and Tabossi 1988; Gibbs 1992; Vega-Moreno 2001). This type of approach, also known as the configuration hypothesis, assumes that idioms are represented in a distributed way and are processed as complex decomposable expressions. Thus, the processing of figurative language will be similar to the processing of literal (semantically compositional) language (cf. Vulchanova, Milburn et al.

2019 for a theoretical discussion), and no dissociations will be observed in individuals with autism.

Two types of accounts have been put forth to explain the well-attested problems with figurative language comprehension in autism. The first type of approach aims to link the deficit to other traits of the autistic phenotype, e.g., the impaired social interaction or as caused by a deficient theory of mind (Happé 1993, 1995). The other type of approach views the deficit in figurative language as directly arising from language competence and skills. Thus, immature linguistic skills (Gernsbacher and Pripas-Kapit 2012) or impaired semantic abilities (Norbury 2005) can also lead to problems in figurative language. On both latter accounts it is expected that no problems will be evident in the processing of figurative expressions among individuals with autism and with intact language competence, as assumed by the configuration hypothesis and by approaches attributing the figurative language problems in autism to deficient language skills. The evidence from the processing and comprehension of figurative language in highly verbal individuals with autism, however, suggests that language skills may differentially impact on figurative language comprehension at different stages of development in that group. A study by Chahboun et al. (2016a) tested metaphor comprehension in two groups of HF participants with autism, children aged 10–12 and young adults (16–26), compared to IQ- and verbal comprehension-matched controls. The results from the two ASD groups indicated an interesting pattern of differential relationship between language competences and performance speed and accuracy depending on age. While for the older group of participants (young adults with ASD) language skills exerted an influence on speed, for the younger participants (children with ASD), language competences influenced accuracy, suggesting that the experimental design with alternating conditions (auditory vs. visual modality; figurative vs. literal relation between prime and target) was more demanding for the children and required the recruitment of core language skills. This study also documented a deviant developmental trajectory for the ASD group with the young adult individuals with autism performing at the same speed as the child control group. Another finding in research in this domain suggests that more transparent expressions, such as idioms that have a biological basis and are more closely linked to human experience, as well as novel metaphors, are processed more easily. Also processing speed and degree of comprehension appear to decrease in the case of less transparent figurative expressions, where the semantic motivation is lost (Rundblad and Annaz 2010; Vulchanova, et al. 2019).

In sum, the verbal profile of autism is characterized by huge heterogeneity, and this is also reflected in relative strengths and weaknesses regarding word learning and word processing in this population. In word learning, there appear to be specific problems in the integration of novel words with already existing lexical knowledge in contrast to somewhat heightened sensitivity to formal aspects of words (phonology, morpho-phonology, orthorgraphy), and strengths in the initial mapping of novel words to new referents, most likely due to intact associative learning mechanisms (Parish-Morris et al. 2007; Baron-Cohen, Baldwin and Crowson 1997). Problems with semantic aspects of words are also reflected in qualitative differences in the activation of lexical knowledge for the purpose of language understanding. Despite preserved structural language skills and sometimes strengths in grammar, even highly verbal individuals with autism are faced with problems in figurative language comprehension and display a delayed developmental trajectory (Chahboun et al. 2016b).

2.4 Reading deficits (Dyslexia)

Reading deficits manifest themselves as problems specific to the orthographic aspects of words characterized as poor decoding (reading) and/or writing skills. It is commonly assumed that dyslexia is caused by an impairment of a phonological nature, which results in problems in the mapping of visual symbols (letters/orthography) to phonology (sound). Whether the problems reside in impaired phonological representations or limited access to these representations is still open to debate (Ramus et al. 2013). Reading deficits have also been associated with impaired phonological processing, and poor memory span. Like with other developmental disorders, dyslexia has a greater than chance overlap with other disorders, such as LI, ADHD, and dyscalculia (Germanò, Gagliano and Curatolo 2010; Pennington and Bishop 2009).

The cognitive markers of dyslexia/reading difficulty across orthographies appear to be stable. Phonological and phonemic awareness has been identified as a robust indicator of reading skill. However, its influence decreases over time and as the child acquires reading skills. Rapid automatized naming of objects, colors, letters and numbers is the other widely documented competence linked to reading skill, and children with a reading difficulty are typically shown to perform poorly on these tasks. Despite the robust association between rapid automatized naming and reading fluency, its nature is subject to debate. Regardless of the details of perspective, it is logical to assume that rapid automatized naming is a process of accessing the phonological codes associated with words and directly taps the form of words (phonological part of the lexical entry, Levelt 1989). In addition, it taps how automatized the association between the lemma and the morpho-phonological form is. The relevance of the mental lexicon and the strength of associations between form and meaning in words are also highlighted in models of reading acquisition which describe the process of becoming literate as a process of adding an orthographic lexicon to the already existing oral lexicon (Ziegler et al. 2014). According to the self-teaching hypothesis, each successful decoding encounter with an unfamiliar word provides an opportunity to acquire word-specific orthographic information that is the foundation of skilled word recognition. Thus, phonological decoding acts as a self-teaching mechanism or a 'built-in teacher'.

Thus, apparently, also in reading, language complexity plays out, and more aspects of lexical items are involved than just, say, phonological information. Research on dyslexia suggests that morphology may be impaired in addition to phonology in this group and that their word recognition problems may also reside at the level of morphological processing (Schiff and Raveh 2006). Emerging evidence contributes to the view that also morphological competence may be relevant to the process of orthographic decoding in reading (see Berthiaume and Daigle 2014 for a review), and that spared morphological awareness can act as a protective factor in children and adults with a reading deficit. A study of morphological awareness in participants with dyslexia, by Law, Wouters and Ghesquière (2015), found a morphological awareness deficit in the dyslexia group. This study also demonstrates that morphological awareness significantly predicts a greater proportion of the variance in reading and spelling skills in the dyslexia group, and furthermore that intact morphological skills contribute to acquiring compensation in adults with dyslexia. In summary, the structure of words at different levels of granularity (individual sounds, syllabic structure, morphological structure) and how this structure is encoded in the word orthography impact on the acquisition of reading skills in typical readers and may present problems for individuals with a reading deficit (Seymour, Aro and Erskine 2003).

2.5 Poor comprehenders

Poor comprehenders (PCs) are children who experience reading comprehension problems in the presence of adequate word decoding (reading) skills. This group has received attention only recently and has often gone undetected, as a result of the widely held view of a strong relationship between decoding ability and reading comprehension. Yet, decoding and reading comprehension have been found to have different independent predictors (e.g. Elwér, Keenan, Olson, Byrne, and Samuelsson 2013), and a recent meta-analysis aimed at determining what factors influence the strength of the relationship between decoding skill and reading comprehension skills in English, suggests that the relationship between these two abilities is moderated by age and listening comprehension (García and Cain 2014).

Oral (listening) comprehension is supported by both lower-level skills, such as vocabulary knowledge and grammar competence, and verbal memory, as well as higher-level skills, such as inferencing and literal language interpretation. These skills have been found to be reliable predictors of later reading comprehension in typical children (Silva and Cain 2015). Among them, inference skills, grammar and literal comprehension measured prior to school entry independently contribute to reading comprehension in the first year of school (Silva and Cain 2015).

Both vocabulary breadth and vocabulary depth have been shown to predict reading comprehension skills. However, interestingly, word knowledge influences text understanding by predicting higher-level comprehension skills, such as inferencing (Cain and Oakhill 2014). While it would be normal to expect problems primarily on the side of vocabulary knowledge and semantic (conceptual) knowledge in poor comprehenders, other factors that affect oral and reading comprehension ought to be considered as well. Thus, a recent study found that, compared to the typical children, the group of poor comprehenders was characterized by a weakness in morpho-syntax (i.e., finiteness marking of verbs) which could not be explained by overall semantic factors (Adlof and Catts 2015). More recent evidence is suggestive of problems in the domain of grammar. Thus, compared to a group of average comprehenders, the children with poor comprehension demonstrated a weakness in meta-linguistic tasks involving morphology and syntax (Tong, Deacon and Cain 2014). Thus, poor comprehension appears to have an overlap with language impairment in that various aspects of the language system are affected and in that children with poor comprehension exhibit impairment in both semantic, as well as morphological aspects of words. This may explain why this group can be classified as a subset of the category of language impaired children. This is confirmed by findings of impaired phonological (verbal) memory in the group of poor comprehenders, suggestive of concomitant language impairment rather than the direct cause of the comprehension problem (Nation et al. 1999). Also, on the component model of language-related deficits (Ramus et al. 2013), the population with LI only are identified as children with problems in oral language only (i.e., poor comprehenders), while children who, in addition, experience problems with written aspects of language (e.g., word orthography) are characterized by co-morbidity with dyslexia ((S)LI + dyslexia group).

3 Comparing the profiles

An interesting pattern of strengths and weaknesses thus emerges across the profiles of the language-related developmental deficits reviewed here. For instance, the problems experienced by children with language impairment appear to be orthogonal to the weaknesses in the profile of highly verbal individuals with autism. While in LI, the most consistently observed problems apply to online computation operations and constructing morphologically complex forms, in HFA the formal aspects of words (phonology, morpho-phonology) are a relative strength. Regarding semantic skills, deficits in that domain are more frequently reported in HFA, while in LI the picture is more complex, with some evidence of a deficit primarily in vocabulary growth. Interestingly, both children with developmental language deficits and children with autism appear to have problems with the consolidation of novel labels and the integration of new words in the mental lexicon. Also, in both populations, word processing (activation and competition) appear to be deviant, suggesting differences in the structure and operation of the mental lexicon in comparison with typical populations.

Another orthogonal pattern emerges between children with dyslexia and poor comprehenders. While in dyslexia, the problems reside in word decoding as a result of problems in mapping visual symbols (orthography) to sound and, quite likely, problems with the grain (internal) structure of words, in poor comprehenders, the problems are primarily of a semantic and conceptual nature and also relate to aspects of oral language competence, including grammar (morphology). These observed patterns of selective impairments of specific aspects of words and specific mechanisms which support word learning (consolidation, integration) and use (word activation) reflect the complexity of the language system itself and are suggestive of subtle dissociations within the sub-modules of language structure, rather than of dissociations between language and cognition, as previously assumed.

Acknowledgement: The second author received funding from the Spanish National Research Agency and Ministry of Science, Innovation, and Universities [Grant NO. PGC2018-096094-B-I00].

References

Adlof, Suzanne M. & Hugh W. Catts. 2015. Morphosyntax in poor comprehenders. *Reading and Writing* 28 (7). 1051–1070.

Baron-Cohen, Simon, Dare A. Baldwin & Mary Crowson. 1997. Do children with autism use the speaker's direction of gaze strategy to crack the code of language? *Child Development* 68 (1). 48–57.

Bartke, Susanne & Julia Siegmüller. 2004. *Williams Syndrome across Languages*. Amsterdam & Philadelphia: John Benjamins.

Bedore, Lisa M. & Laurence B. Leonard. 1998. Specific language impairment and grammatical morphology: A discriminant function analysis. *Journal of Speech, Language, and Hearing Research* 41 (5). 1185–1192.

Bedore, L. M., & Leonard, L. B. 2001. Grammatical morphology deficits in Spanish-speaking children with specific language impairment. *Journal of Speech, Language, and Hearing Research*, 44, 905–924. Doi: 10.1044/1092-4388(2001/072).

Bellugi, Ursula, Amy Bihrle, Terry Jernigan, Doris Trauner & Sally Doherty. 1990. Neuropsychological, neurological, and neuroanatomical profile of Williams syndrome. *American Journal of Medical Genetics* 37 (S6). 115–125.

Berthiaume, Rachel & Daniel Daigle. 2014. Are dyslexic children sensitive to the morphological structure of words when they read? The case of dyslexic readers of French. *Dyslexia* 20 (3). 241–260.

Bishop, Dorothy V.M. 1997. Is specific language impairment a valid diagnostic category? Genetic and psycholinguistic evidence. *Philosophical Transactions of the Royal Society of London. Series B: Biological Sciences* 346 (1315). 105–111.

Bishop, Dorothy V.M. 2004. Specific language impairment: Diagnostic dilemmas. *Classification of developmental language disorders: Theoretical issues and clinical implications*. 309–326.

Bishop, Dorothy V.M. 2013. Cerebral asymmetry and language development: cause, correlate, or consequence? *Science* 340 (6138). 1230531.

Bishop, Dorothy V.M. Robert P. Carlyon, John M. Deeks & Sonja J. Bishop. 1999. Auditory temporal processing impairment: Neither necessary nor sufficient for causing language impairment in children. *Journal of Speech, Language, and Hearing Research* 42 (6). 1295–1310.

Bishop, Dorothy V.M, Tony North & Chris Donlan. 1996. Nonword repetition as a behavioural marker for inherited language impairment: Evidence from a twin study. *Journal of Child Psychology and Psychiatry* 37 (4). 391–403.

Bobrow, Samuel A. & Susan M. Bell. 1973. On catching on to idiomatic expressions. *Memory & cognition* 1 (3). 343–346.

Brackenbury, Tim & Clifton Pye. 2005. Semantic deficits in children with Language Impairments. *Language, Speech, and Hearing Services in Schools* 36. 5–16.

Brock, Jon 2007. Language abilities in Williams syndrome: A critical review. *Development and Psychopathology* 19 (1). 97–127.

Brock, Jon, Courtenay Norbury, Shiri Einav & Kate Nation. 2008. Do individuals with autism process words in context? Evidence from language-mediated eye-movements. *Cognition* 108 (3). 896–904.

Cacciari, Cristina & Patrizia Tabossi. 1988. The comprehension of idioms. *Journal of Memory and Language* 27 (6). 668–683.

Cain, Kate & Jane Oakhill. 2014. Reading comprehension and vocabulary: is vocabulary more important for some aspects of comprehension? *L'année Psychologique* 114 (4). 647–662.
Caramazza, Alfonso. 1997. How many levels of lexical processing are there in lexical access? *Cognitive Neuropsychology* 14 (1). 177–208.
Chahboun, Sobh, Valentin Vulchanov, David Saldaña, Hendrik Eshuis & Mila Vulchanova. 2016a. Predictors of metaphorical understanding in high functioning autism. *Lingue e linguaggio* 15 (1). 29–58.
Chahboun, Sobh, Valentin Vulchanov, David Saldaña, Hendrik Eshuis & Mila Vulchanova. 2016b. Can you play with fire and not hurt yourself? A Comparative study in figurative language comprehension between individuals with and without Autism Spectrum Disorder. *PLoS ONE* 11 (12).
Clahsen, Harald. 1989. The grammatical characterization of developmental dysphasia. *Linguistics* 27. 897–920.
Clahsen, Harald, Susanne Bartke & Sandra Göllner. 1997. Formal features in impaired grammars: A comparison of English and German SLI children. *Journal of Neurolinguistics* 10 (2–3). 151–171.
Coady, Jeffry A. & Julia L. Evans. 2008. Uses and interpretations of non-word repetition tasks in children with and without specific language impairments (SLI). *International Journal of Language & Communication Disorders* 43 (1). 1–40.
Collisson, Beverly Anne, Bernard Grela, Tammie Spaulding, Jay G. Rueckl & James S. Magnuson. 2015. Individual differences in the shape bias in preschool children with Specific Language Impairment and typical language development: Theoretical and clinical implications. *Developmental Science* 18 (3). 373–388.
Conti-Ramsden, Gina M. 2003. Processing and linguistic markers in young children with specific language impairment (SLI). *Journal of Speech, Language, and Hearing Research* 46, 1029–1037.
Conti-Ramsden, Gina M., Nicola Botting & Brian Faragher. 2001. Psycholinguistic markers for specific language impairment (SLI). *Journal of Child Psychology and Psychiatry and Allied Disciplines* 42 (6). 741–748.
Conti-Ramsden, Gina M. & Anne Hesketh. 2003. Risk markers for SLI: A study of young language-learning children. *International Journal of Language and Communication Disorders* 38 (3). 251–263.
Dautriche, Isabelle, Daniel Swingley & Anne Christophe. 2015. Learning novel phonological neighbors: Syntactic category matters. *Cognition* 143. 77–86.
Dollaghan, Chris. 1998. Spoken word recognition in children with and without specific language impairment. *Applied Psycholinguistics* 19 (2). 193–207.
Dollaghan, Chris & Thomas F. Campbell. 1998. Non-word repetition and child Language Impairment. *Journal of Speech, Language, and Hearing Research* 41 (5). 1136–1146.
Dromi, Esther, Laurence B. Leonard, Galit Adam & Sara Zadunaisky-Ehrlich. 1999. Verb agreement morphology in Hebrew speaking children with specific language impairment. *Journal of Speech, Language and Hearing Research* 42 (6). 1414–1431.
Dumay, Nicolas & M. Gareth Gaskell. 2007. Sleep-associated changes in the mental representation of spoken words. *Psychological Science* 18 (1). 35–39.
Eigsti, Inge-Marie, Loisa Bennetto & Mamta B. Dadlani. 2007. Beyond pragmatics: morphosyntactic development in autism. *Journal of Autism and Developmental Disorders* 37 (6). 1007–1023.

Eigsti, Inge-Marie, Ashley B. de Marchena, Jillian M. Schuh & Elizabeth Kelley. 2011. Language acquisition in autism spectrum disorders: A developmental review. *Research in Autism Spectrum Disorders* 5 (2). 681–691.

Ellis Weismer, Susan, J. Bruce Tomblin, Xuyang Zhang, Paula Buckwalter, Jan Gaura Chynoweth & Maura Jones. 2000. Nonword repetition performance in school-age children with and without language impairment. *Journal of Speech, Language, and Hearing Research* 43 (4). 865–878.

Elwér, Åsa, Janice M. Keenan, Richard K. Olson, Brian Byrne & Stefan Samuelsson. 2013. Longitudinal stability and predictors of poor oral comprehenders and poor decoders. *Journal of Experimental Child Psychology* 115 (3). 497–516.

Estes, Annette, Dennis WW Shaw, Bobbi F. Sparks, Seth Friedman, Jay N. Giedd, Geraldine Dawson, Matthew Bryan & Stephen R. Dager. 2011. Basal ganglia morphometry and repetitive behavior in young children with autism spectrum disorder. *Autism Research* 4 (3). 212–220.

Friederici, Angela. 2006. The neural basis of language development and its impairment. *Neuron* 52 (6). 941–962.

Frith, Uta, & Francesca Happé. 1994. Autism: beyond "theory of mind". *Cognition* 50 (1–3), 115–132.

Frith, Uta, & Maggie Snowling. 1983. Reading for meaning and reading for sound in autistic and dyslexic children. *British Journal of Developmental Psychology* 1 (4). 329–342.

Gaffrey, Michael S., Natalia M. Kleinhans, Frank Haist, Natacha Akshoomoff, Ashley Campbell, Eric Courchesne, & Ralph-Axel Müller. 2007. Atypical participation of visual cortex during word processing in autism: An fMRI study of semantic decision. *Neuropsychologia* 45 (8). 1672–1684.

García, J. Ricardo & Kate Cain. 2014. Decoding and reading comprehension: a meta-analysis to identify which reader and assessment characteristics influence the strength of the relationship in English. *Review of Educational Research* 84 (1), 74–111.

Gaskell, M. Gareth & Nicolas Dumay. 2003. Lexical competition and the acquisition of novel words. *Cognition* 8 (2). 105–132.

Gauger, Laurie M., Linda J. Lombardino & Christiana M. Leonard. 1997. Brain morphology in children with specific language impairment. *Journal of Speech, Language, and Hearing Research* 40 (6). 1272–1284.

Germanò, Eva, Antonella Gagliano & Paolo Curatolo. 2010. Comorbidity of ADHD and dyslexia. *Developmental neuropsychology* 35 (5). 475–493.

Gernsbacher, Morton Ann & Sarah R. Pripas-Kapit. 2012. Who's Missing the Point? A Commentary on Claims that Autistic Persons Have a Specific Deficit in Figurative Language Comprehension. *Metaphor and Symbol* 27 (1). 93–105.

Gibbs Jr, Raymond W. 1992. What do idioms really mean? *Journal of Memory and Language* 31 (4). 485–506.

Gold, Rinat & Miriam Faust. 2010. Right Hemisphere Dysfunction and Metaphor Comprehension in Young Adults with Asperger Syndrome. *Journal of Autism and Developmental Disorders* 40 (7). 800–811.

Gopnik, Myrna. 1999. Familial language impairment: More English evidence. *Folia Phoniatrica et Logopaedica* 51 (1–2). 5–19.

Gray, Shelley. 2003. Diagnostic accuracy and test-retest reliability of nonword repetition and digit span tasks administered to preschool children with specific language impairment. *Journal of communication disorders* 36 (2). 129–151.

Gray, Shelley. 2004. Word learning by preschoolers with specific language impairment: Predictors and poor learners. *Journal of Speech, Language, and Hearing Research* 47. 1117–1132.

Hamblin, Jennifer L. & Raymond W. Gibbs. 1999. Why you can't kick the bucket as you slowly die: Verbs in idiom understanding. *Journal of Psycholinguistic Research* 39(1), 25–39.

Happé, Francesca. 1993. Communicative competence and theory of mind in autism: A test of relevance theory. *Cognition* 48 (2). 101–19.

Happé, Francesca. 1995. Understanding minds and metaphors: insights from the study of figurative language in autism. *Metaphor and Symbolic Activity* 10 (4). 275–295.

Happé, Francesca. 1997. Central coherence and theory of mind in autism: Reading homographs in context. *British Journal of Developmental Psychology* 15 (1). 1–12.

Happé, Francesca & Uta Frith. 2006. The weak coherence account: detail-focused cognitive style in autism spectrum disorders. *Journal of Autism and Developmental Disorders* 36 (1). 5–25.

Henderson, Lisa, Anna Powell, M. Gareth Gaskell & Courtenay Norbury. 2014. Learning and consolidation of new spoken words in autism spectrum disorder. *Developmental Science* 17 (6). 858–871.

Huang, Yi Ting & Jesse Snedeker. 2011. Logic and conversation revisited: Evidence for a division between semantic and pragmatic content in real-time language comprehension. *Language and Cognitive Processes* 26 (8). 1161–1172.

Jackendoff, Ray. 2002. *Foundations of language: Brain, meaning, grammar, evolution*. Oxford, UK: Oxford University Press.

Jarrold, Christopher, Samantha J. Hartley, Caroline Phillips & Alan D. Baddeley. 2000. Word fluency in Williams syndrome: Evidence for unusual semantic organization. *Cognitive Neuropsychiatry* 5 (4). 293–319.

Joanisse, Marc F. 2004. Specific Language Impairments in children: Phonology, semantics and the English past tense. *Current Directions in Psychological Science* 13 (4). 156–160.

Joanisse, Marc F. & Mark S. Seidenberg. 1998. Specific Language Impairment: A deficit in grammar or processing? *Trends in Cognitive Sciences* 2 (7). 240–247.

Joanisse, Marc F. & Mark S. Seidenberg. 2003. Phonology and syntax specific language impairment: Evidence from a connectionist model. *Brain and Language* 86 (1). 40–56.

Jolliffe, Therese & Simon Baron-Cohen. 1999. A test of central coherence theory: Linguistic processing in high-functioning adults with autism or Asperger syndrome: Is local coherence impaired? *Cognition* 71 (2). 149–185.

Kan, Pui Fong & Jennifer Windsor. 2010. Word learning in children with primary language impairment: a meta-analysis. *Journal of Speech, Language, and Hearing Research* 53. 739–756.

Kirk, Cecilia & Katherine Demuth. 2005. Asymmetries in the acquisition of word-initial and word-final consonant clusters. *Journal of Child Language* 32 (4). 709–734.

Kjelgaard, Margaret M. & Helen Tager-Flusberg. 2001. An investigation of language impairment in autism: Implications for genetic subgroups. *Language and Cognitive Processes* 16 (2–3). 287–308.

Kornilov, Sergey A., E. L. Grigorenko & N. V. Rakhlin. 2012. Morphology and developmental language disorders: New tools for Russian. *Psychology in Russia: State of the Art* 5. 371–387.

Kornilov, Sergey A., James S. Magnuson, Natalia Rakhlin, Nicole Landi & Elena L. Grigorenko. 2015. Lexical processing deficits in children with developmental language disorder: An event-related potentials study. *Development and Psychopathology* 27 (2). 459–476.

Law, Jeremy M., Jan Wouters & Pol Ghesquière. 2015. Morphological Awareness and Its Role in Compensation in Adults with Dyslexia. *Dyslexia* 21 (3). 254–272.

Leonard, Laurence B. 1998. *Children with Specific Language Impairment*. Cambridge, MA: MIT Press.

Levelt, Willem JM. 1989. *Speaking: From Intention to Articulation*. MIT Press, Cambridge, MA.

Levy, Yonata & Talma Bechar. 2003. Cognitive, lexical and morpho-syntactic profiles of Israeli children with Williams syndrome. *Cortex* 39 (2). 255–271.

López Beatriz & Susan R. Leekam. 2003. Do children with autism fail to process information in context? *Journal of Child Psychology and Psychiatry* 44 (2). 285–300.

Lord, Catherine & Paul Rhea. 1997. Language and communication in autism. In D.J. Cohen & F.R. Volkmar (eds.), *Handbook of autism and pervasive developmental disorders* (2nd ed.), 195–225. New York: Wiley.

Lord, Catherine, Edwin H. Cook, Bennett L. Leventhal, and David G. Amaral. 2000. Autism spectrum disorders. *Neuron* 28. 355–363.

Lukács, Ágnes. 2005. *Language Abilities in Williams Syndrome*. Budapest: Akademiai Kiado.

Mani, Nivedita & Kim Plunkett. 2010. In the infant's mind's ear: Evidence for implicit naming in 18-month-olds. *Psychological Science* 21 (7). 908–913.

Marchena, Ashley, Inge-Marie Eigsti, Amanda Worek, Kim Emiko Ono & Jesse Snedeker. 2011. Mutual exclusivity in autism spectrum disorders: Testing the pragmatic hypothesis. *Cognition* 119 (1). 96–113,

Marshall, Chloe R. & Heather K.J. van der Lely. 2007. The impact of phonological complexity on past tense inflection in children with Grammatical-SLI. *Advances in Speech Language Pathology* 9 (3). 191–203.

McClelland, James L. & Karalyn Patterson. 2002. Rules or connections in past tense inflection: What does the evidence rule out? *Trends in Cognitive Sciences* 6 (11). 465–472.

McMurray, Bob, Cheyenne Munson & J. Bruce Tomblin. 2014. Individual differences in language outcomes are related to variation in word recognition, not speech perception: evidence from eye movements. *Journal of Speech, Language and Hearing Research* 57 (4). 1344–1362.

McMurray, Bob, Vicki Samuelson, Sung Hee Lee & J. Bruce Tomblin. 2010. Eye-movements reveal the time-course of online spoken word recognition language impaired and normal adolescents. *Cognitive Psychology* 60 (1). 1–39.

Micai, M., Vulchanova, M. & Saldaña, D. 2019. Do Individuals with Autism Change Their Reading Behavior to Adapt to Errors in the Text? *Journal of Autism and Developmental Disorders* 49: 4232. https://doi.org/10.1007.

Mostofsky, Stewart H., Melissa C. Goldberg, Rebecca J. Landa & Martha B. Denckla. 2000. Evidence for a deficit in procedural learning in children and adolescents with autism: implications for cerebellar contribution. *Journal of the International Neuropsychological Society* 6 (7). 752–759.

Nation, Kate. 1999. Reading skills in hyperlexia: A developmental perspective. *Psychological Bulletin* 125 (3), 338–355.

Nation, Kate. 2014. Lexical learning and lexical processing in children with developmental language impairments. *Philosophical Transactions of the Royal Society B* 369 (1634). 20120387.

Nation, Kate, John W. Adams, Claudine A. Bowyer-Crane & Margaret J. Snowling. 1999. Working memory deficits in poor comprehenders reflect underlying language impairments. *Journal of Experimental Child Psychology* 73 (2). 139–158.

Nation, Kate, Paula Clarke, Barry Wright & Christine Williams. 2006. Patterns of reading ability in children with autism spectrum disorder. *Journal of Autism and Developmental Disorders* 36. 911–919.

Neville, Helen J., Debra L. Mills & Ursula Bellugi. 1994. Effects of altered auditory sensitivity and age of language acquisition on the development of language-relevant neural systems: Preliminary studies of Williams syndrome. In S. Broman (Ed.), *Cognitive deficits in developmental disorders: Implications for brain function*, 67–86. Hillsdale, NJ: Erlbaum.

Norbury, Courtenay Frazier. 2005. The relationship between theory of mind and metaphor: Evidence from children with language impairment and autistic spectrum disorders. *British Journal of Developmental Psychology* 23 (3). 383–399.

Norbury, Courtenay Frazier, Helen Griffiths & Kate Nation. 2010. Sound before meaning: word learning in autistic disorders. *Neuropsychologia* 48 (14). 4012–4019.

Norbury, Courtenay Frazier, Debbie Gooch, Charlotte Wray, Gillian Baird, Tony Charman, Emily Simonoff, George Vamvakas & Andrew Pickles. 2016. The impact of nonverbal ability on prevalence and clinical presentation of language disorder: evidence from a population study. *Journal of Child Psychology and Psychiatry*. 57 (11). 1247–1257.

Parish-Morris, Julia, Elizabeth A. Hennon, Kathy Hirsh-Pasek, Roberta Michnick Golinkoff & Helen Tager-Flusberg (2007). Children with autism illuminate the role of social intention in word learning. *Child Development* 78. 1265–1287.

Penke, Martina. 2008. Morphology and Language Disorder. In M.J. Ball, M.R. Perkins, N. Müller & S. Howard (eds.), *The Handbook of Clinical Linguistics*. Oxford, UK: Blackwell Publishing Ltd.

Pennington, Bruce F. & Dorothy VM Bishop. 2009. Relations Among Speech, Language, and Reading Disorders. *Annual Review of Psychology* 60. 283–306.

Perfetti, Charles. 2007. Reading ability: Lexical quality to comprehension. *Scientific Studies of Reading* 11 (4). 357–383.

Perfetti, Charles & Lesley Hart. 2002. The lexical Quality Hypothesis. *Precursors of functional literacy* 11. 67–86

Pinker, Steven. 1998. Words and rules. *Lingua* 106 (1–4). 219–242.

Qiu, Anqi, Marcy Adler, Deana Crocetti, Michael I. Miller & Stewart H. Mostofsky. 2010. Basal ganglia shapes predict social, communication, and motor dysfunctions in boys with autism spectrum disorder. *Journal of the American Academy of Child & Adolescent Psychiatry* 49. 539–551.

Ramus, Franck, Chloe R. Marshall, Stuart Rosen & Heather KJ van der Lely. 2013. Phonological deficits in specific language impairment and developmental dyslexia: Towards a multidimensional model. *Brain* 136 (2). 630–645.

Rapin, Isabelle, Michelle A. Dunn, Doris A. Allen, Michael C. Stevens & Deborah Fein. 2009. Subtypes of language disorders in school-age children with autism. *Developmental Neuropsychology* 34 (1). 66–84.

Rescorla, Leslie & Paige Safyer. 2013. Lexical composition in children with Autism Spectrum Disorder (ASD). *Journal of Child Language* 40 (1). 47–68.

Rice, Mabel L. 2007. Children with Specific Language Impairment: Bridging the Genetic and Developmental Perspectives. In E. Hoff & M. Shatz (eds.), *Handbook of Language Development*, 411–431. Blackwell Publishers.

Rice, Mabel L. & Lesa Hoffman. 2015. Predicting vocabulary growth in children with and without specific language impairment: A longitudinal study from 2;6 to 21 years of age. *Journal of Speech, Language, and Hearing Research* 58 (2). 345–359.

Rice, Mabel L., Kenneth Wexler & Patricia L. Cleave. 1995. Specific language impairment as a period of extended optional infinitive. *Journal of Speech and Hearing Research* 3 (4). 850–863.

Rossen, Michael, Edward S. Klima, Ursula Bellugi, Amy Bihrle & Wendy Jones. 1996. Interaction between language and cognition: Evidence from Williams syndrome. In J. H. Beitchman, N. Cohen, M. Konstantareas, & R. Tannock (eds.), *Language, learning, and behavior disorders: Developmental, biological, and clinical perspectives*, 367–392. New York: Cambridge University Press.

Rouhizadeh, Masoud, Emily Prud'hommeaux, Jan van Santen & Richard Sproat. 2014. Detecting linguistic idiosyncratic interests in autism using distributional semantic models. *Workshop on Computational Linguistics and Clinical Psychology: From Linguistic Signal to Clinical Reality*, 46–50. Baltimore, Maryland USA, Association for Computational Linguistics.

Roy, Brandon C., Michael C. Frank, Philip DeCamp, Matthew Miller & Deb Roy. 2015. Predicting the birth of a spoken word. *Proceedings of the National Academy of Sciences* 112 (41). 12663–12668.

Rundblad, Gabriella & Dagmara Annaz. 2010. The atypical development of metaphor and metonymy comprehension in children with autism. *Autism* 14 (1). 29–46.

Saalasti, Satu, Tuulia Lepistö, Esko Toppila, Teija Kujala, Minna Laakso, Taina Nieminen-von Wendt, Lennart von Wendt & Eira Jansson-Verkasalo. 2008. Language abilities of children with Asperger syndrome. *Journal of Autism and Developmental Disorders* 38 (8). 1574–1580.

Sabisch, Beate, Anja Hahne, Elisabeth Glass, Waldemar von Suchodoletz & Angela D. Friederici. 2006. Lexical-semantic processes in children with specific language impairment. *Neuroreport* 17 (14). 1511–1514.

Schiff, Rachel & Michal Raveh. 2006. Deficient morphological processing in adults with developmental dyslexia: Another barrier to efficient word recognition? *Dyslexia* 13 (2). 110–129.

Scott, Paul, Carolyn B. Mervis, Jacquelyn Bertrand, Bonita P. Klein, Sharon C. Armstrong & Andrew L. Ford. 1995. Semantic organization and word fluency in 9- and 10-year-old children with Williams syndrome. *Genetic Counseling* 6. 172–173.

Sears, Lonnie L., Cortney Vest, Somaia Mohamed, James Bailey, Bonnie J. Ranson & Joseph Piven. 1999. An MRI study of the basal ganglia in autism. *Progress in Neuro-Psychopharmacology and Biological Psychiatry* 23. 613–624.

Seymour, Philip HK, Mikko Aro & Jane M. Erskine. 2003. Foundation literacy acquisition in European orthographies. *British Journal of Psychology* 94 (2). 143–74.

Silva, Macarena & Kate Cain. 2015. The relations between lower and higher level comprehension skills and their role in prediction of early reading comprehension. *Journal of Educational Psychology* 107 (2). 321.

Smith, Neilson Voyne & Ianthi-Maria Tsimpli. 1995. *The Mind of a Savant: Language Learning and Modularity*. Oxford: Basil Blackwell.

Snowling, Maggie & Uta Frith. 1986. Comprehension in "hyperlexic" readers. *Journal of Experimental Child Psychology* 42 (3). 392–415.

Spaulding, T. J., Hosmer, S. & Schechtman, C. (2013). Investigating the interchangability and diagnostic utility of the PPVT-III and PPVT-IV for children with and without SLI. *International Journal of Speech and Language Pathology* 15. 453–462.

Stevenson, Ryan A., Justin K. Siemann, Brittany C. Schneider, Haley E. Eberly, Tiffany G. Woynaroski, Stephen M. Camarata & Mark T. Wallace. 2014 Multisensory temporal integration in autism spectrum disorders. *Journal of Neuroscience* 34. 691–697.

Swingley, Daniel & Richard N. Aslin. 2007. Lexical competition in young children's word learning. *Cognitive Psychology* 54 (2). 99–132.

Swinney, David A. & Anne Cutler. 1979. The access and processing of idiomatic expressions. *Journal of Verbal Learning and Verbal Behavior* 18 (5). 523–534.

Tanenhaus, Michael K., Michael J. Spivey-Knowlton, Kathleen M. Eberhard, & Julie C. Sedivy. 1995. Integration of visual and linguistic information in spoken language comprehension. *Science* 268 (5217). 1632–1634.

Titone, Debra A. & Cynthia M. Connine. 1999. On the compositional and non-compositional nature of idiomatic expressions. *Journal of Pragmatics: An Interdisciplinary Journal of Language Studies* 31(12). 1655–1674.

Tong, Xiuli, S. Hélène Deacon & Kate Cain. 2014. Morphological and syntactic awareness in poor comprehenders: another piece of the puzzle. *Journal of Learning Disabilities* 47(1). 22–33.

Tyler, Lorraine K., Annette Karmiloff-Smith, J. Kate Voice, Tassos Stevens, Julia Grant, Orlee Udwin, Mark Davies & Patricia Howlin. 1997. Do individuals with Williams syndrome have bizarre semantics? Evidence for lexical organization using an on-line task. *Cortex* 33 (3), 515–527.

Van der Lely, Heather K.J. 2003. Do heterogeneous SLI deficits need heterogeneous theories? SLI subgroups, G-SLI and the RDDR hypothesis. In Y. Levy, & J. Schaeffer (eds.), *Towards a definition of specific language impairment*, 109–134. Mahwah, NJ: Lawrence Erlbaum Associates.

Van der Lely, Heather K.J. 2005. Domain-specific cognitive systems: Insight from grammatical specific language impairment. *Trends in Cognitive Sciences* 9 (2). 53–59.

Van der Lely, Heather K.J. & Pinker, Steven. 2014. The biological basis of language: Insight from developmental grammatical impairment. *Trends in Cognitive Sciences* 18 (11). 586–595.

Van der Lely, Heather K.J., Stuart Rosen & Alan Adlard. 2004. Grammatical language impairment and the specificity of cognitive domains: Relations between auditory and language abilities. *Cognition* 94 (2). 167–183.

Van der Lely, Heather K.J. & Michael T. Ullman. 2001. Past tense morphology in specifically language impaired children and normally developing children. *Language and Cognitive Processes* 16. 113–336.

Vega-Moreno, Rosa Elena. 2001. Representing and processing idioms. *UCL Working Papers in Linguistics* 13. 73–109.

Volden, Joanne, & Catherine Lord. 1991. Neologisms and idiosyncratic language in autistic speakers. *Journal of Autism and Developmental Disorders* 21 (2). 109–130.

Vulchanova, Mila, Chahboun, Sobh, Galindo-Prieto, Beatriz & Vulchanov, Valentin. 2019. Gaze and Motor Traces of Language Processing: Evidence from Autism Spectrum Disorders in Comparison to Typical Controls. *Cognitive Neuropsychology*, DOI: 10.1080/02643294.2019.1652155.

Vulchanova, Mila, Evelyn Milburn, Valentin Vulchanov, and Giosuè Baggio. 2019. Boon or Burden? The Role of Compositional Meaning in Figurative Language Processing and Acquisition. *Journal of of Logic, Language and Information*. https://doi.org/10.1007/s10849-019-09282-7

Vulchanova, Mila, David Saldaña, Sobh Chahboun & Valentin Vulchanov. 2015. Figurative language processing in atypical populations: The ASD perspective. *Frontiers in Human Neuroscience* 9 (24).

Vulchanova, Mila, Joel B. Talcott, Valentin Vulchanov & Margarita Stankova. 2012a. Language against the odds, or rather not: The weak central coherence hypothesis and language. *Journal of Neurolinguistics* 25 (1). 13–30.
Vulchanova, Mila, Joel B. Talcott, Valentin Vulchanov, Margarita Stankova & Hendrik Eshuis. 2012b. Morphology in autism spectrum disorders: Local processing bias and language. *Cognitive Neuropsychology* 29 (7–8). 584–600.
Ullman, Micheal T. 2004. Contributions of memory circuits to language: the declarative/procedural model. *Cognition* 92 (1–2). 231–270.
Walenski, Matthew, Stewart H. Mostofsky & Michael T. Ullman. 2014. Inflectional morphology in high-functioning autism: Evidence for speeded grammatical processing. *Research in autism spectrum disorders* 8 (11). 1607–1621.
Wright, Beverly A., Linda J. Lombardino, Wayne M. King, Cynthia S. Puranik, Christiana M. Leonard & Michael M. Merzenich. 1997. Deficits in auditory temporal and spectral resolution in language-impaired children. *Nature* 387 (6629). 176–178.
Ziegler, Johannes C., Conrad Perry & Marco Zorzi. 2014. Modelling reading development through phonological decoding and self-teaching: Implications for dyslexia. *Philosophical Transactions of the Royal Society B: Biological Sciences* 369 (1634). 20120397.

Index

Abductive inference 30
Auto correlation function plot 108
Affixation 478
– affix homonymy 488
– root-and-pattern affixation 601
Alexia 130
– alexia with agraphia 130
– alexia without agraphia 130
Allomorphy 538, 669
A-morphous morphology 462
Analogy 216, 315
– analogical gang 217
– analogical modeling 214
    – analogical modeling of language
        (AML) 214, 315
    – generalized context model (GCM) 214
    – Tilburg memory-based learner
        (TiMBL) 214, 315
– analogical proportion 214
ANOVA 88, 530
– factorial design 118
– post-hoc test 91, 96
– repeated-measures ANOVA 89, 116
Antonymy 355, 377, 394
Aphasia 127
– agrammatic aphasia 134
– anomic aphasia 131
– jargonaphasia 135
– neoassociationist approach 131
Augmented addressed morphology
    (AAM) 208, 555
Autism 689–695

Behavioral profile 44
Bilingualism 507
– activation transfer 518
– bilingual competence 515
– bilingual interactive activation model
    (BIA) 515, 520
– cognate 511–512
– cross-language processing 515
– interference 533
– non-cognate 516
– revised hierarchical model (RHM) 520

Binomial data 89
Binyan 607, 613, 615
Blending 296, 423–424, 656
Broca's area 129
– left third frontal gyrus 129

Cell-filling problem 35
Circumfixation 669
Code switching 513
Cognitive ability 597
Cognitive linguistics 372
Cognitive model 182
Cognitive neuropsychology 132, 564
– anatomo-clinical correlation 131
– dissociation 132
    – abstract-concrete dissociation 142
    – double dissociation 133, 564
    – noun–verb dissociation 134
    – simple dissociation 132
    – verb-noun dissociation 140
– functional approach 132
Cognitive semantics 372–377
Co-morphology 539
Competition 38, 55, 59, 63, 72, 514
Complex adaptive system 259
Compounding 336, 337, 605, 640
– compound constituent 339
– compound head 342
– compound modifier 342
– dual nature 338
– intensifying compound 426
– linear order 643
– metaphorical compound 425
– phrasal compound 425
Computation 203
– computation and storage 208–212,
    455–457
Computational linguistics 26
Computational model 298, 315, 323
Computational morphology 243–249
Computational neuroscience 29
Concept 367, 370–372, 384, 385, 389
– conceptualization 373
– conceptual link 520

Open Access. © 2020 Vito Pirrelli et al., published by De Gruyter. This work is licensed under a Creative Commons Attribution-NonCommercial-NoDerivatives 4.0 International License.
https://doi.org/10.1515/9783110440577-018

– conceptual space 375, 385
– conceptual structure 370, 375–376
– lexical concept 371
Connectionism 33, 35, 281, 384, 499, 580
– connection 34, 40
  – connection strength 35, 520
– delta rule 260
– distributed connectionism 471
– input connection 52
– recurrent connection 51
– temporal connection 53
Construction morphology 213, 313
– schema 313
Context 602, 692
– context distribution 604

Decoding 572
Deductive reasoning 30
Derivational morphology 295, 615, 684
– derivation-inflection continuum 72
– non-prototypical derivation 415
– prototypical derivation 415–416
Direct correspondence hypothesis 9, 14
Discovery procedure 273
Distributed morphology 362, 365, 463
Distributional semantics 356, 381, 382, 583, 620
– distributional hypothesis 179
  – strong distributional hypothesis 381
  – weak distributional hypothesis 381
– vector space modeling 179
– word embedding 381
Dyslexia 572, 574
– deep dyslexia 564
– neglect dyslexia 565
– reading deficit 695–696

Emergence 35, 595
– of compounding 347
– emergent property 35
– of morphological awareness 571–579
Emotion 408
English past tense 192, 484
Entropy 63, 66, 252, 603
– conditional entropy 72, 272
– derivational entropy 568

– inflectional entropy 64, 65, 568
– Kullback-Leibler divergence 65
– low conditional entropy conjecture (LCEC) 272
– morphological entropy 568
– paradigm entropy 64, 65, 252
– relative entropy 240, 568
– relative prepositional entropy 582
Etymology 517, 525, 526, 542, 550, 552
– etymological strata 541
Event-related potential 144, 560
– lateralized readiness potential 146
– N400 145
Exemplar model 213
Experimental design 96, 111, 464
– factorial design 118

Finite state transducer 244
Form-meaning association 569
Functional representation for affixes in compositional semantic space (FRACSS) 583
Frequency 193, 239, 240, 249, 251–254, 264, 267, 268, 347, 600, 602
– frequency distribution 63–70, 253–254, 264–267, 497, 603–604
– relative frequency 199
– token frequency 606
– type frequency 606
Frequency effect 179, 479, 480, 559, 565, 686
– morpheme frequency 559
– stem frequency 559
– suffix frequency 559
– word frequency 613

Generalized additive (mixed) modeling (GAMM) 96, 98, 117
– non-linear interaction surface 100, 103
– non-linear random smooth 99, 109
– summary 99
Generative morphology 472
Grammar 612
– architecture 463
– artificial grammar 54
– compartmentalized grammar 540

– development 594, 613
– generative grammar 363
– grammar evaluation 244
– grammar impairment 683–688
– hypothesis testing 249
– lexicon-grammar 212, 392, 612–616, 638, 673
– morphology in grammar 310
Grammaticalization 235, 241, 281
Grammar bias 638

Homonymy 374
Hyperlexia 691
Hyponymy 374

Idiom 41, 46, 242, 284, 298, 459, 514, 693
Inactive morphology 540
Indirect correspondence 4
Inductive reasoning 30
Inflectional complexity 271
– enumerative complexity 271
– Kolmogorov complexity 272
– processing-based complexity 274
– Shannon complexity 272
Inflectional morphology 229, 456, 489, 615, 684
– contextual inflection 229
– inflectional class 230
– inherent inflection 229
– morphopragmatic inflection 430
– non-prototypical inflection 415
– prototypical inflection 414
Inflectional paradigm 36, 238, 567
– discriminative dimension 236
– implicational or predictive dimension 236
– low conditional entropy conjecture (LCEC) 272
– paradigm regularity 276
– principal part 36
– stem indexing 245, 248
Inflectional regularity 267, 276, 461, 500
– regular/sub-regular inflected form 690
Inflectional word formation rule 469
Information theory 602–603
Inheritance tree 475
Integrative model 3, 24, 39, 70, 297, 521

Interactive activation model 509
Interactive function 373
Interdisciplinarity 14, 297, 412, 634
Interfixation 344, 424
Inter-level interaction 29

Language
– adult-directed speech 3, 599
– adult language 596
– child-directed speech 3, 348, 419, 427, 605, 620
– child language 595–596
– child speech 348, 419
Language acquisition 595–596, 681
– age of acquisition 605
– conceptual learning 599
– dynamical learning 620
– emerging generalization 598
– inflection acquisition 249, 264
– intake 606
– language input 606, 608
– lexical acquisition 594, 599–600, 616–619
   – word consolidation 682
   – word integration 682
– lexical concept 599
– mean length of utterance 594
– mean size of paradigm 594
– morpho-lexical acquisition 594
– negative evidence 597
– novel word 146, 583, 691, 695
– starting small 597
– uptake 606
– usage-based account 605
– u-shaped learning curve 51
Language change 200
Language contact 512–515
Language development 595, 596
– blind-alley development 598
– developmental language disorder 683
– developmental trajectory 687
– grammar development 613
– lexical development 594
– morphological development 601
– universal maturational constraints 597
Language feature 33, 45, 50, 179, 195, 206, 229, 231, 234, 317, 383, 475, 476, 685
– concept feature 384

- feature competition 514
- morphosyntactic feature 465
- pragmatic feature 418
Language impairment 683–688
Language resource 167
- behavioral data 84
- CHILDES 177
- clinical resources 173
- corpus 176, 581
- crowdsourcing 173
- dictionary 181
- elicited rating 169
- experimental data 170
- grammar 181
- lexical database 170, 177
- time course data 84, 96
Language typology 600
Language unit 11, 13, 25, 297
Learning 28
- classical conditioning 582
- discriminative learning 37–38, 252, 604
    - cue 317
    - naive discriminative learning (NDL) 39, 196, 308–310, 317–318, 322
    - outcome 317
- error-driven learning 37, 39
- gradual learning algorithm 207
- implicit learning 51
- learning-oriented process 580
- learning rate 54
- minimal generalization learning (MGL) 206
- minimum description length (MDL) 244
- non-monotonic learning 597
- paired-associate learning 687
- Rescorla-Wagner learning 40
Lemma 12, 134, 248, 367, 393, 695
Lexical access 4, 33, 34, 49, 60, 491, 510, 511, 519, 560, 686, 687, 691, 693
- bottom-up approach 515
- decomposition route 209
- race model 34
- resting activation level 536
- whole-word route 209
Lexical blocking 250, 415, 439, 470
Lexical decay 687
Lexical decision 26, 41–44, 114, 149, 172, 298, 479–483, 510, 556–559

Lexical entry 70–71, 468–483
Lexicalism 500
- lexicalist hypothesis 248
Lexicalization 369, 387, 458, 674
Lexical morphology 564
Lexical neighborhood 34, 201
Lexical bias 638, 649
Lexical organization 32, 134, 279, 688
- entrenchment 43, 55, 56, 68
- self-organization 25, 35-36, 251, 514
- strength 514, 637
Lexical phonology 192
Lexical storage 193–203
Lexical typology 347
Lexicon 474, 595, 612
- bilingual lexicon 508
    - integrated lexica hypothesis 508
    - non-selective access 508
    - parallel access 534
- featurally underspecified lexicon 195
- hierarchical lexicon 247, 314
- lexicon architecture 133, 219, 508, 533–534, 555
- lexicon-grammar 212, 392, 612–616, 638, 673
- morphological lexicon 32–33, 595
Lexome 40
Lichtheim's concept center 130
Linguistic intuition 2, 169, 173–175, 377, 583
Linguistic terminology 595
Linguistic theory 182, 298–300, 394, 468
Linking hypothesis 6
Literacy acquisition 571
Local processing bias 690
Logit transformation 89
Logogen 33

Machine learning 29, 31, 257
Marr hierarchy 28
Maximization of opportunity principle 4, 304
Mean-centering 114
Megastudy 171
Memory span 284, 695
Mental lexicon 3, 31–39, 69, 129–144, 153, 191–196, 312, 323, 348, 367–371, 479–494, 554–559, 595, 635, 680

Meta-linguistic task 697
Minimalist morphology 462
Morph 231
- cumulative exponence 231
- exponence relation 233, 465
- extended exponence 231
Morpheme 24, 50, 232, 233, 297, 299–305, 307, 309–311, 315, 324–325, 457, 553
- empty morpheme 37
- linking morpheme 315, 347
- morpheme boundary 62, 66, 268–270, 322
- morpheme decomposition 468–472
- morpheme interference 556
- morpheme segmentation 233
- synthetic morpheme 464
- zero morpheme 37
Morphological awareness 538, 571, 696
Morphological borrowing 513
Morphological decomposition 209, 461, 464, 468
- decomposability 459
- non-decomposable 462
- segmentability 462
Morphological family 63, 345, 524, 606
- morphological family size 239, 322, 508, 526, 569
Morphological integration 537
- reanalysis 538
Morphological process 348
Morphological regularity/irregularity 474, 596
- exception 70, 204–205, 311–312
- irregular paradigm 61–62, 246, 266–270, 684
- semi-regular alternation 213
Morphological segmentation 459
Morphological structure 477, 556
- semantic interpretability 557
Morphological theory 32, 474, 490
- abstractive approach 32, 240, 257, 299
- constructive approach 32, 240, 257
- item-and-arrangement 13, 297, 500
- item-and-process 13, 297, 500

- rule-based 302, 311, 478
Morphophonology 191, 462, 465, 616
- morphophonological accommodation 653
- morphophonological representation 498
Morphopragmatics 405, 406
- alterative 424
- aphasia 439
- augmentative 414, 427, 428
- diachronic variation 422
- diminutive 408, 409, 411–413, 427
- downgrading 409
- elative 424
- evaluative 417, 426
- excessive 413, 431
- fictiveness 418
- honorifics 426, 429
- hypocoristics 437
- iconicity 433
- illocutionary force 417
- Jakobsonian principle of equivalence 431
- non-seriousness 418
- onomatopoeia 438
- pejorative 424, 428
- pluralis maiestatis 430
- reduplication 432, 436
  - echo word 437
  - extragrammatical 432, 435, 437
  - grammatical 432
- upgrading 409
Morphosemantics 405, 410
Morphosyntax 462
- morphosyntactic representation 498
Multisensory temporal integration 691
Mutual attention 605

Naïve discriminative reader 581
Naming disorder 128
- phonological disturbance 128
- semantic impairment 128
Nanosyntax 475
Natural language processing (NLP) 177
Natural morphology 251
Neo-constructionism 465, 500
Neural correlates of phonological processing 138
- frontal lobe 138
- inferior frontal gyrus 139

– temporal lobe 138
Neural correlates of semantic
    processing 138
– angular gyrus 140
– frontal operculum 139
– fusiform gyrus 140–141, 143
– inferior frontal gyrus 139
– left superior parietal cortex 141
– superior temporal gyrus 140
– temporal cortex 143
Neural network 33, 381, 385
– discriminative recurrent neural
    network 264
– perceptron 582
– recurrent neural network 51, 260
Neuroimaging 137
– functional neuroimaging 137
  – functional magnetic resonance imaging
    (fMRI) 137–138
  – positron emission tomography (PET)
    137–138
Neuromodulation 147
– direct electrical stimulation 152
– transcranial direct current stimulation
    (tDCS) 150
  – language recovery 152
– transcranial magnetic stimulation
    (TMS) 148–150
  – offline and online paradigms 148
  – "placebo" control condition 149
  – real condition 149
  – repetitive TMS 148
  – virtual lesion 148
Nonce word 215
– pseudoverb 207
– pseudoword 170
Nonliteral (figurative) language 693
Non-verbal IQ 687
Non-word repetition 685

Optimality theory 206
Organized-unitary-content hypothesis
    (OUCH) 137
Orthography
– orthographic alteration 567
– orthographic cue 519
– orthographic decoding 696

– orthographic overlap 517
– orthography-semantics consistency 570
– transparent orthography 573
  – orthographic-phonological alteration 576
Outlier 122

Paradigm 637
– inflectional paradigm 231, 239, 252, 473
– paradigmatic relation 526
– word paradigm 523
Parallel system borrowing 540
Parental input 605
Pattern detection 605
Perception
– perceptual recognizability 512
– perceptual salience 600
– visual/perceptual feature 136
Periphrasis 241
Perisylvian language network 684
Phonaestheme 307, 308, 322, 323,
    470, 569
Phonology 139, 192
– phonological processing 695
– phonological regularity 219
– phonological representation 695
– phonological sensitivity 681
Politeness 429
Portmanteau 424
Pragmatics 405
– cognitive pragmatics 411
– lexical pragmatics 410
– sociopragmatics 412, 413
Pre-literate child 571
Priming 298, 306–308, 323,
    479, 481, 558
– cross-modal priming 481
– cross-script priming 511
– form-meaning association 577
– identity condition 483
– masked priming 484, 518, 561, 567
– morphological priming 483, 531
– partial priming 492
– prime 528
– priming asymmetry 524
– semantic priming 688
– target 481
– translation priming 531

Principal component analysis (PCA) 113
Principle of contrast 37, 259
Procedural deficit hypothesis 690
Processing
- parallel distributed processing (PDP) 24, 27, 33
- processing and storage 15, 38, 53
Psycholinguistics 26, 32–35, 480
- computational modeling 29–31

QQ-norm plot 111

Reading 554, 696
- latency in reading 573
- morpheme-based reading 574, 575
- novel word reading 564–565
- reading accuracy 573
- reading acquisition 571
- reading comprehension 697
  - poor comprehender 696–697
- word decoding 696
Readjustment rule 466
Regression analysis
- assumption 87, 104
- collinearity 111
  - essential collinearity 112
  - non essential collinearity 112
  - suppression 112
- contour plot 103
- counterbalancing 120
- covariate 84
- linear regression model 86
  - dependent variable 86
  - intercept 87
  - linear mixed-effects modeling 92, 116
    - fixed effect 92
    - random effect 92
  - slope 87
- model comparison 94, 101
- model criticism 104
- non-linear regression model 98, 117
- power of the model 105
- smooth function 98
Relevance
- communicative 601
- of frequency effect 303
- of morphotactic structure 234

- of similarity
- for word access 681
- for word productivity 217
Replacive morphology 460
Rescorla-Wagner equations 318, 582
Residual 87, 104, 108
- autocorrelation 108, 110
- distribution of residuals 111
Residualizing 113
Response competition 51
Ridge regression 114

Salience 2, 71, 251, 377, 636–637
Saussurean sign 459
Semantics 616
- coercion 390–394
- color term 386–389
- componential analysis 538
- compositionality 234, 300, 340–342, 500, 563
- conceptual approach 355
- demotivation of meaning 458
- interpretability 557
- meaning construal 372
- non-compositionality 365–366, 458
- polyseme 375
- polysemy 355, 361, 367, 371, 376
- radial category 421
- relational approach 354
- semantic field 357
- symbolic approach 355
- similarity 356, 379–383, 558
- transparency 340, 341, 563
- usage-based approach 374
Semiological function 373
Separation hypothesis 234, 305–307, 461
Shape bias 687
Social interaction 406
Socio-economic status 608
Speaker's perspective 456
Speech act 406, 419, 421
Speech error 635
- addition error 665
- contextual 635
  - selection problem 636
  - sequencing problem 636
- non-contextual 635

– regularization 663
Speech perception 681
Speech reduction 197
Speech situation 406, 419
Statistical model 29, 84, 104–115, 382–385, 582
Stimulus 169
Storage 15, 38, 53, 191, 455, 688
– declarative memory system 489
– procedural memory system 489
– storage and computation 208–212, 455–457
– storage and processing 15, 38, 43
Stratal phonology 211
Stress 202
– compound stress 202
– stress preservation 199
Structural language 689
Structuralist semantics 357–362
Suppletion 460
Surface realization 463
Synonymy 355, 376, 377, 394
– parasynonym 357
– synonym 392
Syntax 616
– syntactic head 475
– syntactic paradigm 255

Temporal self-organizing map (TSOM) 51, 262
– Best matching unit (BMU) 52, 262
– integated activation pattern (IAP) 57
– 'what' information 54
– 'when' information 54
Text comprehension 572
– listening comprehension 697
– reading comprehension 572
Tilburg memory-based learner (TiMBL) 214, 315
Time-scale effect 14
Topological distance 54
Transposed letter effect 558

Underlying structure 463
Underspecification 195
Ungrammaticality effect 479

Variation 199
– pronunciation variation 197
Vocabulary
– breadth 682
– depth 682
– expressive vocabulary 686
– receptive vocabulary 686
Voicing 207
Vowel alternation 198
– ablaut 666
– breaking 200
– umlaut 200

Weak central coherence hypothesis 690
Wernicke's area 129
– left superior temporal gyrus 129
Williams syndrome 688–689
Word and paradigm morphology 25, 35, 38, 236, 237, 461
Word class 134, 616
– adjective 616
– noun 617
– verb 617
– word-class sensitivity 650
Word coactivation 507, 534
Word cohesiveness 641, 647
Word competition 34, 507, 637, 645, 655, 681
– phonological competition 682
Word comprehension 681
Word family effect 507
Word-finding difficulty 128
Word formation
– word formation pattern 313
– word formation rule 469
WordNet 180
Word processing 264
– dual processing hypothesis 686
  – dual mechanism model 210
  – (parallel) dual route model 208–209
  – race model 250
– form-then-meaning account 562
– form-with-meaning account 562
– full-listing model 555
– full-parsing model 554
– novel word 151, 205, 212, 347, 555

- processing uncertainty 276
- uniqueness recognition point 34, 60, 278
  - complex uniqueness point 60, 270
- morpho-orthographic processing 562
- prefix-stripping 555
- task-dependent effect 563
Word production 33, 72, 134, 259, 304, 339, 520–524, 586, 681
- late Insertion 463
- selection 675
- sequencing 675
- spell out 463

Word productivity 194, 337, 345–346, 674
Word recall 58
Word root 247–248, 366, 458, 468, 557, 575, 601, 607–610
Word stem 61–68, 193–194, 245–248, 469, 490–492, 559, 573–575, 646–654
- stem family 276–277, 568–569
Word structure 35, 71, 268, 297, 322, 684
Word tree 56, 263
Word usage 254, 273, 355–367, 582, 602
Working memory 138, 256, 284